Governing America

Governing
America

H.T. Reynolds
University of Delaware

David Vogler
Wheaton College

HarperCollins*Publishers*

Sponsoring Editor: Lauren Silverman
Development Editor: Jinny Joyner
Project Editors: Paula Cousin/Melonie Parnes
Art Director: Teresa Delgado
Text and Cover Design: D.D.I.
Cover Photo: © Dany Crist, 1989/Uniphoto
Photo Research: Lisa Hartjens/Imagefinders
Production: Willie Lane/Sunaina Sehwani
Compositor: Waldman Graphics
Printer and Binder: Arcata Graphics/Hawkins
Cover Printer: Lehigh Press

GOVERNING AMERICA

Library of Congress Cataloging-in-Publication Data
Reynolds, H. T. (Henry T.)
     Governing America / H. T. Reynolds, David Vogler.
        p.   cm.
     Includes index.
     ISBN 0-06-045393-1 (Student Edition)
     ISBN 0-06-500039-0 (Teacher Edition)
     1. United States—Politics and government.   I. Vogler, David J.
II. Title.
JK274.R613   1991
320.973—dc20   90-38379
                                                                        CIP

91 92 93 94   9 8 7 6 5 4 3 2 1

Brief Contents

Detailed Contents

A Closer Look Boxes

Preface

In the middle of the nineteenth century, Walt Whitman penned several lines that could introduce a book about American politics at any time in this country's history:

> Do I contradict myself?
> Very well then I contradict myself
> (I am large, I contain multitudes.)

We believe that America's contradictions are the lifeblood of its political system. Our own experience in the classroom and in politics has convinced us that the best way to teach politics is to recognize that clashing interpretations are what make the study of government so fascinating and exciting. We also think that students in an introductory course should not simply accumulate disembodied facts but should attempt to integrate, interpret, and evaluate this information. Whether they ultimately become activists, legislators, executives, judges, administrators, campaign workers, or simply constituents, students of American politics need to learn how to reconcile competing explanations and principles. It is these beliefs and experiences that both led us to write *Governing America* and dictated its main theme.

THE CENTRAL THEME: WHO GOVERNS?

F. Scott Fitzgerald once said that the test of a first-rate intelligence is the ability to hold two opposed ideas in mind at the same time and still function. We are convinced that students can not only manage but actually prefer works that promote critical thinking to those that simply present a nuts and bolts catalogue of facts. As its central theme our book raises the fundamental question of who governs and describes three different and often contradictory answers—the democratic, pluralist, and power elite models of government. This theoretical approach, we believe, facilitates the study of American government while at the same time it triggers the critical analysis needed to understand and participate in its governance.

One author is an elected official in town government and has worked in Congress and in congressional campaigns; the other has been actively involved in political campaigns at the state and local levels and has served on a task force on county government reform. These experiences in politics have persuaded us that the models analyzed in *Governing America* are not abstractions created by political theorists and forced to fit the real world of American politics. Rather, they reflect such fundamental values as accountability, competition, freedom, equality, compromise, and fair play, which lie at the heart of politics in the United States and which are recognized and used by citizens and political leaders at all levels of government.

Other textbooks also raise the question of who governs. Yet it is surprising how many of them lose sight of the topic after the initial discussion. We have endeavored to keep this question constantly in mind and to use information about the political system to help answer it. Needless to say, we do not mention the theme on every page or in every section. Still, the matter of who governs is never far from view, and we try to relate each chapter to this higher question. In this respect we also differ from those books that take for granted the inherent importance of each discrete piece of information about American politics without integrating these pieces into the larger picture of who does and should participate in governing.

CONTENT AND ORGANIZATION

Governing America is a mainstream text in content and organization. It includes chapters on the major topics covered in most introductory courses in American government. One chapter, however, is not found in most other texts: Chapter 2 describes the social and economic conditions of American life, to give the student a feel for the environment in which political events take place. The organization of the book thus traces the theme of who governs from the social, economic, and philosophical underpinnings of American politics to the complex world of policymaking in the 1990s.

Although we pursue a central theme, each chapter is self-contained. This means that instructors can skip around, as they often do, to tailor the book to their particular needs and can continue to use their present course outlines. Furthermore, when an important concept reappears we provide a brief review so that readers can understand the concept within that context, without having to refer back to other sections of the book.

PEDAGOGY

A number of goals have guided our writing of this book. One has been to avoid the cluttered, cut-up appearance that makes many textbooks difficult to follow. We have designed graphs, charts, and tables to present data clearly and have directly linked them to the discussion in the text. In addition, we frequently suggest ways students, on their own, can confirm or challenge assertions made in the text. The boxed features called "A Closer Look" in each chapter raise pertinent questions and provide additional information central to the topics of the chapter rather than cluttering the book with trivia.

The extensive use of examples throughout the book reflects our belief that it is always better to show the impact of ideas than it is to tell the reader about them. Another objective is to *use* concepts after they have been introduced and defined. Readers need to know that what they are learning really does matter for comprehending government and politics.

To help students organize the material, checkpoints throughout the chapter review topics covered in the major sections. Each chapter concludes with a summary of the major ideas. Finally, we have included citations of the most

up-to-date political science research (as well as classic studies) and made suggestions for further reading in each chapter so that students can pursue topics they find of particular interest.

SUPPLEMENTS

A comprehensive selection of teaching and learning resources have been developed to supplement *Governing America*.

Laser Disc

American Government: Issues and Images is an original laser disc, also available on video tape. This two-sided video disc, developed in consultation with American Government professors and a multi-media courseware developer, contains over 100 motion picture excerpts from newsreel collections, network news and cable archives, and state historical societies. The video disc has been specifically designed for classroom use and includes pedagogically focused clips from campaign commercials, convention debates, and both historic and recent footage of domestic and foreign policy issues. An accompanying User's Guide links each excerpt to the *Governing America* text.

Student Resource Handbook

Jett Conner, the Chairman of the Political Science Department at Metropolitan State College in Denver, has authored a Student Resource Handbook which provides an interactive review of text material. Each chapter of the Handbook contains learning objectives, a chapter summary, a list of key terms, and sample essay questions. In addition, a "Thinking Critically" section raises issues or questions which require students to respond using analytical reasoning. Another special chapter feature, a "Debating the Issues" section, rephrases a central theme from each text chapter as a debate topic, asking students to resolve the issue by formulating arguments and drawing upon chapter materials in support or rebuttal of their positions.

Instructor's Resource Manual

Larry Elowitz, the Chairman of the Political Science Department of Georgia College, has written an Instructor's Resource Manual which is provided free of charge to instructors. Each of the manual's chapters contain learning objectives, chapter outlines, and lists of key terms, personalities, and concepts. Special features of the manual include suggested classroom activities, research assignments, and "Issue Sketches" intended to promote class debates. Each chapter contains a composite chapter quiz composed of multiple-choice, completion, true/false, and short-essay questions. An answer key to the quizzes completes the Manual.

Test Bank

The test item file, written by Keith Nicholls of Arizona State University, consists of 2,000 multiple-choice, true/false, and completion test questions. Each question is coded with the correct response and referenced to the page in *Governing America* on which the correct answer is indicated. The Test Bank is provided free of charge to instructors.

Testmaster

In addition to the traditional printed format, the complete Test Bank is also available free of charge on *Testmaster,* HarperCollins' computerized test-generating system. Flexible and easy to use, *Testmaster* may be obtained for use with the IBM-PC and most compatibles and the Apple IIe and IIc.

Supershell Student Tutorial Software

A computerized Student Tutorial Guide, written by Robert E. England, Chairman of the Political Science Department at Oklahoma State University, is also provided free of charge to instructors. *Supershell* was developed to help students retain the key concepts and ideas they have read. This versatile drill-and-practice software contains multiple-choice, true/false, and short answer questions for each chapter in the text. Diagnostic graphics provide immediate student reinforcement and make recommendations about areas in which further study might prove beneficial. Students may print out narrative chapter outlines or consult an easy-to-use tutorial guide. In addition, a flash card program is included to drill students on the terms in the text's glossary.

Harper Data Analysis Package

William Parle, of Oklahoma State University, has prepared a student data analysis package for the IBM-PC which performs several basic statistical functions, including: univariate frequency distributions, bivariate frequency distributions, and bivariate frequency distributions controlling for the effects of a third variable. Free to instructors, the package comes with a "real world data" set which allows for a realistic program demonstration, a complete "Help" menu and "Help" files, a data dictionary feature, a set of screen instructions, and a User's Manual.

Writing a Research Paper in Political Science

Daniel E. Farlow, of Southwest Texas State, has authored an informative, practical student guide discussing how to write research papers for political science courses. This supplement is available free to adopters.

The 1988 Elections in America

Written by Larry J. Sabato, of the University of Virginia, this popular supplement provides an in-depth analysis of the events surrounding our most recent national election. Copies are provided free of charge to instructors.

Grades

Grade-keeping and class-management software, free to instructors, maintains data sets for up to 200 students. It is suitable for the IBM-PC and most compatibles.

Transparencies

Transparency acetates of figures in the text are free to instructors who are interested in helping students interpret the presentation of important visual data. These transparencies facilitate the integration of student assignments with classroom lectures.

Media Program

A comprehensive media program includes a wide selection of well-regarded films and videos for classroom use. *The Media Handbook,* designed to help instructors integrate the films and videos with the text and their teaching plans, outlines various audio-visual options and suggests follow-up discussion questions.

Instructors may choose from many excellent programs. *The Power Game,* Hedrick Smith's popular four-part PBS documentary on the elected (and unelected) government in Washington, and *Eyes on the Prize,* the award-winning six-part series on the civil rights movement, are both available through the HarperCollins media policy. Also available is "The Thirty-Second President," Bill Moyers' examination of the office in an age of soundbites, from his PBS series *A Walk Through the Twentieth Century. The Challenge of the Presidency,* a one-hour videotape, combines David Frost's thoughtful interviews of former presidents Reagan, Carter, Ford, and Nixon. Adopters of *Governing America* may also receive a unique *Newsreel Video,* a selection of authentic newsreel footage that captures the key American political events of the past six decades.

ACKNOWLEDGMENTS

Like all books, this is the work of many more people than those listed as the authors. We want to thank our students at the University of Delaware and Wheaton College for helping us to develop many ideas and our teachers at the University of North Carolina, Chapel Hill, for showing us the many different ways of looking at American politics.

Some of the data presented in *Governing America* were made available in part by the Interuniversity Consortium for Political and Social Research. Neither the collector of the original data nor the Consortium bears any responsibility for the analysis or interpretations presented here. The authors also wish to thank the Public Agenda Foundation and John Doble for material presented in the chapter on public opinion.

We cannot overstate the contribution of Jinny Joyner, our development editor, to this project. Her substantive insights, editorial acumen, and goodwill are largely responsible for transforming the multiple drafts of all of the chapters into a cohesive book.

Many people at HarperCollins have played key roles in supporting and improving this project. Political science editor Lauren Silverman provided important editorial direction in the development of the book. The advice and support of editorial director Marianne Russell were a great help at many stages of the project. Project editors Paula Cousin and Melonie Parnes and photo researcher Lisa Hartjens worked hard to make the book attractive to both students and instructors.

H. T. Reynolds thanks Nancy K. Davis, Eileen Brennan, Beverly Clarke, Madeleine Anduze, and John Roberts for their assistance in preparing the manuscript. Elizabeth Doble deserves credit for making the world of publishing a bit more comprehensible. He is most of all, enormously grateful to Lisa, Alan, and Anne and to his colleagues at the University of Delaware for their support, encouragement, and especially patience.

David Vogler thanks the many Wheaton students who helped him gather materials for the book over the years: Tammy Padgett, Sarah Wikenczy, Michelle Weldon, Jessica Graf, Suzanne Murphy, Ellen Conlin, Anne-Marie Lasowski, Christine McLeod, Diane Michaels, and Helen Morgan. Professor Jay Goodman has been a great source of insights into American politics, as he has for thousands of Wheaton students over the years. Also at Wheaton, Kathie Francis, Nancy Shepardson, and Kathy Kollett patiently typed endless drafts of chapters. He can never repay Alice and Bill for all those hours of family time that went instead into writing and rewriting, nor thank them enough for their support throughout the project.

Finally, we thank the many reviewers who read and critiqued several drafts of the manuscript. We recognize that these colleagues have their own full schedules of teaching, research, and writing, and we deeply appreciate the many ideas and suggestions that they have given us. For their help in reviewing the manuscript, we thank:

Janet K. Boles, Marquette University
James Bolner, Sr., Louisiana State University
R. Lewis Bowman, University of South Florida
Ronald J. Busch, Cleveland State University
David T. Canon, Duke University
Edward G. Carmines, Indiana University
George F. Cole, University of Connecticut
Jett Conner, Metropolitan State College
Richard W. Crockett, Western Illinois University
Gavan Duffy, Syracuse University
George C. Edwards, III, Texas A&M University
Peter Eisinger, University of Wisconsin
James C. Foster, Oregon State University
Larry Gerston, San Jose State University
Walter I. Giles, Georgetown University
Richard J. Hardy, University of Missouri, Columbia
Conrad Joyner, University of Arizona
Thomas Keating, Arizona State University
William E. Kelly, Auburn University

Michael D. Martinez, University of Florida
Michael W. McCann, University of Washington
Donald McCrone, University of Washington
Robert D. Miewald, University of Nebraska, Lincoln
Alan D. Monroe, Illinois State University
Keith Nicholls, Arizona State University
Laura Katz Olson, Lehigh University
Albert R. Papa, University of Pittsburgh, Greensburg
Steven C. Poe, University of North Texas
David H. Provost, California State University, Fresno
Sandra Quinn-Musgrove, Our Lady of the Lake University
Leroy N. Rieselbach, Indiana University
Francis E. Rourke, Johns Hopkins University
Barbara Rowland, Northern Arizona University
Claude K. Rowland, University of Kansas
Richard K. Scher, University of Florida
Earl L. Shaw, Northern Arizona University
Lana Stein, University of Missouri, St. Louis
Cheryl Swanson, Southwest Texas State
Charles Walcott, Virginia Polytechnic Institute
Benjamin Walter, Vanderbilt University
Clifford J. Wirth, University of New Hampshire
Martha Zebrowski, Rutgers University, Newark

H. T. Reynolds
David Vogler

Part One

The Framework of Government ★

Who Governs America?

Chapter 1

Is the United States a democracy? Maybe. Maybe not. Most Americans believe their government is among the most democratic in the world. But lots of serious and intelligent thinkers believe that the political system does not come as close to being democratic as most people think. In fact, many are convinced that relatively small organized groups, or even a single power elite, run the country. ■

Surveying the sweeping changes that engulfed Eastern Europe and the Soviet Union in late 1989, Robert Kaiser, an editor for the *Washington Post*, minced no words: "What we are seeing is the manifestation of a disastrous failure—the failure of the Soviet system." He didn't seem to be exaggerating, since the Russian empire from the Baltic Sea to the Caucasus Mountains appeared to be crumbling like "a dry Saltine cracker."[1] Citizens in East Germany, Poland, Czechoslovakia, Hungary, Rumania, and elsewhere clamored for freedom and liberty and an end to communism. In December the Berlin Wall, the malevolent symbol of the divisions between East and West, was torn down.

Soviet leader Mikhail Gorbachev accepted, even encouraged, many of these developments. In a sense he had little choice, because within

Citizens demanding political rights and an end to Soviet domination march in Prague, Czechoslovakia. Many Americans, such as Secretary of State James Baker, interpreted the radical changes in the governments of Eastern Europe as proving "Freedom works! Communism doesn't!"

the Soviet Union's own borders people cried for open markets, free elections, less state interference in the economy, and a dismantling of the oppressive and corrupt communist party. Several republics went farther; they insisted on national autonomy and independence. Such vast and rapid transformations of power behind the Iron Curtain left outsiders gasping in wonderment.

Although it was much too early to tell where these events would lead, many Americans nevertheless congratulated themselves on having won the Cold War. Countless observers couldn't help believing that the Soviet Union, once despised as an "evil empire," was steadily marching down the road toward capitalism and American-style democracy. "Socialism is dead," Nobel prize winning economist Milton Friedman declared.[2] President George Bush had anticipated this interpretation a year before when, speaking from what he called "democracy's front porch" (the West Portico of the Capitol) he said of the United States: "For the first time in this century—for the first time in perhaps all of history—man does not have to invent a system by which to live. We don't have to talk into the night about which form of government is better."[3]

Many of his fellow citizens shared these self-congratulatory sentiments. After all, their constitution guaranteed fair and open elections, a free press, the right to peaceful assembly, freedom of speech, religious tolerance, and stringent checks on the abuse of governmental power. Their economy, moreover, produced one of the highest standards of living anywhere. In the previous 40 years, while Soviet society choked on political repression and economic stagnation, Americans prospered and elected presidents as liberal as John F. Kennedy and as conservative as Ronald Reagan. No wonder Americans looked with pride and self-assurance on their political and economic order.

Yet in politics enthusiasm should always be tempered with caution and introspection. Not only can the reforms in Eastern Europe and the Soviet Union easily come unglued, but the United States also faces its own share of problems. Granted, our form of government may be the envy of the world, but even its staunchest admirers know that it is not perfect. Thus, as we approach the twenty-first century, it might be prudent to ask just how democratic America really is. To raise this issue is to pose the most fundamental question anyone can ask about a political system: Who governs it?

Who governs America? It seems such a simple question, and you do not have to search very far for answers:

- "The people govern, obviously!"
- "No, political bosses do."
- "On the contrary, the country is run by big business."
- "Don't you mean lobbyists in general?"
- "It's controlled by the Rockefellers and Kennedys."
- "That's an overstatement. Lots of groups have power."
- "Actually, no one governs. It's just chaos."

There are many points of view, and most of them doubtlessly contain a grain of truth. Yet, in spite of its complexity, the question of who really governs America has elicited three broad answers.

One reply is that the United States, being a democracy, is governed by the people. Others find this response too simplistic; they claim that the nation is run by a multitude of organized groups, not by the people as a whole. Still others assert that government is in the hands of a single power elite, a small group that makes all of the important decisions. Since the question of who governs is basic to an understanding of American politics—indeed one might say it is the central political question of the times—it is worth exploring each of these three answers in detail.

Before doing so, however, one point has to be absolutely clear: *Government in one form or another inevitably emerges in any society*. It is important to understand why.

THE NECESSITY OF GOVERNMENT

Think for a moment about a major national issue like the budget deficit. It arises when the federal government spends more than it takes in. Because the cause is so easily identified, it would

One of the distinguishing characteristics of government is that it is the only institution that can legitimately use force to maintain law and order.

seem that the problem could just as easily be cured: Reduce spending, raise taxes, or both. But, as everyone knows, problems are not solved that simply in the real world, where such solutions invariably entail costs as well as benefits to specific groups. The elderly do not want Social Security and Medicare, two of the largest items in the budget, cut. But at the same time, nearly all workers oppose higher taxes. Therefore, when it comes to reducing the budget deficit, everyone wants someone else to bear the burden. Former Senator Russell Long of Louisiana reportedly claimed that his constituents always told him, "Don't tax me. Don't tax my friend. Tax the person behind the tree."

And so it is with all public controversies: They are essentially fights over who wins and who loses. Politics is conflict and without conflict there is no politics. Harold Lasswell, an eminent political scientist, perhaps said it best when he defined politics as "who gets what, when, how."[4]

Governments exist to regulate conflict; they prevent us from destroying ourselves as we struggle to work out our differences. Thomas Hobbes, a seventeenth-century English philosopher, believed that individuals left to pursue their selfish interests would ultimately destroy one another in a war "of every man against every man."[5]

In order to escape this chaos, Hobbes argued, people had to surrender their independence to a sovereign power (that is, a government). Even though Hobbes wrote nearly 400 years ago during a period of enormous social and political upheaval, his ideas remain applicable today. Regardless of whether we think government should be large or small, powerful or weak, we can at least agree that some arrangement is needed to manage conflict.

Moreover, individuals resort to violence all the time to settle their quarrels. Yet only government has a legal right to do so. Indeed, one might distinguish government from other social institutions by its legitimate monopoly on the use of force to resolve disputes among its citizens or between them and itself.

Apart from keeping us from cutting each other's throats, government also has the responsibility to do things that individuals acting on their own could not or would not do for themselves and their communities. In these days of intercontinental ballistic missiles, how can the head of a household alone ensure the family's safety? How can parents using only their wits and muscles educate their children, provide them with parks, playgrounds, schools, and zoos? How can they recruit, train, manage, and pay teachers, fire fighters, postmasters, soldiers, and trash collectors? How, in short, can people construct a viable society unless they cooperate

The Tragedy of the Commons and the Need for Government ★★★

Like farmers everywhere, planters in Obion County, Tennessee, want to maximize their profits.[a] One of the most profitable crops in the 1970s and 1980s were soybeans, and, attracted by the high prices they brought, farmers abandoned livestock, turned under pasture lands, and planted beans by the thousands of acres, even on hillsides and in marshes, areas normally left uncultivated.

Unfortunately, as the farmers in this western Tennessee county discovered to their dismay, what is in an individual's immediate self-interest often leads to collective harm in the long run. Here, the problem was the soybean itself. Its shallow root system breaks up the soil, leaving it vulnerable to wind and water erosion. After years of overplanting the land slowly but inevitably dies, and when it is gone, it profits no one.

This phenomenon wreaked havoc in Obion County where each year prime farmland washed down the Mississippi River at the rate of 100 tons per acre. Soil conservationists worried that unless something was done the region would soon turn into a dust bowl.

"Unless something was done"—therein lies the farmers' dilemma. Faced, on the one hand, with soaring operating costs and crushing mortgage payments, they find it hard to look beyond this year's crop. On the other hand, the need for conservation is obvious. Garret Hardin called this dilemma "the tragedy of the commons." An individual farmer would prefer to shift the cost of preserving the soil to others by having *them* plant fewer soybeans, thus raising the price and decreasing erosion. But of course all farmers feel this way, and so none of them stops.

It is tragic because "each man is locked into a system that compels him to increase [soybean production, for example] without limit— in a world that is limited."[b] The pursuit of private gain, as rational as it may be for an individual, ultimately leads to catastrophe.

Is there a solution? Only if individuals give up some of their freedom and act collectively through an agency that has the authority to control at least some of their behavior. A government is just such an agency. The Department of Agriculture, for instance, can require farmers to do things they would not do on their own: hold land out of production, stop planting on hills, rotate crops, plow in contours, and use smaller harvesters. Or it can spend money to reclaim land. Or both. Whatever the case, the goal is to achieve a common objective that is beyond the means and will of the individual farmers to attain.

[a]Based on an article in *Washington Post*, February 7, 1982, p. 20.
[b]Garret Hardin, "The Tragedy of the Commons," *Science* 162:1243–1248; reprinted in Herman E. Daly, ed., *Toward a Steady-State Economy* (San Francisco: Freeman, 1973), p. 138.

to produce the thousands and thousands of goods and services that they need to lead safe and productive lives? As A Closer Look (p. 7) suggests, government seems both inevitable and desirable.

Government, then, is an instrument of collective action. It helps citizens reach common ends. Although one may disagree about what needs to be done or who should do it, government is frequently the logical, and sometimes the only, choice. Furthermore, once an activity has been placed in the public domain, government, and government alone, has the authority to carry it out with force if necessary.

In the language of political science this power has been called the "authoritative allocation of values for a society,"[6] but the Preamble to the American Constitution puts it more simply:

> We the People of the United States, in order to form a more perfect Union, establish Justice, insure domestic tranquility, provide for the common defense, promote the general Welfare, and secure the blessings of Liberty to ourselves and our Posterity, do ordain and establish this Constitution for the United States of America.

Knowing that government is inevitable and indispensable still leaves open the question of who runs it. As mentioned above, three answers have been proposed: democracy, pluralism, and elitism.

Checkpoint

- Governments exist to maintain law and order.
- They also undertake collective actions that people acting separately cannot or will not do for themselves.
- Governments possess a legitimate monopoly on the use of force in carrying out their responsibilities.

✓

DIRECT AND INDIRECT DEMOCRACY

When asked, probably everyone on the street will say that the United States is a democracy. Indeed, the belief in democracy pervades our culture. Democratic symbols appear repeatedly in civics books, patriotic songs, newspaper editorials, Fourth of July speeches, and television commercials. Whatever its faults, most people agree, America is still the "land of liberty," and to question that faith is to question all that they have been taught since preschool.

Yet precisely because the idea is so firmly entrenched, it deserves careful scrutiny. In politics, as in most aspects of life, what seems self-evident often turns out to be more doubtful on closer inspection. If America is a democracy, then it presumably meets certain conditions, the two most important of which are freedom *and* self-government.

Principles of Democracy

DEMOCRACY AS FREEDOM   Democracy is often equated with freedom—for example, the freedom to speak one's mind, to join a political party, to disagree openly with public officials, and to advocate unpopular causes. Freedoms rest on the notion that citizens have rights that governments ought not abuse. The police must have the power to investigate crimes, but people have the right to their privacy; the law has to be obeyed, but defendants have the right to a speedy trial at which they are represented by counsel. These sorts of rights are frequently called **civil liberties.**

Some philosophers extend the concept of rights into the realm of economic and social life, arguing that freedom includes the right to adequate food, clothing, housing, medical care, and protection from psychological manipulation. After all, they ask, can civil liberties be enjoyed by someone who is starving or whose mind is controlled by propaganda?

Whatever one includes within the definition of freedom, a nation's level of democracy is fre-

Civil liberties are an essential ingredient of democracy. No nation can be considered democratic unless its citizens— even those espousing hateful ideas (like the American Nazis)—have freedom of expression. But democracy requires more than political freedoms: it means government by the people.

quently judged by the nature and scope of its liberties. Doing so makes sense, since it is hard to see how a government can be democratic if its subjects do not have basic freedoms. The converse, however, does not hold: The fact that people enjoy rights and liberties does not necessarily mean that they live in a democracy. Being able to criticize President Bush's economic policies in a letter to the editor is an important test of democracy; but being able to take part in the making of those policies is an even more important one. It is essential, then, not to confuse political freedoms with political power. This is where the second condition of democracy, self-government, comes in.

DEMOCRACY AS SELF-GOVERNMENT The word *democracy* means *government by the people.* And the people do not govern unless they control

in some sense what government does. This definition rests on three principles:

- **Popular sovereignty**. A country's citizens are the ultimate source of political power, and their wishes, not those of a privileged individual, elite, or class, determine public policy. Laws, in other words, are legitimate only to the extent that they represent the informed consent of the people.
- **Political equality**. In deciding what policies will be adopted, each person's preferences count the same; no one's opinion carries more weight than anyone else's, even though some individuals are smarter or richer or stronger than others.
- **Majority rule**. When disagreements about policies arise, as they always do, the alternative supported by the most people prevails.

The key, then, lies in the connection between public opinion and public law: In an ideal democracy, the wishes of its citizens determine the policies and rules that are to be followed. Liberties are obviously indispensable, since they provide opportunities for meaningful participation. In the end, however, it is the involvement of men and women in decision making that defines democracy. Because the principles of equality and majority rule often clash, no one can expect to win every time, but individuals at least deserve to have their views taken into account. No matter what other virtues a system has, it is democratic only insofar as all its citizens have the opportunity to participate in making the laws that govern them.

Beautiful in its simplicity and compelling in its logic, the democratic ideal nevertheless raises troublesome questions. How, for instance, does one reconcile majority rule with individual liberties? Can the majority abolish freedom of speech? Does it have the right to outlaw certain religious practices? Suppose a majority favors banning handguns, but does not feel very strongly about the matter. Should it have its way over a minority that adamantly opposes gun control? Or suppose the majority is very poorly informed. Should it govern anyway? Problems of this sort have troubled philosophers for hundreds of years, and we cannot solve them in these pages. But, as we proceed, keep in mind how complex the concept of democracy is.

Direct Versus Representative Democracy

In an ideal democracy people would gather together to debate issues of mutual concern and pass laws. This sort of **direct democracy** is common in town meetings of small New England communities. Yet in spite of the emergence of modern communications, this method of governing does not seem practical for an industrial society with more than 250 million inhabitants spread over thousands of square miles. How could they ever meet at one time in one place to debate and vote on controversies as complicated as nuclear arms control and budget deficits? The idea of having Americans settle these matters in a town hall meeting appears woefully unrealistic.

A more workable alternative is **representative democracy**. The members of a representative democracy choose agents who act on their behalf. This form of government is democratic because sovereignty still resides in the people, because everyone has an equal voice in the selection of the leaders, and because the policies the representatives adopt reflect the will of the majority of citizens. Not necessarily true

Most important, the representatives who make and administer policy are accountable to their constituents. **Accountability**, in fact, is the heart of the system: If the nurse, the carpenter, and the lawyer cannot govern on their own, they at least have the right to demand that their leaders do it for them in a way that serves their interests, or, if there is disagreement, the interests of the majority. Should representatives violate this trust they can be replaced.

The mechanism that keeps public servants accountable is free and periodic elections, which give the voters a chance to judge officeholders not only on their promises for the future but on their past performance as well. Whenever incumbents fail to carry out the people's will, they can be voted out of office at the next election. Representation thus preserves the principles of

In a representative democracy, citizens usually do not make decisions directly but have the right to choose policymakers and hold them accountable in periodic elections.

popular sovereignty, political equality, and majority rule while avoiding the unwieldiness of direct democracy.

This form of government is not foolproof, however. Representatives are presumably guided by public opinion, but all too often opinions are so fragmented that it is impossible to tell who wants what. Or demands may contradict one another, as when the inhabitants of a city ask for increased police protection and lower property and sales taxes. Another problem: Should representative government simply give people what they want or what in its judgment the citizens really need? Foreign aid is not popular with the person in the street, but presidents, Democratic and Republican alike, maintain that it enhances the country's long-run interests. Finally, do we want our leaders to merely count votes in support of proposed policies, or do we also want them to weigh the quality of the alternatives? It is an important question. Unless one wants robots as leaders, they have to have leeway to exercise judgment—but how much leeway?

Is the United States a Representative Democracy?

Despite these theoretical difficulties, the American Constitution created a representative form of government. Its authors, skeptical of the masses' ability and self-discipline to govern and fearful that direct democracy would degenerate into mob rule, established a **republic**. A republic is a system in which power is exercised by elected officials, not by the people themselves.

Although authority in the early Republic supposedly resided in the populace, it was in fact vested in a minority of citizens. Propertyless workers, tenant farmers, blacks, Native Americans, the poor, and women were all barred from voting and other forms of participation. By the early twentieth century, though, the right to vote had been progressively expanded. Indeed, conventional wisdom today holds that the expansion of the suffrage (the right to vote) has succeeded in making the United States the world's largest, most vigorous representative democracy.

Whether this claim stands up to close scrutiny remains to be seen, but elections—the central feature of representation—certainly do dominate our political life. After all, we elect more office-holders than any country on earth. Altogether we vote on more than 500,000 public officials, from president of the United States to register of the wills in New Castle, Delaware. In 1988, Americans elected a president, 34 senators, 435 representatives, and 12 governors, as well as state legislators, judges, mayors, sheriffs, and town commissioners by the score. Campaigns have become a growth industry; many hundreds of millions of dollars are spent every two years on elections. All of this activity, according to many observers, is evidence of a healthy representative democracy.

As one bit of proof they cite the 1980 election. Polls showed that voters were upset by inflation, big government, and the apparent decline in America's military strength, conditions they blamed partly on the Democrats who had been in power for the previous four years. Ronald Reagan's election, the switch in control of the Senate from the Democrats to the Republicans, and the subsequent changes in economic policy such as the 25 percent cut in income taxes convinced many that the people have the power to alter dramatically the course of government.

Still there are grounds for doubt. Remember that for representative government to work several conditions have to be satisfied. First, voters must be responsible. Going to the polls once every two or four years is not enough. In addition, they have to pay attention to politics, to participate regularly, to be familiar with major policies and know how various alternatives affect their interests, and to find out where the candidates and parties stand on the main issues. Second, and equally important, the system itself has responsibilities. The electoral process, for example, has to produce qualified candidates who clearly state their platforms. Different points of view have to be heard. The press and parties have to help inform the electorate. What good is the right to vote if there are no meaningful alternatives or you cannot find out much about the choices that you do have?

Representative government, then, does not exist just because a constitution gives its citizens the right to vote or because elections are held periodically. The heart and soul of the system lie not in forms but in content, in what men and women actually do. We sometimes forget that it is a two-way street in which both voters and institutions have obligations.

Applying these standards to the United States, one sees an enormous disparity between the ideal and the reality. Even a quick glance at voting statistics shows the width of the gap. Only about half of the eligible electorate bothers to vote in presidential elections, and turnout in congressional and state and local contests is even lower, frequently dropping to less than 40 percent.

Equally disturbing, we live in a time of persistent trade imbalances, huge budget deficits, environmental degradation, an epidemic of drug abuse, and the threat of nuclear annihilation. But in choosing among candidates to deal with these matters, people often feel that they are picking at best between Tweedledee and Tweedledum, or at worst between the lesser of two evils. Finally, as campaigns deteriorate into mudslinging contests, the doors of government swing open to narrow-based, single-issue interest groups that frequently place the desires of their members above national needs.

Thus, when the United States is described as a democracy, even a representative one, there is room for doubt. These concerns lead others to offer different explanations of how the system really works.

Checkpoint

- Civil or political liberties are essential for democracy. According to some theorists, social and psychological freedoms are just as important.
- Democracy implies more than having rights, however; it means government by the people.
- Democracy rests on three principles: popular sovereignty, political equality, and majority rule.
- Direct democracy means that the people themselves make collective decisions; in a representative system elected officials who are accountable to the people do.
- For representative democracy to work, both citizens and institutions have responsibilities.
- Although the United States has the trappings of representative democracy, much evidence suggests that it works imperfectly.

PLURALISM

Pluralism is the theory that groups, not the people as a whole, govern the United States. These organizations, which include among others unions, trade and professional associations, environmentalists, civil rights activists, business and financial lobbies, and formal and informal coalitions of like-minded citizens, influence the making and administration of laws and policy. Since the participants in this process constitute only a tiny fraction of the populace, the public acts mainly as bystanders.

Indeed, some pluralists believe that direct democracy is not only unworkable; it is not even necessarily desirable. Besides the logistical problems of having every citizen meet at one time to decide policies, political issues require continuous and expert attention, which the average citizen does not have. Robert Dahl, a noted pluralist, suggested in one of his early writings that in societies like ours "politics is a sideshow in the great circus of life."[7] Most people, he explained, concentrate their time and energies on activities involving work, family, health, friendship, recreation, and the like. Other pluralists go further. They worry that the common person lacks the virtues—reason, intelligence, patience—for self-government and that direct democracy leads to anarchy and the loss of freedom.[8]

Nor do pluralists think that representative democracy works as well in practice as in theory. Voting is important, to be sure. But Americans vote for representatives, not for specific policy alternatives. A candidate's election cannot always be interpreted as an endorsement of a particular course of action. Politicians frequently win office with only a "plurality" of the votes—that is, they receive more votes than their opponents—but not with a *majority* of the total *eligible* electorate. President Reagan, for example, received approximately 51 percent of the ballots cast in 1980, but his total constituted only about a quarter of the votes of all potential voters, since only 55 percent of those eligible to participate actually went to the polls. Furthermore, a first choice among candidates is not necessarily the same as a first choice among policies. The people who elected President Reagan did not all agree with his positions on social security, taxes, national defense, foreign policy, and the environment. Many of them, in fact, were probably voting *against* his opponent rather than *for* Reagan himself.

If Americans do not decide major controversies themselves or indirectly through elections, how are such matters resolved? Pluralists are convinced that public policy emerges from competition among groups. Since relatively few people participate actively in this process, power, it might seem, would be concentrated in few hands. Before drawing any dire conclusions about the possible undemocratic nature of this form of government, however, it is necessary to look at political power as pluralists see it.

The Pluralist View of Power

Everyone recognizes **political power** when they see it: Congress raises taxes; the president sends troops to Panama; the Supreme Court declares the death penalty constitutional; a police officer tells a motorist to pull off the road. In each instance a group or person makes others do something they would not otherwise do.[9] Seen from this perspective, the definition of power seems simple enough. Yet the term is loaded with implications that must be fully grasped if one is to understand pluralism.

RESOURCES In the first place, power is not an identifiable property that humans possess in fixed amounts. Rather, people are powerful because they control various **resources**. Resources are assets that can be used to force others to do what one wants. Politicians become powerful because they command resources that people want or fear or respect. The list of possibilities is virtually endless: legal authority, money, prestige, skill, knowledge, charisma, legitimacy, free time, experience, celebrity, and public support. Civil rights activists in the 1960s relied mainly on their numbers and the legitimacy of their cause to get their way, whereas corporate executives frequently depend on their access to officeholders, control of information, and campaign contributions. Whatever the case, pluralists emphasize that power is not a physical entity that individuals either have or do not have, but flows from a variety of different sources.

POTENTIAL VERSUS ACTUAL POWER Pluralists also stress the differences between potential and actual power. **Actual power** means the ability to compel someone to do something; **potential power** refers to the *possibility* of turning resources into actual power. Cash, one of many resources, is only a stack of bills until it is put to work. A millionaire may or may not be politically influential; it all depends on what the wealth is spent for—trips to the Bahamas or trips to Washington. Martin Luther King, Jr., for example, was certainly not a rich person. But by using resources such as his forceful personality, organizational skills, and especially the legitimacy of his cause, he had a greater impact on American politics than most wealthy people. A particular resource like money cannot automatically be equated with power because the resource can be used skillfully or clumsily, fully or partially, or not at all.

Three of the major tenets of the pluralist school are (1) resources and hence potential power are widely scattered throughout society; (2) at least some resources are available to nearly everyone; and (3) at any time the amount of potential power exceeds the amount of actual power.

SCOPE OF POWER Finally, and perhaps most important, no one is all-powerful. An individual or group that is influential in one realm may be weak in another. Large military contractors certainly throw their weight around on defense matters, but how much sway do they have on agricultural or health policies? A measure of power, therefore, is its **scope**, or the range of areas where it is successfully applied. Pluralists believe that with few exceptions power holders in America usually have a relatively limited scope of influence.

For all these reasons, power cannot be taken for granted. One has to observe it empirically in order to know who really governs.[10] The best way to do this, pluralists believe, is to examine a wide range of specific decisions, noting who took which side and who ultimately won and lost. Only by keeping score on a variety of controversies can one begin to identify actual power holders.

The pluralists' view of power underlies their interpretation of how the American political system operates, a topic to which we now turn.

Although Martin Luther King, Jr., was not a wealthy person like real estate tycoon Donald Trump, he was able to mobilize various political resources to advance the civil rights of blacks. Pluralists believe that resource mobilization, not wealth, determines political power in the United States.

The Characteristics of Pluralism

Perhaps the key characteristic of American government, according to pluralists, is that it is dominated not by a single elite but rather by a *multiplicity* of relatively small groups, some of which are well organized and funded, some of which are not. Although a few are larger and more influential than the others, the scope of their power, far from being universal, is restricted to relatively narrow areas such as defense, agriculture, or banking.

A second characteristic is that the groups are politically autonomous, or independent.[11] They have the right and freedom to do business in the political marketplace. How well they fare depends not on the indulgence of a higher authority but on their own skill in rallying political resources. Because a diverse society like ours contains so many potential factions, political autonomy guarantees constant, widespread, and spirited competition among these organizations.

Third, intergroup competition leads to countervailing influence: The power of one group tends to cancel that of another so that a rough equilibrium results. Group memberships overlap as well. Members of one association, in other words, might belong to another, even competing, group. Overlapping memberships reduce the intensity of conflicts because loyalties are often spread among many organizations.

A fourth characteristic is the openness of the system. It is open in two senses. First, most organizations are seldom if ever completely shut off from the outside. They continuously recruit new members from all walks of life. Second, the availability of unused resources constantly encourages the formation of new groups. Stimulated by threats to their interests or sensitized to injustices, or for whatever reason, individuals frequently unite for political action. In the process groups mine untapped resources. This happened in 1989 when a Supreme Court decision gave states greater latitude in restricting abortions.[12] The Court's action so scared and angered pro-choice groups that they accelerated their organizing efforts to prevent states from enacting stiffer antiabortion laws.

Pluralists judge society not by its actual equality but by its equality of political opportunity. Americans, they contend, have a comparatively equal chance to participate in government. By mobilizing resources (collecting signatures on a petition, for example) they can make existing groups share their influence, or they can create new organizations that will compete with established ones.

The fifth characteristic of the system is the endless quest by groups and office seekers for public support. Even though the masses do not govern directly, their opinions are a resource that can be used by one organization against another. In a country where the belief in popular control of government is so deeply ingrained, people feel compelled to sell their causes to the public and are frequently judged winners or losers by their standings in the polls. What else explains the millions of dollars spent on advertising? What else accounts for the demand for public relations consultants? Why else is so much attention lavished on public opinion surveys? The answers lie in the widely shared belief that a group with popular backing has an important advantage over one that lacks it, even if the masses do not actually take part in decision making.

The public also exerts influence by choosing leaders, most of whom back and are backed by organized groups. So important is this responsibility that one scholar defined democracy as "an institutional arrangement for arriving at political decisions in which [groups] acquire power to decide by means of a competitive struggle for the people's vote."[13]

The final characteristic of pluralism is consensus on the "rules of the game." Consensus, or widespread agreement, among political activists and leaders on democratic principles and values holds the system together. These people accept regular and open elections, the right to vote, majority rule, political equality, free speech, the right to assemble, and the other rules that make peaceful and orderly politics possible. They tolerate differences of opinion. And, of utmost significance, they abide by the outcomes of elections.

Some pluralists contend that, since this acceptance of democratic norms is higher among leaders than the general public, political disagreements are best settled at the top, where they can be dealt with fairly and dispassionately.

Keeping the intolerant and shortsighted masses at bay helps ensure the system's safety and stability.[14] The theory, in short, argues that American government stays free because its main participants, the individuals who actually make policy, agree on a code of conduct that is not always shared by the public at large.

Since it is fair to say that pluralism is the most widely accepted interpretation of American government, it might be useful to consider a concrete example to clarify the theory's main points.

A Case Study of Pluralism: The B-1 Bomber

The decision to design and produce the B-1 bomber has been one of Washington's longest standing controversies. The B-1 battle, which began more than 20 years ago and continues today, contains many of the traits of traditional American politics: election promises and back-room deals, grass roots organizations and corporate money, public relations campaigns and private lobbying, lofty rhetoric about national security and crass selfishness. It has been, as is often the case, a David and Goliath struggle. On one side has stood Rockwell International Corporation, a mammoth aerospace firm with more than $1 billion in annual sales, and its ally in the Pentagon, the United States Air Force. Opposing these giants has been a loose coalition of pacifists, clergy, environmentalists, scientists, and scholars, inspired and led initially by the tiny American Friends Service Committee (AFSC), a Quaker-sponsored peace organization.

What have they been arguing about? Beginning in the early 1970s the air force claimed that its strategic bomber, the B-52, was obsolete. Although modernized several times, the B-52 remained a large, noisy behemoth that lacked the maneuverability to penetrate Russian air defenses. Demanding a plane based on current technology, the air force proposed an awesome (and expensive) weapon. The B-1, with a range of 6000 miles, was to have a low profile (a radar image only a seventh the size of the B-52's), a rapid takeoff capability, and the latest in electronic warfare equipment. It would be able to carry conventional or nuclear bombs or cruise missiles while flying over 750 miles an hour at treetop level. On the drawing board, at any rate, it was a plane Buck Rogers would be proud to fly.

The plane's detractors, however, maintained that the Defense Department was buying a white elephant. Put aside its cost—more than $150 million for each plane. Put aside its vulnerability—it could be attacked by "look down, shoot down" enemy aircraft. Put aside cheaper alternatives—many of the B-1's missions could be performed by refurbishing the B-52 or assigning them to fighter bombers. Put aside all these considerations, the critics pointed out, and the fact remained that the B-1 would be out of date almost before the first one lifted off the ground. For within a few years of its deployment, a newer, ultrasophisticated "stealth" bomber (eventually labeled the B-2) would be available. The newer plane would incorporate techniques that would make it nearly invisible to enemy radar.* Of what use would the B-1 be then? What the air force wanted was really nothing more than an expensive interim antique that would drain funds away from more urgent priorities.

To build or not. It was a question of great national significance, with thousands of jobs, billions of dollars, and enormous institutional resources hanging in the balance. But just as significant was what the handling of the issue revealed about the workings of government in the United States. It particularly well illustrates the strengths and weaknesses of the pluralist interpretation of who governs.

When in the late 1960s the air force began planning for the B-52's replacement, the B-1 attracted relatively little opposition.[15] But by 1974, as appropriations for the plane climbed to $500 million, individuals in and out of government began to question its wisdom. In October the Friends Service Committee convened a meeting of like-minded groups to establish the National Campaign Against the B-1. Operating on a shoestring budget, the organization marshaled the free time, energy, and knowledge of hundreds of volunteers who wrote letters, at-

tended marches and vigils, and lobbied public officials. The coalition's leaders thus forged a new force that confronted the titans in favor of the B-1.

As is often the case in pluralist politics, the battle was fought mainly by groups—in this case, the National Campaign on one side, Rockwell and the Pentagon on the other—and, like so many important but technical controversies, was waged out of view of the public. It was a contest of resource mobilization: Both parties recruited new members; both created information networks; both lobbied uncommitted legislators. At first sight it might have seemed an unfair contest: Rockwell and the air force versus a loose collection of Quakers, environmentalists, scientists, pacifists, and other citizens in the National Campaign. But true to the pluralist concept, resources come in different packages. Rockwell and its subcontractors doubtlessly spent more money, but the coalition held more rallies, circulated more studies, contacted more research institutions, and knocked on more doors.

After two years, the B-1's opponents scored a major victory. In July 1976 Jimmy Carter, a candidate for the Democratic presidential nomination, announced his opposition to the new bomber, and several months after taking office, canceled its production. Many thanked (or blamed) the National Campaign for this decision: "Without their efforts it is very unlikely that the B-1 would have been an issue, and in that sense they performed a very important function. . . . They got Carter to take a stand on the B-1 when he knew little about it, and got him involved in a way that otherwise would not have happened."[16]

President Carter's action did not end the controversy—not by a long shot, as we will see—but it has been taken as evidence that pluralism works. In this instance a small group working against heavy odds successfully mobilized various resources to thwart a large industrial corporation and its allies in and out of government. It seemed to show that groups emerge to check and balance existing centers of power. And although the public did not participate directly, as in a direct democracy, neither was it under the thumb of a closed ruling body. Vigorous competition among organizations kept the system

---

*Ironically, the stealth bomber itself has run into enormous criticism, and many military analysts and legislators think it, too, is a waste of money.

free and open. Note, finally, that both sides played according to well-established rules of the game.

Of course, not every group in society succeeds; many, in fact, do not even try. Yet the wide availability of unused resources ensures that success happens often enough to keep the ruling groups on their toes.

Is American Government Pluralistic?

Is pluralism really how the United States operates in general? Although differing on details, many journalists, social scientists, and politicians would probably agree that it does work in roughly this fashion, at least most of the time. But pluralism has its critics too. They charge, first, that it does not adequately describe who governs and, second, even if it did, pluralism is an undesirable form of government.

PLURALISM IS A FAULTY DESCRIPTION The principal objection to the pluralist interpretation is that it overstates the opportunities to use political resources. Certainly all kinds of resources are potentially available, but some appear to be superior to others. Money, for instance, is a resource that can buy many others. The chief executive officer of a corporation like Rockwell International can purchase information, free time, advisers, access, prestige—the very things, in short, that make one successful in politics and that many people have difficulty acquiring.

More devastating to the theory, critics assert, is the severe inequality in the distribution of resources. Needless to say, the clergy can vote and hand out leaflets, but can they really compete for power with industrial giants like Rockwell International? Does a small Quaker committee have the same impact in the marketplace of ideas as the Pentagon and its allies? True, the "movers

The giant aerospace firm, Rockwell International, along with other defense contractors and the Pentagon, lost in the early rounds of the struggle with the National Campaign Against the B-1 to stop development of the bomber. Many political scientists interpreted Rockwell's loss as evidence that pluralism works, but several years later the Reagan administration revived the B-1 program.

and shakers" in government cannot and do not ignore the common person. But paying attention to the public is not the same as sharing power with it. The top layers of society, according to pluralism's critics, have a distinct advantage. Political scientist E. E. Schattschneider put the matter simply: "The flaw in the pluralist heaven is that the heavenly chorus sings with a strong upper-class accent."[17] Politically valuable resources, in other words, tend to be concentrated among the rich and already powerful members of society. Those at the bottom have much less to work with. Thus, if success in the political arena depends on mobilizing resources, some groups will always have an unequal advantage.

The B-1 story is again instructive. President Carter's cancellation order seemed to give the National Campaign victory over its adversaries, Rockwell and the Pentagon. They were not vanquished, however, and neither was the B-1. Having been dealt a devastating blow, the air force switched tactics. It began pushing for a strategic weapons launcher (SWL) to carry cruise missiles. (Launched from the ground, submarines, or airplanes, cruise missiles are rockets that can travel a thousand miles or more with nuclear or conventional warheads.) Not surprisingly the SWL's specifications were designed in such a way that the B-1, now promoted as a missile carrier, would be the logical choice.[18] Congress, perhaps unaware of the ploy, appropriated $30 million for the project, and the B-1 continued to live in the shadows until a more sympathetic administration came along.

It didn't have to wait long because Ronald Reagan, a staunch proponent of increased military spending, won the presidency in 1980. Early in his term he persuaded Congress to allocate $4.8 billion to the B-1, and by 1990 more than 90 had rolled off the assembly line. Why did Rockwell and its supporters ultimately triumph?*

---

*With the advantage of hindsight it appears that it was a flawed victory. The B-1 has encountered countless technical problems since it became operational, and many military analysts doubt that it can perform its missions satisfactorily. The entire fleet was grounded in 1989, for example, after one plane's movable wings ruptured a fuel tank. *New York Times*, March 29, 1989, p. 1.

Pluralists respond that in the give and take of politics everyone has to expect victories and losses. After winning in the early going, the B-1's opponents simply lost in the later rounds. Critics, on the other hand, claim that the fight was fixed from the beginning. Yes, the plane's opponents theoretically had the freedom to organize and fight. But what chance did they really have against an enormous company with friends in the legislature, subcontractors in nearly every state, and a cabinet department that ranks among the world's largest employers and that has classified data at its fingertips proving that the B-1, and nothing else, would meet the Soviet menace?

Such lopsided contests, critics contend, mock pretensions about competing groups, potential power, resource mobilization, and the rest of the pluralist dogma. Unused resources do not give people potential power. On the contrary, the concept only legitimizes the vast inequalities in influence in American political life, by creating the illusion that everyone who wants to can participate in decision making. The hard fact is that we live in a country dominated by a few extremely powerful groups. And, in fact, without abandoning the idea that politics is characterized mainly by competition among organized groups, many pluralists have conceded that the system frequently works to the disadvantage of the lower classes and the poor.[19]

PLURALISM IS MORALLY BANKRUPT A second criticism is that pluralism contains a contradiction. The system, it appears, functions best when ordinary citizens govern the least. For this reason, the theory has been called "democratic elitism."[20] It is an interesting contradiction, for how can a government of elites be considered democratic?

The answer, pluralists reply, is that the system is neither autocratic nor totalitarian; that is, leaders do not possess unlimited authority. Instead, the groups that ultimately make decisions draw members from all segments of society and govern by rules that most of us would consider fair. Furthermore, there are hundreds of these organizations at all levels of government—local, state, and national—none of which totally dominates the others. And the vast majority of citizens, while perhaps not in direct control, nevertheless have an indirect voice through the attention paid to public opinion. Last, and most significant, pluralistic politics is an open and dynamic process in which unused resources are available to both established groups and their potential opponents. If one group goes too far, others can take up the slack to bring it back in line.

Skeptics, however, point out that even if pluralism works as well as claimed, it still leaves 90 to 95 percent of Americans on the sidelines as spectators rather than participants. What are needed are institutions that encourage public involvement. Individuals are not truly free until they learn how to make decisions and accept responsibility for their choices. Holding leaders accountable is not enough: insofar as possible, the people themselves should formulate the policies that their nation will follow. A pluralistic type of government does not encourage this sort of involvement. With its emphasis on group competition, pluralism does not motivate personal development. Lane Davis summarizes the point this way:

> Popular participation is reduced to the manageable task of choices in elections. This kind of participation is, at best, a pale and rather pathetic version of the responsible and active participation which was the aspiration of classical democracy.[21]

Checkpoint

- Pluralism defines power as getting someone to do something he or she would not otherwise do.
- Power flows from the manipulation of resources like money, prestige, and skill. Consequently, pluralists see a difference between potential power (having access to resources) and actual power (using the resources).
- The scope of power is usually limited.

- According to pluralist theory, American governments' main characteristics are: dispersal of power among many groups; free and open competition among groups; a stable system of checks and balances; mobilization of unused resources; appeals to public opinion and voters; and adherance to democratic norms and practices.
- Pluralism has been criticized on the grounds that it fails to see that resources are unequally distributed and is indifferent to the passive role the public plays.

THE POWER ELITE

Thomas Dye, a political scientist, and his students have been studying the upper echelons of leadership in America since 1972. These "top positions" encompassed the posts with the authority to run programs and activities of major political, economic, legal, educational, cultural, scientific, and civic institutions.[22] The occupants of these offices, Dye's investigators found, control half of the nation's industrial, communications, transportation, and banking assets, and two-thirds of all insurance assets. In addition, they direct about 40 percent of the resources of private foundations and 50 percent of university endowments.[23] Furthermore, less than 250 people hold the most influential posts in the executive, legislative, and judicial branches of the federal government, while approximately 200 men and women run the three major television networks and most of the national newspaper chains.[24]

Facts like these, which have been duplicated in countless other studies, suggest to many observers that power in the United States is concentrated in the hands of a single power elite. Scores of versions of this idea exist, probably one for each person who holds it, but they all interpret government and politics very differently than pluralists. Instead of seeing hundreds of competing groups hammering out policy, the

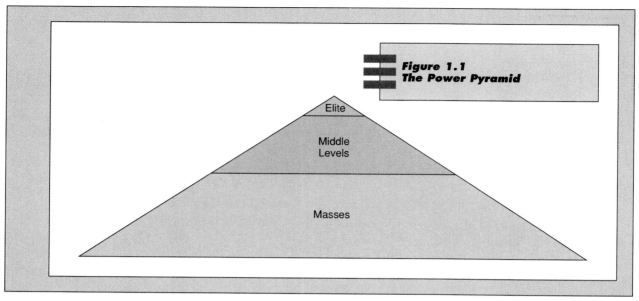

Figure 1.1
The Power Pyramid

Elite

Middle
Levels

Masses

The power elite school believes that a small power elite makes most significant decisions.
The middle level, which consists of members of Congress, state and local governments,
the media, and interest groups, deals mainly with relatively minor policies. The general
public has little direct impact on policy formation.

elite model perceives a pyramid of power (see Figure 1.1). At the top, a tiny elite makes all of the most important decisions for everyone below. A relatively small middle level consists of the types of individuals one normally thinks of when discussing American government: senators, representatives, mayors, governors, judges, lobbyists, and party leaders. The masses occupy the bottom. They are the average men and women in the country who are powerless to hold the top level accountable.

The power elite theory, in short, claims that a single elite, not a multiplicity of competing groups, decides the life-and-death issues for the nation as a whole, leaving relatively minor matters for the middle level and almost nothing for the common person. It thus paints a dark picture. Whereas pluralists are somewhat content with what they believe is a fair, if admittedly imperfect, system, the power elite school decries the grossly unequal and unjust distribution of power it finds everywhere.

People living in a country that prides itself on democracy, that is surrounded by the trappings of free government, and that constantly witnesses the comings and goings of elected officials may find the idea of a power elite farfetched. Yet many very intelligent social scientists accept it and present compelling reasons for believing it to be true. Thus, before dismissing it out of hand, one ought to listen to their arguments.

Characteristics of the Power Elite

According to C. Wright Mills, among the best known power elite theorists, the governing elite in the United States draws its members from three areas: (1) the highest political leaders, including the president and a handful of key cabinet members and close advisers; (2) major corporate owners and directors; and (3) high-ranking military officers.[25]

Even though these individuals constitute a close-knit group, they are not part of a conspiracy that secretly manipulates events in their own selfish interest. For the most part, the elite respects civil liberties, follows established constitutional principles, and operates openly and peacefully. It is not a dictatorship; it does not rely on terror, a secret police, or midnight arrests to get its way. It does not have to, as we will see.

Nor is its membership closed, although many members have enjoyed a head start in life by virtue of their being born into prominent families.* Nevertheless, those who work hard, enjoy good luck, and demonstrate a willingness to adopt elite values do find it possible to work into higher circles from below.

If the elite does not derive its power from repression or inheritance, from where does its strength come? Basically it comes from control of the highest positions in the political and business hierarchy and from shared values and beliefs.

TOP COMMAND POSTS In the first place, the elite occupies what Mills terms the top **command posts** of society. These positions give their holders enormous authority over not just governmental, but financial, educational, social, civic, and cultural institutions as well. A small group is able to take fundamental actions that touch everyone. Decisions made in the boardrooms of large corporations and banks affect the rates of inflation and employment. The influence of the chief executive officers of the IBM and DuPont corporations often rivals that of the secretary of commerce. In addition, the needs of industry greatly determine the priorities and policies of educational and research organizations, not to mention the chief economic agencies of government.

The power of the elite has also been enhanced by the close collaboration of political, industrial, and military organizations. As Washington has been called upon to play a more active role in domestic life, from regulating the business cycle

to inspecting children's sleepwear, government has come to depend on the corporate world to carry out many of its activities.† Conversely, industry now relies heavily on federal supports, subsidies, protection, and loans to ensure the success of its ventures. To be sure, business people and politicians constantly carp at each other. But the fact remains that they have grown so close that they prosper together far more than they do separately.

At the same time, the Cold War elevated the prestige and power of the military establishment. The United States has come a long way from the days of citizen-soldiers to its present class of professional warriors whose impact far transcends mere military affairs. The demands of foreign affairs, the dangers of potential adversaries, the sophistication and mystique of new weapons, and especially the development of the means of mass destruction have all given power and prestige to our highest military leaders.

As a group, then, this ruling triumvirate of politicians, corporate executives, and military officers has, by virtue of the positions they hold, unprecedented authority to make decisions of national and international consequence. But the mere occupancy of these command posts does not fully explain the effectiveness of their power. Of equal significance is their common outlook on life and their ability and willingness to act harmoniously on basic issues.

SHARED ATTITUDES AND BELIEFS Leafing through the pages of *Time* or *Newsweek* one quickly realizes that the members of the so-called power elite constantly squabble among themselves. Such disagreements, which have become part of the background noise of national politics, occur so frequently as to be taken as proof that not one but a multiplicity of elites exist.

According to Mills and others, however, these differences are vastly overshadowed by agreement on a world view.[26] This **world view** is a set of values, beliefs, and attitudes that shapes the elite's perceptions of government and prevents deep divisions from arising.

---

*Professor Dye, for example, concludes that 30 percent of the top echelon come from what he defines as the "upper class," a stratum containing only 1 percent of the population. Dye, *Who's Running America? The Conservative Years* 4th ed. (Englewood Cliffs, N.J.: Prentice-Hall, 1986), p. 194.

---

†See Chapter 13 for more details.

The Pattern of Presidential Appointments: Insiders or Outsiders? ★★★

A good way to understand the power elite model is to consider the cabinets of recent presidents. First, listen to Carter, a Democrat, campaigning in 1976:

> The people of this country know from bitter experience that we are not going to get . . . changes merely shifting around the same group of insiders. . . . The insiders have had their chance and they have not delivered. . . . The time has come for . . . Americans to have a president who will turn the government of this country inside out.[a]

Now look at a few of the people he named to his cabinet:

- Secretary of State Cyrus Vance: A successful and wealthy corporation lawyer and board member of the Rockefeller Foundation, IBM, Pan Am, and *The New York Times*, Vance served both Presidents Kennedy and Johnson as an official in the Defense Department.
- Secretary of Defense Harold Brown: Before becoming president of the California Institute of Technology, Brown was secretary of the air force in the Johnson Administration and worked for Presidents Nixon and Ford on strategic arms control negotiations.
- Secretary of the Treasury W. Michael Blumenthal: A self-made millionaire director of the Bendix Corporation, Blumenthal was a U.S. trade representative during the Kennedy-Johnson years.

President Reagan, another self-styled out-

sider, also promised to bring new blood to the executive branch. But like Carter's "outsiders," most had previous government experience, most were lawyers or executives in charge of large companies, and all had traveled in the upper reaches of power and influence for years. Two examples:

- Secretary of Treasury Donald Regan: The former head of Merrill, Lynch, one of the nation's largest stockbrokers, Regan was in addition vice-chairman of the New York Stock Exchange and a member of the Business Roundtable, a powerful corporate lobbying organization.
- Secretary of Defense Caspar Weinberger: Once an official of the Bechtel Group, Inc., a huge multinational construction company, Weinberger had previously served as director of the Office of Management and Budget and secretary of Health, Education and Welfare under President Nixon. In addition, he served on the boards of directors of Pepsico, Quaker Oats, and other companies.

Even though he was vice-president at the time of his election, George Bush promised during the campaign to bring "wholesale change" and "new faces" to Washington. Yet he too chose men and women who had been working for years in the inner circles of power:

- Secretary of Treasury Nicholas Brady: A graduate of Yale and Harvard, Brady

From top to bottom: Cyrus Vance, Caspar Weinberger, Nicholas Brady. People like these men have been working in the upper circles of government for years and lead some social scientists to believe that decision making is controlled by a power elite.

H. J. Heinz and owns stocks and other assets worth millions of dollars.

- Secretary of State James A. Baker III: Heir to a Texas family fortune, Baker attended Princeton University and the University of Texas and joined one of Houston's largest law firms. He was a deputy secretary of commerce during the Ford administration and then served first as President Reagan's chief of staff and later as secretary of the treasury. Like Brady, Baker holds several million dollars in assets.

- National Security Advisor Brent Scowcroft: Scowcroft, who graduated from West Point, became President Richard Nixon's military aide in 1969 and then deputy to National Security Advisor Henry Kissinger. Scowcroft has been called "one of Washington's permanent fixtures," an "old hand," one of the "wise men," and an "establishmentarian."[b]

This list is selective and does not prove that Democrats and Republicans are the same or that there are no differences between conservative and moderate presidents. But believers in the power elite theory use these background characteristics to demonstrate that presidential appointments usually involve people with years of government and corporate experience and with extensive formal and informal contacts with other establishment personalities. They are individuals who, if not born into the upper crust of society, were very much a part of it at the time of their appointments. In a nutshell, the people who rule the world of large industry and finance rule the world of politics and vice versa.

[a]Quoted in Roger Morris, "Jimmy Carter's Ruling Class," *Harper's*, October 1977, p. 37.
[b]Henry Allen, *Washington Post National Weekly Edition*, January 9–15, 1989, p. 15.

was chairman and chief executive officer of Dillon, Read, & Co. at the time of his appointment. He served on the boards of directors of several large corporations including Purolator Courier, NCR, and

Members of the elite agree on the basic outlines of the free enterprise system including private property, the unequal and concentrated distribution of wealth, and the sanctity of private economic power. They take giantism in the world of commerce for granted. More important, they are united in their belief that the primary responsibility of government is to maintain a favorable climate for business. Other governmental responsibilities, such as social welfare and concern for the environment, are secondary to that task.

What produces the acceptance of this world view? Participants in the elite tend to read the same newspapers, join the same clubs, live in the same neighborhoods, send their children to the same schools (usually private and the ones they themselves attended), and belong to the same churches and charities. They work and play together, employ one another, and intermarry. They share, in a word, a life-style that brings them together in mutually reinforcing contact.

Moreover, they undergo similar apprenticeships. Dye finds that 54 percent of the top corporate leaders and 42 percent of our highest political officials went to just 12 private colleges including Yale, Harvard, Princeton, and Stanford.[27]

But it is while advancing through their professions that the unity of thought begins to emerge. By the time men and women reach the top of the corporate or professional ladder, their common experiences have given them a shared way of looking at economics and politics so that they experience and react to events in the same ways. When they enter public service these people cannot, as Mills explains, shed their heritage:

> The interesting point is how impossible it is for such [political appointees] to divest themselves of their engagement with the corporate world in general and with their own corporations in particular. Not only their money, but their friends, their interests, their training—their lives in short—are deeply involved in this world. . . . The point is not so much financial or personal interests in a given corporation, but identification with the corporate world. To ask a man suddenly to divest himself of these interests and sensibilities is almost like asking a man to become a woman.[28]

This inability to "divest" oneself of one's past is perhaps what once led a former chairman of General Motors to declare "What's good for GM is good for America."

Presidential appointments to top cabinet posts illustrate the shared attitudes and common experiences of the power elite. Candidates for the presidency regularly blame the nation's problems on current officeholders and always promise to put "new" people with fresh ideas into their administrations. But, as A Closer Look shows (p. 22), the newcomers invariably come from the highest levels of the corporate, political, and military world.

Having seen how the governing elite derives its strength, it is important to consider how this power is exercised in the political arena. What roles do the three parts of the pyramid—the elite, the middle level, and the masses—play in American politics?

Distribution of Political Power

THE ROLE OF THE ELITE   Imagine a tree in the dead of winter. With its leaves gone its outline is clearly visible. At the bottom, of course, is the trunk—cut it and the whole tree topples. Higher up three or four main branches support lesser branches, which in turn support still smaller ones until one comes to the twigs at the edges. Cutting the twigs does not change the tree very much. As one saws off branches lower down, however, the shape—and possibly the existence of the tree—is affected. In other words, to determine the direction and extent of growth of the tree, one cannot simply prune off a few boughs at the top but has to cut main limbs or the trunk.

Public policies can be thought of in the same way. There is a hierarchy among them in the sense that some (corresponding to the trunk and main branches) support others. **Trunk decisions** represent basic choices—whether or not to create a welfare system, for example—that, once decided, necessitate making lesser choices—whether the poor should be given cash or food stamps or both. Whoever makes the trunk decisions sets the agenda for subsequent debates about secondary or branch and twig policies.

Return once more to the B-1 controversy. As

important as it seemed, the B-1 in the eyes of power elite theorists is only a twig. In order to appreciate their contention, ask why the United States needs bombers in the first place. Why not rely on land-based missiles and submarines to deter the Soviet Union?

The answer lies in a prior decision to maintain a "triad," a nuclear retaliatory force consisting of land-based missiles, submarines, *and* bombers. Having three separate weapons systems, American defense planners concluded, provides an extra margin of safety in the event of a confrontation with the Russians. Are they right? Do we need three types, or could we get along with two? This is an important question—far more important than whether we develop a new bomber or keep an old one—and who decides it structures the debate on this and a host of other issues. Suppose, for a moment, the United States had decided that bombers were unnecessary. The B-1 debate would then be moot and resources allocated to it could be devoted to other purposes such as conventional arms or schools or tax reductions.

Yet the triad is itself only a branch policy; it rests on an even more fundamental policy, **containment**.* Early in the post-World War II era, the United States had to develop a policy toward the Soviet Union. Some urged a conciliatory approach that would recognize Russia's legitimate security concerns. Others took a harder line. Fearing the spread of international communism, they advocated the use of diplomatic, economic, and especially military means to contain what they perceived to be inexorable Soviet expansionism. The first alternative emphasized cooperation, the second containment; the first implied relatively modest national security efforts, the second enormous expenditures for arms and foreign aid.

Ultimately the United States adopted the strategy of containment, which was the backbone of American foreign policy until the 1990s.

Containment represented a trunk decision, while most other defense policies such as the triad or the B-1 are either branches or twigs. Containing the Russians put us on a long and arduous path, over which we trod for nearly half

a century. National defense swallowed a huge portion of the federal budget; it called for the maintenance of an enormous peacetime army; it led us into alliances with nations in the farthest corners of the globe, including some of the most corrupt and dictatorial regimes on earth; it demanded massive military aid programs; it consumes the talents of our scientific establishment and the attention of our national leaders. Plainly, containment, unlike the B-1, was no ordinary policy but a fundamental commitment of American resources and energies.

Who decides trunk decisions? According to the power elite theory, the top of the pyramid does. The middle levels of government (the Congress, the courts, the states) worry mainly about how best to implement them. This seems to have been the case in the period after World War II when containment first emerged. Most of the key decisions were made behind closed doors in the White House, the State Department, and the Pentagon. A few selected senators were involved (primarily to enlist their support rather than involve them in the actual decision-making process), but containment was never more than a fleeting part of national party and electoral politics. Instead, once the policy had been formulated at the top it was sold to the public.

THE MIDDLE LEVEL Where does this put the workaday politicians, the inhabitants of the middle level of politics? Sadly, the elite school reports, their influence has largely dissipated over the years, leaving them with only the outer limbs and twigs to manage. It is certainly true that government in the middle is colorful and noisy and attracts the attention of the popular press. But for the most part its activities hide an important point: Far from competing with the power elite, professional politicians today have lost their ability to control the nation's destiny.

Elite theorists think that most of the participants in the middle are actually motivated by rather selfish and parochial interests. Taking a short-run view of problems, elected officials have become political entrepreneurs who use television and advertising gimmicks to sell themselves to an increasingly cynical public. In their hands policy becomes a means to an end, getting reelected, rather than an end in itself.

---

*Containment is explained more fully in Chapter 20.

Most important, they have lost the will and capacity to grapple with national and international issues. They seem all too eager to leave these questions to presidents and their inner circles. Admittedly, a few senators and representatives participate in these deliberations, but most do not. And neither do state and local officials. Thus, instead of debating the merits of containment or the triad, they are content to argue about how much of the B-1 will be built in their own hometowns.

Thirty years ago, C. Wright Mills lamented on this state of affairs:

> More and more of the fundamental issues never come to any point of decision before the Congress, or before its most powerful committees, much less before the electorate in campaigns. . . . When fundamental issues do come up for Congressional debate, they are likely to be so structured as to limit consideration, and even to be stalemated rather than resolved.[29]

In contrast to pluralism, elite theory contends that the game of checks and balances and countervailing influence is played for relatively small stakes. Because ordinary politicians are excluded from the higher circles, where fundamental choices are decided, the agenda is predetermined for them.[30] They are free to deal with issues that the power elite finds nonthreatening; the big questions the elite saves for itself.

THE PUBLIC What disturbs power elite theorists most, however, is the demise of the public as an independent force in civic affairs. Instead of initiating policy, or even controlling those who govern them, men and women in America have become passive spectators, cheering the heroes and booing the villains, but taking little or no direct part in the action. Citizens have become increasingly alienated and estranged from politics, as can be seen in the sharp decline in electoral participation over the last several decades. As a result, the control of their destinies has fallen into the lap of the power elite.

Today, of course, it is hard to deny the apathy and disinterest among average citizens. But whereas pluralists view this passivity as understandable (people are too preoccupied with other concerns to take part in public affairs), if not beneficial (too many individuals placing demands on government can clog the system), elite theorists see it as the inevitable consequence of important decisions being made at the highest levels. People lose interest to the degree that they lose control. Moreover, in spite of Independence Day platitudes about good citizenship, the elite

President Harry Truman's administration embarked on the policy of containment of the Soviet Union. Power elite theorists argue that a few individuals made this decision behind the scenes and then sold it to the public. Here Truman meets with a few members of his inner circle. From left to right: George C. Marshall, Paul G. Hoffman, and W. Averell Harriman.

The price of containment: containing the Soviet Union eventually led the United States into military involvement in Korea, a war that cost more than 30,000 American casualties.

does not really encourage mass participation. Such involvement would make its control too uncertain.

The containment strategy adopted after World War II illustrates this point. As noted previously, the initial policies, which were developed largely behind the scenes, called for drastic changes in the way the United States conducted foreign affairs. In the years after 1947 the United States fought a major war in Korea and began spending billions and billions of dollars at home and overseas for national security.

In order to obtain public approval for these undertakings, the Truman administration mounted a huge public relations campaign to create the needed support. As it and subsequent administrations emphasized the seriousness of the threat, the people were led to believe that they faced a ruthless enemy determined to take over the world by subversion if possible and by force if necessary. Yet they had almost no opportunity to hear a full debate between the proponents of containment and alternative policies. Nor did they decide the matter themselves. That the outcome might have been the same is not the issue. What matters is that the chance to make a trunk decision was effectively lost. Americans were consumers, rather than creators, of the policy.

Herein lies a supreme irony of American politics, Mills and his supporters claim. Foreign policy is a trunk. From it grow a host of decisions with far-reaching political, economic, social and moral implications. Since foreign relations affect everyone every day in every way, how can a country be democratic if it takes these matters out of the hands of its citizens? How can people be free unless they discuss and debate the things that affect them the most? The B-1 controversy, for all of its thunder and lightning, is not nearly as important as containment, which at the most critical moments was hardly mentioned in the halls of Congress or in election campaigns.

Elite theory tells us why this silence has lasted for so long: The power elite establishes the basic policy agenda in such areas as national security and economics. Of course, since it only sets the general guidelines, the middle level has plenty to do implementing them, but the public has been virtually locked out. Its main activities— wearing campaign buttons, expressing opinions to pollsters, voting every two or four years—are mostly symbolic. The people do not directly affect the direction of fundamental policies.

Is America Governed by a Power Elite?

Is elite theory correct? Are Americans governed by an omnipotent, unified bloc that imposes its will on national politics?

At first glance it does not seem to be a very compelling idea. We come across instances of political conflict all the time, and the people at the top seem to lose as often as they win. If business had its way on everything, there would be no pollution regulations, no child labor laws, no minimum wages, or no occupational safety standards. And as any admiral or general knows, Congress regularly cuts military appropriations. In view of these considerations, how can anyone take the idea of a power elite seriously?

"Ah, but these facts miss the point," the elite school replies. "The apparent setbacks are mostly symbolic, not real. Although social reforms reduce the unfortunate side effects of capitalism, they do not alter the basic distribution of wealth and power in the United States. The upper class may complain, but after half a century of government intervention in the economy, it remains very much in command. The masses, even though less materially deprived than in the past, still have little direct political control. Besides, improvements in the quality of life really cement capitalism in place by making workers healthier, more productive, and less rebellious."

This answer continues to leave questions unresolved, however. Who exactly is in the power elite? One doubts, for example, that generals, however many stars on their shoulders, have much voice in financial policy. It seems strange, then, for Mills to include them in the top leadership echelons.

Moreover, how does one distinguish among types of decisions? What is trivial to one observer may be vital to another. Rules governing factories may be "twigs," unless one happens to work in a noisy, dirty industry. Then they are of major concern. There is, in addition, a circularity in the elite position. It first claims that elites make major policies. When one points to the choices made by the middle level of government (health, safety, and welfare regulations, for example), elite theory dismisses them as twigs and branches. But on what grounds does it make this separation? How does one distinguish a trunk from a branch? Examples contrary to elite theory can always be rejected as not being sufficiently important.

And even granting that one can tell the trunks from the branches and twigs, does a power elite always make the former? The history of the American recognition of Israel suggests that the answer may be no.

After World War II, Jews everywhere pushed for the partition of the Middle Eastern region called Palestine into separate Jewish and Arab states. Muslim countries were bitterly opposed to the plan and promised to fight any efforts to create an Israeli nation. By early 1948, as the controversy was rapidly coming to a boil, war between the Arabs and Jewish inhabitants and immigrants to the area seemed inevitable.

The Truman administration was divided on whether Palestine should be partitioned or not. On one side, high-ranking officials in the State and Defense departments generally opposed the idea of a partition and the creation of a separate Jewish nation. Major American oil companies joined in this stance because they worried that conflict would jeopardize their commercial interests. But 1948 was an election year, and President Truman faced formidable opposition for reelection. Jewish voters constituted an important part of the Democratic party, and Truman came under intense pressure from domestic and international Zionists (that is, those who championed Israel's cause) to recognize and aid a new Israeli government. Many of the people who took this position were prominent citizens, but only a few would qualify for membership in a power elite.

It was no small matter, no twig: America's future in the area, which even then was considered vital to national security, hung in the balance. The decision, however it went, would affect Americans for decades.

Truman was pulled by both sides. At one point he lamented to a friend, "I have about come to the conclusion that the situation is not solvable as presently set up."[31] His top diplomatic advisers, supported by the oil companies, warned him of the dangers of supporting the Zionists. Yet to do otherwise would jeopardize his reelection campaign.

In the end Truman recognized Israel. When a provisional Jewish government was formed in Palestine in the spring of 1948, the United States quickly granted it diplomatic recognition and economic assistance. Scholars still argue about Truman's decision, but it seems clear that it was not made by a power elite. On the contrary, it seems to fit the pluralist model much better because of the group nature of the struggle.

The Weather
Today—Sunny, warmer, high in low 70s.
Tomorrow—Fair, warmer. Yesterday
—High 70 at 4:30 p. m., low 45 at 4:25
a. m. (Details on Page B-11)

Phone NA. 4200

The Washington Post

FINAL

Phone NA. 4200

NO. 26,266 — By The Washington Post Company. | Entered as Second Class Matter, Postoffice, Washington, D. C. | **WASHINGTON: SATURDAY, MAY 15, 1948** | CARRIER DELIVERY PER MONTH | Daily & Sunday $1.35 City Zone $1.50 elsewhere / Daily Only 90 / Sunday Only 45 | SINGLE COPY PRICE | Daily (city zone) / Sunday (elsewhere)

U. S. Recognizes Jewish State of Israel

5 Convicted In Looting Of $100,000 From Union

Faust Moreschi,
Other Officers
Of Hod Carriers
Face 2 Years, Fine

By Joseph Paull
Post Reporter

The five remaining defendants in the $100,000 labor...

He Wood
Mortimer Snerd Traveling To Golf Meet on Pig Train

Reelection Is Predicted By Truman

Tears Into GOP In Speech Before Young Democrats; 500 Cheer Loudly

By Edward T. Folliard
Post Reporter

President Truman made a scornful attack on the Republican Party by name last night, and calmly predicted that he would remain in the White...

New Jewish Flag Raised in Washington

Truman Acts Soon After New Nation Is Created

British Terminate Palestine Mandate; Efforts for Truce To Be Continued

By Ferdinand Kuhn, Jr.
Post Reporter

The United States last night recognized the new state of...

Despite the opposition of the State Department and large petroleum corporations, President Truman formally recognized the newly established nation of Israel, a decision that led many observers to question the power elite theory.

Checkpoint

- The power elite school argues that the United States is dominated by a single power elite.

- The elite, consisting of top politicians, corporate leaders, and certain members of the military establishment, draws its power from its control of major political, economic, legal, scientific, cultural, media, and educational institutions.

- The power elite is unified by a common world view, a basic set of attitudes and beliefs about how government and the economy do and should work.

- According to elite theory, it is important to distinguish between fundamental or trunk policies and branch and twig decisions.

- Beneath the power elite is the middle level of government consisting of senators and representatives, state and local politicians, lobbyists, the courts, and the political parties. This level deals with a predetermined agenda of relatively minor matters.

- The common people at the bottom of the power pyramid are mostly spectators whose involvement in government tends to be symbolic and ritualistic.

- The power elite model has been challenged on several grounds including vagueness in the definition of the elite, ambiguity in the types of decisions, and the fact that not all trunk decisions seem to be made by an elite.

WHO GOVERNS AMERICA?

Who governs America—the people, competing groups, or a power elite? It is not an easy question to answer. Part of the difficulty lies in the complexity of the theories. Each of them, for example, contains both *empirical* and *normative* components. That is, they claim to describe how American government *does* work and how it *should* work. As Table 1.1 indicates, pluralists believe that group competition keeps the United States more or less democratic, *and* they seem content with this system. Elite theorists, on the other hand, spy a power elite behind major decisions *and* wish that policy could be made more democratically. In this latter respect they are similar to democratic theorists who advocate direct, or at least stronger representative, democracy. The first step in studying American government, then, entails keeping separate what you want from what you think actually exists.

Even with this distinction in mind, judging the different models is not a simple task. Each of them presents a persuasive case. More impor-

tant, at this stage it may not even be wise to accept one to the exclusion of the others. The authors think that each theory contains many grains of truth, which is why in the following chapters we discuss how each approach applies to whatever aspect of government is being considered. You too may find that political institutions and practices combine elements of all three models or that a particular explanation convinces you in one instance but not in others.

Our goal, therefore, is not to present the theories as selections on a menu. You don't have to pick one over the others. Instead, use them as yardsticks. Try looking at elections through the eyes of first a pluralist, then a member of the power elite school, and finally a democratic theorist. Do the same for Congress, the courts, the bureaucracy, and all the other parts of the political system. In so doing, you may discover things that are otherwise easily overlooked.

The 1990s are an excellent time to think about the political system. The far reaching changes in the Soviet Union, Eastern Europe, and China mentioned at the chapter's beginning give Americans an opportunity to rethink fundamental for-

Table 1.1

Comparison of the Three Models of American Government

Model	Component: Empirical: How American Government *Does* Work	Normative: How American Government *Should* Work
Democratic:	Recognizes that the political system contains democratic elements, but in many respects it does not fit the ideal of either direct or representative democracy.	Strongly prefers as much direct democracy as possible and a strengthening of modes of personal political participation.
Pluralist:	Competition among groups keeps America stable and relatively democratic.	Despite shortcomings, the present system is a good one. Only relatively minor reforms needed.
Elite:	A power elite makes trunk decisions; middle levels deal with mostly minor policies; mass participation is largely symbolic.	Advocates more direct democracy or, at least, strengthened representative government.

eign and domestic policies. If the Cold War gradually turns to a warm peace, the United States may abandon its long-standing policy of containment. But what will take its place and who will decide? If the superpowers agree to substantial cuts in their conventional and nuclear forces, the economy may reap a "peace dividend," a sizable reduction in military spending that could be put to other uses. But what other uses? And, again, who will make the choices? If, on the other hand, international tensions increase, who will determine America's response?

However these events unfold, it will be instructive to see which interpretation of American government best fits the facts. After all, President Bush may have been right—we don't need to argue about which form of government is best. Nevertheless, to have a realistic and complete understanding of how American government works you have to observe it in action, to watch it grapple with basic conflicts and problems, and constantly to ask who is governing.

SUMMARY

In any society some form of government emerges to regulate conflict and provide collective goods.

Democracy means government by the people. Political freedoms such as the right to vote are essential but by themselves they do not define democracy. For a nation to be democratic in an ideal sense, its citizens also have to participate in the making of the laws that govern them. Direct democracy is not practical in large heterogeneous societies, and instead, representative government seems a more practical alternative. The key to a representative system is accountability: The people must be able to hold their leaders accountable. Although the United States has the trappings of representative democracy, many indicators suggest that the system works imperfectly at best.

Pluralism asserts that political decisions arise from the competition among groups. There are enough of these organizations and sufficient access to unused resources that no one group totally dominates the others. Furthermore, it is an open and dynamic system in that elites come and go, and there are opportunities for nearly every segment of society to participate in the process.

The power elite school argues that the major policies are made by a single power elite. It consists of the men and women who control the major economic, cultural, scientific, military, and political institutions in society. The nature of their positions, adherence to a shared set of attitudes and beliefs about government and economics, and control of the political agenda assure this elite's domination of the political system.

KEY TERMS

Civil liberties
Popular sovereignty
Political equality
Majority rule
Direct democracy
Representative democracy
Accountability
Republic
Pluralism

Political power
Resources
Actual power
Potential power
Scope of power
Command posts
World view
Trunk decisions
Containment

FOR FURTHER READING

Peter Bachrach, *The Theory of Democratic Elitism* (Boston: Little, Brown, 1967). A very readable and provocative critique of pluralism.

Robert Dahl, *Dilemmas of Pluralist Democracy* (New Haven, Conn.: Yale University Press, 1982). A statement of the modern pluralist position.

G. W. Domhoff, *Who Really Rules?* (Santa Monica, Calif.: Goodyear, 1978). A description of power elite theories.

John Manley, "Neo-Pluralism: A Class Analysis of Pluralism I and Pluralism II," *American Political Science Review* 77 (June 1983):368–383. A critical review of modern pluralist thought.

Henry Mayo, *An Introduction to Democratic Theory* (New York: Oxford University Press, 1960). An elementary introduction to democratic principles and the problems of applying them in industrial societies.

C. Wright Mills, *The Power Elite* (New York: Oxford University Press, 1959). Although written more than 30 years ago, this book is still one of the best statements of the power elite theory and contains ideas that are relevant for today.

Jack Walker, "A Critique of the Elitist Theory of Democracy," *American Political Science Review* 60 (March 1960):285–295. An excellent analysis of pluralism and elitism.

The Social and Economic Contest

"One nation under God." "The great melting pot." "Land of opportunity." Familiar phrases like these suggest that, whatever their backgrounds, Americans share a common purpose, and the United States is a place where everyone can succeed. These are comforting images, but how accurate are they? A close look at the population and the economy suggests that America is a racially, ethnically, geographically, and economically diverse society. These differences, and the conflicts they provoke, constitute the driving force of American politics. ■

Imagine taking a trip through the vast American continent. Go east and west, north and south, to the largest metropolis and the smallest village. Visit schools, factories, farms, churches, shopping malls. Throughout this journey you never seem to be an outsider, for it is remarkable how similar the people seem. Most of them speak the same language, pledge allegiance to the same flag, obey the same laws, and worship in the same churches. Differences exist to be sure, but there is an undeniable similarity in the clothes they wear, the sodas they drink, and the game shows they watch on television. In habits, tastes, fashions, preferences, attitudes, and countless other ways Americans display an amazing resemblance to one another.

Indeed, isn't this sameness one of the nation's greatest sources of national pride? Don't most citizens believe that their country is a melting pot—a kettle that turns diverse peoples into a community of kindred spirits? And isn't it also common to see the United States as a big family—a bit raucous and unruly at times, but a family nevertheless?

Yet underneath the surface there is, as everyone probably realizes, less homogeneity—fewer common interests and values—than first meets the eye. Contrary to the melting-pot image, Americans have not been blended so much as scrambled together.

A systematic study of American politics begins with a careful look at both the similarities and differences of the people who inhabit this land. This is the "who" part of Harold Lasswell's definition of politics as "Who gets what, when, how."[1] Such an examination explains a great deal about the issues that constitute the daily fare of politics, for virtually every domestic controversy—from abortion to tax reform to budget deficits—arises out of conflicts among various economic, social, and ethnic groups.

But it is not enough to describe only people. To take account of the things they fight about—the "what" of politics—we need to consider the economic system as well. A nation's politics is inextricably tied to its economic life. Thinkers from Plato to Marx have emphasized the connection, and talking about government without discussing the economy is like drawing an automobile without wheels or a chassis.

Put simply, this chapter deals with the social and economic context of government. In looking at the population and economy, one soon discovers who has political resources—which, as Chapter 1 stressed, are a politician's wherewithal—the time, money, skills, and prestige that provide leverage in conflict. Knowing how these resources are distributed throughout society tells a great deal about who is potentially powerful and thus about who really governs.

THE POPULATION OF THE UNITED STATES

The first striking feature of the American population is its size: The United States is a nation of roughly 250 million inhabitants scattered over 3,618,700 square miles. The sheer size guarantees that government will have its hands full promoting the general welfare and ensuring domestic tranquility. But the most interesting and relevant aspects of the population are its diversity and the changes in its composition. The growth of some groups and the decline of others underlie many political issues. Nowhere is this fact better illustrated than in the aging of the populace.

Age and Politics

Although Americans value youth and spend millions of dollars annually on health spas, beauty products, diet foods, and contemporary fashions trying to look young, the population *as a whole* inexorably grows older. The median age in 1960, for example, was about 29 years; by 1987 it increased to 32 years and is expected to rise to 40 by the year 2020.[2] Equally important, the size of certain age groups, or **cohorts**, is changing. In the late 1980s, babies and toddlers comprised about 7 percent of the population while citizens 65 and older constituted more than 12 percent. The Bureau of the Census expects this difference to grow in the coming decades. As Figure 2.1 illustrates, the ratio of senior citizens to children will become greater during the next 60 years. Notice too that although the truly elderly—those over 85—were only a tiny fraction of the population in 1980, they will steadily increase in numbers in the twenty-first century. The causes are obvious: The birth rate is going down at the same time that fewer older people are dying.

These changes have some sobering political implications. The 12 percent of the population that is over 65 receives more than half of all government expenditures for social services (such as medical care, housing, and pensions).[3] Where does this money come from? Some analysts argue that it comes largely from the taxes paid by the younger generation still in the labor force. Reflecting this concern, one reporter concluded, "... the old are being enriched at the expense of the young, the present is financed with tax money expropriated from the future, and one of the legacies children appear to be inheriting from their parents is a diminished standard of living."[4] Senator Daniel Patrick Moynihan of New York agreed, saying, "We may be the first society in history of which it can be said that children are worse off than their parents."[5]

Age affects politics in other ways. The cohort known as the "baby-boomers"—children born between 1946 and 1964—initially crowded maternity wards, schools, and colleges and are currently competing for affordable housing, promotions, and other necessities. As these baby-boomers retire in the next century, the burden of paying for their health care and other services could possibly fall on the next generation, which is not as large because it was the product of a time of lower birth rates. The small size of the post baby-boom cohort also means a shrinking pool of young men and women from which the military, universities, and businesses can recruit.

Others are not as troubled by the different sizes of the generations, because each cohort will pay for most of its retirements out of its current savings. Besides, even if there are more elderly to care for, there will be at the same time fewer children to look after.[6] But whoever is right, the changing age composition of the population will inevitably put additional demands on the political system.

Women and Politics

Another aspect of population change is the role of women in society. It is not that there are more of them—the ratio of males to females has remained relatively steady in the last 30 years—but rather that women's expectations about themselves and their place in the family, the economy, and society are changing.

For one thing, more and more women are remaining single, delaying marriage, postponing pregnancies, living alone, and working. A few statistics tell the story. By the end of the 1980s,

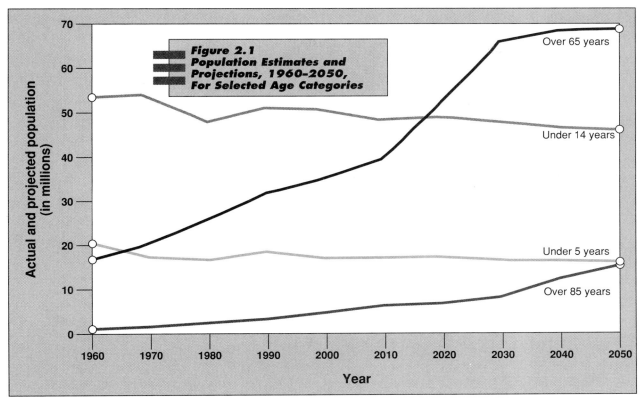

**Figure 2.1
Population Estimates and
Projections, 1960-2050,
For Selected Age Categories**

The lines show the increase (both actual and projected) in number of people in various age categories. The number of those over 65 will grow steadily well into the twenty-first century, whereas the number of children under 5 will decline a bit.

Source: U.S. Bureau of the Census, Current Population Reports, Series P-25, No. 1018, *Projections of the Population of the United States* (Washington, D.C.: Government Printing Office, 1989), p. 7.

the average age at which women married for the first time was almost 24 years, up from 20 years in 1960.[7] At the same time, roughly one in three women were either single, widowed, living without a spouse, or divorced.[8] Equally important, one in two females were in the labor force in 1988, compared with one in three a few decades earlier.[9] (See Figure 2.2 on page 36.) Nor were these workers primarily single women. Sixty-five percent of mothers with children worked in 1987; in fact, more than half of working mothers had children less than 6 years old.[10]

Accompanying these developments has been a rising awareness and resentment of sexual discrimination. The recent attention lavished on "Supermom," who juggles a career, mother-

hood, housekeeping, and a social life, has enabled women to air grievances caused by wage differentials, unequal treatment by insurance and retirement policies, sexist advertisement, pornography, bias in the classroom, and harassment on the job. Yearly earnings of full-time female employees in 1987, to take one example, were 40 percent less than what men received, a gap that had not changed much since 1955. These disparities, moreover, exist even when age, education, and type of occupation are taken into account.[11]

Mothers who work have special concerns. They need to find affordable day care for their children. (In 1987, only 10 percent of private businesses with 10 or more employees provided

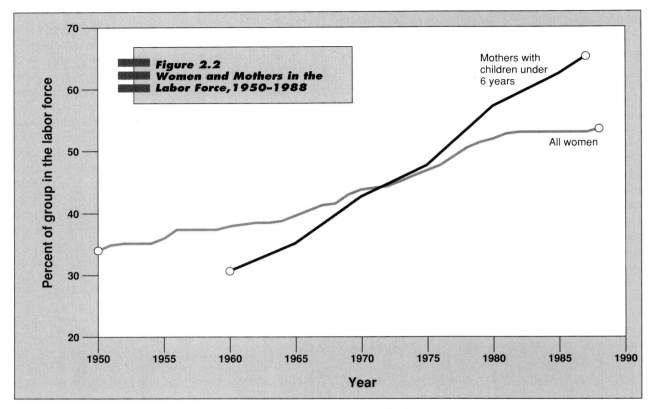

Figure 2.2
Women and Mothers in the
Labor Force, 1950–1988

Mothers with
children under
6 years

All women

*In 1950 about a third of all women worked; by the late 1980s the proportion had grown to
more than 50 percent. There has been an even sharper increase in the percentage of
working mothers with children under six years of age. Today nearly two out of three
women with young children work.*

Source: Department of Labor, Bureau of Labor Statistics, *Handbook of Labor Statistics*
(Washington, D.C.: Government Printing Office, 1985), p. 64; and U.S. House of
Representatives, Committee on Ways and Means, *Background Material and Data on
Programs* (Washington, D.C.: Government Printing Office, 1990), p. 920.

any kind of child care benefits.[12]) Potential mothers also need to know that they won't be penal-
ized in the workplace by their pregnancies and
want flexible and adequate maternity and family
care leaves. The Pregnancy Discrimination Act
of 1978 supposedly guarantees pregnant women
equal treatment in the workplace, but compliance is uneven. The Equal Employment Opportunity Commission, a federal agency, receives
over 3000 complaints a year about discrimination of this kind.[13]

These issues have become so serious that both
the major parties addressed them in their 1988
campaign platforms. Gender issues like these

have encouraged women to organize into such
groups as the National Organization for Women
(NOW) to press government to address these
problems.

By far the most publicized gender issue is the
controversy over abortion. In 1974 the Supreme
Court ruled in *Roe* v. *Wade* that states could not
prevent women from obtaining abortions. In the
eyes of its opponents (both men and women) the
decision was tantamount to granting a license to
kill innocent humans. Its supporters, however,
regard the right to an abortion as a personal freedom that gives women control over their bodies.
Whatever the merits of the argument, the

Supreme Court's action has radically altered contemporary politics. There have been continuous protest demonstrations and innumerable efforts to overturn the Court's decision. President George Bush and antiabortion organizations have even called for a constitutional amendment if necessary to halt the practice.*

The increased consciousness and political activism of women have undeniably brought gains. The Supreme Court has its first female member, Sandra Day O'Connor, while another woman, Geraldine Ferraro, was the first to run for the vice-presidency in the 1984 election. Women comprise a sizable segment of state and national legislatures, although far below their share of the population. An editorial in the *New York Times*, however, puts these achievements in perspective:

> . . . anyone tempted to think that the millennium has arrived had better skip the thought. Because for millions of American women this is a terrible time. . . . They earn 62 cents for every dollar earned by men. Only 10 percent of them earn more than $20,000 a year. That means one has to search pretty hard to find a woman who heads a department, a business or a college.[14]

Geography and Politics

One of the fascinations of American history has been the part that geography has played in its major struggles: North versus South in the Civil War and after; western and southern farmers versus eastern industrialists in the populist and progressive era around the turn of the century; city versus farm in fights over temperance, party reform, and social values. Of course, these battles are understandable when one remembers that a region or city or community stands for one's economic interests, living habits, beliefs, customs—in short, one's whole way of life.

What makes the phenomenon even more com-

plex and interesting is that Americans seldom stay put for long. In 1985 about half of the people interviewed by the Census Bureau said that they had moved in the last five years; about 19 percent had gone to a new county and nearly 10 percent to a new state entirely.[15] Given all this moving about, one might imagine that after a few decades the country would have become homogenized like a dye diffusing through a glass of water. Yet conflicts based on geographical differences seem as divisive as ever.

One reason is that people are not moving at random. During the last few years, the "Frostbelt" states stretching from Illinois and Michigan in the upper Middle West to New England in the East have lost about one percent of their populations while states below the Mason-Dixon line and west of the Mississippi River, the "Sunbelt," have gained a percent or two (see Figure 2.3). Furthermore, whites have left large cities in the Northeast and Midwest in droves, fleeing mainly to the suburbs and small towns, especially in the South and West. Blacks and other minorities, meanwhile, have inherited the core of metropolitan areas such as Detroit (63 percent nonwhite in the latest census tabulations), Baltimore (55 percent), Cleveland (44 percent), Chicago (40 percent), Philadelphia (38 percent), St. Louis (46 percent), Atlanta (67 percent), and Washington, D.C. (70 percent).[16]

This mobility has tipped the political center of gravity to warmer climates. Representation in the House of Representatives is apportioned by population: States with the largest populations get the most representatives. After the 1990 census has been tabulated, New York and Pennsylvania are almost certain to lose three seats in Congress, and Ohio, Michigan, and Illinois two apiece. The big gainers should be California (plus five seats), Texas (plus four), and Florida (plus three). Several other states will either gain or lose one or two seats.[17] Since many political issues (energy, transportation, natural resources, environment, for example) are regional and since votes in the House give a state power, the Sunbelt seems destined to have greater influence on national policy.

Changes in the population of cities and suburbs also have politically significant implica-

---

*They apparently gained a small measure of success when, in 1989, the Supreme Court seemed to back away a bit from its earlier decision. *Webster* v. *Reproductive Health Services*, 109 S.Ct. 3040 (1989).

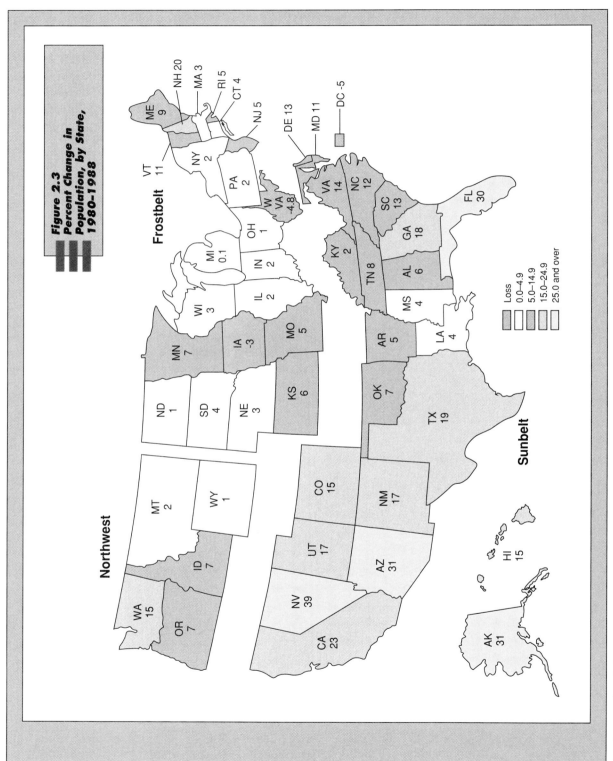

**Figure 2.3
Percent Change in
Population, by State,
1980–1988**

Frostbelt

Northwest

Sunbelt

ME 9
VT 11
NY 2
PA 2
W VA -4.8
OH 1
MI 0.1
IN 2
IL 2
WI 3
MN 7
IA -3
MO 5
ND 1
SD 4
NE 3
KS 6
MT 2
WY 1
CO 15
NM 17
UT 17
AZ 31
NV 39
CA 23
WA 15
OR 7
ID 7
TX 19
OK 7
AR 5
LA 4
MS 4
AL 6
TN 8
KY 2
GA 18
SC 13
NC 12
VA 14
FL 30
HI 15
AK 31

NH 20
MA 3
RI 5
CT 4
NJ 5
DE 13
MD 11
DC -5

Loss
0.0–4.9
5.0–14.9
15.0–24.9
25.0 and over

Populations of Sunbelt and Western states are growing faster than those of the Frostbelt. Source: U.S. Bureau of the Census, Current Population Reports, Special Studies, Series P-23, No. 164, How We're Changing (Washington, D.C.: Government Printing Office, 1990), p. 2.

tions. There are, in the first place, racial and ethnic imbalances. Cities have historically attracted ethnic groups, and in keeping with this tendency, about half of the Hispanic population, the nation's fastest-growing minority, lives in just 10 metropolitan areas.[18] Moreover, the income base of cities is shrinking: In 1987 the median income of families residing in central cities was only two-thirds of the corresponding figure for the suburbs of large metropolitan areas.[19] Many large cities that a quarter of a century before were vibrant and prosperous manufacturing and financial centers nearly went bankrupt in the 1970s and continue to grapple with problems of high unemployment; deteriorating housing; crumbling roads, subways, and sewers; and declining tax bases. One result is the growth of poverty in urban areas. In spite of decreasing population (or perhaps because of it), the poverty rate in central cities was nearly 17 percent in 1982, compared to 7.5 in their outlying areas.[20]

We could continue in this vein indefinitely, but the point is clear. Both in terms of region (Sunbelt versus Frostbelt) and place of residence (city versus suburb), Americans have gradually separated themselves into potentially antagonistic camps with differing concerns. Northern and midwestern urban centers, in particular, house increasingly dependent populations that consume government services but lack the economic resources to pay for them. The more affluent and less densely populated suburbs and southern regions resist the expansion of federal and state programs to help the poor. Many forecasters predict that these areas will grow more politically conservative in the years to come.

Ethnicity and Politics

Adolf Hitler supposedly said, "In general, no such thing as an American people existed as a unit; they were nothing but a mass of immigrants from many nations and races."[21] He, of course, took this as evidence that Americans were less pure and strong than Germans. Yet however wrong his judgment, he did hit the nail squarely on the head: The United States is a land of the sons and daughters of immigrants. Figure 2.4 (page 40), depicting the waves of different peoples who have flocked to these shores during the last 150 years, makes this point, but so do the players in major league baseball: Franco, Canseco, O'Brien, Viola, Righetti, Flannery, Saberhagen, Incaviglia, Dykstra, Hrbek. And although the influx has slowed in the last several years, America still attracted over 600,000 immigrants in 1986, many of them from Spanish-speaking countries of Latin America.[22] (This to-

The ethnic diversity of the American population can be seen in the names on the rosters of major league baseball teams such as the Baltimore Orioles.

tal includes only the ones known to the Bureau of Immigration and Naturalization; it is undoubtedly too low.)

Decades of immigration have created a diverse population—diverse in religion, language, dress, living habits, customs, and, naturally, political interests. It is no secret that racial and ethnic subpopulations have given politics much of its color, charm and excitement—and undeniably its bitterness as well. Ethnicity has shaped public affairs in most parts of the United States, but especially in the urban East and Midwest as group after group has tried to assimilate into the economic and social order. Ironically, over the course of history politicians have competed for the support of immigrants as much as they have fought against their acceptance. Even today candidates try to build coalitions of black, Irish, German, Scandinavian, Italian, East Euro-

pean, Hispanic, and Asian voters.

Of the conflict spawned by ethnicity, none has been as pernicious and as long-lasting as that based on race, and the struggle for equality in politics, economics, and society in general continues to dominate American politics. That progress has been made is undeniable. It may surprise some readers to discover that just shortly before they were born, blacks in many parts of the country were denied access to public libraries, swimming pools, parks and beaches, lunch counters, bowling alleys, theaters, and hotels; that they could not play on basketball or football teams in the Atlantic Coast or Southeastern conferences; and that in many counties and cities they were not allowed to vote, much less hold office. Young people today sometimes take civil rights for granted, overlooking the long brutal fight it took to win them.

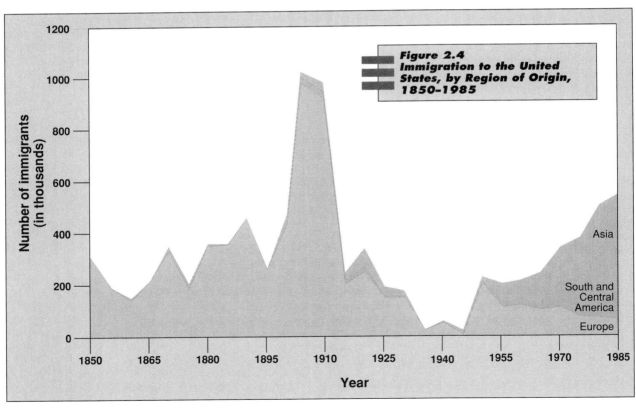

Immigration peaked in the early 1900s but has been growing again in the last few decades. Most immigrants now come from Asia and Central and South America.

Source: U.S. Bureau of the Census, *Historical Statistics of the United States Colonial Times to 1970,* Series c89-c119; and Bureau of the Census, *Statistical Abstract of the United States,* various editions.

Huge numbers of blacks like these youngsters live in inner city slums. Despite demands for equality of opportunity and progress in civil rights, black Americans still trail whites in virtually every category of economic and social well being.

There is also a tendency to believe that the struggle is over. But even if political equality has been achieved (and not many whites and even fewer blacks think that it has), it is not the same as social and economic equality. As Table 2.1 makes plain, there is a long way to go. In fact, blacks trail whites in just about every aspect of life that matters: health, employment, education, and income. Table 2.1 reveals among other things that:

- The infant mortality rate among blacks is twice the rate for whites.
- About three-quarters (76 percent) of whites complete four years of high school or more, but only about 60 percent of blacks do.
- Whites tend to live longer and healthier lives.
- More than twice as many blacks are unemployed as whites.
- Approximately half of black children live in families with only a mother present, a proportion more than three times as large as for whites.

Even these figures hide the magnitude of the disparities. Whites whose *incomes* (salaries, wages, dividends, and so forth) are almost double those of blacks also have 10 times as much *wealth*—the ownership of property, stocks, bonds, real estate, and savings.[23]

Differences like these, which many people attribute to generations of racism and discrimination, continue to fuel many of the political fires in America. White citizens sometimes seem impatient with demands for racial justice, but they are destined to have to live with them because blacks are becoming a permanent force in politics, as demonstrated by the elections in 1989 of Douglas Wilder of Virginia, the nation's first black governor since Reconstruction, and David Dinkins, New York City's first black mayor. In state after state, blacks are more organized and mobilized than ever before and appear to hold the balance of political power. Whether or not they can translate this position into jobs, housing, and income security remains to be seen, but the struggles to achieve these goals will be at the top of the national agenda in the coming years.

Table 2.1

Social and Economic Indicators by Race, Selected Years

			Year		
		Race	1960	1970	1987
Education:	Percent with 4 years of high school or more	White	—[a]	54	77
		Black	—	31	63
Health:	Infant deaths per 1000 live births	White	—	15[b]	9[c]
		Black	—	27[b]	18[c]
	Expectation of life at birth, both sexes (in years)	White	71	72	76[d]
		Black	63	64	70[d]
	Percent of persons with elevated blood pressure	White	19	20	19[e]
		Black	37	37	28[e]
Income and Employment:	Median income of householders (in thousands of current dollars)	White	7.4	9.1	27.4
		Black	4.3	5.5	15.5
	Percent of labor force unemployed	White	—	4	5
		Black	—	9[f]	13
	Percent of families below poverty level	White	15	8	9
		Black	48[g]	30	30
Families:	Percent of children under 18 living with only mother	White	—	8	15
		Black	—	30	51

[a] — = data not available.
[b] 1974–1976.
[c] 1984–1986.
[d] Preliminary.
[e] 1976–1980.
[f] 1973.
[g] 1959.

Source: U.S. Bureau of the Census, *Statistical Abstract of the United States: 1989* (Washington, D.C.: Government Printing Office, 1989), pp. 130, 131, 377, 441, 455; National Center for Health Statistics, *Health, United States, 1988,* DHHS Publication No. (PHS) 89-1232 (Washington, D.C.: Government Printing Office, 1989), tables 13, 15, 55; and U.S. Bureau of the Census, Current Population Reports, Series P-60, No. 162, *Money Income of Households, Families, and Persons in the United States: 1987* (Washington, D.C.: Government Printing Office, 1989), p. 10.

So too will the demands of Hispanics, at once America's oldest and newest minority. Although they have been part of the United States since its founding, only recently have they become our fastest-growing immigrant group. In 1970, about 9 million people told the Census Bureau that they were of Hispanic origin; by 1987 the number had climbed to over 19 million.[24] Part of the increase results from immigration and part from the Hispanics' high birthrates. By the mid-1990s, nearly 1 out of 12 Americans will come from a Spanish-speaking background.[25]

Hispanics as a group are rapidly becoming a force to contend with in the political arena. Although they do not register and vote at the same rate as whites, their participation is nevertheless pivotal in many states in the Southwest and New York and New Jersey. Just as politicians can ill afford to ignore black and Jewish voters, they have to listen to Hispanics.

What will this group demand? Economic deprivation affects them as much as any minority. Table 2.2 presents a bird's-eye view of the situation in 1987.[26]

Hispanics now constitute America's fastest growing minority and have become a major political force in many parts of the country.

Table 2.2

Social and Economic Indicators by Non-Hispanic and Hispanic Populations

	Non-Hispanic Population	Hispanic Population
Median family income	$30,231	$19,995
Percent unemployed	7	10
Percent with less than 5 years schooling	3	12
Percent with 4 or more years of college	24	9
Percent of families below poverty level	10	25
Percent female householders, no husband present	16	23

Hispanics also encounter racial prejudice and growing backlash over language. The federal government tacitly supports Spanish by providing bilingual education, ballots, income tax forms, and the like. Some states and communities have resisted these programs, many of which can be costly. In fact, by the late 1980s 16 states had passed laws or constitutional amendments making English their official language.[27] And many companies now require their Hispanic employees to speak English on the job, even if they are not dealing with customers at the time.[28]

In recent years, however, the most bitter struggle has been over immigration. Organized labor contends that the employment of alien workers depresses wages and working conditions for American citizens, while border states claim that the uncontrolled influx of immigrants from Central America burdens their school and welfare systems. Hispanic groups, on the other hand, worry that immigration bans increase the likelihood of discrimination against Americans from Spanish-speaking backgrounds. In 1986 Congress passed legislation that granted amnesty to certain illegal immigrants who had lived here for a number of years and provided for fines on employers who knowingly hire illegal aliens. Unfortunately, not many people think the law will stem the tide of illegal immigrants from Mexico and elsewhere, and the issue remains as divisive as ever.

Whatever the case, it seems clear that Hispanics are now taking their place beside the Irish, Poles, Italians, Scandinavians, Germans, blacks, and others in the mainstream of American politics.

Checkpoint

- The size and distribution of the population partially determines the scope and intensity of political conflict in the United States.
- The most politically significant demographic changes include:

- Aging of the population: The proportion of young people grows smaller compared to the elderly.
- Changes in sex roles: Since the early 1970s, more and more women, including mothers and wives, work full or part time, a situation that has led to calls for affirmative action, equal pay for equal work, an end to sexual harassment, more generous child care policies, and paid maternity leaves.
- Geographic mobility: The traditional centers of power in America—large cities in the Northeast and Midwest—are losing ground to the suburbs and states in the South and West.
- Ethnic diversity: Many minorities have become assimilated into society, but others—mainly blacks and Hispanics—have been partially left out, causing racial antagonisms that will doubtlessly continue to influence the course of American government into the next century.

SOCIAL CLASS AND POLITICS

Both pluralists and elitists agree that those in the bottom strata of society generally have less influence than citizens higher up the social ladder. Thus, knowing about the class system tells us a great deal about who governs. Four points about the classes in America stand out:

- Like most countries in the world, this nation contains distinct social classes with different and frequently incompatible economic and political interests.
- Some classes have access to more political resources than others and hence continually have more potential power.
- Yet political parties in America generally do not act on behalf of particular classes but

instead represent loose, cross-cutting coalitions of groups.

- As will be seen in Chapter 3, most Americans not only have weak class identifications but commonly deny the relevance of class to politics.

Stratification in America

Social class membership can be defined by a person's standing on one or more of these indices: *occupation, education,* and *income.* By any of these measures the United States is a cornucopia. Certainly the standard of living has risen dramatically in the last century; there is virtually universal education; and millions and millions of Americans are gainfully employed. America, nearly everyone believes, is a land of unlimited prosperity and opportunity where the very notion of social class—implying, as it does, "haves" and "have nots"—seems inappropriate.

But take a closer look.

The Bureau of Labor Statistics recently found that the work force consists of about 25 million professionals, technicians, managers, executives, and administrators. At the same time, it counted 15 million service employees, and 5 million laborers and helpers.[29] Even among the millions classified as *professionals,* there is enormous variation in social standing, wealth, and prestige since this category includes schoolteachers, librarians, nurses, and dental hygienists as well as lawyers, doctors, engineers, and accountants.

Now look at occupation from another perspective. About half of the working population is labeled white-collar, and only about a third is blue-collar (the rest are service and farm workers).[30] Since white-collar workers presumably use their minds while blue-collar laborers toil with their backs, and since the composition of the labor force has become increasingly white-collar in the last 50 years, it is easy to believe that America has become a middle-class society. Yet this interpretation ignores the fact that many white-collar jobs like secretarial work can entail menial, boring, stressful, and low-paying tasks that leave the employee as physically and mentally exhausted as any steelworker.[31]

Similar remarks apply to education. Because of free public schooling, the level of education has risen steadily in the last 100 years, even among the least advantaged groups in society. According to government estimates, the median number of school years completed by adults in 1987 was 12.7, up from 8.6 years in 1940.[32] Formal illiteracy (the ability to comprehend simple written English) has dropped from about 11 percent at the turn of the century to 1 percent in 1985. In addition, the 3400 colleges and universities in the United States enrolled more than 12 million students in 1990.[33] As a result of a variety of public and private programs, practically anyone can obtain some kind of advanced or vocational training.

There is another side of the coin, though. Although most Americans finish high school, nearly one in four do not: In fact, 7 percent have less than eight years of formal schooling.[34] Yes, formal illiteracy is down, but **functional illiteracy**—the inability to read help-wanted ads, fill out a loan application, or understand a ballot—remains depressingly high. The Department of Education has estimated that more than 26 million English-speaking Americans are so functionally illiterate that they cannot write a check or properly address an envelope.[35] A survey of reading comprehension, to cite another instance, found that in a sample of 13-year-olds about 15 percent had trouble understanding the directions on a Jell-O box.[36] Another report revealed that "only a small percentage" of young adults could perform well on tasks such as using a bus schedule or understanding the main point in a newspaper editorial.[37]

If education is a political resource that leads to power, then the better-educated segment of the population has a decided advantage, and pure democracy with its emphasis on equality and mass participation may be unattainable in the present circumstances.

Wealth and income, however, tell the story of class most forcefully. Table 2.3 shows that if one ranks all the families in the United States by income, the lowest 20 percent earned less than 5 percent of the total in 1986. The next three groups, constituting 60 percent of families—presumably the American middle class—took home close to 52 percent of the income, while the top

Table 2.3

**Percentage Shares of Aggregate Income
Received by Each Fifth and Top 5 Percent of Families,
1950–1986**

Year	Poorest Fifth	2nd Fifth	3rd Fifth	4th Fifth	Richest Fifth	Top 5%
1950	3.5	10.3	17.6	25.2	43.41	16.5
1955	4.0	10.4	17.8	25.6	42.2	14.3
1960	3.7	9.7	16.5	25.2	45.6	16.2
1965	4.7	10.8	16.6	24.7	43.2	15.1
1970	4.5	10.6	16.8	24.8	43.4	15.4
1975	4.7	10.1	16.7	25.1	43.3	15.4
1980	4.1	9.5	16.0	25.2	45.3	16.3
1986	4.6	10.8	16.8	24.0	43.7	17.0

Source: U.S. Bureau of the Census, Current Population Reports, Series P-60, No. 132, *Money Income of Households, Families, and Persons in the United States: 1980* (Washington, D.C.: Government Printing Office, 1982), p. 59, and No. 159, *Money Income of Households, Families, and Persons in the United States: 1986* (Washington, D.C.: Government Printing Office, 1986), p. 39.

20 percent received more than 43 percent. The richest 5 percent of families received 17 percent of all of the nation's income. Moreover, despite massive federal programs to help the poor, there has been very little *redistribution* of income in the past 40 years.

Several years ago, Paul Samuelson, a Nobel Prize-winning economist, described the distribution of income this way:

> If we made an income pyramid out of a child's blocks, with each layer portraying $1000 of income, the peak would be far higher than the Eiffel Tower, but almost all of us would be within a yard of the ground.[38]

What about the blocks at the bottom? The figures presented in Table 2.3 hide even more pronounced disparities. Using a different way to measure household income, a congressional study found that certain types of families—those headed by single mothers, for instance—took a financial beating between 1973 and 1987. Family income (adjusted for inflation) among the poorest households fell 20 percent, while those at the top gained more than 25 percent. This growing gap between the rich and poor, Representative Thomas J. Downey said, is "inimical to the health of democracy."[39] The distribution of income is clearly uneven, but it actually understates the extent of inequality because income as defined above does not include many other significant forms of wealth, such as ownership of stocks, bonds, real estate, undistributed corporate profits, and fringe benefits. In 1976, the richest one-half of one percent of households in America possessed 37 percent of corporate stock, 26 percent of bonds, 9 percent of real estate, and 14 percent of all total assets, a concentration of wealth much greater than generally found in Europe.[40] This inequality continued into the 1980s.[41]

Consequently, although the typical American is well off compared to most of the world's inhabitants, there is great variation in economic standing and security. The average person's wealth consists mainly of salary or wages and perhaps equity in a home.[42] Counterbalancing these assets are installment debts for automobiles and appliances and, of course, house mortgages. One social critic claims that at least the bottom quarter of society—one out of four families—are net debtors.[43] It might be added that much of the current success of the middle class results from wives going to work, not from real improvements in its income.[44]

Many social scientists now question the viability of the American middle class. Barbara Ehrenreich, a member of the Institute for Policy Studies, a Washington-based think tank, wonders if the United States is not "becoming a more divided society: over the last decade, the rich have been getting richer; the poor have been getting more numerous, and those in the middle do not appear to be doing as well as they used to."[45] As evidence she cites the usual economic statistics, but relies in addition on more tangible indicators to make her case:

> The stores and chains that are prospering are the ones that have learned to specialize in one extreme of wealth or the other. . . . Whether one looks for food, clothing or furnishings, two cultures are emerging: natural fiber vs. synthetic blends; hand-crafted wood cabinets vs. mass-produced maple; David's cookies vs. Mister Donuts.[46]

Dr. Ehrenreich, like dozens of other commentators, foresees trouble in the demise of the middle class because it historically buffered the antagonisms between the rich and poor. "If the extremes swell," she warns, "and if the economic center cannot hold, then our identity and future as a nation may be endangered."[47]

Poverty Amidst Plenty

The discussion of income leads to the subject of poverty. The very word seems decidedly un-American, for the existence of poverty denies some cherished beliefs about our society as the land of abundance and opportunity, a place where affluence and good living are celebrated in every form of popular culture. So inconsistent is the notion of poverty with the national self-image that people tend to trivialize it, to make jokes about welfare Cadillacs, to glorify it in tele-

vision programs like "The Little House on the Prairie"; to blame it on laziness, incompetence, or bad luck (but never on the economic system); and sometimes to justify it as a preparation for life's struggles.

But poverty may be more widespread and devastating than is commonly realized. If anyone doubts the point, a short quiz might be instructive. Answer true or false:

1. Only a handful of people—certainly less than 5 million—live in poverty in the United States.
2. The rate of poverty has steadily decreased in the last 40 years.
3. Most poor people are black.
4. Poverty exists mainly in large cities.
5. The majority of people living in poverty are able but unwilling to work.

1. *False.* The Bureau of the Census reports that in 1988, 13.1 percent of the population lived below the officially defined poverty line. *That translates into more than 30 million men, women, and children.*[48] Furthermore, the incidence of poverty changed hardly at all from 1980 to 1987. (See Figure 2.5.)

One can argue about the definition of the term. The Census Bureau's standard is money income. Many economists regard this definition as misleading because the poor are eligible for "in-kind" benefits such as food stamps, public housing, and medical assistance, which when added to salaries and wages increase a person's well-being. Yet even when these benefits are taken into account, the rate drops only two to five percentage points, meaning that by virtually anyone's count millions of our fellow citizens live in poverty.[49]

2. *False.* Poverty declined from 22.4 percent in 1959 to 11.1 percent in 1973, remained approximately constant during the 1970s, and then climbed to 15 percent in the early 1980s.[50] (See Figure 2.5.) And even though the economy recovered after a severe recession in the first Reagan administration, the level of poverty dropped only 2 or 3 percent in the following years.[51] Poverty, it seems, hangs on through good times and bad.

3. *False.* In absolute numbers the vast major-

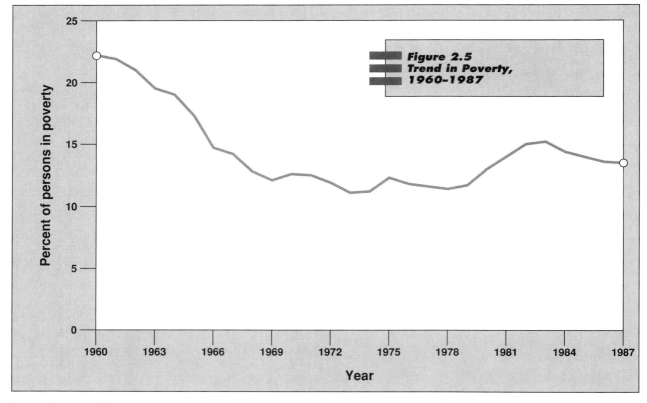

Poverty decreased from 1960 until the early 1970s, when it began to rise.

Source: U.S. Bureau of the Census, Current Population Reports, Series P-60, No. 161, *Money Income and Poverty Status in the United States: 1987* (Washington, D.C.: Government Printing Office, 1988), p. 2.

ity of the poor are white non-Hispanics: approximately 21 million whites, 10 million blacks, and 5 million individuals of Spanish-speaking origin. It is quite true, however, that the *rate* of poverty is higher for blacks than whites. In 1987, 11 percent of the white population lived below the officially defined poverty level whereas the corresponding figures for blacks and Hispanics were 33 and 28 percent, respectively.[52] Thus, as Michael Harrington notes, poverty in America is both integrated and segregated.[53]

4. *False.* Rural poverty exceeds the rate of large metropolitan areas and is almost as high as in inner-city ghettos. Moreover, the *increase* in poverty in outlying areas in the past decade was greater than in central cities.[54]

5. *False.* Roughly half of those living in poverty are either too old or too young to work. Of the 30 million people counted as poor in 1988, 11 million were children under 15 and 3.5 million were 65 or older.[55] Moreover, the poor do work. More than 48 percent of poor householders worked in 1988 and about 16 percent had year-round jobs.[56] It is mainly in families headed by females that there is no one in the work force, usually because the woman has young children at home, lacks experience, and has few marketable skills. The fact that one-quarter of the families receiving public welfare have someone working full time leads social scientists to believe that poverty results partly from low wages, not unwillingness to work.[57]

The significance of these numbers for the study of American politics is that a huge underclass occupies the bottom of society. Preoccupied with keeping body and soul together, its members have relatively few resources needed to compete effectively in the political arena. The Census Bureau reports, for instance, that eight out of ten individuals living in families with incomes of greater than $50,000 were registered to vote in 1988, but less than half of those whose family income was under $15,000 were registered.[58]

These facts do not prove whether the United States is a purely democratic, pluralist, or elitist society, but they do suggest that whoever is in control, it is not the poor.

Contrary to popular belief, more whites than nonwhites live in poverty. It is true, however, that the rate of poverty among minorities is greater than among whites.

Social Class, Poverty, and Politics

Although the United States is a wealthy country, the facts presented above suggest that it is not the affluent middle-class society portrayed by the television hits "The Bill Cosby Show" or "Dallas." Instead, it is divided into strata based on occupation, education, income, and wealth. Stratification, in turn, has important implications for politics.

Members of different social classes have different experiences, problems, needs, and interests as Table 2.4 shows. Statistically speaking, the higher one's social class, the healthier and happier one's existence is likely to be. Compared with the top groups, people with low incomes, poor educations, and less skilled occupations are more likely to suffer debilitating illnesses such as heart disease, diabetes, anemia, and arthritis; to be disabled by accidents in the workplace; to miss visiting a dentist regularly; to be laid off or unemployed at some time during the year; to be victimized by violent crimes; not to be covered by a pension plan; and to possess fewer luxuries.

Life at the bottom, in other words, is less safe, healthy, and pleasurable. For many citizens—not all certainly, but for many—the American dream of success and prosperity can quickly turn into a nightmare. A single major injury or unexpected prolonged period of unemployment can wipe out a family's savings, postpone a child's college education, or shatter hopes for a secure retirement.

The data in Table 2.4 imply that different classes have different political interests, whether they know it or not. If prestige, income, leisure time, skill, celebrity, access to the media, and control of organizations all are convertible into power, there must logically be great disparity in this kind of power between the bottom layers of society, where these resources are hard to find and utilize, and the top, where they are more abundant. Social class need not be a concrete barrier to effective participation, but the unequal distribution of resources in different social strata does give the upper classes more *potential* power than those lower down.

Table 2.4

Social Class Differences in Health, Economic Security, and Material Well-Being

HEALTH

Prevalence of Selected Chronic Diseases (Per 1,000 persons)[a]

Income	Heart Disease	Diabetes	Anemia	Arthritis
Less than $3,000	114.1	45.0	27.5	—
$3,000–4,999	98.0	35.9	22.0	218.6
$5,000–6,999	54.0	23.8	17.1	—
$7,000–9,999	39.9	17.3	14.3	135.1
$10,000–14,999	32.8	14.4	12.3	91.0
$15,000 or more	35.2	12.9	10.2	79.3

Unable to Carry on Major Activity Caused by Chronic Condition

Family Income	Percent
Less than $10,000	9.4
$10,000–14,999	6.0
$15,000–19,999	4.3
$20,000–34,999	2.7
$35,000 or more	1.6

Never visited a dentist (Age-adjusted)

Family Income	Percent
Less than $10,000	13.4
$10,000–14,999	13.6
$15,000–19,999	12.0
$20,000–34,999	10.0
$35,000 or more	7.1

SAFETY AND SECURITY

Comparison Between Clerical and Other Occupations (Clerical Workers = 100)[b]

Occupation	Accident Rate	Workdays Lost	Chronic Illness
Professional, technical	121	80	100
Clerical	100	100	100
Operatives (blue-collar)	435	127	130
Laborers	714	129	155

Victimization Rates (Whites) per 1,000 Population 12 Years and Over

Family Income	Rape	Robbery	Assault	Crimes of Violence
Less than $3,000	3.1	7.6	49.4	60.2
$3,000–7,499	1.7	8.1	31.4	41.1
$7,500–9,999	1.2	7.4	34.1	42.7
$10,000–14,999	1.3	5.9	26.3	33.4
$15,000–24,999	0.7	4.0	25.4	30.1
$25,000 or more	0.6	4.4	25.1	30.2

Social Class Differences in Health, Economic Security, and Material Well-Being
continued

EMPLOYMENT AND INCOME

Unemployment Rates for Selected Groups of Workers, 16 Years and Over, 1982

Occupation	Percent
Total White-Collar	5.6
Professional	3.8
Managers and administrators	3.9
Sales	6.3
Clerical	7.9
Total Blue-Collar	16.5
Craftsmen	12.2
Operatives	21.2
Laborers	19.4
Service	11.2

Average Weekly Earnings for Selected Occupations

Occupation	Median Earnings
Professional	$505
Skilled crafts	408
Technical and sales	320
Operators and laborers	301
Service workers	201
Farm workers	217

Workers Currently Eligible for Pension Benefits

Monthly Earnings	Percent Covered
Under $500	12.8
$500–999	27.9
$1,000–1,499	44.8
$1,500–1,999	55.2
$2,000 or more	66.8

LEISURE AND CONSUMER GOODS

Availability of Recreation Areas

Family Income	Percent with Outdoor Yard or Play Area
Less than $6,000	65
$6,000–9,999	68
$10,000–14,999	80
$15,000–24,999	83
$25,000–49,999	84
$50,000 or more	90

Social Class Differences in Health, Economic Security, and Material Well-Being
continued

Household Expenditures on Selected Appliances, 1971	Average Dollar Expenditures Per Household			
	Family Income	Washing Machines	Color TV	Hi-Fis and Radios
	Less than $3,000	4	9	10
	$3,000–4,999	10	20	13
	$5,000–7,499	13	33	19
	$7,500–9,999	14	40	25
	$10,000–14,999	17	51	34
	$15,000–24,999	19	55	41
	$25,000 or more	28	57	45

[a]Rates are for these years: heart disease, 1972; diabetes, 1973; anemia, 1973; arthritis, 1976.
[b]Rates are adjusted to show how manual and professional occupations compare with clerical jobs. Accident rate: average number of persons aged 17 and over injured while at work, per 1000 in labor force, June 1961–June 1963; workdays lost: days of work lost due to disability, per 1000 in labor force, 1975; chronic illness: persons with one or more chronic illnesses, with limitation of activities, per 1000 in labor force, July 1961–July 1963.

Sources: U.S. Bureau of the Census, *Social Indicators III* (Washington, D.C.: 1980), pp. 101, 558; National Center for Health Statistics, *Health, United States, 1988*, DHHS Pub. No. (PHS) 89-1232 (Washington, D.C.: Government Printing Office, 1989), pp. 93, 110; Giorgio Gagliani, "How Many Working Classes," *American Journal of Sociology* 87 (September 1981):270; U.S. Department of Justice, *Criminal Victimization in the United States, 1980* NCJ-7610, NCS-N-19 (Washington, D.C.: September 1980), p. 32; Colien Hefferan, "Unemployment: The Effects on Family Income and Expenditure," *Family Economics Review* no. 1 (1983):3; U.S. Bureau of the Census, *Statistical Abstract of the United States: 1988* (Washington, D.C.: Government Printing Office, 1988), p. 394; U.S. Bureau of the Census, Current Population Reports, Series P-70, No. 12, *Pensions: Workers Coverage and Retirement Benefits, 1984* (Washington, D.C.: Government Printing Office, 1987), p. 4; Judah Matras, *Social Inequality, Stratification, and Mobility*, 2nd ed. (Englewood Cliffs, N.J.: Prentice-Hall, 1984), p. 38.

If this statement is true, if the top wields more potential influence than the bottom and if these layers have different interests—one might logically expect to find deep class divisions in America, because one way for people in the lower class to gain influence would be to unite against those higher up. As in Europe, political parties would explicitly advocate programs aimed at specific classes. But for reasons discussed in Chapter 3, such conflicts do not occur in the United States. Most Americans express relatively little class hostility or even awareness of class. Nearly everyone identifies with either the middle or working class—hardly anyone says "upper" or "lower" when asked to select a social class.

Blue-collar laborers, for example, feel little hostility toward the rich. They may be well aware of inequalities in wealth and opportunity, but this knowledge has not generated the deep resentments commonplace in other parts of the world.

Equally significant, whatever class antagonisms exist in this country have rarely, if ever, crystallized into concrete ideologies or actions. Political parties and candidates usually do not make strong class appeals, preferring instead to seek support from a broad spectrum of voters. In the 1988 presidential campaign, for instance, Michael Dukakis and George Bush spent most of their time arguing about nonclass issues such as patriotism and law and order. Only at the last minute, when the election seemed lost, did Dukakis make a few explicit class-related appeals to workers, but these were sporadic and not part of his general campaign strategy.

Checkpoint

- Whether measured by income, education, or occupation, social classes are a fact of life in America.
- Poverty is widespread: Approximately one out of ten Americans are destitute by virtually anyone's standards.
- Even the working and lower-middle classes endure hardships that upper-status individuals largely avoid.
- Because of differences in their economic circumstances, the top, middle, and bottom segments of society have different, frequently conflicting interests.
- The wealthy have greater access to political resources than the poor, making it likely that the governing body is drawn mostly from the upper crust of society.
- In spite of these differences, class conflict is almost unknown in the United States.

THE ECONOMIC SYSTEM

The economy of the United States is a vast and varied mixture. It is mixed in what it produces, by and for whom, where, in what manner, and how efficiently. But it is mixed in two other essential respects as well: (1) the role of the government and (2) the size of the participating groups.

The Government and the Economy

Ask anyone to write a paragraph describing the American economy, and words and phrases such as "free enterprise," "marketplace," "capitalism," "private property," "buyers and sellers," and "initiative and hard work" will undoubtedly appear. The terms are accurate because they underline the private nature of the economic system: Goods and services are produced and sold as the result of millions and millions of transactions taking place in an open market. There is little central control or planning. The invisible hand of supply and demand apparently determines what is made, at what price, and for whom. For the most part, individuals have to rely on their own motivation, energy, and wits to succeed. In theory, anyway, this system is both efficient and fair since it creates the things that society needs while giving everyone who is willing to work an opportunity to get ahead.

Yet if the description ended here it would be woefully incomplete, for it would not have mentioned the central part that government plays. Far from having a "private" economy, America has a **mixed economic system** in which the public sector has become the largest and perhaps most important component. However much one may yearn for the good old days when the "business of America was business," there is no denying that the economy now combines private enterprise and government, which are so interdependent that neither can exist without the other. Failure to recognize this mixture of private and public components clouds the understanding of the American political system and who governs it.

Government has come to assume three general responsibilities: (1) managing the business cycle (called macroeconomic policy), (2) protecting the general welfare, and (3) promoting and subsidizing various economic interests. The first two functions are widely known; the third, less frequently noted, is just as significant.

MACROECONOMIC POLICY At least since the Pilgrims landed at Plymouth Rock, the American economy has undergone alternating periods of boom and bust, years of prosperity and growth followed by depression and hard times. The recovery following the deep recession of 1981–1982 is only the most recent example of these ups and downs. It took the Great Depression of the 1930s, the lowest of the lows, to establish once and for all the idea that government cannot and should not sit idly by while factories shut down, banks close, farms fail, and millions of men and women walk the streets looking for employment. Vast, decisive, and continuous intervention is needed to moderate the business cycle and alleviate its effects on both individuals and businesses.

The federal government tries to stabilize the economy by using **macroeconomic policy**. Macroeconomic policy takes two forms: controlling the amount of money in circulation (*monetary policy*) and increasing or decreasing total demand for goods and services through spending and taxation policies (*fiscal policy*).* On paper at any rate, the government's activities help reduce inflation and unemployment while encouraging growth and productivity.

Thus, instead of being an autonomous, self-regulating private enterprise system, the economy depends for better or worse on decisions made in Washington. More important still, there is hardly any debate about *whether* the government should undertake this responsibility, but only about *how* to do it. Sounding like backseat drivers, political parties bicker incessantly about how fast or slowly to drive the economic car, but they never suggest jumping out and walking.

PROTECTING THE GENERAL WELFARE   The government's involvement does not stop with macroeconomic policies. It also looks after the safety and welfare of its citizens. Indeed, it is here that government is most visible and, some would say, most intrusive and out of control. In pursuing these activities, federal, state, and municipal agencies and bureaucrats reach into virtually every aspect of our lives:

_____

*See Chapter 18 for a more complete explanation of macroeconomic policy.

- The national government, of course, provides for the common defense by spending roughly $300 billion annually and employing more than 3 million soldiers and civilians.[59]
- Together with the states, it manages the world's largest pension funds, the Social Security system, and related retirement programs.
- Public agencies provide a "safety net" to catch those unfortunate souls who for reasons of age, illness, disability, or bad luck fall off the economic ladder. The net is woven out of unemployment insurance, food stamps, housing subsidies, welfare payments, job retraining, health care, and countless other programs that each year require billions in tax revenues.
- The national government in particular keeps a watchful eye on the food and drugs we consume, the products we buy, the air we breathe, the water we drink, and, in fact, just about everything else that touches us.
- It also attempts to defend our civil liberties, to prevent racial and sexual discrimination, to ensure equal treatment for the handicapped, and to guard us against criminals, swindlers, trespassers, and charlatans.

Needless to say, all of these programs and activities create controversy. Critics of public involvement in private economic life say that the government often makes life worse rather than better. Yet despite the hue and cry, there is surprising support for most of its *specific* programs. Few people favor "big" government in the abstract, but the public endorses many very expensive activities and often wants more of the same.

The main lesson to be learned, however, is that government in general has become an integral part of the economy. Each year the government spends the equivalent of more than $4000 for every man, woman, and child in the country and is now trillions of dollars in debt. The federal budget for 1990 exceeded $1 trillion, including $176 billion just for interest payments on its debt.[60] Public spending at all levels equals about one-third of the nation's total economic output, and it employs directly or indirectly al-

Promoting the general welfare: This federally funded Head Start project in Beverly, MA, serves homeless children.

most one out of four Americans.[61] In 1983, nearly three out of every ten people lived in a household that received some form of direct assistance from a local, state, or federal program.[62] The government, in short, is not a mere appendage to the economic system that can be lopped off by axing a few welfare programs.

PROMOTING ECONOMIC INTERESTS Most public programs are expensive, and probably more than a few are misguided or wasteful. But the plain fact is that nearly every segment of the economy has come to depend in one way or another on them. If they suddenly vanished, many institutions would collapse like card houses, and individuals and groups from every walk of life would clamor to have them restored.

Hundreds of industries, for example, are supported through a vast array of tariffs, quotas, export agreements, federal grants and loan guarantees, and government purchases. Public funds build, operate, and maintain facilities such as harbors, canals, airports, and irrigation systems that benefit specific interests such as shippers, airlines, and farmers.

Furthermore, federal regulations—the object of so much derision in editorials and on the cam-

paign trail—actually promote and protect particular sectors of the economy. Imagine what would happen if the Federal Communications Commission did not control access to a community's airways. The number of radio and television stations would proliferate until sooner or later their signals would interfere with each other, leaving the owners and their audiences worse off than before.

The government's major impact on the economy, however, is indirect and hence less visible. It is there nevertheless. National and state agencies underwrite huge amounts of research and development; they provide statistical services to business, weather forecasts to farmers, technical advice to manufacturers, and education and training to millions of men and women who form the backbone of the labor force. One example of this assistance is the National Bureau of Standards (NBS), a division of the Department of Commerce that "develops standards, measurement techniques, reference data, test methods, and instrument calibration services. This work lays the foundation upon which [private] advanced technology companies can perform more applied research and product development."[63] Corporation executives concede that having federal research facilities like NBS is crucial to their success.

American taxpayers also built the infrastructure upon which the private sector depends. To take a single instance, the National Highway Act of 1956, which created the interstate highway system, was originally justified on national security grounds, but it has clearly helped both the housing and automobile industries. The vast network of highways to ferry people to and from their jobs allowed the suburbs to grow. Instead of relying on mass transportation like buses and subways, as many now wish had been done, the nation chose to build a system of multilane highways, much to the advantage of the construction, rubber, petroleum, cement, trucking, and automobile industries. Car manufacturers and truckers receive less obvious forms of aid. Some economists ask, for example, how much of law enforcement costs are attributable to the existence of automobiles and how much states and municipalities lose as a result of land being taken off the tax rolls for roadways.

Occasionally the government's role in the economy is very direct. Over the years Washington has stepped in to rescue ailing private businesses, including some of the biggest. The federal government aided the savings and loan industry, Lockheed Aircraft Corporation, the Continental Illinois Bank (the country's seventh largest at the time) and, as A Closer Look explains, the Chrysler Corporation.

Americans may be free market capitalists at heart, but in an age of interdependence, when the financial collapse of a single giant corporation or bank can bring ruin to entire communities, pragmatism seems always to win over ideology. Citizens complain about wasteful and clumsy bureaucracy, but the prospect of losing thousands of jobs frequently leads even the staunchest defender of the private enterprise system hat in hand to Washington for help. Ronald Reagan, the most conservative president in half a century, used, like others before him, the power of government to manage the economy. During his two terms, his administration spent

The construction of the interstate highway system, funded mainly by the federal government, gave an enormous boost to private industries such as automobile, trucking, housing, cement, rubber, and petroleum.

A Closer Look

The Chrysler Bailout ★★★

Chrysler Corporation, facing imminent bankruptcy in 1979, asked the United States government to guarantee more than a billion dollars in loans. Congress was initially hostile to the idea. Chrysler, after all, had gotten itself into trouble and, in a free enterprise system, shouldn't it have to get itself out or face the consequences just like any other company? Skepticism about the loan was softened, though, by a Treasury Department estimate that if the huge car maker went broke, it could ultimately cost the economy nearly $3 billion and 75,000 jobs.[a] Faced with this harsh reality, the lawmakers eventually passed a bill guaranteeing the loans. No money was to come from the Treasury—it was all to be borrowed privately—except, and this is a big exception, if the company had to default, the taxpayers would be left holding the bag.

In order to save a mammoth corporation, therefore, the United States government risked more than $2 billion in public funds. That Chrysler survived and the Treasury did not lose a cent (it actually made millions of dollars) should not obscure the point that the national and state governments are increasingly viewed as economic saviors.[b]

[a]John Brooks, "The Annals of Finance (Chrysler Loan Guarantee)," *The New Yorker*, January 7, 1985, p. 44.
[b]Robert B. Reich and John D. Donahue, *New Deals: The Chrysler Revival and the American System* (New York: Times Books, 1985).

billions to assist financially strapped farmers; placed import restrictions on automobiles, sugar, motorcycles, steel, computer chips, and other products to aid the domestic producers of those products; took over troubled banks; and watched as the national debt more than doubled to $2 trillion and the level of federal spending (as a percent of the gross national product) climbed past 24 percent.

Once again, the major idea is that the United States has a *mixed* economy. In order to comprehend current events one has to realize that government is not an alien force imposed on a hapless and unwilling citizenry, but rather an institution that does things demanded by groups that often profit from them. Needless to say, its tasks can always be performed more efficiently and fairly, and its role in the future may change considerably. Nonetheless, those public and private leaders who hide or deny the closeness of their relationships deceive their listeners, because these connections are the essence of the modern political economy.

Economic Concentration

The American system is mixed in another way as well: There are vast differences in the size of its participating groups, and these differences, in turn, have political ramifications.

The **gross national product (GNP)**—the total value of all goods and services produced—was more than $5 trillion in 1990. Most people take part in this vast market as workers and consumers. Although a few of us may own or manage a shop or a farm or perhaps even a chain of stores, we have a roughly similar impact on the economy's overall performance. Whatever the differences in our income, education, life-style, and tastes, none of us dominates, much less controls, any sizable portion of economic activity.

By contrast, a few members of our society possess a great deal more clout. In economic life, what they do and say *does* matter. Their decisions to buy or sell, to produce or not to produce, to raise or lower prices, or to move or stay in one location affect not only themselves but countless thousands, perhaps millions, of other individuals. When Citicorp, America's largest bank, raises its interest rate, we all feel a twinge in our wallets because of the impact on interest rates in general. When General Motors lays off workers, our own jobs seem less secure because it has plants all over the country whose laborers are suddenly not patronizing our own establishments.

The biggest actor on the stage is the federal government. But there are private players of comparable stature. Table 2.5, for example, lists the 10 largest (in terms of assets) corporations in America. These few entities own and control billions of dollars of assets and hundreds of thousands of employees.

Table 2.5

The Ten Largest Corporations in America, 1988 (Ranked by Assets)

Corporation	Assets (Billions)	Employees (Thousands)
Citicorp	$231	91
General Motors	173	775
Ford Motor	161	367
American Express	131	104
Fed. Nat'l. Mortgage	124	3
General Electric	128	295
Salomon	118	9
Chase Manhattan	107	42
BankAmerica	99	54
JP Morgan & Co.	89	15

Source: *Forbes*, April 30, 1990.

To appreciate fully their potential power, compare them with state governments. The combined revenues of California and New York are smaller than the usual sales of either General Electric or American Express.[64] Michigan employs only a fraction of the workers that its biggest companies, Ford, Chrysler, and General Motors, do. Comparisons of this sort persuade numerous observers that state governments are at a disadvantage when dealing with giant corporations on controversial matters.

Another way of estimating the impact of various participants in the marketplace is the "concentration ratio," the extent to which the largest firms dominate the production of goods and services. Americans commonly think of the market as free and open to everyone. Indeed, there are roughly 12 million proprietorships (individually owned businesses and farms), 1.7 million partnerships, and 3 million corporations in the United States.[65] Yet most of these establishments are relatively small: Two-thirds of the partnerships and nonfarm small businesses have receipts of less than $25,000.[66] At the other end of the scale, approximately 1 percent of the largest active corporations earn three-quarters of all corporate net income.[67]

There is more to the story. *Forbes* magazine annually identifies the nation's richest citizens. In 1989, for example, it listed about 60 billionaires whose combined net worth exceeded $80 billion. Altogether, the richest 400 individuals named in the publication owned many hundreds of billions of dollars in assets. Yet, as the economist Lester Thurow once pointed out, these people actually control much more than the magazine's data suggest. Through various financial maneuvers they have power over "$2,200 billion [that is, more than $2 trillion] in business assets—about 40 percent of all fixed nonresidential private capital in the United States."[68] These financial empires extend, in short, far beyond large estates and companies to encompass about half of the private business sector in the economy.

What lessons can be learned from these facts and figures? What difference does size make for democracy and the question of who governs?

The resources of the largest corporations and wealthiest families give them the power to make decisions of such scope and magnitude that they affect the nation as a whole. Should these decisions not be made more democratically? Although we usually think that economic decisions in the private domain are rightfully made by owners and managers, there is a world of difference between a mom-and-pop store and a huge corporation employing thousands of workers in dozens of states. If the neighborhood gas station moves or closes, only a few people, mainly its employees and customers, are affected. But when Bethlehem Steel turns off its blast furnaces or IBM relocates its corporate headquarters, thousands of individuals, even those with no direct link to the companies, feel the pinch. Plainly stated, a private decision made by a giant company has enormous public implications.

None of these remarks proves the elitist interpretation of government. Even with all the wealth and concentration, there is plenty of competition in the political arena. Individuals and groups organize against the largest corporations. It is done all the time. Still, if wealth and control over huge amounts of resources count for anything—and they surely do, as both elitists and pluralists agree—then there is obviously a huge disparity in potential power in the United States.

This disparity presents a challenge for a free society, because a democratic system rests, as Chapter 1 suggests, on equality. But can equality be meaningful if some people have so much more than others? Is "one person, one vote" a truly realistic yardstick when one individual's property is measured in thousands of dollars while another's is measured in millions or even billions? The problem, in brief, is the difference between *formal* equality, which is fine in theory, and the actual ability to get things done in the real world.

Checkpoint

- Far from being a "private" economy, America has a mixed economic system, in which the public sector plays a crucial role.

- The government uses two macroeconomic tools, fiscal and monetary policy, to help regulate the business cycle.

- The government also looks after the safety and welfare of its citizens through hundreds of agencies and programs.

- Since public expenditures directly and indirectly support commercial economic activity, business greatly depends on federal and state subsidies for its welfare.

- A handful of giant corporations and extremely wealthy families dominate the economy, a situation that some argue undermines the principle of political equality.

TRENDS IN THE ECONOMY

No account of the economic system is complete without a glance at where it has been and where it is headed. Monitoring these trends allows one to anticipate not only the issues of the coming decade but also the combatants and likely winners and losers. These developments also show how really mixed the economy is: Some parts are growing, others are shrinking, and all of it is in constant flux. It will be apparent in this survey that (1) service industries are rapidly eclipsing manufacturing, (2) the labor force is undergoing a corresponding change, and (3) industry in the United States faces ferocious foreign competition.

Manufacturing Versus Service Economy

America has always prided itself on its industrial might, perhaps rightly so: For over a century it led the world in the production of basic resources and commodities like steel and grain as well as consumer goods such as appliances and automobiles. Making *things*, Americans have always believed, has given them their unsurpassed standard of living. Yet many people fail to realize that the ratio of manufacturing to nonmanufacturing activities is steadily declining. Over the past quarter century the provision of *services* has displaced the production of goods as America's main livelihood.

Services encompass all kinds of activities without which modern life would be impossible: *distribution services* (wholesale and retail trade, communications, transportation); *producer services* (marketing, banking); *consumer services* (health care, hair styling); and *nonprofit and government services* (education, police). What these occupations have in common is that they involve people doing things for other people, rather than creating products.

Figures 2.6 and 2.7 (pp. 62–63) show the rising impact of the service sector. Its share of the gross national product and total employment has risen dramatically in the last 30 years, whereas the proportion contributed by goods-producing sectors (agriculture, mining, construction, and manufacturing) has fallen.

To underscore this point, consider that New York City's largest export is legal advice, not

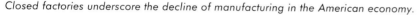

Closed factories underscore the decline of manufacturing in the American economy.

From goods to services: The "era of information" is symbolized by the high-tech office.

clothing; that health and medical services employ more people than the metal, machinery, and electronic industries combined;[69] that New Jersey's fastest-growing industry is casino-hotels, and its second is computer and data-processing services.[70] Finally, look back at Table 2.5, which lists the nation's 10 largest corporations. Only three—General Motors, Ford, and General Electric—make goods; the rest provide services.

Another signpost of the economy's transformation is the leveling off in demand for many basic commodities such as steel, cement, paper, and aluminum. Although more effective use of raw materials explains part of the decline, an equally compelling explanation is the shift from industry to services. One group of economists labeled this change a move from the "Era of Materials" to the "Era of Information." They interpret it as possibly analogous to humanity's passing from, say, the Iron Age to the Bronze Age.[71]

What do these developments mean for politics? For one thing, in the wake of intense foreign manufacturing competition and hundreds of domestic plant closings, especially in the "smokestack" industries such as steel, it has become fashionable among Democrats and Republicans alike to call for increased competitiveness through the reindustrialization of America.

Reindustrialization schemes usually envisage cooperation among government, labor, and management to set research, development, and manufacturing goals and priorities, which are in turn backed by generous public support through tax incentives, loans, development grants, research, import quotas, and billions of dollars of other benefits. The idea is to ensure that the economy can continue to turn out products as efficiently and inexpensively as in the past when the United States dominated world trade.

Yet as the data cited above suggest, these efforts may be misguided. The industrial giant assumed by reindustrialization plans no longer exists and, in fact, has been gone from the scene for quite a while. Eli Ginzberg and George Vojta, two economists, write ". . . [R]eindustrialization of an economy dominated by services is an exercise in futility. Americans must unshackle themselves from the notion that goods alone constitute wealth whereas services are nonproductive."[72] Large-scale investments of federal resources in manufacturing, they add, will only postpone the inevitable while at the same time depriving potentially profitable sectors of needed support.

A service-centered economy, furthermore, may not be as weak a competitor in the international marketplace as it appears at first sight. In 1988, while foreigners were shipping us more merchandise than we sold them, the difference was partly offset by our exporting $186 billion

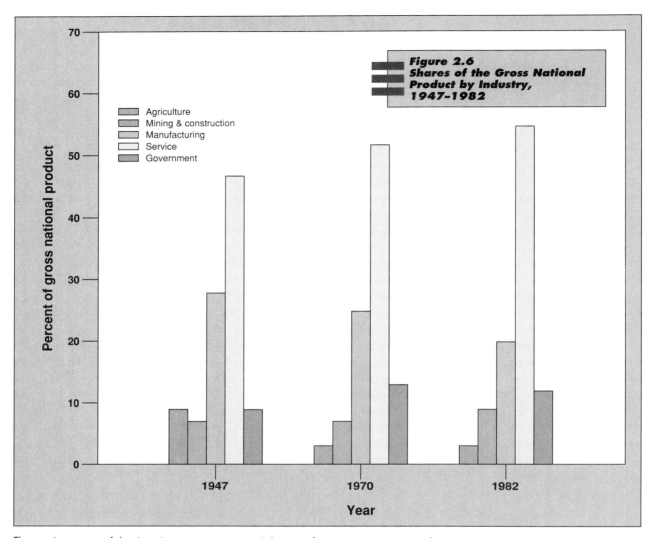

The service sector of the American economy outweighs manufacturing as a percent of gross national product.

Source: Department of Labor, Bureau of Economic Analysis, *The National Product and Income Accounts of the United States* (Washington, D.C.: Government Printing Office, 1986).

in services, ranging from fees paid to bankers to royalties from the sales of popular music to rentals on movies.[73]

This point leads to another approach to the problem: Instead of pouring money into physical plants, some economists recommend investing in "human" capital, namely the skill, dexterity, knowledge, and health of the population. If services, not goods, are becoming the backbone of the economy, if they propel its expansion, and if they depend on the capacities of individuals, why not put energies and resources into educa-

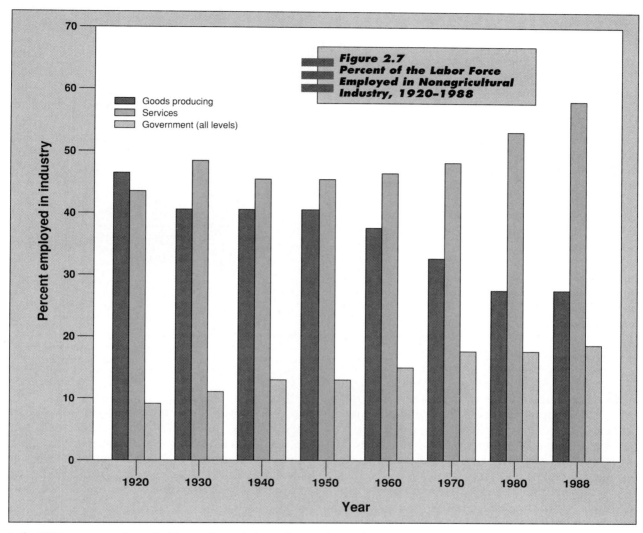

Figure 2.7
Percent of the Labor Force Employed in Nonagricultural Industry, 1920–1988

Goods producing
Services
Government (all levels)

In the 1920s more people worked in goods producing industries than in the service sector. Today the trend has reversed.

Source: Department of Labor, Bureau of Labor Statistics, *Handbook of Labor Statistics* (Washington, D.C.: Government Printing Office, 1985), pp. 174–175; and *Employment and Earnings* 36 (January 1989): p. 83.

tion, training, research, and health? Instead of coming to the rescue of outmoded iron forges and textile looms, why not build schools and laboratories? Instead of propping up crumbling factories, why not support those activities in which America enjoys a comparative advantage?

However the debate about reindustrialization ends, it should be clear that thinking of the American economy as a machine that turns out products rather than services is misleading. This remark is underscored by examining the changes in the composition of the work force.

The Changing Labor Force

The typical American worker is no longer a white male who carries a lunch box into a factory. For the past 40 years people have been steadily moving away from mills, assembly lines, and farms and into salesrooms, banks, law offices, schools, research facilities, day-care centers, and fast-food chains. In 1920, roughly half of the working population earned a living producing goods, but by 1988 the proportion had fallen to less than 30 percent. (See Figure 2.7.)

These trends are likely to continue. The New York Stock Exchange predicts that manufacturing jobs will continue to decline as a share of overall employment.[74] The Bureau of Labor Statistics estimates that the fastest-growing occupations between 1986 and the year 2000 will be medical assistants, home health aides, computer programmers and analysts, X-ray technicians, legal and dental assistants, and guards.[75] Notice that no one on this list produces durable goods such as refrigerators or television sets.

More interesting still, white males, the prototypical breadwinners in society, no longer constitute a majority of the labor force. In January 1989, for example, just under half of civilian jobholders were women. Blacks and Hispanics added several more percentage points, leaving white men in the minority.[76] This trend is explained partly by changing attitudes toward sex roles and partly by the fact that most newly created jobs are in the service sector where women and minorities experience less discrimination—indeed, many service positions such as sales and clerical work have traditionally been filled by females.

An unfortunate side effect of these trends is declining wages. Average hourly earnings in service industries, especially in retail business where many young and unskilled people are finding employment, pay only two-thirds of what construction and manufacturing jobs do.[77] This explains why a study prepared for the Joint Economic Committee of Congress found that two out of five of the 9.2 million new jobs created between 1979 and 1985 paid less than $7400 a year.[78]

Another labor group that is dwindling in size is farmers and farm laborers. In the 1930s nearly a quarter of all Americans lived on farms; now

Duane Hansen's sculpture of a construction worker. The typical American worker is no longer a white male employed in manufacturing or construction. Women and minorities together now constitute a larger portion of the work force.

the proportion is less than 3 percent. Although the amount of land in cultivation remains about the same and agriculture produces more than ever, the number of people actually feeding chickens and planting corn has dropped during this period from 12 million to less than 4 million.[79]

Finally, union membership has dropped from its heyday in the 1950s and 1960s. In 1970 about one-third of American workers belonged to unions; 17 years later less than 20 percent did.[80] The decline in unionization is partially explained by the gradual migration of workers to the South and West, where unions are not as established or popular as in the North, and by the rise of the service economy, which has always been less organized than smokestack industries.

Whatever the causes, the downward spiral in membership greatly concerns labor leaders, who used to compete successfully for the ear of presidents, senators, and representatives, especially Democratic ones. Now, organized labor is engaged in an uphill struggle to maintain its influence in the halls of government, particularly since rank-and-file members have become more independent in their political thinking. One bright spot perhaps is the steady increase in white-collar unionization among, for instance, teachers, fire fighters, and municipal employees.

Internationalization of the Economy

In the mid-1980s, this country's net foreign debt—the difference between what it owed foreigners and what they owed it—exceeded $400 billion; that figure could grow to $1 trillion by 1995.[81] Numbers like these, which have come as a rude shock to many citizens, vividly demonstrate the last trend in this survey of economic developments: the *interdependence* of the American and world economies.

To appreciate this situation you do not have to read government documents or university research reports but simply go into any department store and note the shelves stocked with products marked "Made in Hong Kong"—or Japan, Korea, Taiwan, Germany, Mexico, or any of dozens of other far-off places. Then go outside to the parking lot and count the Toyotas, Hondas, and Nissans. Or, talk to the farmers in Kansas who explain that their livelihoods depend on the state of the economy in Russia and China where they sell their wheat and soybeans. The United States, in a word, has become increasingly immersed in the global economy.

This international interdependence takes getting used to because Americans have grown up believing that their economy was the strongest and most productive ever devised by humans. During the last century America has, despite a few ups and downs, made virtually everything it needed, and what could not be produced at home was easily purchased abroad with the earnings from sales to foreigners. Advanced technology, skilled workers, a well-developed communications and transportation network, and domestic tranquility ensured levels of productivity that gave Americans a competitive advantage in international trade. Year after year, the United States enjoyed a favorable **balance of trade**, the value of exports versus the value of imports. Furthermore, the returns on overseas investments annually brought additional billions of dollars. After World War II, when most of the world was economically prostrate, it was easy to live under the illusion that the economy was totally self-sufficient; that it could manufacture, sell, and consume whatever it wanted; and that the rest of the world could be ignored.

That illusion, if it was ever true, now certainly has to be abandoned. Foreign merchants compete equally not only in the international arena but in America's own backyard as well. In the 1970s America's *merchandise* trade surplus began to slip away and by 1976 disappeared altogether (see Figure 2.8). In 1976 the **merchandise trade deficit**—the value of goods imported from abroad minus the value of our exports to other nations—was $8 billion; by July 1989 it had grown to $108 billion.[82] Even more alarming to some observers was the prospect that the United States was becoming a debtor nation, a predicament many thought was reserved for less developed countries like Brazil and Mexico. But the truth is that foreigners have recently been lending and investing more money here than Americans have sent overseas.*

Like most things in life, there is a good and a bad side to these developments. On the positive side, foreign trade now accounts for a sizable chunk of the gross national product. Export industries—computers, aircraft, construction and farm equipment, lumber, precision instruments, and especially agriculture—employ millions of people. Scores of others find work as a consequence of imports. Take Japanese automobiles, perhaps the most obvious symbol of the tide of imports. People have to advertise, sell, deliver, and service these cars; someone has to produce and install parts for them; they need to be washed, insured, parked, and protected; and, of course, no matter how fuel efficient, they need to be filled up at the local gas station. The point, then, is that imports *create* jobs, just like exports do. Furthermore, as large as the foreign debt is, it is a small fraction of the total GNP. Unless it grows drastically or the economy collapses, we should be able to pay it off.

At the same time, international trade causes hardships, resentments, and fears, particularly

---

*As we will see in Chapter 18, economists attribute part of this problem to the huge budget deficits the government incurred during the 1980s.

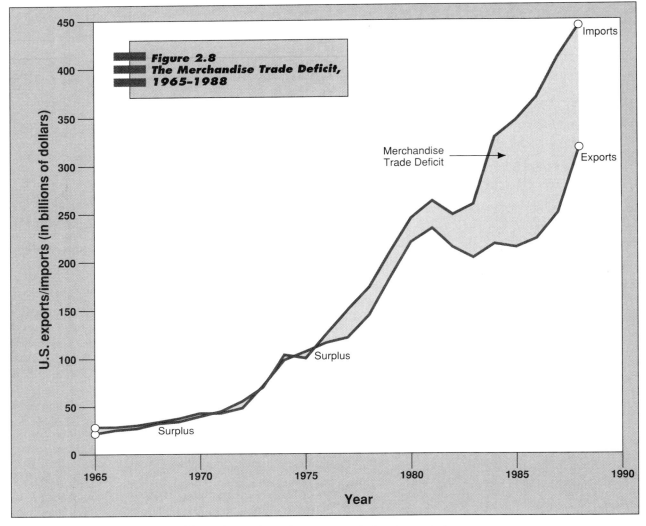

**Figure 2.8
The Merchandise Trade Deficit,
1965–1988**

U.S. exports/imports (in billions of dollars)

Imports

Exports

Merchandise
Trade Deficit

Surplus

Surplus

Year

*Starting in the mid-1970s, the United States began importing more goods than it exported.
This merchandise trade deficit grew throughout the 1980s.*

Source: U.S. Bureau of the Census, *Statistical Abstract of the United States: 1988*
(Washington, D.C.: Government Printing Office, 1989), p. 768; and *Survey of Current
Business*, March 1989, p. 30.

among the displaced workers in the noncompetitive industries. Many companies have seen their sales and profits plummet in the face of intense foreign competition, and, of course, employment in these industries suffers as well. The importation of steel, shoes, textiles, automobiles, and electronic gadgets has caused ever more strident cries for **protectionism**, that is, for legislation to protect American industry from foreign competition. Such bills have been repeatedly introduced into Congress.

In 1988, for example, Congress passed a mammoth trade bill that called for retaliation against countries that ran large trade surpluses in the United States and were judged to be engaged in unfair trading practices. Many observers regarded this legislation as a milestone in America's postwar international economic behavior because it was a step toward the erection of tariff barriers. Although this type of legislation is popular in the "rust belt" states of Michigan, Ohio, Illinois, and Indiana, which have been hard hit by the loss of manufacturing, the law's opponents fear that protectionism will ultimately do more harm than good because other countries will surely retaliate against our exports. For

Japanese automobiles on their way to the United States. Probably the most visible symbol of the internationalization of the economy is the massive imports of foreign made automobiles, especially from Japan.

every job saved in Detroit, two might be lost in Topeka, Kansas, where the local economy depends heavily on grain exports. In addition, the critics point out that part of the trade deficit resulted from the high value of the dollar, a condition that is subject to change. (A few years ago, for example, dollars were worth more relative to other currencies, and as a result Americans found foreign goods comparatively inexpensive and bought more than they sold.)

Protectionism will no doubt remain on the front pages for the next several years. As a nation ages, its economy ages too. Change is inevitable,

and there will inevitably be winners and losers in the process. As things now stand, traditional heavy industries will probably decline more while newer ones based on high technology or services replace them. What is needed is not necessarily protectionism or reindustrialization but economic growth. Growth, in turn, means educating and retraining workers, encouraging research and development, disseminating information, and improving the health and welfare of our citizens.

How this should be done and who should do it is the real political issue of the future.

Checkpoint

- The principal changes in the American economy are:
  - The shift from manufacturing to service industries as the main source of wealth and income

- The decline in traditional blue-collar occupations and farm labor and the growth in female employment
- Intense international economic competition that is beginning to dominate the domestic political agenda

SUMMARY

Many demographic features divide the nation: the aging of the population; demands by blacks, Hispanics, and women for equality; and the migration of affluent and politically active citizens from cities to suburbs and from the North and Midwest to the South and West. Although these cleavages seldom lead to violence, they are the animating force behind most current events.

Like any industrial country, the United States has social classes, that is, groups separated by income, education, and occupation. Because of differences in status, opportunity, life-style, health, and other indicators of well being, classes have differing, often antagonistic, needs and interests. The various layers of society, furthermore, have access to different amounts of political resources. Poverty continues to be widespread in America. During the 1950s and 1960s the rate declined substantially but then increased in the 1970s and has remained above ten percent, even though the federal and state governments spend billions on antipoverty programs each year. In spite of the potential for conflict, relatively little open class strife exists in the United States.

The days of pure capitalism have long since gone, and the economy today is a mixture of private enterprise and public involvement. The government regulates the business cycle and tries to protect the public from economic and social hardships. Many segments of the economy are characterized by great concentration in ownership and management of productive resources.

Significant economic changes affect production and employment. America has shifted from a predominantly industrial to a service economy: It increasingly produces services rather than goods. This change is revealed by the relative decline in traditional male-dominated blue-collar jobs. Perhaps the most frightening trend in the economy has been the impact of foreign competition. In the span of just 20 years the United States fell from the status of an economic superpower to a debtor nation that has trouble competing with many countries in Europe and Asia. A common response calls for protectionism to stem the tide of foreign-made goods. Other analysts, believing that this approach is shortsighted, argue that America should invest in human capital, such as health and education, that will allow it to compete in service industries and high technology.

KEY TERMS

Cohorts
Social class
Functional illiteracy
Mixed economic system
Macroeconomic policy
Gross national product (GNP)

Reindustrialization
Balance of trade
Merchandise trade deficit
Protectionism

FOR FURTHER READING

Harrison Bennett and Barry Bluestone, *The Great U-Turn* (New York: Basic Books, 1988). A good description and explanation of recent economic trends in the United States.

Reynolds Farley and Walter R. Allen, *The Color Line and the Quality of Life* (New York: Russell Sage, 1987). The most up-to-date and comprehensive comparisons of white and black living conditions.

Andrew Hacker, ed., *U/S A Statistical Portrait of the American People* (New York: Viking Press, 1983). A wonderful compendium of facts about the American people.

Michael Harrington, *The Other America* (Baltimore: Penguin Books, 1963). Although written in the 1960s, this book perhaps more than any other opened America's eyes to the existence of widespread poverty within its borders.

Robert Reich and John B. Donahue, *New Deals: The Chrysler Revival and the American System* (New York: Times Books, 1985). A fascinating story of how the economic and political systems at one and the same time work together and at cross purposes.

James A. Sweet and Larry L. Bumpass, *American Families and Households* (New York: Russell Sage, 1987). Using census data, the authors describe and explain important changes in family and household composition.

Lester Thurow, "The Surge in Inequality," *Scientific American*, May 1987, pp. 30–37. A respected economist shows how declining productivity is slowly reducing the wages and standard of living.

U. S. Department of Commerce, *Statistical Abstract of the United States* (various editions) (Washington, D.C.: Government Printing Office). These volumes appear annually and contain a wealth of information about the population and economy of the United States.

A Declaration by the Representatives of the UNITED STATES OF AMERICA, in General Congress assembled.

When in the course of human events it becomes necessary for one people to dissolve the political bands which have connected them with another, and to ~~advance of the~~ ~~which they~~ as sume among the powers of the earth the separate and equal ~~equal & independent~~ station to which the laws of nature & of nature's god entitle them, a decent respect to the opinions of mankind requires that they should declare the causes which impel them to the ~~the~~ separation.

We hold these truths to be self-evident; ~~sacred & undeniable~~ that all men are created equal ~~& independent~~ that ~~from that equal creation they derive~~ they are endowed by their creator with ~~& inherent & inalienable~~ rights; that among ~~which~~ these are ~~the preservation of~~ life, & liberty, & the pursuit of happiness; that to secure these rights ~~ends~~ ge

American Political Philosophy

Chapter 3

Americans pride themselves on their country's deep-seated tradition of freedom of expression. But free speech has never produced a wide variety of political ideologies. Instead, a single philosophy, general-welfare liberalism, dominates political discourse in the United States. This body of thought contains two main strands, which twist around one another like the fibers in a rope. One part emphasizes individual rights and limited government, while the other stresses government action to promote the common good. The predominance of a sole belief system, however, does not prevent conflicts from arising. The rope periodically unravels, and people argue bitterly about which strand we should cling to. ∎

The fire began around 4:30 in the afternoon of March 25, 1911, a Saturday. Apparently touched off in piles of scrap material, the flames quickly engulfed the ninth and tenth floors. Within minutes the Triangle Waist Company, New York City's leading manufacturer of popular shirtwaist blouses, was ablaze.

The company's nearly 500 employees, mostly Jewish and Italian immigrants, were preparing to leave for the day. "I was just fixing my hair and putting on my coat," Pauline Cuoio Pepe later recalled. As smoke and heat filled the hallways, panicked employees rushed to escape. "There were about 100 people right next to the door," Mrs. Pepe said, "but it was closed."[1] In fact, most of the exits were locked, an attempt, investigators alleged afterward, to prevent workers from pilfering the company's merchandise. Many did manage to scramble onto the sole outside fire escape, but, being overburdened, it immediately collapsed, spewing bodies onto the pavement many flights down. The malfunction of the building's only two elevators left everyone else trapped.

Although fire engines arrived quickly, their ladders extended only to the sixth floor. The des-

The Triangle Waist fire in 1911, which killed more than 140 girls and women, was one of many tragedies that caused Americans to rethink government's proper role in regulating the economy.

perate victims, their clothes and hair burning, started jumping from windows and ledges to their deaths on the sidewalks below as firemen watched helplessly. *The New York Times* captured the horror of the scene:

> Then one poor little creature jumped. There was a plate glass protection over part of the sidewalk, but she crashed through it, wrecking it and breaking her body into a thousand pieces. . . . Then they all began to drop. The crowd yelled "Don't jump!" but it was jump or be burned.[2]

After half an hour the worst was over: 146 people had died, almost all of them girls and young women 16 to 23 years old.

Considered the worst industrial accident in New York history, the Triangle fire did more than consume young lives: It seared the nation's conscience, caused it to rethink its political philosophy, and helped bring deep and far-reaching social and economic reforms.

THE IMPORTANCE OF IDEAS IN POLITICS

Prior to 1900 the doctrine of **laissez faire** prevailed in America. Laissez faire is the philosophy that government should refrain from interfering in the economy. Beyond maintaining law and order, neither Washington nor the state capitals had any business telling manufacturers and merchants how to conduct their affairs. A company could protect its goods by locking employees in their workplace; it could maximize profits by hiring women and children for pennies a day in 12-hour shifts including Saturdays; it could hold down costs by skimping on health and safety equipment and facilities. (The building housing the Triangle Waist Company had one fire escape, two narrow and winding stairwells, and wooden doors that opened in instead of out.)

Acceptance of laissez faire dominated the early industrial revolution. According to its tenets, the marketplace, along with people's self-interest and charitable spirits, would promote the general welfare. Government rules and regulations were unnecessary and unwanted.

Industrialization, however, brought with it severe economic dislocations and untold human miseries. By the turn of the century, citizens of all social ranks began to reconsider government's proper role in society. Perhaps, they reasoned, laissez faire worked in a preindustrial era when families were more self-sufficient; when small shops, not massive assembly lines, produced most of the nation's goods; when colossal corporations and trusts did not monopolize transportation and trade; and when life seemed less dehumanized, bureaucratized, and harsh. But in an age of large-scale industry, laissez faire was becoming as outmoded as the horse and buggy.

The Triangle Waist Company tragedy and countless others like it thus ushered in a new set of ideas about political responsibility. Look at your classroom or dormitory. Even if they are old and rickety, chances are they contain metal, unlocked fire doors, clearly marked exits, fire extinguishers, smoke detectors, sprinklers, fire walls, and a host of other safety features mandated by state, local, and national regulations. Such precautions are so commonplace that everyone takes them for granted. But they did not get there by happenstance. They are the culmination of a major transformation in attitudes and expectations about government's legitimate functions.

Clearly ideas about government's responsibilities have changed drastically in the past 100 years. These days hardly anyone expects representatives to sit idly by while depressions, bank failures, inflation, epidemics, natural disasters, and other catastrophes befall their constituents. On the contrary, most of us have come to demand more from political institutions.

Today, then, a different philosophy of government reigns supreme. In order to understand the political system, and especially to know who does and does not have influence in it, we need to examine this philosophy.

It may be surprising to begin the study of American politics with a look at ideas rather than institutions. But a nation's political creed largely determines the shape, scope, and level of its government's activities, and in this sense ideas are an important form of power. They do as much damage as bombs and as much good as penicillin; they can compel behavior as effectively as a police officer; they determine the content of public policy as decisively as lawmakers; and they can squelch change or incite revolution. A nation's morality and political ideals create its policy agenda, legitimize its social and economic institutions, define standards of justice, and, of most significance, determine who governs and how they rule.

These statements are particularly true in free and open societies like ours, where authorities seldom rely on brute force to get their way. The skillful use of language and symbols works just as well. In America, as anywhere else, some individuals and groups benefit more than others from the way the prevailing political philosophy distributes authority.

The Political Philosophy of the United States

A political scientist, Theodore Lowi, coined the phrase "public philosophy" to describe a set of values and attitudes that "dominates all other sources of belief in the formulation of public policy."[3] Although his understanding of what constitutes the prevailing public philosophy differs from ours, we agree that a single viewpoint guides domestic politics.

This proposition may startle some readers. In a land of free speech and virtually unlimited sources of information, it may be hard to believe that one philosophy overwhelms all others. To be sure, a diversity of ideas exists, but underlying this diversity is a widely accepted core of principles with an unmistakable uniqueness and identity. So universally held is this belief system that American history has been largely devoid of clashing ideologies such as socialism and fascism.[4]

We call this set of beliefs, values, and ideals **general-welfare liberalism.** The phrase underlines its two major components, liberalism and general welfare.[5]

CLASSICAL LIBERALISM The label "liberalism" presents a linguistic difficulty. As used in this chapter, it differs from its contemporary usage. Here, liberalism refers to a philosophy that dates back to seventeenth- and eighteenth-century European and British philosophers. Their writings emphasized personal freedoms, political equality, the rule of law, private property rights, limited government (because the state was considered a threat to these rights), and great faith in human progress. Called **classical liberalism** to distinguish it from the modern definition, it is, in essence, a philosophy of individual political freedom. Today's liberal, by contrast, favors a strong, active central government that supplies its citizens with a broad range of services and benefits such as health care, housing, education, and income maintenance.

GENERAL WELFARE The general-welfare part of the public philosophy holds that the government has the right and obligation to protect and promote the people's welfare. Thus, collective action through public institutions is not only necessary but desirable. At times, it even justifies limiting individual rights for the common good.

Agreement on the main principles of general-welfare liberalism runs far and wide on this continent: Americans accept it almost instinctively. At the same time, because the creed has two diverging branches, there is plenty to argue about. One part advocates individual liberties and limited government; the other stresses an active government that provides for the public welfare. All too often these ideals collide. Cities and states, for example, constantly wrestle with the problem of reconciling the community's interests—say, lower medical and insurance costs—with personal preferences—not to wear seat belts. Or, to take a different case, the courts have to weigh the rights of the distributors and consumers of X-rated movies against demands for community decency. This tension between the general-welfare ethic and the belief in liberalism, as well as the inherent ambiguity in the meaning of the terms, are what drive current politics.

Checkpoint

- Ideas are a form of power because they can compel people to do things they would not otherwise do.

- Early in its history the United States was governed by the doctrine of laissez faire, a philosophy of hands-off government.

- Laissez faire has now been superseded by general-welfare liberalism.

- The liberalism part emphasizes individual rights and freedoms, while the general-welfare component stresses the need for governmental action to promote the public good.

- Americans agree on the broad outlines of the philosophy, but the specific parts are sufficiently ambiguous and contradictory that disputes frequently arise about what government should and should not do.

THE ORIGINS OF GENERAL-WELFARE LIBERALISM

A sweeping philosophy like general-welfare liberalism did not spring up fully grown overnight. It developed gradually from the accumulation of past practices, attitudes, beliefs, and experiences. Its roots, in fact, extend back beyond the struggle for independence to seventeenth- and eighteenth-century Europe, especially England and Scotland. The settlers who landed at Plymouth Rock and Jamestown brought with them in addition to their livestock and housewares a cultural heritage, and they tended it as faithfully as their corn, cotton, and tobacco. True, the ideas were substantially modified by the colonial experience—even to the extent of justifying separation from the homeland, Great Britain. But the precepts that found their way into the Declaration of Independence and the Constitution were not strictly American inventions.[6] To appreciate the various influences on American political thought, therefore, one has to travel back and forth across the Atlantic Ocean.

Very roughly speaking, the newcomers to the North American continent transported with them two philosophical impulses: the assertion of individual rights and an affirmation of civic virtue and responsibility. The first, now called classical liberalism, tends to dominate historical accounts of the Revolution. But the second, though less well known, was also important in the young nation, and it too eventually helped to shape the public philosophy.

Classical Liberalism: Emphasis on Individual Freedoms

The intellectual fervor of eighteenth-century Europe, called the Age of Reason or the Enlightenment, taught that fixed laws governed nature. Human minds could discover and study these laws through reason but could neither create nor destroy them. For Enlightenment philosophers it was a short step from this premise to the assertion that human affairs too were guided by immutable principles. Simply by virtue of its existence, humanity was endowed with **natural rights**—liberties that no king or pope or parliament could justly deny it. "Man is born free," Jean Jacques Rousseau boldly proclaimed in *The Social Contract*, meaning that liberty is a natural condition. This notion flourished in the New World. And although the founders disagreed vehemently about the exact definition of freedom, they never doubted its validity or worth.

Hence, they had mixed feelings about government. John Locke, the English philosopher, argued that a government is essentially a "contract" between citizens and a ruler whose sole responsibility is the protection of individual rights. All of a government's powers are subordinate to this responsibility, and, being a compact or agreement among individuals, it derives its legitimacy from—and only from—them. The logic implied that the subjects could annul or cancel the agreement whenever they felt the government put their natural rights in jeopardy.

Colonists debating the meaning of liberty and the principles of government.

Elaborated and modified by the frontier experience and the separation from Britain, these concepts found popular expression in the Declaration of Independence. "Men," Thomas Jefferson wrote there, are "created equal" and "endowed" by God (not the King!) with "unalienable rights" including "life, liberty, and the pursuit of happiness." In keeping with the Lockean tradition, Jefferson added that political authorities only derive their "just powers from the consent of the governed." Thus, "whenever any form of government becomes destructive of [individual freedoms] it is the right of people to alter or abolish it, and to institute new government. . . ." All of these claims were "self-evident" to everyone except the English monarch, George III, who, Jefferson charged, had "repeatedly" violated them by, among other injustices, imposing unfair and unrepresentative taxes, arbitrarily seizing property, interfering with commerce and trade, and denying the colonists their natural rights.

The liberties Jefferson and his compatriots sought to preserve against British "tyranny" are familiar: freedom of speech, religion, press, and assembly, and the right to be secure in one's person and possessions. Private ownership of property was, of course, an important item on the list. The Lockean tradition held that people were not truly free unless they could own, use, and dispose of property as they saw fit.

The concern with personal freedoms implied that government's power and duties had to be circumscribed. The main threat to liberty, Jefferson and his colleagues thought, came from concentrated political power. This preoccupation with protecting political rights by limiting government found its way into the Constitution, which, as we see in Chapter 4, creates a series of mechanical barriers to the concentration of power.

But these institutional devices can only go so far. Hence, James Madison suggested a complementary device: a "compound" or **extended republic**. If the polity is large and diverse enough, he reasoned, it would contain a multiplicity of interests which in the long run would cancel out one another's influence and lead to the protection of interests. Humanity's natural inclination to pursue self-interest, in other words, offered a convenient mechanism for ensuring stability and restraint because no class or group would become overly powerful if it had to contend with others. In addition, as the number of factions multiplied, it would become harder for them to "discover their own strength and act in unison with each other."[7]

Madison's solution, to express it bluntly, was

to pit groups against one another in the hopes that their struggles would be self-limiting. The vigorous pursuit of private gain on the part of many factions would, he hoped, lead in the end to the public good: "[His] answer was to counteract passion with passion, ambition with ambition."[8]

Yet however important liberty and equality were in framing government, their meaning was subject to varying interpretations. In fact, as A Closer Look (p. 76) suggests, those who hark back to a mythical golden age of freedom might be surprised by how regulated life could be at the time of independence.

Civic Virtue as a Method of Securing Liberty

Strictly formal or legal limitations on government left some founders uneasy for they felt that constitutional tinkering by itself could neither prevent autocrats from usurping power nor provide a smoothly functioning state. Instead, they believed that freedom could only flourish in relatively small republics governed by virtuous men (they, of course, had males in mind at the time). What was essential, they thought, was a cadre of dedicated public servants who embodied **civic virtue**: statesmanship, personal sacrifice, wisdom, prudence, and commitment to the community good. Strong and righteous leadership, not rugged individualism or the selfish pursuit of personal interests, would best guarantee freedom for all.

Historians debate the importance of civic virtue on political thought in the United States. For decades most of them assumed that Locke's legacy of individualism, possessive materialism, and limited government shaped our intellectual development.[9]

Recently, though, several intellectual historians have emphasized the significance of civic virtue as a guiding principle in the Revolutionary War period. It is a misreading of American intellectual history, these scholars claim, to see only Locke when other influences were at work as well.[10] They argue that the founders knew the Republic could not be secured by simply unleashing individual rights and interests. On the

contrary, these early leaders maintained a strong sense of community, a feeling they derived from their readings of classical literature. As one historian puts it, they were moved by a conception of "man as a political being whose realization of self occurs only through participation in public life, through active citizenship. . . ."[11]

How far this ideology motivated the founders has still not been settled. Nevertheless, it seems clear that many were concerned with more than simply protecting private interests; that they coupled freedom with duty; and that they, like us, would be troubled by a company that would endanger the lives of several hundred women and girls simply to prevent the theft of a few blouses.

Indirect Versus Direct Democracy

Paradoxically, for all the founders' misgivings about centralized power, they were equally suspicious of the masses. Turning the reins of government over to the people would be ill considered, James Madison advised in *The Federalist Papers*. Not only is it necessary to "guard against the confusion of the multitude," but an even worse danger of unrestrained democracy is despotism by the majority. Madison was just as concerned about protecting minorities from abuse by majorities as he was about restraining government itself:

> In framing a government which is to be administered by men over men, the great difficulty lies in this: you must first enable the government to control the governed; and in the next place oblige it to control itself. A dependence on the people is, no doubt, the primary control on the government; but experience has taught mankind the necessity of auxiliary precautions.[12]

These "auxiliary precautions" consist of numerous constitutional roadblocks in the path of direct control of government by the people, such as the electoral college for selecting presidents, an independent judiciary and, until the passage of the Seventeenth Amendment in 1905, the indirect election of senators.

A Closer Look

The Meaning of Liberty in the Early Republic★★★

One of the amusements of listening to current political discussions is the frequent invocation of the founders to support opposing sides of an argument. It is, of course, natural to call upon Washington, Jefferson, Madison, Hamilton, and the rest because, after all, didn't they write the documents that gave us our freedom? And hasn't our generation lost sight of the simple and eternal truths they bequeathed?

It is a comforting strategy inasmuch as it appeals to history and common sense. But it is too simple and too misleading because the definition of liberty in colonial America was not as straightforward and clear as we might think. Although the Republic's creators had unbridled faith in freedom and equality, they certainly did not share a common understanding of its key terms.[a]

The meaning of equality was particularly contentious. "All men are created equal," Thomas Jefferson declared, but as a slave owner and property holder he did not intend his words to be taken literally. Many of his contemporaries thought equality meant equality of *opportunity*, implying that differences in status were tolerable, while for a few the term suggested equality of *condition*, a more radical concept. As a matter of fact, many eminent citizens in the early Republic doubted that self-government could be sustained for long unless everyone was more or less socially and economically equal.

More was at stake than definitions, however. No one, not even the most outspoken libertarian, advocated *unlimited* rights. Every behavior that was claimed as a natural liberty was saddled with qualifications, restrictions, and exceptions. Most of these limitations were

---

By His EXCELLENCY

GEORGE WASHINGTON, Esquire,

GENERAL and COMMANDER in CHIEF of the FORCES
of the UNITED STATES OF AMERICA.

BY Virtue of the Power and Direction to Me especially given, I hereby enjoin and require all Perfons refiding within feventy Miles of my Head Quarters to threfh one Half of their Grain by the 1ft Day of February, and the other Half by the 1ft Day of March next enfuing, on Pain, in Cafe of Failure, of having all that fhall remain in Sheaves after the Period above mentioned, feized by the Commiffaries and Quarter-Mafters of the Army, and paid for as Straw.

GIVEN *under my Hand, at Head Quarters, near the Valley Forge, in Philadelphia County,* this 20th *Day of December,* 1777.

G. WASHINGTON.

By His Excellency's Command,
ROBERT H. HARRISON, Sec'y.

LANCASTER; PRINTED BY JOHN DUNLAP.

During the War for Independence George Washington requisitioned supplies for his troops at Valley Forge. Laws and ordinances such as this one were common both before and after the Revolution and illustrate the fact the colonists did not believe in absolute freedom. Instead, most rights were limited in various ways.

based on tradition, but many seemed motivated by the imperatives of communal life. Law and precedent, for example, did not exempt private property from public control. Various rules outlawed gambling, prostitution, ostentatious dress and consumption, and other acts that might offend or disrupt community standards.[b] Landownership, to take another case, did not convey absolute rights but was a mixture of privileges and obligations. Statutes in New York City, for instance, required homeowners to hang lanterns from the top-floor windows in order to provide street lighting in the "Darke time of the moon," while the residents of Philadelphia had to plant " 'pines, unbearing mulberries, water poplars, lime or other shady and wholesome trees' so that the town might be 'well shaded from the violence of the sun in the heat of summer and thereby be rendered more healthy.' "[c]

In the same spirit, neighbors could enter another person's land to "fell dead trees and to dig peat for building or heating," and colonial charters considered navigable rivers to be public highways and fisheries "along which anyone had the right to use the banks for toting barges and preserving fish."[d]

Finally, each colony regulated commerce by means that today would be called wage and price controls. By an act of 1718, for instance, New Hampshire limited the fee for grinding grain to "one sixteenth part, and no more," with the exception of "Indian corn, for which the Mill shall take One Twelfth."[e]

More than property was regulated. Political freedoms were more narrowly defined than we sometimes think. As in England, states restricted different sects in varying degrees.

Jews and Catholics did not have full rights until much later. Likewise, freedom of speech and the press were hardly considered grants of absolute and unrestricted expression. According to the historian Forrest MacDonald, a state like Virginia felt no hypocrisy or shame at the time of the Revolution in sending its citizens into battle for freedom from the tyrannical British at the same time that it was "clamping harsh restrictions upon the utterance or publication of opinions that were contrary to the cause of independence or were critical of Congress, the state governments, or public officials."[f]

The present generation can learn at least two lessons from these experiences. First, no matter how obvious a "freedom" appears, it inherently contains ambiguities since a right almost by definition involves a behavior that others might find objectionable or harmful. "Truths," in other words, are seldom self-evident. And, second, no one in the 1770s or 1780s advocated absolute freedoms. On the contrary, they believed that a viable democracy depended on self-restraint and the goodwill of its citizens.

[a]Forrest MacDonald, *Novus Ordo Seclorum: The Intellectual Origins of the Constitution* (Lawrence: University of Kansas Press, 1985), p. 10.
[b]Ibid., pp. 15–16.
[c]Lawrence M. Friedman, *A History of American Law* (New York: Simon & Schuster, 1973), p. 66.
[d]MacDonald, *Novus Ordo Seclorum*, pp. 31, 34.
[e]Friedman, *American Law*, p. 65.
[f]MacDonald, *Novus Ordo Seclorum*, pp. 45–46.

Thomas Jefferson believed the best about human nature. In his view, men and women only needed a nurturing political environment in order to be responsible citizens.

The Founding Fathers, in a word, did not create a direct or participatory democracy, but a *republic*. In a republic, as discussed in Chapter 1, elected officials and representatives, rather than the citizens themselves, make public policy. A republic's power flows from the consent of the governed, and the popular will (on paper, at any rate) controls and disciplines its leaders.

Part of the reasoning behind indirect as opposed to direct democracy was the considerable controversy about human nature. Most social evils, as John Quincy Adams, Alexander Hamilton, and others believed, were traceable to imperfections in the average person's character. Avarice, shortsightedness, impatience, and the insatiable quest for gain on the part of the masses would, they feared, inevitably ruin society. The affairs of state were best left in the hands of virtuous elites whose primary concerns would be the well-being of the commonwealth and who would act as a buffer between the people and power.

Others, like Thomas Jefferson, felt that repressive institutions, not human frailties, stood in the way of successful government. Given a nurturing environment, men and women would become responsible citizens, and government's proper function was to ensure the conditions for liberating people's potential goodness.

Americans still debate this matter. Chapter 8, for example, explores the quality of public opinion, contrasting one group of scholars who accuse the masses of being moody, temperamental, and misinformed with others who assert that the ordinary people are as reasonable and civic-minded as their leaders.

Checkpoint

- Two ideas influenced the formation of the American republic: classical liberalism and civic virtue.

- Classical liberalism was the philosophy that individuals had political rights and that government's main responsibility was to protect those liberties.

- Accordingly, government's powers must be limited as it was considered the main threat to individual freedom.

- Madison also believed that liberty would be preserved in a "pluralist" society in which groups competed with one another.

- The idea of civic virtue held that liberties could only be preserved by entrusting the reins of political power to a group of conscientious people who put the needs of the community as a whole above personal wealth and ambition.

- Distrusting the masses, the founders created a republic in which power is exercised by elected officials, not by the people themselves.

POLITICAL PHILOSOPHY IN THE NINETEENTH CENTURY

As the 1800s unfolded, many classical liberal principles, particularly individual rights and limited government, came to the fore. The belief in civic virtue, which held that these liberties should be used for the common good, receded into the background but did not disappear entirely; it left an impression that eventually found its way back into our public philosophy.

The Interpretation of Rights

A central feature of classical liberalism was its espousal of *political* freedoms. It did not come to grips with what later generations would identify as economic and social rights. The Bill of Rights (the first 10 amendments to the Constitution) protects us against "unreasonable searches and seizures," but does not guarantee us a job so that we can earn something to be protected; it guards us against "cruel and unusual punishments," but not against starvation; it gives us "freedom of speech," but not health care, shelter, and clothing. Nineteenth-century liberalism looked at freedom rather narrowly. A millionaire, a mill worker, and a vagrant would all be deemed equally free if they had the right to vote or attend a church of their own choosing.

INDIVIDUALISM   Early liberal conceptions of rights placed the individual, not the community or the public interest, in the center of the political universe. It was a logical placement because human dignity and moral and intellectual development of the individual were among the Enlightenment's most cherished ideals. Leave people alone, let them develop their natural capacities to the fullest, make them accept responsibility for their own salvation—these were the goals that inspired Americans in the beginning of the industrial revolution.

It appeared to be an appropriate model for a society that spent the next 100 years taming the frontier. The faith in individualism, which grew

into a consuming adulation, was, according to legend, repaid a thousand times by the pioneers who subjugated Indians, forded rivers, survived droughts and blizzards, and ultimately carved a thriving civilization out of a hostile wilderness. Freedom and individualism, not a meddlesome government, created the boundless prosperity for the settlers and their progeny that we enjoy today.

American history is filled with ironies, but few are more striking than the slow transformation of the classical liberal ethic with its emphasis on political equality and independence into an unbridled, acquisitive, even rapacious, individualism that left citizens more unequal and dependent than ever. "Civic virtue," one historian writes, "came to be measured in terms of personal ambition and devotion to the acquisition of wealth. . ." rather than selfless duty to the community.[13] Continuing in this vein, he notes that:

> Instead of sacrificing their private desires in the interests of community, nineteenth-century Americans relentlessly engaged in the individual pursuit of wealth and even justified such activity as the sole legitimate foundation for a free society.[14]

THE ROLE OF GOVERNMENT   Limited government was an imperative in the early 1800s. There were, to be sure, fierce debates about exactly how limited it should be. Commercial interests, under the leadership of Alexander Hamilton, wanted the central government in Washington to be an engine for economic development and modernization. Others, like Jefferson, accepted the desirability of growth but maintained that it could best be achieved by liberating farmers and artisans, not by centralizing power.

At no time, however, did anyone advocate anything remotely resembling the activist general-welfare state that we have today. That concept did not emerge until the turn of this century. In the meantime, a greatly transformed classical liberalism, known as laissez faire, ruled nineteenth-century America.

Pioneers and homesteaders who tamed the frontier reinforced the image of individualism, the belief that self-sufficiency, hard work, initiative, and not government assistance were all that one needed to succeed in America.

The Rise of Laissez Faire

In the years after the Civil War political thought coupled private ownership with individual rights, a merger that lent itself to the growth of a free enterprise, capitalist economy. Classical liberals had no conception of modern-day capitalism. Theirs was an era of small farms and cottage (home-based) industry, when goods and services were exchanged face to face. They could not foresee that this philosophy would ultimately legitimize the acquisition of huge quantities of property and its conversion to capital. Not surprisingly, therefore, nineteenth-century industrialists, bankers, and entrepreneurs marched under the banner of classical liberalism.

Later, especially in the years after the Civil War, a variant of classical liberal thought, laissez faire, emerged. This theory of political economy applied the principles of individualism to human affairs with a vengeance.

A moral code as well as a theory of economics and government, laissez faire taught that all of society benefits if its members are free to pursue their separate self-interests. Instead of leading to conflict, self-interested competition actually produced harmony. Why? Because if in the economic realm buyers and sellers are left alone, they will in the long run produce and consume what they need and want. Men and women, after all, are the best judges of their own desires. In a leap of faith, proponents of laissez faire also argued that the community good is simply the sum of individual preferences. Therefore, whether enlightened or not, the impulse to maximize one's own pleasures and profits adds to society's total welfare.

An absolutely essential ingredient of this system is free and open markets characterized by competition. The laws of supply and demand—and laissez faire theorists considered them laws—ensured that prices, rents, wages, profits, and interests would eventually reach their proper level. Equally significant, the goods and services required by society would be automatically provided since someone is always prepared to produce them, given sufficient demand. Economic freedom and competition, in short, create as if by an "invisible hand" an optimal amount of production and exchange.

If one accepts these premises, government's role is obvious: It should stay totally out of economic affairs, a position consistent with a classical liberal's belief in limited political authority.

For the business class, the message could not have been clearer: Governments are inefficient, slow, and plodding; the market is orderly, prompt, and decisive. Bureaucrats make mistakes, cause delays, and contribute to over- and underpricing; the market correctly regulates output and balances costs and profits. Public planners are unresponsive to both consumers and producers; the market satisfies both.

The logical consequence of laissez faire is a "negative state," a government with minimal duties.[15] Apart from protecting its borders and preventing internal disturbances, the central government had little else to do. And certainly taxing manufacturers or wage earners to help the poor made no sense: "If it [government] takes from him who has prospered to give to him who has not, it violates its duty towards the one to do more than its duty towards the other."[16]

Gradually, a transformation of classical liberalism occurred in the nineteenth century: Rights that were thought of as belonging to individuals were transferred to formal associations in general and to corporations in particular. Not only farmers and shopkeepers as individuals had rights, but so too did *organizations* of farmers and businesses. In a subtle twist of interpretation of the founders' ideas, disembodied corporations and trusts, however large and powerful, came to be considered as entities like individuals with "natural" rights requiring protection.

In the hands of corporate and financial magnates, laissez faire legitimized the accumulation of vast fortunes, the creation of a dispossessed proletariat, and incessant corporate warfare. It justified behavior like the Triangle company's

The use of child laborers like this 12-year-old girl working in a Vermont cotton mill proved to many that laissez faire capitalism was inhumane and immoral and justified government regulation of industry.

treatment of its immigrant workers. Most important, it succeeded in keeping government at bay. According to the theory of laissez faire, public programs to alleviate human misery were at one and the same time unneeded and harmful.*

However harsh these views may seem, they prevailed for most of the time up to World War I. Governments, whether at the national, state,

---

*As a matter of fact, laissez faire's most ardent apologists seem to the present generation as miserly and coldhearted as any collection of thinkers in American history. William Graham Sumner, a sociologist and educator and a man called a "social Darwinist" for his conviction that even in industrial civilization life boiled down to a struggle for survival, claimed in essay after essay that the strong will live and the weak perish: "Let it be understood that we cannot go outside of this alternative: liberty, inequality, survival of the fittest; not-liberty, equality, survival of the unfittest." And what was to become of the unfit? "The fact that a man is here is no demand upon other people that they shall keep him alive and sustain him." (Quoted in Sidney Fine, *Laissez Faire and the General-Welfare State* (Ann Arbor, Mich.: Univ. of Michigan Press, 1956), p. 82). An interesting account of laissez faire philosophy is Richard Hofstadter's *Social Darwinism in American Thought* (New York: George Braziller, 1959).

or local level, took little responsibility or initiative in protecting workers, women, children, the sick, or the elderly. Such efforts were deemed unnatural, immoral, and counterproductive. Helping the destitute was a task best left to churches and organizations. States and municipalities did operate orphanages, poorhouses, and hospitals. But they were on such a small scale that they could not serve the legions of needy cases created by industrialization.

As late as 1908 only 30 states had laws prohibiting the employment of children under 18 in factories; only 15 set maximum 10-hour days for women; only 8 forbade night work for children under 18; and none required medical examinations as a condition of employment, occupational disease reporting, and 8-hour workdays for women in factories.[17] More than 7000 fatalities occurred in mines and railroads in 1907, a total that almost equals half of *all* job-related deaths in a typical year during the 1970s.[18] In one year alone, 1899, more than 2200 railroad workers were killed and another 35,000 injured.[19] Pennsylvania's anthracite coal mines averaged about 400 fatal accidents annually in the 1890s.[20]

Does one need more proof of the power of ideas?[*]

The Demise of Laissez Faire

During laissez faire's reign, other approaches to government waited in the wings. As we noted a

few pages back, Alexander Hamilton had advocated an active central government. And as a matter of fact, the federal government in Washington soon established a national bank, enacted protective tariffs, underwrote bridge and canal construction, deeded millions of acres of land to the railroads, began to subsidize agriculture and the training of skilled workers, and pacified the West. Military purchases during the Civil War provided an enormous boon to the economy.

Yet most of these activities aided business and contributed relatively little to the middle and working classes, who were left to fend for themselves. As the century wore on, industrialization seemed to create hardships as fast as it produced growth. Giant trusts drove small companies out of business, farm prices rose and fell like a roller coaster, and cities deteriorated into slums. All these developments, coupled with the concentration of wealth and power in the grasp of a few financiers and industrialists, sometimes called "robber barons," brought laissez faire under attack.

Psychologists and philosophers questioned the philosophy's empirical basis; economists rejected the facile assumptions about the efficiency and fairness of the "invisible hand"; and religious leaders rejected its tenets as immoral, inhuman, barbaric, and un-Christian.[21] These doubts and discontents slowly coalesced into a plethora of reform movements: populism, progressivism, social gospelists, and, for a fleeting moment in the early twentieth century, socialism. Most agitated for reform of corporate law—enactment of antitrust legislation is one example—but a few demanded public ownership of utilities and large corporations. For some the answer was professional management of government—a return to the civic virtue expounded in the late 1700s. Still others cried for greater federal regulation of the economy, such as control of railroads. Whatever their concerns and solutions, the reformers were united in the conviction that government could not remain a passive bystander while social and economic ills rode roughshod over thousands and thousands of men and women.

Changes in attitudes and practices were slow in coming, many requiring 30 or 40 years before

---

[*]The information reported in the previous paragraph has not been easy to collect. The statistics a nation records reflects its values and priorities. While laissez faire was in ascendancy, the U.S. government was not overly concerned with the health and safety of the labor force. That this proposition is valid may be seen by examining early volumes of *The Statistical Abstract*, which in the early 1900s was published by the Bureau of Foreign and Domestic Commerce. If your library collects government documents, an interesting project would be to compare the kinds of information reported in the earlier *Abstracts* with what appears in the later editions. It would be a way to see firsthand how national priorities have changed over the years. Chances are, for example, that the older versions contain few or no statistics on poverty, illiteracy, infant mortality, and accidents—matters that were considered private concerns—and a lot of trade and commercial data.

"The White Angel Bread Line": Dorothea Lange's classic photo depicts the psychological as well as physical toll the Great Depression of the 1930s took on millions of men and women. The depression convinced most Americans that the federal government should actively pursue policies to moderate the ups and downs of the business cycle.

reaching fruition. By the time of the Great Depression in the 1930s, however, a new philosophy of government had begun to take root. It was, needless to say, not proclaimed on a single day by a single administration. Nor was it a complete rejection of classical liberalism. Instead, it was an adaptation of earlier principles to the requirements of the twentieth century.

Checkpoint

- Philosophy of government in the early Republic interpreted rights as political—not economic or social—freedoms and placed enormous value on individualism, the ability to prosper on one's own.

- Laissez faire, a doctrine that rejected government interference in the economy, dominated America after the Civil War.

- Under its aegis the industrial revolution flourished, producing both economic growth and enormous human suffering.

- As conditions became intolerable, however, laissez faire fell into disfavor.

THE MAIN IDEAS OF GENERAL-WELFARE LIBERALISM

General-welfare liberalism steers a middle ground between unbridled classical liberalism (laissez faire) and the more extreme ideologies, such as socialism, that had become popular in Europe. An amalgam of individual rights and active government, it consists, as described in the beginning of the chapter, of two main parts.

The general-welfare component assigns government three important social and economic functions to smooth the rough edges of capitalism. First, it calls for government to manage the overall economy in order to minimize unemployment and inflation and encourage growth, an activity called macroeconomic policy in Chapter 2. Second, government is asked to provide needy individuals with basic goods and services. Proponents of general-welfare liberalism interpret poverty not as a personal weakness but as resulting in large measure from the failure of economic institutions, and public institutions have a duty to compensate the victims of this malfunctioning. Politicians debate furiously about who deserves help and how much is required, but they usually agree on the general principle of government assistance. Government's third function is to enact measures to protect the public from the perils of industrial life—unemployment, environmental pollution, dangerous products, consumer fraud, catastrophic illnesses, hazards in the workplace, and natural disasters—with which they as individuals acting alone cannot reasonably be expected to cope. This aid is not a matter of assisting the destitute; even well-off citizens are entitled to these protections.

The philosophy's second major component, liberalism, reaffirms classical liberalism's central values. We continue to live in a "private" society in which individualism, political liberties, personal property, limited government, and capitalism hold sway. The government has indeed swelled in size and purpose, but in most key respects the ideas voiced by the Republic's founders influence *how* the political apparatus carries out its responsibilities.

Consider what general-welfare liberalism does and does not encourage:

- Private property remains firmly protected. Although its use is restricted, the emphasis is on public *regulation*, not ownership. Owners are free to reap the profits of their blouse factories so long as they provide for the health and safety of their employees.
- We continue to adhere firmly to the notions of political equality and equality of opportunity. Virtually no significant party or group advocates equal wealth or common ownership of possessions.
- Differences in income, assets, and talents may be envied or resented but are always tolerated. What we demand (in theory, at any rate) is equality before the law; one person, one vote; an equal chance to succeed; and so forth.
- In this connection the unequal distribution of wealth goes unchallenged. Indeed, one of the most important facts about general-welfare liberalism's conception of government is that its programs are not paid for by taking from the rich and giving to the poor. As we saw in Chapter 2, the distribution of wealth today is about what it was 80 years ago. America, in short, pays for its public services with taxes on the population as a whole, from economic growth, and by distributing resources within rather than between social classes.
- As stressed repeatedly, the ideas (though not necessarily the *practice*) of individualism and distrust of government dominate our public philosophy. Comic strips illustrate our propensity to believe the worst about politicians and bureaucracy. The ongoing debate about mandatory seat belt use shows that we still feel that no one has the right to tell us how to live our lives, even if the advice is sound. Although Dan Staples regularly wears a seat belt, he voted to repeal a Nebraska law requiring drivers and

front-seat passengers to buckle up: "I don't want some one telling me whether I should wear a seat belt or not. . . . To me, it's a matter of personal choice."[22]

- As mammoth as the central government has become, it is still viewed as a partner with, not a substitute for, the free enterprise system. Farming, for instance, remains tightly in the hands of family and corporate farms, but depends heavily on the Department of Agriculture for crop subsidies, irrigation and flood control, scientific research, weather forecasts, and county extension agents.

- Although Americans have come, reluctantly perhaps, to recognize the need for collective action, they still cling to their biases against centralized power. They attempt wherever possible to keep public programs close to home and operate them through private institutions and channels.

- The well-known heritage of distrust of monarchs and tyrannical majorities continues to define perceptions of the polity's proper form. And a major contradiction inevitably arises. In seeking to put flesh on the goal of "life, liberty, and the pursuit of happiness," general-welfare liberalism assigns the political system many obligations that demand coherent and consistent action. But how is such action possible in a constitutional arrangement that divides and separates power, creates multiple layers of authority, each with a check over the other, and emphasizes gradual changes rather than rapid action? Ironically, as the size and scope of the federal and state establishments have mushroomed, they have nevertheless stayed as fragmented as the founders intended.

- The marketplace remains the backbone of the economy. Even though business and labor periodically suggest a closer collaboration with the state to meet the challenges of foreign competition, and even though, as we noted, nearly every economic sector receives some kind of government assistance, there is virtually no national economic planning in this country.

- Individual initiative and responsibility are still key social values. Contrary to popular impression, general-welfare liberalism does not advocate ministering to every citizen from cradle to grave. The rich and poor are expected to succeed on their own. The public philosophy distinguishes between success, which is a personal achievement, and suffering, which *may* be a public concern, especially if it is thought to be caused by factors like a major depression. No one, in other words, should be denied a reasonable chance for a decent life, but taking advantage of the opportunities is left up to the individual.

To sum up, general-welfare liberalism represents an accommodation of classical liberalism,

A Closer Look

Consensus on
General-Welfare Liberalism ★★★

That general-welfare liberalism is a public philosophy (that is, it enjoys nearly universal acceptance), can be deduced from the words of the leaders of both political parties. Listen, for example, to this election debate sponsored by the League of Women Voters between Democrats and Republicans:

Marlene Sanders [Moderator]: That takes us to another section which we're calling "The Role of Government." And we've been talking about that all along . . . but perhaps you can be a little more philosophical for a moment. Senator Dole, what are the reasonable expectations people should have in terms of what services government should provide . . . just in general, how much can we look to government for?

Senator Robert Dole [Republican of Kansas]: I think a great deal, and I think we all start off on the same basis, at least now speaking for Republicans. If we have an obligation, there are certain groups in society that need federal assistance whether they're handicapped, whether they're low income, whether they're elderly. And so I would say at the outset that we have a responsibility, and we can't shrink from that responsibility.[a]

Although Senator Dole quickly added "we have to be realistic," his response to this "philosophical" question differed hardly at all from his Democratic opponent, Representative Thomas Foley, who replied

. . . the moral test of government is how it treats those in the dawn of life—children; how it treats those in the twilight of life—the aged; and how it treats those in the shadow of life—the sick, and the needy, and the handicapped.

Between them, Senator Dole and Representative Foley brought within the purview of the government's care a huge portion of the population—the elderly, children, poor, and the sick.

Agreement on the basic political creed, of course, does not mean that the legislators have nothing to debate. Each tenet, each concept of general-welfare liberalism, is loaded with ambiguity. Yes, they agree, for example, that the government should provide for those in the "shadow" of life. But exactly how much care do the sick need?

The reader can test the validity of these remarks by analyzing the content of campaign speeches and debates. Close inspection of this material usually reveals agreement on fundamental political principles.

[a]The League of Women Voters' Educational Fund, "Congressional Leadership Debates," October 19, 1982, pp. 19–20. The commitment of elites to general-welfare liberalism is also systematically documented in Allen H. Barton, "Determinants of Economic Attitudes in the American Business Elite," *American Journal of Sociology* 91 (1985): tables 1(a) and 3.

with its emphasis on political equality, personal rights, private property, and individualism, to the harsh realities of corporate capitalism, a system that raised the standard of living in the United States to unprecedented heights while subjecting hundreds of thousands of individuals to financial insecurity and physical and emotional strain.

Agreement on this approach to government runs far and deep in this country as A Closer Look suggests.

Checkpoint

- General-welfare liberalism combines political liberty and capitalism with a recognition that government has a responsibility to foster economic growth and prosperity and reduce the hardships of modern industrial society. It is an attempt to balance the rights of individuals with the rights of the community.

- The doctrine's general-welfare component calls for an active government to improve the common good as well as ensure individual safety and well-being. The liberalism part, on the other hand, reaffirms traditional American beliefs in personal liberties, private property, limited government, and individualism.

- Because the doctrine contains conflicting and ambiguous standards, it inescapably leads to conflict. The nation thus spends its time arguing over how best to reconcile the contradictory elements and to apply them to concrete problems.

GENERAL-WELFARE LIBERALISM IN PRACTICE

Having looked at the doctrine of general-welfare liberalism as a whole, let us see how it affects several areas of American politics.

Class Consciousness and American Exceptionalism

One of the continuing mysteries of American politics is its absence of social class warfare. The United States, as the data in Chapter 2 reveal, is a multilayered society. A relatively small number of wealthy individuals sits at the top. Under them, in descending order, come managers, executives and professionals, a huge stratum of white- and blue-collar workers, service and farm laborers, and several million poor. It is not a pyramid because the middle layers are larger than the top and bottom. Nevertheless, by whatever yardstick one chooses, these classes are easily measured and identified.

Yet, as also asserted but left unexplained in Chapter 2, America has experienced comparatively little class strife during its 200 years of existence and practically none since 1950.[23] Workers and owners unquestionably fight bitterly about wages, hours, and fringe benefits. And people at the lower end of the scale envy and emulate the rich and powerful. Still, deep class antagonisms are more or less alien to our political culture. Neither the upper nor lower classes manifest distinctive **class consciousness**, the feelings of solidarity with one's own social and economic peers and antipathy to those above or below. Nor do various classes have distinctive ideologies. Labor, for example, seems as hostile to socialism as do industrialists and bankers. Indeed, as this chapter has argued, most layers of society accept the broad outlines of general-welfare liberalism.

Since the American economy is as developed as any country where conflicts between classes are commonplace, the unique situation here has been called American exceptionalism. **American exceptionalism** means that despite the existence of objective social classes, there is relatively little class conflict and no widespread acceptance of socialism in the United States.[24]

In order to experience class conflict, the members of a class have to identify with their social stratum, believe that its needs conflict with other classes, and be prepared to organize politically along class lines to advance their interests.[25] Although most Americans recognize inequalities in

survey identified with the "average" middle or working class. Hardly anyone thinks of being in the "upper" or "lower" class.

Another study found that relatively few manual laborers, the backbone of socialist movements overseas, identified with the working class; on the contrary, they tended to select "middle class," the same category white-collar employees, executives, and professionals picked.[27] The same report also measured other dimensions of class consciousness. Among other items, the authors presented their subjects with this statement: "Do you think that the interests of management and workers are basically opposed or are their interests basically the same?" Only slightly more than a third of the sample replied "opposed" and different occupational groups, executives as well as blue-collar workers, gave essentially the same responses, leading the authors to conclude that ". . . the politics of economic position in America, while it involves disagreement over the equitable division of economic rewards, is not a matter of fundamental conflict among cohesive social groups."[28]

American exceptionalism tells us a great deal about our public philosophy, because general-welfare liberalism is both its parent and child. In the first place, the lack of class consciousness, with its absence of alternative ideologies, has made acceptance of the public philosophy all the easier. With no viable competitors, general-welfare liberalism has had the stage to itself. But in the second place, the pervasive influence of the creed surely contributes to exceptionalism. Realistic and tough-minded, the working class nevertheless has internalized the creed's fundamental beliefs about opportunity, hard work, and justice: Workers may at times entertain doubts about economic and social institutions, but they have been reluctant, especially in the past several decades, to resolve them by political means along class lines.

Organized labor, to take one widely cited example, decided nearly 40 years ago to fight its battles in the economic, not political, arena. Its basic tactics have been strikes and boycotts of owners—head-on confrontations with management—rather than organized crusades against capitalism. By 1960, in fact, nearly all of labor leadership had become "vociferously antisocial-

In spite of real differences in economic and social standing, many Americans do not identify with a social class and class conflict is not a central part of American politics. Both the affluent and the middle and lower classes generally share the same bedrock values of general-welfare liberalism.

wealth and influence,[26] ethnic, religious, and regional loyalties far outweigh class attachments in importance in American politics. Table 3.1 suggests, for example, that few people seem to invest class labels with much meaning or emotion. The vast majority in this public opinion

Table 3.1

Social Class Identification of Americans, 1988

Self Class Identification	Percent
Lower	5
Working	45
Middle	47
Upper	3
Total	100.0
	(1476)

Question: "If you were asked to use one of four names for your social class, which would you say you belong in: the lower class, the working class, the middle class, or the upper class?" (The number in parentheses is the sample size.)

Source: Based on data from National Opinion Research Center, *General Social Surveys, 1972–88.*

ist and anticommunist, a position it shares with most workers."[29] Unions do, of course, lobby in Congress and contribute to the Democratic party. But their primary weapon has been the strength of their organizations relative to their employers. Unlike most industrialized countries, national labor parties or national labor newspapers do not exist here.

Sidney Verba and Kay Lehman Schlozman identify a set of attitudes that partly explains this situation. Studying the opinions of unemployed and working-class individuals, they came across a "gap" between personal experiences (being laid off, for example) and "general social ideology": ". . . there seems to be a very limited association between personal economic circumstances and policy preferences. [T]he links between social ideology and policy preferences seem tenuous or nonexistent."[30] Unemployed, dispossessed, and marginal workers, in other words, have not been galvanized into a unified proletariat that translates its grievances into distinctive political demands such as a radical change in capitalism.

These responses further illustrate the inclination to solve problems individually or through private organizations, with the government seen as a savior of last resort.

Limited Government and the Welfare State

Another component of general-welfare liberalism affects the form and content of government in the United States. Recall that classical liberalism (classical, not the modern version) asserts that "the government that governs least governs best." Paradoxically, despite the enormous size of the federal and state establishments, America has not completely abandoned this principle. On the contrary, it is still very much with us.

The human devastation caused by the industrial revolution led many nations, like ours, to take governmental action to deal with it. Britain, France, Germany, Italy, Belgium, and the Scandinavian countries have all built extensive social welfare systems. A **welfare state** provides income transfers, such as social security payments and unemployment compensation, and services such as medical, dental, and hospital care, to ensure a minimal level of well-being and equity for its citizens.[31]

What is interesting is that the efforts of other countries exceed ours by considerable amounts. Even though the United States possesses comparable wealth and productive capacity, these nations devote a larger portion of their resources to health care, education, housing, pensions, unemployment insurance, and other benefits, and they collect more taxes to pay for them, as Figure 3.1a–c demonstrates. Although the United States spends as much of its wealth on health care as any country, most of this money is raised and distributed through private channels; only 40 percent involves public programs (see Figure 3.1a). Nearly all Europeans, to take another case, are covered by public hospital insurance, whereas most Americans are covered, if they have coverage at all, by private programs (see Figure 3.1b). Notice also that tax revenues represent a relatively small portion of the nation's economic output compared with the other industrial nations (see Figure 3.1c).[32] These data support Charles Andrain's observation that despite its vast riches, the United States still has the "least developed" welfare system among the most highly industrialized countries.[33]

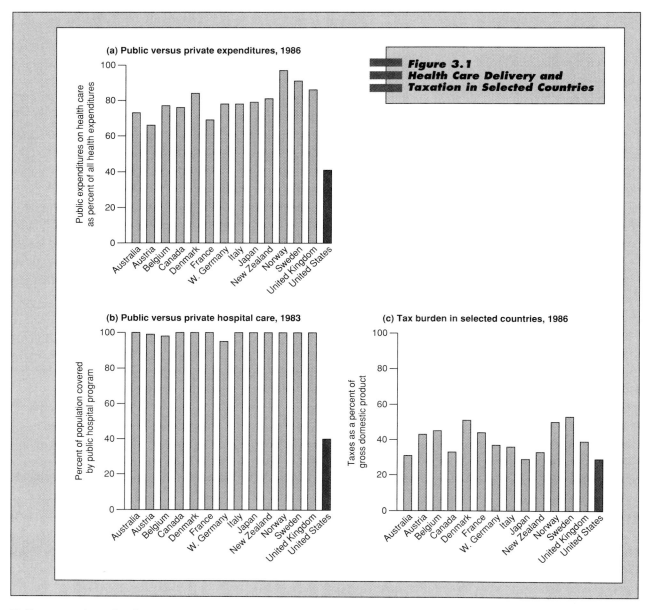

(a) Public versus private expenditures, 1986

(b) Public versus private hospital care, 1983

(c) Tax burden in selected countries, 1986

**Figure 3.1
Health Care Delivery and
Taxation in Selected Countries**

Unlike most industrialized nations, the United States administers health care through private channels. In addition, taxes constitute a lower proportion of its national product. These data suggest that general-welfare liberalism limits the role government plays in society.

Source: George J. Scheiber and Jean-Pierre Poullier, "International Health Spending and Utilization Trends," *Health Affairs* 7 (Fall 1988): 107; OECD, *Financing and Delivering Health Care* (Paris: Organization for Economic Co-operation and Development, 1987), p. 55; and Bureau of the Census, *Statistical Abstract of the United States: 1989* (Washington, D.C.: Government Printing Office, 1989), p. 827.

Why is this the case? The structure and character of America's welfare state have many causes, of course. But a decisive factor has been the opposing tendencies of the public philosophy.[34] One half of the doctrine restrains the other. Americans believe in *both* limited government *and* public management of the economy; they desire personal freedom and opportunity *and* protection from their unrestrained use; they spend their tax dollars year after year on health, education, and welfare *and* are exasperated at times by the very programs they pay for.

Public policy, then, is in the midst of a tug-of-war between two equally compelling urges—the urge to protect individual liberties and the urge to advance the general welfare. From this perspective, the comparisons shown in the figures make sense: We spend less on social programs than most countries at a comparable stage of development partly because we have not made up our mind about which urge we want to heed, demonstrating again that the public philosophy determines what government does and who benefits from its activities. Paul Volcker, former chairman of the Federal Reserve system and a prominent Wall Street banker, describes this philosophical schizophrenia this way:

We Americans have always been ambivalent about government. . . . Instinctively, we still have a lot of feeling that government is best that governs least; nonetheless we are quick and caustic with our complaints and our rhetoric when government doesn't produce what we expect of it. And as we've grown in size and in the complexity of our society, for better or worse we've asked and expected more of government.[35]

Individualism and Poverty

The tension between the general-welfare part of the creed and the traditional homage paid to individualism contributes to another fascination of American politics: the ambivalence about the causes and cures of poverty.

Even as agreement on government activism developed and prodded the nation toward an ever-growing welfare state, individualism—the belief in the virtue and power of self-reliance—never vanished from the national consciousness. Although we may acknowledge the impersonal causes of personal economic hardship, deep down many Americans cannot avoid partly blaming the victims themselves for their plight. After all, people suffering from poverty refute some cherished myths: America is the land of limitless opportunity, where success awaits anyone willing to work hard enough, where private initiative and free enterprise have created the highest standard of living in the world, and where freedom is its own reward.

Because of these deeply held beliefs, a conference of Catholic bishops found that "punitive attitudes" toward the poor frequently surface:

Americans have a tendency to blame poverty on laziness, to stigmatize welfare recipients, to exaggerate the benefits actually received by the poor and to overstate the extent of fraud in welfare payments. The belief persists that the poor are poor by choice, that anyone can escape poverty by hard work, and that welfare programs make it easier for people to avoid work.[36]

An excerpt from a letter to the editor, typical of probably thousands written each year, reflects the beliefs identified by the bishops:

We wonder why the country is in debt. My guess is that one reason is that too many able-bodied people are on welfare. There are help-wanted signs everywhere you go. Why not have welfare recipients take a urine test . . . whenever they come to pick up a check? I bet our welfare rolls would decrease greatly. . . . The ones who do stay on welfare after that should be given jobs to earn their keep (licking envelopes, digging ditches).[37]

These perceptions about fraud and abuse affect the administration of the welfare system. Nearly every program, whether at the state or national level, is saddled with means tests, eligibility requirements, investigations of clients' living habits, and numerous other regulations, most of which assume that chiselers and freeloaders crowd the welfare rolls.

This attitude toward the poor can also be seen in **workfare** legislation, which requires welfare recipients to accept job training and employment as a condition of receiving public aid. Based on the dictum that "work is better than welfare,"[38] the ostensible purposes of the policy are to provide occupational skills, to encourage the poor to work, and to benefit the community as a whole. In this light, workfare seems entirely unobjectionable.

The underlying motive, though, is all too transparent: Workfare's proponents believe that too many recipients of public assistance, who want something for nothing, will not work unless made to. There is also a widely held perception that welfare has become generous to the point of discouraging self-sufficiency. Pierre S. DuPont, former governor of Delaware and a contender for the 1988 Republican presidential nomination, captured the common thinking about welfare when he made workfare a central plank in his campaign platform: "Our policy in this country must be: If you don't work, you don't get paid."[39]

The result of these attitudes, several policy analysts argue, is to create stingy and demeaning social welfare programs. This state of affairs results partly from the context of ideas and is another example of how a nation's basic values and assumptions mold its policies.[40] Because of their strong attachment to individualism and their acceptance of the general-welfare ethic, Americans exhibit a kind of split personality succinctly captured by a headline in the *New York Times*: "Public Found Hostile to Welfare Idea but Backs What It Does."[41]

Checkpoint

- The public's acceptance of general-welfare liberalism helps prevent the emergence of open class conflict. Although America does have social classes, many people do not have a strong class consciousness, nor do they see the need to organize along class lines to make political demands.

- The absence of class conflict is known as American exceptionalism, because it is the exception to the rule found in most industrialized countries.

- Americans tend to have mixed feelings about welfare. Because they realize that capitalism is at times cruel and unfair, they are committed to the notion of general welfare to help the truly needy. This support is tempered, however, by traditional beliefs in limited government and individualism. Partly as a result of these misgivings, the United States has one of the least generous welfare systems in the world.

- Many people are quick to think the worst of the poor, and these doubts show up in policies requiring recipients to earn their keep and prove their need.

GENERAL-WELFARE LIBERALISM: WHO GOVERNS?

The acceptance of general-welfare liberalism has enormous implications for the question of who governs. In the first place, it preempts alternative ideologies that might call for the redistribution of wealth. Second, it enhances the power of highly organized private groups, creating greater inequities between haves and have-nots on a whole range of issues. Since these implications are so important, we need to examine each more closely.

The Effects of Limited Choices

Think for a moment about this question: As a typical citizen exposed to the normal sources of information about government and politics in the United States, how many truly different ideologies regularly compete for your attention? We do not mean differences between Democrats and Republicans, as meaningful as these choices may be. We refer instead to broad-gauge belief systems such as socialism.

You would probably be hard pressed to mention even one, because the widespread acceptance of general-welfare liberalism has pushed its competitors far from view. To illustrate this point, here are excerpts from the 1980 platforms of several political parties living deep in the shadow of American politics:

- A goal of the Socialist party is workers' control of all industry through democratic organization of the workplace, with workers making all of the decisions now made by management.[42]
- Specifically, we [the Libertarian party]:

    recognize the right of any individual to challenge the payment of taxes on moral, religious, legal, or constitutional grounds; oppose all personal and corporate income taxation . . . support the repeal of the Sixteenth Amendment [permitting Congress to tax incomes] . . . support the eventual repeal of all taxation. . . .[43]

- The Citizens party calls for building a new economy, one in which workers and consumers exercise democratic control over the economic decisions that, today, separate the promise of American society from its reality. . . . The people must have an effective voice in deciding such essential questions as what goods and services shall be produced; where and how they shall be produced; what prices shall be charged; and toward what ends the wealth of the nation shall be invested.[44]
- The Communist party:

    Enact the six-hour day with no cut in pay, no speed-up or forced overtime.
    End all taxes on the first $25,000 of family income. Guarantee $15,000 minimum income for a family of four.
    Put the oil monopolies and all energy production under public ownership.[45]

The list could continue indefinitely, but the message is clear: Many of us would consider these planks idealistic, extreme, unworkable,

Lenora Fulani, who ran for president in 1988 on the New Alliance ticket, advocated "empowering the poor and the oppressed" among other radical causes. She won about 200,000 votes out of 90 million cast that year. Her candidacy illustrates the difficulties that third parties have overcoming the deep consensus on general-welfare liberalism.

possibly harebrained; most seem decidedly un-American and far removed from the mainstream of our political traditions. Socialists' calls for the end of private ownership of huge corporations and vast holdings of wealth run headlong into the belief that private ownership of property is a natural right. Libertarian demands for an end to taxation fly into the teeth of the general-welfare ethic: How else can we pay for food stamps, environmental protection, and health and safety inspectors? The Citizens party seems to want to replace the marketplace with some kind of public decision-making apparatus. Almost all of these ideas push past the outer limits of the prevailing public philosophy and hence shake our assumptions about government's proper structure and function.

The embrace of general-welfare liberalism by both major parties considerably limits our choices by confining the policy agenda within narrow bounds. Roughly speaking, the more alternatives citizens have to select from, the greater their freedom, other things being equal. The last qualification is added because unlimited choice may create mass confusion or, if the sides are too polarized, lead to civil unrest.[46] Still, if a democracy means people choosing for themselves, then to the extent that the political culture shrinks the range of options the people begin to lose control over the selection of policies that affect their lives. Public ownership of the oil companies may be a bad idea. Yet how can anyone know for sure unless it is openly and thoroughly debated?

Beliefs About Equality and Redistribution

Consensus on general-welfare liberalism constrains the political agenda in another way: It favors *political* equality ("everyone is equal in the eyes of the law") over *economic* equality (an equitable distribution of wealth). As a measure of the power of this idea in American life, Sidney Verba and Gary Orren collected data showing that, although the United States ranks first on many indicators of political equality, it trails most industrialized countries on economic equality.[47]

A nation's economic and social problems, such as unemployment or poverty, can be addressed in several ways, one of which is to *redistribute* wealth: Tax the rich to aid the jobless or poor. But, as already mentioned, neither Democrats nor Republicans favor equalizing income or wealth to pay for welfare and regulatory programs. The public philosophy stresses private property, initiative, and reward for hard work. Groups at the bottom of the social ladder are free to climb up, but not at the expense of those already at the top. Appeals for a leveling of wealth or public ownership of industry invariably fall on deaf ears.

One of the most interesting aspects of American politics is how the lower and middle classes have come to accept this situation as proper and natural. Robert Lane, a political scientist, once characterized the phenomenon as "the fear of equality."[48] He asked a group of blue- and white-collar workers how they would "feel about a change in the social order such that they and their friends might suddenly be equal." "Most," he learned, "wouldn't like it. They would fear and resent that kind of equality."[49] Among many qualms, his subjects felt equality of condition would lead to a loss of motivation and a desire to get something for nothing, as Rapuano, "a checker in a meat-and-provision company," explains:

> If every one had the same income of a man that's earning $50,000 a year, and he went to, let's say, ten years of college to do that, why, Hell, I'd just as soon sit on my ass as go to college and wait till I could earn $50,000 a year too.[50]

A more recent study echoes Lane's conclusion: "Americans of every political stripe accept the premises of the capitalist system. They agree that rewards should be based on success in the competitive market; the distribution of wealth should be based on skill and effort."[51]

Assumptions about capitalism underlie these sentiments: Hard work and merit are rewarded, the rich earn their status; without property rights society would disintegrate into anarchy; whatever its faults, the system is basically fair; and success awaits anyone with the fortitude to grab it. Yet each of these beliefs is an assumption or a hope, not a fact etched in stone, and is quite contentious. Workers in France or Germany or Italy would probably vigorously dispute each of them.

Who is right and who is wrong is not really the concern here. We simply want to illustrate that ideology—general-welfare liberalism—has political consequences. A two-step chain of thought shows how. First, by embracing the fundamental beliefs and tenets of capitalism, people essentially accept the status quo. But under the status quo, the resources that bring one power are unevenly distributed. Groups and individuals at the top have more than those at the bottom. They command more wealth, prestige, skill, free time, and access to influential officeholders. Hence, even if the masses are unaware of this fact, their acceptance of the dominant public philosophy is tantamount to accepting an unequal distribution of political influence. It virtually guarantees that the country will not be governed along the lines of an ideal democracy.

The Effects of Private Power

Americans, numerous observers have noted, share a distinctive outlook on power and power holders: They readily recognize and distrust power in the hands of public officials. Paradoxically, however, they fail to perceive the political nature of power when it is wielded by nongovernmental bodies. Indeed, private organizations are commonly regarded as "the guarantor of liberty."[52]

Because of their faith in private associations as opposed to public agencies, Americans have a unique approach to problem solving: They seek "private" solutions to local, state, or even national issues. Consequently, they rely heavily on nongovernmental organizations not only to safeguard liberty, but to carry out many ostensibly political functions.* President George Bush underscored the point during his 1988 presidential campaign by referring to a "thousand points of light." He meant, as he later explained in his

---

*See Chapter 13 for more discussion.

This Mobil Oil Corporation ad, which ran in the New York Times and other major newspapers, argues that the president should have a line item veto. Although everyone enjoys freedom of speech, wealthy individuals and corporations have the means to reach far greater audiences.

inaugural address, that "all of the community organizations that are spread throughout the nation" should take the lead in housing the homeless, feeding the hungry, and preventing drug abuse.[53]

When public involvement in the economy becomes unavoidable, the first impulse of most Americans is to create a *partnership* between government and other sectors such as business, labor, and education, thereby giving each of these institutions a strong voice, if not veto power.

Naturally, then, private organizations— banks, corporations, trade associations, unions, interest groups, clubs, professional societies, and the other groups that are the heart and soul of pluralism—enjoy special status and legitimacy in the popular mind and exert enormous influence in politics. The upshot is that in the political arena the strongly organized segments of society with resources (for example, unified and devoted members, expertise, money, prestige) flourish, while unaffiliated or poorly organized individuals having few sources of strength suffer by comparison. It is a common complaint about American government, for example, that large but loosely organized majorities consistently lose to firmly entrenched minorities, partly because the creed legitimizes exactly this kind of arrangement.[54] Moreover, the public's control over these private entities is quite weak.

General-welfare liberalism, therefore, has an important impact: Whom does it encourage to become powerful? Well-organized and financed groups. Whom does it discourage? Disorganized, amorphous masses.

Emphasis on Procedural Rights

The norms contained in the liberalism component of the public philosophy emphasize "procedural" rights, the sort of liberties enumerated in the Bill of Rights, such as freedom of expression and the right to a speedy and public trial. These guarantees suit groups and individuals with the time and resources to take maximum advantage of them. Unfortunately, the weak or destitute often enjoy them in name only. Freedom of speech, to take one example, nominally protects all citizens, whether rich or poor. Yet do the General Electric Corporation and a disgruntled consumer really compete fairly in the marketplace of ideas? Suppose a homeowner believes GE is making a hazardous product that should be immediately withdrawn from the market. True, both parties are entitled to present their cases to the public, but which side is more likely to be heard? Which has the status and clout to get its message across to the public? Which is more likely to win in the political arena? In politics, where getting the people's attention can mean the difference between success and failure, does the consumer or corporation have the advantage?

Take another problem. Courts presumably dispense justice blindly without regard to race, sex, religion, or social rank. But, as a practical matter, do the millionaire socialite and the migrant farm worker, both accused of the same crime (drug possession, say), stand equally before the law? Again the critics are doubtful.

Stress on procedure over substance, on form over content, points to an important aspect of general-welfare liberalism. Winning in politics is not simply a matter of having rights, although they are certainly indispensable. It also requires the resources that are unequally distributed throughout society to take advantage of these rights. Consequently, the power elite school argues, in the absence of an even distribution of resources, general-welfare liberalism effectively benefits those at the top of society more than the classes lower down.

These remarks lead to an interesting question. If general-welfare liberalism is at the core of a balance between two philosophies, will the tipping point shift? Will liberalism, with its focus on individual rights, begin to outweigh the general-welfare component? Many observers of contemporary politics wonder if the change is not already under way.

Checkpoint

- Consensus on general-welfare liberalism severely limits the range of ideas to which we are exposed. As a result, only certain alternatives and possibly not the best ones find their way onto the political agenda.

- The principles embedded in general-welfare liberalism have the effect of favoring the status quo and rationalizing and legitimizing the inequalities in influence.

- Another characteristic of America's public philosophy is its effects on perceptions of power. As a nation we almost instinctively distrust public authority but fail to recognize the impact of private power on our lives.

- The lower classes, the poor, and, especially, unaffiliated individuals suffer by comparison with those segments of society that are highly organized and command enormous resources. These organized and powerful groups are in a better position to take advantage of their procedural rights.

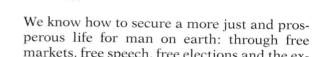

THE END OF GENERAL-WELFARE LIBERALISM?

During his eight years in office, it seemed at times that President Reagan proposed nothing less than a full-scale abandonment of general-welfare liberalism:

> . . . we recognized the limited role that government properly plays. The Federal Government cannot provide prosperity or generate economic growth; it can only encourage private initiative, innovation, and entrepreneurial activity that produce economic opportunities. An overly active Government actually hinders economic progress.[55]

His administration's goals, which he characterized as revolutionary, included dramatic reductions in personal income taxes, huge spending cuts in domestic programs, the elimination of bureaucratic regulation, a restoration of traditional values—God, country, and family—and the return of many federal functions to the private sector or to state and local governments. Past presidents have advocated less government, but none demanded so much change so rapidly.

Many observers interpreted George Bush's election in 1988 as a continuation of the decline of general-welfare liberalism. Bush's inaugural address echoed many of his predecessor's sentiments:

> We know how to secure a more just and prosperous life for man on earth: through free markets, free speech, free elections and the exercise of free will unhampered by the state . . . The old solution, the old way, was to think that public money alone could end these problems. But we have learned that is not so.[56]

President Reagan's and Bush's landslide elections and popularity proved to numerous party leaders and journalists that the public philosophy is changing. Leading Democrats are convinced that the endorsement of social welfare programs costs them in the polls and they accordingly need to adopt new priorities. Both parties in Congress have joined to slow down growth in federal expenditures. As Chapter 18 shows, passage of the Gramm-Rudman-Hollings Act of 1985, legislation that mandates significant cuts in domestic and defense spending, dramatically illustrates the desire to rein in and rethink Washington's proper role in the economy.

Yet before burying general-welfare liberalism, we need to examine more closely what the national government is doing. The current administration, for example, still sends Congress budgets containing billions and billions of dollars for social security, medical care, education, housing, research, and nutrition, not to mention open and hidden subsidies for American industry, labor, and agriculture. Chapter 2 pointed out, for example, that the Bush administration and Congress agreed on a multibillion-dollar plan to bail out the savings and loan industry.

Thus, although changes are afoot, one nevertheless detects a sizable gap between what party leaders claim and promise and what they actually deliver. Even if the welfare state has lost weight, it is a welfare state nonetheless. John Palmer of the Urban League contends that Reagan's years in the White House, contrary to popular impression, merely cemented general-welfare liberalism more firmly in place:

> The Reagan Administration has thus far served primarily to consolidate the public philosophy that emerged in the New Deal and

post-New Deal years in so far as Americans have sorted out the role of government in the formation and maintenance of our public values.

We have accepted the idea that the government owes an assurance of economic stability to the middle class and, somewhat more doubtfully, we have validated the notion of a "safety net" for the most dependent of our people.[57]

It is inconceivable that Reagan or Bush would react to a tragedy like the Triangle fire differently than any of their predecessors or contemporaries. Nevertheless, a real question remains about how far and in what direction the nation has moved from agreement on general-welfare liberalism. It may be that elite beliefs and opinions about the government's proper role in society are not congruent with public opinion.

Checkpoint

- The electoral successes of Ronald Reagan, who espoused an anti-government philosophy, suggested to some observers that consensus on general-welfare liberalism was waning. Yet in spite of Reagan's triumphs and the election of George Bush, Americans still seem wedded to the combination of an activist government and individualism that distinguishes their public philosophy.

SUMMARY

A public philosophy is a body of concepts and beliefs about government that shapes the content and scope of public policies. Its nearly universal acceptance means that it dominates public thinking about politics. The public philosophy in the United States is general-welfare liberalism. It consists of two parts, classical liberalism and general welfarism.

Originating in seventeenth- and eighteenth-century political theory, classical liberalism asserts that individuals have natural rights and that the powers of government, which tend to threaten liberty, must be limited. These views lay behind the founders' conceptions of the proper form of government. At the same time, many of them were also cognizant of the necessity of civic virtue, the notion that freedom could not be preserved unless statesmen acted wisely and selflessly to promote the common good. This idea was a precursor to providing for the general welfare.

During the 1800s, as the country moved from an agrarian to an industrial society, a variant of classical liberalism, laissez faire capitalism, became the prevailing ideology. Laissez faire erected a wall between the government and the economy. The invisible hand of the marketplace would supposedly solve economic problems. If individuals succeeded, fine; if they failed, it was their fault. The state's sole responsibility was to ensure law and order. As the industrial revolution proceeded, however, its hardships gradually discredited laissez faire. Although the free enterprise system, the market, and private ownership continued to be the preferred economic institutions, they were increasingly regulated by the government for the common good.

The blending of this new attitude toward an active state with the earlier ideas about limited government resulted in general-welfare liberalism. Limited government, individualism, and personal freedoms remain cherished ideals, but they are restrained by a collective consciousness.

The effect of general-welfare liberalism in practice has been to soften class distinctions and forestall class conflict, a situation known as American exceptionalism. The conflicting components of welfarism and liberalism have also resulted in a less generous system of public assistance than in other countries and in ambivalent attitudes toward poverty.

General-welfare liberalism has political implications for who governs. Its general acceptance crowds out competing ideologies, reinforces traditional beliefs about rewards for merit, and legitimizes private power and organizations, even when they have public consequences. As a result, those in the upper classes tend to control resources that convey political influence and power and enjoy procedural protections of the system more than others.

Many observers believe that despite the laissez faire tone of Republican rhetoric, the policies of the last two presidents still lie very much within the spirit of general-welfare liberalism.

KEY TERMS

Laissez faire

General-welfare
  liberalism

Classical liberalism

Natural rights

Extended republic

Civic virtue

Class consciousness

American
  exceptionalism

Welfare state

Workfare

FOR FURTHER READING

Bernard Bailyn, *The Origins of American Politics* (New York: Random House (Vintage Books), 1968). A classic study of the intellectual foundations of the American republic.

The Federalist, ed. by Jacob E. Cook (Middletown, Conn.: Wesleyan University Press, 1961). *The Federalist Papers* were written by James Madison, Alexander Hamilton, and John Jay to explain and encourage the adoption of the Constitution. They are an excellent window onto the political thought of the Founding Fathers.

Sarah K. Gidonse and William R. Meyers, "Why the Family Support Act Will Fail," *Challenge*, September/ October 1989, pp. 33–46. This article explains how commonly held views about poverty affect poverty and workfare policies.

Louis Hartz, *The Liberal Tradition in America* (New York: Harcourt Brace Jovanovich, 1955). This classic work argues that American politics has been characterized by consensus on classical liberalism.

Richard Hofstadter, *Social Darwinism in American Thought* (Boston: Little, Brown, 1955). Hofstadter's is an excellent description of nineteenth-century political thought, especially laissez faire.

Theodore Lowi, *The End of Liberalism*, 2nd ed. (New York: Norton, 1979). Besides describing the meaning of "public philosophy," Lowi argues that the acceptance of general-welfare liberalism (he does not use this term) has had unfortunate consequences for American society.

Grant McConnell, *Private Power and American Democracy* (New York: Random House (Vintage Books), 1966). Like Lowi, McConnell critiques the prevailing ideology. This is still one of the best books on American politics.

Gordon Wood, *The Creation of the American Republic: 1776–1789* (Chapel Hill: University of North Carolina Press, 1969). A prize-winning study of the ideas that underlie the Declaration of Independence and the Constitution.

Part Two

The Constitutional Setting ★

The Constitution

The nation's first constitution, the Articles of Confederation, was not working, so delegates to the Constitutional Convention met in Philadelphia in 1787 to provide for a stronger central government. But just how strong that government should be was a subject of intense debate and led to many compromises in the structuring of the new government. Its fundamental principles are separation of powers and checks and balances, federalism and national supremacy, a republican form of government, and civil liberties. ■

In 1971, Jagdish Chadha, an Indian national born in Kenya, was finishing his graduate course work at Bowling Green State University in Ohio. During his years at Bowling Green, Chadha had played on the tennis team, served as head resident in his dormitory, and worked summers to help pay tuition. Certainly, there was nothing in his college career to suggest he would initiate a landmark constitutional decision by the Supreme Court a dozen years later.

Jagdish Chadha's problems began after he had realized his dream of a college education in the United States: As he said, "I had nowhere to go." Kenya had a system of restrictive, expensive, and short-term work permits that made return to the country of his birth out of the question. He had a British passport, but entering Britain under an annual quota of 1500 East African Asians would mean a year's delay. Meanwhile his student visa allowing him into the United States had expired.

After moving to California, Chadha went to the U.S. Immigration Office in Los Angeles to see about getting a visa or work permit. But when immigration officials saw that Chadha's student visa had expired, he was ordered to appear at a hearing and prove that he would suffer "extreme hardship" if he were deported. At this hearing the immigration judge suspended Chadha's deportation.

The Immigration and Nationality Act requires the U.S. attorney general to notify Congress of all suspensions of deportations and to provide supporting information. Using a device called the legislative veto, Congress reserved the power to veto suspension of deportation decisions as a way of ensuring that the executive branch carries out the intent of the immigration law. In practice, however, Congress vetoes less than 5 percent of the decisions reported by the attorney general.

Chadha's suspension decision was sent to Congress as one of 340 cases. The chairman of the House Judiciary Committee introduced a resolution opposing the suspension decisions in 6 of the 340 cases; Chadha's was one of the six. The resolution fit with a broader effort to prevent foreign students from using nonimmigrant visas as a way to gain permanent resident status without being subject to annual immigration limits. The House passed the veto resolution, Chadha's deportation hearing was reopened, and he was ordered to be deported. "When I heard about the veto, I just knew it was wrong," recalls Chadha. "I went to the local law school library and read everything I could find about the constitutional concepts of fairness."[1]

Chadha found a local immigration lawyer who agreed that the legislative veto was both unfair and unconstitutional. They filed a petition in federal court claiming that the immigration act's veto provision violated the constitutional principle of separation of powers—that is, the dividing of powers among the executive, judicial, and legislative branches of government. Article I of the Constitution requires that all bills be presented to the president for his signature or veto after they have passed the House and the Senate. In contrast, the deportation suspension veto passed by the House took effect without any action by the Senate or the president. Moreover, the House veto nullified executive branch decisions.

In 1983, the Supreme Court affirmed a lower court decision that the House veto *was* unconstitutional. In the majority opinion, Chief Justice Warren Burger wrote:

> The records of the Constitutional convention reveal that the requirement that all legislation be presented to the President before becoming law was uniformly accepted by the Framers. Presentment to the President and the Presidential veto were considered so imperative that the draftsmen took special pains to assure that these requirements could not be circumvented.[2]

The Washington Post

© 1983 The Washington Post Company

FRIDAY, JUNE 24, 1983

Supreme Court Strikes Down 'Legislative Veto'

Hill's Hard-Won Gains Of a Decade Wiped Out

By David S. Broder and Cass Peterson
Washington Post Staff Writers

Decision Alters Balance Of Power in Government

By Fred Barbash
Washington Post Staff Writer

The Chadha case generated such conflicting views on the meaning of the Constitution between two Supreme Court justices that one observer compared them to "church leaders who are at odds about how the Bible should be interpreted in today's world."

The Court's ruling in effect invalidated legislative veto provisions in more than 200 laws giving Congress power to pass resolutions (without presidential approval) that would nullify policies or actions of the executive branch. One of the Court's two dissenters, Justice Byron White, made a vigorous dissent. He characterized the decision as "probably the most important case the Court has handed down in years."

"Today's decision strikes down in one fell swoop provisions in more laws enacted by Congress than the Court has cumulatively invalidated in its history," said White. In addition, he felt the Court's decision undermined the central democratic principle of accountability. "I fear it will now be more difficult to insure that the fundamental policy decisions in our society will be made not by an appointed official but by the body immediately responsible to the people."[3]

The differences between Justice White and Chief Justice Burger went far beyond the case of Jagdish Chadha or a particular provision of the immigration act. At the heart of their disagreement were conflicting views of the meaning of the Constitution in the twentieth century. "They were like church leaders," one observer wrote, "who are at odds about how the Bible should be interpreted in today's world."[4]

Determination of what the Constitution says and what the framers meant lies at the heart of many current political debates. Arguments over who should govern in which areas often go back to the words of the Constitution and the recorded intentions of the framers.

The Constitution was the direct product of a convention that met in Philadelphia from May to September 1787. Fifty-five delegates selected by 12 of the 13 state legislatures worked through most of that sweltering summer to produce the final document, which 39 delegates signed.

Who were the people at the Philadelphia convention and why were they there? What did they consider to be the failings of the first American constitution, the Articles of Confederation, which had been in effect for six years? What opinions on who governs and who should govern did they bring to Philadelphia in 1787? The answers to those questions are provided by looking not only at the language of the Constitution itself, but also at such sources as the notes of the convention kept by James Madison of Virginia; the collection of 85 essays known as *The Federalist Papers* written in 1787 and 1788 by Madison, Alexander Hamilton, and John Jay in support of the Constitution; and the subsequent work of a number of constitutional scholars and historians. As you will see, not everyone agrees on what those answers were.

THE LESSONS OF THE ARTICLES OF CONFEDERATION (1781–1789)

If asked "Who governs America?" the delegates to the Philadelphia convention would have most likely answered: "Nobody." This was the chief failing of the national government established by the country's first constitution, the Articles of Confederation. The essence of that failing was succinctly stated by James Madison, an influential delegate to the Philadelphia convention: "You must first enable the government to control the governed; and in the next place, oblige it to control itself."[5] The Articles of Confederation did not meet the first requirement stated by Madison: It did not enable the government to control the governed.

The structure of government created by the Articles of Confederation was one based on supremacy of the states. While the states agreed on the need for joint action for military defense and foreign policy, they were fearful of creating too strong a central government; in addition there was mutual distrust between large and small states and commercial and farm states. These problems, along with a conflict over western boundaries, prevented general agreement on the national government of the articles until 1781, five years after the nation's declaration of independence. And that agreement was only reached by leaving most conflicts unresolved.

The central organ of government under this first constitution was a unicameral (one-house) Congress. Representatives were selected by state legislatures, and the population of a state determined the number of its representatives. Each state, however, had only one vote in Congress; at least nine states had to approve any action taken by Congress. Although the national legislature was charged with the conduct of foreign policy and war and given power to borrow and coin money, the Articles of Confederation created a structure that was more a compact among independent states (in the words of Article III, "a firm league of friendship") than it was a true national government.

Congress, under the Articles of Confederation, had no power to tax and no power to regulate commerce. These two deficiencies, in particular, contributed to an inability to govern. The only way that Congress could raise money to meet a national debt of $40 million after the Revolutionary War was to set voluntary contribution quotas for the states; the states came up with only $2.5 million. The articles provided no way for Congress to force the states to contribute or to raise money directly from a national tax.

The attempt by many state governments to deal with economic problems such as debt repayment and the promotion of trade often resulted in policies that intensified existing social and economic conflicts. The legislatures of seven states, for example, approved the issuance of paper money and limits on debt repayments, which helped farmers and other debtors but made it even more difficult to find creditors willing to invest in government or commercial ventures. Because Congress lacked authority to regulate commerce under the articles, the trade policies of states often produced conflict. For instance, when Massachusetts closed its ports to British ships, the cargo was unloaded in neighboring states and shipped overland. Massachusetts retaliated by establishing a tariff on goods coming from those states, and a conflict over international trade became an interstate conflict. In addition, a widespread system of state taxes to protect industries of those states from outside competition made trade relations between states more like those between nations.

The result of this general indebtedness and interstate commercial warfare was economic depression and forceful demand for change. In 1786, a general trade convention of five states meeting in Annapolis, Maryland, issued a report calling for the Philadelphia convention to address "important defects in the System of the Federal Government of a nature so serious as . . . to render the situation of the United States, delicate and critical."[6] Just how critical the situation had become was made clear to everyone a few months later in Shays' Rebellion. In this uprising economically pressed farmers and war veterans in western Massachusetts took up arms and marched against the courts that were forcing them to foreclose on their farms.

Historian Max Farrand has noted that the document most used by the Committee of Detail in drafting a new constitution was the old one, the Articles of Confederation.[7] The national government created by the first constitution failed, but it was a constructive failure: It taught those who fashioned the new constitution that "you must first enable the government to control the governed."

Particular sections of the Constitution clearly reflect the lessons learned from this experience. Article I gives Congress power to tax and regu-late commerce. But governing involves more than having responsibility for carrying out a particular function. Alexander Hamilton wrote about this other component of governing in *Federalist 15*, one of several essays that dealt with the defects of the Articles of Confederation:

> Government implies the power of making laws. It is essential to the ideas of a law, that it be attended with a sanction; or, in other words, a penalty or punishment for disobedience. If there be no penalty annexed to disobedience, the resolutions or commands which pretend to be laws will, in fact, amount to nothing more than advice or recommendation.
>
> This penalty, whatever it may be, can only be inflicted in two ways: by the agency of the courts and ministers of justice, or by military force; by the COERCION of the magistracy, or by the COERCION of arms.[8]

Article VI provides the national government with the first type of coercion discussed by Hamilton: "This Constitution, and the Laws of the United States, which shall be made in Pursuance thereof . . . shall be the supreme Law of the

Daniel Shays led an armed revolt by economically pressed farmers and war veterans in western Massachusetts only months before delegates convened in Philadelphia to correct defects in the national government. Shays' rebellion demonstrated just how critical the need for a new form of government had become.

Land; and the Judges in every State shall be bound thereby." The power of coercion of arms is clearly given to Congress in Article I, which says that the national legislature shall have power "to provide for calling forth the Militia to execute the Laws of the Union, suppress Insurrections and repel Invasions." While there was disagreement at the Philadelphia convention about the type of government that would be best, and there have been different interpretations of what the framers did want in a new government, there is general agreement on what they did *not* want. They did not want another national government incapable of governing. This was the valuable lesson of the Articles of Confederation.

Checkpoint

- The Articles of Confederation (1781–1789) were this country's first constitution. Under the articles the national government had limited powers.

- The central organ of government was a one-house Congress, in which each state had one vote.

- Congress had authority to conduct foreign policy and war and to borrow and coin money, but did *not* have power to tax or to regulate commerce.

- Congress had no way to enforce its decisions either through the court system or by use of troops.

- The weakness of the national government under the articles provided lessons for those who drafted a new constitution at Philadelphia in 1787. Economic depression, commercial warfare between states, and armed resistance to government decisions underscored the need to learn those lessons and correct the defects of government under the Articles of Confederation.

CREATING THE CONSTITUTION

In February 1787, the Confederation Congress passed a resolution calling on the states to appoint delegates to a convention in Philadelphia in May "for the sole and express purpose of revising the Articles of Confederation" and reporting changes to Congress and the state legislatures. In fact, seven states had already called for a convention and appointed delegates by the time Congress acted. At the earlier convention in Annapolis, Maryland, in September 1786, delegates from five states had discussed the need for the national regulation of trade. Its final report, written by Alexander Hamilton of New York, had noted that the power to regulate trade was so broad in scope that it "may require a correspondent adjustment of other parts of the Federal System."[9]

State delegations to the Philadelphia convention ranged from Pennsylvania's eight to New Hampshire's two, with each state having one vote. Twelve of the 13 states sent delegations. Rhode Island refused to send delegates or otherwise participate in the convention and expressed a concern shared by other small states that states with large populations would dominate a stronger central government. Although the convention followed the congressional practice of each state having one vote, regardless of population, the differences in state populations were striking, as Table 4.1 shows.

The 55 delegates at Philadelphia represented a wealth of experience. Eight of them had signed the Declaration of Independence and most had been active in the Revolutionary War. The average age of the delegates was only 42, but the convention membership included 7 governors and 39 members of Congress. Eight delegates had experience in drawing up state constitutions. In addition to their public positions, most of the delegates were lawyers, doctors, planters, or merchants. More than half had attended college.

Some of the notable leaders at the convention were George Washington, James Madison, and Edmund Randolph of Virginia and Benjamin

Table 4.1

State Populations at Time of Constitutional Convention

State	Total Population	Slaves
Virginia	750,000	290,000
Massachusetts	475,000	none
Pennsylvania	430,000	4,000
N. Carolina	394,000	100,000
New York	340,000	21,000
Maryland	320,000	103,000
S. Carolina	250,000	107,000
Connecticut	240,000	3,000
New Jersey	185,000	11,000
New Hampshire	140,000	158
Georgia	83,000	30,000
Rhode Island	69,000	950
Delaware	60,000	900

Source: Compiled by the authors from data in Carl Van Doren, *The Great Rehearsal* (Baltimore: Penguin Books, 1986, originally published in 1948), p. 16. Total population includes slave population. Numbers have been rounded. Actual population figures for 1787 are not known; these are approximate figures, based on the first census in 1790.

Franklin, James Wilson, and Gouverneur Morris of Pennsylvania. It is also worth noting some of the political leaders of the day who were *not* at the convention in Philadelphia: Thomas Jefferson was U.S. minister in France and John Adams held the same post in England. Virginia had selected Revolutionary War leaders Patrick Henry and Richard Henry Lee as delegates, but they both refused to serve. Two Massachusetts heroes of the Revolution, Samuel Adams and John Hancock, had not been appointed delegates and were only reluctant supporters of the Constitution at the state ratifying convention the following year.

Congress set May 14, 1787, as opening day for the Constitutional Convention. Virginia and Pennsylvania, two of the large commercial states most active in calling the convention, were the only states whose representatives showed up on time. Those delegates in attendance agreed that formal sessions would not begin until a majority of seven states were represented. But they also engaged in daily private discussions that served to reinforce the influence of states with large populations over the opening agenda. The convention's first session was delayed 11 days. When

Although many people today would include Thomas Jefferson, John Adams, and Patrick Henry among the Founding Fathers, they were in fact some of the political leaders of the day who were not at the Constitutional Convention in 1787.

the delegates were able to convene on May 25, they unanimously elected George Washington presiding officer and adopted rules of procedure. Two procedural rules were particularly important. The first was the rule of state representation, by which each state had one vote and decisions could be made by a majority of states present. In addition, votes could be postponed until the following day at the request of a single state. Before the start of the convention, Pennsylvania delegates had suggested that the large-population states unite to deny small-population states equal voting power at the convention. Virginia delegates, fearing the disruptive effects of such a proposal, talked their large-state colleagues out of introducing the proposal when the convention opened.

A second important rule made all proceedings of the convention secret. To protect delegates from outside pressures and from making public commitments that could hinder compromise, the convention met behind closed doors and voted against having recorded votes. The secretary kept an official journal (not printed until 1819), but convention rules said that nothing spoken in debates could be copied, published, or otherwise communicated outside.

Phases of the Convention

The work of the convention progressed through four broad phases between May 25 and September 17, 1787.[10]

FIRST PHASE (MAY 25–JULY 26)   The convention reached most of its crucial decisions early. This phase included the general agreement to go beyond Congress's call for a convention "for the sole and express purpose of revising the Articles of confederation" and to write a *new* constitution. Virginia's proposal for a new government structure was the main topic of debate during this period. A compromise over representation in Congress, an agreement between the large and small states reached on July 16, narrowly prevented a breakdown of the convention. At the end of the first phase, the convention had passed 23 resolutions outlining the general structure of a new national government.

SECOND PHASE (JULY 26–AUGUST 6)   The convention elected a Committee of Detail to draft a "constitution conformable to the resolutions passed by the Convention." To give the committee time to do its work, the delegates voted on

Delegates to the Constitutional Convention worked throughout the summer of 1787 behind closed doors in this room—Independence Hall in Philadelphia.

July 26 to adjourn until August 6. The Committee of Detail consisted of five delegates, representing the states of Connecticut, Massachusetts, Pennsylvania, South Carolina, and Virginia. The committee produced a 23-article Constitution from the 23 resolutions passed by the convention, but it did more than simply translate general points into particulars. For example, the committee took the vague and very general powers of Congress outlined in the resolutions and transformed them into a list of specific powers such as the power to tax, to regulate interstate commerce, and "to make all laws that shall be necessary and proper for carrying into execution the foregoing powers."

THIRD PHASE (AUGUST 6–SEPTEMBER 10)
The delegates met every day for five weeks after reconvening on August 6. In this phase they specified the governing powers of each branch of the new structure and reached a second major compromise on the method of selecting a president. The convention unanimously supported Committee of Detail provisions granting Congress the power to tax and to regulate commerce. Not a single state or delegate voted against the broad grant to Congress in the "necessary and proper" clause proposed by the Committee of Detail. There was no debate and again not a single vote against the provision in Article VI making the Constitution, national laws, and treaties the supreme law of the land. Although the convention almost broke up for a second time over the issue of electing the president (discussed below), there was a clear consensus among the delegates in favor of a strong national government. The unanimous support for the key provisions noted above led constitutional historian Leonard Levy to conclude: "Consensus, rather than compromise, was the most significant feature of the convention, outweighing in importance the various compromises that occupied most of the time of the delegates."[11]

FOURTH PHASE (SEPTEMBER 10–SEPTEMBER 17) The convention appointed another committee of five—the Committee of Style—to put the articles agreed upon into final order and perfect the language. On September 12, this committee presented a draft constitution to the convention. Four of the five states represented on the earlier Committee of Detail also had a delegate on the Committee of Style; delegates from Connecticut, Massachusetts, Pennsylvania, and Virginia joined one from New York to form this second important committee. James Madison (Virginia) and Alexander Hamilton (New York) both served on the Committee of Style, but it was Gouverneur Morris of Pennsylvania who wrote most of the final draft. The committee made one substantive change in the Preamble to the Constitution. The wording of the Preamble adopted by the convention was "We the people of the states of Connecticut, Delaware, Georgia" (and so on, through all 13 states) "do ordain, declare, and establish the following Constitution for the Government of Ourselves and our Posterity." When the convention approved that language it was assumed that the Constitution, like the Articles of Confederation, would have to be accepted by all 13 states to become effective. However, on August 31, the convention had adopted a provision stating that ratification by 9 states was sufficient to establish the Constitution. If only 9 states were to ratify the Constitution, a Preamble listing all 13 would be inaccurate. Trying to guess which 9 to include was also not a satisfactory answer. So the Committee of Style changed the Preamble to "We the people of the United States. . . ." As Historian Carl Van Doren pointed out, "The change was primarily in the interests of accuracy. But what had been done for the sake of accuracy had the effect of making it appear that the Constitution was by and for the united people, not by and for the confederated states."[12]

The convention spent three days going through the Committee of Style's draft of the Constitution and made only minor changes in the committee draft. On September 17, the convention approved a last-minute change from 40,000 to 30,000 in the number of residents represented by each member of the House of Representatives. The convention then approved the Constitution on a motion introduced by Benjamin Franklin but written by Gouverneur Morris in a form that disguised the fact that some delegates were unwilling to sign the final document. All the states except South Carolina (which cast no vote because its delegates were divided) voted for the motion that the Constitution be signed as "Done in Convention by the unanimous consent of the states present." Thirty-nine of the 42 delegates still in attendance signed the Constitution. Elbridge Gerry of Massachusetts and George Mason and Edmund Randolph of Virginia refused to sign. The convention sent the 5000-word Constitution to Congress, which voted on September 28 to transmit the Constitution to the states for ratification.

The Major Compromises

We noted earlier that the Constitutional Convention almost broke up twice during the summer

of 1787: once over the issue of representation in Congress and again over the method of selecting a president. Both of those issues produced a division between the large and small states at the convention. A brief review of how the delegates reached compromises on these issues will demonstrate the importance of the population differences among the states.

THE COMPROMISE ON REPRESENTATION

While waiting for the other delegations to arrive, Virginia's James Madison drafted 15 resolutions outlining a national government. Those resolutions served as the convention's first order of business after electing officers and establishing rules of procedure. For the next two weeks, the delegates debated the *Virginia Plan*, as these resolutions are collectively known.

The Virginia Plan called for a strong national

The Constitution was signed "Done in Convention by unanimous consent of the states present"—a motion that disguised the fact that some delegates had refused to sign the final document.

government with an **executive, legislative,** and **judicial branch**. Congress would consist of two chambers, one elected by popular vote and the second elected by the first from nominations submitted by state legislatures. Seats in the national legislature would be allocated on the basis of a state's population or wealth (the value of all land and buildings). The strongly national Virginia Plan also called for a government that would be independent of the states and act directly on the people, a radical departure from the existing government and Congress's mandate for the convention. The Virginia Plan enabled those who favored a strong national government to gain the initiative at the convention and to establish the basic framework of the Constitution.

On June 15, William Paterson of New Jersey (a small-population state) introduced nine resolutions, known as the *New Jersey Plan*, as an alternative to Virginia's proposals. More a revision of the Articles of Confederation than a proposal for a new structure of government, the New Jersey Plan would have maintained Congress as a one-chamber legislature in which each state had one vote. The New Jersey Plan also included provisions that would greatly strengthen the national government.

On June 19, the convention made one of its crucial early decisions by rejecting the New Jersey Plan in favor of the Virginia Plan. Table 4.1 is helpful for understanding the voting pattern. The populous states of Virginia, Massachusetts, Pennsylvania, North Carolina, South Carolina, and Connecticut were joined by the less populous state of Georgia in support of the Virginia Plan. Three states—New York, New Jersey, and Delaware—voted for the New Jersey Plan, and Maryland was divided. (If you are counting votes here, keep in mind that Rhode Island never sent delegates to the convention and the New Hampshire delegates—greatly delayed by the state's not paying their expenses—did not arrive in Philadelphia until July 23.)

Some of the small-state delegates who opposed the Virginia Plan made it clear that their opposition was to the proposed method of congressional representation and not to the proposed structure or powers of the national legislature. Delaware's John Dickinson, for example, pointed out that he and other delegates from less populous states actually favored a Congress with two chambers and considered themselves to be "friends to a good national government." "But we would sooner submit to a foreign power," Dickinson said, "than submit to be deprived of an equality of suffrage in both branches of the legislature, and thereby be thrown under the domination of the large states."[13]

The convention debated the issue of congressional representation throughout the summer. Early on, the convention had reached a stalemate when the vote on a motion to give each state equal representation in the upper chamber produced a five-five tie, with one state divided. The convention then elected a special committee, comprised of one delegate from each state, which worked over the July Fourth holiday to make recommendations. It came up with a compromise: (1) The first branch of the legislature would have one representative for every 40,000 residents, counting three-fifths of the slaves (the three-fifths rule had been used by Congress in a 1783 revenue bill). Any bill to raise revenue had to originate in the first branch. (2) All states would have equal votes in the second branch of the legislature.

The special committee's recommendation provoked heated debate and threats to adjourn the convention. On July 16, the convention narrowly supported (5–4) the compromise, variously known as the Great Compromise, the Connecticut Compromise (Connecticut delegate Roger Sherman had introduced a similar proposal in early June), or the Federal Compromise. Carl Van Doren has explained why the compromise on congressional representation was really a much broader compromise on federalism:

The small states, by giving up their claim to equal representation in the popular branch of the legislature of the United States, had given up their attachment to a mere confederation.

The large states, by giving up their claim to proportional representation in the Senate, had given up any hopes they may have had for a consolidated government.

The States would now survive as states in a federal system to which they conceded the right to make, execute, and interpret federal laws, while themselves retaining the right to govern themselves within their own borders.[14]

THE COMPROMISE ON PRESIDENTIAL SELECTION

The agreement on representation paved the way for a second important compromise over the method of selecting a president. The delegates had little difficulty in deciding to have a single executive and determining the powers of the office. But the question of how to select the president was an issue on which the convention reversed itself several times over the course of three months. In June the convention voted to have a single executive elected by Congress for a seven-year term. On July 19, the convention voted to have the president chosen by electors who would be appointed by the state legislatures. Five days later, the delegates voted to go back to the earlier system of election by Congress. In late August the issue of presidential election was referred to a special committee, and on September 4 the committee recommended going back to a system of electors. Under the proposed electoral system, as modified by the entire convention before being adopted, each state would choose a number of electors equal to the state's representation in Congress (senators and representatives); state legislatures would determine the method of choosing electors. These electors, forming the **electoral college**, would then vote for president, and the candidate with

the majority of votes would be president. If no candidate had a majority, the House would choose from among the five candidates with the most votes, with each state delegation having one vote.

This compromise gave large states an advantage in that the number of electors a state had was proportional to population, and small states an advantage in that each state had one vote in choosing a president when there was no majority of electors. Like the convention's earlier compromise on congressional representation, the compromise on presidential selection helped to establish American government as a federal system—a topic we look at more closely later in this chapter and in Chapter 5.

The Final Document

There were seven articles in the Constitution that the convention sent to Congress on September 17. Articles I, II, and III created the legislative, executive, and judicial branches of the national government, granted specific powers to Congress, gave broad executive authority to the president, and established the jurisdiction of the federal judiciary. Article IV established the relationship among states, the procedure for admitting new states, and the protections afforded states by the national government. Article V provided for amending the Constitution. Article VI

More than two centuries after it was written, the Constitution continues to symbolize a shared ideology and agreement on principles of government that greatly influence all debates about how America is or should be governed today.

Table 4.2

Comparing the
Articles of Confederation and the Constitution

Articles of Confederation (1781)	The Constitution (1787)
No executive branch	Independent president with extensive powers
No federal judiciary	A Supreme Court and inferior federal courts
Unanimous consent of states required to amend	Simpler amending process requiring consent of ¾ of states
All states have an equal vote	States have equal votes in Senate; proportional vote according to population in House of Representatives
States superior to central government in federal scheme	National government superior to states
Sovereignty located in the states	Sovereignty located in the people
Congress lacked powers to • regulate interstate and foreign commerce • raise taxes • control currency • enforce its laws • enforce treaty provisions	Congress has power to • regulate interstate and foreign commerce • raise taxes • control currency • enforce its laws • enforce treaty provisions
No provisions for checks and balances or separation of powers	Clear system of checks and balances through separation of powers

Source: Melvin I. Urofsky, *A March of Liberty: A Constitutional History of the United States,* vol. I: to 1877 (New York: Knopf, 1988), p. 93.

contained the **supremacy clause,** which declared the Constitution, national laws, and treaties to be the supreme law of the land. Article VII stated that ratification by nine states would be sufficient to establish the Constitution. Table 4.2 shows how the new constitution differed from the old one.

We discussed earlier how a consensus on the need for a stronger national government determined many of the key decisions of the Consti-

tutional Convention. The shared ideology and agreement on principles of governing discussed in Chapter 3 also had a great effect—on the Constitution that came out of Philadelphia in 1787 and on the ratification process that followed the convention. We will take a closer look at the fundamental principles of the Constitution later in this chapter, after we have had a look at the battle for ratification and considered the question of who governs under the Constitution.

Checkpoint

- The Constitutional Convention that met in Philadelphia in the summer of 1787 proceeded through four broad phases, with the important contributions of two committees—the Committee of Detail and the Committee of Style—taking place in two of those phases.

- The Virginia Plan, which called for a strong national government and a two-chamber Congress with representation based on population or wealth, was the first proposal to be considered by the convention. The New Jersey Plan—a counterproposal by the less populous states to the Virginia Plan—called for a single-chamber Congress in which each state had one vote.

- The compromise on congressional representation, in which one chamber of Congress would be based on population and the other on states' having equal votes, settled a fundamental difference between large- and small-population states and paved the way for a similar compromise on the method of selecting the president.

- The Constitution created by the convention consisted of seven articles, which corrected the most serious flaws of the Articles of Confederation.

THE BATTLE FOR RATIFICATION

In deciding on a process for accepting the Constitution, the delegates at Philadelphia once again drew on their experience with the Articles of Confederation. Because the articles had required approval by every state legislature, the reluctance of the Maryland legislature to endorse them had resulted in a four-year delay in implementation. In contrast, Article VII of the Constitution only required nine states to ratify. Since many of the problems leading to the convention at Philadelphia were a result of policies enacted by state legislatures, the framers called for approval by special state *conventions*. Not surprisingly, this procedure for ratifying the Constitution was one that favored its adoption.

Ratification did not take long. Congress sent the Constitution to the states on September 28, 1787. By December 7 of the same year, Delaware had ratified the Constitution. In little over a month, Pennsylvania, New Jersey, Georgia, and Connecticut followed suit. Approval by Massachusetts, Maryland, and South Carolina came rapidly, and the ninth state, New Hampshire, ratified on June 21, 1788.

The speed with which ratification took place, however, should not be taken to mean that there was little or no opposition to the Constitution. The vote to approve in some state conventions was a close one (187 to 168 in Massachusetts, 30 to 27 in New York). The New York convention did not ratify until July 1788, and only then after an intensive campaign by Madison, Hamilton, and Jay in the 85 *Federalist* essays published in New York newspapers from the fall of 1787 to the summer of 1788. Ratification in Massachusetts, Virginia, and New York came only after supporters of the Constitution (known collectively as Federalists) agreed to amend the Constitution with a **Bill of Rights** (the first ten amendments to the Constitution, establishing fundamental civil liberties).

In economic terms, those who opposed ratification—known as Anti-Federalists—drew their support primarily from the have-not classes of debtors and small farmers. For example, a delegate to the Massachusetts convention warned colleagues about "lawyers, men of learning, and moneyed men," who "expect to be managers of this Constitution and get all the power and all the money into their own hands."[15] In political terms, the Anti-Federalists often expressed their opposition in calls for stronger state governments, a more limited national government than that provided in the Constitution, and more direct popular control over government officials.

A detailed study of ratification by Jackson Turner Main led him to conclude that a majority of the public was in fact against ratification in most states. But the superior economic position and political organization of the Federalists gave them control over most newspapers and the resources for mobilizing supporters in the election of delegates to state conventions.[16] Michael Parenti has this to say about democracy and ratification of the Constitution:

> Above all, it should be pointed out that the Constitution never was submitted to popular ratification. There was no national referendum and none in the states. Ratification was by state conventions composed of elected delegates, the majority of whom were drawn from the more affluent strata. The voters who took part in the selection of delegates were subjected to a variety of property restrictions.[17]

Limited suffrage and low turnout in the elections for delegates to state ratifying conventions meant that those voting for adoption of the Constitution represented about 16 percent of the adult males in the United States at the time, or about 5 percent of the population in general.[18] Hamilton, in *Federalist 22*, said that one of the problems with the government established under the Articles of Confederation was that "it never had a ratification by the PEOPLE." He maintained that the Constitution would have a greater validity because it rested "on the solid basis of THE CONSENT OF THE PEOPLE," on what Hamilton termed "that pure, original fountain of all legitimate authority."[19] The Articles of Confederation were ratified by state legislatures and the Constitution by state conventions whose delegates were elected on the basis of their position on that document. In that sense, ratification of the Constitution may be regarded as democratic. Given the restrictive nature of those elections in the ratification process, however, it is difficult to say that a majority of the people governed in ratifying the Constitution in 1787 and 1788.

Checkpoint

- The procedure for ratification of the Constitution differed from that of the Articles of Confederation in that approval by 9 states—rather than all 13—was sufficient for ratification, and special conventions—rather than state legislatures—represented the states on the issue.

- Ratification in Massachusetts, Virginia, and New York was achieved only after supporters of the Constitution agreed to amend the Constitution with a Bill of Rights.

- The Constitution was never directly ratified by the people of the United States. Instead, about 5 percent of the population elected delegates to state conventions, which then voted whether to approve the Constitution.

THE CONSTITUTION: WHO GOVERNS?

Who governs? Answers to that question tell us which individuals and groups have the most influence over policy and who gets what from government policies. They tell us about the *type* of government, more than simply whether one exists. Because the Constitution has helped to determine those answers for 200 years, it is important to raise those questions about the Philadelphia convention itself. Which groups and philosophies of government prevailed at the 1787 convention, and who governed under the constitutional structure that emerged? Debate over those questions continues today. Constitutional scholars and historians have presented evidence to support democratic, pluralist, and power elite explanations of the convention and the Constitution.

The Case for Democracy

A series of essays published in 1980 under the title *How Democratic Is the Constitution?* includes a number of answers to that question. In one essay, Ann Stuart Diamond wrote: "The founders intended to create, and did create, a wholly democratic Constitution."[20] She views as democratic certain aspects of the Constitution that others regard as clearly antidemocratic, such as the electoral college for selecting a president and states having two senators regardless of size. Diamond and those who share her view maintain that such provisions serve to protect individual liberties from precipitous government action or provide a more direct link to majority opinion than would alternatives (such as Congress selecting the president). Proponents of this view contend that individual rights, popular sovereignty, political equality, and majority rule—the democratic ideas discussed in Chapter 1—can be found in the structure of government created at Philadelphia.

Some of the framers also stressed the democratic nature of the new Constitution. Nathaniel Gorham, a Massachusetts delegate, described the new structure as "a perfectly democratical form of government."[21] In *Federalist 10* James Madison wrote of the dangers of a "pure democracy," or direct democracy, but in *Federalist 39* he extolled the indirect democracy of the republican form of government established by the Constitution. Madison's definition of a republic includes the principles of democracy discussed earlier:

> A government which derives all its powers directly or indirectly from the great body of the people, and is administered by persons holding their offices during pleasure, for a limited period, or during good behavior.
>
> It is *essential* to such a government that it be derived from the great body of the society, not from an inconsiderable proportion, or a favored class of it.
>
> ... It is *sufficient* for such a government that the persons administering it be appointed, either directly or indirectly, by the people; and that they hold their appointments by either of the tenures just specified.[22]

James Madison is generally recognized as the chief proponent of the philosophy of government embodied in the Constitution. Scholars disagree, however, over whether that philosophy is closer to a pluralist or power elite theory of government.

The language here is clearly democratic, but not everyone agrees that the framers had democratic intentions and that the Constitution established a democracy. Writing in the same volume as Diamond, Michael Parenti advances the thesis "that the intent of the framers of the Constitution was to *contain* democracy, rather than give it free rein, and dilute the democratic will, rather than mobilize it."[23] The assessment of noted historian Richard Hofstadter is similar:

> A cardinal tenet in the faith of the men who made the Constitution was the belief that democracy can never be more than a transitional stage in government, that it always evolves into either a tyranny (the rule of the rich demagogue who has patronized the mob) or an aristocracy (the original leaders of the democratic elements).[24]

The Case for Pluralism

Because of his active convention role, his record of debates, and his essays on the nature of government in the *Federalist* papers, James Madison is generally acknowledged as the chief proponent of the philosophy of government reflected in the Constitution. Some scholars consider pluralism to be a more accurate description of his philosophy than democracy.

In *Federalist 10*, Madison identified a multiplicity of economic interests all of whom were pursuing their own interests. Andrew Hacker has suggested that Madison's focus on the conflict among different economic interests or classes made him a "premature Marxist" in the eyes of some. But to others, Hacker points out, Madison "was simply describing what we now call 'pluralism,' a society broken into many groups and interests, all of which pursue their separate goals."[25] And Frank M. Coleman writes: "Madison's vision of the political process appears to lie closest to the pluralist interpretation. Modern pluralism emphasizes, as Madison did, that politics is a matter of conflict management among a plurality of social and economic groups."[26]

Support for a pluralist interpretation of the Constitution relies primarily on the new government's great division of powers and variety of representation as well as on two of Madison's most famous essays, *Federalist 10* and *51*. In *Federalist 10* Madison discussed the many economic interests that develop in any society: "those who hold and those who are without property," "those who are creditors and those who are debtors," "a landed interest, a manufacturing interest, a mercantile interest, a moneyed interest." Madison wrote that "the regulation of these various and interfering interests forms the principal task of modern legislation."[27] In *Federalist 51*, Madison discussed the advantages of a political system in which those many economic interests in society are both represented and checked in a government structure characterized by a separation of powers and federalism.

The similarity between Madison's description of society and government and the pluralist view of widely scattered political resources is clear. The idea of a political marketplace in which government acts as referee among competing interest groups can certainly be inferred from Madison's writings. Once again, however, we find disagreement among constitutional scholars. Gordon S. Wood is one of those who rejects the pluralist interpretation:

Despite his keen appreciation of the multiplicity of interests in a commercial society, Madison was not presenting a pluralist conception of politics. He did not envision public policy or the common good emerging naturally from the give-and-take of hosts of competing interests.

Instead he hoped that these competing parties and interests in an enlarged republic would neutralize themselves, which in turn would allow rational men to promote the public good.[28]

The Case for Power Elite Theory

A third view explains the Philadelphia convention and the structure of government produced there as the work of an economic and political elite. The classic statement of this position is Charles Beard's *An Economic Interpretation of the Constitution of the United States*, first published in 1913. By studying the financial status of the framers, Beard found that they were mostly men of wealth, that the value of their wealth had declined precipitously under the weak central government, and that its value was threatened even more by the economic policies adopted by many states. Forty of the 55 delegates had invested in the public securities used to finance the Revolutionary War, and the value of those stocks and bonds had plummeted to less than 10 percent of their face value by the late 1780s. Delegates to the Philadelphia convention also included land speculators, moneylenders, owners of large plantations, and those engaged in manufacturing or commerce.[29] To hold on to that wealth, these men presumably needed a strong central government that could raise money through taxes in order to pay off the national debt and protect creditors against economic instability brought about by the policies of state governments.

Specific provisions of the Constitution are directed to this economic protection. Section 8 of Article I gives Congress power to tax and "to pay the Debts . . . of the United States, to coin money and regulate its value" and broad powers later interpreted to include the power to create a national bank. Section 10 of the same article prohibits state governments from coining money, issuing bills of credit, or passing any law "impairing the Obligation of Contracts." Article

IV declares: "All Debts contracted and Engagements entered into, before the Adoption of this Constitution, shall be as valid against the United States under this Constitution, as under the Confederation."

The elitist interpretation of the Constitution is based not only on the background of the framers and particular provisions of the Constitution, but also on the arguments used by the framers themselves. Madison argued that representative government would put into office those "who possess the most attractive merit and the most diffusive and established characters," in contrast with those commonly found in direct democracies, whom Madison described as "men of factious tempers, of local prejudices, or of sinister designs."[30] In the same essay Madison showed his economic preferences in condemning "a rage for paper money, for an abolition of debts, for an equal division of property, or for any other improper or wicked project."[31] His language makes it clear that the framers intended to construct a government that would allow "rational men to promote the public good."

Based on the framers' discussions of types of leaders and also types of policies considered desirable in the new government, Gordon Wood describes the Constitution as "an intrinsically aristocratic document designed to check the democratic tendencies of the period."[32]

Power elite analyses of the Philadelphia convention go beyond the economic context of 1787, framers' intentions, and the language of the Constitution. They also discuss the effects of this elite control on later generations. Michael Parenti, for example, concludes that the delegates would be greatly satisfied with the enduring nature of their work:

> By offering well-protected havens for powerful special interests, by ignoring substantive rights and outcomes, by mobilizing the wealth and force of the state in a centralizing and property-serving way, by making democratic change difficult, the Constitution has served well an undemocratic military-industrial corporate structure.[33]

Just as contemporary observers look at American politics today and come to dramatically different conclusions about who governs, so too do different people have quite different ideas about the intentions and results of the framers of the Constitution. While the nature of the government structure created by the framers is subject to debate, there is general agreement on the fundamental principles of government embodied in the Constitution and its Bill of Rights.

Checkpoint

- Who governs under the Constitution? Those who make the case for democracy suggest that the key democratic ideas of individual rights, popular sovereignty, political equality, and majority rule are all present in the structure of government created by the Constitution.

- Madison's essays written in defense of the Constitution seem to support a pluralist view, in which government acts as a referee in the conflict among a wide array of economic interests.

- The case for a power elite explanation of the Constitution points to the economic backgrounds and financial positions of those who created the Constitution and the characteristics of government that have made it possible for elites to continue to govern today.

FUNDAMENTAL PRINCIPLES OF THE CONSTITUTION

The Constitution embodies certain fundamental and enduring principles: the separation of powers and checks and balances, federalism and national supremacy, a republican form of government, and civil liberties. Table 4.3 summarizes the meanings of these concepts.

Table 4.3
The Constitution's Fundamental Principles

Separation of Powers
The arrangement by which the political system is divided top to bottom and side to side into competing jurisdictions. For example, the national government is divided horizontally into the legislative, executive, and judicial branches. The structure of government is also divided vertically into the national government and the state governments.

Checks and Balances
The means by which the separate branches and the national and state governments can offset powers of the other branches or level of government. The instruments for accomplishing this principle include the presidential veto of legislation, the presidential appointment of judges with Senate approval, Supreme Court rulings on the constitutionality of presidential actions and laws passed by Congress, and the role of the states in amending the Constitution.

Federalism and National Supremacy
The formal arrangement for dividing government responsibility between a national and smaller component governments and for ensuring that the component governments are represented in the larger one. National supremacy holds that any lawful exercise of power by the national government takes precedence over any conflicting action by a state government.

Republican Form of Government
A government in which elected officials representing citizens, rather than the citizens themselves, make public policy. Distinguished from a pure democracy in which citizens directly govern themselves.

Civil Liberties
The protection of persons, ideas, and property from arbitrary interference by government officials. The Bill of Rights provides more than 25 specific civil liberties including freedom of speech, the press, and religion; protection against unreasonable searches; and procedural guarantees for those accused of a crime.

There is intense disagreement about the effects of some principles, but everyone agrees that they are there. The Supreme Court, the president, Congress, and state governments refer to them in determining who should govern in which policy areas. The principles are found sometimes in the explicit words of the Constitution and at other times in the overall structure it creates. Regardless of how they are expressed, these fundamental principles lie at the heart of the U.S. Constitution. To change them would be to change the basis of the Constitution itself. One way to identify them and to appreciate their importance is to consider how they apply to disputes in contemporary American politics. As you will see, Supreme Court decisions provide the most prominent discussions of these principles.

Separation of Powers and Checks and Balances

Recall the *Chadha* case described in the opening of this chaper in which the Supreme Court ruled that the one-house legislative veto was unconstitutional. The principles of **separation of powers** and **checks and balances** were the key determinants in that case. Chief Justice Burger's opinion for the Court discussed both principles:

The Constitution sought to divide the delegated powers of the new federal government into three defined categories, legislative, executive and judicial, to assure, as nearly as possible, that each Branch of government would confine itself to its assigned responsibility. The hydraulic pressure inherent within each of the separate Branches to exceed the outer limits of its power, even to accomplish desirable objectives, must be resisted. . . .

The bicameral requirement, the Presentment Clauses, the President's veto, and Congress' power to override a veto were intended to erect enduring checks on each Branch and to protect the people from the improvident exercise of power by mandating certain prescribed steps. To preserve those checks, and maintain the separation of powers, the carefully defined limits on the power of each Branch must not be eroded.[34]

Supreme Court nominee Robert Bork who was subsequently rejected by the senate,
testifies before the Senate Judiciary Committee in 1987. The Senate's role in the
appointment of federal judges reflects the constitutional principle of checks and balances.

Chief Justice Burger provides support for these principles by citing the language of the Constitution itself, scholarly accounts of the Constitutional Convention, and three of *The Federalist Papers*. But one of the dissenting Justices in *Chadha* also cited the convention debates and *The Federalist Papers* to reach a quite different conclusion.

One reason for the continuing debate on the meaning of these two principles is to be found in the nature of the principles themselves. Articles I, II, and III of the Constitution clearly state that all legislative power shall be vested in Congress, executive power in a president, and judicial power in the courts. Within each of those articles, however, we find an actual sharing of these powers by the different branches of government. Most of Article I deals with Congress, but it also gives the president an active legislative role. Article II, while it deals chiefly with the powers of the executive, also gives the Senate the power to create executive departments. Article III outlines the powers of the judicial branch, but also gives Congress the power to create federal courts and to regulate the appellate jurisdiction of the Supreme Court. The powers delegated to

the three branches by the Constitution, in other words, are overlapping powers. Tension and boundary disputes among the branches have the effect of both limiting the ability of the national government to govern and giving vitality to the constitutional structure.

Many of the most intense conflicts over who should govern in America today draw energy from the principles of separation of powers and checks and balances. Presidents and Congress regularly disagree about their respective roles in foreign policymaking. The Supreme Court strikes down as unconstitutional acts of Congress, such as those establishing a legislative veto and a procedure for making mandatory budget cuts. The Senate rejects a presidential nominee for the Supreme Court or the cabinet. All three branches advance different positions on civil rights laws and affirmative action. The effects of these constitutional principles on contemporary politics can be seen on an almost daily basis throughout American politics.

A separation of powers depends on the different branches of government having different constituencies. The Constitution meets this requirement by creating four: The president, Supreme Court, House of Representatives, and Senate were to be chosen in different ways and for different terms so that they would represent different constituencies. Without these different constituencies there would be no point in separating government functions and no impetus for one branch to check the power of the others.

Separation of powers and checks and balances are clearly instruments for limiting the power of government. The constitutional structure designed in accordance with these principles is one that includes democratic, pluralist, and elite elements. The representation in the House most clearly exemplifies the democratic principle of majority will. The multiple centers of power created under the Constitution and limited powers of government favor pluralism. The selection of Supreme Court justices and the original methods for selecting the president through the electoral college and senators by state legislators gave power to elites. The overall effect of these two principles is most clearly illustrated when leaders from parliamentary or other political systems ask U.S. officials to tell them the government position on a particular issue. Such a question is likely to elicit another: Which government position? That of the House? The Senate? The Supreme Court? The current administration? The checks and balances and the separation of powers that are provided by the Constitution often make it difficult to say who, if anybody, governs in the American political system.

Federalism and National Supremacy

The Constitution limits the power of governing not only by separating powers among national institutions but also by recognizing different levels of that power. National institutions have only those powers of government provided for in the Constitution. The Constitution is the source of those powers. All other powers of government, unless they are explicitly prohibited in the Constitution, are those of state and local governments. As independent and sovereign states, whose powers predate the Constitution, state governments exercise "police powers," or all

those needed to ensure the health, safety, and general welfare of citizens. The Constitution is not the source of state powers and hence contains no list of what those powers are.

The power to govern is divided between the national and state governments under **federalism**, but such a division does not make for equality between the two, for another fundamental principle of the Constitution is that of **national supremacy**. Article VI (the "supremacy clause") forcefully states that principle by declaring the Constitution, U.S. laws in accordance with that Constitution, and treaties to be "the supreme Law of the Land, . . . any Thing in the Constitution or Laws of any State to the Contrary notwithstanding."

The framers of the Constitution, as we have seen, wanted to correct what they saw as flaws in the structure of government created by the Articles of Confederation. They were interested, therefore, not simply in an abstract notion of federalism but in making sure that the national government would have certain powers not granted under the Articles and that state governments would not have some powers they then exercised. Certain passages of the Constitution are quite clear on this division of powers. The first article of the Constitution says what the national government can and cannot do and what the state governments cannot do. That, of course, leaves the question of what the states *can* do. And here the Constitution is not so clear. The Tenth Amendment, adopted by the first Congress and ratified in 1791, provides one answer: "The powers not delegated to the United States by the Constitution, nor prohibited by it to the States, are reserved to the States respectively, or to the people." But that still leaves the question of precisely what those powers are. In what areas do states have the power to govern? What functions of government belong to the states?

In Chapter 5, we will look at some recent answers the Supreme Court has given to the question of what state governments can and cannot do under the Constitution. The Court decision that best illustrates the principles of federalism and national supremacy, however, came 32 years after the Constitutional Convention in the case of *McCulloch* v. *Maryland* in 1819.

McCULLOCH* v. *MARYLAND In 1816 Congress had established a national bank to provide a uniform monetary system throughout the country. One of its 18 branches was located in Baltimore, Maryland. Some states felt that the bank was adversely affecting the economy with its credit policies and so passed laws that taxed and otherwise attempted to control the bank. Maryland required the Baltimore bank to abide by certain restrictions or pay an annual tax of $15,000, with penalties for nonpayment that could cost the bank millions of dollars. The bank ignored Maryland's law on the grounds that it was unconstitutional, whereupon Maryland sued the cashier of the bank, James McCulloch. The central issue underlying this dispute was whether the national government had the power to charter banks and therefore control credit policies.

The Supreme Court addressed two central questions in the case of *McCulloch* v. *Maryland*: (1) Does Congress have the power to establish a national bank? And if so, (2) can a state tax a branch of the national bank located in that state? The Court, in a unanimous decision, said yes to the first question and no to the second. The Court's opinion was written by Chief Justice John Marshall, who had been an important ally of Madison and a supporter of the Constitution at the Virginia ratification convention in 1788.

Does Congress have the power to establish a national bank? Those arguing "no" said the powers of the national government included only those expressly delegated to it by the Constitution or additional powers that were indispensable to carrying out one of the specified powers. Since the power to establish a national bank was not enumerated in Article I and could not be considered "necessary" for carrying out the powers that were listed there, it was not constitutional. The "necessary and proper" clause of Article I, you will recall, had been added to the Constitution by the Committee of Detail and unanimously adopted by the Convention with little debate. That made it difficult to determine what "necessary and proper" meant to the framers, or even if there had been agreement about its meaning.

Marshall's conclusion that Congress did have the power under the Constitution to establish a national bank is drawn from an understanding of the Constitution as a whole and from the organization of its parts. Unlike the Articles of Confederation, Marshall pointed out, the Constitution contained no phrase excluding implied powers and requiring that "everything granted shall be expressly and minutely described." To describe in detail every power and to prescribe "the means by which government should, in all future time, execute its powers," would have been to change, entirely, the character of the instrument, and give it the properties of a legal code." "We must never forget that it is *a constitution* we are expounding," Marshall said.[35]

Constitutions provide the broad outlines of government powers, not every detail on how to carry out those powers. To illustrate, Marshall used the power granted Congress in Article I "to establish post offices and post roads." The Constitution said nothing about the national government also having the power to carry the mail along post roads from one post office to another or to punish those who rob the mail, but those were implied powers of the more general grant in Article I. In a similar fashion, the power to establish a national bank was an implied power of the more general grants in Article I to pay debts, borrow money, and regulate the value of money.

But was the creation of a national bank "necessary" for carrying out those powers? Marshall said that the meaning of "necessary and proper" could be deduced from the structure of the Constitution itself. If the framers had intended the "necessary and proper" clause to *limit* the national government to those powers that were indispensable to carrying out a specified power, Marshall argued, they would have put it in the section specifying the limits on the national government. Instead, "the clause is placed among the powers of Congress, not among the limitations on those powers," clearly indicating that it is meant "to enlarge, not to diminish the powers vested in the government."

Can a state tax a branch of the national bank located in that state? The Court said no. Marshall based his opinion once again on the overall meaning of the Constitution as well as particular provisions in it. The issue was whether states could use their taxing powers to control what the national government could do. As Marshall pointed out, "the power to tax involves the power to destroy." State taxes could render useless the national government's power to establish a national bank. Furthermore, to say that states may tax a national bank would be saying, in effect, that "they may tax the mail, they may tax the mint, they may tax patent rights." States would then be "capable of arresting all the measures of the (national) government, and of prostrating it at the foot of the states." To say that the Constitution permitted states to do that, Marshall said, would be "changing totally the character" of the Constitution.

The Constitution does not specifically provide that the national government is exempt from state taxes. But Article VI does say, you will recall, that the laws of the United States shall be the supreme law of the land and shall take precedence over any state law to the contrary. Marshall described national supremacy as "a principle which so entirely pervades the constitution, is so intermixed with the materials which compose it, so interwoven with its web, so blended with its texture, as to be incapable of being separated from it, without rending it into shreds."

Marshall found another reason why states could not tax the Bank of the United States in the constitutional principle of a republican form of government. If Congress taxes state banks, it is taxing its own constituents, Marshall said, because "the people of all the states and the states themselves are represented in Congress." But when states' legislators vote to tax a national bank they are taxing "institutions created not by their own constituents, but by people over whom they claim no control." To illustrate the point in the bank issue, the people of Maryland would be represented in a congressional decision to tax banks in Maryland and other states, but the people of Delaware, Virginia, Massachusetts, and so on were not represented in the Maryland legislature when it decided to tax the Bank of the United States. The principle of a republican form of government demands that there be no taxation without representation.

Charles Black, a distinguished scholar of constitutional law, called *McCulloch* v. *Maryland*

Chief Justice John Marshall, the author of the Supreme Court decision in McCulloch v. Maryland. That decision was one of the fullest early expressions of national supremacy. Marshall said that if the Court had decided the case the other way it would have reduced the Constitution to the weakness of the Articles of Confederation.

"perhaps the greatest of our constitutional cases." Supreme Court Justice Felix Frankfurter said that Marshall's statement "we must never forget that it is *a constitution* we are expounding" was "the single most important utterance in the literature of constitutional law." Marshall himself recognized the importance of the case when he wrote that if the case were decided the other way "the constitution would be converted into the old confederation."[36]

The Court's decision in *McCulloch* v. *Maryland* represented a turning point in the development of American federalism, which we discuss in Chapter 5. In this section we have looked closely at Marshall's opinion in *McCulloch* not only for the principles of federalism and national supremacy he discussed, but also because Marshall's arguments demonstrate how these and other fundamental principles are interwoven throughout the text of the Constitution and how they define the meaning of the Constitution itself.

A Republican Form of Government

In Chapter 1 we pointed out that the Constitution established a republican form of government, in which power is exercised by elected officials representing the people rather than by the people themselves. To show the republican nature of the government created by the Constitution, Madison discussed in *Federalist 39* how the people control the government by directly electing the House of Representatives and indirectly choosing the Senate and the president.* Even judges, said Madison, represent a "remote choice of the people themselves."[37] Additional support for this republican principle is seen in the Constitution's specifications for terms of office, provisions for impeachment, prohibition of titles of nobility, express guarantee to the states of a republican form of government, and provision for the Constitution to be ratified by the people.

Alexander Hamilton reinforced Madison's republican argument in *Federalist 22*, where he wrote that "the fundamental maxim of republican government" is that "the sense of the majority should prevail."[38] Yet it is clear that the separation of powers, checks and balances, and federal structure of the government make it more difficult for the "sense of the majority" to prevail. In addition, the Constitution in its original state removes three of the four institutions of government (president, Senate, Supreme Court) from *direct* control by a majority of the people.

This gap between the republican principle so clearly stated by Hamilton, Madison, and other supporters of the Constitution and the actual government structure it creates leads political scientist Joseph Bessette to suggest:

Either the framers engaged in deception employing democratic rhetoric to defend a less

than democratic document, or they shared an understanding of majority rule according to which certain kinds of restraints on the popular will did not violate the basic principle itself.[39]

A "DELIBERATIVE DEMOCRACY"   Bessette's research led him to accept the second point. The republican form of government created in the Constitution and described in *The Federalist Papers* is not that of direct democracy, which the framers viewed as unstable and ultimately tyrannical, but rather one of "deliberative democracy." According to this notion, representatives of the people deliberating over policy in the many forums provided by the Constitution are likely to produce policies that better serve majority interests than would policies chosen by the people themselves. In *Federalist 10* Madison describes how a republican form of government can "refine and enlarge the public views" (Hamilton's "sense of the majority") "by passing them through the medium of a chosen body of citizens."[40]

The republican principle of the Constitution then rests on the two ideas of representation and deliberation. Government institutions in a republic must first *represent* "public views" or a "sense of the majority" before refining or enlarging them through *deliberation*. The extent to which this is done in our constitutional system, of course, is a topic of debate among those who see that system as essentially democratic, pluralist, or controlled by a power elite. If we accept the idea of a deliberative democracy, it provides a new perspective for understanding aspects of the constitutional structure such as separation of powers, checks and balances, and federalism. By dividing the power of governing among different branches and levels of government, the Constitution requires extensive deliberation among public officials before a policy is adopted. For instance, a president does not have an absolute veto; many people would regard that as undemocratic. Presidents must give their reasons for vetoing a bill, and a two-thirds vote in both houses of Congress can override any veto. This is one means that the Constitution provides for deliberation in the policy process.

A recognition that the republican principle of

---

*Until amended in 1913, the Constitution specified that senators were to be chosen by state legislatures.

The republican form of government of the Constitution establishes a "deliberative democracy," in which elected representatives such as these members of the house, "refine and enlarge the public views," rather than a direct democracy, in which the majority opinion directly determines public policies.

the Constitution and the *Federalist* is one of deliberative democracy does not end the debate over the democratic character of the principle, however. Nor can we turn to the Supreme Court for an authoritative interpretation of the republican principle. In the 1849 case of *Luther* v. *Borden*, the Court was asked to define the republican form of government guaranteed to every state in Article IV.[41] The Court said that whether a particular state government was republican was a "political question" to be decided by Congress and the president. The Court reached that decision because the Constitution gives Congress the authority to determine which government is the established government of a state and whether it is republican, and Congress in 1795 gave the president statutory authority to call out the militia when a republican government in any state was threatened by insurrection. The Court has followed this doctrine about the meaning of a republican form of government in all cases since then. It is a question to be decided by the political branches of government—by the legislative and executive—not the judicial.

DIRECT DEMOCRACY   One alternative to a republican form of government is that of direct democracy. Direct democracy in the United States today has taken the form of procedures that permit voters themselves to make state laws in state elections. The **initiative** is a mechanism by which a certain number of citizens (usually between 5 and 15 percent of the total registered voters) sign a petition to place proposed legislation or a constitutional amendment on the ballot for the voters to approve or disapprove. The **referendum** permits voters to veto legislation passed by the legislature, again through a petition to place the measure on the ballot for voters to approve or disapprove within a fixed period of time (usually 90 days). The laws in 23 states currently provide for legislation through initiative, and most states have some form of referendum procedures. But do these procedures of direct democracy in effect destroy a state's *republican* form of government? This issue came before the Supreme Court in 1912. Following the "political question" doctrine of *Luther*, the Court said that the answer to that question and the definition of a republican form of government was one for Congress, not the Supreme Court, to make.

The United States has never had a nationwide referendum; it is one of only a few democracies never to engage in this form of direct democracy. The arguments against national referenda draw on the values of deliberative democracy and a republican form of government that we find in our constitutional system. One such argument maintains that the policies adopted in a direct democracy are more likely to threaten the individual liberties and rights of minorities than are the policies of a deliberative republican form of government.[42]

Civil Liberties

The principle of civil liberties is closely tied to those of separation of powers, federalism, and a republican form of government because the latter are regarded as ways of protecting the former. But there is also an important difference between them. Hamilton's argument in *Federalist 22* was that the structure of government created in the Constitution drew its authority from the consent of the people, "that pure, original fountain of all legitimate authority." Civil liberties, on the other hand, exist outside of, and often in opposition to, the public will. The essence of these individual liberties, of the concept of "inalienable rights," is that they are rights that cannot be taken away by public authority or the consent of the people. Madison, following John Locke, emphasized the right of property as one of those inalienable rights. There was a clear consensus among delegates to the Philadelphia convention that individual liberties, and most especially private property, must be protected under the Constitution. Given this concern, why was no bill of rights included in the Constitution framed in 1787? Most states, by contrast, had a bill of rights as part of their constitutions.

Hamilton sought to answer that question in *Federalist 84*. The importance of the principle of civil liberties is made clear in his essay. Hamilton first pointed to a number of provisions in the Constitution specifically dealing with civil liberties: the limit on punishment for impeachment

(I,3,7); prohibition on jailing persons without charging them with a crime and bringing them to trial (habeas corpus), on laws that pronounce an individual or group guilty of a crime or make an action a crime after it has already been committed (bills of attainder and ex-post-facto laws), and on titles of nobility (I,9); guarantee of jury trial (III,2,3); a precise and limited definition of treason (III,3,1); and the limit on punishment for treason (III,3,2).

A second argument advanced by Hamilton, and by Madison in other essays, is that civil liberties are protected by the overall structure of government created in the Constitution. "The truth is," wrote Hamilton, "that the Constitution is itself, in every rational sense, and to every useful purpose, A BILL OF RIGHTS."[43] This is so, he said, because the structure and administration of the government make clear the political privileges of citizens, and because personal liberties are protected by the immunities and procedures outlined in the Constitution. Hamilton also argued that since the national government was limited to those powers delegated in the Constitution, there was no need to add a bill of rights saying that the government could not do those things that it could not do anyway. If the Constitution gives Congress no power to regulate the press, this argument goes, there is no need for a bill of rights saying Congress shall make no law abridging the freedom of the press.

Hamilton lost this particular argument. As we have seen, the promise to add a bill of rights to the Constitution was a necessary concession for ratification by conventions in Massachusetts, Virginia, and New York. In September 1789 the First Congress proposed 12 amendments, 10 of which were ratified by the states in 1791 to become the Bill of Rights. It is the first 10 amendments more than the original Constitution that form the cornerstone of civil liberties in the United States. The Bill of Rights includes the fundamental political rights of free speech, freedom of the press, the right to assemble and to petition the government, freedom of religion, and the right to be protected from unreasonable searches and seizures. It guarantees that certain procedures will be followed to ensure the fair treatment of those accused of a crime.

That a Bill of Rights was added to the Constitution, however, should not obscure the principle of civil liberties reflected in the original Constitution. The limited government powers of the Constitution serve to protect individuals against all government action. A number of important civil liberties cases decided by the Supreme Court have been based on specific provisions found in the articles of the Constitution. These include not only those discussed by Hamilton, but also the important right of contract (I,10,1) and a right to travel (based on the commerce clause, I,8,3).[44] A full evaluation of civil liberties guaranteed by the Constitution is found in Chapter 6, but it is clear from this brief review that the principle of civil liberties is found both in the original Constitution and in the later Bill of Rights. Moreover, the civil liberties protected by the Constitution include not just those specifically mentioned in the Bill of Rights and other parts of the Constitution. They also include, in the words of the Supreme Court, "fundamental principles of liberty and justice which lie at the base of all our civil and political institutions."[45]

- Federalism and national supremacy dictate that the national government be given the means for carrying out powers granted to it under the Constitution, while at the same time recognizing a limit to those powers.

- The republican form of government established by the Constitution is one in which power is exercised by elected officials rather than by the people themselves. The process of governing under the Constitution is one of deliberative democracy, including both representation and deliberation.

- Both the Constitution itself and the first ten amendments, known as the Bill of Rights, provide civil liberties, rights of the people that government cannot take away.

Checkpoint

- The Constitution embodies certain fundamental principles of governing: separation of powers and checks and balances, federalism and national security, a republican form of government, and civil liberties. These principles are found both in the explicit words of the Constitution and in the overall structure it creates.

- Separation of powers limits the power of government by dividing responsibility for governing among the different branches of the national government and the national and state governments. Checks and balances provide the means for ensuring that one branch does not overpower another.

THE CONSTITUTION AND POLITICAL CHANGE

The U.S. Constitution is the oldest written constitution in the world. How can a constitution written 200 years ago for a nation of 13 states and 4 million people serve to guide those who govern a nation of 50 states and 250 million people? One answer is that the Constitution has changed with the nation: The fundamental principles of the Constitution have been retained but adapted to the demands of governing in the twentieth century.

There is general agreement on that point but disagreement over the reasons for the Constitution's durability and the direction of that change. Those who regard American government as democratic are likely to point to the changes reflected in a number of constitutional amendments that extended the right to vote. Pluralists are likely to stress the consensus on democratic principles and expansion of civil liberties by various political groups as reasons for constitutional stability in the United States. Those who believe American government to be controlled by a power elite are likely to point to the great expansion of executive power in this century, changes made possible by the elastic language of Article II.

Changes in the Constitution come about either because the document itself is altered through the amending process or because particular parts of the Constitution are given new meaning. The Supreme Court cases discussed earlier show that the meaning of even fundamental constitutional principles such as the separation of powers, checks and balances, and federalism can provoke intense conflict today. (See A Closer Look, p. 132, for a list of some crucial constitutional issues debated today.) That conflict and the resolution of conflict in accepted ways help to adapt the eighteenth-century document to the politics of today. We conclude this chapter with a brief outline of the two methods used to adapt the Constitution to political change.

Amendments and the Amending Process

In 1982, the proposed Equal Rights Amendment to the Constitution failed because only 35 of the required 38 state legislatures had ratified the amendment passed by Congress. On November 15, 1983, a proposal for a second Equal Rights Amendment fell six votes short of the two-thirds needed for passage in the House of Representatives. On June 28, 1983, the Senate defeated by 49 to 50 a proposal for a constitutional amendment that said "A right to abortion is not secured by this Constitution." In 1985, 32 state legislatures had passed petitions for Congress to call a constitutional convention for a balanced-budget amendment to the Constitution. Approval by just two more states would have required Congress to call the first constitutional convention since that of 1787.[46]

These cases illustrate the two different ways to amend the Constitution. Both methods reflect the principle of federalism in calling for action by both Congress and the states. Article V provides that Congress, by a two-thirds vote in both

houses, may propose amendments that become law if ratified by the legislatures or special conventions in three-fourths of the states. An alternative method provided by the article is for two-thirds of the state legislatures to petition Congress to call a constitutional convention. The ratification process for amendments proposed by a convention is the same: approval by three-fourths of the states. (See Figure 4.1.)

Congress has a role in both amendment procedures, but the first method gives the national legislature the substantive policy role of proposing amendments, whereas the second limits Congress to procedure. It is therefore noteworthy that every amendment to the Constitution has been a product of the first method. Although both methods require state approval of proposed amendments, the first method more clearly exhibits the principle of national supremacy discussed earlier. Some amendments, such as the Thirteenth, Fourteenth, and Fifteenth adopted after the Civil War, have in fact been part of a major shift of power from the states to the national government.[47]

The provisions for calling a convention have had an impact on constitutional change, even though they have never directly produced a successful amendment. There have been over 300 petitions from states for a constitutional convention over the years. The likelihood of such a convention has been great enough at times to inspire Congress to itself act on amendments. Congressional approval of the Bill of Rights in 1789 and the Seventeenth Amendment in 1912 came after a call for a convention seemed imminent.

Much of the debate over recent proposals for a convention has focused on rules and procedures because there has never been a constitutional convention called under Article V, and the article itself is silent on the subject. Questions have been raised about who should convene the assembly, how many delegates should attend, and what majority of votes should be required. Most people agree that amendments to the Constitution should be limited ones that maintain the integrity of the constitutional structure itself. A bill proposed in the House would require delegates to take an oath not to try to change the Constitution except for the purpose stated in the

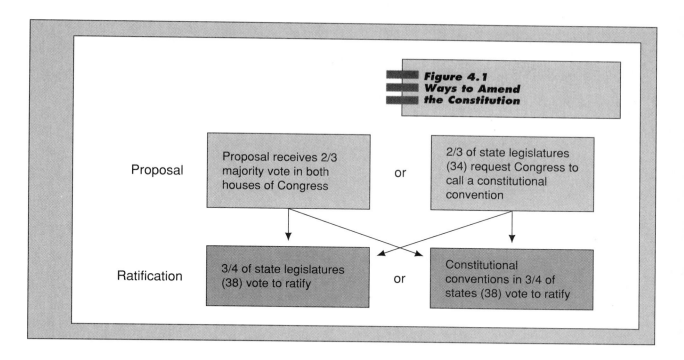

**Figure 4.1
Ways to Amend
the Constitution**

Proposal | Proposal receives 2/3 majority vote in both houses of Congress | or | 2/3 of state legislatures (34) request Congress to call a constitutional convention

Ratification | 3/4 of state legislatures (38) vote to ratify | or | Constitutional conventions in 3/4 of states (38) vote to ratify

petitions calling the convention.[48] But a group of convention opponents, organized as Citizens to Protect the Constitution, cited the limited charge of revising the Articles of Confederation given to the 1787 convention as evidence that attempts to impose limits on such an assembly would be futile. Opponents feared a "runaway convention, which would seek to impose its own political, social and economic agenda."[49] Debate over a constitutional convention has clearly demonstrated great support for the Constitution itself and for an amendment process that requires extensive deliberation and extraordinary majorities to change it. The most recent effort to call a convention has stalled, but it is an issue that will continue to be raised in American politics.

Executive, Legislative, and Judicial Changes

Amendments can change the actual words of the Constitution. But the Constitution has also been adapted to the economic, political, social, and technological changes of the past 200 years by leaving the words the same but interpreting them in a way to fit a changing society. The Su-

preme Court's power of **judicial review** makes it the institution responsible for telling the others what the Constitution means. Judicial review is the power to declare laws and executive acts unconstitutional. The Supreme Court exercises this power over national, state, and local legislatures and executives. For example, in the nineteenth century the Court said that the Fourteenth Amendment's equal protection clause did not rule out state laws permitting "separate but equal" facilities and institutions for blacks and whites and then in this century said the clause prohibited states and local school boards from having racially separate schools. (The discussion of the judiciary in Chapter 17 provides a full discussion of the development of this important Supreme Court role of interpreting the Constitution.)

While the Supreme Court provides the authoritative interpretation of the Constitution in American politics, both Congress and the president have also been responsible for changes in the meaning of the Constitution. Congress must sometimes interpret the meaning of sections of the Constitution in passing legislation because the Supreme Court does not provide advisory

A Closer Look

Crucial Questions on the Constitution ★★★

To commemorate the 200th anniversary of the U.S. Constitution, two constitutional scholars made up a list of the 13 major constitutional issues we wrestle with today.

1. Too much—or too little—power? Are the limits placed on the federal government's powers by the Constitution realistic and enforceable?

2. Does federalism work? Is the Constitution maintaining an efficient and realistic balance between national and state power?

3. Is the judicial branch too powerful? Are the courts exercising their powers appropriately as interpreters of the Constitution and shapers of public policy?

4. Balancing liberty and security: How can republican government provide for national security without endangering civil liberties?

5. Suspects' rights: How can republican government protect its citizenry and yet uphold the rights of the criminally accused?

6. "All men are created equal:" What kinds of equality are and should be protected by the Constitution and by what means?

7. Women's rights: Does the Constitution adequately protect the rights of women?

8. Safeguarding minorities: Does the Constitution adequately protect the rights of blacks, native Americans, ethnic groups, and recent immigrants?

9. The Constitution faces outward: Does the president possess adequate power—or too much power—over war-making and foreign policy?

10. Too many checks and balances? Does the constitutional separation of powers between the president, the Congress, and the judiciary create a deadlock in governance?

11. "Government by the people:" Does the evolving constitutional system, including political parties and interest groups, strengthen fair and effective representation of the people or undermine it?

12. The Constitution and the economy: Can the Constitution be utilized more effectively to provide economic security and promote the well-being of all Americans?

13. Constitutional flexibility: Should we make changing our fundamental charter of government simpler and more democratic?

Source: James MacGregor Burns and Richard B. Morris, "The Thirteen Crucial Questions," This Constitution: A Bicentennial Chronicle, *vol. 1, September 1983, published by Project '87 of the American Historical Association and the American Political Science Association.*

opinions, telling legislators beforehand whether a particular constitutional interpretation is correct. Congress must therefore act and then wait to see if such action is accepted as constitutional by the Court. For example, Congress expanded the meaning of the Constitution when it based the Civil Rights Act of 1964 on the power to regulate interstate commerce granted to Congress by Article I of the Constitution. In that particular instance, the Supreme Court was quick to uphold this as a legitimate interpretation of the commerce clause. The War Powers Resolution of 1973, which sought to give Congress some control over sending United States troops abroad, provides another example of how Congress can give modern definition to the Constitution.

Presidents have been able to greatly expand their executive power because Article II does not list precise limits on that power, as Article I does for Congress. This is most obvious in the case of presidential war powers. Even though the power to declare war is given to Congress in Article I, the concept of "defensive war" developed in 1801 by the Jefferson administration permits a president to exercise a wide range of war powers even without such a declaration by Congress. Expansive interpretations of the president's constitutional powers on military matters, foreign policy, and domestic legislation have created the strong presidency of the twentieth century.

An important difference between the formal procedure for amending the Constitution and the changes through interpretation discussed here is that the states have a role in the former but not the latter (except indirectly through representation in the Senate and the electoral college). Federalism is a central principle of the Constitution and thus of the amendment process. No area of American government more clearly illustrates the degree of political change possible within this constitutional framework than does the relationship between the national and state governments.

The question of who governs in American politics cannot be answered without first answering questions about federalism. A constitutional scholar who later served as president, Woodrow Wilson, stressed the centrality of the link between the Constitution, federalism, and political change when he wrote: "The question of the relation of the States to the federal government is the cardinal question of our constitutional government." Further, said Wilson, it was a question that could not "be settled by the opinion of any one generation, because it is a question of growth, and every successive stage of our political and economic development gives it a new aspect, makes it a new question."[50] Chapter 5 looks at this "cardinal question."

Checkpoint

- The U.S. Constitution is the oldest written constitution in the world. Over the past 200 years, the fundamental principles of the Constitution have been retained but adapted to changes in the nation by amendments and through new interpretations.

- The Constitution establishes an amendment process that requires proposed changes in the document to be approved by extraordinary majorities in both Congress and the states. Although the Constitution provides for calling a constitutional convention to propose amendments, all amendments to the Constitution have been proposed by the alternative method—a two-thirds vote of both houses of Congress. The ratification process requires that three-fourths of the states approve proposed amendments.

- The Supreme Court provides the authoritative interpretation of the Constitution, but the president and Congress also interpret the Constitution in carrying out their executive and legislative functions. The principle of federalism is less evident when the Constitution is altered through interpretation because the states do not have the formal responsibility given them in the amendment process.

SUMMARY

Six years of attempting to govern under the Articles of Confederation had convinced most political thinkers of the need for a strong national government with the power to govern. The Constitutional Convention of 1787 corrected the most glaring weaknesses of the articles by creating a Constitution that gave the national government the power to tax, to regulate interstate commerce, and to enforce its policies. At the same time, the convention limited the powers of government by providing a federal system and three branches of government with a separation of powers and checks and balances.

Ratification of the Constitution reflected the same economic and political divisions evident in the call for a Constitutional Convention. Nine of the states ratified by June 1788, but only after Federalist supporters of ratification promised to include a Bill of Rights.

Democratic, pluralist, and power elite explanations of the convention and the Constitution focus, respectively, on the key democratic ideas of the Constitution, such as individual rights and popular sovereignty; the role of the government as referee for competing economic forces; and the ways in which the Constitution advanced the economic interests of those who created it.

There is widespread agreement on the fundamental principles of the Constitution: separation of powers and checks and balances, federalism and national supremacy, a republican form of government, and civil liberties. But there is continuing debate on how these principles apply to American politics.

The Constitution provides a framework for amending the Constitution in response to political change. Executive, judicial, and legislative interpretations also serve to adapt the Constitution to change.

KEY TERMS

Executive branch
Legislative branch
Judicial branch
Electoral college
Supremacy clause
Bill of Rights

Separation of powers
Checks and balances
Federalism
National supremacy
Initiative
Referendum

FOR FURTHER READING

Charles Beard, *An Economic Interpretation of the Constitution of the United States* (New York: Free Press, 1965) (first published in 1913 by Macmillan). This is the classic power elite explanation of the writing and ratification of the Constitution.

Max Farrand, *The Framing of the Constitution of the United States* (New Haven: Yale University Press, 1913). An interesting account of who was at the Constitutional Convention and what they did there.

Robert A. Goldwin and William A. Schambra, *How Democratic Is the Constitution?* (Washington, D.C.: American Enterprise Institute for Public Policy Research, 1980). A lively collection of essays that provide democratic, pluralist, and power elite answers to the title question.

Alexander Hamilton, John Jay, and James Madison, *The Federalist* (New York: Modern Library, n.d.). A collection of 85 essays written in 1787 and 1788, which discuss the theory behind the Constitution and the advantages of the proposed new system over that which existed under the Articles of Confederation.

Michael Kammen, *The Origins of the American Constitution: A Documentary History* (Baltimore: Penguin Books, 1986). A collection of selected public documents and personal correspondence showing the development of the ideas behind the Constitution and the framers' thoughts about what they had created.

Leonard W. Levy, *Original Intent and the Framers' Constitution* (New York: Macmillan, 1988). An interesting account of the framers' ideas about constitutional interpretation and how judicial review by the Supreme Court keeps the Constitution relevant to modern political issues.

Forrest McDonald, *A Constitutional History of the United States* (New York: Franklin Watts, 1982). A counterargument to Beard's thesis that the Constitution was written by and for an economic and political elite.

Herbert J. Storing, *The Anti-Federalist* (Chicago: University of Chicago Press, 1985). An abridged version of Storing's work that demonstrated the importance of Anti-Federalist thought for understanding the Constitution.

Carl Van Doren, *The Great Rehearsal* (Baltimore: Penguin Books, 1986). A lively day-by-day account of negotiations at the Constitutional Convention.

Federalism

Federalism is a fundamental principle of governing in the U.S. Constitution. Even so, people disagree over which powers should be exercised by a central government and which by governments closer to home, a conflict that helped to shape the very creation of American government and continues today. Federalism is also a way of describing how the national and state and local governments share responsibility for governing and how different states and municipalities interact with one another. Today the national government is able to greatly influence state and local governments through a centralized system of federal grants. ■

On March 24, 1989, the tanker *Exxon Valdez* ran aground south of Valdez, Alaska, triggering the largest oil spill in U.S. history. Eleven million gallons of crude oil poured into Prince William Sound and spread toward the Gulf of Alaska. Oil from the spill eventually polluted more than 700 miles of pristine coastline, and newspapers and television carried pictures of oil-soaked birds and poisoned otters across the nation and around the world.

The culprit in this case was the Exxon Corporation, whose tanker captain was charged with negligence in allowing the oil to discharge. But who was to punish this corporate culprit and deal with the aftermath of the catastrophic spill—was it the responsibility of state government or the national government? Alaska has laws on the books to punish offenders in negligent oil spills, but so does the federal government in such acts as the Clean Water Act and the Trans Alaska Pipeline Act. Alaska presumably should monitor cleanup in its own territory, but such extensive pollution just as presumably calls for national aid and manpower. Two weeks after the spill (too late in the view of some observers) President George Bush announced that he was ordering troops and equipment to Alaska to assist cleanup efforts. "Let me be clear we are not federalizing this operation," he told reporters. "There is no demand from reasonable people to federalize this operation."[1]

Bush meant by this that he did not intend for the federal government to take responsibility for damages and clean up. But the question in many people's minds was: just who was in control? And whose standards, state or national, would apply in establishing Exxon's liability and fines? The questions extended even to the details of the lawsuits. For example, attorneys for the fishing industry sued Exxon under Alaska negligence and liability laws for economic losses caused by the oil spill. But any actions taken to recover damages to ducks, herring, or salmon would fall under the laws of the national government, which acts as trustee for *migratory* wildlife. Otters and shellfish, which like to stay at home, are the responsibility of the state of Alaska.

Ten years earlier a similar oil spill had threatened the coastal district of Congressman Gerry Studds, a Democrat from Massachusetts. Ever since, he has been trying to change the hodge-podge of national and state laws on oil spills. "Common sense says you want a uniform national system," Studds maintains, but his efforts to establish clear liability and a cleanup fund were regularly defeated by those who thought that would be preempting state laws.[2]

One of those critics was a former governor of Alaska. In May 1985 then-Governor Bill Sheffield sent a letter to Representative Studds and the House Subcommittee on Coast Guard and Navigation. "Local and state governments are best

A waterbird on the Alaskan coast shows the effects of the Exxon Valdez oil spill 35 miles away. Does it make sense for the national government to act as a trustee for some wildlife, such as this bird, and state governments for others, such as otters and shellfish?

able to address local environmental problems," Sheffield wrote. "Through local knowledge and political institutions, control of oil pollution cleanup and restoration can be conducted more efficiently and completely under the supervision of state and local officials."[3]

Why do state governments and the national government have different standards on oil spill liability, cleanup costs, and fines? Does it make sense for the national government to act as trustee for some wildlife and state governments for others? Did concern for states' rights delay the national government's response to this environmental tragedy? Should the responsibility for cleaning up oil spills and other pollution rest with the national or state government? All of those questions are about federalism and how the federalist structure affects the governing of America.

FEDERALISM IN THE AMERICAN POLITICAL SYSTEM

In a **federal system** the responsibility for governing is *divided* between a national government and smaller component governments. The U.S. government is responsible for defense and foreign policies, for example, whereas state and local governments exercise primary responsibility for education and law enforcement. Within their spheres of responsibility, the individual states are sovereign. There are also areas of shared responsibility, such as transportation, where both the national government and state and local governments govern. This federal structure is in contrast to a **unitary system**, in which the central or national government has the ultimate responsibility for policymaking in all areas. Sweden, France, and Great Britain are examples of a unitary structure of government. A unitary system can have regional and local governments, such as the departments and communes of France, and those governments might enjoy some autonomy in regional or local problems. The central government, however, grants this autonomy (and can take it away), whereas in the United States state and local officials exercise authority that is theirs by right, independent of the national government.

The structure of a federal government also provides for the *representation* of the smaller governments in the national government. The House of Representatives in Congress directly represents the people of the United States, but the Senate represents the states *as states*. That is why the framers originally specified that senators be selected by state legislatures, and it is why there are two senators from each state, regardless of population. The electoral college system of choosing a president also gives states representation as states in the national government.

A division of powers and representation of the smaller units within the larger unit are important, but they do not define federalism. There must be some guarantee that this arrangement is more than just temporary or a delegation of authority from national to regional government. A *written constitution* provides such a guarantee; it is a formal arrangement for dividing powers and providing representation. Under American federalism, the Constitution delegates certain powers to the national government, prohibits certain powers to the states, and (through the Tenth Amendment) reserves the remaining powers to the states. A comparative study of 21 contemporary democracies found that the six federal political systems among them all had written constitutions whereas the three nations with unwritten constitutions were all unitary.[4] (See A Closer Look for other characteristics federal systems share.)

Federalism can take many different forms and is not just limited to democracies. Table 5.1 sug-

gests some common reasons why a country would adopt federalism. It seems a particularly appropriate structure for governing large areas. The first five nations listed represent some of the largest countries in the world. In other countries—Mexico, Nigeria, Switzerland, Yugoslavia—the presence of administrative districts developed under colonialism and a population with a variety of language, ethnic, and religious differences are additional reasons for adopting federalism.

What about the United States? Size alone would point toward adoption of a federal system to govern America. But there were many other reasons as well why the colonies and new states chose federalism in the eighteenth century. In order to understand the governing of America today it is helpful to know what some of those reasons were. Many of the same political forces that led to the adoption of a federal system in the United States help shape American federalism today.

Table 5.1

Federalism in Comparative Perspective

Country	Federal Units[a]	Major Languages	Primary Reason for Federalism	Extent of States' Power
USSR	15 republics	Several	Nationalities/size	Weak
Brazil	27 states	One	Size/colonial history	Weak
Canada	10 provinces	Two	Size/language	Moderate
India	22 states	Many	Language/size	Moderate
United States	50 states	One	Colonial heritage/size	Moderate
Mexico	32 states	One	Colonial administration/size	Weak
Nigeria	19 states	Several	Tribalism/size/language/colonialism	Weak-moderate
Switzerland	26 cantons	Several	History/language	Strong
West Germany	10 states	One	Postwar occupation/regionalism	Strong
Yugoslavia	6 republics	Several	Language/ethnicity/religion	Moderate

[a]For some countries, state totals may include federal districts and/or other types of subdivisions.

Source: James A. Curry, Richard Riley, and Richard Battistoni *Constitutional Government: The American Experience* (St. Paul, Minn.: West, 1989), p. 195.

A Closer Look

What Federal Systems Have in Common ★★★

A comparative study of 21 contemporary democracies found that the six federal political systems among them share the following characteristics:[a]

1. Each has a written constitution prescribing the division of power and structure of representation.
2. There is a bicameral, or two-chamber, national legislature. One chamber directly represents the people and the other chamber the component governments.
3. The national constitution may not be changed without the consent of the component governments, but the component governments can change their own constitutions unilaterally.
4. The smaller of the component units of government are overrepresented in the federal chamber of the national legislature. That is to say, the share of legislative seats held by the smaller units exceeds their share of the population. To illustrate, every state has two senators in the U.S. Senate, regardless of state population. Currently, that means that voters in the least populated 30 states elect 60 percent of all senators, even though they represent only 25 percent of the total population.
5. Government is decentralized. One way to measure the degree of centralization is to look at the share of taxes collected by the

central and component governments. The average central government tax share in unitary governments among the 21 democracies was 83 percent, while in federal systems it was 58 percent.

Australia, Austria, Canada, Germany, Switzerland, and the United States share these five characteristics of federalism. While some of the unitary democracies had one or more of these characteristics, none had all five. Unitary democracies included Israel, Italy, France, England, Japan, and Sweden.

Knowing these characteristics of federalism can help us understand American politics. For example, the process for amending constitutions, the third characteristic listed above, helps explain why state constitutions on average have 100 amendments, whereas the U.S. Constitution has one-fourth as many with 26; or why an Equal Rights Amendment can pass the Senate and House of Representatives by overwhelming margins (84 to 8 and 354 to 23), be supported by nearly 60 percent of the public in national opinion polls, yet fail, after a ten-year campaign, to be added to the Constitution because only 35 of the necessary 38 states ratified the proposed amendment.

[a]Arend Lijphart, *Democracies: Patterns of Consensus Government in Twenty-One Countries* (New Haven, Conn.: Yale University Press, 1984), pp. 170–186.

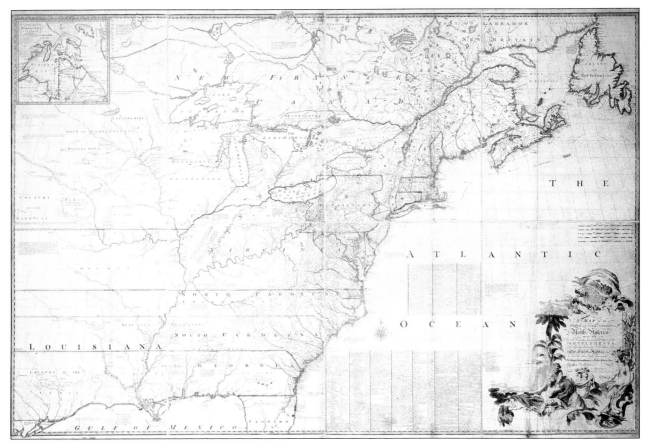

1755 Map of North America. The six tribes of the Iroquois Confederacy—a centuries-old federal union—occupied most of the strategic territory west of the English settlements along the Atlantic coast and the French settlements to the North. During the time of the American Revolution the Iroquois Confederacy influenced the thinking of Benjamin Franklin and other early proponents of federalism.

The Historical Basis of Federalism

American federalism is actually older than the United States. At the start of the American Revolution in 1776, a successful federal union among the Seneca, Onondaga, Oneida, Mohawk, and Cayuga Indian nations was more than 300 years old. When a sixth American Indian nation (the Tuscaroras) joined in the early eighteenth century, the Iroquois Confederacy, as the six nations were known, occupied most of the strategic territory between the British and French settlements in North America.

The Iroquois Confederacy had many of the elements we associate with modern federalism. Each of the six nations managed its own internal affairs. Any joint action or policy involving those outside the confederacy required approval by a Grand Council, in which each nation was represented. The individual nations debated issues internally before taking them to the Grand Council. The rules of debate and decision included a complex system of checks and balances, resembling in many ways the bicameral legislature and executive veto found in modern American federalism.

In 1744, a distinguished Iroquois chief named Canassatego closed a Pennsylvania treaty council with a plea for the colonies to form a federal union in order to keep their promises about controlling settlers and guaranteeing trade. Ten years later, Benjamin Franklin presented a similar proposal to delegates from Maryland, New England, New York, and Pennsylvania meeting in Albany to discuss relations with the Iroquois and the need for unity against the French. Franklin modeled his Albany plan on the Iroquois Confederacy. In the debate on his proposal, he praised "the strength of the League which has bound our friends the Iroquois together." The Albany conference approved Franklin's federal proposal, but it was rejected by the colonial legislatures for giving too much power to a central government and by the British government for giving too much power to the colonies.[5]

FACTORS FAVORING FEDERALISM Many factors contributed to the eventual adoption of federalism by the United States, including a century-long tradition of localism in the British colonies, the cooperative effort required in wars with France, Spain, and England, and the territorial disputes and economic rivalries among colonies before the Revolutionary War and among states afterward. These conflicting needs required the construction of a system that allowed state and local governments to govern on issues close to home and a centralized national government strong enough to pull the smaller units together on larger economic and military issues.

Ironically, at the same time the Revolutionary War was causing the colonists to unite in a common effort, internal conflict was being fueled by a demand for the right to local control. The desire for local autonomy even produced separatist movements within states and within cities and towns. To illustrate, in April 1775, when American militiamen fired "the shot heard round the world" in Concord, Massachusetts, secessionists from Concord had already established a new town of Acton within the old town borders. At the state level, the drive for local autonomy was reflected in separatist movements that within a decade of the end of the war had successfully carved Kentucky out of Virginia and Vermont out of New York. (See Figure 5.1 on page 142, which illustrates the borders of these new districts.)

The pull of separatist movements provoked intense political conflict and occasionally led to violence. Those who opposed separation put forward both economic and political reasons for maintaining the original boundaries. Concord

again illustrates the point. Residents living near Concord center had gone to war with England in order to gain independence and local control, yet they also knew that secessions diminished Concord's political and economic standing and increased the costs to the remaining citizens of supporting the town minister and meetinghouse. Historian Robert Gross notes the irony of the situation: "For all their insistence on maintaining government close to home, Concordians were reluctant to extend their principles to a minority of their neighbors."[6] One effect of separatist movements, then, was to make people aware of the limits to local autonomy.

There was a similar irony to territorial disputes within and between states. On the one hand, the interstate rivalries and distrust generated by boundary conflicts made cooperative efforts and union more difficult to achieve. On the other, these conflicts demonstrated the need for a higher authority to resolve border disputes and maintain peace.

THE FIRST ATTEMPT AT FEDERALISM: THE ARTICLES OF CONFEDERATION The importance of territorial disputes to the development of American federalism is evident in what happened to the first attempt at collective organization under the Articles of Confederation. Eight days after the signing of the Declaration of Independence in July 1776, a committee of the Continental Congress issued a report entitled "Articles of Confederation and Perpetual Union." Sixteen months later, Congress approved the articles and sent them to the states for approval. As we saw in Chapter 4, the articles set up a confederation of states in which the central government had limited powers. In a confederation, the central government does not act directly on individuals but on states, and the states have to approve the policies of the national government. The articles could not take effect until every state had ratified them, something that was not achieved until March 1781, nearly five years after the introduction of the draft proposal in Congress.

Why did it take so long for the states to approve the Articles of Confederation? The chief

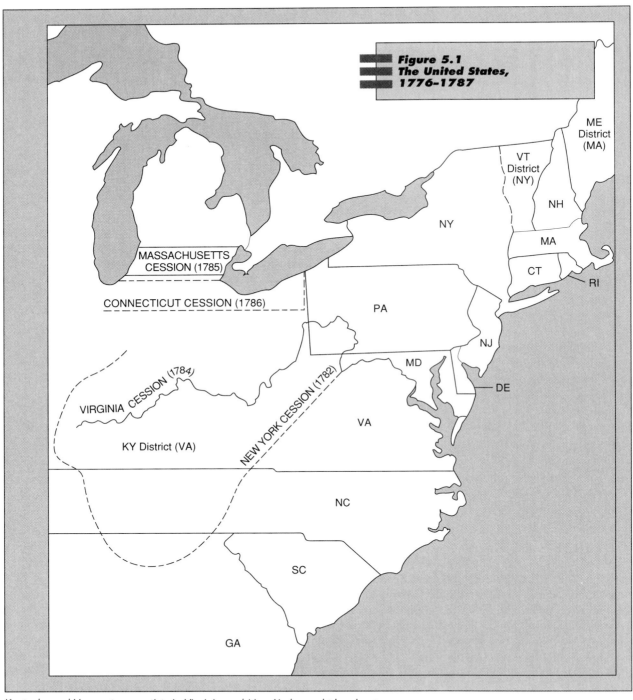

**Figure 5.1
The United States,
1776–1787**

Kentucky and Vermont separatists in Virginia and New York sought local autonomy, an
important factor in the development of early American federalism.

Source: Adapted from Peter S. Onuf, *The Origins of the Federal Republic* (Philadelphia:
University of Pennsylvania Press, 1983), p. 2.

reason was that states with limited land and fixed boundaries—Maryland, Delaware, and New Jersey—would not approve the articles until there was a resolution of the issue of the western boundaries of states such as Virginia and New York—states with a great deal of land and unclear boundaries.

The articles were ambiguous on this issue. One article recognized Congress as the final authority in disputes between states, but another article asserted that "Each state retains its sovereignty, freedom and independence." The formal procedure for settling boundary and jurisdictional disputes between states called for a special court under the supervision of Congress, but it was used only once. Direct negotiations between states turned out to be the most common way of ending their disputes. Several states simply ceded their western territory to Congress (see Figure 5.1). The passive role of Congress in settling these conflicts demonstrated the weakness of the central government under the articles. At the same time, the cooperative efforts of the states in working out their differences implied an acceptance of a common interest and paved the way for the more powerful central government of the Constitution.[7]

By the time of the Philadelphia convention of 1787, federalism was both a widely accepted principle and a somewhat tarnished form of government that had been in existence for six years under the Articles of Confederation. The framers of the Constitution sought to create a federal system, but one different from the loose confederation of the articles.

The Constitutional Basis of Federalism

The Articles of Confederation and the Constitution both provided the formal arrangements of American federalism. One can get a sense of the difference between these two by asking *who* is making the formal arrangement: Who is agreeing to the division of powers and system of representation in that written constitution?

The Articles of Confederation were quite clear about this. The articles began: "We the undersigned delegates of the states." And the final article said ratification was the responsibility of state legislatures, "the legislatures we respectfully represent." In contrast, the Preamble of the Constitution said "We the people of the United States" (not "we the states") are agreeing to a new Constitution. Instead of referring the Constitution to state legislatures for approval, Article VII called for the ratification of the *conventions* of at least nine states.

It would seem, then, that the formal arrangement of the articles was among states and the formal arrangement of the Constitution was among the people of the United States. But if the latter is true, why not ratify the Constitution through a direct popular vote? The answer given by James Madison in *Federalist 39* was that the Constitution established a *federal*, not just a *national* government. Ratification belonged to the people, "not as individuals composing one entire nation, but as composing the distinct and independent states to which they respectively belong." Even though ratification was through state conventions rather than state legislatures, Madison argued, "each state, in ratifying the Constitution, is considered as a sovereign body."[8]

COMPETING THEORIES OF FEDERALISM

Madison's answer helps explain why scholars have found competing theories of federalism in the Constitution. The theory of **state-centered federalism,** or compact theory, is based on the idea of the Constitution as a compact drawn up by independent and sovereign states. The authority of the national government, according to this theory, is limited to that conceded it by the states in the Constitution.

A contrasting theory of federalism suggests that both state and national authority come from the same source: the people. According to this theory of **nation-centered federalism,** since the American people as a whole agreed to the national powers outlined in the Constitution, national powers take precedence over the powers of state government.

Alexander Hamilton, treasury secretary in the administration of George Washington, and John Marshall, chief justice of the United States from

1801 to 1835, were two of the strongest early advocates of nation-centered federalism. James Madison and Thomas Jefferson, who resigned as Washington's secretary of state at least in part because of the administration's nationalist policies, advanced the state-centered, compact theory of federalism. Debate over the issues of creating a national bank and limiting political dissent illustrated the differences between these two views of federalism.

In 1791, President Washington asked Treasury Secretary Hamilton and Secretary of State Jefferson for their opinion as to whether the Constitution gave the national government authority to establish a Bank of the United States. Hamilton said yes; Jefferson said no. Washington followed Hamilton's advice. The national bank issue later provoked a major Supreme Court case on federalism when the state of Maryland challenged the constitutionality of the Second Bank of the United States, which Congress had established in 1816.

This landmark case of *McCulloch* v. *Maryland* (1819), described in Chapter 4, was the most important federalism case in American history. Chief Justice Marshall's opinion upholding the constitutionality of the national bank is a forceful statement of nation-centered federalism. Like Madison in *Federalist 39*, Marshall looked at the process of ratifying the Constitution in state conventions but came to a quite different conclusion about what that meant. "It is true," Marshall wrote, "they assembled in their several states—and where else should they have assembled? No political dreamer was ever wild enough to think of breaking down the lines which separate the states, and of compounding the American people into one common mass." But ratification by state conventions did not make votes on the Constitution "measures of state governments." The American people "did not design to make their government dependent on the states." Instead, "the government proceeds directly from the people." Marshall concluded that the national government "is emphatically, and truly, a government of the people. In form and in substance it emanates from them. Its powers are granted by them, and are to be exercised directly on them, and for their benefit."[9]

The state-centered view of federalism, on the other hand, emerged in the intense political conflict provoked by the Sedition Act of 1798. Fearing that the violence and rejection of authority of the French Revolution were entering American politics, Congress passed the Sedition Act, which made it illegal to criticize the president, Congress, or the national government. Thomas Jefferson and his supporters, who were the targets of the Sedition Act, argued that the law violated First Amendment guarantees of free speech and free press. But Jefferson's opponents not only controlled Congress and the executive but also the federal courts, making legal challenges of the Sedition Act ineffective. Jefferson and Madison tried a different approach by secretly drafting resolutions for the Kentucky and Virginia legislatures challenging the authority of the national government to pass the Sedition Act.

The Kentucky and Virginia Resolutions outlined a doctrine of **interposition**, which claimed a state's right to "interpose" itself between an unconstitutional law and the people of that state and to nullify that law. This doctrine saw the Constitution as a "compact to which the states are parties." Therefore, any attempt by the national government to exercise a power not granted in the compact would be "unauthoritative, void and of no force." Kentucky and Virginia could not get other state legislatures to pass similar resolutions, and Jefferson's election as president in 1800 effectively defused the conflict. Only nine years later, Jefferson's opponents relied on the compact theory and doctrine of interposition to protest certain actions of the Jefferson administration.

The state-centered theory of federalism emerged again in attempts by South Carolina in 1832 to nullify unfavorable tariff laws passed by Congress and in 1861 when seven southern states seceded from the United States and adopted a written constitution that declared: "We, the people of the Confederate States, each state acting in its sovereign and independent character," were establishing a new federal government. In 1956, state-centered federalism and the compact theory were evident in resolutions passed by the legislatures of eight southern states declaring

Who are the parties to the formal agreement of the Constitution? That seemed like a simple question until we saw how supporters of nation-centered federalism and state-centered federalism drew different answers from the same document.

Nation-centered and state-centered federalism provide contrasting views on the formal arrangement of the Constitution. Research by political scientist Samuel Beer has led him to suggest a third view incorporating aspects of the two other views: **representational federalism**. This theory of federalism is based on the idea that the agreement or formal arrangement of the Constitution is among the people, who are represented in *both* the national and state governments. Instead of providing a clear delineation of state and national powers, the Constitution established different levels of government that share an electorate. Answers to questions about who should govern in particular policy areas are to be found not in the precise language of the Constitution, but in the nature of representation in that system. We will see later in this chapter how representational federalism is at the heart of federal-state relations today as well as some Supreme Court decisions.

WHAT THE CONSTITUTION SAYS Specific provisions of the Constitution provide the basis of American federalism. Sections 9 and 10 of Article I stipulate what the national government cannot do and what the states cannot do. Section 8 of Article I says what the national government *can* do by listing specific powers, such as collecting taxes and regulating commerce, and concluding with the words "to make all laws which shall be necessary and proper for carrying into execution the foregoing powers and all other powers vested by this Constitution in the government of the United States." This has become known as the **elastic clause** because it has been used to stretch the powers of the national government as needed.

Article VI provides that the Constitution and laws of the United States made in pursuance of the Constitution are "the supreme law of the land." This is known as the **supremacy clause**. Both the elastic clause and the supremacy clause

A fear of mob violence in American politics led Congress to pass the Sedition Act of 1798. The Kentucky and Virginia Resolutions drew upon state-centered federalism and the doctrine of interposition to challenge the national government's authority.

unconstitutional the Supreme Court's ruling in *Brown* v. *Board of Education* (1954) that schools should be desegregated. Alabama's resolution spoke of "the states being the parties to the constitutional compact" and the Constitution of the United States being "formed by the sanction of the several states" acting in their sovereign capacity. (See A Closer Look on p. 146.)

A Closer Look

The State-Centered View: The Constitution as a Compact Among States ★ ★ ★

VIRGINIA RESOLUTION, 1798

That this Assembly doth explicitly and peremptorily declare, that it views the powers of the federal government as resulting from the compact to which the states are parties, as limited by the plain sense and intention of the instrument constituting that compact, as no further valid than they are authorized by the grants enumerated in that compact; and that, in case of a deliberate, palpable, and dangerous exercise of other powers, not granted by the said compact, the states, who are parties thereto, have the right, and are duty bound, to interpose, for arresting the progress of the evil, and for maintaining, within their respective limits, the authorities, rights and liberties, appertaining to them.

ALABAMA RESOLUTION, 1956

Whereas the Constitution of the United States was formed by the sanction of several states, given by each in its sovereign capacity; and

Whereas the states, being the parties to the constitutional compact, it follows of necessity that . . . they must decide themselves, in the last resort, such questions as may be of suffi-

cient magnitude to require their interposition, and

Whereas . . . : The Supreme Court of the United States asserts, for its part, that the states did . . . upon the adoption of the Fourteenth Amendment, prohibit unto themselves the power to maintain racially separate public institutions; the State of Alabama . . . asserts that it and its sister states have never surrendered such rights; and

Whereas this assertion upon the part of the Supreme Court of the United States, . . . constitutes a deliberate, palpable, and dangerous attempt by the court to prohibit to the states certain rights and powers never surrendered by them; and

Whereas the question of contested power asserted in this resolution is not within the province of the court to determine, . . . the judgment of all other equal parties to the compact must be sought to resolve the question; . . .

Source: Virginia Resolution in Philip B. Kurland and Ralph Lerner, eds., The Founders' Constitution *(Chicago: University of Chicago Press, 1987), Vol. V, pp. 135–136. Alabama Resolution in Richard Bardolph,* The Civil Rights Record *(New York: Crowell, 1970), pp. 378–380.*

Armed force is one way to settle conflicts over the line dividing state and national government. The ruins of the Navy Yard in Norfolk, Virginia, in this 1864 photograph reflect the devastation of the Civil War—the most prominent, but not the only, forceful settlement in the history of American federalism.

are used by nation-centered proponents to urge national power. States' rights advocates refer to the Tenth Amendment: "The powers not delegated to the United States by the Constitution, nor prohibited by it to the states, are reserved to the states respectively, or to the people."

Who decides if Congress is exercising a specific power granted in the Constitution or a power that is "necessary and proper" for carrying out one of those powers? How do we know whether a national law is "in pursuance" of the Constitution and therefore superior to a conflicting state law? Which powers of government are "reserved" to the states? In 1791 and again in 1816, Congress interpreted the "necessary and proper" clause to mean that the Constitution gave Congress the power to establish a national bank. In 1798, the Kentucky and Virginia legislatures concluded that the Sedition Act was not "in pursuance" of the Constitution and was therefore void. In 1974, Congress decided that it could set wage and hour standards for state and local government employees, while opponents argued that was a power "reserved" to the states by the Tenth Amendment.

The Constitution establishes a frontier between state governments and the national government, but it does not provide precise boundaries within that frontier. If Congress makes those boundary decisions, it is likely to expand into state government territory. If the states determine where the borders of state and national authority lie, they can effectively limit what the national government can do by claiming a state power protected by the Tenth Amendment. Like any boundary dispute, conflict over the line dividing state and national authority can be settled by force, by referring the dispute to a higher authority recognized by both sides, or by the parties reaching a joint agreement on their own. The conflicts of American federalism have been settled in all three ways. The Civil War was the most prominent but not the only forceful settlement in the history of American federalism. The next section examines how the higher authority of the U.S. Supreme Court resolves federalism conflicts, and the following section on intergovernmental relations looks at the joint agreements developed through representational federalism.

Checkpoint

- In a federal system responsibility for governing is divided between a national government and smaller component governments.

- The example provided by the centuries-old Iroquois Confederacy, the tradition of localism, the need for cooperative effort in war, and the territorial and economic disputes among the colonies all contributed to the adoption of a federal system in the United States.

- The weaknesses of the Articles of Confederation and the ongoing territorial disputes among states made it clear to the framers of the Constitution that a more centralized federalism than the confederation of the articles was needed to govern America.

- The Constitution established a federal system of government, but it has been interpreted in different ways. Nation-centered, state-centered, and representational federalism have all been described as the federalism of the Constitution.

SETTLING DISPUTES: THE SUPREME COURT AS REFEREE

In 1974 Congress passed a law that set wage and work hour standards for state and local government employees. But state and local officials protested this action as interference in the sovereign powers of state governments given constitutional protection by the Tenth Amendment. This dispute bounced around in the courts until 1985, when the Supreme Court ruled that the law Congress passed was constitutional (revers-

ing an earlier decision voiding the law). The 1985 ruling upset most state and local officials, including Arizona Governor Bruce Babbitt:

> I always viewed the Supreme Court in the role of referee, standing out on the field in a striped shirt, mediating the contest between the state and Federal governments.
> What this decision does is have the referee leaving the field and heading for the shower.[10]

The five justices in the majority in the 1985 case would most certainly deny that they were leaving the field. That they were referees of federalism, however, was beyond question. *Marbury* v. *Madison* (1803), a case we examine closely in Chapter 17, established early on that it was the Court that interpreted the Constitution, and as we saw in Chapter 4, *McCulloch* v. *Maryland* (1819) made it clear that this included interpreting the meaning of federalism under the Constitution.

Dual Federalism: A State-Centered Approach

For about 100 years after Chief Justice John Marshall's death in 1835, the Court interpreted federalism according to the concept of dual federalism, a state-centered approach. Under **dual federalism** the state and national governments had distinct spheres of governing, and each level was supreme within its own sphere. For example, the national government had the power to regulate interstate commerce under Article I, while the Tenth Amendment reserved to the states the power to regulate commerce within a state.

The Supreme Court acted as referee under dual federalism, but the referee had what sports fans today call a "quick whistle." The Court was quick to call a foul if either the state or national government sought to regulate commerce. State attempts were struck down as interference in the national government's sphere, and national regulation was said to intrude on the police powers of state government, which were protected by the Tenth Amendment.

Dual federalism, like state-centered federalism, protected states' rights in the important issue of slavery. Chief Justice Roger Taney's opinion in *Dred Scott* v. *Sandford* (1857) illustrates two important tenets of dual federalism.[11] First, it made a distinction between state and national citizenship and concluded that a person might be a citizen of a state without having the protections afforded citizens of the United States. Second, the Court ruled that national legislation prohibiting slavery in certain areas (the Missouri Compromise) violated the Fifth Amendment because it deprived people of property without due process of law. That left the slavery issue up to the states, not the national government.

The Court's attempt to settle the slavery issue in 1857 was notoriously unsuccessful, as the beginning of the Civil War three years later made clear. The Court held on to the concept of dual federalism, however, and it provided the basis of a number of decisions on government regulation of business. Until Congress passed the Interstate Commerce Act in 1887 and the Sherman Antitrust Act in 1890, business regulation was a state rather than national concern. But the absence of national laws was an incentive for businesses to claim they were engaged in interstate commerce and thus subject to regulation by Congress rather than state governments. Congressional passage of the commerce and antitrust laws turned that argument on its head. Business interests now could best escape regulation by appearing to be a local activity governed by the state, and *not* part of interstate commerce.

For example, after Congress passed the Sherman Antitrust Act to prohibit companies from forming monopolies or combinations in restraint of trade, the American Sugar Refining Company (a combination of companies that controlled 98 percent of all U.S. sugar refining) escaped prosecution when the Supreme Court ruled that Congress did not have power to regulate "manufacture" or production, such as sugar refining, because it was not interstate commerce. That power, the Court said, belonged to the states, and the line between the commercial power of national government and the police power of the state "should always be observed."[12]

A Nation-Centered Approach

When President Franklin Roosevelt took office in 1933 he initiated the New Deal—a series of federal programs meant to cope with the dire effect of the Depression and prevent its reoccurrence. Roosevelt's activist philosophy eventually took hold in the Supreme Court through his appointees, and the Court began to abandon dual federalism in favor of a nation-centered approach. The power of Congress to regulate commerce, which had been narrowly interpreted under dual federalism, now seemed to have no limits. For instance, the Supreme Court ruled in 1942 that the power to regulate interstate commerce extended even to an Ohio farmer who grew wheat for consumption on his farm. The Court said that even though the wheat never went to market, it supplied a need "which would otherwise be reflected by purchases in the open market. Homegrown wheat in this sense competes with wheat in commerce."[13]

The words of the commerce clause in Article I of the Constitution had not changed between 1895 and 1942, but the meaning of federalism clearly had. The Court's broad reading of the commerce clause was similar to that of Chief Justice John Marshall during the earlier period of nation-centered federalism.

After 1942, it was not until 1976 that the Supreme Court overturned a federal law on the grounds that Congress had exceeded its powers under the commerce clause. In *National League of Cities* v. *Usery* the Court ruled that Congress had done so when it amended the Fair Labor Standards Act to cover not just federal employees but state and local government employees as well. In this decision the Court returned to the earlier practice of drawing lines. Certain areas of responsibility traditionally belong to the states, it held, and any congressional interference with a state's ability to make basic employment decisions in those areas is unconstitutional.[14]

But the Supreme Court was closely divided in this case, five to four. One dissenting justice claimed the Court majority had repudiated principles "settled since the time of Chief Justice

John Marshall." Nine years later, as we have seen, the Court directly overruled the 1976 decision and upheld the constitutionality of the act setting wage and hour standards for state and local employees. The vote in this case, *Garcia* v. *San Antonio MTA* (1985), was again five to four.

The Representational Approach

The theory of federalism adopted by the Court in *Garcia* is representational federalism. Recall that this view looks to the system of representation and the shared electorate of state and nation for an understanding of who decides what. Justice Harry Blackmun, in the majority opinion, said that instead of relying on subjective standards like "traditional" functions and looking in the Constitution for lines between state and national powers, the Court should look to the *structure* of government and the political process. The representation of states, as states, in the federal government is what protects them from interference by the national government.

San Antonio bus driver Joe Garcia's suit to gain overtime pay triggered a nine-year battle in the courts and a landmark Supreme Court decision incorporating the theory of representational federalism.

What happened in the months following the *Garcia* decision demonstrates just how representational federalism works. State and local officials went to Washington to ask for changes in the law. Nine months after *Garcia* Congress did revise the law so that states and municipalities could once again have a hand in regulating the wages and hours of certain of their employees, such as police officers. Ultimately, then, the dispute was settled not in the courts but in the legislature, where each state was represented.

Of course, the *Garcia* decision by no means settles the meaning of federalism in the Constitution. Two five-to-four votes within nine years indicates the unresolved nature of the question. In *Garcia*, a biting opinion by dissenting Justice Lewis Powell showed how intense the disagreement on the Court was. Powell accused Blackmun and the rest of the majority of "genuflecting to the concept of Federalism" and then rejecting "almost 200 years of the understanding of the constitutional status of federalism." He said the decision relegated the states "to precisely the trivial role that opponents of the Constitution feared they would occupy." Justice Sandra Day O'Connor, in another dissenting opinion, expressed concern that the federal system of the Constitution was becoming more like "a unitary, centralized government."[15]

Who decides what federalism means? The discussion to this point suggests the Supreme Court does. At different times, the Court has found nation-centered, dual, and representational federalism in the Constitution. The effect of the Court's *Garcia* decision on state and local governments demonstrates the importance of the referee to the contests of federalism. But the prompt congressional response to that decision shows that it is the national, state, and local players, and not the referees acting alone, that determine the outcome of those contests. The meaning of American federalism cannot be determined simply by looking at the Constitution or listening to what the Supreme Court has to say. We must also look at the relationship between the different levels of government in the United States, at how they treat each other. The meaning of federalism in this sense is the topic of the next section.

Checkpoint

- Supreme Court justices are the referees of federalism. In disputes between the national and state governments, it is the Supreme Court that decides what the Constitution says about who governs what.

- The concept of dual federalism, which characterized Supreme Court decisions for about 100 years (1835–1937), recognized distinct spheres of national and state government, with each supreme in its own sphere. The major impact of dual federalism was to limit government regulation of business.

- The Supreme Court endorsed the concept of nation-centered federalism in upholding New Deal programs in the late 1930s, a trend that continued until the 1970s.

- More recently, the Court has described the federalism of the Constitution as representational federalism. In this approach, the Constitution itself does not draw lines between national and state government powers. Instead, it establishes a system of government for determining who governs what and assures that both national and state interests are represented in that government.

INTERGOVERNMENTAL RELATIONS

Nearly a month after the 1989 Alaska oil spill, Exxon chairman Lawrence Rawl blamed state and federal officials for the cleanup delays. The Coast Guard and state environmental officials had to approve any use of chemical dispersants, and the overall cleanup plan had to be approved by "14 or 15 different agencies" at the state and national level, Rawl said. "It was incumbent on those officials to give us a prompt response instead of none. I don't know what their problem was."[16]

The same week, a U.S. senator complained that a number of states—including California, New Jersey, Ohio, and Maryland—had failed to use more than $750 million in federal funds available to them for antidrug programs. But state officials complained that applying for the federal funds was difficult because of the complicated formula for allocating funds to the states.[17]

A month earlier, New York Senator Daniel Patrick Moynihan had expressed frustration that hundreds of millions in federal funds he had obtained for constructing Westway highway along the Hudson River in Manhattan had not been used 15 years after the old highway had collapsed. Federal and state environmental agencies had delayed the work in order to protect the endangered striped bass, which breed among the old pilings in the Hudson River. Industrial pollutants (PCBs) in the river bed were harmful to the fish, so Senator Moynihan had obtained $20 million in federal funds to dredge up the industrial waste. That money had not been spent be-

The use of available federal funds for constructing New York City's Westway highway was delayed to protect endangered striped bass, which breed among the old pilings in the Hudson River. A frustrated senator complained: "You can't build Westway because of the fish, which you can't eat because of the PCBs, which you can't clean up because there's no place you may put them."

cause the state had not been able to locate a suitable disposal site for the waste. Moynihan summed up the situation this way: "You can't build Westway because of the fish, which you can't eat because of the PCBs, which you can't clean up because there's no place you may put them."[18]

The relationship between the state and federal governments in these cases is a complex one of funding and regulation. This sharing of resources and program administration by different levels of government is known as **cooperative federalism,** despite the delays and frustrations often encountered in these situations.

Because cooperative federalism emphasizes the shared electorate of nation and state and works through government structure, it is a natural outgrowth of representational federalism. Political scientist Morton Grodzins once described the separation and independence of government functions in dual, state-centered federalism as a "layer cake" and the blending of government functions of cooperative federalism as a "marble cake."[19] The ingredients of cooperative federalism—the types of national assistance to the states—have remained pretty much the same over the years, but there has been wide variety in how they are mixed.

Forms of Federal Assistance

The national government assists state and local governments through: (1) grants, (2) federal income tax deductions for interest on state and local bonds and for state and local taxes, (3) loan guarantees, and (4) direct expenditures such as purchases and salaries, which can greatly affect state and local economies.[20] Table 5.2 provides a general picture of the mix of these four types of federal aid.

Because the financial stakes are so high, decisions about federal aid and expenditures can generate intense political conflicts. A Reagan administration proposal to eliminate the deduction for state and local taxes (earning the federal government about $34 billion a year) provoked the longest and most heated fight over the Tax Reform Act of 1986. The states won that particular battle, but debate over the deduction is far from over. Federal expenditures in the states in the

Table 5.2

Forms of Federal Assistance, Various Fiscal Years (in billions)

Federal grants	$108.4 (1987)
Tax exemptions (also termed tax expenditures)	46.9 (1987)
Loans and loan guarantees	2.6 (1987)
Federal expenditures among the states (salaries and wages; benefit payments; procurement; special programs)	745.6 (1984)

Source: *Budget of the United States Government, Fiscal Year 1989,* "Special Analysis H," pp. H16, 20; U.S. Department of Commerce, Bureau of the Census, *Federal Expenditures by State for Fiscal Year 1984* (Washington, D.C.: 1985).

form of military installations or research facilities are a perennial topic of American politics. For example, in 1989 competition among states for the $11 billion superconducting supercollider project produced extensive lobbying by states and their congressional delegations until Texas landed the project.

The federal grant system, however, is the form of federal aid that best illustrates cooperative federalism. All forms of federal assistance provide state and local governments with resources, but grant programs also include the shared administration of these programs, which is the hallmark of cooperative federalism. Tables 5.3 and 5.4 provide an overview of the federal grant system.

Table 5.3 shows the tremendous growth in federal grant spending from 1950 to 1980 as well as the decline relative to total federal spending since then. Total spending went from just over $2 billion in 1950 to more than $100 billion in the 1980s. In 1950 federal grants accounted for one of every ten dollars spent by state and local governments; that figure climbed to one of every four dollars in 1980. Since then, the proportion of federal outlays and of state and local spending represented by grants declined, a result of Reagan administration policies to be discussed shortly. The breakdown by function in Table 5.4

Table 5.3
Federal Grant Outlays, 1950–1987

| Year | Total Grants (in billions) | Federal Grants as a Percent of | |
		Federal Outlays	State and Local Expenditures
1950	$ 2.3	5.3	10.4
1955	3.2	4.7	10.1
1960	7.0	7.6	14.6
1965	10.9	9.2	15.2
1970	24.1	12.3	19.2
1975	49.8	15.0	22.7
1980	91.5	15.5	25.8
1985	105.9	11.2	21.0
1986	112.4	11.4	20.6
1987	108.4	10.8	18.2

Source: *Budget of the United States Government, Fiscal Year 1989,* "Special Analysis H, Federal Aid to State and Local Governments," p. H21.

Table 5.4
Distribution of Federal Grants by Function, 1960–1987

| | Percentage of Total Federal Grant Spending | | | |
	1960	1970	1980	1987
Natural resources and environment	2	2	6	4
Agriculture	3	3	1	2
Transportation	43	19	14	16
Community and regional development	2	7	7	4
Educational, training, employment, and social services	7	27	24	17
Health	3	16	17	24
Income security	38	24	20	28
General-purpose fiscal assistance	2	2	9	a
Other general government	a	1	1	5
Total	100	100	100	100

a0.5% or less; because of rounding, percentages may not total 100.

Source: *Budget of the United States Government, Fiscal Year 1988,* "Special Analysis H, Federal Aid to State and Local Governments," p. H20.

shows a tremendous decline in transportation grants and a dramatic increase in grants for health services—a reflection of changing political trends discussed later in this chapter.

The Federal Grant System

Federal grants may take the form of categorical grants, block grants, or general support grants known as revenue sharing. President Lyndon Johnson's "Creative Federalism" of the 1960s, President Richard Nixon's "New Federalism" of the 1970s, and President Ronald Reagan's proposal for a new type of "New Federalism" in the 1980s all represented different ways of combining the three types of grants. Some knowledge of the types of grants is necessary for understanding the current state of American federalism.

CATEGORICAL GRANTS   Assistance programs that provide federal funds for specific purposes are known as **categorical grants.** These grants restrict use of the funds to a particular program or specific function of government, such as community mental health staffing, vocational rehabilitation, and wastewater treatment. The oldest type of grant program, it was first used early in the nineteenth century to provide educational funds to states. Currently, there are more than 400 categorical grant programs, including Medicaid, highway construction, and Aid to Families with Dependent Children (AFDC).

This type of grant is most commonly used to support a government service whose benefits extend beyond the borders of a particular city or state. Without federal assistance to fill in the gap, those services are likely to be underfunded by state and local governments. Some of the largest categorical grant programs redistribute income in providing benefits to the most disadvantaged groups in society.

The federal government gained a tremendous fiscal advantage over state and local governments with the introduction of the federal income tax in 1913. Some of the new revenue was allocated to the states through health care and highway construction grant programs. The

Great Depression triggered another major expansion of categorical grants in the 1930s, particularly in the areas of public works and welfare. The largest growth in categorical grants came in the activist government administration of Lyndon Johnson. Johnson's Creative Federalism instigated more than 200 categorical grant programs between 1963 and 1967.

The federal government attaches restrictions and requirements to all of its grant programs. Categorical grants, however, have more of these strings attached than do other forms of federal assistance. Typically, these conditions prohibit discrimination in use of the funds, require that health and safety standards be met, assure environmental protection, and establish administrative procedures that must be followed in using the funds. Categorical grant programs may also require state and local governments to match federal funds with their own. A 1981 study of ten local governments in five states found more than 1000 conditions and requirements attached to the categorical grants those communities received from the federal government.[21]

BLOCK GRANTS   **Block grants** provide federal assistance in a *general area*, such as health, law enforcement, or education. Congress establishes a formula for allocating the funds among the states and localities, but the recipients determine how the funds will be used within the general area.

The Johnson administration established the first block grants in the areas of health care and law enforcement. Subsequent Republican presidents took block grants much further. Under the banner of "New Federalism," President Richard Nixon proposed replacing 129 existing categorical grant programs with six block grant programs. President Ronald Reagan won congressional support in 1981 for combining 77 categorical grant programs into nine block grants as part of his New Federalism. President George Bush's campaign platform in 1988 pledged to continue the federalism of the Reagan administration.

The block grant approach appeals to Republican presidents because they value decentrali-

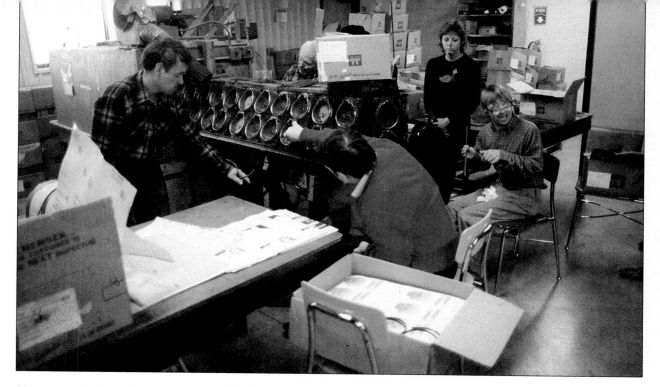

Many categorical grants support programs for disadvantaged groups in society, such as this vocational rehabilitation program for the mentally impaired.

zation and a reduction in the role of the federal government. State and local officials also prefer block grants to categorical grants because of the freedom they have to spend funds as they wish in a general area. While the degree of federal government control is less in block grants than in categorical grants, the recipients must still comply with federal regulations governing nondiscrimination, health, safety, and other aspects of the program.

The national government also exercises control over block grants through the formula that determines how funds will be allocated. For example, Congress provided nearly $1.5 billion for state and local antidrug programs over a two-year period. But it also established a complex distribution formula based on a state's tax revenues, previous spending on antidrug programs, population under the age of 18, urban population, and number of drug addicts. Many state officials said one of the reasons why more than $750 million in available funds had not been used in 1989 was that Congress made its allocation formula too complicated and then kept changing it.

REVENUE SHARING Under the program of **revenue sharing**, the federal government distributed funds to state and local governments without requiring that the money be spent on particular programs or even for certain broad functions like education or health. These general support grants were established in the State and Local Fiscal Assistance Act of 1972. Up to 1980 revenue sharing provided approximately $6 billion to state and local governments each year. One-third of the total went to the states and two-thirds went directly to local governments. Funds were distributed on the basis of population, per capita income, and state and local taxes, but the distribution formula also guaranteed that all 50 states and each of the 39,000 local governments received funds under revenue sharing.

Revenue sharing is based on the premise that there is revenue to share. In fact, it was a federal surplus in 1837 that initiated the first revenue sharing when the federal government passed the excess funds on to the states. But when the federal deficit climbed over $200 billion in the 1980s, revenue sharing lost its appeal even to those who favored decentralization and a re-

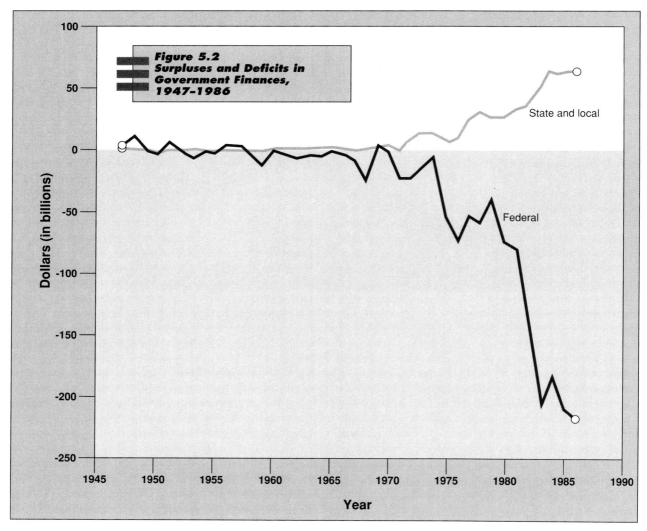

Figure 5.2
Surpluses and Deficits in
Government Finances,
1947–1986

State and local

Federal

Dollars (in billions)

Year

Source: Office of Management and Budget, *Budget of the U.S. Government, Fiscal Year 1988,*
Historical Tables, Table 15.6. Harold W. Stanley and Richard G. Niemi, *Vital Statistics on*
American Politics (Washington, D.C.: Congressional Quarterly Press, 1988), p. 282.

duced federal role. Moreover, at the same time federal deficits were growing, most state and local governments were experiencing a healthy fiscal condition (see Figure 5.2). In 1986 Congress voted to eliminate all revenue-sharing funding.

The federal government distributed $84 billion in revenue-sharing funds to state and local governments between 1973 and 1987. Rather than applying revenue-sharing funds to new programs or projects, state governments used the money primarily to maintain existing programs and to stabilize taxes. Local governments did use revenue sharing for new construction projects, but they, too, applied most of the funds to maintaining services such as police and fire protection and to stabilizing or reducing taxes. Revenue sharing had little impact on the budgets of large states and cities, but it did help smaller towns and rural areas.[22]

Because revenue sharing was distributed to all state and local governments, rather than simply targeted at those with the greatest need, it did little to equalize the taxing and spending capacity of states and cities throughout the country. Some critics of revenue sharing have also suggested that the program contributed to inefficiency in state and local governments by making it possible for them to spend "outside" money without having to raise state or local taxes. Ronald Reagan made that point in criticizing revenue sharing in 1975: "When tax increases are proposed in state assemblies and city councils, the average citizen is better able to resist and make his influence felt."[23]

Table 5.5 shows the mix of categorical, block, and revenue-sharing grants for selected years between 1972 and 1987. The changes in the mix of federal assistance shown there reflect the politics of federal aid, in which presidents, governors, mayors, members of Congress, state legislators, federal and state bureaucrats, and a wide range of interest groups struggle over the amount and forms of federal assistance. The "New Federalism" proposed by President Reagan during the

1980s illustrates the dynamics of intergovernmental relations in the United States.

"New Federalism"

One scholar described President Ronald Reagan as "the first president since Franklin D. Roosevelt to challenge not just the workings of the intergovernmental system but the prevailing federalist ideology of his time."[24] In 1982 Reagan proposed a **"New Federalism"** aimed toward achieving three goals: (1) a clearer division of state and national government functions; (2) a devolution of responsibilities to governments that are closer to the people; and (3) reduced spending by governments at all levels.

The Reagan administration was more successful in achieving its third goal than it was in achieving the first two. (See Table 5.3). The increasing emphasis on block grants early in the Reagan administration reflected the principle of decentralization, of giving state and local officials more control over spending. You can see in Table 5.5, however, a reversal in that trend. Toward the end of the Reagan administration, categorical grants had returned to their earlier position of dominance in the federal assistance program.

The centralizing trend evident in this return to categorical grants, along with the increasing number of conditions Congress added to block grants and the termination of revenue sharing, have led one political scientist to conclude that "ambitious reform proposals such as President Reagan's New Federalism have gotten nowhere."[25]

Why did the latest version of New Federalism fail to achieve lasting changes in the structure of intergovernmental relations in the United States? That question goes hand in hand with questions about why the Supreme Court has changed its views on American federalism over time and why federalism was initially chosen as the structure of American government. To answer any of those questions, we need to have some ideas about who benefits from the different forms of federalism and from federalism in general. Once again, the three views of American politics can help us to answer those questions.

Table 5.5

Mix of Grants, Selected Years, 1972–1987

| Year | Percent of Outlays | | |
	Categorical Grants	Block or Broad-Based Grants	Revenue Sharing
1972	90.1	8.3	1.6
1975	76.7	9.2	14.1
1980	79.3	11.3	9.4
1983	79.1	13.9	7.0
1987	86.0	12.1	1.9

Source: *Budget of the United States Government, Fiscal Year 1989,* "Special Analysis H," p. H23.

Checkpoint

- The sharing of resources and program administration by different levels of government that characterizes intergovernmental relations today is known as cooperative federalism.

- Cooperative federalism is implemented through a system of federal grants, which consists of: (1) categorical grants providing funds for a particular program or specific function of government, (2) block grants providing funds in a general area such as education, and (3) revenue-sharing or general support grants which, until the program was ended in 1986, the recipient governments could use as they saw fit.

- The "New Federalism" proposals of the Nixon and Reagan administrations sought to decentralize the intergovernmental system, but the federalism of the 1980s remained a centralized system dominated by categorical grants.

FEDERALISM: WHO GOVERNS?

The Federalism Working Group of the Reagan administration issued a report in 1986 stating that 50 years of U.S. Supreme Court decisions undercutting the power of the states had fundamentally altered the nature of federalism in the United States. The director of the study, Assistant Attorney General Charles Cooper, suggested in an interview that those who wrote the Constitution would have been appalled by Supreme Court decisions such as *Garcia*: "If you had suggested to the framers of the Constitution or to the ratifying conventions that the commerce clause would be sufficiently muscular to permit Congress to tell state governments how much they must pay state employees, the Con-

stitution—or at least the interstate commerce clause—would never have been enacted as the nation's fundamental charter." It was not the principle of federalism that was at fault for these Court decisions, Cooper said, for "federalism is policy neutral." The real problem, he felt, was that "federalism is often argued by people for the sole purpose of trying to halt policies that they do not favor or trying to advance policies that they do."[26]

The general principle of federalism might appear to be policy-neutral, but interpretations of the principle most certainly have not been neutral. Different views of federalism have been linked with policy preferences throughout American history. The nation-centered federalism of Hamilton and John Marshall supported the activist economic development programs advanced by Hamilton as treasury secretary. The state-centered federalism of the Kentucky and Virginia Resolutions was a direct response to the political conflict surrounding the Sedition Act of 1798, but Jefferson moved closer to nation-centered federalism after being elected president in 1800. Tariff policies and the issue of slavery generated the state-centered doctrines of nullification and secession. Dual federalism protected businesses and corporations from both state and national economic regulation. The many varieties of cooperative federalism, changes in the system of federal assistance, and proposals for major reforms have all reflected broader policy goals and issues of governing, such as Richard Nixon's goal of decentralizing government in order to improve it and Ronald Reagan's goal of reducing government at all levels.

How one interprets federalism is also connected with broader values of democracy and with the recurring question of who governs. Depending on what aspects of federalism one emphasizes, federalism can be seen as serving each of the three models of government.

Democracy

In 1983, the Republican Congressional Committee ran an advertisement in the *New York Times* under the headline: "Does Washington Know Best—Or Did Jefferson?" The ad began with a quotation from Thomas Jefferson on the need for local control of schools and applied that theme to the 1980s:

> Education has always been a responsibility we've chosen to keep close to home. That's why local school districts were formed in America 150 years before the Constitution was ratified. It's why, even in this age of centralization, there are still 16,000 local school districts in America and one school board member for every 2,000 voters. . . . Republicans believe that while Washington has a role to play in education, Jefferson had the right idea. Local control has always been—and still remains—an article of faith for us. Education is no exception.[27]

In 1989, the issue of decentralized schools was again being widely discussed. This time, however, the focus was on what many educators and parents saw as the *negative* aspects of decentralized education. An international study publicized in 1989 found American students ranked last in math and science skills among the 12 nations in the study.[28] Many educators blamed the decentralized nature of American schooling. They said the lack of any coherent and coordinated framework for teaching math and science made it difficult to maintain standards. Here is the way a Nobel Prize-winning physicist identified the problem: "We have some 16,000 independent school systems, and they simply receive too little guidance in terms of a unified science curriculum."[29]

These two views on decentralized schooling illustrate a pattern we have seen throughout the development of American federalism. Americans in the eighteenth century valued local autonomy yet recognized a need to join together, and today we still recognize the benefits of both decentralization and centralization. The argument for decentralization, however, has most consistently been tied with the value of democracy.

People tend to believe that local governments are more democratic than large centralized governments because local governments are closer to the people and more easily controlled by them. This belief has been around for a long time. The French theorist Montesquieu, Thomas Jefferson, and a number of Anti-Federalists advanced the idea that democracy works best in small political systems. "Divide the counties into wards," Thomas Jefferson wrote in 1816, because "in government, as well as in every other business of life, it is by division and subdivision of duties alone, that all matters great and small, can be managed to perfection."[30]

In a survey conducted in 1981, a national sample of Americans were asked: "Of every tax dollar that goes to the federal government in Washington D.C., how many cents of each dollar

Town officials (including one of the authors of this book) follow Uncle Sam in a July Fourth parade in Massachusetts. A belief that the accessibility of decisionmakers and widespread opportunities for participation make democracy work best at the local level continues to shape American federalism.

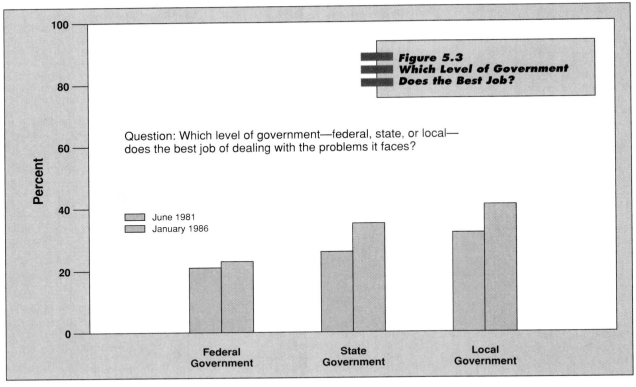

Source: Survey by CBS/New York Times, *Public Opinion*, March/April 1987, Washington, D.C.: American Enterprise Institute for Public Policy Research, p. 27.

would you say are wasted?" The median response was 42 cents. In contrast, respondents said 29 cents of each dollar was wasted at the state level and 23 cents at the local level.[31]

As Figure 5.3 shows, people believe local government does a better job of dealing with problems than either the state or national governments. This view became even more widely accepted during the Reagan years, which emphasized the limited, decentralized government of Jeffersonian democracy.

Justice Lewis Powell devoted much of his dissenting opinion in the *Garcia* case to the connection between federalism and democracy. Powell argued that the federalism of the Constitution was based on a belief in "the far more effective role of democratic self-government at the state and local levels." He cited arguments to this effect in the *Federalist* papers as evidence that the framers believed that democracy works best at

the local level where people have first-hand knowledge of local problems and easy access to public officials. In arguing that the same is true today, Justice Powell quoted the conclusion of a 1979 participation study: "Participation is likely to be more frequent, and exercised at more different stages of a governmental activity at the local level, or in regional organizations, than at the state and federal levels."[32]

Pluralism

Pluralism is often used to characterize both the federalism of the Constitution and contemporary intergovernmental relations. For example, Richard Leach has written that most delegates to the Constitutional Convention had been accustomed for so long to having a number of small units in their political, religious, economic, and social organizations that at the time of the convention they "were pluralist by long habit."[33] In *When Federalism Works*, Paul Peterson and his associates point out that most students of American federalism believe cooperative federalism and the shared administration of policy to be "entirely consistent with the country's pluralist traditions" of different levels of government checking one another.[34]

One can argue that dividing the responsibility for governing among national and subnational units inherently supports pluralism. The creation of independent and relatively autonomous arenas makes it unlikely that any one group or individual can govern in all of them. The different tiers of government in a federal system also create a number of points of access to government and influence over policy. A particular interest or group that is frozen out of power at one level can seek to gain it at another. A party that suffers electoral defeat at the national level can still hope to control the government of some states and cities. A federal system promotes pluralism by distributing political resources and opportunities to a wide range of interests and groups.

Madison's plea for a strong national government in the federal system rests on pluralist arguments. He found that the constituency of this level of government included such a variety of interests and factions that none of them could control the government. That was so, Madison argued, because the large number of factions in the national sphere made it more difficult for them to act in unison (a point discussed in Chapter 3). The smaller constituencies of state and local governments, on the other hand, made those governments more vulnerable to control by a single interest or coalitions. In contrast to those who argue for decentralization in the name of democracy, pluralists are likely to see some merit in the centralization of American federalism that took place in this century.

The distribution of resources through the grants program also reflects pluralist values. For example, Nixon's revenue-sharing program was meant to replace many categorical grants. But eventually the many interests who benefited from specific grant programs were able to reinstate a number of the categorical grants. Pluralism is also reflected in the formulas for distributing funds under categorical and block grants and in the efforts of organized interests to have a say in determining those formulas. For many years a group representing the interests of Frostbelt states focused on obtaining favorable distribution formulas for northern states. Its success, and a general feeling among some southerners that "the Yankees are very ingenious in getting the formulas worked out to their definition," led the Sunbelt states to form their own interest group to change the distribution formulas to their own advantage.[35]

Pluralism has also been connected to some of the problems of federalism today. The failure of New York City to use millions of dollars of federal aid, discussed earlier in this chapter, is a case in point. Why had federal grants for the Westway highway project, mass transit improvements, and drug education programs never been applied to those programs? Brooklyn Congressman Charles Schumer felt the problem was that "there are just so many centers of power" reflected in the vast number of government officials, boards, committees, and commissions that had to give their approval before the grant money could be spent.[36]

The Power Elite

Senator Daniel Patrick Moynihan had a different explanation for why federal grant money was not being used by New York City. According to him, the problem was not pluralism and the "many centers of power" identified by Representative Schumer. "To the contrary," Moynihan said, "it's the capacity of elites to prevent things from happening through access to the rules and to the courts."[37]

Federalism is said to nurture pluralism by providing many centers of power and therefore many points of access to the system for a wide range of interests. But those centers of power can also be considered veto points, where political elites can defeat programs favored by a majority.

We have seen that public opinion polls consistently show that people believe state and local governments are better at solving problems than is the federal government. Why, then, is the federal grant system still dominated by categorical grants, which give federal decision makers more power over the use of funds than do block grants or revenue sharing?

A number of political elites have a stake in maintaining a federal grant system dominated by categorical grants: national political elites in Washington, policy professionals, state and local government bureaucracies, and the larger intergovernmental bureaucracy that administers those grants. The national political elites with perhaps the clearest stake in categorical grant programs are members of Congress. The narrow focus of categorical grants permits representatives and senators to obtain benefits that best meet the needs of their constituencies and to claim credit for bringing federal assistance to the district or state. Once a program is established, members of Congress can continue to gain credit by intervening on behalf of constituents who are having problems in obtaining program benefits. Neither block grants nor revenue sharing help senators and representatives in the same way because they give state and local officials more say over the distribution of funds and make it more difficult for national legislators to claim credit for benefits to constituents. According to this explanation, then, members of Congress vote to maintain categorical grant programs because it is in their own self-interest.[38]

Another elite influential in limiting the Reagan administration's proposals for decentralizing the federal grant system were policy professionals: administrators with professional training and expertise in a particular field such as health care, education, or housing. One study of Reagan's New Federalism proposals found that decentralization met the most effective resistance in those areas in which policy professionals were best established—education and health care—and that the most decentralization took place in housing, where policy professionals had much less influence.[39]

Finally, the large number of categorical grant programs established since the 1960s have created a large state and local bureaucracy to administer those programs. Although they are located in states and cities, these officials have closer ties with their national counterparts in the

same program than they do with elected state and local officials. John Chubb found that "in most states, the bulk of federal assistance is untouched by any general political official except the governor," and that decisions about the distribution of benefits and administration of grant programs were influenced more by the intergovernmental bureaucracy than by elected officials at the state or local level.[40]

The stake that all these political elites have in categorical grants helps to explain why efforts to decentralize the federal grant system have been unsuccessful. It reinforces power elite beliefs discussed in Chapter 1 about how state and local political leaders are left with making relatively unimportant "twig" decisions about governing, while the important decisions are made at the national level by political elites.

Checkpoint

- The general principle of federalism might appear to be policy-neutral, but different views of federalism have been associated with policy preferences throughout American history.

- The democratic view of federalism is generally associated with decentralization and a belief that local government is best.

- A federal structure supports the pluralist values of independent and autonomous arenas of government and multiple access points for influencing government decision making.

- National political elites, policy professionals, and administrators working in intergovernmental programs all have a stake in the federal grant system and particularly in categorical grants.

SUMMARY

A number of factors contributed to the establishment of a federal structure of government in the United States. The example provided by the Iroquois Confederacy, a tradition of localism, and the need for cooperation among colonies in fighting wars and settling disputes were all important factors. The Articles of Confederation established an alliance among states but failed to provide a central government capable of resolving the important economic and political conflicts of the day. The federalism of the Constitution is one in which the central government has more power than it did under the articles. Provisions of the Constitution have been used to support both nation-centered and state-centered interpretations of American federalism.

The Supreme Court applied a concept of dual federalism for about 100 years, from 1835 to 1937. The major effect of dual federalism was to limit government's regulation of business. Since then, the Supreme Court has interpreted the Constitution to support nation-centered and representational federalism.

American federalism today is characterized by a sharing of resources and program administration known as cooperative federalism. Cooperative federalism is implemented through a system of federal grants consisting of categorical and block grants, and, until recently, revenue sharing. Categorical grants continue to be the most popular form of federal grants.

The nature of American federalism provides some support for all three models of governing America. Those who believe that local government is most democratic favor a decentralized federalism. Pluralists recognize the many points of access and influence that exist in a federal system. Those who believe that a power elite governs America point to the failure of the decentralizing proposals of both the Nixon and Reagan administrations.

FOR FURTHER READING

Donald Axelrod, *A Budget Quartet: Critical Policy and Management Issues* (New York: St. Martin's Press, 1989). A good discussion of how federal grants structure intergovernmental budgeting.

Herman Bakvis and William Chandler, *Federalism and the Role of the State* (Toronto: University of Toronto Press, 1987). A collection of essays about how federalism works in a number of political systems.

John E. Chubb, "Federalism and the Bias for Centralization," in *The New Direction in American Politics,* ed. John E. Chubb and Paul E. Peterson (Washington, D.C.: Brookings Institution, 1985). A discussion of the ways in which federal grants have created a new, centralized structure of federalism in the United States.

Timothy Conlan, *New Federalism* (Washington, D.C.: Brookings Institution, 1988). Discusses the differences between the new federalism of Nixon and Reagan and analyzes why they both failed to produce major changes in American federalism.

Daniel Elazar, *American Federalism: A View from the States* (New York: Harper & Row, 1984). A general treatment of the development and operations of federalism.

Bruce Johansen, *Forgotten Founders* (Ipswich, Mass.: Gambit Publishers, 1982). A history of the Iroquois Confederacy and the influence it had on the structure of government created in the Constitution.

Richard Leach, *American Federalism* (New York: Norton, 1970). Discusses competing theories of federalism and how they relate to the American experience.

Paul Peterson, Barry Rabe, and Kenneth Wong, *When Federalism Works* (Washington, D.C.: Brookings Institution, 1986). A study of policy implementation in the federal grant system.

KEY TERMS

Federal system
Unitary system
State-centered
  federalism
Nation-centered
  federalism
Interposition
Representational
  federalism

Elastic clause
Supremacy clause
Dual federalism
Cooperative federalism
Categorical grants
Block grants
Revenue sharing
New Federalism

Civil Liberties

Chapter 6

The civil liberties guaranteed Americans in the Constitution and Bill of Rights are among our most cherished possessions. But over time we have seen that these protections are not absolutes. What if an individual's freedom of expression deeply offends or even endangers others? What if protecting the rights of the accused puts innocent people at risk? What if protecting a person's religious preferences appears to favor one religion over another or over no religion? The rights of individuals and the good of society frequently need to be balanced, and this can be a delicate task. ■

On a dark night in February 1988, three Boston drug detectives were about to raid an apartment believed to be the base of a drug-dealing operation. Suddenly, a shotgun blast through the closed door killed one of the detectives, a 36-year-old father of two. After a year of court battles over witnesses and informants, a judge dismissed the charges against a suspect arrested shortly after the shooting. The judge reached that conclusion after one of the detectives admitted that he had lied about buying cocaine at the apartment while undercover and had invented a nonexistent informant in order to get a search warrant for the raid.

Boston Mayor Ray Flynn responded to the judge's decision by denouncing lawyers who use "technicalities" to get clients off. A friend of the slain police officer complained that a suspected drug dealer and murderer was "slipping through the cracks because of a technicality."[1] A case like this raises many important points about civil liberties in the United States.

First, the conflicts between the two strands of general-welfare liberalism discussed in Chapter 3 were clearly evident in how people reacted to dismissal of the charges. The president of the Boston police patrolmen's union drew on one strand of general-welfare liberalism, the government's obligation to promote the general welfare of the community: "It's so important for the people to stand behind the police who are fighting this drug war on the streets."[2] The individual

freedom and right to privacy represented in the second strand are reflected in the response of the president of the Boston Bar Association to Mayor Flynn's statement about technicalities. Lawyers, he said, are "as interested in winning the war on drugs as the mayor is. But we want to do it with our constitutional rights intact."[3]

Second, the specific rules for obtaining a search warrant—the "technicalities" to critics—are derived from that part of the Fourth Amendment to the Constitution which says: "No warrants shall issue, but upon probable cause, supported by oath or affirmation, and particularly describing the place to be searched, and the persons or things to be seized." English and American law recognized a general right to privacy even before the Bill of Rights, and there were restrictions on government searches and seizures in eight state constitutions predating the U.S. Constitution.[4]

Third, civil liberties in the United States and the liberalism component of this country's public philosophy emphasize procedural rights. The Fourth Amendment protects against unreasonable searches and seizures by establishing procedures for obtaining a search warrant. The number of search warrants issued to the Boston police department's drug control unit had more than doubled between 1985 and 1987. This fact led some to speculate that many other search warrants had been issued on the basis of false information and that the procedural violations in the 1988 case would not have emerged if it had been a routine drug bust rather than a police slaying.[5]

Fourth, in thinking of civil liberties it is easy to conjure up images of Patrick Henry's ringing declaration, "Give me liberty or give me death" or British soldiers ransacking the homes of American colonists. We do not think of liberties as applying to drug dealers who shoot police officers through closed doors. That is why it is important to remember a point made by Supreme Court Justice Felix Frankfurter in another search warrant case: "It is a fair summary of history to say that safeguards of liberty have been forged in controversies involving not very nice people."[6]

What are the civil liberties enjoyed by all Americans—good or bad—and where do they come from? How do they affect governing America?

THE NATURE OF CIVIL LIBERTIES

Civil liberties protect people, opinions, and property from *arbitrary* government interference. **Civil rights**, which we discuss in Chapter 7, protect individuals and groups from arbitrary treatment by the government *and by private individuals* in the society by calling on the government to make policies that provide that protection. The two terms are sometimes used interchangeably, but the distinction between them is important to a number of points about governing America. Civil liberties protect individual freedom by saying what government *cannot* do. In contrast, civil rights require government action to provide equal protection in politics and in the broader society. Civil liberties reflect the limited government of classical liberalism, whereas civil rights are more closely connected with the collective good of the community—the general-welfare component of general-welfare liberalism.

Civil liberties limit government interference, but they do not rule it out completely, as the term *arbitrary* in our definition suggests. A right

to privacy does not mean that government officials can do nothing about a crime if it is committed in the privacy of one's home. The Fourth Amendment protects people against "unreasonable" searches and seizures, not *all* searches and seizures.

The fundamental civil liberties of the Constitution and the Bill of Rights include the right to be freed from jail unless charged with a crime (habeas corpus), religious freedoms, free speech, protection from unreasonable searches and seizures, the right to a jury trial, protection against self-incrimination, restrictions on bail, the prohibition of cruel and unusual punishment, and guarantees of "due process of law." In addition, the U.S. Supreme Court has said that the Constitution protects other civil liberties, such as a broad right to privacy and the right to travel, even though it does not specifically identify those rights.

The original Constitution protected various civil liberties, but it is certain amendments to the Constitution that deserve most of our attention in discussing civil rights and liberties. This chapter will focus on the first ten amendments—the Bill of Rights—all of which are concerned with individual freedom, and the Fourteenth Amendment, which was used to apply these freedoms to the states.

Checkpoint

- Civil liberties protect people, opinions, and property from arbitrary government interference. They say what government *cannot* do.

- The fundamental civil liberties are found in the original Constitution and in the first ten amendments, the Bill of Rights. They give us our basic freedoms and the rights guaranteed to those accused of a crime.

THE BILL OF RIGHTS AND THE FOURTEENTH AMENDMENT

The Bill of Rights

The first ten amendments, known collectively as the Bill of Rights, were proposed by the First Congress and ratified in 1791. The first eight amendments enumerate 27 different civil liberties in the form of restrictions on the national government (see Table 6.1). The Ninth Amend-ment says that there are additional implied rights of the people, which cannot be denied on the grounds that they are not listed in the first eight amendments. The Tenth Amendment states that those powers not delegated to the national government by the Constitution are powers that belong to the state governments or to the people.

Seven of the 11 state conventions that ratified the Constitution in 1787 and 1788 also suggested amendments to that document. When the First Congress began work in 1789, it had more than

---

Table 6.1

Specific Guarantees of the Bill of Rights

1. No law respecting an establishment of religion.
2. No law prohibiting the free exercise of religion.
3. Freedom of speech.
4. Freedom of the press.
5. Right of peaceable assembly.
6. Right to petition government.
7. Right to bear arms.
8. No peacetime quartering of soldiers without owner's consent.
9. No wartime quartering of soldiers except as prescribed by law.
10. Protection from unreasonable searches and seizures.
11. Specific requirements and standards for warrants.
12. Grand jury indictment for capital or infamous crime.
13. No double jeopardy.
14. No compulsion to testify against oneself.
15. No deprivation of life, liberty, or property without due process.
16. No taking of private property without just compensation.
17. Right to speedy and public trial.
18. Right to trial by impartial and local jury.
19. Right to be informed about nature and cause of accusation.
20. Right to confront opposing witnesses.
21. Right to subpoena favorable witnesses.
22. Right to have assistance of defense counsel.
23. Right of jury trial in civil suits.
24. No retrial of civil jury trial except by common law rules.
25. No excessive bail.
26. No excessive fines.
27. No cruel and unusual punishments.

The free exercise of religion is one of 27 specific civil liberties guaranteed by the Bill of
Rights, something that anyone who has been to an airport lately knows firsthand.

200 to consider. Many of these amendments had been offered by opponents of the Constitution—the Anti-Federalists—but it was James Madison, then serving as a Federalist congressman from Virginia, who played the key role in getting legislative action on the proposals. In the end, Congress proposed 12 amendments, 10 of which were ratified by the states in 1791 to become the Bill of Rights.

Once ratified, the first ten amendments were little used. For example, more than 120 years elapsed between ratification of the First Amendment and its first significant test in the Supreme Court.[7] Few cases called for Supreme Court interpretation or enforcement of the Bill of Rights during this period. After the first ten amendments were ratified, the Bill of Rights "turned into a kind of Rip Van Winkle, asleep for more than a century."[8]

A Supreme Court decision in 1833 was a notable exception to this general pattern, and it pertained to property rights, perhaps the most jealously guarded of our civil liberties in the first 150 years of our history as a nation. In this case, Baltimore merchant John Barron claimed that sand and gravel deposits from the city's street-paving program had made it impossible to use his wharf, violating the Fifth Amendment proscription against taking private property for public use without just compensation. Barron was awarded $4500 in compensation by a trial court, but the Supreme Court eventually dismissed Barron's constitutional claim. In *Barron* v. *Baltimore*,[9] the Court said that the Bill of Rights restricted only the *national* government, not states and cities. Chief Justice John Marshall supported the Court's unanimous conclusion by referring to the political history and debate over a bill of rights at the time the Constitution was ratified, the existence of state constitutions that limited the powers of state government, and the language of the Constitution itself.

To understand the importance of *Barron* v. *Baltimore*, look again at the specific guarantees in Table 6.1. Most of the activities on that list, fall under the purview of state and local governments. The individual citizen's contact with government in these areas is more likely to be with state and local officials than with those of the national government.

Today, about half of all cases decided by the Supreme Court are civil liberties or civil rights cases in three areas: the procedural guarantees to those accused of a crime, other civil liberties such as freedom of expression and religion, and civil rights cases involving the claims of disadvantaged groups for equal treatment. Furthermore, the Supreme Court has declared unconstitutional almost ten times as many state laws and local ordinances as it has national laws.[10] Most of the liberties guaranteed in the Bill of Rights now also restrict state and local governments. This change in the meaning of the Bill of Rights is the result of a series of changes in the pattern of governing, and the primary instrument of those changes has been the Fourteenth Amendment.

The Fourteenth Amendment: A "Second Bill of Rights"

A look at Section One of the Fourteenth Amendment will show why that amendment has been called "a second Bill of Rights":[11]

> No state shall make or enforce any law which shall abridge the privileges or immunities of citizens of the United States; nor shall any state deprive any person of life, liberty, or property, without due process of law; nor deny to any person within its jurisdiction the equal protection of the laws.

The primary purpose of the amendment, adopted in 1868, was to secure the civil rights of newly freed blacks. There has been a heated debate among Supreme Court justices and historians about other intentions of those who framed the amendment in the Thirty-ninth Congress, particularly whether the due process clause of the Fourteenth Amendment was intended to apply the Bill of Rights to the states. Does the Fourteenth Amendment incorporate the restrictions on the national government in the earlier amendments and extend those restrictions to the states?

The first Supreme Court case that could answer that question came five years after ratification of the Fourteenth Amendment, in the *Slaughterhouse Cases* of 1873.[12] The case had

nothing to do with the civil rights of blacks, nor did it involve free speech or any of the other issues likely to come to mind today when we think of civil liberties. Instead, it had to do with the claim of New Orleans butchers that a Louisiana law granting a 25-year monopoly to one company violated the key guarantees of the Fourteenth Amendment: privileges and immunities of citizens of the United States, due process of law, and equal protection of the laws.

In a decision based mostly on a very narrow reading of the "privileges and immunities" clause, the Supreme Court rejected the butchers' claims. The Court said that the clause protected certain political rights, such as peacefully assembling and petitioning the federal government, but that fundamental economic and property rights (those being claimed by the butchers) were guarantees of state—not national—citizenship and thus not included among the privileges and immunities protected by the Fourteenth Amendment.

The best explanation of the Court's close (5–4) decision in the *Slaughterhouse Cases* is that a Court majority was unwilling to upset widely accepted patterns of governing and federalism by ruling that the Bill of Rights restricted state governments or by bringing economic rights under constitutional protection.[13] However, by the end of the nineteenth century the Court had interpreted the due process and equal protection clauses of the Fourteenth Amendment as limits on state regulatory power, and those decisions consistently reflected the laissez faire philosophy and concept of dual federalism discussed in Chapters 3 and 5. An amendment intended primarily to secure civil liberties and civil rights for blacks had come to have a meaning that mostly benefited white businessmen.

Selective Incorporation of Civil Liberties

In 1925, the Supreme Court finally addressed the question of whether the Fourteenth Amendment extended the restrictions on the national government found in the Bill of Rights to state governments as well. The Court, in *Gitlow* v. *New York*, said that freedoms of speech and of the press "are among the fundamental personal rights and 'liberties' protected by the due process clause of the Fourteenth Amendment from impairment by the States."[14] Since then, the Supreme Court has followed a process of selecting which guarantees of the Bill of Rights are incorporated into the due process clause of the Fourteenth Amendment as restrictions on state governments as well as the national government. This process, which has taken place in a series of cases over a period of time, is known as **selective incorporation**.

The end result has been close to total incorporation of Bill of Rights guarantees. The Supreme Court has ruled that 20 of the 27 specific guarantees listed in Table 6.1 apply to state governments as well as the national government. Specific Bill of Rights guarantees that have *not* been incorporated are the right to bear arms, the proscription against peacetime and wartime quartering of soldiers, the requirement of a grand jury indictment for capital or infamous crimes, the right to a jury trial in civil suits, and

The right to bear arms is one of the few civil liberties of the Bill of Rights that has not been extended to restrict state governments as well as the national government through the process of selective incorporation.

the protections against excessive bail or fines. They have been left out primarily because there has been no case where they might apply or because they have not been considered essential to due process.[15]

Supreme Court Justice Hugo Black tried to argue that the due process clause of the Fourteenth Amendment incorporated *all* of the specific guarantees of the Bill of Rights and that the Supreme Court should support a position of total incorporation in a single case and be done with it. But the constitutional principle of federalism supports the autonomy of state policymaking in certain areas, and an across-the-board application of the Bill of Rights' restrictions to state governments might seem to violate that principle. In addition, an incremental application of the Bill of Rights to the states over several decades fits with a pattern of Supreme Court decision making that calls for decisions to be accepted gradually by the public and by other institutions of government.

One result of selective incorporation is that some rights have achieved more importance than others. In judging the constitutionality of state laws, the Supreme Court in this century has been more severe in cases infringing on political rights than on those restricting economic rights. As Justice Benjamin Cardozo has noted, some civil liberties were "implicit in the concept of ordered liberty."[16] He singled out freedom of speech as the first among all civil liberties. Thus, in reviewing state laws the Court has applied a "double standard." Some rights are **fundamental rights** and must prevail over state interests unless these interests are compelling. Other rights are less important and would be subordinate to state laws that had a merely "reasonable" or "rational" (as opposed to compelling) basis.

The Bill of Rights and the "Second Bill of Rights" of the Fourteenth Amendment establish most of the fundamental civil liberties affecting the governing of America. Certainly none seem more fundamental than freedom of expression and religion and the procedural rights of the accused. Yet, as we will see in the next two sections, even these basic civil liberties are controversial and cannot be thought of as absolutes.

Checkpoint

- The first ten amendments to the Constitution, collectively known as the Bill of Rights, were proposed by the First Congress and added to the Constitution in 1791. For the first 100 years or so the Bill of Rights was used infrequently in court cases.

- The Fourteenth Amendment (1868) has been called a "Second Bill of Rights" because its due process clause has extended most of the restrictions on the national government in the Bill of Rights to state and local governments as well. These civil liberties have been selectively incorporated into the Fourteenth Amendment over the years until today there is almost total incorporation.

FREEDOM OF EXPRESSION AND RELIGION

Freedom of Expression

Everyone recognizes the central importance of the freedom of expression, but not everyone agrees on the meaning of that freedom. A review of Supreme Court decisions in this area led one constitutional expert to conclude: "The Court has committed itself less firmly to the First Amendment than to nearly any other of the individual rights specifically guaranteed by the Constitution," and another to describe the product of those decisions as "an extensive and at times bewildering array of phrases, slogans and standards."[17]

Consider the following standards advanced by Supreme Court justices in a number of First Amendment cases in this century: Laws that limited speech were said not to violate the First Amendment if the speech posed a "clear and present danger" or a "clear and probable danger," represented a "bad tendency," or was an "incitement" to violently overthrowing the government.[18] Supreme Court justices have also used a "balancing" test that weighs the interests of the individual and society and have considered the "time, place, and manner" of the speech or expression.[19] The Court has struck down laws limiting speech because of "vagueness," because of their "chilling effect," because there were "less drastic means for achieving the same purpose," and because the government had attempted, through "prior restraint," to prevent the publication of information that is considered damaging.[20]

No single rule governing freedom of expression has emerged from Supreme Court decisions in this area. That is at least partly due to the wide range of activities and considerations associated with the freedom of expression. Is "political" expression more protected than other forms, and if so, how is it defined? Is an audience's right to hear as firmly grounded in the First Amendment as the rights of a speaker? Are all types of "symbolic" expression (armbands, hairstyle, dress mode) protected? Does it matter whether a speech or demonstration takes place on the steps of city hall, on the campus of a private college, or in front of someone's home? When a newspaper runs a story calling someone a liar, does it make a difference whether that person holds public office or is a private citizen? Does the freedom of expression include an individual's right to give a candidate for office unlimited campaign contributions? Does it include the right to burn the flag? (See A Closer Look, pp. 172–173). When a town seeks to close down a pornographic bookstore or movie theater is it violating the owner's First Amendment rights? When the government withdraws a grant from an artist whose creations are considered offensive, is the artist's freedom of expression being denied? Is an attempt by the government to prevent a newspaper from publishing a story (prior restraint) more clearly a violation of the First Amendment than its seeking punishment after the story has been published?

A Closer Look

Flag Burning and the Constitution ★ ★ ★

On June 21, 1989, the Supreme Court overturned the conviction of Gregory Lee Johnson for burning an American flag in front of the Dallas City Hall as a protest against the 1984 Republican National Convention in that city. Johnson was convicted of violating a Texas law against desecrating the flag and sentenced to one year in prison and a $2000 fine. In overturning his conviction, the Court said that the Texas statute violated the First Amendment because, in making it a crime to "knowingly cast contempt" upon a flag by burning or otherwise defacing it, the statute was prohibiting the expression of the idea behind the act of flag burning and not simply the act itself. The Court ruling also had the effect of voiding similar laws of 47 other states and the national government, which made flag burning a crime *because* of the ideas it expressed.

In the majority opinion for a closely divided Court, Justice William Brennan said that flag burning is a symbolic form of speech and that "a bedrock principle underlying the First Amendment" is the rule "that the Government may not prohibit the expression of an idea simply because society finds the idea itself offensive or disagreeable."

The Court majority also said that attempts to accord special status to the flag or other symbol by saying that it can only be used to express one point of view, such as patriotism, restricted the freedom of expression guarantees of the First Amendment. "Could the Government, on this theory, prohibit the burning of state flags?" Brennan asked, "Of copies of the Presidential seal? Of the Constitution?" If the Supreme Court had to make judgments about those symbols, he continued, "How would we decide which symbols were sufficiently special to warrant this unique status? To do so, we would be forced to consult our own political preferences, and impose them on the citizenry, in the very way that the First Amendment forbids us to do."[a]

The Court's decision provoked a strong reaction across America. In Washington, President Bush denounced the decision and called for a constitutional amendment to outlaw flag burning. Within a week of the Court's ruling more than 200 members of Congress had sponsored resolutions calling for such an amendment. Ordinary citizens debated the topic in schools and bars and stated their positions with bumper stickers and letters to local newspapers. Here are some of the things they were saying:[b]

If people feel the need to burn our flag to express their pathetic points, I say they should be asked, no, *made* to leave our country and get a taste of what it is like to live in another country.

If people cannot communicate their feelings more clearly or effectively than by burning a flag, ignore them. The lack of attention will trouble them, whereas the latest reaction only fuels their anger. They will never destroy what the flag represents.

How far will we go? To what extent will this so-called freedom of expression be tolerated? Will Congress allow us to add another crack to the Liberty Bell? Do we have the right to scribble graffiti on the Washington monument? Are we free to scratch our thoughts on the Vietnam War Memorial?

Our veterans fought and many died for the flag. No, not for the flag, but for the freedom it represents. Think about it. They sacrificed to preserve a country so free, you can burn its national emblem. That's why the Supreme Court, instead of insulting our veterans, vindicated them.

As it turned out, in October 1989 Congress passed a law that made it a federal crime to "knowingly mutilate, deface, physically defile, burn, maintain on the floor or ground, or trample upon" any U.S. flag. (This statute omitted the phrase "cast contempt on.") A week later, the Senate defeated a proposed constitutional amendment that declared: "The Congress and the States shall have power to prohibit the physical desecration of the flag of the United States."[c]

But in June 1990 the Supreme Court ruled the Federal Flag Protection Act of 1989 unconstitutional because it suffered from the same fundamental flaw as the Texas law overturned earlier.

How do you feel about this issue?

If you were a member of the Congress or a state legislator, would you support a constitutional amendment to outlaw desecration of the flag, or would you favor accepting such actions as protected symbolic speech?

[a]*Texas* v. *Johnson*, U.S.; 109 S.Ct. 2533 (1989).
[b]Letters to the Editor, Wilmington, Delaware *News Journal*, July 30, 1989, pQ3.
[c]Joan Biskupic, "Flag Measure Will Become Law Without Bush's Signature," *Congressional Quarterly Weekly Report*, October 14, 1989, p. 2720; and Robin Toner, "Senate Rejects Amendment Outlawing Flag Desecration," *New York Times*, October 20, 1989, p. 16.

In 1964, the Supreme Court said that the central meaning of the First Amendment was to protect political speech even if it included false statements, as did the 1960 newspaper advertisement that triggered the landmark Supreme Court decision in New York Times v. Sullivan *(1964).*

The "bewildering array" of standards in this area, then, is a reflection of the many different questions that arise when the First Amendment is applied to governing. Over the years, a number of Supreme Court justices have attempted to cut through the many distracting questions that come up in First Amendment cases in order to identify the basic values underlying the freedom of expression.

Justice Oliver Wendell Holmes wrote in 1919 that preventing any prior restraint of speech by the government may have been "the main purpose" of the First Amendment.[21] In 1951, Chief Justice Fred Vinson said that "the basis of the First Amendment is the hypothesis that speech can rebut speech, propaganda will answer propaganda, free debate of ideas will result in the wisest government policies."[22] In 1964, Justice William Brennan said that the great controversy over the Sedition Act of 1798, which prohibited criticism of the government, had "crystallized a national awareness of the central meaning of the First Amendment."[23] The court opinion in a major case on campaign finance law in 1976 described political expression as lying "at the core of our electoral process and of First Amendment freedoms."[24] In a 1985 Supreme Court decision on the same topic, Justice William Rehnquist wrote: "There can be no doubt that the expenditures at issue in this case produce speech at the core of the First Amendment."[25]

A common theme running through the above remarks by Supreme Court justices is that the First Amendment most clearly guarantees freedom of expression when that expression is a form of political participation. This can be seen in the 1964 case of *New York Times* v. *Sullivan*, which broadened the First Amendment protection of those accused of libel by a public official. The case arose from a 1960 *New York Times* advertisement placed by Alabama civil rights leaders. The full-page ad described several incidents of police misconduct against civil rights activists in Montgomery, Alabama. L. B. Sullivan, the city's commissioner of public affairs who was responsible for the police at the time, sued the sponsors of the ad and the newspaper, claiming that there were a number of factual errors in the advertisement and that even though he was not named in the advertisement, he had been defamed by it.

An Alabama jury agreed and awarded Sullivan $500,000 in damages under a libel law similar to that in most states, which requires a defendant to prove that all of the published facts are true in such a case. In reversing the state court decision, the Supreme Court said that the First Amendment protects criticism of official conduct, even when it contains errors of fact, and that a rule requiring the critics to prove all statements to be true amounted to self-censorship. The Court then established a new standard that requires a public official to prove that a defamatory statement was made with "actual malice," with knowledge that it was false, or with reckless disregard of whether it was false or not.

There are two important strands to the majority opinion in *New York Times* v. *Sullivan*: (1) the idea that the central meaning of the First Amendment was to protect political speech and (2) the "actual malice" standard for libel suits. But these two standards have been subject to varying interpretations.

Some constitutional experts interpreted the first strand as expansive because it supported the idea that criticism of public officials and public policy constitutes political or public speech, a form of expression given absolute protection by the First Amendment command: "Congress shall make no law abridging the freedom of speech."[26]

But others used the political speech distinction to support a limiting view of the First Amendment. In 1971, for example, federal judge Robert H. Bork said: "Constitutional protection should be accorded *only* to speech that is explicitly political. There is no basis for judicial intervention to protect any other form of expression, be it scientific, literary, or that variety of expression we call obscene or pornographic."[27] (Judge Bork backed away from that position during the Senate hearings on his nomination to be a Supreme Court justice in September 1987.)

The second strand of the *New York Times* decision—requiring proof of actual malice in a defamatory statement—has also been interpreted in different ways. One scholar felt that the decision had "extended the line of protection past the constitutional minimum all the way to facts, even false facts, to encourage the debate that we deem valuable."[28] Another scholar concluded that use of the actual-malice standard during the past 25 years had simply brought the Supreme Court and other courts into the business of regulating the press and had done little to reduce the number of libel suits. He suggested that the Supreme Court

> . . go back to *New York Times* v. *Sullivan*, reread Brennan's stirring language about a commitment to "Uninhibited, robust and wide-open debate," and then declare simply that the First Amendment protects that debate without qualification. They should jettison the actual-malice test and let Americans debate freely and openly.[29]

New York Times v. *Sullivan* was one of the most important First Amendment decisions ever handed down by the Supreme Court. It sought to determine and apply "the central meaning of the First Amendment." Yet the development of First Amendment law since 1964 and subsequent Supreme Court decisions support the general conclusion about freedom of expression made at the beginning of this section: It is difficult, if not impossible, to come up with a single standard that can be applied in all cases and will protect the wide variety of speech and behavior that come under the overall heading of freedom of expression.

Freedom of Religion

The Supreme Court concluded its 1985 term with a series of major decisions on religion. The Court overturned an Alabama statute permitting a moment of silent prayer or meditation at the beginning of the school day, struck down a Connecticut law giving workers an unqualified right not to work on the Sabbath, and declared unconstitutional programs in Michigan and New York that sent public school teachers to parochial schools for remedial or enrichment instruction. The Reagan administration had filed briefs on what turned out to be the losing side in all of those cases. Shortly after the decisions were handed down, U.S. Attorney General Edwin Meese told an American Bar Association convention that the Court's decisions in those cases, reflecting a "strict neutrality" interpretation of the First Amendment, would have struck the Founding Fathers as "bizarre." The purpose of those who wrote that amendment, said Meese, was "to prohibit religious tyranny, not to undermine religion generally." He urged the justices to "resurrect the original meaning of constitutional provisions" instead of reading their own values and policy preferences into the Constitution.[30]

Religious freedom is protected by both an **establishment clause** and a **free exercise clause** in the First Amendment: "Congress shall make no law respecting an establishment of religion, or prohibiting the free exercise thereof." The two clauses at times appear to be in conflict. An example often used to illustrate this is the case of the Amish and compulsory education. If a state exempts Amish children from compulsory education laws so as not to interfere with the free exercise clause, it might be charged with officially favoring one religion over another and thus violating the establishment clause. To say that the free exercise clause prevents government from penalizing any religious practice and the establishment clause from officially assisting any religion does not eliminate the tension between the two clauses.

The idea of "strict neutrality," the target of Attorney General Meese's criticism of the Court above, represents one solution to the inherent conflict between the two clauses. According to this interpretation, government must be neutral, both among religions and between religion and nonreligion. In the words of Thomas Jefferson, expressed in a letter to Connecticut Baptists in 1801 and often cited by the Supreme Court, the First Amendment was intended to erect "a wall of separation between church and state."[31]

Since 1971, the Supreme Court has applied three standards or criteria for maintaining this wall of separation and determining neutrality under the establishment clause:[32] (1) Does the law serve a secular legislative purpose? The Court concluded, for example, that the Alabama law had no purpose other than to return voluntary prayer to the schools, while there was an educational purpose to the Michigan and New York programs of public school teachers in parochial schools. The Court, in the latter cases, thus turned to the second criterion, which is: (2) Is the principal or primary effect of the statute one that either advances or inhibits religion? In reviewing the Michigan program, the Supreme Court discussed its effects of indoctrinating students, symbolically uniting church and state, and indirectly subsidizing religious education. For those reasons, the Court concluded that the programs "have the primary or principal effect of advancing religion and therefore violate the dictates of the Establishment Clause of the First Amendment."[33] The third standard used by the Court is: (3) Does the law foster excessive government entanglement with religion? The parochial school programs were said to violate this standard because they required the ongoing presence of state employees who monitored classrooms.

This third standard was used to overturn a Massachusetts law that gave churches the option of denying a liquor license to any establishment within 500 feet of the church. In his majority opinion, Chief Justice Warren Burger said: "The core rationale underlying the Establishment Clause is preventing a fusion of governmental and religious functions."[34] Fusing those two functions in one body would substitute the unilateral power of a church for the deliberation of an elected legislative body.

The principle of neutrality and the three standards used to uphold that principle suggest a clarity and consensus about religious freedom

If a state exempts Amish children from compulsory education laws, is it violating the establishment clause of the First Amendment by favoring one religion over another? But if a state requires that Amish children attend public school rather than a church school such as this one, against their religious beliefs, is it violating the free exercise clause of that same amendment?

that are lacking in the area of freedom of expression. But there is no agreement on all issues of religious freedom. In fact, while Chief Justice Burger wrote the Court opinion in the Connecticut case having to do with working on the Sabbath, he dissented in full from the Court majority in the Alabama prayer and New York parochial school cases and in part from the Michigan case majority. The standards of "secular purpose," "principal or primary effect" and "excessive government entanglement" have different meanings to different people.

Moreover, the inherent conflict between the establishment and free exercise clauses of the First Amendment will continue to generate disputes and Supreme Court cases far into the future. As Glenn Abernathy points out, what is neutrality to some is government interference and hostility to others:

> To some, government is neutral toward religion if it does not support or even permit religious exercises in public schools during the school day. It is neither promoting sectarian religion nor is it prohibiting the child from engaging in religious observance, so long as it takes place outside the ambit of public school activities.
>
> To others, the denial of permission to use a portion of the school day for religious exercise is to *interfere* with religious freedom and therefore is outright governmental hostility.[35]

Checkpoint

- Everyone agrees that freedom of expression is one of the most important civil liberties guaranteed by the Constitution, but there has not been similar agreement on a standard for maintaining that freedom. One problem is that there are so many forms of expression. Most scholars, however, regard the protection of political speech as a basic value of the First Amendment.

- Freedom of religion is another fundamental civil liberty in the United States. Although the Supreme Court has reached agreement on standards of neutrality in cases involving the establishment of religion, the inherent conflict between the establishment and free exercise guarantees of the First Amendment continues to generate disputes in this area.

RIGHTS OF THE ACCUSED

The Bill of Rights establishes the **rights of the accused**—chief civil liberties guaranteed to those accused of a crime—in four amendments:

- *Fourth Amendment*—Protects people, their houses, papers, and effects against unreasonable searches and seizures and requires that search warrants be based on probable cause that a crime has been committed or is being committed, that warrants be supported by oath or affirmation, and that the warrant describe the place to be searched and the persons or things to be seized.

- *Fifth Amendment*—Requires grand jury indictment for major crimes, protects a person from being tried twice for the same offense (double jeopardy), says that a person cannot be forced to be a witness against himself or herself (self-incrimination), and protects a person's being deprived of life, liberty, or property without due process of law.

- *Sixth Amendment*—Guarantees the accused a speedy and public trial by an impartial jury and says that those accused of a crime have a right to be informed of the charges against them, to be confronted with the witnesses against them, to call witnesses in their favor, and to have an attorney.

- *Eighth Amendment*—Outlaws excessive bail or fines and cruel and unusual punishment.

Knowing what these rights are and where they come from raises as many questions as it answers. What is an "unreasonable search"? What type of information is needed to establish "probable cause" that a crime was committed? What procedures are required in "due process of law"? How soon after arrest must a person be tried for it to be a "speedy" trial? How can you tell if a jury is "impartial"? At what point does bail or a fine become "excessive"? If the Bill of Rights is going to make a difference in the treatment of those accused of a crime, these terms have to be translated into clear standards and procedures. That difficult and never-ending task falls to the Supreme Court, just as it does with

the freedom of expression and religion. We can get a sense of how important and how difficult it is to translate civil liberties into rules of procedure by looking at two areas: the search and seizure requirements of the Fourth Amendment and the protection against self-incrimination of the Fifth Amendment.

The Fourth Amendment and the Exclusionary Rule

As we have seen, the Fourth Amendment requires certain procedures to obtain a search warrant. Police officers or other government officials must submit a statement to a court officer (either a judge or a magistrate) and swear under oath that the information in the statement is true. A court officer cannot issue a warrant unless there is probable cause to believe a crime has been or is being committed. The search warrant must describe the place to be searched and the persons or things to be seized.

The Boston detective who obtained the search warrant for the drug raid discussed at the beginning of the chapter swore that a police informant named John had been inside a third-floor apartment in the building where the raid took place and had seen a man named Stevie selling cocaine. Stevie was described as a Hispanic man about 5 feet 6 inches tall. A few minutes after the detective was shot through the door of the third-floor apartment, the police went to a first-floor apartment (there was a connecting back stairway) and arrested a black man from Jamaica named Albert Lewin. Lewin is over 6 feet tall. There were no witnesses to the shooting. The police also arrested six others at the same time but dropped charges against all six in exchange for their testimony against Albert Lewin.

Lewin's defense attorney questioned the discrepancy in the warrant's description of Stevie and his client and asked that the police informant be made available for questioning. A year went by without the police producing an informant, and it was only after a judge had dismissed the charges against Lewin for lack of evidence that one of the police officers admitted that he had lied about the informant in the application for the warrant.[36]

A police officer reads a search warrant to suspects arrested in a drug raid. The exclusionary rule requires that police officers follow certain procedures in searches, but the Supreme Court has also recognized a flexibility in applying, and exceptions to, the search warrant requirements of the Fourth Amendment.

Should criminals go free because of police mistakes? Then again, if the police can get away with lying in order to get a search warrant, what good is the Fourth Amendment? However you answer these questions, you can cite a Supreme Court justice who reached the same conclusion. One side can repeat Justice Benjamin Cardozo's famous question whether "the criminal is to go free because the constable had blundered," and join Chief Justice Warren Burger's complaint 45 years later that there had been "thousands of cases in which the criminal was set free because the constable blundered."[37] The other side can agree with Justice Oliver Wendell Holmes's conclusion that "it is a less evil that some criminals should escape than that the Government should play an ignoble part," and share Justice William Brennan's belief that some criminals go free *not* "because the constable had blundered, but rather because official compliance with Fourth Amendment requirements makes it more difficult to catch criminals."[38]

The chief means of enforcing the Fourth Amendment (since 1914 in federal courts and since 1961 in state courts) has been the **exclusionary rule**, which says that prosecutors may not use illegally seized evidence in criminal trials.[39] In other words, that evidence is excluded from use in a trial. The rule gives police officers an incentive to follow proper procedures in obtaining a search warrant by making it unlikely that they will get a conviction in a criminal trial unless they do. When a police officer makes up information and creates a fictional informant to get a search warrant, as the Boston detective did, evidence obtained on the basis of that warrant has been obtained illegally and cannot be used in court.

In 1984, the Supreme Court adopted a "good faith" exception to the exclusionary rule.[40] In a case that turned on the reliability and credibility of an informant, the Court ruled that evidence obtained through a search warrant that later turned out not to be based on probable cause could be accepted in Court as long as the police had acted with objective *good faith* in obtaining the warrant. Since the purpose of the exclusionary rule is to deter police violations of the Fourth Amendment rather than to control the judges and magistrates issuing a warrant, the Supreme Court concluded that evidence should not be excluded if the police *believed* a search to be legal.

What has been the effect of the exclusionary rule? Critics of the rule point to cases like the Boston police slaying and say the exclusionary rule turns criminals back onto the streets. It is difficult to measure with any precision how the exclusionary rule affects police behavior. But most empirical studies have found that it produces far fewer case dismissals or exclusions of evidence than is commonly believed. The exclusionary rule is most often used in cases that involve drugs or weapons. But even in those areas, the exclusionary rule has been successfully used to exclude evidence in only about 2 percent of all cases.[41]

Sometimes it is impractical or impossible for police officers to go through the warrant process and still respond to criminal activity. The Supreme Court has recognized this over the years by permitting five general exceptions to the search warrant requirements of the Fourth Amendment:

1 **Consent.** A person voluntarily and knowingly agrees to a search even though the police do not have a valid warrant.

2 **Search pursuant to a lawful arrest.** These searches are limited to preventing the arrested person from destroying evidence or obtaining a weapon.

3 **Plain view.** Evidence within plain view of a police officer may be used as long as the police officer was justified in being there in the first place.

4 **Hot pursuit.** When the police are chasing someone from the scene of a crime, they need not risk losing that person by going to get a search warrant before pursuing him or her and searching the immediate area.

5 **Automobile.** Warrantless searches of parts of an automobile and its contents are permitted un-

der certain conditions when the police were justified in stopping the automobile in the first place. Many Fourth Amendment cases before the Supreme Court today have to do with warrantless searches.[42]

The Fifth Amendment and Self-Incrimination

The case of Ernesto Miranda illustrates several of the general points about civil liberties discussed at the beginning of the chapter: the tension between individual rights and the general welfare of the community; the procedural rules, or "technicalities," that are used to implement civil liberties; and Justice Frankfurter's point that safeguards of important civil liberties have been developed in cases involving "not very nice people."

In 1963, police arrested Ernesto Miranda, a 21-year-old resident of Phoenix, Arizona, and charged him with kidnapping and raping an 18-year-old girl. Miranda was identified by the victim in a lineup and questioned by two police officers. After two hours of questioning, Miranda signed a handwritten confession, at the top of which was a typed statement that the confession was made voluntarily, without threats or promises, and "with full knowledge of my legal rights, understanding any statement I make may be used against me."[43] The written confession was introduced as evidence at a trial, and Miranda was convicted of kidnapping and rape and sentenced to 20 to 30 years in prison.

In 1966, a closely divided (5–4) Supreme Court reversed Miranda's conviction on the grounds that he had been denied the Fifth Amendment protection against self-incrimination. The Court said that confessions or other information given in response to a police interrogation of suspects in custody could be admitted only if the police informed the suspects, prior to questioning, that:

1 They have the right to remain silent.

2 Anything they say may be used against them in court.

3 They have a right to have an attorney present.

A public safety official holds up a "Miranda card" carried by police in Miami, Florida. A Supreme Court ruling enforced the Fifth Amendment by requiring that police officials fully inform suspects of their rights before questioning them.

4 An attorney will be provided free if the suspects cannot afford one.

5 The suspects may waive these rights, but only if the waiver is done voluntarily, knowingly, and intelligently.

6 All questioning must be halted if the suspects ask that it be stopped.[44]

The *Miranda* decision caused a public uproar. Many people, including dissenting justices, believed that the Court was tipping the balance between individual rights and the welfare of the community too far in favor of the individual. For that reason, it is worth noting what happened to one individual—Ernesto Miranda. Miranda's common-law wife reported that when she visited her husband in jail, he admitted kidnapping and raping the girl. This new evidence led to a second trial and Miranda was again convicted and sentenced to 20 to 30 years in prison. Miranda was

parolled in 1972, after serving nine years of his sentence. He drifted in and out of trouble for a few years and in 1976 was stabbed to death after a barroom argument over a poker game. He was 34 years old. When the police arrested a suspect in the killing, they read him his rights from a "Miranda card," the term police use for the cards listing the six warnings established by the court in 1966.[45]

Many Americans today are aware of *Miranda*'s constitutional guarantees, known as the ***Miranda* rule.** Detective novels, movies, and television shows routinely include scenes of police reading suspects their rights. Indeed, a national survey ten years after the Court's *Miranda* decision found that more than 90 percent of all 13-year-olds in this country knew about a person's right to remain silent when questioned by the police.[46] But what effect has the *Miranda* rule had on police behavior and on crime control?

The findings are similar to the results of Fourth Amendment studies discussed earlier: Requiring police to issue *Miranda* warnings has had little impact on their ability to obtain voluntary confessions and on the dismissal of cases for civil liberties violations. Nearly half of all persons suspected of a felony (a serious crime punishable by a year or more in prison) voluntarily confess to the crime, and few of the challenges to confessions on grounds that the *Miranda* rule was violated are successful.[47]

In 1984, the Supreme Court recognized a "public safety" exception to the *Miranda* rule illustrated in the case that brought the issue to the Court. A police officer chased an armed rape suspect into a supermarket, briefly lost sight of him in the store, and after apprehending the suspect found an empty shoulder holster. Before reading the suspect his rights, the officer asked him where the gun was, and the suspect pointed to some cartons. The Supreme Court permitted use of the statement and the weapon as evidence because "the need for answers to questions in a situation posing a threat to public safety" outweighed the need to protect the individual's rights by issuing the *Miranda* warning.[48]

The implementation both of the Fourth Amendment's guarantees against unreasonable search and seizures and of the Fifth Amendment's prohibition on self-incrimination illustrate an important characteristic about civil liberties: They are not absolutes. Protecting the rights of the individual is not based on ignoring or dismissing the rights of society, the social welfare dimension of general-welfare liberalism. It may seem that only individuals or only criminals benefit from these rights. These civil liberties are designed to protect individuals from arbitrary interference by the government, but they also protect the stake that everyone in society has in determining truth and achieving justice. Supreme Court Justice Frankfurter has pointed out the importance of fair procedures to meeting those goals as well:

> No better instrument has been devised for arriving at truth than to give a person in jeopardy of serious loss notice of the case against him and opportunity to meet it.
>
> Nor has a better way been found for generating the feeling, so important to a popular government, that justice has been done.[49]

Checkpoint

- The chief guarantees of those accused of a crime are provided in the Fourth, Fifth, Sixth, and Eighth Amendments.

- The exclusionary rule implements the Fourth Amendment proscription against unreasonable searches and seizures by excluding illegally obtained evidence from a trial, thereby providing an incentive for police officers to comply with the Fourth Amendment. In 1984, the Supreme Court recognized a "good faith" exception to the exclusionary rule.

- The primary method of enforcing the Fifth Amendment protection against self-incrimination has been the *Miranda* rule, established in 1966, which requires police officers to inform suspects of six specific rights before questioning them. Again in 1984, the Supreme Court recognized a "public safety" exception to the Miranda rule.

- Studies of the effects of the exclusionary rule and the *Miranda* rule indicate that they have not resulted in a high rate of dismissal of criminal charges, as critics of Supreme Court rulings in this area feared they would.

PRIVACY AND OTHER RIGHTS "RETAINED BY THE PEOPLE"

Some civil liberties are not specifically referred to in the Constitution but are nevertheless construed to belong to the people. We will take a close look at the implied right to privacy and in particular the question of whether that includes the right to an abortion.

The Abortion Issue

Few issues in American politics generate the intense feelings and sharp conflicts of the abortion issue. In the 1988 presidential election, the Democratic party candidate Michael Dukakis lost the support of many traditionally Democratic voters because they disagreed with his pro-choice (in favor of the right to an abortion) position.[50] In April 1989 more than 300,000 people took part in an abortion rights demonstration in Washington, D.C. Antiabortion activists countered by setting up a "Cemetery of the Innocents" consisting of white crosses to symbolize the 4400 abortions they said took place every day in the United States. A national public opinion poll released in the same month found 49 percent favoring keeping abortion legal; 39 percent saying it should be legal only in cases involving rape, incest, or when the mother's life is in danger; and 9 percent favoring a total ban on all abortions.[51]

The Supreme Court was the focus of much of the attention and activity over the abortion issue. In 1973 the Court ruled in *Roe* v. *Wade* that a right to an abortion was part of a fundamental right of privacy—part of the liberty guaranteed in the Fourteenth Amendment ("Nor shall any state deprive any person of life, liberty, or property without due process of law"). In the majority opinion, Justice Harry Blackmun said that the right was not unqualified and had to be weighed against important state interests in regulation. The Court recognized two state interests: protecting the health of the mother and protecting potential life.[52]

But because the right to privacy is a fundamental right, the state interest has to be compelling, not just rational or reasonable, to justify state interference with a woman's decision about abortion. The Court's task was to determine at just what point the two state interests of protecting the mother's health and the fetus's potential life become compelling. The answer that Justice Blackmun came up with was a *trimester framework*, which balanced the mother's right to privacy against state interests:

1st trimester: Right to privacy prevails over state interference since abortion is not a health threat to the mother and fetus is not viable (able to live outside the mother's womb).

2d trimester: Abortions are riskier, so state interest in protecting mother's health justifies regulations.

3rd trimester: Fetus is viable, so state interest in protecting potential life of fetus justifies regulations and even bans on abortions (unless protection of the mother's life and health necessitates an abortion).

The Texas law reviewed in *Roe* v. *Wade* made no distinctions between early-pregnancy and late-pregnancy abortions, and it permitted abortions only for the purpose of saving the mother's life. The Supreme Court applied the reasoning underlying the trimester framework to declare the Texas statute unconstitutional. Since 1973, the Court has upheld the right to an abortion recognized in *Roe*, but it has also followed up on the Court's conclusion that the right is not unqualified. Table 6.2 outlines some of the major cases in which the Court has balanced interests and qualified the right to abortion since *Roe*.

The decisions of the Court have become closer and closer since the 7–2 *Roe* v. *Wade* vote. In 1983 the vote was 6–3 in favor of abortion rights; in 1986, 5–4; and in the 1989 *Webster* decision, the vote swung narrowly the other way in upholding a state regulation of abortion (5–4). It was in this decision that Chief Justice William Rehnquist held that "the key elements of the *Roe* framework—trimester and viability—are not found in the text of the Constitution or in any place else one would expect to find a constitutional principle."[53]

Table 6.2

The Right to an Abortion: Supreme Court Decisions, 1976–1990

1976, Planned Parenthood v. *Danforth*—Husband or parent of minor cannot veto decision on abortion by wife or daughter.

1977, Maher v. *Roe*—States do not have to use public funds to support abortions that are not medically required.

1979, Bellotti v. *Baird*—States can require that minors obtain written permission from parents or a judge before having an abortion.

1980, Harris v. *McRae*—Upholds a congressional ban on using federal Medicaid funds for abortions except to save mother's life. Also says states are not required to use public funds for abortions even when medically necessary.

1983, Akron v. *Center for Reproductive Health*—States and cities cannot interfere with a woman's right to abortion by requiring that abortions after the first trimester be performed in a hospital, that there be a waiting period between signing a consent form and an abortion, and that

physicians warn patients about possible emotional disturbance and inform them that an unborn child is a human life from the moment of conception.

1986, Thornburgh v. *American College of Obstetricians*—States cannot interfere with a woman's right to abortion by requiring that a second physician be present in all nonemergency abortions, that physicians file reports on all abortions, and that physicians meet a specified degree of care for abortions in the third trimester.

1989, Webster v. *Reproductive Health Service*—States may prohibit public employees from performing or assisting in abortions not necessary to save mother's life, may ban the use of public buildings for performing abortions, and may require doctors to perform viability tests.

1990, Hodgson v. *Minnesota*—States may require minors to notify both parents, as long as there is a judicial alternative.

Sources of Right to Privacy

Look again at Table 6.1 listing the specific guarantees of the Bill of Rights. A **right of privacy** is not among the 27 specific guarantees, nor is a right of abortion. There have been no amendments since the Bill of Rights was adopted in 1791 to establish or recognize a right of privacy or abortion. Yet the Supreme Court has said not only that the Constitution protects those rights, but also that they are fundamental rights, which government can limit only when there are compelling reasons for doing so. Where do we go to find the guarantees to privacy and of abortion?

The Supreme Court provided one answer in a 1965 decision striking down a Connecticut law prohibiting the use of contraceptives. In that case, Justice William O. Douglas referred to a

"right of privacy older than the Bill of Rights," a right that was implicit in some of the specific guarantees in the Bill of Rights.[54] The First Amendment, for example, protected a freedom of association and a zone of privacy where ideas could be exchanged without government interference. Privacy was also implicit in the Third Amendment's prohibition against quartering soldiers, the Fourth Amendment's protection against unreasonable searches and seizures, the Fifth Amendment's strictures against self-incrimination, and the Ninth Amendment's reference to rights retained by the people ("the enumeration in the Constitution, of certain rights, shall not be construed to deny or disparage others retained by the people").

Not all of the justices in the Connecticut birth control case agreed with Justice Douglas on the constitutional source of a right of privacy, even though the vote was 7 to 2 in favor of recognizing such a right. Some of the justices thought the liberty guaranteed in the Fourteenth Amendment was sufficient to establish a right of privacy, which is what Justice Blackmun said in his opinion in *Roe* v. *Wade* in 1973. Much of the disagreement had to do with the meaning of the Ninth Amendment. The 1965 Connecticut case marked the first time in American history that the Court had used the Ninth Amendment, at least in part, to overturn a statute.[55]

Justice Douglas's concurring opinion in *Roe* v. *Wade* further elaborated on and defined the right of privacy. Douglas said the right to privacy consisted of (1) autonomous control over the development and expression of one's intellect, interests, tastes, and personality; (2) freedom of choice in the basic decisions of one's life respecting marriage, divorce, procreation, contraception, and the education and upbringing of children; and (3) freedom to care for one's health and person, freedom from bodily restraint or compulsion, freedom to talk, stroll, or loaf.[56]

The right of privacy, like the freedom of expression and rights of the accused, is an area of civil liberties giving rise to as many questions as answers. Is a right of privacy tied to owning property? Does it protect places, people, or relationships? Does privacy mean basically a right to be left alone, to protect an individual apart from society, or does it protect a person's autonomy—a right to determine how she or he will interact with others in society? Is privacy simply an instrumental right, a means of protecting freedom of expression rather than an end in itself? Those are questions that the Supreme Court and others in the political system will be debating and deciding long into the future.

Some constitutional scholars and Supreme Court justices have criticized the Court's decisions on abortion and privacy as decisions based on the justices' political values rather than on the Constitution. Debate over the meaning of the

In the 1987 hearings on the nomination of Robert Bork (right) to the Supreme Court, Senator Joseph Biden (left) argued for an expansive view of the Ninth Amendment, while Bork said the Ninth Amendment was not intended to add new rights to the Constitution. This debate reflected a fundamental disagreement about the source and meaning of civil liberties in the United States.

Ninth Amendment in some ways parallels the debate over the "elastic" clause, which gives Congress power to legislate what is "necessary and proper" for the carrying out of government (see Chapter 4). Did the framers of the Bill of Rights intend the Ninth Amendment to be expansive, a way of recognizing rights not specified in the Bill of Rights, such as the rights of privacy or travel? Or was it better understood as part of the compromise over a Bill of Rights needed to get states to ratify the Constitution? That is, was it simply a restatement of the principle that limited the federal government to those powers delegated to it by the Constitution?

Both the limited and expansionist views of the Ninth Amendment were evident in the 1987 Senate hearings on the nomination of Robert Bork to the Supreme Court. The differences in these two positions extend beyond the specific issues of privacy and abortion. At the heart of the debate is a fundamental disagreement about the source and meaning of civil liberties in the United States. Judge Bork believed that the Ninth Amendment was not intended to add new rights to the Constitution, a position he supported with historical evidence in his testimony. Bork's position was that the Constitution protected only those civil liberties stated in the Constitution and the Bill of Rights, and that judges were applying their own subjective values when they said the Ninth Amendment protected additional rights. In a 1984 speech cited by several witnesses at the Senate hearing, Judge Bork said that uncertainty about the meaning of the amendment might force a judge to treat it as "nothing more than a water blot on the document."[57]

Senate Judiciary Chairman Joseph Biden took the opposite view: "When we delegated rights . . . we expressly said . . . the Bill of Rights doesn't cover them all. That Ninth Amendment, to me, is, and should be, expansive." Biden expressed a belief that civil liberties were not limited to those stated in the Constitution, that "we are just born with certain rights," and that those rights have "nothing to do with whether or not the State or the Constitution acknowledges I have those rights."[58]

Checkpoint

- The right to an abortion and a broad right of privacy have been recognized by the Supreme Court as fundamental rights, even though they are not specifically included in the Bill of Rights or the unamended Constitution.

- The right to an abortion is not unqualified. In a series of Supreme Court decisions since 1973, the Supreme Court has upheld a fundamental right to an abortion, but it has also occasionally qualified that right by balancing individual rights against state interests and the general welfare.

- The right of privacy has generated a great deal of controversy and debate on its origins and meaning.

- Differences of opinion about privacy and abortion rights reflect broader differences about the role of the Constitution and the place of civil liberties in American politics today.

CIVIL LIBERTIES: WHO GOVERNS?

The dialogue between Senator Biden and Judge Bork makes it clear that the Constitution helps frame political choices but does not make them. To apply civil liberties in making those choices, it helps to consider the justifications given for those liberties in the first place. The three models of government once again provide a useful way of organizing information and applying the principles of civil liberties to American government.

Democracy

Democracy is often described as including majority rule and individual rights. But what happens if a majority in a democracy votes to deny or severely restrict the right to vote to a certain group in society? Or if that majority decides to recognize Protestantism as the "official" religion of the United States? To ban radical newspapers because they are subversive? To put people in jail if they take part in a march on the Pentagon? The democratic dilemma in these situations is that majority rule may undercut individual rights, that a democratic process may produce oppressive policies.

The relevance of conflicts between majority rule and civil liberties to governing contemporary America is seen in public opinion polls on what Americans believe about civil liberties. Table 6.3 provides a first look at this issue by briefly indicating the degree of public support for a civil liberty often regarded as the most fundamental one in a democracy: freedom of speech.

Table 6.3 shows what all similar studies have found: that there is a high degree of public support for free speech in the abstract but much less support for the right of specific disliked groups to speak freely. The Nazi party represents one such group in Table 6.3, but there is a similar lack of support for other groups considered to be outside the social or political mainstream: atheists, socialists, communists, and homosexuals. These and other findings in national surveys led the authors of this study to conclude that few people realize that how committed we are to liberty depends on our willingness to extend that liberty to dissenters and others who challenge conventional opinion, to those who "conform least to expected standards."[59]

One response to the lack of support for civil liberties among the mass public is to rely on the more tolerant and more active political elites for a defense of individual rights, a subject we discuss below. Another is to engage in line drawing—to say that majority opinion should determine most government policies but not all of them. As Supreme Court Justice Robert Jackson has noted, majority rule must sometimes be checked:

> The very purpose of a Bill of Rights was to withdraw certain subjects from the vicissi-

---

Table 6.3

Levels of Public Support for Free Speech

1. "I believe in free speech for all no matter what their views might be."

Agree:	90%
Disagree:	10%

2. "If the majority votes in a referendum to ban the public expression of certain opinions, should the majority opinion be followed?"

No, because free speech is a more fundamental right than majority rule: 49%

Yes, because no group has a greater right than the majority to decide which opinions can or cannot be expressed: 23%

Neither/undecided: 18%

3. "Should a community allow the American Nazi party to use its town hall to hold a public meeting?"

Yes:	18%
No:	66%
Neither/undecided:	16%

Source: Herbert McClosky and Alida Brill, *Dimensions of Tolerance* (New York: Russell Sage, 1983), pp. 50–53.

---

tudes of public controversy, to place them beyond the reach of majorities and officials and to establish them as legal principles to be applied by the courts.

One's right to life, liberty, and property, to free speech, a free press, freedom of worship and assembly, and other fundamental rights may not be submitted to vote; they depend on the outcome of no elections.[60]

The position articulated by Justice Jackson is one solution to the dilemma of majority rule versus individual rights. It assigns the most important policymaking responsibility for civil liberties to the courts, the political institution most removed from majority control. It also identifies certain civil liberties as "fundamental rights" beyond the reach of majorities. But once again, choices have to be made. Who decides which rights are fundamental and on what grounds?

As we have seen, the Supreme Court added a number of fundamental rights to Jackson's list. These now include rights of privacy, the vote, travel (with interstate travel recognized as more "fundamental" than foreign travel), marriage, and child rearing.[61] As more rights are added to the list of fundamental rights and thus insulated from control by a political majority, is the Supreme Court undercutting the democratic principle of majority rule? Are justices deciding cases on the basis of their own values and policy preferences rather than those of the majority? Is a political system democratic when important policy areas are considered exempt from the principle of majority rule?

A number of constitutional scholars have joined Supreme Court justices in trying to answer that question. They have sought to find a democratic principle that could justify placing certain policy areas beyond the reach of majorities. Justice Harlan Stone once argued that the courts should be less willing to accept majority decisions when they produce policies that restrict "those political processes ordinarily to be relied upon to protect minorities."[62] Constitutional scholar John Hart Ely views Stone's argument as a democratic justification for civil liberties. Democracy is threatened, says Ely, whenever a majority in power seeks to remain in power by closing off normal channels of political change or denies a place in the system of representation to a minority group. In those cases, the justification for the Supreme Court's overruling a majority is that of correcting a malfunction in the democratic process.[63]

Pluralism

A pluralist perspective makes us aware of some additional aspects of civil liberties in American politics. And as is sometimes the case, there are areas of considerable overlap between the pluralist view and those of democracy and elitism. Ely's theory, for example, justified Supreme

Court intervention when the normal political "market" is malfunctioning, when the openness and universal access we associate with pluralism are threatened by the policies of a majority. Elites also have an important civil liberties role in a pluralist system. Because the power elite's support of civil liberties is generally stronger than that of the mass public, pluralists often characterize political elites as "carriers of the creed," who effectively maintain those liberties. (But for another view, see A Closer Look on pp. 190–191.) Table 6.4 shows some of the differences in the level of support for civil liberties among political elites and the general public.

Because the differences in Table 6.4 may also be a reflection of knowledge, education, occupation, ideology, feelings about particular groups, or other social and political factors, the researchers also measured the effects of these other influences and found that the elite-mass differences persisted even when the two samples were matched. They believe that "the data, taken as a whole, provide support for the view that the elites have been more exposed to, and have a better understanding of, the libertarian tradition."[64]

Such findings support the notion that private threats to civil liberties may be greater than those posed by the governing elite, that people need protection *by* government as well as protection *from* government. The authors of *The Federalist* made this argument almost two centuries ago when they pointed out "that liberty may be endangered by the abuses of liberty as well as by the abuses of power; that there are numerous instances of the former as well as of the latter; and that the former, rather than the latter, are apparently most to be apprehended by the United States."[65]

The pluralist perspective particularly highlights two aspects of civil liberties policymaking. The first is the idea that crucial decisions about civil liberties should be made by a neutral "referee," who is outside of the normal, everyday political process. Since pluralists regard most political activity to be that of competing groups pursuing their own interests and the executive and legislature as reflective of those group interests, pluralists turn to the courts as the only in-

---

Table 6.4

Support for Civil Liberties by Mass Public and Political Elites

	Percentage Answering "B" (Supporting Civil Rights and Liberties)	
	Mass Public	Community Leaders
1. "A humor magazine which ridicules or makes fun of blacks, women, or other minority groups: (A) should lose its mailing privileges; (B) should have the same right as any other magazine to print what it wants."	57	74
2. "Should demonstrators be allowed to hold a mass protest march for some unpopular cause? (A) no, not if the majority is against it; (B) yes, even if most people in the community don't want it."	41	71
3. "Forcing people to testify against themselves in court: (A) may be necessary when they are accused of very brutal crimes; (B) is never justified, no matter how terrible the crime."	40	67
4. "The freedom of atheists to make fun of God and religion: (A) should not be allowed in a public place where religious groups gather; (B) should be legally protected no matter who might be offended."	26	53

Source: Adapted from Herbert McClosky and Alida Brill, *Dimensions of Tolerance* (New York: Russell Sage, 1983), p. 246.

stitution capable of objective civil liberties policymaking.

A pluralist perspective also helps us see the connection between the broader society and civil liberties. Tolerance and the protection of civil liberties may be a product of the structure of society as much as of government processes. Some historians attribute the religious and political diversity of early America, for example, not to an ideology of freedom or tolerance in the society as a whole, but rather to the existence of many separate, segregated religious and political communities.[66] In this century, a pluralist view of politics was associated with a shift in Supreme Court decision making in free speech cases. The standard in such cases moved from a focus on the relationship between an individual and the state to one that looked at the effects on other groups in society and the idea that free speech required a "balancing" of competing interests.[67] Pluralism provides both a standard for measuring free speech and a defense for tolerance as a way of holding together the many different and conflicting interests in the modern state.

A pluralist framework was evident in much of the activity both before and after the Supreme Court's abortion decision in 1989. The record number of briefs filed in that case by individuals and groups who were not parties in the case and the demonstrations in Washington were attempts to lobby the Supreme Court justices making the decision. After the decision was announced in July, organized groups intensified their campaigns to influence state lawmakers considering new abortion statutes and Supreme Court justices reviewing abortion cases in the Court's next term.

A Closer Look

Civil Liberties: Theory and Practice ★★★

Do you believe in free speech? Of course you do. Do you think that all people should have the equal protection of the laws? Naturally. Should people be able to criticize the government and political leaders without being fined or jailed as a result of that action? It goes without saying.

How would you feel if you heard that a radical group was planning to come to the local post office and, as a protest to U.S. involvement in Central America, to read aloud the names of undercover CIA operatives in that region? What if you decided to run for local office and after investing all of your savings and six months in the campaign, you lost a close race because the local paper published a vicious personal attack filled with false statements.

Civil liberties policies translate the principles of liberty and participation found in the Constitution into government policies. However, national surveys like those reported in Tables 6.3 and 6.4 show over and over that there is strong public support for civil rights and liberties in the abstract, but much less support for concrete applications of those principles to the real political world.

A period in the 1950s serves as a benchmark for measuring the fragile nature of tolerance in American politics: the McCarthy era.

On February 9, 1950, Joseph McCarthy, the Republican senator from Wisconsin, charged that the Department of State knowingly employed more than 200 Communists. He left the unmistakable impression that treason in the highest levels of government, more than anything else, accounted for foreign policy re-

versals and the increasing success of the Soviet Union in world affairs.

Carried by every wire service in the country, McCarthy's words created an instant furor. Prominent representatives and senators of both parties joined McCarthy in denouncing Communist infiltration of government, industry, the media, and education. They held well-publicized hearings to ferret out subversion. During these meetings people from all walks of life—civil servants, labor leaders, movie stars, authors, professors—were called upon to testify against themselves and their friends and colleagues.

As accusations and recriminations filled the air, tolerance of civil rights and liberties fell by the wayside. With no effective way to rebut the charges against them, many of the accused lost their jobs, saw their reputations slandered, and suffered the indignity of being labeled traitors or worse.[a]

Even though Senator McCarthy lent his name to an era, the term is really a misnomer because the abuse of civil rights it signifies began before he arrived on the scene and lingered long after he left. But whatever word one chooses, it is regarded as one of the darkest periods in American history, comparable to the Salem witch trials in its irrationality, fear, and lack of respect for civil rights and liberties.

Why did McCarthyism and the McCarthy era occur?

Many scholars, focusing on its supposedly mass base, have interpreted McCarthyism as a failure of the public to understand and support the basic freedoms of the Constitution. It

Senator Joseph McCarthy uses a map to illustrate his charges of Communist party infiltration throughout the United States, while special counsel Joseph Welch, with whom McCarthy bitterly clashed over the question of Communists in the army, expresses his disbelief.

represents, in other words, a breakdown of democracy caused by the insufficiently tolerant and enlightened common people.

Other historians, along with several political scientists, take a different tack. They regard McCarthyism as a product mainly of elite behavior. Parties, candidates, and interest groups, members of Congress, the president and his advisors all tried with varying success to manipulate anticommunism for their own ends. Far from being demanded by the outraged, ignorant, alienated, or intolerant common people, fear and panic over Communist subversion were essentially the creations of political leaders.[b]

To sum up, we might look at civil liberties this way: Sizable portions of the population harbor, for whatever reasons, misgivings about unpopular, exotic, or alien ideologies and causes and seem all too willing to deny their adherents the freedoms and protections lying at the heart of the Bill of Rights.

It is doubtful, however, that episodes of hysteria and intolerance such as McCarthyism represent ground swells of opinion from below, forcing public officials to act against their better judgment. On the contrary, the flow of causality goes from the top down. Elites periodically have attempted to achieve domestic and foreign policy objectives by preying on or even creating mass anxiety and anger. One can perhaps go further: Plans to limit civil liberties are almost invariably engineered in high places and then sold to the public as necessary for national security or the protection of the American way of life.[c]

[a]Studies that describe the effects of McCarthyism include Robert Griffith, *The Politics of Fear* (Lexington: University of Kentucky Press, 1970); and Thomas C. Reeves, *The Life and Times of Joe McCarthy* (New York: Stein & Day, 1982).
[b]Robert Griffith, *The Politics of Fear*, pp. 115–116.
[c]Robert Griffith and Athan Theoharis, *The Specter* (New York: New Viewpoints, 1974), p. xi. Michael Rogin agrees: "The data, in sum, do not suggest intense, active, mass involvement in a McCarthyite movement." Michael Rogin, *The Intellectuals and McCarthy* (Cambridge, Mass.: MIT Press, 1967), p. 241.

The forced relocation of Japanese-Americans on the West Coast during World War II, such as this California family awaiting evacuation in 1942, is an example of how elites can ride roughshod over civil liberties.

All of these cases have led some to conclude that the support of political elites for civil liberties is conditional. Elites are less supportive of these rights when the exercise of them is regarded as threatening to the existing system. This particular elitist position leads to a conclusion "that liberties are available to American citizens only as long as and to the extent that their practice represents no fundamental challenge to the overall system of power and privilege."[69]

We have seen that there are two quite different conclusions about the role of elites in civil liberties. The polarity of those two views can be a useful tool for evaluating some of the policies discussed in this chapter. Policies regarding freedom of expression, for example, are shaped by one set of elites seeking to restrict free speech in the face of perceived threats to the system and another set of elites upholding the principle of free speech, regardless of the threat it poses.

The Power Elite

The view of political elites as defenders of civil liberties in the face of public threats has been so widely accepted that John Brigham could write in 1984: "We do not hear much about the dangers to our liberties from those who hold the balance of economic and military power."[68] However, Brigham points to the forced relocation of Japanese-Americans on the West Coast during World War II as an example of how civilian and military elites can ride roughshod over civil liberties. The FBI's extensive campaign of harassment and disruption carried on against black civil rights leaders and antiwar activists in the 1960s and 1970s is said by some to illustrate the same pattern. Others point out that political elites tried to eliminate political opposition at the time of the Watergate scandal of the Nixon administration. The anti-Communist hysteria of the McCarthy era in the 1950s may have been more a reaction of the elite than of the mass public (see A Closer Look on pp. 190–191).

Checkpoint

- The democratic model focuses our attention on levels of tolerance in the mass public, arguments for removing some policy areas from majority control, and the need to check attempts by a ruling majority to limit minority participation in the democratic process.

- Two aspects of civil liberties highlighted by a pluralist perspective are the importance of a neutral referee for making decisions in this policy area and the link between a diverse pluralist society and the need to protect civil liberties.

- Some describe political elites as carriers of the democratic creed, while others point to the conditional nature of elite support for civil liberties in the United States.

SUMMARY

Civil liberties protect people, opinions, and property from arbitrary government interference. Civil rights protect individuals and groups from arbitrary treatment by the government and by private individuals in society.

The first ten amendments, known collectively as the Bill of Rights, include 27 specific civil liberties in the form of restrictions on the national government. Today, these civil liberties greatly affect how America is governed, but for nearly a century after their adoption they were little used. The Fourteenth Amendment has been called a second Bill of Rights because its due process clause has extended most of the restrictions on the national government in the Bill of Rights to state governments as well. The process of selectively incorporating certain civil liberties into the Fourteenth Amendment led the Supreme Court to establish a "double standard," by which some liberties are considered more important than others.

Freedom of expression is considered to be one of the most important civil liberties of the Bill of Rights, but there has been little agreement on the standards for maintaining that freedom. A Supreme Court ruling in 1964 referred to a "central meaning of the First Amendment," but even that decision has been subject to different interpretations. The Supreme Court has developed clearer standards in freedom of religion cases, but an inherent conflict between the establishment and free exercise clauses of the First Amendment complicates this area of civil liberties.

The exclusionary rule and the *Miranda* rule are the chief methods of enforcing the Fourth and Fifth Amendment guarantees against unreasonable searches and seizures and self-incrimination.

The Constitution does not explicitly include a right of privacy or an abortion right, but a series of Supreme Court decisions have recognized both as fundamental guarantees of the Constitution. The Court has found a right of privacy implicit in other civil liberties, such as freedom of association and protection against unreasonable searches, and in the Ninth Amendment. The right to an abortion grows out of the broader privacy right. Because the abortion right is not unqualified, however, the Court balances that right against state interests in protecting the health of the mother and the unborn. Most recently, the Court has upheld state interests in laws restricting abortions and appears ready to reexamine the trimester framework for balancing interests.

The democratic, pluralist, and power elite perspectives offer different ideas about who in society is most supportive of civil liberties and who represents the greatest threats to them. The democratic perspective calls attention to the threats posed by those in power limiting political participation, while pluralists see those elites as carriers of the creed and point to the lack of support for civil liberties by the general public. The power elite school is more likely to emphasize the conditional nature of the support for civil liberties by political elites.

KEY TERMS

Civil liberties	Free exercise clause
Civil rights	Rights of the accused
Selective incorporation	Exclusionary rule
Fundamental rights	*Miranda* rule
Establishment clause	Right of privacy

FOR FURTHER READING

Henry Abraham, *Freedom and the Court*, 5th ed. (New York: Oxford University Press, 1988). A readable and current review of Supreme Court interpretations of the civil liberties guaranteed by the Constitution.

Robert A. Goldwin and William A. Schambra, *How Does the Constitution Secure Rights?* (Washington, D.C.: American Enterprise Institute, 1985). A collection of provocative essays about the roots of civil liberties and political order in the United States.

Herbert McClosky and Alida Brill, *Dimensions of Tolerance: What Americans Believe About Civil Liberties* (New York: Russell Sage, 1983). A landmark study of the beliefs about and attitudes toward civil liberties among the mass public and political elites.

Michael Paul Rogin, *The Intellectuals and McCarthy: the Radical Specter* (Cambridge, Mass.: MIT Press, 1967). Rogin's book broke new ground on the basis of support for McCarthyism in the 1950s and the ongoing debate over the relative degree of support for civil liberties among the mass public and political elites.

Thomas L. Tedford, *Freedom of Speech in the United States* (New York: Random House, 1985). A good overview of the history and development of freedom of speech in the United States.

Samuel Walker, *Sense and Nonsense About Crime*, 2d ed. (Monterey, Calif.: Brooks/Cole, 1989). A book about crime in America that dispels many of the myths about the effect of civil liberties on criminal behavior.

Civil Rights

Chapter 7

We think of equality as an essential characteristic of democracy. Yet the Constitution did not fully embrace the value of equality, the central component of civil rights, until the adoption of the Fourteenth Amendment in 1868. Even then, it was another century before blacks could claim their full civil rights. Their struggle for equality has provided a model for other victims of discrimination. ∎

In the fall of 1988, two Stanford freshmen turned a symphony recruiting poster into a blackface caricature of Beethoven and put it near a black student's room. The previous year, another student was moved to another dormitory after repeatedly yelling antihomosexual slurs at a member of the dormitory staff. To protest the ouster, a group of students wearing ski masks held a silent vigil, an action that some said reminded them of the Ku Klux Klan. What should be done about racial and other forms of harassment on a college campus? Is it freedom of expression protected by the First Amendment? Or should students and college officials respect the civil rights of the minority groups and work together to outlaw all forms of harassment?

Incidents at other campuses in recent years caused students all over the country to raise the same questions. At the University of Michigan, racial jokes were played over the university radio station and anti-Semitic remarks printed in a student newspaper. At Smith College in Massachusetts, the 68 students living in one house voted to search one another's rooms and examine one another's handwriting after four black residents received racist letters containing personal details unlikely to be known by an outsider. At Arizona State University, 500 students demonstrated and shouted antiblack slurs to protest the assault of a white student by black students. A computer-printed, but misspelled, flier circulated through Brown University in Rhode Island carrying a message to "keep white supremecy alive."

Between 1986 and 1989, incidents involving anonymous hate letters, racist graffiti and jokes, and interracial brawls were reported on 175 college campuses throughout the United States. The National Institute Against Prejudice and Violence, which keeps track of these incidents, has found that 20 to 25 percent of the members of minority groups, both on and off campus, face at least one incident of racial harassment a year.[1]

Many colleges and universities adopted or were considering antiharassment policies to prevent future incidents of this type and promote tolerance on campus. Tufts University in Massachusetts adopted a policy to protect students from discrimination and "offensive speech" in dormitories but recognized an unrestricted freedom of speech in public areas, campus publications, and material relevant to class discussions. At Stanford a student group proposed changing the code of student conduct to prohibit any personal attack directly addressed to someone, intended to hurt or harass that individual, which expressed in words, pictures, or symbols hatred and contempt for human beings of a particular sex, race, color, handicap, religion, sexual orientation, or national or ethnic origin. "You have to set up something that tells students what the limits are, what they can do and what they can't," a student leader said.[2]

The "offensive speech" debate on college campuses illustrates the tensions between civil liberties and civil rights and a broader conflict between the two strands of general-welfare liberalism discussed in earlier chapters. A Wisconsin state representative who had introduced legislation requiring antiharassment policies at all branches of the University of Wisconsin emphasized the community's welfare in saying: "We agree that divergent philosophies should be allowed on a college campus, but you cannot yell fire in a crowded theater. You cannot cause a hostile atmosphere on campus."[3] On the other

Smith College students hang a dormitory banner in response to racial incidents on campus. The "offensive speech" debate on college campuses throughout the United States dramatically illustrates the underlying tensions between civil liberties and civil rights.

hand, the executive director of the American Civil Liberties Union, an opponent of antiharassment policies, focused on individual liberty in his remarks:

> When you pass a rule which represses speech, you are avoiding dealing with the underlying problem and you're passing a rule whose sweep is going to be broader than the things you're trying to contain.[4]

Equality is the core of civil rights. Antiharassment policies are designed to ensure the equal treatment of all students. In Chapter 6, we traced the development of the value of liberty, of freedom from government interference, and the impact of that value on American politics. In this chapter, we do the same for the value of equality.

EQUALITY AND THE CONSTITUTION

The Original Constitution

You won't find the word *equal* in the original Constitution or even in the Bill of Rights. The Constitution of 1789 most certainly did not require that individuals be treated equally. Con-

sider, for example, the following provisions:

> Representatives and direct taxes shall be apportioned among the several states which may be included within this Union, according to their respective numbers, which shall be determined by adding to the whole number of free persons, including those bound to service for a term of years, and excluding Indians not taxed, *three fifths of all other persons*. [Article I Section 2]

> The migration or *importation of such persons* as any of the states now existing shall think proper to admit, shall not be prohibited by the Congress prior to the year one thousand eight hundred and eight, but a *tax or duty may be imposed on such importation*, not exceeding ten dollars for each person. [Article I, Section 9]

> No person *held to service or labour* in one state, under the laws thereof, escaping into another, shall, in consequence of any law or regulation therein, be discharged from such service or labour, but shall be delivered up on claim of the party *to whom such service or labour may be due*. [Article IV, Section 2]

These provisions of the Constitution upheld slavery in the United States. Article I's formula for determining congressional representation, counting each slave as three-fifths of a person, was part of the compromise between the populous slaveholding states of the South and the states with fewer slaves and a smaller total population. Article I also guaranteed that the importation of slaves could not be outlawed before 1808 and permitted Congress to get tax revenues from the slave trade. Article IV upheld fugitive slave laws.

How is it that the same nation that declared "all men are created equal" as a self-evident truth in 1776 could adopt a Constitution just over a decade later that so clearly violated the principle of equality? Why, in the words of American historian John Hope Franklin, did the founders speak "eloquently at one moment for the brotherhood of man and in the next moment deny it to their black brothers"?[5]

One answer can be found in the different purposes of the Declaration of Independence and the Constitution. The Declaration sought to rally support for a revolution—it was a document to fight by; the Constitution sought to establish a workable government among people and states with important differences—it was a document to govern by. Another answer is that liberty, not equality, was the key value of the American Revolution, and that those who wrote the Constitution gave most of their attention to threats to liberty rather than to guarantees of equality. A third answer looks to the eighteenth-century meaning of equality; at that time the statement that "all men are created equal" conveyed a limited notion of white males having equal standing in courts of law.

But the best explanation for why the original Constitution makes no reference to equality is found in what did *not* appear in the Declaration of Independence. Thomas Jefferson's initial draft of that document, written in June 1776, charged England's King George III with waging "cruel war against human nature itself, violating its most sacred rights of life and liberty in the persons of a distant people who never offended him, captivating and carrying them into slavery in another hemisphere."[6] The Continental Congress dropped the section of Jefferson's draft condemning slavery in order to retain the support

of certain southern representatives and to gain unanimous approval of the Declaration in July 1776.

Some of the delegates to the Constitutional Convention in 1787 spoke against slavery as vehemently as Jefferson had in 1776. But delegates from South Carolina and Georgia said they would never agree to a Constitution that banned the importation of slaves. The Convention attempted to resolve this dilemma as it did others: It referred the issue to committee. Article I, Section 9 incorporates the major points of the committee compromise by allowing the importation of slaves for 20 more years and setting a maximum tax that Congress could impose on such importation.

It is also worth noting that the Constitution never used the terms *slave* or *slavery*. Instead, it refers to a person "held to service or labour" and talks about the importation of "such persons as any of the states now existing shall think proper to admit." Frederick Douglass, an antislavery crusader of the nineteenth century, compared these provisions to the scaffolding of a building under construction: They supported slavery just enough to allow the creation of a new structure of government, but they could be removed once the stability of the new government was assured.[7] In a recent book on the subject, constitutional scholar Leonard Levy comes to a similar conclusion about the intentions of the framers:

> In a society that inherited a system of human slavery, the Framers compromised by accepting political reality; they could not abolish slavery and still form a stronger Union, but they did what was feasible.
>
> Nowhere in the Constitution is any person described in derogatory terms. Nowhere is slavery even acknowledged as a human condition.[8]

The original Constitution only temporarily resolved the dilemma of the Convention. Not everyone agrees with historian John Hope Franklin's conclusion that the Founding Fathers "set the stage for every succeeding generation of Americans to apologize, compromise, and temporize" on the principle of equality.[9] But it is hard to deny that it took a long time for the "scaf-

President Abraham Lincoln reviews the Emancipation Proclamation with his cabinet. The 1863 proclamation declared all persons held as slaves in the rebellious states to be "forever free."

folding" of the Constitution to be removed and for equality to become an explicit value of the Constitution. In fact, it was to be 80 years and the adoption of the Fourteenth Amendment in 1868 before that happened. In the meantime the Supreme Court put its weight behind slavery.

The Dred Scott Decision

The words and intentions of the framers were ambiguous enough to permit others to conclude that the document and those who wrote it supported slavery. Nowhere is this more evident than in *Dred Scott* v. *Sandford*, a Supreme Court decision handed down in 1857. The Supreme Court ruled in that case that Dred Scott, a slave who had been taken into a state (Illinois) and territory (now Minnesota) where slavery was outlawed, was not a citizen of the United States and therefore could not sue for his freedom in a federal court. The Supreme Court further ruled that legislation prohibiting slavery in northern territories violated the Fifth Amendment by depriving slaveholders of property without due process of law.

Dred Scott was a political decision that went far beyond the legal issues of the case. Responding to intense political pressure, including that of a newly elected Democratic president, James Buchanan, the Court attempted to provide a definitive answer to the question of slavery. But instead, the Court upset the delicate balance and series of compromises that political leaders had fashioned to lessen the tensions between the twin goals of equality and the preservation of the union of states under the Constitution. The decision also destroyed the delicate balance between the northern and southern wings of the Democratic party and, by further aggravating sectional and ideological differences, moved the country toward the start of the Civil War four years later.

Chief Justice Roger Taney had no difficulty finding support for his majority opinion in *Dred Scott*. He said that legislation, history, and even "the language used in the Declaration of Independence" showed that slaves and their descendents were not considered as part of the people forming a government. Chief Justice Taney concluded not only that "the right of property in a slave is distinctly and expressly affirmed in the Constitution," but also that "this is done in plain words—too plain to be misunderstood."[10]

Dred Scott has been described as "the most frequently overturned decision in history."[11] The decision was politically overturned by a bloody Civil War (1861–1865), in which more than 600,000 Americans died, and by President Abraham Lincoln's Emancipation Proclamation in the middle of the war (January 1863), which declared "forever free" all persons held as slaves in the rebellious states.

Northern political leaders concerned about the legal status of Lincoln's proclamation and the fact that it applied only to southern slaves proposed a constitutional amendment that would do more. The Thirteenth Amendment, adopted in 1865, made the institution of slavery upheld in *Dred Scott* obsolete: "Neither slavery nor involuntary servitude, except as a punishment for crime whereof the party shall have been duly convicted, shall exist within the United States, or any place subject to their jurisdiction." A second section of the Thirteenth Amendment gave Congress enforcement power.

When it became evident that the legal proscription against slavery in the Thirteenth Amendment was having only a limited effect on the status of southern blacks, Congress passed the Civil Rights Act of 1866, which directly overruled *Dred Scott* by declaring: "All persons born in the United States and not subject to any foreign power, excluding Indians not taxed, are hereby declared to be citizens of the United States." The act then specified the rights enjoyed by citizens "of every race and color, without regard to any previous condition of slavery or involuntary servitude." These included the right to make and enforce contracts; to bring lawsuits; to buy, sell, and inherit property; and "to full and equal benefit of all laws and proceedings for the security of person and property as is enjoyed by white citizens."[12]

The Role of the Fourteenth Amendment

In passing the Civil Rights Act of 1866, Congress was moving the national government into a pol-

icy area that both tradition and the Constitution suggested belonged to the states. Even supporters of the act agreed that a constitutional amendment would provide a firmer basis of congressional authority to protect the civil rights of black citizens. The Fourteenth Amendment, adopted in 1868, incorporated into the Constitution the provision: "All persons born or naturalized in the United States, and subject to the jurisdiction thereof, are citizens of the United States and of the State wherein they reside." Section One of the amendment protects the civil rights of citizens in three provisions, known as the "privileges or immunities," "due process," and "equal protection" clauses. We cited these clauses in Chapter 6, but they are so important for civil rights it is necessary to look at them again:

> No state shall make or enforce any law which shall abridge the *privileges or immunities* of citizens of the United States;
>
> Nor shall any state deprive any person of life, liberty, or property, without *due process* of law;
>
> Nor deny to any person within its jurisdiction the *equal protection* of the laws. [Italics added.]

Notice that Section One protects the privileges and immunities of *citizens* of the United States, and then refers to *persons* rather than citizens in the due process and equal protection clauses. A number of explanations have been offered for this use of the term *person*· The language comes directly from the due process clause of the Fifth Amendment; "person" rather than "citizen" was used to underscore the amendment's focus on the rights of newly freed blacks; and the term was used to protect corporations, which are recognized as "persons" in legal proceedings.

Another question is what rights constitute the "privileges and immunities of citizens of the United States" protected in the Fourteenth Amendment. We saw in Chapter 6 how the Supreme Court, since 1925, has been interpreting the meaning of "due process of law" through selective incorporation of the rights set out in the Bill of Rights. Finally, what does "**equal protec-**

tion of the laws" mean? Does it outlaw all racial segregation? Is it limited to public laws that discriminate against blacks? Does it only guarantee equal standing in a court of law? Does equal protection extend only to blacks or does it also protect women, Hispanics, gay persons, the handicapped, and others who are the victims of unequal treatment?

The Supreme Court has provided authoritative answers to these and other questions about the meaning of the Fourteenth Amendment and, in doing so, has had a great impact on equality in America. The Court, as well as constitutional scholars and historians, have also tried to determine the intentions of those who wrote and voted on the amendment. This is a most difficult task, because many state legislatures reconsidered and reversed their votes. However, both supporters and opponents of the Fourteenth Amendment agreed that it was a broad recognition of rights, that it changed the relationship between the national and state governments, and as a prominent supporter said, amended the Constitution "to give it unity of purpose (and) harmony with the Declaration of Independence."[13] The value of equality, so evident in the Declaration, was now an explicit value of the Constitution.

In 1988, a leading constitutional scholar described the Fourteenth Amendment as "probably the most controversial and certainly the most litigated of all amendments adopted since the birth of the Republic."[14] The due process clause of the amendment provides the basis of most cases taken to court in the area of civil liberties; the equal protection clause has a similar effect in the area of civil rights.

In addition to providing the basis for civil rights suits demanding equal treatment, the equal protection clause has a broader effect on society. Civil rights protect individuals and groups from arbitrary treatment by government and private individuals as well. But the legal effect of the equal protection clause of the Fourteenth Amendment is that no *state* may deny any person the equal protection of the laws; it says nothing about the actions of private individuals. For many years the Supreme Court interpreted

this very narrowly in striking down laws that required equal treatment by private individuals. Over time, however, the Court eased its interpretation of **state action** and the value of equality permeated into the private areas of society. This can be seen in the case of antiharassment policies on college campuses, for example. The value of equality reflected in the Fourteenth Amendment applied to rules about racist graffiti and jokes at private colleges, not just public ones where the link to state action is clear.

In the section that follows we will trace the course of civil rights gained by blacks over the last century and see how the Fourteenth Amendment lies at the heart of any discussion of civil rights today.

Checkpoint

- Equality is the central issue of civil rights.
- The Constitution of 1787 did not require that individuals be treated equally. In fact, certain provisions of the original Constitution upheld slavery in the United States.
- The view of slavery reflected in the Supreme Court's decision in *Dred Scott* v. *Sandford* (1857) was made obsolete by the Civil War and the subsequent adoption of the Thirteenth Amendment (1865), which outlawed slavery, and the Fourteenth Amendment (1868), which provided fundamental civil rights.
- The Fourteenth Amendment is particularly noteworthy for adding the value of equality to the Constitution and continues to be at the center of civil rights today.

RACIAL EQUALITY

In June 1989, the Supreme Court handed down four civil rights decisions making it more difficult for minorities and women to win discrimination suits. Two of those decisions were Supreme Court interpretations of the 1866 Civil Rights Act, and one of those two involved the distinction between public and private discrimination. The Court ruled that the 123-year-old law could not be used to bring damage suits against state and local governments for racial discrimination and that the statute's guarantee of equality in making and enforcing contracts applied only to hiring practices, not to discriminatory treatment once on the job.[15] Anticipating the intense criticism that was to develop over these decisions, Justice Anthony Kennedy said: "Neither our words nor our decisions should be interpreted as signaling one inch of retreat from Congress' policy to forbid discrimination."[16] A lawyer for the National Association for the Advancement of Colored People (NAACP) offered a contrary assessment. The decisions, he said, showed "it's now the Court against the legisla-

ture," and reflected a division between Congress and the Supreme Court not seen in more than 50 years.[17]

The current state of racial equality in the United States and the significance of recent Supreme Court civil rights rulings can only be appreciated by understanding about the history of racial equality since the Civil War. We will examine three important eras in American politics: (1) the Reconstruction era (1865–1877); (2) the era of segregation (1880s–1954); and (3) the "second Reconstruction," a period that began in 1954 with the Supreme Court decision to desegregate schools and some think might have ended with the Court's civil rights rulings in 1989.[18]

Reconstruction (1865–1877)

The Thirteenth Amendment freed 4 million black slaves in 1865, but they were not yet citizens. Mississippi became the first state to establish the status of the newly freed slaves by passing a **Black Code**—a collection of laws that restricted the living and working conditions of blacks almost as severely as slave codes had be-

Selling a freedman to pay his fine at Monticello, Florida, 1867. After the Civil War, every southern state passed Black Codes, which restricted the living and working conditions of free blacks almost as severely as had earlier slave codes.

fore the Civil War (see A Closer Look on pp. 206–207). Every southern state enacted a Black Code during this period, which effectively relegated free blacks to a status of unpropertied farm laborers with few political rights.

Publication and circulation of these Black Codes in early 1866 generated pressure from northern political leaders for civil rights legislation. Congress passed the Freedmen's Bureau Bill in February 1866, giving the army responsibility for protecting the civil rights of blacks in the South. In March, Congress passed the Civil Rights Act of 1866, declaring blacks to be citizens and outlining the civil rights of all citizens. The law was aimed directly at the southern Black Codes. Not only did it specify rights and guarantee blacks the "full and equal benefit" of all laws, as noted earlier, but it also held that blacks "shall be subject to like punishment, pains and penalties, and to none other, any law, statute, ordinance, regulation, or custom to the contrary notwithstanding."[19] President Andrew Johnson vetoed the Civil Rights Act on the grounds that protection of civil rights was a state, not a national, responsibility. Congress not only overrode the veto but also proposed the Fourteenth Amendment, incorporating into the Constitution the provisions of the Civil Rights Act and making clear the authority of the national government in this area. In 1870, the Fifteenth Amendment was adopted, giving to blacks the right to vote.

The Thirteenth, Fourteenth, and Fifteenth Amendments, known as the **Reconstruction amendments**, have been described as a "second American Constitution."[20] They changed the Constitution in a way previous amendments had not. The first 12 amendments do not alter the powers of the national government spelled out in the Constitution. The next three *do* by granting Congress the power to enforce the amendments by appropriate legislation. The original Constitution intended to keep slavery out of national politics by leaving it a state responsibility; but the Thirteenth Amendment now gave Congress power to enforce its ban on slavery anywhere in the United States. The Fourteenth Amendment gave the national government the power to prevent states from interfering with the civil rights outlined in the amendment, and the Fifteenth Amendment gave Congress power to prevent states from denying or abridging the right of citizens to vote on account of race, color, or previous slavery. (Table 7.1 provides a chronology of the important civil rights laws and amendments passed in the Reconstruction era.)

The Reconstruction amendments *are* like the Bill of Rights in one sense, however. In Chapter 6, the Bill of Rights was described as "a kind of Rip Van Winkle, asleep for more than a century." Although the Reconstruction amendments had an immediate impact on how America was governed after the Civil War, once the Reconstruction era ended, the amendments also became a kind of Rip Van Winkle as far as expanding civil rights was concerned. After 1875, Congress did not pass another civil rights law for nearly 80 years—until 1957.[21]

The end of the Reconstruction era of American politics is often considered to be the Compromise of 1877, when Republican presidential candidate Rutherford B. Hayes won Southern Democrats' support in a disputed election by promising to return responsibility for civil rights to the individual states.[22] An era of segregation followed in which the Supreme Court's interpretation of the Reconstruction amendments (particularly the Fourteenth Amendment) set back rather than advanced the cause of civil rights and the value of equality in the United States.

Era of Segregation (1880s – 1954)

The Civil War and the Reconstruction amendments put an end to slavery and Black Codes—the most extreme forms of inequality—but they did not establish racial equality in the United States. The era of segregation that began in the 1880s[23] was characterized by a retreat on the national level from the commitment to civil rights; the development of state policies in the South requiring the **segregation,** or separation, of whites and blacks (known as *de jure* segregation because it was "by law"); and the continuation of *de facto* ("by fact") segregation in northern states, in which the separation of blacks and whites was more often a result of residential pat-

Table 7.1

Civil Rights Laws of the Reconstruction Era

Year	Law or Amendment	Major Provisions
1863	Emancipation Proclamation	Declared that slaves residing in Confederate states were free
1865	Thirteenth Amendment	Outlawed slavery throughout U.S.
1866	Freedman's Bureau Act	Made U.S. military responsible for protecting black civil rights
1866	Civil Rights Act	Granted citizenship to blacks and specified civil rights of all citizens
1868	Fourteenth Amendment	Defined U.S. citizen and protected rights through privileges and immunities, due process, and equal protection clauses
1870	Fifteenth Amendment	Declared that right to vote cannot be denied on account of race or color
1870	Civil Rights Act (Enforcement Act)	Enforced voting rights of the Fifteenth Amendment and outlawed conspiracies to deny rights
1871	Civil Rights Act (Ku Klux Klan Act)	Enforced Fourteenth Amendment by providing civil and criminal sanctions for denying such rights as registering to vote, serving on a jury, or holding office
1875	Civil Rights Act	Guaranteed equal rights in public accommodations (inns, theaters, trains, carriages)

terns and social customs than of segregation laws.

One explanation for southerners' continued resistance to black equality after the Civil War can be found in a letter Thomas Jefferson wrote years earlier. In 1776, you will remember, Jefferson had characterized slavery as "a cruel war against human nature itself." Yet as a Virginia landowner he also had as many as 200 slaves of his own. Jefferson recognized the dilemma. "We have a wolf by the ears," he said of slavery in a letter he wrote in 1820, "and we can neither hold him, nor safely let him go. Justice is in one scale, and self preservation in the other."[24] Jefferson's dilemma helps to explain why even those southerners who recognized the injustice of slavery resisted the idea of racial equality after the war. White racism was based on a strong belief in the intellectual and moral superiority of whites, coupled with what whites saw as the preservation of their lives, property, and status in society.[25]

Segregation was manifested in state laws that

required separate facilities for blacks and whites in the late nineteenth century, voting laws that effectively denied blacks access to the ballot despite the Fifteenth Amendment, and Supreme Court rulings that upheld segregation under a "separate but equal" doctrine that lasted to the middle of the twentieth century. Together, these policies made racial equality an issue to be decided by individual states, much as the Constitution had treated the issue of slavery in the eighteenth century.

"JIM CROW" LAWS   In the South, segregation was most evident in laws requiring separate facilities for blacks, known collectively as **"Jim Crow" laws** (Jim Crow being a derogatory term for a black person used in minstrel shows of the 1830s and 1840s). Three weeks after Congress passed the Civil Rights Act of 1875 requiring equality in public facilities, Tennessee enacted the first permanent Jim Crow law. The Tennessee statute gave owners and employees of hotels, public carriers, and places of amusement permission to exclude persons "for any reason whatever."[26] In 1881, Tennessee passed a second Jim Crow law, which moved beyond *authorizing* private discrimination to *requiring* separate facilities for blacks in first-class railway cars.

In the five years between 1887 and 1892, 9 southern states enacted Jim Crow laws; by 1907, 14 states had laws requiring separate facilities for blacks and whites on railway cars. What started in transportation was soon extended to other areas. By the early twentieth century, detailed legislation in most southern states required separation of the races from birth (hospitals) to death (cemeteries) and just about everything in between, from schools and public housing to drinking fountains, telephone booths, and circuses (see A Closer Look, pp. 206–207). In Atlanta courtrooms, black witnesses were even sworn in on separate Bibles from whites.[27]

VOTING RESTRICTIONS   The empowerment and protection of black voters was a key element of Congress's Reconstruction policy after the Civil War. Although black voters and elected officials were in the minority in most southern states throughout Reconstruction, they were an important part of the governing coalition in

those states. But by 1910, every southern state had found ways to disfranchise blacks (to take away their right to vote) despite the clear command of the Fifteenth Amendment. Whites did this by establishing voter "qualifications," which effectively denied blacks the vote. The most common devices were:

1   Literacy tests. Voters were required to demonstrate an ability to read, write, and in some cases interpret the meaning of laws or the Constitution in **literacy tests**. In 1890, two-thirds of the adult blacks but less than one-quarter of the adult whites were illiterate in those states with literacy tests (Alabama, Georgia, Louisiana, Mississippi, North Carolina, South Carolina and Virginia).[28]

2   Grandfather clauses. Certain clauses in literacy tests permitted anyone whose ancestors could vote at a particular date (most often, January 1, 1867—before the law passed requiring southern states to permit blacks to vote) to vote, regardless of how well the person did on the test.

3   Poll taxes. These taxes, usually one or two dollars a year, might seem trivial by today's standards, but they were also cumulative and could be selectively enforced through exemptions; blacks could be denied the right to vote until all back taxes had been paid.

4   Residency requirements. Four southern states had a two-year residency requirement for voters, and the other southern states had a one-year requirement. Selective enforcement and high black mobility accounted for the discriminatory racial effect of these requirements.

5   White primary. A number of southern states disfranchised blacks through the **white primary,** permitting only white voters in the Democratic primary. In the solidly Democratic states of the South this was the only election that mattered.

All of these methods of disfranchising blacks eventually were eliminated by congressional action, Supreme Court decisions, and—in the case of the poll tax—a constitutional amendment. But many of those changes did not come until much later. By early in this century, whites were able to limit or deny black political participation, as the case of Louisiana dramatically illustrates. In 1896, more than 130,000 blacks were registered to vote in Louisiana; by 1904, there were just over 1300.[29]

Jim Crow laws and voting restrictions clearly demonstrate southern opposition to racial equality. But two Supreme Court decisions during this period show that the retreat from civil rights and racial equality of the Reconstruction era was not limited to the South: the *Civil Rights Cases* (1883) and *Plessy* v. *Ferguson* (1896). Both cases involved the Fourteenth Amendment, and both have had lasting effects on equality in America.

THE CIVIL RIGHTS CASES In the *Civil Rights Cases*, the Supreme Court consolidated five separate cases in which blacks charged that their being denied entry to hotels and theaters in California and New York and a railway car in Tennessee violated the Civil Rights Act of 1875. The 1875 statute required: "That all persons within the jurisdiction of the United States shall be entitled to the full and equal enjoyment of the accommodations, advantages, facilities, and privileges of inns, public conveniences on land or water, theaters, and other places of public amusement."[30] The key questions before the Court were: Did the Fourteenth Amendment give Congress the power to regulate public accommodations? Did the refusal of entry or service in them impose a "badge of slavery or servitude" upon blacks and therefore violate the Thirteenth Amendment prohibition on slavery and involuntary service? Did such a refusal abridge the "privileges or immunities" of black citizens or deny them "the equal protection of the laws" guaranteed by the Fourteenth Amendment? If the answer to these questions was yes, then under the provisions of these two amendments, Congress had power to enforce them by appropriate legislation.

But the Supreme Court quite clearly (8–1) answered no to these questions. Justice Joseph Bradley's majority opinion addressed the Thirteenth Amendment issue by stating that "an act of refusal has nothing to do with slavery or involuntary servitude," and that "it would be running the slavery argument into the ground to make it apply to every act of discrimination which a person may see fit to make as to the guests he will entertain, or as to the people he will take into his coach or cab or car, or admit

Voter "qualifications" throughout the South effectively denied blacks the right to vote despite the commands of the Fifteenth Amendment. On this form applicants were required to answer a question calling for a "reasonable interpretation" of the Mississippi Constitution.

to his concert or theater, or deal with in other matters of intercourse or business."[31] In other words, Congress had the power to prevent slavery, but this was not slavery.

The Court also answered no to the Fourteenth Amendment question, although for a different reason. That amendment, Justice Bradley pointed out, says no *state* shall abridge privileges and immunities or deny due process and equal protection of the laws. But Congress has no power to pass legislation in this area "until some state law has been passed, or some state action through its officers or agents has been taken, adverse to the rights of citizens sought to be protected by the Fourteenth Amendment." Congress did not have power under the amendment to pass a law against private discrimination, Bradley argued, because "individual invasion of individual rights is not the subject-matter of the amendment."[32]

A Closer Look

Slave Codes, Black Codes, and Jim Crow Laws ★★★

The Emancipation Proclamation and the Thirteenth Amendment freed black slaves, and the Fourteenth Amendment made them citizens. But a comparison of earlier Slave Codes with Black Codes passed after the Thirteenth Amendment was adopted in 1865 and with Jim Crow laws passed after the Fourteenth Amendment was adopted in 1868 demonstrates how southern whites sought to limit the freedoms and the status of blacks in American society.

EXCERPTS FROM THE SLAVE CODE OF ALABAMA (1852)

- The state or condition of negro or African slavery is established by law in this state; conferring on the master property in and the right to the time, labor and services of the slave, and to enforce obedience to all his lawful commands. [Chapter IV, Section 2042]
- No slave can own property, and any property purchased or held by a slave, not claimed by the master or owner, must be sold by order of any justice of the peace. [Chapter IV, Section 1018]
- No slave must go beyond the limits of the plantation on which he resides, without

a pass or token from his master or overseer, giving him authority to go and return from a certain place. Violators must be punished, not exceeding twenty stripes [lashes] at the discretion of any justice. [Chapter IV, Section 1008]
- Not more than five male slaves shall assemble together at any place off the plantation, with or without passes or permits to be there, unless attended by the master or overseer of such slaves, or unless such are attending the public worship of God. [Chapter IV, Section 1020]

EXCERPTS FROM BLACK CODE OF MISSISSIPPI (1865)

- All freedmen, free negroes and mulattoes in this state over the age of eighteen years, found with no lawful employment or business, or found unlawfully assembling themselves together either in the day or night time, and all white persons so assembling with them on terms of equality, or living in adultery or fornication with a freedwoman, free negro, or mulatto, shall be deemed vagrants. [Chapter VI, Section 2]
- In case any freedman, free negro or mulatto shall fail for five days after the im-

position of any fine or forfeiture upon him or her for violation of any of the provisions of this act, to pay the same, that it shall be, and is hereby made the duty of the sheriff of the proper county to hire out said freedman, free negro or mulatto, to any person who will, for the shortest period of service, pay said fine or forfeiture and all costs. [Chapter VI, Section 5]

- That all the penal and criminal laws now in force in this state, defining offenses and prescribing the mode of punishment for crimes and misdemeanors committed by slaves, free negroes or mulattoes, are hereby re-enacted and declared to be in full force and effect, against freedman, free negroes and mulattoes, except so far as the mode and manner of trial and punishment have been changed or altered by law. [Chapter XXIII, Section 4]

EXCERPTS FROM SOME TYPICAL JIM CROW LAWS (1909–1928)

- No textbook issued or distributed under this act to a white school child shall ever be reissued or redistributed to a colored school child, and no textbook issued or distributed to a colored school child shall ever be reissued or redistributed to a white school child. [Acts of Kentucky, 1928]
- The superintendent shall use as guards such convicts as may, in his judgment, be trusted with such service; provided, that none but white men be used to guard white convicts. [Acts of Arkansas, 1909]
- White convicts shall not be required to eat at the same table or sleep with any persons of the negro race. [Acts of Arkansas, 1913]
- Tent shows are to maintain separate entrances for different races. Any circus or other such traveling show exhibiting under canvas or out of doors for gain shall maintain two main entrances to such exhibition, and one shall be for white people and the other entrance shall be for colored people, and such main entrances shall be plainly marked "For White People," and the other entrance shall be marked "For Colored People," . . . [Laws of South Carolina, 1917]

Source: The Alabama Slave Code, Mississippi Black Code, and Kentucky and Arkansas Jim Crow laws, Richard Bardolph, The Civil Rights Record (New York: Crowell, 1970), pp. 6–10, 37–41, and 195–196. The South Carolina circus statute is from Charles Lofgren, The Plessy Case (New York: Oxford University Press, 1987), p. 202.

Most southern states required "separate but equal facilities" for everything from schools and public housing to drinking fountains and waiting rooms.

Justice John Marshall Harlan, a former slaveholder from Kentucky and the only Supreme Court justice voting to uphold the 1875 Civil Rights Act, wrote a blistering dissent that filled 40 pages. Harlan argued that the state action requirement of the Fourteenth Amendment was met because those who run public accommodations must be licensed by the state, that Congress also had power under the commerce clause to regulate the activities listed in the Civil Rights Act, and that the rights under consideration involved legal equality, not social equality. Harlan criticized the majority opinion as "too narrow and artificial," and as one that sacrifices "the substance and spirit" of the Thirteenth and Fourteenth Amendments.[33]

Subsequent decisions of the Supreme Court have expanded the limits of the state action doctrine, but the limit itself continues today as the major legacy of the *Civil Rights Cases* ruling.

Equality under the Constitution now meant legal or political equality, not social equality, and primary responsibility for civil rights shifted once again to the states.

"SEPARATE BUT EQUAL": *PLESSY V. FERGUSON*

Most southern states began passing Jim Crow laws after the *Civil Rights Cases*, with a rush of legislation coming after 1887. Since state laws requiring separate facilities for blacks would clearly be state action, how could those laws escape being ruled unconstitutional under the Fourteenth Amendment? The answer to that question can be found in another constitutional doctrine of great importance to civil rights in America: the doctrine of **separate but equal**.

Of the nine states that passed Jim Crow laws for railway cars between 1887 and 1892, five used the phrase "equal but separate" to describe the standard for white and black facilities.[34] A

Louisiana statute of 1890 was typical. The first section of the statute, entitled "An Act to Promote the Comfort of Passengers," said:

> All railway companies carrying passengers in their coaches in this state shall provide equal but separate accommodations for the white and colored races, by providing two or more passenger coaches for each passenger train, or by dividing the passenger coaches by a partition so as to secure separate accommodations.[35]

A coalition of blacks, civil rights organizations, business interests (seeking constitutional protection from state regulation), and railroads (wanting to be free of the economic burden of supplying two of everything) challenged the constitutionality of the Louisiana law. In *Plessy* v. *Ferguson* (1896), the Supreme Court ruled that the Louisiana statute violated neither the Thirteenth nor the Fourteenth Amendment.

That the Louisiana statute did not conflict with the Thirteenth Amendment was "too clear for argument," according to Justice Henry Billings Brown, because the legal distinction it made between blacks and whites "has no tendency to destroy the legal equality of the two races, or reestablish a state of involuntary servitude." But the Fourteenth Amendment did apply, for there was clearly state action in the Louisiana statute. However, Brown said, the racial distinctions in the Louisiana statute were designed to promote the comfort of travelers and preserve peace and order. The Court ruled that the Louisiana law did not deprive blacks of *legal* or *political* equality, and it is that type of equality, not *social* equality, that is protected by the Fourteenth Amendment. "If one race be inferior to the other socially, the Constitution cannot put them upon the same plane," Brown concluded.[36]

Justice John Marshall Harlan, the dissenter in the *Civil Rights Cases*, once again wrote a forceful dissenting opinion. "The thin disguise of 'equal' accommodations will not mislead anyone," Harlan said, and he predicted that the Court's decision would "prove to be quite as pernicious as the decision made in the *Dred Scott* case," because it would encourage those who sought to undercut the Fourteenth Amendment. In language that was to be often quoted by later justices, Harlan declared that "in view of the Constitution, in the eye of the law, there is in this country no superior, dominant, ruling class of citizens. There is no caste there. Our Constitution is color-blind, and neither knows nor tolerates classes among citizens."[37]

We have noted that racism was not limited to the South. While it is true that the Jim Crow law upheld by the Court in *Plessy* came from Louisiana, 30 of the 45 states at that time (including New York, Kansas, Indiana, and most western states) had "separate-but-equal" laws governing public schools.[38] For nearly 60 years the separate-but-equal doctrine upheld in *Plessy* governed race relations in the United States.

Second Reconstruction (1954–1989?)

Reconstruction lasted 12 years (1865–1877), the era of segregation at least 70 years (1880s–1954), and the period of civil rights advances often called the Second Reconstruction at least 35 years (1954-1989). The constitutional amendments of the Reconstruction era laid the groundwork for many of the key congressional acts and Supreme Court decisions of the Second Reconstruction era. In this section, we briefly consider some of the landmark decisions on racial equality in four areas: schools, public accommodations, voting, and affirmative action.

SCHOOLS The 1954 Supreme Court decision in *Brown* v. *Board of Education*, outlawing racial segregation in public schools, marks the beginning of the Second Reconstruction. This ruling is so important because the Court unanimously rejected the separate-but-equal doctrine of *Plessy* v. *Ferguson*.

The case of *Brown* v. *Board of Education* was brought to the Supreme Court by the National Association for the Advancement of Colored People (NAACP)—an organization founded in 1910 to advance the cause of racial equality. The NAACP brought 50 cases to the Supreme Court between 1915 and 1958 and had been successfully chipping away at the separate-but-equal doctrine for almost 20 years before *Brown*. The doctrine proved to be vulnerable in two ways. First, it could be shown that the separate facilities were not physically equal. Second, the idea of measuring equality in this way was itself called into question.

Although *Plessy* was a case involving public transportation, the separate-but-equal doctrine also governed public education in America. But the separate schools for blacks and whites were far from equal. For example, South Carolina spent $24 per white student and $3 per black student in 1915, and spending for whites in six southern states was three times that for blacks in 1931.[39] But the NAACP strategy for attacking the separate-but-equal doctrine was one that concentrated more on the concept of material equality. The NAACP argued, for example, that a separate law school for blacks in Texas would not be equal to the all-white University of Texas Law School, even if the two schools were equal in volumes in the library, physical plant, and spending per student. In *Sweatt* v. *Painter* (1950), the Court agreed that measuring equality required looking at such factors as the reputation of the faculty, the influence of alumni, the standing in the community, and prestige—"qualities which are incapable of objective measurement but which make for greatness in a law school."[40] Those are qualities that could be easily understood by Supreme Court justices—most of whom attended prestigious law schools—and they demonstrated a fundamental weakness in the separate-but-equal doctrine.

Four years later, the Supreme Court applied this standard of "intangible considerations" to public schools. Chief Justice Earl Warren identified the central question before the Court in the *Brown* case: "Does segregation of children in public schools solely on the basis of race, even though the physical facilities and other 'tangible' factors may be equal, deprive the children of the minority group of equal educational opportunities?" Warren cited psychological studies that showed how racial segregation was linked to feelings of inferiority in black children, which reduced their motivation and hindered their educational development. "Whatever may have

been the extent of psychological knowledge at the time of *Plessy*, this finding is amply supported by modern authority," Warren wrote. "Any language in *Plessy* contrary to this finding is rejected. We conclude that in the field of public education the doctrine of 'separate but equal' has no place. Separate educational facilities are inherently unequal."[41] The Supreme Court ruled in *Brown* that segregated public schools were unconstitutional because they violated the equal protection clause of the Fourteenth Amendment.

The Supreme Court has consistently upheld the principle laid down in the *Brown* decision ever since. But the implementation of school desegregation has been long and complicated. A year after *Brown*, the Court declared that local school boards would be responsible for desegregation—subject to federal court supervision—and that schools must be desegregated "with all deliberate speed."[42] Years of massive southern resistance to school desegregation then led a frustrated Supreme Court to require in 1969 that school systems be integrated "at once."[43] In 1971, the Court upheld mandatory school busing to achieve racial integration.[44] Three years later, in a case that involved school busing in and around Detroit, Michigan, however, the Supreme Court upheld the distinction between de jure and de facto segregation noted earlier. The state action limit to federal remedies under the Fourteenth Amendment—the key principle in the *Civil Rights Cases* in 1883—again limited the federal government to prohibiting de jure segregation, where it could be shown that policymakers or administrators intended to discriminate on the basis of race.[45]

At the time of the *Brown* ruling in 1954, two-thirds of the black students in the United States went to all-black schools. Thirty years later, in 1984, that figure was down to one-third.[46] In 1954, Linda Brown was a sixth-grade student in Topeka, Kansas, whose parents had joined other black parents to sue the Topeka Board of Education for having schools that were racially segregated—the case that became *Brown* v. *Board of Education*. Thirty years later, the same Linda Brown, now Linda Brown Smith, had joined other black parents to sue the Topeka Board of Education to correct racial imbalances in the city's school system (one elementary school was 54 percent black while another was less than 1.5 percent black). Here is how an attorney for Linda Brown Smith and the other black parents described the Topeka school system 30 years after *Brown*: "It's integrated, but it's not desegregated."[47]

Federal courts and state and local political leaders have ended the most blatant de jure segregation targeted in *Brown*. Almost all school systems, like Topeka's, are "integrated" in the sense that there is a single school system for black and white students. But economic inequalities and residential patterns (particularly in and around large cities both North and South) can segregate the schools *within* systems. That is why racial equality in schools is linked to racial equality in the broader society and why education continues to be an important part of the civil rights agenda in the 1990s.

PUBLIC ACCOMMODATIONS In June 1989, President Bush invited civil rights leaders to the White House for a ceremony marking the twenty-fifth anniversary of the signing of the Civil Rights Act of 1964. One of the invited guests was Rosa Parks of Montgomery, Alabama. Her presence at the ceremony was an indication of her importance to that legislation.

The year after the *Brown* decision, Rosa Parks, a black seamstress, refused to give up her seat to a white rider and move to the rear of a Montgomery bus. Her action set into motion a year-long black boycott of the segregated bus system, which ended only when the Court struck down the Montgomery law as a violation of the Fourteenth Amendment's equal protection clause (see Chapter 10).[48]

There was no direct link between the Supreme Court decision in *Brown* and the Montgomery boycott, but "the idea in *Brown* and the action in Montgomery" have been described as "the vision and the practice" that made this the initial struggle of the civil rights movement.[49] The success of the Montgomery boycott triggered similar actions throughout the South. In February 1960, four black college freshmen invented the "sit-in," another form of nonviolent protest, by sitting in protest at a Greensboro, North Caro-

Rosa Parks at a Washington, D.C. tribute to her role in the civil rights movement, February 1990.

lina, lunch counter after being denied service. Within a month, civil rights activists had staged similar sit-ins in 50 cities throughout the South and established the Student Non-violent Coordinating Committee (SNCC) to coordinate protest activities. In the spring of 1963, Birmingham, Alabama, authorities used cattle prods, water hoses, and police dogs against black demonstrators, triggering a wave of demonstrations in 800 cities both North and South.

In August 1963, a "March on Washington for Jobs and Freedom" drew more than 200,000 civil rights supporters to the nation's capital. President John Kennedy invited ten of the March on Washington leaders to the White House that evening to count the likely votes in Congress on a major civil rights proposal he had submitted earlier that year.[50] Congress had already responded to the civil rights movement by passing the Civil Rights Acts of 1957 and 1960, the first civil rights laws since the Reconstruction measures more than 80 years earlier. Both laws sought to protect Fifteenth Amendment voting rights by strengthening federal enforcement powers and making it easier to bring voting discrimination suits. The legislation proposed by Kennedy in 1963 included a major section on public accommodations, the precise area in which the Supreme Court had denied congressional authority in the *Civil Rights Cases* of 1883.

Congress passed the Civil Rights Act of 1964 on July 2, a year after President Kennedy had introduced the bill and seven months after his assassination. The public accommodation provisions of the law were similar to those Congress had approved in 1875: Racial discrimination was outlawed in hotels, restaurants, theaters, and similar establishments. How did Congress get around the "state action" limit of the Fourteenth Amendment, which the Supreme Court had used to strike down the public accommodations provisions of the 1875 act? The law relies primarily on the power granted Congress in Article I to regulate interstate commerce. Here is how Attorney General Robert Kennedy tackled the question in Senate hearings in August 1963:

> We base this on the commerce clause which I think makes it clearly constitutional. In my personal judgment, basing it on the 14th Amendment would also be constitutional.
>
> I think that there is argument about the 14th Amendment basis—going back to the 1883 Supreme Court decision [*Civil Rights Cases*], and the fact that this is not state-action, that therefore Congress would not have the right under the 14th Amendment to pass any legislation dealing with it.
>
> I think that there is an injustice that needs to be remedied. We have to find the tools with which to remedy that injustice. There cannot be any legitimate question about the commerce clause. That is clearly constitutional.[51]

In December 1964, the Supreme Court put its stamp of approval on this interpretation of the commerce power. The opinion for a unanimous Court noted "the disruptive effect that racial dis-

crimination has had on commercial intercourse," and said, "Congress was not restricted by the fact that the particular obstruction to interstate commerce with which it was dealing was also deemed a moral and social wrong."[52]

VOTING   Certain places have symbolic importance to the civil rights movement in the United States. In the spring of 1965, Selma, Alabama, took its place alongside Montgomery (the bus boycott), Greensboro (the first sit-in), and Birmingham (police violence against demonstrators) as an important symbol. After the Civil Rights Act of 1964 had become law, many civil rights leaders began to concentrate on the right to vote. When efforts to register black voters in Selma were unsuccessful because of the resistance of white officials, Martin Luther King, Jr., and other civil rights leaders organized a protest march from Selma to the state capital 50 miles away in Montgomery. At the time of the Selma march, blacks accounted for about half of Alabama's population but only 1 percent of its registered voters.[53]

State troopers broke up the march with whips, cattle prods, nightsticks, and tear gas, and scenes reminiscent of Birmingham filled television screens across the country. Eight days later, President Lyndon Johnson called for voting rights legislation in a televised address to a joint session of Congress. In August, Congress passed the Voting Rights Act of 1965, judged by many to be "the most radical civil rights bill of its time."[54]

The Constitution makes this area of civil rights a complicated one, for the original Constitution does not grant a right to vote. Delegates to the Philadelphia convention in 1787 debated at some length the idea of limiting the right to vote in federal elections to property owners. Every state at that time restricted voting to those who owned property and paid taxes, but the property qualifications differed from state to state.[55] Unable to reach a uniform standard of voter qualifications, the delegates left the issue up to the states. Article I, Section 2 of the Constitution requires that voters in elections for the U.S. House of Representatives have "the qualifications requisite for electors of the most numerous branch of the state legislature," and Ar-

Selma to Montgomery march to register black voters in Alabama in 1965. Blacks made up about half of Alabama's population at this time, but only 1 percent of the state's registered voters.

ticle I, Section 4 says: "The times, places and manner of holding elections for senators and representatives shall be prescribed in each state by the legislature thereof; but the Congress may at any time by law make or alter such regulations, except as to the places of choosing senators."

The Constitution did not include a right to vote until the Fifteenth Amendment was adopted in 1870. Even then the Supreme Court said in 1875 that Article I made it clear that the responsibility for determining voter *qualifications* rested with the states and that even the amended Constitution "does not confer the right of suffrage upon anyone."[56] The Court later backed away from that position by upholding the conviction of Ku Klux Klan members found guilty of interfering with a black person's right to vote and invalidating some of the state methods used to prevent blacks from voting.

But until Congress passed the Civil Rights Act of 1957, the only way for blacks to protect their right to vote was through the federal courts, an expensive and exceedingly slow process that did little to increase black registration and voting. The Civil Rights Acts of 1957 and 1960 gave the U.S. attorney general authority to bring suits against those who interfered with the right to vote on racial grounds and established procedures to facilitate black registration. Certain provisions of the Civil Rights Act of 1964 sought to expedite voting rights hearings and to limit states' use of literacy tests. But this remedial case-by-case approach had done little to boost black registration. From the mid-1950s to the mid-1960s, black registration increased by only one-tenth of one percent in Louisiana and 2 percent in Mississippi. Throughout the South, white registration was consistently 50 percentage points higher than black registration.[57] Civil rights leaders wanted legislation that would force the federal government to take an active, positive role in registering black voters and promoting black participation.

The Voting Rights Act of 1965 was based on the authority given Congress by the Fifteenth Amendment, and it targeted the southern states with discriminatory practices where less than 50 percent of the voting-age population was registered or voted in 1964. For those areas, the act: (1) banned literacy tests and similar devices for limiting registration, (2) authorized the U.S. attorney general to send federal voting examiners to observe elections and in some cases actually register voters, and (3) prohibited the introduction of any new voting law or practice without the approval of the attorney general or a federal court in Washington. The Voting Rights Act also forbade any electoral procedures that have the effect of diminishing or diluting black voting power anywhere in the United States, not just the South.

When the original Voting Rights Act expired in 1975, Congress renewed it for seven years, made the literacy test ban permanent, and extended coverage to other minorities. In 1982, Congress extended the act for 25 years with two additional changes: One established procedures for states and cities to get out from under federal regulations by proving an absence of discrimination, and the other said the proof of discrimination would depend on the *results* or *effects* of voting procedures rather than their *intent*.

The Voting Rights Act of 1965 had a dramatic effect on black voter registration in the South (see Table 7.2). In Selma, Alabama, where it all started, the percentage of eligible blacks registered rose from 10 percent to 60 percent within two months of the arrival of a federal registrar, and statewide, more than 160,000 new black voters were registered in Alabama within a year.[58]

Another indication of the changes brought about by the Voting Rights Act of 1965 is the number of blacks holding elected office. Prior to 1965, that number in the South was estimated to be fewer than 100; by 1974 there were ten times that many, and by 1981 nearly 2500 blacks held elective office in the southern states.[59]

Table 7.2
Black Voter Registration, 1964 and 1976

State	Percentage of Black Voting-Age Population Registered to Vote	
	1964	1976
Alabama	23	58
Georgia	44	56
Louisiana	32	64
Mississippi	7	67
South Carolina	39	61
Virginia	46	61

Source: James Curry, Richard Riley, and Richard Battistoni, *Constitutional Government: The American Experience* (St. Paul, Minn.: West, 1989), p. 367.

The success of black candidate Jesse Jackson in a number of presidential primaries in 1984 and 1988 and the opposition of many southern senators to the Supreme Court nomination of Robert Bork in 1988 because of his narrow interpretation of civil rights demonstrate the changes in American politics triggered by civil rights policies in voting.

AFFIRMATIVE ACTION Programs that seek to remedy the effects of past discrimination and to prevent it in the future are known as **affirmative action.** Most of these programs are aimed at getting a broader representation of all groups and racial and cultural diversity in employment and education. By requiring positive action to correct past discrimination, affirmative action goes further than equal opportunity and antidiscrimination policies, which simply require that all individuals and groups be treated equally.

In 1989, the president of Temple University's White Student Union said that he and other members of this organization just wanted "equality to be the rule," and that scholarships and jobs "should be given on merit alone." They believed that "white people are being discriminated against by affirmative action." Reginald

Wilson, a senior scholar at the American Council on Education, said the Temple students were not alone in those beliefs. He noted that affirmative action programs, high tuition costs, and the fact that most college students today lack a direct knowledge of the civil rights movement had all contributed to the increase in racial incidents on campuses in the late 1980s: "You can often hear white students say, 'My old man is paying through the nose to send me to school, while they [blacks] get Pell grants and talent search grants.'"[60]

Title VI of the Civil Rights Act of 1964 prohibited discrimination on the basis of race, color, or national origin in any federally financed program and authorized federal agencies to cut off funds to recipients who did not comply. Title VII prohibited discrimination on the basis of race, color, religion, and sex in any firm with 25 or more employees. In 1965, President Lyndon Johnson issued executive orders to implement the new civil rights policy, and in 1967 the Department of Labor required government contractors to submit detailed written plans that established goals and a timetable for hiring a certain number of blacks, Hispanics, Orientals, native Americans, and women in each job category. The Department of Labor order defined an affirmative action program as "a set of specific and result-oriented procedures" designed to overcome inequalities caused by past discrimination.[61] In 1970, the Department of Health, Education, and Welfare (HEW) issued "guidelines" for colleges and universities receiving federal funds to follow in hiring and admissions and threatened the withdrawal of federal grants for noncompliance.

Critics of affirmative action said "specific and result-oriented procedures" and "guidelines" really meant that employers and admissions offices had to establish *quotas*, setting aside a certain number of jobs or places in school for minorities and women. This was reverse discrimination, according to critics, and it violated the principle that the Constitution is "color-blind" or "race-neutral"—that race should not be a factor in making decisions.

The proponents of affirmative action pointed to the wide acceptance of programs in America's past that gave preferential treatment to some groups, such as veterans who were given preference in jobs and housing after World War II. These supporters said that centuries of discrimination could not be overcome simply through policies that give the victims of discrimination "equal opportunity" to compete for jobs or education. As President Johnson said in announcing an executive order on affirmative action: "You do not take a person who, for years, has been hobbled by chains and liberate him, bring him up to the starting line of a race and then say you are free to compete with all the others, and still just believe that you have been completely fair."[62]

Once again, the question of racial equality created a dilemma for those who govern. On one hand, affirmative action required that race, sex, and ethnic background be taken into consideration and that there be inequality in admissions and hiring decisions. On the other hand, the Fourteenth Amendment said that all citizens were guaranteed the equal protection of the laws. By the mid-1970s, whites who felt they had been the victims of reverse discrimination began to initiate lawsuits claiming violations of that amendment. One of those suits led to the Supreme Court's first major ruling on affirmative action in *Regents of the University of California v. Bakke* in 1978.

Allan Bakke, a white male, claimed that the University of California Medical School at Davis had violated the Fourteenth Amendment and the Civil Rights Act of 1964 because it had admitted students with lower grades and admissions test scores under a special program that set aside 16 of 100 admissions every year for minority applicants. The California Supreme Court upheld Bakke's claim and ordered his admission to the medical school. The Supreme Court ruling in the *Bakke* case has been called "The Decision Everyone Won," and its key findings have been summarized as: "Bakke won, quotas lost, and affirmative action by universities was upheld."[63] Justice Lewis Powell wrote the majority opinion for a Court that was evenly split (4–4) on the key issues. Powell joined one side to overturn the quotas used in the admissions program and uphold the California Supreme Court ruling that

Allan Bakke (top right) graduates from the University of California Medical School at Davis in 1982, four years after the Supreme Court's first major affirmative action ruling, in which "Bakke won, quotas lost, and affirmative action by universities was upheld."

Bakke be admitted and joined the other side to say that schools could use race as a consideration in admissions in order to secure a more diversified student body.

The U.S. Supreme Court has ruled on affirmative action programs more than a dozen times since the *Bakke* decision. It has upheld the constitutionality of some affirmative action programs and struck down others. In these decisions, a majority of the Court has agreed that policies or programs that classify people by race, gender, or ethnic origin need to be reviewed closely by the courts, but also that affirmative action programs carefully tailored to help minorities and women overcome the effects of past discrimination will be upheld.

Two of the five Supreme Court rulings of 1989 regarded by many as a turning point in the history of civil rights in America and by some as the end of the Second Reconstruction were affirmative action cases. In January 1989, the Supreme Court overturned an affirmative action program for awarding public construction contracts in Richmond, Virginia, on the grounds that there was no evidence of actual discrimination in that area.[64] In June 1989, the Court permitted white fire fighters in Birmingham, Alabama, to challenge an eight-year-old, court-

approved affirmative action program for increasing the number of blacks hired and promoted; previously, court-approved programs of this type had been considered immune from legal challenges.[65] Some members of Congress sought to reverse these rulings through the Civil Rights Act of 1990.

It remains to be seen whether the "Supreme Court Rulings Spell End of an Era for Affirmative Action," as the headline in one newspaper read, and whether racial incidents like those discussed at the beginning of the chapter marked a new era of racism. But the disappointment and anger many blacks felt over these and other issues was expressed forcefully by Harvard Law School Professor Derrick Bell. He pointed to the declining percentage of black males in college, the fact that white high school graduates have a median income higher than black college graduates, the increase in racial incidents on college campuses, ongoing discrimination in housing and bank loans, infant mortality rates among American blacks that rival those in developing countries, and Supreme Court decisions that make it harder for blacks to win in the courts. "It seems like blacks don't do too well at the end of centuries," Bell said:

In 1787, the Constitution made them three-fifths of a man and said fugitive slaves can be sent back to their master.

In 1883, the Supreme Court wiped out all the public accommodations and political rights laws of Reconstruction.

Now, 100 years later. blacks are still nowhere near equality, and here comes the Supreme Court again, telling us America is cool.

They're telling us there's no racism. It seems like every 100 years, we get some rights for 15–20 years.[66]

Checkpoint

- Three periods of great importance to racial equality in the United States were Reconstruction, the era of segregation, and the Second Reconstruction.

- The post-Civil War Reconstruction era (1865–1877) brought major advances in the status of black Americans, including the Thirteenth, Fourteenth, and Fifteenth Amendments—which ended slavery, guaranteed equal protection, and gave blacks the vote—and civil rights laws.

- The era of segregation (1880s-1954) was characterized by "Jim Crow" laws that enforced racial segregation throughout society, voting restrictions that denied blacks access to the ballot, and the constitutional doctrines of state action and separate but equal, which provided legal protection for segregation policies.

- The Second Reconstruction (1954–1989?) produced major advances in racial equality in education, public accommodations, voting, and employment. But recent Supreme Court decisions have led some to conclude that this era might be coming to an end.

WOMEN AND OTHER VICTIMS OF DISCRIMINATION

At the beginning of this chapter we talked about incidents of racial and other forms of harassment on college campuses. In 1988, the University of Michigan adopted an antidiscrimination policy and provided punishments ranging from a reprimand to expulsion from school. A university publication defining discriminatory harassment gave as an example a male student remarking in class that women are inferior to men in a given field. A graduate student in psychology then sued the university on the grounds that the antidiscrimination policy violated his First Amendment right to free speech. He cited the example of a male student's remark about women and claimed that research in his field of psychology often considered the possible influence of sex and other characteristics on mental performance. But talking about such research in class, he argued, would be similar to the male student's remarks in the example and would thus be considered a violation of the university's antidiscrimination policy.[67]

The broadcasting of racially offensive jokes on a student radio station in 1987 was the most visible incident leading the University of Michigan to adopt its antidiscrimination policy. But the value of equality underlying the movement toward racial equality in the United States also requires that equality extend to others who historically have been discriminated against because of their sex, sexual orientation, age, or physical handicap. For that reason, the antidiscrimination policies of Michigan and other schools prohibit the harassment of women and other frequent victims of discrimination as well as blacks.

The similarities between race and sex in American politics are instructive. Unlike wealth or education, a person's race or sex is not something the individual can change (except for a limited number of sex-change operations). A person who so desires cannot undertake a "self-improvement" program of work or education to change either trait. In addition, race and sex have historically been used to determine a person's political, economic, and social status in America, to the detriment of both blacks and women. Those who governed early America implicitly excluded blacks from the Declaration of Independence's claim in 1776 that "all men are created equal," but explicitly left out women. In fact, four years after the Fifteenth Amendment had given blacks the right to vote in 1870, the Supreme Court ruled that the Constitution did not give women a right to vote—a decision that stood until the Nineteenth Amendment added women's suffrage to the Constitution in 1920.[68]

In 1973, Supreme Court Justice William Brennan referred to the vote and other issues in describing what he called this country's "long and unfortunate history of sex discrimination," which Brennan said had "put women not on a pedestal but in a cage."

> Throughout much of the 19th century the position of women in our society was, in many respects, comparable to that of blacks under the pre-Civil War slave codes.
>
> Neither slaves nor women could hold office, serve on juries, or bring suit in their own names, and married women traditionally were denied the legal capacity to hold or to convey property or to serve as legal guardians to their own children.
>
> And although blacks were guaranteed the right to vote in 1870, women were denied even that right—which is itself "preservative of other basic civil and political rights"—until adoption of the Nineteenth Amendment half a century later.[69]

There are important differences between race and sex in American politics as well. One is that women are a majority of the general population and of voters in national elections. Another difference is that sex classifications are sometimes used in legislation to *promote* the interests of women, whereas racial classifications—at least prior to affirmative action—were almost always discriminatory. Some examples of "benign" classifications to promote women's interests have been property tax exemptions for widows, time limits for promotion in the military, and alimony laws.

The black civil rights movement has provided a model for those seeking equality for women and others in society.[70] It made political leaders and the courts sensitive to the issues of equality and provided standards for judging other forms of discrimination as well. The civil rights movement's use of demonstrations, boycotts, and other forms of public protest in the 1960s were tactics women's rights advocates had been using since the nineteenth century. But the NAACP's success in using *litigation* to achieve political goals was instructive for women and other groups seeking equality.

Constitutional and Legislative Protection for Women

The Fourteenth Amendment failed to extend specific guarantees to women. For this reason and because it marked the first time the word *male* was introduced in the Constitution (in determining the basis of congressional representation in states denying the vote to "any of the male inhabitants"), feminist leaders opposed the adoption of the amendment. In 1866 feminist Elizabeth Cady Stanton predicted "if the word male be inserted in this amendment it will take a century to get it out again."[71] She was just about right; it took 105 years. A Supreme Court decision in 1971 was the first time the Court used the equal protection clause of the Fourteenth Amendment to overturn a law that discriminated against women. Since then it has often been used to protect women.

Title VII of the Civil Rights Act of 1964 also protects women's rights in American politics. Representative Howard W. Smith, a powerful Democratic congressman from Virginia who opposed the act, had proposed adding the word *sex* to the list of discriminations prohibited to employment, in the hope that this addition would make the bill so controversial that it would not pass. However, in the rush to pass the bill after President Kennedy's assassination, the wording stayed. In the first year of the Equal Employment Opportunity Commission (EEOC), which Title VII had set up to hear cases on employment discrimination, more than one-third of the complaints were charges of sex discrimination.[72] The

Equal Rights Amendment supporters march in New Orleans. Proposed by Congress in 1972, the ERA died three states short of ratification in 1982.

major task of the feminist movement at that time was to get the EEOC to take sex discrimination as seriously as it considered racial discrimination.[73]

Title VII has been credited with paving the way for Congress to finally pass a proposal for the **Equal Rights Amendment** (ERA) in 1972, which had been proposed, but never passed by Congress, dozens of times since its first introduction in 1923. After Title VII had invalidated all protective labor laws for women, labor unions dropped their opposition to the ERA. In March 1972, Congress sent to the states for ratification the following amendment:

1. Equality of rights under the law shall not be denied or abridged by the United States or by any state on account of sex.
2. The Congress shall have the power to enforce, by appropriate legislation, the provisions of this article.
3. This amendment shall take effect two years after the date of ratification.

Thirty of the required 38 states had ratified the Equal Rights Amendment by the end of 1973,

but that same year saw the emergence of a vigorous national "Stop ERA" campaign. Between 1974 and 1977 five more states ratified the amendment, and Congress extended the ratification deadline from 1979 to 1982. No state voted to ratify the ERA after 1977, however, and in 1982 the ERA died three states short of ratification.

Scholars point to a number of reasons why the ERA failed: the difficulty of the amendment process itself, which requires proponents to build a consensus both nationally and in at least 38 states; the inherent weakness of the voluntary organizations supporting the ERA; the opposition by a majority of Americans to major changes in men's and women's roles in society; the exaggerated arguments adopted by both proponents and opponents; the way in which controversial issues such as abortion and women fighting in combat became linked with the ERA (see A Closer Look); and Supreme Court rulings in the 1970s, which broadened the protection of women under the Fourteenth Amendment and made the need for an Equal Rights Amendment seem less pressing to some.[74]

A Closer Look

Interpreting the Constitution: The ERA and Women in Combat ★★★

Between 1972 and 1982, when the question of ratifying the Equal Rights Amendment was before state legislatures, public opinion polls consistently showed most Americans to be strongly against the idea of sending women into combat. ERA opponents knew that and made the most of the issue. Phyllis Schlafly, who led the fight against the ERA, said: "ERA will require mothers to be drafted on exactly the same basis as fathers, and no matter how many there are, it is no step forward to require that half of our casualties be women."[a] A leading congressional opponent of the ERA, Senator Sam Ervin, a Democrat from North Carolina, vividly warned that if the ERA were to pass, "the daughters of America" would be "sent into battle to have their fair forms blasted into fragments by the bombs and shells of the enemy."[b]

In 1970, Representative Shirley Chisholm, a Democrat from New York and a leading ERA supporter, said that the amendment not only *would* require women to be drafted and assigned to combat, but that it *should*: "Each sex, I believe, should be liable when necessary to serve and defend this country."[c] The authors of an article interpreting the ERA, which was published in the *Yale Law Journal* in 1971 and which greatly influenced the thinking of most ERA proponents on this issue, also concluded that women could no longer be ex-cluded from the military draft and combat duty if the ERA were to pass.

Would adoption of the Equal Rights Amendment require that women be drafted and sent into combat? In 1981, the Supreme Court ruled that a provision of the Military Selective Service Act that required males but not females to register for the military draft did not violate the equal protection guaran-tees of the Constitution. In the majority opin-ion in this case, Justice William Rehnquist ob-served: "The case arises in the context of Congress' authority over national defense and military affairs, and perhaps in no other area has the court accorded Congress greater de-ference."[d] The Court decision suggested that Congress would decide the women-in-combat issue and that the Supreme Court would maintain a tradition of deferring to Congress on national defense issues. But ERA support-ers in the states considering ratification never effectively communicated that position. At-tempts to do so lacked credibility, according to Jane Mansbridge: "While most pro-ERA pamphlets suggested that the ERA would not require Congress to send women into combat, the pamphlets never explained *why* this might be so in legal terms."[e]

Meanwhile, Phyllis Schlafly, Sam Ervin, and other ERA opponents hammered away at the women-in-combat issue, and there is no

Did ERA supporters make a political mistake in their handling of the women-in-combat issue?

doubt that the issue caused problems for those supporting the amendment.

Did ERA supporters make a political mistake in their handling of the women-in-combat issue? Should they have done more to let people know about the Supreme Court's deference to Congress on military matters? Should they have accepted a military exclusion to the amendment, as some in Congress had suggested? Or do you think that accepting a military exclusion would give in to antifeminist myths about women's physical inferiority and need for protection, and in doing so undermine the whole purpose of an Equal Rights Amendment in the first place?

[a]Phyllis Schlafly, quoted in Gilbert Y. Steiner, *Constitutional Inequality* (Washington, D.C.: Brookings Institution, 1985), p. 70.
[b]Sam Ervin, quoted in Jane Mansbridge, *Why We Lost the ERA* (Chicago: University of Chicago Press, 1986), p. 264.
[c]Shirley Chisholm, quoted in Steiner, p. 54.
[d]*Rostker* v. *Goldberg*, 453 U.S. 57 (1981).
[e]Mansbridge, p. 83.

Supreme Court Interpretations of Women's Rights

Three Supreme Court cases serve to show the similarities between the development of the law on sexual equality and racial equality.

In February 1870, Myra Bradwell printed an opinion by the Illinois Supreme Court in the *Chicago Legal News*, a law journal she had started two years earlier. Bradwell added a note to the opinion suggesting that what the Supreme Court decision in the *Dred Scott* case was to the rights of blacks, "this decision is to the political rights of women in Illinois—annihilation."[75] The case she printed was her own. Myra Bradwell had taken and passed the Chicago bar exam in 1869, but the Illinois Supreme Court refused to give her a license to practice law. The court said that Bradwell could not honor a contract between an attorney and a client because, under a long-standing legal doctrine then in effect in Illinois and most states, women lost their right to enter into contracts when they married.

Mrs. Bradwell appealed to the U.S. Supreme Court, which upheld the right of Illinois to deny her permission to practice law. In the *Dred Scott* decision in 1857, Chief Justice Roger Taney had talked of a separate political world made up of citizens and said that blacks had been excluded from that world. In 1873, Justice Joseph Bradley wrote an opinion in this case, *Bradwell* v. *Illinois*, which rested on a similar distinction between a public sphere and a private sphere and excluded women from the public sphere:

> The natural and proper timidity and delicacy which belongs to the female sex evidently unfits it for many of the occupations of civil life. The constitution of the family organization which is founded in the divine ordinance, as well as in the nature of things, indicates the domestic sphere as that which properly belongs to the domain and functions of womanhood.[76]

The separation of civil life and family life evident in *Bradwell* and the consignment of women to the latter helps to explain the Supreme Court decision the following year denying that the Constitution gave women the vote and decisions into this century upholding the exclusion of women from jury duty. As recently as 1961 (although the decision has since been overturned), the Court upheld a Florida statute automatically excluding women from compulsory jury duty and observed: "Despite the enlightened emancipation of women from the restrictions and protections of bygone years, and their entry into many parts of community life formerly considered to be reserved to men, woman is still regarded as the center of home and family life."[77]

The Supreme Court decision in *Reed* v. *Reed* in 1971 is a second case that illustrates the development of civil rights law on sexual equality. This was the first time that the Supreme Court said a law discriminating between men and women violated the equal protection clause of the Fourteenth Amendment. At issue was an Idaho law that required courts to appoint fathers rather than mothers as executors of a dead child's estate when both were otherwise equally qualified. In equal protection cases other than those involving race, the Supreme Court had applied a test that generally upheld state laws as long as there was a rational explanation for the classification. But in *Reed* v. *Reed* the Supreme Court unanimously voted to overturn the Idaho law, even though the law had a rational purpose of reducing the work load of the state courts by limiting challenges to the appointment of executors. The Supreme Court decision came as the Senate was debating the Equal Rights Amendment, and it marked the beginning of an era in which the Court would rule most laws that distinguished men from women unconstitutional under the Fourteenth Amendment.[78]

A third case important to the development of women's rights is *Craig* v. *Boren* in 1976. The case involved an Oklahoma statute that set different legal ages for selling beer to men and women (21 and 18 years, respectively). Applying the Fourteenth Amendment, the Supreme Court overturned the Oklahoma statute as a denial of equal protection to males between 18 and 20 years old. Attorneys for Oklahoma argued that the state law was directed toward the legitimate goal of protecting public safety. Statistics showed that men between 18 and 20 years old were more likely than women to drink beer, drive after drinking, and be arrested for drunken driving. Justice William Brennan's opinion for the majority in *Craig* said "classifications by gender must serve important governmental objectives and must be substantially related to achievement of those objectives."[79] The Court recognized the importance of the public safety objective but said it could not accept a conclusion that discrimination by sex helped to achieve that objective. The *Craig* standard is known as the "intermediate test" because it is not as strict as the standard the Court uses in reviewing cases of racial discrimination, but it is stricter than the standard used in cases involving discrimination based on age, sexual orientation, wealth, or physical handicap.

Other groups in America have sought to follow the civil rights examples of blacks and women in American politics. The Supreme Court's commitment to equal protection under the Fourteenth Amendment has led others to seek redress for discrimination based on age, sexual orientation, illegitimacy, status as an alien (noncitizen), or a physical handicap. To date, the Supreme Court has not consistently granted these other victims of discrimination the same degree of equal protection it has blacks and women. But affirmative action programs and antidiscrimination policies such as those discussed at the beginning of the chapter now regularly extend to these groups as well.

Civil Rights and Civil Liberties: An Important Distinction

Many of these groups won recognition of their civil rights by learning from the experiences of black Americans and applying the tactics developed in the black civil rights movement. The black experience in America also sheds light on an essential difference between civil liberties and civil rights—a point that we hope has become clearer in the course of your reading Chapters 6 and 7. Shortly after the end of the Civil War, you will recall, there was a period when four million blacks who had been slaves were

now free but were not yet citizens. They were threatened by a new type of slavery in the form of the Black Codes, social customs, and economic practices. Blacks would not remain free if the federal government simply freed them and left them alone. Only positive action by the federal government would truly change the status of blacks in society, and it came in the form of the civil rights act and constitutional amendments.

Contrast that with the civil liberties policies discussed in Chapter 6. Many of the rights discussed in that chapter are essentially what Supreme Court Justice Louis Brandeis once called "the right to be let alone—the most comprehensive of rights and the right most valued by civilized men."[80] The rights of free expression and privacy discussed in Chapter 6 illustrate the importance of the government letting people alone. But the black experience after the Civil War shows that freedom sometimes requires that government *not* just let people alone, that positive action in the form of civil rights laws is required to maintain that freedom. One scholar makes a similar point in discussing women's rights: "A mere right to be left alone reinforces the traditional liberal dichotomy between the public and private spheres, between the state and the family."[81] That distinction justified the discrimination against women we have reviewed in this chapter.

In 1969 the gay civil rights movement in America was energized by gays fighting back after a police raid on The Stonewall Inn in New York City's Greenwich Village. Twenty years later, a gay-rights activist talked about the changes in that civil rights movement. Her comments, in our judgment, capture the essence of this difference between civil liberties and civil rights:

We began by fighting representatives of government. We still are, in a sense, but I think our demands have changed. The demand at Stonewall was to get off our back.

The demand today is not that government should get off our back but that government should be involved in helping. Now we're saying, "Government, give us the protections we need to live safely in society."[82]

Checkpoint

- Sexual discrimination in the United States has limited the political, economic, and social standing of women in ways that are similar to those of racial discrimination.

- The Civil Rights Act of 1964 and the Supreme Court decision in *Reed* v. *Reed* in 1971 were turning points in the development of legislative and constitutional protection for women.

- Three Supreme Court decisions (*Bradwell*, *Reed*, and *Craig*) demonstrate the changing standards used to judge sexual discrimination and the extension of equal protection guarantees to women over the course of 100 years.

- The Supreme Court continues to review discrimination based on age, sexual orientation, illegitimacy, alien status, and physical handicap, but has not granted these other victims of discrimination the same degree of equal protection it has blacks and women.

- An important distinction between civil liberties and civil rights is that civil liberties limit government action and leave people alone, whereas civil rights *require* the government to act in order to maintain freedom and assure equality.

CIVIL RIGHTS: WHO GOVERNS?

In July 1989, the producer of a documentary film on the civil rights movement responded to the restrictive civil rights rulings of the Supreme Court that year by saying that African-Americans must be prepared to "go to the streets."

If the streets don't work, you go to the vote. If the vote doesn't work, you go to the boycott.

The civil rights movement of the '50s and '60s had a powerful adaptability that we perhaps never realized and perhaps have forgotten.

Sure we need to go to Congress, but people forget that the civil rights movement was also hundreds of economic boycotts.[83]

Supreme Court rulings in 1954 and 1989 marked the beginning and perhaps the end, respectively, of the period of black civil rights advances known as the Second Reconstruction. There were important Supreme Court decisions throughout this era, but there were also other arenas and other forms of political action that shaped the civil rights movement: economic boycotts, sit-ins, street marches, congressional lobbying, presidential speeches and legislative proposals, executive-legislative bargaining, and the implementation of civil rights policies by government officials and private agencies. The three models of governing can help us understand the different stages of the civil rights movement and the variety of political action it included.

Democracy

Later in the book (Chapter 10), we examine the ways in which the civil rights campaign of the 1950s and 1960s was a *grass roots movement*—a form of political participation in which groups of citizens use both conventional and unconventional means (such as lobbying Congress and marching in the streets) to generate visibility, credibility, and popular support in order to force governments to act on the group's goals. Those who believe the democratic model best explains American politics point to the success of grass roots movements to bolster their views. Rosa Parks's attendance at the White House ceremony in 1989 to mark the twenty-fifth anniversary of the signing of the Civil Rights Act symbolized the grass roots nature of the civil rights movement. It reflected a bottom-up rather than top-down view of governing America. The civil rights movement, according to this view, gained a great deal of initial momentum from the actions of a single individual and continued to grow, with more and more people participating in different ways, until those who govern were left with no choice but to pass a civil rights law.

The civil rights movement at times had direct effects, such as economic boycotts or other forms of direct action that created crisis situations in cities and towns and forced the local business community and political leaders to deal with those crises. In addition to these direct effects, the civil rights movement followed the democratic principle of building a public majority in favor of civil rights legislation. Although most Americans opposed the use of unconventional tactics such as sit-ins and demonstrations, media coverage of violent responses by whites to these forms of political action and the positive image of the 1963 March on Washington had created a civil rights majority by 1964.[84]

The democratic model can also help explain the outcome of the campaign to ratify the Equal Rights Amendment in the 1970s. National polls taken between 1970 and 1982 showed that, on average, 57 percent of the public favored the ERA, 32 percent opposed it, and 11 percent had no opinion. These surveys also indicated no clear national trend toward or away from supporting the ERA.[85] But surveys also showed a substantial majority of Americans, including those in favor of the ERA, supported the traditional role of women as homemaker and child rearer. Jane Mansbridge concluded that Americans can favor abstract rights even when they oppose substantive change:

> The campaign against the ERA succeeded because it shifted debate away from equal rights and focused it on the possibility that the ERA might bring substantive changes in women's roles and behavior.[86]

We noted earlier that women and other victims of discrimination in American society have looked to the black civil rights movement of the 1950s and 1960s as a model of successful action. It is the democratic vision of the civil rights movement that these other groups seek to replicate: a grass roots movement that is successful in achieving major policy goals because it has created a supportive public majority.

Pluralism

We can gain further insight into the civil rights movement in the United States by considering it from a pluralist perspective. Two characteristics of pluralism seem particularly relevant to civil rights: (1) multiple sets of political activists operating in different political arenas and (2) a stable political process of continual bargaining among public officials and interest group representatives.

The "powerful adaptability" of the civil rights movement mentioned at the beginning of this section is a response to the multiple points of political action in a pluralist system. Even before civil rights leaders turned to sit-ins and demonstrations in the early 1960s, there was more than one arena of government where they could try to influence policy. What civil rights leaders could not get from the executive and Congress, they were able to get from the courts. The NAACP achieved a courtroom victory in the landmark *Brown* v. *Board of Education* decision in 1954, whereas earlier attempts by the NAACP to get Congress and state legislatures to pass antilynching laws and establish fair employment practices had met with failure.

President John Kennedy's response to the marches and demonstrations of the grass roots civil rights movement in 1963 illustrates the second characteristic: the pluralist view of politics as bargaining among political and interest group leaders. Although, as we noted earlier, President Kennedy did invite some of the leaders of the March on Washington to the White House for a strategy session, he had been concerned for some time that the march might do more harm than good to his civil rights proposals in Congress.[87] He warned civil rights leaders:

> The problem is now before the Congress. Unruly tactics or pressures will not help and may hinder the effective consideration of these measures.
>
> If they are enacted, there will be legal remedies available; and therefore, while the Congress is completing its work, I urge all community leaders, Negro and white, to do their utmost to lessen tensions and to exercise self-restraint.[88]

Kennedy's response to the mass politics and direct action of the civil rights movement was also reflected in his administration's efforts in 1961 to shift the focus of the Student Nonviolent Coordinating Committee (SNCC) from direct action to voter registration. Political scientist Bruce Miroff has suggested that a consistent theme ran through all of the Kennedy administration's responses to the civil rights movement: the attempt to channel the energies of civil rights leaders into conventional pluralist activities, such as voter registration and lobbying Congress, and to buy time for the bargaining among executive and legislative leaders that would produce a compromise bill.[89]

The Power Elite

The democratic and pluralist models are used most often to explain the successes of the civil rights movement, such as the *Brown* decision and the landmark civil rights legislation of the 1960s. But some scholars have attributed those civil rights victories to the changing attitude of white economic elites in the 1950s. Frances Fox Piven and Richard Cloward, for example, say that the rapid development of machine technology and the increased ability of corporations to manage markets during this period reduced the need for cheap black labor and for using racism in the workplace as a way of keeping wages low and slowing unionization. Those changes occurred at the same time that large numbers of unskilled blacks were arriving in northern cities, and corporate elites came to view unemployed blacks as a threat to investments in those cities. Piven and Cloward conclude that the power elite began to speak out against racial discrimination in the 1950s because changes in the economic role of blacks had "undermined the traditional economic uses of racism" and because the "discriminatory attitudes and practices were beginning to create economic and related problems of their own."[90]

The power elite framework also helps explain what some see as a lack of success in the area of civil rights. A major study of black social, political, and economic trends since 1945 reinforces a limited view of civil rights progress in recent years. The study found substantial gaps between blacks and whites in infant mortality rates, poverty, and access to quality education and health care. There had been significant improvements in race relations and the status of blacks since 1945, according to the study's director, but "the status of blacks relative to whites has stagnated or regressed since the early 1970s."[91]

Why do black Americans today continue to be disadvantaged economically and socially? One explanation echoes the reason given for the preservation of slavery in the original Constitution and the regression in civil rights after Reconstruction: Key decisions were controlled by a ruling class or dominant elite whose power was based on the control of economic resources. To have abolished slavery in the original Constitution would have cut the economic legs from under southern members of the power elite, and to have continued Reconstruction policies after 1877 would have severely limited or made impossible the nationwide economic expansionism of the late nineteenth century.

From the power elite perspective, apparent victories for blacks in *Brown* v. *Board of Education* and other cases

> . . . simply imprisoned blacks within a cage of formal equality and failed to address the social and economic disadvantages of black Americans.
>
> What good, according to this way of thinking, does it do to give blacks equal access to a housing market they cannot afford or to an employment market for which they are unprepared?[92]

The power elite perspective on civil rights reminds us of a point discussed in Chapter 3: The American political philosophy of general-welfare liberalism favors *political* equality over *economic* equality. Given that emphasis, it is no surprise that the greatest gains in civil rights have been the political ones of voter registration, voting, and holding political office, and that the greatest resistance to civil rights policies, as evident in recent Supreme Court setbacks have had to do with affirmative action programs designed to overcome economic inequalities in the workplace.

A power elite perspective offers little hope for further civil rights advances in America, but it does help us recognize the central importance of economic equality to civil rights progress in the future. Feminist political leaders stress the importance of economic equality by advancing the doctrine of **comparable worth**, which states that a person's salary should be based on his or her job's value to society rather than whether the person in that job is usually a man or a woman. Comparable worth would require that women in lower-paid jobs traditionally thought of as "women's work" (secretaries, nurses, librarians) be paid the same as men in higher-paid jobs traditionally considered "men's work" (mechanics, truck drivers). A meeting of black political leaders in New Orleans in April 1989 also stressed the central importance of economic equality. For as black political leader Jesse Jackson told that assembly:

> What does it matter if we have 35 mayors presiding over cities which can't borrow money to build and develop?
>
> There is always nobility in fighting for racial and social justice but we are suffering from economic anemia and the absence of a capital flow.[93]

The doctrine of comparable worth recognizes the importance of economic equality and states that a person's salary should be based on his or her job's value to society rather than whether the person in the job is usually a man or a woman.

Checkpoint

- The democratic view of civil rights stresses the grass roots nature of the civil rights movement and its success in building a public majority for civil rights legislation.

- Pluralists emphasize the successful bargaining among civil rights leaders and public officials in the judicial, executive, and legislative political arenas.

- The power elite school sees economic reasons for the changes in racial attitudes among elites and points to the lack of real progress toward economic equality in the United States.

SUMMARY

The Constitution of 1787 did not require the equal treatment of individuals in society and, in fact, supported the institution of slavery. The adoption of the Thirteenth, Fourteenth, and Fifteenth Amendments after the Civil War ended slavery and added the value of equality to the Constitution.

There have been three periods of great importance to racial equality in the United States. The Reconstruction era (1865–1877) advanced racial equality through constitutional amendments and civil rights laws. The era of segregation (1880s–1954) was characterized by racial segregation in both government and the larger society. The Second Reconstruction (1954–1989?) saw major advances in racial equality in education, employment, politics, and public accommodations.

The Civil Rights Act of 1964 and a Supreme Court decision in 1971 were important steps toward reducing sexual discrimination in the United States, which has limited the political, economic, and social status of women in ways similar to racial discrimination. The Supreme Court continues to examine cases of discrimination based on age, sexual orientation, illegitimacy, alien status, and physical handicap, but this has not led to the same degree of equal protection that it has for blacks and women.

Democratic explanations of civil rights in America focus on the grass roots nature of the civil rights movement and its success in creating a supportive public majority in the 1960s. Pluralists are more likely to focus on the bargaining process among public officials and interest groups in a number of political arenas. Those who see a power elite in control of American politics focus on the economic reasons for a change in racial attitudes among elites and on the lack of real progress in achieving economic equality.

KEY TERMS

Equal protection
State action
Black Code
Reconstruction
  amendments
Segregation
"Jim Crow" laws
Literacy tests
White primary
Separate but equal
Affirmative action
Equal Rights
  Amendment
Comparable worth

FOR FURTHER READING

Richard Bardolph, *The Civil Rights Record* (New York: Crowell, 1970). A collection of original documents and commentary that traces the history of black Americans and the law.

Fletcher Blanchard and Faye Crosby, *Affirmative Action in Perspective* (New York: Springer-Verlag, 1989). Analyzes the impact and effectiveness of affirmative action programs.

Sara Evans and Barbara Nelson, *Wage Justice* (Chicago: University of Chicago Press, 1989). Looks at the effects of the women's movement on the workplace and evaluates comparable-worth policies.

Richard Kluger, *Simple Justice* (New York: Random House [Vintage Books], 1977). A case study of the landmark *Brown* v. *Board of Education* decision.

Jane Mansbridge, *Why We Lost the ERA* (Chicago: University of Chicago Press, 1986). Analyzes the campaign for the Equal Rights Amendment and what it teaches us about gender politics in America.

Howard Meyer, *The Amendment That Refused to Die* (Boston: Beacon Press, 1978). Looks at the history and meaning of the Fourteenth Amendment for governing America.

Part Three

The People and Government ★

Every body should have Freedom.

The United States capital building

The Formation and Expression of Public Opinion

Chapter 8

- ★ Democracy and Public Opinion: Two Views
- ★ Analyzing Public Opinion
- ★ Political Socialization: The Learning of Attitudes
- ★ Measuring Attitudes: Public Opinion Polls
- ★ The Expression of Public Opinion: Who Governs?

**H**ow much influence should public opinion have in American government? The answer depends partly on how informed and wise you think it is. Many observers believe that the people, being fully capable of self-government, can make enlightened decisions if given the chance. Others are more skeptical; they believe that average citizens tend to be poorly informed, indifferent to national affairs, and too preoccupied with personal interests and problems to be trusted with much political power. To decide which side is right one has to take a hard look at the content, quality, sources, measurement, and expression of public opinion. ■

In June 1985, the Public Agenda Foundation, a not-for-profit research organization, convened a panel of citizens to ask them about nuclear proliferation, the spread of atomic weapons to more and more countries throughout the world. Representing a cross section of people living in and around Baltimore, the group was told to pretend that the President and Congress sought its advice. In particular, the participants were asked:

What should be America's policy about what we will call proliferation; that is, about the bomb going to other countries that don't have it? What should we do? What should be our policy?[1]

The responses provide a microcosm of the quality and content of public opinion in the United States:

Lou: Well, I feel we were the first. We learned our way. Let these people learn their way . . . the thing of it is you have to use that term, "man your battle station," [by] which I'm referring to . . . you have to be ready for protection on your own part. But

as far as secrets go or how to put this thing together, you keep everything within.

Don: I think that we should actively—I don't know what I mean by "actively" at this point—but we should actively try to discourage other people, other nations from developing this particular technology . . . I'm looking at the list [of countries that might acquire nuclear arms] and thinking "jeez" I don't want those crazies to have it. But, on the other hand, they're looking at us and saying "those crazies already have it." The fewer fingers on the button the safer we are.

Marcie: I think the United States should worry about theirself and keep their own secrets. Keepin' it ourself and the heck with . . . let 'em do it on their own.

Kelly: I'm not really sure of the question . . . let's keep it ourselves.

Carolyn: We can't stop . . . if, you know, we have a car—I'm just simplifying things—we build a car, we have cars, you can't stop other countries from wanting this type of transportation. They want to go ahead with it. That's on the level you asked. On my level, I say and I've always said this, that whoever drops it that's the end anyhow. That's it. So, I mean, once it's off, it's off. That's it.

At first, asking carpenters, clerks, and football coaches for their advice on a subject as complex as nuclear proliferation seems a waste of time. These replies suggest that the average man or woman is not sufficiently informed, articulate, logical, or farsighted to render meaningful counsel to a head of state or legislature. (The participants, for example, tended to underestimate the number of nations having access to nuclear technology and overestimate the ease with which they could convert it to weapons.) It is apparently a question about which they have little information, and their answers tend to come from the gut ("once it's off, it's off"; "let 'em do it on their own"; "I'm not really sure"). Better leave the matter to the experts, one is inclined to think.

On second thought, however, this reaction is far removed from the ideals outlined in Chapter 1. In a representative democracy, for example, public opinion guides and controls decision makers. On an issue as vital to national security as nuclear proliferation, what the electorate believes and wants should be foremost in the minds of elected officials. Far from delegating this power to a handful of specialists, the people ought to play a prominet role in decision making.

To know who does and who can govern, therefore, requires a hard look at public opinion. What do the masses want? How informed are they? Do their preferences and ideas measure up to the standards set by democratic theory? If not, why not? Even if many individuals currently lack civic virtues, can society be reformed so that they can obtain the education and motivation to participate more fully in community and national affairs, or are they always going to remain on the sidelines?

DEMOCRACY AND PUBLIC OPINION: TWO VIEWS

From the birth of the American Republic, its citizens have been at the same time idolized and cursed, respected and distrusted, admired and feared, praised and damned. The question of the people's capacity for self-government certainly troubled the Constitution's authors. Cynical about human nature, Alexander Hamilton split his compatriots into two camps:

> All communities divide themselves into the few and the many. The first are the rich and well born; the other the mass of the people. The voice of the people has been said to be the voice of God; and however generally this maxim has been quoted and believed, it is not true in fact. The people are turbulent and changing; they seldom judge or determine right. Give therefore to the first class a distinct, permanent share in government. They will check the unsteadiness of the second. . . .[2]

Aghast at the prospect of "ochlocracy" (mob rule), Hamilton strove to limit access to the levers of power. Direct democracy, he once declared, was a "disease" and a "poison."[3] Were he alive today, he would no doubt pale at the idea of plain folk participating in life-and-death decisions like nuclear proliferation.

Countless others have shared Hamilton's skepticism. Walter Lippmann, one of the foremost journalists of the twentieth century, worried that democracies inevitably decay. The reason? Unrestrained public opinion. Statesmanship, Lippmann argued, requires wisdom, patience, discipline, deep knowledge of national and world affairs, and willingness to weigh the long-range consequences of an act against its immediate benefits—virtues that the public lacks. Hence, popular opinion and enlightened leadership invariably collide. Unfortunately, Lippmann concluded, the public was often "destructively wrong at . . . critical junctures" of American history and was sufficiently powerful that politicians had no choice except to "placate, appease, bribe, seduce, bamboozle, or . . . manipulate'' their constituents.[4] This pandering to the masses created a "morbid derangement" of government, a potentially fatal "malady" unless people realized that society remains free only so long as its leaders have sufficient latitude to exercise their judgment.[5]

Others, however, hold the populace in higher esteem. Thomas Jefferson wrote to a friend in 1816: "We both consider the people as our children. But you love them as infants whom you are afraid to trust without nurses; and I as adults whom I freely leave to self-government."[6]

Jefferson also has allies. One astute observer of American politics, V. O. Key, Jr., agreed that democracies might decay but questioned whether the cause lay with the public. Look instead, he recommended, at political leaders:

> . . . democracies decay, if they do, not because of the cupidity of the masses, but because of the stupidity and self-seeking of leadership echelons. Politicians often make of the public a scapegoat for their own shortcomings; their actions, they say, are a necessity for survival given the state of public opinion. Yet the opinion itself results from the preachings of the influentials of this generation and of several past generations.[7]

Skeptics Versus Optimists

Out of this debate two schools of thought emerge. One, the **skeptics**, maintain that human frailties make mass participation in politics both impractical and undesirable. Ordinary people simply lack the requisite knowledge, skills, and motivations to act responsibly.[8] They place immediate gratification of wants ahead of the long-run interests of the commonwealth. Conceding that the populace is the ultimate source of political authority (popular sovereignty, in the language of Chapter 1), these doubters nevertheless believe that the affairs of state are best left to trained, experienced, and dispassionate public servants. Periodic elections, interest groups, the media, and town meetings suffice to keep leaders in line. A large dose of apathy is healthy for the country, in fact, since the masses can be overly demanding and tempestuous and, unless reined in, are likely to trample political institutions. In a nutshell, this school takes a dim view of the public's capacity for self-government.[9]

The skeptics' arch rivals, the **optimists**, recognize the public's many shortcomings but still insist that most citizens have more intelligence and decency than critics realize. Furthermore, the common people's flaws result not from inborn weaknesses but from defective social and political institutions that limit information and discourage participation. The body politic can govern itself responsibly if given the chance, and therefore "average" men and women should become more, not less, involved in public affairs.

The debate between the two schools is particularly heated in the area of foreign affairs. The disagreement is worth exploring because so much of what government does involves international relations and because it is an area the common person often avoids.

The Moody American and Foreign Policy

What do average people know and think about the world? When Gabriel Almond posed that question more than 30 years ago, he arrived at an unsettling answer. Americans, Almond concluded, react to foreign policy in a moody, rather than thoughtful, way. The mood may vary from indifference to fatalism to anger, but it was almost always a "superficial and fluctuating response."[10] Almond did not intend to be uncharitable to his compatriots; he simply believed that they were so involved with their immediate private concerns that they lacked the time and energy to stay abreast of world events.[11] Nevertheless, writing as if describing a smoldering volcano that periodically erupts in a storm of fire and ash, he described the public mood as "essentially . . . unstable" and prone to "dangerous overreactions."[12] Others have shared his concern. George Kennan, a principal architect of U.S. foreign policy after World War II, said:

> . . . a democracy is uncomfortably similar to one of those prehistoric monsters with a body as long as this room and a brain the size of a pin . . . he is slow to wrath—in fact, you practically have to whack his tail off to make him aware that his interests are being disturbed;

Protestors demonstrating against U.S. aid to the government of El Salvador. Scholars and politicians debate whether the average citizen is sufficiently informed and qualified to participate directly in major decision areas like foreign policy.

but once he grasps this, he lays about him with such blind determination that he not only destroys his adversary but largely wrecks his native habitat.[13]

Another postwar diplomat, W. Averell Harriman, feared that his fellow citizens would simply wash their hands of world affairs and "go to the movies and drink Coke."[14]

Hard numbers seem to back up these impressions. Charles W. Kegley and Eugene Wittkopf cite data indicating considerable ignorance of and disinterest in foreign affairs: 28 percent of the respondents in 1964 did not know that the Communists controlled the mainland of China; in 1950 and again in 1966 only about one-third of the samples could identify the secretary of state; and less than half of the individuals interviewed in 1978 said they were "very interested" in reading about international relations.[15]

To the skeptics the lesson is unmistakable. Since the masses are simultaneously tempestuous and poorly informed, their involvement in decision making would only muddy the water. Better that they stay out of the way so leaders have the room to conduct the delicate negotiations essential for successful diplomacy.

Optimists, however, challenge the mood the-

ory. Changes in public attitudes are quite reasonable and understandable, they say, and should not be attributed to shifts in "mood." Instead, specific international events and political circumstances "quite naturally" shape citizens' views of what policies to pursue.[16] Similarly, William Caspary and John Mueller, two political scientists working independently, contend that the masses have consistently backed their government's foreign policy. In Caspary's words, "American public opinion is characterized by a *strong* and *stable* 'permissive mood' toward international involvements."[17]

A key question then, is: How much can ordinary citizens actually do to influence the decisions that ultimately shape their lives and futures? Since the skeptics and optimists answer so differently, it is extremely important to find out who is right. Public opinion lies at the heart of democratic theory. To understand who governs and indeed decide how much democracy is possible in a large industrial nation, one must start with common people's attitudes and beliefs, not the Congress or the bureaucracy or the courts. First, though, it is helpful to have a conceptual framework for analyzing attitudes, because the public's opinions are not as easy to fathom as they first seem.

Checkpoint

- Public opinion is the heart and soul of an ideal democracy. In order to decide how well the American system works, one has to look at the attitudes and behavior of the common citizen.

- Controversy exists about the quality of public opinion. Skeptics fear that the masses are too unruly, shortsighted, and unpredictable to be entrusted with much power. Others are more optimistic. They believe that ordinary citizens have, or can develop, the skills to participate intelligently in public affairs.

- Opinions vary on the public's capacity to understand and take part in foreign policymaking. The masses have been called moody because their opinions seem to shift so drastically and rapidly, but others believe the swings are understandable in light of what is going on in the world and what leaders are saying and doing about these events.

ANALYZING PUBLIC OPINION

Public opinion is the collection of millions of individual attitudes, much as a flock of geese consists of thousands of separate birds. Like a flock, public opinion at times seems coherent, organized, and heading toward a specific destination; at other times it mills about, going nowhere in particular. Before trying to make sense of the whole, however, it is perhaps best to examine the individual birds.

A Framework for Studying Public Opinion[18]

Simply stated, an **attitude** is a *tendency to favor or disfavor an object, such as a person or policy.*[19] Because people like or dislike things in varying amounts, it makes sense to label attitudes (or opinions—we use the terms interchangeably) "strong," "weak," or "indifferent." In some instances support for a program is a mile wide and an inch deep, while in others people believe in a cause so passionately that they will lay down their lives for it.

Note also that an opinion is directed toward an **attitude object**. The point may appear obvious, but it is surprising how often even experts lose sight of the fact that opinions refer to objects and how easily two or more objects get mixed together, making the interpretation of responses difficult.

Attitudes do not materialize out of thin air. No one wakes up in the morning loving or hating President Bush having gone to bed the night before totally indifferent to him. Rather, people have an opinion for reasons, and it is as important to discover the underlying reasons as it is to measure the feeling itself. One way to picture an attitude is to imagine it resting on a set of beliefs about an object and evaluations of these beliefs. A **belief** represents what a person thinks is true of the attitude object, while an **evaluation** is a judgment about the belief (is it favorable or unfavorable?).

An example reveals that this idea is not very complicated. Figure 8.1 shows how two different people might think about George Bush. In Figure 8.1(a) a hypothetical individual has favorably evaluated beliefs about Bush and the overall impression is thus positive. Figure 8.1(b) shows the beliefs and evaluations of someone who is ambivalent about the President; some beliefs are favorable, others less so, resulting in a neutral opinion. Individuals, in other words, can have both favorable and unfavorable beliefs.

Notice that beliefs and evaluations of beliefs are an individual matter. What one person knows for certain may be a matter of dispute to another. Each diagram, therefore, describes a specific man or woman. Note also that beliefs may be right or wrong. Objectively speaking, it is possible to misperceive a candidate's personality traits or real position on issues. If, to take a farfetched case, 60 percent of adults think Bush is a Democrat, one naturally wants to know why so many people are wrong. In any event, every citizen acts on the basis of perceptions or beliefs,

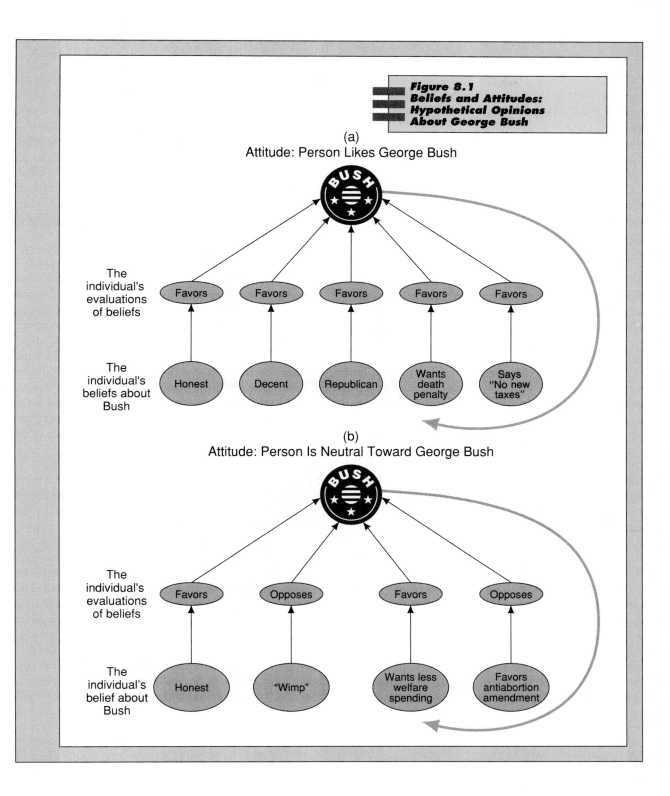

Figure 8.1
Beliefs and Attitudes:
Hypothetical Opinions
About George Bush

(a)
Attitude: Person Likes George Bush

The individual's evaluations of beliefs

The individual's beliefs about Bush

(b)
Attitude: Person Is Neutral Toward George Bush

The individual's evaluations of beliefs

The individual's belief about Bush

so whether they are true or not they have to be taken into account. Finally, attitudes themselves can affect beliefs, as shown by the curved arrows in each figure. This "feedback" can lead to **selective perception**, the tendency to see, hear, and remember what one wants to see, hear, and remember.[20] Thus, someone who admires President Bush is likely to believe the best about him; someone who detests him, the worst.

To summarize, attitudes do not exist in a vacuum but are the product of beliefs and evaluations. Beliefs may be held with varying degrees of certainty. Depending on both the object and the individual, an opinion is tied to a handful of beliefs (say, five to ten), some or all of which may be favorable or unfavorable. This analysis leads to these generalizations:

- To the extent that a person firmly holds a large number of positive beliefs about an object, he or she will have a favorable attitude toward it. (The opinion will be favorable regardless of the accuracy of the beliefs.)
- Conversely, if the beliefs are mostly negative, the attitude will be unfavorable.
- Finally, if few or no beliefs exist, or if the positive ones roughly equal the negative ones, the individual will be more or less neutral.

Applying the Framework to Public Opinion

Why take this excursion into psychology? Without a road map, public opinion frequently resembles a dark and mysterious forest. (Even with such a guide it is often contradictory and confusing.) Here is a typical example. A series of polls sponsored by the Advisory Commission on Intergovernmental Relations asked random samples of Americans: "Suppose the budgets of your state and local governments have to be curtailed, which parts would you limit most severely?" Of the programs listed, only about 9 percent of the respondents chose "aid to the needy." One could interpret the result as an overwhelming endorsement of government assistance to the poor. But when the question was rephrased to read "public welfare programs,"

the proportion calling for cuts shot up to 40 percent.[21]

Are the results inconsistent? Do they show that Americans do not know their own minds? Not necessarily. In the first place, the attitude objects differed considerably. One question referred to "welfare" whereas the other mentioned "the needy."

Second, and more significant, the beliefs underlying these two attitudes may have been drastically different. Since pollsters do not normally measure the beliefs, one can only guess, but it seems likely that many individuals equate *welfare* with fraud, waste, mismanagement, unwillingness to work, getting something for nothing, indolence, and a host of other vices. Seen in this light, eagerness to reduce welfare spending seems perfectly understandable. But the mention of the needy perhaps triggers images of disabled veterans, hungry children, the elderly, the homeless, and orphans. Which of these sets of perceptions is more accurate is not the issue. The point is that the second set of responses may flow from a different set of beliefs than the first.

Figure 8.2 shows how a hypothetical respondent might view the matter. If we measure only attitudes, not the underlying beliefs, then we miss the factors that make the opinions less contradictory.

Another reason for stressing the structure of attitudes is that they should not be taken for granted. The beliefs that produce them must come from somewhere, and it is essential to find out where. This quest leads to the realm of "belief creation," the process by which people acquire their perceptions. It is logical to ask, for instance, *why* so many individuals think that welfare programs are overrun with chiselers. Who told them so?* Is it really true? The attitude framework demonstrates that beliefs deeply affect attitudes; knowing about the sources or causes of beliefs is as important as knowing about the opinions themselves.

---

*Chapter 3 suggests that unfavorable attitudes toward welfare programs stem partly from the widespread acceptance of general-welfare liberalism. To appreciate this point, make a list of the things that you think are true of people receiving welfare. Then, check these beliefs against the information in Chapters 2 and 17.

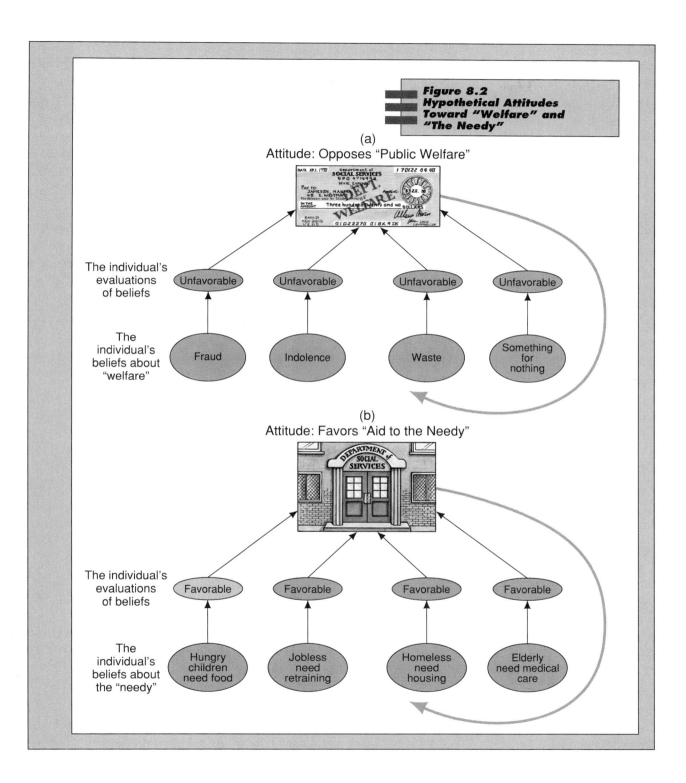

Figure 8.2
Hypothetical Attitudes Toward "Welfare" and "The Needy"

(a)
Attitude: Opposes "Public Welfare"

The individual's evaluations of beliefs: Unfavorable | Unfavorable | Unfavorable | Unfavorable

The individual's beliefs about "welfare": Fraud | Indolence | Waste | Something for nothing

(b)
Attitude: Favors "Aid to the Needy"

The individual's evaluations of beliefs: Favorable | Favorable | Favorable | Favorable

The individual's beliefs about the "needy": Hungry children need food | Jobless need retraining | Homeless need housing | Elderly need medical care

Checkpoint

- An attitude is a predisposition to like or dislike something, such as a candidate, a political leader, a policy, or an institution.

- Attitudes rest on beliefs about the object and evaluations of these beliefs. Some beliefs may be favorable, some unfavorable. In order to make sense of public opinion it is necessary to take beliefs into account.

POLITICAL SOCIALIZATION: THE LEARNING OF ATTITUDES

Once social scientists realized that attitudes rest on a foundation of beliefs, they began searching for the sources of perceptions about government and politics. The search eventually led back to childhood, to the preschool and kindergarten years, when boys and girls first discover the existence of a president, a flag, a nation, an entire world beyond their homes and neighborhoods.

In the 1960s behavioral scientists vigorously studied children and politics because nearly everyone assumed that the "political self is made, not born."[22] Although genes and physiology set limits, a young mind was considered a blank slate upon which society ultimately wrote its traditions, values, and history. What children carried into adulthood must have, according to this line of reasoning, started with **socialization**, the process of learning a society's norms, customs, and roles. The **agents of socialization**—the institutions that transmit social and political values and beliefs—include the family, schools, peers, the mass media, and the community.

This training obviously continues throughout life. But because 5- to 10-year-olds are so impressionable, because they depend heavily on others for information, because their cognitive and emotional capacities develop unevenly, and because socializing agents like the family are so pervasive, scholars felt certain that basic political identities began developing in those early years.[23]

Moreover, socialization was originally thought to have consequences for entire political systems as well as for individuals. By learning and accepting a culture, a child turns into a loyal citizen ready to participate in the polity. When the process functions smoothly, each new generation grows up accepting the outlines of the existing order which, in turn, fosters governmental stability and harmonious social relationships. In this kind of climate, institutional changes occur gradually and peacefully. But in some societies socialization may be ineffective in producing universal loyalty to a nation or a specific type of government and, in extreme cases, may even work against the current regime, leading to demands for radical changes in the status quo. Such demands often create upheaval, as in China and Eastern Europe in the late 1980s. Thus, political training, socialization theorists used to argue, helps either to preserve or to upset the existing polity.[24]

These propositions, however, are not as evident and simple as they once appeared,[25] and the more social scientists observed and interviewed children, the more they realized that boys and girls are not passive subjects who unquestioningly absorb everything they are told. Instead, they display an uncanny ability to discern truth from slogans, reality from fantasy, and fact from fiction. Moreover, the relationship between socialization and political stability and instability has been hard to establish.

In spite of these problems, socialization still demands attention, since it partially explains a salient fact about politics in the United States: The public's behavior seems to be a bundle of contradictions. Citizens are free to participate in campaigns and elections, yet relatively few do so. Education and information are readily available, yet political misinformation abounds. Most voters idolize the Constitution and resist fundamental changes in it, yet they tend to distrust officeholders and on occasion seem willing to in-

In 1989, Chinese students demanded fundamental economic, social, and political reforms. Despite decades of sustained and overt socialization efforts, the communist government in China had failed to build support for its regime and had to stop the demonstration with force.

fringe on the civil liberties of unpopular groups. Americans usually rail against big government and impersonal bureaucracy, yet they just as adamantly demand the very programs that make bigness and bureaucracy inevitable.

A review of several developments in socialization research may unravel one or two of these mysteries. It also underscores the controversy raised at the beginning of the chapter: To what extent do cultural and political institutions encourage average citizens to accept the responsibilities of self-government?

What Children Learn About Politics

Influenced by their families, schools, peers, the mass media, and other agents of socialization, humans develop a political awareness at an early age, perhaps earlier than commonly thought. Indeed, as A Closer Look (see pp. 242–243) suggests, children have a keen sense of the controversies going on around them. Their knowledge may be limited and stereotypical, but they still recognize major political actors and the drama and bitterness of politics.

The youngsters in A Closer Look tell us a number of things about socialization. First, 9-, 10-, 11-year-old boys and girls absorb as if by osmosis the surrounding dominant culture. Second, their reactions—the bitterness and joy, the resignation and confidence, the despair and optimism—accurately mirror, one suspects, their social, economic, and political circumstances. Schools, for example, reinforce, or at most counterbalance only slightly, the child's own percep-

A Closer Look

Children Talk About Politics ★★★

Robert Coles, a psychiatrist and author, has spent most of his career listening to children talk about themselves, their hopes and fears and dreams, and especially about their nation, its government and leaders and their place in it. Here is what a few of them told him:

A 9-year-old black boy, a Mississippi share-cropper's son: Maybe; I don't know. [He has been asked whether he would vote if he were old enough; the interview took place in the 1960s when the vast majority of blacks in the South were barred from voting.] My daddy says what's the use, because even if everyone of us voted, the whites would still run Mississippi and still own everything.... The teacher told us the President is a good man ... and he's trying to do good by the white, and by the colored. To tell the truth, I don't believe her. My sister laughed when I told her about what the teacher said. My sister said that if I believe everything I hear teachers say, and the gov-

ernor, and the President—then I'm still a baby.... Well, I told her I try on something I hear, to see if it fits, but I know when it doesn't, and I throw it away real fast, because I'll tell you, if you're colored, you'd better learn the difference between a piece of real meat and streak o'lean [salt pork]. ... And I'll bet it's mostly streak o'lean that they hand out to you, a sheriff or a governor or a President. If they'd be handing out good meat, it would be better. But like my daddy says, there's nothing you can expect to get for the asking from white people, so it's good the civil rights people are getting the governor mad and worrying the President, even if the teachers say we should obey the law and salute the flag and America isn't second to any country. If you're not white, you're second, and a lot of whites, they're second, too; and my sister says that's the scene and if you don't know what scene you're watching you're dumb, dumb, dumb.

tions. The sharecropper's son, even at age 9, displays a great deal of alienation. On the other hand, the little girl from Boston, the product of a well-to-do family, knew about President Nixon's involvement in the Watergate scandal but did not let this knowledge shake her faith in the system: "The President made a mistake. It's too bad. You shouldn't do wrong; if you're President, it's bad for everyone when you go against the law. But the country is good."[26]

Finally, as individuals grow up they unquestionably acquire more sophisticated and perhaps realistic ideas about politics and occasionally develop radically different outlooks on life. Yet

early socialization experiences leave an indelible mark on most of us, and in order to understand how and why people acquire the beliefs and attitudes they do, we need to explore this process in more detail.

NATION, LOYALTY, AND STABILITY In spite of their suspicions of "politics" and "politicians," the vast majority of Americans love their country. They revere its institutions, willingly obey its laws, and dutifully attend to its rituals. Speaker after speaker may berate the Supreme Court's decisions, but no one advocates its abol-

A 9-year-old son of a lawyer: The man who's elected [President] will be a good man; even if he's not too good before he goes to Washington, he'll probably turn out good. This is the best nation there is, so the leader has to be the best, too.

A 9-year-old girl living in an affluent Boston suburb: It's better to be born here [in America]. Maybe you can live good in other places, but this is the best country. We have a good government. Everyone is good in it—if he's the President, he's ahead of everyone else, and if he's governor, that means he's also one of the people who decide what the country is going to do. . . . If there is a lot of trouble some place, then the government takes care of it.

A 12-year-old Hopi Indian girl: We are nothing to the white people; we are a few Hopis, but they are millions of Americans, millions of them. My father told me that their leader . . . ends his speech by saying that God is on their side; and then he shakes his fist and says to all the other nations: You had better pay attention, because we are big, and we will shoot to kill, if you don't watch out. . . . Everything, everyone is the white man's; all he has to do is stake his claim. They claimed us. They claimed our land, our water; now they have turned to other places. My uncle, who knows the history of our people, and of the United States, says it is a sad time for others; but when my little brother began to worry about the others, our uncle sighed and said: "At least our turn is over. Don't be afraid to be glad for that." They are not really through with us, though. They come here—the police, the red light going around and around on their cars: visitors to our reservation from the great United States of America. "There they are," my father always says. He tells us to lower our eyes. I have stared at them and their cars, but I will never say anything, I know that. If their President came here, I would stay home or come to look at him, but not cheer. I have seen on television people cheering the President. In school they show us pictures of white men we should cheer. I never want to. I don't think the teachers expect us to *want* to; just to pretend. So we do.

Source: Children's quotations from the book, The Political Life of Children; *copyright © by Robert Coles. Used by permission of Atlantic Monthly Press (Boston, 1986), pp. 29–30, 32, 33, and 43 (Author's italics.)*

ition. Congress might provide Johnny Carson and Arsenio Hall with enough jokes for a lifetime, but an independent legislature, one of the main components in our system of separation of powers and checks and balances, enjoys universal support. Since no dictator or secret police enforce this level of respect and loyalty, where does it come from?

Partly from socialization, political scientists think.[27] Allegiance to one's community and nation emerges at an early age and, in the absence of a major upheaval like a civil war or a depression, remains intact for life. Not every segment of society shares this enthusiasm—listen once more to the black and Hopi children—but most Americans start out believing the United States is the "best nation" and "It's better here."

For those who treasure order and stability, these positive socializing agents and experiences bring a wealth of benefits. If citizens accept their government's institutions, procedures, and decisions, they don't form the kind of cleavages that can lead to turmoil and bloodshed. Take something as commonplace as elections. In this country, whatever disappointment the losers suffer, they do not take their anger into the streets; instead they accept the legitimacy of the outcome and begin planning for the next election.

Children generally develop positive attitudes toward authority figures, a phenomenon called the benevolent leader syndrome.

By the same token, the winners do not celebrate their victory by throwing their opponents in jail.

Given this tradition, it is difficult for many Americans to understand those countries where voting is often just a pretext to stage demonstrations, assassinate opposition leaders, bomb campaign headquarters, or embark on terrorist raids. In such settings the political system receives less popular acceptance partly because people identify with ethnic, religious, regional, or ideological factions more than with the central government.

Of course, one's view of peace and stability depends on where one stands. Learning loyalty to a government is easy for the son of a well-to-do lawyer or the daughter of an affluent Boston family. But what about the Hopis? The one we heard from contended that they are forced to live permanently at the bottom of the social and economic ladder.

With these ideas in mind, social critics sometimes damn those institutions and practices that cement the status quo firmly in place. For them, preventing justified change is as damaging to the human spirit as political upheaval. Writing in the depths of the Great Depression, Reinhold Niebuhr, an American theologian, condemned the "hypocrisy and self deception" of those who feared violence and radical change but who at the same time lived comfortable and secure lives while millions of their fellow citizens endured "misery and "semi-starvation."[28] Stated differently, how much you value the *stabilizing* effects of socialization depends on how happy you are with the way things are.

AUTHORITY: THE BENEVOLENT LEADER   The social scientists who first mapped the child's political mind came across mainly positive beliefs and attitudes about political authorities. Like the lawyer's son and the girl living near Boston, 7- to 11-year-old children invariably seemed to idolize the president, the mayor, the police officer. They saw these figures as kind, caring, and all-powerful leaders who dedicated themselves to protecting their country and helping others. Listen to some of the grade-school students Fred Greenstein, a political scientist, interviewed.[29]

The president does good work. [Sixth-grade boy]

The mayor sends men to build parks for us and make our city a good one. [Fourth-grade girl]

I think that he [the president] has the right to stop hard times before they start. [Fifth-grade girl]

The president gives us freedom. [Eighth-grade girl]

The mayor helps everyone to have nice homes and jobs. [Fourth-grade boy]

The president worries about all the problems of all the . . . states. [Seventh-grade boy]

Greenstein labeled this pattern of perceptions and sentiments the **benevolent leader** syndrome to emphasize how the youngsters view public of-

"Sanitizing history?": Helen Keller's struggle to overcome blindness and deafness and her success as a writer and speaker are widely celebrated in textbooks while her feminist, socialist, and pacifist thoughts go largely unmentioned.

ficials as essentially benign and caring. His findings contrasted sharply with the frequently hard-boiled and cynical attitudes adults harbor about politicians.

The discrepancy between young and old, in fact, led to endless speculation about its causes. Were mothers and fathers shielding their offspring from the unsavory side of politics? Did schools gloss over corruption and ineptitude? Were communities so determined to foster patriotism that they insisted on making saints out of mortals? Did children's psychological development go through stages that prevented them

from seeing a president or a mayor as anything other than a parent figure?

All these propositions were put forward and tested at one time or another, and each seemed to contain a grain of truth. Educators, for example, have been charged with covering up the unpleasant aspects of the lives of famous citizens in an attempt to perpetuate traditional American values and myths. Jonathan Kozol, a proponent of this viewpoint, illustrates the proposition by showing what schoolchildren learn about Helen Keller.

If an eighth-grade class consults the *World Book Encyclopedia*, a common reference work found in most school libraries, it learns that Helen Keller, born in 1886, was blind, deaf, and mute from infancy and that with the assistance of Anne Sullivan she overcame these handicaps to become a famous author, lecturer, and friend and confidante to presidents, kings, queens, and other celebrities. (A broadway play and movie, *The Miracle Worker*, chronicled her triumphs.) As presented in standard sources, her life celebrates the belief in the power of individual courage and determination, an especially compelling lesson in the United States where the theme of unlimited opportunity dominates the popular culture.

Each of these "facts" is true. But they hardly cover Helen Keller's whole story. What is not revealed in civics books is that she was also what today would be called a radical, pacifist, and feminist.[30] Among her other pronouncements she declared: "The foundation of society is laid upon a basis of . . . conquest and exploitation . . . [and] is bound to retard the development of all"; and "The output of a cotton mill or a coal mine is considered of greater importance than the production of healthy, happy-hearted [and] free human beings." The economic system, she maintained, was safeguarded by organizing the "workers into an army which will protect [the capitalists'] interests." Voting? "We the people are not free. Our democracy is but a name. We vote? What does that mean? We choose between Tweedledum and Tweedledee."[31]

Kozol suspects that schools and textbook publishers consciously "decontaminate" historical figures such as Helen Keller by presenting only the bland, trivial, noncontroversial—the really "safe"—parts of their lives and thoughts by concealing their more extreme and upsetting words and deeds. It is one thing, Kozol suggests, to describe to adolescents Keller's fortitude and determination in the face of adversity—traits very desirable in a capitalist society; it is quite another to ignore her political doctrines that call into question that society's economic, social, and political foundations.

Is Kozol's interpretation of the benevolent leader syndrome too farfetched? Do schools censor history? Do they try to cover up dissent and dissatisfaction and portray America as essentially a happy family?* Plenty of social scientists think Kozol goes too far and offer less drastic explanations of the benevolent leader phenomenon.

In the first place, not all the lessons children learn are sugar-coated. Timothy Cook analyzed award-winning children's books published between 1941 and 1981 to find out what messages they conveyed about authority.[32] These works, he concluded, do not paint a glowing picture of society or its leaders. In fact, far from being kind, helpful, and all-powerful, "[p]olitical authority is treated with suspicion rather than deference."[33] Since the protagonists in the stories are apt to face an impersonal, unfriendly, and threatening world, they have to rely on their own wits, not benevolent leaders, to solve their problems. More than anything, then, the books' "lessons" pertain to self-reliance and self-sufficiency and thus reinforce individualism, a pillar of general-welfare liberalism (see Chapter 3).

Other social scientists pointed out that the research that unearthed positive feelings about political authorities first appeared at a particular time and place. Greenstein and his associates began their studies in the late Eisenhower years (1956–1960), a time noted for its domestic tranquility and prosperity. In these happy times it was only natural that school-aged children would have positive, favorable beliefs and attitudes about the nation's leaders; there was little strife to cause them to think otherwise. In addition, Greenstein's subjects were drawn mainly from white, middle-class society. Their parents thrived under a government whose officials seemed to be men and women of honesty and goodwill.

Would children interviewed during more unsettling times exhibit the same positive attitudes and beliefs? Although the evidence is mixed, it appears that the Vietnam War and the Watergate scandal that caused President Nixon to resign shook, but did not destroy, young people's faith in their leaders and government. In a follow-up investigation conducted at the height of Nixon's impeachment struggles, Greenstein observed a "capacity to criticize the president" and to recognize that he might try to evade the law. Nonetheless, only 5 percent of his new sample had unfavorable images of the President as compared to 45 percent positive, 44 percent neutral, and 2 percent mixed.[34]

Taking a third position that casts doubt on both Kozol's "decontamination" thesis and Greenstein's benevolent leader hypothesis, Coles finds that the children he talked with have sensitive political antennas and are able to discount much of what is "idealized" by parents and teachers. His conversations with preteenagers convince him that they are sufficiently alert to "historical pieties" and they can "connect what they see or hear to a larger vision—a notation of those who have a lot and those who have very little."[35]

Coles's point is supported by research on the sons and daughters of poor whites in Appalachia and of blacks in urban ghettos.[36] Even while they are still quite young, these children mirror the hostility and despair of their surroundings. Greenstein himself came across a youth—an 11-year-old black—who contrasted sharply with his white middle-class peers:

Boy: I said [of the President] he's stupid and he don't know what he's doing.

Interviewer: What does he do?

Boy: . . . He doesn't let people do what they want to do. He's always putting people in jail or somethin'. . . . He's suppose to help people, and he suppose to

---

*It might be interesting to find out by comparing the information about famous Americans found in middle and high school libraries with what is available in colleges.

Interviewer: keep peace in the world, but he isn't doing that . . .

Interviewer: Suppose a foreign child asks you what is the President of the United States?

Boy: A rat.[37]

The Family and Political Learning

Because children are so immersed in family life, one might expect them to inherit their parents' political values. To some extent they do.

Political scientists regard party identification or partisanship—the feeling of closeness to a party—as a kind of sun around which a person's attitudes and beliefs revolve. It illuminates perceptions of candidates, issues, and events; it is a source of constancy in an ever-changing climate of politics; and it provides energy and motivation to participate. In the 1950s and 1960s, when asked about their party preferences, most teenagers mentioned the same one as their parents. (See Figure 8.3 on p. 248.) The son of a Democrat tended to consider himself a Democrat as well or perhaps an independent who leaned toward the Democrats. The children of independents tended themselves to be middle-of-the-road, while Republicans followed in their parents' footsteps. Inheritance of party identification, in short, used to be one of the givens in the study of political behavior.

The data in Figure 8.3 come from the early 1970s, however, and in recent years families have been less successful in transmitting party identification. One report, for instance, found that whereas 25 years ago about three out of four people adopted their parents' partisanship, the proportion had dipped to less than two in three by the middle of the 1970s.[38] Thus, although most young Americans have roughly the same political leanings as their parents, the relationship is less strong than it used to be. Researchers also discovered that opinions on economic and social issues can affect the development of political affiliations. The daughter of staunch Republicans, for example, may abandon her family's party if she feels closer to the Democrats on matters like abortion and women's rights.[39]

A Generation Gap? Nevertheless, this pattern does not necessarily represent a trend toward a **generation gap**, or the overt rejection of parental political philosophy and values. Indeed, social scientists as a rule find relatively little intergenerational political conflict in the United States. If the generations war against each other, they normally pick different battlegrounds such as life-styles, dress, tastes in music, and grooming habits. An eleventh-grader is not likely to join a radical political movement because his father refuses to lend him the car on Saturday night. Even during the war in Vietnam, when college campuses were alive with antiwar demonstrations and draft card burnings, most of the participants were not rebelling against their parents' values. The bulk of the protesters, in fact, came from "liberal" families.[40]

Although young people's tastes in music, clothes, and appearance sometimes upset their parents, there is almost no political rebellion between the generations in the United States.

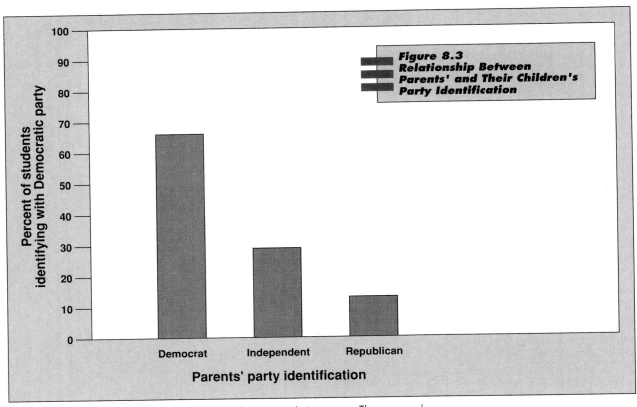

**Figure 8.3
Relationship Between
Parents' and Their Children's
Party Identification**

Adolescents tend to have the same party identification as their parents. The sons and daughters of Democrats, for example, tend to identify with the Democratic party.
Source: Adapted from data presented in M. Kent Jennings and Richard G. Niemi, *The Political Character of Adolescence* (Princeton, N.J.: Princeton University Press, 1974), p. 41.

None of these remarks means that one generation is simply a political clone of the previous one. Each age cohort (that is, people of the same age) grows up with its own distinctive traits and experiences. M. Kent Jennings and his colleagues at the University of Michigan interviewed a sample of high school seniors and their fathers and mothers in 1965. They then doggedly tracked the respondents for the next 17 years, reinterviewing them in 1973 and again in 1982. This persistence allowed them to compare one generation with another—children and their parents—and at the same time observe the maturation of teenagers into young adults. Among other results, the Michigan team discovered that:

- The younger generation was and continues to be less committed to political parties (as suggested by the rise in the number of self-classified independents).
- Partly as a consequence of their weaker attachment to parties, these people are more apt to vote a split ticket (vote for both Republicans and Democrats instead of casting a straight party ballot) and to support third-party candidates.
- The level of partisanship of the young increased with time but still has not reached their parents' level.[41]

This pattern, if it persists, spells bad news for the major parties. Democrats and Republicans will have fewer dedicated loyalists and may therefore have to face greater split-ticket voting, more maverick candidates, declining financial backing, increased swings in electoral support, and less party line voting in Congress. The real beneficiaries of the new generation's tepid partisanship may be third parties and interest groups, organizations that grow in stature and potency as traditional parties weaken.

In short, it appears that youngsters do not automatically inherit their mothers' and fathers' political views. Families no doubt pass along very broad orientations toward government, such as the acceptance of particular parts of general-welfare liberalism, but the transmission of specific attitudes and beliefs is far from perfect. The widespread lack of interest in government and current events may explain why. Parents who are apolitical simply don't take the time and trouble to instruct their offspring in their political views; other areas of life seem more important. Consequently, political socialization, in the words of one social scientist, "does not teach children just what they ought to be; at best, it teaches them what they ought *not* to be."[42]

ARE THE YOUNG BECOMING CONSERVATIVE?
One frequently hears that new voters (those born after 1964) are, to the extent that they express political leanings, more conservative than the "flower children" who came of age during the turbulent 1960s or workers who lived through the Great Depression of the 1930s. The new generation supposedly seeks secure, well-paying jobs and believes that big government and welfare spending stand in the way of those aspirations. It also disapproves of the apparent decline in the United States' international prestige and competitiveness. Proponents of this thesis offer President Reagan's appeal among first-time voters as evidence of this conservatism among the young.

To test this proposition and at the same time give many readers an opportunity to compare their attitudes with Americans of their own age, consider Table 8.1 (p. 250). If young adults are more conservative than older people today or than young people a generation ago, they have managed to hide the fact from pollsters. As the table suggests, the vast bulk of the young adopt middle-of-the-road positions that do not differ greatly from the older respondents. About 40 percent, for instance, consider themselves "moderates" (nearly the same proportion as the older group), and the number of liberals just about equals the number of conservatives. Furthermore, "strong" partisans, whether Democrat or Republican, are a minority.

Similarly, on a battery of spending issues the 23-or-younger category takes moderate positions and even seems liberal on some items. Many feel that the nation spends too much on defense but too little on the environment or health care. Like most Americans, they exhibit little of the enthusiasm for cuts in government spending that one usually associates with conservatism.

Schools and the Creation of Leaders and Followers

Anyone who studies the American electorate soon realizes that many people with firm beliefs and attitudes seldom translate them into action. Whatever their state of mind, nearly half of the voting-age population fails to vote and only a handful take part in election campaigns. However angry or satisfied, informed or misinformed, less than one out of ten Americans ever calls or writes a senator or representative.*

Indeed, politics in America is perhaps best described as a spectator sport: A few players run up and down the field while the vast majority sit in the stands cheering or booing or daydreaming. When it comes to complicated issues such as nuclear proliferation, most citizens seem by turns uncertain, powerless, bored, mystified, and alienated. They prefer to leave decision making to experts.

But who picks the experts?

The educational system is an obvious place to look for the answer. Here, conventional wisdom asserts, is where elites are made. From the democratic perspective, education is indispensable for building character, instilling leadership qualities, and promoting the values of freedom and equality.

Research supports this interpretation, because study after study shows that higher levels of formal education are associated with political participation, tolerance of dissent, knowledge of

---

*See Chapter 10 for more complete statistics.

Table 8.1

Selected Political Attitudes by Age, 1988

		Age	
		23 or Younger (%)	24 or Older (%)
Party Identification	Strong Democrat	16	16
	Democrat & independent— leaning Democrat	32	35
	Independent	12	12
	Republican & independent— leaning Republican	30	27
	Strong Republican	10	10
Ideological Identification	Liberal	27	28
	Moderate	39	37
	Conservative	34	35
Protecting the Environment[a]	Too little	69	68
	Right amount	25	28
	Too much	6	4
Improving Nation's Health[a]	Too little	70	68
	Right amount	29	28
	Too much	2	4
Improving Condition of Blacks[a]	Too little	39	37
	Right amount	44	46
	Too much	18	17
Military and Defense[a]	Too little	21	15
	Right amount	41	43
	Too much	38	42
Social Security[a]	Too little	54	55
	Right amount	41	39
	Too much	7	6

[a]Question: "We are faced with many problems in this country, none of which can be solved easily or inexpensively. I'm going to name some of these problems and for each one I'd like you to tell me whether you think we're spending too much money on it, too little money, or just about the right amount."

Source: Based on data from the National Opinion Research Center, University of Chicago, *General Social Survey, 1988*.

current events, interest in elections and government, efficacy (the belief that one's involvement in public affairs is both possible and worthwhile), and a host of other indicators of good citizenship.[43] A person with at least some college training is almost certain to be more knowledgeable and active than people who did not graduate from high school. Educated men and women, in short, possess the characteristics vital to successful self-government.

Yet significant questions remain: Since education is universally available and since the majority of the population has a high school or college diploma, why are only a comparative handful of people involved in public affairs? Why do activists become active? Does everyone start with an equal chance and some drop out simply because they choose to? Or is there a mechanism that "sorts" the masses into leaders and followers?

One line of reasoning contends that schools, intentionally or not, systematically segregate children, turning a few into political activists while making spectators out of the rest. Equally dismaying to many commentators, social class rather than merit underlies the selection process.

Nearly everyone has attended or knows of high schools that separate students into college prep, vocational, and general education tracks. Edgar Litt found a similar sorting mechanism in the Boston area. Litt, a sociologist, compared the civics curriculums in three communities: (1) an upper middle-class neighborhood whose adults are both affluent and politically active; (2) a lower middle-class place with moderate levels of participation; and (3) a working-class section of mostly nonpolitical inhabitants.[44] Based on a review of textbooks, instructional materials, and prevailing community norms in each district, he concluded that students were being politically segregated and trained to play different roles in politics. Students in the working-class community were offered "training in the basic democratic procedures without stressing political participation." In the lower middle-class schools, students received similar training along with an

Some social scientists believe that schools socialize students to play different political roles. Young people at the bottom of the social ladder are encouraged to be more passive than those at the top, who learn leadership skills.

emphasis on the responsibilities of citizenship but "not on the dynamics of public decision-making." Litt found that "only in the affluent and politically vibrant community . . . are insights into political processes and functions of politics passed on to those who, judging from their socioeconomic and political environment, will likely man those positions that involve them in influencing or making political decisions."[45]

Litt's point is that effective citizenship involves more than learning state capitals or the name of the governor or the number of Supreme Court justices. It requires peering into the soul of politics, knowing that its lifeblood is power, that individuals and groups win and lose bitterly fought battles, that the real rules are not always the written ones, that appearance and reality constantly converge and diverge like a camera going into and out of focus, that organization charts of the legislative process do not tell even half the story of how laws are passed. Most of all, effective civics education means acquiring the understanding and confidence that issues— whatever their technical complexities—are comprehensible in at least general terms, that they are political in nature, and that being political they can and should be decided democratically, not by "specialists" and "authorities."

Sadly, Litt concludes, communities and schools track their pupils not on achievement or intelligence criteria but on the basis of social class membership. Others have expanded this theme. What Richard Merelman calls a "hidden curriculum" lies beneath the day-to-day lessons most children sit through. It teaches "hierarchy, not democracy."[46] Robert Hess and Judith Torney discover that schools emphasize "compliance" to the law while understating the skills needed to participate effectively in government. In their words, the educational process tells students that they have the right and obligation to vote, but "does not offer . . . sufficient understanding of [the] procedures open to individuals for legitimately influencing the government."[47]

Perhaps the most provocative claims about how American education turns most pupils into passive followers is Samuel Bowles and Herbert Gintis's *Schooling in Capitalist America*. These two economists maintain that the primary pur-

pose of public schools is to train workers to accept and perform occupations required by capitalism, not to enlighten them so that they can take part meaningfully in democracy.[48] Schools, according to them, are the handmaids of capitalism, not democracy. They breed conformity, acceptance of hierarchy, obedience, and apathy, traits that may be helpful in the office or on the assembly line but that effectively discourage popular participation. In this light it is little wonder that individuals manifest confusion, misinformation, and temerity when asked to talk about nuclear proliferation: The real message behind their instruction has been to acquiesce to experts and not try to analyze a controversy and decide on their own.

Anyone feeling that Bowles and Gintis and others stretch the argument too far might ponder this point. Most of the cries for educational reform made over the last ten years are really motivated by economic concerns: The United States needs better schools so that it can compete against technically advanced nations such as Japan. Taxpayers, for instance, hear that "a high-quality educational system is a vital part of the infrastructure of nations that seek to remain competitive in a technologically driven global economy."[49] One almost never comes across demands for educational improvement as a means to increase voter turnout or enhance citizenship.[50]

Most readers of this book have recently gone from high school to college and are thus in an excellent position to reflect on these matters. Spend a moment asking what schools really taught. Did they encourage students to question (not reject, but question) authority? To challenge conventional myths and symbols, however comforting and reassuring? To explore radical, even hateful, ideas for any bits of truth they might contain? Did they supply them with the confidence and skills necessary to understand public policy?

More to the point, compare these school experiences with the experiences of students who dropped out or started working on construction jobs or joined the marines or just hung out. What lessons did they learn in school? Most likely they learned how to spell *Democrat* and *Republican* rather than what the parties stand for. Most likely they memorized the names of candidates rather than discovered that campaigns frequently involve a great deal of sound and fury but little substance. Most likely they watched cartoon characters march a bill through a diagram of the Congress on the way to becoming a law rather than read about what goes on behind closed doors where lobbyists and representatives hammer out deals and trade votes for favors.

Checkpoint

- The study of childhood socialization, the process of learning a society's norms, values, customs, and roles, helps explain why different individuals develop their attitudes and beliefs.

- Many youngsters, especially those from middle- and upper-class backgrounds, acquire positive feelings about political authorities, while the children of minorities and disadvantaged families are more likely to display cynicism and hostility.

- Some critics claim families and schools try to "sanitize" public figures and institutions and, in so doing, make students less aware of their true qualities and history.

- There is relatively little political conflict between the generations in the United States: Survey data suggest that young people have roughly the same views as older individuals, especially on social and environmental issues.

- Schools seem to play a role in sorting children into leader-follower roles. Civics education for upper-status children encourages them to be politically active, whereas students from the working class may learn to be mainly spectators or only occasional participants.

MEASURING ATTITUDES: PUBLIC OPINION POLLS

Public opinion polls have become the main tool of journalists, politicians, and scholars to peer into the mind of the average American. Indeed, polls are as important to social scientists as test tubes are to chemists. Furthermore, their results justify all sorts of claims about the public, including its capacity to govern. Since knowledge of public opinion leans so heavily on polls, it is essential to understand what they can and cannot do.

A **public opinion poll**, or sample survey, involves asking a limited number of people about their preferences. Because pollsters incorporate only a tiny fraction of the population in their tabulations, one might doubt their validity. This common criticism turns out to be groundless. Surelite Match Company does not evaluate its product by striking every match to see if it burns. Besides the obvious problem of consuming the entire inventory, the procedure would be exceptionally costly and time consuming. Instead, the company tests a *random sample* of matches, the number being only a small proportion of their output. If the testers find that 2 percent of the sample matches are defective, they generalize to the entire batch, saying that approximately 98 out of every 100 strike properly. Thus, a sample leads to information about the whole from which it is drawn. The secret is not the size, but the quality of the sample: It has to be truly *representative* to be informative.

Pollsters apply exactly the same principle. Rather than asking everyone in the country about tax reform, they interview a randomly chosen sample of adults. Most polls reported in the media contain between 500 and 2000 respondents. Even though these figures represent a minuscule part of the population, the results can be legitimately generalized to the public at large. There is a margin of error—sampling error, the experts call it—but by drawing a representative sample and using statistical theory, pollsters can measure this error.[51] When a newspaper reports that 57 percent of its sample favors raising the minimum wage, the "true" percent-

A Closer Look

The Science and Art of Polling ★★★

To be useful, a poll or survey has to be based on a *random sample* of a population. (Here the word *population* refers to a specific group of individuals such as "all males over 18 living in Iowa"; it does not necessarily mean all of the people in the United States.) *Random* means that the sample is drawn in such a way that each member of the population has a known probability of being included. In the ideal case, each person would have an *equal* chance of being chosen, but for practical and technical reasons it is usually not possible to attain the ideal. As a consequence, polling firms use approximate methods such as first drawing a sample of counties, then of areas within each of those counties, then blocks of houses within these areas, and so on until the required number of individuals can be contacted.

Polls are also expensive, especially when they involve face-to-face interviews. Many organizations, therefore, use telephone surveys. Computer programs select residential phone exchanges (in proportion to the population of the region) and then add random digits to make a list of complete phone numbers. Random digits help make sure households with unlisted numbers are included. The lists can then be given to interviewers who will make the calls or even to another computer that automatically dials the number and records the information.

Obtaining a truly representative sample of Americans is no easy chore. Sizable segments of the population are either transient (students away at college, young men and women in the armed forces, or families on vacation) or institutionalized (patients in hospitals or prisoners in jail). Equally troublesome, some geographical areas, such as rural communities, are underrepresented because they are hard to reach or because polling firms have trouble recruiting interviewers to visit them. Women are frequently overrepresented because more females than males tend to be home during the day or answer the phone at dinner time.

Surprisingly, the size of the sample does not affect its validity. The larger the sample, however, the more confidence one can have in a particular estimate. (In technical terms, the larger the sample the smaller the sampling error.) To take a common case, suppose the objective of the poll is to predict the outcome of an election. With a sample of 500 people, the prediction might be 6 or 7 percentage points too high or too low. The guess will not necessarily be invalid, just lacking in preci-

age might be a bit higher or lower, but the paper's report is accurate to within, say, 3 or 4 percent. (A Closer Look provides more information on how representative samples are chosen.)

Thus, surveying is a sound research tool. For any particular question the pollster may not know to the hundredth of a percent how the voters feel, but sampling a representative population provides more than just a ballpark guess.

Problems in Polling

Despite the adequacy of the method, polls are still not infallible. At least three factors—timing, question wording, and opinion intensity—affect their validity and interpretation.

TIMING Social scientists know that a president's popularity soars during an international

sion. Having a larger sample reduces the margin of error (to perhaps 3 or 4 percent) and so increases one's confidence in the prediction of the election results.

As the text indicates, even though polls are based on statistical theory and presented in technical jargon, they lend themselves to misinterpretation. Here are a few tips to keep in mind when reading the results:

- Try to ascertain the complete breakdown of *all* the responses, including even the seemingly insignificant ones such as "depends" or "don't know." These numbers indicate how well the respondents comprehended the questions and how divided they really are. Hearing that 62 percent of a sample opposes a constitutional amendment prohibiting abortion is not especially helpful (and can be misleading) if the "undecided" and "not sure" categories are missing. One is in the dark, for example, about the 62 percent: Is it 62 percent of the *total* sample or 62 percent of those expressing an opinion? They are not the same. If one out of four people leave the question blank, then the 62 percent is not two-thirds of the population but a much smaller proportion. Unhappily, locating this information is not always easy, because pollsters do not always provide it.

- Examine questions for compound objects. Here is a typical case: In an effort to count how many Americans supported U.S. involvement in world affairs, respondents were requested to agree or disagree with the statement, "We shouldn't think so much in international terms but concentrate on our own national problems and building up our strength and prosperity here at home."[a] When responding, a person could have in mind staying out of international affairs or "building up our strength" which, to confuse matters even further, might mean military *or* economic strength.

- Always note dates, sample sizes, and the poll's sponsor. These facts often convey as much information as the data themselves. It is a fact of life, for instance, that organized groups underwrite national surveys not to further anyone's understanding of people's attitudes but to promote their causes by claiming that the public supports them.

[a]Lloyd A. Free and Hadley Cantril, *The Political Beliefs of Americans* (New York: Touchstone Books, 1968) p. 197.

crisis. No matter how blundering or ineffectual the commander-in-chief's actions may be, Americans tend to "rally around the flag."[52] In the aftermath of an American bombing raid on Libya in 1986, President Reagan's approval rating, already very high, soared to 70 percent. Although only one in five respondents had any hope that the raids would stop terrorism, the confidence in the President's handling of foreign affairs reached an all-time high for him.[53] These results do not suggest that people are fickle but simply demonstrate that ordinary citizens, just like elites, respond to dramatic headlines. The timing of a poll, then, can affect its results.

QUESTION WORDING The old saying, "Ask a dumb question, get a dumb answer," illustrates the second factor affecting the interpretation of survey data: question wording. Every competent pollster realizes how sensitive respondents are to the way questions are framed.[54] In a clear example, the *New York Times* and CBS inquired about abortion. Their interview started with the question: "Do you think there should be an amendment to the Constitution prohibiting abortions, or shouldn't there be such an amendment?" The amendment was resoundingly defeated by 62 to 29 percent. Later on, however, the *same* individuals were asked: "Do you believe there should be an amendment to the Constitution protecting the life of the unborn child, or shouldn't there be such an amendment?" This time around, 50 percent supported the proposal while only 39 percent opposed it.[55]

A contradiction proving the masses are confused and mercurial? On the contrary, this case shows the significance of beliefs and evaluations.

The wording of a question often influences the answer. About half of Americans supported free speech when asked if the government should "forbid" speeches against democracy . . .

. . . but only a quarter of Americans supported free speech when the question was changed—by one word—to ask whether the government should "allow" speeches against democracy

Courtesy of Discover, May 1984.

By altering the wording, a poll, usually inadvertently, arouses different beliefs that are attached to and support an opinion. An amendment "prohibiting abortion" is one thing; it becomes something quite different when connected with "protecting the life of the unborn child." Presumably the second question in the *Times*/CBS questionnaire expanded or perhaps created new beliefs about abortions. Also, its wording suggests an appropriate response, for who is against unborn children? In view of its "reactive" nature, this item does not give a clear picture of where Americans stand. One could naturally make the same charge about the first question. The lesson is that poll results, no matter how scientifically dressed up, have to be interpreted thoughtfully, a point brought home by A Closer Look.

OPINION INTENSITY   Social scientists have discovered a third complication in reading polls: people hold opinions with varying degrees of conviction, or **opinion intensity**. Those individuals who feel strongly about an issue give consistent answers when asked about it at different times. Others, though, feel less intensely and appear to change their minds randomly as time passes.

This shallowness causes serious problems for researchers trying to find out what voters want. Robert Erikson and his colleagues cite research suggesting that pollsters can easily be fooled into thinking the public prefers a policy when in fact it probably has no real knowledge or beliefs at all.[56] In one study, a sample was asked about the Agricultural Trade Act of 1978, an obscure piece of legislation that the investigators assumed no one would know. Nearly a third of the people did venture an opinion, even though their attitudes probably rested on no beliefs. A second sample answered the same question but with the phrase "or do you not have an opinion" added to the choices. When put this way, 90 percent of the responses fell in the "no opinion" category. Erikson and other scholars interpret results like these as demonstrating that people will sometimes conjure up "doorstep," or made-up on the spot, attitudes because they fear appearing uninformed or disinterested.[57]

How common are attitudes that rest on few or no beliefs and are not held with much conviction? Opinion analysts disagree, but the phenomenon is doubtlessly widespread. Thus, one should be justifiably cautious when looking at polls that deal with technical, vague, or little-known issues.

Checkpoint

- Opinion polls are based on random samples selected from a relevant population. The samples can be relatively small so long as they are representative of the population.
- The timing of polls is crucial, because opinions, especially toward political leaders, tend to change along with events.
- Question wording is even more important. How a question is phrased determines the attitude object and hence the beliefs and evaluations it evokes.
- Opinion intensity is still another consideration. Many people will answer a question without having a strong opinion or even an informed one.

THE EXPRESSION OF PUBLIC OPINION: WHO GOVERNS?

Americans hold opinions on a vast array of subjects. One may regard these attitudes as informed or misinformed, practical or utopian, profound convictions or seat-of-the-pants responses. Yet the deeper question is the influence these opinions have on public policy: In what ways and to what extent does government listen to the voice of the people? Asking this question, of course, takes us to the heart of democratic theory and the issue of who governs. Let's consider

some plausible descriptions of the connection between public opinion and public policy.

Direct Influence

In a direct democracy citizens themselves govern; in a representative system they govern indirectly through their elected representatives who are held accountable in periodic elections. In either case, though, the public's preferences should theoretically have a **direct influence** on the polity's laws, goals, and priorities. How well does the United States fit this standard?

At first glance, the query appears to be self-answering. "Even a dictatorial regime," V. O. Key, Jr., wrote, "cannot remain oblivious to mass opinion."[58] So it seems obvious that in a society characterized by open discussion and free elections politicians have no choice but to heed their constituents' wishes. Ignoring or even inaccurately gauging the electorate's mood can cost legislators their jobs. For additional evidence, look at what the people want and what they receive. Poll after poll shows how favorably regarded many social welfare policies have become over the years, and Congress has dutifully allocated billions of dollars to them. What better proof, then, that public opinion is in command!

On paper, this interpretation agrees nicely with democratic theory. It may nonetheless be overly simplistic and unrealistic, and it is worth examining three additional explanations of the linkage between public opinion and policy.

Contingent Influence

A number of controversies burn in the public's mind: unemployment, pollution, abortion, crime, and drug abuse, to mention only a few. Other issues, such as agricultural subsidies or genetic engineering, are more complicated or mysterious or touch relatively few people and hence generate few or no opinions. On these matters the vast majority of voters are usually indifferent and fall into the "middle-of-the-road," "don't know," or "undecided" categories. Attitudes, as mentioned above, can be characterized by their strength, or intensity.

Political preferences can be arrayed along another dimension as well: the extent of agreement. On a few issues *consensus*, or overwhelming agreement, prevails. Nearly everyone supports social security, for example. Other controversies, however, create *polarization*, or the division of the public into opposing camps.

In view of this diversity, a set of general propositions about the influence of mass attitudes on decision making comes to mind: On issues about which people feel intensely and are in substantial agreement, representatives have little leeway; they can ignore their constituents' wishes only at their peril. Social security is an example of a program that few politicians dare tamper with. In such cases, the public shapes policy. On the other hand, when the populace is divided, confused, or indifferent, leaders have much more room to maneuver and special-interest groups readily get their way. Finally, if opinions are polarized into two or more less evenly divided factions, policymakers may avoid the issue altogether for fear of antagonizing one group or the other.

This classification, it goes without saying, is not exhaustive. Yet it demonstrates that the effects of public opinion are *contingent* upon the prominence of the issue and how attitudes are distributed throughout society. Hence, we use the term **contingent influence** to describe the connection between what citizens want and get from government. A few governmental activities affect so many individuals that their preferences are decisive, while on a wide range of subjects fragmentation, lack of concern, or misinformation weaken—if not eliminate—the links between the electorate and its elected officials.

Gun control illustrates the contingent nature of the impact of public opinion. Polls consistently show broad backing for gun control legislation. Yet for years senators and representatives have refused to crack down on gun owners or manufacturers. The reason? The majority in favor of restrictions on firearms is not sufficiently aroused and mobilized to challenge the "gun lobby," a coalition of groups that feel passionately about the issue and are willing to fight tooth and nail to prevent the enactment of any gun laws. In these circumstances, officeholders find it expedient to listen to the zealous minority rather than the apathetic majority.

A different kind of research backs up the contingency influence idea. In the late 1950s, Warren Miller and Donald Stokes conducted a unique study in which they interviewed a sample of members of the House of Representatives *and* their constituents. This procedure allowed them to correlate hometown preferences in three policy areas—civil rights, social welfare spending, and foreign affairs—with the attitudes and votes of the representatives themselves.[59] They discovered that the salience, or importance, of an issue to voters increased the impact of people's preferences on the behavior of their representatives. In the area of civil rights, the matter of greatest popular concern at the time, the lawmakers were likely to know and follow their constituents' wishes. But in the realm of social welfare spending (like aid to education), party affiliation rather than constituency pressure best explained congressional behavior, while in the international arena—a matter of even lower salience to the average voter—representatives could make up their own minds without the folks back home breathing down their necks.

Other studies carried out since then arrive at roughly the same conclusions, although they differ on important details.[60] Among the factors that increase a constituency's hold on its representatives are: how closely elections are held to the time legislators cast their votes on an issue, the electoral competitiveness of the representatives' districts, and the degree to which officeholders feel they *should* listen to the people rather than act on their own as "trustees."[61]

Although pluralist political scientists do not use the phrase *contingent influence*, they would undoubtedly agree that it fits their theory like a glove. Pluralism, remember, contends that the essence of politics is group struggle; the public, for the most part, stays on the sidelines. Of course, on certain occasions an overwhelming consensus develops behind a policy, as in the case of social security, and the people's voice will be decisive. But these instances are relatively rare. More often (as in the case of gun control) the populace is insufficiently knowledgeable or motivated to challenge interest groups, which have the political arena to themselves. In these cases organizations and politicians thrash out their differences without feeling direct constitu-

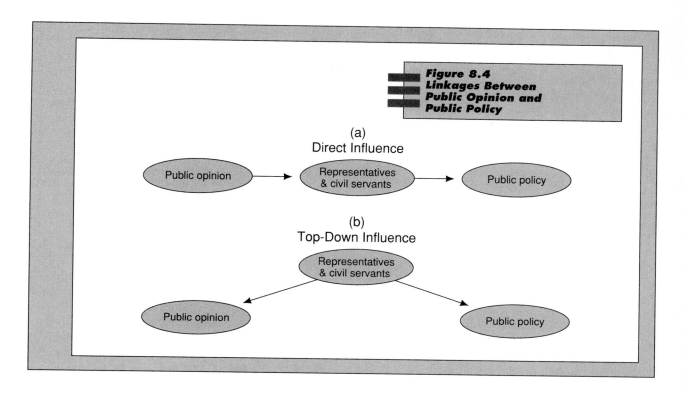

**Figure 8.4
Linkages Between
Public Opinion and
Public Policy**

(a)
Direct Influence

(b)
Top-Down Influence

ency pressure. Briefly stated, pluralists agree that the impact of public opinion is contingent on the nature of the issue.

Top-Down Influence

Many scholarly papers written on the influence of public opinion contain a diagram like the one in Figure 8.4(a).[62] The specific form and labels of the diagrams differ from study to study, of course, but the arrows—indicators of influence—invariably point from left to right, suggesting that voters control to some degree their elected and appointed officials. Yet the elite school of American government asks if the arrows don't point in the opposite direction, at least on major issues (Figure 8.4(b)). Do political leaders in those cases shape public opinion? Is the direction of influence **top-down**? If so, one has to be slightly pessimistic about the existence of real democracy in the United States.

How accurate is Figure 8.4(b)? Everyone knows that legislators actively try to shape their constituents' perceptions and opinions. Although some campaign funds go for polling, to find out what the voters are thinking, the lion's share pays for advertising—for selling candidates and their platforms. These sales pitches are considered a natural and desirable part of the electoral process.

What is less well known is that the same selling mentality characterizes policymakers as well. *The Capital Source*, published by *National Journal*, lists the addresses and telephone numbers of dozens of cabinet departments and federal agencies. In every instance the booklet includes the name and number for a "public affairs" office. This unit supposedly exists to inform the people about the bureau's activities. But, as often as not, its real function is *selling* policies to the public. Nor are these small-time operations. Taken together, they spend millions of dollars and employ thousands of workers, not to measure and record attitudes but to mold them.[63] The government's effort to promote the peaceful uses of atomic energy illustrates these attempts.

In the late 1940s the Atomic Energy Commission (AEC), the agency charged not only with providing nuclear weapons to the military but also with promoting the peaceful uses of the atom, began worrying about the public's reactions to the new technology. A Gallup survey conducted after World War II discovered that even though 43 percent of the sample agreed that "in the long run, atomic energy will do more good than harm," nearly a quarter of the respondents disagreed and 35 percent remained uncertain.[64] If the people were not intimidated by atomic fission, neither were they enthusiastic about it. Concerned that communities across the United States might resist industrial applications of nuclear technology, the AEC began a campaign to create a receptive public that would "assume [its] atomic-age responsibilities."[65]

Presumably these "responsibilities" meant going along with the agency's projects and not becoming paranoid about fallout, radiation, and catastrophic accidents. It was an era, after all, when many engineers envisioned using nuclear devices to excavate canals and harbors and to propel automobiles and airplanes.

Both the government and the affected industries committed substantial resources to the task of shaping the public's thinking. The AEC created a Division of Public and Technical Information that underwrote traveling exhibits, books, pamphlets, movies, audiovisual displays, and speakers—all devoted to demonstrating the positive side of atomic energy.[66] In Hyattsville, Maryland, a testing ground for the project, high school students staged a drama featuring characters such as Miss Molecule and Mr. Atomic Energy while grade school pupils heard "simplified talks on the atom's peacetime potential."[67]

A major nuclear reactor contractor, the General Electric Corporation, with the assistance of the AEC, distributed over 250,000 copies of a comic book, *Dagwood Splits the Atom.* Its leading figures included Mandrake the Magician, who reduced Blondie and Dagwood to the size of an atom as Popeye and Maggie and Jiggs looked on in amazement. The cartoons were adorned with comforting drawings of power plants, factories, medical laboratories, and ships utilizing the miracles of atomic fission.[68]

How successful were these efforts? Although it is difficult to prove a cause-and-effect connection, polls conducted in subsequent years suggested that the public was getting the message. In 1956, more than two out of three respondents said they were not afraid to have an atomic power plant located in their community.[69] This support continued well into the 1970s when another poll reported that 71 percent felt that it was either "somewhat" or "very important" to generate electricity with nuclear energy.[70]

Since that time two well-publicized nuclear accidents—one at Three Mile Island in Pennsylvania and the other in Chernobyl, Russia—have dampened if not reversed popular support for the peaceful use of the atom.[71] Nevertheless, the main point still stands: Government bureaus frequently serve as more than neutral agencies collecting and handing out "objective" information. They, like lobbyists and candidates, are actors in the political arena whose goals include *shaping* as well as responding to the public's desires. By framing a debate in a fashion that serves their purposes, they can effectively create or change beliefs and hence attitudes about issues. In view of these considerations, the flow of influence from the top down in Figure

The General Electric Corporation, with the blessing of the Atomic Energy commission, printed and distributed comic books to help convince the public of nuclear power's advantages and safety. Copyright © 1948 King Features Syndicate/Hearst Entertainment.

8.4(b) seems descriptive of how many policies are made and administered in the United States.

Symbolic Influence

In *The Symbolic Uses of Politics*, Murray Edelman, a respected political scientist, turns the familiar and reassuring picture of political leaders responding to their constituents' desires on its head.[72] He asks, in effect, how people come to want what they want and what it takes to convince them that they are getting it.

For Edelman, the most "conspicuously 'democratic' institutions are largely symbolic and expressive. . . ."[73] Campaigns, televised debates, polls, elections, referenda, letters to the editor, demonstrations, and other activities that seem to prove the electorate has an effective say in government actually have a different and more important function—*reassurance*. These events and activities give people the sense that political involvement is really meaningful and that their leaders listen and respond to their desires, regardless of whether they actually do or not. This reassurance also dispels doubts about the legitimacy and justice of public policies that may be enacted in the name of the people as a whole but that in fact benefit relatively few. In this sense, participation has only a **symbolic influence** on policymaking.

Edelman's view seems pessimistic, but actually, he does not see the political arena as a sinister place where elites secretly manipulate citizens. Instead, symbolic reassurance is part and parcel of everyday politics. At the risk of oversimplification, the process works this way: An event such as a mine disaster, the discovery of toxic wastes in a community's drinking water, or the collapse of a highway bridge sparks a public outcry for corrective action. What normally follows is an outpouring of official pronouncements, government studies and reports, public hearings, solemn statements to the press by politicians and candidates, and even the passage of highly publicized laws. Edelman calls these steps the "intensive dissemination of symbols." But in many, if not most, instances these expressions of outrage and the remedial actions do not change the underlying situation.[74] The most bal-

lyhooed provisions are largely symbolic, while the ones carrying the most weight remain in the shadows. As a consequence, "reforms," which give common people a sense of accomplishment and reassurance, actually promise more than they deliver. When the issue fades from public attention, the groups that might have been threatened by changes in the law escape relatively unscathed.

The Clean Air Act of 1970, the legislation enacted in the wake of highly publicized fears about the destruction of the environment, illustrates the concept.* In the years before its passage, environmentalists and others staged numerous widely publicized protests while the media described one potential ecological catastrophe after another. All of these events aroused widespread public anxiety and stimulated demands for action. Promising a great deal, the Clean Air Act appeared responsive to these concerns: It set limits on industrial pollutants, ordered automobile manufacturers to design cleaner exhaust systems, and required cities and states to establish timetables for reducing ozone, hydrocarbons, and other toxic elements. Senator Edmund Muskie, the bill's chief sponsor, pledged that "all Americans . . . shall have clean air to breathe within the 1970s," and the law itself reads in part: "air in all parts of the country shall have no adverse effects on any American's health."[75]

It would be misleading and unfair to say that the act has had no effect. Car and truck emissions are cleaner, and industries have spent billions on pollution control. Yet by 1990, 20 years after it became law, the goal of healthy air had not been achieved, but had instead become the new goal of comprehensive Clean Air legislation passed by Congress that year. As visitors to New York, Denver, Los Angeles, Houston, and dozens of other large metropolises know, cities continue to choke in smog. A study released in 1989 by the Coalition for Clean Air found that "ninety-four of the nation's urban areas with a collective population of 136 million [about half the popu-

---
*Actually the law was first put on the books in 1967. Its renewal, however, made so many changes that it is commonly referred to as a 1970 law.

Smog hangs over Houston, Texas. In spite of promises made by the Clean Air Act, air pollution in nearly all metropolitan areas continued to worsen in the 1970s and 1980s, leading some political scientists to wonder if the act was not mainly a symbolic gesture.

lation of the United States] violate the Clean Air Act health standards for ozone."[76] Acid rain, caused by sulfur and nitrogen emitted from smokestacks and automobile tailpipes, annually destroys thousands of acres of forests and freshwater lakes; the release of carbon dioxide, a gas implicated in the warming of the atmosphere (the "greenhouse" effect), has not been controlled; and only a few of the hundreds of cancer-causing toxic chemicals that Congress said would be eliminated at their source are being regulated.[77]

The situation leaves one wondering if the Clean Air Act has not had more of a symbolic than substantive impact. In thinking about this question we might also consider how the symbolic-politics idea relates to the question of who governs.*

Symbolic influence is clearly not satisfactory to democratic theorists, who want either direct or indirect citizen control of policymaking. Plu-

ralists, on the other hand, regard legislation like the Clean Air Act differently. There is nothing symbolic about it, they say. Indeed, it proves how public policy emerges from protracted group struggle. In the case of the clean air legislation, environmental and scientific organizations played a major role in persuading Congress to enact air quality standards that many industries bitterly opposed.† Granted, proponents did not get the tough standards and strict enforcement that they sought. But at the same time, as noted above, progress has been made. Thus, this policy, like countless others, demonstrates the pluralist notion that politics involves compromise and gradual change, that it has few consistent winners (and especially no power elite),

---

*In 1990 Congress toughened many provisions of the Clean Air Act, partly in response to the charge that the old standards were not doing the job. An interesting project would be to see if these reforms have had a symbolic or real impact on environmental policy.

---

†Here is a method pluralists might use to prove their point. Incidentally, it is a technique the reader might try applying to this or another public controversy. The 1970 index to the *New York Times*, available in most libraries, lists under the heading "Clean Air" all of the year's stories about the struggle to renew the bill. As one scans these summaries, it quickly becomes apparent that dozens of organizations from across the political spectrum fought in the battle. Not all of them won, of course, but this exercise may impress you with the role that groups, even small ones, seem to play in policymaking.

Table 8.2

How the Theories of American Government View the Influence of Public Opinion on Public Policy

Theory	Question	Types of Influence			
		Direct	Contingent	Top-down	Symbolic
Democratic	Is it desirable?	Yes!	No	No	No
	Real impact?	Yes	—	—	—
Pluralist	Is it desirable?	Perhaps	Yes!	No	No
	Real impact?	On some issues	Yes!	Few issues at most	No
Elitist	Is it desirable?	Yes	No	No	No
	Real impact?	No	Only on minor issues	Yes!	Yes!

and that for the participants who fight the day-to-day struggles, the process is hardly symbolic.

The elite school replies that symbolic influence accurately describes how the masses are manipulated and fooled by the trappings of democracy while major decisions are made at the highest levels. Enactment and renewal of the Clean Air Act only gives the illusion of popular control. Whatever changes manufacturers were forced to make were done at their own speed and on their own terms; whenever an industry felt the need for delay, it usually got it from a compliant Congress and bureaucracy.

Far more important to the elite school, however, is the fact that large industries, with the acquiescence if not the blessing of top-level political leaders, still dictate fundamental industrial policies that make clean air a problem in the first place. Consider transportation. The public may think automobile makers are being regulated. Yet the nation's transportation system still depends overwhelmingly on cars and trucks. The option of increasing mass transportation in order to reduce pollution rarely reaches the na-

tional agenda. Given the size and power of the automobile companies and their allies in the petroleum, rubber, steel, and cement industries, it is unlikely that America will soon extricate itself from its dependence on passenger cars and trucks. Polluted air is likely to be with us for a long time and will disappear only when industry finds it economically feasible to change to other modes of transportation. For elitists, the Clean Air Act is merely an exercise in futility.

The Influence of Public Opinion Summarized

Let's step back to review how the three schools of American government—democratic, pluralist, and elitist—might view these models of public opinion. As we saw at the end of Chapter 1, two questions immediately arise. First, what do the schools of thought believe is the *desirable* type of connection between leaders and followers? Second, which model best describes the *real impact* of public opinion? Table 8.2 summarizes the various alternatives. Notice that this table only approximates the positions taken by the theories, because they are all so complex and each has so many adherents. No one sees the world exactly the same way. Nevertheless, we can appreciate the major philosophical and empirical differences in what the theories see and desire for America.

No doubt all sides to the controversy contain a grain of truth, and at this point it is certainly not essential to decide whether one or the other is completely right or wrong. The main point is simply that the connection between what the people want and what the people get is extremely complex.

Checkpoint

- "Pure" democratic theory believes that public opinion should directly influence public policy.

- The contingent-influence explanation holds that whether or not leaders follow public opinion depends on such factors as how strongly and how widely the attitudes are held.

- The top-down view asserts that political leaders attempt to shape mass attitudes on many major issues.

- Another theory holds that the influence of public opinion is largely symbolic. Numerous political rituals convince people of the importance of their opinions and participation when in fact they have relatively little actual impact on decision makers, especially on trunk policies.

SUMMARY

According to democratic theory, the public should directly or indirectly determine the content of policy. Yet questions have been raised about how qualified and willing the American people are to accept this responsibility. One school of thought (the skeptics) argues that ordinary citizens lack the knowledge, temperament, and motivation to be entrusted with the reins of governmental power. Another school (the optimists), however, maintains that the people are more capable of governing themselves than their detractors suggest.

Public opinion is the range or collection of the individual attitudes of the populace. Beliefs and evaluations of these beliefs determine attitudes' direction (favorable or unfavorable) and intensity. Thus, to appreciate why a person develops a set of opinions one has to examine the underlying beliefs.

Political opinions and their associated beliefs develop at a surprisingly early age through a process called socialization, the learning of a society's culture, norms, roles, and customs. Children's attitudes and beliefs about politics tend to reflect their familial and educational experiences. Many critics argue that schools, intentionally or not, separate students into leaders and followers and that the educational system does not encourage democratic citizenship in all citizens.

Social scientists, journalists, and others measure public opinion with polls or surveys based on random and representative samples of populations. Factors such as the timing of the poll, question wording, and intensity of opinions greatly affect the results, so the data must be interpreted with caution.

Various models attempt to explain the connection between public opinion and the making of public policy. The direct-influence model, which coincides with democratic theory, asserts that the public's desires determine what decision makers do. Unfortunately, this simple model does not seem applicable to a broad range of issues. The contingent-influence theory suggests that policy depends on the intensity of the public's attitudes and the extent of its agreement about an issue. This model fits nicely with pluralist arguments. Power elite theorists argue that the top-down and symbolic-influence ideas best describe the real connection between mass attitudes and policymaking.

KEY TERMS

Skeptics
Optimists
Public opinion
Attitude
Attitude object
Belief
Evaluation
Selective perception
Socialization

Agents of socialization
Benevolent leader
Generation gap
Public opinion poll
Opinion intensity
Direct influence
Contingent influence
Top-down influence
Symbolic influence

FOR FURTHER READING

Herbert Asher, *Polling and the Public: What Every Citizen Should Know* (Washington, D.C.: Congressional Quarterly Press, 1988). A very readable look at the methods, uses, and abuses of public opinion polls.

Robert Coles, *The Political Life of Children* (Boston: Atlantic Monthly Press, 1986). Coles has spent years interviewing children, especially ones from disadvantaged backgrounds. His is one of the best works on the political thinking of American children.

Robert Erikson et al., *American Public Opinion*, 3rd ed. (New York: Macmillan, 1988). An excellent introduction to various aspects of public opinion, including socialization.

Fred I. Greenstein, *Children and Politics* (New Haven, Conn.: Yale University Press, 1965). Greenstein, one of the pioneers in the study of political socialization, describes with numerous examples how children see the world of politics.

V. O. Key, Jr., *Public Opinion and American Democracy* (New York: Knopf, 1961). Although some of the data are out of date, this is still one of the most insightful books on public opinion ever written.

Norman R. Luttbeg, ed. *Public Opinion and Public Policy*, 3rd ed. (Itasca, Ill.: Peacock, 1982). An excellent collection of articles on the connection between public opinion and public policy.

Malcolm X, *The Autobiography of Malcolm X* (New York: Ballantine Books, 1964). Malcolm X rose from a life of petty crime, drug dealing, and pimping to become a major figure in what some whites call the black revolution in America. This book shows the development and evolution of his political consciousness.

The Mass Media

Chapter 9

**A**lthough the United States has perhaps the freest press in the world, it is not necessarily the most informative. News coverage frequently stresses conflict, drama, violence, and human interest angles and underplays substantive issues and policies. This emphasis creates problems because citizens, who rely heavily on the mass media for their knowledge about government and politics, may not be getting the information they need to understand and participate in decision making. ■

T he headline in the August 1, 1989, edition of the Wilmington, Delaware *News Journal* must have shocked and outraged its readers:

SHIITES: WE HANGED A U.S. HOSTAGE

The accompanying article reported in grim tones that a Lebanese group, the Organization of the Oppressed on Earth, claimed it had hanged William R. Higgins in retaliation for Israel's abduction of a Muslim cleric. Higgins, a marine lieutenant colonel, had been kidnapped more than a year earlier while serving with a United Nations peacekeeping force in southern Lebanon. According to the story, another American, Joseph Cicippio, also faced execution if Israel did not release its prisoner. The remainder of the account described the release of a poor-quality videotape showing a body hanging from a ceiling, mentioned the possibility that Higgins might have been killed months before, and gave the reactions of President George Bush, members of Congress, and the victims' families and friends.

The report seemed perfectly factual and objective. It could not, of course, help arousing feelings of outrage and frustration, since the murder and the threat against Cicippio appeared so brutal and senseless. Nevertheless, the report stuck

to the facts, telling only what happened and quoting authoritative sources. The *News Journal*'s subscribers no doubt believed that they were getting a truthful, unbiased, and complete picture of the event. In this respect, it was the kind of journalism they expected.

But just how accurate and informative was the account? It might pay to look a bit more closely at what the *News Journal* said and did *not* say.

First, the headline smacks of ethnocentrism. The Shiites are a Muslim sect with millions of adherents living throughout the Middle East. The story contained no evidence that Shiites as a whole, or a majority of them, or even a minority, participated in or condoned the execution. The group responsible was, in fact, a faction of another relatively small organization called the Hezbollah, or Party of God, and acted on its own and certainly not on behalf of any government or religion. (Hezbollah itself was internally divided on the value of taking hostages.[1]) Seen from this perspective, the headline seemed as unfair as one that might read, "Catholics: We Killed British Officer," to describe the actions of the Irish Republican Army (IRA), a clandestine Catholic movement that uses force in an attempt to drive the British army out of Northern Ireland.

The mass media are virtually the public's only source of information about national and international affairs. But it is essential to ask how informative they really are, especially in regard to complex matters like Middle Eastern politics.

More significantly, however, the dispatch left a number of key questions unanswered, and they remained unanswered for the next ten days, when coverage of the Higgins affair eventually stopped. Most troubling of all was the absence of any explanation of the *context* of the kidnappings and murder. What conditions spawn and nurture bands like the Organization of the Oppressed on Earth? Do their members have legitimate reasons for hating the United States? How do their long-range objectives affect American interests? More generally, a civil war has been raging in Lebanon for a decade. What are its causes? Does the situation pose a threat to our national security? What is U.S. policy toward the different sides? Is this policy working? Are there alternatives? What are their pros and cons?

These questions demanded an answer because most citizens reading about Higgins and Cicippio probably agreed with ex-marine Daniel Fuller, who said, "It's time to set diplomacy aside . . . [I]t's time to take off the gloves and go knuckle to knuckle."[2] Although such reactions are understandable, they may be misguided. There was much more to the story than the immediate facts surrounding Higgins's murder and the threats against Cicippio. These incidents were part of a long, complex history of U.S. involvement in Middle Eastern affairs, and without a grasp of this background, it was difficult for citizens to form reasoned judgments about what their government could and should do.[3]

Coverage of the Higgins tragedy illustrates a crucial point about the press and the public: The **mass media**—newspapers, television, radio, magazines, books—largely determine the common person's understanding of and responses to national and international affairs. After all, few people have any direct knowledge about what goes on beyond their neighborhoods and places of work. Instead, they rely heavily, if not entirely, on what others tell them. Most citizens are, in this way, totally dependent creatures. That is precisely why mass communications are so important for understanding government and politics.

THE PUBLIC AND THE MASS MEDIA

Society creates information in such abundance and so cheaply that it is readily available to everyone. Books, newspapers, magazines, television, radio, videocassettes, and now even computers are not the luxuries of a privileged class but the commonplace goods of men and women everywhere. It is easy to be optimistic about this development because it means that people have at their fingertips a huge store of facts and figures about the outside world. Each day, the *News Journal*, like most papers, takes its readers to Washington, New York, Moscow, Tokyo, China, the Middle East, and hundreds of other places all over the world. The August 1 edition, for example, described events ranging from the routine (major banks announced the lowering of lending rates) to the tragic (a man drowned trying to save his companions on a sinking fishing boat) to the humorous (a heavy smoker chained himself to his house in a last-ditch effort to break his habit). Typical of most papers its size, the *News Journal* that day contained more than three dozen reports in the first section alone.

In theory, with all this information at their disposal Americans have the resources to be alert, responsible citizens. They can gather data on virtually any issue, weigh its pros and cons, and decide what course of action to follow. More important, knowing what is going on in government gives people an opportunity to control their representatives. The growth of mass communications, in other words, should greatly enhance democracy by leading to a fully informed citizenry.

Any technical development can be abused, however. For the media can misinform as well as inform, create conformity as well as independence, manipulate as well as enlighten. Knowledge, as thinkers from Francis Bacon to George Orwell have said, is power, and whoever controls the production and distribution of information is powerful indeed, especially since what citizens know about the world comes to them secondhand and cannot be verified directly.

In order to discover who really governs the United States, one needs to explore these possibilities. What role do the mass media play in society? Do they determine the political agenda—the issues that are debated in the arena of politics? Do they increase or diminish democracy? Do they spread power around as pluralists argue? Or do they concentrate it in a few hands as the power elite school contends?

Answering these questions is as important as knowing how Congress or the courts or the bureaucracy work. Why? Because as George Gerbner, a long-time student of the effects of television, says, "If you can write a nation's stories, you needn't worry about who makes its laws."[4] What he means is that journalists, editors, commentators, and publishers are the eyes and ears of the body politic, and they determine to a large degree its awareness of the world and hence what it deems desirable and possible. As Chapter 8 explained, attitudes are based on beliefs. What people think about the Middle East, for instance, depends partly on their perceptions of its inhabitants, their history, culture, and religion. (In this case, research shows, for example, that Americans have vague and mostly negative impressions of Arabs and Muslims.[5]) These beliefs come from a variety of sources, including family, friends, fellow workers, and neighbors. But, as political scientist Benjamin Page and his colleagues note, the mass media provide a huge portion of the information:

. . . whatever they learn about politics, most people must rely heavily upon the cheapest and most accessible sources: newspapers, radio, and television, especially network TV news.[6]

Public Dependence on the Mass Media

That television, radio, newspapers, and other forms of mass communication pervade everyday life is well known. The numbers, nevertheless, are sobering and informative. In 1988, 98 percent of American homes housed at least one television set.[7] Nor are these sets idle. The majority of those interviewed in a survey reported watching television for more than three hours on "an average day."[8] A typical child graduates from high school having spent 11,000 hours in the classroom and 15,000 hours in front of the television.[9] Figure 9.1 clearly indicates that nearly every American sees a televised news show at least three or four times a week and more than half watch one *every* day. As for the print media, there are more than 1700 daily newspapers in the United States and another 7000 weeklies, foreign-language papers, advertising supplements, and the like. Circulation of the dailies exceeds 60 million.[10] In addition, about 11,000 periodicals appeared in 1988, while over 2 million books were published that year.[11]

The specific numbers are not as important as the conclusion they lead to: Americans cannot escape bombardment by the mass media. Given the sheer volume of messages being sent, one would expect that just about every point of view, from the most conservative to the most radical, finds its way into the marketplace of ideas. Superficially at any rate, people have the freedom and opportunity to explore new ideas, to validate competing claims, to experience what is remote from their personal lives, and to have their own opinions aired.

Pluralists, it would seem, are right. In a society that publishes the *Conservative Digest*, the *Militant*, *Dissent*, the *Socialist Review*, *Contemporary Marxism*, and the *Progressive*, among countless other opinion magazines, journals, papers, and books, virtually any group can make its voice heard. Surely the quantity and quality of information available to the common person must act as a brake on the government, thus supporting the pluralist notion that even if the United States is not a perfect democracy, it cannot be too far from the ideal.

Before accepting this conclusion, though, we should think about a point the power elite school considers critical: who owns and controls the sources of all this knowledge.

Concentrated Ownership

A familiar theme in the folklore of American democracy is the small-town newspaper publisher who, with shirt sleeves rolled up, single-handedly unearths corruption in city hall and exposes swindlers before they bilk widows out of their

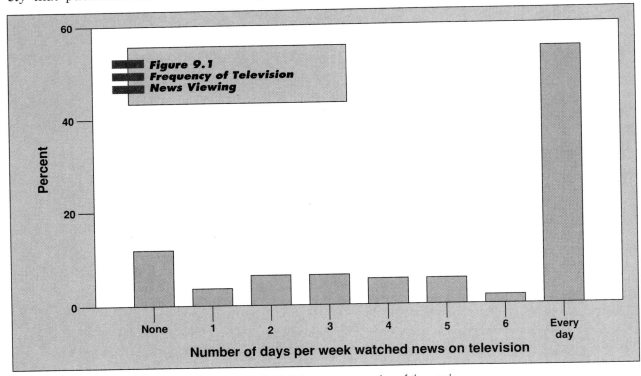

Figure 9.1
Frequency of Television News Viewing

The vast majority of Americans watch some form of television news every day of the week.

Source: Based on data from the Center for Political Studies, University of Michigan, *American National Election Study, 1988.*

Many observers, particularly in the power elite camp, argue that relatively few corporations dominate the media and thus restrict the kinds of information Americans receive.

pensions. Seen in innumerable movies and television dramas, the image is of a small, family-owned paper taking on the "big boys." What stands out is the paper's *independence*: It prints the news as it sees it. Multiplied a thousand times over, the independents supposedly defend democracy by keeping the public informed and the politicians on their toes.

Today's reality is disturbingly different. Family-owned newspapers, for instance, are largely a memory of bygone days. The number of dailies dropped from 2600 in 1909 to about 1700 in 1990; this decline is all the more remarkable given the growth in the population. (See Figure 9.2, on p. 272.) As the dailies fell by the wayside, the ownership and operation of the remainder came into fewer and fewer hands. Huge corporations have replaced local owners. Twenty companies now sell more than half of the more than 60 million papers distributed each day in the United States. (In fact, 1 percent of all newspapers circulate about 34 percent of this total.[12]) One Wall Street analyst estimates that 155 chains own 1175 of the country's dailies.[13]

To appreciate the degree of concentration, take a close look at the masthead (the top portion of the front page) of a typical local paper. Chances are it is not an independent company but belongs to a chain. (The *News Journal*, for instance, belongs to the Gannett Corporation, which publishes 83 other newspapers through-

out the country, including *USA Today*.) And while on the subject, ask whether the local paper has any competition. Most do not. Since the 1920s there has been a steady decline in competition so that by the mid-1980s only 2 percent of American cities had rival newspapers.[14] (The *News Journal*, which has a morning and an evening edition, is Wilmington's only paper.)

It is also instructive to look at where papers get their national and international news. Rarely is such news reported by their own correspondents and columnists. Instead, they generally rely on a handful of wire services such as the Associated Press, the New York Times News Service, or Gannett News. (The Higgins story came from the Associated Press.) In effect, then, what the citizens of Wilmington, Delaware read is much the same as what people in Santa Fe, New Mexico, or Salem, Oregon, or Des Moines, Iowa read. The huge number of different titles carried on mastheads of newspapers around the country does not mean that each town has its own source of independent information.

Enormous conglomerates also command the television, radio, magazine, and book-publishing industries. The major networks dominate television programming, although cable companies offer additional choices. These networks are information giants. In the late 1980s, CBS alone owned assets in excess of $4 billion and employed more than 7000 workers.[15] ABC joined

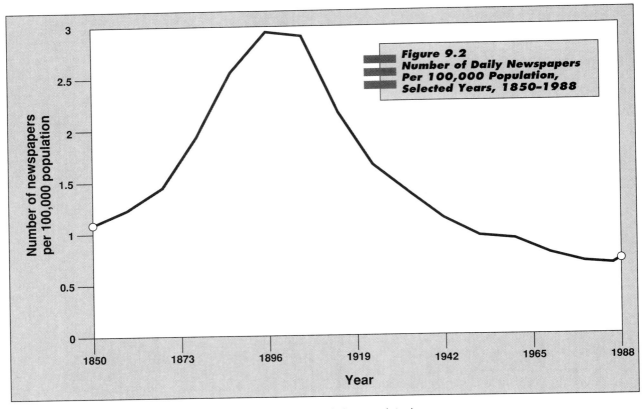

After 1850 the growth in the number of newspapers kept pace with the growth in the population. This expansion in the press stopped in the late 1800s, however, and today the number of daily newspapers continues to decline even though the population is increasing.

Source: U.S. Bureau of the Census, *Historical Statistics of the United States*, Part 1, p. 8 and Part 2, p. 810; and U.S. Bureau of the Census, *Statistical Abstract of the United States: 1989* (Washington, D.C.: Government Printing Office, 1989), p. 549.

with Capital Cities Communications in 1987 to create a television and communications empire with annual sales of close to $5 billion.[16] McGraw-Hill, with book publishing and other interests, has 16,000 employees on its payroll and close to $2 billion in assets.[17] Similarly, information acquisition and transmission are by and large in the hands of corporations like AT&T and IBM, and there are only a few syndicated polling firms, the organizations that tell the public what it is thinking.

The king of the hill in mass communications, however, is the mega-corporation Time Warner Inc. Created in 1989 by the merger of Time Inc. and Warner Communications, the media giant brings together under one roof magazines like *Time*, *Sports Illustrated*, and *People*; entertainers like Madonna, Fleetwood Mac, U2, Phil Collins, and Van Halen; television hits like "Dallas" and "Falcon Crest"; and cable programming like HBO.[18] A reporter likened Time Warner to a huge assembly line: Raw materials in the form of writers, journalists, singers, and producers enter at one end while information in nearly every conceivable medium pours out the other.[19]

To muddy the waters further, the owners and managers of these mammoth structures sit on one another's boards of directors. Gannett shares directors with, among others, McGraw-Hill (book publishers), New York Telephone Company (communications), 20th Century Fox (entertainment), and Merrill Lynch (stockbrokers).[20] Men and women from a variety of corporations sit on the boards of NBC, Knight-Ridder newspapers, Time Warner, and most of the other leaders in the communications industry. Due to these interconnections, one journalist calculates that "there are in fact only 50 corporations whose presidents hire and fire the people responsible for presenting new ideas to 220 million Americans."[21]

Is this centralization dangerous? Is there room for independent thought and divergent opinions? Will conformity drive out diversity? Can the media represent a broad spectrum of ideas, or do they reflect only the values, needs, and interests of large corporations?

A blanket answer is not possible because, as in most controversies of this nature, there are two sides to the coin. On one side, new forms of communication, such as cable television, electronic mail, satellites, and computer bulletin boards, are constantly being born. Their emergence diversifies the available forms of information. In addition, although large enterprises own the vast majority of media outlets, they seem mainly interested in profits, not editorials. Reporters and editors often say that the companies leave them alone to present the news as they see fit. Few of them feel much pressure to bend to the whims of corporate directors. Even the largest book publishers produce works espousing an endless variety of viewpoints, including many that are highly critical of capitalism.

Pluralists point out that the public's right to know and to hear different voices is protected by the Constitution, congressional statues, and tradition. Most important of all, freedom of expression is so deeply embedded in the American experience that even the most radical doctrines, if they are persistently advocated, eventually see the light of day.

Yet critics, particularly those in the power elite camp, are not reassured. Many corporations have access to, if not outright ownership of, a major communications outlet. When compared with individuals or small groups or even large, disorganized ones, this access gives them a huge, perhaps unfair, and unquestionably unequal advantage in the political arena. Ben Bagdikian, a

student of the press for many years, puts the matter this way:

> . . . the imbalance between the great voices of the mass media and the small voices of individual enterprises is so vast that it is more difficult than ever for society to hear minority voices in the majority thunder.[22]

Private ownership is not the issue—it is essential. What is dangerous is *concentrated* ownership. Information is a major resource in politics, and according to the elite interpretation, it is hypocritical to speak on the one hand of democracy and equality while on the other tolerating gross inequalities in the control of the production and distribution of knowledge.

There is another point. Society supposedly relies on news organizations to check and balance other forms of political power. But if these entities are themselves woven together, can they play this role? If the media are part and parcel of the corporate sector, can they act as a brake on it? If profits are the ultimate goal, can they be depended on to provide a balanced, fair, thorough, and comprehensible picture of the world? If the sale of airtime and advertising space are the imperatives, will truth, depth, and subtlety give way to oversimplification and blandness?[23]

Checkpoint

- Citizens do not normally experience politics firsthand but must depend on the mass media for their information. Thus their beliefs about government and politicians are formed largely by television, newspapers, magazines, and books.

- As one would expect in a free society, the public has easy access to an enormous variety of information sources. Nearly everyone reads a newspaper or watches television during the day.

- There is a great deal of concentration in the ownership and management of the media. A few large corporations control the bulk of the communications industry.

• This situation arouses controversy. Some observers argue that despite the concentration, censorship and manipulation of ideas are rare. Others, however, worry that corporate giants inevitably limit the public's understanding of issues.

THE PRESENTATION OF THE NEWS

Contemporary America faces a dilemma. People rely almost entirely on outside sources for their information about politics and government. Yet the objectivity of these sources is frequently questioned. Are they truthful and unbiased? Whose interests do they serve? Do they fragment power, as the pluralists suggest, or do they simply reinforce it, as the elitists contend? To answer these questions, it is helpful to look at how the media present the news to the public.

The Myth of Objectivity

Newspaper reporters and television commentators repeatedly profess their belief in **objectivity**. Their mission, they assert over and over, is to report the news as it happens—not as anyone wants it to happen, but as it actually occurs. "The unvarnished truth." "Tell it like it is." These are the watch words of professional journalism. Frank Stanton, a former president of CBS, told a congressional committee that "what the media do is to hold a mirror up to society and try to report it as faithfully as possible."[24]

According to this interpretation, which has been called the **mirror metaphor**, the media do not fabricate or distort the news; they merely report events, whether beautiful or ugly, as they happen. Objectivity requires that journalists adhere to the principles of independence, fairness, balance, honesty, and courage. They must maintain this stance in the face of growing concentration in the ownership and control of mass communications and brave the wrath of irate

politicians or the general public who do not like what they are hearing or reading.

That the press adheres to the standards of objectivity, truth, and independence seems at first sight self-evident. Most newspapers are not openly partisan. They save their opinions for the editorial page, which is clearly marked as such. Reporting is straightforward. Here, for example, is a news item reprinted in part from the same edition of the *News Journal* that carried the Higgins and Cicippio story:

> Defense Minister Yitzak Rabin, acknowledging that Israeli actions had threatened Western hostages in Lebanon, offered Monday to release Lebanese Shiite Moslem leader Abdul Karmim Obeid and all other Shiite prisoners Israel holds in exchange for the hostages. . . .
>
> Official sources confirmed that Israel had decided to seize Obeid as part of an effort to free three captive Israelis in Lebanon and had acted without consulting the United States or other governments, despite the possible impact on Higgins and other hostages.
>
> Speaking to reporters late Monday, Rabin said that Israel had expanded its offer of an exchange to include all Western hostages because the other captives now "are also threatened in the wake of Israeli action."[25]

Nothing unfair or biased here. The article simply repeats what the Israeli defense minister said about the hostage situation.

To be sure, news organizations are from time to time the objects of charges that they emphasize violence, are too liberal, or criticize more than they praise. In fact, most public leaders cross swords with the press more than once in their careers. Former President Nixon devoted endless hours to plotting against journalists he believed were his enemies. His predecessor, Lyndon Johnson, also frequently tangled with members of the press. Yet these feuds only further convince reporters that they are merely doing their job of telling the truth and letting the chips fall where they may.

Reporters and ordinary citizens alike cling tightly to the belief in objectivity because it reassures them that nothing is being held back; nothing is slanted. Since an abundance of objec-

CBS anchorman Dan Rather engaged in a heated interview with George Bush during the 1988 presidential primaries. Exchanges like this convince many people that the media keep politicians on their toes and help restrict their power.

How might American interests be affected by them? What is the cause of that struggle between the different parties? After reading this piece, does a citizen have an adequate "picture of reality"?

Surprisingly, the *News Journal* story, which came from a wire service and was presumably read by millions of people across the country, addressed none of these concerns. Not one. Indeed, measured against Lippmann's criterion of showing the hidden facts of an issue and how they relate to one another and to other issues, the report seems seriously deficient.

A key question is how typical this kind of reporting is. If the knowledge can easily be obtained elsewhere, it is possible to conclude with the pluralists that citizens have the tools to govern themselves more or less democratically. If, on the other hand, there are serious shortcomings, we might agree with the power elite camp that the people, because they have insufficient *meaningful* information, wield less power than they could and should.

How the Press Covers and Presents the News

A little thought about the mirror metaphor quickly leads to the conclusion that it cannot be totally correct. News coverage, whether by television, radio, magazines, or newspapers, must inevitably be *selective*, selective not simply in which stories it reports but in *how* it presents them as well. Selectivity is essential to journalism. Can the evening news, a 30-minute program, give an account of everything that has transpired during the day? Obviously not. Instead, reporters, camera operators, writers, editors, and directors must act as gatekeepers, and the ordinary viewer does not know what is being let in and kept out.[27]

Equally important, the men and women who present the news are human beings who, in spite of their good intentions, occasionally succumb to anger, jealousy, anxiety, impatience, ambition, and other emotions that cloud their objectivity. They belong to large, complex organizations that have their own diverse, often conflicting, goals and needs. A correspondent in

tive information permits people to be responsible and active citizens, democracy is protected.

Still, one wonders how far the argument can be pushed. Writing in 1922, Walter Lippmann, one of America's most respected journalists, said that "news and truth are not the same thing and must be clearly distinguished." He continued, "The function of news is to signalize an event, the function of truth is to bring to light the hidden facts, to set them in relation with each other and make a picture of reality. . . ."[26]

Lippmann's point is that there is an enormous difference between being objective—that is, fair and unbiased—and being informative—that is, telling people everything they need to know in order to act responsibly.

Consider the item about Israel's willingness to trade its prisoner for Western hostages. The offer is, of course, objectively reported. But does the story contain enough information for the reader to understand Israel's motives and how they relate to American interests? Obeid was apparently seized as a bargaining chip, but who were the Israelis trying to free and why? Were any of the pros and cons of these exchanges discussed?

Washington may be interested in getting all the "facts" behind a story, but the publisher in Denver who has to pay the bills may want something less than the total picture. Sooner or later compromises have to be made.[28]

Presenting the news to the public is not merely a matter of "telling it like it is." It is very much a human activity. Reporters do not willfully distort their stories, but the way they describe issues and events nevertheless affects the public's understanding of them.

TIME AND SPACE CONSTRAINTS   As mentioned above, the August 1, 1989, edition of the *News Journal*, a paper similar to the ones read by millions of Americans, contained more than 30 national and international news items. The number seems large until one realizes that the average length per item was only 200 words. The longest article (the one about Higgins) contained no more than 1000 words, less than an average college term paper, and most reports consisted of a single, one-sentence paragraph. Advertisements, in fact, took up about a third of the first section. (Mattress ads, for instance, covered more space than the lead story.)

Brevity is an even more serious problem for television and radio news, which have been described as snapshot-and-headline services. After subtracting time for commercials, network evening news programs have only 20 minutes or so to cover the day's events. If they mention 15 subjects, a not uncommon number, they have less than two minutes for each. Most stories, though, are reported in less than 45 seconds.

Far from being a mirror that reflects government and politics back to the citizenry, then, news organizations are searchlights that illuminate some objects while leaving others in the dark. What gets exposed?

Before that matter is taken up, an important distinction must be drawn between the **popular press** and the **activist press**, which differ greatly in the detail and sophistication of their news coverage. This analysis mainly concerns the popular press, the sources like the *News Journal* used by the average person. Detailed accounts of national and international affairs are available in papers such as the *New York Times* and *Washington Post* or on public television programs aimed at politically active and influential audiences.

THE OFFICIAL POINT OF VIEW   A network executive once said, "The news you print is actually the news you cover . . . the question is how far do you fling the net."[29] From an organizational point of view, it is most efficient and economical to cast the net only in the places where something is likely to be caught: legislatures, government offices, foreign capitals, and scheduled press briefings—places where authoritative speakers will be doing the talking. Consequently, broadcasters and journalists tend to congregate in capitals and large cities from where they can always fan out if the need arises.

Besides, the norm of objectivity places heavy emphasis on the **official point of view** or utterances and deeds of government officials and experts. If, say, a small-town minister or teacher expresses an opinion about the Middle East, it is usually considered just that, an opinion. Certainly no one would think of publishing it. But if exactly the same thought is expressed by a senator or a cabinet secretary, the press is apt to consider it a pronouncement worthy of presentation on the six o'clock news.

W. Lance Bennett, who has carefully studied the way news is conveyed to the public, claims that the media avoid "wide-ranging coverage of diverse viewpoints and experiences in favor of extensive coverage of official positions and mainstream perspectives."[30] He cites one study that shows that government officials (domestic and foreign) are the source of three-quarters of all reports in two of America's leading newspapers, the *Washington Post* and the *New York Times*.[31] The study concluded that less than 1 percent of all news stories originated from the reporters' *own* investigations, while more than 90 percent relayed "calculated messages" of people with a vested interest in a particular point of view. A huge number were based on situations in which the "newsmakers [had] either complete or substantial control."[32] Notice that in the article about the hostages quoted earlier, the *only* source cited is an Israeli official.

Another survey of stories on the front pages of

The press interviews Senator Richard Lugar of Indiana. Studies show that the vast majority of news stories come from government officials, not reporters' own investigative efforts. Consequently, what the public reads and hears is largely what politicians want them to read and hear.

the coverage of major issues. In the beginning, doubts about American involvement in Vietnam came mainly from a handful of individuals, most of whom were private citizens. That the strife in Vietnam was extremely complex, that America's interests in its outcome were never entirely clear, that the enemy might have greater strength and resolve than anyone imagined, that the United States might be blundering into a quagmire from which there would be no easy escape, and that alternative policies existed were hardly ever discussed in the evening news or the daily newspapers prior to 1964.[34] Instead, as an NBC correspondent says of the first years of the war, "To the extent that we in the media paid any attention at all to that small, dirty war . . . we almost wholly reported the position of the [U.S.] government."[35]

Daniel Hallin, who cataloged network broadcasts from 1965 to 1973, summarized this reliance, saying that the media relied heavily on official information and carefully avoided judging U.S. policies and statements.[36] Michael Parenti, a severe critic of the media, puts the point more bluntly: ". . . during the early years of the conflict the press reported the war largely the way the U.S. government wanted it reported, raising no serious objections about U.S. intervention."[37]

The war eventually became the object of critical attention, but only *after* the United States was deeply committed. By then the debate on its merits was too late to prevent American involvement. Skeptics like Hallin and Parenti and others feel that by stressing the government's stand and not airing other ideas, the media greatly delayed public discussion that might have encouraged the Kennedy or Johnson administrations to reassess their policies.[†]

Official interpretations of issues and policies appear in print and on the air so much not only because the news media find it convenient to cover them. Politicians, like members of any large organization, skillfully cultivate the press and maintain a well-oiled public relations ap-

both popular and activist newspapers discovered that nearly one out of three sources of the news items were "affiliated" with the national government; another 14 percent represented state and local governments, while private citizens accounted for only 4 percent of the total. (See Table 9.1, p. 278.) These results led the investigators to conclude that "front-page news stories in both the national and local press and the wire services rely heavily on government sources who are primarily men in executive positions. . . . Most reporting relies on routine channels, such as press conferences and press releases."[33]*

The war in Vietnam dramatically demonstrates how the official point of view prevails in

---

*The reader might want to check this assertion by looking for the sources of information presented in stories in a recent newspaper or television newscast. Look not at what the item is about or who wrote it but who provided the reporter with the information.

†If anyone doubts this conclusion, an interesting project would be to compare newspaper coverage of the Vietnam War in selected papers in the years, say, 1963, 1965, and 1968.

Table 9.1

Sources of Information in National and Local Newspapers

Source of Information	National Reporters (%)	Local Reporters (%)	Wire Service (%)	Total (%)
U.S government	32	16	36	31
State/local government	12	32	11	14
Foreign government	12	a	13	10
Citizen affiliated with institution	25	36	19	24
Private citizen	4	6	4	4
Other[b]	16	10	18	16

[a]Less than 1 percent.
[b]Includes foreign citizens.
Source: Adapted from Jane Delano Brown et al., "Invisible Power: News Sources and the Limits of Diversity," *Journalism Quarterly* 63 (Spring 1987): 49. (Percents do not add to 100 because of rounding.)

paratus. The Defense Department, perhaps the most spectacular example, spends millions of dollars each year disseminating information about its programs and activities.[38] It holds frequent briefings, supplies films and photographs, issues background reports, conducts tours of military bases, and, when it suits its purposes, even leaks secret documents. All this material serves the Pentagon's interests and at the same time simplifies the media's work. Furthermore, because it emanates from a supposedly authoritative source and because reporters often do not have expertise in these areas, the information is passed on to the public as the unvarnished truth.

No one should take any of these remarks to mean that the government controls the press. Politicians sometimes wish they could tell reporters what to write and have on occasion tried to do so. On the whole, however, freedom of the press is well protected by law and tradition. Compared with their counterparts in other democracies, American journalists have remarkable latitude. The *New York Times*, in one famous case, published the "Pentagon Papers," a classified analysis of the origins of the Vietnam War, despite intense pressure from the White House

and Defense Department, which took the matter to the Supreme Court. In what is now considered a landmark decision, the Court upheld the *Times'* right to publish the material.[39] Probably few other democracies would be as lenient.

Moreover, there is no conspiracy of silence in this country; the media are not passive observers. They continually doubt, criticize, and antagonize public officials. Yet the fact remains that for a host of reasons the media depend heavily on official interpretations of events. As Bennett explains: ". . . most news stories reserve for official sources the first, the last, and many words in between. Much of the daily news is devoted to official actions and reactions."[40] Stated another way, the news that most Americans consume does not mirror the world as it really *is* but as people in positions of power and leadership want them to see it.

PERSONALIZATION News stories tend to emphasize individuals' trials and tribulations, the "human angle."[41] In the days following the Higgins and Cicippio episode, the *News Journal* ran a series of articles describing the personal feelings of not only the victims' families and friends

A Closer Look

Personalizing the News ★★★

On Sunday, November 23, 1986, "Meet the Press" interviewed Senators Sam Nunn of Georgia and David Durenberger of Minnesota. One segment of the program covered the revelation that the Reagan administration had been secretly selling arms to Iran and possibly diverting the proceeds to the Contras, an anti-Communist rebel force fighting to overthrow the leftist government of Nicaragua. The uproar created by these revelations raised many questions about American policy in both the Middle East and Central America.

The interviewers on "Meet the Press," though, did not ask about the substance of the issues: Should the United States have embargoed arms shipments to Iran? Was it wise to help the Contras? How sensible were the President's policies in these regions?

Instead, 16 of the 18 questions dealt with the President's staff. Who, the reporters wanted to know, should be fired? Here is a sampling of what they asked:

Okay. Would the number one challenge, in your view, Senator, be first, a shakeup?

Well, the architect of that position was Admiral Poindexter. Should he stay?

Are you saying [William] Casey [director of the Central Intelligence Agency] should be replaced now, too?

Senator Nunn, do you have confidence in William Casey and Admiral Poindexter?

Other questions dealt with the President's competence, not the content of his policies:

When you say, Senator Nunn, bring in some "wise men," are you saying that the President is not wise?

Let me ask you this: Does the President of the United States know what he's doing in foreign policy?[a]

The best way to find out if the news overpersonalizes its coverage is a firsthand check. Read a local newspaper or watch the evening news on television—the kind of source nine out of ten Americans rely on—and each time a story is presented ask whether it enlightens the public about an issue's causes and long-run implications or whether it describes someone's personal feelings about the matter. Count the number of "substantive" news reports—the ones that deal with broad policy concerns—versus human interest accounts such as catastrophes, misfortunes, or illnesses.

[a]"Meet the Press," November 26, 1986. Transcript printed by Kelly Press Inc., Washington, D.C.

but also of senators, representatives, State Department officials, and many others. (On August 2, the day after Cicippio's life was threatened, for instance, the paper carried a front-page account "Cicippio family: 'We're being held hostage, too.' ")

Personalization, the emphasis on the personal aspects of news stories, is especially prevalent in the coverage of political battles where winners and losers are easily identified. Early in 1985 the House of Representatives approved funding for additional MX missiles, a very controversial and expensive weapons system. President Ronald Reagan lobbied hard for the program, but many

The media are frequently charged with emphasizing dramatic or violent stories and neglecting stories that have policy content.

Democrats, especially Thomas ("Tip") O'Neill, then speaker of the House, vigorously opposed it. Here are the headlines and lead paragraphs from three newspapers:

MX: REAGAN 219, O'NEILL 213
USA Today, March 27, 1985

The House delivered a slender, hard-fought victory to President Reagan on Tuesday voting 219–213 to approve spending $1.5 billion for 21 more MX missiles. The vote was a major reversal for Democratic Speaker Thomas P. O'Neill and other House leaders who had worked hard to defeat the MX.

News Journal, March 27, 1985

The House of Representatives gave President Reagan a narrow but significant triumph tonight when it voted 219 to 213 to release $1.5 billion earmarked for the purchase of 21 additional MX missiles.

New York Times, March 27, 1985

Reagan's "victory," not the missiles' strategic merits, is the center of attention and encourages the reader to regard that as the most important aspect of the story.

The press thus explains issues not on their own terms but as they affect various individuals; it dissects events not for their ideological content but for their personal drama. The question most often addressed is not, What are the merits of this policy? but, Who will it benefit and who will it harm? Whether something is newsworthy or not is gauged not by its economic or social ramifications but by how much interpersonal conflict it arouses.

Another way to verify these assertions is to watch television interview shows such as NBC's "Meet the Press" or CBS's "Face the Nation." The example in A Closer Look illustrates the emphasis on personality in contemporary journalism.

David Paletz and Robert Entman succinctly capture the essence of personalized news: "Prime news generally involves prominent, powerful people in action, or more desirable from the media's point of view, in conflict."[42]

DRAMA AND ACTION A journalist can report a political incident from many angles. It is possible, for example, to focus on its causes, its connections to other events, its immediate ramifications, or its historical meaning. But the news media, and television in particular, seem to take a different perspective: ". . . the exciting and controversial, the 'visual' and above all, the quick will survive the editorial process; the complex, difficult and abstract will wind up on the cutting room floor."[43] Or, as a British critic notes, "Professional television pressures work constantly toward portraying action and not thought, personalities and not issues, what is visually happening and not the boring explanations of why."[44] Patrick Buchanan, former President Reagan's director of communications, stated the proposition differently: "The principal press bias is not a liberal bias. It's a bias for a good fight. The press loves to see a fight start, and it hates to see it end."[45]

The stress on drama, conflict, and violence is easily seen in the lead story of television news shows or the front page of the local daily. After all, what appears first—airplane crashes, bombings, earthquakes, murders, typhoons, and armed conflict or substantive public policy controversies?

Even more significant, the emphasis on the sound and fury of politics becomes part of how even routine situations are reported. Consider CBS news coverage of a congressional hearing during which the secretary of defense, Caspar Weinberger, asked for no further cuts in military appropriations. Instead of describing the secretary's position or the counterarguments it raised, CBS showed a heated exchange of insults between Senator Donald Riegle and Mr. Weinberger. Senator Riegle's denunciation of the secretary's judgment as "dangerous to the country" drew the retort, "You have accomplished your principal purpose, to launch a demagogic attack on me in time for the afternoon and evening editions."[46] The content and form of CBS's presentation implied that images of two angry men were more newsworthy than an analysis of what they were arguing about in the first place.

Another common tendency is to report violence without explaining the underlying motivations or grievances. The coverage of Higgins's hanging by the Organization of the Oppressed on Earth, as we have seen, did not delve into the factors that ultimately led to his being held hostage. It may be true that the killers are no more than a band of insane terrorists, but it is still important to know what conditions produce and sustain such groups.

Domestic confrontations between protesters and authorities are invariably handled the same way. By dwelling on frenzied crowds battling police with rocks and bottles, the news satisfies its craving for sound and fury but obscures the issues that sparked the confrontation.[47] A good example is the way television presented student antiwar protests during the late 1960s and early 1970s. According to Edward J. Epstein, "only . . . one type of campus story was routinely covered: the confrontation between police and students. . . ."[48]

Many of the factors that determine how the media cover news in general also govern their approach to political campaigns and elections.

Checkpoint

- Journalists and editors strive to be objective, but it is nearly impossible to report the "news as it happens." Because of the number and nature of events, reporters must necessarily select what and how they report stories.

- Instead of gathering facts on their own, journalists frequently rely on what they are told by political leaders, press secretaries, public relations departments, and other officials.

- The media tend to personalize the news by emphasizing the human interest aspects of a story rather than its policy implications.

- Newspapers, and especially television, frequently stress the dramatic components of events without explaining their underlying causes.

COVERAGE OF POLITICAL CAMPAIGNS

Elections are the centerpiece of democracy. Through voting, people can voice their opinions, express their hopes and aspirations, discipline their leaders, and ultimately control their nation's destiny. According to democratic theory, elections are the public's source of power, but in order to use its muscle effectively the public has

Latest poll shows Weld pulling away from Pierce

By Mitchell Zuckoff
GLOBE STAFF

William F. Weld opened his first significant lead yesterday over Steven D. Pierce in their race for the Republican gubernatorial nomination, according to a new poll.

The Boston Globe/WBZ-TV poll found that Weld had the support of 51 percent of likely Republican primary voters, versus 41 percent for Pierce, the party's endorsed candi-

for independent voters, who he believes may be looking for a candidate who is moderate on social issues and conservative on fiscal ones. He slammed both Democratic gubernatorial candidates and made a case for sending a message by voting in the GOP primary.

"John Silber is out of touch. He has said consistently if the CLT petition passes he would seek an injunction in court against it. That's just nuts. There's no legal basis for it,"

WILLIAM F. WELD
Says he can provide change

Describing the close race for the Democratic gubernatorial nomination in Massachusetts in 1990, this story illustrates that the emphasis on campaign coverage is often on who is ahead and who is behind.

to know where candidates and parties stand on public policy issues. Besides the people themselves, two groups have major responsibilities in this regard.

Those running for office must state their positions. Otherwise, there is no real choice and elections lose their meaning. (Chapter 11 shows how and why candidates regularly shirk this obligation.) But they are not solely responsible for the success of the system. The mass media have a duty to report thoroughly and accurately what the contestants stand for.

This role is perhaps the media's major challenge. All news is important, but campaign coverage is crucial because of its capacity to empower the electorate. What voters know about campaigns comes to them almost entirely secondhand from newspapers, television, and magazines. Table 9.2 shows, for example, that voters in 1988 rarely met candidates face to face but learned about them indirectly from television and newspapers. Therefore, in assessing how well the political system works in America, it is essential to inspect the media's treatment of elections.

In reporting on campaigns, the news media bring their usual procedures and tendencies to the campaign trail. In other words, far from mirroring all that politicians say and do, journalists select the information to be reported. Because time and space constraints do not allow speeches

and rallies to be described in their entirety, certain parts are mentioned, others ignored.

Thus, once again the basic question is not whether the media are selective—they have to be—but what they include and exclude, and how these choices affect voters' beliefs and behavior.

Campaigns as Sporting Events

**HIGH STAKES IN NEW ORLEANS
CAN BUSH GET BACK ON TRACK?
THE DEBATE: HARDBALL
BUSH COMES ON STRONG
HOW BUSH WON**

One wonders if these headlines from 1988 editions of *Newsweek* and *Time* described an athletic contest or a presidential election. Using metaphors is perfectly good journalism, yet Thomas Patterson, along with countless others, believes that the media take the metaphor literally: "The dominant theme of presidential news coverage is winning and losing."[49] He finds that:

> In its coverage of a presidential campaign, the press concentrates on the strategic game played by the candidates in the pursuit of the presidency, thereby de-emphasizing questions of national policy and leadership.[50]

Instead of examining issues, reporters tend to describe **campaign hoopla**: the size of crowds, surges and declines in the polls, organizational triumphs and failures, endorsements won and

Table 9.2

How Citizens Come into Contact with Candidates for Congress

	Incumbent Representative (%)	Opponent (%)
Met personally	16	9
Saw at a rally or meeting	13	4
Heard on radio	30	25
Read about in newspapers	65	61
Saw on television	60	45

Questions: There are ways in which U.S. Representatives can have contact with the people in their districts. . . . Have you come in contact with or learned anything about [name of representative] through any of these ways? How about [name of opponent] who also ran for the U.S. House of Representatives from this district?

Source: Based on data from the Center for Political Studies, University of Michigan, *American National Election Study, 1988.*

lost, and above all the ebb and flow of momentum. Elections are likened to horse races in which attention centers on who is ahead, who is behind, who is gaining, who has dropped out.[51] What gets lost in the excitement is why the race is being run at all.[52]

The numbers in Table 9.3 demonstrate the point. Analyzing *Time* and *Newsweek* articles, Patterson shows that the "horse race" aspect and campaign maneuvers account for close to half of the election content in these magazines. Issues, as they are normally understood, receive only a fraction of the coverage. Over the years media scholars have repeatedly confirmed these sorts of findings.[53] One observer, himself a politician and campaign strategist, summarized the situation this way: "Political coverage has become too much like a pregame sports show, elevated to the color and drama of the athletic event."[54]

What is attractive about a sporting event? Its action—the faster, the better; its drama; its tension; its unexpected plays; and the uncertainty of the outcome. Perhaps these are the reasons

Table 9.3

Themes in Coverage of the 1988 Campaign, Stories Appearing in *Newsweek* and *Time*

Type of Coverage	Percentage of Election Coverage
Horse race (e.g., who is winning)	32
Campaign issues (e.g., scandals)	13
Images (e.g., leadership ability, style)	22
Candidate background (e.g., ideology)	16
Policy issues (e.g., budget deficit)	17

Source: Thomas E. Patterson, "The Press and Its Missed Assignment," in *The Elections of 1988,* ed. Michael Nelson (Washington, D.C.: Congressional Quarterly Press, 1989), p. 98.

A Closer Look

Issues Versus Personality in Campaign Coverage ★★★

In 1976, Jimmy Carter, the Democratic nominee for president, granted an interview to Robert Scheer, who was writing for *Playboy* magazine. At the end of the session, as the two men walked out Carter's front door, the candidate delivered a spontaneous monologue during which he said, "I've looked on a lot of women with lust. I've committed adultery in my heart many times. This is something that God recognizes I will do—and I have done it—and God forgives me for it."[a]

Needless to say, this offhand remark created an instant sensation. Carried by every wire service and network in the country, it stirred up a week-long political storm that nearly destroyed Carter's candidacy. It was one of the more memorable incidents of the election period and is, in fact, about all that most people remember about the *Playboy* interview.

It is debatable whether this confession deserved all the fuss it received. Carter did, however, say something else in the course of the interview that was at least as significant and,

ironically, touched on the media's priorities:

> Issues? The local media are interested all right, the national news media have absolutely no interest *at all* . . . the traveling press have zero interest in any issue unless it's a matter of making a mistake. . . . There's nobody in the back of the plane who would ask an issue question unless he thought he could trick me into some crazy statement.[b]

For students of American government, this last statement is more informative than the furor over "lust in the heart," because it underscores the press's propensity to give not the whole truth but of necessity only a portion of it. What it chooses to present are frequently the surface elements of election campaigns— the personal and sporting aspects—while it downplays candidates' and parties' stands on major public disputes.

[a]*Playboy*, November 1976, p. 86.
[b]*Ibid.*, pp. 66. Carter probably did not realize how close to the truth he was.

why reporters tend to treat elections as athletic contests: Doing so makes them seem more interesting and appealing.

Still, a price has to be paid. Patterson, for example, believes that the electorate is flooded with the wrong kind of information.[55] The media do not enlighten voters but leave them mystified about complex issues. The anecdote in A Closer Look illustrates the preoccupation with campaign hoopla.

Candidates and the Media

It is not entirely fair to blame news organizations for issue avoidance. Office seekers themselves are often all too eager to duck controversies and show off their personalities and images instead. Many of them, along with members of the press corps, do not believe that voters are knowledgeable or interested enough to care about specific policy questions. Candidates do much better, they tell each other, to speak in easily understood symbols than to deal with the complexities of the economy. As Chapter 11 explains, they also obscure their positions on contentious issues because of their fear of alienating potential voters. Whatever the reason, Richard Joslyn found, after carefully analyzing hundreds of spot advertisements, that relatively few ads disclose candidates' stands on issues.[56]

In fact, many candidates and their staffs believe that the media should be used mainly to promote and advertise campaigns, not to inform or educate the electorate. If any law of politics is true, it is surely that unmanaged news is the politician's worst enemy. Campaign strategists work with three principles in mind: First, because they know that people lean heavily on television to learn about candidates, television exposure outranks substance in importance. Second, due to space and time constraints, television news shows "stories" that can be told in one or two minutes and that depict people doing something visually exciting. Finally, newscasters hate "talking heads"—speakers droning on and on about some complex issue. What they want, instead, are short, pithy statements—**sound bites**, professionals call them—that can be aired in 30 to 45 seconds. An example: While criticizing his opponent's allegedly soft stand on defense, Bush told audiences, "I wouldn't be surprised if [Dukakis] thought that a naval exercise is something you find in Jane Fonda's workout book."[57] Short and to the point, the remark could easily be squeezed into any broadcast, however brief.

Integrating this knowledge into their campaign strategies, office seekers attempt to manipulate press coverage for their own purposes. What is surprising is how successful they are. By carefully staging the location, timing, and context of their appearances, presidential candidates can virtually dictate how they will be reported on the six o'clock news. Former President Reagan was the master of this art, but his successor quickly caught on. Perhaps Bush's most brilliant effort to maneuver the media to his advantage came early in the 1988 campaign. In what CBS admitted was a "floating political theater," the vice-president sailed around Bos-

ton Harbor, the very heart of Dukakis's turf, pointing out to hordes of reporters, camera operators, and photographers all the trash and slime in the malodorous water. Then the sound bite: "My opponent's solution—delay, fight, anything but clean up. Well, I don't call that leadership, and I certainly don't even call it competence."[58] As Bush's advisers confidently predicted, the three networks dutifully aired the event on their evening news broadcasts; only one, ABC, tried to explain the extremely complicated history of the mess in the harbor and that

"Hey, do you want to be on the news tonight or not? This is a sound bite, not the Gettysburg Address. Just say what you have to say, Senator, and get the hell off."

Drawing by Ziegler; © 1989 The New Yorker Magazine, Inc.

Dukakis might not be totally to blame for it.

Although Bush's advisers may have been superstars in this game, they are certainly not its only players. Pseudo-events—staged visits to nursing homes, polluted beaches, orphanages, slums, drug rehabilitation centers, factory gates, and toxic waste dumps—are the lifeblood of electoral politics. They are popular with candidates precisely because everything is supposedly under their control; the "image" is not disturbed by placard-waving protestors or tricky questions from hostile reporters. This is how the game is played, and the press knows it.

Given this knowledge, however, one wonders why the news media go along. Speaking of President Reagan's ability to stage campaign events to suit his needs, Tom Brokaw of NBC said, "He's the best I've ever seen." David Brinkley conceded, "He certainly tries to use us, because he is so good at it—and he knows it. But we know it."[59] Despite this awareness, the networks generally report campaigns as the professionals want them reported.

In an article entitled "How Television Failed the American Voter," David Halberstam summed up the media's acquiescence:

> If they covered professional football . . . in the same way it would go something like this: During the season they would not cover any games live but would instead give 75-second reports on the previous day's game. This would continue right through to the Super Bowl. Nor would they deign to cover the Super Bowl itself. After the game, however, they would cover—live and in color—the three-hour champagne celebration in the winner's locker room.[60]

Campaign Debates

"Okay," one might respond to these remarks, "the news is not perfect, but what about debates? Don't most candidates, including those running for the presidency, have to debate their opponents face to face? Aren't these affairs broadcast live by radio and television and published verbatim in newspapers? Isn't there a lot of give and take with no place to hide when a mistake is made? Don't the cameras and microphones expose falsehood, temerity, weakness, and lack of candor?"

Debates are commonplace these days, and, on paper anyway, they should well serve democracy by placing candidates and their programs in the limelight. Each presidential election year, for example, there are several debates—Democratic and Republican presidential primary contenders staged more than a dozen in 1987 and 1988—so one might believe that the manipulation of the media is somewhat blunted.[61]

Yet appearance does not always match reality, since these affairs are not as spontaneous and freewheeling as they seem. In 1988 both the Bush and Dukakis camps laid down the ground rules, specifying the number of debates, the format for questioning, and the length of time for answers and rebuttals. No *direct* exchanges between the men were allowed; instead, a panel of three reporters interviewed each man. The candidates so controlled the planning that they had the final say on the timing (Bush's advisers insisted on the end of September and early October, when competition from the Olympics and World Series might dilute coverage of a Dukakis "victory"); positioning of the candidates (each man would stand, but Dukakis could use a box if he wanted to look taller); and the panelists (no one wanted hostile questioners).[62]

To see how self-serving such arrangements can be, imagine two contenders for the heavyweight boxing championship of the world meeting privately to decide the number and length of rounds, the dimensions of the ring, and the names of the judges. Then, when the fight starts, instead of punching each other they begin sparring with the referee.

Many observers are convinced that candidates participating in debates deliver canned speeches that have little or nothing to do with the questions they are asked; that they deal in platitudes, symbols, and images; that they evade controversies; that they frequently contradict their past statements; and that interviewers seldom have a chance to point out these evasions or inconsistencies. The overriding objective is to sell oneself, not one's program. Richard Joslyn's analysis of the 1960, 1976, and 1980 presidential debates concludes that policy discussions consist of general, vague, and widely agreed upon objectives such as full employment and the elimination of government waste; as a result, debates add little to the public's understanding of specific programs.[63]

Whatever programs and policies do get discussed in debates, the press tends to downplay them in favor of discussions of "winners and losers." Rather than asking if the candidates' pronouncements hold water, journalists are more apt to analyze how each side prepared, how it came across in the heat of the battle, and especially how its future chances were affected. The media are encouraged in this postmortem analysis by "spin doctors," campaign aides who immediately after the debate appear in interviews and press conferences to clarify or emphasize certain points, to explain away damaging statements, and especially to insist that their candidate won.

George Bush received this sort of "first aid" after his first debate with Dukakis. He had stepped in hot water when a panelist asked him if in the event abortions were outlawed, women receiving them should be jailed. Clearly rattled, the vice-president muttered "I haven't sorted out the penalties," leaving open the possibility that he might favor prosecution. But the next day his campaign manager, sensing danger in such a position, assured reporters that Bush was not really suggesting that these women would be treated as criminals.[64] The press reported this clarification, and the issue quickly disappeared.

As it turns out, comparatively few voters seem to be swayed by debates. Their most common effect, in fact, is to reinforce initial preferences. A less common result is the creation of new opinions among those who were previously undecided. Only rarely does a listener switch sides as a consequence of listening to a debate.[65] Polls bear out these propositions. Seventy-seven percent of the people interviewed by a Gallup poll after the first Bush-Dukakis debate in 1988 claimed that the debate did not change their voting plans.[66] Similarly, Arthur Miller and Michael MacKuen found that, although the 1976 debates between Jimmy Carter and Gerald Ford may have stimulated curiosity and raised political awareness, they nevertheless mainly reinforced preexisting preferences.[67]

Still, the small portion of the electorate that does switch can be decisive in a close election. This possibility explains why candidates invest so much time and energy preparing for debates.

ARE THE MEDIA SERVING THE PUBLIC? One may, of course, wonder if this description of how the media cover the news is not overly critical. Is it not true, for instance, that the press is in business to make money, and the way to do that is to give people what they want? Certainly, the news contains violence and drama, but that is what concerns most Americans. Granted, technical issues are not given prominence, but how many citizens would comprehend them anyway? The average voter understands personality better than foreign affairs or economic doctrine, so it is sensible, is it not, to talk about people rather than ideas? In short, how much *can* the electorate know, and how much does it *want* to know? We take up this topic next.

Television cameras being readied for a debate between George Bush and Michael Dukakis in the 1988 presidential election. Presidential debates have become media events in which the participants are judged more on their style and appearance than on the substance of what they say.

Checkpoint

- The media's coverage of elections parallels their coverage of politics in general. Instead of dissecting candidates' platforms and promises, newspapers, magazines, and television tend to liken the contests to sporting events, putting the emphasis on who is ahead and why.

- Reporters are not totally to blame for this situation, however, since candidates tend to avoid controversial issues and try to manipulate press coverage to their own advantage.

- Political debates commonly resemble press conferences rather than in-depth exchanges of views. The media, aided by candidates' "spin doctors," by and large ignore the substance of debates and concentrate instead on who won.

EXPLAINING NEWS COVERAGE

The news that most Americans consume clearly does not mirror life but reports only certain parts of it. What accounts for the selection of the stories and the manner of their presentation?

Many people—particularly conservatives, and some scholars—complain that national news is biased in various ways. They claim it favors liberals, denigrates traditional values, exaggerates social and economic injustices, ignores what is good in America, and is quick to find fault in most of our cherished institutions. Others suspect that television and newspapers unwittingly undermine political authority and create cynicism in the public.[68] Samuel Huntington, a political scientist at Harvard University, believes that the media have so persistently criticized national authority that Americans have become distrustful and resentful of it.[69] George Keyworth, a science adviser to President Reagan, shares this perception, claiming that "much of

the press seems to be drawn from a relatively narrow fringe element of the far left of society . . . and . . . is trying to tear down America."[70]

How much truth there is in these charges is a matter of dispute. Reporters as individuals do tend to favor environmental protection, the rights of women, blacks, homosexuals, and other minorities, and more permissive life-styles—all of which are generally considered liberal positions. The majority vote for Democrats over Republicans for national office.[71] In these respects they differ, but not drastically, from the general public.

On a more fundamental level, however, the men and women who report the news are fully committed to the free enterprise system. Few of them question basic economic or political institutions. They fully approve of the separation of powers, federalism, judicial review, private property, the Bill of Rights, individualism—in short, the bedrock values upon which American society is built. True, they support government regulation of the economy, but this attitude hardly distinguishes them from most citizens.[72] And keep in mind that newspaper owners tend to be conservative.[73]

Furthermore, no systematic study has shown the mass media to be overtly politically biased.[74] Articles in the news sections are usually rather bland accounts of what candidates do, not critical assessments of their stands on issues. In addition, several analyses contradict Huntington's thesis that the media undermine authority: If they have any effect, it is to legitimize the status quo and the establishment.[75] A survey of election night coverage arrives at the same conclusion: The media reinforce beliefs about the uniqueness and benevolence of the American political system.[76]

Like everyone, journalists have faults. But these weaknesses by themselves do not account for the selection of news stories or the manner of their reporting. Instead, various external pressures and constraints largely determine how reporters present their material.

Economic Considerations

Most sources of public information, such as the *News Journal*, are part of a profit-making enter-

Covering major political events, such as the 1988 Republican convention in Houston, Texas, requires a great deal of expensive equipment. The high costs of covering special events forces newscasters to limit the depth of their coverage of everyday news.

prise. They strive to be fair, factual, and representative, but they also have to make money to stay alive. Driven by these two responsibilities, news and profits, they constantly face potential conflicts. Newspapers provide many services to their readers besides political coverage: Advertisements direct buyers to one-day sales; the movie section tells what is playing at the mall; sports pages reprint last night's box scores; horoscopes guide personal decisions. Readers want to know about a nephew's wedding as much as President Bush's travels. Indeed, if one looks carefully at a typical American newspaper, it becomes plain that politics is only part, and occasionally only a small one, of its business.

Economic constraints bind television as well. Network executives see the nightly news as an integral part of "audience flow."[77] After arriving home from work and finishing dinner and the dishes, people tune in first the local, then the national news. One theory holds that once a viewer selects a channel, he or she will continue watching it until bedtime. Even if a program does not attract new viewers, it cannot, from the network's perspective, afford to drive them away. Thus, a network demands an "entertaining" news hour. As John Hart, a network correspondent for 25 years, remarked, "Resources are gathered and spent, talent hired, executives promoted, broadcasts shaped . . . with an eye to seizing the audience."[78]

With money going toward style, format, and personalities, the best news may be too expensive to produce, thereby forcing broadcasters to rein in the scope and depth of their coverage. Monetary considerations explain a great deal about how the news is presented. Selectivity, for example, is one effect of having a limited number of camera operators and technicians available to film the daily quota of news stories. These crews tend to congregate in Washington, where they can easily cover the Supreme Court, the bureaucracy, the Congress, and above all else, the presidency.[79] At the same time, the networks and wire services cannot afford to deploy many correspondents overseas, especially in Third World countries. (The number of foreign-based journalists dropped sharply after World War II; there are now probably fewer than a thousand.[80]) In order to cover international affairs, news organizations retain "stringers"—freelance reporters—or use what William Dorman calls "parachute journalism": When a crisis develops, correspondents quickly fly to the scene and just as quickly leave when it passes.[81] Because these men and women tend to be generalists, without a firsthand knowledge of the language, history, and culture of the places they visit, reports tend to be superficial. This perhaps explains why the coverage of the Higgins and Cicippio tragedy did not include much background information. In any event, the electorate's knowledge of the world depends heavily on where the networks and newspapers find it profitable to deploy cameras and reporters, and not on totally "objective" determinations of news worthiness.

Official interpretations dominate the news for exactly the same reasons. Public officials, experts, celebrities, and other authorities are comparatively easy to locate and interview; their activities are predictable; their words are credible; and they work in capitals and central cities where the media are housed. In view of economic constraints, it is no wonder that the government and public officials, not investigative reporters, are the source of so much news.

Economic considerations also explain why action, drama, and emotion take up enormous amounts of time and space. Television editors and writers believe that in order to maintain their audience, their reports have to be both visually interesting and psychologically appealing. Stories are best told with conflict and emotion, not with abstractions or disembodied statistics. What keeps a family glued to the television set, a lecture on defense policy or an F-16 dive-bombing a jungle village?

The consequences of these economic constraints, many observers worry, is that the people receive at most a superficial and fragmented view of events and issues. The parts do not add up to the whole. Americans realize, for example, that terrible violence is occurring in Lebanon; after all, they see *episodes* of artillery duels and terrorist bombings night after night. But do they understand the root causes of this violence? Put more crudely, thousands of Americans die violently each year. Why, then, did Higgins's death make the front page? Without answers, the Middle East must be a totally incomprehensible place to the man and woman in the street.

Assumptions About Audiences

Salespeople know that the key to success is a firm grasp of the market. Discover what consumers want and make a fortune; misjudge their preferences and go out of business. (This principle assumes, of course, that the organization is not big enough to *create* wants, but can only satisfy them.) The axiom applies to the mass media

as much as to any profit-making institution. After all, reporters, editors, publishers, and broadcasters are all selling a product—news—and how they package that product depends on their beliefs and perceptions of the marketplace.

What do the media think the public desires? Perhaps the reasoning goes this way: If people really wanted to be informed instead of entertained, they would watch public television or CNN; if they wanted in-depth briefings about the Middle East, they would buy the hundreds of new books on public affairs that appear each year; if they wanted to know where candidates stand on issues, they would read campaign brochures.

Instead, according to experts in and out of the media, the masses have a short attention span, a fascination with action, and a craving for simplicity. They want stories, not discussions; fantasies, not reasons; conflict, not analysis. They want to see terrorism in action, not study the conditions that cause it.

A political scientist with years of experience studying mass reactions to the media feels the public's capacity to absorb complicated information is limited:

> To gain the attention of average Americans, who lack deep political interest, the media must tell political stories simply and interestingly. But most important political stories are not simple, and many have little appeal for general audiences. Most cannot be condensed to fit the brief attention span of a public that is not highly motivated to pay attention.[82]

Network executives and newspaper publishers think they have data to back up this unflattering portrait. Ratings suggest that what makes a news broadcast profitable is not its intellectual content but the personality of the newscaster (why else do network anchors make seven-figure salaries?), its visual effects, its timing, its story lines, its ability to evoke emotions like fear, outrage, anxiety, sympathy, and happiness. One does not need ratings to make the argument. Go into any doctor's office: what do the patients read, *Foreign Affairs* or *People Weekly*?

At first glance, then, the executives and owners seem to have a strong case. They present the news as they do because it is what the people want. On the other hand, this situation may be a chicken-and-egg problem. If voters have for most of their lives been given rather superficial coverage—the sauce and not the meat of politics—and if in addition their government seems remote, mysterious, and beyond control, then naturally they may prefer entertainment to political debates. Having been constantly exposed to campaign ballyhoo, they may by now feel that that is all there is to elections. Besides, what good is it to understand an issue if you are convinced that your opinions will be ignored anyway? Suppose citizens' feelings of efficacy—the belief that political participation does matter— were higher and the news more informative. Then their curiosity and motivation might be aroused, which might, in turn, create a larger audience for informative programs.

To restate this argument, the way news is presented may be a cause (just one of many, to be sure) as well as a result of public apathy. But even this line of reasoning may concede too much. One poll, for example, found that its respondents believed television news gave too much attention to "politics" (presumably hoopla, not substance), homosexuals, and crime and not enough to "foreign affairs," "Congress," "the economy," and "poor people."[83]

The Press Corps

Journalists are intelligent, honest, and hardworking. Yet, as we just observed, almost every reporter belongs to a large organization that has its own requirements, values, and concerns. However much a writer wants to explore the nuances of Middle Eastern politics or the intricacies of the budget deficit, the medium sets limits that have to be heeded.

In addition, members of the press have limited time and energy, and most are not experts on policy but generalists who rely heavily on what others tell them. Not having expertise means that they cannot always ask the most pertinent question or critically evaluate the response. This lack of specialization encourages them to report on the things they do understand, such as political feuds, dramatic episodes, and human interest events.

The press corps, furthermore, has mutually dependent relationships with public officials and private authorities who are the source of so much news. No one doubts that at times reporters and civil servants are bitter adversaries. Nevertheless, there is perhaps less independence than commonly supposed.

For instance, the press has been taken to task for its failure to uncover the so-called Iran-Contra scandal, an episode in which members of President Reagan's administration secretly and unlawfully sold arms to Iran and then diverted portions of the funds to the contras, a rebel group that sought the overthrow of the government of Nicaragua.[84] Although dozens of officials in the White House, the State and Defense Departments, and the Central Intelligence Agency knew about parts of the operation, the public did not learn about any of it until an obscure Lebanese magazine, *Al Shiraa*, published the report of the arms sales in late 1986. Only then did the mass media in the United States pick up the story. American journalists were further stunned a few weeks later when Attorney General Edwin Meese announced that portions of the arms sales had been channeled to the contras. The president of the American Society of Newspaper Editors later conceded that "The press was lax in this case. The press failed, and its failure allowed the policy to continue . . . part of this scandal must be laid at the doorstep of the press."[85]

Why was the Iranian arms deal not exposed by syndicated columnists, network correspondents, or other members of the press? One theory holds that the top journalists are too close to and dependent on the establishment to uncover corruption in high places.[86] The men and women whose "beat" encompasses the top rungs of an administration daily rub elbows with their subjects and sooner or later establish personal relations that make distance and objectivity difficult. Until recently, private misconduct (such as excessive drinking or adultery) of public leaders frequently went unreported.[87]

Moreover, to be too intrusive or aggressive puts a reporter's access to political figures at risk. Politicians partly control who interviews them, who rides in the press bus, who receives inside tips, who has a pass to a briefing, and who might be mentioned for an appointment to an important post at some future date. Journalists, in other words, have strong incentives for getting along with the very people they cover. The cooperation that occurs is, as Ben Bagdikian notes, "perhaps a natural result in an equation where one side controls information and the other has to report it."[88] This interpretation of investigative reporting points to a general characteristic of political journalism that runs counter to common belief: The press has personal ties to the upper echelons of government that can make independence and objectivity difficult to achieve.

Checkpoint

- The mass media operate under constraints that affect the presentation of the news.

- Although individual reporters may be more liberal than the public as a whole, there is little evidence that they consciously slant their reports or undermine basic institutions and values. Indeed, many scholars think that the press has, if anything, a "status quo" bias.

- Reporting cannot escape economic considerations. News organizations are profit-making enterprises and accordingly cannot devote limitless resources to news coverage.

- The media also tailor their product to what they think their audiences will understand and accept. For the most part, they assume that people prefer action, drama, and human interest over abstract ideas.

- Most reporters are generalists who have to rely heavily on what others tell them. This fact makes them susceptible to cooptation by the very institutions they are supposed to cover independently and objectively.

THE MASS MEDIA: WHO GOVERNS?

It is commonplace in the social sciences to liken the news to a window: If it is large and open people can see far and wide, but if it is narrow and partially closed their field of vision is shortened. How big is the window in the United States? Naturally, the three models of American government give different answers.

Pluralists think it is huge. In the first place, they reason, Americans enjoy a freedom of the press that is the envy of the world. This freedom coupled with the plethora of media outlets gives groups, however small, ample opportunity to express their views and participate in policymaking. Don't forget that for pluralists it is the equality of *opportunity* to gain power, not equality of actual power, that matters. Access to the media means that we always have a competition of ideas. Finally, as A Closer Look suggests, anyone willing to take the time can become fully informed about every level of government.

Both the democratic and elite perspectives seem to agree that the window is really a peephole. The media, they complain, emphasize the wrong aspects of events and controversies. Describing the media's general impact on public perceptions and attitudes, one scholar summarizes the case this way:

> The personalized [and dramatized] view of politics gives people little, if any, grasp of political processes or power structures. Without a grasp of these things it is virtually impossible to understand how the political system really works. As a result, the political world becomes a mystical realm populated by actors who either have political "force" on their side or do not.[89]

By distorting beliefs about the world of politics, the popular press inadvertently pushes government into the shadows where it seems mysterious and beyond control. In so doing, it reinforces the established political authority, obscures alternative policies (by making them appear deviant and hence not worthy of consideration), creates apathy and alienation, and for all

A Closer Look

Alternative Sources of Information ★ ★ ★

With a bit of effort, any reasonably intelligent and motivated person can probe behind the headlines to explore the background and context of public policy and government. You do not have to be a specialist or devote endless hours to the process.

All papers have editorial pages. Read them as thoroughly as any section. True, the opinions expressed in editorials, letters, commentaries, and analyses are biased, but that does not make them worthless. In fact, they are often very helpful since their authors try to convince their readers by supplying the kind of logic and data that do not appear on the front page.

For the same reason it is worthwhile reading opinion magazines—liberal, conservative, socialist, libertarian alike— because, although they are by definition one-sided, they attempt to buttress their arguments with detailed information. When the *Nation*, a liberal weekly, rails against President Bush it gives reasons for its criticisms, some of which are logical, some of which are not, but most of which add to your store of knowledge of politics. In the same way, the *National Review* or the *American Spectator*, two conservative magazines, distrust Democrats, and you can learn a great deal by reading about their concerns.

For less partisan or more thorough coverage turn to major national newspapers such as the *New York Times*, the *Washington Post*, the *Philadelphia Inquirer*, the *Los Angeles Times*, and the *Baltimore Sun*, to name a few. Television is also an excellent source, *provided* that you are willing to get up Sunday morning for the interview programs, to tune in documentaries instead of game shows, and especially to give public television a chance. Virtually every community has a PBS station, which carries the "MacNeil-Lehrer Hour" (compare this evening news program with the network versions), "Frontline," and news specials by the score. Coupled with National Public Radio's "All Things Considered," these programs offer insights into politics that are informative and balanced.

Notice that it is not necessary to *increase* time spent on public affairs. It is rather a matter of switching to different forums: "MacNeil-Lehrer" as opposed to "60 Minutes," the *New York Times* versus *USA Today*, the *New Republic* or the *National Review* instead of *Vogue*. The point is that by simply reordering one's time and sources it is possible to become well informed.

these reasons, hinders responsible citizenship.

Not unexpectedly, power elite theorists go even further. They point out that the concentration of ownership and management of the popular press described earlier in the chapter stifles real political competition. In a large, industrial society nearly everyone depends on outside sources for information about government and politics. But with the sources of this information concentrated in such few hands, the ideas and power of the dominant elite are hardly ever challenged.

Who is right? One way to find out is to pick an issue and try to analyze it first by seeing how it is portrayed in the popular press. Then, compare that treatment with what is found in the activist press. As you do this, you will help yourself answer the question, Who governs?

Checkpoint

- Pluralists believe that the innumerable news outlets in the United States prevent any political group or segment of society from gaining excessive power.

- Democratic theorists believe that easy access to a variety of types of information is essential for popular control of government. But, like members of the power elite school, they are skeptical that the average American receives this information.

perts, rely heavily on the goodwill of the people they are supposed to cover. This reliance, some observers assert, prevents them from probing into the nooks and crannies of a story.

Pluralists argue that there are ample sources of information and that groups have numerous outlets for their views. The abundance of media outlets makes America relatively democratic. Democratic and elite theorists are not as optimistic. Despite freedom of the press, the media are not as informative as they could and should be.

KEY TERMS

Mass media
Objectivity
Mirror metaphor
Popular press
Activist press

Official point of view
Personalization
Campaign hoopla
Sound bites

SUMMARY

Americans rely almost exclusively on the mass media for their information about government and politics. Newspapers, television, magazines, and books set the political agenda and greatly influence the beliefs that underlie attitudes. There is an enormous number of media outlets in the United States and great variation in the kinds of information available to the public. Concentration in the ownership and management of these information sources, however, raises fears in some quarters that the public does not have unrestricted access to independent and competing ideas.

Selectivity inevitably creeps into news coverage, which as a result frequently emphasizes official viewpoints, personal and human interest angles, and drama, conflict, and violence. Substantive issues and policies are underplayed.

The media liken election campaigns to sporting events and emphasize who is ahead and who is behind. The candidates' stands on issues are not covered as thoroughly as campaign hoopla. Debates between the candidates do not compensate for the lack of issue coverage because the participants usually make only bland statements and the press does not probe their policy positions.

Personal, economic, and organizational factors constrain the media: Since television stations and newspapers are profit-making enterprises, they cannot allocate endless resources to news coverage. Reporters, who are frequently generalists and not ex-

FOR FURTHER READING

Timothy Crouse, *The Boys on the Bus* (New York: Ballantine Books, 1972). A classic account from the inside on how reporters covered the 1972 presidential campaign.

Robert M. Entman, *Democracy Without Citizens* (New York: Oxford University Press, 1989). Describes the crucial connection between the media and democracy.

Edward Jay Epstein, *News from No Where* (New York: Random House (Vintage Books), 1974). Shows how economic, organizational, and political constraints affect the presentation of the news.

George Gerbner et al., "Charting the Mainstream: Television's Contributions to Political Orientations," *Journal of Communications* 32 (Spring 1982): 100–127. This and other articles by Gerbner are among the best for showing the effect of the media, especially television, on perceptions of the world.

Doris A. Graber, *Mass Media and American Politics*, 3rd ed. (Washington, D.C.: Congressional Quarterly Press, 1988). A good introduction to various aspects of the media and politics.

Mark Hertsgaard, *On Bended Knee* (New York: Farrar, Straus & Giroux, 1988). A first-rate account of how the press is co-opted by the political establishment.

Thomas Patterson, *The Mass Media Election* (New York: Praeger, 1980). A superb account of how the American press covers elections.

Political Participation

**N**umerous civic leaders and scholars worry that something is seriously wrong in the United States because the rate of political participation is disturbingly low. Nearly half of the eligible electorate does not vote, and even fewer people take part in other types of activities such as contacting public officials or working in election campaigns. Other observers are not so concerned, however; they cite many opportunities for participation and note that widespread apathy has not prevented the formation of grass roots political movements that have brought important social and political changes. ∎

Life at Firebase Elsmere in 1989, like duty in many military outposts, had its ups and downs. The spartan living quarters consisted of two ramshackle tents and a portable latrine; a kerosene stove provided the only heat; entertainment came mostly from a transistor radio, a few books and magazines, or a game of solitaire. The tents' "decorations," mainly combat insignias and slogans ("Don't Mess With the U.S.A." and "Boycott Jane Fonda, American Traitor Bitch"), did not hide the hardship of living away from the comforts of home. Apart from a few engagements such as the "Spring Offensive," the days and nights at the base were filled with routine chores, idle conversation, and the hope that the effort would ultimately be worthwhile. In these respects, living at Firebase Elsmere was typical of military service anywhere.[1]

What made this camp unique, however, was that it was not an official army post. Manned solely by a dozen or so volunteers (many of them Vietnam veterans), the base sat on the front lawn of the Veterans Administration (VA) Hospital in Elsmere, Delaware. One could see through the tent flaps across Kirkwood Highway, a congested suburban thoroughfare, to a row of retail stores and a quiet residential neighborhood beyond. The encampment, in fact, seemed as out of place as a picnic table in the middle of a battlefield. Yet the men who garrisoned the base were serious and vowed not to pull out until they accomplished their mission.

And what was the mission? The veterans established the base to protest federal budget cuts in VA hospitals and health services. A petition circulated to "The United States Government" asserted that medical care for veterans had been slashed by more than $800 million, and it asked that the money be restored or possibly increased. They only wanted what the nation "promised" them in return for their service.

Although by 1990 Firebase Elsmere had been staffed continuously for more than two years, it is difficult to measure its success. Some volunteers sense public indifference to their plight. On the other hand, they collected several thousand signatures on a petition, won the endorsement of the town of Elsmere, received a resolution of approval from the Delaware General Assembly, and had the backing of the state's congressional delegation, which claimed to support supplemental funding for the VA.

Even though most of the people who drove or walked past the command post may have sympathized with the veterans, probably quite a few wondered if the tactics were not a bit extreme or bizarre. Living month after month in a couple of tents on the lawn of a VA hospital appeared to be a hard way to make a point. "Why not just write your congressman?" one pedestrian asked. Other onlookers—after two years there were very few—thought the encampment was an exercise in futility. "No one pays attention anyway," they said.

TYPES OF POLITICAL PARTICIPATION

Yet whether or not the public approves of their methods, the behavior of the men at Firebase Elsmere is a form of political participation, just as voting is. **Political participation** is any activity intended to affect the making and content of public policy. Although no hard-and-fast rules exist, social scientists classify the *types* of participation on a continuum running from "conventional" to "unconventional."[2]

At one end are those behaviors generally considered legitimate and appropriate for a free country. They include electoral activities—such as voting, wearing buttons, displaying yard signs, listening to debates, going to rallies, or working for a candidate—as well as efforts aimed at policymakers (writing a representative, calling state legislators, or attending a town meeting, for example). Even though many Americans may not do all of these things themselves, as we will see, they nonetheless regard them as traditional and acceptable ways of influencing decision making.

At the unconventional end of the scale are acts that may offend or confound the public's notions about what is necessary and proper in an open society or may even be illegal. These activities run the gamut from sit-ins, boycotts, demonstrations, and civil disobedience (refusal to pay taxes or obtain a parade permit, for instance) to acts of violence such as bombings, assassination, and kidnapping.

Unconventional participation is noteworthy not for the number of participants, but for their degree of commitment. During the 1960s and early 1970s, when America seemed to be a hotbed of social and political unrest, relatively few men and women actually took part in the protests. One study polled approximately 1500 respondents during the late 1960s but could find only a handful who said they had participated in a march or demonstration.[3] Even on college campuses, where resentment against the war, racial discrimination, and other social and economic injustices ran high, only a small minority of students ever burned draft cards or sat in administration offices.[4] Figure 10.1 shows just how reluctant most Americans are to resort to unconventional activities to make a political statement: Very few have engaged or would engage in these acts of unconventional political protest.

The varieties of political participation: Political participation ranges from conventional activities, such as working for a candidate, to acts of violence.

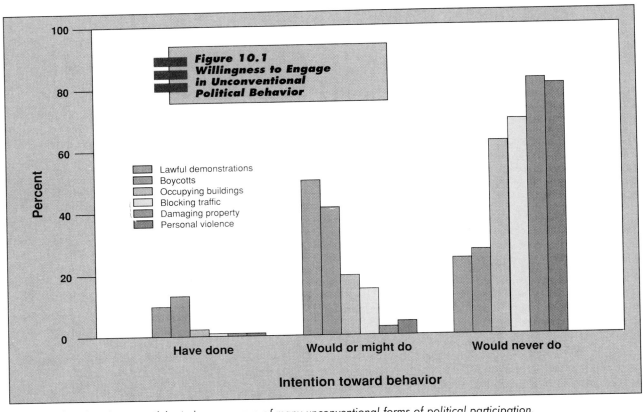

Figure 10.1 Willingness to Engage in Unconventional Political Behavior

Relatively few Americans participate in or approve of many unconventional forms of political participation. Almost no one, for example, has ever engaged in or supports activities such as blocking traffic or destroying property to make a political statement.

Source: Based on data in Samuel H. Barnes and Max Kaase, *Political Action* (Beverly Hills, Calif.: Sage, 1979), pp. 548–549. Used by permission of Sage.

Indeed, unconventional participation is so uncommon that polling organizations and research centers almost never ask about it anymore.*

*The National Opinion Research Center (NORC) at the University of Chicago, for example, annually conducts a survey of Americans' social and political values and activities. During the 1970s, when memories of large-scale anti-Vietnam and civil rights protests were still fresh in people's minds, the NORC asked its respondents if they had ever taken part in some form of direct political action, but by the end of the decade the organization stopped asking the question presumably because so few people answered in the affirmative. See, for example, National Opinion Research Center, *General Social Surveys: 1972–1989 Codebook* (Chicago: National Opinion Research Center, 1989), p. 242.

Yet the small numbers should not obscure the level of commitment that activists feel. Many of them routinely put their livelihoods and lives on the line for a cause. Hundreds of demonstrators, including children and handicapped people, were arrested in Seabrook, New Hampshire, in June 1989 after they scaled a chain link fence surrounding a nuclear power plant they wanted shut down.[5] In the same month, 50 antiabortion protestors faced a year in jail and a $5000 fine for trespassing on a family-planning clinic where abortions were performed. The judge agreed to suspend the sentence only if the defendants promised not to commit any more violations. When only a handful made the promise, the somewhat stunned judge commented, "In nine years on the bench, I've never seen people tell me they are ready to go out and commit their crimes again."[6]

The conventional-unconventional yardstick entails a good deal of subjective judgment. How one views a particular deed depends to some degree on who is doing it and for what purpose. Marches by the Nazi party invariably draw the wrath of community leaders, who often attempt to outlaw them, while a rally to protest apartheid in South Africa generally meets with approval. In other words, in many (but certainly not all) cases, Americans will tolerate the means if they believe in the ends.

Whatever one thinks of a particular kind of behavior—such as pitching a tent in front of a VA hospital—the act can have intended and unintended political consequences. In order to understand who is having an impact on American government, therefore, we need to examine the various types of participation, keeping track of both the rates and effects of the different kinds. Let's look first at voters and nonvoters, since elections play a pivotal role in politics. Then, we turn to other forms of political behavior.

Checkpoint

- Political participation is activity intended to influence the making and content of public policy.

- Social scientists often measure the types of participation on a conventional-unconventional scale. Conventional behaviors are widely accepted and associated with democratic processes.

- Unconventional activities straddle or step over the limits of accepted morality or legality. Few people engage in unconventional participation, but those who do are highly committed.

VOTING TURNOUT IN THE UNITED STATES

A regular customer in Farell's Bar and Grill in Brooklyn, New York, pointed to a detective and said "He don't vote." Going down the line of patrons, the man repeated, "He don't vote. He don't vote. He don't vote. Hardly anyone in here votes anymore." Every now and then, as the customer spoke, an expensive political advertisement appeared on the television set above the bar, but no one seemed to pay any attention to it.[7]

By almost any standard, voting turnout in the United States is low. In the 1988 presidential election about 90 million Americans voted, but this total still left another 90 million nonvoters, slightly less than half of the voting-age population.[8] Participation at city, county, and state and congressional levels is even lower. The 1986 House and Senate elections, for instance, attracted barely 46 percent of the eligible electorate,* and this percentage was high compared with some years.[9] Yet these overall figures, bad as they are, hide the shocking apathy that exists within many states. In certain regions, especially in the South, turnout in general elections has averaged less than 35 percent. Voting in primary elections—elections to choose a party's nominee—seldom exceeds 40 percent and often falls as low as 15 or 20 percent. Indeed, it is probably safe to conclude that nine out of ten Americans do not bother to vote in all of the major elections to which they are entitled.

Moreover, as Table 10.1 shows, turnout in most European and English-speaking countries greatly exceeds the American rate. In a few of these nations voting is required by law, but for the most part the higher rates are voluntary. As

*Keep in mind the distinction between "voting-age population," which is the total number of adults over 18, and the "eligible" population, which consists of those old enough to vote and not disqualified because they are not citizens, have committed a felony, been declared mentally incompetent, do not meet state or local residency requirements, or are ineligible for some other reason. U.S. Bureau of the Census, *Voting and Registration in the Election of November 1986* (Washington, D.C.: Government Printing Office, 1987), p. 42.

Table 10.1

Voting Turnout Rates in Selected Countries, 1970–1988
(Average Percentages for Indicated Years)

United States	
Presidential (1972–1988)	53
Congressional[a] (1974–1986)	39

Austria (1971–1983)	91	Luxembourg[b] (1968–1979)	84
Sweden (1970–1985)	90	Netherlands (1971–1986)	84
W. Germany (1972–1983)	89	Norway (1973–1985)	82
Iceland (1971–1983)	88	Israel (1973–1984)	78
Italy (1972–1983)	88	Gt. Britain (1970–1987)	75
Belgium[b] (1971–1985)	86	Canada (1972–1984)	73
Denmark (1971–1984)	86	Japan (1972–1983)	70
France[c] (1974–1981)	85		

[a]"Off-year" or non-presidential election years.
[b]These countries have compulsory voting.
[c]French presidential elections.

Source: Adapted from Table 5–1, Walter Dean Burnham,
"The Turnout Problem," in *Elections American Style*, ed. A. James Reichley
(Washington, D.C.: Brookings Institution, 1987), p. 107, and Bureau of Census data.

one can see in the table, about nine out of ten Swedes, West Germans, and Austrians vote in national elections, whereas only about one out of two Americans do. We will see later in the chapter that these cross-national differences arise largely because of dissimilarities in election laws.

Nevertheless, the low rates of turnout are especially disconcerting in view of the long struggle our ancestors fought to obtain the right to vote.

The Right to Vote

Suffrage—the right to vote—was at the time of the Revolution limited mainly to white male property holders. Women, blacks, native Americans, and the poor were all excluded by law and custom. Indeed, much of the political history of the United States during its 200 years of existence has been the story of the progressive enfranchisement of one group after another. By 1860 virtually every state had adopted universal manhood suffrage (Americans led the rest of the world in this respect). The Fifteenth Amendment (1870) gave the vote to black males, and the Nineteenth Amendment, adopted in 1920, enfranchised women. The Twenty-sixth Amendment, ratified in 1971, lowered the voting age in federal elections from 21 to 18 years.

As Chapter 7 pointed out, the long, arduous fight by blacks for the vote provides the most dramatic example of the expansion of the suffrage. In the aftermath of the Reconstruction era, blacks technically had the right to vote but were effectively excluded from electoral politics in the South. Employing such tactics as poll taxes, literacy tests, intimidation, and violence, whites kept nearly all nonwhites away from the polls for close to 100 years. Pushed by the civil rights movement, the courts and Congress slowly lowered barriers to voting. Finally, the Voting Rights Act of 1965 vastly increased registration among blacks in the South. As much as any piece of legislation in American history, this act represented the end of a long, difficult effort to give nearly every adult in America the vote. As seen below, many of our fellow citizens do not take advantage of the opportunity, but, on paper at least, the system has been thoroughly democratized.

Turnout in Historical Perspective

Given the hard-fought battles to expand suffrage, it is disconcerting to realize that the trend in turnout over time has been generally downward. As Figure 10.2 suggests, our great-grandparents were more likely to have voted than we are. In the late nineteenth century it was not uncommon for 75 to 85 percent of the eligible electorate in a state to go to the polls. Since then, however, participation has steadily dropped off in both presidential and congressional elections. Scholars call this downturn **demobilization** and debate its causes. It is worth pausing to listen to the arguments because they directly pertain to

views about the common person's capacity for self-government and to the question of who does and should govern.

CORRUPTION, STATISTICS, AND TURNOUT
One side points out that prior to the turn of the century corruption was rampant as the political parties outdid each other in stuffing ballot boxes, buying votes, and herding legions of bewildered and uninformed immigrants to the polls. Voting laws were loosely enforced and registration requirements virtually nonexistent. People could appear at the polls and vote merely by being spoken for by another individual. The parties themselves printed and distributed the ballots—always in distinctive color and occasionally with a noticeable odor—and then tabulated the returns on their own.[10]

Ballot peddling was commonplace. Prices var-

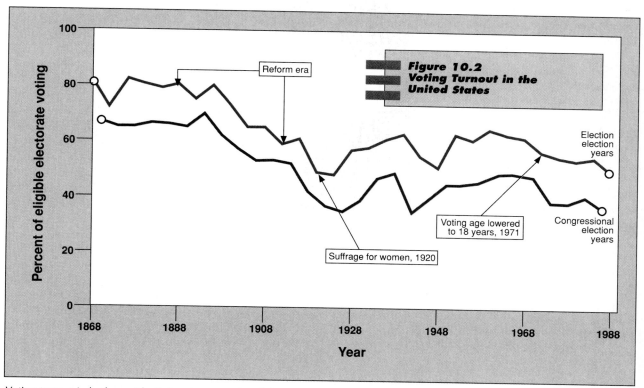

Voting turnout in both presidential and congressional (years in which there is no presidential race) elections has generally declined since the 1880s. The decline in turnout has occurred despite the passage of laws and constitutional amendments removing legal barriers to voting for various groups such as blacks and women.

Source: U.S. Bureau of the Census data.

ied according to the needs of the seller and the desperation of the candidates. In some locales a vote went for as little as a swig of whiskey; in others it might cost as much as $20 or $30.[11] It is said that politicians in Sussex County, Delaware, spent $60,000 purchasing votes in 1894 even though the county cast only 8000 ballots.[12]

In these circumstances, it is easy to see how greed and fraud, not civic-mindedness, swelled the ranks of the electorate. When one takes into account all the corruption, citizens before the turn of the century look decidedly less virtuous than the statistics indicate.

Various reforms ended some of the most blatant abuses. The most far-reaching were registration laws giving independent electoral boards, not the parties, the power to certify eligibility to vote. Another reform took the distribution and counting of ballots out of the hands of the parties. Before 1900, polling places were poorly supervised and votes could hardly ever be cast in secret. The introduction in the late 1800s of the **Australian ballot**—a ballot printed at public expense and listing all the candidates for office—ended this practice. These ballots are cast secretly in official polling places run under the supervision of nonpartisan commissions.

According to the first theory of demobilization, then, as the corruption was curbed, the high rate of voting naturally started to fall.[13] This theory also contends that in the years prior to the ratification in 1920 of the Nineteenth Amendment giving females the right to vote, many states had been enfranchising women on their own. As a result, the pool of qualified voters began expanding rapidly. Yet suffrage did not necessarily give women the experience and motivation to vote, and it was years before they participated at the same rate as men. This sudden infusion of nonvoting women into the ranks of eligible voters caused a nosedive in turnout statistics, but the different voting-age population base makes comparisons with earlier years somewhat misleading.[14]

INSTITUTIONAL CHANGE AND TURNOUT

The other side of the debate believes that the decline in turnout reflects a larger, more ominous explanation: *Institutional* changes caused the demobilization of the public. Historians and political scientists claim that voters in the late nineteenth century were interested and concerned with politics; that they had the capacity and motivation to respond to parties and candidates; and that, not having television, automobiles, or video games, they were willing to listen to campaign oratory, discuss national affairs with one another, and go faithfully to the polls on election day. Elections had, in short, both civic and entertainment value.[15]

Political parties, furthermore, were well organized to mobilize their followers. True, there were abuses. Bosses certainly bought votes and rewarded their cronies with jobs. But what really explains the success of parties in getting the masses to vote was their organizational skills, their internal cohesion and discipline, their relevance to people's needs, their control of information, and especially their ability to clarify and simplify the chaotic world of government. As the historian Robert Marcus suggests, most women and men probably considered identification with a party more of a virtue than a vice and often perceived political action as the moral equivalent of war.[16] It was, in short, a time when blacksmiths and wheelwrights, shopkeepers and teachers, farm hands and factory laborers were enthusiastic about politics. They were not model citizens to be sure—far from it—but at the same time they exemplified a civic spirit that seems lacking today.

What happened, then, to the old-time enthusiasm for politics? This second school of thought cites three factors: (1) the decline of party competition throughout many parts of the country, (2) the enactment of tough voting registration laws, and (3) the replacement of partisan newspapers by independent, "objective" journalism.

In the period after 1896, several regions of the country gravitated toward one-party politics, the northern and central states becoming solidly Republican, the South even more solidly Democratic. Many historians and political scientists believe that as party competition declined, so too did turnout; parties became unable to excite and mobilize their followers. In the absence of party competition people naturally lose interest in politics and lack a reason to vote.[17]

A political rally in a small New York town around 1900. Many social scientists believe that around the turn of the century average citizens were much more interested and involved in politics than they are now.

At the same time, many states began passing stringent voter registration and campaign laws. Aimed at stopping corruption, the regulations nevertheless presented formidable barriers to mass participation and further depressed turnout, especially among the less educated lower and working classes.[18]

Finally, the character of the popular press started changing around the turn of the century in ways that eventually discouraged many people from going to the polls. During most of the nineteenth century newspapers were openly partisan, a fact that one historian argues had certain benefits: It "made politics seem important, simplified issues, encouraged the public to judge men and [policies] with the yardstick of partisanship, and urged voters to display their political beliefs."[19]

These newspapers were gradually replaced by ones emphasizing "objectivity," independence, and sensationalism. Although the new brand of journalism was technically neutral, it did little to encourage political involvement because it trivialized issues; made government seem remote, corrupt, or unimportant; and hence left its readers unconcerned about voting.

The Electorate Today

Regardless of the causes, the earlier activism, if it ever existed, has gradually dissipated. There is today almost unanimous agreement that a large portion of the public is apathetic, cynical, and even slightly hostile toward candidates and parties. A key question arises: Why?

Social scientists and historians give two answers.[20] First, to the extent that there is a problem, it can be traced to the people themselves. If they do not vote, are not informed, or do not care, the fault lies in them. Something about their attitudes or personal circumstances cause their indifference and coolness to politics.

Another possibility, though, is the existence of various institutional forces that have intentionally or unintentionally discouraged good citizenship and contributed to the demobilization of the electorate. Instead of criticizing the average person, take a hard look at electoral laws, candidates, and the conduct of campaigns to see how they affect turnout. Political demobilization—apathy, disinterest, and nonvoting—may result as much from them as from the public's own shortcomings.

Checkpoint

- Participation in American elections is low both compared to other nations and in historical perspective.

- In the early Republic, the right to vote was limited mainly to white male property holders. Over the years, usually after bitter battles, voting rights have been extended to minorities, women, and 18-year-olds.

- Voting turnout has decreased steadily since the turn of the century.

- Scholars propose two explanations for the downturn. The first asserts that widespread corruption made turnout rates appear higher than they really were and that the sudden infusion of nonvoting women into the electorate intensified the drop-off.

- The other theory holds that citizens used to be more concerned and motivated than they now are and that this decline in interest has been caused by strict registration laws, one-party politics in many states, and the demise of partisan journalism.

- The low rate of voting turnout today can be explained by personal *and* institutional factors.

EXPLAINING VOTING AND NONVOTING

The search for the causes of voting and nonvoting leads first to individual characteristics such as social traits, party loyalty, and other attitudes. They are not the whole story, though, so we will also take up the effects of institutional factors such as election laws.

Individual Factors and Turnout

DEMOGRAPHIC CHARACTERISTICS OF VOTERS AND NONVOTERS A good way to sort out voters from nonvoters is to look at their socioeconomic differences. As Table 10.2 suggests, people in different social classes vote at different rates: The higher a person's status—measured by income, education, employment, or other demographic attributes—the more likely she or he will be to register and vote. The gaps between upper and lower income groups, between college graduates and high school dropouts, and between employed and unemployed workers approach 40 percent.

Voting is connected with other social traits as well. Older men and women, for instance, participate more regularly than young adults (see Table 10.2 again). Incidentally, the sudden expansion of the eligible electorate caused by the Twenty-sixth Amendment, which lowered the voting age to 18, may account for part of the recent decline in turnout. After all, young people, being mobile and less rooted in a community, vote less frequently than their elders: Not even half of them were registered in 1988, and less than one in three voted. As in the case of the rapid enfranchisement of women, the sudden increase in the number of potential voters was not accompanied by a surge in actual voting.

Table 10.2 also indicates that blacks vote slightly less often than whites, while Hispanics are considerably below the national average. Race in and of itself does not account for the different rates, however. The differences are largely attributable to demographic factors, and when we compare whites and blacks with the same economic status, education, and age, we find that their levels of turnout are nearly identical.[21] The same generalization holds for Hispanics: Since so many of them are young and poorly educated they appear to participate less frequently than the majority population. But once one factors in socioeconomic status (age, income, and education, and so forth), they are as active politically as white citizens.

Finally, politics used to be mostly a man's world. Today, however, both sexes register and

Table 10.2

Registration and Voting According to Selected Social Characteristics, 1988

		Percent Who	
		Were Registered	Voted
Income	Under $5,000	48	35
	$5,000–$9,999	53	41
	$10,000–$14,999	57	48
	$15,000–$19,999	63	53
	$20,000–$24,999	67	58
	$25,000–$34,999	72	64
	$35,000–$49,999	78	70
	$50,000 and over	82	76
Education	Elementary	47	37
	High school:		
	1–3 years	53	41
	4 years	65	55
	College:		
	1–3 years	73	65
	4 years or more	83	78
Employment Status	Employed	67	58
	Unemployed	50	39
Race	White	68	59
	Black	64	51
	Hispanic	36	29
Age	18–19	43	32
	20–29	52	41
	30–44	66	58
	45–64	75	68
	65 and older	78	69
Sex	Male	65	56
	Female	68	58

Source: U.S. Bureau of the Census, *Voting and Registration in the Election of November 1988* (Washington, D.C.: Government Printing Office, 1989), pp. 4, 13.

vote at the same rate. Unfortunately, the increase in women in the electorate has not yet led to equality in the halls of power.*

Who, then, is most likely to vote? A middle-aged college graduate in a profession that provides a steady income, flexible schedule, free time, self-confidence, and experience. And who is least likely to vote? An unemployed high school dropout who drifts from town to town looking for a job and a future.

---

*In 1990, for example, men outnumbered women 8 to 1 on the Supreme Court, 48 to 2 in governorships, 98 to 2 in the Senate, and about 17 to 1 in the House of Representatives. In this country's long history there has never been a female president (or vice-president) or a secretary of state, treasury, or defense or more than one member of the Supreme Court.

THE CONSEQUENCES OF CLASS DIFFERENCES IN TURNOUT   Do members of different social classes have different interests? No doubt. And herein lies a crucial problem for contemporary American government. If public policy partially reflects the demands of the voters and if, in turn, the electorate consists of some groups and not others, can democracy be said to be truly representative? It's a serious question because laws and policies are not perfectly neutral but favor certain segments of society over others. The poor and uneducated do not register or vote regularly, so whatever success they have in the political arena generally depends on someone speaking *on their behalf*, not on their speaking *for* themselves. This difference leads many political scientists to believe that those who are most active in government benefit most from it. Put differ-

ently, because turnout has an upper-class bias,[22] one can reasonably wonder if laws and policies do not tend to favor those at the top of the socioeconomic ladder.

PARTISANSHIP AND TURNOUT   Psychological involvement also explains turnout. One measure of such involvement is **party identification**. In contrast to party registration, which is a legal condition, party identification, or **partisanship**, as it is frequently called, refers to the feeling of closeness or attachment to a political party.[23] For some individuals the ties to a party are particularly strong; for others they are weak or nonexistent. Pollsters classify respondents as strong partisans, moderate or weak partisans, and independents. Thus, two friends may both call themselves Republicans, but one feels especially

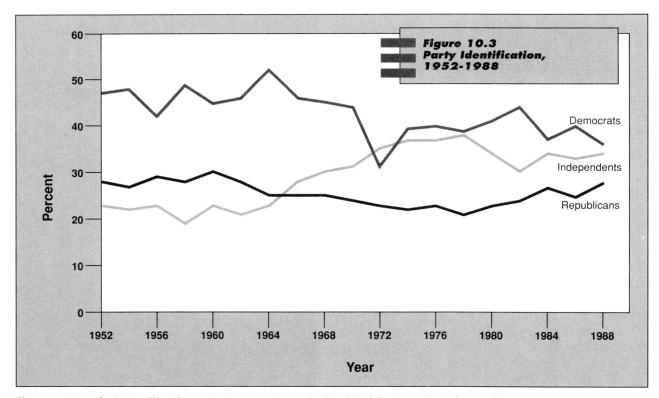

Figure 10.3 Party Identification, 1952-1988

The proportion of adults calling themselves Democrats has declined slightly since 1952, whereas the percentage of self-identified independents has increased. During the same time the percent of Republicans has remained roughly the same.

Source: Based on data tapes from the Center for Political Studies, University of Michigan, *American National Election Studies*, various years.

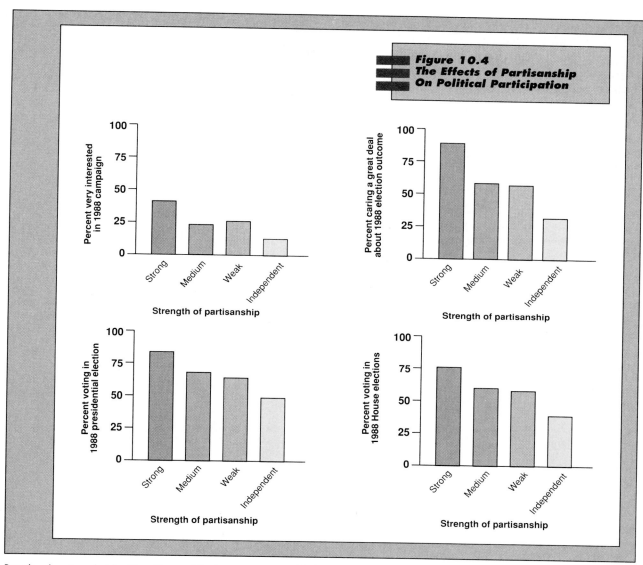

**Figure 10.4
The Effects of Partisanship
On Political Participation**

People who strongly identify with a political party are more likely to be interested in an election, to care about its outcome, and to vote than those who have only a weak attachment to a party or are independent.

Source: Based on data from the Center for Political Studies, University of Michigan, *American National Election Study 1988.*

close to the party while the other has merely a weak attachment. Figure 10.3 shows the percentage of Americans who have identified with one of the two major parties or classified themselves as independents since 1952. Roughly two-thirds of the respondents in the samples feel relatively close to one of the major parties. The number of self-classified independents grew considerably after 1964 and now constitutes about one-third of the population.

How do partisans—those who identify with a party—compare with independents? Generalizations can be misleading because recent research shows that there are different kinds of independents, and their behavior and attitudes are not easily summarized.[24] Popular belief holds that independents carefully study issues and candidates and "vote for the person, not the party." In view of this conventional wisdom, it is perhaps surprising to learn that partisans—those most committed to a party—are better citizens than commonly thought, while many independents, however virtuous they claim to be, are not quite as good.

Naturally, people who feel close enough to a party to care about its well-being take the trouble to vote for its candidates. This is often more than can be said of independents: Many of them are rather apathetic and disinterested; tend to stay at home in congressional, state, and local elections; do not regularly go to the polls in "off" or nonpresidential election years; and are no more informed on issues than partisans. Figure 10.4 demonstrates a few of these tendencies. Note, for instance, that about 80 percent of the "strong" partisans—the people most firmly allied with one of the two major parties—voted

in the 1988 presidential election, whereas only about 50 percent of the self-styled independents did.* This pattern holds for lesser elections and other indicators of political involvement.

POLITICAL EFFICACY AND TURNOUT For a country that prides itself on the strength and vigor of its political institutions, large numbers of Americans apparently feel that time and energy invested in politics are wasted. In the language of social research, they lack **political efficacy**, the belief that "political action does have, or can have, an impact."[25] Efficacy is usually measured by asking people if "public officials care much" about what they think and if the

---

Note: The data reported in this and other figures come from public opinion polls in which many people say they voted when, in fact, they did not. That is why the turnout rates in the figures seem to be higher than the actual level.

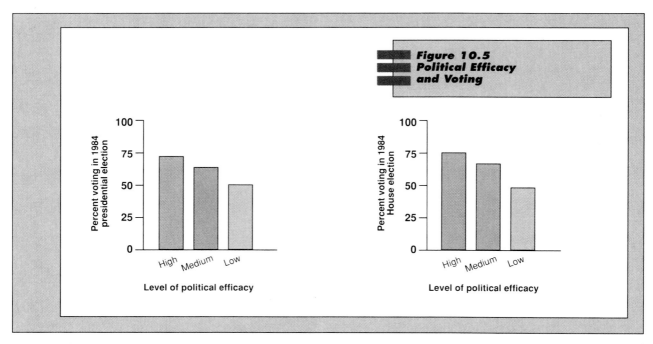

**Figure 10.5
Political Efficacy
and Voting**

Citizens with a strong or high sense of political efficacy—the feeling that involvement in politics is important and rewarding—are more likely to vote than those with a weak or low feeling of efficacy.

Source: Based on data from the Center for Political Studies, University of Michigan, *American National Election Study 1984.*

common person has "any say in what government does." This feeling is related to participation, as Figure 10.5 shows: Those who believe that their opinions count and that elected officials listen to them (the "high" end of the scale) tend to vote more regularly than those at the lower end, who feel their voices go unheard. Another study found that a sizable portion of the decline in turnout over the last 20 years can be attributed to a general decrease in efficacy.[26]

Social traits, partisanship, and efficacy are not the only factors affecting interest and turnout in elections, however. Electoral laws and campaign techniques also play a role.

Institutional Factors and Turnout

REGISTRATION REQUIREMENTS Among the most obvious barriers to participation are laws regulating registration and elections. Most states in the United States require **registration** as a prerequisite to voting. Prior to election day, those who want to vote must appear before an official registrar to establish their eligibility. These rules and procedures are clearly designed to prevent fraud, but in the process of eliminating that evil they create new difficulties.

For the most part, the Constitution leaves the states free to conduct elections as they see fit. A few national standards exist. Poll taxes and literacy tests—once obstacles to registration, particularly for blacks—have been eliminated and Constitutional amendments have given women and 18-year-olds the right to vote. In a 1972 ruling, the Supreme Court effectively reduced residency requirements—the time one has to reside in a state before being allowed to vote there—from a year to about a month.[27]

For the most part, however, states vary greatly in their laws and practices. Some places make the procedure rather difficult, others easy.[28] In 1982 in Matthews County, Virginia, for example, the local registrar maintained an office behind a furniture store where it was apparently hidden from all but the most determined searchers. Halifax, another Virginia county, contained only one office, even though parts of the county were 50 miles away.[29] This pattern is found in other states where the "closing" date, the last day to register, can be 30 or 40 days before the election; where registration offices remain open only a few hours a week (and never in the evenings or on weekends); and where registrars do not go out to the potential voters but insist that applicants visit them.

In other areas the process is much simpler. Indeed, several states such as Maine, Minnesota, and Wisconsin permit registration on election day, while North Dakota does not even require it in the first place.[30] Elsewhere the offices stay open at night and on weekends during campaign periods, and election officials travel to shopping centers, libraries, colleges, and churches to enroll prospective voters.

As one might guess, the severity of the requirements affects turnout: Studies show that participation is highest in the states with the easiest rules, even when demographic characteristics such as education are taken into account.[31] It is no accident that turnout in North Dakota and Wisconsin is among the highest in the nation. These findings agree with the experience of European countries where registration requirements are virtually nonexistent and turnout is high.[32] The relationship is so pronounced, in fact, that many social scientists consider electoral laws to be an important cause of nonparticipation.

Realizing the significance of these legal impediments, reformers have frequently tried to eliminate or modify them. Proposals have included registration by postcard, by presentation of a valid identification card, or by giving registration information in applications for drivers' licenses.[33] A few states and communities have begun allowing residents to register in government offices like motor vehicle or health departments.

In the past, plans to liberalize the rules governing registration have met stiff opposition in Congress, where members of both parties feared that changes in the laws would lead to widespread corruption. Republicans also worried that the higher participation levels might favor the Democrats, who perhaps enjoyed a slight edge among nonvoters.[34]

TIMING OF ELECTIONS The timing of elections presents prospective voters with another problem. National and most state and local elections are held on the first Tuesday in November, a time working people frequently find inconvenient, especially since many polls close about 8:00 P.M. Faced with rush hour traffic jams, dinners to serve and eat, homework to check, and meetings to attend, many individuals have difficulty finding the time to vote.

In contrast to the United States, European countries tend to make elections national holidays or hold them on weekends or over several days. Inasmuch as turnout is higher there, it has been proposed that election day be moved to Saturday or Sunday or both. So far Congress has rejected these reforms, again mainly for political reasons.

NONPARTISAN ELECTIONS AND STRAIGHT-TICKET BALLOTS Election laws affect participation in other, more subtle ways. Some states and communities hold **nonpartisan elections**, in which candidates run as individuals without a party label. But for many citizens, party labels provide a shortcut method for choosing among candidates. In some circumstances, knowing only that an office seeker is a Republican or a Democrat allows one to infer a great deal about the candidate's stand on issues. It may not be the most rational way to pick, but many citizens find party labels a useful guide to the complicated, chaotic world of politics. What happens when this guide is taken away? Research suggests that participation in nonpartisan elections is lower than in partisan races where candidates list their party affiliation.[35]

In the same vein, there is evidence that **straight-ticket ballots**, which permit one to select a party's entire slate with one mark, elicit greater participation than ballots requiring a separate vote for each office.[36] It appears, then, that simplifying the electorate's tasks increases participation.

ELECTION LAWS AND PARTICIPATION All these findings and arguments underscore the fact that participation is costly. There is a tendency among many of us with college educations to take voting for granted. The most you have to do, we tell one another, is hop in a car, drive to the polls, and vote. There's nothing to it. But life is not that simple for people who don't own an automobile, who are ill or infirm or elderly, who are pressed for time after work, who are suddenly called out of town, who have a sick baby at home, or who do not speak English and cannot understand registration rules. For them and countless others, political participation demands perhaps more than they can give.

An important test of democracy is whether it can bring the costs of good citizenship within the price range of its least educated and poorest members. That the United States has a long way to go in this respect may be surmised from the low turnout in its elections.

Registration and voting laws are not the whole story, however. How campaigns are run also affects turnout, but we defer that point to Chapter 11.

Checkpoint

- Demographic characteristics partially explain participation in elections: Individuals with high standards of living and education are more likely to vote than members of the lower class. Older men and women turn out more regularly than younger people.

- Voting is also linked to partisanship, the feeling of closeness with one of the major parties. Partisans are more active than many self-professed independents.

- Individuals with a high sense of political efficacy, the conviction that one's participation matters, tend to vote more faithfully than those with a lower level of efficacy.

- In order to vote in the United States, a citizen in most states must first register. Some states make registration relatively easy, while others have rather stiff regulations. Turnout is generally higher in the areas with the less demanding rules.

- National elections are held on the first Tuesday in November of the election year, a time many workers find inconvenient.

- Nonpartisan elections, in which candidates run for office without a party label, and ballots prohibiting straight-ticket voting tend to discourage turnout, since many voters rely on party identification, especially when choosing among lesser-known candidates.

OTHER FORMS OF CONVENTIONAL PARTICIPATION

If the rate of voting in the United States is low, participation in other political activities is even more so. A 1988 survey, typical of dozens of others done over the years, found that the vast majority of respondents do not work in campaigns, contribute money to candidates, or try to contact elected officials (see Table 10.3). For example, only about one in ten wore a button or displayed a bumper sticker, probably the easiest way to support a party or candidate. Even fewer performed more demanding tasks such as handing out leaflets or making a campaign contribution.

Although these figures perhaps disappoint civic leaders, they compare favorably with most European nations. Yes, Americans do tend to vote less regularly than foreigners. But this difference results in large measure from registration requirements; most other nations do not have these rules. With respect to other forms of conventional political activity, we seem more involved. A cross-national study conducted by Samuel Barnes and Max Kaase, in fact, indicated that political apathy here was lower than elsewhere "by a wide margin."[37]

Many of the same personal factors that explain turnout also account for variation in other modes of conventional participation. Individuals at the upper end of the demographic scales such as education or income tend to be more active than those farther down.[38] By the same token, psychological variables—political efficacy, for instance—are related to political involvement

A relatively small number of people take part in campaign activities. Those who do tend to be somewhat older, better educated, and more affluent than nonparticipants.

A Closer Look

The Costs of Political Participation: A Case Study ★★★

Many of the families living near Route 273 in Cecil County, Maryland, chose the area for its rural charm and beauty. The road, a portion of which the county's comprehensive plan designates as a "scenic highway," cuts through gently rolling hills, lush pastures, and groves of hardwood trees. Drivers frequently see deer, hawks, Canada geese, and other wildlife in the meadows and streams. Some of the farmhouses that border the road date to the 1700s.

As in many regions, however, suburban sprawl threatens the area's rural character. That's why when two men proposed converting an abandoned gas station on Route 273 into an automobile repair shop, a half dozen home owners organized an ad hoc committee to fight the plan. They used the standard tools of citizen organizations: informal meetings,

letters and phone calls to local officials, attendance at public hearings, and so forth. Since the site was not originally zoned for commercial use, the group first took the matter to the planning board, hoping it would recommend against changing the zoning. Unfortunately, the planners sided with the builders. The issue then went to the county commissioners, who also agreed that the garage could be built. As a last resort, the committee hired a lawyer in order to appeal the commissioners' decision in court. Once more, the committee lost, and within a year the repair shop was bustling with activity.

This minor episode, typical of thousands that occur throughout the United States each year, illustrates a few of the benefits and costs of conventional participation. On the positive side, democratic theorists argue that political

---

Table 10.3

Participation in Selected Political Activities

Percent of Respondents Who Said They . . .	
Attempted to convince someone how to vote	29
Attended a meeting at which an incumbent spoke	13
Displayed campaign buttons, bumper stickers, etc.	9
Attended a campaign meeting or rally	7
Worked for a party or candidate	3
Contributed money to a campaign	6
Contacted representative or representative's staff	12

Source: Based on data from the Center for Political Studies, University of Michigan, *American National Election Study 1988.*

involvement leads to feelings of community attachment and personal satisfaction. Although few in numbers, the group's members certainly derived a sense of satisfaction from the fight to preserve their community's quality of life. By pressing the matter as far as they could, moreover, they also hoped to encourage other developers to think twice before starting major commercial projects in the area. Most important, the participants believed that keeping elected and appointed officials on their toes helped maintain local democracy.

These efforts, though, entailed costs. Legal fees alone exceeded $200 per person, an expense that strained each of their budgets. (Even minor expenditures like the $21 for a photocopy of zoning ordinances were a burden.) But the most taxing costs were more subtle. Time, for example, was a real problem. Besides the difficulty of tracking down and studying zoning laws, committee members could only meet evenings, whereas the planners and commissioners held their hearings in midday. The conflicting schedules meant that many in the group had to choose between not attending the meetings or missing work. Or consider information. For some this was their first experience in county politics, and they had to learn from scratch. There were, it seemed, endless nuisances that made participating difficult. (One individual spent 25 minutes trying to find a parking place near the courthouse.) Equally important, the controversy jeopardized interpersonal relations. The garage's owners were respected community residents. Thus, even though many homeowners in the the area worried about the precedent of permitting a commercial establishment on Route 273, they were reluctant to take action. Doing so, they feared, would antagonize friends and neighbors. As one said later, "The shop is no big deal so why should I get Dave mad at me?"

Each of these "costs" probably seems trivial until you realize that they rapidly accumulate to the point where participation can take a sizable chunk out of a person's free time and energy. Unless the issue is of overwhelming importance or the rewards are clear and immediate, only the most dedicated citizens are likely to pay the costs regularly.

Source: Based on one author's observations.

(see Table 10.4 on p. 314). Understandably, someone who agrees that "public officials don't care much what people like me think" has little reason to expect campaigning or contacting a representative to be worthwhile.

Yet even among the most affluent, literate, partisan, and efficacious strata of society, levels of participation are quite low. Since virtually no legal barriers stand in the way, one wonders why so few men and women take part in politics. The answer lies partly in the costs and benefits of participation. Citizens have to divide their time among various activities. Their choice depends on the expected benefits versus the anticipated costs. At first sight, of course, most forms of participation seem inexpensive: Writing a representative only requires a few minutes and a stamp. But as A Closer Look suggests, calculations of this sort are not that simple. For many individuals the rewards of participation come slowly, are difficult to appreciate, or do not satisfy immediate personal needs. Costs, on the other hand, are often more tangible; they can be felt in one's pocketbook or crowded schedule.

We shouldn't let the small number of activists in politics mislead us, however, because they can still have a major impact, as the next section indicates.

Table 10.4

Political Participation by Demographic and Psychological Characteristics

| | | Percent who: | |
		Worked for a Party or Candidate[a]	Contacted Representative[b]
Education	Less than high school	0	7
	High school	2	11
	Some postsecondary or college	4	14
	College	8	17
Income	Less than $15,000	1	9
	$15,000–$44,999	2	12
	$45,000 or more	8	17
Partisanship	Independent	2	9
	Weak	4	13
	Moderate	2	12
	Strong	5	14
Efficacy[c]	Low	2	11
	Medium	3	7
	High	5	15

[a]Did you do any . . . work for one of the parties or candidates?
[b]Have you (or anyone in your family . . .) ever contacted [your] representative?
[c]Based on responses to the statement: "I don't think public officials care much what people like me think."

Source: Based on data from the Center for Political Studies, University of Michigan, *American National Election Study, 1988.*

Checkpoint

- Apart from voting, the vast majority of Americans do not regularly take part in conventional political activities such as working in election campaigns or contacting public officials.

- Participation is related to demographic and psychological factors: Those with more education, political efficacy, and partisanship tend to be most active. But even so, the rates of political involvement are low.

- An additional reason for the low level of political involvement is that many individuals find that the benefits do not outweigh the costs in time and energy.

Grassroots political movements resort to conventional and unconventional tactics to express their beliefs and publicize their causes.

GRASS ROOTS MOVEMENTS IN AMERICAN POLITICS

Passing motorists perhaps regarded the men at Firebase Elsmere as a forlorn lot fighting for a cause about which 95 percent of Americans knew little or nothing. Yet most people have probably seen similar vigils before, and the firebase typified an important phenomenon in current politics: the role of grass roots political movements. A **grass roots movement** is a group of citizens organized on a local level to promote or attain a political objective. Using both conventional and unconventional means, these organizations try to generate visibility, credibility, and popular support in order to force governments to accept their goals. A movement typically consists of a small core of activists—often individuals with little or no previous political experience—and rank-and-file members with varying degrees of commitment to the cause.

Journalists and social scientists use the label *grass roots* because the leaders are usually not public officials and because the movements often originate and operate in towns and communities far from the nation's main centers of power. Some of these bodies are also called *single-issue* organizations because they commonly pursue rather narrow objectives. (Antiabortionists, for example, may march under the banner of "right to life," but their sole concern is halting abortions, not capital punishment, animal experimentation, or world hunger.)

Whether their purpose is narrow or broad, they usually blend conventional forms of participation with direct action such as marches and demonstrations. Quite a few grass roots associations have grown to the point where they are part of the permanent political scene, but many more wither away after just a few years of existence.[39]

Whatever the success or failure of particular groups, grass roots politics has become a prominent feature on the political landscape. Indeed, although it has been part of American history since 1776, this type of citizen participation has grown dramatically in the last 30 years. One report indicates that as many as 1300 local groups are engaged in environmental activities alone.[40] Much of the impetus for this growth came from the fame and accomplishments of the civil rights movement.

The Civil Rights Movement: A Study in Grass Roots Politics

The civil rights movement, an effort to end racial segregation and achieve political equality, social justice, and equal economic opportunity for all races, illustrates the characteristics and tactics of grass roots organizations. (Chapter 7 addresses the legal and constitutional dimensions of the battle for equal rights.) It is obviously not possible to recount in detail the long, brutal struggle for civil rights that continues to this day,[41] but a quick look shows why, how, and with what effect ordinary citizens can band together to achieve sweeping changes.

Historians date the civil rights movement from the Eisenhower era (1952–1960), when blacks and their white allies began taking to the streets to call for an end to segregation.* In making these demands, the participants faced enormous hurdles. At the outset, the movement's leadership was young and inexperienced and, apart from local churches, had only a modest organizational base. A far more formidable obstacle, though, was the political climate. In the South, where segregation was most visible and firmly entrenched, whites maintained an iron grip on the reins of power. From the highest elected officials such as Governor George Wallace of Alabama, who proclaimed in his inaugural address, "Segregation now! Segregation tomorrow! Segregation forever!," to small-town bullies like J. B. Stoner ("I've been fighting Jews and niggers full time more or less since starting

---

*Actually, the struggle to overthrow racial segregation started much earlier but had not made much headway until the mid-1950s.

in 1942"[42]), opposition to racial integration was unrelenting. Moreover, the South's moribund political structures—one-party government and low voter turnout—left the region poorly equipped to deal with demands for change.[43] Segregationists in those days frequently answered cries for freedom and equality with arrests, beatings, arson, bombs, and murder.

Civil rights leaders found verbal support at the national level, but neither Congress nor presidents showed much inclination to translate this sympathy into concrete action. President John Kennedy, for example, did not vigorously push civil rights legislation for fear of antagonizing southern representatives and senators who chaired key congressional committees and had the power to block his foreign and domestic programs.[44]

As A Closer Look indicates (p. 318), the fledgling civil rights movement faced a major problem: how to make the political system listen to its grievances. Blacks felt especially frustrated and cheated because 100 years of "politics as usual" had left racism virtually untouched. Granted, the Supreme Court in its landmark *Brown* decision (1954) declared segregated schools unconstitutional, but states in both the North and South simply ignored its orders to integrate them. True, the Democratic party had made modest civil rights proposals in its platforms, but they were never enacted into law, and southern states, solidly Democratic at the time, refused even to consider them. The time was ripe for a different approach.

Beginning in 1955 with the Montgomery, Alabama, bus boycott, blacks and a few whites in dozens of towns and villages across the South gradually organized and took action. With most conventional avenues of participation blocked, they turned to unconventional tactics—sit-ins, marches, demonstrations, boycotts, prayer vigils, and civil disobedience. These methods had two consequences: First, they put enormous pressure on community leaders to abolish segregationist laws and practices; and second, by forcing the nation to confront the inconsistency between racism and the American creed, they generated considerable public support outside of the South.

Although the tactics of the civil rights movement were firmly rooted in the principles of nonviolence taught by Jesus, Gandhi, and Thoreau, many southerners found its methods unorthodox and hence somewhat confusing and frightening, and they fought ferociously to preserve segregation. When legal maneuvers failed, segregationists resorted to intimidation and violence. In spite of the physical and psychological toll this opposition exacted, the marchers, boycotters, and demonstrators eventually achieved notable successes, including the 1964 Civil Rights Act and the Voting Rights Act of 1965. Even though the United States still does not enjoy complete equality of opportunity in politics, it has at least abandoned the most pernicious symbols of racism and given blacks a measure of political power. These are not small achievements for a movement that began in humble circumstances with meager resources.

Why Grass Roots Movements Succeed or Fail

A prototypical grass roots movement, the civil rights campaign of the 1950s and 1960s left a legacy that went beyond race relations. Hundreds of groups espousing causes spanning the political spectrum have been inspired by its philosophy and have emulated its strategies. Many of these organizations continue to be active and widely known—feminists, environmentalists, gay-rights activists, pro-choice advocates and anti-abortionists, to name only a few—while others either left the scene after making their mark (the anti-Vietnam War effort is a prime example) or exist only in the shadows of American politics, as does the vigil at the Elsmere VA hospital. Rather than cataloging each and every one, an impossible task in any event, it is more informative to explore briefly the reasons for their triumphs and failures. Five explanations come to mind.

A RALLYING CRY To grow and prosper, a movement has to be based on shared interests, grievances, or values that give potential members an incentive for joining.[45] Blacks were mo-

bilized by racial discrimination; women by unfair employment, credit, and educational practices and sexual harassment; environmentalists by air and water pollution, the destruction of wildlife habitats, and resource depletion; evangelicals by the seeming breakdown in public morality. In each case, these concerns served as a *rallying cry* creating bonds of mutual interest. In addition, the underlying cause has to persist over time and be tangible, specific, and immediate, since general issues like "consumer protection" and "good government" are harder to organize than specific ones.[46]

The nuclear freeze movement illustrates these points. At the beginning of the 1980s, many peace activists, scientists, religious leaders, and others felt the nuclear arms race threatened world peace. While both the United States and the Soviet Union rapidly expanded their arsenals, arms control talks hit a dead end and a nuclear confrontation did not seem out of the question. The freeze movement emerged out of this concern with a clear proposal around which supporters could rally: a mutual and verifiable halt (or "freeze") to the production and deployment of nuclear weapons. Like other movements, the campaign began at the local level. It achieved its first victories when several states, counties, and towns throughout the United States passed freeze resolutions or nonbinding requests that the Reagan administration negotiate with the Soviets an immediate end to the manufacture of nuclear weapons. The matter became a major issue in the 1982 congressional elections and reached a climax in May 1983 after the House accepted a watered-down version of the freeze proposal.[47]

Yet at just the time the campaign was reaching national prominence, it began to lose steam. The reason lay partly in the changing political climate. President Reagan, for example, toned down his harsh anti-Soviet rhetoric, and the two superpowers resumed serious arms control talks, culminating in a treaty to eliminate intermediate-range nuclear missiles. Thus, even though both countries continued to maintain huge atomic stockpiles, the urgency and severity of the arms race *appeared* to lessen. Without a palpable cause to fight for, the freeze movement lost

A Closer Look

The Montgomery Bus Boycott ★★★

After work on a December day in 1955, Rosa Parks, a black tailor's assistant, boarded a bus in Montgomery, Alabama. In those years public transportation in the South, along with every other service and accommodation, was racially segregated, and custom *and* law required Mrs. Parks to sit in the back of the coach along with the other "coloreds." When she first got on, however, the bus was not crowded, and she found a seat in the middle, a sort of neutral zone where blacks could sit until whites needed the space. After three stops, more white passengers did board, so the driver asked her to move. Mrs. Parks refused. As she remembered later, "I told them [the police] I didn't think I should have to stand up. After I had paid my fare and occupied a seat, I didn't think I should have to give it up."[a]

The police immediately arrested Mrs. Parks, took her to jail where she was booked, fingerprinted, photographed, interrogated, and placed in a cell. She was released only when a minister and lawyer posted bond and her husband drove her home. All of this because she refused to go to the back of a bus.

For Mrs. Parks, along with others in the black community, it was the last straw. The arrest and detention were the kind of indignities that caused generations of blacks to seethe with anger. But they faced an awful dilemma. On the one hand, for people who had to serve in the military, pay taxes, and obey the law just like everyone else, racial separation was oppressive to the soul and devastating to the pocketbook. On the other hand, there seemed no way to redress these grievances. Whites monopolized political power, and conventional forms of protest like voting or complaining to local officials were either unavailable or futile. Thus, led by local clergy and other activists, the community resorted to a new and different tactic: a boycott of the city's bus system. Leaflets soon circulated through black neighborhoods saying: ". . . don't ride the bus to work, to town, to school, or any place, Monday, December 5. Another Negro woman has been arrested and put in

momentum and gradually disappeared. To be sure, other groups continue to work for arms control, but the freeze idea has left the stage.

ORGANIZATIONAL STRENGTH   Resentments, anger, fear, frustration, good intentions, or any other emotion have to be aggregated and channeled into action if they are to have a lasting political impact. Grass roots movements, therefore, need an organizational base in order to exist. Churches served as the mainstay of the early civil rights movement until formal institutions such as the Southern Christian Leadership Conference (SCLC) and Student Non-violent Coordinating Committee (SNCC) were formed. What is important is that the organization establish a pool of resources—contributions, experienced leaders, phone banks, mailing lists, offices, and the like—to sustain the membership for what is usually a prolonged struggle. Feminists, for instance, have been successful in part because they are backed by interest groups (such as the National Organization for Women) that appeal to middle- and upper-class citizens and consequently can raise funds for offices, lawyers, advertising, direct mailing, and so forth. Ironically, one might conclude, grass roots movements do not succeed until they grow out of their grass roots origins.

jail because she refused to give up her bus seat. . . . Come to a mass meeting . . . at the Holt Street Baptist Church for further instructions."[b] At the meeting citizens were urged to carpool, take taxis, even walk if necessary to avoid using public transportation.

City and business leaders, of course, fought back, prosecuting dozens of the boycott's leaders, including Martin Luther King, Jr., a young and then relatively unknown Baptist minister from Atlanta. In addition, the police announced that patrol cars would follow every bus to prevent boycotters from intimidating any potential passengers from boarding. The city also attempted to forbid black cab drivers from lowering their fares to increase ridership. Die-hard segregationists bombed homes and churches and threatened workers with dismissals. Despite all of these efforts, however, the boycott continued for 381 days and ended only when Montgomery, prodded by a federal court ruling the city's segregated bus system unconstitutional, grudgingly gave in and integrated its buses.

The episode illustrates some of the motives, tactics, and success of a grass roots campaign. Although the participants constituted only a fraction of the state's population and had to

To protest racial segregation of buses in Montgomery Alabama, blacks staged a year-long boycott of the city's public transportation system. The nearly empty buses demonstrated the power of this tactic.

endure enormous hardships, they still achieved a major objective. But they did so only by going from the conventional to the unconventional end of the participation scale. This lesson was not lost on hundreds of groups in the following years.

[a]Quoted in Howell Raines, *My Soul Is Rested* (New York: Putnam, 1977), p. 46.
[b]Ibid., p. 46.

LEGITIMACY OF THE CAUSE Both the public and politicians find it difficult to ignore people fighting for what are universally perceived to be just causes, such as political equality, clean air and water, freedom from sexual harassment, and an end to the arms race. The greater the legitimacy of its goals, then, the more likely a movement will be successful in the political arena, other things being equal.[48] One can perhaps better appreciate this point by looking at a counterexample: abortion.

Each side in the controversy over abortion makes effective use of compelling slogans and symbols. Pro-choice advocates talk about women's "right to choose," "control of their bodies," and "privacy," while the opponents counter with demands for "the protection of the unborn" and "the right to life." Because both appeals seem to rest on strong moral foundations, neither side has managed to gain the upper hand in the struggle for the hearts and minds of the public and policymakers. Consequently, the right to an abortion lives a precarious existence in the United States, having come under fire from the courts, Congress, the White House, and state legislatures; at the same time, women can still obtain abortions. Precisely because each side presents convincing arguments, the dispute over abortion will undoubtedly continue throughout the 1990s.

The power of symbols: Groups exploit symbols to advance their cause in the political arena. Abortion is a particularly contentious issue partly because both sides utilize emotionally compelling slogans and symbols, such as these crosses representing the unborn.

LEGITIMACY OF TACTICS   If public acceptance of the goal is important, so too is the acceptance of the means to that end, as reactions to anti-Vietnam protests illustrate. While the United States sank deeper into the quagmire in Southeast Asia, poll after poll detected an increasing discontent and frustration with American policy. But these same polls also revealed widespread condemnation of both the activists and their methods. For the most part, the antiwar demonstrators were peaceful and law abiding. Nevertheless, just enough well-publicized flag and draft card burnings, attacks on ROTC buildings, and classroom disruptions occurred to cause the electorate to dislike the protesters as much as the war itself. Adding fuel to the fire, the participants' appearance (long hair and flamboyant clothing) and freewheeling life-styles seemed to many to mock traditional American values. When a 1970 survey asked respondents what they thought about students and faculty who took part in campus demonstrations, a mere

10 percent supported them while the overwhelming majority favored using force to stop them.[49] One might conclude from this case that to be successful a movement has to be respectfully disrespectful.

CONTENT OF THE GOALS   Economists sometimes describe controversies as **zero-sum games**: If group A wins, group B loses, and vice versa. In more technical language, the sum of the "payoffs" is zero: There is no way that *both* sides can win. Politicians have a hard time deciding what to do in these disputes, since helping one side means taking away from the other. A movement that hopes to succeed should avoid goals that result in zero-sum payoffs.

The civil rights movement discovered these principles after its initial successes. However much southerners resented desegregating restaurants, drinking fountains, rest rooms, public parks, swimming pools, theaters, and motels, they soon found that they could live with the changes because they really had not lost anything; at worst they had to share facilities with blacks, and at best they had new customers for their services. But as demands shifted from integrated accommodations to equality in the workplace and classroom, resistance stiffened.

To understand why, consider a hypothetical company. If it reserves, say, four of ten new jobs for minorities, it has four fewer jobs for whites. In a community with high rates of unemployment, this practice can easily create bad feelings. Or, to take another situation, if a medical school has room for only 20 new students and sets aside five for black and Hispanic applicants, it obviously has five fewer openings for whites. Admission to medical school is highly competitive, so these enrollment procedures inevitably create hostility among whites. In general, unless employment or educational opportunities can be expanded to meet everyone's needs, which is almost never the case, one group will feel, rightly or wrongly, that it is losing out to the other.

In the past 20 years, civil rights and women's groups have fought for affirmative action programs and quotas (see Chapter 7). Because many white males interpret these policies in zero-sum terms (they, of course, do not use that term), they feel threatened and have appealed to the courts, Congress, and the political parties to end them. Their efforts have met with some success, particularly since the Justice Department under the Reagan and Bush administrations has been cool to racial quotas in hiring and education.

The Government's Response to Political Protest

Most Americans would probably applaud the kind of fortitude displayed by the men at Firebase Elsmere. We may not share their goals or approve of their specific methods, but most of us would agree that direct action is sometimes necessary in politics. On occasion, however, federal and state governments have viewed certain groups as threats to national security and have taken extraordinary, and sometimes illegal, steps to stop them. As a matter of fact, the United

States has a long and unpleasant history of trying to suppress unpopular causes.[50] One wave of official repression occurred in response to the civil rights and anti-Vietnam war movements during the 1960s and early 1970s.

After passage of the Voting Rights Act of 1965, the civil rights movement gradually split into several fragments. Most black leaders remained loyal to the principles of nonviolence and continued to work within the established political framework, but a few groups took more militant stands. The Black Panther party, for example, called for "black power," which meant to them black control of schools, police, social services, and local government in black neighborhoods, but which many officials in Washington interpreted as a call for revolution and separation. Furthermore, because ghetto riots devastated such cities as Los Angeles, Detroit, and Washington, D.C., because a few blacks engaged in widely publicized shootouts with the police, and because the Panthers and other organizations adopted a defiant rhetoric that whites were not used to hearing, it was easy for some officials to believe that racial extremism was beginning to jeopardize social and political stability. A secret report* prepared in the summer of 1970 by an interagency committee consisting of the heads of the Federal Bureau of Investigation (FBI), the Central Intelligence Agency (CIA), and other national security bodies warned President Nixon that the Black Panthers' goals included "revolution, insurrection, assassination, and other terrorist-type activities" and that they "regularly stockpiled" weapons.[51]

Militant blacks were not the only object of suspicion. Both Presidents Johnson and Nixon became convinced that Communists and radicals inspired and sustained the antiwar movement and that it posed a grave menace to the country's security. The report cited above also claimed

---

*This document was the infamous "Huston Plan," approved and then revoked by President Nixon, that would have, in the words of an eminent journalist, permitted the government to reach "all the way to every mail box, every college campus, every telephone, every home" in America. Theodore H. White, *Breach of Faith* (New York: Atheneum, 1975), p. 133.

Poster distributed by the Committee to End the War. The Vietnam War aroused intense hostility among countless Americans, including artists who used their creative skills to protest American military involvement in Vietnam. The government countered this type of dissent through spirited and sometimes illegal means.

that "the movement of rebellious youth ... is having a serious impact on contemporary society with a potential for serious domestic strife." The students, the document concluded, sought to "... confront all established authority and provoke disorder. They intend to smash the U.S. educational system, the economic structure, and, finally, the government itself."[52]

Although some campus protests were disruptive and occasionally violent, anyone who observed or participated in the mainstream antiwar movement would know how overblown these charges were. Nevertheless, many high-ranking government authorities accepted them

at face value and used legal and illegal means to deal with the perceived threat. President Johnson, for instance, pushed for cuts in federal aid to students convicted of rioting and instituted a criminal conspiracy trial against two well-known peace activists who were accused of encouraging students to evade the draft.[53] Similarly, the Nixon administration resorted to grand juries and criminal prosecutions to harass antiwar dissidents.

When these lawful means did not dent antiwar and black activism, illegal methods came into play. The activities ran the spectrum from wiretapping, covert photography, electronic eavesdropping, secretly opening mail, recruiting informants, breaking and entering offices, disrupting meetings, using phony press credentials, and even inciting unlawful behavior. All of it was done without search warrants or court orders and involved numerous branches of the government from the FBI and the Internal Revenue Service to the Postal Service and the military.[54]

Had these efforts been directed at a few, demonstrably dangerous groups they would still have violated fundamental, constitutionally guaranteed rights. But, in fact, thousands of innocent Americans became victims. The Internal Revenue Service, to take just one of dozens of cases, established a unit to investigate political protesters. It eventually compiled dossiers on 8000 individuals and 3000 organizations, including the American Library Association, the Ford Foundation, the Urban League, and the Conservative Book Club.[55]

The CIA and FBI opened thousands of letters—even some addressed to prominent citizens and members of Congress.[56] The FBI suspected the Southern Christian Leadership Conference, the nonviolent civil rights association led by Martin Luther King, Jr., of secretly advocating racial conflict and the overthrow of the government. J. Edgar Hoover, the bureau's director, distrusted and hated King so much that he kept a confidential dossier on his activities, including his extramarital affairs.[57] In the mid-1970s, Senate investigators unearthed a bizarre plot by the bureau to force King to kill himself. The civil rights leader received a tape recording—obtained by electronic surveillance of his hotel rooms across the country—of his encounters with different women, along with a note reading, "King, there is only one thing left for you to do. You know what it is. . . . There is but one way out for you. You better take it before your filthy, abnormal fraudulent self is bared to the nation."[58]

King rejected the blackmail attempt, as did his wife after she received a copy. The incident nonetheless illustrates the extent to which federal agencies have gone to discredit, harass, and destroy protest movements they find dangerous. These brief examples, which represent just the tip of the iceberg, also show that the government does not simply act as an impartial referee for disputes among groups but frequently tries to affect the outcomes as well.

Grass roots movements have had varying degrees of success in American politics. Their overall impact, however, is part of a more significant question: How does political participation in general affect who governs?

Checkpoint

- Grass roots movements are locally organized efforts to attain a political objective.

- Their success depends on several factors including (1) the existence of a compelling rallying cry, (2) their organizational strength, (3) the legitimacy of their cause, (4) the perceived legitimacy of their tactics, and (5) the content of their goals.

- The government has on occasion used legal and illegal methods to stop movements it found objectionable.

POLITICAL PARTICIPATION: WHO GOVERNS?

Political participation is obviously central to the question of who governs, and its role in each of the models—democratic, pluralist, and elitist—differs.

Democracy

In an ideal democracy people govern themselves directly. For this kind of system to work, citizens need to be informed, interested, and active in government. It is not enough to vote periodically. On the contrary, they have to make public affairs part of their daily lives. Even in a representative democracy, in which elected officials pass and administer laws, men and women still have to be continuously vigilant in order to know whom to reward and blame for government's successes and failures.

Many democratic theorists believe that political participation does more than keep civil servants on their toes. It becomes its own reward. Being active in the community, rationally discussing issues, making decisions, and accepting their consequences are essential aspects of life in a democracy and lead to individual self-development. The English philosopher and economist, John Stuart Mill, felt that involvement in local government would widen a citizen's horizons and thus lead the person to "weigh interests not his own" but to consider "the common good."[59] Seen from this perspective, participation is beneficial not simply because it restrains those who govern but also because it adds to the education and morality of the governed. Furthermore, the more people get involved in politics, the more confident they become, and the more likely they are to continue doing it.[60]

These theorists feel that all institutions in society—schools, businesses, factories, farms, unions, political parties, and voluntary associations—should be democratized. After all, many of us spend considerable time in these organizations, and they can provide a training ground for participation in the larger political arena. As Carole Pateman, a political philosopher, puts it,

"One might characterize the participatory model as one where maximum [participation] is required and where [the result] includes not just policies . . . but also the development of the social and political capacities of each individual. . . ."[61]

Pluralism

In contrast to democratic theorists, pluralists have mixed feelings about political participation. On the one hand, they acknowledge that citizens have to be moderately involved, particularly during elections, for the political system to remain reasonably free and stable. Pluralist theory argues that competition among groups keeps society democratic, and one way groups compete is to vie for the public's backing. Voting plays a crucial role, since in choosing among the contenders, the electorate has ultimate control over *who* governs. Likewise, direct action, such as in the civil rights movement, is an integral part of the process of intergroup competition that maintains the balance of power in society.

On the other hand, many pluralists tend to be hard-nosed about participation. They note, in the first place, that most citizens are rather apathetic, especially when judged against the standards of ideal democracy. As we have seen, a large proportion of the population does not go to the polls regularly, only minuscule numbers are politically active on a daily basis, and very few display the commitment and dedication of the men at Firebase Elsmere. This passivity is understandable, pluralists claim, because people have to earn a living, run households, and satisfy personal needs. These pursuits, which are basic to human existence, take time and energy away from other activities: As Giovanni Sartori points out, disinterest in politics is "nobody's fault . . . and it is time we stopped seeking scapegoats."[62]

Moreover, whatever its causes, the lack of massive public involvement has certain advantages for the polity as a whole. Some pluralists worry that if citizens become too active, too passionate, too demanding, the political system may become dangerously overburdened, just as plug-

ging too many electrical appliances into a single outlet can overload a circuit and start a fire. Too much participation is as bad as too little, for it leads to disruption, polarization, and instability.[63] The optimal level is just enough to keep elections working smoothly and one group from dominating the rest.

The Power Elite

One thing elite and pluralist theorists agree on is that the level of political participation in the United States is relatively low. What they disagree about are the causes and consequences of this apathy.

Whereas pluralists tend to see passivity as resulting from personal choice (men and women are busy with other activities) or individual shortcomings (lack of education, for instance), the elite school blames institutions such as schools, the mass media, the major parties, election laws, and "issueless" political campaigns. Since we already touched on this debate earlier in the chapter and elsewhere (see Chapter 8), we turn for the moment to the second disagreement, the consequences of nonparticipation.

Elite theorists maintain that what passes for participation in America is either symbolic behavior or deals with mainly "twig" or trivial matters. In spite of their potential power, elections do not really have much impact on the fundamental controversies that confront the nation: the direction of the economy, foreign policy, nuclear weapons, energy policy, and the like. From the elite perspective, many, if not most, presidential and congressional campaigns are based on name-calling, slogan mongering, and superficial differences. Notice, too, that many movements aim at redressing individual grievances like racial or sexual discrimination, not at altering the general direction of government.

The public's passivity appalls the elite school for a more fundamental reason: Widespread apathy plays into the hands of the governing elite, who are free to make trunk decisions. After all, if half of the eligible electorate fails to vote and a mere one out of ten citizens contacts his or her representatives, those at the top can make basic economic and foreign policy decisions by themselves.

The elite school also sides with those democratic idealists who say that participation can be more than an instrument of popular control of leaders and has an intrinsic value of its own. An active *public*, as opposed to the passive masses, takes an interest in community and national problems, works to solve them, and in so doing achieves a level of personal satisfaction not attainable by standing on the sidelines letting others make decisions.[64] Hence, far from fearing broad participation at all levels of government, the elite theorists bemoan its absence.

Checkpoint

- Those who support the ideal model of democracy believe that participation has two functions: (1) It lets citizens decide their own fates, and (2) it leads to individual moral and intellectual development.

- Pluralists observe that large numbers of Americans are not active in politics but believe that this situation is a mixed blessing. To some extent it is the inevitable consequence of human nature, and besides, if everyone were intensely involved in all aspects of government, the system might not be able to satisfy the demands placed on it.

- The elite school recognizes that many Americans are not as active as they could be, but blames social and political institutions. Like the democratic theorists, elite theorists wish more citizens would get involved.

SUMMARY

Political participation is activity intended to influence the making and content of public policy. It is usually measured on a conventional-unconventional continuum. Conventional behaviors are widely considered appropriate for a democratic system. Unconventional activities generally exceed the public's standards of acceptable political behavior or are considered illegal. Few people engage in unconventional participation, but those who do are highly committed.

Compared with other nations, turnout in American elections is low. It has also declined steadily in the twentieth century. The right to vote was originally limited to white male property holders. Over the years, however, voting rights have been extended to minorities and women. Two competing theories explain the decrease in voting over the last 100 years. The first maintains that widespread corruption and the inclusion of nonvoting populations made turnout rates appear higher than they really were. The other theory holds that citizens used to be highly motivated and conscientious, but various institutional and electoral changes have dampened their enthusiasm for politics.

Two explanations for low turnout today focus on personal and institutional factors. The individual traits that explain whether people vote include demographic characteristics such as income, education, and age, and psychological variables like partisanship (the feeling of attachment to a political party) and efficacy (the belief that one's participation is worthwhile). Institutional arrangements also explain variation in turnout. A major obstacle is registration. Some states make the process relatively painless, while others have rather stiff regulations. Turnout is generally higher in the areas with the less demanding rules. The timing of elections on the first Tuesday in November, nonpartisan elections, and the absence of provisions for straight-ticket voting also discourage many individuals from voting.

The vast majority of Americans do not regularly engage in conventional political activities such as working in campaigns or contacting public officials. Conventional participation is related to demographic and psychological factors: Those with more education, political efficacy, and partisanship tend to be active. But even among the highest groups, rates of participation are quite low. One explanation is that many individuals find the benefits of participation not worth the time and energy.

Grass roots movements, organized efforts by citizens to attain political objectives, have become important forces in American politics. Whether or not grass roots movements succeed depends on a variety of conditions: the existence of a persuasive rallying cry, organizational strength, the cause's legitimacy, the acceptability of the tactics, and the nature of the objectives. The government has occasionally reacted with legal and illegal methods to undercut movements it perceived to be dangerous.

Democratic theorists believe that political participation is significant because it keeps leaders accountable and helps build moral character. Pluralists contend that the public's lack of involvement in politics is understandable since people have so many nonpolitical interests. Besides, apathy has certain advantages, especially since mass participation might overburden the political system with demands it could not satisfy. The elite school knows that Americans are not politically active but argues that political institutions cause this passivity. Like the democratic theorists, elite theorists wish more citizens would become involved.

KEY TERMS

Political participation	Political efficacy
Suffrage	Registration
Demobilization	Nonpartisan elections
Australian ballot	Straight-ticket ballots
Party identification	Grass roots movement
Partisanship	Zero-sum games

FOR FURTHER READING

Jo Freeman, *Social Movements of the Sixties and Seventies* (New York: Longman, 1983). This collection of essays combines case histories with theory to show how social and political movements function in America.

Joyce Gelb and Marian Lief Palley, *Women and Public Policies*, rev. ed. (Princeton, N.J.: Princeton University Press, 1987). Besides describing the background of the feminist movement, this book offers insights into grass roots movements in general.

Morton H. Halperin, *The Lawless State* (Baltimore: Penguin Books, 1976). A superb and disturbing look at the abuse of civil liberties by government agencies.

Lester W. Milbrath and M. L. Goel, *Political Participation*, 2nd ed. (Skokie, Ill.: Rand McNally, 1977). An excellent place to start the search for explanations of participation.

Frances Fox Piven and Richard A. Cloward, *Why Americans Don't Vote* (New York: Pantheon Books, 1988). The authors blame low turnout on registration laws, which they believe work to the disadvantage of poor people.

Howell Raines, *My Soul Is Rested* (New York: Putnam, 1977). The story of the civil rights movement told through the very moving words of its participants.

Elections, Voting and Campaigns

Elections, theoretically the mainsprings of democracy, function best when the public votes responsibly and candidates and parties provide clear and meaningful choices. On both counts, however, the political system exhibits a mixed bag of tendencies. The electorate seems at times to lack the knowledge and interest to vote intelligently, and yet the way candidates run their campaigns often leaves voters confused, angry, bored, or frustrated. Money, moreover, is pouring into campaigns so profusely that many observers wonder if elections are not being bought and sold. ■

You are an incumbent U.S. representative. For several years you have been troubled by the continuing federal budget deficit. You have proposed several measures to reduce it, but so far none has been accepted by Congress. Facing a tough reelection campaign this fall, you would like to take the issue to the voters, particularly since your opponent refuses to say specifically how the deficit should be cut. Although you believe that making tough economic choices is essential, your staff adamantly opposes your stressing the point in the campaign. "People don't vote on issues," they keep telling you. "Don't go out on a limb that will make the folks back home angry or scared or both. Play it smart. Stress your advantages: experience, personality, integrity." They give you the name of one of Washington's most successful public relations firms. It's late in the day and you have to decide. A recent poll shows you just 8 percent ahead of the challenger. Do you make the budget crisis an issue or do you call the consultant?

Now you are a media consultant. With offices in both New York and Washington, your firm has helped elect senators, representatives, and

governors all over the country. A congressman has just called asking for help with a close reelection campaign. He wants his messages to stress the budget deficit, including possible cuts in defense spending and social security benefits. He feels it is time the voters faced the issue squarely. But you know better. "Whenever you try to educate the public," you have always said, "you get into trouble. Keep the message simple, and don't say anything controversial or complicated. Better yet, bash the opposition!" For a substantial fee you will produce a series of 30-second spots showing the candidate at work or at home with his wife, three daughters, and the family dog. Another series will call the opponent soft on crime. These are the images that get votes. Of course, like everyone else, you are concerned about the deficits, but, Hell, this is politics, isn't it? Still, the congressman is doubtful. What do you do? Go along with him or insist on the spots?

Finally, you are a 35-year-old dental hygienist, housewife, and mother. It's election day. But for you it is a Tuesday just like any other: after work there's the laundry, groceries, and, it seems, a million other things to do. You also want to visit your mother who is ill, but she lives an hour and a half away. You wonder if you are going to have time to vote. It's not that you don't care about politics. As a matter of fact, you have worried a lot lately—there has been so much talk about drugs, the environment, all those banks going out of business, and whatnot. Yet none of the candidates seems to be saying anything specific. One of them has lots of ads on television. They do not tell you much, though. They either show him sitting in front of a fireplace with his wife, kids, and a dog, or else calling his opponent weak and indecisive. You have to choose. Do you vote (and, if so, how) or do you drive out to see your mother?

Choices like these are the daily fare of electoral politics in America. They are not easy, even when people act with the best intentions, because all the alternatives have merit and the stakes are so high. Yet it is important to understand how and why people make them. For only when we understand the ins and outs of elections will we begin to know who really governs America.

THE PROMISE: ELECTIONS AND SELF-GOVERNMENT

Free and open elections are the heart and soul of democracy. They supposedly provide a way for the public to translate its will into law. They also have the equally important role of making government accountable to the people. Unless the electorate has the power to throw incumbents out of office, it risks succumbing to tyranny. Even pluralists, who doubt that America is or can be an ideal democracy, still believe that regular elections are essential for selecting and disciplining competing leaders.

Voting, finally, can play another role: As mentioned in Chapter 10, it provides a means for participation in community affairs and teaches men and women to cooperate, to search for compromise, to regard the public interest as important as private ones, and to accept responsibility for decisions. By linking the citizen to the commonwealth, elections strengthen both.

For all these reasons, Americans have elevated

their belief in the ballot almost to the status of religious faith. Despite the misgivings of the Founding Fathers, who feared placing too much power in the hands of the common people, elections have become an integral part of the constitutional order. Before considering how well these ideals agree with reality, however, let's briefly examine the electoral system's main components.

The Electoral System

THE ELECTORAL COLLEGE   As mentioned in Chapter 4, the president of the United States is selected by the electoral college, a somewhat peculiar institution that simultaneously grants and denies Americans the right to elect their president directly. The parties in each state pick a slate of electors who are pledged to support the party's nominees for president and vice-president.* The number of electors in a state equals the total number of its congressional delegation, that is, the number of senators *and* representatives. The District of Columbia also gets 3 electors, making 538 in all (see Figure 11.1, p. 330). Although ballots usually list only the names of candidates and their party affiliation, a vote for president is really a vote for a party's slate of electors. The electors chosen in all the states constitute the electoral college.

The candidate receiving a **plurality**, or the most votes, in a state wins *all* its electoral votes.[†] Shortly after the election in November, the electors meet in their respective state capitals to cast their ballots. They almost always vote for the candidate to whom they are pledged; throughout the years there have been only a handful of "faithless" electors.[‡] Since there are a total of

---

*Electors are usually relatively obscure but faithful party activists, not necessarily the outstanding community leaders the Founding Fathers envisaged.

[†]In Maine, the only exception to the winner-take-all principle, two of the state's four electors are chosen on a statewide basis while the other two are picked by whichever party wins in each of the congressional districts.

[‡]In 1988, for example, an elector in West Virginia was supposed to vote for Michael Dukakis for president but actually voted for his running mate, Lloyd Bentsen.

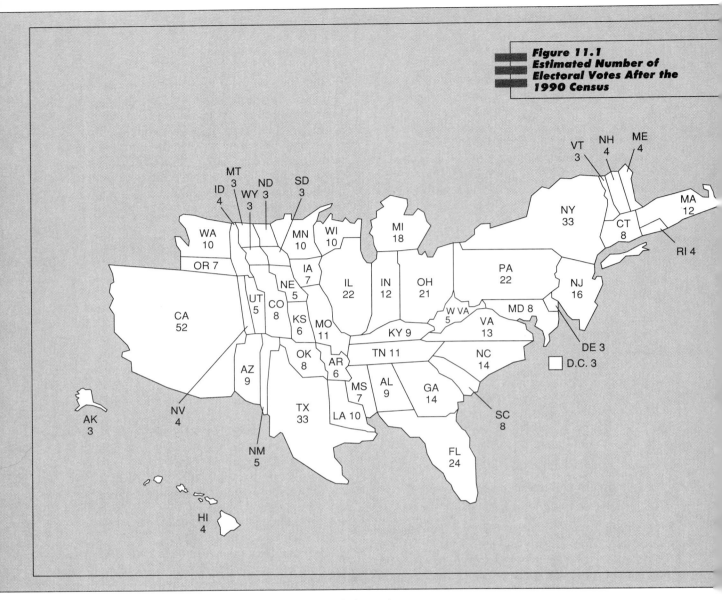

**Figure 11.1
Estimated Number of
Electoral Votes After the
1990 Census**

States are depicted in proportion to their projected number of electoral votes.
Source: U.S. Bureau of the Census data.

538 electoral votes, a candidate with a majority of 270 or more wins the presidency.

Third parties, however, can drain enough electoral votes away from the main contenders to deny anyone a clear majority. The decision is then made by the House of Representatives, which chooses from the top three contenders. In this situation, each state casts one vote for the person preferred by the state's congressional delegation.

Most of the time the electoral college is invisible to the voters, who believe that they are casting ballots for particular candidates rather than for slates of unseen, unknown electors. And it has worked tolerably well over the years. The last time an election went to the House of Representatives was in 1824, when it picked John Quincy Adams over Andrew Jackson (who, incidentally, won more popular votes than Adams).

Nevertheless, the system has plenty of critics. The winner-take-all feature is decidedly unfair, they say, and, worse, encourages candidates to seek electoral rather than popular votes. It is entirely possible for a nominee to win narrowly in a few populous states with huge blocs of electoral votes while losing decisively in many smaller ones. This candidate could, as a result, win the presidency yet trail in total popular votes. That this outcome has not occurred often—the last time was in 1888—does not make the prospect any more desirable.

The critics also complain that the system opens the gates to third parties. The Constitution's framers may have intended the House of Representatives to decide presidential contests,* but today the idea seems outrageous. Now everyone thinks that the people themselves should select the president. So long as there are only two parties and the electors vote as they promise, the system works well. But third-party candidates, such as George Wallace in 1968 and John Anderson in 1980, can throw a monkey wrench into the machinery. If they win enough electoral votes to deny one of the major parties a clear-cut victory, the House has to decide, and the numerous constitutional and political uncertainties make this an extremely unattractive alternative.

Moreover, throwing the election into the House potentially gives a minority party too much leverage. Wallace, for example, never thought he could capture the presidency outright when he ran in 1968. Instead, as he emphasized repeatedly, his goal was to deny victory to either the Democratic or Republican candidates, thereby positioning himself to trade his support for concessions on major public policies. Although many European countries live quite comfortably with this kind of politics, most observers here dreaded this eventuality. Fortunately for them, Wallace's total of 46 electoral votes was not enough to deadlock the election.

In view of this close call, there have been renewed efforts to reform the system by letting popular rather than electoral votes decide the winner.[1] As of yet, however, Congress has not been able to agree on a suitable constitutional amendment to submit to the states for approval.

---

*Not anticipating the rise of two major political parties, the framers may have assumed that a crowded field of presidential contenders would regularly require the House of Representatives to decide elections. See Theodore J. Lowi, *The Personal President* (Ithaca, N.Y.: Cornell University Press, 1985), pp. 31–32.

DIRECT, WINNER-TAKE-ALL ELECTIONS Unlike the president, who is chosen indirectly through the electoral college, the voters *directly* elect all 100 senators and 435 members of the House of Representatives. (State legislatures originally chose senators, but the Seventeenth Amendment, ratified in 1913, turned their selection over to the people.) Furthermore, state constitutions create layer after layer of officials, and elections for these posts give each voter dozens of additional candidates to choose from.

In most of these elections, the person with a plurality of votes wins, even if the total is not an absolute majority of ballots cast. Unlike some European countries that have "proportional" representation, the parties do not share seats in proportion to the number of votes they receive. One, and only one, representative goes to the legislature from each district. Hence, these winner-take-all contests are called **single-member plurality** elections.

As simple and fair as these rules seem, they have raised numerous difficulties over the years. A Closer Look (pp. 332–333) points out, for example, that legislative districts are commonly drawn in peculiar shapes to favor one party over another, a practice called **gerrymandering**.

Another problem is that election districts used to contain unequal numbers of voters, a situation known as **malapportionment**. As a result, sparsely populated areas tended to have the same or more representatives than cities. This situation meant that rural areas tended to dominate government at the expense of urban and suburban places and that, contrary to the tenets of democracy, some votes counted more than others. Malapportionment has been reduced over the years by Supreme Court decisions that ruled that legislative districts in a state should have as nearly the same size populations as possible.[2]

THE RESPONSIBLE ELECTORATE? The electoral system would, one might think, enhance democracy. For one thing, nearly all public officials are directly or indirectly accountable to the electorate; for another, countless laws, court decisions, and constitutional amendments have affirmed and reaffirmed every American's right to cast a secret ballot. Yet Chapter 10 demon-

A Closer Look

Mapmaking and Political Power ★★★

The practice of drawing congressional and state legislative election districts to favor one party over another—frequently called gerrymandering, after Governor Elbridge Gerry of Massachusetts who signed a bill in 1812 creating a salamander-shaped district—is one of the least visible but most important activities in American politics. To appreciate its significance, consider the House of Representatives. Its total membership is set at 435, with each state receiving seats in proportion to the size of its population. Populous states like California get more representatives than sparsely populated ones like Wyoming. Since people move from place to place, each state's share of the total is recalculated every ten years. Invariably, some gain and some lose representatives. Furthermore, the population *within* states shifts around so that regardless of whether a state's representation increases, decreases, or stays the same, its district boundaries still have to be periodically redrawn.

Ideally, every district would be a compact geographical area that followed sensible borders. Ideals, however, do not interest political mapmakers; power does. And how they design the maps greatly determines the balance of power between the two parties.

Take a hypothetical state with a population of 1.2 million and entitled to four representatives. If half the residents vote Democratic and half Republican, you might expect each party to send two representatives to Washington, as in Figure 11.2(a). Yet partisans are not spread around randomly but live in pockets. A clever cartographer can take advantage of this situation by packing most of, say, the Republicans into one district that they win overwhelmingly and carving the rest of the state into three more districts that have slight Demo-

cratic majorities. The result? Even though both parties cast the same number of votes, Democrats outscore Republicans three to one in House seats (Figure 11.2(b)).

Accomplishing this feat, though, often requires the map's designer to create odd-shaped districts. The serpentine districts shown in Figure 11.2(b) are imaginary, but in the real world they occur all the time. Several years ago Iowa had a district that resembled a monkey wrench, New York one that looked like a horseshoe, and Pennsylvania one that reminded viewers of a "dumb bell."[a]

The mapmakers, who hold the keys to the parties' fortunes, do not belong to impartial agencies but are the governors and the state legislators of the 50 states. After each decennial census, state governments usually have to draw new lines for both congressional and state legislative districts. Those in power at the time of reapportionment are in a perfect position to help their parties. One of the keys to success in American politics, then, is control of state government at the time the Census Bureau publishes its revised population tallies.

The struggle to dominate statehouses will be especially complicated and contentious in the early 1990s because both parties realize the outcome will partially determine their strength for the next ten years. The experience of the previous decade shows why. California, to take just one case, gained two additional representatives after the 1980 census. Democrats, who controlled both the governorship and the legislature, redrew the district boundaries in such a fashion that they captured five more seats than they would have gotten had more neutral criteria been applied.[b] Republicans looking at the electoral

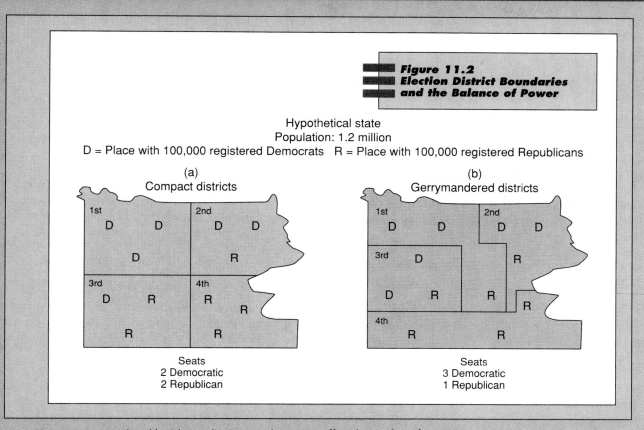

Figure 11.2
Election District Boundaries and the Balance of Power

Hypothetical state
Population: 1.2 million
D = Place with 100,000 registered Democrats   R = Place with 100,000 registered Republicans

(a)
Compact districts

(b)
Gerrymandered districts

Seats
2 Democratic
2 Republican

Seats
3 Democratic
1 Republican

How congressional and legislative districts are drawn can affect the number of seats in Congress or the state legislature that each party receives.

map saw their districts strung out like "Christmas tree ornaments."[c] The Sixth congressional district had an especially odd shape: It consisted of four separate areas two of which were isolated from the others by San Francisco Bay. It was drawn in this fashion to guarantee that the Democratic incumbent would have enough Democratic voters to win another term.[d] This process, repeated in other states under Democratic control, helped the Democrats perpetuate their majorities in Congress and state governments. Republicans are consequently prepared to spend millions of dollars to win as many state contests as possible in the early 1990s, while the Democrats

are just as determined to hold the line. These battles will be particularly hard-fought in the Sunbelt, where states such as Arizona, Texas, Florida, and California will gain congressional seats, and in the Frostbelt, where New York, Michigan, Ohio, and other states will lose them.

[a]William Safire, *Safire's Political Dictionary* (New York: Random House, 1978), p. 256.
[b]*National Journal*, January 21, 1989, p. 157.
[c]*New York Times*, September 3, 1989, p. 3.
[d]Congressional Quarterly, *State Politics and Redistricting, Part I* (Washington, D.C.: Congressional Quarterly Press, 1982), p. 148. Ironically, the representative resigned his seat immediately after the creation of the new district.

To what extent are voters swayed by a candidate's physical appearance? Many political commentators believed that Paul Simon, a candidate for the 1988 Democratic presidential nomination, lacked the personal appeal and charisma to succeed on television, even though his ideas were sound.

Not everyone shares this assessment of the public, but a surprising number of scholars, journalists, politicians, and even average citizens do. It is worthwhile exploring whether or not they are right. Democracy requires a **responsible electorate**: voters who stay active, alert, and informed and who choose among candidates on rational grounds. If Americans do not meet this test of responsibility, we need to find out why. It is necessary, therefore, to take a dispassionate survey of the *reality* of voting and elections in the United States. Proceeding in two stages, we first take stock of *personal* characteristics, like social group memberships and attitudes that affect political choices, and then turn to *institutional* features, such as campaign management, that are just as important in explaining voting behavior.

strated a crucial point about American politics: Literally millions of men and women in the United States do not vote. Rather than rushing to grasp the reins of power, much of the public seems apathetic and bored. Equally troublesome, numerous political commentators question the quality of the electorate, which seems preoccupied with candidates' images and styles, seems to know next to nothing about issues, and seems to value a strong personality more than a strong idea. How many times has it been said that Abraham Lincoln could not win office in modern times because he was too awkward and unkempt to master the modern media? Does this exaggerate? Perhaps. But *Newsweek* reporters claimed that Paul Simon, a senator from Illinois who wore a bow tie and horn-rimmed glasses, was doomed from the start in his quest for the 1988 Democratic presidential nomination, partly because he "looked more like Pee-wee Herman than John F. Kennedy" and insisted on being himself, which "to the ubiquitous television cameras . . . wasn't good enough."[3]

Checkpoint

- Elections theoretically allow citizens to hold representatives accountable and to take part in national and community affairs.

- Under the electoral college system, which applies only to presidential elections, each state has a number of electors equal to the number of its representatives and senators. A presidential candidate receiving a plurality (or the *most* votes) in a state collects *all* of that state's electoral votes and wins the presidency with a majority of the electoral ballots.

- Legislators at the state and national level are chosen in plurality elections from single-member districts.

- Many observers wonder whether Americans vote responsibly.

THE REALITY:
HOW VOTERS DECIDE

What goes through the minds of voters while standing in the voting booth? Some seem motivated by self-interest:

What happens in Nicaraguan jungles doesn't interest me, and what happens in Middle Eastern deserts doesn't interest me. My wife and I are hoping to buy a house, so I'm worried about interest rates. [Newspaper editor][4]

Others look for strong leaders:

America is in the same position as Chrysler was just a while ago. It needs new leadership that will make it able to compete again. [Tavern owner][5]

Party labels matter for some:

I'm more or less for Dukakis. I've been a regular Democrat all my life.... [Retired mail carrier][6]

Ethnicity occasionally counts:

We're Italian but we have a lot of Greek friends and I'd like to see a Greek get in. [New Jersey woman][7]

Voters often feel that they are choosing among the lesser of two evils:

[Bush] is a wimp and he always will be, but I don't have any choice. Dukakis has programs I just don't support. [Pipefitter][8]

Keeping things as they are is important to many:

I better not rock the boat; so I'll go with a Republican again this time. [Woman in Michigan][9]

A few appear filled with resentment and frustration:

Bush is a bozo. He can't talk straight. When he talks on an issue, I can't figure out what the hell he's saying. [Computer programmer][10]

Ideology and issues may be decisive in some cases:

I grew up thinking the Republicans were for the rich and the Democrats for the little guy; but I heard from a friend of mine that Dukakis is for the gay-rights bill. If Dukakis is that far on the liberal side, he will do more harm than good. [Retired police officer][11]

Political scientists have argued long and hard about how to classify sentiments like these. One can interpret them as evidence of the populace's lack of knowledge, even irrationality. Indeed, as seen in previous chapters, many observers conclude that the average man or woman is not knowledgeable or motivated enough to deal with the complexities of modern government. People all too often vote for pretty faces or catchy slogans or party labels without taking the time to study issues, investigate candidates, or consider the long-run implications of their choices. If one accepts this line of reasoning, there is surely reason to be pessimistic about the public's capacity for self-government.

Others find more prudence and intelligence in the common person and agree with V. O. Key, Jr., who wrote:

... voters are not fools. To be sure many individuals act in odd ways, yet in the large the electorate behaves about as rationally and responsibly as one should expect, given the clarity of the alternatives presented to it and the character of the information available.[12]

How does one resolve this dispute? Are voters rational or not? Over the years social scientists have identified several personal factors that seem to affect how people vote, but they still disagree about their relative importance. The disputed variables include (1) demographic characteristics, such as race, occupation, and religion, (2) party identification, (3) attitudes and beliefs about issues, and (4) candidate images.

Demographic Characteristics and the Vote

Demographic attributes like income and education explain to a degree how people vote. In the wake of the Great Depression of the 1930s, the Democratic party, under the leadership of Pres-

Table 11.1

How Different Demographic Groups Vote

		1988 Presidential Election		1988 House Election	
		Bush (%)	Dukakis (%)	Republican (%)	Democrat (%)
Sex	Men	57	43	41	59
	Women	50	50	41	59
Race	White	59	41	45	55
	Black	8	92	8	92
Religion	Protestant	58	40	—	—
	Catholic	49	50	—	—
	Jewish	24	74	—	—
	"Born again" White Protestant	71	27	—	—
Age	Less than 24	56	44	32	68
	25–29	51	49	34	66
	30–39	53	47	42	58
	40–49	50	50	39	61
	50–59	53	47	43	57
	Over 60	55	45	45	55
Region	East	45	53	—	—
	South	58	40	—	—
	Midwest	52	47	—	—
	West	54	43	—	—
Union household?	Yes	41	59	32	68
	No	56	44	43	57
Income	Less than $15,000	43	57	32	68
	$15,000–$24,999	51	49	43	57
	$25,000–$34,999	50	50	42	58
	$35,000–$44,999	49	51	39	61
	$45,000 or more	69	31	51	49
Education	8 years or less	39	61	24	76
	9–11 years	43	57	32	68
	High school grad	50	50	37	63
	Post-high school training	58	42	47	53
	Junior college	59	41	38	62
	College & advanced degree	58	42	48	52

Source: Based on data from Center for Political Studies, University of Michigan, *American National Election Study, 1988*, and *National Journal*, November 21, 1988, p. 2855.
Note: A dash means data not available. Percents may not add to 100 percent due to rounding.

ident Franklin D. Roosevelt, forged a loose coalition of big-city blue-collar workers, Catholics, Jews, blacks and other ethnic groups, southerners, and intellectuals. It was an unwieldy and quarrelsome alliance but was nevertheless large enough to dominate American politics for nearly half a century. The Republican party by contrast historically drew support from small towns and rural places, the business community, professionals (doctors, lawyers, accountants, and so on), white-collar workers, Protestants, and residents of New England and the Midwest. Thus, in the years from 1932 to 1964 one could predict fairly well how people would vote by knowing their social and economic backgrounds.[13]

Today the connection between social characteristics and voting decisions is not as clear cut. Table 11.1 shows that part of the Roosevelt coalition remains intact. Blacks, Jews, and the poorest and least educated classes voted overwhelmingly for Michael Dukakis in 1988. But note also that support for the Democrat rapidly faded among lower-middle class groups. Large numbers of blue-collar and ethnic voters, who were once stalwart Democrats, generally backed Bush, as did southerners.

So many changes in the voting habits of various demographic categories have occurred over the last two decades that scholars and journalists wonder if a *realignment*, or regrouping of the components of the parties, is not under way.[14] Others contend that trends in voting suggest not the realignment of the electorate, but its *demobilization*, the tendency of individuals to abstain from voting or split their ticket when they do vote, and not to show much concern for campaigns and elections.[15] Whatever the case, it is now more common to explain voting choices in terms of attitudes toward parties, candidates, and issues rather than social status.

Party Identification and the Vote

One of the most important of these attitudes is *party identification* or *partisanship*, which means the feeling of closeness to a political party (as seen in Chapter 10). Although the press talks a great deal about the decline in party loyalty, most adults still identify to some degree with one of the major parties. Granted, there has been a steady increase in the number of independents, a growth that has come at the expense of Democrats and Republicans alike. But roughly two out of three Americans still identify with a party and less than a third can be called pure independents.

Consistent with the logic of party identification, strong Democrats back Democrats and strong Republicans support Republicans. In 1988, for example, 98 percent of the strongest Republicans voted for George Bush (see Figure 11.3, p. 338). And there were relatively few defections among partisans in Senate and House elections. Seen from this perspective, the American public is divided into three camps: a large force of Democrats on one side, a somewhat smaller number of Republicans on the other, and a growing bloc of independents in the middle.[16]

INDEPENDENT VERSUS PARTISAN VOTERS
Independents occupy a special place in the folklore of American politics: They are widely perceived as open-minded individuals who vote for "the person, not the party." Chapter 10, however, cast doubt on this assumption by underlining the propensity of independents to vote less faithfully than strong party identifiers, to pay less attention to campaigns, and to care less about their outcomes. In addition, since they are also likely to split their ballots—voting for, say, a Republican for president but a Democrat for the Senate or House (see Figure 11.4, p. 339)—they help create the division of power that has characterized (some would say plagued[17]) the national government for the past 25 years.

If these decisions were based on careful analysis and a desire to ensure a balance between the parties, one might applaud this behavior. But research indicates that independents are no better informed than staunch party regulars.[18] In fact, some scholars believe that transitory events such as a scandal or international crisis affect independents' decisions more than a deep understanding of issues or a critical comparison of party platforms.

What, then, of those partisans who back their

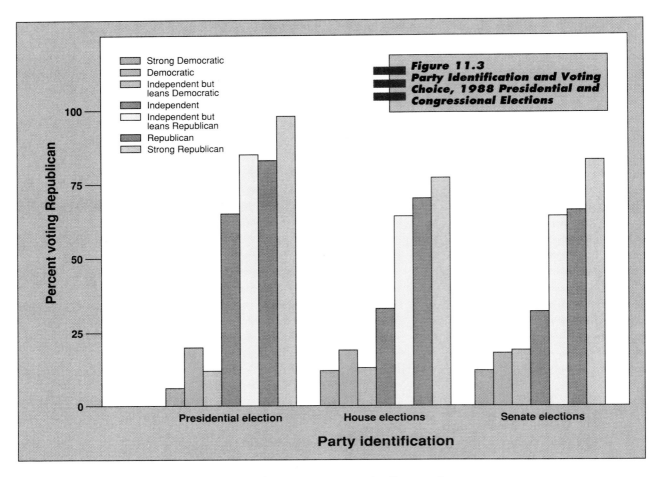

Party identification is strongly related to how people vote. Strong party identifiers usually support their party's presidential and congressional candidates.

Source: Based on data from the Center for Political Studies, University of Michigan, *American National Election Study, 1988.*

party through thick and thin? Isn't that a rather mindless form of civic duty? In theory, voting a straight party ticket might not be as lazy or irrational as it first seems. Many citizens find politics a baffling business: There are so many sides to so many issues that it is nearly impossible even for experts to sort them out. Ballots list literally dozens of choices; information about candidates and their stands on issues is scarce and difficult to obtain. Even if people care about government, it is not easy to keep up.

In such a situation, political parties can greatly simplify matters. If you feel that *on the whole* one party rather than another will best serve your interests, then it might be reasonable to support that party consistently rather than trying to find out everything on your own. Voting a party line may lead to errors since you will occasionally vote for an idiot or a crook or worse. Theoretically, though, by sticking to one party you might be able to serve your interests while reducing the cost of becoming informed.[19]

Because this sort of argument offends editors and civic leaders, who advise "vote for the person, not the party," think for a minute about the federal budget deficit. Newspapers print claims

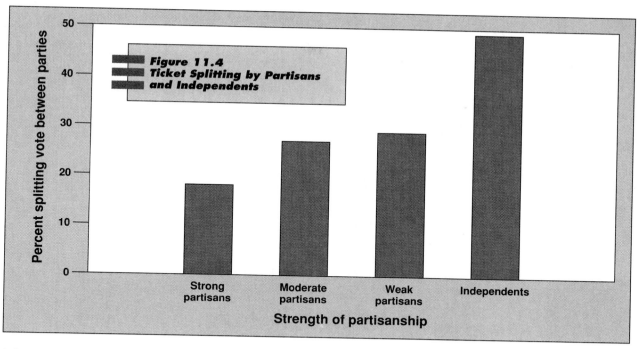

**Figure 11.4
Ticket Splitting by Partisans
and Independents**

Independents split their ballots (voting for both Republican and Democratic candidates), whereas strong partisans (those who identify strongly with a party) tend to vote along party lines.

Source: Based on data from the Center for Political Studies, University of Michigan, *American National Election Study, 1988.*

and counterclaims: "Cut taxes." "No, raise them." "Freeze Social Security benefits." "No, that's unfair." "Lower interest rates." "No, leave them alone." "Defense spending should be reduced." "No, it creates jobs." Given this muddle, can we blame anyone for looking for signposts? If the Democrats in general stand for one economic philosophy and Republicans for another, and if, in addition, your needs are best met by one of these two philosophies, then voting consistently for that party makes sense. Moreover, voting for the "best" person is a waste of time unless that person belongs to a *winning* coalition that supports your interests. An individual legislator, no matter how honest, experienced, or qualified, cannot balance the budget. Only a group of legislators acting in concert can. And what better means to organize them than through a political party?

The fly in the ointment comes, of course, when the parties fail to clarify their stands on such

important issues as the management of the economy. In the United States there are broad differences between Democrats and Republicans, but the parties represent such large and unwieldy coalitions, their internal discipline is so weak, and their platforms are so vague that much of the electorate has trouble recognizing which party will best serve its general interests. In the final analysis, whether or not party line voting is a sound strategy depends on the political system: If the parties truly differ and if a voter can accurately relate his or her interests to one of them, party voting may be sensible; if not, it may be counterproductive.

Issues and Voting

Does the close connection between party identification and voting mean that the electorate does not take specific issues into account when choos-

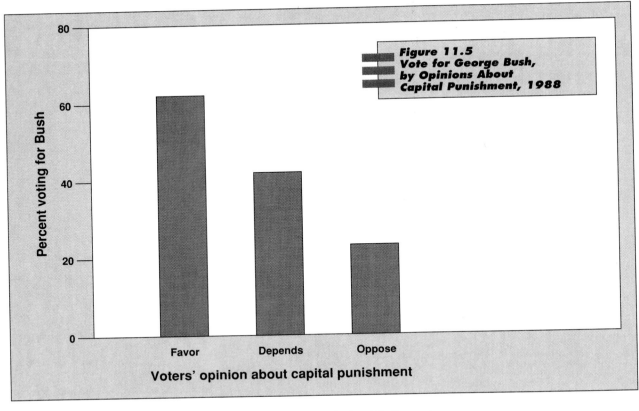

**Figure 11.5
Vote for George Bush,
by Opinions About
Capital Punishment, 1988**

Those who favored capital punishment tended to vote for George Bush, while those who opposed it voted for Michael Dukakis.

Source: Based on data from the Center for Political Studies, University of Michigan, *American National Election Study, 1988.*

ing among candidates? This question is sometimes rephrased more bluntly: Are voters rational? The topic has sparked endless debates in newsrooms, campaign headquarters, and universities. Yet, despite volumes of scholarly books and articles on the subject, the matter remains as unsettled today as ever. Part of the problem lies in the meaning of rationality, a term no one seems able to define satisfactorily, and part in the varied and unfathomable nature of human behavior. A simple place to start is the consistency between attitudes and behavior. If voters are rational, according to one line of reasoning, their stands on issues will determine how they vote. Rational voters presumably favor candidates who share their views on important issues and reject those who do not. It seems simple enough. Yet the question remains: How many

Americans fit this mold?

The answer depends on the kind of issue. Edward Carmines and James Stimson distinguish between "easy" and "hard" issues.[20] Among other features, an easy issue is "symbolic" rather than technical and has been on the political agenda for a long time. Hard issues are more technical, and it is difficult to tell where the parties and candidates stand on them. According to Carmines and Stimson, issue voting will be more common when easy rather than hard issues are involved.[21]

For example, men and women who strongly favored the death penalty—a relatively unambiguous, easy issue to have an opinion about—tended to vote for George Bush, who also favored it, instead of for Dukakis, who opposed it (see Figure 11.5). But take a more difficult issue: how

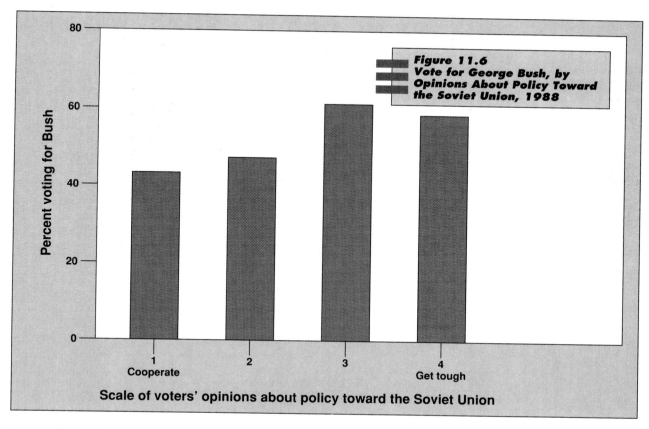

Figure 11.6
Vote for George Bush, by Opinions About Policy Toward the Soviet Union, 1988

In terms of candidates preferences those who favored getting tough with Russia did not differ greatly from those who favored more cooperation. These data suggest that this particular issue did not influence the voters' choices.

Source: Based on data from the Center for Political Studies, University of Michigan, *American National Election Study, 1988.*

America should deal with the Russians. On this matter there is more room for doubt and candidates tend to be less clear on how they intend to proceed. In such cases the electorate's attitudes are less clearly connected to their voting preferences (see Figure 11.6).

Many political scientists use the congruence between opinions on issues and candidate preferences as a barometer of issue voting: If the correspondence is close, they infer that the electorate is reasonably rational, at least in this sense; if the association is weak, they conclude that voters use other, presumably less rational, criteria such as candidate images.[22]

But before accepting this approach to rationality, we ought to keep several points in mind.

For one thing, a few voters decide on the basis of a single issue. Many gun owners feel so strongly about their right to "bear arms" that they will vote against *any* candidate who advocates gun control, no matter what other qualifications the person may have. Although their opinions and their votes coincide, what are we to make of these **single-issue voters**? Are they rational?

Second, remember that a citizen's impression of a candidate rests partially on *perceptions* of where that candidate stands on different issues. These beliefs may or may not be accurate, but they form the basis of opinions (see Chapter 8). Consequently, we need to measure not simply a person's own position but also where he or she

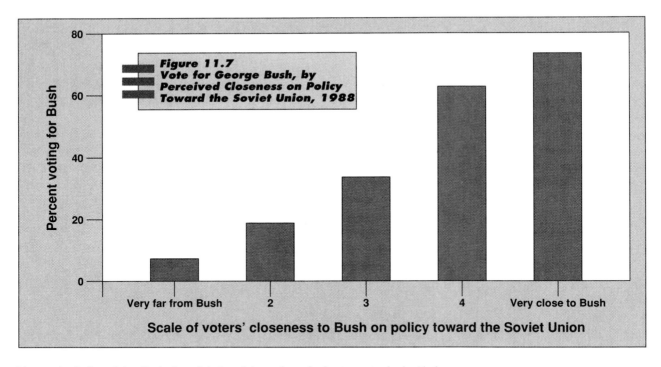

Figure 11.7
Vote for George Bush, by Perceived Closeness on Policy Toward the Soviet Union, 1988

Voters who believed that Bush shared their opinions about the best way to deal with the Soviet Union tended to vote for him. Those voters who felt distant from Bush on this issue tended to vote for Dukakis.

Source: Based on data from the Center for Political Studies, University of Michigan, *American National Election Study, 1988.*

believes the candidates stand on the matter.

Hence, we can approach the issue vote problem this way. Consider an imaginary voter, Mary. Call Mary an issue voter if she picks the candidate she believes is closest to her own positions. **Proximity**, or perceived closeness, is the key.[23] If Mary favors getting tough with the Russians *and* she thinks, for whatever reason, that Dukakis shares this view and that Bush does not, then, other things being equal, she will vote for Dukakis. If, on the other hand, she feels that Bush, not Dukakis, most agrees with her, then she should vote for Bush. In the event that she perceives that both candidates are equally far from her position or that they do not differ, then she will either have to abstain or choose on some other grounds. In a nutshell, this approach to issue voting takes into account not only the voters' own opinions but also their perceptions of where the candidates stand.

Using perceived closeness or proximity as the standard, it appears from Figure 11.7 that many Americans do act reasonably responsibly once their perceptions of the candidates' positions are taken into account. More than three-quarters of the respondents who felt very close to Bush on this issue voted for him, while close to 90 percent of those who felt distant chose his opponent. Not everyone fits the pattern. Yet some social scientists think that proximity scales like the one in Figure 11.7 accurately predict, if not explain, the behavior of most citizens.[24] These findings, in turn, have naturally led to a certain amount of enthusiasm about the competence, if not rationality, of the common person: Perhaps Key was right—people are not fools.

Unfortunately, there is still room for doubt. In the first place, the voters in Figure 11.7 might be *rationalizing* the choices they made for other reasons, such as liking a candidate's personality and

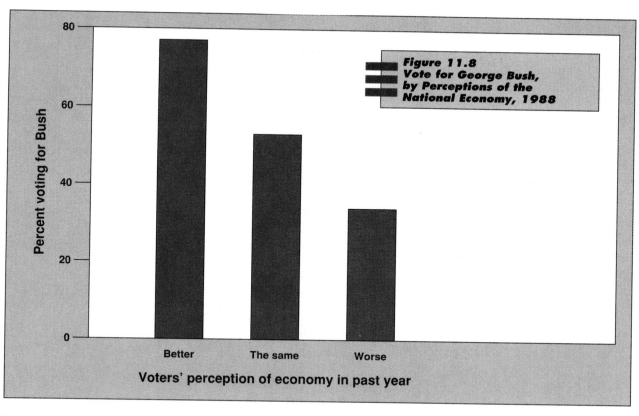

**Figure 11.8
Vote for George Bush,
by Perceptions of the
National Economy, 1988**

People who felt that the economy had improved in the previous year tended to support George Bush. Those who believed that the economy was worse tended to support Bush's opponent.

Source: Based on data from the Center for Political Studies, University of Michigan, *American National Election Study, 1988.*

style. Humans in general tend to project traits they consider favorable onto people they like. This tendency, called "projection," applies to public opinion as well.[25] Furthermore, we might hesitate applying the label *rational* to a voter whose beliefs are demonstrably wrong. Suppose that someone who opposes the death penalty believes Bush shares this view and accordingly votes for him on those grounds. The vote might be consistent with the attitude, but would it be rational? Bush, after all, made his support for capital punishment a major plank in his platform, and thinking that he opposes it is clearly incorrect. One wonders how many voters misperceive the candidates' stands.

But misperception may not be solely the individual's fault. A test of an electoral system is how well it clarifies candidates' positions on important issues. Chapter 9 suggested that the media's coverage of campaigns, which emphasizes the "horse race" aspects rather than their issue content, makes it hard for the electorate to know who stands for what. We will see in the next section that the management of campaigns creates similar problems. So, even if large numbers of voters misperceive the candidates' positions, the fault may not be entirely theirs.

RETROSPECTIVE VOTING Because so many issues can be "hard," it is perhaps unreasonable to expect many voters to make the sophisticated calculations described above. Therefore, they may use simpler methods to decide how to vote. Party identification is one; retrospective voting is another.

According to the theory of **retrospective voting**, men and women have trouble predicting the nation's future but clearly understand where it has been. Hence, they vote *retrospectively*: they look back over the past couple of years to judge how things have been going.[26] If inflation has roared out of control, voters notice the price increases in their grocery bills and blame the incumbents. If, on the other hand, the country has prospered, they appreciate this and reelect current officeholders. For this reason the electorate has been described as a "rational god of vengeance and reward."[27]

Figure 11.8 (p. 343) illustrates the point by showing the close connection between people's assessments of the national economy in the year before the election and their votes. Individuals who felt the economy was doing better or at least staying the same backed the incumbents, the Republicans, while those who felt it was getting worse no doubt wanted change and voted for the challenger. This is not the most sophisticated way to choose, but it does reflect common sense.

In his 1988 presidential campaign Michael Dukakis went to considerable lengths to dispel his image as cold and aloof. Dukakis was perhaps spurred on by the common belief that voters choose on the basis of images rather than issues.

Candidate Images and Voting

Social characteristics and partisanship may predispose individuals to support certain ideas or groups but are not necessarily the *immediate* determinants of their choices. Instead, candidate images—how an individual perceives the contenders' personal qualities—appears to be a more direct influence. The authors of *The American Voter*, a milestone in voting research, asked respondents in a national survey what they liked and disliked about the 1956 presidential candidates and their parties.[28] Based on the answers to these open-ended questions, they constructed a scale of "partisan" attitude that was an overall assessment of the candidates and their parties. This partisan attitude, the investigators found, was highly correlated with how people voted. It was, in fact, a better predictor than party identification or issue preferences.[29]

In the years following the publication of *The American Voter* in 1960, many of its readers interpreted the results as proving that images rather than substance motivated the typical citizen. Large numbers of voters, it was believed, were swayed by superficial personality traits—charm, physical appearance, and the like—and could barely articulate the reasons for their preferences.

This lack of information and sophistication among the public led (and still leads) many political observers to think that office seekers, no matter how politically inexperienced or inept, can win if public relations firms neatly package them. The frequent electoral success of newcomers to office, such as celebrities and sports stars, reinforced this perception. Needless to say, all of this theorizing left the common person with a black eye. If the electorate picks its leaders on the basis of images, not issues, can it be called responsible?

More recent research continues to show the significance of images but at the same time demonstrates that many voters use these perceptions in relatively sophisticated ways. Researchers at the University of Michigan, for example, found that images often contain judgments about candidates' past performances or future policies.[30] Moreover, a coherent structure underlies these evaluations; they are not necessarily disorganized, spur-of-the-moment impressions but are assessments about the candidates' competence, reliability, and leadership skills.[31]

One can even justify "image" voting. After all, personal traits—especially honesty, competence, perseverance, and reliability—*are* appropriate criteria for choosing among office seekers. In a dangerous world overrun with nuclear weapons, drug cartels, and international terrorism, who wants a weakling in the White House? Moreover, information about where candidates stand on even major controversies is frequently difficult to obtain.[32] Thus, in many campaigns voters are forced to rely on more readily available information such as how the candidates present themselves in the media and other public forums.

What Explains Voting?

Arguments about the competence of the American public no doubt leave many readers baffled. Certainly these competing theories confuse even the experts. Nevertheless, it is obvious that citi-

zens are complex creatures and calling them rational or irrational oversimplifies their behavior. Most political scientists now believe that no single factor alone accounts for voting decisions. Rather the variables described above—social status, party identification, issues, and images of the candidates—form a web, with candidate evaluations, issues, and partisanship being close to the center and demographic attributes farther out. Even though the impact of some variables is immediate and the influence of others is indirect, they are all important in understanding why people vote as they do.[33]

At this juncture, however, another point arises. Perhaps Americans do not vote as regularly and wisely as they should. Perhaps many of them are disinterested or lazy. Perhaps they should study the candidates and issues more thoroughly. Perhaps they are too captivated by images. All of this may be true. But if we stop here we risk losing sight of a crucial point. Behavior never takes place in a vacuum but in a *context*. Voting is shaped by specific institutions,

How do voters choose among candidates? It appears that voters are influenced by a number of variables—both personal and environmental.

including electoral laws, the mass media, and campaign styles and strategies. These factors are quite separate from individual qualities, and it makes little sense to analyze voters without taking these institutional factors into account. In fact, the context of elections partially explains the electorate's actions. Before concluding that people are or are not competent to govern, therefore, we need to examine the political environment as thoroughly and scrupulously as the voters themselves.

Checkpoint

- In the past, certain demographic groups generally voted for the Democratic party, while Republicans drew strength from other segments of society. Today the traditional voting blocs are less cohesive.

- Party identification is strongly related to how people vote. Strong partisans back their party, whereas independents and weak partisans swing back and forth, splitting their tickets or not voting in any but the most exciting contests.

- There is evidence that many Americans take issues into account when deciding how to vote. Sometimes the connection is direct. Usually, though, it is necessary to measure not only a person's own opinion but also where he or she *thinks* the candidates stand.

- Some people choose candidates on the basis of retrospective judgments about the economy's performance in the past year.

- Many people also vote on the basis of candidate images. Such behavior does not necessarily mean that they are blinded by superficial or emotional characteristics, since a candidate's image frequently reflects traits that are important for success in office.

THE REALITY: HOW CAMPAIGNING AFFECTS VOTERS

A cursory glance at *Campaigns & Elections*, a slick bimonthly magazine aimed at political consultants and pollsters, quickly reveals the direction modern campaigns are taking. Nearly every article deals with some aspect of telemarketing, fund-raising, computers, direct mailing, or polling. Titles in the March/April 1988 issue, published at the height of the candidate selection season, included "Planting the Money Tree," "Case Study I: Saving Money With a PC," "Hiring the Perfect Press Secretary," and "Keeping Tabs on Your Opposition: A New Opposition Research Software Package." Full-page advertisements describe computer programs that automatically schedule campaign appearances, keep track of expenses, coordinate voter drives, and supervise mass mailings. Others show readers where they can buy the services of media consultants, graphic artists, computer programmers, public relations firms, attorneys and accountants, and a host of other professionals.

Running for office has clearly become a high-technology business. Today's office seekers depend heavily on sophisticated equipment and paid consultants to get elected. This change in style is not without consequences, unfortunately, because campaign management can adversely affect voting behavior. Although television, polling, computers, automated phone banks, and other innovations appeal to candidates, they are a mixed blessing for the electorate.

High-Tech Campaigning

THE USES OF TECHNOLOGY IN CAMPAIGNS

Television, the most conspicuous symbol of modern campaigning, brings political images and controversies into every living room in America. Each year politicians spend millions of dollars filling the airwaves with their profiles and messages. Besides utilizing regular commercial channels, they also take advantage of cable systems that allow them to tailor appeals to specific audiences. A candidate who broadcasts on a

THE MARKETPLACE

The Marketplace is *C&E's* handy guide to political products and services. Listings are sold on an annual basis (six issues). Call Lynne Bonney-Busby at 202/331-3222 or 800/237-7842.

One-line listing—$150/year; each additional line—$75.
Boldface listing—$200/year; each additional line—$175.
ALL CAPS listing—$200/year; each additional line—$175.
One-inch-deep display ad—$720/year.

(*)=Member of the American Association of Political Consultants (**)=Corporate Member of the American Association of Political Consultants (D)=Democrat (R)=Republican

ADDRESSING, MAILING & INSERTING

Campaign and Opinion Research Analysts (*), 118 E. Cornerview Rd., Gonzales, LA 70737 504/647-1767

ADVERTISING/PUBLIC RELATIONS

The Bynum Consulting Group (D*), 162 Madison Ave, Suite 601, New York, NY 10016, 212/213-9300
Civic Service, Inc. (**), 1050 Connecticut Ave., NW, #870, Washington, DC 202/785-2070
CHARLES LEVINE COMMUNICATIONS, 64 USSISHKIN ST., JERUSALEM, ISRAEL (POB 7834) Tel. 972-2-351925, Fax 972-2-228063
Professional (**), Promotional Services, 1200 Harger Rd., #717, Oak Brook, IL, 60521
Sonis and Assoc. Advertising (**), 1521 Killearn Center Blvd., Tallahassee, FL 32308

ASSOCIATIONS

Association of Independent TV (**), 1200 18th St., NW, Ste 502, Washington DC, 20036

University of Oklahoma Foundation, Inc. (**), 100 Timberdell Rd., Norman, OK 73019

CAMPAIGN SOFTWARE

Below, Tobe & Assoc. (**), 7801 Norfolk Ave., #102, Bethesda, MD 20814 301/656-4966
Campaign Coordinator, 425 Bush Street, PH, San Francisco, CA 94108 415/986-2044
Capital Data Services, 1200 Eaton Ct. NW, Washington, DC 20009 202/333-8800
Data + Imagination, Inc., 5430 Van Nuys Blvd., Ste. 207-A, Van Nuys, CA 91401 818/784-3460
FYI, 955 Eudora, Ste. 207, Denver, CO 80220 Fund Raising Management, Easy to use, inexpensive 303/322-5599
Grass Roots Software Systems, 2800 Shirlington Rd., Ste. 716, Arlington, VA 22206 703/998-5861
Hannibal/Landslide-LSW, Inc. 8240 Professional Place, Landover, MD 20785 800/255-4579 or 301/459-2323
HEADLEE SYSTEMS, INC. - Total Campaign Tracking & Communication (TC^2), 38215 W. Ten Mile Rd., Suite 2, Farmington Hills, MI 48024 313/476-7015
People & Contacts, P.O. Box 11830, Fort Worth, TX 76110-1830 800/727-3897
Politech/SD Associates, 1201 Asylum Avenue Suite 418, Hartford, CT 06105 203/278-3434
Political Contact Technologies, 3027 Rosemary Lane, Falls Church, VA 22042
Q.E.D. Systems Inc. (R), 1210 Glenwood Ave., Minneapolis, MN 55405 612/377-1616
A complete political software system for statewide races up to 250,000
Real Good Software, 300 N. Washington St., Falls Church, VA, 22046 703/237-2577

COALITION DEVELOPMENT

Today's campaigns rely heavily on computer programmers, financial analysts, media consultants, pollsters, and other experts. Some observers worry that these specialists oversimplify or obscure important policy issues and help trivialize campaigns.

channel aimed mainly at Hispanics can air a message favoring bilingual education, an idea that might not appeal to the general viewing public.

But television is only the tip of the iceberg. No serious candidate, for example, would consider running without the benefit of a public opinion poll. Polls open doors to wealthy contributors who need evidence that the aspirant has a chance; they encourage and excite volunteers; they provide strategic information about where to allocate resources and time; and they bring credibility to the nominee. As with television commercials, polls are becoming more and more sophisticated. "Tracking," or day-by-day polling, is a case in point. Several years ago it took a week or more to collect and analyze the results of a sample survey. Now polls can be conducted on a daily or even hourly basis. These tracking

polls give an instantaneous snapshot of where the candidate stands with the voters.

A good example occurred in the 1982 Missouri senatorial race between John Danforth, the Republican incumbent, and Harriet Woods, his Democratic opponent.[34] Danforth's pollster called 150 to 200 potential voters each evening for several weeks before the election. When in mid-October he found a sudden surge in support for Woods, he urged a change in strategy. Prior to this time, Danforth, an ordained minister, had insisted on a positive, upbeat campaign. But Woods's hard-hitting ads, which suggested that the wealthy senator did not care about the jobless and elderly, were apparently having an effect because the race began to get close. The Danforth camp thus hurriedly prepared new commercials with an "edge" on them. At the same time, the Woods organization, lacking poll data of its own and short on money, scaled back its television advertising. Almost immediately Woods started losing ground. And despite another surge at the end of the month she eventually lost.

Both camps agreed afterward that the Republican's ability to monitor opinions daily gave him a decisive advantage. "We would talk every day in our campaign about what we ought to be doing," a Woods adviser said later, "but we only had money for two polls all fall, so we were constantly looking back at data 10 days old trying to guess where and how it might have changed. We just didn't have what they had."[35]

A variation of polling is the **focus group**, a dozen or so randomly selected citizens brought together for an in-depth probe of their opinions on issues, assessments of campaign events, and reactions to radio and television commercials. Republicans made good use of focus groups in 1988 when they discovered, almost by accident, that Dukakis could be wounded by negative advertising. Two gatherings in Paramus, New Jersey, revealed that so-called Reagan Democrats (people who normally vote Democratic but backed Reagan in 1984) expressed hostile reactions to some of Governor Dukakis's past actions, such as his veto of a bill making the Pledge of Allegiance mandatory in Massachusetts public schools. Even though the veto had been cast in the 1970s for constitutional reasons, the focus group leaders sensed the issue might play well with the public and convinced Bush to emphasize it in his speeches and television ads.[36] The strategy worked with deadly effectiveness: By portraying Dukakis as being out of step with traditional American values, the vice-president's camp drove up Dukakis's negative ratings in the polls.

Technology influences politics in countless other ways. Not long ago politicians kept lists of supporters on three-by-five cards. Contacting them during a campaign was an arduous task requiring battalions of ward bosses and precinct workers. Even the most successful candidates could reach only a small proportion of their potential followers. Today electronics makes the job child's play.

One company, P/M Corporation, maintains a list of 140 million households. It cross-references these names against 200 other lists, giving its staff the power to target potential donors based on precise economic and social characteristics. The company claims, for instance, that 90 percent of Volvo drivers are wealthy liberals, whereas Jaguar owners favor conservatives.[37] Firms like this one program computers to type personalized letters with the recipient's name used throughout. Appeals are crafted to fit particular audiences: The elderly read about a candidate's devotion to social security and Medicare, while Catholics learn of his opposition to abortion. The messages can also be delivered by computer-driven telephones with the capacity to call 35,000 people in an hour.[38]

THE DOWNSIDE OF TECHNOLOGY IN CAMPAIGNS However inevitable, high-tech campaigning has had mixed consequences. Certainly it permits candidates to reach more people than ever before, which may stimulate interest (although there has been no increase in turnout in the past decades). But if these techniques have benefits, they have drawbacks as well. For one thing, they appear to debase political discourse. The heavy reliance on television leads to 30-second spot advertisements, a fine format for selling wine coolers or dog food, but not for discussing budget deficits or international trade.

Second, polling and direct-mail solicitation tend to encourage office seekers to be all things to all people, with the result that they stand for very little. Men and women in political life have always tried to avoid making enemies, but today this art has become a science. "Dramatic" and "courageous" pronouncements are often in reality carefully orchestrated moves based on sophisticated polling. During the 1980 presidential election campaign, Ronald Reagan pledged to nominate a woman to the Supreme Court. Since no female had ever served on the Court, it appeared a bold and forthright commitment. In truth, however, Reagan made it with a firm grip on the public's pulse. Richard Beal, a campaign consultant, had surveys in hand proving that there were no pitfalls: "We knew it was an all-win situation."[39]

Michael Dukakis's 1988 advertisements demonstrate the point from another angle. In radio broadcasts directed largely at black audiences in the Northeast that tended to be concerned about crime and illegal firearms, Dukakis berated Bush's opposition to tough gun control laws. Meanwhile, in Texas, where gun control is as popular as rattlesnakes, one of his commercials said, "Only one candidate for President has voted for Federal gun control. Only one. George Bush."[40] Maneuvers of this sort are not lost on the electorate, who must wonder how many pledges are sincerely made.

Third, the newer forms of campaigning drive up the cost of running for office. Only well-funded campaigns can afford the computers, mass mailings, focus groups, teleconferencing, tracking polls, and media exposure that seem essential for success. Finally, not only are campaigns costing more, they are lasting longer. Television and electronic fund-raising let political novices run for high offices but require them to start early so they can generate name recognition and collect enough contributions. (The increased length, in turn, raises the price the contestants have to pay.) Most of the contenders for the 1988 presidential nominations began running more than three years in advance. Members of the House of Representatives, it is said, start their reelection drives the day after taking office. And presidents spend the last two years of their first term worrying about the next election.

Where does this endless campaigning leave voters? All too frequently tired, bored, and frustrated. Equally significant, the changing campaign techniques have driven candidates into the arms of a new breed of adviser, the professional consultant.

Consultants and "Political Ambiguity"

As long as men and women have run for elective office they have sought advice. For the most part they received it from friends or relatives who had spent years working in politics. These old-style politicians relied on intuition, experience, common sense, judgment, and hard work. If they were a bit nonsystematic and imprecise, they nevertheless displayed a remarkable insight into

the temper of the times; if they kept lists of supporters in shoe boxes, they still knew how to get them to the polls.

Consultants today are different. Not only do they advise their clients about specific matters such as polling, but many have become total managers who take over and run entire campaigns, beginning with fund-raising coffees and ending with the postelection office cleanup.[41] Indeed, it has been observed more than once that candidates are becoming mere appendages to the consultants who supposedly serve them. Rather than simply collect data or offer advice, these managers dictate itineraries, coordinate financing, produce advertising, and most important of all, decide what the candidates will say. A reporter described Bush's 1988 campaign organization this way: "The candidate is another division [although] an important one, but most of the thinking and strategy and preparation in the Bush effort takes place at the headquarters building."[42]

And what is the new generation of consultants advising its clients to say? Richard Scammon and Ben Wattenberg set the tone in the early 1970s in a widely read and influential book, *The Real Majority*.[43] Reportedly writing for Democrats, the authors advised their readers to adopt "centrist" positions on issues in order to avoid rocking the boat by taking clear-cut stands on controversies. Stay firmly in the middle of the road, they warned, or run the risk of losing to someone who does. A political scientist, Benjamin Page, calls this strategy **political ambiguity**, meaning the decision of office seekers to avoid clearly stating their positions on major issues.[44]

This kind of thinking is not new to American politics. Politicians have always hedged their bets. Lately, though, not revealing one's hand on controversial issues has soared in popularity. Under the tutelage of their advisers, candidates seeking votes rely more and more on personality, image, style, and platitudes instead of specific statements on issues. President Jimmy Carter's pollster once told him: "Too many good people have been beaten because they tried to substitute substance for style."[45] Carter's media consultant, Gerald Rafshoon, echoed this advice saying, "Issues per se are not what move people to make their choice. . . . The issue is the candidate's

Senator Earl Clements campaigning in Kentucky in 1956. Campaigns used to be relatively simple, relying on face to face contacts and direct appeals to the voters. They made little use of sophisticated technology.

character, leadership, and integrity."[46] Similarly, Lee Atwater, a mastermind behind George Bush's election, told reporters that he learned early in his career that "Republicans in the South could not win elections by talking issues."[47] Several of Michael Dukakis's aides told the *New York Times* that the governor delighted them by not making any firm or detailed commitments during his drive for the nomination and that they wanted him to stress his "character," "leadership," "coolness," and "predictability."[48]

Countless others have heeded the advice to straddle the fence.[49] A common complaint during the last decade has been that candidates and parties do not stand for anything. Exasperated by the candidates' failure to address major national problems, David Broder, a syndicated columnist, observed that the 1988 campaign "is about to expire from lack of mental oxygen," and was "a conspiracy of silence."[50] A leading political scientist, Walter Dean Burnham, was equally disgusted, calling campaign ads "real junk food."[51] But Jack Germond and Jules Witcover, two veteran political reporters, have been most scathing of how presidential contenders conduct themselves. Writing about the 1984

presidential election, they assert:

> The real losers . . . were the people of the United States, and that was the case without regard to which candidate they had supported. They had just dozed through a process that is supposed to be the ultimate of democratic exercises—the choice of one candidate over another for the most powerful office in the free world. But they had settled for an empty contest full of images on their television screens that told them essentially nothing about the decisions that would be made for their future. . . . Moreover, because the campaign was so devoid of content, the results told them nothing reliable about the shape of American politics in the years ahead.[52]

Of course, it is not just columnists and academicians who are turned off by fence straddling. We saw in Chapter 10 that turnout has dropped precipitously over the years. Perhaps part of the reason is captured by a New Yorker who noted, "If you're voting, you should have a positive reason. There's an old saying: People vote with their feet. If you want me to vote, you have to come up with a better choice."[53]

The reason that candidates and parties stay

In recent years, as Michael Dukakis' Boston campaign headquarters illustrates, campaigns have become high-tech operations that use sophisticated computers and electronic communications techniques.

firmly in the middle of the road lies partly—but only partly—in the way elections are conducted in this country. In a two-party, plurality, winner-take-all system, both sides risk losing at least some voters if they take a stand on a divisive issue. The more contentious the issue, the greater the risk. The goal, after all, is to build a winning coalition, and the best way to gain supporters is not to lose them.[54] Hence, the electoral system encourages ambiguity. A candidate does not offend anyone by advocating a balanced budget, a strong national defense, and fine schools; but votes can easily be lost by *specific* calls for higher taxes, more MX missiles, and competency testing of teachers.

This explanation is not the whole story, however. The strategy of ambiguity is also encouraged by polling, which always shows that potential enemies exist on any controversy;* by reliance on brief television advertisements that preclude detailed policy statements; by the entry of so many newcomers into politics who need to build coalitions quickly; and by the pervasive distrust of the public's capacity to understand complicated issues.

Note, too, that many of the influential consultants are drawn from the ranks of public relations specialists and media professionals.[55] Perhaps their previous experience coupled with their unfamiliarity with the complexities of public policy naturally lead them to embrace non-issue campaigning. David Broder thinks: "Too many of the successful candidates in recent years have had only political operatives and media manipulators . . . riding with them in the front section of the plane. These folks too often lack the wisdom or the standing to help the candidates think through questions beyond the tactics for the next day or week."[56]

Negative Campaigning

Besides leaving voters without a meaningful choice, reliance on consultants without policy expertise all too often leads to **negative campaigning,** in which personal attacks, not public policy, characterize campaign messages. Although smears have been part and parcel of elec-

---

*When Susan Estrich, Dukakis's campaign manager, was asked how decisions were made, she replied "Nothing is visceral. Let's be honest. . . . Very little is done viscerally here. We polled. We had extensive focus groups. . . . At least in the general election we polled constantly." Quoted in *Campaign for President: The Managers Look at '88*, edited by David R. Runkel (Dover, Mass.: Auburn House, 1989), p. 157.

A Closer Look

Campaigning in the Mud ★★★

Listen to what some of the candidates were saying about one another in the 1986 congressional elections:

- A California television station ran an advertisement showing a teenager smoking marijuana, a convict, and a scantily clad prostitute "endorsing" a veteran state senator. "Thank you, Senator Greene," the prostitute says, "You're our best friend."[a]
- Linda Chavez, a candidate for the Senate in Maryland, called her opponent, Barbara Mikulski, a "San Francisco liberal," "anti-male," and an employer of a "fascist, feminist, and Marxist." One of Chavez's mailings depicted a bright red imprint of pursed lips with a caption "Kiss Your Traditional Values Good-Bye."[b]

By 1988, this type of mudslinging reached the presidential level. George Bush, in particular, has been singled out for going too far, although his opponent, Michael Dukakis, responded in kind by the end of the campaign. Among the most notorious (and some would say effective) types of pro-Bush advertisements were these:

- A television commercial showing inmates walking through a steel revolving door while the voiceover asserts: "As

Governor, Michael Dukakis vetoed mandatory sentences for drug dealers. He vetoed the death penalty. His revolving door prison policy gave weekend furloughs to first-degree murderers not eligible for parole. While out, many committed other crimes like kidnapping and rape, and many are still at large."[c] (Nowhere did the ad define "many.")

- A spot ad showing Dukakis riding in a tank with a helmet that even his supporters agreed made him look like Snoopy or Alfred E. Newman. The announcer, meanwhile, told viewers that the governor opposed "virtually every defense system we developed" and "America can't afford to take that risk."[d]
- In a thinly disguised appeal to racial fears, a letter to California Republicans asked "why is it so urgent that you decide now? . . . Here are two [reasons]." On one side of the letter was a picture of Bush and President Reagan, on the other a photo of Jesse Jackson towering over the much shorter Dukakis. The letter continued that if Dukakis "is elected to the White House, Jesse Jackson is sure to be swept into power on his coattails."[e]

Candidates kept at it in 1989:

- James Florio, Democratic candidate for governor of New Jersey, aired an ad stat-

Mudslinging has become an integral part of many campaigns. In 1989, both candidates for governor of New Jersey used Pinocchio images in their television advertisements to accuse the other of lying.

ing in part, "Imagine—it's almost un-believable—a candidate for governor with toxic waste barrels on his own property."[f]

- Florio and his opponent, Jim Courter, both produced television commercials showing the other man's face growing a Pinocchio nose to convince viewers of their opponents' mendacity.[g]

- Republican John Rice of Alabama minced no words when comparing him-self to his opponent: "He's lying, he's lib-eral, he's gutless and I'm not."[h]

[a]Paul West, "Oh, What Dirty Campaigns," Wilmington, Delaware *News Journal*, November 2, 1986, p. 9E.
[b]*Baltimore Sun*, November 2, 1986, p. 3C.
[c]*Washington Post*, October 5, 1988, p. 18.
[d]*New York Times*, October 19, 1988, p. 6B.
[e]Ibid.
[f]*New York Times*, October 16, 1989, p. 6B.
[g]Ibid., p. 1B.
[h]*New York Times*, October 24, 1989, p. 24.

tions since the Republic's founding, they seem to have soared to new heights in the last decade, as A Closer Look on pp. 352–353 illustrates.

Negative campaigning has become popular partly because candidates and their advisers are convinced that it works: "The sad truth is that negative advertising works," according to Washington consultant Roger Stone, who continues: "The voters tell us they don't like it, but they respond to it. Therefore, what politician is unilaterally going to disarm?"[57] A political scientist concurred, saying of a series of negative ads that had apparently helped Dukakis win an important primary, "It just reconfirms my view that negative ads matter. Candidates who ignore them do so at their own peril. You've got to fight fire with fire."[58] Dukakis's own campaign manager agreed with this view, "I think people are really used to negative advertising. It's effective. It's become a fixture.... We've moved beyond the point where anyone takes heat for running negative."[59]

The Effects of Modern Campaign Practices

Are the consultants right? Maybe. But whatever its justification and causes, the reliance on ambiguity and negative advertising has important consequences for voters and how we assess their competence. If candidates really do agree on policy, we can hardly criticize them for not taking opposing positions. If, on the other hand, their evasion of issues stems simply from their hopes of getting elected, they create problems for themselves and the electorate. For by not debating substantive issues, they are left to forage for things to do and say. Often they emphasize images and platitudes, attack their opponents, and substitute slogans and jingles for discussion and debate.

Americans are routinely condemned for choosing their leaders on the basis of images, not substance. But given the dominance of image making and issue avoidance, how else can they choose? Voters are blamed for their apathy. But how much interest can there be in look-alike candidates, in superficial policy pronouncements, in

vitriolic attacks, in slogans, and in elections without meaningful differences?

There is evidence that the new style of electioneering dissatisfies large segments of the public. Walter Dean Burnham predicted that "... [the voter] is likely to find himself being forced to make choices—especially in presidential elections—which do not permit him to do more than vote for the lesser of evils ... he is very likely indeed to conclude that voting makes no great difference...."[60]

Checkpoint

- Campaigns are increasingly relying on computers, television, polling, direct mail, automated phone banks, and other high-tech devices.

- Although these developments help candidates streamline their operations, they have serious consequences, including driving up the cost of running for office and undermining the quality of political debate.

- Campaigns are now in the hands of consultants who, although skilled at modern communications and public relations, are not necessarily experienced in policy areas.

- Candidates frequently follow a strategy of political ambiguity: They deliberately avoid clarifying their stands on major issues.

- Although politicians have always smeared one another, the frequency, sophistication, and ugliness of negative campaigning have grown in recent years.

- When issues are trivialized or ignored and image is promoted over substance, voters perhaps should not be blamed for their apathy or lack of sophisticated voting habits.

THE REALITY: THE INSTITUTIONAL CONTEXT OF ELECTIONS

It is obviously unfair to lay all the blame for the electoral system's shortcomings at the doorstep of candidates and their advisers. Campaigns, after all, consist of more than nominees seeking votes. They affect and are affected by countless organizations, institutions, and practices, some of which lie beyond anyone's control.

Chapter 9, for example, contended that the mass media have a mixed record of presenting information to the electorate. All too often television, radio, and newspapers portray elections as horse races by telling their audiences who is ahead in the polls, raised the most money, traveled the farthest, collected the most endorsements, attracted the largest crowds, and ran the slickest commercials. What the media fail to do, study after study concludes, is describe the candidates' specific stands on issues.

Unfortunately, as Chapter 12 points out, political parties do not pick up the slack. They have become less and less effective in educating and mobilizing their rank-and-file members; less and less effective in organizing interests; and especially less and less effective in recruiting, training, and disciplining leaders who are committed to the party's program. Candidates today create independent organizations that have their own staffs and fund-raising capabilities.[61] If parties are an important instrument in electoral democracy, then the relative weakness of the American party system explains as much of the decline in participation as individual characteristics do.

The sheer size, complexity, and impersonality of modern government also play a part. The Constitution, with its separation of powers and checks and balances, makes understanding the political process difficult enough. Add to this labyrinth the volume of business transacted by federal, state, and local agencies. Take into account the intricacies of power relationships and the tangle of ideas, personalities, and passions that permeate the halls of Congress, the White House, the courts, the bureaucracy, the state capitals, and town governments throughout the country. Think also of the breadth and depth of the crises facing the nation and of the claims and counterclaims, each supported by mountains of statistics, these controversies engender. Consider, finally, that most major problems—nuclear annihilation, ecological catastrophe, drug abuse, AIDS, budget deficits, crime—persist year after year without anyone seeming to be able to dent them, much less resolve them.

In light of these realities, is it any wonder that many citizens rely on party, easy issues, and images when deciding how to vote?

Money and Elections

Elections supposedly embody the key principles of democracy: popular sovereignty, majority rule, and political equality. As one might expect, however, gaps between the ideal and the reality exist. Money causes especially difficult problems. Ideally each individual's vote counts as much as the next person's, no matter how great the differences in their intelligence or education or income. The "one person, one vote" rule is easy enough to enforce—that is what registration laws are for. But no one has found a way to ensure *actual* political equality, and in a society characterized by great disparities in wealth, its absence is a fact of life.

The extent of these differences is most noticeable in campaign financing, another important part of the institutional context of elections. Will Rogers, the American humorist, once said, "You have to be loaded just to get beat."[62] The high cost of running for office in the United States bears him out. Although the numbers have been repeated many times, they become more mind-numbing with each retelling:

- Herbert Alexander, an authority on campaign financing, estimates that the presidential contenders in 1988, including the ones who ran for their party's nomination, spent more than $500 million.[63]
- Add to this total the roughly $257 million spent by candidates for the House of Representatives and the $201 million doled out by those running for the Senate.[64]

- A typical House contestant in 1988 paid about $162,000 for expenses; Senate campaigns were more costly, averaging about $958,000 apiece.[65]
- These summaries, however, hide some astounding totals: Senator Pete Wilson (Republican of California) had receipts of $11 million; Senator Lloyd Bentsen (Democrat of Texas who was also running for the vice-presidency) collected $8 million; Representative Joseph Kennedy, nephew of Senator Edward Kennedy, took in $1,419,819, even though his opponent spent less than $20,000.
- At least he had an opponent. In 1988, approximately 49 incumbent representatives ran unopposed but still received, on average, $312,000 in campaign contributions.[66]
- Running for state and local office is in many instances only slightly less expensive and sometimes more so. Three-quarters of the way through his campaign, Ronald Lauder, running for the 1989 Republican nomination for mayor of New York City, reported spending at least $8.5 million, about $85 for every likely voter.[67]

Money does not buy elections—there are too many rich losers for that to be the case[*]—but there is nevertheless a widespread fear that candidates, who are increasingly relying on television, highly paid consultants, and other forms of high-tech campaigning, are being overwhelmed by the necessity of raising huge sums of money. This need, in turn, creates a dependency on wealthy individuals and groups that gives the donors unfair advantages and influence. At the same time, the high price of campaigns undoubtedly discourages many talented but less affluent individuals from running for office. Moreover, because incumbents have an easier time raising money, few of them, especially in the House, face serious challenges. For all

these reasons, campaign financing potentially subverts the principle of political equality.

Campaign Reforms

Concerns about the impact of money in politics have sparked repeated cries for reform. Beginning in the early 1970s in the wake of the Watergate scandal, Congress passed several campaign finance measures. The Federal Election Campaign Act (1971) and amendments to it (1974, 1977) sought to limit the amount of money flowing into elections. Here are the law's major provisions:

1 **Public financing.** Eligible presidential candidates receive public funds for primary and general election expenses. Funds are also available for national party committees to stage their nominating conventions. In return for accepting public funding, the candidates must agree not to spend more than the total. Public financing is available *only* to presidential candidates.

2 **Public disclosure.** Congressional as well as presidential candidates are required to disclose periodically the names of major campaign contributors, expenses, and other financial activities.

3 **Contribution limitations and prohibitions.** Individuals may give $1,000 to each candidate per election; $20,000 to a national party; and $5,000 to other political committees or organizations. Total contributions in a calendar year may not exceed $25,000. The law prohibits direct contributions to candidates from corporations, banks, labor unions, government contractors, and foreign nationals, and it also prohibits cash contributions in excess of $100 and donations supplied by one person in the name of another.

4 **Political action committees.** The law permits individuals, companies, unions, and other organizations to establish political action committees (PACs) that can collect donations from members and distribute them to candidates.

5 **Enforcement.** A six-member, bipartisan Federal Election Commission (FEC) enforces the law's provisions.

---

[*]Think of these Senate candidates who spent so much on losing efforts in 1988: George Voinovich (Ohio), $8.2 million; Peter Dawkins (New Jersey), $7.6 million; and Leo McCarthy (California), $7.0 million. Federal Election Commission news release, February 24, 1989.

On paper at any rate, the campaign act, as well as state regulations, brought sweeping changes to campaign financing. The most important reform in many observers' minds was the provision for federally funded presidential elections. The funds reimburse candidates for their nomination and general-election expenses. As a condition of receiving the grants, the recipients agree to limit their spending to a set amount. In 1988, each candidate received $46.1 million for the general election, plus additional sums for primaries and nominating conventions.

Government subsidies meant that the public, not corporations, unions, or millionaires, would bear the cost of running the campaigns. Although the law has shortcomings—third-party candidates are particularly disadvantaged in obtaining assistance—its main goal is to reduce the influence of wealthy contributors.

Campaign Finance Reform in Practice

Despite the hopes placed on them, campaign finance reforms have not worked completely as intended. The reality is that money still pours into elections at an unprecedented rate, and the worst abuses have not been corrected. In 1988, for instance, Bush and Dukakis both spent millions more than the nominal limit set by the act.[68] Congressional races consumed additional millions of dollars. Analysts attribute the problem to a variety of causes: (1) "independent" committees, (2) "soft" money, (3) growing indebtedness to political action committees, and (4) the constant preoccupation with raising campaign funds.

INDEPENDENT COMMITTEES The campaign act as amended in 1974 originally limited the amount of money that any federal candidate could spend, but in 1976 the Supreme Court struck down this portion of the law, arguing that it unconstitutionally infringed on freedom of speech.[69] According to the Court's interpretation, popularly known as the "money talks" decision, an individual can spend unlimited amounts of his or her *own* money. Thus, candidates for the

House and Senate are free to raise and spend as much money as they can, and presidential candidates can likewise do so if they do not accept public funds.

The Court's decision also legitimized the establishment of **independent committees**, which can solicit and spend money on behalf of a presidential candidate so long as they work independently of the official campaign headquarters. These independent operations have grown enormously in size. For instance, Dukakis's 1988 campaign in Illinois was really directed by Campaign '88, an offshoot of the state Democratic party.[70] Employing more than 100 workers, it eventually managed to solicit about $2 million from unions, businesses, and individuals who were free to make these contributions because Campaign '88 was ostensibly independent of Dukakis's official organization.

Needless to say, Democrats were not the only ones to use this ploy. Bush had similar organizations in many states, and his predecessor, Ronald Reagan, received the benefit of millions of dollars in independent committee expenditures in 1980 and 1984, especially from ideologically conservative groups.

SOFT MONEY Public financing of presidential races would supposedly shield the candidates from the pressure of large donors and from potential conflicts of interest. Unfortunately, Congress in the late 1970s inadvertently created a loophole in the law. In order to encourage state "party-building" activities such as voter registration and get-out-the-vote drives, it permitted individuals and groups to make gifts to local party organizations that needed money for these purposes.

In fact, however, these activities end up benefiting the top of the ticket and are tightly controlled from the national headquarters. Moreover, donations to these state units—called **soft money**—did not have to be reported and were unregulated by the Federal Election Commission. So, besides the proceeds from independent committees, the presidential candidates continue to receive huge sums in soft money from private sources. Both parties were unusually candid about the situation, admitting after the

1988 elections that they had raised millions this way and even naming the hundreds of contributors who had spent up to $100,000 each.[71]

POLITICAL ACTION COMMITTEES The reforms also legalized political action committees (PACs). Prior to 1974, federal laws prohibited corporate and union donations to political campaigns. Direct contributions continued to be illegal after 1974, but businesses, labor organizations, trade associations, public interest groups, and other groups are now allowed to establish PACs. **Political action committees** solicit and distribute contributions to candidates who sympathize with their purposes, interests, or ideology. Businesses and unions can use their own

funds to run PAC headquarters, hire staff, and pay for fund-raising costs, but any money actually given to a candidate must be collected from individual contributors.

PACs have become a potent force in American politics. By 1990 more than 4000 of these bodies represented almost every economic, social, and political interest in society. Financial institutions, corporations, unions, professional and trade associations, agricultural organizations, and many ideological groups are especially well represented. In the 1978–1979 period they gave $61 million to candidates; by 1986, the total had swollen to over $200 million, and the totals for 1988 were even higher.[72]

PACs (discussed in greater detail in Chapter 13) have aroused a great deal of criticism from across the political spectrum. The main concern is that they are buying influence in Congress. Others blame PACs for protecting incumbents because they tend to give more to current officeholders, who are in a position to help the donors, than to challengers, who may never come to power anyway.

PREOCCUPATION WITH FUND-RAISING Legislators find themselves in a quandary. Elections are expensive, and one of the most irksome conditions of their employment is the never-ending quest for campaign contributions. Lawmakers start searching immediately after winning their first election and never really stop. Since they are becoming proficient at the task, many amass huge war chests well in advance of their next campaigns.

The reforms enacted in the 1970s failed to relieve these pressures. Instead, incumbents spend considerable time hosting fund-raising parties, phoning and writing potential contributors, speaking before PACs and other lobbyists, and consulting with professional fund-raisers. These efforts do pay off—several senators up for reelection in 1990 had collected hundreds of thousands of dollars as early as 1988[73]—but there are unfortunate side effects. One is that challengers, who usually do not receive their party's nomination until a few months before the election, begin at a huge financial disadvantage. Equally important, "fat cats," the men and women who can afford large donations and often expect spe-

"WHAT'S IT DONE TO THE CONTENTS OF *THIS* BOX?"
November 2, 1982

HERBLOCK, Through The Looking Glass (W. W. Norton, 1984)

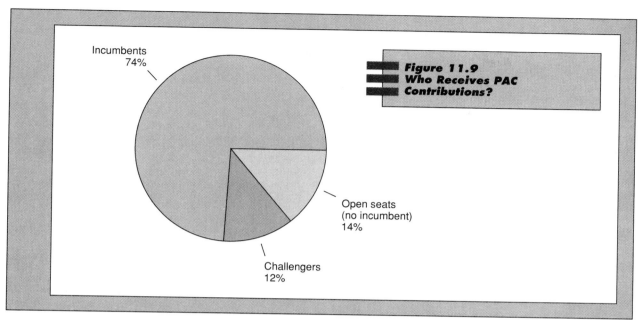

Incumbents
74%

**Figure 11.9
Who Receives PAC
Contributions?**

Open seats
(no incumbent)
14%

Challengers
12%

*About three-quarters of all PAC contributions go to incumbents (current officeholders).
Relatively little goes to challengers.*

Source: Federal Election Commission, Press release, April 9, 1989.

cial access and treatment in return, remain as potent as ever.

Elizabeth Drew illustrates these problems by showing how Fred, an imaginary contributor, can legally circumvent the spirit and letter of the law. First, he donates the maximum of a thousand dollars to his favorite candidate, then $20,000 to the national party, and then up to $5,000 to whatever PACs he sees fit. (He has to make sure the total doesn't exceed the $25,000 limit set by the law.) Next, he "requests" similar donations from his wife, his parents, his brothers and sisters, his in-laws, his children if they are old enough (the law has not clarified how old they have to be), his friends, his partners, and his business associates. Finally, he can organize fund-raising parties at which this cycle of giving is repeated by others. The upshot is that even though there are limits on individual contributions, Fred can still be a fat cat.[74]

In a society that treasures individual rights, there is probably little that can be done about Fred's activity. He is merely spending his time and money on behalf of causes or people he admires. Yet the equation of the use of wealth with

free speech collides with the principle of political equality. The danger is that Fred's influence may go far beyond his one vote, and no one knows for certain how much power the Freds of America really have.

Not surprisingly, the recipients of the donations minimize their impact. House Speaker Thomas S. Foley once said: "The money is not insignificant. But I object to the simplicity of saying that a vote is bought when Members receive money from people who like their view. But that doesn't mean the vote is because of the contribution."[75] Other insiders, such as Leon Billings, former executive director of the Democratic Senatorial Campaign Committee, agree and feel that the system runs as it always has: "I don't see that the politics of the institution have changed much with the PACs or that the AMA [American Medical Association] or labor, for example, are more influential."[76]

Skeptics, on the other hand, are certain that excessive money inevitably leads to unfair advantages. An aide to President Jimmy Carter conceded, "You'll try to do a favor for someone you know to be a big fund raiser."[77] Charles

Keating, Jr., a bank executive who had run afoul of federal banking regulations in 1988, reinforced these fears when, asked if his $1.3 million in direct and indirect contributions to five senators had influenced them to "take up [his] cause," he replied, "I want to say in the most forceful way I can: I certainly hope so."[78]

Even if votes in Congress are not traded for cash, critics nonetheless worry that virtually limitless campaign money undercuts the marketplace of ideas. If elections go to the highest bidder, certain philosophies or programs may never be sold.

Reforming the Reforms

Can anything be done? Many observers feel that plugging a few loopholes would be tremendously helpful. The most obvious reform is to extend public financing to congressional elections, coupled with limits on or the elimination of PAC contributions. These proposals have aroused opposition, however, because many campaigns, especially those mounted by challengers, are actually underfunded. One expert notes that anyone hoping to unseat a member of the House of Representatives needs at least $500,000 to have any chance.[79] Thus, public financing and spending limits might protect incumbents, who have a decided edge in name recognition, staff, experience, and access to the media.

Politics further complicates the prospects for reform. Republicans have historically outcompeted Democrats in raising funds and would logically be expected to oppose spending limits implied by public financing. But at the same time, they have experienced great difficulty dislodging Democrats from the House of Representative because current officeholders generally collect more contributions than challengers. Figure 11.9 (on p. 359) shows, for example, that three-quarters of PAC donations go to incumbents. For this reason limitations on spending might benefit Republican challengers who want to unseat Democratic House incumbents but cannot raise the huge amounts needed to do so. Democrats are in exactly the opposite position: In theory they should support strict financial controls, but many of their House members are doing quite well under the present system. Why should they

change it, they wonder. As a consequence of these political machinations, attempts to reform campaign finance laws have been stalemated.

Others feel that the problem is television. Because it drains campaign budgets, why not prohibit political advertising and provide candidates with free broadcast time, perhaps in chunks of half an hour or more? Besides lowering costs, this policy, followed in many European democracies, might elevate the quality of political debate. Once again, however, politics intrudes: Current officeholders and wealthy individuals who can afford to purchase airtime bitterly oppose these sorts of media reforms.

Checkpoint

- Voters are affected by the institutional context of elections. In particular, their knowledge of and participation in elections reflect (1) the quality of media coverage, (2) the strength of political parties, and (3) the remoteness, complexity, and impersonality of government.

- The infusion of money into campaigns causes political inequities. Campaign finance laws enacted in the early 1970s tried to control the impact of money on elections by limiting contributions, requiring disclosure of their sources, providing public financing of presidential contests, and establishing a Federal Elections Commission. The laws also legalized political action committees.

- Independent committees, soft money, and PACs have to some extent gutted the purposes of the campaign act.

- Many observers continue to be troubled by the vast amount of money spent on elections. Since relatively few individuals and groups have access to great wealth and since they contribute so heavily to campaigns, the principle of political equality is being undermined.

Many observers hailed George Bush's overwhelming defeat of Michael Dukakis in 1988 as a mandate to carry out Republican policies. Yet in view of the relatively low turnout and the mixed motives of voters, the mandate idea may not be valid.

ELECTIONS: WHO GOVERNS?

Democracy

Town hall democracy assumes that citizens themselves debate and decide public policy alternatives. Unfortunately, most Americans do not live in small, closed communities, and this ideal is not practical, especially for resolving national controversies. Hence, we have to rely instead on representatives. But in a perfectly functioning representative democracy, decisions would still reflect public opinion. If candidates clearly and forthrightly debate alternatives and take opposing stands on them, a vote for a person becomes in effect a vote for a policy, and the winners can rightly claim to have a **mandate**, an authorization from the people to enact and carry out a particular course of action. The problem is that elections do not work this simply in real life.

The victors, of course, almost always say they have a mandate. Certainly former President Ronald Reagan did. By most standards his victory in 1980 was a landslide: He won 51 percent

of the popular vote, far more than Jimmy Carter's 44 percent, and carried 44 states with 489 electoral votes. Since Reagan advocated conservative policies, Democrats as well as Republicans took his success as evidence of a national swing to the right. As soon as he was in office, Reagan asked Congress for a three-year, 25 percent tax cut, enormous reductions in domestic spending, a huge military buildup, and a curtailment of federal regulation of business. He and his supporters justified these requests by reference to the mandate given them by the voters. Republican Senator Paul Laxalt, a close Reagan ally, said of the President's program, "That's what the election was all about. It's part of the Reagan mandate."[80]

Similarly, after George Bush crushed Michael Dukakis in 1988, the newly elected president claimed that he too spoke for the people and immediately proposed a cut in the capital gains tax (a tax on the profits from the sale of assets such as real estate or stocks and bonds). One of his supporters wrote in the *New York Times*: "The matter should have been decided last year, when George Bush campaigned for the [lower] rate.... Michael Dukakis oppose[d] the cut...."

Since Mr. Bush won, he presumably has a mandate."[81]

Yet polls call into question claims about "mandates."[82] In Reagan's case, Arthur Miller, a political scientist at the University of Michigan, notes that "less than half the Republicans and independents and only a third of the Democrats who voted for Reagan favored his . . . tax-cut proposal."[83] In addition, whatever the voters thought about Reagan as a person, they nonetheless continued to back most federal health, education, and welfare programs. True, nearly everyone did want increased defense spending, but these "military increases were supported *in addition* to domestic programs."[84]

We have also shown that the electorate does not always vote on the basis of issues or ideology. Indeed, a variety of considerations enter into its calculations: A voter may like a candidate's personality or style but not necessarily his or her platform. Moreover, since laws can only be made by the president and the Congress working together, since there are 535 senators and representatives, and since they run independently of one another, even to the point of fighting with members of their own party, it is hard to find an overarching meaning in election results.

Nonvoting further clouds the picture. Because so many people abstain, winners usually poll less than a majority of the eligible electorate. Therefore, even if all of a candidate's backers favored a proposal, they would not necessarily constitute a majority of the public as a whole.[85] Finally, far from allowing voters to choose among competing philosophies or settle trunk decisions, many, if not most, of today's campaigns have degenerated into petty quarrels among men and women who argue about trivialities, sling mud, trust technicians more than policy experts, and spend millions of dollars looking attractive but saying little of substance. For all these reasons, votes cannot automatically be interpreted as endorsements of specific policies.

Pluralism

If elections do not provide mandates, what purpose do they serve? For pluralists, they have two important functions. First, voting offers citizens a peaceful method for choosing their leaders. This is not the same as making decisions themselves, but it may be the next best thing. After all, the power to reward and punish elected officials prevents them from acting irresponsibly or arbitrarily. Second, elections are one of the arenas of group conflict that characterize pluralist democracy. They provide an outlet through which organizations can invest their resources, especially money and volunteers, so as to create access and nudge decision makers closer to their points of view.

Power Elite

These arguments do not convince the power elite school. It thinks that under present circumstances voting is largely symbolic. The hoopla and excitement of campaigns and postelection celebrations reassure individuals that they are part of the governing process when in fact elites make major decisions far from the public's view. Elite theorists ask what fundamental economic or foreign policies are decided as the result of an election. In the 1988 presidential and congressional races, for example, candidates talked about the federal budget deficit, but who offered a coherent plan to close it? Did the Democrats stand for one approach, higher taxes perhaps, and the Republicans another, like cuts in domestic spending? Were there clear-cut differences on any other *major* issues? The power elite theory believes the answers are no. Judged from this perspective, elections mainly legitimize the present system of government because they foster the essentially false belief that the people are in charge of it and that it works democratically.

Who is right, the pluralists or elitists? To help decide, try this during the next election: Listen carefully to the candidates. Do they offer a specific and distinct platform, or do they speak mainly in vague generalities and platitudes? Imagine what, if any, difference the outcome will make to you, your family, your social class, your nation. This personal assessment may be rewarding because it helps answer the question of who governs.

Checkpoint

- If elections functioned as democratic theorists wanted, they might serve as mandates to guide elected officials. But nonissue voting and low turnout, among other factors, cloud the interpretations of election results.

- Pluralists view elections as a means of peacefully choosing leaders and as arenas for group conflict.

- Power elite theorists see elections as largely symbolic—they reassure voters that they are part of the governing process, whereas in reality elites make the fundamental decisions.

SUMMARY

Elections have been called the mainspring of democracy because they permit citizens to hold elected officials accountable and provide a means for political participation. Under the electoral college system the president is chosen indirectly, but other officeholders are selected in single-member districts in winner-take-all elections. Elections provide citizens with the opportunity for self-government, but one can question how well Americans accept this responsibility.

Certain social groups (such as urban blue-collar workers, blacks, Catholics, and Jews) used to vote mostly Democratic, while others (farmers, professional, service, and white-collar workers, for instance) supported Republicans. Today these voting patterns are less pronounced. Party identification partially determines how some individuals vote. Depending on whether the parties clarify their positions, party voting may or may not be rational. If issue voting is used as the yardstick, many Americans seem to be reasonably rational, especially if one takes into account the nature of the issues and people's perceptions of where candidates stand. A portion of the electorate apparently uses the economy's performance as a kind of shortcut for deciding which candidates to back. Many

people rely on candidate images. Doing so may be reasonable, because a candidate's image frequently reflects important traits that lead to success in office.

Campaigns now depend heavily on sophisticated and expensive tools such as computers, television, polling, direct mail, and other technical innovations. These developments perhaps help candidates streamline their operations, but they have also increased the cost of running for office and lowered the quality of the discussion of issues. Many of today's candidates depend heavily on political consultants, men and women who may be experts at communications and image making but not necessarily at developing public policy. In addition, candidates are frequently encouraged to follow a strategy of ambiguity, that is, not clearly stating their positions on issues. Another disturbing trend is the use of negative advertising, which in 1988 reached the presidential level. In view of these developments, one should probably not totally fault voters for being misinformed or apathetic.

The institutional context of elections, including the quality of media coverage, the strength of political parties, and the remoteness, complexity, and impersonality of government, also makes responsible voting difficult. Campaign finance laws attempted to regulate elections by limiting contributions, requiring disclosure of their sources, providing public funding of presidential contests, and establishing a federal commission to supervise these provisions. But the reforms have not succeeded in stemming the flow of money into campaigns. Independent committees, soft money, and PACs in particular trouble many observers. The enormous growth in campaign costs and expenditures puts the principle of political equality at risk.

Democratic theorists view elections as *potential* mandates for particular policies, but in fact they do not usually function this way; pluralists consider them as another arena for group conflict; and power elite theorists discount voting as largely a symbolic ritual.

KEY TERMS

Plurality
Single-member plurality
Gerrymandering
Malapportionment
Responsible electorate
Single-issue voters
Proximity
Retrospective voting
Focus group

Strategy of political
  ambiguity
Negative campaigning
Independent committees
Soft money
Political action
  committees
Mandate

FOR FURTHER READING

Elizabeth Drew, *Election Journal* (New York: Morrow, 1989). Drew, one of Washington's most perceptive and sharp-tongued journalists, follows the 1988 campaign from the primaries to the postelection analysis.

William H. Flanigan and Nancy H. Zingale, *Political Behavior of the American Electorate,* 6th ed. (Dubuque, Iowa: Brown, 1988). A clear discussion of various aspects of voting behavior including turnout, party identification, ideology, issue voting, and the impact of the mass media.

Jack W. Germond and Jules Witcover, *Whose Broad Stripes and Broad Stars* (New York: Warner Books, 1989). Two veteran reporters describe the 1988 presidential race, presenting provocative opinions as they go. This is the latest in a series of election books by the same authors.

Michael Nelson, ed., *The Elections of 1988* (Washington, D.C.: Congressional Quarterly Press, 1989). A series of essays on all facets of presidential and congressional elections.

Gerald M. Pomper, ed., *The Election of 1988* (Chatham, N.J.: Chatham House, 1989). Essays on various aspects of the 1988 presidential and congressional elections.

A. James Reichley, *Elections American Style* (Washington, D.C.: Brookings Institute, 1987). A superb collection of essays dealing with American elections from the decline in turnout to parties to PACs.

David R. Runkel, ed., *Campaign for President: The Managers Look at '88* (Dover, Mass.: Auburn House, 1989). In a wonderful inside view of campaigns and elections, campaign managers for George Bush and Michael Dukakis discuss their strategies with reporters.

Larry Sabato, *The Rise of Political Consultants* (New York: Basic Books, 1981). A fascinating analysis of how political consultants affect contemporary elections.

Chapter 12

**P**olitical parties have long been regarded as essential to a democracy by providing a link between the electorate and elected officials and a means of ensuring accountability. But many see a decline in the strength of political parties in the United States and question whether parties can perform these tasks. Can interest groups, personal campaign organizations, the media, or other institutions perform those functions just as well? What would a party-less United States look like? Who would govern it? ■

O n November 20, 1989, President George Bush went to Illinois and Rhode Island to campaign for two of his party's candidates in the 1990 races for the Senate. In Chicago, Bush told an enthusiastic crowd that Republican Congresswoman Lynn Martin would be a great asset for his administration and for the party in the Senate. Martin had served as a national cochairwoman of Bush's presidential campaign in 1988, and the President described her as someone "who has been right on issue after issue."[1] Later the same day, President Bush strongly endorsed Rhode Island Representative Claudine Schneider. Bush told a Republican audience in Providence that Schneider would be an outstanding Republican senator because she had always been a "pacesetter" for the Republican party and for the nation.[2]

Less than a week before this campaign trip, however, President Bush had a different sort of meeting with Representatives Martin and Schneider. They had gone to the White House to try to convince the President to change his position on abortion. That fall President Bush had vetoed three spending bills because they provided federal funds for abortion in cases of rape and incest. Representatives Martin and Schneider had voted for funding abortions in each case. In fact, their position was the same one George Bush had taken when he had first sought the Republican nomination for president in 1980. But Bush had later adopted the more restrictive

abortion position of his running mate Ronald Reagan and had been elected president in 1988 on a Republican party platform that supported a "fundamental right to life" and opposed "the use of public revenues for abortion."[3]

The President prevailed on all three bills, but the intense debate within the Republican party over the abortion issue raised questions about party loyalty and the role of political parties in governing America. The issue was widely viewed as a key reason for Republican losses in state elections in New Jersey and Virginia in November 1989. The Republican governors of Illinois and New Jersey told a meeting of their colleagues a week after those elections that the party should abandon its position on abortion. New Jersey Governor Thomas Kean, the keynote speaker of the 1988 Republican convention, said: "My own view is that parties should not have a position on abortion. When you try to make an issue of religion or conscience a matter of party policy, you run into trouble."[4]

At a Washington press conference that November, President Bush had this to say about Republicans and the abortion issue: "Well, look, there are many issues. And abortion divides. We have room in our party for people that feel one way—pro-life or pro-choice. Democratic Party, the same way."[5] In Chicago, the President told those who were concerned about Representative Martin's abortion stance:"Our party is broad enough to contain differing views on this."[6] He

President Bush campaigns for Republican senatorial candidate Lyn Martin in Illinois and claims that the Republican party is broad enough to contain differing views on abortion.

told Rhode Island Republicans at the dinner for Representative Schneider: "Sometimes Claudine disagrees with her party, but with Claudine I can always bank on one thing. Exactly where she stands—right by her principles."[7] Officials of the Republican National Committee in Washington quickly followed Bush's lead and began to refer to the Republican party as an "umbrella party capable of absorbing lots of diverse views."[8]

When people describe a political party as an umbrella, or say that it is broad enough to contain differing views on abortion, does that seem to defeat the purpose of having political parties in the first place? What good is a party platform when candidates who run for office as members of that party disagree with the platform? Do certain issues require party loyalty more than others, and, if so, which ones? Shouldn't knowing what party a candidate belongs to help us know what positions he or she will take on important issues? These are just some of the questions that come up when we examine the role of political parties today in governing America.

WHAT IS A POLITICAL PARTY?

Even those who study parties in the United States and in other countries do not agree on how to define a **political party**. Political scientists generally define it in three different ways: ideological, organizational, and functional.[9]

Eighteenth-century statesman and political philosopher Edmund Burke provided an *ideological* definition of party when he said that it was a group of people "united, for promoting by their joint endeavors the national interest, upon some particular principle in which they are all agreed."[10] This point of view stresses commonly held ideas and stands on issues. Not many political scientists would apply the ideological definition to American political parties today, because the diversity of ideological positions and principles within both the Democratic and Republican parties makes it difficult to use ideology as a means for defining party.

Political scientists use an *organizational* definition when they describe a party as "a group of officeholders, candidates, activists, and voters who identify with a group label" or focus on the "hierarchical organization or structure that draws into its orbit large numbers of voters, candidates, and active party workers."[11] Political scientists often identify the people who make up the political party, the "group" in the definition above, by focusing on three elements of the party. First is the **party organization**, those people who hold formal party positions at the local, state, or national level and all the volunteers who help run campaigns and carry on other party activities. Second is the **party-in-government**, those people who have been elected to office and are identified as Democrats, Republicans, or members of another party. Third is the **party-in-the-electorate**, those people who are not active in the party but who think of themselves as Democrats or Republicans and who, at least some of the time, vote that way. There is a great deal of discussion among political scientists, journalists, and political activists about the relative importance of these three parts of the party and the extent to which these different elements can be said to be part of the same structure.

The first two ways of defining a political party

Table 12.1

Minor Party Presidential Candidates, 1988

Candidate	Party	Votes
Ron Paul	Libertarian	431,616[a]
Lenora B. Fulani	New Alliance	217,200
David Duke	Populist	46,910
Eugene McCarthy	Consumer	30,903
James Griffin	American Independent	27,818
Lyndon La Rouche	Independent	25,530
William Marra	Right to Life	20,497
Ed Winn	Workers League	18,662
James Warren	Socialist Workers	15,603
Herbert Lewin	Peace and Freedom	10,370
Earl Dodge	Prohibition	8,000
Larry Holmes	Workers World	7,846
Willa Kenoyer	Socialist	3,878
Delmar Dennis	American	3,476
Jack Herer	Grassroots	1,949
Louie Youngkeit	Independent (Utah)	372
John G. Martin	Third World Assembly	236

[a]To put these numbers in perspective, it helps to know that George Bush won 48,881,278 votes and Michael Dukakis won 41,805,374. Bush received 53.4 percent of the popular vote; Dukakis, 45.6 percent; Paul, 0.5 percent; and Fulani, 0.2 percent.

Source: Adapted from *Congressional Quarterly Weekly Report*, November 5, 1988, p. 3184 and January 21, 1989, p. 139. The New Alliance candidate was on the ballot in 50 states and the District of Columbia, and the Libertarian candidate in 46 states and the District of Columbia. All other candidates were on the ballots of 15 states or less, and five (American Independent, Grassroots, Right to Life, Third World Assembly, and Independent (Utah)) were on the ballot in only one state.

look at it as a shared way of thinking or a shared interaction with others. A *functional* definition focuses on what parties *do*: "An organized effort to win elective office in order to gain political power and control the policies of government."[12] At least two functions of parties are implicit in that definition: running candidates for election to public office and organizing the government so as to produce certain policies. Other party functions associated with those activities are recruiting political leaders, educating and mobilizing voters, nominating candidates, coordinating political activity among the different branches and levels of government, and making government accountable to the public. Organi-

zations other than political parties carry out some of these activities, but the function of most importance to a political party, the one that distinguishes a party from other political organizations, is that of selecting and running candidates in elections.

So far we have talked almost exclusively about the Democratic and Republican parties, but those two are not the only political parties in the United States. In the 1988 presidential election, for example, voters in every state had at least three choices for president, and in most states they had more than three. Table 12.1 shows the names and party affiliations of the 17 minor-party presidential candidates in 1988.

The Democratic and Republican parties may not be the only parties in American politics, but almost all the votes for president in 1988 went to the two major-party candidates, Bush and Dukakis, while candidates from the 17 minor parties garnered only 1 percent of the total vote. Because of this dominance by the two parties, our discussion in this chapter focuses on Democrats and Republicans. But as can be seen from the history of parties in America, there were important predecessors.

Checkpoint

- Political parties can be defined in ideological terms (shared beliefs), organizational terms (groups and structure), and functional terms (party activities).
- Two parties have dominated American politics, but minor political parties exist as well.

THE DEVELOPMENT OF AMERICAN POLITICAL PARTIES

The United States has been home to more than 1100 political parties, but only 15 have had any significant impact on American politics, and 10 of those were "third" parties that received more than 5 percent of the vote in national elections (see Table 12.2, p. 370). Minor parties have made important contributions to governing America by providing havens for dissatisfied voters, creating new electoral coalitions, and supporting policies—such as progressive taxation, economic regulation, and electoral reforms—that later were adopted by a major party and made into law. But minor parties are sometimes called the bees of American politics because they sting and then they die. Only five political parties in the 200-year history of the American political system have either governed or been a serious contender for governing. Of those five parties—the Federalists, Jeffersonians, Democrats, Whigs, and Republicans—only two remain today.

These parties governed or competed for power during five different eras in American political history. These were periods of one-party dominance or two-party competition or transitional periods in which new parties or new electoral groups emerged. By looking at these five party systems we can get an idea of the contributions made by political parties to the development of the American political system.[13]

First Party System (1790–1824): Federalists and Jeffersonians

The world's first political parties emerged with the competition between the governing **Federalists** (Washington, Adams) and the opposing **Jeffersonians** (led by Jefferson and Madison). The latter were also known as Republicans and Democratic-Republicans, but to avoid confusion with modern political parties we refer to them as Jeffersonians. The Jeffersonians enjoyed a period of one-party dominance from 1800 to 1820, but this was followed by a transition period of factionalism within that party from 1820 to 1824.

The Federalists and the Jeffersonians divided on ideological lines concerning the role of the national government. This division was dominant in American politics even before the adoption of the Constitution in 1789 and was manifested in the economic programs of the two parties. The merchants and financial interests of the Northeast and Atlantic states, who wanted a strong central government that would provide economic stability, supported the Federalist party. The small farmers, workers, and "have-nots" who formed the core of the Jeffersonian party argued for states' rights and a decentralized national government.

Neither of these parties were grass roots organizations; both were formed by the existing political elite. Of the two, the Jeffersonian party came closer to our conception of parties today in that it sought to mobilize voters in order to cap-

Table 12.2

Important Third Parties in U.S. History

Year	Party	Platform	Percentage of Total Vote for President
1848	Free Soil	Antislavery	10%
1856	American	Limits on immigration	21
1860	Breckenridge Democrats	Pro-slavery	18
1860	Constitutional Union	Preservation of Union and Constitution	13
1892	Populist (People's)	Banking and land reforms Nationalized transportation Expanded money supply	9
1912	Progressive	Regulation of corporations Direct democracy reforms	27
1912	Socialist	Economic and labor reforms	6
1924	Progressive	Nationalized railroads, water power Labor and farm reforms Antimonopoly reforms	17
1968	American Independent Party	Law and order Racial segregation	14
1980	National Unity	Fiscal conservatism Social liberalism	7

Sources: Adapted from Samuel J. Eldersveld, *Political Parties in American Society* (New York: Basic Books, 1982), p. 41. Others have measured the importance of minor parties by their ability to carry one state in a presidential election (seven minor parties have done so) or by winning more than the mean popular vote (5.6 percent) for third parties. See Frank J. Sorauf and Paul Allen Beck, *Party Politics in America*, 6th ed. (Glenview, Ill.: Scott, Foresman, 1988), pp. 50–51; and William Crotty, *The Party Game* (San Francisco: Freeman, 1985), pp. 38–41.

ture control of the national government. The Federalists, as the first governing party, were organized more to coordinate political activity than to contest elections. A motivation for the formation of both parties, though, was a desire for some predictability and stability in political life, which only an ongoing organization such as a party could provide.

One scholar who studied this first party system suggests that its greatest impact was to increase political participation during this period. This increase is attributed to the disappearance of deference, the feeling that politics was only for the wealthy, that had prevailed in America prior to this time.[14] Party development broadened the conflict between the two sets of political elites.

The decline of the first party system is gener-

ally attributed to the lack of a party contest for the presidency during the succession of Virginia presidents: Jefferson, Madison, and Monroe. This one-party rule by the Jeffersonians reached its height with James Monroe's winning 231 of 232 electoral votes in 1820. By that time the Federalists ceased to exist. But the Jeffersonians began quarreling among themselves.

Second Party System (1824–1860): Democrats and Whigs

The election of 1824 was notable for having four presidential candidates, all from the Jeffersonian party. Andrew Jackson received the greatest number of popular votes but did not get the required majority of votes in the electoral college. The House of Representatives selected second-place John Quincy Adams as president. Supporters of Jackson split from the Jeffersonians and, forming the **Democratic party**, immediately began to organize for 1828. This organization is most important to the development of political parties during this period.

The Democratic party supporters constituted the first mass-based party organization in the United States. The coalition of farmers, westerners, small businessmen, and workers who supported Jackson nominated him through a series of state conventions, local meetings, and closed sessions attended by party activists, rather than through a meeting of the national congressional party members as had been the practice up to then. Unlike the earlier parties, which were as-sociations of political elites, the Jacksonian or-ganization made extensive appeals for mass sup-port. The impact of this mass organization and changes in voting rules expanding suffrage re-sulted in a tremendous increase in voter partici-pation, from a turnout of about 27 percent in 1824 to over 50 percent in both 1828 and 1832.

Two other points about this party system are worth noting. First, the new Democratic party under President Jackson developed **patronage** politics—giving government jobs to party sup-porters (also known as the "spoils system")—to a degree not seen before in American politics. Second, a sectional division helped bring about a new party during this era. In 1824, John Quincy Adams carried all of New England by a heavy margin, Andrew Jackson did the same in the southern and western states, and the real bat-tle between the two was fought in the middle states such as New York, New Jersey, Maryland, and Kentucky. But during Jackson's second term, when it became clear that Vice-President Martin Van Buren of New York was to be Jack-son's choice as presidential candidate, many conservative southern Democrats left their party and formed the **Whig party** in 1834. By 1840, Whig organizations had picked up supporters in the West and New England among those who felt the Democrats were too nationalistic. With Wil-liam Henry Harrison leading the ticket in 1840, the Whigs captured control of the White House and both houses of Congress. For the next 15 years Democrats and Whigs alternated in the presidency.

Third Party System (1860–1896): Democrats and Republicans

Between 1854 and 1860, American political par-ties went through a period of factionalism and instability similar to the earlier period between 1820 and 1828. The issue of slavery divided both parties into northern and southern factions. A number of abolitionist third parties sprang up during this time in the North. In 1854 a coalition of some of these third parties and Whig and Democratic defectors formed the new **Republi-can party**, replacing the Whigs as the second ma-jor party by the election of 1856.

The election of Lincoln as a Republican pres-ident in 1860 and the northern victory in the Civil War had the effect of freezing the party di-visions in the United States along regional lines. The Republican party was the party of the North and the Democratic party was the party of the South, although it diminished to near extinction in the years following the Civil War. That basic sectional division continued into the twentieth century, and the two dominant parties that emerged during this era are, of course, the Democrats and Republicans that we have today.

The third party system is marked by one-party Republican dominance from 1860 to 1874 and then alternating control of Congress and the presidency by the two parties for the rest of this era. In addition to the hardening of sectional di-visions, there were two other developments of importance during this era. One was the emerg-ence of urban political machines in which city party bosses would dispense favors and patron-age in return for votes, particularly among im-migrants. The second was the development of militant parties that could mobilize voters to a greater extent than ever before. Voting turnouts in the elections of 1876, 1888, and 1896 were be-tween 80 and 90 percent.*

---

*See Chapter 10 for varying interpretations of this high turnout.

President William McKinley speaks to a whistlestop crowd during his 1900 reelection bid. McKinley's election four years earlier had helped to usher in the Republican-dominated fourth party system in the development of American political parties.

The Republican party inherited the support of big business from the Whigs. The party's commitment to the forces of wealth and capital led to serious third-party challenges in the latter part of the nineteenth century. These challenges by midwestern farmers in the Granger movement, the Greenback party, the Farmers' alliance, and the People's party reached a high point in 1892 when the presidential candidate for the Populist (People's) party received over a million votes.

Fourth Party System (1896–1932): Democrats and Republicans

As the intense Civil War loyalties began to wane toward the end of the third party system, the Democratic party gained electoral strength. In 1892 the Democrats captured control of the presidency and of the House of Representatives. But

the governing party had to contend with the depression of 1893, with its unemployment rate of 20 percent. The Democratic party's western faction, drawing support from farmers and populists, became the dominant wing of the party during this time.

The 1894 and 1896 elections shifted leadership to the Republican party once again, as the parties underwent a **realignment**, a fundamental change in voting coalitions. Republicans won the support of the growing urban working class, which had been hit especially hard by the depression of 1893. The Republican landslide in the congressional elections of 1894 represented the most massive shift of seats from one party to another in U.S. history. The rise of the Republican party was so strong that the Democrats were shut out of the White House for 16 years.

The fourth party system was, in effect, two distinct one-party systems: the Democratic South and the Republican Northeast and Midwest. That regional alignment followed the sectional divisions growing out of the Civil War, but the basis of the new alignment was economics. The Republican party opposed the regulation of economic activity and favored the unfettered industrial development and modernization of the private sector. The Democrats favored government policies to relieve some of the economic difficulties experienced by many people, particularly in the South.

This era did see the election of a Democratic president, Woodrow Wilson, in 1912 and 1916, but that was due to a split between the progressive and conservative wings of the Republican party. In 1920, Republicans regained control of the White House with the election of Warren G. Harding.

A development during the fourth party system that continues to affect American politics today was the emergence of a major reform movement. The Progressive movement, which reached its height in presidential elections with the candidacy of Theodore Roosevelt in 1912 (27 percent of the popular vote) and Robert LaFollette in 1924 (17 percent of the popular vote), advocated a number of reforms to weaken the control of party bosses. The most important of these was the **direct primary**, an election in which voters select the candidates to run on the party label in the general elections. This reform took the nominating power away from party bosses and put it into the hands of the electorate. About three-fourths of the states had direct primaries by 1917. By denying party leaders control over nominations for office, primaries weakened the party organizations from top to bottom.

Fifth Party System (1932–present): Democrats and Republicans

It was not reforms but another economic depression that led to the demise of the fourth party system. Just as the 1893 depression turned voters away from the governing Democrats, the even more severe depression that began in 1929 turned voters away from the governing Republicans. The party realignment in 1896 consolidated Republican strengths, but the realignment of 1932 saw a major shift of former Republican voters in the Northeast to the Democratic party. New voters in urban immigrant families also aligned themselves with the Democrats.

The New Deal coalition forged by Democrat Franklin Roosevelt in the 1932 and 1936 elections was a combination of regional and class divisions. Democratic support came primarily from the South, from the working class, from urban ethnic voters entering the electorate for the first time, from blacks, and from poor farmers. Outside of the South, class lines were drawn between the parties more sharply than they had been.

The basic partisan divisions formed during the early part of this era are still with us to some extent today, but several factors have weakened the New Deal coalition to the point where many observers wonder if it can ever be regrouped. Many of the urban dwellers, union members, and ethnic voters—working-class whites in general—have gained in affluence and have moved to the Republican party in recent elections. Democratic support for the civil rights programs of the 1960s induced many southern Democrats to abandon their traditional loyalties and support the Republican party.

The breakdown of the New Deal coalition is seen most clearly at the level of presidential voting. Republicans have won more presidential elections since 1944 and won a majority of the popular vote twice as often as Democrats. While such demonstrations of Republican support have led many people to talk about a realignment and new Republican dominance since 1968, voting in congressional elections and the distribution of party identification indicate that a major realignment, such as those of 1896 or 1932, has not yet taken place.

George Bush solicits union votes in Illinois. Many members of the New Deal Coalition, such as union workers, have gained in affluence and moved to the Republican party in recent elections.

Checkpoint

- More than a thousand political parties have existed in United States history, but only five of them have governed or been serious competitors for governing: the Federalists, Jeffersonians, Democrats, Whigs, and Republicans. These parties have competed for political power in five party systems.

- Political competition in the first party system began as a contest among elites (Federalists and Jeffersonians) who differed over the central government's role, but that contest increased political participation in the United States.

- The Jacksonian Democrats of the second party system represented the first mass-based party in American history, which was characterized by a grass roots system of presidential nominations and extensive patronage known as the spoils system.

- The major events of the third party system were the birth of the Republican party and the development of sectional and ideological bases for the Democratic and Republican parties.

- The fourth party system was one of Republican dominance, and the emergence of reforms aimed at weakening the control of urban party leaders.

- The New Deal coalition of Democrats ushered in the fifth party system in 1932, but the electoral base of this coalition has greatly diminished. In recent years, Democrats have dominated congressional elections while Republicans have been more successful in capturing the presidency.

PARTY FUNCTIONS

During these different eras, political parties performed important functions that helped provide both the stability and adaptation needed for the political system to survive. They carried out some of these functions better in some eras than they did in others. While parties in the first party system, for example, recruited leaders, formed government, and coordinated political activity, it was not until the second party system that the function of voter mobilization really took place. The accountability of party and government leaders is suggested by the electoral realignments that followed depressions in 1893 and 1929. American parties were probably strongest during the latter part of the third party system when they were most successful at mobilizing voters and functioning as disciplined organizations.

Let us now take a close look at how well parties are serving these functions today.

Political Recruitment

In any political system, the actual decision making and day-to-day governing is done by a relatively small group of executives, legislators, judges, bureaucrats, and their official staffs and informal advisers. **Political recruitment** is the process through which persons seek to become and are selected to be members of that governing elite. Theodore Roosevelt's desire to become a member of the governing class led him to join the Republican organization two blocks away (see A Closer Look, pp. 376–377). Two years after he joined, a party leader selected Roosevelt to be a candidate for the state legislature. In this particular case the political party organization served as the primary agent of political recruitment.

Of course, not all political activists, candidates, officeholders, or presidents enter politics in this way. Our decentralized and federal system provides a wide variety of decision-making positions on various levels. And the political party is only one of many avenues by which political leaders are chosen. Some candidates, for instance, are self-starters whose candidacy represents their first real political activity. Labor unions, civic associations, or business and professional organizations can be more important than party organizations in beginning some political careers (as A Closer Look shows in the case of Ronald Reagan). Still, studies of state legislators and of members of the House of Representatives have found that on average about one-half of these legislators credited the local party organization with their entry into politics.[15]

Political recruitment is not limited to candidates and officeholders, however. Parties also recruit campaign workers and **party activists**, who participate in campaigns and can expect to have some influence on the decision making of those they help put in office. Just at the level of local or precinct organizations, about 200,000 persons are brought into the ranks of party activists in this way.

The political party is not the sole agent of leadership recruitment in the American system, but it does help perform this essential political function of providing candidates for office and active workers for political campaigns. The lack of entry requirements and the openness of the party organization to all would-be campaign workers also help the political system to be a more democratic one.

Voter Mobilization

Political parties mobilize voters both directly, by getting out the vote, and indirectly, by putting together coalitions of existing interests. Chapter 10 has detailed the low rates of voter turnout today, but we should not interpret these low rates to mean that political parties are not performing their function of voter mobilization. The percentage of the public reporting contacts by local party officials more than doubled from 1952 to 1976, surely a clear indication of the political party's voter mobilization activities.

Parties also help mobilize voters when they attract strong partisans. Research shows that in every election since 1952, people who strongly identify with a party are more likely to vote than are weak partisans and independents.[16] (See also

Chapter 10.) In recent years partisanship has been declining, as we will see later in this chapter. Such a decline obviously affects how well political parties are able to carry on their function of voter mobilization.

By creating electoral coalitions of interest groups, political parties indirectly mobilize voters. When a party's candidates receive the endorsement of a particular group, the turnout rate of members of that group is likely to be higher than if that group has not endorsed the candidates. In 1972, for example, union leaders did not support Democratic candidate George McGovern; in 1976 they did support Democratic candidate Jimmy Carter, and the voting patterns of union households reflected those differences.[17] Early in the 1984 campaign both parties were eagerly courting educational unions and interest groups, which had demonstrated a great ability for mobilizing voters in the two previous elections.

Nominating Candidates

Other kinds of organizations overlap parties in recruiting leaders, mobilizing voters, providing campaign support, and attempting to influence the behavior of officeholders, but the nomination of candidates is regarded as the exclusive province of the political party.

The nominating process for any political office takes three basic forms: caucus, convention, and direct primary. A **caucus** is a closed meeting of party leaders or rank-and-file members to select candidates. Caucuses were the chief method for nominating candidates during the first party system (1790–1824), but today they are used mainly to select delegates to state and local party conventions. A **convention** is a meeting of party delegates at the local, state, or national level, which endorses a range of party policy positions in a party platform and, in some cases, nominates candidates. While the national conventions of both parties formally select the nominees for president and vice-president, only 12 states still use conventions to nominate candidates for statewide offices. State conventions are more commonly used for endorsing candidates for the

A Closer Look

Two Republican Presidents and Their Party ★★★

One of the key functions of political parties in a democracy is the recruitment of political leaders. In their autobiographies, former Republican presidents Theodore Roosevelt (1901–1909) and Ronald Reagan (1981–1989) discussed their entry into politics as Republicans. What can we learn about career patterns and the motivation of political activists by reading these two accounts? The first is about a 22-year-old who was elected to office two years later and went on to become our youngest president, and the second, about an initial move to political activism at the age of 34, a conversion from Democrat to Republican five years later, a first campaign at 54, and election as our oldest president. Roosevelt's autobiography was published one year after he had run unsuccessfully for president as a third-party candidate, and Reagan's book was published one year before his election as governor of California.

THEODORE ROOSEVELT

Almost immediately after leaving Harvard in 1880 I began to take an interest in politics. . . . At that day . . . a young man of my bringing up and convictions could join only the Republican party, and join it I accordingly did. It was no simple thing to join it then. . . . The party was still treated as a private corporation, and·in each district the organization formed a kind of social and political club. A man had to be regularly proposed for and elected into this club, just as into any other club.

. . . The men I knew best were the men in the clubs of social pretension . . . of cultivated taste and easy life. When I [inquired] as to the whereabouts of the local Republican Association and the means of joining it, these men—and the big business

men and lawyers also—laughed at me, and told me that politics were "low"; that the organizations were not controlled by "gentlemen," that I would find them run by saloon-keepers, horse-car conductors, and the like, and not by men with any of whom I would come in contact outside; and, moreover, they assured me that men I met would be rough and brutal and unpleasant to deal with. I answered that if this were so it merely meant that the people I knew did not belong to the governing class, and that the other people did—and that I intended to be one of the governing class.

. . . The Republican Association of which I became a member held its meetings in Morton Hall, a large barn-like room over a saloon. I went around there often enough to have the men get accustomed to me and to have me get accustomed to them, so that we began to speak the same language.

RONALD REAGAN

I was a near-hopeless hemophilic liberal. I bled for "causes"; I had voted Democratic, following my father, in every election. I had followed FDR blindly, though with some misgivings. I was to continue voting Democratic through the 1948 election—Harry S Truman can credit me with at least one assist—but never thereafter. The story of my disillusionment with big government is linked fundamentally with the ideals that suddenly sprouted and put forth in the war years.

. . . Meanwhile I was blindly and busily joining every organization I could find that would guarantee to save the world. . . .

. . . My first evangelism came in the form of being hell-bent on saving the world from

Theodore Roosevelt (left) was warned that a political party organization was not a place for "gentlemen" but said he "intended to be one of the governing class." Ronald Reagan (right) at a 1964 political reception at the Beverly Hills hotel. As he said, "I became an easy mark for speechmaking on the rubber-chicken and glass-tinkling circuits."

neo-Fascism. At that time there were visible dangers of this. I myself observed more than forty veterans' organizations arise; most of them seemed to be highly intolerant of color, creed, and common sense. I joined the American Veterans Committee because of their feeling that the members should be citizens first and veterans afterward—and, as it worked out, I became a large wheel in their operations.

But in the meantime I became an easy mark for speechmaking on the rubber-chicken and glass-tinkling circuits. It fed my ego, since I had been so long away from the screen. I loved it. But, though I did not realize it then, both my material and my audiences were hand-picked, or at least I was being spoon-fed and steered more than a little bit.

. . . I have my movie hat on again—I hope for some little while: I've missed it. . . . Another hat—a really new one—was displayed recently and, while it had some intriguing features, I decided it wouldn't be completely comfortable. A group of my fellow citizens were the designers and they did me a great honor, for which I am humbly grateful, even though the hat didn't fit. Their hat

was the kind you throw into the political ring and they wanted me to do just that, for either governor or senator.

One does what he feels he can do best and serves where he feels he can make the greatest contribution. For me, I think that service is to continue accepting speaking engagements, in an effort to make people aware of the danger to freedom in a vast permanent government structure so big and complex it virtually entraps Presidents and legislators. . . .

It's a curious thing: I talked on this theme of big government during six years of the Eisenhower administration and was accepted as presenting a nonpartisan viewpoint. The same speech delivered *after* January 20, 1961 [the inauguration of President John Kennedy], brought down thunders of wrath on my head, the charge that my speech was a partisan political attack, an expression of right wing extremism.

Source: Theodore Roosevelt, Theodore Roosevelt: An Autobiography *(New York: MacMillan), 1913, pp. 62–64; Ronald Reagan (with Richard G. Huber),* Where's the Rest of Me? The Autobiography of Ronald Reagan *(New York: Karz), 1981 (originally published 1965), pp. 139, 141, 296–297.*

Presidential candidate Richard Gephardt campaigning in the 1988 New Hampshire primary. The power of making nominations now rests in the hands of those who vote in presidential primaries.

party nomination who are then formally chosen in a primary election; 17 states permit parties to use conventions for preprimary endorsements. As we saw earlier, a direct primary is an election in which voters choose who will run on the party label in the general election. A *closed primary* (used in 38 states and the District of Columbia) limits participation to those affiliated with that party, while an *open primary* (used in 9 states) permits voters to choose which party primary to vote in. A *blanket primary* (used in 3 states) permits voters to vote in both party primaries. Political conventions have historically served as the arena for presidential nominations, one in which party leaders have been able to exercise the most control. But this century has seen a fundamental change in the nominating process: the great proliferation of primaries at all levels of government.

All 50 states use some form of primary nomination system for state and local offices. However, the most visible primary system is the one used for nominating candidates for president. **Presidential primaries** are indirect; voters select delegates to a convention rather than directly select candidates themselves. In 1968, 17 states had presidential primaries; in 1988, 37 (see Figure 12.1, on pp. 382–383). In 1968, less than half the delegates to the national conventions in both parties were selected in primaries; in 1988, more than three-fourths of them were chosen that way. The candidate who wins the most primaries generally becomes the party's nominee for president, regardless of past service to the party or experience in national politics. The effect of these primaries is to remove the power of making nominations from the party organization and party leaders and to place it in the hands of those who vote in primaries.

Critics of the primary suggest that the nominees produced by such a system are less likely to be able to govern if elected than nominees chosen by party leaders. They point out that Jimmy Carter and Ronald Reagan, two presidents with little experience in governing at the national level, were both products of the primary nominating system. Primary winners generally succeed by making appeals to a series of groups and constituencies who are important primary election voters, not by resolving conflicting demands, as is required in governing. Moreover, candidates and presidents who emerge from this nominating system owe little or nothing to state and national party leaders, with whom they will have to work in order to govern.

By not controlling the nomination, party leaders lose control over who holds office as well as over the party's issue positions advanced in the general election, and they are in a weakened position to influence officeholders who plan to run again as the party's candidates. Control over nominations is the chief means for a party to link what candidates say in elections with their behavior in office and is thus a key to democratic accountability.

Contesting Elections

The function of contesting elections has been used to define what a party actually is. Joseph Schlesinger says that a political party organization is really a collection of groups of people who are working to elect a particular candidate to office.[18] The cooperative effort of these campaign groups in behalf of candidates with the same party label constitutes what we call party activity.

There is a definite pattern to the level of party activity, with peaks of intense effort during campaigns being followed by varying periods of little or no party activity. The activities most often engaged in by local party workers are election-related ones, such as voter registration, telephone and house-to-house canvassing, and the election day mobilization of supporters. But an effective party organization must also be active between elections if it is to influence elected officials and coordinate the activity of political leaders in these "off" years.

Just as the emergence of primaries is said to have weakened the party organization's control over nominations, so has the professionalization of campaigns in the last 20 years said to have reduced the importance of parties in elections. As Chapter 11 brought out, professional pollsters, campaign managers, advertising specialists, and fund-raisers now perform most of the crucial election tasks of information gathering, information dissemination, and funding once performed by the party organization. Part-time, amateur workers in a local party organization cannot be expected to compete with these professionals in supplying these campaign services. On the national level, however, both parties provide some overall coordination of these professional services and directly provide some of these services to local candidates.

Forming a Government

In a parliamentary system of government, the party that wins a majority, by itself or in conjunction with another party or parties, forms a government, with members of the legislative majority serving as the executive branch of government. In the United States, matters are a bit more complicated. One party may win the presidential election while the other party wins the majority of the congressional elections. In 1988, for example, the Republicans held the presidency, and the Democrats controlled both houses of Congress. In cases of divided control, it is difficult to say what forming a government really means. Indeed, visitors from parliamentary systems sometimes question whether there *is* a government under the U.S. system. Is it the

president? the Congress? the bureaucracy?

Political parties in the United States take some part in forming a government in that they provide the initial organization of the executive and legislative branches after an election. In Congress, the majority party fills the leadership positions from House speaker and Senate majority leader on down to the chairs of the smallest subcommittees. After the 1980 elections, the Democrats organized the House and the Republicans organized the Senate, and then in 1987 the Democrats reorganized the Senate. Votes on organizing the chamber are always straight party line votes (as opposed to voting on legislative issues, which may produce coalitions made up of members of both parties). In the legislative branch, then, political parties do perform an important time-saving organizational function.

Staffing and organizing the executive branch is less a party matter than it is in the legislature. Newly elected presidents and their advisers generally spend months on the task. While party affiliation is a relevant characteristic for some appointments, presidents will occasionally appoint individuals, even at the cabinet level, from the other party.

Because newly elected presidents will draw heavily on their own campaign organization in staffing the presidency, and because presidents also dominate the staffing and organization of their own national party organization, it might be more accurate to say that a president forms the national party than that the party forms the government.

Coordinating Political Activity

The federal and separated structure of government in the United States makes it impossible to govern without some organization or institution to link the activities of the different levels of government and the many actors in the political system. The one institution capable of this linkage and coordination is the political party. Sometimes that link takes the form of a structured organization, such as the national party committee or legislative party organization. At other times the only link might be election on the same party label.

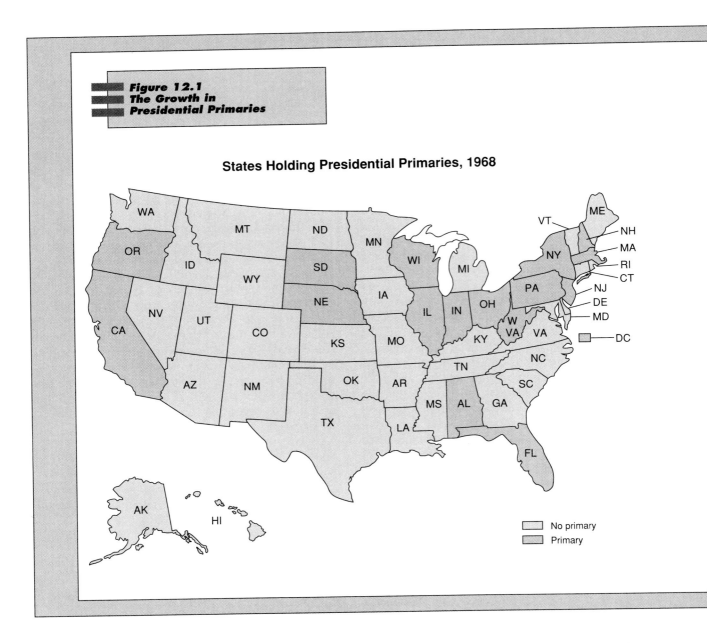

**Figure 12.1
The Growth in
Presidential Primaries**

States Holding Presidential Primaries, 1968

No primary
Primary

American political parties are often criticized for not being more effective in coordinating political activity at the national and state level. How well they perform this function is a subject of some discussion, which we will look at in considering the party-in-government in this chapter. As in the case of the other party functions, other institutions have emerged to share the party role. Interest groups, the mass media, informal groups within Congress, and presidential coali-

tions now all help to coordinate political activity in our system. But only political parties have the capacity to do this with the scope and continuity required of governance.

Providing Accountability

Knowing whom to blame for policies that hurt you or you consider to be wrong and knowing whom to thank when government decisions

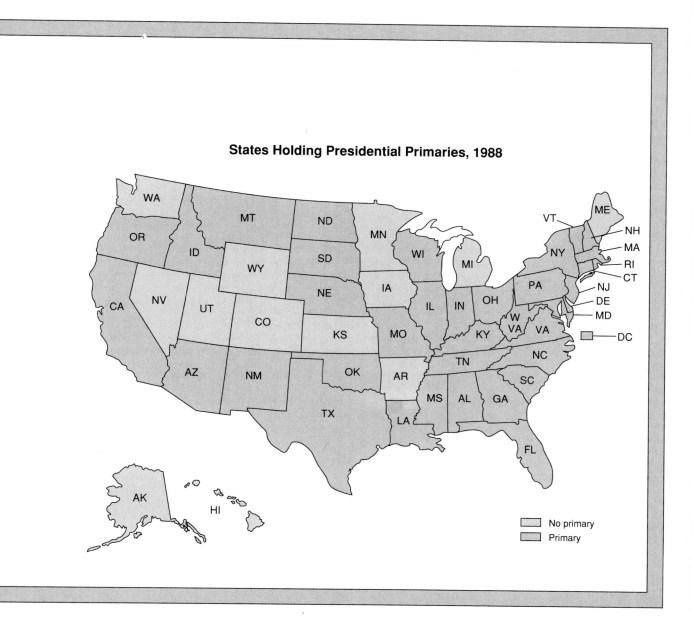

States Holding Presidential Primaries, 1988

No primary
Primary

please you constitute the essence of accountability. The political slogans of "four more years" or "throw the rascals out" express the positive and negative forms that accountability can take.

Accountability depends on a linkage between public officials and their policies at the time of elections. In some elections it is clear that a political party is held accountable for the performance of officeholders. Republican congressional candidates in the 1974 elections, to cite a notable example, suffered a great deal from the linkage in many voters' minds of the Watergate scandal and the Republican party. But sometimes the electorate finds it difficult to pin blame (or praise) on one party's public officials because the policies are proposed or enacted by a **bipartisan coalition**, a group incorporating members from both parties. For example, during Bush's first term, Democratic as well as Republican legislators voted to increase the minimum wage and bail out the savings and loan industry. If you were unhappy with these policies, which party would you hold accountable?

Consideration of the function of accountability brings us back to the electoral functions of parties discussed earlier, especially the nominating and campaigning functions. A strict standard of accountability would require that the party organization control both the nomination and the issue positions of candidates bearing the party label. Consistency among the party's candidates on electoral positions is a prerequisite to consistency among the elected officials of the same party. As we have seen, however, primaries have effectively eliminated the party leaders' control of nominations, and the variety and diversity of constituencies force national party leaders to be tolerant of party candidates who stray from party positions at election time.

The essence of a democratic political system is that the people exercise control over who governs and how they govern, that those who make policy decisions are accountable to voters in regular elections. However, accountability requires more than elections; it requires *organized* elections. The political party organization is set up to do that. Political parties also can provide the link between the policy positions of thousands of candidates and millions of voters, by making the party-in-government a reflection of the party-in-the-electorate. We now look at the democratic linkage performed by the party organization, the party-in-the-electorate, and the party-in-government.

Checkpoint

- Political parties are essential to democracy because they provide a link between the policy preferences of the electorate and the policies of government. In order to do this, parties must organize both the electorate and the government.

- That requires that parties perform seven specific activities or functions: (1) recruiting political leaders, (2) mobilizing voters, (3) nominating candidates, (4) contesting elections, (5) forming a government, (6) coordinating political activity, and (7) providing accountability.

PARTY ORGANIZATION

The party organization for Democrats and Republicans extends from workers and leaders in the smallest units of voting (precincts) up to national committees and national chairpersons. In between these two levels are ward committees, intermediate committees (city, township, and legislative), county committees, congressional district committees, and state committees. There is great variety in the size and relative importance of these units within the 50 states, but a typical party structure is shown in Figure 12.2.

The party organization is not a hierarchy, as one might at first think by looking at Figure 12.2. Indeed, the members at each level generally are selected by those at the level *below*. Although the national and state committees write rules governing the structure and procedures of their constituent units, local party organizations enjoy a great deal of independence from the state and national organization. In that sense, the party organization is a federal structure, like that of the government, but with the state and local party units having more autonomy than state and local governments do.

Local Party Organizations

The smallest political or voting unit—containing between 200 and 1,000 voters—is the **precinct**; there are more than 100,000 of them in the United States. Precinct leaders are elected either in the primary election or at a caucus, to which all registered members of that party can come. The chief activities of the precinct organization

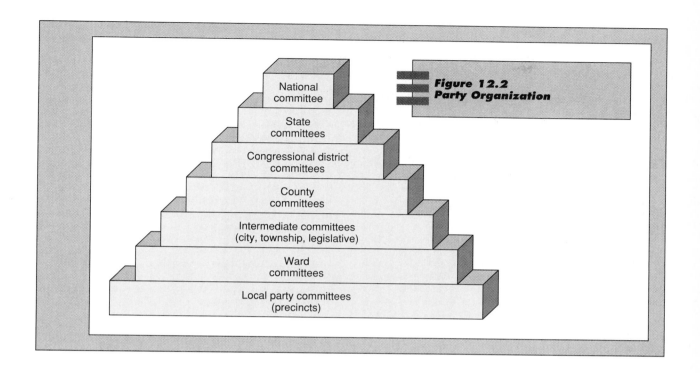

**Figure 12.2
Party Organization**

National committee

State committees

Congressional district committees

County committees

Intermediate committees (city, township, legislative)

Ward committees

Local party committees (precincts)

are election-related, including registration drives, canvassing, and getting out the vote on election day. Larger local units include the ward and the township. It is estimated that there are at least 200,000 local party organizations at the precinct, ward, and township level.[19] The ward is a division of a city for electing a member to the city council. The township is a subdivision of a county, used primarily in the Northeast and Midwest.

The relative importance of party organizations at the city, county, and congressional district level varies a great deal from place to place. While city political machines and bosses once exemplified the party organization at its strongest, more than three-fourths of all cities over 25,000 now have nonpartisan elections and the big-city bosses have faded from the scene. Today the county committee is often the most important party organization within a state.[20] This is true especially in southern and midwestern rural counties, where the county party organization often has a say over who fills important posts such as sheriff and tax collector.

Congressional districts do not fit neatly into a party organization based on state and local governmental units; a particular congressional district will often include parts of a number of counties and state senatorial districts. That is one reason why candidates for Congress must put together ad hoc electoral organizations rather than rely on the party machinery. "If we depended on the party organization to get elected," a Republican member of the House once observed, "none of us would be here."[21] Elections scholar Gary Jacobson has pointed out that "scattered instances of party control over congressional nominations can still be found," but his general conclusion is that this influence is for the most part feeble:

Few congressional candidates find opposition from the local party leaders to be a significant handicap; neither is their support very helpful. The nomination is not something to be awarded by the party but rather a prize to be fought over (when it seems worth having) by freebooting political privateers.[22]

Precinct workers engage in election-related activities, such as registration drives, canvassing (as shown here), and getting out the vote on election day.

Local party organizations can vary greatly in their structure and importance, but the average city or county party organization has the following characteristics: (1) An active chairperson and executive committee make most of the decisions, carry on most activities, and speak for the party; (2) party leaders and staff members are volunteers with limited resources for carrying on the party's work; (3) campaign activities consist primarily of organizing, fund-raising, and contacting voters on behalf of party candidates; and (4) there is intense activity around election time with little or no party activity in between.[23]

Another characteristic of local party organizations, one that is widely discussed by journalists and political scientists, is the apparent decline in their importance since the heyday of the local party machine in the late 1800s and early 1900s and since their more recent successes of the 1950s and 1960s.[24] Reforms such as the direct primary, civil service, competitive bidding for government contracts, and campaign finance laws are said to have led to the decline, if not the demise, of local party organizations. While it is true that local party organizations have lost con-

trol over nominations, still their activity can be gauged by the number of voters contacted by local party activists during a campaign. As we saw earlier in the chapter, voter contact has *increased*. In 1952, 13 percent of the public reported contacts by local party officials; in 1976, 30 percent of the public reported such contacts.[25] A number of other studies of local party organizations reported in the early 1980s have found similarly high levels of activity by those organizations and an increase in that activity in recent years.[26] These recent studies suggest that the local party organization, at least during election time, still has a place in American politics.

State Party Organizations

The basic structure of state party organizations is the same: state chairperson, state committee, state convention, and legislative party organizations. Within that framework, however, there is great variation, particularly in organizational unity and in ideology. State party unity is reflected in fights for state office and in voting for presidential nominees at national party conventions. Some state parties tend to be consistently liberal and others consistently conservative in their support for presidential nominees.

Most observers agree that the proliferation of presidential primaries over the last two decades has greatly reduced the power of state parties in presidential politics. As we have seen, to win votes at the national convention, presidential candidates can go directly to the voters in the state primary rather than to state party leaders. Despite the loss of this major source of state party influence, one study found that state parties have become stronger over the last 20 years. The authors of this study suggest that strong state party organizations are those that maintain a permanent headquarters, provide a regular source of operating funds, and are able to hire professional staff. On all three measures, state parties were found to be stronger in the 1980s than they were in the 1960s.[27]

The fact that the state party organizations have been strengthened while the influence of state party leaders in nominating presidential candidates has been declining is more than a passing bit of irony. As will be seen in the next section, both parties' national committees have tried to build the "grass roots" (state and local) organizations of the two parties. But at the same time, presidential candidates in both parties have a stake in preventing state party leaders from regaining the central role they once played in American politics. Here is what Nelson Polsby had to say about that conflict:

> Within the political parties, the fundamental division of interests is between presidential candidates and their agents on the one hand, and state parties and their leaders on the other.
>
> It is in the interests of prospective presidential candidates for state delegations to be relatively permeable to their influence, for decisions about the identities of delegates to be made in highly visible processes, for commitments to candidates to come early in the selection process.
>
> It is in the interests of state parties and their leaders to maintain their influence over the composition of delegations to the national conventions, to remain neutral as among possible candidates until they can see which way the wind is blowing and arrange for appropriate access for the benefit of the state party.[28]

Polsby suggests that this fundamental conflict between state party leaders and presidential candidates is central to the debate in both parties about past and future reforms in the party structure and candidate selection process. Although all levels of the party organization are involved in this discussion, the national party organizations have initiated most of these changes and reform proposals.

National Party Organizations

The national organization for both Democrats and Republicans consists of (1) the national conventions; (2) the national committees and executive committees; (3) the national chairperson and staff; (4) the House and Senate party organizations, which have important legislative and campaign responsibilities; and, for one party at least, (5) the president and top members

of the administration. Whether the party is that of the president or of the opposition greatly affects the structure of the national party organization. The in party is more centralized because of the dominance of an incumbent president. The party not in power is more likely to have many claimants for the title of party spokesperson, including the party's losing presidential nominee, congressional leaders, the national chairperson, and future candidates for president.

These five elements of the national party organization are not of equal importance for this discussion. We will look at the congressional party as part of the responsible party model later in this chapter. The president's role as party leader is discussed in Chapter 15.

The **national convention** is responsible for nominating the party's presidential and vice-presidential candidates, as well as for passing the rules that determine the structure and procedures to be followed by both national and state parties. In that sense, the national conventions are the highest levels of authority within each party. But these conventions are unwieldy bodies, ranging from just over 2000 delegates (Republicans) to more than 4000 delegates (Democrats)—most of whom are there because they were elected in a primary to support a particular candidate. The size and composition of the delegate body and the long interim between conventions limit their ability to run the party's organization or manage its everyday affairs.

Both parties look to the **national committees** to provide leadership and continuity between conventions. The Democratic National Committee is more than twice the size of the Republican National Committee, with 365 as opposed to 162 members. Since the national committees for both parties are part of a federal structure, they depend on state and local units for membership. An authoritative work on party organization published in 1964 described the national party committees as "large groups of people, variously selected, who come together now and then to vote on matters of undifferentiated triviality or importance, about which they are largely uninformed and in which they are often uninterested."[29] This description is less true than it once was, as the national committees have instigated centralizing, or nationalizing, reforms.

Table 12.3

The Republican Lead in Campaign Technology and Party Services

Technology or Service	Year Adopted by National Party	
	Republican	Democratic
Direct mail (campaign)	1964	1972
In-house television advertising	1970	1984
Direct mail (party fund-raising)	1978	1980
Local party organization effort	1978	1981
Young community leader program	1978	1981
National staff assigned to state parties	1978	1984
Electronic mail network	1982	—

Source: Adapted from Stephen E. Frantzich, *Political Parties in the Technological Age* (New York: Longman, 1989), p. 89.

Procedural reforms in the 1970s created a system in which the national party provides guidelines that state and local party units must follow in selecting delegates to the national convention. This centralization has been more clearly marked in the Democratic party. But even these Democratic reforms have not affected other aspects of the party organization, as one study concludes:

The national party is increasingly permeating all levels of party organization. This much is clear. It is particularly dominant in those procedural areas involving delegate selection. Nevertheless . . . there is little reason to expect that in the foreseeable future the party's central committee is likely to serve as the primary source of party policy or that it will seek to "punish" errant party officeholders.[30]

The nationalization of both parties is seen in another area of great importance in politics: fund-raising. Both national committees are capable of sophisticated fund-raising that produces resources shared by state, local, and national candidates. The Republican National Committee was the first to develop an extensive, computer-based operation for raising and distributing

funds and continues to enjoy a distinct advantage over the Democratic National Committee in this regard. For instance, the national Republican party raised over $100 million for congressional campaigns in 1988, while its Democratic counterpart raised less than $30 million.[31] Democrats are able to narrow the gap through PAC contributions (see Chapter 11) and candidate fund-raising.

The Democratic national organization is also still playing catch-up to the Republican National Committee in applying new campaign technology and providing services to candidates. Democrats made great gains in building the party organization in the 1980s, but the extent to which they were following the lead of the national Republican party is reflected in Table 12.3.

Despite increasing national party influence over convention delegate selection and campaign fund-raising for state and local candidates, the party organization has not come to be a hierarchical structure with power and authority flowing from the national organization down to the precinct level. The fate of the Republican party's 1991 Plan illustrates the point. Much of the Republican technology and resources in Table 12.3 were used to enhance the party's position in state legislatures, which would be responsible for redrawing congressional districts after the 1990 census (see Chapter 11). The creation of 15 to 20 new congressional districts in states such as California, Florida, and Texas would give Republican candidates an opportunity to run for Congress without having to face a Democratic incumbent. The Republicans' 1991 Plan sought to make the most of that opportunity by providing party support to candidates for the state legislatures. For a while, the plan seemed to be working: Republicans picked up more than 600 state legislative seats in both the 1980 and 1984 elections. But the 1988 elections threw cold water on the 1991 Plan. After the elections that year, Democrats controlled both chambers in 28 state legislatures while Republicans actually lost ground and wound up with a two-chamber majority in only 8 state legislatures (13 had split majorities in the two chambers and Nebraska's single-chamber legislature does not organize along partisan lines).

The chief characteristic of the party organization continues to be a *diffusion* of power. At the national level, the party chairperson, congressional party leaders, and the president and presidential candidates all serve as spokespersons for the national party. State and local party leaders maintain their primacy in the areas of candidate recruitment and the mobilization of campaign workers and voters. Yet even the limited nationalization of the party organization that has taken place has upset some observers of American politics. Polsby, for example, feels that "state and local parties that root in local soil have the best chance of surviving and prospering, of winning elections and recruiting good candidates, and bringing to the national nominating process the authentic voices of the people of the several states."[32]

Party Activists

What kind of people are active in the party organizations at the local, state, and national level? One state party chairwoman described her party's regulars this way: "They are young. They are chicano. They are black. They are women." Another characterized the party regulars of the

Democratic National Chairman Ronald H. Brown. At the national level, the party chairperson, congressional party leaders, and the president and presidential candidates all serve as spokespersons for the national party.

1980s as young professionals, middle managers, "people with an M.B.A. who bothered to take a philosophy course."[33]

The types of people active in the party will depend to some extent on which party it is and where, but two characteristics found in most party organizations throughout the country serve to distinguish party activists from the general population. First, most activists come from families in which one or both parents were active in party work and elections, so that as children they were socialized into an active political role. Second, income, education, and occupation levels of party activists are higher than they are for the general population.[34]

Anyone who finds himself or herself stuffing envelopes with campaign literature at midnight or braving vicious dogs in a door-to-door voter registration drive is likely at some point to ask, Why am I doing this? In an earlier era, local party organizations and political machines could provide material benefits, such as jobs or welfare services, to those who were active. But the party activists of today are more likely to be motivated by political ideology and policy goals. An immediate goal of importance might be helping a candidate or candidates to win the election. But to continue this type of work for a political party for any extended period, a person has to believe that it makes a difference which party wins elections and controls the government. This is another way of saying that active participation in political campaigns and party activities is important to the extent that it has an effect on who governs.

Checkpoint

- Political party structure in the United States parallels the federal structure of the government. The parties are decentralized organizations of relatively autonomous local, state, and national units.
- Even though primaries have replaced local and state parties in controlling the nomination of candidates, the party organizations at this level often provide election services and support for candidates.
- A number of reforms over the past two decades have "nationalized" the parties, primarily in the area of selecting delegates to national conventions, but the organization of American parties continues to be more a decentralized, federal structure than it is a hierarchy.
- Party activists tend to be from politically active families, have higher socioeconomic status than the general population, and be motivated by ideology and policy goals.

PARTY-IN-THE-ELECTORATE: DEMOCRATIC LINKAGE

Parties are important to the democratic process because they link the people and the government. This linkage takes place partly because the party organization mobilizes voters and nominates candidates, and partly because elected of-

ficials pay attention to party colleagues and leaders in making decisions. In addition, it takes place because political parties also exist outside of government and outside of their formal organizations. The party-in-the-electorate consists of all of those voters who think of themselves as Democrats, Republicans, or otherwise and whose evaluations of candidates and policies are likely to be affected by their party identification. Few of these people hold any position in a campaign or party organization, and many will occasionally vote for candidates from the other party. Some will be officially identified as members of a party because they voted in that party's primary, yet they will vote for the other party's candidates in the general election. Membership in American political parties is open to everyone. A person does not have to meet any membership requirements or pay dues. Thinking of yourself as a Republican or Democrat, and acting that way at least some of the time, makes you one.

The party-in-the-electorate provides some structure to mass politics. It gives policy mandates to elected officials and holds them accountable for carrying them out. A disorganized electorate, one that serves up an unlimited number of policy alternatives, is one that decision makers can safely ignore. The existence of the party-in-the-electorate reduces the number of policy proposals in the political arena and provides a basis for building coalitions around these proposals.

A trend of great concern to both parties is the decline in partisanship in the electorate or, conversely, the increase in the percentage of the electorate identified as independents. One study ascribes 75 percent of this partisan dealignment to younger voters. These people appear less likely to identify with a party, more likely to desert a party they once identified with, and—contrary to the usual pattern—less likely to become partisans as they grow older.[35] Needless to say, a decreasing party-in-the-electorate makes it harder for parties to mobilize voters.

Paralleling the decline in partisanship is the decline in voter turnout. As Chapter 10 noted, strong party identifiers are much more likely to vote than weak partisans or independents. If at least part of the decline in voter turnout lies with

The leading candidates for the Democratic presidential nomination in 1988 get ready to debate (left to right: Paul Simon, Richard Gephardt, Albert Gore, Michael Dukakis, Jesse Jackson, Bruce Babbitt, and Joseph Biden). As the number of primaries increased after 1968, so too did the number of candidates for the nomination.

changing attitudes about political parties, the question is, Why do people now feel that parties are less important than they used to? What have parties done, or failed to do, that makes them less effective as agents of voter mobilization? One explanation is that changes in how candidates are nominated have helped reduce public interest in parties and participation in elections. "In the course of discouraging coalition-building and encouraging factionalist strategies by presidential candidates," says political scientist Nelson Polsby, "ordinary citizens may in greater numbers feel themselves and their opinions less taken account of by politicians."[36] Changes in how parties nominate candidates for president, the argument goes, have reduced the parties' ability to perform the function of voter mobilization. More specifically, the blame is laid on presidential primaries.

After its defeat in the 1968 election, the Democratic party undertook a series of reforms in its delegate selection process to broaden the base of the party. A direct result of this reform was the increase in the number of presidential primaries. While the impetus for the primaries was to democratize the nomination process, some individuals and institutions soon realized that they could not do without them. State business leaders counted on the additional money that primaries brought into the state. State political leaders enjoyed being wooed by presidential

candidates and having opportunities for national exposure. The mass media had a longer and more visible prenomination campaign to cover. And presidential candidates from outside the party's mainstream, with a limited or special-issue appeal, had a chance for the nomination that they would not have had under the old party-dominated system.

States began scrambling not just to have a primary, but to have a *meaningful* primary. That meant having one that took place before one candidate had already captured enough delegates to guarantee the nomination and take away interest in later primaries. While only 1 state primary had been held by the middle of March in 1968, and 7 by that time in 1984, more than 20 primaries had been held by the middle of March in 1988.

As the number of primaries increased after 1968, so too did the number of candidates for the nomination. This is more evident in the out party, since the party of an incumbent president seeking reelection always has fewer challengers. Nine Republican candidates ran in more than one primary in 1980, and eight Democrats in 1984. The 1988 election marked the first time in 20 years that neither party had an incumbent president running. Six Republicans and eight Democrats were in the early running for president that year.

When the field is large, candidates for the

presidential nomination can win primaries without having to capture a majority of the electorate's vote. Michael Dukakis won the 1988 New Hampshire primary, for example, with 36 percent of the vote and went on to win the nomination easily with 42 percent of the total Democratic primary vote for that year.

This system affects campaign strategies. A candidate in a crowded election field generally has only to mobilize an existing group of supporters to win. There is no need to attempt to build a majority coalition, to unite different factions and interests. Campaigns for the presidential nomination in such a system, then, are a series of appeals made to those narrow constituencies that are important to winning primaries.

Critics suggest that this type of campaign affects both the electability and the ability to govern of the person who emerges as the winner. After listening to the special-interest appeals of several candidates in primaries, for example, a top political strategist observed that "the cumulative demands of these groups end up being four or five times the federal budget."[37] It is often argued that a nomination process that required coalition building would force candidates to be more realistic about what government can and cannot do for these groups. That is part of the reasoning behind recent Democratic reforms that allocate a number of delegate seats to congressional and state party leaders, known as "superdelegates." "Such alliances not only enhance the candidate's electability," says the former head of the Democratic reform commission, North Carolina Governor James Hunt, "they are absolutely essential to effective governance after the election is won."[38]

So far in this chapter we have looked at changes in the party organization and the party-in-the-electorate. While the political party organizations seem to have undergone a nationalization and revitalization over the last decade or two, there are signs that the party-in-the-electorate is less responsive to those party organizations than it used to be. And, most importantly, those changes in the party-in-the-electorate affect the ability of elected officials to govern once in office. We turn now to this third element of the party and linkage process, the party-in-government.

Checkpoint

- The party-in-the-electorate provides structure to mass politics in the United States by giving policy mandates and holding elected officials accountable to them.
- The decline of partisan voters, voter turnout, and party leaders' influence in the nomination process has contributed to a general weakening of the party-in-the-electorate.

PARTY-IN-GOVERNMENT: RESPONSIBLE PARTIES

A belief shared by all elements of the political party is that it matters who wins. If Republican officeholders support the same policies favored by Democratic officeholders, then it makes little sense for parties to organize voters, for candidates to contest elections, or for eligible voters to go to the polls. "We have to have some differences articulated between the two parties, not simply more areas of agreement," House Republican leader Vin Weber told President Bush and his representatives on Capitol Hill.[39]

In a democracy, elected officeholders must be responsible to the electoral majority that put them in office. To do this in any long-term and consistent way requires an organization to coordinate the activities of officeholders who were elected with similar goals or programs. The party-in-government, which consists of public officials of the same party, is the organization charged with this coordination. We expect Republican senators and representatives to agree with other Republican senators and representatives more than they do with Democrats. We expect Democratic presidents to get along with a Democratic congressional majority better than Republican presidents do. Just as the party organization and the party-in-electorate link the mass public with the government, so does the party-in-government link the individuals and institutions of government. In order to determine how well the party-in-government does this, we will look at three aspects: the congressional party, the party as a bridge between the president and Congress, and policy differences between the two parties.

The Congressional Party

E. E. Schattschneider, in his book *Party Government*, emphasized what he termed "the most important single fact concerning the American parties"—their inability to govern. "He who knows this fact, and knows nothing else," Schattschneider contended, "knows more about American parties than he who knows everything except this fact."[40] This revelation comes after a discussion of congressional voting and a conclusion that neither political party is able to hold its members in line on most congressional votes.

Two ways of measuring the influence of party in congressional voting are the incidence of party votes (roll call votes in which a majority of one party opposes a majority of the other party) and party unity scores (the percentage of time the average Democrat and Republican voted with his or her party majority in disagreement with the other party's majority). Studies of congressional voting over the last century show that there has been a long-term decline in the percentage of all votes that are party votes. In the late nineteenth century and the first decade of the twentieth, a majority of one party opposed a majority of the other party on between two-thirds and three-fourths of all roll call votes. For the next 50 years (from 1911 through the 1960s), party votes took place on about half of all roll calls. In the 1970s, less than half of all roll calls (averaging about 40 percent) were party votes; in the 1980s party voting increased in the House of Representatives, reaching nearly 65 percent in 1987, while party voting in the Senate stayed

closer to the 40 percent average of the 1970s.[41]

Studies that look at party unity scores, however, find that there has been much less of a change in support for party. In 1989, for example, the average congressional Democrat voted with his or her party on 81 percent of the partisan votes in Congress; the average Republican, 73 percent. That level of support for party is considerably above the average support score for both Democrats (64 percent) and Republicans (66 percent) during the 1970s.[42] Put another way, these studies indicate that party leaders in Congress can count on about seven or eight of every ten of their own party members supporting them on partisan issues in Congress.

There are two quite distinct ways of interpreting these patterns of behavior. One is to focus on the stable pattern of party support and to recognize that a member's political party is the best indicator of how that representative or senator will vote on any issue. Another is to focus on party defections—the regular pattern of three of every ten legislators who vote against their party—and to recognize the limitations of the congressional party as an instrument for governing. (See A Closer Look, pp. 392–393, for an account of one legislator's defection from his party to join the opposing party.)

President, Party, and Congress

The Constitution provides a separation of powers, a division of responsibilities, between the president and Congress. For 22 of the 37 years between 1953 and 1990, more than half of the time, we have had divided government, with one party in the presidency and the other controlling one or both houses of Congress. Americans like this *partisan* separation of powers and checks and balances, which goes beyond the constitutional principles discussed in Chapter 4. In the 1988 elections, for instance, voters in almost one-third of all congressional districts (135 of 435) sent a Democrat to Congress while supporting Republican George Bush for president.[43] Some of this split-ticket voting, no doubt, reflects the consistent support of voters for incumbent members of Congress (a topic examined more closely in Chapter 14). But some is also due to the voters'

A Closer Look

From Democrat to Republican ★★★

It took just six years for Phil Gramm to go from being Professor Gramm of the Texas A&M economics department to being U.S. Representative Gramm—Democrat from the 6th District of Texas—to being U.S. Senator Gramm—Republican from Texas. The move from professor to political candidate is not unusual in American politics, nor is the move from the House of Representatives to the Senate. What is noteworthy about Gramm's career is the change in his party label from Democrat to Republican.

During the first year of the Reagan administration, House Majority Leader Jim Wright was able to persuade the Democratic Steering and Policy Committee to nominate Gramm and two other members of the Conservative Democratic Forum to the House Budget Committee. The majority leader was familiar with Gramm's record as an outspoken conservative on economic issues, but he felt that by electing Gramm and the other two conservative representatives to the Budget Committee, Democrats might gain the support of conservatives in the House who would otherwise vote with the Republicans and give that party a working majority in the House. Gramm wanted the Budget Committee seat and sent a letter to House Democratic leaders, in which he assured them that he would be a responsible member of the Budget Committee and would support the final passage of the budget on the House floor.

After House Democrats had elected Gramm to the Budget Committee, however, the Texas lawmaker began working with David Stockman, President Reagan's budget director, to develop an alternative budget. Some Democrats on the Budget Committee claimed that

Republican Senator Phil Gramm of Texas. In six years he went from being Professor Gramm of the Texas A&M economics department to being a U.S. Senator, and from Democrat to Republican.

Gramm was keeping Stockman informed of budget decisions and legislative strategies developed by Budget Committee Democrats in closed session, what one House member likened to the "story of the fox in the hen house." The Texas Democrat later served as a floor leader for the Reagan administration's budget, which passed the House with the support of 63 Democratic representatives.

When the Democratic Steering and Policy Committee voted to deny Gramm a seat on the Budget Committee two years later, he said that Democrats were punishing him for "practicing in Washington what I preach at home." "That may be unusual," said Gramm, "but I didn't know it was a crime."[a] Shortly thereafter, he resigned his seat in the House and announced that he would be a Republican candidate in the special election to fill the seat the following month. Ten other candidates entered the special election, but Gramm received more than 55 percent of the votes and became the first Republican to hold that seat in Texas history. Six months later, the state's Republican senator, John Tower, announced that he would retire at the end of his term, and Gramm began the campaign that put him in the Senate.

During his term as a Democratic representative, Phil Gramm voted against the majority of his party on about three-fourths of all the votes on which a majority of House Democrats opposed a majority of House Republicans. Rather than seeing this as disloyalty, however, Gramm contended that he was voting in accordance with his constituents. Whether he was a Democratic representative from the 6th District of Texas, a Republican representative from that district, or a Republican senator from Texas, said Gramm, "I'm gonna dance with them that brung me."[b]

[a]Alan Ehrenhalt, ed. *Politics in America, 1986* (Washington, D.C.: Congressional Quarterly Press, 1985), pp. 1470–1472; and Dale Tate,"Gramm: An Unrepentant Boll Weevil Bolts Party,"*Congressional Quarterly Weekly Report*, January 8, 1983, p. 5.
[b]Quoted in Roger H. Davidson and Walter J. Oleszek, *Congress and Its Members* (Washington, D.C.: Congressional Quarterly Press, 1990), p. 305.

belief in the principle of divided government, a conclusion supported by the findings of a national poll in 1986 in which nearly 70 percent of those polled agreed that "it is almost always best for the country when the White House is controlled by one party and Congress by the other."[44] Those beliefs and voting patterns complicate conceptions of the party-in-government and party responsibility for government policies.

Since political party affiliation is the best single explainer of voting in Congress, we would expect presidents to be able to count on the support of most of their party colleagues in Congress most of the time. Table 12.4, on p. 396, shows the extent of that support over a number of years. (This table shows the *average* support for presidents. Presidents Lyndon Johnson in 1965 and Ronald Reagan in 1981, for instance, enjoyed congressional support far above this average.) According to the table, the party does provide a base of support in Congress for the executive branch, but that support falls far short of being unanimous. Most presidents, most of the time, can count on the support of about two-thirds of their own party colleagues in the legislature—considerably more than the support from members of the opposition. Because party support is never unanimous, presidents often resort to a bipartisan approach to Congress, appealing to both parties. Democratic presidents in the 1960s used this approach with civil rights legislation; presidents of both parties have stressed bipartisanship on foreign policy issues since the end of World War II; and Republican presidents from Eisenhower to Bush have relied heavily on bipartisan appeals to the Democrat-controlled Congress.

The bipartisan approach to major issues was quite evident in the Reagan administration. The creation of bipartisan national commissions to come up with proposals on such issues as social security, the MX missile, and policy toward Central America reduced party differences before the proposals went to Congress—a procedure known as "precooking" in Washington.

While a bipartisan approach is sensible for some presidents and some members of Congress, it also has the effect of blurring the differences between the two parties. A voter who does not

Table 12.4

Congressional Support for Presidents, 1953–1986

	Average Support Score (%)	
	Democratic Presidents	Republican Presidents
House Democrats	68	41
House Republicans	40	64
Senate Democrats	63	43
Senate Republicans	45	69

Source: Calculated from data in Larry J. Sabato, *The Party's Just Begun* (New York: Scott, Foresman, 1988), p. 57.

like the compromise policy cannot register an objection by voting against a particular party. Thus, bipartisanship may strengthen the ties between a president and Congress, but it can also weaken the link between government and the people. One congressional Democrat, a critic of the commission approach, asked: "Why would you expect voters to come out and vote for Democrats, as if we stand for something different?" These remarks echoed those of Democratic President Harry Truman some 30 years earlier: "When the voters have a choice between a Republican and a Republican," Truman said, "they'll pick the Republican every time."[45]

Do Democrats stand for something different? Given the defection rate seen in the congressional party and the use of bipartisan appeals by presidents, one can certainly ask whether the differences between Democrats and Republicans have become so minimal that they have lost their meaning. Can a voter conclude that there are

Table 12.5

QUESTION: "Now I'd like to ask you about some specific issue areas and for each, I'd like you to tell me which political party you think would do a better job—the Democratic party, the Republican party, both about the same, or neither?"

	Percentage Favoring		
Issue Area	Democratic Party	Republican Party	Party Advantage
Helping the poor	58	11	+47 Dem
Helping farmers	50	13	+37 Dem
Protecting social security	43	13	+30 Dem
Limiting nuclear arms race	42	18	+24 Dem
Reducing unemployment	39	23	+16 Dem
Holding taxes in line	28	31	+ 3 Rep
Dealing with drug problem	13	24	+11 Rep
Controlling government spending	22	37	+15 Rep
Controlling inflation	21	41	+20 Rep
Keeping strong national defense	15	50	+35 Rep

Note: Poll was taken in November 1986.

Source: Adapted from Larry J. Sabato, *The Party's Just Begun* (Glenview, Ill.: Scott, Foresman, 1988), p. 143.

policy consequences to which party governs? Does it really make a difference whether the party in government is Democratic, Republican, or both?

Policy Differences

One way of determining whether there are policy differences between the parties is to see if the public *perceives* such differences. A national survey in 1986 found that a majority of Americans (54 percent) believed that there was *"only some* difference between the candidates and policies of the Republican party and the candidates and policies of the Democratic party."[46] However, many of those finding "only some" difference between parties also felt those differences to be significant, and the proportion of the public saying there were "important differences" between the parties increased by 16 percent between the early 1970s and the mid-1980s.[47] Table 12.5 shows some of the important differences the public sees between the two major parties.

These poll results suggest that the public does see policy differences in the matter of who governs. Students of public opinion and elections know that these perceived differences between the two parties are based on more than campaign promises and party platforms; they have some basis in the types of policies advanced by those parties when they govern. But it is difficult to measure these policy differences directly. One study of specific pledges made in party platforms between 1944 and 1978 found that almost three-fourths of these policy promises were fulfilled.[48] Another study found that periods of major policy change throughout U.S. history were linked with strong differences between party platforms and with electoral realignment.[49]

What these studies suggest is that it *does* make a difference which party governs, that there are policy consequences to which party wins elections. There are many points of slippage and breaks in the link between the people and government, the executive and legislature, and individual officeholders of the same party. But it is clear that American political parties do help to perform some of the functions that are essential to democratic government, even if, as a number of contemporary observers suggest, parties are not performing those tasks as well today as they did in the past.

Checkpoint

- Democracy requires organization of the party-in-government and responsible parties that can link the separate branches of government.

- On the one hand, congressional parties do provide a relatively stable base of support for presidents of the same party. On the other hand, bipartisan appeals and commissions make it more difficult for voters to assign responsibility for policies.

- Despite the many points of slippage in the links between voters and those who govern, between the executive and the legislature, and among individual officeholders of the same party, it does make a difference which party wins elections and governs in the United States.

PARTIES: WHO GOVERNS?

What would American politics be like without political parties? Who would govern and how? At a time when political scientists and journalists were described as "conducting a death watch over the American parties,"[50] the noted historian Arthur Schlesinger, Jr., painted a grim picture of a party-less United States:

Political adventurers will roam the countryside like Chinese warlords or Iranian ayatollahs, recruiting personal armies, conducting hostilities against some rival warlords and forming alliances with others, and, as they win elections, striving to govern through ad hoc coalitions in legislatures.

The crumbling away of the historic parties would leave political power in America concentrated in the adventurers, in the interest groups that finance them and in the executive bureaucracy.[51]

Whether you think Schlesinger is being melodramatic or making an important point will depend on your views about the role of political parties in governing America. Throughout this book we have been considering different answers to the question of who governs. The three models of government help us to order the information about political parties in this chapter and to evaluate their role in governing America.

Democracy

On the first page of *Party Government*, E. E. Schattschneider had this to say: "This volume is devoted to the thesis that the political parties created democracy and that modern democracy is unthinkable save in terms of the parties."[52] In the case of American parties, Schattschneider's judgment was based on a belief that political parties had created a workable government out of an outdated and unworkable structure of checks and balances and separation of powers. Parties did this by organizing the mass public into recognizable electorates and by transforming national elections into public mandates on policies.

The interdependence of political parties and democracy has been treated in many books in the nearly 50 years since *Party Government*, and some of these have found that those same political parties that were instrumental in developing democracy in this country have been greatly weakened by continuing democratizing trends, particularly the use of primaries to nominate party candidates. As one scholar of parties and elections has written: "The development of mass-based political parties in the United States provided the key driving force behind the modern democratization of electoral power. Yet this democratization itself has actually diminished the strength, the vitality, and the stature of the political parties to which it owes its life."[53]

The chief goal of a political party in a democracy is to make sure that elected officials are responsive to those who put them in office. Political parties can provide that type of democratic accountability only when all three elements of a political party are working. The party organization must be able to mobilize voters and exercise some control over nominations. The party-in-the-electorate must be strong enough to shape the policy and candidate preferences of voters. The party-in-government must coordinate the activities of those who govern in order to produce the policies favored by an electoral majority.

The party-in-the-electorate is central to the democratic model because it is only through the organization of party and the vote that those who have little or no power as individuals are able to make those who govern responsive to them. That is why the decline of the party-in-the-electorate discussed in this chapter and the decline in voter turnout discussed in Chapter 10 are considered so important. Nonvoting tells us something about the state of political parties in the United States. And as Walter Dean Burnham has observed, voter turnout is "an important indicator of the relative health of democracy in any political system based upon elections and the consent of the governed."[54]

Pluralism

A central idea of the democratic view of political parties is that parties make it possible for voters to give elected officials mandates. We discussed President Reagan's claim to a mandate in the 1980 and 1984 elections at the end of Chapter 11. The outgoing president made a similar claim for the winning Republican ticket in 1988. George Bush and Dan Quayle had gone to the people asking for a mandate on taxes and defense and foreign policy, Reagan said, and "that mandate has been unmistakenly delivered."[55]

In 1961, reporters asked another president whether his election represented a mandate. Having just been elected by a popular-vote margin of less than one percent, John Kennedy replied: "Mandate, 'schmandate.' I'm on this side of the desk and you're on that side."[56] Kennedy's response reminds us that while *some* elections can be considered mandates requiring those who govern to respond to voters' policy preferences, *all* elections put somebody in office (and on "this side of the desk").

The pluralist view of American politics puts particular emphasis on this aspect of elections. By winning an election, public officials take their place at the bargaining table of American politics—whether they won by one vote or one million votes. In this view, elections are important more for the positions they bestow than for the programs they demand of those who govern.

The focus on positions rather than electoral mandates was also evident in a strategy Republican National Committee Chairman Lee Atwater actively pursued early in the Bush administration. This strategy was to convince Democratic officeholders in certain areas to switch to the Republican party, thereby making electoral challenges unnecessary. By July 1989, more than 120 Democratic officials, including two congressmen, had switched to the Republican party. At a White House reception honoring these party converts, Representative Tommy Robinson of Arkansas was asked why he did not resign his seat and run in a special election with his new party label. After first producing groans among reporters by saying that sounded like "a typical Democratic question," Robinson expressed a view of elections in sharp contrast to the party program notion discussed earlier:

> Let me say this. I represent 550,000 people in the 2nd district of Arkansas—Democrats, Republicans, independents and people, quite frankly, that don't care about any of the three above. I am not going to resign.[57]

Arthur Schlesinger's depiction of a United States without parties reflects another idea about parties often expressed by pluralists. Interest groups, which lie at the heart of pluralism, are similar to political parties in many ways: They seek to mobilize citizens and voters; they raise money and provide campaign assistance; and they seek to influence government officials. But political parties also differ from most interest groups in the breadth of their membership and political goals; parties seek benefits for all citizens rather than just members of the party.

President Bush welcomes Tommy Robinson, one of the former Democratic office holders who switched to the Republican party, at a White House press conference in July, 1989. The pluralist focus on positions rather than electoral mandates was evident in the Republican strategy to convert Democratic officials, including two congressmen, to the Republican party.

In that way, political parties counterbalance the demands of special-interest groups and PACs in American politics. Political scientists sometimes describe "a world without parties" as extreme pluralism, a world in which special interests and PACs are out of control and resemble the "political adventurers" depicted by Schlesinger.[58]

The Power Elite

"As a general rule," the American humorist Robert Benchley once wrote, "Republicans are more blonde than Democrats."[59] Those who view American politics from a power elite perspective consider most party differences in the United States to be similarly trivial. Look in the index of C. Wright Mills's *The Power Elite* or Thomas Dye's *Who's Running America?*—a more recent statement of Mills's thesis of a power elite—and you will find no entry for "political parties," "Democrats," or "Republicans." They are just not that important, from this perspective.

Political parties have the *potential* for bringing

about political change, according to this view, because they are perhaps the only instrument by which the powerless can organize and mount electoral challenges to those who govern. But capitalism and the private power of corporations force both major parties to draw water from essentially the same corporate wells. Howard Reiter characterizes the result of this process as "a buttress for corporate capitalism":

> . . . a political system in which power is concentrated in the corporate sector, and the public is anesthetized both by a party system that fails to offer the kinds of major ideological and class differences found elsewhere in the world, and by the mass media which concentrate on trivia. . . .
>
> To make matters worse, those Americans who are sympathetic to social change too often devote their energies to a reformism that undercuts the effectiveness of political parties, damaging perhaps the only mechanism which can both represent those with few material resources and organize to carry out social change.[60]

What about third parties? If the two major parties are indeed limited to the degree that power elitists say they are, third parties might be regarded as the only way of changing the status quo of American politics. Bernard Sanders, the socialist mayor of Burlington, Vermont, said the message of the 1988 presidential election— "the old Democratic-Republican tweedle-dee, tweedle-dum"—clearly demonstrated that "this country needs a third political party." He called for one that would represent the needs and interests of working people, the elderly, farmers, minorities, environmentalists, peace activists, and "all people who believe they are not represented by status quo politics."[61]

In July 1989, the National Organization of Women (NOW) raised the idea of forming a third party to support women's rights. Two weeks later, most of the leaders attending a convention of the National Women's Political Caucus vehemently rejected the third-party idea. Maxine Berman, a Michigan state legislator, summed up the feelings of many women leaders: "To divert yourself from the established power structure,

which will go on and continue to make decisions anyway, to pull yourself out of it, is absolutely stupid."[62]

Checkpoint

- All three elements of a political party (party organization, party-in-the-electorate, and party-in-government) serve the goal of democratic accountability, but the party-in-the-electorate is the key to assuring that those who govern are responsive to those who put them in office.
- Pluralists tend to downplay the idea of elections as policy mandates and focus more on how elections affect the bargaining process and how political parties broaden interest representation in American politics.
- Most power elite theorists say that political parties have the potential for bringing about political change, but that American parties fail to offer real ideological and class differences or challenge the prevailing ideology of corporate capitalism.

SUMMARY

There are three ways of defining a political party: ideological (shared beliefs), organizational (groups and structure), and functional (activities).

Although there have been more than 1000 political parties in the course of American history, 5 parties and party systems have dominated the governing of America.

Political parties participate in governing America by (1) recruiting political leaders, (2) mobilizing voters, (3) nominating candidates, (4) contesting elections, (5) forming a government, (6) coordinating political activity, and (7) providing accountability. Three elements of political parties share the task of performing these functions and providing democratic linkage: the party organization, the party-in-the-electorate, and the party-in-government.

Political parties in the United States are decentralized and consist of relatively independent local, state, and national organizations.

The party-in-the-electorate, long considered an essential element of democracy in the United States, has been weakened by a decline in party identification and turnout among voters.

The party-in-government is characterized on the one hand by congressional parties, which provide a relatively stable base of support for presidents of the same party, and on the other hand by divided government, which requires presidents to make bipartisan appeals for legislative support.

Those who view the system from the perspective of the democratic model focus on elections as mandates; pluralists emphasize interest representation and elections as contests for positions, not policy action; and the power elite model draws attention to a lack of fundamental differences between the two major parties.

KEY TERMS

Political party
Party organization
Party-in-government
Party-in-the-electorate
Federalists
Jeffersonians
Democratic party
Patronage
Whig party
Republican party
Realignment

Direct primary
Political recruitment
Party activists
Caucus
Convention
Presidential primaries
Bipartisan coalition
Precinct
National convention
National committees

FOR FURTHER READING

David S. Broder, *The Party's Over* (New York: Harper & Row, 1972). An analysis of the breakdown of the two-party system and reform proposals for party revival.

William Nesbit Chambers and Walter Dean Burnham, *The American Party Systems: Stages of Development* (New York: Oxford University Press, 1975). A collection of original essays on the five party systems discussed in this chapter.

Stephen E. Frantzich, *Political Parties in the Technological Age* (New York: Longman, 1989). Discusses the ways in which computers and television have changed the political parties' traditional role as communicator and helped to revitalize party organizations.

L. Sandy Maisel (ed.), *The Parties Respond: Changes in the American Party System* (Boulder, Col.: Westview Press, 1990). A collection of essays by party scholars and political participants about the significant changes that American political parties have undergone in recent years.

David R. Mayhew, *Placing Parties in American Politics* (Princeton, N.J.: Princeton University Press, 1986). A "bottoms-up" look at traditional party organizations in the 50 states and the differences they have made to these states' politics.

Howard L. Reiter, *Parties and Elections in Corporate America* (New York: St. Martin's Press, 1987). A radical critique of politics and the party system in the United States.

Larry J. Sabato, *The Party's Just Begun* (Glenview, Ill.: Scott, Foresman, 1988). Analyzes the revival of party organizations and the continuing decline of the party-in-the-electorate and proposes reforms for party renewal.

E. E. Schattschneider, *Party Government* (New York: Holt, Rinehart and Winston, 1942). A classic examination of why political parties are essential to democracy.

Frank J. Sorauf and Paul Allen Beck, *Party Politics in America*, 6th ed. (Glenview, Ill.: Scott, Foresman, 1988). A comprehensive review of the political science literature on political parties.

Interest Group Politics

Chapter 13

nterest groups, private organizations that attempt to influence public policy, spark endless controversy. Detractors accuse them of promoting their members' selfish needs over national priorities and blame them for corrupting all levels of government. Other observers, however, feel this reputation is undeserved. Groups do far more good than harm by creating avenues for individual participation, by providing public decision makers with information and services, and by keeping potentially powerful segments of society in check. Whichever side in this debate is right, interest groups are certainly among the most prominent actors on the political stage. ■

Charls Walker is the kind of person you want to know if you have a problem with Congress or the federal bureaucracy. A former under secretary of the treasury, coauthor of a book on taxes, and a seasoned lobbyist for more than two decades, Walker daily rubs elbows with key senators and representatives, dines with cabinet officers, and maintains first-name relationships with corporate executives, nationally syndicated columnists, presidential advisers, and other members of the Washington establishment. When an industry wants to convince legislators to support a bill or when banks need assistance dealing with a federal agency, he is one of the first people they call.

During the course of an interview several years ago with Elizabeth Drew, a reporter for the *New Yorker* magazine, he described how he dealt with one organization's political difficulties. Notice that, as he talks, Walker drops the names of influential politicians like someone throwing confetti:

> Well, I talk to Jim. [Jim is James Schlesinger, President Jimmy Carter's secretary of energy.] Two days after we decided to take on the Lone Star Steel thing . . . I go out to play golf with Ashley [Lud Ashley, Democratic representative and chair of a House committee on energy], and then our families meet for some drinks and barbecue. The phone rings and Lud comes back twenty minutes later and

says "Jim [Schlesinger again] wants to talk to you." I told Jim I was getting into the energy thing and that I want to talk to some of his people and he says to talk to one of his deputies, and gives me a name, and we went over and talked to him and asked him to change his mind. He did not, and we went over and talked to someone at Treasury. I didn't talk to Jim again until late July. It was friendly but a little bit tense. He wanted to know how I sized up the situation. He knew I was in close touch with Senator Long [Russell Long, Democrat of Louisiana and chair of the Senate Finance Committee] and others. The next Sunday we had dinner, and we've been talking ever since. I keep telling him not to worry about the Moffett group [Representative Tobey Moffett, Connecticut Democrat]. I say "Hell, Jim. If you get a hundred Republican votes you didn't have before, what do you need with the Moffett group?" A couple of weeks ago, Russell asked me to come to his apartment . . . Russell and I went upstairs and talked tactics and strategy for about forty five minutes.[1]

During the interview Walker was interrupted by a call from Senator Herman Talmadge, at the time the second-ranking member of the Finance Committee: "Mornin' Senator, how are you sir. I got a problem I want to run by you."[2]

Charls Walker, an influential tax consultant and lobbyist, represents dozens of corporations in Congress and the federal bureaucracy. He typifies a type of representation called interest group politics.

With all his connections and experience, Walker, the quintessential *insider*, would clearly be a valuable ally in any political struggle. (Wouldn't it be nice to receive a phone call from a senator so that you could "run a problem by" her or him?) But the chances of ever benefiting from his services are slim, unless you happen to own a large corporation or bank. Walker Associates, a political consulting firm with offices midway between the White House and Capitol Hill, represents mainly large corporations and financial institutions, although members of its staff have participated in presidential campaigns.

But this doesn't mean you could not find someone to help you. The nation's capital swarms with men and women like Charls Walker whose jobs are to speak on behalf of their clients in the inner sanctums of power. They are part of what is commonly called the *interest group system*, a web of organizations and individuals that some say represents Americans as effectively as Congress.

The study of this form of representation bears directly on the question of who governs. Nearly everyone has an opinion about the desirability of interest groups. Democratic theorists obviously feel that citizens should make public policy and wonder if businesses like Walker's do not have too much influence. Pluralists, on the other hand, regard interest groups as balance wheels that keep government free and stable and thus supplement traditional political institutions. The elite school sees them as a noisy sideshow that occupies the middle rungs of power where the groups draw attention away from the real influentials who make trunk decisions. Yet whether one views them as the shame or glory of American government, knowledge of interest group politics is indispensable for trying to understand how American government really works.

THE NATURE OF INTEREST GROUPS

Interest groups, sometimes called *pressure groups* or *special interests*, are private organizations that try to influence public policy. Even if they claim to act in the name of a high purpose (such as national security), they usually work mainly to advance the specific needs of their members.

These groups may be organizations of like-minded individuals, (e.g., the National Rifle Association (NRA)); people united by common social or economic concerns, (e.g., the National Organization for Women (NOW) or the Home Builders Association of America (HBA)); individuals who share an occupation or trade, (e.g., the American Medical Association (AMA)); or a coalition of groups, (e.g., the Business Round Table, an alliance of several dozen large corporations). Whatever the case, their main political purpose is to influence laws and policies that affect their members.

Interest Groups Versus Political Parties

Interest groups differ from political parties in three significant respects:

1 Whereas parties strive to control government as a whole—to manage the affairs of state—interest groups deal with a relatively narrow range of issues. They do not want to balance the federal budget or rewrite the entire tax code; instead they merely attempt to protect the interests of their constituents.

2 Unlike parties, interest groups do not nominate candidates for office, although they certainly try to affect the outcome of elections. The NRA and NOW, for example, normally do not pick a nominee to run for the presidency under their own labels; they try instead to influence the choice the Democrats and Republicans make.

3 Finally, and most important, interest groups are basically *private* and hence are not accountable to the general public. Their members, not society as a whole, judge their performance in the political sphere.

These are crucial differences for evaluating who does and should have power in the United States. It is much easier and more important for citizens to maintain control over parties than over private organizations.[3] To stay in power parties must periodically earn the approval of the electorate, but no such requirement exists for interest groups, which depend only on the goodwill of their followers. However steadfastly private organizations like the NRA or NOW stand by their members, they can at best only supplement parties, which, on paper at any rate, offer the electorate meaningful policy choices and assume responsibility for implementing them.

Briefly stated then, interest groups are private formal organizations that have a comparatively narrow range of concerns and attempt to influence the course of public policy but not to control government in its entirety.

Number and Kinds of Interest Groups

Anyone who strolls around downtown Washington quickly realizes that it contains more than just government office buildings. Almost every street houses a private organization of one sort or another. The White House, the Supreme

Dr. Sidney Wolfe, a staff member with Public Citizen, a public interest group. This type of organization claims to speak for broad segments of the public, not just the specific interests of its members.

Court, and the Congress are immersed in a sea of interest group headquarters representing every segment of American society from multinational corporations to gun owners to beekeepers. The 1989 edition of *Washington Representatives*, a listing of "persons working to influence government policies and action to advance their own or their client's" causes, contained more than 12,500 entries, including 3,750 officers of trade and professional associations, 1,500 corporate representatives, and 2,500 advocates of "special causes from ERA to environment, from handgun control to prison reform, from saving

Table 13.1

Groups Represented in Washington, D.C.

	Groups Having Washington Representatives
Corporations	3017
Trade associations, other business	1182
Foreign commerce and corporations	429
Professional associations	455
Unions	112
Public interest groups	270
Civil rights/minority organizations	89
Social welfare/poor	40
New entrants (elderly, gay, handicapped)	73
Government units—U.S.	277
Other foreign	132
Others	541
Total	6617

Source: Based on Table 1 in Kay Lehman Schlozman, "What Accent the Heavenly Chorus? Political Equality and the American Pressure System," *Journal of Politics* 46 (1984):1012. By permission of the author and the University of Texas Press.

whales to saving unborn children."[4] In another tally, political scientist Kay Lehman Schlozman, who did not claim to do an exhaustive survey, found over 6,000 interest groups that either had their own offices in Washington or were represented by law or consulting firms that did (see Table 13.1).[5]

Economic conflict has always spawned organized groups, and those based on business, labor, agriculture, trades, and professions are firmly entrenched in politics. So too are associations built on other significant social divisions such as civil rights. These days, moreover, just about every conceivable interest, activity, or dispute leads to the establishment of an association that makes demands on government. Consider for a moment just a few of the groups busy in the committee rooms of Congress or hallways of executive departments: National Welfare Rights Organization (NWRO), American Civil Liberties Union (ACLU), American Association of Retired Persons (AARP), National Abortion Rights Action

League (NARAL), Accuracy in Media (AIM), Polish American Congress (PAC), National Wildlife Federation (NWF), People for the American Way (PAW), Zero Population Growth (ZPG). Besides these traditional types of organizations there are ideological groups ranging from the liberal Americans for Democratic Action (ADA) to the conservative Committee for the Survival of a Free Congress (CSFC).

A newer type of organization that has proliferated in the last two decades is the **public interest group**. These bodies claim to speak for the public as a whole (or significant parts of it, such as consumers or hospital patients) rather than for the narrow interests of a small rank-and-file membership. Common Cause, which advocates open and honest government, Ralph Nader's conglomeration of safety, health, and consumer groups (such as the Center for the Study of Responsive Law), and the National Taxpayers Union are among the best-known examples. They purport to act on behalf of general concerns—open government, safe toys, or reduced federal spending—but they still fit the definition of interest group because in both form and spirit they are private entities trying to influence public policy.

An even newer member of the cast is the political action committee (PAC). As Chapter 11 explained, a PAC is a special kind of group: Usually, but not always, affiliated with a parent body such as a corporation, union, or trade association, it collects funds and funnels the money into election campaigns in the hope of winning the goodwill of candidates. Having poured millions of dollars into campaigns in the last 16 years, these organizations are now a force to be reckoned with in American politics.

The presence of interest groups in such number, strength, and variety raises two questions: (1) What explains their emergence, growth, and success in politics? (2) More important, what consequences do they have for control of government? In particular, who wins and loses because of them?

Checkpoint

- Interest groups are private organizations that attempt to influence public policy, but unlike political parties they do not nominate candidates for office or try to run the government as a whole.

- Several thousand groups, representing every segment of American life, are politically active.

- Two new types of organization are public interest groups, which claim to represent the public as a whole, not just a particular segment of it, and political action committees, which raise and donate money to election campaigns.

THE PROLIFERATION OF INTEREST GROUPS

Alexis de Tocqueville, the astute nineteenth-century French observer of American society, noted: "In no country in the world has the principle of association been more successfully used or applied to a greater multitude of objects than in America."[6] Even though written more than 100 years ago, Tocqueville's remark is as applicable now (if not more so) as it was then. What explains this phenomenon?

An economist, Mancur Olson, advances the hypothesis that the older and more stable a democracy becomes, the more likely interest groups will multiply and grow in strength.[7] His proposition certainly holds for the United States, a large and socially and economically diverse nation whose Constitution, history, traditions, and political creed all encourage individuals to unite and fight for what they believe to be their rights. That they do so more "privately" than "publicly" is one of the most significant facts of politics and government in this country.

The First Amendment to the Constitution guarantees "the right of the people to peaceably assemble and to petition the government for the redress of grievances." This guarantee is only a small part of the picture, however, for it is the structure of the system itself that gives organized groups their importance. By splitting power among three independent (if not equal) branches and between the federal and state levels, the Constitution opens many doors to anyone who wants to influence policy. Why bother trying to control the entire system when there are so many independent power centers that can protect and promote one's particular concerns?

The answer can be seen in the struggle over tax reform. As part of his 1986 tax reform package, President Ronald Reagan proposed closing a loophole that gave businesses the right to deduct meal and entertainment expenses from their tax bills. Ending this exemption not only antagonized business leaders but also infuriated restaurant owners and their employees, who feared the change would eventually cost them income and jobs. If businesses could no longer take deductions for treating clients to lunch, they reasoned, the food industry was bound to suffer.

Fortunately for them, the president can only propose legislation. *Both* houses of Congress must pass the necessary bills, *and* the bureaucracy and courts have to implement and enforce them. Thus, the food and entertainment lobbies had many fronts to fight on. They logically started with the legislature, where power is also fragmented among numerous committees and subcommittees, each having authority to delay, modify, or even block the president's program. After the committees finished drafting the reforms, the bills had to pass both chambers as a whole. Getting 435 representatives and 100 senators to agree on anything is no easy task; convincing them to accept a bill as complicated and controversial as tax restructuring was especially difficult.

In situations like these, preventing change is much easier than passing sweeping reforms. By doing favors, creating alliances, supplying information, and mobilizing opinion, an industry such as the restaurant owners and workers can often win with a strategy of divide and conquer. It is not necessary to convince the entire Congress, only enough members to keep the objectionable parts of the bill bottled up in committee or, failing that, watered down. (In fact, this is what the restaurant lobbies managed to accomplish: The final bill allowed 80 percent of meal and entertainment expenses to be deducted.[8])

Yet the restaurateurs do not have to stop here. If unacceptable legislation slips through the first line of defense, it can be fought in the courts or bureaucracy. The Internal Revenue Service (IRS), for example, often has surprisingly wide latitude in interpreting and enforcing tax legislation, and more than a few businesses and individuals have gone to the agency for favorable rulings.

The Constitution, in short, puts political power in many hands. Unlike England, the United States does not have a *unitary system* of centralized government in which control is consolidated in one body headed by a person such as a prime minister. American presidents are powerful, to be sure, but at the same time they need the cooperation of other independent power

Table 13.2

Membership in Voluntary Organizations in 1988

	Percent Responding
No memberships	29
1	26
2	19
3	10
4	7
5 or more	9
Total	100

Question: "Here is a list of various organizations. Could you tell me whether or not you are a member of each type?"

Source: Based on data from National Opinion Research Center, *General Social Surveys, 1972–1988*, distributed by the Inter-university Consortium for Political and Social Research, University of Michigan.

centers. These other centers greatly strengthen interest groups because if the groups cannot persuade the White House, they can always carry the fight to another field.

The separation and fragmentation of powers that characterize the American political system partly account for the number, diversity, and strength of interest groups. People gravitate toward institutions that can help them, and since so many exist in the United States, a large number of groups naturally surround them.

Another explanation for the proliferation of interest groups lies in Americans' distrust of centralized public authority.[9] One survey asked individuals what they could do if Congress or a local government were considering a law or regulation that they thought was unjust or harmful.[10] The most common answers included acting individually (directly contact a public official, for instance) or working through a group (though not necessarily an organized one). Almost no one—one percent or less—would work through a political party.[11] A salesman succinctly expressed the prevailing feeling: "Get up a petition. Get together with people who have the same objection."[12]

Getting together with "people who have the same objection" has always been one of our most obvious traits, as Tocqueville noted when he wrote the "right of association . . . is now incorporated with the manners and customs of the people."[13] These customs and manners, which are part of what we have called general-welfare liberalism (see Chapter 3), contain large doses of skepticism of political power and a fierce determination to protect individual rights. Although they identify with political parties, Americans nevertheless support private organizations as a main instrument for advancing their interests in politics. Parties are broad, collective entities that emphasize compromise and cooperation, whereas interest groups exist to serve the specific, immediate, and frequently narrow needs of their members.

These sentiments perhaps explain why so many Americans belong to voluntary associations. As the data in Table 13.2 indicate, more than two-thirds of the sample said they belong to at least one organization such as a union, service group, or garden club. Many of these organizations do not play a prominent part in policymaking, but their popularity underscores the adage that Americans are a "nation of joiners."

Thomas Nast's cartoon, drawn in 1876, illustrates the traditional American view of lobbyists as scoundrels who often try to bribe politicians in exchange for favors.

Checkpoint

- Two factors explain the number and strength of interest groups in American politics:
  - The constitutional system of checks and balances fragments power, giving interest groups multiple points of access to press their claims.
  - Americans tend to distrust public authority and whenever possible prefer private associations to solve their problems.

INTEREST GROUP POLITICS IN PRACTICE

Interest groups have always received mixed reviews. Critics see them as corrupt, selfish, greedy, untrustworthy, and, especially, undemocratic because they give unfair advantages to economically and socially powerful classes. Pluralists, on the other hand, view them as indispensable mechanisms for preventing one part of society from dominating the rest. James Madison argued in *The Federalist Papers* that in a large and diverse nation numerous "factions" (his term for groups) inevitably arise and check and balance one another, thereby helping formal political institutions prevent any segment of society from acquiring excessive power. Thus, although pluralists admit that interest groups sometimes get out of hand and do not always adequately represent the different strata of society, these groups nevertheless ensure political liberties and promote political stability.[14]

Who is right? It is a hard question. Before trying to answer, however, let's first survey what groups do. After studying how they perform in these areas we can better assess their role in American government. Their main activities include lobbying and raising campaign funds.

Lobbying

In the early 1970s a series of scandals in the Nixon administration shocked the nation. Of the many wrongdoings that surfaced, none seemed as unfair and illicit as attempts by large corporations to buy political influence. The Lockheed Corporation, to take a notorious example, confessed to making illegal campaign contributions to President Nixon's reelection committee, presumably in return for special treatment from the White House. Several years later the FBI uncovered widespread bribery in Congress and in many state and local governments. In the midst of this scandal, called Abscam, Americans witnessed night after night on the evening news videotapes of lawmakers exchanging promises of political favors for large sums of cash.

These episodes, merely the latest in a long string of exposés stretching back to the nineteenth century, reinforce people's suspicions about politics.[15] The term that seems to evoke these doubts most frequently is *lobbyists*, people depicted by generations of political cartoonists as fat, greedy-looking characters chomping on cigars while stuffing $100 bills into lawmakers' coat pockets. The word lobbying conjures up images of wining and dining, arm twisting, gift giving, all-expenses-paid trips, and occasionally money under the table. Lobbyists, in the popular lore, are unsavory at best and downright corrupt at worst.

But for whatever bits of truth the conventional wisdom holds, it is too narrow, too misleading, and certainly too simplistic to adequately describe the way interest groups function. Simply stated, **lobbying** means *any* effort by a group or individual to influence government's policies and actions. There are many ways to do it, including, among others, mobilizing public opinion, contacting decision makers face to face, cultivating friendships, and using relationships with former employers in government.

MOBILIZING OPINION   Lobbyists have a variety of weapons in their arsenals but few as potentially lethal as the ability to mobilize public opinion. By organizing and sponsoring letter-writing campaigns, vigils and marches, visits to Congress or state capitals, petitions, research reports, telephone banks, press conferences, and coverage by the media, interest groups hope and expect to convince legislators and bureaucrats that the people back home support their causes. The organizations often speak for only a small slice of the public. But, by producing enough letters, phone calls, marchers, and television coverage, a group can create the appearance of massive support, and in politics appearance is often as important as reality.

The 3 million-member National Rifle Association (NRA) is famous for its skill at rallying the faithful and persuading lawmakers of the folly of opposing its demands. When Congress, a state legislature, or even a city council proposes restrictions on gun ownership, the NRA mounts letter and telephone campaigns that leave few policymakers untouched. Backed by millions of dollars in contributions, it buys newspaper and magazine advertisements, prints millions of bumper stickers ("Guns Don't Kill, People Do"), floods town meetings with supporters, registers voters (and sees that they go to the polls), collects endorsements from celebrities (Roy Rogers: "They'll have to shoot me first to take my gun"), and, in the rare instances when it loses at the legislative level, sends its lawyers into court.[16]

Even though public opinion polls show widespread support for gun control laws, the NRA is sufficiently active and determined that few politicians ever vote for them. As one example of its clout, it spent close to $2 million and mailed 10 million letters in 1988 in a successful effort to defeat a congressional proposal requiring a seven-day waiting period for the purchase of a handgun.[17]

Countless other groups copy tactics like these, though not always with the same success. Sometimes the attempts to create publicity and arouse support take rather dramatic twists. Earth First!, a small environmental group, advocates civil disobedience and "guerrilla theater" to popularize ecological issues. Its members once swept through a national forest driving large nails into

When the Maryland legislature put a hand gun control measure on the ballot in 1988, hunters and gun owners associations fought tooth and nail to defeat it. As with many interest groups, their principal weapon was mobilizing public opinion.

trees to make them unusable to the timber industry. (The nails would destroy saw blades.)[18] Another environmental organization, Greenpeace, routinely stages "media events" to dramatize its concerns. In the fall of 1989, three of its members scaled a DuPont Company water tower in Deepwater, New Jersey, from which they unfurled an enormous banner shaped like a blue first-prize ribbon. The "award," which read "#1 Ozone Destruction," was designed to protest DuPont's production of chlorofluorocarbons, chemicals implicated in the destruction of atmospheric ozone.[19]

Most of the time, though, lobbyists use more ordinary methods. The last two decades have seen the arrival of movements espousing the rights of women, farmers, gays, animals, and the homeless, to mention just a few of the dozens of causes that dot the political landscape. In each instance, these organizations strive by various means to achieve the impression that vast numbers of Americans endorse their purposes.

PERSUADING DECISION MAKERS Although public servants have strong convictions, they still keep an open mind on many matters and will, given the proper inducements or sufficient reasons, change their opinions. That is why interest groups regularly send lobbyists to congressional and administrative hearings to give "expert" testimony about the groups' concerns. They also frequently appear in court, not necessarily as plaintiffs or defendants but as interested third parties. A favorite device is the **amicus curiae brief,** a statement and supporting documentation submitted to a court by someone not directly involved in the litigation. These briefs give groups a way to present evidence and information to judges in the hope of swaying their decisions. In addition, interest groups sponsor test cases and pay for legal fees because the judicial branch is frequently the best (or even only) forum in which to advance their causes.[20]

Equally important, civil servants and elected officials have to contend with conflicting, sometimes irreconcilable, claims in a relatively short time. Besieged on all sides, they constantly look for justification and backing for their actions. Here is where interest groups come to the fore. Using whatever resources they can marshal, they attempt to supply the reasons, inducements, friendships, or whatever else it takes to persuade a skeptical, confused, or reluctant decision maker.

As anyone who observes the Washington scene realizes, members of Congress need help. Lots of help. To pass a bill a legislator has to draft and

Face to face contacts, cultivating personal relationships, and providing services are among lobbyists' most potent weapons.

redraft it several times, collect data, find cosponsors, identify potential allies and foes, attend committee hearings, and watch over its fate on the chamber floor. At the same time, it is necessary to deal with hundreds of constituents whose problems range from lost Social Security checks to requests for autographed pictures. And since many of the world's most vexing issues come before the House and Senate, a member of Congress needs to spend hours studying and debating complex and abstract legislation. On top of this, most legislators have to devote endless days seeking reelection.

The need for assistance provides an opening for the lobbyist. Indeed, many Congress watchers think that the provision of services is by far the most effective form of influence.

Does a senator require a speech by tomorrow afternoon? A good lobbyist is more than willing to write it. Is a representative being pestered for reasons why a revision of the tax code should not pass? A concerned lobbyist will supply 10 or 12. Is a committee chair having trouble lining up support for a pending bill? Lobbyists can make a few phone calls. Would a trip back home to pacify constituents help a member facing a tough reelection fight? A lobbyist will try to find a corporate jet.

Doing favors can be a powerful tool in the hands of a skilled lobbyist precisely because it brings advantages to both sides. Besides helping public officials get their work done quickly and smoothly, the information and services lobbyists provide help raise issues that might not otherwise be addressed. Most of the time, moreover, no improprieties occur and the activities are entirely legitimate.

Of course, when private parties become too closely bound to lawmakers, conflicts of interest can arise. Entertaining, for example, is a standard tool of the lobbying trade. Large interest groups routinely buy season tickets to Washington Redskins football games, host sumptuous dinners in four-star restaurants, charter yachts for excursions up and down the Potomac, or sponsor other gatherings where public officials and private individuals can meet informally. Any pressure exerted is subtle. The lobbyist wants to make an impression, cultivate a friendship, create an atmosphere, or win a sympathetic ear, not bludgeon a guest into submission. As one lobbyist points out: "You don't talk shop at social events . . . you'd be a social boor if you sat there and talked business." Instead, she explains, the goal is to build rapport ". . . so I can talk freely when it's time to discuss business" later.[21] Another said "I don't think it's good to lobby . . . on the golf course. On the 19th hole you can go in and visit and discuss your issue."[22]

How many IOUs these affairs generate is an open question since the provision of services or favors can go pretty far. All-expenses-paid trips, for example, frequently straddle, if not cross, the line of propriety. Early in 1989 the Tobacco Institute, an association sponsored by cigarette manufacturers and tobacco growers, invited 27 members of Congress to spend up to four days at a posh resort in Palm Springs, California.[23] The legislators, most of whom traveled with their spouses and children, attended a few panel discussions but had plenty of free time for golfing, swimming, tennis, and dining in the resort's elegant restaurants. The club was not inexpensive—a suite cost up to $300 a night, meals averaged $25 an entree, and greens fees on the golf course exceeded $40. But these expenses did not come out of the lawmakers' pockets. The Tobacco Institute picked up the tab, plus airfare, and gave most guests another $1000 to $2000 in honorariums or speaking fees.

Was the Tobacco Institute simply being civicminded, or was it getting something in return for its generosity? The way Congress operates makes it impossible to tell; representatives vote for and against bills for many reasons. Nevertheless, at the time, Congress had before it several proposals, including higher cigarette taxes and broader bans on advertising, that would adversely affect the tobacco industry. The Tobacco Institute probably felt it would not hurt to have a few friends on Capitol Hill.

FRIENDSHIP AND ACCESS The old saying, "It's not *what* you know, but *who* you know that counts," contains more than a grain of truth, especially in Washington where lobbyists are judged by the number of influential people they know personally. In the political arena, making friends, winning trust and respect, and gaining the attention of insiders are essential for success.

Perhaps the unofficial champion of these skills is Charls Walker, the tax and business lobbyist introduced at the beginning of the chapter. What are the keys to Walker's success? Golf, drinks, barbecues, 45-minute phone conversations—all

Former Senator John Tower's nomination as George Bush's secretary of defense demonstrates the problem of the revolving door. After leaving the Senate, Tower received lucrative consulting fees from several defense contractors. Later, when Bush asked him to head the defense department, the Senate refused to approve the appointment partly on the grounds that his financial dealings with military industries would compromise his ability to administer the Pentagon impartially.

with members of the Washington establishment. Charls Walker and those like him use their access and friendships at least as much as their substantive knowledge of the budget and taxation to make their points.

Having connections is valuable in its own right—policymakers lend a sympathetic ear— but it is also important because it lets the lobbyist build alliances. Since power is scattered throughout so many institutions, no one working alone can hope to accomplish much. Form a coalition, however, and mountains can be moved.

A reputation as an effective insider, in addition, feeds on itself. As the network of contacts grows, so too does the lobbyist's *credibility*. Credibility is essential because to be influential one has to be perceived as influential. Groups are anxious to hire individuals they believe can lead them to the inner circles of power.

THE REVOLVING DOOR Walker's career illustrates another phenomenon: the hiring of former public officials by private firms to represent the

A Closer Look

Michael Deaver Goes Through the Revolving Door ★ ★ ★

For 20 years Michael K. Deaver had been one of Ronald Reagan's closest and most trusted confidants. He helped Reagan win the California governorship in 1966 and the presidency in 1980. But more than a political ally and adviser, Deaver was also a longtime family friend. The president rewarded this loyalty by naming him deputy chief of staff in the White House. If anyone had Reagan's ear, it was surely Michael Deaver.

When Deaver resigned his White House post in 1985 to establish a public relations and lobbying firm, he quickly signed up dozens of major corporate clients (such as Rockwell International, CBS, and Philip Morris) and several foreign governments, including Saudi Arabia, South Korea, Mexico, and Canada. Since these companies and governments, all having business with the U.S. government, wanted to be represented by someone with clout, many observers attributed Deaver's

rapid success to his close personal relationship with the president. Long after his resignation, for example, he kept his White House pass and received the President's confidential daily schedule.[a] A fellow lobbyist described Deaver's main attraction: "Access to the president when they want it; that's his only product."[b] Deaver himself once boasted, "There's no question, I've got as good access as anybody in town."[c] Because he could reach the highest levels of the executive branch, his clients viewed him as the perfect person to represent them.

Deaver's practice flourished for a while—*Time* magazine featured him on its cover—but his activities eventually ran afoul of the spirit and letter of the law. Federal statutes prohibit ex-government employees from lobbying their former agencies for one year. These rules also bar current officeholders from participating in decisions affecting outside parties while at the

company before their former government colleagues. Prior to starting his own consulting company, Walker served as deputy secretary of the treasury in President Nixon's administration. Consequently, his clients are presumably eager not only for Walker's knowledge of government and economics but his associations with his former fellow workers. This well-known practice has its own name, the **revolving door**. It seems to be a natural and sensible method for getting interests represented. A Closer Look, however, shows that it occasionally leads to trouble.

Monitoring the revolving door takes Solomon-like wisdom, since the line between objective service and conflict of interest is difficult to draw. Consider the story of John Tower, former senator from Texas and President George Bush's first nominee for secretary of defense. After Tower retired from the Senate in 1985, military contractors, eager to exploit his years of experience on defense appropriations committees and his numerous contacts in the Pentagon and on Capitol Hill, offered him enormous consulting fees: $120,000 from Rockwell International (builders of the B-1 bomber), $265,000 from Brit-

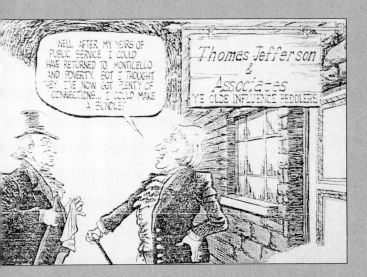

NELL AFTER MY YEARS OF
PUBLIC SERVICE, I COULD
HAVE RETURNED TO MONTICELLO
AND POVERTY, BUT I THOUGHT
HEY I'VE NOW GOT PLENTY OF
CONNECTIONS... I COULD MAKE
A BUNDLE!

Thomas Jefferson
&
Associates
YE OLDE INFLUENCE PEDDLERS

same time discussing prospective employment with these organizations. Deaver apparently violated both regulations. While still in the White House, he helped prepare a U.S.-Canadian meeting on acid rain; then as soon as he entered private practice, he lobbied the President and his staff on this matter at the request of the Canadian government. Furthermore, his company hired ex-employees of the Office of the United States Trade Representative to plead the cases of foreign businesses before their former agency.[d] A federal court ultimately convicted him for lying under oath about these lobbying activities.

Despite Deaver's misfortunes, the practice of leaving government to work for corporations or foreign governments continues to be a main lobbying technique.

[a]*Washington Post National Weekly Edition*, May 12, 1986, p. 8.
[b]Quoted in *National Journal*, May 3, 1986, p. 1052.
[c]Elizabeth Drew, "Letter from Washington," *New Yorker*, May 26, 1986, p. 93.
[d]Ibid., pp. 94–95.

ish Aerospace, $116,000 from Martin Marietta, $70,000 from Textron, and $247,000 from LTV.[24] The problem, however, was that despite being so well paid, he apparently spent little time actually doing anything for these firms. When Bush picked him to be defense secretary, reporters and certain members of Congress wondered if he could really be impartial on military procurement matters. After all, he would be judging contracts proposed by the very companies that had been so generous to him. Partly for these reasons, the Senate refused to confirm his appointment.* Yet Tower, Bush, and others were dismayed by what they considered the unfairness of this decision because, in fact, he had done nothing illegal.

Fund-Raising: PACs

Interest groups influence government in ways other than direct lobbying. For one thing they have become adept campaign fund-raisers—so much so that distributing money to candidates

_____
*Tower's nomination was also rejected because of alleged personal indiscretions.

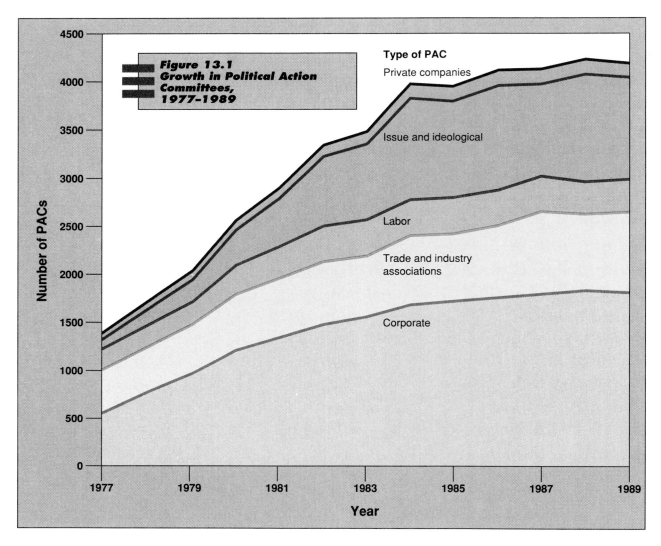

**Figure 13.1
Growth in Political Action
Committees,
1977–1989**

Type of PAC

Private companies

Issue and ideological

Labor

Trade and industry
associations

Corporate

Number of PACs

Year

1977   1979   1981   1983   1985   1987   1989

*The number of political action committees of all types has grown since 1977, but those
based on issues of ideological concerns have grown especially rapidly.*

Source: Federal Election Commission, Press release, July 28, 1989.

and parties is now perhaps their principal method for advancing their causes.

The vehicle for raising and dispensing the cash, as we saw earlier, is the political action committee, a body that solicits money from its members for a campaign fund, which it then shares with candidates who are sympathetic to its interests or whose friendship is worth having. As noted in Chapter 11, campaign finance re-forms enacted in the early 1970s have given an enormous boost to the formation of PACs. They have grown from about 600 in 1974 to more than 4000 today (see Figure 13.1). Virtually every private interest in America is represented.

Money can be donated directly—the limit is $5000 per candidate per election—or spent in-dependently in unlimited amounts on a candi-date's behalf. The $5000 limit presumably keeps

PACs in check, although there are ways around this rule, as when a group provides a candidate with poll results at a greatly discounted rate. By making contributions to different candidates in different elections, various segments of society can raise and spend millions of dollars to influence elections.

Although most PACs (about 80 percent) are connected with a parent organization, quite a few are unaffiliated with any sponsoring group. The best known of this type are ideological PACs, such as the National Conservative Political Action Committee (NCPAC), which supports conservatives.

A third type, the personal political action committee, is founded by an individual who, in most instances, has aspirations for higher office. Former Representative Jack Kemp, a contender for the 1988 Republican presidential nomination, created Kemp Associates. For $5000, a contributor could meet with Representative Kemp in "small informal dinners" and "come to know on a first-name basis the top politicians" in Washington.[25] Kemp Associates, like similar personal PACs, passed the contributions on to other candidates in hopes of building a coalition that would support his political aspirations.

PACs are changing the political landscape, perhaps permanently and, many believe, for the worse. One reason is that elected officials are increasingly becoming beholden to interest groups for campaign support. This makes them dependent on a myriad of organizations and causes rather than a central body like a political party that a president can lead. The loyalty of members of Congress, in other words, is more fragmented these days than in the past.

The purpose of PAC spending is, obviously, to influence legislation by determining the people who will make it. These groups follow various strategies in deciding who receives their largesse. Many give pragmatically: They endorse well-entrenched incumbents of whatever party in order to protect their vested interests; they do not seek to change the direction of public policy as a whole. For similar reasons, businesses, however conservative, frequently support liberals; they need friends wherever they can find them.[26] A related tactic is to reward senators and rep-

resentatives who have stood with the group in the past—"thank you money" it is called.

Still another ploy is to give to both sides. Fred Wertheimer, president of Common Cause, a public interest group, said PACs "contribute to both candidates because they want their investment to be a sure thing . . . [they] want to be assured of access in January no matter which candidate wins in November."[27]

Ideological groups, on the other hand, apply a political litmus test. They only back candidates who share their ideology and purposes. This approach induces them to gamble, as when they support an acceptable long-shot challenger against an entrenched but repugnant incumbent. In the same spirit, labor leaders (although not always the rank-and-file members) often endorse Democratic candidates in the belief that Democrats sympathize with workers more than Republicans.

In any event, interest groups acting through PACs are having a growing impact on elections and public decision making. Whether this development is good or not is widely debated. But, before deciding, we should look at another form of interest group activity: their direct participation in the making and implementing of the laws and regulations that govern us all.

Interest Groups and Shared Government

Most citizens believe that only the legislative, executive, and judicial branches of government make and enforce the nation's laws. Yet reality turns out to be more complicated. Another branch, one only dimly perceived by most Americans, shares authority with the constitutionally established institutions. It consists of private groups taking on public duties and functions, and it provides interest groups with additional means for influencing policy.

In the past 30 to 40 years, as the federal government's responsibilities have grown by leaps and bounds, it has come to rely more and more on nongovernmental people and organizations to help develop and administer its programs.[28] Economists and political scientists call the reliance on outside parties—banks, corporations, unions, hospitals, nonprofit foundations, and trade associations, to name just a few—*privatization*.[29] Perhaps a more descriptive term is **shared government** because these outsiders, in effect, act as partners with public officials in creating, administering, and enforcing policy. Since this arrangement saves the taxpayers money and provides services more efficiently, presidents and Congress have over the last several decades delegated enormous responsibilities to private groups, thereby creating what amounts to another layer of government. Its powers and duties are every bit as real as those wielded by traditional authorities.

Private participation in policymaking and administration seems to be the price that has to be paid for many new public programs. Different interests in society are not always strong enough to deny an idea whose time has come, but they frequently have the strength to obtain a piece of the action. If chemical manufacturers cannot stave off demands for clean air and water, their lobbyists can at least help write environmental protection codes; if the medical profession cannot prevent the coming of public health insurance, its representatives can ensure that the payments go to private physicians and dentists; if contractors cannot block public housing, they can at least construct the dwellings themselves.

Shared government takes several forms: legislation, administration, and enforcement.

LEGISLATION   In 1985, representatives of the maritime shipping industry (the International Longshoremen's Association, the Joint Maritime Congress, and the Council of American Flag Ship Operators, among others) met with agricultural organizations (including the Cotton Council, the Millers' Federation, and the Association of Wheat Growers) to discuss rules governing the shipment of grain to overseas markets. Ship owners and sailors wanted produce carried in American vessels, while farmers demanded that it be hauled as cheaply as possible. They got together to try to work out a compromise.

There was nothing extraordinary about their meetings except that (1) they met five times in a room adjoining Senate Majority Leader Robert Dole's offices; (2) John Gordon, Dole's assistant,

presided over the sessions; (3) their purpose was to draft legislation that neutral observers felt could end up costing the American people millions of dollars in subsidies; and (4) once they reached agreement on a bill, it was sent to Congress for approval.[30] In an inversion of the textbook account of how laws are passed, the shippers and growers sent a bill to Congress for action rather than Congress proposing legislation that interested parties could comment on.

Citing another example, the *Washington Post* flatly asserts:

> The Carlton Group [a coalition of lobbyists representing the U.S. Chamber of Commerce, the National Association of Manufacturers, the National Association of Wholesale Distributors, and several large corporations] wrote the initial version of the business provisions of the tax cuts enacted in the first year of the Reagan administration, provisions that were extremely lucrative for the group's members. . . .[31]

". . . wrote the initial version. . . ." Once again the popular image of Congress is turned on its head. Private parties acting as legislators propose a bill that eventually becomes law and sometimes profits them handsomely.

No one claims that Congress bends to the whims of outside groups. It can and almost always does write the final legislation to its own liking. But because of its work load, time constraints, and the complexities of the problems, it relies heavily on private groups to take the initiative in drafting and refining legislation. These groups try, of course, to fashion the bills to suit their requirements. Still, for the most part everyone—senators, representatives, their staffs, and certainly the groups themselves—see this delegation of responsibility as entirely sensible and just. Whether it is remains to be seen.

ADMINISTRATION   Power sharing plays a similar role in the administration of economic and social policy. Both Congress and the president realize that the public bureaucracy cannot oversee every detail of all of the thousands of programs that have been put on the books since World War II. They entrust authority and discretion to private operators who grant loans for college tuition, retrain displaced workers, build public housing, counsel pregnant teenagers, distribute surplus cheese to the poor, refurbish historic landmarks, irrigate arid plains, and perform countless other tasks.[32] Recent proposals have envisioned turning the National Institutes of Health, federal prisons, urban subways and buses, air traffic control, national parks, and public schools over to nongovernmental parties. In all these instances, the Treasury would foot the bill while private agencies did the actual work.

ENFORCEMENT In a few areas, public power has always been in private hands. State bar associations and medical societies have the authority to license practitioners; their rulings carry the weight of law. More recently, however, other areas of administration have fallen into the private arena. Law enforcement and the protection of public safety and health have become joint enterprises between traditional political institutions and private organizations.

A good case study of this phenomenon is nuclear energy. Although atomic power plants are owned and operated by private utility companies, their regulation—presumably to safeguard the general welfare—is the responsibility of the Nuclear Regulatory Commission, formerly the Atomic Energy Commission (AEC). Its very name implies that it oversees the nuclear industry, making certain that reactors operate safely. The vision conjured up by the word *regulatory* is one of two adversaries—the industry versus the government—constantly at each other's throats.

In view of this widely held and reassuring image, it is surprising how closely the two sides work together. Far from being enemies, they better resemble partners who have for years fought side by side to encourage the development of nuclear energy. Daniel Ford, in *The Cult of the Atom*, documents instance after instance in which the industry (utility companies, uranium suppliers, reactor manufacturers) played a major role in writing the rules and regulations that supposedly guided their behavior.

One of the AEC's most famous reports, the "Reactor Safety Study," written in the early 1970s in response to the growing concerns of independent scientists and environmentalists

Are nuclear power plants safe? In the past the government relied heavily on the manufacturers and operators of nuclear reactors to help answer the question. Although these businesses had useful information and expertise, their participation in assessing safety raised questions about potential conflicts of interest.

about nuclear power, illustrates the cooperative rather than antagonistic nature of the relationship between the regulator and the regulated. The report's principal author was Dr. Norman C. Rasmussen, who was not an AEC employee but a professor at MIT and a former consultant to the nuclear industry. Early in the project, when safety criteria were being developed, Dr. Rasmussen and his codirector thought that the study "must have reasonable acceptance by the people in the industry."[33] In other words, the commission's findings, whatever they might be, should not be too displeasing to the plant builders and operators.

Then, as the project progressed and the complexity of the safety issues became apparent, the research team increasingly turned to the industry, not the government or independent sources, for technical assistance. Ford reports:

The [nuclear] industry did more than supply raw data for the Reactor Safety Study. The role of industry expanded to the point where it assumed a major responsibility for some of the actual analysis . . . published in [the] final report.[34]

By one standard, such participation makes a great deal of sense. After all, the industry not only has to live with the rules, but it also has the experts, data, and experience necessary for intelligent decision making. On the other hand, intimate cooperation like this can lead to serious conflicts of interest. Suppose a reactor's reliability is being disputed. Isn't there a likelihood that the industry will consider it safe instead of erring on the side of public health and welfare?

In any event, direct participation in government is a basic tool that private interests use, because they have found that the power to help write, administer, and enforce laws is certainly as effective as letter-writing campaigns or taking senators to football games.

Checkpoint

- Lobbying, the attempt to influence the making of public policy, takes various forms: mobilizing opinion and the media, providing lawmakers with information and services, and using access and friendship to persuade decision makers.

- The revolving door is the practice of hiring ex-government officials to represent a group before their former employers.

- Political action committees (PACs) raise and dispense campaign funds. Most, but not all, are sponsored by industries, professional associations, unions, or other organizations with common concerns.

- Interest groups also influence public policy through shared government: private parties helping to draft legislation, administer programs, and enforce regulations.

INTEREST GROUP POLITICS: WHO WINS AND LOSES?

An astonishingly large number of political battles in this country are not waged between Democrats and Republicans but among interest groups. Is this kind of politics healthy? Would it be better to organize disputes along clear-cut party lines in order to give voters a straightforward choice, a choice that would allow them to hold one of the parties accountable for the success or failure of a program like tax reform? Or do interest groups, supposedly being closer to the hearts and minds of Americans, have advantages that outweigh the benefits of party government? There are good arguments on both sides of the question.

The Advantages of Interest Group Politics

Observers from Tocqueville's day to the present have praised interest group politics. In their minds, it demonstrates the genius of the Constitution. By encouraging citizens to organize for the "redress of grievances," the founders created a self-regulating machine. As one part of society grows in strength, others rise to challenge it. Competing "factions," to use Madison's term, constantly check and balance one another, thereby ensuring liberty.

The key to this argument is the opportunity that interest groups provide their members to make their voices heard. If government were dominated by a disciplined or strong party system and if, in addition, one party represented a majority of voters, how could the minority make its case? How would injustices be corrected?

The civil rights movement provides a clear illustration. Beginning with the National Association for the Advancement of Colored People (NAACP) and subsequent organizations such as the Southern Christian Leadership Conference (SCLC)—once led by Martin Luther King, Jr.— the Congress of Racial Equality (CORE), and the Student Nonviolent Coordinating Committee (SNCC), blacks in the 1950s and 1960s mounted a concerted challenge to racial segregation.

EQUAL HOUSING OPPORTUNITY

All real estate advertised herein is subject to the Federal Fair Housing Act of 1968 which makes it illegal to indicate any "preference, limitation, or discrimination based on race, color, religion, sex, handicap, familial status, or national origin or an intention to make any such preference, limitation, or discrimination."

We will not knowingly accept any advertising for real estate which is in violation of the law. All persons are hereby informed that all dwellings advertised are available on an equal opportunity basis.

Many observers give credit to interest group politics for helping to outlaw segregation in employment, housing, and education.

They, of course, used direct action—protest demonstrations, sit-ins, prayer vigils, and the like (see Chapter 10). But they also relied on classic lobbying techniques. Since the Congress and state governments did not initially respond to their demands, civil rights advocates turned to the courts. Lawyers, along with marchers, fought most of the initial integration battles. In the years after World War II, for example, the NAACP, backed by allies such as the American Jewish Congress, the American Federation of Labor, and the Congregational Christian Church, waged a protracted and ultimately successful struggle in federal and state courts to outlaw "restrictive covenants," or agreements prohibiting the sale of property to nonwhites.[35] (They were opposed, it might be added, by white interest groups, mainly neighborhood property associations.)

Race relations in America remain a divisive political and social issue, and pernicious inequalities continue. But despite these shortcomings, the racial situation in the United States differs greatly from what it was just 25 years ago when rest rooms were segregated according to race as well as sex and few blacks ever appeared on prime-time television, not even to sell laundry detergent.

What caused the changes? New laws and attitudes. What produced these? In large measure they were brought about by blacks themselves organizing and pressuring the system. It seems doubtful that Congress or one of the parties would have acted without prodding by civil rights activists.

Interest group politics, its advocates claim, helps many similar social groups. Only a decade ago, for example, homosexuals faced social and economic ostracism, economic sanctions, and physical harm. Today, even though this intolerance remains, they have nonetheless publicly organized to fight for their rights. And they have done so in the most American way: through interest group tactics. There is even a gay PAC, The Human Rights Campaign Fund.[36]

The main advantage of the reliance on interest groups, then, is the opportunities for the redress of grievances they provide to various parts of society, ranging from corporate giants to college teachers. An opportunity, of course, is not a guarantee, and seldom does anyone win all that he or she desires. Still, from the viewpoint of the nation as a whole, these interminable fights between factions lead to stability, to peaceful change, to the protection of individual rights, to a balance of power, and to democracy.

For the most part, the defenders of the system add, interest groups operate aboveboard. You can always find a few rotten apples in the barrel, and the millions of dollars pouring into PAC coffers make even the most hardened politicians uncomfortable. But the abuses seem mild compared to the benefits, especially since lawmakers are adept at playing groups off against one another.

There is, for example, little evidence that legislators are routinely bought outright. Senator Robert Packwood, who played a large role in the passage of the 1986 tax reform bill, had little trouble raising money for reelection, even from individuals who opposed many of the changes he was proposing. In the summer of 1985 he collected $500,000 at a dinner attended by business leaders and lawyers with specific concerns in the tax code. Yet David Broder of the *Washington Post* reports that "what they heard, one [guest] said bitterly, was a 'sermon on leadership'—a speech a Packwood aide laughingly said '200 Oregon high schools have gotten for free.' "[37] Thus, however much the attendees hoped to sway the senator, they must have been sorely disappointed.

A systematic study of PACs concluded that: "Because they scatter their contributions in small, even 'token gifts,' most corporate political action committees seem less like awful political plotters than a 'political United Way.'. . ."[38]

Interest groups, finally, are helpful to government in other ways. They help share the burden of writing, administering, and enforcing laws. This assistance, their advocates claim, leads to efficiency, flexibility, and adaptability—all of which benefit taxpayers. These organizations also convey information to decision makers. Acting as the political system's antennas, groups can tell where trouble is brewing, whose problems have to be addressed, which policies are likely to work, and what institutions or practices have to be altered. They are, in short, feelers that allow government to respond to its constantly changing environment.

To the advocates of interest group politics, through the existence of thousands of formal organizations making demands on government and attempting to influence public policy creates pluralistic democracy. Pluralism, recall from Chapter 1, does not mean that everyone has an equal voice or that the majority preference always prevails on each issue. It means, instead, that leaders and institutions are held in check and that most people have an opportunity to affect policymaking through participation in group activities.[*]

The critics, on the other hand, are not so optimistic.

The Disadvantages of Interest Group Politics

The freedom to form and join groups is an integral component of America's heritage of civil lib-

---

[*]Believers in pluralism readily acknowledge its many flaws. Some, in fact, wish it could be improved to make it more democratic. See, as one example, Robert A. Dahl, *Dilemmas of Pluralist Democracy* (New Haven, Conn.: Yale University Press, 1982), chap. 3.

erties, which no one disputes. On the other hand, the advancement of private interests in the public arena by lobbying, fund-raising, organized persuasion, and the other techniques can, if it goes unchecked, conflict with the basic tenets of democratic government: popular sovereignty, political equality, and majority rule. What disturbs many students of politics is that the recent explosion of special interests has reached the point where it now threatens to undermine these values.

Critics cite several drawbacks to America's heavy reliance on interest groups for representation and policymaking: the abuse of power and money, the underrepresentation of some segments of society, potential conflicts of interest, leadership inequities, the elevation of group over national interests, and the adverse effects on parties.

ABUSE OF POWER   Given the way decisions are made in Washington and state capitals, it is almost impossible to know where acceptable lobbying stops and exerting unfair pressure begins. To an extent it is a matter of judgment. Here is one case to think about.

Like most states, Delaware wants to attract as much business as it can. So, in 1981, it passed a comprehensive bank reform act aimed at encouraging out-of-state banks to relocate within its borders. Among its other features, the bill granted banks wide discretion over credit card operations—including the authority to charge virtually unlimited interest rates and to make variable and even retroactive finance charges—and gave banks that moved to the state generous tax breaks. Based on the building boom that followed, the legislation appears to have been successful: Wilmington, Delaware's largest city, has a new skyline dominated by 20- and 30-story office towers and hotels, and the state's tax coffers have swelled by millions of dollars.

But a law should be judged by more than its results. Motivated by the question, Who governs? one wants to know *how* legislation is framed and passed and who is involved in the process. A report in the *New York Times* notes these facts:

- The man who shepherded the bill through its drafting and legislative phases was apparently working as a consultant for the state at the same time as he served as a lobbyist for Chase Manhattan, one of the main movers behind the bank proposal.

- The law was mainly "drafted in private" by lawyers from two banks, Chase Manhattan and J. P. Morgan. When asked why it was drafted privately and not by state senators, representatives, and concerned public officials, Glenn C. Kenton, Delaware's secretary of state, replied that he and Governor Pierre S. DuPont "shared the 'bias' that banks should charge what they want in fees" and "I didn't see any sense in running that fundamental principle by anybody who doesn't agree with it."

- The bill's authors worked "without any written analysis by any Delaware official . . . ," the public, and the press. In addition, several interested state officers, such as the head of the Division of Consumer Affairs, who would have to deal with many of its provisions, were "intentionally kept in the dark, according to bankers and [other] state officials."

- Although the legislation's supporters claim it had an adequate hearing, it was debated for only three hours and "many legislators say they did not read the 61-page bill before agreeing to sponsor it and did not understand the complicated measure before voting on it."

- Irving Shapiro, at the time chairman of the DuPont Company, Delaware's largest employer, and a "prime catalyst" in the negotiations with the banks, conceded that "the people who had an interest were involved" but added "you couldn't afford to scare the banks away."[39]

This experience and others like it raise a number of questions about interest groups, questions that go to the heart of public participation in a democracy. Whether Delaware's bank reform law was a good or bad law is not the issue. The point is power: Who has it and who should have it. Critics of interest group politics say it is one thing for bankers to plead their case, to suggest improvements in existing laws or propose new ones, or to argue that unless changes are made they will move elsewhere.

It is quite another matter, however, for them to use their financial resources, their accountants and lawyers, their connections to giant corporations, their prestige, and their threats to relocate in order to draft legislation to their own specifications—practically down to the last semicolon and period—and then to have it passed with a minimum of discussion and debate. Think of the power and audacity, the critics say, of a public official who believes that "a fundamental principle" does not have to be run by "anybody who doesn't agree with it." What happens to popular sovereignty and majority rule when the wishes of an industry loom so large in the legislative process that "you couldn't afford to scare" it away?

This example suggests to skeptics, especially in the power elite camp, that the fault of interest group politics is its tendency to lead to improper and inequitable representation; the best idea does not win, the one backed with the most resources does.

MONEY AND POLITICS The potential for damage is especially grave these days because interest groups have become so proficient at raising money. True, most students of government, even the most skeptical, doubt that much money passes under the table. In fact, several prominent political scientists do not think that PAC spending determines how representatives vote; there are simply too many other pressures at work—constituency demands, presidential leadership, ideology, and partisanship.[40]

Nevertheless, campaign donations do create a feeling of indebtedness, as one representative notes: "Anytime someone, whether a person or a PAC, gives you a large sum of money, you can't help but feel the need to give them the extra attention, whether it is access to your time or, subconsciously, the obligation to vote with them."[41] Justine Dart, chairman of Dart Industries, expressed the same sentiment more bluntly: "Talking with politicians is a fine thing, but with a little money they hear you better."[42]

The problem, then, is not bribery but the subtle psychological climate of indebtedness created by interest groups and others spending huge sums for political purposes. This dependency has become so pervasive that many students of

The relentless pursuit of PAC funds: Like Robert Clements (on the left), a candidate for the House of Representatives, many politicians devote enormous time and effort to soliciting PAC contributions. This poses a troubling situation for both candidates and neutral observers, who fear the recipients of the donations will be in an awkward position when the groups later ask for assistance.

government worry about the potential negative consequences.

OVER- AND UNDERREPRESENTATION   One of the presumed advantages of interest group politics is that everyone can participate. And, indeed, as seen earlier, more and more segments of society are becoming organized, sending representatives to Washington and the state capitals, and attempting to shape policy to their advantage. So many individuals and groups play the game that the political arena scarcely seems able to hold them all. Still, the players come in drastically different sizes and weights, and given these differences it seems doubtful that they really compete equally.

In a nutshell the problem is this: Many parts of society, particularly those based in manufacturing, finance, and agriculture, are highly organized and disciplined; they can amass numerous political resources; and they can stay on the scene year after year. Other interests, such as the homeless or impoverished children, are either not organized at all or are so underfunded and poorly staffed that they cannot match their opponents.

The point that the critics of interest politics make about the huge disparities in the size, resources, and cohesiveness of groups is that in American politics, if group competition decides policy, the weaker side—even if it speaks for a majority interest, or however just its cause—will consistently lose. Kay Lehman Schlozman succinctly summarizes the point: "The evidence here indicates that the pressure system is biased not only against groups representing broad publics but also against groups representing those with few resources."[43]

GROUP VERSUS NATIONAL INTERESTS   A more serious concern is the tendency to elevate group needs over national priorities. In an ideal democracy, an issue—tax reform, say—would prompt a prolonged debate about various alternatives that would be accepted or rejected by majority vote. During these discussions, the interests of specific individuals and associations would naturally be heard, but the guiding principle would still be the general good. After all, can a system be democratic if it consistently gives minorities what they want, leaving the majority out in the cold?

This situation is exactly what detractors of interest group politics assert happens: Group needs take precedence over the general welfare. The "few," because they are well organized and strong, win; the "many," because they are disorganized and weak, lose. What is good for a specific interest prevails over what is good for the nation as a whole.

Several years ago, the Anthracite Industry Association, a coalition of 40 to 45 anthracite coal producers, worked with a strategically placed Pennsylvania congressman to persuade Congress to require the Defense Department to purchase American coal for its bases in Europe. Since the coal could be obtained more cheaply in the host countries, this requirement effectively cost the military an extra $15 million a year, money that could have been used for uniforms or ammunition.[44] The main beneficiaries of the provision were obviously the anthracite mines which, because domestic manufacturers and utilities burned the more abundant and less expensive bituminous coal, had few buyers for their product.

The $15 million does not look like very much when measured against the hundreds of billions of dollars the Pentagon annually spends. But $15 million here, $15 million there begins to add up to an enormous sum that taxpayers have to bear. Since so many groups win these sorts of concessions, the cost of government soars. As one Defense official explained of the anthracite requirement, "It's a marked cost to the department and to the taxpayers. . . . We could do this cheaper . . . but we have to live with the political realities."[45]

THE PROBLEM OF REPRESENTATION Not only are interest groups selfish, their critics add, but they frequently misrepresent their members, if they have any members to begin with. The leadership of large formal organizations tends to become self-perpetuating, to lose touch with the rank and file, and to speak for no one but itself. A nineteenth-century European sociologist, Robert Michels, referred to this tendency as the **iron law of oligarchy**.[46] Although he analyzed mainly political parties, oligarchy, which means "government by the few," characterizes many associations. It has been claimed, for example, that certain labor unions are dominated by bosses who care more about their own prestige and "perks" than the needs of their fellow workers. Furthermore, by manipulating information and election procedures, they perpetuate themselves in office indefinitely. The problem is not confined to unions. A former official of the American Association of Retired Persons (AARP) complained that the organization "doesn't have any democratic process to determine members' views. . . . There's no bottom-up process for members to . . . set policies."[47]

It is also true that some groups consist only of leaders. One survey of public interest groups discovered that as many as 30 percent had no members at all.[48] Thus, when a consumer advocate claims to speak on behalf of the buying public, that person should perhaps be interpreted as speaking for what he or she *thinks* is the public's interest, not what the public has actually said through its elected representatives.

If the critics are correct, if groups are so dominated by their organizers that broad constituencies are either misrepresented or ignored, then interest group politics is seriously defective. It is defended, after all, as a means by which people can air their grievances and influence policy. Should this not be the case, much of their justification is gone.[49]

The critics, however, may overstate the matter. To be viable, organizations sooner or later have to pay attention to their followers. A study of five major PACs, for instance, discovered that all depended heavily on the opinions of local branches when deciding whom to support in elections, even when the national leadership had serious reservations about these choices.[50]

SHARED GOVERNMENT AND CONFLICTS OF INTEREST As we saw earlier, shared government—the delegation of public functions and authority to private organizations—has certain advantages. Still, the benefits have to be weighed against the costs.

For one thing, handing power over to private groups places an enormous responsibility on them. Certainly the nuclear power industry's participation in the preparation of the AEC re-

A Closer Look

Monsanto and the EPA: Problems of Shared Government ★ ★ ★

An episode involving the Environmental Protection Agency (EPA) demonstrates the practical and ethical issues raised by shared government. Congress entrusts the EPA with the responsibility of protecting the nation's environment. In order to do its job, the agency has to keep track of thousands of potentially hazardous chemicals. Knowing which compounds are a menace and which are safe is an arduous task requiring a great deal of expertise. Naturally the EPA looks to outsiders for aid.

In 1975, therefore, it awarded a $4 million contract to Monsanto Research Corporation, a subsidiary of the giant chemical manufacturer, the Monsanto Company.[a] Among other things, Monsanto agreed to study the environmental risks of producing and distributing acrylonitrile, a substance widely used in the production of synthetic rubber, plastic, and textiles. After a year's work, Monsanto's researchers, who it should be noted shuttled back and forth from the parent company to the subsidiary, finished their preliminary assessment. Several things stand out about this report.

For one, although certain conclusions were based on data collected from specific plants scattered around the country, the exact information was never included in the draft; instead it was destroyed at the insistence of the Monsanto Company, which claimed to be worried about its proprietary trade secrets. In any event, EPA staff members had no means of *independently* verifying the findings. For another thing, the draft report was first sent, not to the EPA, but to Monsanto's corporate headquarters, where it was reviewed by company lawyers and technicians. It did not reach the EPA until 16 months later. Finally, the report concluded that acrylonitrile production did not threaten public health and did not war-

port on reactor safety raised questions about possible conflicts of interest. As A Closer Look argues, sharing power with public authorities commonly puts its participants in the difficult position of separating self-interest from the general welfare. Even given the best intentions, it is not always easy to do and opens the door to doubt and mistrust.[51]

INTEREST GROUPS AND POLITICAL PARTIES

Numerous social scientists, journalists, and politicians maintain that interest groups weaken political parties. This fact may not trouble most Americans who are suspicious of party politics anyway. But before making a final judgment, briefly consider the advantages of strong parties as opposed to strong groups.

Ideally, political parties, which seek to run the government as a whole, would offer the people broad choices in the content and implementation of public policies. In so doing they would provide the electorate with an effective means to express its will and to hold public servants accountable for their actions. On the other hand, interest groups by definition only serve the narrow, immediate needs of their followers.

rant government regulation. This judgment, supported by an EPA review of the Monsanto Research study, was announced in September 1977 in a document titled "Source Assessment: Acrylonitrile Manufacture (Air Emissions)." Bearing the seal of the EPA, the cover did not mention Monsanto when, in fact, "This official government report was actually the study written by Monsanto Research Corp."[b]

To summarize, Monsanto Research, not the EPA or any other impartial body, studied the chemical and wrote the report that became the basis of federal policy, a policy that affected citizens across the land. Furthermore, the research division withheld data on emissions in various plants and gave the seal of approval to a product that earned $110 million for its parent company in 1975.[c]

To neutral observers, including even administrators in the EPA itself, the assessment was at best self-serving and at worst a positive threat to the nation's health. The Food and Drug Administration, for example, had outlawed the inclusion of acrylonitrile in soft-drink bottles because it had been found to be carcinogenic (cancer-causing) and was leaching into the drinks. And two years later, an EPA regulator asserted "Quite frankly . . . I don't see how they reached that conclusion. . . . It was not reasonable based on the data we have. . . . Our conclusion is that acrylonitrile is one of the biggest sources of hydrocarbons in the chemical industry. It's a major polluter."[d]

[a]*Washington Post National Weekly Edition*, June 22, 1980, p. 15.
[b]Ibid.
[c]Ibid.
[d]Ibid.

Can these two types of organizations coexist? Yes, but generally speaking, to the extent that parties are strong, interest groups will be weak, and conversely, weak parties imply strong interest groups. It is as though the system is not big enough for both.

In the United States, parties seem to be consistently losing ground to well-organized and well-funded special interests. Parties have always been decentralized, especially in comparison with European countries, but recent developments have made them in certain respects even more so.[52] Campaign finance laws, for example, unleashed PACs, which in turn strengthened interest groups by allowing them to disburse money to *individual* candidates. Once in office these individuals are beholden to their backers, not to their parties. Stated differently, groups are helping to create independent **political entrepreneurs**, individuals who build their own election organizations and do not depend on party support to get elected. The emergence of these independent politicians causes parties to languish even further. As a result, they have difficulty drafting coherent, unambiguous platforms that their legislative members pledge to support and help translate into public policy.

One consequence of this absence of cohesion among party regulars is that major items on the national agenda—reducing budget deficits, protecting the environment, curbing drug abuse, plugging the trade gap, and so forth—turn into helter-skelter struggles fought as much between floating coalitions of interest groups as between the major parties. It is difficult in these circumstances for voters to hold anyone accountable for the success or failure of government programs. There are just too many players to follow.

John Brademas, himself a former representative, summarizes the relationship between interest groups and parties this way:

> In this environment, the additional pressures that special-interest groups bring to bear make it more and more difficult for party leaders to put together the working and winning coalitions necessary to produce viable policy for a country of 230 million.[53]

The concern, then, is that interest groups take advantage of and worsen the fragmentation of the parties and thereby dissipate the nation's political energies. The specific problems of certain groups may get solved, but not those of the people as a whole.

Checkpoint

- Many political struggles in the United States are fought among interest groups, not political parties.
- Interest groups have a number of advantages for the political system:
  - Dispossessed members of society can organize to advance their causes.
  - Groups provide services and information to policymakers.
  - Groups contribute to pluralism, the system of checks and balances that keeps power dispersed and liberties secure.

- At the same time, however, the proliferation and prominence of organized private interest groups has potential drawbacks:
  - Some groups, especially the ones with enormous resources, abuse their power.
  - Not all segments of society are represented equally.
  - Groups frequently elevate their own needs over national priorities.
  - Many organizations do not speak for their rank-and-file members and therefore act mainly for the benefit of their leaders.
  - Conflicts of interest sometimes offset the benefits of shared government.
  - Political parties are better suited for establishing equality and majority rule, but they have been badly hurt, if not crippled, by the proliferation of organized interest groups.

INTEREST GROUPS: WHO GOVERNS?

Interest groups occupy a conspicuous place in the United States. Their prevalence and power in the political process means that many decisions, instead of being made by majority rule or in elections, emerge as the result of group conflict. These battles are frequently waged out of the public's view and with weapons such as lobbying, fund-raising, and power sharing that are unfamiliar to most citizens. How democratic is this system? The question is not easy to answer, partly because it depends on what kind of government you see and what kind of government you want.

Democracy

Democratic theorists feel that the people themselves should govern insofar as possible. Groups can play a part by opening avenues for participation. Certain members of the National Rifle Association are perhaps more politically active than they would otherwise be because the organization encourages them to write letters, display bumper stickers, attend rallies, donate money, and meet with elected officials. The downside comes when tightly organized minorities sometimes push aside majority preferences. It is fine for the NRA to mobilize its followers, but democracy suffers if they become powerful enough to intimidate lawmakers and thwart the public's desire for gun control. Democratic theorists also worry about disparities in the size and resources of groups. As in major league baseball, where there are always perennial cellar dwellers, some groups (the poor, for instance) always seem to finish last.

Pluralism

Pluralists, on the other hand, see intergroup competition as the heart and soul of American politics. Specific tactics, such as campaign fundraising, may cause concerns about undue influence, but for the most part the system functions smoothly: Thousands of interests receive a hearing in the political arena, and no segment of society becomes totally dominant.

Take the battle over smoking and public health. The tobacco industry, both growers and cigarette makers, is relatively closely knit and certainly well financed. Its lobby enjoys a reputation as one of the country's most sophisticated, powerful, and effective. Its operating arm, the Tobacco Institute—which employs lawyers, public relations specialists, accountants, and former cabinet officials, White House assistants, and members of Congress—sponsors research, produces press releases, entertains legislators (as we saw earlier), and distributes thousands of dollars in campaign contributions. Yet in spite of these resources, the tobacco industry does not always get its way and, in fact, has been in retreat for several years. Nonsmokers and public health advocates (such as the American Lung Association) have chalked up several memorable victories in their war against tobacco consumption: The Surgeon General requires health warnings on tobacco products and advertisements, smoking is prohibited in many offices and public accommodations and domestic air flights, and cigarette ads have been banished from the airways.

Groups, moreover, perform a host of useful services, from channeling information and expertise to government, to participating in the administration of laws, to allowing disgruntled citizens to let off steam. And even though a particular organization occasionally dominates one area of policy for awhile, interest groups in general have to share power with constitutionally established institutions, political parties, candidates, the media, and other political actors. In fact, the circumstances in which groups have their greatest impact are relatively limited. Other things being equal, they will be most successful when:

- The *scope* of the issues is narrow. That is, groups will be strongest when the policies they are trying to influence touch relatively few people directly.
- The issues are technical or abstract.
- The general public is not aware of a problem or mobilized to deal with it.
- They are able to maintain sufficient resources (money, personnel, prestige, and so on) to fight year after year.
- They have allies in key political institutions such as congressional committees or federal agencies.

This list, pluralists contend, suggests that groups do not have unlimited power.

The Power Elite

The power elite camp readily concedes that interest groups take part in decision making at the local, state, and national level. But even so, the mismatch in the size and resources between groups belies pluralists' contentions about the balance of power in society. Granted, the use and advertisement of tobacco products has been restricted. But despite smoking's well-documented effects on health, which include lung cancer, heart disease, and emphysema, cigarettes continue to be sold by the billions. Indeed, in view of the risks to smokers, a good measure of the tobacco lobby's clout has been its ability to forestall the kinds of government regulations that have outlawed other harmful products. Another tribute to its power is this paradox: One government agency—the Office of the Surgeon General—actively discourages smoking, while at the same time, another branch, the Department of Agriculture—underwrites the production and distribution of tobacco products in both domestic and foreign markets.[54] The industry and its trade association, in other words, have enough influence to cause one arm of the vast federal establishment to wrestle another arm. Here is another paradox: The government is waging a multibillion-dollar, all-out war on drug abuse. Yet nicotine, an addictive chemical that gives cigarettes their flavor, goes unregulated.

Power elite theorists' main criticism of interest group politics, however, is that group activities have only a marginal impact on fundamental or trunk decisions. What the Tobacco Institute and American Lung Association or thousands of other organizations argue about, although of great concern to their members, does not affect the direction and fundamental content of economic and foreign policy. Prohibiting smoking on airlines is not a trivial accomplishment, but it pales in comparison with, say, the signing of an arms control agreement with the Soviet Union or changing monetary policy. The power elite school is convinced that interest groups do not make those kinds of decisions. Instead, they deal in middle-level issues, a visible but not crucial part of the policy hierarchy.

Is Reform Needed?

Interest group politics, as even its staunchest defenders readily admit, is an imperfect form of democracy. Should it be reformed, and if so, how?

Given the United States' commitment to individual liberties, the right of peaceful assembly,

the separation of powers, and the conviction that authority has to be restrained—all of which help explain the existence of so many formal organizations in this country—interest groups are surely here to stay. What one hopes for is that they do not become so powerful that the political system suffers.

Perhaps the most effective safeguard is public awareness. To the extent that citizens know what is going on in Washington and their state capitals, they can protect themselves against abuses by well-financed or underhanded special interests. To the extent that they are ignorant of politics, no reforms are likely to alter seriously the balance of forces or the way the public's business is conducted. In the last analysis, then, if interest group politics presents problems, the best solution to them may be political education.

Checkpoint

- Democratic theorists value interest groups for political participation but worry that they sometimes overwhelm majority preferences and possess unequal resources.

- Pluralists welcome intergroup competition, value the services groups provide the American political system, and argue that groups do not have unlimited power.

- Power elite theorists regard interest groups as taking part in the middle level of politics. They have only a marginal impact on trunk decisions in foreign and economic affairs.

- Interest groups are here to stay; the best safeguard against their excesses is public awareness of their activity.

SUMMARY

Interest groups are private organizations that try to promote the needs of their members by affecting the making and administration of public policy. Unlike political parties, they do not nominate candidates for office or try to run the government as a whole. Thousands of groups, representing nearly every segment of American society, are politically active. Public interest groups and political action committees are two new types of groups.

Two factors explain the proliferation and influence of interest groups in politics. First, the constitutional system of checks and balances that fragments power creates multiple points of access to power holders around which groups can form. Second, Americans tend to distrust public authority and prefer to rely on private organizations to solve problems.

The main weapons used by interest groups include lobbying—mobilizing opinion and the media, providing lawmakers with information and services, using access and friendship to persuade decision makers, and hiring former government officials (the revolving door); raising and distributing money to political campaigns through political action committees (PACs); and sharing governmental authority with public officials.

Interest group politics has a number of advantages. Members of most strata of society can organize to fight for their causes; groups provide services and information to lawmakers and administrators; and interest groups enhance pluralism by helping to check and balance competing social, political, and economic interests. The prominence of so many well-organized private interests has potential drawbacks, however. Some observers fear that they exert too much influence; do not represent every segment of society; frequently elevate their needs over national priorities; act mostly for the benefit of their leaders, not their constituents; allow conflicts of interest to interfere with fair government; and weaken political parties.

Democratic theorists have certain reservations about how interest groups work out in practice. They believe that, although groups may create opportunities for political participation, they can also abuse their power. Pluralists, on the other hand, recognize the potential dangers of interest group politics but still view them as an indispensable part of the American political system. The power elite camp does not believe that interest groups affect fundamental, or trunk, decisions.

KEY TERMS

Interest groups
Public interest group
Lobbying
Amicus curiae brief
Revolving door
Shared government
Iron law of oligarchy
Political entrepreneurs

FOR FURTHER READING

Jeffrey M. Berry, *The Interest Group Society*, 2nd ed. (Glenview, Ill.: Scott, Foresman, 1989). This book describes the formation and operation of interest groups, with chapters devoted to fund-raising, lobbying techniques, and the impact of interest group politics on American government.

Jeffrey M. Berry, *Lobbying for the People* (Princeton, N.J.: Princeton University Press, 1977). A discussion of public interest lobbies.

Jeffrey H. Birnbaum and Alan S. Murray, *Showdown at Gucci Gulch* (New York: Random House, 1987). An entertaining report of how groups fought with varying degrees of success to protect their interests during the battle over tax reform.

Richard Harris, *A Sacred Trust* (Baltimore: Penguin Books, 1966). Although written more than two decades ago, this remains a superb account of the politics and power of the American Medical Association.

Terry M. Moe, *The Organization of Interests* (Chicago: University of Chicago Press, 1980). Moe explains how interest groups attract and organize their members.

E. E. Schattschneider, *The Semi-Sovereign People* (New York: Holt, Rinehart and Winston, 1960). Perhaps one of the best critiques of interest group politics ever written.

Kay Lehman Schlozman and John T. Tierney, *Organized Interests and American Democracy* (New York: Harper & Row, 1986). An excellent book about the role of interest groups in American politics.

Part Four

Governing
Institutions ★

Congress

Chapter 14

★ The Functions of Congress
★ Representation
★ Lawmaking
★ Congress: Who Governs?

Members of Congress are representatives to government as well as participants in governing. The tension between their representing and lawmaking responsibilities structures Congress and shapes the behavior of legislators. Should constituent interests take precedence over the national interest or over a legislator's personal convictions in lawmaking decisions? How can a representative best divide his or her time, energy, and resources between constituent tasks and lawmaking duties? Overshadowing these concerns for most legislators is the constant preoccupation with getting reelected. ■

The Senate Finance Committee was in the final hours of revising the Tax Reform Act of 1986, the most comprehensive tax reform measure in more than 40 years. It was close to 11 o'clock on a Tuesday night, and committee members were exhausted from weeks of working from dawn to midnight on the tax bill. The committee was sharply divided over a section of the bill of great importance to the oil industry but of little concern to the average taxpayer.

Under the leadership of Senators Russell Long, Robert Dole, and Lloyd Bentsen, senators from oil-producing states had introduced a provision that would exempt investors in oil-drilling operations from a section of the bill designed to eliminate tax shelters. Under the old tax laws, investors could reduce their tax bills by taking paper losses in a "tax shelter" investment in such areas as real estate, equipment leasing, oil drilling, and cattle feeding. These provisions in the tax laws encouraged investment by permitting the speculators to get several dollars in tax savings for every dollar they put into a tax shelter.

Oil state senators were concerned that independent oil and gas drillers, who relied heavily on outside investors, might be put out of business by the elimination of tax shelters. The chief opponents of the oil industry exemption, Sena-tors Bill Bradley, George Mitchell, and John Chafee (all representing non-oil-producing states in the Northeast) said the exemption would provide an unfair benefit to oil-producing states and would cost the government $1.4 billion in lost taxes.

Late in the evening, after Senator Mitchell had argued that the exemption was unjustified, Senator Long said Mitchell was "a great lawyer and a great judge. He had a lifetime job as a federal judge, and he sacrificed that to serve in the Senate. Why a man would do that, I don't know." Laughter filled the room, as Long warmed to the oratory for which he was famous in the Senate. Gesturing to the Supreme Court building next door, Senator Long continued:

They have a lady holding a scale. She's blindfolded. She doesn't know whose weight is on the left-hand side and whose is on the right-hand side. And that's how they're supposed to decide cases over there: not knowin' who they're helpin' and who they're hurtin'.

We fellas are lawmakers. We're supposed to know who we're helpin' and do it deliberately, and know who we're hurtin', and do that deliberately. Now the people in the oil and gas b'ness are the most depressed industry in the United States.[1]

The Senate Finance Committee announces agreement on the Tax Reform Act of 1986.
Left to right: Senators George Mitchell, Bill Bradley, John Danforth, Russell Long, and
John Chafee.

Senator Long and the other oil state senators won the battle; the exemption for oil-drilling investors stayed in the tax reform bill. Even those senators bitterly opposed to the exemption voted for the bill when the Finance Committee approved it on a 20 to 0 vote early in the morning of Wednesday, May 7, 1986.

The Tax Reform Act of 1986 closed loopholes worth about $300 billion, increased corporate taxes by $120 billion, and lowered tax rates on individual income. The House and Senate passed the tax reform legislation that fall by wide margins. The votes made it clear that most legislators thought the tax reform law would improve how America was governed. Passing the bill was in the national interest, even for those senators opposed to the oil exemption.

We expect our national legislators to govern, to make decisions they consider to be in the national interest. Yet we also expect those we send to Congress to protect our own needs and those of the state and district they represent. Oil state senators could satisfy both responsibilities by voting for a tax reform bill that served the national interest while it also protected oil inter-ests. But senators from states like New Jersey, Rhode Island, and Maine knew that the tax reform bill put industries in their own states at a disadvantage in comparison with the oil industry.

Should those senators protect state interests and refuse to support the tax reform bill until the oil exemption provision is removed from the bill? Even if that would kill the chances of Congress passing a tax reform act? Members of Congress regularly make choices based on who will be helped and who hurt by legislation. Those are often hard choices, and they are made even more difficult by the expectation that members of Congress will act as both representatives *to* and members *of* the government—that they will seek to protect state and district interests while working for legislation in the national interest.

The twin goals of representation and governing by passing laws greatly affect the behavior of members and the institutional structure of Congress. Judgments about the role of Congress in governing America must consider these dual expectations that we have of members and the institution.

THE FUNCTIONS OF CONGRESS

Article I of the Constitution makes Congress the first branch of government: "All legislative powers herein granted shall be vested in a Congress of the United States, which shall consist of a Senate and House of Representatives." The framers of the Constitution put the powers of the legislative branch before those of the executive or judicial branches, says constitutional scholar J. W. Peltason, because "they expected Congress, except in time of war or emergency, to be the central and directing organ of the government."[2]

Article I places responsibility for making laws squarely on the national legislature. Members of Congress are expected to do more than just pass laws, however; they also must represent the interests of constituents, oversee and check the executive branch, educate the public through debates and hearings, and help individual constituents with government-related problems. Those are the activities that senators and representatives engage in every day. Still, as a member of the House has pointed out, being in Congress means: "Ultimately, you have to govern."[3] On the one hand, we find general agreement about what Congress should be doing and how it should participate in the governing of America. On the other hand, and often overlooked, are the inherent conflict between some of those activities and a disagreement as to which functions of Congress are most important.

Representation

In a republican form of government, citizens elect others to represent their interests. It was in that sense that James Madison, in 1788, described the proposed House of Representatives "as a substitute for a meeting of the citizens in person."[4] In the process of **representation**, members of the House speak for the half million citizens who live in their districts and senators do the same for all of those in their home states.

Representation is often assumed to mean that legislators' votes should be in agreement with the opinions of a majority of constituents. Senators and representatives realize that getting too far out of step with constituents courts electoral defeat, but most members would agree with the Massachusetts representative who said that he

Senator Sam Nunn meets with constituents from Georgia. The central activity of representation for most members of Congress is hearing what constituents have to say and explaining their votes in Washington.

did not believe "that an elected representative is a delegate chosen simply to vote the way the majority of the people in his congressional district want him to vote." He continued: "I do subscribe, however, to the concept that the most legitimate role for a congressman is that of a trustee—someone who is given power and control over certain resources of this country for the benefit of those who empower him: his constituents."[5] The extent to which legislators act as **delegate** or **trustee** will depend on the type of issue under consideration and the type of district they represent. On some issues—farm policy, tariffs, defense contracts, immigration policy—legislators are likely to vote as a delegate of the district. But lawmakers are more likely to act as trustees in deciding how to vote on issues such as social security, tax reform, budget cuts, and foreign policy.

Studying representatives in their districts led Richard Fenno to conclude: "Members of Congress believe, if anything, that two-way communication is more valued by their constituents than policy congruence" (members voting in accordance with constituents' policy preferences).[6] Hearing what constituents have to say and explaining their votes in Washington is the central activity of representation for most members of Congress. A representative put it this way: "I have to be able to go home every week and tell the folks what I am doing and why I am doing it, and I earn the right to come back here and do whatever it is I want to do."[7]

The structure of Congress facilitates the function of representation. Most organized interests know that they cannot win all the legislation they want from Congress, but they also know that they are likely to get a hearing. The openness of Congress, its decentralized structure, and the constituency focus of members all work to the advantage of groups seeking to be heard by those who govern.

Lawmaking

When the First Congress ended its work in 1791, it had considered 167 bills and enacted 117 into law. The record of the 100th Congress (1987–1988) was quite different: more than 11,000 bills had been introduced and a total of 713 had been passed.[8] "I think I'd like to go home now and see my people," a weary legislator told his colleagues in the closing hours of a recent Congress. "I'm sick of you people. I'm tired. I want to go home."[9]

Much of the work of Congress has to do with **lawmaking,** considering and passing legislation. As Richard Fenno has observed: "Representative government requires more than accountability and responsiveness to constituents; it also requires the governing of constituents."[10] This governing, or lawmaking, function makes Congress more than an assembly of delegates who represent our interests in the councils of state. Congress, in fact, is a part of the state. It acts *on* citizens as well as *for* them. We may think of constituents as those who tell representatives and senators what they want done in government. But when Congress passes laws, its members are telling constituents what they can and cannot do. "Every day members make decisions that they know are authoritative for the whole country," Philip Brenner has written, and as a result, "members come to see themselves as rulers of the country."[11] A House veteran of 22 years spoke of the dual nature of the job: "Basically a representative has two responsibilities. He has a responsibility to his district; he is a representative of that district. But at the same time, he has a national responsibility, a responsibility to the whole country . . . to serve the national interest, to help make policy for a country of [250] million people."[12]

The lawmaking activities of Congress raise interesting questions about the democratic, pluralistic, and power elite explanations of governing America. By sharing a responsibility for governing, and by acquiring information and an awareness of a wide range of options, legislators sometimes *create* policies they perceive to be in the public interest; they don't just *respond* to the policy preferences of groups in society. An example of this type of Congress-initiated legislation, the Tax Reform Act of 1986, passed in the face of general public apathy and the opposition of many powerful interests. The act of governing, in other words, can *generate* policy preferences and a sense of the public interest, just as the act of representation *reflects* existing societal preferences and interests.[13]

Administrative Oversight

While the Constitution clearly gives Congress the lawmaking power, Article II does say that the president "shall take care that the laws be faithfully executed." **Administrative oversight** is the process by which Congress seeks to *assure* that those laws are "faithfully" executed. If a law prohibits military aid to a foreign group, for example, the process of administrative oversight should alert Congress to executive attempts to provide that aid in secret. If Congress establishes a fund for cleaning up toxic waste dumps, administrative oversight provides a way to make sure that the Environmental Protection Agency uses the money for that purpose.

Congress has several ways to check on the administration of programs by the executive branch. The most common is the committee or subcommittee investigation and hearing. **Investigative hearings** aim at making administration more efficient, but they sometimes uncover cases where executive officials have actively worked against national policies established by law and even committed crimes in attempting to cover up those activities. The nationally televised Iran-contra hearings in the summer of 1987 provided a dramatic example of congressional oversight. An immediate result of that investigation was President Reagan's decision to change executive branch procedures on covert operations and the notification of Congress about such operations in the future.

The **legislative veto** has been another important instrument of administrative oversight. This veto generally takes the form of a resolution passed by one or both houses of Congress, which overrules or prohibits a decision made in the executive branch. Since the mid-1930s Congress has enacted about 500 laws that give it the power to veto executive decisions. The legislative veto provision of the 1973 War Powers Resolution, which gives Congress a check on the president's power to send troops into combat, is one of the more prominent examples of this instrument.

A Supreme Court decision in 1983 (the *Chadha* case, discussed in Chapter 4) ruled that certain types of legislative vetoes violated the principle of separation of powers and were therefore unconstitutional. But Congress continues to use legislative vetoes: between 1983 and 1989, Congress passed more than 140 laws empowering the legislature to veto executive spending decisions. As congressional scholar Louis Fisher points out, they serve the interests of both the executive and Congress: "the desire of agencies for greater discretionary authority and the need of Congress to maintain control short of passing another public law."[14]

In addition to these formal legislative veto provisions, the executive and legislative branches have used informal agreements to enhance administrative oversight. That was the case in March 1989, when President Bush and congressional leaders reached an agreement to provide nonmilitary funding to the contras in Nicaragua through February 1990, with the understanding that the aid would not continue after November 30, 1989, without the approval of the appropriations and foreign policy committees of the House and Senate.

Congress also uses the "power of the purse" to oversee the executive branch. When agencies fail to carry out congressional goals in administering laws, Congress can threaten to reduce their budget. Within the bills that appropriate funds, Congress often spells out what an agency can or cannot do. An appropriations bill for the Legal Services Corporation, for example, included this language:

> *Provided*, That no part of this appropriation shall be used for publicity or propaganda purposes designed to support or defeat legislation pending before Congress or any State Legislature; *Provided further*, That none of the funds appropriated in this title may be used to carry out any activities for or on behalf of any individual who is known to be an alien in the United States in violation of the Immigration and Nationality Act. . . .[15]

Audits of how agencies spend funds and the annual appropriations process provide members of Congress with the information and opportunity to enforce oversight through the power of the purse.

Congress can also attempt to achieve executive compliance with the spirit and letter of the law by issuing specific directives in committee reports, by delaying Senate confirmation of executive or judicial appointments, and by commissioning independent studies of program performance from legislative support agencies, such as the General Accounting Office. The complex and technical nature of governing in the 1980s, however, requires that Congress give a great deal of leeway to the executive bureaucracy. There is simply no way that Congress can provide clear direction and specific rules for every policy area and every government decision. In fact, Congress regularly grants executive agencies the power to make those decisions along the policy lines indicated in its laws. The goal of administrative oversight is to minimize executive deviations from those goals.

Education

A freshman representative who had won his Florida district just a few months earlier by pledging to fight tax increases and reduce the budget deficit found himself supporting his party's position and voting for a budget program of record deficits and $30 billion in new taxes. Soon after that, at a Chamber of Commerce breakfast back in his district, he was asked to explain that vote. He responded with a long answer in which he described the congressional budget process and explained how his vote would help to get that process moving again. He also described how House-Senate differences on a bill are settled through a conference committee and told his listeners why he thought the compromise bill coming out of that process would mean lower taxes and smaller budget deficits than the House bill.[16]

Senators and representatives are expected to be able to explain their votes in Congress, especially when those votes appear to be inconsistent with constituency interests or opinion, or with campaign promises. Those explanations have an obvious value to representatives seeking reelection and to voters seeking accountability. But in the course of explaining their votes, members are also likely to be educating their listeners about the congressional process. Those who heard the congressman from Florida explain his vote also learned something about the budget process and conference committees.

Woodrow Wilson stressed the importance of education in his book, *Congressional Government* (1885): "Quite as important as legislation is vigi-

In the course of telling constituents what they have been doing in Washington, members of Congress (such as Representative Pat Schroeder, shown here) are also likely to be educating their listeners about the congressional process.

lant oversight of administration; and even more important than legislation is the instruction and guidance in political affairs which the people might receive from a body which kept all national concerns suffused in a broad daylight of discussion."[17] Congressional reforms that require committees, subcommittees, and conference committees to hold open sessions for almost all of their business enhance the public education that Wilson considered so important. The televising of House and Senate floor proceedings has a similar effect. The decentralized structure of Congress provides a wide array of forums in which members can teach their colleagues and the public about substantive issues. And committees and subcommittees often take those forums on the road by conducting hearings in the home districts of members. House and Senate panels set up to investigate or oversee executive action also serve as educators of the public. The millions of Americans who watched the Iran-contra hearings learned about both the substantive issues underlying the arms transactions and the process through which they were carried out.

Constituent Service

"Rightly or wrongly," a House member suggested to his colleagues, "we have become the link between the frustrated citizen and the very involved Federal government in the citizens' lives." This has happened, he said, "because the Federal government is so often hard for them to deal with. They end up writing letters, getting letters back from computers, after a while throwing up their hands, and the last step is the congressional office. . . ."[18]

Constituent service, or casework, is intervention by senators, representatives, and—more commonly—their staffs on behalf of constituents having problems stemming from government action or inaction. It is a form of representation: The legislator represents a particular constituent's interests before the federal bureaucracy.

Lawmaking and representation require a continuing pattern of behavior over time and a general approach to policy issues. By contrast, constituent service is a series of separate and often unrelated actions on behalf of individual constituents. People call their congressmen or con-

gresswomen if their social security check is late, if a veteran is denied eligibility for treatment, if a relative's application for entry into this country has been rejected by the Immigration and Naturalization Service, if a student loan has been drastically cut back or eliminated because of new federal guidelines, and so on. The types of cases most often brought to congressional offices are inquiries about the status of cases being handled by government agencies, requests for services and information, and appeals for favorable or preferential treatment.

Casework demands on a congressional office vary according to the demographic characteristics of a district, such as the proportion of retirees, unskilled laborers, or military employees living there. How long senators or representatives have been in office and whether they "hustle" casework will also help to determine the caseload. Generally speaking, the average weekly caseload for Senate offices is about 300, with the average for House offices being about 100 a week. The annual work load of cases for Congress as a whole exceeds 4 million. The agencies most often involved in congressional casework are Social Security, the Department of Veterans Affairs, the military services, the Justice Department (mostly immigration and criminal law cases), and the Department of Labor.[19]

Members who consider constituent service important allocate time for it, organize their staff to deal with it, and maintain active district offices, where most constituent casework is done. Senators and representatives regularly complain about the amount of time and effort given to casework and the drain that puts on resources needed for other activities, but they also recognize that they reap electoral benefits from good constituent service. The high level of satisfaction of most voters with their own representative's job performance, particularly in responding to constituent needs and problems, is one reason for the regularity with which incumbent members of Congress are reelected.

Making Choices

Congress and its members engage in representation, lawmaking, administrative oversight, edu-

A Closer Look

Why Members of Congress Can Never Win ★★★

The Poet Laureate of the United States, Howard Nemerov, wrote a poem to celebrate the 200th anniversary of the convening of the first Congress in March 1789, which included these lines:

Praise without end for the go-ahead zeal
of whoever it was invented the wheel;
But never a word for the poor soul's sake
that thought ahead and invented the brake.[a]

Members of Congress have long found that they are damned if they do and damned if they don't. Quick action by Congress or a committee is likely to draw criticism similar to that leveled by Senator Gary Hart against a Senate committee's investigation of the Central Intelligence Agency in 1975: "This is like building your boat as you go out to sea." But if Congress puts on the brakes and moves cautiously or delays action, it will find other critics agreeing with Senator Frank Church's characterization of the same investigation as "a hippopotamus rolling a pea."[b]

Nicholas Longworth, speaker of the House from 1925 to 1931, once said that members of Congress can never win:

Suppose we pass a lot of laws. Do we get praised? Certainly not. We then get denounced by everybody for being a "Meddlesome Congress" and for being a "Busybody Congress."

cation, and constituent service, but not all at once. Individual representatives and senators make choices in their daily schedules, and they have different opinions about which of their many jobs are most important. This point was illustrated at an orientation session for new members, where speaker after speaker stressed the importance of paying close attention to the mail. The high regard in which the frank—or free mail—privilege is held on Capitol Hill was made clear to a representative when he asked his father, who had preceded him in the House, for guidance and was told: "Son, I have three pieces of advice for you if you want to stay in Congress. One, use the frank. Two, use the frank. Three, use the frank."[20] New members were advised to personally read as much incoming mail as they

could and to sign their own mail. Toward the end of the session, however, a respected long-term member of the House stood up and told the newcomers: "I don't open my mail, I don't read my mail, I don't answer my mail, and I don't sign my mail. I think my job is to hang around the floor of the House and know what's going on."[21]

Close attention to the mail helps a legislator as a representative. Being on the floor (or in committee) is central to lawmaking. And the great demands on legislators' time require that they constantly make choices. A four-term congressman who said that his main goal was "to contribute to government" commented:

I'm not as enthused about tending my con-

But suppose we take warning from that experience. Suppose that in our succeeding session we pass only a few laws. Are we any better off? Certainly not. Then everybody, instead of denouncing us for being a "Meddlesome Congress" and a "Busybody Congress," denounces us for being an "Incompetent Congress" and a "Do-Nothing Congress."

Suppose, for instance, that we follow the President. Suppose we obey him. Suppose we heed his vetoes. What do we get called? We get called a "flock of sheep." We get called "echoes of the master's voice," a "machine."

Suppose, then, we turn around and get very brave, and defy the President and override his vetoes. What, then, do we get called? We get called "factionists." We get called "disloyalists." We get called "disrupters of the party." We get called "demagogues."[c]

[a]Howard Nemerov quoted in Robin Toner, "Senators Mark Congress's Rich Past Before Facing the Painful Present," *New York Times*, March 3, 1989, p. 22.
[b]Senators Hart and Church quoted in Loch Johnson, *A Season of Inquiry*, (Homewood, Ill.: Dorsey Press, 1988), pp. 76 and 79.
[c]House Speaker Nicholas Longworth, quoted in Marjorie Hunter, "Congress and Dangerfield," *New York Times*, October 16, 1985, p. 24.

stituency relations as I used to be and I'm not paying them the attention I should be.

There's a natural tension between being a good representative and taking an interest in government. I'm getting into some heady things in Washington, and I want to make an input into the government. It's making me a poorer representative than I was.[22]

Representation and lawmaking present the same sort of conflicts for the institution. As former Speaker Nicholas Longworth has pointed out, if Congress maximizes the lawmaking function of efficiently passing legislation, some will denounce it as a "rubber stamp" or "me too" Congress. If it maximizes representation and delays legislation so that all interests can have a say, it runs the risk of being tagged a "do nothing" Congress. (See A Closer Look.) Specific reform proposals also highlight the inherent conflict between representation and lawmaking. Debate over reform often produces one side seeking to improve the efficiency with which Congress performs its lawmaking function, and the other contending that inefficiency is the price the legislature must pay if it is to be truly representative. The tension between representation and lawmaking helps determine a great deal of congressional behavior and greatly influences the structure of Congress as an institution. As we will now see as we look at these two functions in more detail, they generate competing and often contradictory ideas about how Congress can best govern.

Checkpoint

- Members of Congress are expected to engage in a wide range of activities in order to meet their responsibilities of representation, lawmaking, administrative oversight, education, and constituent service.

- Everyone agrees that this is what senators and representatives should be doing, but not everyone agrees on which activities are more important than others. Individual members often have to choose between competing activities in their daily schedules. To meet its lawmaking responsibility, Congress sometimes must limit representation.

REPRESENTATION

The chief responsibility of Congress is lawmaking, passing laws and budgets to support them. But the authority of Congress to do that rests on its being a representative body. Representation encompasses both the selection of men and women to serve in Congress and the actions of those people in Washington and in their home districts and states. We can separate electoral activities and congressional activities for analytical purposes, but the representative aspects of the two are often the same. Activities that help a candidate to get elected and reelected are essentially those that constitute effective representation: the articulation of district interests and the servicing of constituents' needs.

Getting Elected to Congress

When we think of congressional elections, most of us think of some variation of classic scenarios: a young, energetic challenger unseating an aging incumbent who has lost touch with voters in the district; a popular representative or senator going down to defeat after a personal or political scandal; a House or Senate seat moving from one party to the other in response to a presidential candidate or a president's program. Those types of congressional elections provide drama and attract press coverage. But that is not the way most members of Congress get to Capitol Hill.

Members of Congress are more likely to have first won election, not by defeating an incumbent, but by winning an open seat left by a retiring or deceased incumbent. For example, two out of three members of the 101st Congress (1989–1990) first came to Congress that way.[23] What happens in most congressional elections is that *incumbents win*. The reelection of incumbents is the single most important factor in these congressional elections. This incumbency advantage permeates the congressional recruitment process at both the nomination and general-election stages.

NOMINATIONS The first step on the road to Congress is winning the party primary to be that party's nominee in the general election. House members need fear little from challengers within their own party. Less than 2 percent of the incumbents running for reelection to the House are defeated in a primary. Senators have been more vulnerable to primary challengers, but in recent years they, too, have been extremely successful at the nomination stage. The incumbency effect is so strong that the out party often has difficulty even in recruiting strong candidates to challenge an incumbent, especially in House elections. In 1988, for example, 81 incumbent representatives—one of every five incumbents seeking reelection—had no major party opposition at all.[24]

Political scientists have found that the incumbency effect at the nomination stage of congressional elections helps account for the underrepresentation of women in Congress. Although the 101st Congress (1989–1990) held a record number of 29 women legislators (2 senators and 27 representatives), that represents only 5.4 percent of the total membership of Congress.

In a recent book on the recruitment of congressional candidates, Linda Fowler and Robert McClure show how incumbents' reelection success and the shortage of female challengers with political experience have helped create a "gender trap" in American politics.[25] Incumbents, most of whom are male, keep winning, so women in those races never have a chance to catch up. In order to overcome the gender trap in congressional elections, strong female candidates need to focus on "winnable" seats—those where no incumbent is running. But the arithmetic of office holding makes that difficult. In the 1988 congressional races, only 26 of the 435 House seats—less than 6 percent—were open seats. Moreover, open seats attract candidates with political experience, who stand a better chance of winning the party's nomination than an inexperienced opponent. As a group, women in 1989 had far less political experience than men: They held approximately 12 percent of the elected political positions and accounted for only 17 percent of all state legislators in the United States.[26] The difficulty women face in gaining major party nominations in competitive congressional races is the essence of the gender trap identified by Fowler and McClure. The authors conclude that "under the prevailing rates of election, reelection, and retirement in the Congress, the number of women serving in Congress will increase by no more than 1 percent by the year 2001."[27]

THE GENERAL ELECTION Who wins congressional elections and why? Incumbency, as we have seen, is crucial. But other factors—party, campaign spending, issues, candidate characteristics—also help explain the outcomes of congressional elections.

The advantage of incumbents has been very consistent over time, (see Table 14.1, p. 444). In 1988, 408 incumbents sought reelection to the House and 402 succeeded, a success rate of 98.5 percent. In fact, 95 percent of those incumbents won reelection by more than 10 percentage points. Incumbency does not have the same electoral value to senators (see Table 14.1). An average of three out of four incumbent senators running for reelection will be returned to that chamber, compared to the nine out of ten House incumbents who are typically successful.

A reason often given for incumbents' success in congressional elections is the wide array of staff and services available to members, the perquisites ("perks") of office. House challengers would have to raise and spend a million dollars or more to obtain the same level of services.[28] Incumbency also provides an edge in the flow of private funds into congressional elections. Political action committees (PACs) contributed more than $150 million to congressional campaigns in 1988, for example, with incumbent senators receiving four times as much as Senate challengers and sitting House members receiving eight times as much as challengers.[29] There are also electoral payoffs to many of the routine activities of representatives and senators. Incumbents can claim credit for federal programs that benefit the district or state and for the thousands of cases in which they helped constituents. News releases, newsletters and other mailings to constituents, and trips home all help keep the incumbent's name before the public.

Name recognition in congressional elections helps explain both incumbents' success and the advantages that representatives have over senators. For example, a study by Barbara Hinckley found that 92 percent of the voters could recognize and rate the incumbent representative, while only 44 percent could do the same for the challenger. In Senate races, however, 95 percent knew and could rate the incumbent and 85 percent the challenger. Hinckley concluded: "Senate races provide a choice between two candidates known and in contact with voters while many House races do not."[30]

Those differences are at least partly a reflection of the types of campaigns waged by House and Senate challengers. Senate races are more expensive, more highly visible, and more competitive. In the 1988 elections, for example, it took $4 million to win an average Senate race and $400,000 to win an average House race.[31] Twenty-one percent of the Senate seats up for election that year changed party hands compared with 2 percent of the House seats; 44 percent of the incumbent senators won less than 60 percent of the vote compared with 13 percent of the House incumbents.[32]

Incumbency affects the impact that campaign

Table 14.1

Advantage of Incumbency, 1946–1988

Year	Number of Incumbents Seeking Reelection		Percent Reelected	
	House	Senate	House	Senate
1946	398	30	82.4	56.7
1948	400	25	79.2	60.0
1950	400	32	90.5	68.8
1952	389	31	91.0	64.5
1954	407	32	93.1	75.0
1956	411	29	94.6	86.2
1958	396	28	89.9	64.3
1960	405	29	92.6	96.6
1962	402	35	91.5	82.9
1964	397	33	86.6	84.8
1966	411	32	88.1	87.5
1968	409	28	96.8	71.4
1970	401	31	94.5	77.4
1972	390	27	93.6	74.1
1974	391	27	87.7	85.2
1976	384	25	95.8	64.0
1978	382	25	93.7	60.0
1980	398	29	90.7	55.2
1982	396	30	90.6	93.3
1984	410	29	95.1	89.7
1986	393	28	98.0	75.0
1988	408	27	98.5	85.0
Average	399	29.2	91.6	75.3

Source: *Congressional Quarterly Weekly Reports*, November 15, 1986, and November 12, 1988.

spending and party identification have on congressional elections. For challengers, a high level of campaign spending can only help their election. They need to spend a great deal of money in order to even partially counteract the many campaign resources of incumbents. Heavy spending by an incumbent, on the other hand, often goes hand in hand with defeat. That is because an incumbent who has to spend a lot of money likely has serious opposition and a strong chance of losing.[33]

The political party affiliation of candidates and voters also influences the outcome of congressional elections. Between 70 and 75 percent of the voters in a congressional election regularly support the candidate of the party with which they identify (see Figure 11.3). Since more voters identify themselves as Democrats than Republicans, it is not surprising that the Democrats have won an average of 54 percent of the national vote in congressional elections for the past 30 years. However, about one of every five voters in congressional elections defects to the other party, and the number of party defectors has been growing in recent elections. Of those who defect, nine of ten are supporting an incumbent.[34] The declining hold that party has on congressional voters and the pull of incumbency help explain why nearly one of every three congressional districts elected a Democrat to the House while supporting the Republican Bush for president in 1988.[35]

Candidate characteristics and issues also play a part in congressional elections. Studies find that somewhere between 20 and 30 percent of the electorate know enough about the issue positions of both candidates to be considered issue voters.[36] Even then, however, political party and incumbency affect how voters perceive issues and candidates' issue positions, and those perceptions favor incumbents.

Some of the electoral success of House incumbents is due to a lack of competition, a winning by default. But some credit must also be given to the favorable image of representation that most House members are able to create in the minds of voters. Public opinion polls regularly indicate a generally unfavorable rating of the institution of Congress but a high regard for the job being done by one's own representative. When asked to give reasons for this evaluation, most people refer to their own member's performance in representing district interests and the record of Congress as a whole in passing legislation. Representation is the standard for judging individual House members, and lawmaking is the standard for measuring the institution.[37]

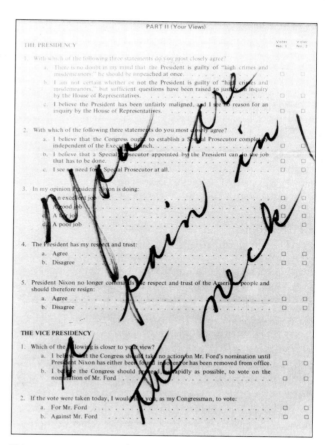

This response to a newsletter poll sent out by Massachusetts Congressman Gerry Studds in the early 1970s says a lot about how one constituent feels but little about how the Congressman should vote. Studds framed this note and hung it on his office wall.

Styles of Representation

When representatives and senators vote, when they introduce legislation and revise bills in committees, when they give speeches and write letters—in whatever they do as members of Congress—they are acting in behalf of others. But *which* others? That answer depends on the legislator's style of representation. The member may feel that he or she should be representing district or state constituents, important special interests, or the national interest. Any issue or activity is likely to involve a combination of these, but they are not always in agreement. Representation involves choice, and it is necessary to look at three styles of representation—

constituent, special interest, and national interest—in order to see what those choices are.

CONSTITUENT REPRESENTATION A member of Congress cannot be sure of voting in accordance with a majority opinion of constituents on most issues, because the senator or representative is unlikely to know what that opinion is.[38] Some members regularly conduct informal newsletter polls of constituency opinion, but they are far from scientific. Statistically accurate public opinion polls are too expensive and too general to be of much use to a legislator. Even when such polls are available, members might find reasons why they are limited as guides to representation: the public's low information level or lack of interest on most issues and the rapidity with which public opinion may change.

On the other hand, representatives and senators who completely ignore constituency opinion might find themselves job hunting. Members do need to have a sense of constituency opinions and interests. In performing this task of representation, legislators develop a complex picture of their constituency and deal with the various components of that constituency in different ways. Richard Fenno's study of House members in their districts found that representatives viewed their constituencies as a series of concentric circles and had different ways of interacting with the four constituencies making up those circles: geographic, reelection, primary, and personal.[39] It is more difficult to apply the same framework to senators' constituencies, because they are larger and more diverse.[40]

When asked about their constituency, most members will respond with a description of the **geographic constituency,** the physical location and boundaries of their congressional district: "It is in Massachusetts—the 10th District, the one that runs down the South Shore below Boston, through New Bedford, and includes all of Cape Cod"; or "My district is in northern California, on the southeastern end of San Francisco Bay, and includes the industrial city of Fremont and the downtown section of San Jose." The geographic constituency refers not just to the physical location but to the internal makeup of the district as well: its ethnic, racial, religious, economic, ideological, partisan, and residential characteristics. Members are certainly sensitive to important economic interests and large demographic groups in the district, and they are quite aware of its general ideological tilt, but the geographic constituency is not an important referent on most issues.

The **reelection constituency** is a smaller group within the boundaries of the geographic constituency, with greater political relevance to the member of Congress. It consists of those people within the district that members felt were supporters—those people who probably voted for them in the last election. Generally, when legislators speak of representing their constituency

they are more likely to be referring to the reelection constituency than the geographic one. The members' knowledge about exactly what generates support may be imperfect, but how they vote and act in Washington will be influenced to some degree by how they anticipate the reelection constituency will react.

Membership in the **primary constituency** requires more than simply voting for the representative; it reflects a more intense and durable form of support. This smaller group includes those people who had a hand in recruiting the representative for office and worked in the first campaign. Representatives naturally feel a special responsibility to their primary constituency. As one House member said: "When I look around to see who I owe my career to, to see those people who were with me in [the first campaign] when I really needed them and when most people thought I couldn't win—these are the people I think I owe."[41] Representatives are going to be alert to the opinions and interests of those they "owe." Primary constituents do not have to engage in active lobbying in most cases. The representative is likely to seek out their opinions on issues of importance to them.

The **personal constituency,** the innermost circle, is the one closest to members themselves— their friends. They may be political friends, or they may simply be people with whom representatives relax or from whom they receive emotional support. The determining requirement for inclusion in this smallest constituency is having the representative's complete trust. These are the friends who will be loyal even in the face of an electoral disaster or a scandal. Representatives may discuss political strategy with members of their personal constituency, but they do not rely on this constituency in deciding how to vote on issues before Congress. The link between legislators and their personal constituency is not the political relationship that they have with their reelection and primary constituencies.

SPECIAL-INTEREST REPRESENTATION "The interests run this city; everyone knows it," was the frank evaluation of a Washington lawyer and congressional lobbyist.[42] A member of the influential House Ways and Means Committee complained that the influence of special interests had caused him to develop a cynical perspective: "I'm asking myself, 'What am I doing here?' If I wanted to be an agent for special interests, I might as well go back to practicing law."[43]

The representation of economic interests has always been regarded as a function of Congress. In 1790, a group of mustard manufacturers from Philadelphia petitioned the First Congress to get a higher tariff on imported mustard. Domestic manufacturers of paint, cotton cloth, and rope sought similar legislation to protect their industries. What is different about the modern form of interest representation, and what contributes to negative assessments of the process, is the extent to which private interests are involved in financing congressional campaigns. Specifically, it is the development of political action committees over the past 20 years or so that has changed the nature of interest representation in Congress.

The tremendous growth in the number of PACs and their increasing importance in providing campaign funds for congressional races were documented in Chapter 13. We will add here the fact that PAC funds follow incumbents. Representative Greg Laughlin, a Democrat from Texas, learned this fact just a few days after his election in 1988. He was one of only six challengers in that year to defeat an incumbent. During the campaign, the political action committee of the National Association of Realtors (known as RPAC) gave $10,000, the maximum contribution, to Laughlin's opponent, incumbent Republican Mac Sweeney. Within a few days of Laughlin's taking office, however, representatives from RPAC stopped by his office with $10,000 in checks.[44] Nationally, PACs contributed nearly one-third of *all* funds raised by House and Senate candidates in the 1988 elections, and almost one-half of *incumbents'* funds. This practice of PACs giving mostly to incumbents is reflected in the fact that campaign spending by House challengers *decreased* by 30 percent (controlling for inflation) between 1980 and 1988, while spending by incumbents *increased* by 50 percent during the same period.[45] "The PACs know that if you bet on every incumbent, you are going to have a 98 percent success rate," points out one political scientist.[46]

In addition to favoring incumbents over challengers, PAC contributions are directed more to congressional leaders and to members sitting on important money committees, such as the tax-writing House Ways and Means and Senate Finance Committees, or on committees with jurisdiction in an area of importance to a particular PAC.[47]

Why give money to candidates who are certain to win anyway? Interest groups have good reasons for supporting incumbents, even those without any election opponent. "We're not buying loyalty, or buying support, or buying anything" with a campaign contribution, said RPAC director, William Thompson. Rather, "the question is: 'Is the member accessible? Does he listen to our point of view?'"[48]

Studies of interest representation in Congress support the general conclusion that campaign contributions buy access more than they buy votes.[49] But even if it cannot be determined whether congressional votes follow money or whether the money follows the votes by going primarily to supporters, Representative Les AuCoin asserted in the summer of 1989: "Something is systematically wrong with Congress today, and it's money, the pursuit of money, the endless pursuit of money, the virtual hourly pursuit of money."[50] There were signs that the public agreed with AuCoin.

Four of the six congressional incumbents defeated in 1988 had been charged with questionable financial practices involving special interests. A leader of the House Democrats, Representative Tony Coelho, said the voters sent a clear message in 1988: "Anybody whose ethics were in question ran into trouble."[51] Six months later, Coelho himself—the number three Democrat as majority whip—and House Speaker Jim Wright announced their retirement from Congress under the cloud of benefiting from improper financial deals. Coelho and Wright were not alone. By the end of the summer of 1989, ten House members (including the chairman of the House Ethics Committee) and one senator were reported to be under investigation by the ethics committees of the House and Senate for benefiting financially from public office.[52] One representative described the image of Congress in the summer of 1989 as "a green slime pool," and a *Washington Post–ABC News* poll taken then found that three out of four Americans believed that Congress cared more about "special interests" than about people like them.[53]

Although highly visible in recent years, congressional ethics is not a new issue. The House and Senate adopted ethics codes in 1968 and made them stricter in 1977 and 1989. Both chambers created ethics committees—the House Committee on Standards of Official Conduct and the Senate Select Ethics Committee—which are charged with investigating members' conduct and enforcing ethical standards. Committee membership is equally divided between Republicans and Democrats and, for understandable reasons, most representatives and senators prefer not serving on these committees, which require sitting in judgment of their colleagues.

Although members of Congress have joked that "ethics means only having to say I'm sorry," and that "we aren't even sure whether the word is singular or plural," senators and representatives are bound by rules of behavior outlined in congressional ethics codes, criminal statutes, party rules, and campaign finance laws.[54] Table 14.2 outlines the major provisions of congressional ethics.

The close ties between members of Congress and special-interest groups and the attention given to congressional ethics raise a fundamental question: Is Congress corrupt? Congressional scholar Norman Ornstein suggests that campaign finance laws and other reforms have reduced corruption but that they reinforce the *appearance* of corruption. With full disclosure, Ornstein says:

> We see the warts. We see that politics has a lot of dirt and messiness to it.
>
> Twenty-five years ago, the doors would close and money would change hands and no one saw it. So we all felt better about it.[55]

Morris Fiorina has written about a "Washington Establishment" made up of members of Congress, bureaucrats, and citizens with special interests all pursuing their respective goals of re-election, program expansion, and receiving government benefits at the least cost. "What we

Table 14.2
Congressional Ethics

1. Full financial disclosure of income, assets, holdings, transactions, and liabilities of all members and staff earning $25,000 or more a year (including spouses and dependents).

2. No gifts worth $100 or more from lobbyists.

3. Limits on outside income: Senators and representatives can collect no more than $2,000 per speech or appearance for a yearly total just under $27,000. House members are banned from receiving any "honoraria" for speeches and appearances beginning in 1991.

4. Prohibition on practicing law or another profession during regular office hours and on using congressional facilities for professional work.

5. Prohibition on former members becoming lobbyists until they have been out of Congress one year.

6. Elimination of unofficial office accounts (known as "slush funds").

7. Prohibition on using campaign funds for personal use (exempts members in office since January 1980).

8. Limit on foreign travel at government expense for members in final weeks of service.

9. No mass mailings using frank (free mailing privilege) within 60 days of primary or general election.

Source: Compiled from information in Alan L. Clem, *Congress: Powers, Processes, and Politics* (Monterey, Calif.: Brooks/Cole, 1989), p. 247; Janet Hook, "Chambers Rules Differ on Outside Earnings," *Congressional Quarterly Weekly Report*, January 21, 1989, p. 114; and Janet Hook, "Stalemates of Last Decade Haunt Agenda for 1990," *Congressional Quarterly Weekly Report*, January 6, 1990, pp. 12–13.

think of as plain and simple corruption is probably as uncommon in today's Congress as it ever has been," Fiorina says, but "the problem with Congress is more serious."

The problem with Congress is that Congressmen conscientiously, openly, and as a matter

The Senate Ethics Committee hears testimony in 1990 on charges that Minnesota Senator Dave Durenberger had violated Senate rules regulating members' outside income. The close ties between most members of Congress and special-interest groups raises a fundamental question: Is Congress corrupt?

of electoral survival assiduously service the special interests of their districts.

And in the absence of the coordinating forces of strong parties or presidential leadership, the general interest of the United States gets lost in the shuffle.[56]

In the next section and in the discussion of lawmaking later on in this chapter, we consider the coordinating activities of political parties and the president and the extent to which Congress serves a general or national interest.

REPRESENTING THE NATIONAL INTEREST A commonly held belief is that presidents represent the national interest and members of Congress local interests. This idea is not new in American politics. Thomas Jefferson made that distinction in his inaugural address in 1801, Woodrow Wilson said the president's voice "is

the only national voice in affairs," and John Kennedy said, "Only the President represents the national interest."[57]

There are obvious political reasons for presidents to advance this notion, but a case can be made for members of Congress too. In *Congress and Democracy*, David Vogler and Sidney Waldman show that Congress emphasizes broad national interests in policy areas such as immigration reform, environmental protection, and defense policy.[58] Case studies of the social security reform bill in 1983 and the Tax Reform Act of 1986 found a similar pattern of representation of national interests and not just those of state or district.[59]

But even if presidents are not the *only* elected officials concerned with the general interest of the country, they do serve to focus congressional attention on that interest. All presidents have three general sources of influence over Congress: party, public support, and legislative skills.[60]

The president wins support for a program by vigorous appeals to fellow party members in Congress, but party support also comes as a natural consequence of a shared point of view between the president and the party members. For example, President Reagan was credited with extraordinary party leadership because nearly all the Republicans in Congress voted for his programs. But as George Edwards points out, there was a preexisting strong consensus among Republicans in Congress on the issues that Reagan emphasized, particularly on his priority issue of tax reduction.[61]

Increases in public support for the president, as measured by public opinion polls, result in additional congressional support. That fact helps explain the presidential strategy of going public, of seeking to convert personal standing in the polls into congressional support.[62] But why should members of Congress care about the president's standing in the polls? No doubt they have one eye on the ballot box: How the folks at home feel about the policy positions of the president can translate into votes. There is also evidence, however, that many senators and representatives feel that Congress *should* respond to national public opinion, and that public support for the president is one indication of that national public opinion.[63]

Presidents also use their legislative skills—bargaining, personal appeals, consultation, agenda setting, vote structuring—to induce members of Congress to share their views about which programs are vital to national needs.[64] A president's opportunity for employing legislative skills is closely tied to the party division in Congress and the level of public support for the chief executive.

Members of Congress want to know the president's position on most issues, just as they want to know the position of constituents and of particular interest groups. And like these other sources of influence, the president's position is a point of reference rather than a determinant of a member's vote. For members of Congress also have their own views about national priorities and which program proposals are most likely to meet the national interest.

Checkpoint

- The authority of Congress to govern rests on its being a representative institution. Elections are the primary instrument of representation.

- In most congressional elections incumbents win, especially in House races, and they win by a wide margin. An incumbent House member running for reelection enjoys a number of advantages in staff support, name recognition, campaign funding, and a positive public image as a representative of the district. Stronger challengers, campaign issues, and party voting make Senate races more of a contest than most House races.

- Congressional representation extends far beyond periodic elections and is a more complex relationship than simply one of legislators doing what their constituents want them to do.

- Congressional representation includes interest groups and the national interest in addition to constituent interests. Within a representative's district are four types of constituency: geographic, reelection, primary, and personal.

LAWMAKING

Sometimes it is not easy to get a straight answer to the question of who is in charge of the government, of who has responsibility for governing. This was the case in a recent election year when much of the news out of Washington had to do with a federal budget deficit of $200 billion. Even though President Reagan had been in office for three years at the time, he still liked to portray himself as an outsider rather than as part of the Washington government. In a speech in

Atlanta, for example, the President said that during his term in office he had been working "to change just one little two-letter word: control by government to control of government."[65]

About the same time, House Speaker and Democratic spokesman Thomas P. O'Neill wanted everyone concerned about budget deficits to understand that it was the President, not Congress, who was responsible for governing the nation. "He's running the Government; we're not running the Government."[66] We see a similar denial of responsibility for governing in many reelection campaigns for senators and representatives. Incumbent and even veteran legislators quite often campaign for reelection by running *against* Congress. Members are eager to take credit for their actions as representatives but place the blame for deficits and unpopular laws on the institution.

Even though the question of who governs sends many government officials running for cover, the general public and political leaders do recognize lawmaking as a major responsibility of Congress. Congressional scholar Randall Ripley has found that the high points of public approval of Congress coincide with congressional productivity in passing bills. When people are asked why they think Congress is doing a good or poor job, their answers focus more on congressional lawmaking than on representation or other activities.[67]

Lawmaking puts different demands on Congress and its members than does representation. Most of the activity surrounding lawmaking takes place in Washington, whereas the focus of representation is the state or district. Representation can often be an individual effort, but lawmaking requires group effort and the building of coalitions. A centralized Congress is most effective at lawmaking, a decentralized one at representation. Representation evokes the idea of "control of government," while lawmaking is by its very nature "control by government."

This section considers the key elements of Congress as a lawmaking institution—the party leadership, the committee structure, rules and norms, and congressional staff. Their role in lawmaking can be best understood if the reader takes a few minutes first to study the general picture of the lawmaking process shown in Figure 14.1, on p. 452.

Party Leadership

Leaders in the House and Senate play important roles at some key stages of the lawmaking process shown in Figure 14.1. Before we see what it is that they do, it is helpful to get the cast of characters straight. The Constitution made no provision for the leaders of the chambers to be chosen by the parties, but this is how it has worked out in practice. On the Senate side, the Constitution provides for the vice-president to be presiding officer, and for a president pro tempore to be chosen from the Senate to preside in the vice-president's absence. Few vice-presidents, however, have paid much attention to this post, unless their vote has been needed to break a tie, and the president pro tempore's position is, for the most part, an honorary one. The real power in the Senate lies in the hands of the **majority leader,** who is chosen by the members of the majority party. The counterpart in the minority party is the **minority leader**. Each leader is assisted by the party **whip**.

The Constitution provides for a **speaker** to preside over the House. Although the speaker is elected by the whole House, the vote proceeds along strict party lines, affirming the candidate of the majority party. The speaker's position is far from honorary but carries with it important powers, as we will see. The Speaker is assisted by a majority leader selected by fellow party members. The opposing party chooses its minority leader, and both parties elect whips.

The party leaders in each chamber organize Congress by determining the size and makeup of the committees, referring bills to committee, setting the rules for floor action, and appointing members to conference committees (which reconcile differing versions of bills voted on by the Senate and the House). Organizing the congressional process is no small task, but party leaders are expected to do much more: They must see that policies favored by their party get passed by Congress and that policies favored by the oppos-

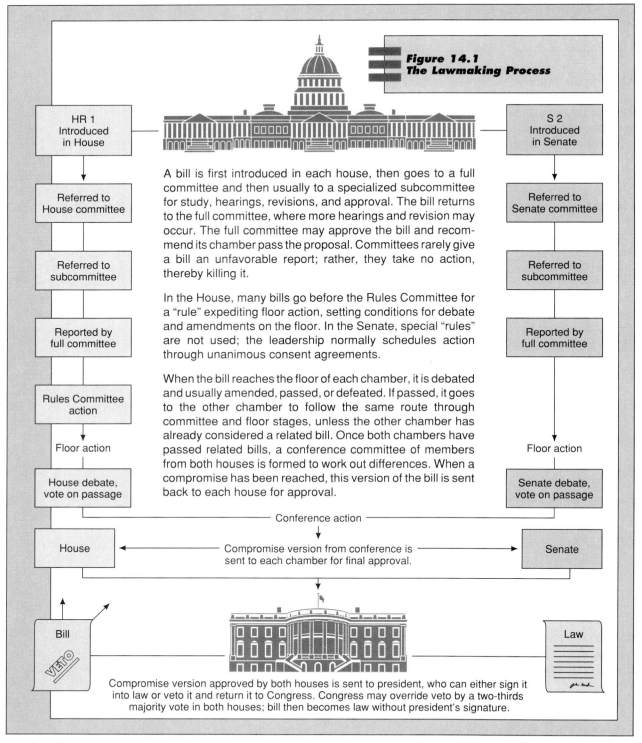

**Figure 14.1
The Lawmaking Process**

HR 1 Introduced in House		S 2 Introduced in Senate

A bill is first introduced in each house, then goes to a full committee and then usually to a specialized subcommittee for study, hearings, revisions, and approval. The bill returns to the full committee, where more hearings and revision may occur. The full committee may approve the bill and recommend its chamber pass the proposal. Committees rarely give a bill an unfavorable report; rather, they take no action, thereby killing it.

In the House, many bills go before the Rules Committee for a "rule" expediting floor action, setting conditions for debate and amendments on the floor. In the Senate, special "rules" are not used; the leadership normally schedules action through unanimous consent agreements.

When the bill reaches the floor of each chamber, it is debated and usually amended, passed, or defeated. If passed, it goes to the other chamber to follow the same route through committee and floor stages, unless the other chamber has already considered a related bill. Once both chambers have passed related bills, a conference committee of members from both houses is formed to work out differences. When a compromise has been reached, this version of the bill is sent back to each house for approval.

Referred to House committee

Referred to subcommittee

Reported by full committee

Rules Committee action

Floor action

House debate, vote on passage

Referred to Senate committee

Referred to subcommittee

Reported by full committee

Floor action

Senate debate, vote on passage

Conference action

House ← Compromise version from conference is sent to each chamber for final approval. → Senate

Bill

VETO

Law

Compromise version approved by both houses is sent to president, who can either sign it into law or veto it and return it to Congress. Congress may override veto by a two-thirds majority vote in both houses; bill then becomes law without president's signature.

This chart shows the most typical way in which proposed legislation is enacted into law. There are more complicated as well as simpler routes, and most bills fall by the wayside and never become law. The process is illustrated with two hypothetical bills— House bill no. 1 (HR 1) and Senate bill no. 2 (S 2). Each bill must be passed by both houses of Congress in identical form before it can become law. The path of HR 1 is traced by a lavender line, that of S 2 by a light green line. In practice, most legislation begins as similar proposals in both houses.

Source: David Vogler, *The Politics of Congress* (Dubuque, Iowa: Brown, 1988), pp. xii–xiii.

ing party are blocked. In order to carry out their party's program in Congress, the party leaders must gather and disseminate information relevant to policies under consideration, schedule the business of the Senate and House, and control the floor proceedings of both chambers. The particular strategies they use have varied over the years with changes in rules and leaders. Some leaders favor a low-key conciliatory approach to passing legislation, while others are more high-pressured and aggressive.

Leadership style became an issue for House Democrats in September 1989, after 64 Democrats defected from their party to support a capital gains tax cut endorsed by President Bush. That vote was considered the first major test of the House Democratic leadership team—Speaker Thomas Foley, Majority Leader Richard Gephardt, and Majority Whip William Gray—which had taken over three months earlier after the resignations of Speaker Jim Wright and Ma-

jority Whip Tony Coelho. The Foley-Gephardt-Gray leadership style was one of conciliation and consensus, in sharp contrast to the aggressively partisan, "hardball politics" of Speaker Wright.

The loss of one out of every four House Democrats on the capital gains cut led many Democrats to question the new leaders' style. "That dog don't hunt," a Georgia Democrat complained, while a colleague from Michigan said his party's leaders had "punted."[68] A third Democrat complained that the consensus style had produced too many meetings and not enough "old-fashioned arm-twisting," and advised Democratic leaders: "At some point you have to stop the meeting and start the headcrashing."[69]

Party leadership styles vary, but all party leaders draw on the same basic set of resources in attempting to influence legislative outcomes: House and Senate rules, tangible rewards, status, and information.[70] The first of these re-

House Democratic leaders meet with the press after losing a party vote on a capital gains tax cut in 1989. One Democratic representative later told party leaders: "At some point you have to stop the meeting and start the headcrashing."

sources, *chamber rules*, primarily benefits the majority party. When a chamber votes to change its rules, it is generally at the urging of the majority party leader as a means of improving the legislative efficiency of the House or Senate. What the changes also do, of course, is improve the majority party's control over the legislative process. House Democratic leaders and the Committee on Rules (which determines how a bill will be debated, amended, and voted on the House floor), for example, developed new rules over the past 15 years that severely restricted House debate and helped the majority party to move legislation through Congress.[71]

Party leaders distribute or influence *tangible rewards*, which include appointments to special committees and commissions, office space, and material support for reelection campaigns. *Status*, the third resource, is also conferred on individual members by party leaders. How a member stands in the hierarchy of each chamber to a certain extent determines that member's ability to bargain with colleagues. Representative Norman Mineta described the effect of party leaders' selecting him to be a deputy whip: "Among my colleagues, I'm given some recognition for having some information, being connected. Like Ivy League eating clubs, . . . well, I'm part of the Speaker's eating club."[72]

Of the resources available to party leaders, however, *information* is probably the most important. In order to cast rational votes on the thousands of issues that come before them each year, legislators need both technical information about substantive issues and political information about the positions of legislators and effects on people. The committee system processes most of the technical information about proposed legislation. But political information about who inside and outside of Congress favors a particular bill and what the likely division is in each chamber is collected and disseminated through the party organization. Party leaders, by virtue of their position, have information about supporters and the bargains needed to create more supporters. To hold the party together in floor votes, party leaders must also disseminate some of this information to their troops. The party organi-

zation is, in effect, both an intelligence network and a communications network.

Party whips are the core elements in this network. Organized on the basis of geographic regions, the whips and their assistants collect information through regular polls. Representatives and senators are obliged to give accurate responses in whip polls, even if they have not arrived at a public position on the upcoming bill and even if they are not telling fellow members their position. Party strategy on legislation begins with the initial assessment of the likely vote on a bill, and this assessment is based on the information provided by the whip polls. The whip organization also disseminates information. Written whip notices summarize the major issues involved in important legislation and provide regular updates on the legislative schedule. Members who are part of the whip organization also give verbal cues on how to vote on particular measures when party colleagues enter the chamber.

All this effort by no means results in legislators always following the party lead in their voting. After watching so many Democrats desert their party leaders on the capital gains tax cut, for example, a senior Republican commented: "It's not that leaders in Congress can't lead. It's that the followers have found they don't have to follow."[73] But win, lose, or draw, party leaders occupy a central position in congressional lawmaking.

Committees

Committees are the workshops of Congress. The committee system provides a decision-making structure that is essential to congressional lawmaking. As Table 14.3 shows, there were 38 standing committees and 224 subcommittees in the 101st Congress. These congressional committees serve the important function of separating the legislative wheat from the chaff. Five of every six bills introduced in the House and Senate never make it out of committee.

Before going to committee, bills have to be introduced. In the Senate, bills are introduced by members on the floor or simply by handing the bill to clerks. In the House, members intro-

Table 14.3

Standing Committees in the 101st Congress (1989–1990)

House Committee	Members	Subcommittees	Senate Committee	Members	Subcommittees
1. Agriculture (B)	43	8	1. Agriculture, Nutrition, and Forestry (A)	19	7
2. Appropriations (A)	57	13	2. Appropriations (A)	29	13
3. Armed Services (B)	52	7	3. Armed Services (A)	20	6
4. Banking, Finance, Urban Affairs (B)	51	8	4. Banking, Housing, Urban Affairs (A)	21	4
5. Budget (C)	35	6	5. Budget (B)	23	0
6. District of Columbia (C)	11	3	6. Commerce, Science, Transportation (A)	20	8
7. Education and Labor (B)	34	8	7. Energy and Natural Resources (A)	19	5
8. Energy and Commerce (B)	43	6	8. Environment and Public Works (A)	16	5
9. Foreign Affairs (B)	43	8	9. Finance (A)	20	8
10. Government Operations (C)	39	7	10. Foreign Relations (A)	19	7
11. House Administration (C)	21	6	11. Government Affairs (A)	14	5
12. Interior and Insular Affairs (C)	37	6	12. Judiciary (A)	14	6
13. Judiciary (B)	35	7	13. Labor and Human Resources (A)	16	6
14. Merchant Marine and Fisheries (C)	43	6	14. Rules and Administration (B)	16	0
15. Post Office and Civil Service (B)	23	7	15. Small Business (B)	19	6
16. Public Works and Transportation (B)	50	6	16. Veterans' Affairs (B)	11	0
17. Rules (A)	13	2	Subcommittee total		86
18. Science, Space, Technology (C)	49	7			
19. Small Business (C)	44	6			
20. Standards of Office Conduct (C)	12	0			
21. Veterans Affairs (C)	34	5			
22. Ways and Means (A)	36	6			
Subcommittee total		138			

Note: Committee classifications in the House—A, exclusive; B, major; C, nonmajor. Committee classifications in the Senate—A, major; B, minor.

duce legislation by dropping a bill into the "hopper," a mahogany box in the front of the House chamber. Once they are introduced, bills are routinely assigned a number—preceded by HR in the House and S in the Senate—reflecting the order in which they were introduced. The bills are printed and made available to members and the public.

The bills are then referred to a standing committee. The speaker of the House and presiding officer of the Senate are officially responsible for referring bills to committee, but it is the House and Senate parliamentarians who routinely carry out that function. The rules of both chambers specify the jurisdiction of committees, so most of the time referral to a committee is a simple clerical task: Tax bills go to House Ways and Means and Senate Finance, farm bills to Agriculture, and so on. Both chambers also permit multiple referrals—sending a bill to more than one committee—because there is some overlap in committee jurisdiction. More than 10 of the standing committees in the House, for example, have some jurisdiction over environmental policies.

When a committee receives a bill it can simply approve it and send it on to the House or Senate floor with or without amendments, reject the bill, or do nothing. The usual course of events for important bills, however, is for the chair of the committee to refer the bill to a subcommittee (following the subcommittee jurisdictions established by the full committee) and for a subcommittee to hold hearings, to make changes (known as "mark-up"), and to report the bill to the full committee. The full committee may then repeat the three stages of hearings, mark-up, and report, but most committees, most of the time, accept the subcommittee's actions and vote to report the bill to the parent chamber.

The large number of subcommittees and committee deference to their decisions had created what congressional scholars termed "subcommittee government" in the 1970s.[74] Congress was so decentralized it was difficult to act on energy policy, welfare reform, and other areas requiring comprehensive policy. The Senate continues to be a decentralized body, but for several reasons (increased party unity, rules changes that strengthened the speaker, and the dominance of the budget issue) the House moved away from subcommittee government and became more centralized in the 1980s.[75] The relative importance of party leaders, committees, and individual members on the floor will continue to change as Congress responds to a changing political environment. But most of Congress's lawmaking work will continue to be done in committees.

Some of the committees in Table 14.3 are more important than others. The committees with higher status are those that can boost the careers of individual legislators and have an impact on congressional decision making. Naturally the committee assignment process at the beginning of each Congress is of great interest for both new members and incumbents who seek to change committees.

The two chambers and the two parties make committee assignments in different ways. Senate Republicans get their assignments from a 14-member Committee on Committees, which is appointed by the Republican party leader. Senate Democrats are appointed to committees by a 25-member Steering Committee, which in turn is appointed by the Democratic party leader. In the House, the Republican Committee on Committees consists of members elected by each state having GOP representation in the House. A smaller executive committee of the Committee on Committees makes the actual assignments, however, with votes weighted by the size of each state's party delegation. Finally, committee assignments for House Democrats are made by the Steering and Policy Committee, which consists of elected and appointed party officials in the House. When the Democrats control the House, the speaker chairs the Steering and Policy Committee, and the speaker alone appoints the Democratic members of the House Rules Committee.

Both chambers have rules that limit the discretion of these assigning committees. These rules operate by classifying committees and limiting membership by category. As Table 14.3 shows, committees in the House fall into three categories: exclusive, major, and nonmajor. A member assigned to an exclusive committee is limited to that one committee, with the exception that he or she can be on the Budget Committee as well. Members not on an exclusive committee are limited to a total of two committees; House Democrats guarantee that one of those two assignments will be to a major committee. House Democrats are also limited to a total of five subcommittees. Senate committees are covered by two categories: major committees and minor committees (see Table 14.3). Senators from both parties are limited to two major and one minor committee and a total of eight subcommittees.

The exclusive committees in the House and major committees in the Senate are at the top of the status hierarchy. The popularity of other committees is something that changes in reaction to changes in the broader political environment. The House Judiciary Committee, for example, was popular after its nationally televised meetings on the impeachment of President Nixon in 1974. By 1980, however, House members were avoiding Judiciary because it was handling electorally dangerous issues such as school busing, abortion, and gun control and because membership on Judiciary was of little help in attracting campaign contributions from PACs. In recent sessions, House members have sought assignment to the money-attracting Banking, Commerce, and Budget committees.

Those responsible for assignments use several informal criteria to match legislators to committees.[76] The first consideration is the members' own preferences. Another is seniority; those who have served longest in Congress are considered first when members are assigned to new committees. Ideology is a criterion in assignment to highly partisan committees, such as Labor. Religion is a factor whose relevance is limited to particular committees; Jewish members, for example, often seek the Foreign Affairs committee. Where a member is from leads to assignment to committees with regional influence, such as Agriculture. Party loyalty, personality, professional background, race, and sex are additional informal criteria sometimes used in making assignments.

Some committees serve the members' own goals better than other committees. Richard Fenno has classified committees according to the goals of power, policy, and reelection.[77] He found the Appropriations and Ways and Means committees to be the best panels for members who sought power within the House of Representatives. A desire to effect particular policy ends drove members to be on Education and Labor and Foreign Affairs. A greater-than-normal concern over reelection and attention to constituency needs predominated among members of the less demanding Interior and Post Office and Civil Service committees. These differences in members' goals can explain many of the differences in assignment criteria, committee structure, style, leadership, and floor success of committees.

Rules and Norms

For a bill to become law, it must be approved by both the House and the Senate. These two chambers are similar in many ways. They are both elected bodies organized by party and committee. Both senators and representatives divide their time between the lawmaking arena of Capitol Hill and the representative arena of the state and district. Informal norms guide the behavior of members in both chambers. But there are also some key differences between the two chambers, as can be seen in Table 14.4, on p. 458.

Most of the differences in Table 14.4 stem from sheer size. Because the House is more than four times the size of the Senate, it cannot operate in the informal way in which the Senate does. The House is more formal, impersonal, and hierarchical than the Senate. The rules of both chambers reflect this fundamental difference, as a brief look at how bills are scheduled and considered on the floor will illustrate.

RULES OF THE CHAMBERS When a Senate or House committee has completed action on a bill, it is placed on a chronological list of bills in the chamber known as a **calendar**. The House has five different calendars: the *Union Calendar* lists bills that raise or spend money; the *House Calendar* lists all public bills not raising or spending money; the *Consent Calendar* lists noncontroversial bills; the *Private Calendar* lists bills that affect only those named in the bill; and the *Dis-*

Table 14.4

House-Senate Differences

House	Senate
435 members	100 members
2-year term	6-year term
Constituency: average district population 520,000	Constituency: entire state, average population 4.5 million (ranges from 300,000 to 20 million)
Low visibility in national media	High visibility in national media
Rules limit individual participation	Rules maximize individual participation
Committee and subcommittee work is important	Committee and subcommittee work not as important
Distribution of power is hierarchical	Distribution of power is more diffuse
Leaders' authority based on formal position	Leaders' authority based on persuasion
Strict leadership control of floor proceedings	Less leadership control of floor proceedings
Less reliance on staff	More reliance on staff
Policy specialists	Policy generalists
Rules facilitate lawmaking	Rules facilitate representation

charge Calendar lists bills that have been pulled out of committee by a House majority. The Senate operates with just two calendars: an *Executive Calendar* of treaties and nominations and a *Calendar of General Orders* for all legislation. To conduct business, both chambers must move legislation from these calendars to the floor. The rules and procedures for doing this are relatively simple in the Senate, but more complex in the House.

Senators call bills from the calendar by unanimous consent or by majority vote. The standard procedure is for the leaders of both parties and the key senators involved in a bill to develop *unanimous consent agreements*. These written agreements indicate the order in which particular measures will be considered on the floor, which senators will control floor time during debate, and guidelines for debate, stipulating such matters as what types of amendments will be acceptable. All members of the Senate routinely provide their unanimous consent to bring legislation to the floor under these rules.

The House has a different set of rules for bringing legislation to the floor. Although the Consent and Private calendars provide a way for the House to dispose quickly of noncontroversial and limited private bills, most important legislation appears on the Union Calendar or House Calendar. Bills are brought from these calendars to the floor through a resolution sponsored by the House Rules Committee. This resolution, known as a *rule*, sets a time limit for debating the bill, allocates that time between those in favor of and those opposing the bill, and establishes a procedure for amending the bill. The House Rules Committee is the instrument through which the majority party leaders regulate traffic to the floor and enable a body with 435 members to debate and decide on legislation in an orderly fashion.

House rules provide for stricter control of the floor than do Senate rules. In debating and amending legislation, the House generally operates under a set of procedures that are triggered by the House resolving itself into the Committee of the Whole. By doing this, the House changes the time limit on debating amendments from one hour to five minutes. This five-minute rule is an integral part of the lawmaking process in the House.

The Senate has no such rule. Debate in the Senate is almost unlimited, and a Senator can talk indefinitely, or **filibuster**, in order to block legislation. The Senate can vote to end debate on a measure, known as *cloture*, but it requires a three-fifths majority (60 of the 100 members). Although reforms in the 1970s put more teeth into a cloture vote, Senate rules still support the idea that members should be relatively unrestricted in debating issues on the floor.

The differences between House and Senate rules illustrate an underlying and fundamental difference between the two chambers. House rules are designed to facilitate the passing of laws; they emphasize the lawmaking function of Congress. Senate rules are designed to maximize representation. The differences in rules and procedures also create a system in which the House acts more rapidly than the Senate to pass legislation. About 70 percent of the bills that go to a conference committee for resolution of House-

Workers set up cots in the Capitol in preparation for a filibuster on a campaign finance bill in 1988. The Senate met for three days of round-the-clock sessions until supporters pulled the bill after failing to win enough votes to limit debate.

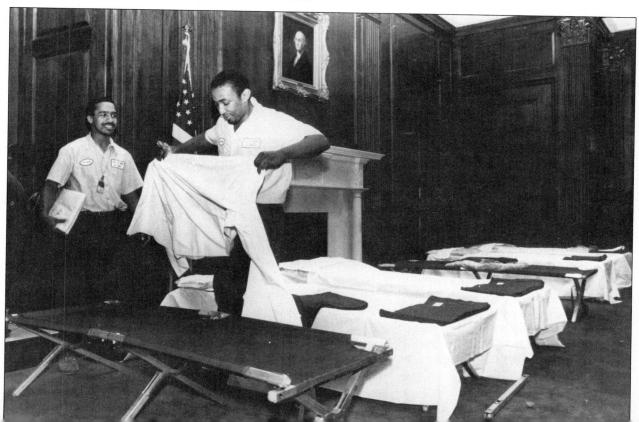

Senate differences have passed the House before they were passed by the Senate.[78]

NORMS House and Senate rules reflect the differences between the two chambers. The informal guidelines, or **congressional norms,** illustrate their similarities. Any organization develops norms of behavior that newcomers to the organization must learn to follow if they are to become effective members. Donald Matthews's study of the Senate uncovered six folkways of the Senate, and other studies of both chambers have confirmed the existence of these folkways and noted changes in them over recent years.[79] The six folkways discussed by Matthews are reciprocity, institutional patriotism, courtesy, specialization, apprenticeship, and legislative work.

The norm of *reciprocity* is central to the congressional bargaining process. All senators permit their colleagues full expression on issues, and representatives defer to the expertise of committee members. *Institutional patriotism* and *courtesy* are folkways that help reduce conflict within Congress. The former provides a shared set of values about the House or Senate that even bitter opponents can agree on; the latter controls conflict by depersonalizing debate so that it is between "the gentleman or gentlewoman from . . ." and his or her "distinguished colleague." *Specialization* is an important folkway for House members. It is closely tied to their committee work and their status in the House. Senators also specialize in particular areas, but the norm is not as tied to committee work and status based on expertise as it is in the House. *Apprenticeship* is a norm that has all but disappeared in the modern Congress. Newcomers and junior members no longer go through an obligatory period in which they let their seniors organize Congress and make the important decisions. The election of particularly activist legislators in 1974 and 1980 and many internal reforms in the last two decades have given junior members the opportunity for full participation in the legislative process.[80] Finally, *legislative work* is a norm that provides rewards in the form of status, influence, or procedural benefits to members who put in long hours on the politically unrewarding and difficult work of developing legislation. All these norms help defuse potentially explosive confrontations and reduce the normal tensions that develop over policy differences. Without the norms, members of Congress would have a much harder time producing legislation.

Congressional Staffs

Members of Congress are supported by large numbers of personal and committee staffs. Representatives receive more than $400,000 to hire up to 22 people as personal staff. Senators' staff allowances, based on state population, range from about $700,000 to $1.4 million; the average size of a senator's personal staff is just under 40, but some senators have more than 70 people. Committee and subcommittee staff are hired by the chair and ranking minority member of these panels, but every senator also hires three committee staff members to cover his or her committee work. Figure 14.2 shows the growth in personal and committee staff since 1955. The number of employees working for the legislative branch is greater than that in some executive departments such as the Department of Labor and the Department of Housing and Urban Development.[81] A question that naturally arises in looking at this expansion of the congressional bureaucracy is, What do all those people do?

Critics of this legislative bureaucracy suggest that it does more to create problems for members of Congress than it does to aid those legislators in their decisions. One senator complained: "Everybody is working for the staff, staff, staff; driving you nutty. In fact, they have hearings for me all of this week." Another senator appeared to agree with his colleague: "If we would fire half the Senate employees we have," he said, "fire half the staff and not permit a paper to be read on the floor of the U.S. Senate, we would complete our business and adjourn by July 4th. When you get more staff and more clerks they spend most of their time thinking up bills, resolutions, amendments. They write speeches for senators, and they come in here on the floor with senators."[82] There are others, however, who suggest that the expanded size of congressional staffs has greatly improved the

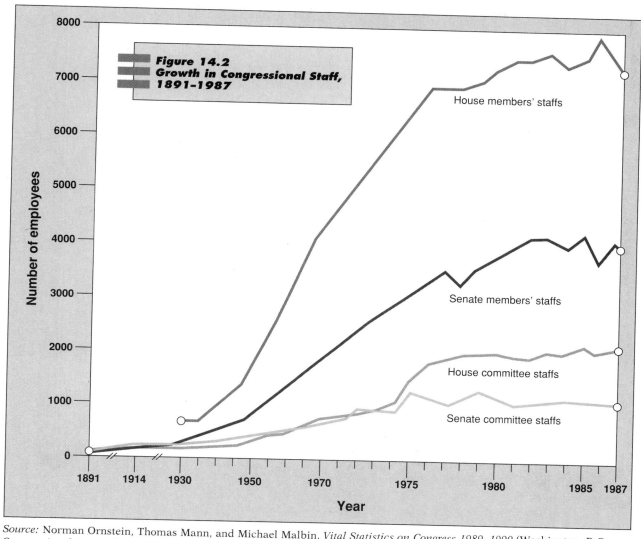

**Figure 14.2
Growth in Congressional Staff,
1891–1987**

House members' staffs

Senate members' staffs

House committee staffs

Senate committee staffs

Number of employees

Year

Source: Norman Ornstein, Thomas Mann, and Michael Malbin, *Vital Statistics on Congress 1989–1990* (Washington, D.C.: Congressional Quarterly Press, 1990), p. 133.

ability of Congress to function in an increasingly complex world. An extensive study led two political scientists to the following conclusion:

> Our contention is that staffs perform much of the congressional work: They perform almost exclusively the constituent-service function; do most of the preliminary legislative research; help generate policy ideas; set up hearings, meetings, and conferences; carry out oversight activities—program evaluations, investigations, etc.; draft bills; and meet

and talk with executive, interest, and constituent groups on substantive matters.[83]

The authors mention the constituent service function as one that is performed almost exclusively by staff. One answer to the question of what staffers do, then, is that they help members get reelected by performing constituent casework. Growth in congressional staff is not restricted to Washington, D.C.: Representatives and senators are stationing more and more of their staff in the district and state.[84] The division

Staff members advise legislators at a committee meeting. The growth in congressional staff has helped members meet many of the demands of law making.

of labor in most congressional offices is one in which district offices are responsible primarily for casework and the Washington office for legislative work.

According to Michael Malbin, Congress sought to achieve four different objectives by increasing its staff as it did over the last several decades.[85] Members of Congress wanted to decrease their dependence on the executive branch and interest groups for information needed in decision making. They wanted to have more impact on national issues. They wanted greater resources for putting new issues on the legislative agenda. Finally, they wanted to gain control over their constantly increasing work load. Malbin suggests that the staff increases in Congress have gone a long way toward helping the institution and members achieve the first three objectives, but they have made the members' work load problem even worse than it had been before.

The work load problem is exacerbated by congressional staffers who play an entrepreneurial role as legislative merchants. They seek out products in the form of ideas for laws, which they then sell to their employers in the form of a bill or article that they can then introduce. The staff system rewards committee and legislative aides who search for proposals that they can bring to their bosses for approval and action.

A simple indicator of the increased work load is the amount of time legislators have for research and reading, time that is essential to a member's being informed on issues. A 1965 survey found that representatives spent about one full day a week on legislative research and reading. A similar survey in 1977 found that the amount of time spent in this way was about one *hour* a week.[86] The increase in staff seems not to have helped members to gain control over their work load and to have more time for research and reading; in fact, it seems to have had the opposite effect.

The growing dependence of members on a large congressional staff has another effect noted by Malbin: Negotiations among staff members have replaced deliberation among legislators in many areas of the legislative process. Malbin studied a number of cases of legislation in which it was the staff rather than the elected members who were doing the legislative bargaining and producing the compromise bill. When the negotiations of staff replace or supplant the direct interaction of members, we have a Congress where the real work of governing is carried on by what Malbin calls "unelected representatives" rather than by legislators who are accountable to the voters.

Congressional Voting

There were more than 1700 recorded votes in the 100th Congress (1987–1988), over 800 in the Senate and over 900 in the House. This is in addition to the hundreds of voice votes cast on the floor and all the votes taken during committee and subcommittee consideration of bills. Members of Congress govern through their votes, and the outcomes of those votes determine the record of Congress and most policies of the government.

How do members of Congress make up their minds on these votes? What factors determine their decisions on the House or Senate floor? Political scientists seeking answers to those questions have followed two courses of study. One is to count votes and analyze the results in terms of party, region, constituency characteristics, the president's position, or the position of certain congressional colleagues. The second approach is to ask members what factors influence them or how they go about making up their minds in voting.

By studying thousands of roll call votes over long periods of time, political scientists have been able to isolate some of the key determinants of congressional roll call voting.[87] The most important influences turn out to be the party affiliation of members, the region of the country from which they come, certain constituency characteristics such as urbanism and proportion of blue-collar workers, ideology, and the president. Of course, the relative importance of these

different influences will vary from issue to issue and member to member.

If you could know only one thing about a member of Congress in order to predict how he or she would vote, the question to ask would be whether the member was a Democrat or Republican. Roll call vote analyses consistently show that *party affiliation* is the single most important influence on congressional voting. As we saw in Chapter 12, seven of every ten members of Congress vote consistently with a majority of their party on votes in which a majority of Republicans opposes a majority of Democrats. Certain constituency characteristics reinforce party voting by members of Congress. For most members, a party vote is also a constituency vote because the Democratic or Republican position on the issue will also be the position held by most of their constituents or the position deemed to be in the best interests of the dominant groups in their districts. The relationship between constituency and party voting can also be seen when we look at senators and representatives who regularly defect from their own party to support the opposition. Southern Democrats and northeastern Republicans—whose constituencies are likely to differ from the typical constituency of their party on urbanization, race, and other characteristics—have historically been less supportive of their party's positions on most major issues than have northern Democrats and midwestern and western Republicans.

The primary regional influence on congressional voting has been the conservative coalition, which emerged in opposition to New Deal programs in the 1930s but became less important in congressional voting in the 1980s. The conservative coalition, defined as a majority of voting southern Democrats and a majority of voting Republicans, appeared as a voting bloc in about one of every five House votes and one of every four Senate votes until the 1980s. This coalition was particularly strong on defense policy, economic concerns, and agriculture policy. Although there was a clear regional basis for the conservative coalition, it was united by a shared conservative ideology as well.

The Reagan administration owed a great deal of its early legislative success to the support of

The electronic voting board in the House of Representatives. "I find that a lot of times, people walk in, and the first thing they do is look at the board, and they have key people they check out."

the conservative coalition, but by the late 1980s the coalition had greatly diminished as a force in congressional voting. Southern Democrats started coming back into the party's fold on many issues as a result of the changed southern electorate brought about through the Voting Rights Act of 1965 and the decline of civil rights as a decisive issue. By 1988, the conservative coalition appeared as a voting bloc on less than one of every ten votes in both the House and the Senate.[88] The conservative coalition reemerged in 1989 and was important to the outcome of the House capital gains tax cut vote. But even with that victory, the coalition's failure to appear on most of the important votes in 1989 made it "a mere shadow of its former self."[89]

The president's influence on congressional voting has been discussed elsewhere in this chapter and is examined in Chapter 15 as well. It depends on a number of factors such as electoral margins, standings in the polls, issues and events, and the party division in Congress.

When members of Congress are asked to name the influences on their votes, they are likely to include some of the same factors as were found by political scientists in their studies of votes. One difference, however, is that the members tend to stress the importance of the human interaction within Congress in determining their voting. According to them, one of the most important influences on how any member votes is his or her colleagues. Here's what one representative has to say:

Many guys vote based on how one of the other members of their state delegation voted, and not necessarily on the merits of the amendment.

I find that a lot of times, people walk in, and the first thing they do is look at the board, and they have key people they check out, and if those people have voted "aye," they go to the machine and vote "aye" and walk off the floor.

I read all that background stuff—the Democratic Study Group stuff—in the morning before I go to vote—now, I go on the floor, unless it has been something that has been amended and substituted, so I don't know what is going on, I will go in and kind of know where I am going.

But I will look at the board and see how members of the state delegation vote, because they are in districts right next to me and they have constituencies just like mine. I will vote the way I am going to vote, except that if they are both different, I will go up and say, "Why did you vote that way? Let me know if there is something I am missing."[90]

Fellow members whose opinions are sought out before a member votes form a **cue network.** In a study of this network in the House of Representatives, members were asked: "Suppose you had to cast a roll-call vote and could know only the position of three of the people or groups on this list?" They were then handed a list of ten groups: the state party delegation, a majority of their party, the president, three ideological groups (the Democratic Study Group, the Republican Wednesday Club, and the conservative coalition), the chair of the reporting committee, the ranking minority member of the reporting committee, a majority of all members, and their party leadership. Members' responses led to a distinction between two types of cue givers: initial and intermediary. Members look to *initial cue givers*, such as committee leaders and the executive branch, because of their expertise. While members recognize the technical expertise of initial cue givers, they may sometimes question the underlying value preferences of these sources. *Intermediary cue givers* consist of colleagues with the same value preferences as the member, who have looked at the technical information and arrived at a collective decision on how to vote. The intermediary cue sources most often cited by members were the state party delegation and party leaders.

This study of cue taking in the House confirms the importance of the political party in Congress and illustrates the fact that members turn to other members for guidance on how to vote. It is very much an internal network. By knowing the position of the cue sources listed, the authors of this study were able to predict the actual roll call vote in the House 88 percent of the time.[91] Thus it appears that the human interaction of members of Congress is an important part of the institution's decision-making process. Legislators are influenced by their colleagues, and deliberation is as important as representation.

Checkpoint

- Congressional party organizations and leaders contribute greatly to the institution's ability to meet its lawmaking responsibilities. Parties organize the structure of each chamber and establish the rules under which it operates. Party leaders are responsible for scheduling legislation and controlling floor action so that members can act on legislation in an orderly fashion.

- The party whip organization provides an information network that helps individual members cast rational votes and assists party leaders in developing legislative strategy.

- Congress works through committees. While the representation of district and state interests is an important factor in determining to which committees members seek to be assigned, it is in their committee work that we most commonly find members acting as members of the national government. Some congressional committees are more important than others, and some serve members' goals better than others.

- The written rules of the House and Senate provide the order—the limits on representation—that are needed to pass laws. Certain unwritten norms also support the lawmaking functions of the institution: specialization, legislative work, reciprocity, and the mild form of apprenticeship still remaining in Congress. The norms of courtesy and institutional patriotism help regulate conflict.

- The growth in congressional staff has permitted members of Congress to focus more on lawmaking than on constituent service, to be less dependent on the executive branch and interest groups for lawmaking information, and to have a greater impact on national issues and more resources for putting new issues on the legislative agenda. But it has not allowed legislators to gain control over an increasing work load.

- Party affiliation and cue networks are the most important influences on how members of Congress vote.

CONGRESS: WHO GOVERNS?

In describing the proposed structure of the House of Representatives to the New York Ratifying Convention in 1788, Alexander Hamilton observed: "Here, sir, the people govern."[92] Would it be accurate to use the same phrase to describe the modern Congress? The democratic, pluralist, and power elite perspectives of governing America provide different ways of answering that question.

Democracy

Congress is widely regarded as the most democratic institution of American government. James Madison's description of the House of Representatives as "the grand repository of the democratic principle of government" in his notes on the Philadelphia Convention makes it clear that those who wrote the Constitution intended Congress to be the chief institution of democracy.[93]

The democratic ideals of popular sovereignty, political equality, and majority rule are most evident in the two-year terms, equal representation (1 vote for every 520,000 people), and voting procedures of the House. The connection between voters' behavior in congressional elections and representatives' behavior in Congress is key to this understanding of Congress as a democratic institution. If constituencies are likely to elect and reelect only those representatives who support policies favored by the constituencies, and if representatives want to be reelected, then representatives have no choice—they must support policies favored by their constituents. As Robert Bernstein has recently pointed out, however, what we know about the behavior of voters in congressional elections and of representatives in Congress provides little support for what Bernstein calls "the myth of constituency control":

> Constituencies do not control the policies adopted by their representatives; they have some influence over what those policies are, but members are by and large free to adopt what they think best. Constituency influence does not flow primarily from electoral threats against those in office, but rather from the initial selection of representatives.

Once selected, liberals are likely to adopt liberal policies and conservatives to adopt conservative policies. The desire for reelection has only marginal impact in shifting members from ideological preferences should those preferences differ from the preferences of their constituencies.[94]

The evidence that led to that conclusion does not mean that Congress is not a democratic institution. Despite the high reelection rates of incumbents, for example, the number of retirements and resignations from Congress add to those who are defeated to make the average tenure of members of Congress less than 11 years.[95] It is this turnover and the opportunity it provides for selecting a new member that establish the electoral connection between members of Congress and their constituents more than it is electoral threats.

The picture that comes to mind when most of us consider Congress and democracy is one of legislators representing district and state interests. In the 1986 tax reform discussion that opened this chapter, for example, it seemed entirely appropriate that oil state senators sought to provide a tax shelter exemption for investing in oil drilling. After all, that is what their constituents sent them to Washington to do. But what if the representation of constituency interests in that case had resulted in no tax reform legislation passing Congress that year, despite a national majority that believed that the tax laws then in effect were unfair? A democracy requires more of Congress than representation; it also requires lawmaking. A national legislature in which all members are concerned only with the interests of their own constituents would find itself unable to pass laws that respond to a national majority or to the national interest.

There is, in other words, a second model of democracy for judging Congress—one based on the ideas of "deliberative democracy" discussed in Chapter 4. It is characterized by legislative debate and deliberation on different perceptions

Members of the 101st Congress deliberating on the floor. A democracy requires more of Congress than the representation of constituency interests; it also requires lawmaking and deliberation on different perceptions of a common or national interest.

of a common or national interest—on the overall impact of tax reform legislation as well as on the effects of particular provisions on members' constituencies. Judgments about Congress and democracy by the general public, congressional scholars, and members themselves are based on both meanings of democracy.[96]

Pluralism

Pluralists see a number of advantages to how Congress operates. Congressional scholars William Keefe and Morris Ogul have written about some of the reasons why pluralists are often the staunchest defenders of Congress:

> If the legislature is lacking in hierarchy, it correspondingly enhances the opportunities for legislators to pursue their individual goals and for private citizens and groups to gain access to the legislative process.
>
> If the diffusion of legislative power makes it perplexing to fix responsibility, it also makes it difficult to undo traditional practices and arrangements.
>
> If legislative procedure makes it difficult for the majority to work its will, it also assures the minority of its right to be heard.
>
> If legislators subordinate broad interests to provincial ones, they nevertheless make government responsive to local needs and viewpoints.[97]

Bargaining is a central part of congressional decision making. The members' commitment to representation and the open nature of the institution guarantee that a wide range of interests will be considered. The representation of group interests that is the essence of pluralism is reflected in the policies passed by Congress, as in the case of the Tax Reform Act of 1986. As we saw at the beginning of the chapter, oil and gas interests succeeded in protecting investors in that industry.[98] But the final bill also contained a large number of provisions designed to help other special interests—labor groups, insurance companies, major corporations.

Some of this interest representation, as we have already seen, can be regarded as the constituency representation expected in a democracy. A pluralist framework, on the other hand, helps explain some of the provisions of the tax law (a tax break for Bermuda, for example) that seem unrelated to the members' representation of geographic constituencies. Instead they seem more connected to the representation of organized interests, as part of the bargaining that characterizes congressional policymaking, and to a philosophy of government that believes interest groups should have an important role in government decisions.[99]

A final point about pluralism and Congress has to do with a criticism of pluralism discussed in earlier chapters—that government serves organized interests but ignores the unorganized. A study of constituency service found that there is less socioeconomic bias to asking one's representative for assistance than there is in other forms of participation such as voting, contributing to a campaign, or expressing an opinion or policy. Members of Congress are able to serve unorganized interests through the casework of constituency service to a degree they do not through congressional policymaking.[100]

The Power Elite

"Power doesn't keep people here," said a House member going into his fourth term. "They come, they realize that they don't have it. But they don't want to switch to something else." A top Democratic leader in a recent Congress agreed: "A hell of a lot of state legislators have more power than most of us do." He felt that members of Congress stayed on term after term because they liked to be at the center of events, even if they had little influence over the outcome.[101]

Some of those who view the governing of America from a power elite perspective would go much further than the two representatives. If you want to find out who governs, they say, do not waste time looking at Congress. What you see on C-SPAN—the televised proceedings of Congress—is one of the carnivals of politics, but it has little to do with who gets what from government. Individual members of Congress may be a part of the governing elite, but the real decisions about governing are made away from the glare of television lights by small groups drawn mostly from industry and the executive branch. "Congress is becoming increasingly irrelevant to politics," according to political scientist Howard Reiter. "This does not mean that there has been a conspiracy to destroy the power of Congress, only that other power centers have not been concerned enough about the decline of congressional effectiveness to take the steps that would be necessary to reverse it."[102]

Not all of those who subscribe to the power elite view, however, dismiss the institution in that way. Mark Green's *Who Runs Congress?* is typical of another elite perspective. According to this view, members of Congress exercise power, but they use it to further the interests of an economic elite:

So who rules Congress? A century ago it was "King Caucus," then King Speaker, then imperial Presidents, then autocratic chairmen—and now King Cash. Members are run by the special interests who enable them to run for office.

The answer, then, to this book's opening three questions—Who owns Congress? Who influences Congress? and Who rules Congress? is the same. Until that changes, the Golden Rule of Politics will prevail in the parliament of the world's greatest democracy—he who has the gold, rules.[103]

Those who believe America is governed by a power elite consider both the power of Congress in governing America and the power of individual members within Congress. The power of the institution of Congress seems limited compared to that of the executive branch and the private sector elite. Thomas Dye addresses the issue of the power of individual members by including about 90 of the 535 members of Congress in America's power elite—or just over 1 percent of the total membership of the national power elite. These 90 members of Congress are party leaders and the chairpersons and ranking members of congressional committees. This congressional elite is important because it influences decisions in which Congress does exercise power and because it serves to facilitate power elite decisions in other areas as well. "Congressional committees are an important link between governmental and nongovernmental elites," according to Dye. "Congressional committees bring department and agency heads together with leading industrial representatives—bankers, cotton producers, labor leaders, citrus growers, government contractors."[104]

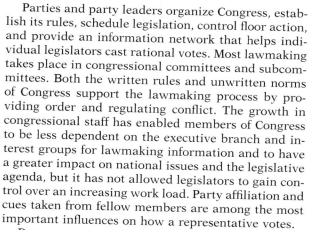

Checkpoint

- The democratic, pluralist, and power elite frameworks provide different ways of looking at Congress and different standards for evaluating the institution. The democratic model emphasizes the accountability of legislators to constituents and focuses on congressional elections.

- Pluralists stress the accessibility of lawmakers and the legitimate role of interest groups in government decision making.

- Those who believe a power elite governs America are likely to discuss how Congress is either irrelevant to elite decision makers or supportive of their rule.

Parties and party leaders organize Congress, establish its rules, schedule legislation, control floor action, and provide an information network that helps individual legislators cast rational votes. Most lawmaking takes place in congressional committees and subcommittees. Both the written rules and unwritten norms of Congress support the lawmaking process by providing order and regulating conflict. The growth in congressional staff has enabled members of Congress to be less dependent on the executive branch and interest groups for lawmaking information and to have a greater impact on national issues and the legislative agenda, but it has not allowed legislators to gain control over an increasing work load. Party affiliation and cues taken from fellow members are among the most important influences on how a representative votes.

Democracy requires that members of Congress be accountable. Constituencies establish that accountability through the initial selection of representatives more than through the use of electoral threats to control behavior. By seeing Congress as an arena for interest group bargaining, pluralists emphasize the representational strengths of Congress more than lawmaking, while the power elite perspective sees Congress as either irrelevant to elite decision making or controlled by outside forces.

SUMMARY

Legislators are both the people's representatives *to* government and members *of* the national government. Those two responsibilities are reflected in the institutional functions of representation and lawmaking, which give rise to a tension that shapes the congressional role in governing America. Other congressional functions include administrative oversight of the executive branch, education of constituents about government processes, and constituent service.

Congressional elections and representative styles determine who comes to Washington and how they connect what they do in Congress with interests at home. Incumbents enjoy the electoral advantages of staff support, name recognition, campaign funding, and a positive public image, which helps explain why they win most congressional elections. But congressional representation extends beyond periodic elections and includes interest groups and the national interest as well as constituent interests.

KEY TERMS

Representation	Primary constituency
Delegate	Personal constituency
Trustee	Majority leader
Lawmaking	Minority leader
Administrative oversight	Whip
Investigative hearings	Speaker
Legislative veto	Calendar
Constituent service	Filibuster
Geographic constituency	Congressional norms
Reelection constituency	Cue network

FOR FURTHER READING

Robert A. Bernstein, *Elections, Representation, and Congressional Voting Behavior* (Englewood Cliffs, N.J.: Prentice-Hall, 1989). A good review of political science research on the behavior of voters and representatives that challenges the myth of constituency control.

Lawrence Dodd and Bruce Oppenheimer, *Congress Reconsidered*, 4th ed. (Washington, D.C.: Congressional Quarterly Press, 1989). A collection of essays by leading congressional scholars on how Congress is changing and why.

Richard Fenno, *Homestyle: House Members in Their Districts* (Boston: Little, Brown, 1978). Gives readers a feel for what representatives do when they are back home.

Morris P. Fiorina, *Congress: Keystone of the Washington Establishment*, 2nd ed. (New Haven, Conn.: Yale University Press, 1989). An account of self-interested constituents, legislators, and bureaucrats that caused quite a stir when first published in 1977. The second edition looks at what, if anything, has changed since then.

David Mayhew, *Congress: The Electoral Connection* (New Haven, Conn.: Yale University Press, 1974). A classic essay on how the motivation for reelection influences the behavior of members and the structure of Congress.

Norman Ornstein et al, *Vital Statistics on Congress 1989–1990* (Washington, D.C.: Congressional Quarterly Press, 1990). A collection of statistics that permits those who follow Congress to discuss patterns and trends at a level previously reserved to followers of baseball.

David Vogler and Sidney Waldman, *Congress and Democracy* (Washington, D.C.: Congressional Quarterly Press, 1985). Analyzes the ways in which members of Congress seek to serve national interests as well as those of the state and district.

The Presidency

Chapter 15

★ Presidential Powers
★ Presidential Selection
★ The Institutional Presidency
★ Presidential Decision
   Making: Who Governs?

The American public tends to blame presidents for just about anything that goes wrong during their term in office and to give them credit for the good things that happen during those years. Presidents are the responsible officers of the national government, but they are more than that—they are symbols of the national condition. When presidents and administration officials talk about the office, however, they are more likely to point to the limits on presidential power and to emphasize the collective effort required to govern America. ■

In November 1986 Americans learned for the first time that Reagan administration officials had been selling arms in secret to Iran, in violation of U.S. policy not to sell arms to terrorist countries. In direct violation of U.S. law, the funds from the arms sale were being secretly diverted to the contras, a rebel group fighting the Communist government of Nicaragua. President Reagan claimed to know nothing of the affair, and he replaced his national security adviser and chief of staff for their involvement. Shortly after the Tower Commission issued a report critical of the administration's actions in the Iran-contra affair, the President had this to say in a nationally televised address to the American people:

> First, let me say I take full responsibility for my own actions and for those of my administration. As angry as I may be about activities undertaken without my knowledge, I am still accountable for those activities. As disappointed as I may be in some who served me, I am still the one who must answer to the American people for this behavior. And as personally distasteful as I find secret bank accounts and diverted funds—well, as the Navy would say, it happened on my watch.[1]

Executive responsibility was also the theme sounded 26 years earlier by President John Kennedy after his administration had suffered a setback in the Bay of Pigs fiasco. In that case, 1200 Cuban refugees who had been trained and supported by the Central Intelligence Agency (CIA) landed at the Bay of Pigs on the coast of Cuba in an attempt to overthrow the government of Fidel Castro. Castro's forces quickly defeated the invasion. A member of the Kennedy administration, who blamed the Bay of Pigs failure on the CIA, got this response from the President: "When I accepted responsibility for this operation, I took the entire responsibility on myself, and I think we should have no sort of passing of the buck or backbiting, however justified." At his first press conference after the Bay of Pigs, Kennedy made the same point: "I'm the responsible officer of the Government." This was followed up by a White House statement:

> President Kennedy has stated from the beginning that as President he bears sole responsibility. He has stated it on all occasions and he restates it now. The President is strongly opposed to anyone within or without the administration attempting to shift the responsibility.

Privately, however, President Kennedy blamed the CIA for the Bay of Pigs failure and took steps that eventually led to the resignation of that agency's two highest officials. We see a different perspective on presidential responsibility in Kennedy's private remarks to those CIA officials about why they had to be replaced. "Under a parliamentary system of government," said Kennedy, "it is I who would be leaving office. But under our system it is you who must go."[2]

We all know that the task of governing America is one that the president shares with Congress, the bureaucracy, the courts, and state and local political leaders. But we also hold the president responsible for most of what government does or does not do during that chief executive's term. Whether that responsibility is associated with the popular mandates of a democratic model, with the pluralist view of the president as chief bargainer, or with the president as the most visible member of a governing elite, our judgments about government rely heavily on our evaluations of presidential performance, and vice versa. The high expectations we have for any new president make the chief executive not only the responsible officer of government but also a symbol of the nation's well-being. In the middle of his term in office, President Jimmy Carter observed: "When things go bad, you get entirely too much blame. And I have to admit that when things go good, you get entirely too much credit."[3] No president knew the second part of that formula better than Carter's successor, Ronald Reagan, who in 1984 claimed credit for a rise in the average national SAT scores.[4]

Presidents have long advanced the notion that those outside the White House have misconceptions about what they really can do. Franklin Roosevelt said that once he became president he understood that Lincoln was a sad man because he couldn't get personal power all at once. John Kennedy commented on how much more powerful Congress looked from the White House than it had when he was a member of the House and Senate. Lyndon Johnson complained that his only power was nuclear—and that he couldn't use that. And Harry Truman once wrote: "All the President is, is a glorified public relations man who spends his time flattering, kissing and kicking people to get them to do what they are supposed to do anyway."[5]

Somewhere between the overly grand notions of presidential power held by the public and the limits on those powers stressed by presidents and other insiders we can expect to find the real powers of the presidency. We begin by turning to grants of power in the Constitution and the evolution of the modern presidency through the 1980s.

PRESIDENTIAL POWERS

George Bush had been president for nearly six months when he held his first prime-time television news conference in June 1989. In many ways it was quite a contrast to news conferences of his predecessor, Ronald Reagan. President Reagan would begin his press conferences by purposefully striding down a long, red-carpeted hallway leading to a lectern placed before the open doorway in the middle of the White House East Room. "The reason we had Reagan stand in front of the open doors," one aide said, "was because it gave life and depth to the body that's there."[6] Another aide compared Reagan's meetings with the press to the classic showdowns of a western movie. "We'd always be in the East Room sitting on the edge of our chairs," he added.[7]

In contrast, President Bush began his press conference by walking through a side doorway to a lectern placed inconspicuously before gold drapes at the front of the East Room. The contrast with his predecessor continued when President Bush candidly answered questions about the United States' response to the violent repression of pro-democracy demonstrations in China the previous week by saying "we aren't going to remake the world." A few minutes later, this exchange took place:

> **Reporter:** Mr. President, the other day you picked up the phone and talked to Richard Nixon about China. I'm wondering, since you know some of the Chinese leaders personally, why you don't pick up the phone and talk to them?
>
> **President:** I tried today. Isn't that a coincidence that you'd ask that question?
>
> **Reporter:** And what did you learn?
>
> **President:** The line was busy. I couldn't get through. They're out—[8]

In a book on the presidency published about

One of President Reagan's aides compared his press conferences to the classic showdowns of a western movie. Another aide said President Bush's first televised press conference "brought his audience behind the Wizard of Oz curtain."

the middle of the Reagan years, political scientist Theodore Lowi observed: "The president is the Wizard of Oz. Appearances become everything."[9] A former Reagan White House official used the same image to explain why Bush's press conference had come as such a surprise. President Bush, he said, had "brought his audience behind the Wizard of Oz curtain."[10]

How did the president come to be seen as the Wizard of Oz—both by those on the outside, who see SAT scores go up and wonder at his powers, and those on the inside, who know that the magic is not magic at all? To begin to answer that question, we look at the core powers the Constitution gives to the president and at how those powers have grown over the years.

Constitutional Grants of Power

The powers of the modern president include five core powers that can be traced to specific provisions of the Constitution and to interpretations of those provisions by the Supreme Court over time: the executive power, the appointing power, the war power, legislative powers, and the treaty power. Many of these powers are shared with Congress, giving rise to rivalries and conflicts between the two branches over the years.

EXECUTIVE POWER Section One of Article II says: "The executive power shall be vested in a President of the United States." Section Three of the same article says of the president, "He shall take care that the laws be faithfully executed." These two provisions form the basis of **executive power**, a grant of power not limited to specific laws passed by Congress or to the other specific presidential powers listed in the Constitution. The key authors of these provisions at the Philadelphia Convention in 1787, James Pinckney, Gouverneur Morris, and James Wilson, intended for executive power to be expansive, a view adopted by the Supreme Court in a number of key decisions.

For example, in 1890, the Court ruled that a bodyguard assigned by the attorney general to protect a threatened federal judge could not be held for the murder of a man who drew a knife on the judge; his shooting was understood to be "an act done in pursuance of a law of the United States." Congress had passed no law concerning the appointment of bodyguards. The Supreme Court in this case said that the "law" under which the bodyguard acted was the attorney general's order, issued with the consent of the president. According to the Court, the executive power given to the president in Article II meant that order had the force of federal law.[11]

Other Supreme Court decisions, however, illustrate that executive power is not unlimited. In 1952, the Court said the provisions of the Constitution did not empower President Truman's takeover of the nation's steel mills in order to prevent workers from striking and to keep the mills running during the Korean War. In 1971, the Court ruled against President Nixon's claim of executive power in seeking an injunction to prevent the *New York Times* and other papers from publishing the Pentagon Papers on the basis that their publication would threaten national security. These papers portrayed years of secret plans to escalate the Vietnam War and mislead the public about that escalation.[12] In both of these cases, the Court recognized the fact that the president does have executive powers granted in Article II, but that those powers have to be balanced against competing constitutional powers of Congress (to pass labor laws, for example) and restrictions on government action outlined in the First Amendment.

APPOINTING POWER An old political saying has it that each appointment creates a dozen enemies and one ingrate. Despite that, the president's **appointing power**—the power to appoint, with the Senate's consent, important officials of the executive branch, judges, and ambassadors—is one of the core powers of the office. The Constitutional Convention had gone back and forth on the issue of whether the Senate or executive should have the power of appointment until the position of shared power reflected in Article II was accepted in the final weeks of the convention.[13]

The usual pattern is for the Senate to confirm, rather than reject, presidential nominees. In fact, the confirmation rate of presidential appointments in the 100th Congress (1987–1988)—99 percent—is typical.[14] Presidents do not have the sole power of appointment, but they can almost always count on the Senate to support their choices. The appointment power becomes most visible in American politics when the Senate *rejects* a high-level presidential appointment, as it did with John Tower's nomination to be secretary of defense in the Bush administration in 1989 and Robert Bork's nomination to the Supreme Court by President Reagan in 1987. Senate rejection of a presidential cabinet nominee is rare—John Tower was the first in 30 years and only the ninth in the history of the country. The rejection of Robert Bork was less exceptional. Historically, the Senate has rejected one of every five nominees to the Supreme Court.

The most heated controversies over the appointment power have centered on the flip side of this power—the authority to fire. In 1789, this issue was a point of debate because amendments to bills establishing the first executive departments (State, Treasury, and War) called for Senate approval before a president could remove these department heads. The only time in American history that a president has been impeached and tried—in the case of Andrew Johnson in 1868—turned on the question of whether the president could remove high officials (the secretary of war in Johnson's case) without first getting Senate approval.

The power to fire is an important administrative tool, and as we saw in the Bay of Pigs and Iran-Contra cases at the beginning of the chapter, it can be an important political resource for the president as well. The language of the Constitution does not by itself answer this question: If the Senate must confirm a particular appointment, does the president need the Senate's approval in order to *remove* that person from office? In 1926, the Supreme Court upheld the president's power to fire executive appointees without having to get the approval of the Senate. The majority opinion in this case was written by a former president, Chief Justice William Howard Taft, who argued that for a president to act effectively as a chief executive he had to have the power to select his own subordinates.

Presidents can still remove officials whose duties are executive, and they can do so for political or policy reasons. But they cannot remove officials whose duties are judicial or quasi-judicial, as are those of regulatory agencies such as the Federal Trade Commission. Congress sets the terms of office for these officials, and only Congress can specify the conditions under which they can be removed before that term has expired.

In 1801, President Jefferson introduced the concept of defensive war to justify his sending troops and ships to Tripoli, even though Congress had not declared war.

WAR POWER Article I gives Congress, not the president, the power "to declare war." At the Constitutional Convention, the Committee on Detail's original language for this section was that Congress would have the power "to make war." This was changed to "declare" after delegates argued that "to make war" meant to conduct the actual operations of war, a power that should belong to the executive, not the legislature. Article II provides for this power: "The President shall be commander in chief of the army and navy of the United States and of the militia of the several states when called into the actual service of the United States."

In giving Congress the power to declare war, the Philadelphia convention seemed to be giving the **war power** (the authority for protecting the nation from its enemies) to Congress rather than the president. That was certainly the interpretation of Thomas Jefferson, who wrote in a letter to James Madison in 1789 that the Constitution had given "one effectual check to the Dog of war by transferring the power of letting him loose from the Executive to the Legislative body, from those who are to spend to those who are to pay."[15]

But the commander-in-chief clause of Article II gave the president war powers, too. The same Thomas Jefferson was acting as president and commander in chief when he sent troops and ships to fight the Barbary pirates in Tripoli in 1801 even though Congress had not declared war. President Jefferson's argument was that a state of war already existed when Tripoli attacked American ships. Jefferson's position that the president had defensive war powers when another country initiated a state of war won quick acceptance in the nineteenth century. Between 1801 and 1901, presidents sent armed forces abroad without a formal declaration of war on 48 separate occasions.

Congressional war powers seemed to have all

U.S. troops invade Panama in December 1989. The issue of congressional and presidential war powers is still a central question of governing America.

but disappeared when U.S. involvement in the war in Vietnam brought the constitutional issue to the forefront. In 1966 a spokesman for the Department of State made clear the Johnson administration's position on the war power of the Constitution:

> No declaration of war is needed to authorize American actions in Vietnam. The President has ample authority to order the participation of United States armed forces in the defense of South Vietnam.
>
> Over a very long period in our history, practice and precedent have confirmed the constitutional authority to engage United States forces in hostilities without a declaration of war.
>
> This history extends from the undeclared war with France and the war against the Barbary Pirates, at the end of the 18th Century, to the Korean War of 1950–53.[16]

The growing unpopularity of the Vietnam War, the number of American casualties (50,000), the high-handed conduct of the war by the executive branch, and its indeterminate outcome led Congress to pass the War Powers Resolution in 1973. That law states: "It is the purpose of this joint resolution to fulfill the intent of the framers of the Constitution and insure that the collective judgment of both the Congress and the President will apply to the introduction of U.S. armed forces into hostilities." The specific mechanism ensuring Congress' collective judgment was the legislative veto, a device by which Congress could block executive action. The 1983 Supreme Court decision overturning the legislative veto in an immigration law obviously raises questions about the constitutional status of the 1973 act, and the issue of congressional and presidential war powers is still a central question of governing America. Debate over the extent and limits of the president's war powers continued to crop up in cases such as the deployment of Marines in Lebanon in the 1980s and the sending of troops and ships to counter Iraqi actions in the Middle East in the 1990s.

LEGISLATIVE POWER   The president's **legislative powers** are based on three Constitutional provisions: the power to recommend legislation, to call special sessions of Congress, and to veto legislation. The sparse language of the Constitution has been augmented by custom and statutes, so that the president's legislative program now largely determines the congressional agenda.

Because Congress is now in session throughout most of the year, the presidential power to call Congress into special session is less important than in years past. President Franklin Roosevelt, for example, convened an extraordinary special session of Congress in March 1933, which passed a flood of New Deal legislation in the famous first hundred days of the new administration.

Section Seven of Article I provides for the presidential veto of legislation. This section clearly shows the intended legislative role of the president. All legislation passed by Congress must be sent to the president for approval—not just bills but "every order, resolution or vote to which the concurrence of the Senate and House of Representatives may be necessary (except on a question of adjournment)." If the president signs a bill, it becomes law. If he sends it back with objections, both the House and the Senate must repass it by two-thirds majorities to override the veto. If the president does nothing, the bill automatically becomes law after ten days, unless Congress adjourns during that time. In that case, the bill does not become a law, and the president has used what is called a pocket veto (the bill is pocketed until nothing can be done with it). Unlike a regular veto, which Congress can override, a pocket veto is absolute. Can the pocket veto be used when Congress is adjourned for a recess (as a number of presidents have maintained) or only when Congress adjourns after a two-year session (as a federal judge ruled in 1985)? That is a matter of some dispute,

which may not be clarified until the Supreme Court rules on it.[17]

How often a president uses the veto depends on such obvious factors as whether the president's party controls Congress and the nature of the executive program, but Table 15.1 reflects the overall infrequency of vetoes: Of the several hundred bills passed by Congress in each session, less than one percent are turned down by the president.[18] Congress overrides only about 7 percent of all presidential vetoes, so the veto is an effective way of stopping Congress from doing something that the president opposes.[19] The *threat* of a veto often serves the same purpose and is an important bargaining chip in the president's dealings with Congress.

Presidents must sign or reject entire bills; they cannot reject just parts of it. Presidents Reagan and Bush have been strong proponents of a constitutional amendment to give the President a *line-item veto*, allowing for veto of certain provisions in a bill or a budget line in an appropriations bill, while approving the rest of the legislation. But Congress has been reluctant to shore up what already seem to be formidable legislative powers of the presidency and has buried line-item veto proposals in committee.

TREATY POWER   The president's **treaty power** is based on Section Two of Article II, which says that the president "shall have power, by and with the advice and consent of the Senate, to make treaties, provided two thirds of the Senators present concur." The original draft of the Constitution, as reported by the Committee on Detail in August 1787, gave the Senate the power to make treaties. But James Madison and others argued that since the Senate was the body for representing states rather than the country as a whole, it should not have the power to make treaties with other countries.

The wording of the Constitution does not make it clear whether the advice and consent of the Senate is to be sought by the president during the actual negotiations for a treaty or after it is negotiated. George Washington was the first and last president to follow the first interpretation. In August 1789, he went to the Senate to

Table 15.1

Presidential Vetoes of Public Bills

President	Regular Vetoes	Overridden	Pocket Vetoes	Total Vetoes
Franklin Roosevelt	372	9	263	635
Truman	180	12	70	250
Eisenhower	73	2	108	181
Kennedy	12	0	9	21
Johnson	16	0	14	30
Nixon	26	7	17	43
Ford	48	12	18	66
Carter	13	2	18	31
Reagan	39	9	39	78

Source: *Congressional Quarterly Weekly Report,* January 7, 1989, p. 33.

get its advice on proposals for a treaty with southern Indian tribes, but became upset when the Senate postponed action on the matter. The Senate role subsequently became one of ratification of treaties negotiated by the executive, in effect a Senate veto power.

Washington's administration quickly established the president as the dominant partner in the treaty-making process. Ten years after the ratification of the Constitution, a man who was later to be one of the great interpreters of that document as chief justice of the United States— John Marshall—said in a House debate over a treaty, "The President is the sole organ of the nation in its external relations, and its sole representative with foreign nations." A constitutional scholar, commenting on the century and a half of experience since Marshall's statement, came to a similar conclusion when he observed that "there is no more securely established principle of constitutional practice than the exclusive right of the President to be the nation's intermediary in its dealing with other nations."[20]

This does not mean, however, that the president operates with a free hand. The Senate has regularly failed to ratify treaties submitted by the president, made so many changes that the treaty was unacceptable to the president, or made substantive changes in the treaty conditions before ratifying it. Consequently, presidents have come to use an alternative device, the **executive agreement**. This agreement is a pact between the leaders of two countries that does not require Senate approval. It provides a way to avoid Congress and to achieve many of the goals normally sought through treaties. Since the end of World War II, about 95 percent of all agreements with other countries have taken the form of executive agreements rather than treaties. (See Table 15.2 on p. 480.)

The Constitution does not provide specifically for executive agreements. The authority for them stems from the president's executive power and power as commander in chief. In a major decision on an executive agreement, the Supreme Court concluded that the Constitution gives "the President alone the power to speak or listen as a representative of the nation" and makes the president "the sole organ of the government in the field of international relations."[21] Congress also authorizes the president to enter into executive agreements. While they do not require Senate approval, executive agreements do depend on congressional funding for implementation.

Table 15.2

Treaties and Executive Agreements, 1789–1988

Years	Treaties	Executive Agreements
1789–1839	60	27
1840–1899	215	238
1900–1932	431	804
1933–1944 (Roosevelt)	131	369
1945–1952 (Truman)	132	1324
1953–1960 (Eisenhower)	89	1834
1961–1963 (Kennedy)	36	813
1964–1968 (Johnson)	67	1083
1969–1974 (Nixon)	93	1317
1975–1976 (Ford)	26	666
1977–1980 (Carter)	70	1476
1981–1988 (Reagan)	117	2837

Source: Harold Stanley and Richard Niemi, *Vital Statistics on American Politics*, 2nd ed. (Washington, D.C.: Congressional Quarterly Press, 1990), p. 255.

From time to time, Congress has sought to restrict the president's freedom to make executive agreements. The Bricker Amendment of 1954 would have required two-thirds Senate approval for executive agreements, but it failed to pass Congress. The Case Act of 1972 requires the secretary of state to submit the text of any international agreement to Congress within 60 days.

Executive Prerogative

It is important to know the constitutional provisions and separate components of presidential power, but you should also know that the whole of presidential power is more than the sum of its parts. An incident that took place during Lyndon Johnson's administration illustrates the point. When President Johnson was preparing to leave a military base one day, an Air Force sergeant saw that he was heading toward the wrong helicopter. "Mr. President," he said, "*that* is your helicopter over *there*." Johnson walked up to the sergeant, hugged him, and said: "Son, they are *all* my helicopters."[22]

The formal powers of the presidency spelled out in the Constitution can provide only a partial explanation of presidential power in the twentieth century. The way the Constitution is worded in Article I and Article II illustrates an important difference in the grant of legislative and executive powers. Article I states: "All legislative powers *herein granted* shall be vested in a Congress of the United States" (italics added). In contrast, Article II says: "The executive power shall be vested in a President of the United States of America." There is no limiting phrase of "herein granted" to the executive power of the Constitution.

For example, the Constitution says that the president shall be commander in chief of the armed forces, but it does not specify the duties, responsibilities, and powers that go with that office. Various presidents have interpreted the commander-in-chief powers to allow them to establish blockades, suspend fundamental civil liberties such as the writ of habeas corpus and substitute military courts for civilian court systems (Lincoln), use troops to break strikes (Hayes, Cleveland, Truman), order 120,000 Japanese Americans to be held in internment camps during wartime (Roosevelt), and even order the burglary of a psychiatrist's files in a case perceived by the president as one of national security (Nixon). We do not turn to the wording of the Constitution for guidance as to the legitimacy of such claims; it is rather the interpretations of those words, or the theories about the distribution of power under a Constitution, that help us understand how such claims of power could have been put forward.

A theory that has provided the basis for presidents' asserting such powers as those listed above is that of **executive prerogative**: the right that is attached to the executive office to perform certain functions without the requirement of public or legislative approval. We can trace the idea of prerogative back to the powers of monarchs. The English philosopher John Locke (who, by the way, was a strong proponent of legislative power) defined prerogative in *The Second Treatise of Government* (1690) as "the power to act according to discretion for the public good, without the prescription of law and sometimes even against it."[23]

When the Constitution is silent on a particular matter (the president's power to fire or the process of negotiating treaties, for example), or when the language of the Constitution is not explicit (the duties of commander in chief), the theory of executive prerogative suggests that there are inherent powers that belong to any executive. Certain functions must be carried on by someone in government. But it is the second part of Locke's statement that has provided the most controversial uses of executive prerogative to expand the powers of the presidency. Sometimes, according to the theory, the executive must act *against* the law. This assertion of power goes beyond one based on the Constitution's silences and has led the Supreme Court to set some limits on presidential power. In major cases in this area stretching over more than a century, the Supreme Court has ruled that Presidents Lincoln, Truman, and Nixon's claims of executive power conflicted with the Constitution and were therefore null and void.

Presidents generally advance their claims of executive prerogative during times of international or domestic crisis. The president must act, it is argued, in order to preserve the very system of government and the existence of the nation. Abraham Lincoln, for example, said that if he could save both the Constitution and the union he would do both, but that his first duty was saving the union. Public opinion polls consistently show that strong leadership is the trait people most want in a president and that people name the generally recognized strong presidents in response to the question of who they wish were president today.[24]

The expansion of presidential power that took place under the aegis of executive prerogative was perhaps the major development of the American political system in the twentieth century. This growth in presidential power, creating what Arthur Schlesinger called the "Imperial Presidency" of the 1960s and 1970s, was part of a broader change in patterns of governing America that had to do with the economic distress of the Great Depression era and the United States'

President Richard Nixon waves goodbye after resigning from office in August, 1974. The abuses of office associated with the Watergate scandal led Congress to place limits on some presidential claims of executive prerogative.

increasing involvement in global affairs, including two world wars.[25]

The exercise of executive prerogative during times of military and economic crisis has not been a steady, uninterrupted buildup of power from administration to administration, however. Rather, executive power has expanded under strong presidents, stayed relatively stable under less active presidents, and retrenched in some areas when strong presidents sought more power than others in the political system were willing to give.

Two major events of recent decades—the Vietnam War and Watergate—shape presidents' claims to executive prerogative today. As we have seen, it was the development of seemingly unchecked presidential war powers during the Vietnam era that finally led to congressional action to check those powers in the War Powers Resolution of 1973. About the same time, abuses associated with the Watergate scandal prompted Congress to rein in the president's domestic powers. In June 1972, a group of men working for the reelection of President Richard Nixon broke into Democratic headquarters in the Watergate building in Washington. Two years later Richard Nixon resigned under the threat of impeachment

A Closer Look

Three Views of Presidents and Governing ★★★

One of the first things we all learn about the political system is who is president, and our early images are those of a benevolent leader—of a president as a good person who helps other people (See Chapter 8). While presidents themselves are more aware than the public of limits on presidential power, they also know that the concept of executive prerogative and its exercise by past presidents support an expansive view of presidential power. Those two views are represented here by the comments of a third-grader and a former president. There is another view of presidential power, however, that suggests the dangers of an unquestioning acceptance of the first two views. Excerpts from the Articles of Impeachment voted by the House Judiciary Committee in 1974 show that even the extraordinary powers of a modern president are subject to the checks and balances of our constitutional system.

A STUDENT IN THE THIRD GRADE

Q: What does the president do?
A: He runs the country, he decides the decisions that we should try to get out of, and he goes to meetings and tries to make peace and things like that.
Q: When you say he runs the country, what do you mean?
A: Well, he's just about the boss of everything.
Q: And what kind of person do you think he is?
A: Well, usually he's an honest one.
Q: Anything else?
A: Well, loyal and usually is pretty smart.
Q: Usually, but not always?
A: Well, they're all smart, but they aren't exactly perfect [pause]. Most of them are.[a]

FORMER PRESIDENT RICHARD NIXON

Q: So what, in a sense, you are saying is that there are certain situations where the President can decide that it's in the best interests of the nation or something, and do something illegal.
A: (Nixon): Well, when the President does it, that means that it is not illegal.
Q: By definition.

for his role in covering up that break-in. Congress then passed campaign finance reform laws to correct the abuses of the Watergate era and a host of other measures designed to check presidential power. Four weeks before he left office, a politically weakened Richard Nixon reluctantly signed the Congressional Budget and Impoundment Control Act of 1974, which provides that Congress can disapprove of a president's impounding funds—that is, deferring the spending of funds appropriated by Congress for a specific project. This law can be regarded as only indirectly related to Watergate, yet it serves as a symbol of efforts to check the president's domestic powers in much the same way that the War Powers Act does in the area of the president's war powers.

It was clear even before the 1986 revelations about clandestine arms sales to Iran and diversion of funds to aid Nicaraguan rebels that these

A: Exactly, exactly. If the President, for example, approves something because of the national security, or in this case because of a threat to internal peace and order of significant magnitude, then the President's decision in that instance is one that enables those who carry it out, to carry it out without violating a law. Otherwise they're in an impossible position.[b]

CONGRESS

Article I—In his conduct of the office of President of the United States, Richard M. Nixon, in violation of his constitutional oath faithfully to execute the office of President of the United States and, to the best of his ability, preserve, protect, and defend the Constitution of the United States, and in violation of his constitutional duty to take care that the laws be faithfully executed, has prevented, obstructed, and impeded the administration of justice.

Article II—Using the powers of the office of President of the United States, Richard M. Nixon, in violation of his constitutional oath faithfully to execute the office of President of the United States and, to the best of his ability, preserve, protect, and defend the Constitution of the United States, and in disregard of his constitutional duty to take care that the laws be faithfully executed, has repeatedly engaged in conduct violating the constitutional rights of citizens, impairing the due and proper administration of justice and the conduct of lawful inquiries, or contravening the laws governing agencies of the executive branch and the purposes of those agencies.[c]

[a]Robert D. Hess and Judith V. Torney, *The Development of Political Attitudes in Children* (Garden City, New York: Doubleday, 1968), p. 42.
[b]Richard Nixon, "Television Interview with David Frost, May 20, 1977," reprinted in Barbara Hinckley, ed., *Problems of the Presidency* (Glenview, Ill.: Scott, Foresman, 1981), p. 256.
[c]Excerpted from Articles of Impeachment voted by the Committee on the Judiciary of the House of Representatives and submitted to the House in its report of August 20, 1974.

laws designed to check presidential power were not completely successful. Even so, they have changed the context of presidential claims of executive prerogative by creating an executive-legislative bargaining situation, much like that established by some constitutional grants.

Are presidents the responsible officers of government, as Presidents Kennedy and Reagan suggested when things go wrong and as President Carter admitted was also true when things go right? The evolution of the modern presidency has been in the direction of expanded powers and of public perceptions of presidential responsibility that goes even beyond those powers. Three views of presidential power are given in A Closer Look. Two of them (the views of a child and of a former president) support expanded powers; the third view illustrates the ultimate congressional check on presidential power—impeachment.

The administrations of six highly rated presidents—George Washington, Thomas Jefferson, Abraham Lincoln, Theodore Roosevelt, Woodrow Wilson, and Franklin Roosevelt— illustrate the importance of leadership styles and the power of persuasion.

The Power to Persuade

A central fact about the presidency noted by Richard Neustadt 30 years ago is that " 'powers' are no guarantee of power." "The President of the United States has an extraordinary range of formal powers, of authority in statute law and the Constitution," Neustadt said, but "despite his 'powers' he does not obtain results by giving orders—or not, at any rate, merely by giving orders." The theme of Neustadt's *Presidential Power* is that "Presidential Power is the power to *persuade*."[26]

A look at presidents who have been rated highly in polls of both scholars and the general public reveals the importance of persuasion powers and leadership styles. The names of six Presidents—Franklin Roosevelt, Theodore Roosevelt, Abraham Lincoln, George Washington, Thomas Jefferson, and Woodrow Wilson— are regularly invoked in these polls.[27] These presidents share certain characteristics. All but Theodore Roosevelt served during a time of war or a time when the legitimacy of the government was threatened. This shows the degree to which presidents are shaped by circumstance and tied to the political world of their time. Presidential scholars have also identified a number of skills or characteristics that these successful presidents possess: stamina, a sensitivity to people's needs, an ability to inspire trust, historical perspective, and an ability to set priorities.[28]

Political scientists Marcia Lynn Whicker and Raymond Moore have attempted to develop a simple and straightforward scheme for judging the personal leadership of presidents in their book, *When Presidents Are Great*. In addition to the traditional qualities exhibited by great presidents of the past, a president today needs *selling skills* in order to generate support in the public, the press, Congress and among world leaders and *managerial skills* in order to manage programs and bureaucracies, particularly in the areas of defense, foreign affairs, social policy, and economic policy:

> The president who is a good salesperson can more easily lead, manipulate, and motivate people.
>
> The president who is a good manager can assemble materials and people to achieve particular goals.[29]

Their term "selling" includes Neustadt's persuasion, and "managing" refers to patterns of decision making and administrative control. In evaluating presidents since Franklin Roosevelt, Whicker and Moore find that some presidents have been ineffective both as salesmen and managers (Gerald Ford and Jimmy Carter), some have been good at selling but ineffective at managing (Lyndon Johnson and Ronald Reagan), one president was a poor salesman but a good manager (Richard Nixon), and four presidents were effective both as salesmen and managers (Franklin Roosevelt, Harry Truman, Dwight Eisenhower, and John Kennedy).

If presidential greatness or successful personal leadership depends on a president being an effective salesman and manager, we want to know what types of political experience are likely to develop those skills and how we can identify presidential candidates who have those skills. These are important aspects of the presidential selection process, which we turn to next.

Checkpoint

- The role of modern presidents in governing America is based on two sources of presidential power. The first consists of grants of power in the Constitution: the executive power, the appointing power, the war power, legislative powers, and the treaty power. These constitutional powers form the core of presidential governance, but they are shared with other institutions of government and are subject to interpretation by the Supreme Court.

- The second source of presidential power is that of executive prerogative, the right of executives to perform certain functions without public or legislative approval. Presidents have claimed these extraordinary powers particularly during times of war and economic crises.

- Successful presidents have developed personal leadership styles that combine the power to persuade with managerial skills.

PRESIDENTIAL SELECTION

As the delegates to the Philadelphia Convention went about their work in the summer of 1787, they considered the broad questions of where our presidents would come from, what sort of person we wanted serving in that office, and how we should select our presidents. Those questions continue to be central to governing America today. Three aspects of presidential selection are addressed in this section: Where have our past presidents come from? How have they been nominated? How have they been elected?

Presidential Backgrounds

The legal qualifications to serve as president are quite simple. The Constitution requires that the president be at least 35 years old, a natural-born citizen, and a resident of the United States for at least 14 years. Millions of American men and women meet those requirements. However, informal qualifications of the presidency that have prevailed up to this point have drastically reduced the size of the pool from which presidential candidates are drawn. Every one of the 40 individuals to serve as president has been a middle-aged or older white male Christian of northern or western European stock (Great Britain, Holland, Germany, and Switzerland). By looking at the political and social backgrounds of presidents we get a clearer picture of the *informal* qualifications of the office.

POLITICAL QUALIFICATIONS The major political qualification for the presidency, based on the careers of past presidents, is that a person should have served in some government position—in particular, an executive position in state government, a legislative position in national government, or as vice-president of the United States (see Table 15.3). Eight of the nine presidents since Franklin Roosevelt not only had previously served in government, they had been *elected* to national or state office. The number of years served in an elected position prior to becoming president ranged from 8 (Carter and Reagan) to 28 (Johnson), but the average for all eight presidents was 17 years. The seeming exception to this pattern is the category of military presidents: Washington, Taylor, Grant, and Eisenhower.

As Table 15.3 shows, one-third of all our presidents have previously served as vice-president, but not all of those went directly to the presidency. The table also shows some change over time in the value of particular positions as a qualification for the presidency. Being governor, for example, seems to have waned as a political asset after Franklin Roosevelt, but it was revived 30 years later with the presidencies of Jimmy Carter and Ronald Reagan. Although the Senate continues to serve as a common source of pres-

idential candidates, their experience in recent campaigns has convinced a number of incumbent senators that it is difficult, if not impossible, to meet the twin demands of a legislative schedule and a full-scale campaign for the presidency.

SOCIAL QUALIFICATIONS "How they grew up to be President" is one of the most often told stories in America. Parents use it as a way to teach their children to study harder in school. The belief that anyone's son or daughter can grow up to be president comforts those who wish a better life for their children. Abraham Lincoln's boyhood home is the central symbol of the log cabin myth in American politics. The message of the myth is equality of opportunity— any person who works hard can grow up to be president.

Does the log cabin myth accurately represent the social backgrounds and careers of presidents? The social backgrounds of presidents include their occupation (other than public service), class, education, ethnic group, religion, region, race, sex, and family status. Sometimes a particular background characteristic stands out, such as the fact that more than half of all our presidents have been lawyers, that they have all been white males, that almost all have been college educated, or that, except for John Kennedy, a Catholic, all have been Protestants.

Table 15.4 (p. 488) portrays the social background of presidents using the measure of class (as determined by father's occupation). Two patterns reflected in the table deserve attention. First, our first six presidents came from upper-class families. Theodore Lowi suggests that merit and breeding were stressed in our early chief executives because the success of the new national government depended on citizens regarding it as a legitimate government.[30] George Washington, for example, replaced King George III as the individual symbolizing the state. Where George III had been "The Father of His People," Washington became "The Father of His Country." The tune of the anthem "God Save the King" stayed the same after 1789, but the lyrics were changed to "God Save Great Washington." Washington's face replaced the King's on coins. The trappings of monarchy that surrounded the

Table 15.3

Last Political Office Held by Presidents

Vice-President	Appointive Federal Office
Succeeded to Office Tyler (1841)[a] Fillmore (1850) Johnson, Andrew (1865) Arthur (1881) Roosevelt, Theodore (1901) Coolidge (1923) Truman (1945) Johnson, Lyndon (1963) Ford (1974) **Won Office in Own Right** Adams, John (1797) Jefferson (1801) Van Buren (1837) Nixon (1969) Bush (1988)	**Military Position** Washington (1789), commander in chief Taylor (1849), general Grant (1869), general Eisenhower (1953), supreme commander of NATO **Secretary of State** Madison (1809) Monroe (1817) Adams, John Quincy (1825) **Other** Harrison, William (1841), minister to Columbia Pierce (1853), U.S. district attorney for New Hampshire Buchanan (1857), minister to Great Britain Taft (1909), secretary of war Hoover (1929), secretary of commerce

Governor	Congress
Polk (1845), Tennessee Hayes (1877), Ohio Cleveland (1885), New York McKinley (1897), Ohio Wilson (1913), New Jersey Roosevelt, Franklin (1933), New York Carter (1977), Georgia Reagan (1981), California	**Senate** Jackson (1829), Tennessee Garfield (1881), Ohio Harrison, Benjamin (1889), Indiana Harding (1921), Ohio Kennedy (1961), Massachusetts **House of Representatives** Lincoln (1861), Illinois

[a]Date refers to the year president first took office.

Source: Adapted from Richard A. Watson and Norman C. Thomas, *The Politics of the Presidency* (New York: Wiley, 1983), p. 108.

first president and the high social status of early presidents helped establish the legitimacy of the new government at a time when Americans still deferred to an elite in political matters.[31]

The election of Andrew Jackson in 1828, the first president with a working-class background, ended the string of upper-class presidents. But a second pattern evident in Table 15.4 is that Jackson has been the exception rather than the rule. Half of our presidents have come from the 3 percent of the population classified as upper class, and seven of ten have had upper-class or middle-class backgrounds. "One thing is clear," says historian Edward Pessen. "The popular assumption

Table 15.4

Social Backgrounds of Presidents, as Measured by Occupation of Father

Upper Class	Middle Class	Working Class
Prosperous Farmers and Planters Washington (1789)[a] Adams, John (1797) Jefferson (1801) Madison (1809) Monroe (1817) Adams, John Quincy (1825) Harrison, William (1841) Tyler (1841)	**Small Businessmen** Van Buren (1837), tavern owner Coolidge (1923), storekeeper Ford (1974), lumber and paint business	**Dirt Farmers** Jackson (1829) Fillmore (1850) Buchanan (1857) Hayes (1877) Lincoln (1861)
Professional Ministers Arthur (1881), Episcopalian Cleveland (1885), Presbyterian Wilson (1913), Presbyterian	**Small Landowners** Truman (1945) Johnson, Lyndon (1963) Carter (1977)	**Blue- and Minor White-Collar** Johnson, Andrew (1865), janitor porter Garfield (1881), canal worker Hoover (1929), blacksmith Eisenhower (1953), mechanic Nixon (1969), streetcar conductor Reagan (1981), shoe salesman
Other Pierce (1853), general Harrison, Benjamin (1889), lieutenant colonel Taft (1909), lawyer Harding (1921), doctor	**Tradesmen** Polk (1845), surveyor Grant (1869), tanner McKinley (1897), ironmonger	
Well-to-do Businessmen Roosevelt, Theodore (1901) Roosevelt, Franklin (1933) Kennedy (1961)		
Governmental Taylor (1849), collector of internal revenue Bush (1989), U.S. senator		

[a]Date refers to the year president first took office.

Source: Adapted from Richard A. Watson and Norman C. Thomas, *The Politics of the Presidency* (New York: Wiley, 1983), p. 110.

belly." In every presidential election cycle, some potential candidates who have met the qualifications decide not to pursue the presidency. In 1984, for example, there were 17 Democratic senators who met most of the qualifications we have been discussing, but only four became active candidates (Alan Cranston, John Glenn, Gary Hart, and Ernest Hollings).[33] Again in 1988, four potential Democratic candidates met the key political requirements—New York Governor Mario Cuomo, Massachusetts Senator Edward Kennedy, New Jersey Senator Bill Bradley, and Georgia Senator Sam Nunn—but decided against being active candidates, at least for that year.

Some of the candidates regarded as qualified to be president who chose not to run in 1984 and 1988 were known to harbor presidential ambition. But ambition must be coupled with *opportunity* in order to produce an active presidential candidacy:

> Presidential ambition sets off a sort of biological clock. The Constitution requires that a president must be at least thirty-five years of age. Realistically candidates do not run much before their mid-forties or after their mid-sixties.
>
> With elections coming at four-year intervals, this allows five shots at the office. At least one chance must be deducted, though, because incumbents are almost always renominated.
>
> . . . Thus presidential opportunity is more like a four-per-lifetime proposition.[34]

In November 1987, one year before the 1988 presidential election, *Congressional Quarterly Weekly Report* listed the field of major-party candidates for president: There were 16, 6 Republicans and 10 Democrats.[35] The qualifications discussed in this section had served to narrow the field of potential presidential candidates from the millions of citizens who met the constitutional requirements of office down to the fewer than 20 who actually made the race. We now turn to the nomination stage of the presidential selection process, which further narrows the field down to the two major-party candidates who face each other in the general election.

"The true Portraiture of his Excellency George Washington, Esq." by J. Norman after C. W. Peale ca. 1783. The trappings of monarchy of George Washington's presidency helped establish the legitimacy of the new government at a time when Americans still deferred to an elite in political matters.

that most of the presidents were of humble birth is wrong."[32]

The informal qualifications for the presidency that have prevailed up to now show that while any child born in the United States can grow up to be president, the chances of some are much greater than others. The winnowing of potential candidates that takes place at birth and in one's choice of career is also present much later in the careers of those who have met all the informal qualifications. Presidential *ambition* is the qualification that is important at this later stage— what candidates often refer to as "fire in the

Nominations: Primaries and Conventions

Since 1860, every president has been a Democrat or a Republican. The two major parties have a clear monopoly on the White House, which is why the nomination stage is regarded as the crucial one in the presidential selection process. The choice in the general election is essentially between two candidates for president. The nomination stage determines who those two candidates will be. As New York's famous machine politician, Boss Tweed, used to say, "Elect who you will to office. Just let me pick the candidates."[36]

Although the party's nominee for president is formally chosen by the national convention, the real decision is made earlier, during the *primaries* (see Chapter 12). By the time the delegates gather to choose a nominee, enough of them have been bound by the outcomes of primaries to make the selection at the convention a mere formality. Table 15.5 shows the increase in primaries and how that increase is translated into convention votes. States without primaries select delegates to the national conventions through state conventions, with local and regional conventions or caucuses selecting delegates to the state conventions.

It is obvious from Table 15.5 that winning primaries is the only way to win the nomination for president today. A corollary to that rule is that winning *early* primaries (and the Iowa caucuses, which select delegates to the state convention even before the first primary in New Hampshire) is crucial to a successful nomination campaign. The importance of early primaries has led to the development of what has been called the invisible primary—low-visibility contests and fundraising, which take place long before the first primary.[37] A year before the 1980 election and three months before the first primary, for example, Jimmy Carter put a lot of effort into defeating Ted Kennedy in a nonbinding straw vote at the Florida Democratic convention.

The long primary season and the importance of the early nomination contests give an advantage to candidates able to raise funds early. In order to qualify for public funding for the nomination campaign, a candidate must raise $5000 in each of 20 states based on contributions of $250 or less. Candidates who are well known nationally or who have access to a particular fundraising constituency are in the best position to take advantage of these rules on public funding. A total of nearly $200 million was spent on the *pre*nomination presidential campaigns for the 1988 election, with the eventual nominees George Bush and Michael Dukakis accounting for $55 million of that total.[38]

In 1988 the nominating process was wide open, with a large field of candidates in both par-

---

Table 15.5

Presidential Primaries and Convention Votes, 1968–1988

		1968	1972	1976	1980	1984	1988
Democratic Party	Number of states with primaries	17	23	29	31	25	31
	Percentage of all convention votes cast by delegates chosen in primaries	49%	66%	75%	71%	55%	77%
Republican Party	Number of states with primaries	16	22	28	33	24	33
	Percentage of all convention votes cast by delegates chosen in primaries	45%	53%	66%	75%	57%	77%

Source: Stephen E. Frantzich, *Political Parties in the Technological Age* (New York: Longman, 1989), p. 116.

ties and no incumbent president running for the first time in 20 years. This raised concerns that an untested candidate without political experience would win the nomination or that the primary vote would be so divided that a candidate might win the nomination of his party without having widespread support. But political scientist Gerald Pomper points out that "in nominating Michael Dukakis and George Bush, [the political parties] chose two men who were experienced politicians with extensive records of public service."[39] Studies have shown that most major-party nominees since 1936 have been the front-runners in public opinion polls a year before the election and the candidates with the most support in the party's rank and file.[40]

Presidential Elections

Presidential elections are hailed as one of the great exercises in democracy. But the delegates meeting in Philadelphia in 1787 were hardly in favor of such a method of selecting presidents. Asking the people to pick a president, said one delegate, made as much sense "as it would to refer a trial of colors to a blind man."[41] At one point during the proceedings, the Constitutional Convention voted unanimously to have Congress choose the president. But the procedure for selecting a president finally agreed on at the convention—one that came from the Committee on Unfinished Business in September 1787—was that of the electoral college, as we saw in earlier chapters.

The electoral college was intended to act as a check on popular election of the president by giving the actual vote to electors chosen from each state. But as it works today, all the electoral votes of a state go to the candidate who wins a plurality of that state's popular vote. In order to be elected, a presidential candidate must win 270 of the total 538 electoral votes.

Some presidential candidates have developed an electoral college strategy of concentrating on key states that could give them an electoral vote majority even without a majority in the popular vote. The electoral college is just one of the "givens" around which candidates develop campaign strategies. Other givens include party identification, incumbency, and the state of the economy. As we saw in Chapters 11 and 12, these factors serve to establish the general political setting within which presidential elections take place.

Presidential scholar Richard Neustadt has cautioned that the White House "is not a place for amateurs."[42] Only a president with deep experience in politics will know how to use the resources available to make the presidency work. The presidential selection process generally keeps amateurs out of the White House. But it does raise the question of what kinds of professionals it puts in office. Does the selection process test the selling and managerial skills discussed earlier in the chapter? Whicker and Moore point out that presidential campaigns and elections generally tell us more about a candidate's selling skills than his or her ability as a manager:

> With the shift to media campaigns, candidates who are not good salespeople will be less likely to be elected, whereas candidates who appear attractive and communicate persuasively will be more likely to become presidents.
>
> Rarely, however, are the managerial skills of presidential candidates tested before entering the White House on a scale comparable to what is needed once in office.[43]

We consider the managerial aspect of the presidency in the next section on the institutional presidency.

Checkpoint

- The Constitution specifies certain formal requirements of the office of president; unofficial informal qualifications have tended to limit the pool of candidates to middle-aged or older white male Christians of northern or western European stock who have served in some governmental position or had a military career. Most presidents have come from an upper-class or upper middle-class background.

- The national party conventions formally nominate presidential candidates, but in the last two decades they have simply ratified the choice determined by state primaries.

- The electoral college, voters' party identification, incumbency status of candidates, and state of the economy all affect presidential campaign strategies and outcomes.

- Some political observers are concerned that the presidential selection process tests candidates' selling skills more than their managing skills, both of which are needed in office.

THE INSTITUTIONAL PRESIDENCY

Although Ronald Reagan accepted presidential responsibility for the Iran-contra affair, he "went to some lengths," as Wilson Carey McWilliams has pointed out, "to disclaim *personal* responsibility, and his language—'Mistakes were made'—directed blame to a subjectless organizational process."[44] Much of the personal responsibility or blame for the program of selling arms to Iran and using the proceeds to support Nicaraguan rebels fell on White House aide Oliver North. In May 1989, a federal court jury in Washington, D.C., found North guilty on 3 of 12 felony charges stemming from his role in the Iran-contra affair. After the trial, jury foreman Denise Anderson told a reporter that she was "disappointed in our whole system":

> At a certain point, I wanted to stand up and say, "Get the rest of these people down here! This doesn't make any sense." But they probably would have locked me up. . . .
>
> You have to remember, Reagan was over the top of everything, just like God is over the top of all of us.[45]

The institutional presidency includes "the rest of these people" that the jury foreman wanted in the courtroom. The **institutional presidency** consists of those officials and staff members whose job it is to assist the president in information gathering, decision making, and the implementation of decisions. The recent growth of the institutional presidency can be traced to Franklin Roosevelt's administration. Concluding that "the President needs help," a report commissioned by Roosevelt recommended establishment of an Executive Office of the President and an increase in the number of administrative assistants to the president. Congress created the Executive Office two years later in 1939 and has subsequently expanded it until today it includes more than 1500 people. One unit of the Executive Office is the White House Office, consisting of the president's personal staff. The number of staff members grew from fewer than 50 under Roosevelt to a high of 560 under Nixon, and back down to just over 350 under Bush.

The institutional presidency has grown over the years for a number of reasons: a general increase in the scope and activity of the federal government; presidential distrust of the bureaucracy; the representation of interest groups and special constituencies within the presidency; the expansion of media and public relations functions; and the needs of particular presidents. But the single most important reason for this growth is the widespread acceptance of the role of the president as general manager of the government. Some presidents have attached more importance to this role than others—Nixon and Carter much more than Ford and Reagan, for example. George Bush emphasized the management role early in his administration by blitzing his staff with handwritten or hand-typed blue note cards inscribed "From the President." His press secretary described the blue note cards and the 15 or more phone calls the President made each day as essential ingredients of Bush's "management technique."[46]

Nixon developed the government management role in its broadest sense after his landslide reelection in 1972. Nixon's "administrative presidency" was one in which the president and his staff sought to control policy implementation as

President Bush prepares to make one of the 15 daily phone calls that his press secretary described as an essential ingredient of his management technique.

well as policy formulation. This required a large presidential staff that would assume many of the functions of the permanent bureaucracy. A career civil servant once described the institutional presidency, at its height in the Nixon administration, as "too many people trying to bite you with the president's teeth."[47] We will look at four sets of people—and teeth—in this section: the cabinet, the Executive Office of the President, the White House Office, and the vice-president.

The Cabinet

President Bush wanted cabinet government to be one of the areas that distinguished his administration from the Reagan administration. He moved quickly to establish a strong **cabinet**—the group of advisers and department heads selected by the president to assist him in making decisions and running the government. Bush had been in office only four months when a Republican leader close to the White House contrasted

cabinet government under Bush with that under Reagan in this way:

> Rather than having a centralized Administration run by staff from out of the White House, you now have peers of the President in Cabinet positions making the kinds of decisions that ministers in a parliamentary system often make.[48]

In a parliamentary system, such as Britain, the prime minister selects colleagues from the legislature to form a government. In the United States, though, it is the government that forms the cabinet. The president nominates individuals to head certain executive departments, and the Senate must approve these appointments. In direct contrast with a parliamentary system, no member of the legislative branch may simultaneously serve as a member of the cabinet.

The U.S. Constitution, however, says nothing about a cabinet, nor anything about there being "peers of the President" within the executive branch. Article II does say that the president "may require the opinion, in writing, of the principal officer in each of the executive departments upon any subject relating to the duties of their respective offices." But the Constitution provides no authority for the president's delegating executive authority to other executive officers.

In American politics, the term *cabinet government* generally means that the president gives the heads of executive departments leeway in running their departments and that the president meets regularly with these department heads as a group to seek their advice on government matters. Table 15.6, on p. 494, shows the departments represented in the cabinet. In addition to these positions, presidents and Congress sometimes give cabinet rank to other officials, such as the budget director or the United States trade representative, and the vice-president also joins in cabinet meetings.

Not all members of the cabinet are equal. The status and influence of particular members will vary from presidency to presidency, but a useful distinction—one that seems to hold for all administrations—is that of the inner cabinet and the outer cabinet. The inner cabinet consists of the secretaries of state, treasury, defense, and

Table 15.6

Cabinet

	Department	Year Established (Established in Present Form)
Inner Cabinet	State	1789
	Treasury	1789
	Justice	1789 (1870)
	Defense	1789 (1949)
Outer Cabinet	Interior	1849
	Agriculture	1862 (1889)
	Commerce	1903 (1913)
	Labor	1903 (1913)
	Health and Human Services	1953 (1979)
	Housing and Urban Development	1965
	Transportation	1966
	Energy	1977
	Education	1979
	Veterans Affairs	1989
	Environment	proposed 1990

Source: Richard Rose, *The Postmodern President* (Chatham, N.J.: Chatham House, 1988), p. 166.

justice. The nature of their jobs brings these officials into contact with the president on a regular basis. Members of the outer cabinet see the president less often and generally are not as directly involved in policymaking with him.[49]

CHOOSING A CABINET Political scientist Nelson Polsby suggests that presidents have five options to follow in appointing a cabinet. They can appoint:

1 Clientele-oriented officials, who have ties with one or more of the important groups in a particular area (secretaries of agriculture and commerce often fit this category)

2 Specialists who understand the technology and programs in a particular area

3 A Washington careerist or generalist

4 Presidential allies who have long-standing ties with the chief executive

5 Symbolic representatives whose distinction comes from what they are rather than what they have done in the past or what or who they know (women, blacks, and Hispanics, for example)

Polsby suggests that the composition of the Carter administration, for example, revealed that administration's emphasis on technical solutions to problems and its isolation from the traditional groups of the Democratic party.[50]

USING A CABINET Presidents almost always begin their administration believing that they will use their cabinets better than past presidents have, and generally wind up the same way: using cabinet members on an ad hoc policymaking basis rather than as a governing body. Individual members of the cabinet can be influential, but the cabinet as a unit generally ranks below the White House staff and policy units in the Executive Office as a participant in decision making. There are a number of reasons for that. The separate policy areas of the cabinet and their ungainly size make collective policymaking impractical (a former secretary of commerce noted: "There was no one at the table who could be of help to me except the President, and when I needed to consult him I did not choose a Cabinet meeting to do so."[51]). Also, in every administration, conflict often develops between presidential assistants in the White House Office and cabinet members. Finally, many cabinet members, especially those in the outer cabinet, are prone to "marrying the natives," becoming spokespersons for their departments more than they are the president's men or women. A former vice-president pointed out that when cabinet secretaries act as advocates for their departments they become "vice presidents in charge of spending, and as such are the natural enemies of the President."[52]

The Bush administration began to show signs of conflict between the White House staff and cabinet officials even while many were praising the operation of cabinet government. After two secretaries had gone directly to the press to announce administration policies on health issues and a public housing drug program, the White House chief of staff was described as "fuming" and another member of the President's staff privately branded the cabinet as "undisciplined" and "runaway."[53]

Executive Office of the President

The original purpose of the **Executive Office of the President** (EOP) when it was established in 1939 was to assist the president in fiscal affairs and planning, primarily through the Bureau of the Budget and the National Resources Planning Board. Since 1939 more than 40 units have been incorporated into the EOP for varying periods of time; today 13 remain in operation (see Table 15.7, p. 496). Two of the most important organizations added to the EOP are the Council of Economic Advisers, created in 1946, and the National Security Council, established in 1949.

The Council of Economic Advisers consists of three members, usually professional economists, and a support staff of about 35 persons. The council is responsible for gathering and analyzing economic data, making projections and recommendations to the president, and preparing

the president's annual economic message. Its importance is very much tied to the fact that it is an independent body; it does not represent the viewpoint of any of the operating executive departments.

The National Security Council (NSC) was established to give the president a viewpoint on military and foreign policy matters independent of the Joint Chiefs of Staff, the Pentagon, and the State Department. The NSC started as a planning and coordinating body but gradually began to assume operational responsibilities, implementing rather than just formulating plans. It was this operational role that led the NSC into its involvement in the Iran-Contra affair in the Reagan administration. The Bush administration sought to avoid the dangers of an operational NSC staff acting in isolation from the State and Defense departments by emphasizing its coordinating role and by staffing key positions with people who had worked together in the past. After being criticized for a slow response to an attempted coup in Panama in October 1989, the President and his advisers extended this coordination of effort by creating a crisis management organization made up of the second-ranking officials in the National Security Council, the Defense Department, the State Department, and the Central Intelligence Agency. This crisis management group, known as the Deputies Committee, provides cross communication among agencies and reviews information before it goes to the President. Two months after its creation, this group helped support the U.S. military action that deposed President Manuel Noriega of Panama in December 1989.

The Office of Management and Budget (OMB), which was created in 1970 by reorganizing the Bureau of the Budget, is another major organization of the Executive Office. It is the agency primarily responsible for executive oversight and coordination of the president's legislative program, the allocation of resources within the executive branch, and the preparation of the president's budget. The old Bureau of the Budget had a reputation for neutrality and technical expertise serving the institution of the presidency rather than any particular president. But the distinction between institutional staff and personal staff has become blurred since the reorganiza-

Table 15.7

The Executive Office of the President, 1990

Unit	Date Established
Office of the Vice President	1789
White House Office	1939
Office of Management and Budget (OMB)	1970 (reorganized from Bureau of the Budget)
Council of Economic Advisers	1946
National Security Council	1949
Office of Policy Development	1981 (reorganized from Domestic Policy Staff)
Office of the United States Trade Representative	1963
Council on Environmental Quality	1969
Office of Science and Technology Policy	1976
Office of Administration	1977
National Critical Materials Council	1984
Office of National Drug Control Policy	1988
National Space Council	1989

Source: *The United States Government Manual 1989/90* (Washington, D.C.: Government Printing Office, 1989), pp. 85–100.

tion of the bureau in 1970, and the OMB has become politicized. When Carter's OMB prepared the 1981 budget, for example, it included a long section listing the "Major Accomplishments" of the administration. The central political role of the OMB was also apparent in 1989, when OMB director Richard Darman took the lead in negotiating a broad agreement with congressional leaders on the fiscal 1990 budget.

Presidents have come to use the Executive Office to build a counterbureaucracy in order to control the regular bureaucracy. Many of the key agencies within the EOP have changed from information-gathering and coordinating agencies into operational units, in which commitment to the president and the president's program are as important as technical expertise. Two former officials in the Carter administration (one of whom had worked in the OMB) described

the Executive Office as "the chief instrument for converting the executive branch into a coherent administration," but also made clear the limitations of the organization:

> Unfortunately, the EOP was not designed for this role. In fact, it hardly seems to have been designed at all; it just grew.
>
> Even its name is deceptive: the EOP is not an executive office. Rather, it is a bloated and disorderly grab bag of separate and mutually suspicious staffs, units, councils, boards and groups with strikingly different histories, purposes and problems.[54]

A president needs some way to control the counterbureaucracy of the Executive Office, and all presidents turn to the element of the EOP designed to serve the president personally—the White House Office.

White House Office

George Reedy, press secretary and special assistant to President Lyndon Johnson, once wrote: "The life of the White House is the life of a court. It is a structure designed for one purpose and one purpose only—to serve the material needs and desires of a single man."[55] Thirteen years later, a national journalist picked up on the same theme of a monarch and his court:

> Inevitably, each successive court takes part of its character from the monarch who assembled it. John Kennedy's men, as a group, combined the intellectual edge, the political smarts, and personal arrogance of their leader. The Nixon crew shared its boss's boldness of purpose, his cunning and what turned out to be the fatal void where basic values should have been. The Carterites rivaled their President in good intentions, pious naïveté and an inability to differentiate between the politics of election and that of governance.[56]

Most of the men and women who make up the president's court have a staff position in the **White House Office.** Presidents also rely on key advisers holding down positions in other EOP offices and executive departments. The formal duties and routine schedules of these presidential advisers vary, but a characteristic they have in common is that other people believe them when they say what one Washington insider described as the three magic words: "the President wants."[57] Table 15.8 shows top positions of the White House Office in the Bush Administration.

Every President has a different way of using the White House staff. President Reagan, for example, relied on White House aides to serve as a buffer between himself and those responsible for implementing policy; he preferred that policy issues be presented to him in the form of recommended decisions. In contrast, President Bush regularly reaches outside formal channels to seek information and prefers to read briefing books and background papers himself rather than depend on advisers' summaries and recommendations. His own experience as a presidential aide and adviser and 20 years of study led Richard Neustadt to the conclusion that:

Table 15.8
Key Positions of White House Office, 1990
Chief of staff
Counsel to the president
National security adviser
Press secretary
Assistant to the president for legislative affairs
Assistant to the president for economic and domestic policy
Deputy to the chief of staff

... no continuity of pattern, no stability of doctrine, and precious little lore survives from one Administration to the next about a matter so important to a President as where to put advisers, how to use them, whom to seek. Staffing the Presidency now is a game played catch-as-catch-can, with very few rules.[58]

All presidents draw on their campaign staff in filling positions in the presidency, especially the White House Office. It is natural for a president to turn to those people who have run a successful campaign and ask them to help run the government. But one of the few "rules" about staffing the presidency calls for the inclusion of at least some people with experience in governing, as well. As Johnson and Nixon learned, a president can become isolated from the rest of the political system and wind up dealing directly only with White House aides. When this happens, presidential decisions are likely to be made on incomplete information. White House assistants with past ties in government, however, can draw on that experience and on their contacts throughout government to broaden the base of knowledge for presidential decisions. Such aides are also likely to have a more realistic view of what presidents can or cannot do as general managers than aides less schooled in government operations.

An effective White House staff provides the president with the information needed for decision making. Some presidents achieve that goal by promoting conflict among the White House staff. Franklin Roosevelt and John Kennedy, for example, deliberately gave overlapping responsibilities to their assistants, which led these aides to bring their arguments and supporting information directly to the president. Other presidents feel that the goal of reliable information is best achieved by filtering out the "noise"—the unnecessary information—in the system in order to focus on fundamental policy choices. Presidents Eisenhower and Nixon followed this pattern. Reagan delegated extensive authority to his aides and distanced himself from the details of management, focusing instead on a few selected major decisions. This "minimalist" approach appeared to have filtered out important and valuable advice as well as "noise," as was evident in the Iran-Contra case. As we have seen, President Bush has sought a middle ground between Carter's excessive attention to the details of governing and Reagan's detached governing through aides. Whatever their style, presidents spend a good part of each day with members of the staff (see A Closer Look on p. 500).

The flow of information within the White House and the way the staff structures that information is the key to understanding the White House staff. Questions about the number of presidential assistants to appoint, what their backgrounds should be, whether to appoint a chief of staff, and what the job descriptions of assistants should be all center on the type of information a president seeks. A senior White House staff member in both the Reagan and Bush administrations commented on the centrality of information and the difficulties of obtaining it:

> There's no time really to learn from what's been happening. Society may be trying to do something or get somewhere over many years, but there's all this noise in the system, all this flux.
>
> There is such a short attention span, so little institutional memory. Who really studies the literature? Far too few. As a civilization we haven't yet institutionalized an effective capacity to learn—to learn about governance.[59]

The Vice-Presidency

The single most important bit of information about the vice-presidency is reflected in Table 15.3: 14 of our 40 presidents had previously been vice-president, and 9 of the 14 assumed the presidency on the death of the incumbent. One of those nine, Lyndon Johnson, once said that a vice-president "is like a raven hovering around the head of the president, reminding him of his mortality."[60] Most vice-presidents have made similar comments about the office and the peculiar relationship it creates between its inhabitant and the president. One point all former vice-presidents agree on is that our political system provides for only one president. There is no room for a co-president or an assistant president.

Vice-presidents today are initially selected by one person—the presidential candidate. Leaving the choice of a vice-presidential candidate up to the national party convention, as Adlai Stevenson did in 1956, is a rare occurrence unlikely to happen again. In selecting a vice-presidential candidate, most presidential nominees pay lip service to the notion of choosing a person who would make an able president. But the choice really rests on other considerations. Chief among them is the electoral strength that a potential vice-presidential candidate would bring to the ticket. This is often expressed as seeking a *balanced ticket*, and the balancing can refer to geographic regions of the country, to ideological factions within the party, and even to age—as when George Bush chose Dan Quayle. Thus, a northeastern John Kennedy with a reputation as a liberal Democrat sought to balance the ticket with Texas Democrat Lyndon Johnson—a pattern repeated by Michael Dukakis in 1988 in choosing Texas Senator Lloyd Bentsen as his running mate. Southerner Jimmy Carter selected Minnesota's Senator Walter Mondale in 1976. Conservative Republican Ronald Reagan chose as his running mate George Bush, whose party associations were with the more moderate factions of the Republican party. Bush, in turn, chose a young conservative, Dan Quayle, as his running mate in 1988.

Another quality sought in a vice-presidential candidate is skill as a political campaigner, especially with a style or appeal that complements

President Bush and Vice President Dan Quayle lunch weekly at the White House. As Quayle notes, "I have the right to go into his office anytime I want to."

that of the presidential candidate. Since the president and vice-president are elected or defeated together, the presidential candidate obviously looks for someone who will strengthen the chances of winning.

In most administrations throughout American history, the vice-president had no influence over or participation in major decision making. But the experience of the Carter, Reagan, and Bush administrations suggests that a vice-president can do more than campaign, attend funerals of foreign leaders, and ask the president how he's feeling today. Carter's vice-president, Walter Mondale, described his duties after a year in office: "I see my role as a general adviser on almost any issue, as a troubleshooter, as a representative of the President in some foreign affairs matters and as a political advocate of the Administration."[61] President Reagan assigned Vice-President Bush general responsibility for certain policy areas, such as the drug interdiction program, but de-emphasized the selling aspects of the job. The Bush administration revitalized salesmanship in what was described as "the Quayle Model"—a combination of policy responsibilities ("I have the right to go into his office anytime I want to," Vice-President Quayle told reporters) and high visibility as a conservative spokesman for the Bush administration.[62]

Checkpoint

- The president's role as general manager of the government has led to the creation of the offices and staff known as the institutionalized presidency and to its steady growth since 1939.

- Four components of the institutionalized presidency are the cabinet, the Executive Office of the President, the White House Office, and the vice-presidency.

- Presidents who would manage and govern find that they first must manage those who share the responsibilities of governance in the executive branch.

A Closer Look

The President's Workday ★★★

Something you might want to consider before running for president is the fact that most presidents begin their day by getting up early and going to class. The first item on a president's daily schedule is an intelligence briefing. Presidents do not have exams and term papers, of course, but they are expected to do their homework. The teachers who brief them aren't expected to give presidents a grade, but word does get out on those who don't do their assigned work. President Reagan found that out when newspapers reported that he had "once confessed to startled aides that he had watched 'The Sound of Music' on television rather than read his briefing books for the economic summit at Williamsburg in 1983."[a]

We show here a typical workday in the life of a president of the United States. Presidents' personalities and management styles will greatly affect how they structure their workdays. President Nixon's aide responsible for his daily schedule reported that he always made sure to schedule "the President's alone time, from 2 to 3 o'clock almost every day."[b] But a member of the White House staff under

Nixon's predecessor, Lyndon Johnson, had this to say about President Johnson: "He could not bear to be by himself, not for an evening or for an hour. Always there were people, in his office, at his house, in the swimming pool, even in the bathroom."[c]

A characteristic of all president's schedules, however, is the high proportion of their workday that is spent with White House staff. On this particular April day, President Bush spent about half of his scheduled working hours with White House aides—a pattern seen in the work schedules of other presidents.[d]

[a]Gerald M. Boyd, "The Bush Style of Management," *New York Times*, March 19, 1989, p.1.
[b]Alexander Butterfield in Larry Berman, *The New American Presidency* (Boston: Little, Brown, 1987), p. 265.
[c]Doris Kearns, *Lyndon Johnson and the American Dream* (New York: Harper & Row, 1976), p. 8.
[d]Berman, *The New American Presidency*, pp. 263–272; and Richard Rose, *The Postmodern President* (Chatham, N.J.: Chatham House, 1988), pp. 151–153.

Schedule of the President

Tuesday, April 18, 1989

8:00 A.M. (15 min)	Intelligence briefing	Oval Office
8:15 A.M. (30 min)	National security briefing	Oval Office
8:45 A.M. (30 min)	Meeting with Governor Sununu (chief of staff)	Oval Office
9:15 A.M. (15 min)	Personal staff time	Oval Office
9:30 A.M. (5 min)	Photo with Mr. and Mrs. Parker Banzhaf (Florida campaign supporters)	Oval Office
9:35 A.M.	Personal staff time	Oval Office
9:50 A.M.	The President departs to address the National Conference of Building and Construction Trades Department, AFL-CIO, at the Washington Hilton Hotel	South Lawn
10:35 A.M.	Arrives White House	South Lawn
10:45 A.M. (20 min)	Staff time	Oval Office
11:15 A.M. (30 min)	Meeting with conservative evangelical leaders	Roosevelt Room
11:45 A.M.	Personal staff time	Oval Office
12:00 noon (60 min)	Lunch with Secretary of Defense Cheney and General Scowcroft (national security adviser)	Oval Office
1:05 P.M.	The President departs for the Department of Agriculture to address USDA's Live Farm Radio Broadcast	South Lawn
1:40 P.M.	Arrives White House	South Lawn
1:45 P.M. (30 min)	Personal staff time	Oval Office
2:15 P.M. (15 min)	Signing ceremony for bipartisan accord on Central America	Rose Garden
2:30 P.M. (15 min)	Personal staff time	Oval Office
2:45 P.M. (30 min)	Meeting with Dr. Burton Lee (President's physician)	Oval Office
3:15 P.M. (60 min)	NSC Meeting	Cabinet Room
4:30 P.M. (30 min)	Meeting with Secretary of Health and Human Services Sullivan	Oval Office
5:00 P.M. (15 min)	Meeting with Governor Sununu	Oval Office

PRESIDENTIAL DECISION MAKING: WHO GOVERNS?

The Constitution makes Congress the chief poli-cymaker in the American political system, but as we have seen, it also gives the president an active role in shaping domestic and foreign policies. Today, as a presidential scholar points out, the advantage may have passed to the chief execu-tive: "Seizing on the initiative which the Consti-tution provides, and which their central per-spective, institutional structure, and political support facilitate, presidents have become chief policymakers."[63] The democratic, pluralist, and elite models offer different perspectives on pres-idential policymaking.

Democracy: The Importance of Public Opinion

All presidents are concerned with public opin-ion. "Public sentiment is everything," said Lin-coln, "With public sentiment nothing can fail, without it nothing can succeed."[64] Representa-tive Newt Gingrich, the Republican whip of the House, made a similar point in 1990, shortly after public opinion polls showed that President Bush had higher approval ratings after one year in office than any president since John Kennedy. Asked what Bush would do about a pending Democratic proposal to cut Social Security pay-roll taxes, Gingrich said: "If the President's pop-ularity is at 80 percent, I think the President can do whatever he wants."[65] Political science stud-ies confirm the importance of public opinion. For example, the level of support presidents receive in Congress is directly related to their standing in the public opinion polls.[66] But public opinion matters not just for presidential prestige; the es-sence of the democratic model is the link be-tween public opinion and public policy, and presidents can help provide that link. "Going public" is one of the primary strategies of pres-idential leadership today.[67]

Given the importance of public opinion to the president's success in office, and to the workings of democracy, it is no wonder that presidents are concerned with understanding the patterns of public approval and—if possible—with keeping their approval ratings high. Two aspects of pres-idential popularity are of greatest importance to the president: long-term trends and short-term fluctuations. Together, these patterns illustrate a fundamental rule of politics: "Friends come and go, but enemies just accumulate."[68]

LONG-TERM TRENDS   Newly elected presi-dents usually enjoy a brief "honeymoon" period followed by a steady decline in their standings in the polls. This is the most common long-term trend in presidential popularity (see Figure 15.1). For most presidents, the approval rating starts fairly high and declines at a rate of 6 per-cent a year.[69] This decline is perhaps the natural result of presidential decisions that alienate former supporters and disappoint unreasonable public expectations. Regardless of the causes, however, most presidents know that they begin their term of office with the highest level of sup-port that they are ever likely to see. Public ap-proval of both Presidents Reagan and Bush, however, deviated from the usual pattern. A New York Times/CBS poll in January 1989 found that 68 percent of the public approved of the way Re-agan had handled the job since 1981—the high-est rating given any president at the end of his term since World War II.[70] And public approval of George Bush increased from about 60 percent in the early months of his administration to 80 percent in January 1990, after he had been in office for one year.[71]

One response to the normal pattern of public approval is for a president to get as much of the executive program through Congress as quickly as possible. That was the essence of President Lyndon Johnson's observation: "I keep hitting hard because I know this honeymoon won't last. Every day I lose a little more political capital. That's why we have to keep at it, never letting up. One day soon, I don't know when, the critics and the snipers will move in and we will be at stalemate. We have to get all we can, now, before the roof comes down."[72] A different approach is for a president to avoid controversy and divisive issues in order to maintain high popular ap-proval. President Eisenhower, for example, has been described as a president who "hoarded his popularity as a deterrent to those who might try

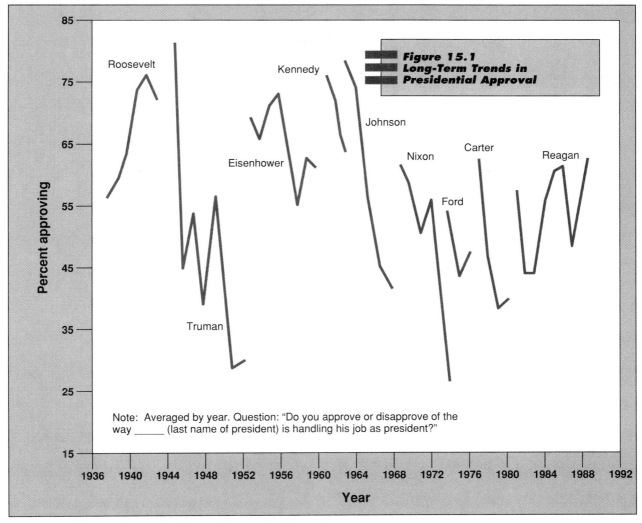

**Figure 15.1
Long-Term Trends in
Presidential Approval**

Note: Averaged by year. Question: "Do you approve or disapprove of the
way _____ (last name of president) is handling his job as president?"

Source: Harold W. Stanley and Richard G. Niemi, *Vital Statistics
on American Politics,* 2nd ed. (Washington, D.C.: Congressional
Quarterly Press, 1990), p. 256.

to strike down his policies or to undermine him personally."[73] In 1990, a Republican strategist expressed a concern that President Bush was not using his high standing in the polls to push the party's policy agenda and that "popularity like this breeds inertia."[74]

SHORT-TERM FLUCTUATIONS   Short-term fluctuations occur during all presidencies. The pattern of the Reagan administration shown in Figure 15.2 is typical (see p. 505). As the figure shows, international events or the state of the economy explain most short-term surges and declines in the president's public prestige. Of course, presidents do seek to manipulate the economy, but there are serious limits on their ability to do so. It is the real economic conditions, and not the president's actions, that determine public approval ratings. International

President Lyndon Johnson used to worry that "every day I lose a little more political capital."

President Dwight David Eisenhower "hoarded his popularity as a deterrent to those who might try to strike down his policies or to undermine him personally."

events are even less under the president's control.

If presidents are often unable to control events, they can at least seek to influence how those events are perceived. Most recent presidents have included advertising specialists and public relations experts among the White House staff. All presidents since Eisenhower have had extensive White House press operations whose purpose is to make sure that media coverage of presidential activities is favorable. This concern about favorable press coverage stretches so far as to influence decision making involving substantive policies. After sitting in on a number of staff meetings in the Reagan administration, a Washington journalist said that:

> . . . one concern permeated all those sessions: how events had played or would play on the air and in print. What items on the schedule should be turned into "photo ops"? Should the President have a question period with the press today? If he does, what story should be "sold"? Is the briefing material ready to prepare Reagan for his next magazine interview?[75]

Lloyd Cutler, who served as counsel to the president in the Carter administration, made a similar observation some years after leaving office: "I was surprised by how much the substantive policymaking decisions in the White House are affected by press deadlines and, in particular, by the evening television news."[76]

AGENDA SETTING   A president's appeal for public support not only helps provide the linkage required of the democratic model, but also serves to set the agenda for the bargaining that characterizes the pluralist model. As former presidential assistant George Reedy has suggested, "The president's ability to place his views before the public is important primarily because he can usually set the terms of the national debate—and anyone who can set the terms of a debate can win it."[77] A recent study of presidential government refers to the importance of the president's role as a "national highlighter" whose task is not to settle all issues but to focus attention on a few issues of great national importance.[78] And an analysis of Ronald Reagan's great success in getting his economic policies through Congress in 1981 cites this reason for his

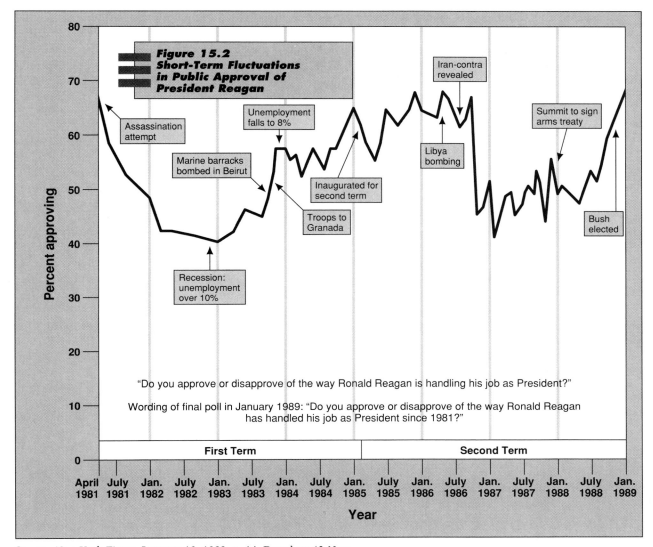

Source: New York Times, January 18, 1989, p. 14. Based on 62 New York Times/CBS News polls and 5 New York Times polls. When two polls conducted in the same month gave identical results, only one value is shown.

success: "President Reagan picked as his first priority the issue on which he found a strong consensus and a palpable conservative trend—the urge to cut back government and the sense of a pocketbook squeeze at all levels of society."[79] Successful agenda setting by a president must be based on the policy priorities held by the general public.

Pluralism: The Importance of Coalition Building

Clinton Rossiter's *The American President* was one of the most widely read books on the subject in the 1950s and 1960s. Rossiter opened his book with a quote from Macbeth that seemed to capture the burdens of the office: "Methought I heard a voice cry, 'Sleep no more!' " Shortly before President John Kennedy's death in 1963, he sent to Rossiter some lines from Shakespeare's Henry IV, which he felt more accurately reflected the true difficulty with the office:[80]

Glendower: I can call spirits from the vasty deep.

Hotspur: Why, so can I, or so can any man; But will they come when you do call for them?

To be effective policymakers, presidents need to call—and people need to come.

A president's success in governing depends on the ability to convert an electoral coalition into a governing coalition. A coalition is an interdependent set of groups with a shared attitude or attitudes. An **electoral coalition** is a set of groups in which the shared attitude is support for a certain candidate or party and includes a nominating coalition and a general election coalition. A **governing coalition** is a set of groups that support particular officeholders and their programs or policies. Table 15.9 illustrates the key elements of these two coalitions.

Putting together an electoral coalition requires a candidate to call enough spirits to win the nomination or election and to have those spirits come when they are called—at least on

Table 15.9
Electoral and Governing Coalitions

Electoral Coalition	Governing Coalition
Nominating coalition	Congress
General-election coalition	Bureaucracy
	Political party
Party factions	General public
Interest groups	Foreign governments
Ethnic, racial, class groups in general population	Media
	Interest groups
	Institutional presidency

Source: Adapted from Lester G. Seligman and Cary R. Covington, *The Coalitional Presidency* (Homewood, Ill.: Dorsey Press, 1989), p. 12.

election day. Putting together a governing coalition requires those spirits to stay around for awhile so that a president is able to get a program through Congress. However, changes in the way presidents get nominated today make it unnecessary to form the normal electoral coalitions, which, in turn, makes it difficult to develop a governing coalition once in office.[81]

Jimmy Carter's presidency illustrated how the nature of the electoral coalition affects the attempt to build a governing coalition. In 1976 Carter was elected as an "outsider"—a president whose nomination and election owed little to congressional and national party leaders and who was committed to changing how the business of governing was carried on in Washington, D.C. This approach applied to coalition building, as it did to all aspects of governing. Rather than involving members of Congress in the initial stages of policy formulation—as, for example, Lyndon Johnson and Gerald Ford had done—Carter relied on the White House Office of Public Liaison to build "outside" coalitions of interest groups and individual constituents to demonstrate support for the president's programs after they had been sent to Capitol Hill.[82] The Carter administration's outside approach to coalition building was successful at times, most notably in winning approval of the Panama Canal treaties in 1977. This approach was pluralist in its group focus, but by leaving Congress out of the process, the Carter administration was unable to develop a governing coalition that could resolve difficult issues such as the budget and energy policy.

The initial stages of the Reagan administration, particularly the budget cuts of 1981, suggested that Carter's successor had succeeded in assembling a governing coalition. A recent assessment suggests, however, that the Reagan administration had proven "more adept at creating the *appearance* of governing":

Reagan could not sustain a consensus on his budgetary priorities or much of his foreign policy.

His achievements in the latter stages of his presidency have been either, as tax reform revealed, the result of building exclusive coalitions or, as the Iran-Contra case revealed, a result of unilateral action by the White House rather than coalition-building leadership.[83]

George Bush assumed office in 1989 with less party support in Congress than any newly elected or reelected president in U.S. history.[84] That made the task of transforming an electoral coalition into a governing coalition even more difficult than it had been for earlier presidents; it virtually dictated a bipartisan insider approach to coalition building. House Budget Committee Chairman Leon Panetta described President Bush's approach to Congress this way:

> The ability to acknowledge one another and speak on a one-to-one basis and stroke one another is extremely important to our process of government.
> And that's what he's good at.[85]

The Power Elite: The Importance of Crisis Management

Agenda setting and coalition building are the aspects of policymaking on which presidents spend most of their time. Presidential involvement in these activities in any one policy area can extend over an entire four-year term. There is a never-ending quality to this task. The process simply begins again after every presidential victory in Congress. There are times, however, when the slow-motion nature of policymaking speeds up dramatically.

Crisis situations act like a shot of adrenalin to presidential policymaking. The general public and political leaders turn to the president for action. The lights in the West Wing of the White House burn all night. As you recall from the discussion earlier in this chapter, the exercise of prerogative powers and a general acceptance of broad presidential authority are most likely to take place during emergencies. We remember presidents and presidencies in terms of their crises—unanticipated events, either foreign or domestic, that so change the political relationships among groups or nations that a governmental response of some sort is required. In most cases, but not all, crises are further characterized

by a short time frame. They usually demand rapid decision making by political leaders.

Successful coalition building in routine presidential policymaking involves a constant expansion of the decision-making circle. The policymaking process in a crisis works the opposite way. The requirements of speed, secrecy, expertise, loyalty to the president, accurate information, and reliability all lead to decisions being made by a relatively small group that includes the president. It is partly because of the small size of the decision-making group that a problem arises from the need for information. How can a president be assured of having complete information that permits a full evaluation of all possible options?

Distortions in the information flow to crisis decision makers appear to come from two primary sources. First, the decision makers are likely to have particular biases, so bureaucratic politics and the role of some key decision makers as department or service advocates can lead to some bias in all information. If the president can tap enough different sources of information, bias in one direction can be canceled out by bias in another.

The second common source of information distortion comes from the nature of small-group interaction itself. Psychologist Irving Janis has studied the tendency of small, cohesive decision-making groups to produce a group consensus that inhibits dissent and limits the number of options and type of information that the group will consider. He found this phenomenon, which he called **groupthink,** to be present in some crisis decision making in the Korean War, the escalation in Vietnam, and the Bay of Pigs.[86]

Alexander George has made a detailed analysis of the quality of information and advice given to the president during a number of crisis decisions.[87] He concludes that the most common malfunctions of the informational and advisory system have been the following: (1) The president and his advisers agree too quickly on the nature of the problem and the correct response. (2) Possible explanations and options are excluded. (3) There is no advocate among the president's advisers for an unpopular policy action. (4) The advisers debate the options among them-

President John Kennedy meets with advisers during the Cuban missile crisis in October, 1962. The President took steps to avoid the groupthink that influenced his earlier decision to invade Cuba at the Bay of Pigs in 1961.

selves and then present the president with a unanimous recommendation. (5) The advisers agree on what needs to be done, but fail to convey that to the president. (6) The decision makers rely on a single channel of information. (7) Only the advocates of a proposal evaluate its key assumptions and premises. (8) The president ignores one or two advisers if he disagrees with them. (9) The president is so impressed by the consensus among his advisers that he fails to determine the basis of that consensus.

George found that these malfunctions of the system affected the outcomes of several key crisis decisions made by presidents and their advisers in the past. He suggests that the best way for a president to assure reliable information and advice is through a system that he calls **multiple advocacy**. The chief requirement is that the different participants in the system be relatively equal in their competence and expertise, the information available to them, their staff support, their status with the president, and their bargaining skills. Another requirement of multiple advocacy is that presidents actively participate

in decision making by the group, that they monitor and regulate the advisory system.

In the first two forms of presidential decision making discussed in this section, a president expands the number of participants by "going public" and building a governing coalition. In a crisis situation, however, the number of participants is strictly limited and those outside of the immediate decision-making circle are kept uninformed. This is what happened when the Social Security System was in danger of running out of money in 1983. "After winnowing the list of key players," Paul Light said in describing the nine decision-making participants in that crisis, they "had to find a place to hide."[88] Presidential scholar Bruce Buchanan says that the decision-making model of the 1983 Social Security reforms is one that presidents and Congress will turn to more and more in making unpopular decisions.[89]

Proponents of this form of elite decision making see it as the only way to provide the energy in government needed to overcome a stalemate. The general public's opposition to both increasing taxes and reducing Social Security benefits in 1983, for example, created a stalemate that could not be overcome by either the president's going public or building a coalition. Alexander Hamilton was one of the strongest advocates for energy in the executive at the time the Constitution was adopted, but he was also aware of the dangers of that energy in a republic. In *Federalist 70*, Hamilton wrote that since everyone

> . . . will agree in the necessity of an energetic executive, it will only remain to inquire, what are the ingredients which constitute this energy?
>
> How far can they be combined with those other ingredients which constitute safety in the republican sense?[90]

Checkpoint

- The democratic framework calls attention to the importance of public approval as a resource. The normal long-term trend in public approval requires a president to act early to get a program across. All presidents also seek to influence the short-term fluctuations in public approval by educating the public on what they do.

- The pluralist model alerts us to the way in which presidents must assemble a broad-based stable governing coalition in order to be effective. But the diminishment of coalition-building skills in running for election has made that task more difficult.

- The power elite explanation of governing best describes crisis policymaking, when the demands of secrecy, speed, expertise, loyalty to the president, and accurate information lead to a small decision-making group that includes the president.

SUMMARY

The central role of the president in governing America is the result of five core constitutional powers and their historical expansion: the executive power, the appointing power, the war power, legislative powers, and the treaty power. The concept of executive prerogative—the right of executives to perform certain functions without public or legislative approval—has also been an important source of presidential power. The constitutional powers and executive prerogative granted to all presidents are no guarantee of presidential power. That results from a president's ability to persuade others to support his policies or to carry out his orders. To be effective, a president needs selling skills to generate support in the public, Congress, the press, and among world leaders; and managerial skills to manage programs and bureaucracies.

The Constitution specifies a few legal qualifications to be president, but unofficial informal qualifications have greatly limited the presidential pool. Generally, presidents and candidates have been middle-aged or older white male Christians of northern or western European stock who have had government or military experience. Presidential campaign strategies and electoral outcomes are influenced by the electoral college, voters' party identification, incumbency status, and the state of the economy. Some political observers feel the presidential selection process tests the selling skills of candidates more than their managing skills.

The presidency is more than the individual who holds that office; it also includes the officials and staff whose job it is to provide decision-making support for the chief executive and to manage the government. There are four main components to the institutional presidency: the cabinet, the Executive Office of the President, the White House Office, and the vice-president. The expansion of this institutional presidency during the past 40 years has meant that presidents spend a great deal of their time managing the managers.

Applying the question of who governs to the presidency, we have found answers that correspond to all three models: democracy and the presidential resource of public approval, pluralism and the need to build governing coalitions, and the elite decision making that takes place in foreign or domestic crises.

KEY TERMS

Executive power	Cabinet
Appointing power	Executive Office of the
War power	President
Legislative powers	White House Office
Treaty power	Electoral coalition
Executive agreement	Governing coalition
Executive prerogative	Groupthink
Institutional presidency	Multiple advocacy

FOR FURTHER READING

Bruce Buchanan, *The Citizen's Presidency* (Washington, D.C.: Congressional Quarterly Press, 1987). An analysis and guide for citizens on improving the standards for choosing among presidential candidates and judging the performance of those in office.

Thomas E. Cronin, *Rethinking the Presidency* (Boston: Little, Brown, 1982). A collection of provocative essays on the development of the office and the exercise of presidential power.

George C. Edwards III, *At the Margins: Presidential Leadership of Congress* (New Haven, Conn.: Yale University Press, 1989). An empirical study of the legislative influence of recent presidents, which challenges many of the myths surrounding the topic.

Fred I. Greenstein, *The Hidden-Hand Presidency* (New York: Basic Books, 1982). A fresh look at the easy-to-miss but effective leadership techniques of President Eisenhower and how other presidents might learn from him.

Samuel Kernell, *Going Public: New Strategies of Presidential Leadership* (Washington, D.C.: Congressional Quarterly Press, 1986). Examines the thesis that presidents are increasingly turning away from the traditional bargaining approach to policymaking in favor of direct appeals to the American people.

Richard E. Neustadt, *Presidential Power and the Modern Presidents*, 3d ed. (New York: Free Press, 1990). An updated and revised analysis and primer on how presidents can maximize personal power.

Donald L. Robinson, *"To the Best of My Ability": The Presidency and the Constitution* (New York: Norton, 1987). A highly readable analysis of the major constitutional issues of the presidency.

Bert A. Rockman, *The Leadership Question* (New York: Praeger, 1984). An examination of presidential leadership and the conflict between strong leadership and key values in the American political system.

Barry Schwartz, *George Washington: The Making of an American Symbol* (New York: Free Press, 1987). A fascinating account of the transformation of Washington into an American myth and of the president into an important national symbol.

Marcia Lynn Whicker and Raymond A. Moore, *When Presidents Are Great* (Englewood Cliffs, N.J.: Prentice-Hall, 1988). An examination of presidents who succeeded and presidents who failed, and why.

The Bureaucracy

Chapter 16

Government bureaucracy is sometimes thought of as the machinery of government. But it is not a neutral machine that simply implements the policy choices made by those who govern. Bureaucrats participate in governing America: They influence other decision makers; they have discretion in implementing policies; they reflect particular interests and respond to constituencies much as elected officials do. The political nature of the bureaucracy, the fact that it does influence policy, necessitates political control of it. ∎

A Georgia congressman once did some investigating and found that in a year in which Congress had enacted 404 public laws, the *Federal Register* (the official document of rules and regulations issued by U.S. government agencies) listed 7496 rules and regulations from 67 agencies. It was clear, said the congressman, that the federal bureaucracy had "evolved into a fourth—nonconstitutional—branch of government with a thick tangle of regulations that carry the force of law without the benefit of legislative considerations."[1]

Throughout the 1980s, the number of pages of rules and regulations in the *Federal Register* was considerably higher than the number of pages of laws passed by Congress during the same period. The One-hundredth Congress, for instance, passed laws totaling less than 5,000 pages while the rules and regulations in the *Federal Register* for that same time (1987–1988) filled more than 100,000 pages.[2] A similar point was made in 1985 by a list that was being circulated around some government offices in Washington, D.C.:[3]

Lord's Prayer	56 words
Twenty-third Psalm	118 words
Gettysburg Address	226 words
Ten Commandments	297 words
Department of Agriculture order on the price of cabbage	15,629 words

In 1985, the Reagan administration sought to gain control over the rules and regulations issued by federal government agencies. An execu-

tive order established a unit within the Office of Management and Budget (OMB) to review and approve rules or regulations proposed by any executive agency. The order was intended to make the administration's policy consistent and to enable Reagan "to guide and supervise the implementation of administrative policy."[4]

The administration's action, however, stirred considerable debate. Critics charged that it would centralize controls in a small office that was unresponsive to either the public or Congress. One legislator worried that the government's regulatory program would be "an isolated policy developed by the Office of Management and Budget under authority of an executive order."[5]

What is remarkable in the debate is what both sides agreed on. Both recognized the policymaking nature of the regulations issued by the federal bureaucracy. And both sides understood that there would inevitably be a tilt in the implementation of policy, whether toward Congress or toward the White House. In other words, implementation would not be neutral. A recognition that the bureaucracy helps shape government policy, that the machinery of government affects both those who ostensibly run it and the resulting product, is an important first step in understanding bureaucracy.

Any discussion of the bureaucracy is likely to evoke strong feelings. One scholar writes: "No fear has been more constant in modern politics—shared by revolutionaries and reactionaries alike—than the apprehension that bureaucrats might become a power elite and dominate the

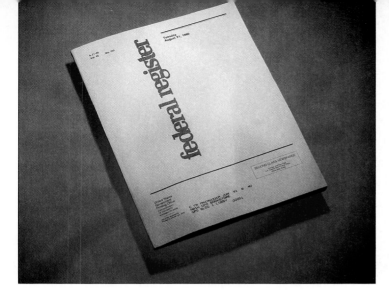

The federal bureaucracy generates about 20 pages of rules and regulations in the Federal Register for every page of laws passed by Congress.

governmental process in which they are meant to play a subordinate role."[6] Another suggests: "Everyone has trouble with bureaucracy. Citizens and politicians have trouble controlling the runaway bureaucratic machine. Managers have trouble managing it. Employees dislike working for it. Clients can't get the goods from it. Teachers have trouble getting an overall grip on it. Students are mystified by the complexity of it."[7]

A majority of Americans in a 1986 CBS News/*New York Times* poll said the federal government "creates more problems than it solves." A respondent detailed this attitude more fully in another public opinion survey taken in 1987:

> There's just thousands and thousands of white collar workers in Washington who do nothing but shuffle paper and don't do anything that's of any value to anyone. . . . It's just flab, it's just waste.[8]

In many ways, people are justified in their concern with the government bureaucracy. Consider its size and growth, public perceptions of wasted tax dollars and inefficiency, the image of cold and impersonal bureaucrats, the demand for record keeping and paperwork, rules and regulations that seem to make no sense. A belief that is central to these concerns, one that was exemplified in the debate over the Reagan administration's changes in 1985, is the idea that bureaucrats have an active role in governing America, one that goes far beyond the routine implementation of policies made by others.

These concerns bring to our attention some of the key questions regarding the role of the bu-

reaucracy in governing America. What is the structure of the federal bureaucracy and the policymaking roles of its different elements? What were the dimensions and causes of bureaucratic growth that recent political leaders have sought to reverse? How do other governing institutions seek to gain and maintain political control of the federal bureaucracy?

These are questions this chapter seeks to answer. First, however, we should arrive at an understanding of just what bureaucracy is.

THE NATURE OF BUREAUCRACY

A **bureaucracy** is a formal organization in which specialists organized in a hierarchy carry out policies by using standardized procedures. A public bureaucracy is a type of formal organization that carries out government policies. The essential structural features of a public bureaucracy also serve to define it:

hierarchy—A ranking of roles within the organization with those higher up in the organization having higher status and more responsibility and privileges than those lower down.

specialization—A division of labor in which jurisdictions and specific tasks are assigned to certain offices.

formalization—A process whereby written job descriptions specify the duties of each position and communication among offices is in the

Public bureaucracies are everywhere, providing essential services such as national defense and assisting needy individuals in society.

form of written memoranda, which are maintained in files.

merit and seniority—A person's entry into the bureaucracy is based on a standardized way of evaluating skills, while promotion within the bureaucracy depends on merit and length of service in that organization (seniority).

size—No fixed number determines when an organization becomes a bureaucracy, but a bureaucracy is generally large enough that those at the top of the hierarchy know less than half of all other members of the organization.

nonmarketable output—Public bureaucracies generally do not produce a product or service that is readily available in the marketplace. Therefore, the efficiency and output of the bureaucracy cannot be evaluated by the market standards of profit and loss. As a result, bureaucracies are often evaluated by the quantity rather than the quality of their work.[9]

Certain generalizations about public bureaucracies can serve as a starting point for understanding their contemporary role in governing America.[10] First, bureaucracies are everywhere.

All modern societies use this form of organization for dealing with collective problems. Second, bureaucracies dominate policy implementation. They also have varying degrees of importance at earlier stages of governing, such as formulating policies. Third, bureaucracies serve different functions. Some provide essential governmental services, such as national defense and foreign relations, or distribute benefits, such as food stamps or medical care. Others promote particular economic interests, such as farmers or organized labor. Still others regulate private industries such as television, food, and drugs.

A fourth point is that bureaucracies function in a large and complex world of government. This complexity is reflected in the wide array of relatively autonomous government agencies, the different organizations sharing responsibility for programs, and the interaction of public and private agencies in implementing policies. Another valid generalization is that old bureaucracies rarely die, and new ones are constantly being born. A study of the "immortality" of government organizations found that 85 percent of the government organizations in existence in 1923 were still around 50 years later, that most had the same status in the federal government that they did earlier, and that nearly 250 new agencies had come into being during the same period.[11] In 1976 President Jimmy Carter promised to reduce the number of federal agencies from an estimated 1900 to 200; he left office four years later with the size of the federal bureaucracy relatively unchanged.

Finally, bureaucracies are not neutral, nor are they fully controlled by any external officials or organizations. Executive officials and members of Congress begin with the premise that the policy preferences and values of bureaucrats influence policies and seek to exercise some control over that process. The OMB regulation review illustrates this point.

An early and influential explanation for the increasing dominance of governmental bureaucracy in the twentieth century was offered by German sociologist Max Weber in 1920. Bureaucracies, said Weber, enjoyed a technical superiority over other types of organizations. The expertise of full-time professionals in a formal bureaucracy produced "precision, speed, unambiguity, knowledge of the files, continuity, discretion, unity, strict subordination, reduction of friction, and of materiel and personnel costs," which could not be matched by organizations made up of part-time nonprofessionals operating in informal decision-making groups. "The fully developed bureaucratic mechanism compares with other organizations exactly as does the machine with the non-mechanical modes of production."[12]

Checkpoint

- A bureaucracy is a formal organization in which specialists organized in a hierarchy carry out policies by using standardized procedures. Its essential features are hierarchy, specialization, formalization, merit, seniority, size, and nonmarketable output.

- Certain generalizations can be made about governmental bureaucracies: They are used in all modern societies; they dominate policy implementation; they serve different functions; they operate in a large and complex world of government; once formed they rarely die, and new ones are constantly being born; they are not neutral or fully controlled by external officials.

THE STRUCTURE OF AMERICAN BUREAUCRACY

Franklin Roosevelt successfully changed the structure of the federal government more than any other president. During his second term, Roosevelt sent his budget director a memorandum showing that the President kept his sense

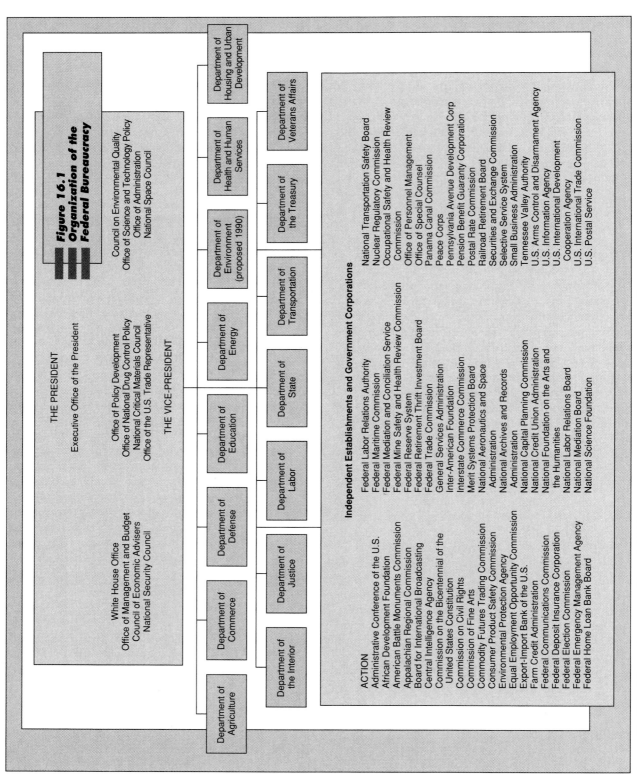

Figure 16.1
Organization of the Federal Bureaucracy

THE PRESIDENT

Executive Office of the President

White House Office
Office of Management and Budget
Council of Economic Advisers
National Security Council

Office of Policy Development
Office of National Drug Control Policy
National Critical Materials Council
Office of the U.S. Trade Representative

Council on Environmental Quality
Office of Science and Technology Policy
Office of Administration
National Space Council

THE VICE-PRESIDENT

Department of Agriculture
Department of the Interior
Department of Commerce
Department of Justice
Department of Defense
Department of Labor
Department of Education
Department of State
Department of Energy
Department of Transportation
Department of Environment (proposed 1990)
Department of the Treasury
Department of Health and Human Services
Department of Veterans Affairs
Department of Housing and Urban Development

Independent Establishments and Government Corporations

ACTION
Administrative Conference of the U.S.
African Development Foundation
American Battle Monuments Commission
Appalachian Regional Commission
Board for International Broadcasting
Central Intelligence Agency
Commission on the Bicentennial of the United States Constitution
Commission on Civil Rights
Commission of Fine Arts
Commodity Futures Trading Commission
Consumer Product Safety Commission
Environmental Protection Agency
Equal Employment Opportunity Commission
Export-Import Bank of the U.S.
Farm Credit Administration
Federal Communications Commission
Federal Deposit Insurance Corporation
Federal Election Commission
Federal Emergency Management Agency
Federal Home Loan Bank Board

Federal Labor Relations Authority
Federal Maritime Commission
Federal Mediation and Conciliation Service
Federal Mine Safety and Health Review Commission
Federal Reserve System
Federal Retirement Thrift Investment Board
Federal Trade Commission
General Services Administration
Inter-American Foundation
Interstate Commerce Commission
Merit Systems Protection Board
National Aeronautics and Space Administration
National Archives and Records Administration
National Capital Planning Commission
National Credit Union Administration
National Foundation on the Arts and the Humanities
National Labor Relations Board
National Mediation Board
National Science Foundation

National Transportation Safety Board
Nuclear Regulatory Commission
Occupational Safety and Health Review Commission
Office of Personnel Management
Office of Special Counsel
Panama Canal Commission
Peace Corps
Pennsylvania Avenue Development Corp
Pension Benefit Guaranty Corporation
Postal Rate Commission
Railroad Retirement Board
Securities and Exchange Commission
Selective Service System
Small Business Administration
Tennessee Valley Authority
U.S. Arms Control and Disarmament Agency
U.S. Information Agency
U.S. International Development Cooperation Agency
U.S. International Trade Commission
U.S. Postal Service

Source: The United States Government Manual 1989/90 (Washington, D.C.: Government Printing Office, 1990), p. 21.

of humor despite long battles with the federal bureaucracy:

> I agree with the Secretary of the Interior. Please have it carried out so that fur-bearing animals remain in the Department of the Interior.
>
> You might find out if any Alaska bears are still supervised by (a) War Department (b) Department of Agriculture (c) Department of Commerce. They have all had jurisdiction over Alaska bears in the past and many embarrassing situations have been created by the mating of a bear belonging to one Department with a bear belonging to another Department.[13]

More than 80 departments, agencies, commissions, and government corporations make up the executive branch of the U.S. government (Figure 16.1). Some of these organizations are quite familiar, while others carry on in relative obscurity. To make sense of the vast system depicted in the figure, it helps to see how bureaucracy as a whole differs from another branch of government and then to look at differences and similarities among the bureaucratic organizations and to categorize them in those terms. In that way, instead of trying to know and understand individual bureaucracies, we are able to focus on patterns of behavior and problems associated with more general types.

How Bureaucracy Differs from Congress

Certain general characteristics of all governmental bureaucracies distinguish them from other institutions, and from Congress in particular. Perhaps the most fundamental difference is how people get into those organizations in the first place. Members of Congress are elected to represent a specific geographical district. Bureaucrats are appointed or hired by those higher up in the organization. That means legislators and bureaucrats have differing notions of constituency, of who they must please in order to stay in office. Another main difference is that elected public officials are responsible for determining public policies; appointed officials are respon-

sible for implementing them. Selection by appointment and responsibility for policy implementation help determine those structural characteristics found in most bureaucracies: hierarchy, technical decision making, and low visibility.[14]

The typical bureaucratic hierarchy has a departmental secretary or commissioner on top, a limited number of assistant secretaries and under secretaries just below, and a series of levels of civil servants below that. The hierarchical structure is one in which authority flows downward and information and accountability upward. A difference between this executive hierarchy and the levels of influence found in a legislative committee system or party network goes back to the initial selection process discussed earlier. Senior members of Congress do not hire and fire other members of the institution. That power rests with constituents outside the organization.

A bureaucracy also differs from a legislature in that the former is expected to make decisions based on technical information and expertise, while the latter makes decisions on the basis of values and political considerations. The line separating the two, however, is tenuous. Congressional staff members provide legislators with a wealth of technical data, and bureaucrats know they must cultivate political support. Decisions in both types of institutions reflect a mixture of technical expertise and political considerations. The structure of bureaucracy, however, is geared more to technical decision making, as can be seen in such policy areas as weapons development, food and drug regulation, and the space program.

Legislative and bureaucratic decision making also differ in their relative visibility. Congress opened up its own party caucuses, committee and subcommittee meetings, and House-Senate conferences in a series of reforms in the 1970s. It also increased the visibility of much bureaucratic decision making by requiring open hearings, citizen input in the regulatory process, periodic reports to Congress, and a response to citizen requests under the 1974 Freedom of Information Act. Even though both structures are now more open, the visibility of decision making in a bureaucracy is still much lower than that in a legislature. The structure of a legislature permits public access at every stage of decision making. In bureaucracies, even after the many reforms of the 1970s, most decisions are still made outside of the public eye.

How Bureaucracies Differ from One Another

The structural characteristics of hierarchy, technical expertise, and low visibility distinguish any bureaucracy from Congress. But not all bureaucracies are the same. And just as the general differences in structure between the legislature and bureaucracy reflect the distinct political roles of those two organizations, so too does the structural variety that is found among bureaucracies. Bureaucracies differ from one another in their functions, the main problems they face, their history, constituencies, hierarchy, agreement on procedures, degree of professionalism, accessibility, centralization, and extent of competition in a policy area.[15]

FUNCTION Some bureaucracies deliver services in the form of health care, housing, job training programs, and the like, while others perform what is essentially a banking function in administering grant programs. Bureaucrats who deliver services come into direct contact with citizens and local political conditions and, as a result, often exercise discretionary authority in a decentralized structure. Administering grants, on the other hand, allows for a more centralized structure.

PROBLEM Each bureaucracy has a main problem it is believed to face in order to carry on its function. Does it have to develop resources in order to fund a new weapons system or a public housing project? Does it need to be more responsive to particular groups such as women or the elderly? Must it build or reestablish public trust in the delivery of medical services or intelligence gathering? Should it reform or restructure in order to reflect a changing political climate or new policy priorities? The particular mix of problems

that policymakers regard as important will be reflected in bureaucratic structure.

The relationship between problem and structure is illustrated by the establishment of the Resolution Trust Corporation (RTC) in 1989. Legislation designed to rescue failed savings and loan institutions created the RTC to take over more than 500 insolvent savings associations and to sell or liquidate $300 billion worth of troubled assets. The problem was how to accomplish this fairly and how to make the RTC accountable in its spending of $50 billion in public funds. Congress set up an unusual bureaucratic structure: It made an independent and neutral agency, the Federal Deposit Insurance Corporation, responsible for managing the RTC, and also created an RTC Oversight Board, made up of officials appointed by and responsible to the president, to set general policy guidelines and approve RTC transactions. "As far as I know, there has never been an animal like this set up in government," RTC Chairman L. William Seidman said. "We're really sort of the body and they're the mind," he said of the oversight board.[16]

HISTORY The Departments of State and Treasury were created in 1789, 200 years before the Department of Veterans Affairs. "Old" bureaucracies are often described as less flexible and less responsive to new political forces and policy ideas than are "new" bureaucracies (such as Health and Human Services, Transportation, Energy, and Housing and Urban Development). The development of any bureaucracy is a result not only of the growing institutionalization that comes with age, but also of the purpose for which it was formed, for example, to conduct foreign policy or provide for the national defense (State and Defense), to represent certain interests in government (Commerce and Labor), or to coordinate a wide range of programs in a broad policy area (Health and Human Services and Education).

CONSTITUENCIES While all bureaucracies depend to some extent on outside groups in order to achieve goals and maintain political support, there are differences in the nature of those constituencies. For a clientele department such as

The savings and loan crisis of the late 1980s and 1990s raised special problems that led to the creation of an unusual bureaucratic structure, the Resolution Trust Corporation. "As far as I know," said the first head of that corporation, "there has never been an animal like this set up in government."

Agriculture, Labor, Commerce, or Veterans Affairs, the constituency is easily recognizable and supportive. At the other extreme is a department such as Health and Human Services, whose many constituencies (for example, providers and receivers of health care, state and local health and welfare officials, and interest groups representing those with special needs) are often in conflict with one another. In some cases the primary constituency is another part of the government rather than any outside group. The important constituency of the State Department and the Central Intelligence Agency (CIA), for example, is the president and Congress.

HIERARCHY The structure of every bureaucracy is, on paper, a hierarchy, but organizations differ in how much control is actually exercised by those higher up in the hierarchy, which is also a reflection of how centralized the bureaucracy is. Military bureaucracies exhibit the most formal and centralized hierarchies, while organi-

zations with many functions (such as the Departments of Health and Human Services and Education) or clientele organizations (Labor, Commerce, Agriculture) are likely to be more decentralized and informal. A bureau that has strong constituencies of its own is also less bound by formal structure. The independence of the Federal Bureau of Investigation (FBI) within the Department of Justice illustrates that point. The presence of many skilled professionals in an organization also contributes to decentralization. The extent to which a bureaucracy is centralized and hierarchical will also affect how it interacts with others, for decentralized bureaucracies provide many more points of access for legislative and interest groups.

AGREEMENT ON PROCEDURES Organizations differ in how to achieve bureaucratic goals. Some bureaucracies have clearly established procedures. An Internal Revenue Service audit, for example, consists of a fixed pattern of actions.

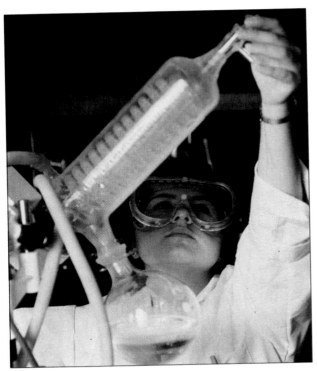

Professionalism is an important characteristic of some government bureaucracies such as the National Institutes of Health.

Members of that organization "go by the book" or "follow the drill" in order to achieve a particular goal. There is much less agreement in bureaucracies whose goal is education, job training, or drug rehabilitation, however, because of differing opinions on the best way to achieve those goals. The lack of consensus in such organizations can produce fluctuations in policies, difficulties in management, and an openness to suggestions from outside.

PROFESSIONALISM Organizations differ in the degree of professionalism exhibited by their experts. Doctors, military officers, and scientists, for example, have extensive training and specialized knowledge. They have clearly established operating procedures and resist attempts by nonprofessional managers to carry out those procedures themselves or to change them. At the same time that they maintain their independence and distinctiveness from nonprofessionals within the organization, these professionals also establish links with their fellow professionals outside the organization. All these factors affect the hierarchy of an organization and the degree of access offered to outside groups. Professionalism is an important characteristic of government bureaucracies such as the National Institutes of Health, the Joint Chiefs of Staff, and NASA. It has less effect on bureaus and agencies within, say, the Departments of Commerce or Labor.

ACCESSIBILITY Some bureaucracies are open to the policy suggestions and participation of private citizens and outside officials. Others are closed to outsiders, sometimes to the point of absolute secrecy. Many of the characteristics described above—function, problem, hierarchy, agreement on procedures, and professionalism— determine how accessible an organization is to outside individuals and groups. The activities that the Defense Department or CIA carry on to accomplish military and intelligence goals obviously require a great deal of secrecy. The relative lack of outside access to NASA and the Nuclear Regulatory Commission stems in part from the technical nature of those organizations' work. On the other hand, a need to pay attention to constituencies and statutes that mandate citizen participation through public hearings lead other organizations to be quite accessible to outside groups and officials. The openness of bureaucracies in the Departments of Commerce and Agriculture reflects the emphasis they place on constituency service. Environmental laws account for much of the high accessibility that has been associated with the Environmental Protection Agency (the proposed Department of Environment).

CENTRALIZATION The organizational chart or hierarchy of a bureaucracy is not always a clear indicator of where most of the organization's activities are or where decision-making responsibility lies. The structure of the Treasury Department, for example, includes field offices scattered throughout the country, yet it is a centralized organization because most decision-making authority rests in Washington. The programs and policies of many other organizations, however, are built around the joint efforts of the national, state, and local governments. The federal nature of programs in health care, housing, and education helps produce the decentralized structure found in the Departments of Health and Human Services, Housing and Urban Development, and Education. Federalism, then, can have an important decentralizing effect on the structure of some governmental bureaucracies. Organizations differ not only in the degree to which a hierarchy concentrates authority at the top, but also in whether the focus of activity and authority is in Washington, D.C., or geographically distributed.

COMPETITION   Does the responsibility for carrying on a particular governmental function rest primarily with one organization, or is it widely shared among many? Once again, we find that different organizations have different answers to that question. At one extreme are organizations such as the FBI and CIA, which at times have had spheres of activities in which they were either alone or clearly dominant. The other extreme is illustrated when a number of agencies compete in a policy area. In the Carter administration in the late 1970s, for example, the Departments of Housing and Urban Development, Health and Human Services, Transportation, Commerce, and Labor all sought authority over different aspects of urban policy. The intensity of that bureaucratic competition led President Carter to centralize control over those programs in the White House staff.

Even when the primary responsibility in a particular policy area belongs to one department, competition can arise. The State Department's authority in the area of foreign policy, for example, does not prevent other organizations, such as the National Security Council, the CIA, and the Departments of Defense, Agriculture, Commerce, Justice, and Treasury, from having some responsibilities for aspects of foreign policy.

Types of Bureaucracies

These different traits show the great structural variety found under the general heading of bureaucracy. But because many of these characteristics are interrelated, it is possible to construct two distinct types of bureaucracies, as shown in Table 16.1 (p. 522).

Most of the characteristics of type A bureaucracies are seen in the State, Treasury, and Defense departments; the National Security Council; the CIA; independent regulatory commissions; and scientific research agencies. Bureaucracies that more closely resemble type B include the Departments of Agriculture, Commerce, Health and Human Services, and Housing and Urban Development. Many government bureaucracies, of course, contain elements of both types. The differences seen in Table 16.1 represent tendencies rather than absolute and fixed characteristics.

What difference does it make if we call the State Department or some other bureaucracy a type A rather than type B? Reducing the number of organizations under scrutiny from 80 or more to two types in itself has advantages, but the purpose of this kind of classification goes beyond that. The overriding question about governmental bureaucracy, as we noted at the beginning of the chapter, is one of political control.

The two types of bureaucracy present quite different problems of political control. For type A organizations, the control question is one of avoiding bureaucratic dominance. An established, closed, centralized, highly professional, and hierarchical organization is likely to be efficient, but difficult for outside political officials or the general public to control. Type B bureaucracies are open to direction or even control by executive and legislative officials, interest groups, and the public, but the many competing claims made on them are likely to make them less efficient than type A organizations. As a result of these differences, efforts to exercise some political control over type A bureaucracies generally are attempts to make those organizations more open and democratic, while political control over type B bureaucracies is sought through making those organizations more efficient.

Table 16.1

Two Types of Bureaucracies

Type A Bureaucracies	Type B Bureaucracies
1. History—old, established bureaucracy with single dominant mission	1. History—newly created bureaucracy with many agencies and tasks
2. Constituencies—inactive or single dominant one	2. Constituencies—many, diverse, conflicting ones
3. Hierarchy—strong	3. Hierarchy—weak
4. Agreement on established procedures	4. Competing ways of doing things
5. Professionalism—high	5. Professionalism—low
6. Accessibility—low or closed	6. Accessibility—open
7. Centralization—Washington focus	7. Centralization—state and local government roles
8. Competition—low	8. Competition—high

Source: Adapted from Douglas Yates, *Bureaucratic Democracy* (Cambridge, Mass.: Harvard University Press, 1982), p. 141.

President Lyndon Johnson discusses Vietnam strategy with his National Security Council, a Type A bureaucracy. The problem of political control of this type of bureaucracy is one of avoiding bureaucratic dominance.

Checkpoint

- Bureaucracies differ from other political organizations such as Congress in many ways: the appointment rather than election of members, hierarchy, technical decision making, and the low visibility of most decision making.

- Government agencies differ from one another in their history, function, the problem they address, constituencies, hierarchical structure, agreement on procedures, professionalism, accessibility, centralization, and degree of competition.

- A comparison of the U.S. government agencies along those dimensions reveals two general types of governmental bureaucracies in the United States, which require quite different solutions to the problem of democratic control of the government. Type A bureaucracies need to be made more open and type B bureaucracies more efficient.

THE GROWTH OF GOVERNMENT

A central political issue in the past decade or so has been that of government spending. Concern over the federal deficit is felt on both sides of the political spectrum and dominates the politics of all other issues, from national ones such as defense and tax policies to state and local issues such as highways and education. The federal deficit is a particularly difficult problem for elected officials because it presents them with two politically unattractive alternatives: Raise taxes or reduce levels of funding for government programs.

A presidential panel of corporate executives, however, identified a third alternative. The 1984 report by the President's Private Sector Survey on Cost Control, known as the Grace Commission after its chairman, J. Peter Grace, said that the deficit could be virtually eliminated by the year 2000 "without raising taxes, without weakening America's needed defense build-up, and without harming in any way necessary social welfare programs."[17] This could be achieved,

said the commission, by eliminating waste in government through the application of sound business practices. In other words, the government should be run more like private business, and the principles of management in the private sector should be used to make governmental bureaucracy more efficient. The commission report included 2478 specific recommendations, which it said could produce savings of $424 billion over three years.

An independent study of the Grace Commission report jointly conducted by the Congressional Budget Office and the General Accounting Office concluded, however, that savings would be about a third of those estimated by the commission and that over 95 percent of the Grace Commission's projected savings of $424 billion would involve *policy changes*, such as changing eligibility requirements for social welfare programs and reducing federal benefits.[18] A Washington public interest lobbying group branded the Grace Commission recommendations "a thinly disguised assault on social welfare programs."[19] Whatever the case, they clearly called for more than reforming management and personnel practices of the bureaucracy.

The Grace Commission report and its aftermath reflect three general points about governmental bureaucracy in American politics. First, the appointment of such a commission indicates that presidents, other public officials, and the general public share a concern about the size of government and the problems of waste and inefficiency in government. Second, standards from the private sector, such as cost-effectiveness, are to be used to evaluate the performance of governmental bureaucracy. The Grace Commission even asked whether certain goods and services now provided by the government could better be provided by private industry. Third, the nature of the recommendations and the reaction they provoked demonstrate again that administration is not neutral, that bureaucracy and politics are intertwined. We must, in fact, look to political factors in order to understand that twentieth-century phenomenon, the growth of government.

Patterns of Government Growth

The long-term trend of government growth is reflected in increases in government spending and the number of government employees. Figure 16.2 provides an overall picture of the growth in government. Two trends particularly stand out in the figure. The first is the great expansion in the size of government. The second is that growth has been concentrated at the local and state levels of government. These levels have needed to hire personnel to implement the many grant programs that characterize modern federalism and were discussed in Chapter 5.

The public policies of certain administrations are also clearly linked with some of the changes shown in Figure 16.2. The social welfare programs of Johnson's Great Society, for example, helped make government employment the fastest-growing sector of the nation's labor market during the mid-1960s. President Reagan's commitment to reducing the size of government helped bring about the slight reduction (about 50,000 employees) in the federal work force between 1980 and 1981, but at the end of his administration the total number of federal employees was the highest since World War II.[20]

The overall long-term growth and the infrequent periods of decline underscore a link between politics and bureaucracy. Rather than attributing bureaucratic growth solely to natural laws or inexorable social and economic forces, we may look for political explanations for these patterns of government growth. What types of evidence and arguments would we find in a democratic explanation of these patterns of bureaucratic growth, and how would they differ from those found in pluralist or power elite explanations?

Explaining the Patterns of Government Growth

Asking the question of who benefits from bureaucracy is a first step in explaining its particular forms and its growing political dominance. Answers to that question, like so many others about American politics, depend to a great extent on one's general views about governing America.

THE DEMOCRATIC VIEW The core democratic notion of popular sovereignty would suggest that governmental bureaucracy has expanded and taken on its present form in response to public needs and public opinion. In this view, public demands for social services, economic support, regulation, and the distribution of benefits have all expanded governmental bureaucracy. Various government agencies then develop constituencies and political support, which reinforce their growth. This combination of public opinion "pushes" and bureaucratic "pulls" has characterized government growth since the last century.

But public opinion polls, as we mentioned earlier, regularly portray a public disenchanted with bureaucracy. How can a democratic view of bureaucratic growth be reconciled with these antibureaucratic public attitudes? One answer consistent with the democratic view would be that the 1980–1981 decline in the size of government is a direct result of such attitudes. Another answer is that these survey results, in fact, send mixed signals. For the same public opinion polls that show support for a smaller government also

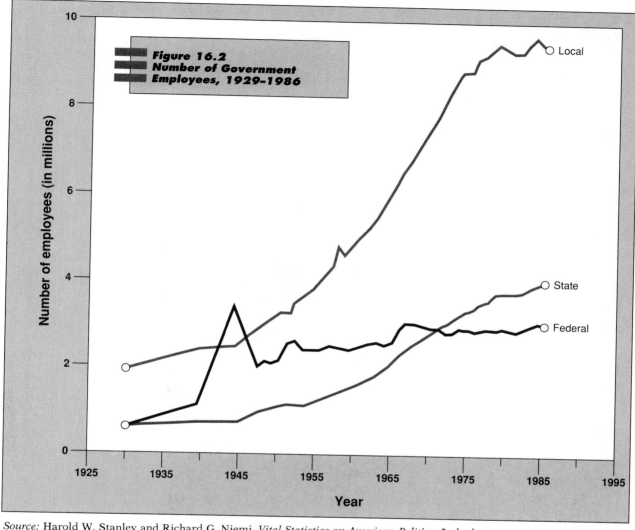

**Figure 16.2
Number of Government
Employees, 1929-1986**

Source: Harold W. Stanley and Richard G. Niemi, *Vital Statistics on American Politics,* 2nd ed. (Washington, D.C.: Congressional Quarterly Press, 1990), p. 292.

reveal support for specific government activities and programs.[21]

Public attitudes about governmental bureaucracy, then, do help explain recent patterns of government growth. Support for antibureaucratic sentiment expressed in Carter's presidential campaign in 1976 and Reagan's in 1980 and 1984 and for reforms and deregulation of the type favored by the Grace Commission can be found in the public's general feelings about government spending, size, and waste. On the other hand, public support for *specific* government programs and current spending levels in particular areas of policy helps substantiate democratic explanations of government growth patterns.

THE PLURALIST VIEW Pluralists often portray bureaucratic growth as a result of group bar-

The Dead Letter Office of the Department of the Post Office in the 1880s. It was bureaucracies such as this that nineteenth-century reformers sought to remove from partisan politics by creating a merit-based civil service in 1883.

gaining and describe government bureaucracy as a "broker and mediator, working out and facilitating the acceptance of policy compromises on the part of competing groups."[22] As the number of interested groups has increased, the bargaining process has had the effect of decentralizing bureaucracy— dispersing rather than concentrating responsibility for formulating and implementing policy. This dispersement can be seen in the growth in government bureaucracy in recent years at the state and local level. Robert Dahl views bureaucratic decentralization as part of a pattern of government in America:

In the context of decentralized bargaining parties and a decentralized bargaining legislature, it was perhaps inevitable that despite the powerful efforts of many Presidents and the somewhat Utopian yearnings of many administrative reformers, the vast apparatus that grew up to administer the affairs of the American welfare state is a decentralized bureaucracy. This is merely another way of saying that the bureaucracy has become a part of the "normal" American political process.[23]

The burgeoning and decentralized bureaucracy developed in response to changes in American society. Nineteenth-century reformers campaigned to remove the administration of policies from partisan politics, which led to creation of a merit-based civil service in 1883. The emergence of large corporations, particularly in the railroad, steel, and oil industries, during the same period caused the government to create agencies to act as market regulators and mediators of conflicting economic interests. A third development during that time is of particular importance to pluralist explanations of the growth of government: the increasing specialization of society. Groups with common concerns and interests gave rise to executive branch departments that served as their "representatives." The Department of Agriculture and Department of Commerce are examples of government agencies that formed around group interests.[24]

The pluralist view focuses on governmental bureaucracy as one of many actors in a decentralized system of political bargaining. According to this view, **subgovernments**, or **iron triangles**, consisting of key legislators and congressional staff, representatives of private groups and interests, and members of the government agency or agencies with responsibility in that area, make most of the routine decisions about governing America, such as the level of price supports farmers receive for certain crops or funding for public works projects.[25] When they engage in the bargaining that characterizes these subgovernments, bureaucrats act as mediators among different interests, as agents for those private interests they may "represent" in government, and as members of an organization with interests of its own. All members of these subgovernments share an interest in maintaining the existing decision-making structure, which may explain why governmental bureaucracies rarely die.

Both pluralist and democratic explanations of growth patterns focus on public support for government activities. Democratic explanations portray a government responding to general public support for particular programs, while pluralist explanations describe subgovernments in which the line between government and the private sector is often difficult to see. Some critics of pluralism have suggested that it depicts governmental bureaucracy as essentially a cash register that adds up the resources of competing private interests and announces policies based on those totals.[26] An important question raised by pluralist explanations is whether the representation of interests in subgovernments is sufficiently broad and equitable to meet pluralist standards. Is subgovernment representation biased to favor certain groups? Do distinct bureaucratic interests make the neutral cash register analogy incorrect?

THE POWER ELITE VIEW Power elite explanations have sought answers to those two questions and in the process have taken many different forms. Some resemble pluralism in focusing on the bureaucracy's representation of private interests, but they differ in contending that only a *few* interests are represented in those subgovernments. Other power elite explanations regard governmental bureaucracy as much more than a neutral broker or mediator; they see it as a powerful institution with interests of its own.

C. Wright Mills identified a shift in political initiative and decision-making power from the legislative to the executive branch during the 1950s, which resulted in key political decisions being made "in the executive chambers, and in the agencies and authorities and commissions and departments that stretch out beneath them."[27] Thirty years later, Thomas Dye points out, the professional federal executives who supervise this vast system "comprise a powerful bureaucratic elite," particularly the secretaries, assistant secretaries, and under secretaries of the cabinet departments, the top officials of the armed services, the administrators of important agencies in the Executive Office of the President, and members of key regulatory commissions and boards.[28]

Most political observers today accept the existence of a bureaucratic elite and the governmental structure described by Mills and Dye. Without necessarily adopting a power elite view of American politics, a number of scholars attribute government growth to elite behavior, especially among political and economic elites. According to Ralph Hummel, economic elites pressed government to take on the task of regulating, monitoring, and stabilizing the economy.[29] Morris Fiorina has suggested that all members of Congress, even those most critical of the federal bureaucracy, contribute to its growth. "So long as the bureaucracy accommodates congressmen, the latter will oblige with ever larger budgets and grants of authority. Congress does not just react to big government—it creates it."[30] Presidents have also contributed to the growth of government through their attempts to gain political control of the civil service. Their appointment of politically dependable assistants in the upper-management levels of the bureaucracy has created a "top-heavy" structure.[31]

Bureaucratic elites themselves also contribute to government growth. They see many advantages in expansion: Growth makes it easier to recruit and retain capable workers, enhances the power and prestige of leaders, helps reduce internal organizational conflicts and morale problems, and may improve both the quality of an organization's performance and its chances of survival.[32] William Niskanen even likened the desire of a bureaucracy to maximize its budget

to a private firm's desire to maximize profits.[33] The presence of these incentives in every organization and the interdependence of government organizations helps to account for what Rourke has termed "the contagion effect of bureaucracy."[34]

This combination of external and internal pressures suggests that the growth of governmental bureaucracy is a political phenomenon and not some immutable law of nature. The size of government has expanded or contracted because those with political resources in American society wanted it to. Democratic and pluralistic explanations alert us to forces outside the government that contribute to that growth, while elite explanations remind us that people *in* government benefit from the expansion of government.

Checkpoint

- The pattern of government growth in the United States is one of long-term expansion interrupted by periodic declines.

- Democratic explanations for the patterns of government growth point to public support for specific government programs, coupled with an aversion to "big government" in general.

- Pluralists focus on the role of government agencies as brokers and mediators among competing interests in society and explain growth as a result of the development of civil service, the regulatory role of government, and the representation of specialized interests within government departments.

- Power elite explanations for the growth in government focus on the benefits that a governmental bureaucracy can provide for both private economic interests and the political elites of the executive and legislative branches of government.

POLITICAL CONTROL OF THE BUREAUCRACY: WHO GOVERNS?

Governing through bureaucracy has become a fixture of contemporary American politics. The most obvious alternative is governing by physical force. The bureaucracy provides a way for government to regulate private behavior in a predictable way and without a constant reliance on physical coercion. The general acceptance of bureaucracy as the instrument of governance, however, has not eliminated a concern discussed at the beginning of the chapter: How can those who govern control the machinery of government? Every president has wrestled with this issue. As we saw earlier, President Reagan's executive order attempted to bring more of the bureaucracy under the direct control of the Office of Management and Budget. But at no time has the issue of political control assumed more importance than during the Nixon administration.

In April 1972, after more than three years in office, President Nixon was disappointed in how little progress had been made in the implementation of his policy goals. He complained to a top White House aide:

> We have no discipline in this bureaucracy. We never fire anybody. We never reprimand anybody. We never demote anybody. We always promote the sons-of-bitches that kick us in the ass.[35]

President Nixon and his advisers concluded that it would be necessary to take over the bureaucracy politically during his second term by appointing Nixon loyalists to key positions in the executive departments and to weed out those with a constituency other than the President. "It works in the Vatican, it works in the Mafia, it ought to work right here," President Nixon remarked to aides as they discussed the plan.[36]

The problem of control is anticipated in *Federalist 51* where James Madison notes: "In framing a government which is to be administered by men over men, the great difficulty lies in this: you must first enable the government to control the governed; and in the next place oblige it to control itself."[37] In the twentieth century, bureaucracy is the chief instrument by which the government controls the governed. The question of how that government controls itself can therefore take the form of how the legislative, executive, and judicial branches of government control the administrative branch. As you would expect, there are democratic, pluralist, and power elite answers to this question of political control. Any proposal for controlling the bureaucracy, however, must be based on an understanding of how and why bureaucracies gain influence in the first place.

Sources of Bureaucratic Influence

INFORMATION Gathering and processing information are activities at the core of governing. From the initial policymaking stages of identifying a problem and alternative courses of action to the monitoring and evaluating of policies that have been implemented, the ability of individuals and institutions to influence policy greatly depends on the information they have. Before proposing changes in income tax laws, for example, political leaders in Congress and the executive branch need information on who gets what under the present system as well as predictions from economic experts about the likely effects of various proposals. The information that the president and Congress have about the impact of military operations has a direct and obvious effect on what they decide should be done next.

The connection between information and influence can be seen in the hierarchy of organizations. The flow of information in a hierarchy is to the top, which means that officials at the upper levels have more comprehensive information than those below them. The authority of superiors is partly based on this claim to superior information. Subordinates are expected to obey, not just because of organizational rules and norms, but because those above them are in a position to know more.

Claims to information also lie at the heart of many conflicts between institutions. Statutes requiring executive branch reports to Congress are intended to improve the legislators' information, and thus their influence, relative to bureaucratic officials. Most of the activity that comes under the heading of congressional oversight of the bureaucracy is, in fact, a legislative search for information. There are parallels to the congressional search for more and better information within the executive branch itself. The expansion of the Executive Office of the President has taken place primarily to provide the president and his advisers with more information.

POLICY SHAPING AND IMPLEMENTATION
Bureaucrats have influence early in the governing process when they help determine the realistic options available to policymakers. The way bureaucracy can shape policy options is illustrated by President Johnson's decision in 1965 to commit large numbers of American troops to the ground war in Vietnam in contrast to President Eisenhower's earlier decision, in 1954, against such a commitment. Because of President Kennedy's great expansion of our conventional war forces in the intervening years, President Johnson had a military organization that allowed him to commit ground troops; President Eisenhower did not have that option.[38] The general point is that those who govern are limited by the ability of bureaucracies to implement particular policy options.

The discretion that bureaucracies often have in implementing policies is another source of influence. Officials in any organization are said to have **discretion** when they are permitted to choose among different courses of action. In passing laws, Congress usually leaves the "details"—the definition of particular standards and the exact procedures for achieving certain policy goals—to those who administer those laws. This discretionary authority can give bureaucrats great influence over policies. Take the example of the Social Security Administration's implementation of the disability program. A key determinant of a person's eligibility for disability benefits is whether that person can still work, that is, have a "substantial gainful activity." But Congress did not define "substantial gainful activity" in amounts of dollars that a person is earning. It is up to officials in the Social Security

Administration to determine what level of gainful activity is enough to deny a person's claim for disability benefits. The importance of those decisions cannot be overstated. In fiscal 1982, for example, the Social Security Administration paid out over $21 billion to more than 4 million disabled workers and processed 1,250,000 claims for disability benefits.[39]

The sources of bureaucratic influence—information, policy shaping, and implementation—are so closely linked to the very nature of bureaucracies that political leaders who seek to control a bureaucracy can never eliminate them (see A Closer Look, on pp. 532–533). Any attempt to exert political control, therefore, is likely to take the form of generating independent sources of information and limiting the discretionary authority of administrators. As we will now see, the three views of how America is governed focus on different aspects of political control, establish different goals, and provide different methods for achieving them.

The Democratic View: Control Through Accountability

The accountability of public officials and their responsiveness to the general public lie at the heart of democracy. Elections are the primary instruments for linking the policy decisions of those who govern with the interests and demands of the public. But unelected officials in governmental bureaucracy are not directly accountable to the public in the same way. The question of democratic control of the bureaucracy thus becomes one of how to make the unelected bureaucrats accountable and responsive to elected officials who are their nominal "superiors." Robert Dahl points out that because "bureaucracies are almost never mere agents of legislatures and executives," the democratic control of bureaucracy is always a matter of degree rather than an absolute:

> Officials in bureaucracies are motivated by concerns for their own power, status, income, security, popularity, policies, and ideology. Consequently, their goals rarely coincide fully with the laws and policies determined by their superiors.

Because bureaucratic officials generally have access to enough resources for them to acquire considerable autonomy vis-à-vis their superiors, and strong incentives for doing so, they cannot usually be fully controlled by their superiors.[40]

Another reason democratic control of the bureaucracy is difficult to achieve is that the requirements of democracy and bureaucracy are so at odds. Table 16.2 summarizes the conflict.

Table 16.2
Democracy and Bureaucracy

Democracy Requires	Bureaucracy Requires
Equality	Hierarchy
Rotation in office	Seniority
Freedom	Command
Pluralism	Unity
Citizen participation	Participation of experts
Openness	Secrecy
Community	Impersonality
Legitimacy based on elections	Legitimacy based on expertise

Source: Samuel Krislov and David H. Rosenbloom, *Representative Bureaucracy and the American Political System* (New York: Praeger, 1981), p. 15.

There is a catch here, however. A distinction has to be made between the characteristics of the bureaucracy itself and of the broad political setting in which the bureaucracy operates. Attempts to make bureaucracies themselves more democratic would not necessarily produce greater democratic control. Such changes might in fact *reduce* democratic control by making bureaucracies less responsive to direction from elected officials. The characteristics of hierarchy, command, unity, and even secrecy actually enable bureaucracies to more rapidly and fully respond to the direction provided by elected officials.

Some of the differences between type A and type B bureaucracies shown in Table 16.1 help illustrate the point. At first glance, type B bureaucracies would seem to fit a democracy better than type A, for the type B characteristics of many constituencies, weak hierarchy, low professionalism, and open accessibility seem closer to the democratic characteristics of majority rule, rotation in office, citizen participation, and openness. The problem, however, is that the same characteristics that make a bureaucracy more democratic internally can reduce the accountability and responsiveness of the bureaucracy to elected public officials.

A debate on missiles within a type A bureaucracy (the Defense Department) in the Bush administration and a scandal in a type B bureaucracy (Housing and Urban Development, or HUD) in the Reagan administration illustrate how a type A bureaucracy may be more accountable than the seemingly more democratic type B bureaucracy.

The Defense Department debate was over the means for moving missiles around to prevent them from being a fixed target. The question was whether to fund rail carriers for 50 MX missiles or invest in smaller Midgetman missiles that can be transported on trucks. In March 1989, the Air Force Chief of Staff, General Larry Welch, told reporters that he had been speaking to influential members of Congress in support of the air force position, which favored rail carriers for the MX missiles. Defense Secretary Dick Cheney wasted no time in publicly rebuking General Welch, saying that he would not permit generals or any other Defense Department subordinates to "get out in front" on matters of policy.[41] Cheney's message was clear: The Defense Department was accountable to President Bush and responsible for carrying out the policies of the administration.

The Housing and Urban Development scandal, which became public knowledge in 1989, illustrates how accountability can be lost in a type B bureaucracy. The federal government lost an estimated $2 billion through mismanagement and fraud in housing programs during the tenure of HUD Secretary Samuel Pierce in the Reagan administration. A HUD program known as Sec-

Defense Secretary Dick Cheney sent a clear message that he would not permit generals to "get out in front" on matters of policy.

tion 8 Moderate Rehabilitation, which provided long-term rent subsidies to developers who fix up substandard housing for low-income families, was used to channel millions of dollars to consultants and developers with political connections.

Ironically, at the same time that Secretary Pierce's subordinates were lobbying Congress for funds for Section 8, the Reagan administration was trying to terminate the program. How was the HUD bureaucracy able to continue a program that the President wanted terminated and permit mismanagement and fraud to go undetected? In explanation, critics point to a number of characteristics of a type B bureaucracy: a weak hierarchy, decentralization, low professionalism, and many diverse constituencies. An independent investigator for the agency said

A Closer Look

Bureaucracies: Governing Machines and Human Beings★★★

The decisive reason for the advance of bureaucratic organization has always been its purely technical superiority over any other form of organization. The fully developed bureaucratic mechanism compares with other organizations exactly as does the machine with the non-mechanical modes of production.

Precision, speed, unambiguity, knowledge of the files, continuity, discretion, unity, strict subordination, reduction of friction and of materiel and personnel costs—these are raised to the optimum point in the strictly bureaucratic administration.[a]

In this quotation from "Bureaucracy," Max Weber was writing about the ideal bureaucracy, which he compared to a machine. But bureaucracy is not just a mechanism; it is made up of human beings, who often have differing ideas of how to do things. The real test of the bureaucratic "machine" comes in a time of crisis, when government must act quickly. The Cuban missile crisis of 1962, which took place over a period of two weeks, provided such a test for the bureaucracy of the United States Navy.

In October 1962, the United States confirmed that the Soviet Union was installing missiles in Cuba capable of reaching the American mainland. President Kennedy met this challenge with a decision to blockade Cuba and turn back Soviet ships. But as Graham Allison points out, Kennedy expressed concern that the navy might blunder into an incident.

Sensing the President's fears, Secretary of Defense Robert McNamara decided to explore the organization's procedures and routines for making the first interception. Calling on the Chief of Naval Operations (Admiral George Anderson), McNamara put his questions harshly. Precisely what would the Navy do when the first interception occurred? Anderson replied that he had outlined the procedures in the National Security Council meeting and that there was no need to discuss it further. Angered, but still calm, McNamara began to lecture the admiral. According to Elie Abel's reconstruction of that lecture, McNamara firmly explained that:

"The object of the operation was not to shoot Russians but to communicate a political message from President Kennedy to Chairman Khrushchev. The President wanted to avoid pushing Khrushchev to extremes. The blockade must be so conducted as to avoid humiliating the Russians; other-

A Soviet ship approaches the U.S. naval blockade of Cuba in 1962. A frustrated Defense Secretary told the admiral in charge: "I don't give a damn what John Paul Jones would have done. I want to know what you are going to do now."

wise Khrushchev might react in a nuclear spasm.

"By the conventional rules, blockade was an act of war and the first Soviet ship that refused to submit to boarding and search risked being sent to the bottom. But this was a military action with a political objective. Khrushchev must somehow be persuaded to pull back, rather than be goaded into retaliation."

Sensing that Anderson was not moved by this logic, McNamara returned to the line of detailed questioning. Who would make the first interception? Were Russian-speaking officers on board? How would submarines be dealt with? At one point McNamara asked Anderson what he would do if a Soviet ship's captain refused to answer questions about his cargo. At that point the

Navy man picked up the Manual of Naval Regulations and, waving it in McNamara's face, shouted, "It's all in there." To which McNamara replied, "I don't give a damn what John Paul Jones would have done. I want to know what you are going to do now." The encounter ended on Anderson's remark: "Now, Mr. Secretary, if you and your Deputy will go back to your offices, the Navy will run the blockade."[b]

[a]Max Weber, "Bureaucracy," in *From Max Weber: Essays in Sociology*, ed. H. H. Gerth and C. Wright Mills (New York: Oxford University Press, 1958, p. 214).
[b]Graham T. Allison, *Essence of Decision: Explaining the Cuban Missile Crisis* (Boston: Little, Brown, 1971), pp. 131–132.

there "appeared to have been little accountability or oversight by headquarters and regional offices," and former Secretary Pierce conceded: "Perhaps we should have watched the program better than we did."[42]

Members of Congress seek to make the governmental bureaucracy accountable to them through congressional oversight activities such as frequent hearings, specific guidelines and directives in legislation, and control over budgets. But the greatest efforts in this direction are found in the executive branch. In order to govern, presidents need more than a Congress that passes their programs. They also need a bureaucracy that will implement those programs in the way they intended.

The upper levels of the federal bureaucracy consist of approximately 700 political executives appointed by the president and 7000 career officials from the civil service, a cadre of permanent government employees. Presidents seek to fill the ranks of the first group with individuals who share their policy goals and who will exert influence over civil servants in that direction. In the Reagan administration, for example, one of the tasks of the deputy under secretary of education was enforcing political discipline. He would review speeches and testimony of senior civil servants and require them to include strong support for the President's proposals in the area of education. "When the message they get from political appointees is clear," said this official, "the real professionals in the department will do their job. But the signals have to be absolutely clear."[43]

In the Bush administration, the Office of Management and Budget serves as an instrument for controlling the bureaucracy and making sure that administration policies are followed. This practice was revealed in dramatic fashion in May 1989, when Dr. James Hansen, director of NASA's Goddard Institute told a congressional panel that OMB had ordered him to change his testimony that gases produced by human activities are primarily responsible for the "greenhouse effect," or global warming, to a statement that such a conclusion "remains scientifically unknown."[44]

The Bush administration also sought to extend its control over the Treasury Department

and others in the executive branch by developing what a former top White House aide described as "the greatest concentration of economic policy coordination within the White House we've seen."[45] President Bush relied heavily on the Council of Economic Advisors and his assistants in the White House Office in formulating policy on an airlines strike, savings and loan rescue, and foreign debt in 1989.

The slow manner in which the Bush administration went about filling assistant secretary and deputy assistant secretary positions in the executive departments also extended the President's control of the bureaucracy. Responsibility for much of the policy development normally associated with these vacant positions gravitated to White House aides and a policy structure in which "President Bush will make the final policy decisions . . . on any major issues."[46]

Accountability is the theme that runs through these approaches to political control. As chief executive, the president is the focus of most attempts to increase accountability through centralization. The remarks of members of Congress in the debate over the 1985 executive order cited at the beginning of this chapter suggest that democracy requires bureaucratic accountability to Congress as well. Democracy and control of bureaucratic structure are often linked in another way. Efforts to "democratize" governmental bureaucracy through representation often grow out of a pluralist view of American politics.

The Pluralist View: Control Through Representative Bureaucracy

A quite different approach to the problem of political control is to create what is called **representative bureaucracy**. Its basic premise is a "belief that a bureaucracy that mirrors a society in its social, economic, and cultural composition will be much more sensitive to the needs of citizens of that society, and much less likely to be arbitrary or abusive when it is exercising power over its own kind of people."[47] A representative bureaucracy reflects several of the characteristics associated with type B bureaucracies in

Table 16.1, particularly the open and accessible structure and the trade-off of professionalism for representativeness. The concept of representative bureaucracy is one that seeks to reflect in the bureaucracy the pluralism of the broader political system.

This approach to political control is closely tied to the democratic requirement that government be responsive to majority opinion, but it differs from the democratic approach in reducing the need for external controls and centralization. Attempts to make the bureaucracy more representative, in fact, are likely to lead in the opposite direction, toward decentralization. Accessibility, rotation in office, high levels of citizen participation, and open decision making are all characteristics of a representative bureaucracy.

To determine how representative a bureaucracy is, we can look at the people who make up the organization, the private groups that have access to and influence over it, and the opportunities for citizen participation in the organization's decision-making process.[48]

PERSONNEL The idea that those who administer laws and governmental policies should be representative of the population at large has long been accepted in the United States. It is a theme that extends from the practice of awarding government positions to a wide range of political supporters and rotation in office, which characterized the "spoils system" introduced by President Andrew Jackson in 1829 (the term coming from the expression "To the victor belong the spoils"), to the 1970 declaration of the Civil Service Commission that "organizations of the Federal Government should in their employment mix, broadly reflect, racially and otherwise, the varied characteristics of our population."[49] Recruitment and executive development programs have, over the years, been designed with that goal in mind. Another value guiding those programs, however, is that of *merit*—of obtaining the most competent and best qualified persons for government positions. Because merit is often measured by education and skills that are not evenly distributed throughout the population, a merit-based bureaucracy is not always a representative one.

How representative is the bureaucracy of the U.S. government? Hugh Heclo's study of executive politics in Washington led him to this conclusion:

> Taken as a whole the U.S. federal bureaucracy appears open and broadly representative of the American population in education, income, and social status (as indicated by father's occupation). But the higher their civil service rank, the more U.S. officials approach the statistical elite qualities observed among political executives.

And those political executives, says Heclo, are "disproportionately white, male, urban, affluent, middle-aged, well educated at prestige schools, and pursuers of high-status white-collar careers. They are unlikely to be female, nonwhite, wage-earning, from a small town, or possessors of average educational and social credentials."[50] The upper reaches of the bureaucracy, the levels of policymaking and governing, then, are not as representative as are the lower levels of governmental bureaucracy.

The real value of a representative bureaucracy, especially to pluralists, lies in its bringing a wide range of experiences and viewpoints into government. But since employees of an organization are likely to develop shared or similar values, some people attempt to overcome that problem by making the structure of bureaucracy itself representative.

STRUCTURE Theodore Lowi has characterized the "clientele departments" of the federal government—particularly Agriculture, Commerce, and Labor—as "government sponsorship of pluralism," and agencies "set up not to govern, but to be governed."[51] The entire structure of these departments is based on the representation of economic interests. But most organized interests do not have a whole department to themselves. In these cases, it is the subgovernment structure, the iron triangle described earlier, that makes governmental bureaucracy representative. Organized interests are represented not only by private groups in these subgovernments but also by government policymakers from the executive and legislature. Bureaucrats develop the support of private groups in order to assure their own survival or to increase their influence within government. Bureaucrats in the Department of Education will cultivate support from teacher groups; those in Health and Human Services, the support of doctors; those in Housing and Urban Development, the support of community leaders; and so on.

The combined political resources of interest group, executive, and congressional representatives in these subgovernments has made them effective in dominating government policymaking in certain areas, usually those of narrow economic concern such as a particular agricultural crop (tobacco, sugar) or water projects (dams, harbors). The closed nature of these subgovernments and their favoring of special interests has drawn some criticism. But political scientists have found that the iron triangle lost much of its dominance in the 1980s due to a combination of factors: a proliferation in the number of public interest groups, a shift in congressional decision making from committees to the House and Senate floor, and the president's efforts to gain political control of the bureaucracy.[52]

CITIZEN PARTICIPATION One way of overcoming the representational biases of organized interest groups is to establish points of access in the administrative process, enabling members of the general public to be heard. In the 1960s, such accessibility was built into major social legislation, including programs providing for antipoverty community action, health services, and model cities. Most environmental laws of the 1970s included similar provisions for citizen participation. These statutes required the creation of citizen committees, which would sometimes act as advisers to those administering the program and at other times be responsible themselves for implementing policies in certain areas.

The most common form of citizen participation is the advisory body. The proliferation of citizen requirements had produced more than 900 advisory bodies throughout the federal bureaucracy by the mid-1980s.[53] This approach does permit administrators to hear the views of individuals and groups who lack the political resources to gain access at other stages of the policy process. But how much these programs actually broaden the scope of representation is open to question.

The generally low turnout of voters to elect neighborhood representatives in community action programs, for example, often limited the actual representation on those boards to already existing local political groups or to those initiated by local program administrators. Decisions about who would be represented and how were often left up to those running the federal programs. As a result, some critics have suggested that citizen participation works primarily to strengthen the influence of bureaucrats: It co-opts those with local political power into supporting the program, and it gives administrators a claim to being representative, which is useful in dealing with Congress.[54]

A representative bureaucracy requires decentralization in order to achieve the widest possible participation of a variety of government employees, interest groups, and the general public. But the more decentralized an institution is, the longer it takes to make decisions and implement policies. A third approach to the question of control of the bureaucracy is associated with the elite view of American politics and emphasizes the notion of neutral efficiency.

The Elite View: The Need for Neutral Efficiency

According to elite theorist C. Wright Mills, "the civilian government of the United States never has had and does not now have a genuine bureaucracy." One characteristic of a genuine bureaucracy, according to Mills, is political neutrality. The development of technical expertise and stability that is found in a true bureaucracy, that helps to make it a "most efficient form of human organization," can only be achieved when bureaucracy is separated from partisan politics. But in the United States, said Mills:

> There is no civil-service career that is secure enough, there is no administrative corps that is permanent enough, to survive a change-over of political administration. . . .
>
> Neither professional party politicians nor professional bureaucrats are now at the executive centers of decision. Those centers are

now occupied by the political directorate of the power elite.[55]

Mills's view raises the question of how to *create* a genuine bureaucracy more than how to extend control over such a bureaucracy. And since the most widely recognized values of a genuine bureaucracy are political neutrality and efficiency, those standards are the focus of elite perspectives on the bureaucracy. Mills sees an efficient bureaucracy as a way of checking the power elite. However, the value of efficiency is also regularly invoked by both the political and corporate leaders identified by Mills as members of the power elite. How can the same standard be put forward by both influential elites and those who seek to reduce the power of those elites?

The term efficiency seems at first to be a neutral one. In common usage, **efficiency** is the ability to produce a desired effect with the minimum amount of effort, cost, or waste. As a standard, it differs from accountability, which suggests a policy direction, and from representation, which points toward a decentralized structure. The efficiency of an organization can be measured by its ability to produce any desired effect, whether we agree with that goal or not.

The Grace Commission report discussed earlier evaluated governmental bureaucracy by the standard of efficiency. That report made clear that the efficiency of the public bureaucracy could best be determined by comparing it with performance in the private sector and by evaluating it in business terms. Giving this meaning to efficiency makes it less of a neutral standard. To achieve the largest savings recommended by the Grace Commission, Congress would have to change the requirements that determine who is eligible for such programs as Medicare, food stamps, and student loans. Clearly, these recommendations involve changing the goals of those programs rather than simply finding more efficient ways of achieving those goals.

Is the business model an appropriate way of judging the efficiency of governmental bureaucracy? Critics of the Grace Commission report think not. They point out that governmental organizations are expected to pursue other values

just as important as efficiency: accountability, responsiveness, and representational equality. Some characteristics associated with bureaucratic inefficiency, such as duplication of effort, high demands for paperwork, and a large middle-management staff, actually help bureaucracies achieve the values of accountability and representation. Business organizations do not have the same pressures for achieving those two values; they are free to concentrate more on the goal of efficiency.[56]

A second point raised by critics of the Grace Commission is that the business model itself may be undesirable. The Grace Commission reported that the federal government wasted $141 billion annually, but the research of two public interest advocates led them to conclude that private corporations waste $862 billion annually. They attributed "avoidable waste" in the private sector to such factors as price-fixing, environmental damage, and excess bureaucracy.[57] The question of exactly how much waste actually occurs in the public and private sectors is not the central point here. Rather, the question is whether the private sector does in fact provide a model of efficiency that public bureaucracies can and should follow.

Calling for a more efficient governmental bureaucracy might not seem to be an attempt to control the bureaucracy in the same way as are attempts to increase accountability or make the bureaucracy more representative. Efficiency in government is a value shared by the general public and political leaders regardless of ideology. But a call for efficiency is often associated with the general goal of *reducing* the size of government. The pursuit of efficiency alone may not be an attempt to exert political control over the bureaucracy, but invoking the value of efficiency as a way of reducing the size of bureaucracy clearly is such an attempt.

A chief concern of power elite theorists is that the machinery of government can take over government policymaking in much the same way that computers take over society in science fiction stories.[58] That is why bureaucratic neutrality is important and why the search continues for a neutral standard to replace the goal of efficiency that is based on business models.

Checkpoint

- Since the key political resource of bureaucracy is information, both legislative and executive attempts to gain political control of the bureaucracy take the form of gaining control over information.

- Another source of bureaucratic influence is policy shaping and implementation, a process which both the legislative and executive branches also attempt to control by reining in bureaucratic discretionary authority.

- Making the bureaucracy responsive to elected officials who are in turn accountable to the public is the primary method of democratic control of the bureaucracy.

- Pluralists seek a representative bureaucracy as the key to political control. They believe that a bureaucracy whose personnel, structure, and avenues of citizen participation make it representative of the larger society will require little overt political control. In contrast to the centralization necessary for accountability in the democratic model, the representative bureaucracy of pluralists is a decentralized structure.

- Both critics of the power elite and the political and corporate leaders who make up that elite focus on efficiency as the standard for determining political control of the bureaucracy, but they give quite different meanings to the term *efficiency*.

SUMMARY

A bureaucracy is a formal organization in which specialists organized in a hierarchy carry out policies by using standardized procedures. Bureaucracies are used in all modern societies, operating in the large and complex world of government. They serve many different functions and tend to dominate policy implementation. Once formed they rarely die, and new ones are constantly being born. Bureaucracies tend not to be neutral or fully controlled by external officials.

Bureaucracy differs from Congress in the appointment rather than election of members, hierarchy, technical decision making, and low visibility of that decision making. Government agencies also differ from one another along various dimensions. The way the agencies differ produces two general types of bureaucracy: type A (established, closed, hierarchical, centralized, highly professional) and type B (open, decentralized, less hierarchical and professional, subject to competing claims).

Government growth in the United States has been one of long-term expansion with periodic declines. Democratic explanations for this pattern of growth focus on public support for specific programs coupled with an aversion to big government in general. Pluralists point to the increase of competing interests in the political arena and their representation in executive governments. Power elite theorists hold that both private economic interests and elites in the executive and legislative branches of government seek benefits from bureaucracy and see advantages in maintaining and expanding it.

Sources of bureaucratic influence include the use of information and policy shaping and implementation. From the democratic point of view, control over the bureaucracy needs to be obtained by making it responsive to elected officials who are accountable to the voters. Pluralists seek a representative bureaucracy as the key to political control. Elite theorists focus on neutral efficiency as a means of control. Members of the power elite also seek efficiency but not necessarily through neutral standards.

KEY TERMS

Bureaucracy
Subgovernments
Iron triangles
Discretion

Representative
    bureaucracy
Efficiency

FOR FURTHER READING

Anthony Downs, *Inside Bureaucracy* (Boston: Little, Brown, 1967). Develops a theory of bureaucratic decision making based on the premise that officials are significantly motivated by self-interests.

Samuel Krislov and David H. Rosenbloom, *Representative Bureaucracy and the American Political System* (New York: Praeger, 1981). Presents the case for enhancing the political representativeness of governmental bureaucracy.

Frederick C. Mosher, *Democracy and the Public Service* (New York: Oxford University Press, 1982). A look at the often competing demands of democracy and effective government administration.

Richard P. Nathan, *The Administrative Presidency* (New York: Wiley, 1983). An examination of presidential efforts to gain political control of the federal bureaucracy in the Nixon and Reagan administrations.

Francis E. Rourke, *Bureaucracy, Politics and Public Policy*, 3rd ed. (Boston: Little, Brown, 1984). An examination of the effects of two antibureaucratic trends in recent American history: presidential efforts to gain political control of the executive branch and the movement toward deregulation and a reduction in government services.

Harold Seidman and Robert Gilmour, *Politics, Position, and Power*, 4th ed. (New York: Oxford University Press, 1986). An analysis of the effects of changes in the role of government, from the direct provider of services to indirect regulator.

Max Weber, "Bureaucracy," in H. H. Gerth and C. Wright Mills, *From Max Weber: Essays in Sociology* (New York: Oxford University Press, 1958). A translation of Weber's classic essay of 1920, which examines the bases of political power of bureaucrats and bureaucratic organizations.

Douglas Yates, *Bureaucratic Democracy* (Cambridge, Mass.: Harvard University Press, 1982). A study of the ways in which the competing goals of efficiency and democracy shape the politics of bureaucracy and how to make the existing system more democratic.

The Judiciary

Affirmative action, abortion, drug testing, school busing, street crime, pornography—all of the hottest topics in politics today seem to wind up on the doorstep of the federal and state courts that make up the judiciary. The Supreme Court's power to strike down laws and executive actions that the Court deems unconstitutional has also pulled the judiciary into the center of major political controversies about governing America. Key actors in the judiciary—police, attorneys, judges, juries—participate in governing by exercising discretionary authority. ∎

For 11 years, from 1974 to 1985, the administration of the school system of Boston, Massachusetts, was in the hands of a federal judge. The voters of Boston continued to elect a School Committee during those years, but it was U.S. District Judge Arthur Garrity, Jr., not the School Committee, who was responsible for "establishing school hours, hiring and firing personnel, ordering roofs repaired and hallways painted." In his book about busing in Boston, J. Anthony Lukas illustrates the degree to which the judge was involved in the details of running the schools: "One day he instructed South Boston High to purchase twelve MacGregor basketballs and six Acme Tornado whistles. Nor did he neglect to instruct a school that was being converted from elementary to middle grades to raise the height of its urinals."[1]

Judge Garrity's involvement in running the Boston schools began with a 150-page opinion issued in June 1974, in which he found that the School Committee had carried out a systematic program of segregation and that the entire school system of Boston was unconstitutionally segregated. When a closely divided (3 to 2) School Committee refused to submit a desegregation plan six months later, Judge Garrity took steps toward developing a plan of his own. Eventually, he ordered the busing of 25,000 students in the Boston school system, a decision that unleashed a storm of protest. When Judge Garrity refused at one point to answer a phone call from Boston's mayor, the mayor reacted angrily: "He issues his damn order, then retires to his sub-

urban estate and refuses to talk with the only guy who can make it work."[2] The judge received thousands of letters, some of them calling him a "Nazi," a "nigger lover," and a "child murderer." A carefully lettered sign appeared on the Boston Common one morning with this message:[3]

> THE CITY IS OCCUPIED
> A BOYCOTT EXISTS
> A TYRANT REIGNS
> LAW IS BY DECREE

A high school senior's paper for a history class written in the bicentennial year, 1976, drew parallels with the American Revolution two centuries earlier: "The dictatorship our ancestors fought to defeat has been reestablished here. We are living in a new tyranny. Garrity is the same as King George. He is appointed for life. Nobody can say nothing to him. His decisions are like laws. They are as unjust as taxation without representation."[4]

Any student in the Boston schools in the late 1970s, if asked who governed, would likely respond that Judge Arthur Garrity did. It was the judge who was making decisions that would profoundly affect students, parents, and many other residents of Greater Boston for years to come. The U.S. district court was more than a place for settling disputes and correcting past wrongs. It was a place for making social policy. And Judge Garrity was doing more than sitting in judgment. He was governing.

U.S. District Judge Arthur Garrity, Jr. "One day he instructed South Boston High to purchase twelve MacGregor basketballs and six Acme Tornado whistles."

Judge Garrity was not the only judge who has taken on the governing role. Judge Russell G. Clark stirred controversy in the Kansas City School District by raising property taxes in the district after voters repeatedly refused to approve taxes to pay for school improvements that he had ordered. Cries of "No Taxation Without Representation" took Judge Clark's decision all the way to the Supreme Court in 1989.

The judiciary, like the bureaucracy, is different from the political branches of government— the executive and the legislature. Senator Russell Long's statement cited in Chapter 14 illustrates that difference: Judges are expected to decide cases by applying rules, without regard to whom they are helping or hurting, but lawmakers are expected to deliberately help some people and hurt others when they make decisions. Congress and the president make policy, but the

courts are expected to settle disputes by applying the rules laid down in government policies. The Boston and Kansas City experiences demonstrate, however, that while American courts do enforce the laws, they are also more than a neutral branch of government making sure that executive or legislative policy directives are carried out. The judiciary regularly engages in policymaking.

THE ROLE OF COURTS IN AMERICAN POLITICS

The judiciary's dual role of enforcing policies developed by the legislature and executive and of making policy itself is implicit in the structure of American government. It goes back to a principle of constitutional government discussed earlier in this book, a principle best expressed in James Madison's observation that in framing a government, "the great difficulty lies in this: you must first enable the government to control the governed; and in the next place oblige it to control itself."[5] The provision in Article VI of the Constitution that the Constitution, federal laws, and treaties shall be "the supreme Law of the Land" and "the judges in every state shall be bound thereby" makes it clear that the judiciary is a chief instrument for controlling the governed, for making sure that the rules established in government policies are obeyed.

Policymaking

The way in which the Constitution provides for the second activity noted by Madison, government controlling itself, opens the way for policymaking by the judicial branch. The Constitution established separation of powers and checks and balances as the chief means for controlling the government. Such a structure leads to recurring questions about who should govern: Congress or the president? The national government or the states? The judiciary is responsible for resolving this debate over which institutions should govern in which areas, a task that directly leads to the courts' role in policymaking. As we will see in this chapter, the power of judicial review, the authority to declare executive or legislative policies and actions at the national or state level null and void because they violate the Constitution, is the most visible form of judicial policymaking.

Supreme Court decisions reflect the scope and importance of judicial policymaking. For example, in a landmark federalism case that we discussed in Chapter 5, the Supreme Court recognized Congress's power to regulate state and local employees' wage and hours standards, a decision that would have had the direct policy effect of forcing state and local governments to pay millions of dollars in overtime pay for employees if Congress had not responded to the decision by changing the law.

Other areas where the impact of Supreme Court policymaking has been most evident in recent years include school busing to achieve racial integration, the regulation of abortion, public policies regarding prayers in schools, the right to an attorney in criminal trials, capital punishment, restrictions on travel to certain countries, affirmative action programs in employment practices and college admissions, standards in press coverage of public officials, the eligibility of illegal aliens for education and welfare benefits, regulations governing interstate banking, draft resistance and selective service laws, and limits on a president's authority to withhold information. In all these areas, the Supreme Court has either determined what public policy would be or established guidelines for the making of policy.

Judicial policymaking by the Supreme Court is highly visible and easy to identify. But what about the courts below that level? Is it accurate to say that trial courts at the state and local level are policymakers, that they too govern? A clear difference between Supreme Court decisions and those of trial courts is that Supreme Court decisions regulate the behavior of everyone in a particular policy area, while trial court decisions more commonly affect only those directly involved as parties in a case. These lower courts are like the bureaucracy in that they apply policies made elsewhere to cases before them. As we saw in Chapter 16, however, the implementation of general policies and enforcement of rules often gives members of a bureaucracy great discretion in interpreting those policies and rules. In a similar way, the judges, lawyers, police, and other actors in the court system can be considered policymakers to the extent that they also exercise discretion in making decisions. A pattern of lower court decisions that benefits some groups in society and hurts others has much the same effect as a policy decision along the same lines made by the executive, the legislature, or the Supreme Court.

Judicial Activism Versus Judicial Restraint

The proper role of the Supreme Court in the political system has been the subject of intense debate throughout American history. On one side of that debate are those who favor **judicial activism**, whereby judges actively promote certain social goals by overturning legislative and executive policies they consider contrary to those goals. On the other side are those who favor **judicial restraint,** which calls for judges to defer to the popularly elected branches of government and to keep their personal political beliefs out of their decisions. A related debate focuses on the authority used for Court decisions. The "strict constructionist" or "interpretivist" position in the authority debate would limit the Supreme Court to interpreting the actual words of the Constitution in its decisions. The opposing "loose constructionist," or "noninterpretivist," side of the argument supports the Court's going beyond interpreting the Constitution and basing its decisions on broad values such as equality or liberty.

Sometimes we find that political conservatives support judicial restraint and liberals judicial activism, as in the case of many of the Warren Court decisions on civil rights, reapportionment, and rights of the accused in the 1960s and 1970s. At other times, conservatives have supported judicial activism and liberals judicial restraint. This happened with cases involving government regulation of business early in this century and in a number of recent cases involving affirmative action programs.

The debate on activism versus restraint frequently makes its way into presidential politics. The Republican and Democratic party platforms of 1988, for example, both endorsed judicial restraint. Republicans promised to continue what they described as the Reagan-Bush administration's record "for naming to the federal courts distinguished men and women committed to judicial restraint."[6] Democrats criticized the Republican administration's record on judicial appointments and claimed that judges had been chosen "more for their unenlightened ideological views than for their respect for the rule of law."[7]

The positions of the two parties reflect the broad appeal of judicial restraint as a value in a democracy, for judicial restraint means that an unelected judiciary seldom overrules policies decided by a president and Congress elected by the people. But judicial restraint means different things to different people. Democrats wanted to appoint Supreme Court justices who would show restraint in overturning civil rights and civil liberties judicial precedents established in the 1960s and recent civil rights laws passed by Congress. Republicans wanted justices who would narrow or reverse many of those earlier decisions, because they were a reflection of what George Bush termed "legislating from the bench."[8]

The activism/restraint debate is related, in part, to the judiciary's dependence on the other branches of government for the implementation of its policy decisions. One reason why so many people favor judicial restraint is that it avoids the enforcement problem. Congressional, presidential, and state actions encounter relatively little court interference. Judicial activism, on the other hand, requires an acceptance of a Supreme Court decision by the branch or level of government responsible for implementing it, which generally means there has to be a compelling justification for the activism.

This discussion of judicial activism suggests how judicial policymaking depends on the relationship between the courts and other government institutions. We turn now to that topic, beginning with a description of the dual court system.

Checkpoint

- Courts below the Supreme Court are concerned primarily with controlling the governed. The power of judicial review exercised by the Supreme Court makes it the chief instrument for the government's controlling itself.

- The Supreme Court actively engages in determining broad policies over a wide range of issues. Decisions in the trial courts of state and local government mainly implement policies and enforce rules.

- Debate over the proper role of the judiciary in American politics focuses on judicial activism (an interventionist role) versus judicial restraint (deferring to legislative and executive policymaking). A related debate is how strictly the Constitution should be interpreted by the Supreme Court.

THE DUAL COURT SYSTEM

The Constitution says the judicial power of the United States shall be "vested in one Supreme Court, and in such inferior Courts as the Congress may from time to time ordain and establish." The first Congress organized the structure of the national judiciary in 1789 by establishing 3 courts of appeals (for the southern, eastern, and middle circuits) and 13 district courts (one in each state). By making this judiciary separate from the existing state courts, Congress created a **dual court system** in the United States. Thus, there are two separate court structures—that of the federal government and those of the states. Because state court structures are not all the same the judiciary could be described, in fact, as 51 separate structures. We present here a gen-

U.S. Courts of Appeals have the power to review decisions made by independent regulatory agencies such as the Nuclear Regulatory Commission's decision to approve the opening of the Seabrook nuclear power plant in New Hampshire.

eral description of state court structure, one that corresponds to the judicial hierarchy found in most state systems.

The dual nature of the court system means that state courts are not subordinate to the federal courts, as they would be in a unified court system. But they are subject to review by the Supreme Court when their decisions concern a federal issue. Article VI of the Constitution made that document, federal laws, and treaties the supreme law of the land and enforceable through the state courts. The Judiciary Act of 1789 also made state court decisions involving a federal statute, treaty, or the Constitution subject to review by the Supreme Court. The supremacy of federal courts on national issues and the binding of state courts to those federal decisions are vital characteristics of our constitutional system. On the other hand, in all cases that involve the laws of a particular state, where there is no federal issue, it is the state courts that make the decision and have the final say. In nonfederal cases, state courts are independent of the federal judiciary. Cases that involve citizens of two states are the one exception; federal courts have what is known as *diversity jurisdiction* in such cases.

Figure 17.1 (p. 546) illustrates the important features of the court system in the United States. A hierarchy of trial courts, courts of appeal, and a supreme court is evident in both the state and federal structures. Each system also has specialized courts with limited jurisdiction: the Tax Court, Court of Military Appeals, Claims Court, and Court of International Trade on the federal level, and a range of state courts, including probate, traffic, juvenile, housing, municipal, police, and family courts. The two structures are joined only where appeals from a state supreme court are subject to review by the Supreme Court. This method of appealing from the highest state court to the highest federal court directly rather than through the federal court hierarchy again illustrates the separate nature of the dual court system. In the dual court system, then, state and federal court structures are best described as parallel structures rather than as a superior federal court system overseeing subordinate state systems.

Jurisdiction and Caseload of the Two Systems

Federal courts hear cases that involve alleged violations of U.S. laws such as civil rights stat-

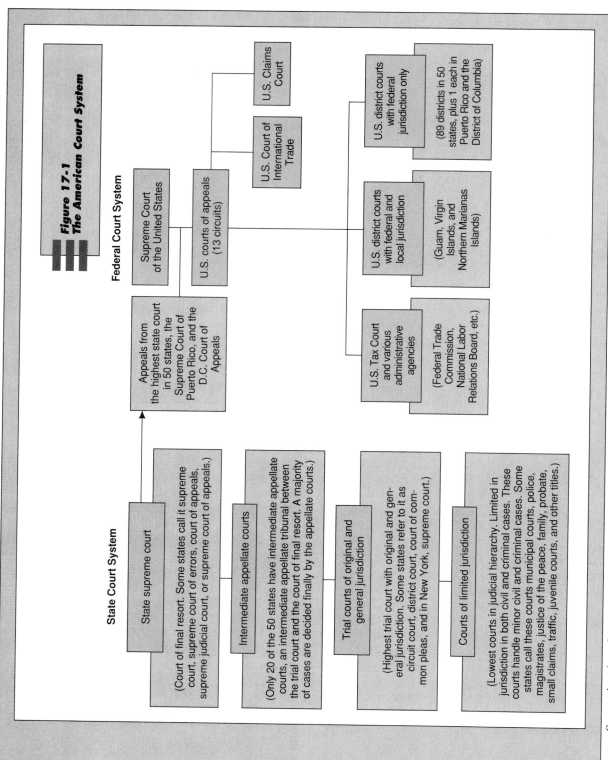

Figure 17-1
The American Court System

Federal Court System

Supreme Court of the United States

Appeals from the highest state court in 50 states, the Supreme Court of Puerto Rico, and the D.C. Court of Appeals

U.S. courts of appeals (13 circuits)

U.S. Court of International Trade

U.S. Claims Court

U.S. district courts with federal and local jurisdiction

(Guam, Virgin Islands, and Northern Marianas Islands)

U.S. district courts with federal jurisdiction only

(89 districts in 50 states, plus 1 each in Puerto Rico and the District of Columbia)

U.S. Tax Court and various administrative agencies

(Federal Trade Commission, National Labor Relations Board, etc.)

State Court System

State supreme court

(Court of final resort. Some states call it supreme court, supreme court of errors, court of appeals, supreme judicial court, or supreme court of appeals.)

Intermediate appellate courts

(Only 20 of the 50 states have intermediate appellate courts, an intermediate appellate tribunal between the trial court and the court of final resort. A majority of cases are decided finally by the appellate courts.)

Trial courts of original and general jurisdiction

(Highest trial court with original and general jurisdiction. Some states refer to it as circuit court, district court, court of common pleas, and in New York, supreme court.)

Courts of limited jurisdiction

(Lowest courts in judicial hierarchy. Limited in jurisdiction in both civil and criminal cases. These courts handle minor civil and criminal cases. Some states call these courts municipal courts, police, magistrates, justice of the peace, family, probate, small claims, traffic, juvenile courts, and other titles.)

Source: Current American Government (Washington, D.C.: Congressional Quarterly Press, 1989), p. 73; Harold W. Stanley and Richard G. Niemi, *Vital Statistics on American Politics*, 2nd ed. (Washington, D.C.: Congressional Quarterly Press, 1990), p. 263.

Table 17.1

Civil and Criminal Procedures

Civil Cases	Criminal Cases
1. Plaintiff sues	1. Government officials apprehend
2. Summons	2. Preliminary examination
3. Pleadings	3. Indictment by grand jury or prosecutor
4. Trial	4. Arraignment and pleading
5. Verdict	5. Trial
6. Judgment and sentencing	6. Verdict
7. Appeal	7. Judgment and sentencing
8. Enforcement	8. Appeal
	9. Execution of sentence

Source: Henry J. Abraham, *The Judiciary*, 7th ed. (Dubuque, Iowa: Wm C. Brown, 1988), p. 4.

utes, tax laws, and business and trade regulations. Trials are conducted at the district court level; appeals courts review a limited number of cases appealed from the district courts and also have the power to review decisions made by independent regulatory agencies such as the Nuclear Regulatory Commission and the Federal Trade Commission. The United States Supreme Court is the court of last resort in the federal hierarchy. As we have noted, state courts have jurisdiction over all cases that involve alleged violations of state laws. Federal court review of state court cases is a limited power that applies only to certain types of cases.

Both federal and state courts deal with **civil cases** (in which one party sues another to recover damages or to change another's behavior) and **criminal cases** (in which the government charges someone with violating a law). As Table 17.1 indicates, a person's entry into the court system and the procedural steps that follow differ for civil and criminal cases. Both procedures, however, provide for an appeal in both the state and federal judiciary. The parties to a case have a right to appeal a decision made at the trial court level, but after that, responsibility for continuing

a case shifts to the court system. The U.S. Supreme Court or a state court of appeals or supreme court can decide whether to review a case at that level. These appeals are a reconsideration of the law involved in a case, not a rehearing of the facts. They are not second trials.

This control over the agenda that most supreme courts have (known as discretionary jurisdiction) and the focus only on legal questions in appellate review result in a filtering out of cases as one moves up the hierarchy of the court structure. In the federal court system more than 250,000 cases at the trial court level dwindle to around 5,000 on the Supreme Court docket.[9]

The differences between the caseloads of state courts and the federal courts are striking. In contrast with the quarter of a million cases filed in the federal courts each year, 80 to 100 *million* cases are filed in the 50 state courts each year—about one case for every two or three people in the United States![10] If we want a picture of what happens to most people caught up in the judicial system, we look to the state court system. But questions about the role of the judiciary in governing America also require that attention be paid to the Supreme Court and the approximately 150 written opinions that annually result from the 5000 appeals to that highest court. The effects of those decisions go far beyond the immediate case and parties in the case.

Political Effects of the Dual Court System

The dual court system of the United States grew out of the federal structure of government embodied in the Constitution. Over the years, as the nation has become more of an economic and social union, the 51 legal and judicial systems that exist side by side have maintained a strong judicial federalism.

At the state level, the dual court system makes possible a "market" for laws:

> The states compete with each other for "customers," by passing competing laws. And one state can frustrate the policy of others by of-

The dual court system in the United States helps to make possible a "market" for laws in which states compete for "customers," such as these gamblers in Las Vegas, Nevada.

fering for sale (so to speak) a cheaper, better, or simply different brand of law.[11]

Nevada and Delaware are two states that have taken great advantage of this market for laws. In the 1920s, Nevada passed divorce laws making it faster and easier for couples to obtain a divorce in Nevada than in any other state. Nevada followed up with laws that legalized gambling, made it possible for couples to get married more easily and earlier than in most states, and authorized counties in the state to legalize prostitution. Customers flocked to Nevada, and gambling soon outpaced mining as the state's top industry. Delaware took similar advantage of the market in laws early in this century by passing lenient corporation laws. The low taxes and loose procedures of those laws led thousands of corporations to be chartered in Delaware, even though their actual places of business remain in other states.[12]

Judicial federalism and the dual court system mean that disputes arising under the laws of Nevada and Delaware will be settled in the respective court systems of those states, unless the case also involves a federal issue that brings the case under federal jurisdiction.

The dual court system also makes it possible for state courts to move in a different policy direction than the federal courts in some areas, thereby lessening the impact of federal court decisions. As conservative Supreme Court justices and federal court judges moved the national judiciary in a conservative direction in the 1980s, for example, one judicial scholar saw evidence of "a new judicial federalism" in the developing trend of many state courts to move in a more liberal direction on such issues as criminal justice, freedom of expression, privacy, and equal protection.[13] A Florida Supreme Court ruling on abortion in October 1989 illustrates this trend. Three months after the U.S. Supreme Court had upheld a restrictive state abortion law, Florida's highest court ruled that a state law requiring minors to get parents' consent for an abortion violated the Florida constitution's privacy clause, which guarantees a citizen "the right to be let alone and free from governmental intrusion into his or her private life."[14]

Checkpoint

- The Constitution does not specify the structure of the federal judiciary below the Supreme Court. When the first Congress established the national structure in 1789, it in effect created a dual court system, in which there are parallel but separate federal and state court systems.

- Federal and state courts handle both civil cases (in which parties sue others to recover damages or change behavior) and criminal cases (in which the goverment charges people with violating a law).

- The dual court system maintains judicial federalism, which makes it possible for states to compete in a market for laws and for state courts to move in a different policy direction than federal courts.

Do you know these judges? Television Judge Joseph Wapner of "The People's Court" was correctly identified by six times as many Americans as was U.S. Chief Justice William Rehnquist.

THE SUPREME COURT AND JUDICIAL REVIEW

In a *Washington Post* national survey in 1989, respondents were asked to name the chief justice of the United States, other members of the Supreme Court, and the judge on "The People's Court" television show. Only 9 percent of those polled could name Chief Justice William Rehnquist. Justice Sandra Day O'Connor was the best-known member of the Court at 23 percent. But 54 percent correctly identified Judge Joseph Wapner of "The People's Court."[15]

The Supreme Court is the preeminent federal court in the nation. And despite the fact that Chief Justice Rehnquist and his colleagues are not as well known as Judge Wapner, the federal courts have a more regular and more visible role in policymaking than do state courts. The brevity and broad language of the U.S. Constitution require judicial interpretation to a greater degree than do the longer and more specific constitutions of most states. Economic issues and the regulation of business produce cases that are national in scope. Civil rights laws passed by Congress over the past two decades have generated a series of cases in which federal courts engage in making policy. The federal courts, as we have seen, have not just implemented but have created policies in the areas of school busing and affirmative action. Within the federal court structure, the Supreme Court is the chief policymaking institution.

The governing power of the Supreme Court is exercised most clearly when the Court engages in judicial review. State courts and lower federal courts regularly take part in activities that Madison identified as the government controlling the governed. The disposition of most cases and the enforcement of judicial decisions take place at this level. The Supreme Court's power of judicial review, on the other hand, is the most important vehicle for meeting Madison's second requirement, that of the government controlling itself. **Judicial review** may be defined as the Court's power "to declare unconstitutional and hence unenforceable: (1) any law; (2) any official action based upon a law; and (3) any other action by a public official that it deems to be in conflict with the Constitution."[16]

The cases that come to mind when we think of the power of the Supreme Court are likely to be exercises of judicial review: ordering a president to surrender White House tapes that would drive him from office; ruling on states' abortion laws; declaring legislative veto provisions unconstitutional; or establishing strict standards for legislative redistricting and reapportionment. In its entire history, the Supreme Court has exercised this power of judicial review in about 1300 cases, with nearly 95 percent of those cases overturning state or local actions.[17]

Marbury v. Madison: The Origin of Judicial Review

The term *judicial review* does not appear in the Constitution. Nor does the discussion of judicial powers in Article III include any statement that the Supreme Court or other courts have the power to declare laws or actions by officials unconstitutional and thus void. Instead, the basis of the Supreme Court's power of judicial review was most clearly articulated 16 years after the Constitutional Convention by Chief Justice John Marshall. Writing the Court's opinion in *Mar-*

bury v. *Madison* (1803), Marshall observed that "it is emphatically the province and duty of the judicial department to say what the law is." Because the law of the Constitution is "superior to any ordinary act of the legislature," this meant that the Court had a responsibility to review legislation and to declare that "an act of the legislature, repugnant to the Constitution, is void."[18]

The *Marbury* case and its assertion of judicial review arose from an intense political conflict over who would govern the United States. After 12 years of governing in the Washington and Adams administrations, the Federalist party lost control of both the presidency and Congress in the election of 1800. In their final weeks in office, however, Federalists sought to retain some share in governing by holding onto the judicial branch. To that end, the lame-duck Congress created a number of new federal judgeships, and lame-duck President John Adams nominated 58 Federalists for those positions. William Marbury was one of 17 nominees whose commissions were not delivered at the time the Jefferson administration took office in March 1801. The new President and his secretary of state, James Madison, for obvious political reasons, failed to deliver the leftover commissions to those Federalist nominees. The Jefferson administration and new Congress also repealed one of the Federalist court laws passed the previous year, effectively closed down the Supreme Court for a year by changing its term, and moved to impeach two Federalist judges, including Supreme Court Justice Samuel Chase.

Federalists still held every position on the Supreme Court. For that reason William Marbury and three other federal judge nominees whose commissions were undelivered turned to that body for an order, in the form of a writ of mandamus, directing Secretary of State Madison to deliver the commissions. The battle lines were clearly drawn over who was to govern, with the Federalist judiciary on one side and the Republican President and Congress on the other. Jefferson wrote at the time that the Federalists "have retired into the judiciary as a stronghold," and he feared that "from that battery all the works of Republicanism are to be beaten down and erased."[19]

Portraits of William Marbury and James Madison hang next to each other in the Supreme Court's John Marshall dining room.

The *Marbury* decision and Marshall's opinion may be regarded, in the short run at least, as a backing off by the Federalists from this escalating party conflict. Marbury, the Federalist petitioner, was *not* granted a writ of mandamus. The legal decision of the Supreme Court in *Marbury* was that Section 13 of the Judiciary Act of 1789, which granted the Supreme Court power to issue such a writ, was unconstitutional and therefore void. Chief Justice Marshall pointed out that since the process of obtaining a writ of mandamus entails going directly to the Supreme Court, it represents original, rather than appellate, jurisdiction. But Article III of the Constitution limits the original jurisdiction of the Supreme Court to specific types of cases, which can be changed only by a constitutional amendment. Statutory attempts to do this, such as Section 13, conflict with Article III, and in such a conflict the "superior" law of the Constitution must prevail.

Marshall's opinion in *Marbury* was based on a discussion of the nature of written constitutions and general principles of governing. As we

mentioned, there are no specific provisions of the Constitution that could be cited as authority for the Court's power of judicial review. Nor did Marshall cite the debates at the Constitutional Convention or the descriptions and rationale for the Constitution found in *The Federalist* (even though Alexander Hamilton had discussed judicial review 15 years earlier in *Federalist 78*).

The Court's assertion of its power of judicial review in *Marbury* raises questions that continue to be hotly debated today. Did that case represent an unjustified intrusion of the Court into the realm of policymaking and governing? Does the Court have the right to overrule presidential and congressional actions made in response to majority opinion? Whenever the Supreme Court decides controversial issues regarding prayers in school or abortion, these and similar questions come up. They appear in public discussions of crime rates and debates over who the president should nominate as Supreme Court justices or federal judges. These are highly charged and intensely political debates.

But there is no disputing the long-term effect of *Marbury* v. *Madison*: Judicial review is the source of most Supreme Court policymaking today.

Characteristics of Policymaking by the Supreme Court

As the case that established the legal basis of judicial review, *Marbury* is one of the most important Supreme Court decisions in United States history. Its value to an understanding of governing modern America, however, goes beyond that, for *Marbury* illustrates some of the chief characteristics found in Supreme Court policymaking even today.

A first characteristic is the relatively passive nature of Court policymaking, at least compared to that of the president or Congress. Article III limits Supreme Court jurisdiction to actual cases and controversies. The Court cannot offer advisory opinions, nor can it initiate policy. This aspect of Court policymaking is perhaps best seen in the chronology of the *Marbury* case. Marbury's petition to the Court was filed in December 1801, six months after the Jefferson administration had taken office and failed to deliver his commission. On December 18, two days after that, Chief Justice Marshall ordered Secretary of State Madison to appear before the Court in the next term, which was to be in June 1802. But while Marbury's case was still pending, the Republican-controlled Congress passed a law in March 1802 eliminating the Court's June and December terms and replacing them with one annual term in February. By the time the Court finally heard arguments and decided the case, almost two years had expired since the incident giving rise to the case had occurred, which meant two years of new national policies under the Jefferson administration. The characteristic of Court policymaking to be noted here, though, is not simply that of delay (some cases take only a month), but rather that the Court must depend on the actions of others to get an issue on its agenda.

A second characteristic of Supreme Court policymaking, one that is dramatically illustrated by *Marbury*, is a dependence on others for the enforcement of a decision once it is made. It was very clear in this case that Secretary of State Madison would not have obeyed an order from a Federalist Supreme Court instructing him to deliver commissions appointing Federalists to these judgeships. It was also clear that the Supreme Court had no means of forcing Madison to do that or of punishing him for not following such an order. The Court's ability to have any part in governing depends on its decisions being accepted and its orders obeyed by other parts of the government.

The actual decision by the Court in *Marbury* is considered a brilliant political stroke because it was self-enforcing. The Court had to depend on neither the executive nor the legislature for the decision to take effect. Nor did the Court itself have to take any positive action; it simply said that it did not have the authority to issue a writ of mandamus because the statutory provision giving the Court that authority was unconstitutional. Nobody else had to do anything.

Although the legitimacy of judicial review today is based on almost two centuries of acceptance since *Marbury*, the enforcement question is still an important one affecting Supreme Court policymaking. The landmark school desegregation case of *Brown* v. *Board of Education* in 1954, for example, required a separate decision the following year on implementation and 20 years of cases having to do with achieving racial equality in education through integration programs such as busing.

A third characteristic of the Supreme Court's role in governing is the influence of elections and the political climate on the Court, even though its members are supposedly insulated from that process by their lifetime appointments. The nature of that link is the central democratic question about the Supreme Court and policymaking. Of course, there have been periods of intense conflict between the Court and popularly elected institutions. One of these took place during Franklin Roosevelt's first term as president when a conservative Court exercised its power of judicial review 12 times between 1934 and 1936 to strike down New Deal legislation. That conflict led Roosevelt to propose increasing the number of justices in his "Court-packing plan" of 1937, which was to make the Court more responsive to

Elections and the nation's political climate influence Supreme Court decisions even though the lifetime appointments of its members insulates the Court from direct political control.

the new political majority. Congress never passed Roosevelt's plan, and the issue was resolved when the Court began to uphold New Deal legislation in 1937. Conflict, then, does occasionally arise, but the normal relationship between the Supreme Court and elected institutions is quite different. Lawrence Baum's review of that relationship led him to conclude: "Only in a single period [1934–1936] has the Court's power to review federal legislation been used to disturb a major line of federal policy."[20]

Judicial review does *not* give the Court authority to substitute its political judgment for that of the executive or legislature, a point made in Marshall's opinion in *Marbury* and by the nature of the Court's later exercise of that power. As Marshall wrote: "The province of the court is, solely, to decide on the rights of individuals, not to enquire how the executive, or executive officers, perform duties in which they have a discretion. Questions, in their nature political, or which are, by the constitution and laws, submitted to the executive, can never be made in this court."[21] This conception of judicial review

as a *limited* power was also reflected in subsequent Supreme Court behavior. For more than 50 years after *Marbury* (until the Dred Scott case in 1857), the Court upheld every act of Congress brought before it for review. That does not mean, of course, that the Supreme Court is always guided by election returns when it decides cases. But it does suggest that the Court is not completely isolated from the democratic forces influencing Congress and the president.

A fourth characteristic of judicial policymaking today that is reflected in *Marbury* v. *Madison* stems from the fact that federal judges are appointed rather than elected. It deals with the question of what are the sources for the court's authority. In Chapter 4, we discussed Alexander Hamilton's point that the authority of government institutions under the Constitution rests on the consent of the people, on what Hamilton termed "that pure, original fountain of all legitimate authority."[22] The president and Congress can refer to their election as the source of their authority, but the Supreme Court can lay no such direct claim. On what grounds, then, can it

A Closer Look

Roe v. *Wade:* The Story of Norma McCorvey ★★★

Supreme Court Justice Oliver Wendell Holmes once described the Court as the "storm center" of political controversy—a description that David O'Brien has adopted as the title of a book on the Court's role in American politics. The book opens with the case that resulted in the Supreme Court's landmark decision on abortion, one of the most controversial issues in American politics.

On a hot night in August 1969, Norma McCorvey, a twenty-one-year-old carnival worker nicknamed Pixie, was returning to her motel on a side road outside Augusta, Georgia. On her way back to her room, she was gang-raped by three men and a woman. The carnival and Pixie moved on to Texas. There, several weeks later, Pixie found herself pregnant. A high school dropout, who was divorced and had a five-year-old daughter and little money, Norma McCorvey unsuccessfully sought an abortion. Texas, like most other states at the time, prohibited abortions unless necessary to save a woman's life. "No legitimate doctor in Texas would touch me," she has remembered. "I found one doctor who offered to abort me for $500. Only he didn't have a license and I was scared to turn my body over to him. So there I was—pregnant, unmarried, unemployed, alone and stuck."[a]

McCorvey (Jane Roe) found someone to adopt her baby and two lawyers to challenge the Texas antiabortion law. In 1971, McCorvey's case was one of the 163 cases that the Court selected from more than 4500 petitions for hearing before it at the time. At one point during the oral argument of the case,

Justice Byron White responded to McCorvey's attorney by noting that she had given "a very eloquent policy argument against" the Texas statute, but admonished: "We cannot here be involved simply with matters of policy, as you know." Justice White wanted to hear more on the constitutional grounds for striking down the law and recognizing a right to abortion.

On the other side, the attorney for Texas pressed two points: that the court system was not the place to resolve the abortion controversy and that the case was not about freedom of choice. He said, "There are situations in which, as the Court knows, no remedy is provided. Now I think she makes her choice prior to the time she becomes pregnant. That is the time of choice." Considering the fact that the case before them involved a rape, one Justice suggested "Maybe she makes her choice when she decides to live in Texas." The attorney's response, "There is no restriction on moving," was almost lost in the general laughter in the courtroom.

During the year that passed between oral argument and the Court's handing down a decision, the case went through a second oral argument, two new justices joined in the decision making, and the complex nature of the issues required the extensive circulation of opinions and comments among the justices before agreement was reached. In January 1973, the Court announced its decision in *Roe* v. *Wade*: The constitutional right of privacy includes a woman's decision to terminate a pregnancy and the Texas statute unconstitutionally violated that right.

The Court's ruling by no means settled the issue but only intensified the abortion controversy. Many cases have since come to the

Norma McCorvey, the Jane Roe of Roe v. Wade. "She reminds us that there is a human being, a flesh and blood person at the root of this case."

Court concerning state restrictions on abortion. As a result of Ronald Reagan's appointments to the Court, the majority upholding the right to an abortion has dwindled from 7 to 4. Many people feel that the Court is poised to overturn *Roe* v. *Wade*. Both pro-choice and antiabortion forces are gearing up for a battle, and Norma McCorvey is still at the center of this controversy.

To antiabortion groups, Norma McCorvey is living proof that those who obtain abortions are misguided or immoral. They point out that McCorvey admitted in 1987 that she had made up the story about being raped 18 years earlier, thinking that would make it easier to obtain an abortion. In addition, antiabortion leaders say that Norma McCorvey had not sought redress on her own but had been re-

cruited to be a test case by two attorneys who got her name from the lawyer she had spoken to about arranging the adoption of her unborn child.

Abortion rights advocates, on the other hand, describe McCorvey as a symbol of "Everywoman"—"unmarried, pregnant, and wanting an abortion at the age of 20," but "too poor to travel to a state where she could have an abortion."[b] A leader of the National Abortion Rights Action League said Norma McCorvey was an important symbol because "she reminds us that there is a human being, a flesh and blood person at the root of this case."[c]

Norma McCorvey won her case in 1973 when the Supreme Court struck down the Texas antiabortion law. Sixteen years after that decision, however, McCorvey began a search to locate the child she had given up for adoption in 1970. And in April 1989, someone fired three shotgun blasts at McCorvey's Dallas home where she slept in the predawn darkness, shattering windows in her house and automobile.

The case will never end for Norma McCorvey or the Supreme Court. As in many controversies, the Supreme Court continues to be the "storm center" of political controversy over abortion, as more human beings—with their own "flesh and blood" stories—try to reach the docket of the highest court in the land.

[a]David M. O'Brien, *Storm Center: The Supreme Court in American Politics* 2d ed. (New York: Norton, 1990), p. 23.
[b]Lisa Belkin, "Woman Behind the Symbols in Abortion Debate," *New York Times*, May 9, 1989, p. 18.
[c]Ibid.

require that the public and the other institutions of government accept Supreme Court decisions as acts of government to be obeyed? We know that the Supreme Court has no army or police to enforce its decisions by physical coercion. That makes it especially important that those institutions with that power of enforcement accept the Court's authority. Why should they?

Marshall's answer in *Marbury* was that a written constitution was worthless unless it was accepted as a higher law that took precedence over statutes and actions of public officials. Either constitutions are accepted as higher law, he said, or they are "absurd attempts, on the part of the people, to limit" government power. To deny the courts the power of interpreting and applying this higher law, said Marshall, "would subvert the very foundation of all written constitutions;" it would reduce "to nothing what we have deemed the greatest improvement on political institutions—a written constitution."[23] This argument also permits the Supreme Court to tap Hamilton's "pure, original fountain of all legitimate authority." Since the consent of the people is reflected in their ratification of the written constitution, later actions that uphold that constitution against statutory or other challenges can be perceived as reflecting that original consent.

Marbury did not, by any means, settle the question of the Court's authority. Court opinions often devote a great deal of attention to establishing the authority for making a particular decision, even though the Court has engaged in judicial review for 200 years. This can be seen in Court references to "the clear meaning" of a particular section of the Constitution, to the "intention of the framers," and to historical analyses of earlier decisions by the legislature and executive. When the Constitution is not clear and the historical record is mixed, the Court must base its decision on other grounds. In the 1954 school desegregation case of *Brown* v. *Board of Education*, for example, the Court first sought evidence as to whether the framers of the Fourteenth Amendment intended it to outlaw segregation in schools. When a search of congressional records could provide no clear answer to that question,

the Court drew instead on sociological and psychological studies on educational inequality as the basis of its decision. Similarly, the 1973 abortion decision of *Roe* v. *Wade* relied heavily on medical data regarding the risks at different stages of pregnancy. In both of these cases, critics of the Court argued that it had gone beyond its authority, that instead of interpreting law made by policymakers, the Court was legislating its own solutions to social problems. (See A Closer Look, pp. 554–555.)

Some bases of authority are preferred over others. The Constitution and clear evidence regarding the framers' intentions are always the strongest grounds for Supreme Court decisions. The *Marbury* case raises the question of whether those who wrote the Constitution intended courts to have the power of judicial review. Max Farrand found a number of references in the Constitutional Convention about the power of the judiciary to declare laws inconsistent with the Constitution to be null and void, evidence that led him to conclude that "it was generally assumed by the leading men in the convention that this power existed."[24] In *Federalist 78*, Alexander Hamilton also wrote about "the right of the courts to pronounce legislative acts void, because contrary to the constitution."[25] On the other hand, William Crosskey has argued that the framers intended the power of judicial review to be restricted only to laws directly interfering with the operation of the judiciary.[26] The continuing debate over the Supreme Court's authority in the *Marbury* decision and many other cases tells us a great deal about the unsettled nature of the judiciary's role in governing America.

The four characteristics of judicial policymaking outlined above indicate how the judiciary differs from the other branches in governing America. They are also useful in evaluating the Court's impact in the United States. The first characteristic, limiting of the Court's agenda to actual cases and controversies, leads to active judicial policymaking in areas such as civil rights, in which individuals and groups are likely to initiate cases, and to much less activity in the area of foreign policy. Despite a heated debate over the constitutionality of the War Powers Resolution of 1973, for example, the Supreme Court is not likely to decide that question. Unlike the president and Congress, whose agendas include all policy areas, the Court's scope of policymaking is more restricted.

The second characteristic—implementation or enforcement—is not unique to the courts. The effectiveness of Congress and the president as policymakers also depends on how policies are implemented. The judiciary, however, must depend on *other institutions* to put those policies into effect. Presidents can fire executive officials who resist or disobey and employ troops to enforce decisions, and Congress has a powerful instrument of enforcement in its control over government spending. But the courts must rely on those and other institutions to accept judicial authority and act in accordance with court decisions. This dependence on others for implementation is one reason why we find the link between elections and judicial policies, which we identified as the third characteristic. It also explains why so much attention is paid to the fourth characteristic of judicial policymaking: the stated authority on which the court's decision is based.

Checkpoint

- The Supreme Court case of *Marbury* v. *Madison* (1803) established the constitutional grounds for judicial review by the Supreme Court, an important power in the Court's policymaking role.
- Some of the key characteristics of contemporary Supreme Court policymaking are its passive or reactive nature, a dependence on others for enforcement, a link with electoral politics, and the exercise of authority based on interpreting a written constitution.

STATE COURTS: THE CRIMINAL JUSTICE SYSTEM

To determine the impact of judicial policymaking, it is best to move from the highest level of the judicial branch, the Supreme Court, to the level where most judicial policies are implemented and government acts directly on the people, the state courts. These courts deal with both civil and criminal cases, but our focus here is on criminal justice, for several reasons. One is the often-noted observation "that the courts . . . have had greater success in altering behavior in the criminal justice area than in any other."[27] Another reason is the importance of crime as a political issue. Public opinion polls during the last 20 years show that people are concerned about crime rates and support increased government spending to combat crime, even more than for education, the military, the environment, space exploration, or social welfare programs.[28]

The concern is not surprising in light of the number of people affected by crime or involved in the criminal justice system. Every year, more than 14 million Americans are victims of serious crimes (murder, rape, robbery, aggravated assault, burglary, larceny, or vehicle theft).[29] At the other end of the criminal justice system are the more than 600,000 men and women in federal and state prisons.[30] The criminal justice system, particularly in state courts, is the government institution primarily responsible for doing something about crime rates and for putting all those people behind bars.

The Criminal Justice Process

Because it is primarily a state responsibility, the criminal justice system in the United States takes different forms in different states. However, whether the case is a misdemeanor (generally defined as a crime punishable by less than a year in jail) or a felony (more serious crime), the end points in the criminal justice process are the same: a return to full freedom, a fine, probation, a suspended sentence, or a commitment to jail or prison. Return to full freedom is gained by either dismissal of the case at an early stage or acquittal after a trial. Similarly, two roads lead to punishment: a guilty plea or conviction after a trial.

The broad goal of the criminal justice system is, of course, to see that those who break the law are punished in a just manner. Much of the behavior in the system is directed toward achieving justice through **adversary proceedings**, in which the opposing sides directly confront one another, with each side vigorously arguing its own case and refuting the arguments and evidence of the other side. "Ideally," says Lawrence Baum, "the trial operates as a kind of marketplace of ideas: if each side presents the strongest possible case, the truth will emerge from the confrontation of those cases."[31] But another goal is efficiency, clearing the court docket as quickly as possible. Every year, about 11 million people are brought into the criminal justice system through police arrest (not counting traffic offenses).[32] The system thus focuses on handling the large volume of cases without sacrificing the goal of achieving justice.

An important characteristic of the criminal justice system is that it is an administrative or organizational process: The chief actors in this system (the police, prosecutors, defense attorneys, habitual defendants, judges, and corrections officials) develop routines and structure their behavior to achieve their goals. This can be seen at every stage of the process, but the part of this process that best illustrates its administrative nature is the guilty plea. Nine out of ten defendants in the criminal justice system plead guilty. In New York City, where 95 percent of defendants plead guilty, it has been estimated that a person charged with a crime would have to wait 25 years for a trial if the practice of pleading guilty were eliminated.[33] Even a minor reduction from 90 to 80 percent in the incidence of guilty pleas would double the work load and costs of the present system.[34] The value of the guilty plea to the criminal justice system, then, is primarily an administrative one. It adds to the police clearance rate (the percentage of reported crimes successfully disposed of by police), which is a standard measure of police efficiency. It saves the time of prosecutors, public defenders, judges, and juries. And it benefits the person who

pleads guilty because it generally reduces the number or severity of criminal charges and results in a more lenient sentence than if the person were found guilty in a trial. Early in the criminal justice process, both prosecutors and defense attorneys engage in **plea bargaining** in order to settle a case in a manner acceptable to both sides. Plea bargaining, not the adversary process of a trial, is the way the vast majority of criminal cases are handled in the United States.

Plea bargaining is efficient, but it has its critics. They say that the procedure is flawed because it is based on a false premise that a guilty plea is a first step in rehabilitation. In fact, according to these critics, plea bargaining reinforces a defendant's beliefs about the unfairness of the criminal justice system; it undercuts constitutional guarantees regarding confessions and search warrants that are enforced by excluding illegally obtained evidence from trials; it gives prosecutors too much discretion; plea bargaining with state's witnesses can lead to distorted information; it reinforces inequalities in the bail system because defendants who are denied bail have a stronger incentive to plead guilty than those who are free on bail; it produces greater leniency as a reaction to increased crime. Finally, plea bargaining can lead innocent people to plead guilty, since a guilty plea and a suspended sentence can sometimes result in an earlier release than a trial and acquittal.[35]

W. Boyd Littrell has called the way in which the criminal justice system seeks to achieve the goals of justice and efficiency **bureaucratic justice**.[36] This concept, which Littrell says guides the behavior of those in the system, is based on a presumption of guilt coupled with a commitment to fairness. The presumption of guilt facilitates the administrative handling of cases, and the commitment to fairness is a way of seeing that individuals are treated equally. A criminal justice system guided by this concept of bureaucratic justice runs counter to the notion that a person is innocent until proven guilty. Nor does it conform to the picture of an adversarial process that most people associate with the judicial system. In many ways, the system is like any bureaucracy that seeks to achieve certain goals in the most efficient manner.

The Influence of Supreme Court Decisions

The Supreme Court has had an important influence on the operation of the criminal justice system. A series of landmark decisions in cases that arose under the due process clause of the Fourteenth Amendment established clear procedural guidelines for the police and other officials in the criminal justice system. These cases, beginning in the 1960s, created what is sometimes referred to as a due process revolution in America. Two of these cases were discussed in Chapter 6: *Mapp* v. *Ohio* (1961), which said that all evidence gathered illegally must be excluded from a trial (the exclusionary rule), and *Miranda* v. *Arizona* (1966), which required police to fully inform persons in custody of specific constitutional guarantees. Another important due process case was *Gideon* v. *Wainright* (1963), which clearly affirmed a person's right to an attorney. These and similar cases decided by the Warren Court in the 1960s have been modified in some cases under the Burger Court in the 1980s to give police more leeway.

Studies of the impact of these decisions show that they have not had the effect of "coddling criminals" or "handcuffing the police," as some have charged. *Gideon* and later right-to-counsel decisions seem to have had the most impact on the criminal justice system, but the effects of other decisions on the behavior of police and other officials have been limited. Recent reviews of the studies led one scholar to conclude that these effects "have been less than fully satisfactory in achieving the Court's goals," and another to report that "there is little evidence that the Court's decisions reforming the criminal justice system have had a large impact on the crime rate, on the ability to obtain convictions, or on protecting the innocent."[37]

Between 1948 and 1978, spending for police in our 400 largest cities tripled, the number of police officers per capita doubled, and the number of judges, prosecutors, prison beds, and prison guards increased at a similar pace. Yet crime rates in those cities were five times higher in 1978 than they had been 30 years earlier.[38] It is easy to see how findings such as these can lead to frustration on the part of American policymakers. What they tell us about the system of criminal justice in America, more than anything else, is that this part of the judiciary is also a political one. It is political in the sense that police, attorneys, judges, and other officials are responsive to a number of constituencies, including one another, in their behavior. If the police ignore *Miranda* and *Mapp* they are likely to have cases thrown out of court by judges, but if they appear not to be aggressive enough in making arrests they are likely to lose the support of public officials and the general public. In order to get a clearer picture of the political nature of the judiciary in America, we need to have a closer look at the participants in the judicial system.

Checkpoint

- The criminal justice system at the state court level is shaped by the twin goals of achieving justice through adversary proceedings and maximizing efficiency through administrative procedures such as plea bargaining.

- The ability of the criminal justice system to achieve both justice and efficiency depends to a great extent on the structure of government and on the behavior of the system's chief constituents, to whom it must be responsive: the Supreme Court and other higher courts, elected public officials, and the general public.

PRINCIPAL ACTORS IN THE JUDICIAL SYSTEM

Early in the sixteenth century, Spain's King Ferdinand warned those who were recruiting settlers for that country's colonies in America: "No lawyers should be carried along, lest lawsuits should become ordinary occurrences in the New World."[39] If the Spanish monarch were to visit some of the 17,000 courthouses scattered throughout the contemporary United States, he might find cases like the following:

- A Boulder, Colorado man sued his parents for $350,000, alleging that they had provided him with inadequate home life and psychological support and were therefore guilty of "malpractice of parenting."
- A woman in the state of Washington, who had been dismissed from the Gonzaga University School of Law because of her grades, initiated a suit asking for either a law degree or $110,000 from the law school. Her argument was that the law school admissions board should have advised her that her chances of graduating from law school were slim, given her mediocre college grades and aptitude test scores.[40]

Over the past several decades America has experienced a litigation explosion. The number of civil suits in both federal and state courts has skyrocketed. We have already seen how the criminal justice system is swollen with cases. Former Chief Justice Warren Burger has expressed concern that these demands are so great that the legal system "may literally break down before the end of this century."[41]

We will look now at the principal actors in the judicial system—those who must shore up the system and attempt to administer justice both fairly and efficiently: the police, lawyers, and judges.

Police

Because a police officer's job is to enforce laws passed by legislatures and city councils and to follow policies decided by executives, we are not used to thinking of them as political decision makers. The limits on police decision making are evident in a case that went all the way to the Supreme Judicial Court of Massachusetts. The case arose from a claim of police negligence brought by a woman whose husband and infant daughter were killed in an automobile collision. Moments before the crash, the police had

stopped the driver of the other car for suspected drunk driving but had let him go because he seemed sober. In bringing her suit against the police, the woman claimed that the police had been negligent in releasing the driver. The court agreed. In its opinion, a court majority said: "The statutes which establish police responsibilities in such circumstances evidence a legislative intent to protect both intoxicated persons and other users of the highway." The police had no discretion under these circumstances, the court said, because "policy and planning decisions to remove such drivers have already been made by the legislature."[42]

The Massachusetts court was attempting in this case to set limits on police discretion in a particular area. Yet the decision also recognized that discretionary judgments are inherent in the job of a police officer. A police officer is constantly required to decide quickly whether certain actions constitute a violation of a law—which may itself be ambiguous—or a threat to themselves or other persons. This discretion, coupled with a legitimate right to use force, is why many scholars describe the police as political decision makers.[43] William K. Muir notes that "the offices of patrolmen are on the curbside instead of off corridors. They are streetcorner politicians."[44]

Police behavior varies greatly in America. That is not surprising, considering the discretion that individual officers have and the fact that close to 20,000 separate law enforcement agencies are scattered throughout the United States.[45] Two leading experts on policing in America recently studied police innovation in several American cities and found a direct connection between the political values of a community and the operations of its police. Most Americans, the authors suggest, have an attitude toward the police that is similar to:

> . . . the working-class English boy in grade school who was asked to write a one-sentence description of the police. To the teacher's considerable consternation, he wrote, "The police are bastards."

The teacher immediately decided that something had to be done about such a nega-

A New York City police officer assigned to a community policing program jokes with a neighborhood resident. Community-oriented policing is based on the idea that good policing is good politics.

tive attitude. So she arranged with the local police to have the class visit a police station, climb in and out of police cars, visit the radio room, and get to meet officers over cups of tea.

Then she again assigned a one-sentence description of the police. Hurriedly leafing through the papers, she found that this time the boy had written, "The police are clever bastards."[46]

The two experts found that police forces could overcome the disdain and distrust many Americans feel toward the police through **community-oriented policing**. This is a new kind of professionalism in which police officers form a partnership with the community in preventing crime, as opposed to the old concept that emphasizes police expertise in crime control, with little or no input from the community. In the community-oriented approach, the police organization is decentralized to assure accessibility to the police in all sections of the city. Foot patrols establish links with neighborhoods and focus on crime prevention. In addition, civilians are drawn into the force to perform clerical, research, training, maintenance, and other tasks, creating further bonds with the community while freeing police officers for tasks they have been trained for.

Community-oriented policing has emerged in many American cities because traditional responses to crime have not been effective. Increasing the number of police officers and motorized patrols, replacing one-person patrol cars with two-person patrols, saturating certain areas with police, and improving the response time to emergency calls have been found to have little effect on crime rates or the proportion of crimes that are solved.[47] What is important—both for solving crimes that are committed (by locating offenders and serving as witnesses) and for crime prevention—is for police to have the support of the community. Good policing, in short, is good politics.

Lawyers

There is approximately one lawyer for every 350 persons in the United States—about 750,000 in total. Since 1950, the number of attorneys has grown twice as fast as the general population. The ratio of lawyers to population in the United States is 3 times that of England, 9 times that of France, and 35 times that of Japan.[48] Many people consider the growing number of lawyers as one of the causes of the litigation explosion discussed earlier. Chief Justice Burger, for example, has warned: "We may well be on our way to a society overrun by hordes of lawyers hungry as locusts."[49] Similarly, Harvard University President (and former Law School Dean) Derek Bok contends that the United States suffers from "too many laws, too many lawsuits, too many legal entanglements, and too many lawyers."[50]

Other commentators have suggested that it is not the number of lawyers that is a problem for justice in America but rather the *distribution* of lawyers' services. To illustrate, Lloyd Cutler, a prominent Washington, D.C., lawyer, has written: "The rich who pay our fees are less than 1 percent of our fellow citizens, but they get at least 95 percent of our time. The disadvantaged we serve for nothing are perhaps 20 to 25 percent of the population and get at most 5 percent of our time. The remaining 75 percent cannot afford to consult us and get virtually none of our time."[51]

Judgments about the number of lawyers in the United States depend partly on whether the focus is on civil or criminal cases. Burger's criticisms, for example, are aimed primarily at lawyers engaged in civil suits who, in his opinion, stir up litigation in order to make money. In criminal cases, however, the number of available lawyers is sometimes thought to be too few rather than too many. This is especially true for poor people. Even with the great expansion in legal services to the poor over the past 20 years, according to the former director of the federal legal assistance program, "private wealth is the primary criterion for access to the legal system."[52]

The influence of lawyers and the legal profession in the judiciary goes beyond the number of working attorneys in that system. As Herbert Jacob points out: "All persons with substantial authority in the courts come from the legal profession, and almost all decisions are made in the presence of lawyers and by them. No other governmental institution is so dominated by a single profession."[53] Judges, lawyers for the plaintiff, and lawyers for the defendant all share a common training and a common legal language.

Descriptions of shared bonds and friendly negotiations between lawyers are easier for most of us to accept in civil cases. In criminal cases, however, we look to the adversary process to achieve justice. The lawyer for one side in a criminal case is a government official from the office of a district, state, or U.S. attorney whose goal is to win a plea of guilty or a conviction. On the other side is a defense attorney committed to a client's interests and therefore aiming for a not-guilty verdict or the best deal in a plea bargain. Yet even here, the common legal training and shared bonds and a shared stake in the judicial organization lead to cooperation as well as conflict. Stuart Scheingold writes: ". . . the level of conflict within the criminal courts is really very moderate. Defense attorneys, prosecutors, and judges are all lawyers . . . and they all have a stake in making the criminal courts function as smoothly as possible."[54] Abraham Blumberg also focuses on what he calls the "bureaucratic practice" of criminal law and on the role of attorneys as "agent mediators" as well as adversaries.[55]

As discussed earlier, the organizational and bureaucratic characteristics of the judiciary are best illustrated by the practice of plea bargaining, which settles nine out of ten cases. A study reported by Blumberg found that it was the defense counsel, rather than the police or prosecutor, who was most effective in getting defendants to plead guilty.[56] Impoverished clients with public defenders (appointed by the court) plead guilty more often than those with private defense attorneys. Because public defenders are likely to have more cases before a particular court than are private attorneys, they play a more central role in the organization of the court. Judges acknowledge that key role in their relatively lenient sentencing decisions.

We recognize the political nature of the job of prosecuting attorney in the United States by making the position of district attorney a locally elected one. State attorney generals are elected in 43 states, and U.S. attorneys, appointed by the president, are dependent on changes in the national administration after an election. The political influence of prosecutors is heightened by the great discretion they have over what criminal charges to bring and against whom. The values of a political community and those reflected in prosecutors' decisions are likely to be similar. The relative importance to the public of issues such as drunk driving, drug abuse, street crime, white-collar crime, or organized crime gets conveyed to prosecutors in elections. That is one way in which lawyers play a role in governing America. Another, we have seen, is by making the decisions that help administer the judicial bureaucracy.

Judges

The Boston school case discussed at the beginning of the chapter illustrated the enormous political power of U.S. District Judge Arthur Garrity, Jr. The influence of an appointed federal judge over education policy in Boston was greater than that of any elected officials: the mayor, governor, school committee, city council, or state legislature. It was a highly visible and dramatic example of a judge governing. It also illustrated a concept that goes back to English judges in the Middle Ages, that of the judge as a "surrogate sovereign." In his book, *How Courts Govern America*, West Virginia Supreme Court Justice Richard Neely has provided this description of the concept:

> Any trial court can order any member of the executive branch within its jurisdiction to do anything—under pain of fine and imprisonment—until a higher court reverses or grants a stay. This is basically the same power which an energetic president or governor would have if he personally oversaw the workings of bureaucracies.
>
> Furthermore, any trial judge can interpret statutory or common law or declare a law unconstitutional—exactly the same thing which

Congress or a state legislature could do either by changing a law or refusing to enact it in the first place.

In every backwoods county seat and in every federal district courthouse, there is a man or woman who can give you as complete relief against incompetent bureaucracy as a governor or even the president him very self. Thus we still have the judge as surrogate sovereign.[57]

Even when judges are not acting as surrogate sovereigns, however, they are powerful participants in governing America. The influence that an individual judge can have is perhaps best illustrated by looking at the highest level of judging in America—the justices of the Supreme Court.

A member of the Senate Judiciary Committee, responsible for hearings on Supreme Court appointees, said in 1987: "The selection of a Supreme Court Justice is just as important as the election of a new President or a new Congress."[58] Why should this be so? Part of the answer is that one vote can tip the balance of the Court on a closely divided issue. Landmark abortion and civil rights decisions of 1989, for example, were decided by one vote. But a Supreme Court justice's influence often extends beyond his or her vote, and to appreciate that influence we need to look at the nature of Supreme Court decision making.

The Supreme Court's official term begins in October and ends with the completion of business in June or July. Most of the term consists of two-week sittings, when the collective work of hearing oral arguments and discussing cases in conferences is done, and two-week recesses, during which the individual justices discuss cases with their law clerks and review and write opinions, functioning as one justice described it "as nine small, independent law firms."[59] The key steps in the Court's decision making are: agenda setting, oral argument, conference, and opinion writing.

Agenda setting is the process by which the justices decide which of the approximately 5000 cases appealed to the Supreme Court each year will be included among the 150 or so on which the Court hears oral arguments and writes opin-

President Bush introduces Supreme Court nominee David H. Souter to the press in July 1990. "The selection of a Supreme Court Justice is just as important as the election of a new President or a new Congress."

ions. Four justices must agree to hear a case for it to go any further. Decisions about which cases to hear occupy much of the justices' fall conferences, but the agenda-setting process continues throughout the term. It is at this point that the Court drops frivolous cases, such as a suit claiming that the federal income tax is unconstitutional because it does not provide a deduction for depreciation of the human body.[60] The vote of a single justice can be extremely important at this stage. In 1970, for instance, three justices agreed to hear a Massachusetts suit challenging the legality of the Vietnam War—one short of the four affirmative votes needed.[61]

Each side in a case is normally allocated 30 minutes to present its case directly to the justices in *oral argument*. The Court will generally hear four cases during the four hours of oral argument, which is usually scheduled from 10:00 A.M. to noon and 1:00 to 3:00 P.M., Monday through Wednesday when the Court is sitting. Justices regularly interrupt the presentation of lawyers during oral argument, trying to shape the course of the argument and influence how their colleagues view the case.

The Supreme Court regularly holds *confer-*ences on Wednesday afternoon and all day Friday when it is sitting. Only justices are permitted in the room, and there is no official record of the conference. The Chief Justice begins the discussion of each case and the other justices follow in order of seniority on the Court. After a tentative decision is reached, the Chief Justice, if in the majority, assigns the task of writing the court opinion to a justice in the majority. When the Chief Justice is in the minority this responsibility is assumed by the most senior justice in the majority. One goal generally achieved in assigning opinions is a relatively equal distribution of the work load. Beyond that, however, the opinion assignment is an intensely political process through which the Chief Justice or senior justice can seek to have his or her own views become the Court's views, to reward or punish justices for other votes, or to otherwise affect coalition building among the justices.

The importance of the *opinion-writing* stage stems from the fact that the decision reached in conference is only tentative: Justices can change their positions up until the Court announces its decision. One study found that 10 percent of the justices' votes shifted from one side to the other between the conference and the announcement of the decision and that at least one justice shifted sides in about half of the cases.[62] The fluidity evident in this stage of Court decision making permits individual justices to have an influence extending beyond their single vote. It helps explain why Justice Rehnquist's opinion in the 1989 abortion ruling incorporated language from earlier opinions in this area by Justice Sandra Day O'Connor, who was considered a key vote in assembling a majority on this issue.[63]

The internal dynamics of Supreme Court decision making illustrate why the selection of justices is as important as selecting those who hold political office:

> Members negotiate over votes and the language of opinions as members of Congress do over legislation. Justices engage in feuds just as administrators do, and these feuds may affect the disposition of policy questions in the same way.[64]

An accurate picture of the role of judges in governing America, however, must include the limits on their power as well. For as Henry Abraham points out:

> Judges are bound within walls, lines, and limits that are often unseen by the layman—walls, lines, and limits built from the heritage of the law; the impact of the cases as they have come down through the years; the regard for precedent; the crucial practice of judicial restraint; the deference to the legislative process; in brief, the tradition of the law.[65]

The doctrine of *stare decisis* ("stand by the decision"), that a principle of law settled in earlier judicial decisions is applicable in later cases, is central to the limits described above and an important legacy of the English common law brought to America. In assessing the impact judges have on governing America, then, we need to be aware both of the impact of individual

Chief Justice William Rehnquist discusses the wording of opinions with his law clerks. Supreme Court Justices "negotiate over votes and the language of opinions as members of Congress do over legislation."

justices and of factors that limit individual judges' behavior.

On the one hand, studies of Supreme Court justices and federal and state judges have found that policy preferences or party differences among justices and judges can best explain their judicial decisions. Baum's research on Supreme Court voting found: "Not only are justices' policy preferences largely responsible for differences in their decisional behavior, but to a considerable degree those preferences are expressed in a moderately simple ideological form."[66] Robert Carp and Ronald Stidham summarize the research findings on judicial decision making for federal and state judges at all levels:

> Democrats more than Republicans are inclined to be supportive of civil rights and liberties, to support government regulation that favors the worker or the economic underdog, and to turn a sympathetic ear toward the pleas of criminal defendants.[67]

The ideological and partisan nature of judges' behavior helps explain why political leaders consider judicial appointments so important. During his two terms in office, President Ronald Reagan appointed three associate Supreme Court justices and one Chief Justice, 78 appeals court justices, and 290 district court justices—nearly half the federal judiciary. Indeed, some political scientists describe Reagan's justices and judges as his most enduring legacy, one that will extend into the next century.[68]

On the other hand, the doctrine of *stare decisis* and the other limits described by Abraham make judges reluctant to stake out new judicial positions or to ignore or seek to reverse earlier judicial decisions even when they disagree with the substance of those decisions. This judicial conservatism extends to the judicial role of surrogate sovereign discussed earlier. "You won't see Reagan's appointees taking over school systems and jails and ordering forced busing," said one judicial scholar.[69] Still, because there is no higher court to reverse them if they stray too far from existing constitutional doctrines, Supreme Court justices are freer to change policy direction and to introduce new legal doctrines than

are federal judges in lower courts. In 1989 references to "a new era" and "watershed term" characterized changes at the Supreme Court level, while the changes at lower levels of the federal judiciary were generally described as "gradual and incremental."[70]

When President Bush took office in 1989, three of the four Supreme Court justices making up the liberal minority (Brennan, Marshall, and Blackmun) were over 80 years old. Bush had a chance to carry on Reagan's conservative judicial policy when he named David H. Souter to the Court on Brennan's retirement in 1990. The direction of the Bush administration was made clear by Attorney General Dick Thornburgh, the official responsible for recommending judicial prospects to the White House:

> It would be unrealistic to expect real differences in philosophy from the Reagan and Bush administrations.
>
> Both are Republicans and share a belief that we should not have activist judges.[71]

Checkpoint

- Demands on the judicial system have greatly increased over the past two decades. This increased work load has affected, in different ways, the governing role of key judicial actors such as the police, lawyers, and judges, and has highlighted the political nature of their behavior.

- A broad discretion and a legitimate use of force permit police officers to function as "streetcorner politicians." Community-oriented policing involves interaction with the community and focuses on crime prevention.

- The influence of lawyers on the judicial system is due not only to their numbers as active players in the judiciary but also to the professional values shared by lawyers and judges and to the role of attorneys as "agent mediators" as well as adversaries.

- Judges at all levels of the judicial system participate in governing America through their individual actions and, for some judges, as part of a Supreme Court majority.
- The Supreme Court justices proceed through four stages in their work: setting agendas, hearing oral arguments, meeting in conference to make decisions, and writing opinions.

THE COURTS: WHO GOVERNS?

The central theme of this chapter is that the courts play a much more vital role in the workings of American democracy than is generally recognized. A similar thesis, one that Frank Coleman calls the "judicial supremacy" interpretation of American politics, suggests that the final political authority in the United States does and should rest with the Supreme Court and its interpretation of the Constitution.[72]

Any evaluation of the role of the judiciary in governing America depends on making connections to generally accepted values. There is no reason to favor the judiciary over the legislative or executive for some kinds of policymaking unless one can show that judicial policymaking is more democratic, necessary to maintaining a constitutional system, or more likely to protect liberty or some other value. Judicial policymaking, like other aspects of governing America, can be evaluated in terms of its relationship to democracy, pluralism, and elitism.

Democracy

How is it possible to call a political system democratic when an unelected body of nine per-

sons can overrule decisions made by an elected president and Congress? That question, says constitutional scholar John Hart Ely, brings us to "the central function" and "at the same time the central problem of judicial review: a body that is not elected or otherwise politically responsible in any significant way is telling the people's elected representatives that they cannot govern as they'd like."[73] Another scholar, Jesse Choper, writes: "Reconciling judicial review with American representative democracy has been the subject of powerful debate since the early days of the Republic."[74] That the debate continues is suggested by the preface of Richard Neely's *How Courts Govern America*, which was published one year after the books of Professors Ely and Choper: "The principal thesis of this book is that American courts, both state and federal, are the central institution in the United States which makes American democracy work, contrary to the assertion that courts are a uniquely undemocratic institution in an otherwise completely democratic society."[75]

A democratic interpretation of judicial policymaking can be supported in two ways. First, over the long run, scholars point out, the major policies of the Court have been consistent with those of the president and Congress.[76] For example, beginning in 1937, the direction of Court policymaking changed to coincide with the New Deal philosophy of the elected branches.

A second way of viewing the judiciary as a democratic institution is to focus on judicial intervention to eliminate undemocratic procedures. In 1938, for example, Justice Harlan Stone contended that the Supreme Court could strike down legislation favored by a majority when the law restricts democratic processes or prevents the participation of certain minorities in those processes.[77] Some of the landmark decisions in civil rights and reapportionment made by the Warren Court in the 1960s were democratic in this sense. They broadened democratic participation by striking down laws and procedures aimed at denying minorities the vote and other forms of participation or at apportioning a majority of the legislative seats to a minority of the population.

Pluralism

Pluralists view the courts as a means of access to government for particular interests and groups who have little or no access to executive or legislative policymakers. Access to the courts may be necessary in order to maintain the group competition, the wide range of interest representation, and the balance that pluralists regard as important. There is an underlying pluralist framework, for example, to Herbert Jacob's observation that the American system "allows certain people who would otherwise be excluded from politics to have a voice in making public decisions. Convicts not only have no right to vote but also are not a very respectable constituency for any legislator or executive. Yet they have played an important role in creating safeguards in criminal law that protect all members of society."[78]

The National Association of Colored People (NAACP) instigated a series of civil rights suits in the 1950s (see Chapter 10). Their success demonstrates how a group that is denied access to the executive and legislature can seek to influence policy by initiating or sponsoring cases in the courts, a process known as **interest group litigation**. In 1963, the Supreme Court said that such litigation is a right protected by the First Amendment, for as Justice Brennan noted, "Litigation may well be the sole practicable avenue open to a minority to petition for the redress of grievances."[79]

A legal concept of great importance to a pluralist interpretation of judicial policymaking is that of **standing**. In order to bring a case into court, an individual or group must have standing. To achieve that status, the person or group must demonstrate a personal stake in the outcome of a case or show that he, she, or it is representative of those with such a personal stake. Decisions about standing are made by Congress as well as by the courts. In 1984 the Supreme Court made an important decision affecting standing in a case involving an affirmative action program for Memphis fire fighters. Justice Byron White wrote in that case that "mere membership in the disadvantaged class" is not enough to establish an affirmative action claim and that "each individual must prove that the discriminatory practice had an impact on him."[80] The Court upheld this narrow interpretation of standing in subsequent cases, and it had a part in the series of civil rights decisions in 1989, discussed in Chapter 7, that inhibited the process of interest group litigation. By *restricting* standing, these decisions reduce the ability of the courts to provide an alternative means of access to policymakers and thereby diminish pluralism in American government.

Pluralism is also important to enforcement. Groups in America can provide the energy needed to put court decisions into effect. When officials drag their heels in enforcing a Supreme Court decision, interest groups challenge the noncompliance in courts.[81] Reapportionment is a policy area where this aspect of pluralism is clear: The enforcement of the Court's one person–one vote principle is a result of ongoing suits for noncompliance and court review by various interest groups.

The Power Elite

Many observers of American politics have explained judicial policymaking in terms of a power elite. The former director of the federal legal assistance program, you will recall, saw elitism in the judiciary because "private wealth is the primary criterion for access to the legal system." American legal scholar Isaac Balbus concluded that the courts were primarily instruments of social control and "that the underlying motives of many court actions are to promote the objectives of dominant economic and political elites."[82]

Federal judges in the United States come primarily from upper- or upper middle-class families that are politically active and that often have a tradition of judicial service. Carp and Stidham describe federal judges as "an elite within an elite" and discuss how that socioeconomic background influences judicial policymaking:

Seldom bitten is the hand of the socioeconomic system that feeds them. Although an occasional maverick may slip in or develop within the judicial ranks, most judges are basically conservative in that they hold dear the traditional institutions and rules of the game that have brought success to them and their families.

While America's elite has its fair share of both liberals and conservatives, it does not contain many who would use their discretionary opportunities to alter radically the basic social and political system.[83]

Those who characterize the judiciary as an elitist institution focus on different aspects. Some point to the unrepresentative nature of membership. Others find elitism in judicial policies that benefit certain groups and classes in society. Still others emphasize the general public's unawareness of most judicial policymaking, so that the interpretation and implementation of those policies are left to national and local elites.

The elitist view of American politics is useful for bringing to our attention a number of important characteristics of the judiciary. While membership at the highest levels of the judiciary is disproportionately upper and middle class, and while judges and justices are insulated from the electorate, the Supreme Court in particular is often in the forefront on policies that primarily benefit low-income groups. These include such issues as the right to a court-appointed attorney for indigent defendants, welfare and public education rights for resident aliens, and affirmative action in employment programs.

Most of those who have studied the judiciary have recognized that there *is* a class bias to the criminal justice system and that it is primarily the poor who get prosecuted in criminal courts. On the other hand, most would also accept Stuart Scheingold's assessment that the bias of the judicial system is really one of the larger society and political system rather than one limited to the internal workings of the judiciary.[84] The many links between the judiciary and the other arenas of American politics make it almost certain that the judiciary will reflect the values found in the broader political system.

Checkpoint

- In order to be consistent with democratic values, court decisions must, over the long run, reflect the issue positions of electoral politics or be deemed essential to maintaining democratic procedures.
- An active judiciary can advance pluralist values by providing access to interests that would otherwise have no influence over governing America.
- The unrepresentative membership of courts, the class bias of the criminal justice system, and the low visibility of judicial policymaking reinforce power elite explanations of governing America.

SUMMARY

America's judiciary is a dual court system, consisting of parallel but separate federal and state court systems. The Supreme Court controls the government and actively engages in policymaking. State courts control the governed by implementing policy and enforcing rules. A continuing debate in American politics pits proponents of judicial activism (an interventionist role) against proponents of judicial restraint (deferring to existing law and executive policymaking).

Marbury v. *Madison* established judicial review by the Supreme Court, which gives the Court a role in policymaking. Some characteristics of that policymaking are the Court's passive or reactive nature, its dependence on others for enforcement of decisions, its link with electoral politics, and the exercise of authority based on interpreting a written constitution.

The criminal justice system pursues the twin—often competing—goals of justice, achieved through the adversarial process, and efficiency, achieved through administrative routines and plea bargaining.

The principal actors in the judicial system are police, lawyers, and judges. Police officers have discretionary powers that give them a policymaking role. The most effective policing seems to be one that interacts with the community in preventing crime. Lawyers inundate the justice system but tend to service the very rich more than the poor or the middle class. They share professional values with one another and with judges, which may undercut the adversarial process. Judges can act as "surrogate sovereigns" in the American political system. The Supreme Court justices have the most opportunity to play a policymaking role. There are four key steps in their work: agenda setting, hearing arguments, making decisions in conference, and writing opinions.

The democratic view holds that court decisions must, over the long run, reflect the positions of electoral politics and maintain democratic procedures. Pluralists view the courts as another means of access to interests that otherwise have no influence over policymakers. Power elite theorists emphasize the unrepresentative membership of courts, the class bias in the criminal justice system, and the low visibility of judicial policymaking.

KEY TERMS

Judicial activism	Plea bargaining
Judicial restraint	Bureaucratic justice
Dual court system	Community-oriented
Civil cases	policing
Criminal cases	Interest group litigation
Judicial review	Standing
Adversary proceedings	

FOR FURTHER READING

Henry J. Abraham, *Justices and Presidents: A Political History of Appointments to the Supreme Court,* 2nd ed. (New York: Oxford University Press, 1985). A lively history of presidential appointments and how the behavior of members of the Supreme Court fulfilled or disappointed those who appointed them.

Lawrence Baum, *The Supreme Court,* 3rd ed. (Washington, D.C.: Congressional Quarterly Press, 1989). A description and analysis of the Supreme Court's political role and the impact of Court decisions on American politics.

Robert A. Carp and Ronald Stidham, *Judicial Process in America* (Washington, D.C.: Congressional Quarterly Press, 1990). A comprehensive analysis of the procedural and human factors that shape the American judiciary.

Lief H. Carter, *Contemporary Constitutional Lawmaking* (Elmsford, N.Y.: Pergamon Press, 1985). An imaginative reexamination of Supreme Court policymaking and how the Court reinforces the values of the political community.

John Hart Ely, *Democracy and Distrust* (Cambridge, Mass.: Harvard University Press, 1980). A theory of judicial review grounded in democratic theory.

Lawrence M. Friedman, *American Law* (New York: Norton, 1984). An analysis of the development and operation of the legal system as a part of the broader social system.

David M. O'Brien, *Storm Center: The Supreme Court in American Politics* 2d ed. (New York: Norton, 1990). A lively description of how the Supreme Court exercises a great influence in governing America and how the power of the Court rests on public support.

Michael J. Perry, *The Constitution, the Courts, and Human Rights* (New Haven, Conn.: Yale University Press, 1982). An inquiry into the legitimacy of Supreme Court policymaking, which makes a strong argument for Court intervention and judicial activism in the area of human rights.

Jerome H. Skolnick and David H. Bayley, *The New Blue Line* (New York: Macmillan, 1988). A study of police innovation in six American cities and an analysis of community-oriented policing.

Part Five

ROMAN
GODDESS OF WAR

APPROPRIATIONS.

-S-128-

Public Policy ★

BUDGET OF THE U. S. GOVERNMENT • FY 1991

BUDGET OF THE U. S. GOVERNMENT • FY 1991

BUDGET OF THE U. S. GOVERNMENT • FY 1991

BUDGET OF THE U. S. GOVERNMENT • FY 1991

Economic Policy

Chapter 18

★ Economic Policies:
  Choices and Trade-Offs
★ Economic Policy
  from Roosevelt to Reagan
★ Economic Policy
  in the 1980s and 1990s
★ The Federal Budget
★ Economic Policymaking:
  Who Governs?

Your welfare and the welfare of everyone you know depends on the health of the economy. Since this statement holds for all Americans, management of the economy surely ranks first among society's tasks. In view of its universal significance, economic policymaking should ideally be as democratic as possible. Yet considerable evidence suggests that small groups, perhaps even a power elite, make a majority of the important decisions. ∎

In the summer of 1981, Congress voted to slash personal income taxes by 25 percent. Its action was a triumph for President Ronald Reagan, who had campaigned for lower taxes in his 1980 campaign. By lowering the rates, Congress confirmed popular beliefs about American democracy: The President strongly advocated a program, the people overwhelmingly supported him, and the legislature responded to their wishes. Here, it seemed, was a perfect example of democracy in action.

Less than two years earlier the government adopted an equally significant policy. Yet this time the circumstances were quite different. On a Saturday afternoon in October 1979, members of the Federal Reserve System's board of governors voted to change the way the nation's money supply was managed.[1] The Fed, as this institution is known, has the power to increase or decrease the amount of money and credit available to the economy. In what one journalist described as a "leap into darkness,"[2] it abandoned its previous efforts to control interest rates and declared that it would henceforth focus almost exclusively on limiting the supply of money.

This policy was every bit as far-reaching as the tax cuts two years later. Limiting the money supply meant that banks had fewer funds to lend and had to charge higher interest rates for them. Faced with mounting interest rates, businesses invested less in plant and equipment, and consumers slowed down their purchases of new homes and automobiles. Industries went into a tailspin. By the first part of 1982 unemployment had reached nearly 11 percent, and certain interest rates reached their highest point since the Civil War. Two analysts at the Urban Institute estimated that the economic downturn cost more than $800 billion in lost output.[3] The Fed, in effect, had triggered a **recession**, a period of greatly reduced economic activity.

Deep recessions like the one in the early 1980s lead to terrible consequences not just for those out of work but for the country as a whole. Studies conducted by M. Harvey Brenner, for example, show that unemployment causes increases in divorce, spouse abuse, alcoholism, anxiety, mental illness, and premature death. Brenner estimates that a 1 percent increase in joblessness brings in its wake a 1.2 percent increase in overall mortality. Translated into numbers, that means perhaps an extra 30,000 deaths per year. Considering that roughly 50,000 American troops died in Vietnam, Brenner's research suggests that an increase in unemployment from, say, 6 to 10 percent produces as many casualties as a major war.[4] Clearly, monetary policy, like tax cuts, entails fundamental national choices.

Yet unlike the congressional debate over taxation, the Fed's moves were made by a nonelected body that is at most only indirectly accountable to the people. Although not secret, its work is followed mainly by economists, bankers, financial analysts, and business leaders. Probably not more than one American in ten even knew about the Fed's action, much less understood its ramifications. And even though senators and representatives complain about the Fed's policies, these complaints are seldom the subject of partisan debate.

People waiting in line to receive unemployment benefits. Action by the Federal Reserve System in 1979 helped plunge the United States into its worst economic tailspin since the Great Depression.

Economic policy, then, raises the question of who governs. Inasmuch as the economy touches every man, woman, and child in the country, it is vital to understand how the fundamental decisions affecting its performance are made. A few may be made according to the tenets of textbook democracy. But for the most part it appears that either pluralism or elitism best describes economic policymaking. To document this conclusion we need to look first at the policies themselves and then see how they are made.

ECONOMIC POLICIES: CHOICES AND TRADE-OFFS

At least since the Great Depression 60 years ago there has been general agreement that Washington has a major responsibility for fostering economic prosperity and stability (see Chapter 3). The demands placed on the federal government run the gamut from controlling the business cycle (the ups and downs in employment and prices) to encouraging stable growth in the pro-

ductivity of labor and capital to regulating commercial activities so as to ensure the public health, safety, and welfare to protecting business and labor from unfair foreign competition. Attaining these goals is clearly a tall order. More important, even though Americans generally agree on the need for public action, they quarrel bitterly about its extent and form.

Economists and politicians all have their favorite approaches. Many favor a combination of taxing and public spending, while others advocate regulating the supply of money. In practice, economic policy involves a mixture of the two, but during the past several decades each method has at one time or another been dominant. Since they often lead to radically different solutions, we need to consider each separately.

Fiscal Policy

By manipulating government spending and taxes in order to stimulate or slow down growth, Washington affects the aggregate or total demand for goods and services. This method of economic management is called **fiscal policy.**

To see how fiscal policy works, consider a period of high unemployment and business stagnation. The national government attempts to revive industry and create jobs by injecting billions of dollars into the economy (called "pump priming"). It does so by cutting taxes, thereby leaving individuals and businesses with more to spend; by purchasing goods and services (such as building bridges, dredging harbors, and buying airplanes); and by making direct payments to individuals (social security or unemployment insurance, for example). In theory at least, the net effect is to raise *aggregate demand*, the total goods and services citizens and businesses can afford to buy. A rise in demand causes industries to manufacture more products, hire additional labor, and invest in new buildings and machinery, all of which helps commerce and trade.

Government spending, moreover, has a *multiplier effect*. The billions of dollars allocated to public projects go into the pockets of carpenters, steelworkers, bricklayers, truck drivers, and thousands of other laborers, who spend the money on food, clothing, housing, medical care, automobiles, and recreation. Workers in these industries, in turn, spend their wages on additional goods and services. Gradually the government's dollars trickle through the economy. The multiplier effect holds for all types of budget transactions, whether in the form of tax cuts, direct payments, or actual purchases. Consequently, federal "pump priming" increases national income by much more than the nominal or face amount of the outlays.

In times of prosperity, on the other hand, demand may exceed supply. The excess causes prices to increase and, unless stopped, leads to **inflation**, a condition in which the value of money decreases as prices rise. When this happens, the government reverses gears by cutting spending, raising taxes, or both. The result is less money in the hands of consumers and business, and less money means lower aggregate demand, which causes prices to level off.

Fiscal policy thus strives to smooth out the business cycle by manipulating the federal budget to maintain just enough demand to keep people working but not so much as to fuel inflation. In essence fiscal policy is a juggling act: By adjusting spending and taxation, the government can in principle maintain high levels of employment and stable prices.

In the past, Democrats, especially members from the liberal wing of the party, have advocated fiscal action to combat unemployment and sustain economic productivity and were willing to risk inflation and incur budget deficits to achieve these ends.

Associated with the British economist John Maynard Keynes, fiscal policy is often called **Keynesian theory**. Although Franklin Roosevelt effectively adopted Keynesian theory in the 1930s and it has been widely accepted ever since, it has nonetheless always created deep misgivings and endless controversy. Several leading economists doubt that the national government can fine-tune the economy by raising or lowering taxes and expenditures. Besides being too ponderous and time-consuming, these methods involve enormous uncertainties. A better approach, they say, is monetary policy.

Monetary Policy

Monetary policy attempts to control the amount of money in circulation or the cost and availability of credit. The objective is straightforward even if difficult to put into practice. If money is readily available because, say, interest rates are low, people can afford to borrow and spend. But unless production keeps pace, there will not be enough goods and services to go around. In the face of the excessive demand, producers and suppliers have incentives to raise their prices. As time goes by, prices spiral upward, leading to uncontrolled inflation during which dollars lose their value. The key to keeping inflation in check is to maintain stable interest rates and not let the money supply grow too rapidly.

Like fiscal policy, monetarism has a downside. Should the government constrict the flow of cash into the economy too severely, consumers and businesses cannot afford to borrow, spending and investments decline, products sit on store shelves, factories close, and new homes, automobiles, and appliances go unsold. As the economy cools off, more and more workers are laid off and the downward plunge picks up momentum. As we saw at the outset, the Fed's decision to curb the supply of money in 1979 led the United States into its worst recession in 50 years. Nevertheless, just as Democrats traditionally favor stimulative policies, conservative Republicans tend to boost monetary policy as the best way to control inflation, which they argue is a greater evil than unemployment.

Fiscal and monetary policies often work at cross-purposes. Generally speaking, monetarists are mainly concerned with keeping the lid on inflation and will tolerate relatively high unemployment to achieve that goal. Fiscal policy, on the other hand, appeals to politicians who want to keep the economy vigorous and growing even at the cost of moderately higher prices.

Checkpoint

- Fiscal policy means adjusting federal taxing and spending to stabilize employment and production, thereby countering the ups and downs of the business cycle:
  - During a recession the government spends more or collects fewer taxes or both in hopes of stimulating aggregate demand.
  - When the economy nears full employment and prices begin to rise, the government raises taxes or cuts spending or both in order to hold demand in check.
  - Fiscal policy tolerates moderate inflation and budget deficits in the interests of full employment.
- Monetary policy tries to manage the economy by manipulating the supply and cost of money. This policy accepts moderate unemployment in the interest of price stability.

ECONOMIC POLICY FROM ROOSEVELT TO REAGAN

Since economic policy affects the welfare of every American and the well-being of the nation as a whole, and since it arouses strong feelings in every public official, policymakers constantly and bitterly battle about its direction and content. In order to understand what these men and women are fighting about, we have to review what they have done in the past.

The New Deal: A Revolution in Economic Policy

Before 1929 Americans by and large accepted the main tenets of laissez-faire capitalism (see Chapter 3). The marketplace, most economists and politicians assumed, was self-correcting, and economic periodic depressions simply had to be endured like droughts and floods. In those days fiscal policy was unknown, and state and local governments had the primary task of looking after citizens in distress. The Great Depression of the 1930s, however, changed people's thinking about the relationship between government and the economy. Had it ended quickly or affected fewer people, Americans might have continued believing in unregulated capitalism. But widespread and persistent unemployment (see Figure 18.1) and the bankruptcy of thousands and thousands of banks, businesses, and farms forced Washington to act.

Congress, under President Roosevelt's prodding, passed a series of bills designed to revitalize business and agriculture and put people back to work. These programs, collectively called **The New Deal**, entailed vast government expenditures on public works projects (such as highway and bridge construction) and income maintenance programs (like Social Security). The money Washington spent on these activities effectively stimulated aggregate demand because part of each dollar that went to a laborer or pensioner eventually found its way back into the economy where it helped create additional jobs and production.

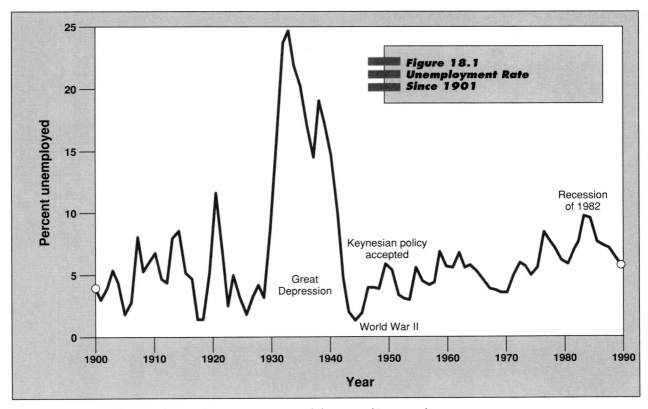

Before World War II, the rate of unemployment swung up and down, reaching a peak during the Great Depression. After the general acceptance of fiscal or Keynesian policy, the variation in unemployment has been smaller, although the rate climbed during the 1970s.

Source: U.S. Bureau of the Census, *Historical Statistics of the United States* (Washington, D.C.: Government Printing Office, 1975), Part 1, Series D86; and Office of Management and Budget, *Economic Report of the President 1989* (Washington, D.C.: Government Printing Office, 1989), p. 352.

As a consequence of spending without collecting sufficient taxes to pay for its programs, the Roosevelt administration consistently incurred budget deficits. These deficits soared even more during World War II, when the annual deficit amounted to more than 20 percent of the gross national product (see Figure 18.2, p. 579). Yet the deficits did not lead to financial ruin; on the contrary, on the eve of Japan's surrender in 1945 the United States enjoyed virtually full employment and a huge increase in its total income.

Economic Policy After World War II

Despite the fact that fiscal policy and unbalanced federal budgets contradicted many traditional American values, the idea of an activist state firmly took root after World War II. Government expenditures as a share of GNP climbed from 16 percent to more than 20 percent by 1980;[5] only occasionally during this period did Congress and the White House manage to bal-

New Deal programs such as this Works Progress Administration project illustrate the revolutionary shift in the government's hands-off approach to the economy to one of actively attempting to maintain high levels of employment and low rates of inflation.

ance the books. For a while at least, this economic policy seemed to bring enormous benefits. The country experienced the greatest economic expansion in its history, and the government reaped the dividends of this bountiful economy to pay for benefits (aid to farmers, for example) to different segments of society without taking away from others by raising their taxes.[6] Political economists call this approach **distributive policy**, since goods and services are distributed to one set of individuals or groups, but not by *re*distributing them at the expense of others. One expert described federal budgeting in the postwar years as a matter of whose "ox is to be fattened," not whose "ox is to be gored."[7]

But policy analysts and historians also describe budget making during the 1950s and 1960s as **disjointed incrementalism**: Each year existing programs usually received a slight increment or increase, and government spending decisions took place without any comprehensive planning.[8] Until 1970 the economy was so robust

and federal programs aided so many individuals and businesses that no one seemed too concerned about the disjointed budget process or the mounting national debt.

By the end of the 1960s, however, clouds began appearing on the horizon. Several developments, beginning with the explosion in social welfare legislation known as the Great Society and America's involvement in the Vietnam War, set in motion a train of events that shook the economy to its roots and left a legacy of problems that continue to confound policymakers today.

The Economy in the Turbulent 1970s

During President Lyndon Johnson's administration Americans found themselves waging two costly wars simultaneously, one against poverty at home, the other against communism in Southeast Asia. Making matters worse, President Johnson did not want to arouse opposition to either venture by raising taxes to pay for them. Vietnam and the Great Society thus strained the budget to the breaking point. The impact of Washington's red ink on inflation could not be ignored. Then, in the ensuing years several more economic shocks followed, including three recessions and skyrocketing oil and food prices. These events not only further fueled inflationary fires, but ironically caused the economy to stagnate as well. The result was **stagflation**, a time of both high unemployment and high prices. Normally one cures the other. But in the 1970s unemployment averaged more than 6 percent (see Figure 18.1) while the consumer price index (CPI), a measure of inflation, rose sharply until 1981.[9]

Stagflation meant that the government could no longer distribute benefits by tapping into economic growth. Tough choices had to be made: Helping one group required taking from another. Even more troubling, economic planners found themselves with less room for maneuver because of changes in the composition of the federal budget.

ENTITLEMENTS For most of its history the federal government spent most of its money on highways, dams, bridges, mail delivery, and other programs with more or less fixed costs. Each year Congress appropriated the required money unless it felt a program had outlived its usefulness and could be terminated. That it rarely made such decisions only reflected the growing economy; Congress believed that, if it

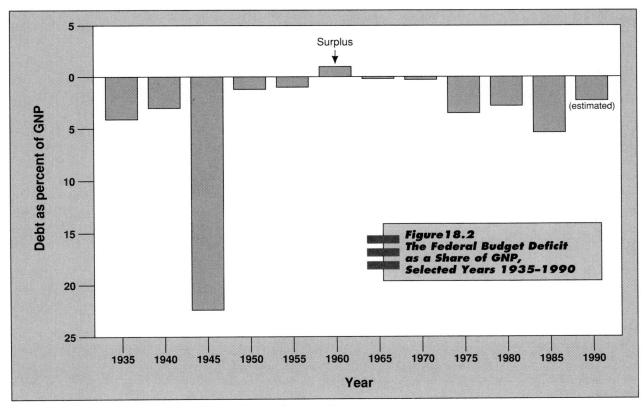

Figure 18.2
The Federal Budget Deficit as a Share of GNP, Selected Years 1935–1990

Source: Office of Management and Budget, *Budget of the United States Government Fiscal Year 1991* (Washington, D.C.: Government Printing Office, 1990), p. A-282.

had to, it could control spending. But in the 1970s the options began to narrow because the composition of the federal budget included more and more entitlements.

An **entitlement** is legislation that requires the government to pay benefits to citizens meeting certain conditions.[10] Senior citizens, for example, are now *entitled* to retirement income and medical care when they retire. Once entitlement legislation is passed, its funding level depends on the state of the economy, demographic trends, and other factors that lie largely beyond immediate congressional control. For instance, Social Security payments increase annually because benefits are tied to the rate of inflation and the number of elderly goes up each year. Entitlements, then, represent "relatively uncontrollable

spending," a budgetary term meaning that the amount of funding cannot be controlled in the usual appropriation process. To decrease funding requires changing the authorizing legislation that creates the programs in the first place.

Entitlements mushroomed after the early 1960s and now constitute almost half the federal budget (see Figure 18.3). Since interest on the national debt also has to be paid and the nation's defenses maintained, most public expenditures today are extremely hard to trim. This means that nondefense discretionary expenditures—the programs that can be cut in the appropriations process and are most talked about in the press and on the campaign trail—actually constitute a relatively small part of the total federal budget (see Figure 18.3).[11]

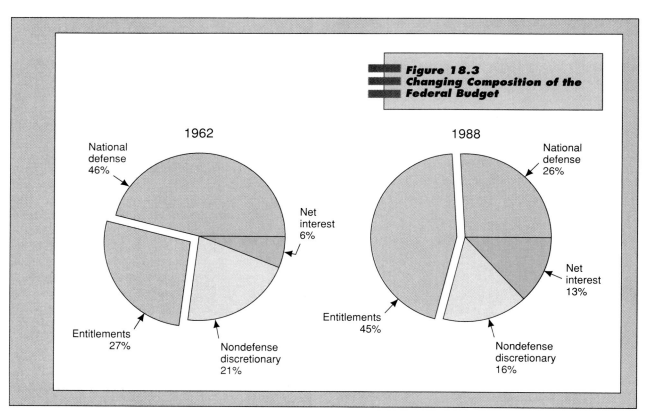

Figure 18.3
Changing Composition of the Federal Budget

1962

National defense 46%

Net interest 6%

Entitlements 27%

Nondefense discretionary 21%

1988

National defense 26%

Net interest 13%

Entitlements 45%

Nondefense discretionary 16%

The proportion of the federal budget earmarked for entitlements or mandatory spending programs has grown considerably since the early 1960s. This growth, together with increased interest payments on the national debt, make budget cuts difficult to achieve.

Source: Congressional Budget Office, *The Economic and Budget Outlook: Fiscal Year 1990–1994* (Washington, D.C.: Government Printing Office, 1989), p. 134.

By the end of 1980 these trends had come to a head: Interest rates hovered near 20 percent; unemployment topped 7 percent; and with inflation at 13 percent, the so-called misery index (unemployment plus inflation) exceeded 20 percent. Equally troubling, Congress and the president seemed unable to discipline themselves to stop the flow of red ink, especially since so much money was tied up in entitlements, defense, and interest payments. None of these developments was lost on the voters, who perhaps out of a sense of desperation, elected a man, Ronald Reagan, who promised them salvation from their economic woes.

Checkpoint

- The depression of the 1930s permanently changed people's ideas about the government's role in the economy. The Roosevelt administration gradually adopted Keynesian or fiscal policy through massive government spending and incurring deficits rather than raising taxes to pay its activities.

- Two characteristics describe rising federal spending up to the 1970s: (1) distribution, not redistribution, of funds by tapping into the expanding economy, and (2) disjointed incrementalism, which allowed Congress to add slightly more to most programs each year without working under a master plan.

- The Great Society and the war in Vietnam strained the budget to the point where inflation became a serious problem and deficits could no longer be ignored. Then several recessions and spiraling prices led to stagflation.

- Stagflation and the growth of entitlements made it harder for the government to follow distributive policies and disjointed incrementalism.

ECONOMIC POLICY IN THE 1980s AND 1990s

The economic turbulence of the 1970s did not surprise President Reagan, who believed that massive public spending was dangerous, misguided, and immoral; that the Democrats' policies boiled down to "tax and spend"; that government regulation hampered industry; that high taxes crushed individual initiative; and that public borrowing to pay for social welfare programs was out of control. Reagan, thus, came to accept a doctrine that fit hand in glove with these beliefs: **supply-side economics**. The secret to restoring prosperity, supply-side economists insisted, was across-the-board tax cuts. Lower tax rates would not only stimulate investment, employment, and productivity, but would pay for themselves in the long run by leading to greater savings, output, and profits and ultimately higher tax revenues as well. Supply-siders also advocated sharp reductions in government expenditures to cut down on public borrowing, which, they claimed, sucked capital away from private investment.

Reaganomics

President Reagan incorporated many of these ideas into his economic plans, commonly known as Reaganomics. **Reaganomics** called for sweeping, across-the-board cuts in income tax, reductions in social welfare activities, curtailment of federal regulation of business, a balanced federal budget, and massive increases in military spending.

Despite the tax plan's dramatic scope and uncertain effects,[*] Congress passed virtually the entire package. At the same time, however, the President found cutting domestic spending much harder to achieve, partly because so much of the budget was tied up in popular entitlement pro-

---

[*] During the 1980 campaign, George Bush dismissed the idea as "voodoo" economics, while Republican Howard Baker, who became Senate majority leader and later White House chief of staff, labeled the plan a "riverboat gamble."

grams.[12] Although the legislature did slow the rate of growth in many discretionary programs, it did not come close to reducing overall spending to the White House's proposed level. Finally, expenditures for national defense accelerated dramatically.

By the end of 1981, therefore, Reaganomics was moving under a full head of steam. Briefly stated, it promised an increase in jobs, more savings and investments, lower interest rates, less inflation, an internationally competitive economy, and a balanced budget. Even in the best of circumstances the promises would have outstripped its performance. But these were not the best of circumstances, as the President and his advisers quickly discovered.

First, the economy did not spring to life as everyone had hoped. In fact, it plunged into the worst recession since the 1930s. Second, in a blow to supply-side expectations, personal savings did not go up but actually fell.[13] Third, the budget never came close to being balanced: The deficit in 1983 exceeded $200 billion, the highest on record.

It would be unfair and misleading to blame Reagan's policies for all of these conditions. As we saw at the beginning of the chapter, the Federal Reserve System clamped down on the money supply as early as October 1979, a year and a half before Reagan took office. This act, as much as anything the Reagan administration or Congress did, dealt the economy a body blow. Furthermore, just as hot water does not start flowing the minute you turn on the tap, the tax cuts and increases in defense spending—both of which were stimulative and should have encouraged employment—did not have an immediate effect.[14] And in any case, the economy gradually recovered after the 1982 recession. By 1985, inflation had dipped to 4 percent while employment, especially in service industries, gradually rose.[15] In the middle of his second term, the President could with some justification claim a return to prosperity.

But just as it is unfair to blame the Reagan administration for the 1982–1983 recession, so too it is incorrect to credit it entirely for the economic turnaround. Bountiful harvests and falling oil prices helped push down the cost of living and revive industry. Equally important, the Fed,

an institution largely insulated from direct presidential manipulation, eased the money supply, thereby causing interest rates to fall. With more money available, both consumers and businesses began to spend more. Indeed, some economists believe that the change in monetary policy, not supply-side economics, provided the impetus the economy needed to get rolling again.[16]

Whatever the case, Reaganomics failed in four major respects: (1) It left a huge *underclass* of Americans, homeless and destitute, who lived far below the comfortable existence of their fellow citizens;[17] (2) the national savings rate did not improve; (3) the trade deficit (the excess of imported goods and services over exports) climbed by leaps and bounds, making the United States a debtor nation for the first time since the turn of the century; and (4) the budget remained grossly out of balance. Reagan's legacy to George Bush was thus a mixture of opportunities and dangers. Outwardly, the country seemed prosperous and stable, enabling the newly elected president to announce that he would follow the course charted by his predecessor. But despite this show of confidence, there were dangers lurking beneath the surface.

Economic Policy in the Bush Administration

In his first year in office, President Bush found himself caught between a rock and a hard place. On the one hand, his 1988 campaign promised Americans a "kinder, gentler" nation. Although he seldom spoke in specifics, Bush did pledge to protect the environment, help families pay for child care, improve education, maintain a strong defense, and wage an all-out war on drugs. On the other hand, his most memorable campaign statement was "Read my lips—no new taxes!" (The candidate even proposed *lowering* the capital gains tax on the sale of stocks, real estate, and other assets.) He thus set himself a difficult task: Make good on his promises while keeping within the confines of severe budgetary constraints, including a law enacted several years earlier requiring that the federal government's books be balanced by 1993. His rhetoric and harsh economic realities thus forced the Presi-

In 1989 President Bush and Congress, with great fanfare, signed a budget deficit reduction agreement. Within a year, however, that plan had fallen apart, and Bush was forced to retract his "no new taxes" campaign pledge.

dent to fulfill his promises mainly with symbolic gestures, not major programmatic changes in the budget. His critics also charged that he resorted to dubious accounting practices—"smoke and mirrors" the press called them—to meet his commitments. Two problems, the war on drugs and the savings and loan crisis, illustrate economic policy early in the Bush administration.

In the summer of 1989, the President unveiled a widely ballyhooed antidrug campaign that seemed at first glance to be a bold new initiative. On closer inspection, however, it asked for only an extra billion dollars, money that would have to be spread over a host of activities including treatment, enforcement, rehabilitation, prevention, and education. Moreover, the funds would have to be raised by cutting other programs, many of which were helping people who might fall prey to drug abuse. The next year he felt he could only ask for another $1.1 billion.[18] Congress promptly declared the proposals inadequate and came up with its own, more expensive, alternatives.

The savings and loan issue demonstrates even more starkly the hardship of reconciling a pressing national need with Bush's "no new tax" pronouncements. As earlier chapters mentioned, many savings and loan banks (S & L's) across the country faced bankruptcy in the late 1980s. Since deposits in these institutions were federally insured, the government had little choice except to act. But estimates of the cost of rescuing the S & L's ran as high as several hundred billion dollars. To meet the challenge, Bush suggested and Congress ultimately accepted a plan to establish a nonprofit corporation that would sell bonds, guaranteed by the Treasury, to funnel money into the ailing savings industry. From Bush's point of view, one of the plan's most attractive features was that it would be "off-budget"; that is, the money would not show up as a government expenditure. But the taxpayers would obviously have to pay the tab if the bond plan fell apart. Furthermore, because the corporation would not be able to raise sufficient capital, additional direct federal funds were nec-

essary. In order not to push the government further into the red, Congress, with the President's blessing, charged these funds to the previous year's budget (the fiscal 1989 budget) rather than to the current budget it was trying to reduce.

These kinds of accounting maneuvers underscore the dilemma staring Bush in the face. Washington was besieged by a torrent of crises and demands: AIDS, hazardous wastes at nuclear weapons plants, deteriorating air and water quality, cries from East European and Third World nations for economic aid, crime, soaring health costs, universal dissatisfaction with public education, and especially the military crisis in the Middle East precipitated by Iraq's invasion of Kuwait. But what could be done? The discretionary slice of the budget pie was shrinking relative to the others. Hence, stalemate, acrimony, and mostly symbolic change dominated the Bush presidency.

Checkpoint

- Reaganomics contained five main features: across-the-board tax cuts, reductions in social welfare programs, increases in military spending, curtailment of government regulation of business, and a balanced federal budget.

- The early years of the Reagan administration were marred by a severe recession, but after 1982 the economy rebounded and inflation, unemployment, and interest rates fell. However, enormous budget deficits and other problems tarnished the successes of Reaganomics.

- The Bush administration has been torn by the need to deal with pressing national problems while trying to cope with severe budgetary constraints.

THE FEDERAL BUDGET

When politicians assert that "government cannot live beyond its means," they strike a responsive chord in the hearts of average citizens. Most of us, after all, have to live within a fixed budget and have been taught since childhood that spending more than we earn is immoral, if not illegal. Of course, everyone borrows from time to time. Yet many do so with trepidation and always with the expectation that debts have to be paid off. It only seems natural to apply the same morality to the government. If it spends and borrows more than it collects in revenues, it risks economic catastrophe that will inevitably doom our children and grandchildren to a lower standard of living.

How accurate are these perceptions? Answering the question requires a careful look at the budget. It differs in many respects from a typical household ledger, and whether or not we have mortgaged the future depends on far more than the simple arithmetic office seekers bandy about.

Where It Comes from: Revenues

The Treasury estimates it will collect about $1.2 trillion in 1991.[19] As Figure 18.4 indicates, the lion's share comes from personal income taxes (roughly $500 billion) and social security taxes and contributions ($398 billion). Corporate taxes ($129 billion) will amount to 11 percent of the total, with the rest coming from tariffs, estate and excise taxes, and other sources.

Since most economists believe that a portion of business taxes is ultimately passed on to consumers, Figure 18.4 shows that for the most part individuals finance Washington's various undertakings. Although they complain, Americans seem willing to bear this burden, especially if the money pays for activities close to their hearts such as social security, environmental protection, and education. In any case, total taxes of all kinds take up a smaller percent of the gross national product here than in most other industrialized countries.*

On paper, the United States has maintained a

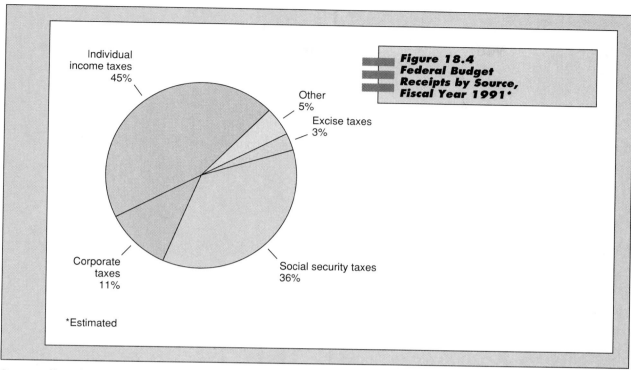

Individual income taxes 45%

Other 5%

Excise taxes 3%

Corporate taxes 11%

Social security taxes 36%

Figure 18.4 Federal Budget Receipts by Source, Fiscal Year 1991*

*Estimated

Source: Office of Management and Budget, *Budget of the United States Government Fiscal Year 1991* (Washington, D.C.: Government Printing Office, 1990), p. A-286.

progressive system of taxation. **A progressive tax** takes proportionally more from the rich than the poor, the theory being that the wealthy not only can afford to pay more but also derive greater benefits from public institutions. (One might argue, for example, that it costs the police the same amount to guard an estate as a bungalow, but the millionaire stands to lose more from a burglary than an average homeowner.) Prior to 1986 the federal tax schedule contained 14 brackets running from 11 to 50 percent. Individuals earning more than $75,000 were in the highest bracket and presumably paid 50 percent of their taxable income in taxes. People making less paid proportionally smaller amounts.

These 14 brackets comprised the *nominal* rates, or what people were supposed to pay. But the tax code contained innumerable exceptions, or loopholes, that allowed individuals and companies to escape paying the full nominal rates. Wealthy landowners, to take one case, could deduct state and local taxes, interest payments on mortgages, business expenses, depreciation on buildings, and other items from their tax obligations. Thus, although they might nominally be in the 50 percent bracket, their actual, or *effective*, rate was usually far lower. By the early 1980s, if one took *all* taxes—national, state, local, and sales—into consideration, the effective rate for the richest 10 percent was 25 percent, about 23 percent for middle-income groups, and 21 percent for the poor.[20] In effect, then, the United States had inadvertently adopted a system of **flat taxes**, because each income group paid roughly the same rate.

---

*In 1986, only the Japanese paid a lower percent of their national product in taxes. U.S. Bureau of the Census, *Statistical Abstract of the United States, 1989* (Washington, D.C.: Government Printing Office, 1989), p. 827.

1 Control number		OMB No. 1545-0008		

2 Employer's name, address, and ZIP code		3 Employer's identification number	4 Employer's state I.D. number

5 Statutory employee ☐	Deceased ☐	Pension plan ☐	Legal rep. ☐	942 emp. ☐	Subtotal ☐	Deferred compensation ☐	Void ☐

6 Allocated tips	7 Advance EIC payment

8 Employee's social security number	9 Federal income tax withheld	10 Wages, tips, other compensation	11 Social security tax withheld

12 Employee's name, address, and ZIP code	13 Social security wages	14 Social security tips

16	16a Fringe benefits incl. in Box 10

17 State income tax	18 State wages, tips, etc.	19 Name of state

20 Local income tax	21 Local wages, tips, etc.	22 Name of locality

Form **W-2 Wage and Tax Statement 1988**
Employee's and employer's copy compared ☐

Copy 1 For State, City, or Local Tax Department

Although most Americans do not realize it, they pay more social security than income taxes.

By the mid-1980s the number and magnitude of loopholes had grown so notorious that the demand for reform became irresistible. Congress, with President Reagan's support, enacted the Tax Reform Act of 1986. The legislation reduced the number of brackets from 14 to 2, one being 15 percent, the other 28 percent, and closed or reduced dozens of tax shelters and deductions in order to make nominal and effective rates approximately the same. In addition, the new law removed nearly 6 million poor from the tax rolls by raising various standard deductions and personal exemptions. Finally, it was supposedly "revenue neutral": In theory, the government would collect as much as ever, but the burden would be more fairly shared.

The jury is still out on how well the reforms are working. Economists generally feel it helps those below or near the poverty line. On the other hand, the law does not affect social security taxes, which continue to take a substantial bite out of earnings.[21] In fact, if the employer portion of the tax is counted, the vast majority of Americans pay more in social security than income taxes.[22] Other tax analysts fear the law's potentially negative impact on business investment and savings. The key to economic strength and international competitiveness, these experts maintain, lies in increasing investment in buildings, machinery, new technology, and human resources, investments that are best paid for by internal savings. But the reforms of 1986 gave most breaks to individuals while terminating many provisions that encouraged corporate investments.[23] There is also a possibility that the reforms will come unglued. Lopping off deductions has hurt many groups, which constantly pressure Congress to restore the loopholes. Pestered by lobbyists, Senator Daniel Patrick Moynihan of New York, one of the guiding lights in the reform effort, complained to reporters: "I feel as if I am being nibbled to death by ducks."[24]

In any event, the difficulties of constructing a workable tax code pale into insignificance compared with the problem of controlling government spending.

Where It Goes: Outlays

President Bush's 1991 fiscal year budget message contained over $1.2 trillion in spending proposals.[25] Politicians and journalists love to describe the number 1 trillion, a one followed by 12 zeros. One columnist compared it to a train:

> If you packed $1 trillion, in the form of $1 bills, into average-sized, 50 foot long railroad boxcars, you could get about $63.5 million into each boxcar. A train carrying $1 trillion would have 15,743 boxcars and be 167 miles long.[26]

Images like this scare nearly everyone. The flow of money out of the Treasury sparks demands from both aisles of Congress to stop it before it is too late. Most citizens agree that the lid could be put on government expenditures if only Congress and the president would put their minds to it, and unless they do, the country faces disaster.

Yet for the last 50 years federal outlays have inexorably grown, no matter who controlled the White House or Congress. One wonders, then, why the budget is such a tough animal to tame. The answer lies partly in the nature of the spending categories.

BUDGET OUTLAYS BY FUNCTION Think of the federal budget as a pie (see Figure 18.5): The biggest single slice goes to national defense, and in the past this portion has for political reasons been cut only marginally, if at all. This situation

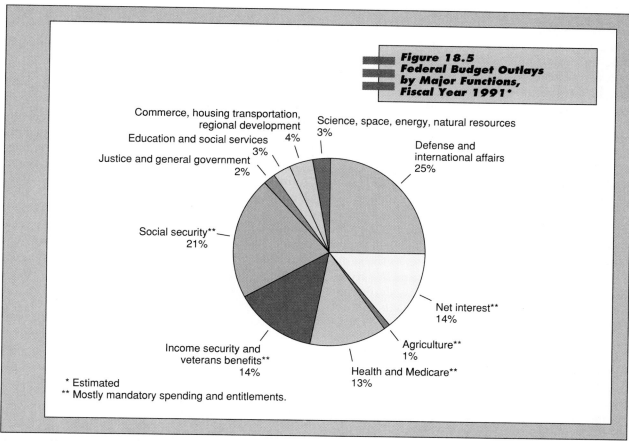

**Figure 18.5
Federal Budget Outlays
by Major Functions,
Fiscal Year 1991***

Commerce, housing transportation, regional development 4%

Science, space, energy, natural resources 3%

Education and social services 3%

Justice and general government 2%

Defense and international affairs 25%

Social security** 21%

Net interest** 14%

Income security and veterans benefits** 14%

Agriculture** 1%

Health and Medicare** 13%

* Estimated
** Mostly mandatory spending and entitlements.

Source: Office of Management and Budget, *Budget of the United States Government Fiscal Year 1991* (Washington, D.C.: Government Printing Office, 1990), p. A-282.

may change if the Cold War thaws sufficiently to produce a substantial "peace dividend." The other big slices—social security, medical programs, and income security (that is, for example, veterans' benefits and federal pensions)—involve entitlements. These activities, which constitute nearly half the total, fall into the "uncontrollable" category mentioned previously. Because Americans regard these programs as fundamental public commitments, because they help so many citizens, and because they enjoy such widespread popularity, both the executive and legislature find it politically dangerous to cut them. Interest payments on the national debt, one of the fastest-growing items, *has* to be paid, so no cuts can be made there.

With entitlements and interest (more than half of all federal budget outlays) largely off limits, policymakers have relatively little leeway to adjust spending levels. Moreover, the remaining portion, which Congress has the option of cutting in the appropriation stage, includes some of the most essential and popular public activities, such as defense, law enforcement, aid to education, and environmental protection. Even if they were chopped in half—an unthinkable option—the savings would amount to no more than a fraction of total outlays.

THE GRAMM-RUDMAN-HOLLINGS ACT For all these reasons politicians have been hard pressed to cap federal spending, and by the middle of the 1980s budget politics had reached an impasse. After the tax cuts of 1981, Washington began running up enormous deficits. At the same time, spending rose under the impetus of entitlements. Equally important, Congress could not agree on what to axe. Each side in each conflict seemed strong enough to veto the other's proposals. Almost no one had the nerve to advocate tax increases. Not even President Reagan, popular as he was, could break the stalemate.

Pushed by desperation and frustration, Congress finally responded by passing the Balanced Budget and Emergency Deficit Control Act of 1985, better known as the **Gramm-Rudman-Hollings Act** after its sponsors Senators Phil Gramm (Republican of Texas), Warren Rudman

(Republican of New Hampshire), and Ernest Hollings (Democrat of South Carolina). Its authors designed the bill to force the president and legislature to do what they were not doing voluntarily, balance the budget.

The act's purpose is to reduce the budget deficit to zero by 1993.* This objective was to be reached in steps: In the first year (1986) the deficit had to be reduced to $172 billion, to $144 billion in 1987, and so on. If the White House and Capitol Hill cannot agree on the cuts by a certain date, they are to be made automatically according to a specific and inflexible formula in a process known as *sequestration*. Although the act exempts certain programs (such as Social Security and interest on the debt), the automatic reductions are to be split evenly between defense and domestic spending, with each category being cut by the same percentage. Policymakers have little or no flexibility in the matter; apart from a few (but major) exceptions, virtually every federal undertaking is on the chopping block.

Critics worry that the bill tosses judgment and discretion to the wind. Truly vital activities will be trimmed as much as nonessential projects. The Pentagon, for example, fears that its cuts will come no matter how hostile the international scene. The military buildup in the Persian Gulf in late 1990 confirmed these fears. Even more significant to some economists, Gramm-Rudman-Hollings makes no provision for economic conditions. In a severe recession, a deficit might be beneficial if it stimulates aggregate demand.† The act's supporters counter by pointing out that Congress had almost bankrupted the country and simply lacked the discipline to change its ways.

How well has the law worked? Nearly everyone agrees that federal spending is lower than it would otherwise have been. Two of its sponsors, Senators Gramm and Rudman, admit it is not perfect but caution: "Just as we don't judge the

---

*The original target date was 1991 but was changed partly because Congress could not meet the deadline.
†Lawmakers can vote to suspend the Gramm-Rudman-Hollings cuts if economic growth is low for two successive quarters.

From left, Senators Warren Rudman, Philip Gramm, and Ernest Hollings, authors of legislation requiring Congress and the president to reduce the federal budget deficit in stages to zero by 1993. If agreement on a level for a given year is not reached by October, across-the-board cuts are made automatically.

success of religion by the number of saints but by whether the world is better off, so we should judge Gramm-Rudman-Hollings."[27]

Yet the Gramm-Rudman-Hollings Act has not been a panacea. Many reductions have been achieved by dubious accounting procedures (a favorite is to speed up certain tax collections), by the sale of government holdings (once they are sold they cannot be resold), by pushing the cost of programs forward or backward in time (on one occasion Congress switched the military payday from the first day of the month to the last), and by moving certain activities off-budget (as in the case of the S & L bailout). Nor has the act forced a consensus between Democrats and Republicans on spending and revenue priorities.

What is important, though, is that both political parties adhere to the act's underlying philosophy: Runaway deficits threaten economic stability and have to be stopped. Since that view dominates discussions of economic policy, it is worth asking how bad the situation really is.

How Bad <u>Are</u> Budget Deficits?

No doubt nine out of ten newspaper editors, civic leaders, and ordinary citizens rank the federal budget deficit along with famine and pestilence. Likening the government to a family, they are convinced Washington lives far beyond its means and sooner or later the roof will cave in. Mainstream economists, though, warn against overly simplistic comparisons of the government and households. Public and private finances differ considerably, and it is easy to misunderstand the nature and consequences of deficits. Indeed, a few economic analysts question the seriousness of deficits and debts. Most economists, on the other hand, still maintain that deficits are a major threat to America's economic health, although not for the reasons commonly mentioned. Since economic policy for the rest of the 1990s will turn on how decision makers handle budget deficits, it is worth hearing both sides of the story.

THE NATURE AND SIZE OF THE PUBLIC DEBT

First, let's not forget that public spending is an important macroeconomic tool. We noted earlier that federal expenditures or tax cuts stimulate aggregate demand. In the middle of a recession, this "pump priming" helps the economy get back on its feet, and running a deficit is generally considered a wise policy.

Second, the size of deficits has to be judged in relative, not absolute, terms. A train carrying a trillion dollars might stretch for miles, but one holding all of America's national income would stretch hundreds of miles farther. One way to estimate the magnitude of the government's indebtedness is to compare it to the gross national product (GNP). As a percentage of GNP, the deficit in 1950 was 1.2 percent; in 1980 it had grown slightly to 2.8 percent; by 1983 it was up to 6.3, but afterwards declined somewhat (see Figure 18.2). Briefly stated, federal deficits at their worst have been only a small fraction of the country's total national product.

Third, the budget is difficult to understand not simply because of its size and complexity but also because of the accounting practices that go into its presentation. The United States maintains a "cash" budget that only reports cash transactions. It does not, for example, record *capital assets*. True, over the years Washington amassed a debt of more than $2 trillion. What tends to be overlooked, however, is that it possesses a vast range of assets worth billions of dollars. The federal government, for example, owns millions of acres of timber and grazing land, offshore oil deposits, hundreds of thousands of square feet of prime office space, and countless other holdings. We should, therefore, measure not simply the accumulated gross national debt, the number most frequently cited in the media, but the *net debt*, the difference between what is owed and what is owned, just as any modern business does. Robert Eisner, an economist, points out that America's net debt is substantially smaller than the gross debt.[28]

Fourth, Eisner describes another shortcoming in the way people typically portray debt figures. The most accurate measure of the public debt is its *market value*. Most homeowners discover that paying off their mortgages becomes easier with each passing year. Why? Because inflation pushes up wages and salaries while monthly mortgage payments stay about the same. Someone who borrowed $30,000 in 1970 felt the payments were an enormous load, but by 1990 the burden of such a mortgage was considerably less.

The same general principle, Eisner argues, holds for the government. The nominal or face value of the national debt has to be discounted because of inflation. He shows that when this adjustment is made, the *real value* of the net federal debt steadily dropped from 1945 to 1980 by about 58 percent.[29]

Finally, economists point out that just as in the private sphere one person's debt is another's wealth, government borrowing adds to overall income. After all, many Americans count government savings bonds among their safest assets. As Eisner and Paul Pieper explain, the public is responsible for the federal debt, but "it is also the public itself which would be paid off and which receives the interest payments."[30]

In short, it is easy to misperceive the problem. People imagine a bill collector suddenly appearing on the steps of the Capitol to declare the country bankrupt and send future generations to debtor's prisons. But government is in a different position than a family or a business. Its creditors—the banks, institutions, and individuals who hold federal securities—belong to the same community from which it extracts its resources in the form of taxes. Up until the 1980s, when foreigners began investing heavily in American assets, Washington did not transfer funds to outside parties; it simply moved them from one group (taxpayers) to another (security and bond holders), both of which lived in the same nation.[31]

THE REAL DANGERS OF DEFICITS Conceding that Eisner and others make valid points, most economists nevertheless worry that when the federal government piles up deficits year after year, especially when the economy is reasonably robust, it causes the country grave problems.

Whenever the Treasury writes a check that it cannot cover with its own funds, it borrows to make up the difference. But, of course, society does not have an unlimited supply of capital from which to borrow. Whatever is available comes from savings, and in a period of large deficits businesses, individuals, and the government all compete for this scarce resource. A respected economist, Charles Schultze, calculates that in the late 1980s private savings of households and corporations constituted about 6.5 percent of our national income. In the absence of deficits, this money could have financed investment in new factories, machines, technology, and the like—assets called capital stock. Yet because the government's books were so far out of balance, the *net* savings—the amount left over after subtracting the government's deficit—comprised less than 3 percent of total income.[32]

This fact greatly troubles Schultze and others since without adequate savings, investment falls, and without investment the capital stock that produces future wealth is not created. Sluggish investment, they fear, will inexorably lead to a decline in our standard of living. We, and especially the next generation, will live less well than our parents unless we revive the nearly stagnant growth in investment and productivity.[33]

Public indebtedness raises problems of another sort. During the Reagan years the deficits caused by huge tax cuts and enormous growth in military spending should have overheated the economy, causing prices to soar. But inflation did not get out of hand. In fact, it fell. No one has a complete solution to this mystery, but part of the answer lies in the massive infusion of capital from overseas. Foreigners found ideal investment opportunities in the United States: They received high rates of return on their money, and political and social stability made them feel their assets were safe. Generous interest rates and stability have therefore attracted billions of dollars in foreign investments. This influx of funds has, in effect, helped pay for the deficit and compensate for the shortfall in investment and savings.

This dependence may turn out to be a time bomb, however. Large-scale foreign investments inevitably mean that a sizable share of our income has to go abroad for interest payments. (This undercuts the argument made above about

Japanese ownership of assets in the United States, such as the purchase of Rockefeller Center in New York City, convinces many economists that America relies too heavily on foreign investments to pay for its budget deficits.

the government owing only to Americans.) Worse still, if Japanese, German, and other investors decide to slow down or stop the transfer of capital, America could be in for a rough landing: We will be confronted with sharply climbing prices and interest rates and a declining standard of living. We will also have to find ways to increase savings and investments, and that means keeping the budget deficit down. But a reduced deficit can be achieved only by painful tax increases or cuts in popular programs or both.

Checkpoint

- The federal government raises the bulk of its revenues from individual and social security contributions.

- In the past, the tax rates were theoretically progressive, meaning that the rich supposedly paid more than the middle class and poor. In fact, however, tax loopholes meant that different income groups paid about the same rates.

- The Tax Reform Act of 1986 reduced the number of tax brackets from 14 to 2 and eliminated many loopholes.

- Entitlements and interest payments on the national debt represent essentially "uncontrollable" expenditures; the discretionary part of the budget is relatively small.

- The Gramm-Rudman-Hollings Act requires automatic, across-the-board cuts in domestic and military spending if the deficit is not lowered to prescribed ceilings in each year.

- Considerable controversy and misunderstanding exist about deficits and the debt. During recessions deficits help revive the economy. The government, furthermore, possesses billions of dollars of assets which partially offset its financial obligations, and, when adjusted for inflation, the national debt seems less onerous than commonly supposed. Besides, government borrowing adds to the public's income.

- Persistent deficits, however, pose dangers. They absorb savings and stifle investment. A sudden reversal of foreign investments, which have partly financed the government's borrowing, would drive up interest rates and prices and threaten America's standard of living.

ECONOMIC POLICYMAKING: WHO GOVERNS?

Because of its widespread effects, economic management tops everyone's list of government's responsibilities. Who, then, makes these fundamental decisions? The best way to find out is to look carefully at the main participants: the president, the Congress, the Federal Reserve System, and the public.

The President

As nationally elected public servants constantly living in the limelight, presidents function as the lightning rods of American politics. Regardless of the problem or its causes, they take the blame for our misfortunes. When unemployment or inflation goes up, all eyes turn toward the Oval Office; when farms and small businesses fail, their owners look to the White House for relief; when the stock market crashes, millions of investors ask the chief executive why; when imports force workers out of their jobs, they ask the president to get tough with foreign producers.

It is, of course, true that presidents wield extraordinary powers. They employ hundreds of economists, accountants, lawyers, and planners; the prestige of their office gives them national visibility; they have access to reams of technical information; they head their political parties and theoretically, at least, command the federal bureaucracy. American presidents, to put it mildly, have their hands on numerous tools for directing economic policy.

Yet making these instruments work together is a herculean task. Bureaucrats, as we have seen, commonly defy presidential directives. More important, presidents frequently find themselves working at cross-purposes with other institutions such as the Congress and Federal Reserve. As a consequence, the presidency usually receives more blame (or credit) than it deserves given the severe constraints on its authority.

THE PRESIDENT'S ECONOMIC POWERS Although the Constitution limits the president's duties to ensuring that the "laws be faithfully executed," the office has gradually assumed a major role in the enactment of those laws. This increase in power is particularly evident in budgeting.

Prior to World War I, presidents had few fiscal responsibilities. Those agencies needing funds took their requests directly to Congress. No overall supervision of spending and taxing existed, primarily because these activities constituted a minuscule part of the economy. Today, by contrast, the president sets the agenda for the entire process. By law the chief executive must submit a "Budget of the United States Government" to Congress. Though this document is considerably modified in the following months, it establishes the tone and framework for economic debates during the year.

In addition to the White House staff, three bodies assist the president in preparing the budget proposal: the Office of Management and Budget (OMB), the secretary of the treasury, and the Council of Economic Advisors.

The OMB has principal responsibility for drafting the president's spending and revenue requests. Although OMB's position depends on what a president wants to make of it, it is potentially one of the most powerful agencies in the bureaucracy. Budget examiners in OMB carefully screen proposals from the federal departments, and they can trim or eliminate items they consider out of line with the president's goals. This command of the budget gives OMB enormous political leverage in dealing with Congress and the bureaucracy.

The Treasury Department performs a wide variety of services, ranging from protecting high-ranking government officials and their families (the Secret Service) to collecting taxes (the Internal Revenue Service) to printing money. Its main function, however, is to manage the nation's finances. When Congress authorizes an increase in the national debt, for example, the Treasury decides what mixture of bonds, bills, and notes to issue.

Most presidents rely heavily on the treasury secretary for assistance in developing policies and selling them to Congress, the public, and even foreign governments. Because they have access to the inner sanctums of the White House

and because they maintain close ties to large corporations and financial communities, these men (no woman has ever held the post) are among the most powerful on the scene.

The third group in charge of assisting the president is the Council of Economic Advisors. Composed mostly of academic economists, the council provides technical advice to the president and prepares the annual "Economic Report," another document that partially sets the policy agenda. Even though the council is usually led by a prestigious economist who commands the attention of the media, this organization's power depends on the wishes of the president. During the Reagan years it stood in the background; in the Bush administration it seems to have more influence.

All these institutions and individuals, together with the prestige of the presidency and its constitutional right to veto appropriations or revenue bills, give the White House enormous leverage in making fiscal policy. Naturally, then, people look to the president for solutions to economic crises. Yet in reality each of these resources can thwart presidential ambitions as much as advance them. Obviously, a president leads a large staff and has access to mounds of data. But at the same time the bureaucracy can be unruly. Most departments and bureaus have strong friends in congressional committees and interest groups. The White House staff or the OMB cannot always easily direct a rebellious agency to cut its budget, since bureaucrats have strategies for protecting pet projects. For example, when OMB asks an agency to cut its spending requests, the agency can propose reductions in programs that it knows are popular in Congress. When the budget finally reaches Capitol Hill, legislators usually restore these funds.

Equally frustrating to presidential control, perhaps, are the fights among the heads of OMB, Council of Economic Advisors, and the Treasury, frequently over basic means and ends. The Reagan administration, for example, was split between those who championed supply-side economics and those who advocated more orthodox approaches.

Hence, instead of ruling by fiat, presidents devote considerable time to cajoling recalcitrant

OMB Director Richard Darman (left) and Treasury Secretary Nicholas Brady (right) have authority to manage the government's fiscal policies. But Brady's expression says it all: politics and economics have made budget planning a daunting if not impossible task.

bureaucrats, refereeing disputes, and negotiating compromises. Moreover, the visibility of the office both strengthens and weakens it. For while presidents can appear before nationwide audiences to plead their cases, they cannot avoid being the center of attention during hard times. Just as major league managers lose their jobs for the failings of their players, chief executives often take the blame for events they did not create and cannot control.

Finally, the veto or even the threat of one is a potent weapon. But Congress can override a veto directly by a two-thirds vote in each chamber, or it can pass a "veto-proof" bill. American presidents, unlike most state governors, lack a *line-item veto*, which would give them the right to reject parts of a piece of legislation, not all of it. Consequently, lawmakers who anticipate trouble winning presidential approval of an appropriation sometimes try to attach provisions that either the president strongly supports or have

widespread public backing. The president is then caught in a dilemma: Accept the package in its entirety, or veto it and lose the desirable as well as objectionable parts.

HOLDING THE PRESIDENT ACCOUNTABLE All these factors—the intractability of the bureaucracy, squabbling among advisers, living in a fishbowl, and the limitations on the use of vetoes—weaken the president's hand. The White House also has to contend with unexpected and uncontrollable events. The voters tossed Jimmy Carter out of office in 1980 partly because of high interest rates, inflation, and unemployment. Yet he alone could hardly have been responsible for *all* of these maladies. Petroleum-exporting countries, for example, nearly doubled the price of oil in a short space of time. This action, as much as anything the Carter administration did, accounted for the huge leap in prices that doomed his presidency.

Considerations like these encourage many observers to believe that pluralism best describes economic policymaking. Indeed, however powerful the White House has become, the shackles on its effectiveness call into question the idea of a power elite. The central role of Congress lends additional credence to this argument.

Congress

Congress's influence on the economy stems from its power of the purse. The Constitution gives the legislative branch the right to collect taxes, to "coin" money and regulate its value, and to borrow from the public.

When spending the taxpayers' dollars, Congress goes through two separate steps: first, an **authorization** establishes a program, identifies its goals, and determines its spending limits. But an authorization does not actually allocate any money. That occurs in the next step, **appropriations**, which provide an agency with the funds it needs to carry out the specific activities. In a manner of speaking, then, Congress has to approve a program twice, once in the authorization stage and once again in appropriations.

Considering their hold on the purse strings, one might think that legislators would have the final word on fiscal affairs. Their influence is formidable to be sure, but they nonetheless experience considerable difficulty in exerting this power. A close examination of the budget process reveals why.

CONGRESS AND THE BUDGET Before 1974 the president sent an annual budget message to Congress, which instead of debating it as a whole assigned different sections to about a dozen appropriations committees. As each committee finished its work, the full House or Senate voted on its specific recommendations. Only at the end of the entire process could outlays be compared with income, and by then it was too late to reconcile any differences. Besides running sizable deficits each year, the slow and cumbersome budget machinery often delayed the passage of appropriations until long after the start of a fiscal year. To bridge these gaps Congress resorted to *continuing resolutions*, temporary legislation allowing departments to continue spending at their current rates until a permanent bill could be enacted.

In the late 1960s, when inflation and deficits became too large to ignore, President Nixon began *impounding* funds, that is, refusing to spend money appropriated by Congress. The practice infuriated both Democrats and Republicans who interpreted it as an unconstitutional intrusion on their powers. Nonetheless, they had to admit the President had a point. House and Senate committees made decisions piecemeal and seldom finished their work on time. The reliance on continuing resolutions and stopgap appropriations as well as the persistent inability to balance the budget upset not just the President but nearly everyone else as well.[34]

THE BUDGET AND IMPOUNDMENT ACT OF 1974 After years of study and several bruising legislative-executive battles, Congress finally passed the **Budget and Impoundment Act of 1974**. Both ends of Pennsylvania Avenue won something. The 1974 act created a Congressional Budget Office (CBO), giving legislators the staff of economists and policy analysts they felt they needed to compete with the president's advisers. It also curtailed the president's authority to impound congressionally appropriated funds.

At the same time, however, the act required Congress to put its own house in order. In particular, it laid down a fixed schedule for decision making and established two budget committees, one in each chamber. Each year these committees draft a **budget resolution**. The resolution spells out Congress's economic goals, sets revenues and spending limits, and instructs various committees to adjust programs within their jurisdictions to the resolution's objectives. A Closer Look gives the details of the budget process as amended by the Gramm-Rudman-Hollings Act (see pp. 596–597).

Both the 1974 act and the Gramm-Rudman-Hollings Act attempted to force Congress to match ends to means and to finish its work on time. Did the reforms succeed?

Nearly everyone agrees that the changes have brought positive results. The Congressional Budget Office and two budget committees (both

A Closer Look

The Congressional Budget Process ★ ★ ★

As amended by the Gramm-Rudman-Hollings legislation, the 1974 Budget Act theoretically requires Congress and the president to make fiscal policy in an orderly and timely manner. Under the act, Congress and the president are supposed to follow a series of steps in developing and enacting the federal budget:[a]

- By mid-January the president submits a budget for the next fiscal year. (A fiscal year starts on October 1.) The president's recommendations must include estimates of total revenues and outlays, indicators of economic performance, and a statement about "current services"—that is, the money needed to keep federal operations running at their present levels.

- Both the Senate and the House must then pass a *concurrent budget resolution* by April 15. This action, which does not require the president's signature, embodies Congress's economic priorities and plans. It specifies total budget expenditures and commitments, recommends revenue targets, estimates the budget surplus or deficit and cumulative national debt, and places dollar limits on specific appropriations.
- The budget resolution also contains *reconciliation instructions* that direct committees to adjust authorizations, appropriations, and taxes to bring them into line with spending ceilings and revenue floors. After the resolution with its rec-

of which have their own sizable staffs) give lawmakers expertise and data comparable to the president's. More important, members now have to look at the budget as a whole, not just the bits and pieces of special interest to them.

At the same time, however, everyone realizes that the process does not function nearly as smoothly as its designers intended or hoped. No matter how streamlined the process may look on paper, power remains dispersed among many committees and subcommittees. This diffusion of power means congressional leaders and the president have difficulty making the various groups work together. Briefly put, the budget reforms enacted since 1974 have not transcended the inherent fragmentation of authority that exists within Congress and between it and the executive.

Because bitter fights between and within parties continue to characterize decision making,

Congress seldom meets the statutory deadlines. It's supposed to pass 13 separate appropriations before the start of the fiscal year (October 1), but in practice, it hardly ever does. Indeed, it gets so far behind that it lumps many appropriations together in a gigantic "omnibus" money bill, catchall legislation that includes funds for several departments and bureaus.

Congress also distorts the reconciliation process. When the budget law was first enacted, a reconciliation bill was intended to be a vehicle for making small adjustments in spending and revenues so that overall budget totals would agree with the targets mandated by the budget resolution. But in 1989, to take a recent case, the reconciliation bill considered by the House—a 2000-page document—included a significant revision in capital gains taxes, repeal of a major health insurance program, a ban on telephone pornography, a new federally funded child care

onciliation instructions passes Congress in the spring, committees and subcommittees get down to the business of writing the particular bills. There are 13 different appropriations bills, each of which requires approval by both houses and the president.

- After the appropriations committees have finished their work, Congress has to pass a *reconciliation bill*. The 1974 act originally intended this legislation to be a simple and routine way to adjust the budget so that its totals matched the goals set out in the budget resolution. By 1981, though, reconciliation bills had become all-encompassing acts that contain an astounding variety of proposals.

- Finally, if by October 1 Congress has failed to agree on a budget that lowers deficits to the levels mandated by the Gramm-Rudman-Hollings Act, sequestration begins.

These steps describe what Congress and the president are *supposed* to do. In practice, things do not work out this neatly, particularly since deadlines come and go without action.

[a]Stanley E. Collender, *The Guide to the Federal Budget Fiscal 1987* (Washington, D.C.: Urban Institute, 1986), chap. 2.

program, a tax on ozone-depleting chemicals, reinstatement of the fairness doctrine (a law requiring broadcasters to give equal time to opposing sides of controversial issues), and dozens of other items.[35] Because of the complex and controversial nature of these issues, none of which were germane to fine-tuning the budget, Congress missed its October 1 deadline. So frequently does Congress behave in this manner that a *New York Times* editorial called the budget process a "crazy way to govern the country."[36]

Crazy or not, budgeting bolsters the pluralists' contention about the dispersion of power throughout the system. The reason Congress has such trouble enacting coherent budgets on time, according to this line of reasoning, is its openness to interest groups. Business, labor, senior citizens, farm, and other lobbies have sufficient clout to protect their members' interests, regardless of budget timetables and guidelines.

Fiscal policy, which represents the sum of spending and taxing decisions, is thus subject to crosscutting pressures. Given these circumstances, one doubts that a power elite could be at work. The same conclusion may not hold for monetary policy, however, since it lies mainly within the jurisdiction of the Federal Reserve System, a shadowy quasi-public institution that elite theorists contend enjoys an almost incestuous relationship with major banks.

The Federal Reserve System

The Federal Reserve System, as mentioned earlier, dominates monetary policy, the control of the supply and cost of money. Since monetary policy affects every sector of the economy, the Fed has to be considered coequal with the president and Congress in macroeconomic decision making.

THE FED'S STRUCTURE   The Federal Reserve System consists of a seven-member board of directors in Washington, D.C., and 12 regional banks, each controlled by its own directors. These regional institutions, owned by commercial banks within their jurisdictions, only do business with the Treasury and their member banks, not with the public at large. They do not lend money for automobiles or homes, and their main assets are U.S. government securities (such as Treasury bonds). The Federal Reserve banks also perform a variety of services for other banks such as check processing and storing and distributing cash.[37] All national and state chartered banks are subject to Federal Reserve supervision and regulation.

The *Federal Reserve Board of Governors* oversees the entire system. The president appoints six of the governors (subject to Senate confirmation) to 14-year terms and the board's chair to a 4-year term. (The president's and chair's terms of office do not overlap, however.)

THE FED'S OPERATIONS   Even though the Constitution authorizes the government to mint money, it would be impractical to control its supply by speeding up or slowing down the printing presses. After all, if enough were printed it would soon be worthless. It is also impractical to tie the value of paper money to precious commodities such as gold or silver, since the supply of these commodities does not always stay even with economic growth. Governments discovered that when these metals didn't keep pace with growth there was usually insufficient currency to finance investment and consumption. Therefore, the Fed relies on its legal authority to manipulate *fiat money*: paper currency, coins, funds in checking and savings accounts, and other legally accepted forms of exchange.

The Federal Reserve System manages the money supply in three ways:

1 **Reserve ratios.**   Banks are required to maintain a certain proportion of their deposits as a "reserve" against potential withdrawals. By

The Federal Reserve building. The Fed, which is charged with managing monetary policy, is one of Washington's most powerful institutions but is relatively little known and understood by the general public.

varying this amount, called the *reserve ratio*, the Fed controls the quantity of money in circulation. Suppose, for example, it orders banks to hang on to an extra 1 percent of their deposits. They would then have 1 percent less to lend. One percent may not sound like a lot, but it translates into billions of dollars that are siphoned out of the economy.

2   **Discount rate.** When banks temporarily overcommit themselves, they occasionally have to borrow from the Fed to secure the necessary funds to meet their reserve requirements. The interest rate charged for these loans is the *discount rate*, and it too affects the money supply. If the Fed raises the discount rate, banks cannot afford to borrow as heavily as before and have to curtail their lending and raise their own interest rates. That results in less money flowing into the economy. Conversely, if the Fed relaxes its discount rate, financial institutions have more dollars for their customers. Seen from this perspective, the discount rate has a snowball effect: Raising it means that other interest rates go up as well and, other things being equal, economic activity slows down; lowering it has the opposite effect.

3   **Open-market operations.** By far the most important of the Fed's activities are *open-market operations*, the buying and selling of government securities. After Congress approves an increase in the national debt, the Treasury Department prepares a mix of bonds, bills, and notes that it auctions to private dealers who are authorized to trade government securities. When it wants to influence economic activity, the Fed buys or sells these assets through its Federal Open Market Committee (FOMC) or open-market desk, as it is commonly known.

The process works this way: If the Fed decides to increase the money supply, its open-market manager buys back treasury securities from private dealers, paying for them by simply crediting their bank accounts. It does not transfer any actual cash. (This power distinguishes it from all other financial institutions and gives it its clout.) The dealers' banks now have more money to lend, and these loans ultimately find their way into more banks, which pass a portion of them on to additional borrowers. The Fed's initial purchase thus has a multiplier effect as money ripples throughout the economy. Of course, the process is reversed when the Fed sells off some of its securities, because it in effect deducts the price from the purchasers' accounts, leaving their banks with fewer deposits.

The main idea is that the Fed's accounting maneuvers, not switching the printing presses on and off, produce increases or decreases in the money supply.

THE FED AND THE POLITICAL SYSTEM How you interpret the Fed in relation to our models of who governs depends on how much independence from political influence you think the system has. On paper the Federal Reserve System appears to be relatively autonomous, since it receives its operating revenues from its constituent banks, not from congressional appropriations, and since its governors, once in office, cannot be dismissed by the president. The governors' long terms mean that an occupant of the White House cannot expect to pick a majority of the governors. The Fed, moreover, conducts its meetings in private and is under no legal obligation to report to the executive branch. Given these conditions, one might think it could escape public accountability altogether.

Yet the Fed is also the creation of Congress, which takes a strong interest in its work and can always amend its charter. Furthermore, as a practical matter, the Fed's officers have to interact daily with senior executives in the Treasury Department, the OMB, and other agencies. The chair frequently testifies before legislative committees and regularly consults with the president's staff. All members of the board of governors realize the value of maintaining support at both ends of Pennsylvania Avenue because they know determined political opposition can undercut their policies. In short, the Federal Reserve's statutory independence does not immunize it from political pressures.

The ill-defined boundaries between the Fed and the rest of the Washington establishment leads to endless debates about its autonomy. Some observers emphasize the Fed's political nature, arguing that it pays close attention to the desires of the White House. Presidents normally want the money supply to flow freely enough to keep the economy booming and will pressure the Fed to achieve that result. Members of the board do not want to antagonize the chief executive and, if pressed, often cave in.

Some political economists go even further: They detect a **political monetary cycle** (PMC), during which the Fed relaxes monetary policy in the months before a presidential or congressional election, hoping that business will pick up and thus make the incumbent president's party shine in the eyes of the electorate. As soon as the campaign ends, however, it tightens the screws again to hold down inflation. According to this interpretation, the Fed rhythmically starts and stops the economy for partisan purposes.[38] If true, the existence of a PMC would suggest that the Fed is at least indirectly accountable to the people, as democratic theorists hope.

Others, however, doubt the Fed's susceptibility to presidential influence and question the whole PMC concept. It seems unlikely, they claim, that the Fed would act so blatantly on anyone's behalf because such partisan behavior would tarnish its reputation in financial circles for competence and objectivity. It is also doubtful whether the Fed has sufficient data and knowledge to fine-tune the supply of money on short notice. Monetarism, in the last analysis, is a broadsword, not a scalpel, and cannot be wielded with the precision assumed by the PMC hypothesis. Finally, several empirical studies dispute the existence of a political monetary cycle.[39] One economist said that he could not uncover a "single episode . . . in the Fed's history to suggest that [it] had bowed to presidential election pressures, and a lot of episodes to suggest that it resists them."[40]

If the Federal Reserve System avoids the tugs of partisanship, what factors do affect its actions? It could be argued that it has many of the trappings of a power elite. Superficially, at any rate, it meets many of the criteria of C. Wright Mills and others outlined in Chapter 1. In the first place, monetary policy is by any reasonable standard a trunk decision. The availability of money and magnitude of interest rates affect employment, prices, savings, investment, growth, and productivity and hence touch the lives of everyone from the smallest consumer to the largest corporation. These policies are developed and enforced by the Fed's board of governors and its operating arm, the FOMC, two tiny, nonelected groups of men and women with close connections to the banking and financial communities. Indeed, the background of the Fed's highest officers is one of its most distinguishing features. Though many of them come from modest origins, they have spent the bulk of their careers in major banks and Wall Street investment firms and many, like former Fed Chairman Paul Volcker, have shuttled back and forth between jobs in these private financial institutions and important positions in the U.S. government.

Spending one's life in banking, business, and commerce creates the sorts of loyalties the power elite school predicts. One expert, who does not necessarily accept the power elite thesis, nonetheless lends it credibility when he writes that "Federal Reserve officials work in a milieu that is significantly shaped by the interests and concerns of the commercial banks."[41]

In brief, as much as fiscal policymaking seems to conform to the pluralist interpretation of American politics, monetary policy approximates the power elite model. Yet before accepting either of these theories, we need to see what influence the public as a whole exerts.

The People

The pluralist and elite schools find plenty of support for their theories in the workings of the presidency, Congress, and the Fed. But what about ordinary citizens? What role, if any, do they play in economic policymaking? In a direct democracy, men and women would decide for themselves which monetary and fiscal policies the nation should follow; in a well-functioning representative system they would choose among candidates who stood for clearly defined and articulated alternatives. How close does the United States come to these ideals?

Many political scientists find a connection between voting and the performance of the economy. As Chapter 11 pointed out, some voters take their own or the country's financial status into account when casting a ballot, a behavior called retrospective voting. If voters do vote retrospectively, officeholders have incentives to attempt to manipulate the economy to create at least the appearance of economic growth and stability. Seen in this light, public control takes the form of anticipated action: Congress and the president act in anticipation of reward for success and punishment for failure.

Taking this line of reasoning a step further, a handful of public opinion analysts see a **political business cycle** (PBC), analogous to the political monetary cycle.[42] According to this theory, in the months before an election incumbents try to create the illusion, if not the reality, of a humming economy by increasing public spending, taxing less, and incurring large budget deficits. In nonelection years, they reverse direction to hold down inflation. Consequently, fiscal policy swings back and forth between expansion and contraction.

Statements about retrospective voting and the political business cycle are only theories. Still, one can easily find supporting evidence. In 1987, for example, Congress realized that it would not be able to meet the deficit reduction targets mandated by the Gramm-Rudman-Hollings Act without slashing spending on many popular programs. Not wanting to abandon the Budget Act completely—that too would have been unpopular—the lawmakers voted to postpone the reductions so that the severest cuts would occur *after* the 1988 elections.[43]

Recall also that the two major parties have different centers of gravity in economic affairs.[44] Democrats, as we pointed out earlier, tend to prefer stimulative policies to encourage employment and productivity even at the risk of higher prices, whereas Republicans generally favor tighter money to prevent inflation and will tolerate moderate unemployment. Considered as a whole, parties do seem to offer a choice to the electorate.

The impact of popular control can be easily exaggerated, though. For every study showing the existence of a PBC, there is another that refutes it.[45] After all, the idea that politicians can easily manipulate the economy is hard to swallow. Fiscal policy is difficult, if not impossible, to manage in a manner that will assist incumbents. The effects of a tax cut, for instance, may be unpredictable, slow in arriving, or counterbalanced by the Fed's actions. Furthermore, there may be disagreement about the best way to expand the economy. Moreover, as we saw in an earlier section, many hands hold the levers of fiscal policy: the president, the committees of Congress, the bureaucracy, interest groups, and lobbies. Making these institutions work together is exceedingly difficult, so how could the economy be manipulated in the way the PBC hypothesis proposes? Therefore, regardless of whether people reward success and punish failure, neither the president nor legislators may be able to exert sufficient control over events to guarantee their reelection.

But even if there is a connection between voting and economic performance, this form of government is a far cry from the tenets of democracy sketched in Chapter 1. It is one thing for political leaders to keep a watchful eye on their constituents; it is quite another for them to be held accountable in a democratic sense. Accountability does not mean that voters intermittently reward or punish officeholders. Instead, accountability rests on reasoned and informed judgments about what is desirable and practical. (The people elected Reagan in 1984 and Bush in 1988 apparently because the economy *seemed* to be in fine shape. Yet plenty of experts saw enormous dangers lurking beneath the surface. Were the voters mindful of these possibilities as they entered the polling place?) Of course, meaningful accountability is not possible unless the parties, candidates, and media thoroughly and clearly air the policy choices.

Using these ideas as a benchmark, many democratic theorists argue that economic policymaking in the United States leaves a lot to be desired. Most Americans do not grasp the main outlines, much less the intricacies, of current economic debates. But their ignorance may not be entirely their fault. An enormous chunk of the policymaking process—monetary policy—takes place far from the public's view. When the Fed tightens money, everyone feels the effects, but only a tiny fraction have more than a vague idea of how and why the change was made. Indeed, the Federal Reserve's board of governors does not answer to the electorate in any direct way. While Fed Chairman Paul Volcker was leading the fight against inflation in the early 1980s, for example, his name seldom, if ever, came up in campaign speeches.

Even in the area of fiscal policy, the public's control of representatives is perhaps more tenuous than the retrospective and PBC ideas suggest. The budget process is so fragmented and complicated that the average citizen cannot be expected to hold particular representatives or senators accountable for its results. And while parties as a whole may stand for different economic philosophies, individual office seekers frequently obscure their positions (recall the "strategy of ambiguity" mentioned in Chapter 11) and utter symbolic appeals ("Good jobs at good wages," for instance) without mentioning the specific and usually painful actions that will have to be taken to reach these goals. And, as we have repeatedly contended, the mass media do not fully inform their audiences about the substance of various government policies. For all of these reasons it is possible that economic policymaking does not fit the democratic model very well.

which it has little or no control; and Congress, through its power of the purse, can thwart presidential plans.

- For years congressional decision making has been slow, cumbersome, and disorganized. In spite of reforms, the process still does not work smoothly. Since the budget process seems so wide open, it fits the criteria of pluralism.

- The Federal Reserve System manages monetary policy. Although it is sensitive to political pressures, the Fed seems to act independently of the White House and the Congress. In many respects its governors fit the mold of a power elite.

- The public has an indirect say in economic policymaking, since elected officials must be mindful of how voters will react to economic conditions. Nevertheless, the democratic model does not fit economic policymaking very well.

Checkpoint

- The main influences on economic policy are the presidency, the Congress, the Federal Reserve System, and the public.

- The president's economic powers stem from access to experts and data, nominal control of the bureaucracy, the visibility and prestige of the presidency, and the veto and other constitutional and statutory powers.

- Yet many of these factors frequently work against presidential ambitions: the bureaucracy, with a mind of its own, is difficult to control; the visibility of the presidency attracts blame for events over

SUMMARY

The federal government attempts to stabilize the economy with both fiscal policy—using taxes and spending to stimulate business and employment—and monetary policy—the control of the supply and cost of money. In the period after World War II, fiscal or Keynesian policy was at the peak of its popularity, and the economy boomed, making possible the rapid growth in social programs. In the 1970s inflation, unemployment, and budget deficits brought a slowdown in these activities.

Reaganomics, President Reagan's answer to the doldrums of the 1970s, consisted of tax cuts, increases in military spending, less government regulation, and reductions in domestic spending. His policies brought mixed results. On the one hand, unemployment and inflation fell, but at the same time budget deficits soared. Partly as a result of the budget constraints left over from the Reagan years, President Bush found making good on his campaign promises and dealing with unexpected events extremely difficult.

Most taxes are collected from individuals in the form of income and Social Security taxes. An enormous part of federal budget outlays is tied up in entitlements, defense spending, and interest on the debt. The discretionary portion is relatively small. Federal budget deficits are a serious but commonly misunderstood problem. Although it is simplistic to compare them to household finances, they do eat into domestic savings and investment, and many economists fear that they threaten America's standard of living.

The president, Congress, and the Federal Reserve System dominate economic policy. One can find support for both the pluralist and elitist theories in the way these institutions operate. Although some political scientists feel the people play an important role in economic policy, mainly by rewarding or punishing officeholders, their control is tenuous because many decisions are made behind the scenes, because the policy process is complex, and because choices are seldom openly and clearly debated.

KEY TERMS

Recession
Fiscal policy
Inflation
Keynesian theory
Monetary policy
The New Deal
Distributive policy
Disjointed
  incrementalism
Stagflation
Entitlement
Supply-side economics
Reaganomics

Progressive tax
Flat taxes
Gramm-Rudman-
  Hollings Act
Authorization
Appropriations
Budget and
  Impoundment Act
  of 1974
Budget resolution
Political monetary cycle
Political business cycle

FOR FURTHER READING

Stanley Collender, *The Guide to the Federal Budget Fiscal 1987* (Washington, D.C.: Urban Institute Press, 1986). An informative guide to the intricacies of the federal budget.

Robert Eisner, *How Real Is the Federal Deficit?* (New York: Free Press, 1986). Essential reading for those who think they know everything about budget deficits. Not all economists agree with Eisner's conclusions, but most respect his work.

Benjamin M. Friedman, *Day of Reckoning* (New York: Random House, 1988). Friedman describes the potentially disastrous consequences of Reaganomics.

Norman Frumkin, *Tracking America's Economy* (Armonk, N.Y.: M. E. Sharpe, 1987). Describes the interpretation of various economic indicators and statistics.

William Grieder, *The Secrets of the Temple* (New York: Simon & Schuster, 1988). A readable, lively, but controversial account of the workings of the Federal Reserve System.

Robert Heilbroner and Lester Thurow, *Economics Explained* (New York: Simon & Schuster, 1982). An enjoyable and simple introduction to economics by two respected economists.

Denise E. Markovich and Ronald E. Pynn, *American Political Economy* (Monterey, Calif.: Brooks/Cole, 1988). Provides a basic understanding of the American economic system.

Rudolph G. Penner and Alan J. Abramson, *Broken Purse Strings* (Washington, D.C.: Urban Institute Press, 1988). Penner and Abramson describe congressional budget procedures and make suggestions for reforms.

David Stockman, *The Triumph of Politics* (New York: Avon Books, 1987). Stockman, President Reagan's first director of the Office of Management and Budget, provides an inside but controversial view of the enactment of Reaganomics.

AND STILL THERE IS NO ROOM AT THE INN

THIRD·WORLD·AMERICA

Social Policy

Chapter 19

★ Major Social Policies Today
★ Evaluating the
   Effects of Social Policy
★ Social Policy:
   Who Governs?

Social policy is characterized by a general agreement that government is ultimately responsible for the welfare of people in society and intense disagreement over how best to achieve that goal. The development of—and ongoing debate over—major social policies such as Social Security, Medicare and Medicaid, food stamps, Aid to Families with Dependent Children, drug policies, aid to education, child care, AIDS treatment, and relief for the homeless reveal the sharp contrasts between the collectivist and individualist strands of the American political philosophy of general-welfare liberalism. ∎

In 1989 Congress took a second look at two acts it had passed the preceding year: the Medicare Catastrophic Coverage Act and the Family Support Act. These acts represented two of the most sweeping social policy reforms in U.S. history. The Medicare legislation had provided the largest expansion of Medicare benefits since the program was established in 1965. Most important, it extended benefits to more than 30 million elderly and disabled Americans for hospital and doctors' care for catastrophic illness. The Family Support Act had extensively overhauled the welfare system by tightening child support enforcement procedures, requiring states to implement job training and education programs, extending welfare payments to poor two-parent households (previously covered in only half the states), and providing child care and medical benefits to the families of those who leave the welfare rolls to take a job.

The reassessment of these acts just one year after they were passed was part of what one analyst called "a sea change in the prospects for social welfare legislation" in the 1990s:

> Elected officials and their staffs, as well as lobbyists and academicians who push for social programs, are asking fundamental questions about the nation's agenda for social policy and the tolerance of middle-class Americans for paying the costs.[1]

Social policy is the general term used for government attempts to improve the welfare of people who would otherwise be hurt by unregulated

social and economic forces. The preamble to the Constitution includes "to promote the general welfare" as one of the goals of government, and most people agree that government is responsible for the welfare of its citizens. However not everyone agrees on the best way to achieve that goal. That was clear in the debate over the health care and welfare reform legislation of 1988, and it will be evident in other areas of social policy discussed in this chapter.

President Reagan's approach to social policy focused on greatly reducing the federal government's role. This philosophy differed markedly from that of an earlier president, Lyndon Johnson, who hoped that his Great Society programs would free the country from "hopeless want." The strong rhetoric and stated goals of the Reagan administration led some observers and participants to characterize its social policy programs as "a large-scale rejection of the goals of the Great Society" and "a full frontal assault on the American welfare state."[2] President Bush called for more federal government involvement in social policy than his predecessor, but he shared an overall belief that economic growth and limited government intervention are the best ways to promote the general welfare.

The different approaches to social policy seen in President Johnson's Great Society programs and those of the Reagan and Bush administrations are, in fact, indicators of broader differences about governing America. The **individualism** reflected in Reagan and Bush administration policies is one of limited government intervention in the private economic market. In this view, government programs can provide a social safety net for those who need help, but the chief protector of a citizen's welfare is economic growth, which is best achieved by keeping government's hands off business. The Great Society programs of the 1960s, on the other hand, reflected **collectivism,** which regards government programs as necessary correctives to economic and political decisions that benefit some citizens at the expense of others.

Opinions about social policy reflect these broader conceptions of economics and politics, and we have organized the discussion of social policy in this chapter with that context in mind. The first section describes some of the major social policies of the United States and discusses recent trends. The second section takes a closer look at a key point of disagreement in the individual-collectivist debate: the *effects* of these social policies. The final section looks at democratic, pluralist, and power elite explanations of the politics of social policy.

MAJOR SOCIAL POLICIES TODAY

A scholar and student of welfare policies in both the United States and Europe has written: "At its core, the politics of social welfare is really an argument about how and where to strike a balance between individualism and collectivism."[3] A pastoral letter drafted by a group of Catholic bishops in 1985 illustrates the point. In urging Americans to rethink attitudes about welfare, the bishops called upon them "to move from our devotion to independence, through an understanding of interdependence, to a commitment to human solidarity."[4] The bishops' call for collectivism came at a time when the Reagan administration sought to move the country in the other direction, toward individualism. In order to understand the current social policy debate or to make judgments about a proper balance between the competing values of collectivism and individualism, it is first necessary to have some knowledge of existing social welfare policies in the United States. This section outlines some of the more important and representative of those

policies: Social Security, Medicare and Medicaid, food stamps, and Aid to Families with Dependent Children (AFDC).

Social Security

The Social Security Act of 1935 created a pension system for retired workers, an unemployment compensation program for those out of work, and an assistance program for the elderly, the blind, and needy children. The 1935 act was a direct response to the unemployment and poverty of the Great Depression. A series of major amendments greatly expanded the scope of the system by adding a Social Security disability program and a health insurance and medical assistance program and by "indexing" the system to the rate of inflation, allowing for automatic benefit increases. Today **Social Security** is the single largest domestic program of the federal government. One in every six Americans receives Social Security benefits, which total more than $240 billion annually.[5] About 90 percent of all workers are covered by Social Security.

The budgetary impact of Social Security and the number of people affected by it are enough to make it of great political importance. Its immense appeal gives it additional political weight. The program is funded by a separate tax on both employers and employees, so people who see these payroll deductions throughout their working life naturally come to view the collection of benefits as a recovery of what they had earlier paid into the system, as a government-sponsored pension program. Beneficiaries do not feel the stigma associated with being "on welfare." Social Security is a pay-as-you-go program, in which current taxes on workers pay for current benefits for retirees. The program, in effect, transfers money from one generation to another, with an understanding that the future benefits of current workers will be funded by taxes on the next generation of workers.

By the 1980s, two-thirds of all elderly people in the United States relied on Social Security for at least half their income; for a fifth of that population, Social Security was the *only* source of income.[6] A national poll in 1985 found that 92 percent of the public considered the Social Se-

1935 Social Security Poster. Those who now receive social security checks regard it as a government sponsored pension program and do not think of themselves as being "on welfare."

curity program a success.[7] The political appeal and public support for Social Security led one congressional aide to describe it as "the third rail of American politics," because any political leader who touched it would get the shock of his or her life.[8]

In 1983, President Reagan and Congress touched that third rail when they increased Social Security payroll taxes and cut benefits. This was the first time in the history of the program that benefits were openly cut, but many observers agreed it was the only way to save the system itself. In 1980 the Social Security system was annually paying out $10 billion to $15 billion more in benefits than it was taking in through taxes. Unless action was taken soon, the Social Security trust fund would technically be bank-

rupt, and the 36 million checks that were due beneficiaries could not be covered from within the system. The Social Security reforms of 1983 came into being only after an extraordinary series of secret negotiations among a nine-member group from Congress and the executive branch.[9] With its $170 billion in tax increases and benefit cuts, the 1983 amendments rescued the Social Security system and, after a while, actually began to generate a surplus in the Social Security trust fund. In 1989, the $52 billion Social Security surplus was used to bring the federal deficit down to $152 billion (on paper at least), a practice that touched off a heated political debate in 1990 over whether it was proper to use the funds in that way and whether payroll taxes should be cut in light of the surplus.[10]

Medicare and Medicaid

Medicare and Medicaid, the two major government programs for providing health care, mix social insurance and public assistance, just as Social Security does. Both health programs were established by the Social Security Amendments of 1965. **Medicare** is a federal program that provides health insurance for the aged and disabled and is funded through a payroll tax. **Medicaid** is a joint federal-state program to give medical care to the poor. The federal government provides funding in the form of matching grants and establishes health care standards, but the primary responsibility for administering Medicaid rests with state governments.

Both programs came about after 20 years of political conflict during which those who opposed them (including the powerful American Medical Association) charged that their introduction would bring "socialized medicine" to the United States. Incorporating Medicare into the existing Social Security program made Medicare more acceptable to many people, however, because it could be regarded as a social insurance program designed to help the elderly. As Figure 19.1 (p. 608) demonstrates, the growth in spending for social insurance programs (Social Security and Medicare) has greatly outpaced spending for public assistance programs (welfare, housing, and food stamps). Several addi-

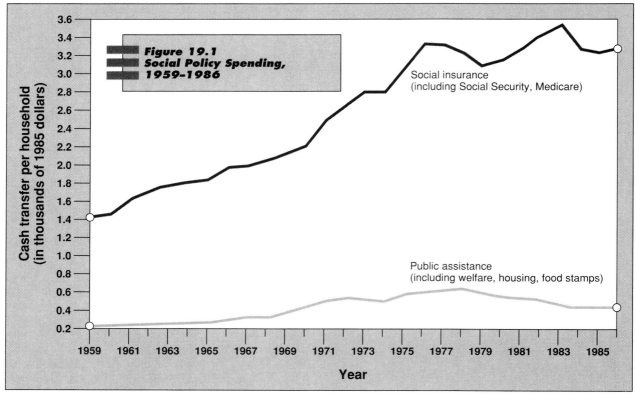

**Figure 19.1
Social Policy Spending,
1959–1986**

Social insurance
(including Social Security, Medicare)

Public assistance
(including welfare, housing, food stamps)

Source: Phoebe H. Cottingham and David T. Ellwood, eds., *Welfare Policy for the 1990s*
(Cambridge, Mass.: Harvard University Press, 1989), p. 46.

tional factors contributed to the rapid expansion of both health care programs: the aging of the population, the increased political activity of senior citizens, the broadening of coverage, and an expanding American economy during the 1960s and early 1970s that helped support the increases.

There is no doubt about the size and reach of the health care effort. Before 1965, only about half of those aged 65 or over had health insurance. In 1990, Medicare provided health insurance for more than 30 million Americans, or virtually all of the aged and disabled. While Medicare coverage does not include all medical costs, it does pay for slightly under half the medical bills of older Americans. The federal-state Medicaid program of health assistance for the poor has a similar broad reach. In 1990, the pro-

gram subsidized health care for 25 million people. Two-thirds of those receiving Medicaid are welfare recipients, and the rest are elderly and disabled people eligible for long-term care.[11]

There is also little doubt that Medicare and Medicaid have improved the health of millions of Americans. Five years after passage of the programs, the percentage of poor never examined by a doctor had been cut in half, and the proportion seeing a doctor at least once a year was similar to that found in higher income groups. The infant mortality rate, which is often used as an indicator of general health, is one-third of what it was in 1950 (although the U.S. rate is still higher than that found in 17 nations, including Japan, Sweden, France, and Canada).[12]

The Medicare Catastrophic Coverage Act of 1988 discussed at the beginning of the chapter

Seniors participate in a day-care program in North Carolina. The majority of social welfare expenditures fund programs for the elderly.

tells us a great deal about the history and future of health insurance programs in America. Congress passed catastrophic coverage in 1988 and then retreated a year later. When senior citizens strongly objected to having to pay for the coverage under the 1988 legislation, many legislators went along with the repeal because, as one member put it, they felt the elderly were being "ungrateful" for all that Congress had done for them over the years.[13] After all, most of the increased social spending under the Great Society programs of the 1960s had been "targeted on the elderly and [had] yielded a dramatic decline in their poverty rate."[14] And today more than 60 percent of all social welfare expenditures goes for Social Security, Medicare, and other programs for the elderly.

Despite these gains, however, the health in-

surance program failed to cover the costs of long-term nursing home care (beyond 100 days)—a major drain on the pocketbooks of elderly Americans. President Reagan proposed the catastrophic coverage bill in 1987 as an alternative to paying for all long-term nursing care and to Democratic proposals for increasing other Medicare bills. The bill proposed by President Reagan estimated the cost of the program at $31 billion for 1989–1993, which was to be financed by a flat premium of just under five dollars a month paid by Medicare beneficiaries. But the Reagan proposal soon became a vehicle for members of Congress to deal with a range of health care problems: They added benefits to cover prescription drugs, examinations for breast cancer, nursing home care for 50 more days than the current law provided, support for those who cared for sick relatives, and protection against bankruptcy brought on by a spouse's nursing home costs. These added benefits raised the estimated costs of the program to $48 billion. When it became evident that a flat fee would not cover those costs, Congress added a surtax (or additional tax) onto the income taxes of those aged 65 or older above a certain income level. About 40 percent of all Medicare beneficiaries had to pay this additional tax, and 5 percent had to pay the maximum tax of $800 a year, or $1600 per couple.

Interest groups representing the elderly had called for catastrophic coverage for years, but many elderly Americans objected to Congress's funding the act through a "seniors-only income tax increase."[15] Congress responded to intense lobbying by seniors' groups by cutting the benefits and repealing the surtax of the catastrophic coverage law. Some legislators regarded this as a positive sign that Congress would eventually address the most pressing issue of health insurance for the elderly: long-term nursing care. Others felt the 1989 experience had reduced the chances that Congress would expand Medicare coverage in the future. Representative Brian Donnelly, who led the fight to change the catastrophic coverage law in the House, said that the experience had clearly shown a "need to rethink the whole damn program."[16]

Food Stamps

The **food stamps** program began as an experiment in 1961 and became a permanent social policy with passage of the Food Stamp Act of 1964. Under this program, those who qualify on the basis of need purchase stamps, and then use them in stores for buying food. The government subsidy in the program is found in the value of the stamps, which is higher than their purchase price. Recipients get more food through using the stamps than they could with cash. Congress greatly expanded the program in the 1970s, and by 1973 it was the major nutritional effort supported by the government. The program has a broad appeal. Liberals see it as a way to end hunger in America; conservatives like the fact that the program is locally administered and

provides benefits in the form of food rather than cash; and food producers and retailers appreciate the customers that food stamps generate.

The food stamps program is a **means-tested program,** because benefits are restricted to those without the means to acquire them on their own. Funding for these programs is based on general government revenues rather than previous contributions by recipients. Such programs involve a redistribution of resources within the society. Social Security and Medicare, by contrast, are referred to as *entitlements*, because they provide a benefit that has been earned and to which anyone is entitled once he or she reaches the age of qualification. They are often thought of as insurance programs in which people receive benefits that they had paid into the system earlier.

Originally, benefits under the food stamps program were restricted to those on welfare. By 1974, however, benefits were extended to anyone whose income was determined "to be a substantially limiting factor in the attainment of a nutritionally adequate diet."[17] In replacing the original welfare requirement, this means test greatly increased the number of people eligible for food stamps. Between 1970 and 1975, the number of people participating in the program tripled, from 6.5 million to 18.5 million. About one of every five persons in the United States was potentially eligible for food stamps. The cost of the program in 1975 was almost ten times that spent in 1970.[18]

Critics sought to scale down the program and assess greater penalties for illegal use of food stamps. Spending for the program was cut by $8 billion during President Reagan's first term. Congress also approved new rules that tightened eligibility requirements during this period, such as effectively ending food stamp benefits for college students and striking workers. In all, approximately 1 million persons—5 percent of the total—lost their eligibility for food stamps as a result of these stricter rules and reduced funds.[19]

Changing public attitudes toward welfare programs and the poor began to emerge in the mid-1980s, however, as more and more Americans became aware of the homeless and of poor children in particular.[20] The Food Security Act of 1985 and subsequent legislation on food stamps

The food stamps program restricts benefits to those without the means to acquire them on
their own.

increased the benefits and liberalized the eligibility requirements of the food stamp program
into the 1990s. The 1985 law also required states
to establish employment and training programs
for food stamp recipients, a linking of work and
benefits that was to become the centerpiece of
the Family Support Act of 1988.

AFDC

The Aid to Families with Dependent Children
program (AFDC) originated in the child welfare
provisions of the 1935 Social Security Act and
has been amended more than 100 times since
then. **AFDC** provides assistance to families with
children under the age of 18 who have suffered
a lack of economic support due to the disability,
chronic unemployment, or desertion of a parent.
AFDC is a means-tested program: A family's income and assets must be below a level established by the state in order to be eligible for assistance.

AFDC is the program most people have in
mind when they refer to those who are "on welfare." Both the federal government and state
governments have a role in the program. The
federal government provides the funds for about
half the total benefit costs of the program, and
state governments have the primary responsibility for determining eligibility requirements
and benefits and for administering the program.

From 1960 to 1970, the number of AFDC participants grew from 3 million to well over 9 million. The magnitude of these increases led many
to talk of a "welfare explosion" and of a need for
policies to regulate that growth.[21] Welfare reform continued to be an important issue in the
1980s, but attention shifted away from claims of

Children in poverty. One study found that one of every four children in the United States had been on the welfare rolls during the mid-1980s.

welfare cheating and controlling a welfare explosion. The total number of AFDC recipients in 1987 was just under 11 million—about the same as it was in 1977. But the number of AFDC recipients as a percentage of the total population had *declined* between 1977 and 1987 (from 5 to 4.5 percent).[22]

What changed between the 1970s and the 1980s, one expert points out, is that "poverty in America has shifted from the aged to children and their mothers," which in turn meant that "the primary motivation for reforming the welfare system is to change the conditions of long-term poverty among children."[23] A Census Bureau study reported in 1989 found that one of every four children in America had been on the welfare rolls during the mid-1980s.[24]

Welfare reform in the 1980s focused on children not only because they represented an increasing proportion of the poor in America, but also because children growing up in poverty were more likely to depend on welfare as adults. A first step toward reducing welfare dependency is to recognize that effective welfare policy must deal with two distinct types of welfare recipients:

1. Short-term recipients who average less than two years on AFDC and move on and off as a transition between jobs or marriages;

2. Long-term recipients who average eight to ten years of dependency and who often begin their welfare experience with giving birth out of wedlock while a teenager.[25]

Welfare policies directed to the first group seek to prevent poverty by providing benefits, while policies aimed at the second group seek to reduce welfare dependency. The two groups and their different needs raise what public policy analyst David Ellwood has identified as the underlying dilemma of welfare policy:

The obvious way to reduce poverty is to raise welfare benefits. But higher benefits almost inevitably increase welfare use and the length of time people are on welfare.

Conversely, the obvious antidote to dependence is to cut back dramatically on welfare. So we apparently must decide whether to worry about current poverty or longer dependency.[26]

Before 1988, most welfare reform proposals had

been unable to resolve the dilemma. Liberals proposed benefit increases to reduce poverty, while conservatives proposed work requirements and job training programs aimed at reducing welfare dependency.

The Family Support Act of 1988 broke this deadlock by including programs aimed at reducing both short-term poverty and long-term dependency, thus gaining support from both liberals and conservatives. Congress took a second look at some of these programs in 1989, after many states had complained that the federal regulations were hindering their ability to maintain or develop effective job training programs. But still, the combination of benefits, education and training programs, and work requirements served to make the Family Support Act acceptable to most conservatives, liberals, and moderates in Congress.

The Family Support Act of 1988 was based on a consensus among welfare experts and those who govern, a shared belief that:

> The welfare system should be transformed from one emphasizing income maintenance to one stressing education and training so that welfare parents could gain and keep jobs that paid enough to support their families.[27]

How Social Problems Are Interrelated

The four social policies we have focused on in this chapter represent the core elements of government efforts to promote the general welfare, but the social policy agenda for the 1990s has been filled with many related problems demanding the attention of those who govern: drug abuse, the homeless, AIDS, child care, and education.

What can the government do about these problems? Answers to that question illustrate once again how these areas are interrelated and how an effective social policy directed toward one of them must consider its connection with other social problems. One connection is what many consider an underlying cause of many of these problems: the breakdown of the Ameri-

can family. A second link can be seen in the debate over whether social policies should focus more on immediate problems or on underlying causes and long-term solutions to those problems.

In 1987, Senator Daniel Patrick Moynihan pointed out that nearly 85 percent of the children receiving AFDC benefits were on welfare because of divorce, separation, or illegitimacy—the result of an "utterly unforeseen, utterly transforming change in American family life which took place in a brief period, roughly 1960–1980."[28] Census data show that the number of one-parent families increased by nearly 150 percent between 1970 and 1987, while the number of two-parent families declined. More than 85 percent of all families with children in 1970 were two-parent families, whereas the comparable figure in 1987 was less than 75 percent. What is most striking about single-parent households, however, is that in approximately nine of every ten cases it is the mother who heads the household.[29] The **feminization of poverty** is a general term that has been used to describe the high incidence of poverty among female-headed single-parent families in the United States (although this term has engendered controversy, as A Closer Look on pp. 614–615 shows).

A recognition that family structure has a lot to do with poverty is evident in many of the welfare reforms of the Family Support Act of 1988: child support enforcement; extension of AFDC benefits to two-parent families; and the child care, medical benefits, and training programs designed to help parents get off the welfare rolls through employment. Social policies that seek to reduce drug use and the rate of school dropouts have also come to reflect the importance of family structure to solving those problems.

Any social policy needs to deal with immediate problems while also working toward long-term solutions that get at underlying causes. With welfare reform, we saw that this requires a decision about whether reducing poverty or reducing dependency is the primary goal. The 1988 Medicare reforms addressed the short-term problems of catastrophic medical costs but failed to address the larger question of paying for long-term nursing care. Social policies for the

A Closer Look

Debate Over the Feminization of Poverty

The first step in developing a social policy agenda is to identify society's most serious social problems. In 1978, sociologist Diana Pearce coined the term *the feminization of poverty* to describe one such problem: the fact that in every year between 1969 and 1978, 100,000 additional women with children had fallen below the poverty line.[a] By the late 1980s, two of every three poor adults in the United States were women, and nearly half of the female-headed households in the United States were poor—as compared to 8 percent of the male-present families below the poverty line.[b]

Impoverished women and children clearly represent a serious social problem in America today, but some have questioned whether identifying this problem as the feminization of poverty helps move society closer to policies to deal with the problem. The authors of a recent book on women and poverty in the United States asked:

Did the long-needed naming of the problem as the *feminization* of poverty—and not the impoverishment of women—tend to put a pink dress on issues that were somehow more serious when they affected men?

Isn't the explanation for poverty more complex than that all women are but "one man away from welfare?" And, aren't the solutions somehow more complicated than either simply "putting women to work" or reforming the welfare system?[c]

To illustrate, Linda Burnham has pointed out that class and race are more significant causes of the impoverishment of black women than is gender, and that "the feminization-of-poverty analysis seriously misrepresents the dynamics shaping female poverty in the United States and misidentifies the sectors of the population most at risk of becoming poor."[d]

Welfare scholar Mary Jo Bane has suggested that the feminization-of-poverty concept has led to conclusions that family structure causes poverty when in fact the lack of employment opportunities, low wages, and low skills often have more to do with poverty among female-headed families than does family structure. Her research found that most of those in female-headed families, and particularly black families, who are poor would have been poor even if both parents had stayed in the family.[e]

Another scholar, Douglas Besharov, has also called the feminization-of-poverty concept fundamentally misleading because it lumps together two distinct groups of female-headed families: families headed by divorced mothers and families headed by never-married mothers. The latter are typically younger, less educated, less likely to work, and less likely to receive child support from the father than divorced mothers. Divorced women are also much more likely to leave the welfare rolls through marriage than are never-married mothers. All these differences help explain why divorced mothers are more likely to rely on welfare only as a temporary measure while never-married mothers more often become trapped in long-term welfare dependency. Indeed, Besharov says, "the evidence is mounting that never-married mothers compose the majority of long-term welfare dependents—a permanent underclass."[f]

Whether the Family Support Act of 1988 distinguishes between the two types of female-headed families and their problems in ways that will permit the early identification of those most likely to become welfare dependent and the tailoring of education and training requirements to those families remains to be seen.

[a]Diana Pearce, "The Feminization of Poverty: Women, Work and Welfare," *Urban and Social Change Review*, February 1978, pp. 28–36.

[b]Rochelle Lefkowitz and Ann Withorn, eds., *For Crying Out Loud: Women and Poverty in the United States* (New York: Pilgrim Press, 1986), p. 3; and U.S. House of Representatives, Committee on Ways and Means, *Background Material and Data on Programs Within the Jurisdiction of the Committee on Ways and Means*, (Washington, D.C.: Government Printing Office, March 15, 1989), p. 953.

[c]Lefkowitz and Withorn, *For Crying Out Loud*, p. 4.

[d]Linda Burnham, "Has Poverty Been Feminized in Black America?" in Lefkowitz and Withorn, *For Crying Out Loud*, p. 83.

[e]Mary Jo Bane, "Household Composition and Poverty," in *Fighting Poverty*, ed. Sheldon H. Danziger and Daniel H. Weinberg (Cambridge, Mass.: Harvard University Press, 1986), pp. 209–231.

[f]Douglas J. Besharov, "Targeting Long-Term Welfare Recipients," in *Welfare Policy for the 1990s*, ed. Phoebe H Cottingham and David T. Ellwood (Cambridge, Mass. Harvard University Press, 1989), p. 147.

Is the traditional American family becoming obsolete? Dramatic changes in family structure have had an enormous impact on social welfare programs.

problems of homelessness, drug abuse, and AIDS also require policies that address the immediate problem—such as shelter programs, drug interdiction policies, and antidiscrimination policies to protect AIDS victims—at the same time that they seek long-term solutions, such as programs for the construction of low-rent housing units, drug education and treatment policies, and research support for the prevention, treatment, and cure of AIDS.

Homelessness and other social problems require policies that address the immediate problem, such as shelter programs, as well as those that seek long-term solutions, such as low-rent housing.

Checkpoint

- The collectivist approach to social policies regards a broad range of government social programs as a necessary corrective to economic and political decisions that benefit some in society at the expense of others.

- The individualist view supports a more limited government role and looks to the private sector and economic growth as the best way to promote the general welfare. Social policymaking in the United States has revolved around the question of where to strike a balance between individualism and collectivism.

- The ongoing debate between proponents of those two views has shaped the development of major social policies such as Social Security, Medicare and Medicaid, food stamps, and Aid to Families with Dependent Children (AFDC).

- Social policies in these areas as well as those directed at problems such as homelessness, drug abuse, education, and AIDS must deal both with underlying causes, such as family breakdown, and with the immediate and long-term consequences of the problem.

EVALUATING THE EFFECTS OF SOCIAL POLICY

Each new social policy is built on beliefs about the *effects* of previous policies. For example, a belief that the social policies of the early 1960s, which focused on individual opportunities through job training and similar programs, had not reduced poverty laid the foundation for the policies of income maintenance and aid to the working poor advanced during the late 1960s and 1970s. The Reagan administration's approach to social welfare was grounded partly on a belief that the Great Society programs had failed. The evaluation of past policies is an important stage in the development of new policies. Much of the debate over social policies grows out of different evaluations of the effects of previous policies.

Varying Interpretations

That there are quite different interpretations of the effects of particular policies is clear just from the titles of two books about social policy. John Schwarz's assessment of 20 years of public policy is called *America's Hidden Success*, while Charles Murray's evaluation of American social policy from 1950 to 1980 is entitled *Losing Ground*. Although they study a number of government programs, both Schwarz and Murray pay particular attention to those programs aimed at reducing poverty. Schwarz finds them to have been successful: "In the space of one generation, the economic growth of the times combined with the government's programs had reduced poverty among Americans by about 60 percent."[30] But Murray writes that "a higher proportion of the American population was officially poor in 1980 than at any time since 1967," and that "the number of people living in poverty stopped declining just as the public-assistance program budgets and the rate of increase in those budgets were highest."[31]

How is it possible to draw such contradictory conclusions about the effects of social welfare policies? Part of the answer lies in how poverty and income are measured. Murray relied on Census Bureau figures that count only cash income, whereas Schwarz included food stamps, Medicaid, and other "in-kind" government benefits as income. The way in which different measures of poverty produce different results was illustrated in a Census Bureau study released in 1989. After concluding that the number of Americans living below the poverty line in 1988 was the same as for the previous year—32 million—the report showed how alternative ways of calculating income could reduce by 3.5 million the number of people below the poverty line.[32]

Even when such differences are eliminated by relying on a single standard measure, it is possible to come to different conclusions about the effects of social policies. The Census Bureau reported that there were 1.8 million fewer people below the poverty line in 1984 than there had been in 1983, a reduction of almost one percent. (A family of four needed a cash income of $10,609 or more in 1984 to be above the poverty line.) A White House official described the poverty figures as a "triumph" for the administration's policies, while Democratic critics of the administration looked at the same report and drew quite different conclusions.[33] The 1984 poverty rate was less than that of the previous year, these critics pointed out, but it was also higher than it had been at any time between 1966 and 1980, and it was 1.4 percent above the 13 percent rate inherited by the Reagan administration when it took office.

Some General Conclusions

Although there are areas of disagreement, studies by a number of scholars have nevertheless provided some general conclusions about the effects of social policies in the United States.

First, there *has* been a reduction in the poverty rate since President Johnson declared a war on poverty in 1965—from 17 percent of the population falling below the poverty line in 1965 to 13 percent in 1988.[34] Even with that reduction, however, certain groups in society continue to have a disproportionate number of the poor among them. Compare the 13 percent poverty rate for the total population in 1988, for instance,

with that for blacks: 32 percent; for Hispanics: 27 percent; and for those living in female-headed families: 34 percent.[35]

Second, this reduction in poverty is not part of a more general redistribution of income or wealth in the United States. A smaller proportion of society today falls below the poverty level, but the gap between rich and poor in America was greater in the late 1980s than it had been a decade earlier.[36] Hugh Heclo attributes this lack of redistribution to the fact that many social welfare policies in the United States are aimed at providing security more than equality, that they seek to alleviate the effects of economic inequalities rather than the causes, and that these programs include benefits for the nonpoor as well.[37] As we have already seen, the social insurance programs account for most of the increase in social spending over the past 20 years and for more than 60 percent of all social spending. And studies consistently show that social insurance programs (Social Security, Medicare, and unemployment insurance) primarily protect the middle class.[38] The overall impact of these social policies is clearly not one of redistributing income and wealth in the United States.*

A third development associated with welfare policies, one discussed earlier in this chapter, is the growing proportion of women and children among the poor and on welfare. Whether welfare policies have contributed to the breakdown of the traditional family and the feminization of poverty has been a subject of much debate. As A Closer Look pointed out earlier (pp. 614–615), policy analysts have found that two distinct groups account for the feminization of poverty and that an effective policy must recognize the differences between the two.

All three of the developments under review here are, of course, shaped by economic policies as well as by social policies. For example, some observers attributed the reduction in poverty between 1983 and 1984 more to the 6 percent real economic growth rate during that period than to any changes in social policy. Another example is the Tax Reform Act of 1986, which provided $30 billion in tax relief to low-income families over

_____
*See Chapter 2.

The gap between rich and poor is greater today than it was a decade earlier even though a smaller proportion of society falls below the poverty level.

a five-year period. A *New York Times* editorial supporting the tax reform measure claimed that it "would do more to relieve poverty than any social welfare measure in 15 years."[39] It is evident that there is a close connection between the economic policies discussed in Chapter 18 and the social welfare policies under consideration in this chapter.

It should be clear by now that policy evaluation is a difficult task. Both sides in the debate over whether the programs of the Great Society succeeded can find evidence to support their position. Whether changes in the poverty rate or in the numbers receiving AFDC are the result of particular social policies or of economic influences is often unclear. Other factors also help determine the impact of a particular policy: the resources committed to that policy, the emergence of new problems that command attention, how well the policy is administered, the reaction of those directly affected by it, disagreement about the causes of the problem being addressed, unanticipated costs, and the fact that opponents of a policy continue to work against it even after it has been adopted.[40] What this means is that the failure of any policy to achieve a stated goal does not necessarily mean that the policy itself is flawed. Any evaluation of the effects of social

policies must take into account the impact of these other influences.

The War on Poverty and the War on Welfare

The Great Society programs, including its war on poverty, did not wipe out poverty and end discrimination, but they did do much to reduce poverty, hunger, malnutrition, and disease; to increase the access of the poor to important social services; and to lower barriers against black Americans. Why, then, did these welfare policies meet with such resistance from both the administration and the public at large in the 1980s? One reason was the election in 1980 of an administration philosophically opposed to the welfare state. Another reason was that in the late 1970s many Americans began to suffer the effects of an unstable economy characterized by high inflation and high unemployment: "In the search for scapegoats and ways to trim public expense that followed predictably, welfare and its clients, especially its black clients, were inevitable and early targets."[41]

That there was a change in philosophy is clear, yet we still must ask how much change in the welfare system actually took place. Did the

President Lyndon Johnson. Has the war on poverty he declared in the 1960s been replaced by a war on welfare?

ideology of individualism reflected in the Reagan and Bush administrations lead to dramatic changes in social policies? Has there been a dismantling of the welfare state and a shift away from the goals of the Great Society? Did the war on welfare supplant the war on poverty? One way to measure the changes brought about by the Reagan administration is to look at the resources committed to particular social policies. Spending for Social Security and Medicare, programs serving poor and nonpoor alike, continued to grow, although at a slower pace than in previous administrations. Cuts in some social programs were offset by the increases in others, so that overall domestic spending did not decline during the Reagan years.[42]

The war on welfare, in short, has not brought a dismantling of most social welfare programs, although its long-term impact on social policy is yet to be determined. The Reagan administration's real success was shifting the terms in which those who govern debate and decide social policy—a framework the Bush administration seeks to preserve. The problem-solving approach of the Great Society was replaced with a budget-cutting approach in the 1980s, and the issue of resources dominates the social policy debates of the 1990s.

Reforms discussed at the beginning of this chapter provide clear evidence that the war on poverty will continue in the United States, while battles over funding, eligibility requirements, and levels of benefits suggest that the war on welfare will also be carried into the future. Whatever the outcome, the politics will be difficult and the fundamental issues never finally resolved. The protracted nature and intensity of conflict in this area led one former secretary of the Department of Health, Education, and Welfare to call welfare "the Middle East of domestic politics."[43] A similar view from the trenches, which captures what is at stake in social policymaking, was expressed by Representative George Miller: "The politics are tough. You have to do this one because you care about the very social fabric of the country in which you live. Other than that there's not a hell of a lot of reason to do it."[44]

Checkpoint

- Studies of the effects of social welfare policies have produced different and contradictory conclusions about whether past policies have worked.

- Some general conclusions about the effects of social welfare policies are apparent to all: Poverty has been reduced over the past three decades; the reduction in poverty is not part of a general redistribution of income or wealth in the United States; a growing proportion of the poor consists of women and children; and it is difficult to sort out the effects of social policies from those of economic policies.

- The war on welfare initiated by the Reagan administration in the 1980s has not changed many of the social programs, but it has changed the terms of the debate on social policy among those who govern. A problem-solving approach has given way to a budget-cutting approach.

SOCIAL POLICY: WHO GOVERNS?

Broad social policies such as those discussed in this chapter grow out of intense political conflicts. Their creation is marked by strong party divisions, high levels of presidential initiative and commitment, intense public interest, active lobbying by special interests, and ideological conflict both within and outside of Congress. Once established, these programs—like any others—develop constituencies and varying degrees of public support. But the politics surrounding them remains charged. That is most evident when presidents and Congress propose changes in these programs' revenues or benefits. The political debate on such proposals is never limited only to the suggested changes in the program. Rather, it raises again fundamental questions about the goals and effectiveness of the overall program.

There is another reason for the great intensity of politics when social policy is involved. Debate over Medicare benefits, Social Security taxes, or welfare reform is different from the debate over national defense programs or tax policies. The government's responsibility for national defense and taxes is a given in American politics, but its role in social policies is not at all clear. Does the government have a *responsibility* to guarantee every person a minimum annual income? Should people who are unable to find employment in private industry be given a government job? Answers to those questions depend not only on views about who should govern but also on notions about what governing means. And that, in turn, rests on fundamental beliefs about human nature and the relationship of the individual to society.

The conclusion of Paul Light that "anyone who wants to understand American politics must first understand social security" might be broadened to include other social policies as well.[45] The actions of political leaders and the general public on social policy are determined by more general ideas about politics and government. These political ideas shape the debate over social policy in American politics. Table 19.1 (p. 622), for example, summarizes the ideological underpinnings of the debate on social welfare.

We see in the table the competing values of collectivism and individualism discussed earlier in the chapter. We also can see that attitudes toward welfare reflect differences over the role of government, individual mobility, economic rights, equality, humanitarian values, and human nature. Richard Coughlin and others who study welfare policies have pointed to this "ideological complexity" as a key to understanding social policy politics. The general public and individual political leaders will often support a liberal position on some welfare issues and a conservative one on others. The public and political leaders value both equality and individual freedom, as we have seen in earlier chapters on civil rights and civil liberties. They believe in the need for both security and economic mobility.[46] This ideological complexity is recognized in all three explanations of social policy politics—democratic, pluralist, and elite—but is particularly important for the democratic view.

Democracy

What accounted for the welfare explosion between 1965 and 1975? Why were proposals for a guaranteed annual income rejected by Congress in the 1970s? Why is social security considered one of the sacred cows of American politics? What are the reasons for requiring welfare recipients to enroll in training and work programs?

A democratic answer to all those questions would begin by looking at public opinion on social welfare issues and at the representative institutions of government. As James Patterson notes, one might explain the great expansion in the welfare rolls by suggesting "that it represented the working out of the democratic process—that an informed, altruistic populace perceived the need and opened up the gates for the poor."[47] Patterson himself rejected that explanation as an oversimplification. He found the relationship between public opinion and social policy much more complex than unqualified support for, or rejection of, policies to help the poor in America.

Large majorities of Americans favor increased spending or current levels of spending in government programs for health care, the homeless, AIDS research, the elderly, and social security;

Table 19.1

Ideological Dimensions of the Social Policy Debate

Generally Pro-welfare Positions	Generally Anti-welfare Positions
Liberalism: Solutions to social problems through government intervention.	**Conservatism:** Preference for private redress of social problems; minimum government intervention.
Collectivism: Origins of and solutions to social problems found in societal intradependence; emphasis on shared responsibility of the collectivity.	**Individualism:** Origins of and solutions to social problems found in willful actions of individuals; emphasis on individual to do what is best for himself.
Social Determinism: Individual success or failure depends mostly on economic and social structural conditions.	**Success Ideology:** Individual success results from ability plus hard work and is a sign of virtue; failure results from laziness, incompetence, and is a mark of vice.
Social Guarantees: The "social rights" of citizens are minimum standards of health, nutrition, income, etc., guaranteed as political rights, regardless of individual productive employment.	**Work Ethic:** Work is a virtue in itself; it provides economic and spiritual sustenance; idleness is a vice leading to moral decay and should be punished.
Absolute Equality: It is the purpose of social policy to reduce inequalities in the distribution of valued social and economic resources by absolute reductions in status and income differentials.	**Equality of Opportunity:** It is the purpose of social policy to provide equal chances for all individuals to achieve the social status commensurate with their individual performance; also called the "free mobility" ideology.
Humanitarianism: It is both moral and beneficial to aid the less fortunate or less able; such action benefits the giver and receiver.	**Survival of the Fittest:** The process of natural selection furthers social and human progress by weeding out the unfit and weak individuals; it is a mistake to interfere with this process.
Social Optimism: Human nature is essentially good.	**Social Pessimism:** Human nature is essentially evil.

Source: Richard M. Coughlin, *Ideology, Public Opinion and Welfare Policy* (Berkeley: Institute of International Studies, University of California, 1980), p. 16.

there has been little change in the pattern of this support since 1973.[48] Yet support for government spending in specific areas of social policy has gone hand in hand with the public's concern about budget deficits and distrust of big government, and with more people describing themselves as conservatives than liberals.

A review of public attitudes toward antipoverty policy reflected in public opinion polls over the past 40 years illustrates the ideological dimensions of the social policy debate discussed earlier. Hugh Heclo found that public attitudes toward antipoverty policy could be summarized as follows:[49]

1   **Americans support the principle of the national government acting to help the poor.** Whether the federal government should be helping the poor is no longer a debatable issue in American politics. In fact, public support for this belief was higher at the end of the Reagan administration than it was when he took office.

2   **At the same time, Americans do not support comprehensive ideological justifications for national government actions in social policy.** Most Americans apply the values of collectivism and equality to political issues and the values of individual competition and inequality to economic issues. Since social policies are seen as both political and economic issues, both sets of values come into play. A comprehensive theory of social policy, whether liberal collectivist theory or conservative individualist theory, would require the rejection of one set of values. It would require, in other words, that Americans reject one strand of the general-welfare liberalism discussed in Chapter 3.

3   **Americans apply a strong needs-based standard in their evaluation of social policy.** The needs-based standard extends beyond helping the poor to supporting government action that would substantially reduce the gap between the rich and the poor.

4   **Americans distinguish among different needs and favor programs designed to permit individuals to meet those needs themselves.** For instance, the public assesses differently a widow's need for child care in order to work, a nonworking mother's need for child care because of an absent father, and an unmarried mother's need for child care because of youth and inexperience. The public endorses social policies aimed at supporting individuals who assume responsibility for themselves (such as the widow who works) but looks with disfavor on policies that directly help the needy with no regard to developing personal responsibility (the young unwed mother).

5   **Paradoxically, Americans favor government action to help the poor but dislike government programs that specifically target the poor.** Mass-based entitlement programs such as Social Security and health care receive the highest support, while means-tested programs that target the poor, such as food stamps and AFDC, receive much less support. One explanation for this difference has to do with Americans' antagonism toward the term *welfare*. As we saw in Chapter 8, there is little public support for government spending on "welfare," but there are high levels of support for spending on assistance for "the needy." And it is programs that target the poor that come to mind in discussing "welfare."[50] Americans' strong support of the concept of work also helps explain these differences. The training programs and work requirements of the Family Support Act of 1988 reflect the belief that social policies should support work rather than replace it as a source of income.

We know that democracy means more than political equality and majority rule; it also means a recognition of individual rights. Does the concept of individual liberties include economic and welfare rights in addition to political rights? Are food stamps and AFDC payments "privileges" granted by the government, or are they "rights" guaranteed to everyone in society? Would a right to food, shelter, and medical care be a fundamental right like free speech or voting, or would it be considered less important than political rights?

Supreme Court decisions since 1970 have upheld a number of welfare claims on equal protection grounds and maintained the open access to the courts for those making such claims. All those decisions provide some support for a welfare rights argument, but they do not settle the matter. The Court has neither clearly recognized a status of right, rather than privilege, for wel-

An unemployed father and his son. Americans take a collectivist view in holding government responsible for ending poverty yet support the individualist position in valuing personal initiative and work.

fare benefits, nor has it afforded the protection of fundamental rights to the economic needs of individuals in the United States.[51]

A democratic framework, then, calls our attention to some important characteristics of the politics of social policies in the United States. The American public takes the collectivist view in holding government responsible for ending poverty and supports the individualist position in valuing personal initiative and work. That helps explain why the American approach to social welfare has been described as "simultaneously pro-government and pro-market," and why the major increase in social spending has taken place not in programs that target the poor, but in programs that seek to help the poor by helping everyone in society.[52]

Pluralism

Social policies in the United States tend to distribute many small benefits across society rather than provide a more limited number of worthwhile benefits directed at those who need them most. The pluralism of American politics provides one explanation for this diffuse, all-inclusive form of social policies. In creating these programs, Congress responds to the many different interest groups within society. Even if interest group activity was not instrumental in establishing a particular program, interest groups are likely to form around a program once it exists. Two different types of interest groups develop around a particular program: the program's beneficiaries or recipients and the governmental or private agencies that administer the program. The groups organized around the Social Security and Medicare programs illustrate both of these types.[53]

The American Association of Retired Persons (AARP) and the National Council of Senior Citizens (NCSC) are important beneficiary interest groups. Both consist of the elderly (sometimes called the gray lobby) and seek to protect or improve benefits received through Social Security and Medicare. The growth in the size and importance of these groups came *after* the creation of both programs. By the 1980s, the two groups had more than 30 million members, and although they disagreed on many specific proposals and differed in political influence, they were two of the most active interest groups involved in the 1983 Social Security reforms and the Medicare Catastrophic Coverage Act of 1988.

The professional organizations of those who deliver health services under Medicare and Medicaid and government officials who administer social welfare programs form interest groups in support of these programs because they derive their income from them. They have a clear financial stake in maintaining or improving government programs.

The relative importance of these two types of interest groups will vary from policy to policy. The gray lobby groups, for example, are better organized and more politically active than beneficiary groups for food stamps and AFDC. The interest groups most active in these areas are often the service delivery groups, who sometimes assume the role of speaking *for* the low-income recipients. Too often, the actual or potential recipients are not represented at all in the interest group system, a criticism of the pluralist viewpoint noted throughout this book.

Pluralist explanations for the growth in social welfare spending and programs, then, are likely to focus on interest group activity. In this view political leaders who support these programs are responding to organized interest groups more than they are to the general public opinion that is the focus of the democratic viewpoint. Table 19.2 shows some of the national interest groups that actively participate in the politics of social welfare policies discussed in this chapter.

Theodore Lowi says the pluralism seen in some recent social welfare policymaking represents "interest group liberalism," or a brokering among competing interest groups. To show how this works Lowi distinguishes between "old welfare," such as the original Social Security program of 1935, and "new welfare," such as food stamps and AFDC, created more recently.[54] The

Table 19.2

Social Welfare Interest Groups

Group	Year Founded	Number of Members
American Association of Retired Persons	1958	30 million
American Public Welfare Association	1930	7,000
American Senior Citizens Association	1982	35,000
American Society on Aging	1954	7,000
Association of Informed Senior Citizens	1981	50,000
Child Care Action Campaign	1983	3,000
National Alliance of Senior Citizens	1974	2 million
National Association of People with AIDS	1985	15,000
National Coalition for the Homeless	1982	9,000
National Committee to Preserve Social Security and Medicare	1982	5 million
National Council of Senior Citizens	1961	5,000

Source: Karen E. Koek and Susan B. Martin, eds., *Encyclopedia of Associations* (Detroit, Mich.: Gale Research Inc., 1990).

Gray Panthers rally in Washington, D.C. This grass-roots organization represents the interests of the elderly. Pluralist explanations for the growth in social welfare spending focus on the actions of interest groups such as this.

policies of **old welfare** treated poverty as an economic problem, a product of capitalism that affected people randomly, and whose effects government sought to mitigate somewhat through programs such as Social Security. The government's role under old welfare was to establish categories of relief and to routinely deliver benefits to people within those categories. Lowi argues that old welfare was successful because it had clearly defined objectives and beneficiaries, a distinct government role in providing benefits, and a specified way of increasing benefits or changing categories in response to changed economic conditions.

New welfare policies, on the other hand, represented a quite different approach to poverty.

The programs of the Kennedy and Johnson administrations were designed not just to mitigate the effects of poverty but to eliminate poverty altogether. These new programs, says Lowi, were shaped by interest group liberalism. Unlike old welfare policymakers, who saw poverty as a strictly economic phenomenon, new welfare policymakers sought "to organize poverty as though it were a human characteristic comparable to any other 'interest' around which interest groups form."[55] The government acted as a broker among many interests.

Lowi shows how the new welfare programs established by the Economic Opportunity Act of 1964 reflected the operation of interest group liberalism. Instead of establishing categories and providing specific benefits, these programs set up a process for making those decisions. Decisions about benefits and priorities were left to the public and private agencies and groups involved in that process. The distinction between government and private groups all but disappeared in new welfare programs. According to Lowi, this delegation of authority and local discretion resulted in uneven application of welfare laws and in fragmented and parochial welfare programs administered by local and even neighborhood agencies. These consequences help explain why there is often great dissatisfaction with new welfare even when spending for these programs is high.

The pluralist view alerts us to the important role of interest groups in shaping social welfare policies in the United States. Interest group activity also helps to account for the continuation and expansion of programs once they have been established, the fragmented nature of those programs, and some of the dissatisfaction with these social welfare policies. Pluralists emphasize the competition among a variety of elites, both public and private, in policymaking. The power elite view sees more uniformity than competition in the actions of political elites.

The Power Elite

Elite explanations of social welfare policy do not attach much importance to public opinion, which is the center of the democratic view. And while those who offer power elite explanations are aware of the existence and importance of interest groups in shaping social policies, they are likely to question the representative quality of those groups and their leaders and to point to the many people in society who have a great stake in those policies but are *un*organized and *un*represented. Two distinct forms of the power elite view of social welfare policies have developed in the United States. One comes from critics of capitalism on the left side of the political spectrum; the other comes from right-wing conservative critics of the welfare state.

According to the first view, the governing power elite creates welfare policies as a form of *social control*, a way of regulating and gaining the allegiance of the unemployed and poor. They point out that nondemocratic, paternalistic societies, such as nineteenth-century Germany, were the first to develop social insurance policies, because political leaders feared that the poor and laboring class might otherwise support socialist or revolutionary movements.[56] Welfare policies were a way for the power elites to control social unrest and avert revolution.

The expansion of mass democracy and capitalism early in this century made policies of social control seem even more necessary to the power elite. Democracy gave unemployed workers and the poor the power to vote, a more immediate and usable power than the threat of revolution or revolt. Capitalism tied national economies to worldwide business cycles that regularly produced high levels of unemployment and unrest. The social control thesis holds that elite-sponsored policies are necessary to maintain the existing political and economic system. It is a top-down explanation, the reverse of that seen in the democratic view.

The social control thesis helps explain the cyclical nature of welfare policies, periods of expansion followed by periods of "reform" to reduce welfare rolls. During times of economic and social unrest, such as the Great Depression of the 1930s and black unrest in the 1960s, the government expands its welfare programs in an attempt to keep the peace among unemployed workers.[57] Another characteristic of welfare policies explained in terms of control is that the benefits provided by those policies must be small enough to make most recipients prefer work to welfare.

Frances Fox Piven and Richard Cloward, in their book *Regulating the Poor*, assert that for a time welfare policies in the United States reflected both the cycles and the minimal benefits predicted by the social control thesis. In a more recent book on the Reagan administration and welfare policies, however, these same scholars argue that since the 1970s the cyclical nature and minimal benefits of earlier policies have disappeared. They contend that too many people now have a stake in existing welfare policies to permit their elimination or serious reduction. In their view, a social control explanation, while helpful for understanding past welfare policies, does not work as well for policies in the 1980s and beyond.[58]

Charles Murray's book, *Losing Ground*, looks at welfare programs from the right-wing end of the political spectrum.[59] He suggests that many or most of the welfare programs begun in the mid-1960s have not been successful in meeting their policy goals. Indeed, Murray argues that by increasing welfare dependency these policies have harmed the poor more than they have helped. He suggests that the flawed welfare policies initiated in the mid-1960s reflected a change in how decision makers viewed poverty.

One of the important changes described by Murray is the emergence of a *structural* view of poverty, one that regarded poverty as a result of flaws in the political and economic system itself, rather than a failing on the part of the individual. According to Murray, this shift from individualism to collectivism in explaining the causes of poverty led to an important change in policy goals. Instead of providing equality of opportunity, social welfare policies focused on providing equality of outcome. They took the form of aid to the working poor and affirmative action programs that would give special preference to victims of discrimination. Equality of opportunity could be achieved by providing jobs; equality of outcome required additional support to the working poor.

How did this change in the approach to social

welfare policies come about? Murray says that it was not the result of a change in public opinion.

> The shift in assumptions occurred among a small group relative to the entire population, but one of enormous influence. The group is, with no pejorative connotations, best labeled the intelligentsia—a broad and diffuse group in late-twentieth-century America, but nonetheless identifiable in a rough fashion.[60]

The most important members of this elite are scholars, journalists, publishers, professionals at foundations and research centers, high-level civil servants, and some politicians. All the members of this loosely constructed group share a professional concern with ideas about social problems and their solutions.

The elite described by Murray is not a power elite in the sense that its members govern. Some members of the intelligentsia do indeed directly exercise political or economic power, but for most, their influence is indirect. They help shape the dialogue about social welfare policy by generating ideas and by writing and talking about those ideas. A broad agreement among members of this elite about the direction social policy should take, a new "elite wisdom," began to emerge in 1964. Within a few years, social welfare policies reflected this goal of equality of outcome and aid to the working poor, ideas that had been rejected by policymakers in earlier times.

The two elite views described above, coming as they do from opposite ends of the political spectrum, tend to support Hugh Heclo's conclusion that a "convergence has taken place between the political right and political left in many democracies. Both tend to see the postwar welfare state as excessively centralized, bureaucratic, professionally self-interested, and insensitive to individual and local needs."[61] The solution to this problem offered by conservatives is an increased reliance on the private sector as a way to increase employment and reduce poverty. Critics from the left are more likely to favor decentralizing, but not abandoning, social welfare programs. These are two quite different approaches to social welfare policy. Both, however, could have the effect of diminishing the influence

of those members of the elite with a stake in existing social welfare programs.

Checkpoint

- The attitudes of both the general public and political leaders toward social policy are complex and are based on a belief in the competing values of equality and liberty, security and economic mobility, and individualism and collectivism.

- The democratic perspective calls attention to two important aspects of the politics of social welfare: a limited support for the concept of welfare rights and a greater emphasis on welfare programs that are not restricted to the poor but are available to the middle class as well.

- The pluralist model of American politics helps explain the fragmented nature of welfare programs in the United States, their long life and expansion once they are started, and the widespread dissatisfaction with many of the programs.

- Power elite explanations of social policy have taken two distinct forms: a social control thesis offered by critics from the left side of the political spectrum and conservative explanations that focus on an elite intelligentsia that formed a consensus on equality of outcome.

SUMMARY

Social policy represents the means through which government seeks to meet a responsibility expressed in the preamble to the Constitution: "to promote the general welfare." Some of our most important social policies are Social Security, Medicare and Medicaid, food stamps, and Aid to Families with Dependent Children (AFDC). Many other social problems—homelessness, AIDS, education, drug abuse—also claim the attention of policymakers. Social policies in these areas must deal with both underlying causes (such as the breakdown in family structure) and immediate and long-range consequences of the problem.

The current debate over welfare policies reflects continuing disagreement over the effects of past policies: Have they worked or not? Some general conclusions are possible: Poverty has been reduced since 1965, but it has not involved a redistribution of wealth and income (the gap between the poor and the rich has widened); the proportion of the poor who are women and children is growing; and it is unclear to what extent policy effects are shaped by economic factors. The politics of social policymaking is, at bottom, a debate over the proper role of government in American society.

Democratic explanations for social policy focus on the direction of public opinion. The pluralists look at the decentralizing effects of interest group activity. Power elite theorists, from both right and left ends of the political spectrum, see social policy as a direct consequence of elite decision making, whether it is used as a form of social control or as a means to pursue equality of outcome.

KEY TERMS

Social policy	Food stamps
Individualism	Means-tested programs
Collectivism	AFDC
Social Security	Feminization of poverty
Medicare	Old welfare
Medicaid	New welfare

FOR FURTHER READING

Phoebe H. Cottingham and David T. Ellwood, eds., *Welfare Policy for the 1990s* (Cambridge, Mass.: Harvard University Press, 1989). A good overview and analysis of the major issues of the debate over welfare policy leading up to the reforms of the Family Support Act of 1988.

Richard M. Coughlin, *Ideology, Public Opinion and Welfare Policy* (Berkeley: Institute of International Studies, University of California, 1980). An analysis of the complex nature of public opinion on welfare policy and how that affects social policymaking in a democracy.

Sheldon M. Danziger and Daniel H. Weinberg, eds., *Fighting Poverty: What Works and What Doesn't* (Cambridge, Mass.: Harvard University Press, 1986). Twenty-three welfare experts assess the social, economic, and political effects of antipoverty programs.

Hugh Heclo, *The Welfare State in Hard Times* (Washington, D.C.: American Political Science Association, 1985). A brief introduction and comparative perspective on government policies to promote the material welfare of citizens.

Michael B. Katz, *In the Shadow of the Poorhouse: A Social History of Welfare in America* (New York: Basic Books, 1986). An interesting review and analysis of welfare policies from colonial times to the 1980s that examines the underlying themes of government policies in this area and why many of these policies have failed to accomplish their goals.

Theodore Lowi, *The End of Liberalism*, 2nd ed. (New York: Norton, 1979). An analysis of how interest group liberalism produced the welfare state and the "new welfare" discussed in this chapter.

Charles Murray, *Losing Ground: American Social Policy, 1950–1980* (New York: Basic Books, 1984). A critique of the Great Society programs, which advances the thesis that those programs have harmed rather than helped the poor and blacks in particular.

Frances Fox Piven and Richard A. Cloward, *Regulating the Poor: The Functions of Public Welfare* (New York: Pantheon Books, 1971). A political and economic analysis of public welfare in the United States and a thorough presentation of the social control thesis discussed in the chapter.

John E. Schwarz, *America's Hidden Success: A Reassessment of Twenty Years of Public Policy* (New York: Norton, 1983). A counterpoint to Charles Murray's *Losing Ground*, this book concludes that the social policies of the previous 20 years have been much more successful than is generally recognized.

Foreign and Defense Policy

For more than 40 years the United States, motivated by fear of Soviet expansionism, erected a huge national security state. Its influence seeped into every aspect of American society, frequently subordinating domestic needs to concerns about war and peace. Then, beginning in the late 1980s, events in the Soviet Union, Central Europe, and elsewhere rocked the foundations of the national security state. In the century's last decade the United States finds itself at a crossroads: How will it adjust to the rapidly changing international environment? Even more important, who will make the fundamental decisions—the people, interest groups, or a power elite? ■

Nineteen forty-five provided the common frame of reference—the compass points of the postwar era we've relied upon to understand ourselves. That was our world. Until now. The events of the year just ended—the Revolution of '89—has been a chain-reaction—change so striking that it marks the beginning of a new era in the world's affairs.[1]

President George Bush's words in his State of the Union message in January 1990 reflected what all his listeners knew was happening in the world. For the past half century the United States and the Soviet Union had been locked in a bitter, protracted Cold War. Each country had spent trillions of dollars arming itself. Although the two nations never engaged in face to face combat, their struggle included virtually every form of diplomatic, political, economic, and propaganda warfare.

Then suddenly, seemingly within months, changes in the Soviet Union and Eastern Europe drastically transformed the international order. Poland, East Germany, Czechoslovakia, Hungary, Romania, and other central European nations threw off the shackles of communism and Soviet domination. East and West Germany, divided for more than 45 years, took halting steps toward reunification. Within the Soviet Union's own borders the winds of political and economic reform blew with gale force intensity. Most hopeful of all, the superpowers traded proposals

for massive reductions in military forces. American foreign and defense policy leaders struggled to keep pace with developments. No wonder a somewhat bewildered congressman said: "Every night for 40 years we walked into the bedroom, opened the closet and looked under the bed to see if we could find a Communist. And one day we walked in, and he was in our bed, smiling. It's very confusing."[2]

Of course, it is still too early to tell if the future will justify Bush's belief that the world has entered a new era. But the changes in international politics raise three key questions: First, what happened in the years after 1945—what were the "compass points" that guided American foreign and defense policy? Second, who made the key decisions that set the nation on the course it followed for so long? Third, and most significant, who will decide what is to be done in the future?

Many Americans are not comfortable dealing with these sorts of issues. They feel that international relations are best left to diplomats and generals. Like it or not, however, what goes on overseas touches every man, woman, and child in the country. All of us live in the shadow of the atomic bomb. And it is not just nuclear annihilation that threatens us. Regional conflicts, trade wars, terrorism, international drug trafficking, global hunger, pollution of the oceans and atmosphere, and a host of other problems have vitally important consequences for everyone.

The significance of foreign affairs: American casualties of an attack on the U.S.S. Stark by an Iraqi warplane in 1988. Although many Americans claim to be ignorant of international relations, most foreign and defense policies have such widespread and deadly ramifications that they constitute trunk decisions.

Consider, too, the more mundane aspects of national security. The Defense Department, which consumes about a quarter of the federal budget, is the nation's biggest consumer, landlord, and employer. Certainly if any part of the government is worth keeping under civilian control, surely it is this one. But foreign affairs reach even more directly into American hometowns. The Korean War cost the lives of about 34,000 U.S. soldiers; the Vietnam War took another 50,000 casualties. Cold statistics like these give meaning to the old saying, "War is too important to leave to the generals."

Foreign and defense policy, finally, typify trunk decisions, those basic choices described in Chapter 1 that set the agenda and scope of politics. A nation's external relations partly shape its domestic life. What government does on the home front—its tax rates and spending priorities—depends on how much is left over after military and diplomatic requirements have been met. Thus, to appreciate who governs, to know who decides "whatever is decided of major consequence,"[3] one necessarily has to study foreign and defense policy.

Chapter 20

FOREIGN POLICY AFTER WORLD WAR II: CONTAINMENT

The years between 1945 and 1948 were as fateful as any in American history. During that period the foreign policy establishment made decisions that still reverberate today. As World War II wound down, officials in the highest circles of government thought long and hard about what kind of international system was possible and desirable.[4] Though they disagreed about particulars, they had to face certain inescapable and unsettling facts.

Europe lay in ruins, an easy prey for an aggressor or, more likely, internal upheaval. The Soviet Union, too, was devastated, but its army controlled Eastern Europe, half of Germany, and had a strategic foothold in Asia. To complicate matters, Soviet leaders had been advocating the overthrow of capitalism for 25 years. Although the United States suffered heavy casualties, it otherwise escaped the war relatively undamaged. With its farms and industries intact and its skilled population healthy and well fed, it was the only non-Communist power on its feet. Simply by virtue of this condition, America seemed destined for world leadership.

But how should the United States exercise this responsibility? What role should it play? And of utmost significance, how should it deal with its wartime ally, the Soviet Union, which, after all, was the only country capable of challenging its supremacy?

The top echelons of government considered two general policies. One advocated cooperation with the Soviet Union. Its advocates believed that the Russians posed no direct threat to the United States, which should try to recognize and accommodate the Soviets' legitimate security interests. The other policy, eventually known as *containment*, assumed that the Soviets' ultimate goal was world domination and called for a firm commitment to hold off their expansionist tendencies. As A Closer Look (pp. 634–635) shows, containment won the day in Washington. It was a fateful decision that shaped the course of American history for the next four decades.

Containment's Four Branches

As applied by the Truman and succeeding administrations, containment consisted of four components or branches: diplomacy, foreign aid, military force, and arms control. All elements have been present to one extent or another during the past 45 years, but most presidents have relied most heavily on the military branch.[5]

THE DIPLOMATIC BRANCH The acceptance of containment caused the United States to establish alliances and bilateral agreements with scores of countries in Europe, the Middle East, Asia, and Latin America (see Figure 20.1 on p. 636). Breaking with America's long-standing policy of **isolationism**—a tradition of neutrality and noninvolvement in the affairs of countries outside the Western Hemisphere—these pacts committed the United States to come to the defense of the victims of "aggression." The North Atlantic Treaty Organization (NATO), the most important of these treaties, inexorably tied the United States to Europe because an attack against one member would be "considered an attack against them all" and would be met with whatever action was deemed necessary, "including the use of armed force."[6]

Complementing alliances such as NATO were vigorous diplomatic maneuvers to shore up governments friendly to the West and to undermine pro-Soviet regimes. Any unstable place that the Soviets might exploit became a cause for concern; any revolution receiving support from Moscow or its allies was considered a menace, even if the Communists played only a minor role and the revolutionaries' grievances were legitimate.

By the same token, anxiety about the expansion of Soviet influence fueled attempts to isolate or undermine left-wing movements whenever and wherever they emerged. Using the Central Intelligence Agency (CIA), the Eisenhower administration helped overthrow popular governments in Iran (1953) and Guatemala (1954) because of their allegedly pro-Soviet or anti-Western leanings. Similarly, Eisenhower withdrew diplomatic recognition of the Cuban government after its chief of state, Fidel Castro, began seizing American property and expressed sympathy for revolutionary movements in other parts of Latin America.

The role of diplomacy, however, is most clearly seen in our relationship with Vietnam. At the end of World War II, forces led by the nationalist leader Ho Chi Minh fought to rid the part of Indochina now called Vietnam of French domination. In the early years of their struggle, Ho and his followers had Washington's sympathy, but as the Cold War unfolded, American policy shifted to the French side. The United States, increasingly viewing Ho as a tool in the Kremlin's plan to dominate Southeast Asia, stepped up diplomatic and economic aid to the French. In spite of this support, the French steadily lost ground and were forced at an international peace conference to partition the area into two zones. Ho controlled the northern half, while the French withdrew to the South. The division was to be temporary, since both sides agreed that free and open elections would take place within two years to unify the country.

In the following years, American influence

A Closer Look

Two Letters and the Origins of Containment ★ ★ ★

In July 1946, Secretary of Commerce Henry Wallace, a former vice-president to Franklin Roosevelt, wrote President Harry Truman a letter recommending that the United States "allay any reasonable Russian grounds for fear, suspicion, and distrust" of our goals.[a] It was necessary, he said, to understand and accept the Soviets' legitimate security interests. Having suffered 10 to 12 million casualties during World War II, the Russian bear was mainly intent on being left alone to lick its wounds. Although it may be a surly and secretive animal, it posed no threat to the United States. Trying to put American policymakers in Soviet shoes, he asked:

> How would it look to us if Russia had the atomic bomb and we did not, if Russia had 10,000 mile bombers and air bases within 1,000 miles of our coastlines and we did not.[b]

Advocating a policy of conciliation, Wallace recommended that we "be prepared . . . to agree to reasonable Russian guarantees of security," to "negotiate a treaty which will [establish] international control and development of atomic energy," to "counteract the irrational fear of Russia," to "enter into economic discussions" without preconditions, and to pursue a vigorous policy of "active trade" with them, a policy that "might well help clear away the fog of political misunderstanding."[c] In a nutshell, Wallace advocated a policy of understanding, mutual respect, and restraint toward the Soviets.

Some months earlier, however, in February 1946, the State Department received different advice about the Russians. George Kennan, a career diplomat with considerable experience inside the Soviet Union, sent a telegram to his superiors in which he warned them to be prepared for a protracted struggle.[d] The conflict would in all likelihood not be violent but would nonetheless require patience and determination to win. Although Kennan agreed with Wallace on some points, he painted a much darker picture of Soviet motives and goals. According to Kennan, the Soviets saw themselves encircled by antagonistic capitalist governments with which peaceful coexistence was impossible. Their fundamental strategy, therefore, was to build up their economic and military strength at the expense of the West. They would attempt to implement this policy by exploiting divisions among capitalist powers, fomenting revolution in underdeveloped nations, imposing their ideology in the areas they controlled, consolidating their internal power, and making "timely and promising" moves against their neighbors.[e] Kennan, briefly stated, saw Russia as a dangerous foe that unless stopped could and would threaten the vital interests of the United States and its allies.

What should be done? Kennan felt that the answer lay in the minds of the men in the Kremlin. Unlike Hitler, they were not reckless, but would back down when confronted with overwhelming force: Russia "can easily withdraw—and usually does—when strong resistance is encountered at any point."[f] By mobilizing sufficient resources and displaying a willingness to use them, the United States

Henry Wallace (left) and George Kennan (right) recommended sharply different policies for dealing with the Soviet Union after World War II. Kennan's advocacy of containment eventually prevailed.

and its allies in Europe could make the enemy abandon its objectives, usually without armed conflict. Our policy, in a word, should be *containment*—to halt or check Soviet expansionism.

The contrasts between Kennan and Wallace could hardly have been clearer. Wallace wanted conciliation; Kennan advised vigilance and toughness. In the end Kennan's view prevailed. The die was cast by late 1947 when President Truman, rejecting Wal-

lace's arguments, began implementing containment.

[a]Letter to Harry S. Truman, July 23, 1946. Reprinted in John M. Blum, ed., *The Price of Vision: The Diary of Henry A. Wallace* (Boston: Houghton Mifflin, 1973), p. 597.
[b]Ibid., p. 591.
[c]Ibid., pp. 587–600.
[d]Reprinted in Barton J. Bernstein and Allan J. Matusow, eds., *The Truman Administration: A Documentary History* (New York: Harper & Row, 1966), pp. 198–212.
[e]Ibid., pp. 198–212.
[f]Ibid.

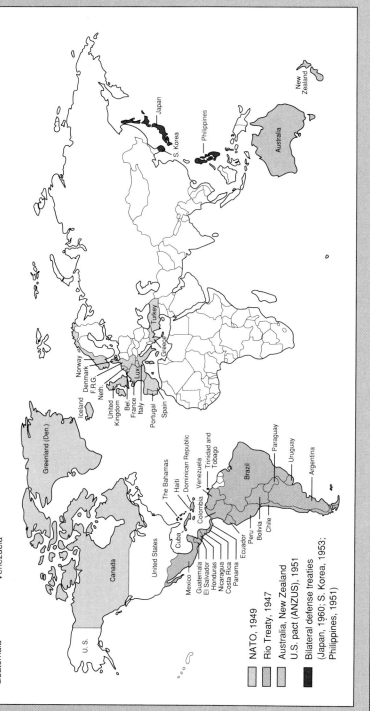

Members of Inter-American Treaty of Reciprocal Assistance (Rio Treaty)

An armed attack against any American State "shall be considered as an attack against all the American States," and each one "undertakes to assist in meeting the attack."

Argentina
The Bahamas
Bolivia
Brazil
Chile
Colombia
Costa Rica
Cuba (suspended)
Dominican Republic
Ecuador
El Salvador
Guatemala

Haiti
Honduras
Mexico
Nicaragua
Panama
Paraguay
Peru
Trinidad and
 Tobago
Uruguay
United States
Venezuela

Members of North Atlantic Treaty Organization (NATO)

"The parties agree that an armed attack against one or more of them in Europe or North America shall be considered an attack against them all; and each party, will assist the . . . attacked by taking . . . such action as it deems necessary including the use of armed force."

Canada
Belgium
Denmark
France
West Germany
Greece
Iceland
Italy

Luxembourg
Netherlands
Norway
Portugal
Spain
Turkey
United Kingdom
United States

Figure 20.1
U.S. Collective Defense Treaties

Members of ANZUS Treaty

Each party recognizes that "an armed attack in the Pacific Area on any of the parties would be dangerous to its own peace and safety," and each party agrees that it will act "to meet the common danger in accordance with its own constitutional processes."

Australia
New Zealand
United States

NATO, 1949
Rio Treaty, 1947
Australia, New Zealand
U.S. pact (ANZUS), 1951
Bilateral defense treaties
(Japan, 1960; S. Korea, 1953;
Philippines, 1951)

Source: United States Department of State, *Atlas of United States Foreign Relations* (Washington, D.C.: Office of Public Affairs, 1985). p. 83.

gradually replaced the French in South Vietnam. Indeed, by the end of the 1950s, Washington supported Ngo Dinh Diem, a pro-Western Vietnamese leader. Even though Diem became steadily unpopular with his subjects and as much as anyone prevented the promised elections from taking place, he seemed preferable to Ho, a man of uncertain political persuasions. Backing Diem's dictatorial and corrupt regime, State Department officials felt, was better than allowing a Communist takeover that would lead to further Soviet expansion in the region.

President Eisenhower described this logic in his famous **domino analogy**: If Indochina fell, he reasoned,

> You have . . . what you would call the "falling domino" principle. You have a row of dominoes set up, you knock over the first one, and what will happen to the last one is the certainty that it will go over very quickly.[7]

After taking over Vietnam, in other words, the Communists, presumably inspired and guided by Moscow, would be in a position to threaten Laos, then Cambodia, then Indonesia, then the Philippines, and so on. The dominoes would only stop falling, if they stopped at all, at the shores of California. This kind of reasoning has led the United States to support dictatorial, but anti-Communist, regimes all over the globe.

THE FOREIGN AID BRANCH Putting containment to work required more than diplomacy. It demanded immense amounts of financial assistance as well. Humanitarian impulses to help alleviate hunger, illness, and misery also happened to dovetail with the demands of foreign policy. Containment's advocates believed that if a country possessed a strong, stable economy, its citizens would be less apt to listen to Marxist ideology. In the struggle to hold back world communism, then, our interests would be served by lending a hand to destitute people.

The economic branch began growing swiftly after 1948. In one of the most ambitious recovery efforts ever taken, the United States committed $19 billion to the European Recovery Program, popularly known as the **Marshall Plan** after one of its authors, Secretary of State George Mar-

shall. The objectives were to rebuild European economies, raise living standards, reduce tariffs, and establish stable currencies. Such a harmonious bloc, the Congress was told, would stand as a bastion against the Soviet Union. It would also, its backers shrewdly pointed out, provide a lucrative market for American exports.*

Europe occupied the center of attention in World War II's aftermath, but gradually the direction of American assistance shifted to less developed regions. By the 1970s, 99 cents out of every dollar of foreign aid went somewhere other than Western Europe. Nevertheless, the primary motivation remained the same: containment of communism.

THE MILITARY BRANCH In the postwar years, leaders in the White House and on Capitol Hill were convinced that they had a military crisis on their hands. A cascade of events—the descent of an "iron curtain" across the middle of Europe, the emergence of a Communist government in China, the USSR's successful detonation of an atomic bomb—convinced President Truman's advisers to reconsider the best way to meet the threat. Their thoughts culminated in a watershed document, **NSC 68**, a report by the National Security Council that reached Truman's desk in April 1950.

NSC 68 concluded that the United States faced a bellicose and implacable foe and therefore had to beef up its military capability.[8] Diplomacy and foreign assistance would by themselves be insufficient. Instead, we had to maintain qualitative and quantitative *superiority* in nuclear arms and strengthen our conventional forces as well.[9] Expanding the defense budget might require postponing desirable domestic programs and require tax increases, but these sacrifices were the cost of freedom. In a nutshell, the report justified making military force containment's primary branch.

---

*The State Department invited the Russians to participate, but on terms that made their acceptance highly unlikely. For example, they were asked to ship goods to Europe even though their own economy had been devastated by the war. Walter LaFeber, *America, Russia, and the Cold War* (New York: Knopf, 1985), p. 59.

Radioactive fallout from atmospheric testing of nuclear weapons convinced both the United States and the Soviet Union to curb these tests. This realization led to the signing of the Partial Test Ban Treaty in 1963.

Acceptance of NSC 68 and related policies implied a commitment to a **national security state**, a government that devotes a huge portion of its attention and resources to national defense. Contrary to its traditions of isolationism and neutrality, the United States would have to accept a huge peacetime standing army, a smaller budget for nondefense purposes, methods for maintaining internal security, higher taxes, personal sacrifice, a toning down of political debate, and the prospect of living in a state of permanent cold war. As the national security state grew, it drastically changed the nature and spirit of American democracy.

THE ARMS CONTROL BRANCH The start of the Cold War and the policy of containment did not mean that the United States and the Soviet Union stopped speaking to each other. American policymakers continued to distrust their Russian adversaries but still sought to make containment less dangerous. After all, the new weapons of mass destruction radically and permanently altered the nature of warfare.

Negotiations on arms control, however, moved at a glacial pace during the 1950s and early 1960s. Washington and Moscow regularly traded arms reduction proposals, but propa-

ganda seemed to motivate most of them.[10] Yet as the arms race continued it became evident that the competition was nudging the world closer to catastrophe.

Atomic testing, for example, polluted the atmosphere with radioactive fallout. Faced with this increasingly obvious threat, the United States and Soviet Union signed a *Partial Test Ban Treaty* in 1963. This agreement outlawed the detonation of atomic devices in the air, on land, or at sea. It permitted only underground tests. Most of the nuclear powers also agreed to the *Non-Proliferation Treaty* of 1968. This pact prohibited states that had already developed the bomb from transferring this technology to nonnuclear nations, while those signatories that had not yet acquired an atomic capability agreed not to do so in the future. The United States, the Soviet Union, and Great Britain signed the treaty, but it has not been accepted by several important countries, notably China, France, Israel, India, Pakistan, and South Africa.

Efforts to limit the arms race did not end here by any means (see Table 20.1). In fact, they intensified in the 1970s and 1980s. But these negotiations and treaties are integrally bound up with contemporary policy, so we defer discussion of them until a later section.

Table 20.1

Major Arms Control Treaties and Agreements Since World War II

Name	Parties	Effective Date	Description
Antarctic Treaty	13 nations, including U.S., USSR	June 23, 1961	Internationalized and demilitarized Antarctica
Hot Line Agreement	U.S., USSR	June 20, 1963	Established direct radio and wire telegraph link between governments of USSR and U.S.
Partial Test Ban Treaty	Original parties: U.K., U.S., USSR; most nations except France and China have signed	Oct. 10, 1963	Banned nuclear weapon testing in atmosphere, outer space, under water
Outer Space Treaty	89 signers, including U.S., USSR	Oct. 10, 1967	Banned weapons of mass destruction from space, demilitarized celestial bodies
Non-Proliferation Treaty	138 nations; notable exceptions: Argentina, Brazil, China, France, India, Israel, Pakistan, South Africa	March 5, 1970	Aimed to prevent spread of nuclear weapons, promote peaceful uses of nuclear energy and nuclear disarmament
Seabed Arms Control Treaty	U.K., U.S., USSR, and others; not France and China	May 18, 1972	Banned weapons of mass destruction from seabed outside 12-mile zone
Accident Measures Agreement	U.S., USSR	Sept. 30, 1971	Prevention, notification of accidental launch
Biological Weapons Convention	U.K., U.S., USSR, and others; not France and China	March 26, 1975	Banned bacteriological and toxin weapons
SALT I—Anti-Ballistic Missile Treaty	U.S., USSR	Oct. 3, 1972	Limited antiballistic missile systems to two sites, prohibited them for territorial defense
SALT I—Interim Agreement on Offensive Weapons	U.S., USSR	Oct. 3, 1972	Set temporary limits on strategic offensive forces
SALT I—ABM Protocol	U.S., USSR	May 24, 1976	Limited ABMs to one site
Threshold Test Ban Treaty	U.S., USSR	Signed July 3, 1974; **not ratified by Senate**	Limited underground nuclear tests to 150 kilotons
SALT II	U.S., USSR	Signed June 18, 1979; **not ratified by Senate**	Would have limited offensive nuclear weapons

Continued

Table 20.1

(Continued)

Name	Parties	Effective Date	Description
Stockholm Accord on Confidence-Building Measures	U.S., USSR, and 33 European nations	Sept. 22, 1986	Provided for notification, observation of conventional military exercises, Atlantic to Urals
Nuclear Risk Reduction Centers Agreement	U.S., USSR	Sept. 15, 1987	Established high-speed communication centers in both capitals
Intermediate-Range Nuclear Forces Treaty	U.S., USSR	June 1, 1988	Banned ground-based nuclear missiles with ranges of 300–3500 miles

Source: Based on "Has Arms Control Worked," *Bulletin of the Atomic Scientists* 45 (May 1989): p. 36.

Checkpoint

- After World War II, American policymakers had to decide how to deal with the Soviet Union. They settled on containment, the policy of actively resisting perceived Soviet aggressiveness.

- The diplomatic branch of containment required the United States to abandon its traditional policy of isolationism, enter into numerous alliances, try to destabilize pro-Communist governments and support pro-Western ones.

- Containment also required the United States to spend billions of dollars on military and foreign aid.

- The policy took on its greatest significance, however, when military force became a primary instrument for implementing containment.

- Despite their bitter rivalry, the Soviet Union and the United States agreed to several arms control measures.

THE MILITARIZATION OF CONTAINMENT

Since containment relied so heavily on conventional and nuclear weapons, an extraordinary amount of America's brainpower went into thinking about how to use them.

Containment with Conventional Arms

In the years since the end of World War II, the United States has become involved in several minor military engagements—sending troops to the Dominican Republic, the island of Grenada, and Panama. But the wars in Korea and Vietnam mark two of the main "compass points" President Bush mentioned in his State of the Union address.

The Korean conflict started when North Korean armed forces (whom American leaders suspected were following orders from Moscow) invaded South Korea in the summer of 1950. The Truman administration felt it had to repel the North Koreans and teach the Russians a lesson, yet at the same time it did not want the war to spread to the rest of Asia or Europe. The best way to achieve these objectives, Truman and his

The militarization of containment eventually propelled the United States into full scale involvement in the War in Vietnam, one of the most divisive conflicts in American history.

advisers thought, was to confine the fighting to the Korean peninsula and use only conventional weapons. They consistently resisted entreaties to bomb bases in China, invade the Chinese mainland, or drop atomic bombs.

This approach, however, aroused considerable criticism, especially when the conflict, which lasted three years and cost thousands of casualties, ended in a stalemate. Truman's critics complained bitterly that limited wars, particularly those fought by Soviet proxies, would bleed America dry. Why not use weapons of our own choosing against the real enemy, they asked?

This question came up again a decade later when the United States began to get militarily involved in Vietnam. President John F. Kennedy was mindful of the criticisms directed at Truman's policies, but nonetheless, like Truman, he appreciated the value of conventional forces as an instrument of containment. One of the key tenets of his national security policy in the early 1960s was a strategy of *flexible response*. In his view, threatening to use nuclear weapons in a small conflict would not seem credible to the enemy, and actually using them would be counterproductive, especially since the Russians were developing their own nuclear capability. Instead, conventional forces—soldiers, tanks, tactical aircraft, and the like—would be needed for most of the situations the United States was likely to encounter.

Vietnam put Kennedy's ideas to the test. As time went by, he and his successor, President Lyndon Johnson, gradually increased the number of military advisers and equipment sent to help the Diem regime. When this extra assistance failed to stem the tide, limited air strikes were ordered; when these did not work, more missions were flown. Slowly, step by step, the United States climbed the ladder of escalation, using just enough force, defense analysts thought, to make the enemy capitulate.

Finally, in 1974, the United States abandoned the struggle, and the North Vietnamese claimed victory. The war in Vietnam left almost everyone in America unhappy. "Doves" felt that besides destroying the country we were trying to save,[*] the United States was too preoccupied with military force and too insensitive to human needs at home and abroad. "Hawks," on the other hand, believed that, as in Korea, we had not conducted the war vigorously enough.

_____

[*]The air force dropped more bombs in that relatively small area than were dropped by the allies during all of World War II. No one knows for certain, but probably more than a million people (most of them civilians) died in the conflict. According to Barry Weisberg, herbicides destroyed 15 percent of Vietnam's forests and 7 percent of its farm land. Cited in Ira Katznelson and Mark Kesselman, *The Politics of Power*, 2nd ed. (New York: Harcourt Brace Jovanovich, 1979), p. 240.

Containment by Nuclear Deterrence

Korea, America's first major attempt at containment by conventional military power, greatly dissatisfied President Dwight D. Eisenhower, who succeeded Truman. A "limited war," the Korean conflict had neither deterred the Communists nor punished them for their transgressions. As a matter of fact, it apparently played into their hands, since with a large population and captive nations to act as their surrogate combatants, they were better prepared to wage these kinds of conflicts.

To get the United States out of this box, John Foster Dulles, who became Eisenhower's Secretary of State, proposed a new strategy for containing communism:

> There is one solution and only one: that is . . . to develop the will [and] the means to retaliate instantly against open aggression by Red armies, so that, if it occurred anywhere, we could and would strike back where it hurts, by means of our choosing.[11]

Although Dulles did not define the word "means," everyone understood it as nuclear weapons. This method for halting Soviet expansion, which came to be known as **massive retaliation**, struck a responsive chord with President Eisenhower, a fiscal conservative, who wanted balanced federal budgets as well as a free world. Coldly stated, the Eisenhower administration sought more "bang for the buck." Since nuclear weapons are cheaper to build and maintain than conventional forces, the doctrine appeared to be the perfect answer to the twin questions of how to keep the Russians at bay while maintaining a vibrant economy. But appearances could be deceiving, as the President and his advisers soon discovered.

NUCLEAR DETERRENCE Eisenhower's stress on massive retaliation ushered in the era of nuclear deterrence. **Nuclear deterrence** assumes that one nation can prevent another from doing something (attacking an ally, for example) by threatening it with certain and devastating retaliation. The *threat*, not its realization, causes the foe to desist. Deterrence creates a state of mind, a fear that an aggressive action will inevitably provoke a catastrophic counteraction.

Despite its apparent simplicity, the concept is more complex than it first seems. After the Russians developed a sizable nuclear capability of their own, American planners began to wrestle with a dilemma: If we launch an all-out attack on them in response to an invasion of Western Europe, they can and will undoubtedly respond in kind. Given the destructive power of nuclear arms, both sides face annihilation. Deterrence, it turns out, is rational *only if the threats are never carried out*; once one nation pushes the button for whatever reason, both are doomed by an act of ultimate irrationality.

Moralists find numerous objections to this state of affairs. Is it ethical, they wonder, to risk the extinction of the human race?[12] On a more practical level, what about accidental war? Should foreign policy depend so heavily on a strategy that could accidentally destroy the planet?

MAKING DETERRENCE WORK There are other considerations. To be effective a threat has to be *credible*. Credibility haunts military theorists who play mind games like this: Suppose we announce to the Russians, "If you invade Belgium, we will destroy ten of your largest cities. And you know we have the weapons to do so." The hope is that Soviet leaders would not consider the risk (the destruction of ten metropolitan areas) worth the gain. But what if they reason this way: "The Americans are only bluffing because they know that an attack on our cities would trigger a similar assault on theirs. Why would they accept the destruction of ten U.S. cities just to save a tiny European country, a place thousands of miles from their territory? When push comes to shove, they'll back down." Deterrence works, in other words, only if the enemy is convinced to take the threat seriously. In order to deter, a country has to maintain both the means *and* the resolve to carry out its threat.

President Kennedy constantly wrestled with the credibility question, which he tried to resolve by modernizing and diversifying the nuclear arsenal and by adopting a policy of "graduated deterrence": Instead of launching a spasmodic, all-out attack on Russian cities and industry—a move that would certainly invite a response in kind—the United States would initially target its nuclear weapons against selected military installations such as missile and air bases, naval depots, and command and control centers. To accomplish this objective, however, the United States had to vastly increase the size and sophistication of its nuclear arsenal.

This strategy would presumably have more credibility than massive retaliation. It appeared to have two additional advantages. First, by destroying a sizable chunk of the Soviet nuclear forces, the United States could limit potential damage to itself. At the same time, the Russians would have an incentive not to devastate our urban centers, for doing so would only cause us to do likewise. Second, and in some observers' minds even more appealing, the approach could put America in a position to "win" a nuclear war. As one defense analyst put it, ". . . if war should come, we want to be able to bring it to a speedy termination on *military terms favorable to ourselves.* . . ."[13]

The belief that a nuclear war can be in some sense "won" has remained part of U.S. strategic doctrine ever since. Officials may publicly decry the horrors of atomic weapons, but administration after administration clings to the notion that, if worse comes to worse, we have to prevail in a nuclear exchange. Not surprisingly, however, they usually do not explain what "prevail" means.

Nuclear deterrence leaves still another problem: the potential vulnerability of our nuclear arsenal to a *preemptive first strike.* Vulnerability constantly plagues national security planners. Suppose the Soviet Union launched a surprise attack on American missiles and bombers. If the strike knocked out 75 percent of our arsenal in a quick blow, a president, having little to retaliate with, might be willing to capitulate to Moscow's demands. In short, a first strike against unprotected forces might weaken the United States' deterrent capacity, leaving it with little choice except to accede to the enemy's demands.

The essence of effective deterrence, then, is an *assured destruction capability,* the ability to ab-sorb an initial blow and retain enough fire power to inflict unacceptable damage on the enemy.[14]

How does one achieve this margin of safety? Essentially, by building more of everything. As noted earlier, the Kennedy administration embarked on an ambitious modernization and expansion program. It requested funds to keep a large portion of its intercontinental bombers airborne and to accelerate the purchase of land- and sea-based missiles. The resulting combination—bombers, intercontinental ballistic missiles (ICBMs), and submarine-launched ballistic missiles (SLBMs)—came to be known as the **triad,** a trio of totally different weapons systems. It would not be enough for the USSR to destroy one leg of the triad; in order to cripple our deterrent it would have to destroy all three.

THE ROAD TO MAD For most of the Cold War period the United States' nuclear arsenal has been clearly superior to the Soviets'. But this advantage never prevented any administration, Republican or Democratic, from pressing ahead with research and development. The Russians did not relent either, and the arms race accelerated in the 1970s. In the course of this contest several new types of weapons emerged. Ironically, as the adversaries spent more and more to achieve security, they acquired less and less of it. The result has been a situation called **mutual assured destruction (MAD):** Whatever one side does, the other can still destroy it.

No sooner had intercontinental missiles become operational than their designers sought to protect them by burying them in underground reinforced concrete bunkers. But hardening silos stimulated countermeasures, which had deadly consequences.

Each side, for example, began manufacturing mammoth ICBMs carrying warheads large enough to obliterate silos with near misses. Nuclear strategists worried about the impact of these weapons on the vulnerability issue. Here's why: If a country thinks its missiles, even those tucked away deep beneath the earth's surface, are vulnerable to a sudden attack, it has an incentive to launch them *before* its enemy can destroy them. During a crisis this "use 'em or lose 'em" sense of insecurity might create a hair trigger mentality and heighten the risk of miscalculation or accident. Thus, far from ensuring invulnerability, hardened silos tended to destabilize the strategic balance and cause an upward spiral in weapons development.

Another development was the deployment of multiple warheads. The first ICBMs carried a single warhead. (The warhead is the part that falls through the atmosphere and explodes on its target. A missile simply lifts the warhead aloft, puts it on a trajectory, and drops back to earth.) The strategic calculus was therefore very simple: one missile, one warhead. But American engineers soon devised a way to place several warheads on a single launcher. Furthermore, each of these warheads could be independently targeted, which is how the acronym MIRV—*m*ultiple *i*ndependently *t*argetable *r*eentry *v*ehicle—

Minuteman warheads shown with their protective nose cone removed. The development of these multiple independently targetable re-entry vehicles (MIRVs) further escalated and destabilized the arms race.

came into vogue. Although the United States pioneered this technology, the Soviets quickly caught on and began "MIRVing" their missiles. Soon it was not necessarily the number of missiles that determined a nation's strength but the number and accuracy of the *warheads* these launchers carried.

Arms control advocates fear that MIRVs might tempt one camp into thinking it could successfully cripple the other with a first strike. After all, since one missile could now do the damage of ten, it would be possible to wipe out the other side's silos and still have launchers left over. As long as both the United States and Russia maintain a mixture of ICBMs, bombers, and submarine launched missiles, it is highly improbable that MIRVs will ever give either one a decisive advantage. Still, the possibility, however remote, makes defense planners nervous and induces them to keep on augmenting and refining their arsenals.

In addition to MIRVs, the superpowers added another lethal weapon to their stockpiles, cruise missiles. A cruise missile resembles a relatively small pilotless drone, the kind of aircraft the air force used for target practice. Unlike ICBMs, which leave the earth's atmosphere, these rockets, guided by sophisticated radars and computers, hug the ground and can travel up to several thousand miles carrying either nuclear or conventional explosives. Because they fly so low they can presumably penetrate air defenses and deliver their payloads with great accuracy. Being relatively small, cruise missiles are easily launched from bombers, submarines, or mobile platforms where they are difficult to spot. Arms control experts deplore these weapons because they are so hard to detect that a treaty banning their deployment would be difficult to verify.

Where have all these moves and countermoves taken us? Have the billions and billions of dollars spent modernizing our awesome nuclear stockpile bought us security? Perhaps. But it is a strange kind of security. Even if both sides ever agree to substantial reductions in their nuclear forces, they will still retain enough firepower to destroy each other a dozen times over. For this reason the United States and Russia have been likened to two people standing in a room waist deep in gasoline. Each holds a match. They can only verbally threaten each other; they can't act. For the death of one leads inescapably to the death of the other. Nothing either one does can change this fact. Survival boils down to the *hope* that threats to retaliate are never carried out.

The logic (or illogic) of MAD partly explains the two superpowers' motivations to seek ways to limit their strategic arsenals. These efforts began in earnest during the period of "detente."

Checkpoint

- The United States has relied on both conventional and nuclear weapons to deter the Soviet Union.
- Conflicts in Korea and Vietnam represented containment by conventional arms. Critics of these limited wars felt the policy wasted America's nuclear superiority.
- Nuclear deterrence means preventing an adversary from taking an action by threatening to retaliate with nuclear arms.
- The Eisenhower administration advocated the doctrine of massive retaliation: threatening to counter Soviet aggression with weapons and at times and places of its own choosing. Worrying that this policy lacked credibility, President Kennedy advocated a more flexible type of deterrence, one that required maintaining a variety of weapons that could be used in a controlled fashion against selected targets.
- The attempt to ensure the survivability of their nuclear forces has prompted both sides to deploy a vast range of new and deadly weapons. The resulting arms race has led to a peculiar kind of security: mutual assured destruction (MAD).

THE ERA OF DETENTE

The foreign policy President Richard Nixon inherited upon taking office in 1969 greatly troubled him and his national security adviser, Henry Kissinger. Most troubling was the lack of an overall global perspective, a strategy that could steer the United States through the perilous and rapidly changing international arena.

It was apparent, for instance, that the world was shifting from bipolarity to *multipolarity*: The emergence of several new powers, including Japan, Western Europe, and China, was replacing the domination of the international system by the two superpowers. In these changing circumstances, America needed fresh approaches, Nixon and Kissinger agreed.

The most far-reaching conclusion these men reached was that cooperation with the Soviet Union was both possible and desirable. By offering inducements as well as punishments, they might encourage the Soviets to change their behavior enough to stabilize international relations. This approach ushered in an era in the 1970s known as **detente**. Detente entailed trying to identify and take advantage of areas of common interest, such as arms control, in order to reduce tensions and the threat of war between the two countries. From the Nixon administration's perspective, detente was another form of containment, the goal being to convince the Soviet Union of the advantages of containing itself.[15]

The SALT Agreements

Operating from these premises, Nixon and Kissinger tried to establish an atmosphere of reciprocity with Moscow. Why not balance concessions in one area with gains in another? The Soviet Union, they knew, wanted an agreement on nuclear weapons and increased trade, especially in grain and advanced technology. The United States sought a graceful way out of Vietnam. Thus, they wondered, why not link the two interests: In exchange for arms control and American exports the Soviets would be expected to cooperate in Indochina. This line of reasoning eventually led to what became known as the

In 1972 President Richard Nixon and Soviet Premier Leonid Brezhnev signed the SALT I Treaty, a milestone in the era of detente.

SALT negotiations. (SALT stands for *Strategic Arms Limitation Talks*.)

SALT I, signed in 1972, contained two main parts: a ban on antiballistic missiles (ABMs) systems and an interim agreement limiting offensive weapons (see Table 20.1). This interim deal, which limited the United States and the USSR for the next five years to certain ceilings on their offensive nuclear weapons, was to be a stepping-stone to a more comprehensive agreement. Unfortunately, it took nearly four more years of hard bargaining before that agreement, SALT II, could be hammered out. A complicated package, it established limits and sublimits on strategic weapons. In essence, the superpowers tried to cap and then reduce their arsenals, but in a manner that allowed them to keep their best systems. In spite of the prodigious negotiations, however, the SALT II agreement did not eliminate major categories of weapons or halt research on newer

and deadlier forms of mass destruction.

President Jimmy Carter and Soviet leader Leonid Brezhnev finally signed the SALT II Treaty in 1979. Although both countries have adhered to its ceilings, the Senate never ratified it. The principal reason for the Senate's refusal to act was the storm of controversy SALT and detente stirred in the domestic political arena.

The Politics of Detente

Presidents Nixon, Ford, and Carter considered detente another way to continue the policy of containment by making the superpower rivalry safer and more stable.[16] Yet as tough as all these presidents were, detente in general and the SALT agreements in particular came under intense fire. Rumblings of discontent emanated from both parties in Congress, from influential news commentators, from the Pentagon, and from various interest groups. Most of these individuals regarded detente as a dangerous fantasy. They contended that the Soviets, who wanted domination, not accommodation, hid behind arms control in an attempt to achieve military superiority. While we showed restraint, they produced more and more sophisticated missiles and aircraft; while we cut defense appropriations, they increased theirs; while we withdrew from Vietnam, they extended their influence into Angola, Ethiopia, and Nicaragua.

Two major events eventually derailed detente. The fall of the shah of Iran, a staunch ally of Washington, and the rise of fundamentalist Muslims under the leadership of Ayatollah Rubollah Khomeini jeopardized America's position in the Middle East. The shah's demise was disturbing enough, but when radical students, with the ayatollah's blessing, stormed the American embassy in November 1979 and seized more than 50 American hostages, the United States *seemed* to have lost its enormous prestige and power.

Then, in December 1979, the Soviet Army invaded Afghanistan to prop up its puppet government there. Many experts considered Afghanistan, a tiny landlocked nation virtually isolated from the rest of the world, of little strategic importance. To some Americans, however, the invasion signaled a prelude to possible Russian intervention in the Persian Gulf, the source of much of the West's petroleum.

In any case, the Carter administration came under blistering attack from both Democrats and Republicans for being too naive about the international Communist menace. Responding to these charges, Carter spent the last months of his presidency redirecting the content and tone of American foreign policy. He withdrew SALT II from consideration by the Senate (he knew it stood little chance of being ratified), embargoed grain shipments to the Soviet Union, forced a boycott of the Summer Olympics in Moscow, and called for huge increases in defense spending.

Even these measures were not enough to quiet the demands for change, and in 1980 the voters elected Ronald Reagan, a man who promised to make America stand tall in the eyes of the world.

Checkpoint

- President Nixon and his national security adviser, Henry Kissinger, continued the tradition of containment but changed the methods for implementing it. The new approach led to an era in the 1970s commonly known as detente, a period during which the United States and the Soviet Union engaged in continuous and far-reaching arms control negotiations in order to reduce tensions between them.

- Detente produced the SALT I and SALT II treaties that attempted to limit nuclear weapons.

- Influential members of Congress, the media, and others, who were concerned that the Soviets hid behind detente while building up their military strength, vociferously attacked the SALT II treaty, and the Senate never ratified it.

FOREIGN AND DEFENSE POLICY IN THE 1980s AND 1990s

When he took office in 1981, Ronald Reagan held a simpler view of Soviet-American relations than his predecessors. Where they saw diversity, complexity, and rapid change, he saw a clear-cut, life-and-death struggle with an implacable foe; where they occasionally detected a mellowing in Soviet attitudes, he detected a "single-minded determination to expand their power";[17] where they perceived Russia as a dangerous but complicated society buffeted by countervailing forces, he perceived it as the "focus of evil in the modern world";[18] where they found benefits in making limited concessions to slow down the arms race, he found grounds for alarm: "the Soviets . . . respect only nations that negotiate from a position of strength."[19]

F-16A Fighting Falcon aircraft over the Pacific Ocean. A cornerstone in President
Reagan's foreign policy was a massive buildup of American nuclear and conventional
weapons.

Defense Spending

To redress the Soviets' arms buildup that took place during the era of detente, Reagan proposed a five-year, $1.6 trillion defense budget. Congress did not appropriate all of the money, but outlays for national security soared from $185 billion in 1982 to more than $300 billion in 1989—a jump of more than 50 percent (see Figure 20.2).[20]

The dollars purchased a lot of hardware: a planned increase to 600 naval vessels, including 15 nuclear-powered aircraft carriers (the largest and most expensive ships in the fleet) and 4 refurbished battleships; 50 MX ICBMs, each carrying up to ten extremely accurate warheads; a revival of the B-1 bomber; a new generation of nerve gases; a doubling of tactical aircraft; and a vast array of sophisticated weapons from antitank missiles to armored troop carriers.

The goal once again was to deter the Soviet

Union if possible and defeat it if necessary.[21] In this respect, the policy did not depart from previous plans, which ever since Kennedy's days have always maintained that the United States has to prevail in any kind of conflict with the Russians. Where the Reagan government broke new ground was in the enormity and scope of its efforts. The military buildup stretched the federal budget to the breaking point and partly explains why deficits are such a pernicious problem in the 1990s.

The Reagan Doctrine

Besides pumping money into the Defense Department, President Reagan advocated a more assertive foreign policy. In this spirit, his administration developed another variation of containment, the **Reagan Doctrine.** The United States, the President announced, would not simply ver-

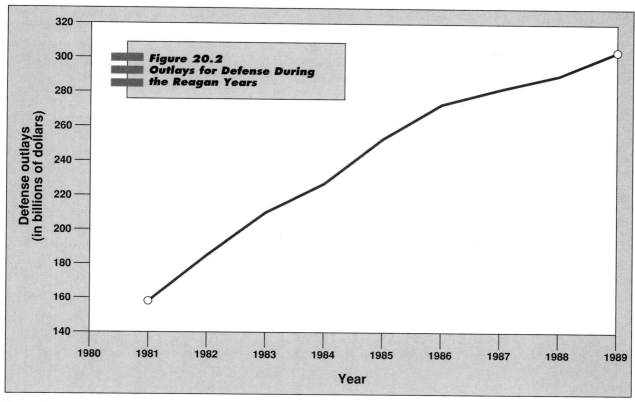

From 1981 to 1989 expenditures for national defense climbed from approximately
$160 billion per year to more than $300 billion per year.

Source: Office of Management and Budget, *Budget of the United States Government
Fiscal Year 1991* (Washington, D.C.: Government Printing Office, 1990),
pp. A293–A294.

bally oppose Communist intrusions in underdeveloped countries but would go on the offensive by backing resistance forces fighting to overthrow Marxist or Soviet-sponsored regimes. This policy meant shipping money and arms to guerrilla movements in countries such as Angola, Cambodia, Afghanistan, and Nicaragua where indigenous forces were trying to topple pro-Soviet governments. By nudging containment away from passive resistance to liberation or "roll back" of communism, the doctrine aroused a storm of protest that came to a climax over Nicaragua.

A coalition of political factions known as the Sandinistas came to power in Nicaragua in 1979 after the overthrow of Anastasio Somoza, a brutal dictator. Washington initially hailed Somoza's downfall, but as the Sandinistas solidified their position, the Reagan administration became increasingly suspicious and hostile. The President tended to regard the Sandinistas as the vanguard of a Communist conspiracy to infiltrate Latin America, especially after they established ties with Cuba and the Soviet Union. In Reagan's mind a government, however constituted, that received aid and encouragement from Moscow jeopardized American interests. He accordingly requested funds for the "Contras," a group of exiled Nicaraguans waging guerrilla warfare against the Sandinistas.

Congress was reluctant to approve this aid. Some senators and representatives regarded the contras as unsavory thugs who routinely abused human rights and trafficked in drugs. Besides, the Sandinistas constituted the lawful government of Nicaragua in the eyes of the international community, and the United States had little moral or legal justification trying to undermine it. Finally, and most important to the critics, American involvement with the contras risked another protracted, indecisive war in a country lying outside its sphere of vital interests—a reminder of Vietnam.

Over the years Congress occasionally granted limited aid to the Contras, but it just as frequently voted to stop the assistance or encumbered it with restrictions. Frustrated by a hostile legislature, the President's staff went underground to help the contras. The White House, for example, gave tacit approval to private fundraising appeals for the anti-Sandinistas. In a rather bizarre series of incidents, administration officials even prevailed upon oil-rich sheiks in the Persian Gulf to funnel millions of dollars in contributions through Swiss bank accounts.[22] These efforts took place without the knowledge of the public or most members of Congress.

Then came the startling revelation late in 1986 that the National Security Council, presumably a policy planning and advisory body, had secretly sold arms to Iran in violation of U.S. law and policy and had diverted part of the proceeds to the contras, at a time when Congress had banned such aid. In the eyes of many observers, the Iran-Contra scandal demonstrated how the Reagan Doctrine inadvertently but perhaps predictably led to hidden government and secret wars and the "privatizing" of foreign policy. As Senator William Cohen, Republican of Maine complained, "We've taken the foreign policy mechanism and pursued it through private channels, going beyond Congress and the normal institutions in the executive branch. . . ."[23]

The Strategic Defense Initiative

In a nationally televised address on March 23, 1983, President Reagan startled his listeners with another bold proposal: a defensive system that could intercept and destroy ballistic mis-

siles before they reached their targets. The anti-missile shield would render MAD obsolete. The United States, the President hoped, could defend itself without threatening or running the risk of blowing up the planet. Given the technical difficulties of such a proposal, his detractors deemed the idea wildly unrealistic and promptly dubbed it "Star Wars" to underscore its science-fictional quality.

Yet the critics underestimated the President's determination. He ordered the Pentagon to develop the **Strategic Defense Initiative (SDI),** its official title, and persuaded Congress to allocate funds for research on its various components. In the following years SDI received billions for research and testing. But after Reagan left office, the program lost momentum, especially since it ran into numerous technical difficulties and a severe budget crunch.

Reagan's Accomplishments

Despite the controversy surrounding the Iran-contra affair and SDI, the public generally gave Ronald Reagan high marks for his foreign and defense policies. Of course, Reagan had his critics. Many complained that the President had no overall foreign policy objective other than an extreme distrust of the Soviet Union, and by equating national security with raw military power he nearly bankrupt the country. But in the public's eyes, his promise to restore America's prestige and credibility succeeded admirably, at least judged by outward appearances. Reagan certainly demonstrated toughness by sending troops to Grenada (a tiny Caribbean island that seemed to be falling under Cuba's sway) and bombing Libya in reprisal for its alleged sponsorship of terrorism. His most noteworthy accomplishment in the minds of his admirers, however, was the reversal of the downward drift in America's military strength.

And while standing firm against the Russians, he nevertheless managed to sign an important arms control agreement, the Intermediate-range Nuclear Forces (INF) Treaty (see Table 20.1). The treaty requires the United States and the Soviet Union to eliminate all intermediate- and short-range missiles along with their launchers, oper-

An artist's rendition of a rocket designed to intercept and destroy Soviet ICBM warheads as part of Reagan's proposed Strategic Defense Initiative (SDI). As the costs and complexity of SDI mounted and the Cold War dwindled, President Bush and Congress cut spending on the program.

ating bases, and support facilities. Ratified in 1988, the agreement is a landmark because of its detail (example: "nozzles of the [SS-4] propulsion system shall be cut off at locations that are not assembly joints") and because for the first time it allows "on-site" verification.[24] American inspectors, for example, can visit Soviet territory to ensure compliance with the treaty's terms.

Besides the INF accord, the Reagan administration held a series of arms reduction talks with the Russians. Called START (for Strategic Arms Reduction Talks), these discussions did not lead to any formal treaties but seemed to reduce tensions between the two powers. The President's admirers regard the INF agreement and START negotiations as highlights in his administration and proof that his policy of firmness paid off. The Soviet Union would not have come to the bargaining table, much less agreed to anything, if the United States had not strengthened its armed

forces. Should the Cold War in fact end, they assert, Reagan deserves a lion's share of the credit.

From Cold War to Cold Peace: Foreign Policy Today

George Bush could hardly do more than pledge to follow in his predecessor's footsteps when he took office in 1990. Yet the Bush presidency looked out on a rapidly changing world, one filled with both opportunities and dangers. These momentous changes appeared to require sweeping new policies. Simply continuing Reagan's policies did not seem to be a viable option.

The biggest transformation was occurring in the Soviet Union, where, under the leadership of Mikhail Gorbachev, the harsh and rigid Soviet state appeared to be thawing at a dizzying pace.

Gorbachev convinced many outsiders that he sincerely wanted to reform Russia's society and economy. Following a policy known as *glasnost*, he granted his people greater voice in government and basic civil liberties. Another policy, *perestroika*, attempted to modernize the economy by encouraging free markets and gradually ending government control of industry and agriculture. To make these measures work, he called for drastic cuts in the Red Army. Equally significant, the Kremlin eased its iron grip on Eastern European nations. At the same time Gorbachev also challenged the United States and Western European nations to join in reducing both nuclear and conventional arms. He backed up these pronouncements by promising unilateral cuts in Soviet forces. An editorial in the *New York Times* summed up what was on many people's minds:

> It's as though America just won the lottery. With Communism collapsing, the United States . . . now stands to save a fortune. . . . What a precious moment; what a Heaven-sent

opportunity for a political leader to capture attention and resources to do great good.[25]

But while thinking about what "great good" could be done, President Bush must have wondered if he was not entering a mine field. True, the end of the Cold War, if it was indeed over, could not have come at a better time. The federal government was up to its eyes in red ink, and any chance to cut defense appropriations was more than welcome. Still, at the same time, many of the President's advisers warned that the Soviets might reverse direction or conflict could erupt in some other part of the world. Proceed cautiously, they told him. The military budget can be trimmed but not by much.

Iraq's invasion and annexation of Kuwait in the summer of 1990 dramatically bolstered this line of reasoning. A tiny nation, Kuwait nevertheless supplied Europe and Japan with substantial quantities of oil. Even more frightening, many officials warned, the Iraqi action was possibly a prelude to an attack on Saudi Arabia, the world's largest petroleum exporter and one of

American troops unloading supplies in Saudi Arabia. The Iraqi invasion of Kuwait and the massive American military buildup in the Middle East illustrate the changing demands on American foreign and defense policy.

America's best friends in the Middle East. The Bush administration responded to Saudi Arabia's request for American troops and imposed a blockade on shipments to and from Iraq. In a matter of months more than 100,000 combat personnel and a vast flotilla of aircraft carriers, destroyers, battleships, and cruisers were in the area. Indeed, by September the buildup was the largest since the Vietnam War.

Events like those in the Persian Gulf forced President Bush to confront a new reality: International affairs can no longer be defined strictly in East-West terms. As scholars and diplomats tried to convince President Reagan for years, there are now too many independent actors in the world arena for the United States to react to every incident or crisis as a potential confron-

tation with the Soviets. (The Soviet Union, as a matter of fact, supported economic sanctions against Iraq.) As Bush rapidly realized, other hazards now fill the foreign and defense policy agenda: the steady spread of nuclear weapons; drought and famine in Latin America, Asia, and Africa; the emergence of new economic powers; escalating trade wars and international monetary instability; chaos and bloodshed in the Middle East; drug smuggling from Latin America; terrorism; and the pollution of the environment on a global scale. These kinds of issues, as much as U.S.-Soviet relations, are likely to occupy policymakers for the rest of this century. Indeed, two of the key questions facing America are what the new policies will be and who will make them.

Checkpoint

- President Reagan, distrusting the Soviet Union and desiring to make the United States as strong militarily as possible, increased defense spending substantially.

- The Reagan Doctrine called for supporting rebels fighting pro-Soviet governments in Third World countries such as Nicaragua.

- President Reagan was also determined to build the extremely controversial Strategic Defense Initiative (SDI), a space-based antiballistic missile defense system that he hoped would extricate us from MAD. But critics said the project was too costly and complex to be feasible.

- During the latter part of his second term, Reagan's mood toward the Soviet Union softened. He and Mikhail Gorbachev signed the INF Treaty requiring the destruction of short- and intermediate-range nuclear missiles and continued strategic arms limitations talks.

- The changing nature of the Soviet system, a possible end to the Cold War, pressures in the Middle East, and other world events present George Bush with enormous challenges and raise questions about the future direction of foreign and defense policy.

MAKING FOREIGN
AND DEFENSE POLICY

Foreign policymaking can be pictured as a series of concentric circles, much like the waves formed by dropping a stone into a pond. The president and his closest advisers occupy the innermost circle, suggesting that they are prime movers in the system. But the outward flow of the waves is not unimpeded, for they collide with various obstacles. The president's ideas inevitably encounter opposition that frequently forces them to be reshaped or dropped.

Moving from the center to the periphery, the main obstacles are the bureaucracy, the Congress, interest groups, defense industries, the media, and, at the edges, the general public. The impact of these institutions, groups, and individuals varies from time to time and issue to issue. Many of the most sweeping decisions (such as the adoption of NSC 68) go largely unnoticed and unchallenged, whereas lesser ones (like aid to the Contras) become front page news.

The Executive Branch
and Foreign Policy

THE PRESIDENT During the 1960s, as America's involvement in Vietnam steadily escalated, the press and scholars used the phrase *the imperial president* to describe the chief executive's apparent omnipotence in foreign affairs. Acting with neither the advice nor consent of the Congress, a succession of presidents seemed to wield diplomatic and military power in other parts of the world with impunity. This dominance troubled observers who worried that unchecked presidential authority not only led the country into ill-conceived adventures but threatened to undermine one of our most sacred constitutional principles, the system of checks and balances. But just how omnipotent is the president?

Sitting atop an enormous national security establishment, presidents have at their command hundreds of diplomats, military officers, scientists, international lawyers, technicians, intelligence operatives, and personal advisers, all of whom provide up-to-the-minute information

and insights about the world. No other person, furthermore, enjoys as much visibility. Presidents can demand on a moment's notice the attention of the news media and speak live before nationwide audiences. In both peace and war, the country looks to the chief executive for inspiration and guidance.

Yet these very factors can also limit presidential power. If presidents control the bureaucracy, it nonetheless frequently thwarts their most cherished ambitions. Experts give advice based on sophisticated research, yet even they make disastrous mistakes. Presidents have the public's attention, but it in turn watches their every move, the failures along with the successes.

Simply put, the instruments that make presidents strong can and do weaken them. With the push of a button a president can literally blow up the planet. But none of them have been able to translate that awesome power into the ability to run the international affairs on a day-to-day basis as they want. In order to appreciate this generalization, let's look briefly at the individuals and agencies that serve the president.

THE DEPARTMENT OF STATE The State Department, headed by the secretary of state, represents the interests of the United States to foreign governments. Its activities range from high-level negotiations with the Soviets to the mundane chore of processing passport applications.

The State Department, like nearly every other governmental entity, has grown into a mini-empire. It employs more than 20,000 workers and spends close to $2 billion annually. In addition to its Washington headquarters, it maintains embassies, consulates, and other offices in more than 260 places scattered over the globe.

The heart and soul of the State Department is its cadre of career diplomats, the foreign service officers (FSOs). These professionals are experts on different regions of the world. Although political appointees occupy the top rungs, they rely heavily on the FSOs for advice. The subculture of the FSOs, which emphasizes tradition, precedent, and conformity, occasionally puts them at odds with the White House, particularly when a president wishes to undertake a bold new initiative with another government.

The strategy room in the Pentagon. The Defense Department supposedly administers the military policies decided by the President and Congress, but, in fact, it has a large voice in developing and implementing foreign policies in general.

THE DEPARTMENT OF DEFENSE The previous generalizations apply equally well to the Defense Department. In creating this department after World War II, Congress wanted to eliminate interservice rivalry, streamline management, and reduce waste and duplication. What it got after several decades was a gigantic organization that ranked among the world's largest employers and consumers. Nor has housing the three military branches in one organization ended their feuding and jealousies. Each still insists on maintaining separate missiles, aircraft, intelligence units, training centers, and, needless to say, uniforms. Critics say this redundancy costs the taxpayers billions of dollars every year without adding to national security.

Perched atop this empire, nominally in control and directly responsible to the president, is the secretary of defense. Below the secretary are the secretaries of the army, navy, and air force (all civilian appointees of the president) and the Joint Chiefs of Staff, the top-ranking officers from each service. The defense secretary also supervises a phalanx of under secretaries in charge of manpower, logistics, political affairs, research and development, and other activities.

On paper, the department's mission is straightforward: protect the United States and its vital interests from armed attack. In view of this role, one would think that the Pentagon would simply carry out orders issued from above. Civilian control of the military, after all, is one of America's oldest traditions. Here again, however, appearance does not match reality.

As the Defense Department has grown, so, too, has its role in *making* foreign policy. The secretary and subordinates within the department do not meekly follow instructions handed down from above. They frequently have the clout to challenge or even reverse their superiors. Indeed, they constitute an integral part of the national security making apparatus itself. The president may wish to close a base in Ohio or cancel the production of a new helicopter. But the military establishment, with strong allies in Congress, the states, the media, and especially the defense industries, often successfully defies these efforts. To take another case, the Pentagon has a virtual veto over arms control proposals. No president, however popular, can make a deal with the Soviet Union without first clearing it with the Joint Chiefs of Staff.

THE NATIONAL SECURITY COUNCIL The National Security Council (NSC), the part of the executive office responsible for advising the president on national security matters, has had a curious history. Its role, power, and prestige vary according to the temperament and style of the occupant of the White House. President Truman relied on his personal associates more than the NSC staff, whereas under Eisenhower it became highly bureaucratized. President Kennedy, who took an active interest in foreign affairs and wanted to keep a close eye on its administration, gave the NSC greater stature than his predecessors. His motives were clear: the State and Defense Departments, being relatively distant and autonomous bureaucracies, were hard to discipline. Locating foreign policymaking closer to his office gave him a greater sense of control.

The NSC reached the apex of its influence under the guidance of Henry Kissinger, President Nixon's assistant for national security affairs. From 1969 until 1973, when he became secretary of state, Kissinger masterminded far-reaching initiatives, including secret talks with the North Vietnamese on ending the war in Vietnam, the opening of relations with Communist China, and the first SALT negotiations. In carrying out his duties, Kissinger overshadowed the nominal secretary of state.

As we saw in Chapter 15, presidents gradually transformed the NSC from an advisory and planning body to an "operational" agency. Two considerations prompted this change. First, everyone in the White House was convinced that the country needed to take decisive action against international terrorists and to support anti-Communist guerrillas in underdeveloped countries. Second, the CIA, the organization that would normally spearhead these efforts, was too restricted by Congress to be effective. Hence, the NSC gradually assumed the role.

During the Reagan administration, for example, the NSC began to undertake various clandestine activities, the most famous being the shipment of arms to Iran and secret funneling of part of the proceeds to the contras (see p. 650).

THE INTELLIGENCE AGENCIES The same law that created the NSC in 1947 also established the Central Intelligence Agency (CIA), the organization that gathers and disseminates information about foreign countries. It attempts, in addition, to coordinate the activities of other intelligence-gathering bodies—each of the armed services, for instance, maintains its own data-gathering machinery—so that the president has an up-to-the-minute picture of international events.

Since its inception, the CIA has become at one and the same time Washington's most glamorous, notorious, and boring institution. Perhaps better known for its failures than its successes, many of which must necessarily go unpublicized, its exploits are legendary. Because of its secrecy, countless myths have sprung up about its influence and deeds. Detractors blame it for everything from coups d'état to droughts; its admirers are just as convinced it has kept the United States free and prosperous.

Its aura of mystery notwithstanding, the CIA leads a rather humdrum existence. Much of its work is routine, dull, and tedious. Most of the agency's 16,000 employees work in Langley, Virginia, not in dimly lit cafes in exotic cities around the world. They spend countless hours reading foreign newspapers, listening to overseas broadcasts, poring over aerial photographs, analyzing international trade reports, interviewing travelers, and studying scientific journals. A trained analyst can assess a country's military potential by looking at its imports, while an area specialist learns as much about a regime's stability from published accounts as from undercover agents. The CIA devotes the bulk of its resources to these crucial but unexciting tasks.

Although cloak-and-dagger pursuits constitute the lesser of the agency's work, they nonetheless make it famous and mysterious. Clandestine operations, however distasteful to democracy, which is predicated on openness, have always been a fact of life in the world arena. But the CIA and similar bodies have periodically overstepped the bounds of their primary missions by violating publicly announced and congressionally approved policies. In their determination not to lose to international communism, past administrations have allowed the agency to stray far beyond its ostensible mandate:[26]

- The CIA either directly or indirectly sought to overthrow legally constituted governments in Guatemala, Chile, Cuba, and Iran, to mention just a few.
- It plotted the assassination of several heads of state, including Fidel Castro of Cuba and Patrice Lumumba of the Congo.
- It recruited, trained, advised, and equipped revolutionaries fighting against the governments of Angola, Cuba, and Nicaragua.
- For years it ran its own airline, Air America, that shipped supplies to anti-Communist guerrillas in Laos, a small country bordering Vietnam.
- It secretly designed and built a high-altitude reconnaissance aircraft.
- It helped police forces in scores of Latin American nations harass, assassinate, and torture their enemies.
- It spied on American citizens protesting the war in Vietnam.
- It tried to mine harbors in Nicaragua.

Activities like these lead some observers to wonder if the CIA is not an underground government with its own foreign policy.

THE CHIEF EXECUTIVE? By now it should be clear that presidents are not total masters of the executive branch. The tension between the president, a temporary and certainly political creature on the Washington scene, and career civil servants explains why foreign policy does not always flow smoothly. Presidents, of course, appoint their cabinet secretaries (contingent upon approval by the Senate). But as Chapter 16

pointed out, department heads often become captives of the bureaus they supposedly manage. Consequently, a secretary gradually begins representing the agency to the White House rather than the other way around. This indirect influence of the professionals makes life difficult for presidents who want things done their way and expect orders to be followed, not debated or ignored. Many of them have complained about their inability to control the bureaucracy. During World War II, President Franklin Roosevelt complained that "To change anything in the N-a-a-v-v-y is like pounding a feather bed. You punch it with your right, and you punch it with your left, until you are finally exhausted, and then you find the damn bed just as it was before you started punching."[27]

One expects dealings with other nations to be difficult, but what is surprising is how hard it is for presidents to put their own house in order. As Strobe Talbott, a correspondent for *Time* magazine, puts it, talks between the United States and the USSR go on at two levels: the first is between the two governments and the second within the confines of the executive branch itself. "The second," he writes, "has on occasion been just as important and difficult as the first."[28]

The president's difficulties lie in the nature of bureaucracy and the separation of powers. Confronting well-established departments and agencies backed by powerful allies in Congress, industry, the media, and interest groups, chief executives must act as brokers as well as commanders, as persuaders as well as bosses, as manipulators as well as superiors. How well they sell their ideas often counts as much as how well they wield their statutory authority.

The Legislative Branch and Foreign Policy

The Constitution's drafters assigned joint responsibility for the general direction of foreign affairs to both the president *and* the Congress. Thus, although the commander in chief of the armed forces resides in the White House, only the legislature can declare war; although the president negotiates and signs treaties, the Senate has to ratify them before they become bind-

"Unfortunately, our hands are tied. Congress won't let us take part in any covert operations that will risk global annihilation."

Drawing by Ed Fisher; © 1989 The New Yorker Magazine, Inc.

ing; although the executive branch develops strategic plans, the Congress controls the purse strings.

This built-in sharing of power inevitably leads to conflict, particularly when a president wants to go in one direction, the Congress in another. Presidents and legislators, even when they share the same party label, have always struggled over foreign relations, but the battles have been especially fierce in the post-Vietnam era.

Prior to 1970, presidents generally took the lead in national security. President Truman sent ground troops to Korea without asking or obtaining a congressional declaration of war. Similarly, Presidents Kennedy and Johnson committed the army and air force to Vietnam largely on their own initiative. And President Nixon not only continued the war, but extended it into Cambodia and Laos while Congress objected but did little to stop him. The legislature often deferred to the president because of the perceived Soviet menace and the need for quick and resolute action to deal with it, and because the executive branch tended to monopolize information and expertise. Besides, members of Congress tended to adhere to the norm of bipartisanship; they thought that debating foreign policy along party lines too often and too openly would only help the nation's enemies.

RECENT CHANGES IN EXECUTIVE-LEGISLATIVE RELATIONS The war in Vietnam, probably more than any event, soured relations between the two branches. That war came to be seen as a misbegotten adventure that might have been avoided had lawmakers been more vocal and forceful in stating their objections.

At the same time, another change was occurring. The representatives and senators elected in the early 1970s were a different breed of men and women than their predecessors. Though they still accepted containment's main tenets, they also believed that the country required fresh approaches and insights to adapt to the changing international environment. Moreover, many of these individuals had arrived at Congress on their own. Having built their own campaign organizations, raised their own funds, and mobilized their own constituents, they were relatively autonomous and insulated from party and presidential leadership. Accustomed to doing things their own way, younger members of the House and Senate manifested a streak of independence that boded ill for harmony between the executive and legislative branches.

The new membership altered Congress in two ways. For one, old patterns of authority broke down. Subcommittees, each with responsibilities and a staff of its own, proliferated. Older representatives and senators had to share power with their junior colleagues. These changes meant that presidents had to bargain with more and more individuals, a situation that diminished their capacity to lead.

A second transformation, however, was even more devastating to presidential domination of foreign and defense policy: Congress began to assert its constitutionally mandated prerogatives in decision making. During the past two decades, for example, it has passed several bills intended to limit the president's use of military force or covert operations. The War Powers Act (1973), as Chapter 15 explained, is the best known of these laws. The House and Senate committees on intelligence, which try to oversee covert operations, are additional examples.[29]

Such measures are defended as essential for giving the legislature a voice in the conduct of foreign relations. Presidents and their national security staffs, on the other hand, bitterly resisted these efforts on the grounds that 535 men and women, who are often misinformed and seldom agree on anything, cannot act quickly and decisively enough to take the kind of action international affairs requires.

CONGRESS' INFLUENCE ON FOREIGN AND DEFENSE POLICY Despite its best efforts, Congress is still not an equal partner with the pres-

ident. To be sure, it often clashes with the White House, and no president, no matter how popular, wins on every issue. Yet even with its expanded role, the legislative branch still does not decide the broad direction of foreign policy. That power remains largely in the hands of the president and the national security apparatus. Instead, what Congress usually does is react to, rather than set, the agenda. Even in carrying out this limited responsibility, it tends to see mostly trees, not the forest as a whole.

Consider, for example, the type of analysis Congress can make when drawing up the defense budget. It can either focus on *financial* oversight—how efficiently funds are being spent—or on *policy* oversight—whether a particular program serves the national interest.[30] Policy oversight, it seems clear, is by far the more important. Legislators can debate endlessly about how carefully the Defense Department spends its dollars. But the more profound questions—the logically prior ones—concern the roles various weapons play in American foreign policy. Do they really contribute to defense? Will they upset arms control? Are they likely to provoke the Soviet Union to take countermeasures, which will leave us about where we started, only poorer? Digging even deeper, they can ask if basic assumptions about deterrence and the Cold War still remain valid. And why stop there? Why not conduct a full-blown discussion on containment itself? Should it be abandoned, given the changes in the Soviet Union and Eastern Europe?

How does Congress spend its time? One specialist believes that in general:

> Congress continues . . . to look mostly at the details of defense spending but rarely at the big picture. . . . In my judgment the congressional treatment of defense has suffered from so great a preoccupation with next year's budget that it has tended to crowd out consideration of the more basic questions and the longer term perspective.[31]

Several well-known senators share these beliefs:

> The budget cycle drives the Congress, and Congress drives the executive branch to such

an obsession that we don't have time to think about strategy. We never had a strategy hearing since I've been in the Senate. (Sam Nunn, Democrat of Georgia)

. . . I think Congress has become mesmerized with the budget process to the detriment of other responsibilities and considerations. . . . We have failed to have the kinds of debates that are essential on national issues such as foreign policy and defense.[32] (William Roth, Republican of Delaware)

To sum up, neither the House nor the Senate deals very much with trunk policies. By concentrating on the nuts and bolts of the "budget process," they fail to provide broad guidelines to the executive.[33] As policies come before them, representatives may stamp them with their own preferences and thereby deflect the president from a specific course of action. But they usually do so without having a grand design in mind.[34]

Checkpoint

- The president has primary responsibility for developing and carrying out foreign and defense policy.

- The president's preeminence comes from management of the State and Defense Departments, the National Security Council (NSC), the Central Intelligence Agency (CIA), and other organizations.

- The president does not rule with a free hand, however, because the bureaucracy can create obstacles and the Congress shares in the making of foreign policy.

- Since the early 1970s, Congress's efforts to assert influence over foreign relations has met with mixed results. Congress tends to concentrate on rather narrow matters rather than debating policy oversight.

FOREIGN AND DEFENSE POLICY: WHO GOVERNS?

Foreign policy since the end of World War II has entailed the most consequential decisions ever made by the American polity. In the early 1990s, moreover, the United States is at a crossroads in its dealings with the Soviet Union, Europe, China, Japan, and the rest of the world. In order to know who governs, therefore, one has to think about who ultimately decides foreign and defense policy. What role does the public play? Do competing groups dominate the policymaking process as the pluralists suggest? Or is it in the hands of a power elite?

Democracy

Since democracy means government *by* the people, one would expect them to debate and choose among the basic alternatives that affect their lives. Theoretically, parties and elections are admirably suited to assist in this task. If Republicans and Democrats take opposing stands on major (not just minor) issues, if they clearly articulate these positions, and if they carry out their campaign promises when elected, the electorate has a way of controlling policy.

In practice things have not worked out this neatly. Democrats and Republicans without question tend to differ on many specific twig and branch issues. But in the past so much overlap has existed on trunk policies that it has sometimes been hard to tell where the parties stood. Perhaps this is why, with few exceptions, studies show that foreign affairs affect voters less than domestic controversies.[35] A Closer Look (pp. 662–663), for instance, shows the somewhat passive role that the parties and the public played in the adoption of NSC 68, the document that drastically expanded the definition of vital U.S. interests and helped create a national security state.

One sees in the adoption of policies like NSC 68 an example of the top-down model of influence described in Chapter 8. According to this theory, those in the upper reaches of government try to *shape* public opinion rather than respond

HAS AMERICA BECOME NUMBER 2?

The U.S.-Soviet Military Balance and American Defense Policies and Programs

Committee on
THE PRESENT DANGER
1800 Massachusetts Avenue, N.W.
Washington, D.C. 20036
202/466-7444

The Committee on the Present Danger, formed in the mid-1970s, argued that the United States was losing its military superiority to the Soviet Union. Its success in getting Congress and the executive branch to increase defense spending convinces pluralists that even trunk decisions are made by intergroup competition.

to it. Instead of listening to and acting on a popular outcry for greater national security, leaders created the outcry itself. Containment, NSC 68, detente, SDF, and other major national security decisions did not originate in a sudden burst of mass concern. On the contrary, high-level officials perceived a threat or opportunity, considered different options, made a decision, and then began persuading the country at large to accept it.

Pluralism

In March 1976, a dozen or more leading business executives and former high-ranking government officials met for lunch in the Cosmopolitan Club, a posh Washington restaurant. The participants were deeply troubled by detente. The apparent thaw in the Cold War was, they were all convinced, a mirage. In actuality, the Soviets were taking advantage of the relaxation in tensions to modernize and expand their nuclear and conventional arsenal. Slowly but surely America's military superiority was eroding. Detente so worried the diners that they created a new organization with the portentous name the Committee on the Present Danger (CPD).[36]

Almost immediately after getting under way, the CPD became a potent force on Capitol Hill and the White House. It adamantly opposed detente and called for substantial increases in arms expenditures. Both Presidents Ford, a Republican, and Carter, a Democrat, repeatedly crossed swords with it. Its credibility soared in 1979

A Closer Look

The Selling of NSC 68 ★★★

Although NSC 68 was classified "top secret," the report's contents were freely discussed in Washington's higher circles, and several leading members of Congress and the executive branch expressed deep misgivings about the plan. For example, Senator Robert Taft of Ohio (nicknamed "Mr. Republican") thought NSC 68's recommendations were too passive and too costly: too passive because they accepted the status quo, namely the Soviets' subjugation of Eastern Europe, and too costly because they entailed the creation of a huge peacetime army, a sizable portion of which was to be stationed overseas. Taft, concerned that containment might push the country into economic ruin, warned that "there is a definite limit to what a government can spend in time of peace and still maintain a free economy. . . ."[a]

Confronted with such doubts, President Truman's advisers had to, in Secretary of State Dean Acheson's words, "bludgeon the mass mind of the 'top government' " as well as convince the reluctant public as a whole.[b] Skeptical of the general public, Acheson likened the polity to a body composed of differ-

ent cells, the most important being the "thinking cells":

> The society operates best, improves its chances of survival most, in which the thinking cells work out a fairly long-range course of conduct before the others take over. . . .[c]

Getting the other cells to do their part would take patient cajoling:

> Qualification must give way to simplicity of statement, nicety and nuance to bluntness, almost brutality, in carrying home a point . . . points to be understandable had to be clear. If we made our points clearer than truth, we did not differ from most other educators and could hardly do otherwise.[d]

In other words, selling NSC 68 to the general public required oversimplification, dramatization, even distortion (making statements "clearer than truth"). Otherwise, the people would not support the necessary measures. The Truman administration thus mounted a campaign to sell its ideas first to

when the Soviets invaded Afghanistan and fundamentalist Muslims deposed the shah of Iran, and as soon as Reagan took the oath of office in January 1981, many CPD activists accepted key posts in the new administration.[37]

Pluralists see in the formation of the Committee on the Present Danger and its early successes the tradition of interest group politics that keeps America democratic and stable. When individuals become dissatisfied, they frequently organize to press their case on government. For most of our history interest groups have dealt primarily with domestic matters. Industries, of course,

have always lobbied for tariff protection, but relatively few organizations participated in foreign policymaking. Those that did tended to be nonpartisan and to support the government, not criticize it.

What has changed in the past 20 years is the proliferation of organizations specializing in international security affairs. These groups occupy all points along the ideological spectrum and range from small, essentially one-person operations to highly sophisticated and well-financed research institutions. In the early days of the Cold War, lobbying tended to be infor-

the policy establishment, including senators and representatives, journalists, business and labor leaders, the clergy, educators, and anyone else who might be able to reach the common citizens, and then to the public as a whole. By the 1952 elections, the efforts to create consensus had succeeded. Both parties agreed on containment's main premises, particularly on the emphasis on military force. The Democrats promised:

> . . . to stand unequivocally for the strong, balanced defense forces for this country—land, sea, and air. We will continue to support the expansion and maintenance of the military and civil defense forces required for our national security.[e]

Not to be outdone, the Republican party declared:

> . . . we should develop with utmost speed a force-in-being . . . of such power as to deter sudden attack or promptly and decisively defeat it. This defense against sudden attack requires the quickest possible deployment of appropriate and completely ade-

quate air power and the simultaneous readiness of coordinated air, land and sea forces, with all necessary installations, bases, supplies and munitions, including atomic energy weapons in abundance.[f]

Where, one can ask, was a public discussion of the merits of this far-reaching policy?

[a]Robert Taft, *A Foreign Policy for Americans* (Garden City, N.Y.: Doubleday, 1951), pp. 69–70.
[b]Dean Acheson, *Present at the Creation* (New York: Norton, 1969), p. 374.
[c]Ibid., pp. 374–375.
[d]Ibid., p. 375.
[e]"Democratic Party Platform of 1952," in *National Party Platforms Volume 1*, compiled by Donald Bruce Johnson (Urbana: University of Illinois Press, 1978), p. 475.
[f]"Republican Party Platform of 1952," in ibid., p. 499. To see how close Democrats and Republicans were on NSC 68s compare their platforms with the Progressive party, which believed that "peaceful coexistence of the Soviet Union and the United States is both possible and essential"; rejected the "stockpiling of A-bombs and H-bombs and the militarization of our country . . ."; favored "international inspection of atomic stockpiles and installations"; and opposed "Universal Military Training" and the "Draft Law." "Progressive Party Platform," in ibid., pp. 489–491.

mal—prominent citizens would call on the president or secretary of state to offer advice—but today's associations are adept at fund-raising, generating publicity, contacting senators and representatives, sponsoring letter-writing campaigns, and other lobbying techniques. When the SALT II Treaty was submitted to the Senate, for example, the CPD fought tooth and nail to defeat it:

> During the SALT . . . hearings its members testified on seventeen different occasions before the Armed Services Committees and the

Senate Foreign Relations Committee, participated in four hundred and seventy-nine TV and radio programs and distributed over two hundred thousand pamphlets.[38]

But in accordance with pluralist predictions, the CPD did not have the field to itself. At least a dozen well-organized groups lined up on the other side of the issue. These organizations, including the Council on Foreign Relations, the Trilateral Commission, and the Committee on East-West Accord, wanted to promote better relations with the Soviet Union. They too testified before Congress, printed brochures, and talked to the press. Detente was indeed derailed for a while, but only for a while. By continuing their advocacy, the CPD's opponents helped foster a climate that made negotiations with the Russians politically safe, if not essential. The Reagan administration, as we noted earlier, even concluded a major weapons reduction agreement with the USSR, and President Bush promised to continue the process. These battles over arms control thus satisfy pluralists that even trunk decisions like detente emerge from the give and take of group conflict and that no one segment of society, and certainly not an elite, dominates foreign and defense policy.

The Power Elite

Power elite theorists obviously look askance at these arguments. Consider first, they suggest, the membership of the groups that take part in policymaking struggles. The most influential ones are headed by the United States' most prominent citizens, exactly the kind of people who sit in the command posts of society.

The CPD, for example, drew members from the upper crust of the Washington establishment: Paul Nitze, successful lawyer and adviser to presidents since the Truman years; Walter Rostow, professor and national security assistant to President Kennedy; Douglas Dillon, former secretary of the treasury and New York banker; Charls Walker, one of the Capitol's most influential lobbyists and an ex-official in the Nixon administration (see Chapter 13); and even Ronald Reagan, who joined in 1979. Its participants came mostly from the highest echelons of business, finance, government, and education. The same can be said about its opposition.

David Rockefeller, chairman of Chase Manhattan Bank, founded the Trilateral Commission, which included dozens of influential industrialists, professionals, and top politicians. The Committee on East-West Accord was started by the chairman of PepsiCo and drew supporters from the ranks of large corporations and banks.[39] The Council on Foreign Relations, founded in 1920, is governed by a board of directors drawn from the top rungs of business, universities, the

media, and former government officials, and they regularly brush elbows with the nation's top policymakers. The council's journal, *Foreign Affairs*, is "considered throughout the world to be the unofficial mouthpiece of United States foreign policy."[40]

The power elite school doubts that these groups really represent democratic pluralism. Operating far from public scrutiny, they enjoy little if any mass support; their discourse is technical and arcane; their differences of opinion normally pertain only to twig matters and, in any event, seldom get translated into partisan politics in such a way that the public can understand them; and usually after fighting among themselves they present the fruits of their victories to the people as accomplished facts.

When it comes to foreign policy, according to power elite theorists, there is plenty of politicking, which seems to involve such familiar pluralist activities as bargaining, persuasion, and competition. The problem is that the public does not participate meaningfully in these discussions and, in fact, has only a vague notion of what they are about.

Checkpoint

- The democratic model does not fit foreign and defense policymaking very well, since so many important policies are "sold" to the public without much chance for meaningful popular debate.

- Since interest groups are found on both sides of major controversies like detente, their presence lends support to the pluralist interpretation of American politics.

- The power elite school, on the other hand, contends that these groups, which draw their members mostly from the top layers of society, merely represent different segments of the ruling elite rather than true pluralism.

SUMMARY

Since World War II, the United States has pursued a policy of containment: using diplomacy, economic assistance, military power, and arms reduction agreements as means to prevent Soviet expansion. Military force has been the most prominent and expensive branch. Besides conventional weapons, the United States relies heavily on nuclear deterrence, the threat to annihilate an enemy that aggresses against the United States or its allies.

The Nixon administration initiated detente, a policy of trying to stabilize U.S.-Soviet relations. The arms control agreements that emerged from this process have somewhat reduced tensions. Detente, however, aroused opposition from those who felt it benefited the Soviets more than the United States.

The Reagan administration undertook a massive buildup of American military forces and pursued a strongly anti-Communist foreign policy. Severe budget constraints and rapid changes in the Soviet Union and Eastern Europe appeared to reduce Cold War tensions and put George Bush under great pressure to rethink some of these programs. But the military crisis in the Persian Gulf in late 1990 raised cries of alarm among those who objected to deep defense cuts.

Although presidents' control of the bureaucracy and information, along with their prestige and visibility, put them in a preeminent position in foreign and defense policymaking, they do not possess unlimited power. Bureaucrats often resist or undermine presidential ambitions; the public will withdraw its support if things go wrong in the international arena; and Congress has a voice in defense and foreign policymaking.

Until the early 1970s Congress normally deferred to the president in foreign affairs. But Vietnam and the emergence of a new, independent breed of representatives and senators caused Congress to try to exert more control over the White House's conduct of defense and foreign and defense policy. Still, the legislature frequently lacks sufficient information and gets too bogged down in details to effectively challenge the president.

Rather than having a part in creating foreign and defense policy, the public generally has to live with what top-level officials decide. Interest groups, according to pluralists, have a loud voice in foreign and defense policymaking. But the elite school contends that these groups are really just a facade that hides elite domination.

KEY TERMS

Isolationism
Domino analogy
Marshall Plan
NSC 68
National security state
Massive retaliation
Nuclear deterrence
Triad
Mutual assured
destruction (MAD)
Detente
SALT negotiations
Reagan Doctrine
Strategic Defense
Initiative (SDI)

FOR FURTHER READING

Richard J. Barnet, *The Rockets' Red Glare* (New York: Simon & Schuster, 1990). A fascinating history of how American presidents have sold their foreign and defense policies to the public.

John Lewis Gaddis, *Strategies of Containment* (New York: Oxford University Press, 1982). Gaddis describes the origins of containment and how it has been implemented through the years.

Loch K. Johnson, *America's Secret Power* (New York: Oxford University Press, 1989). A former congressional staff member analyzes the role the CIA plays in American government and society.

Robert Kennedy, *Thirteen Days* (New York: Norton, 1969). A fascinating account of the Cuban missile crisis told by President Kennedy's brother.

James A. Nathan and James K. Oliver, *Force in World Politics*, 4th ed. (Boston: Little, Brown, 1989).

James A. Nathan and James K. Oliver, *Foreign Policy Making and the American Political System*, 2nd ed. (Boston: Little, Brown, 1987). An excellent survey of how American foreign policy is made.

John Newhouse, *War and Peace in the Nuclear Age* (New York: Knopf, 1989). A history of superpower relations in the Cold War period.

Jonathan Schell, *The Fate of the Earth* (Boston: Houghton Mifflin, 1982). Although controversial, this book lucidly poses the moral and practical questions raised by the strategy of nuclear deterrence.

Richard Smoke, *National Security and the Nuclear Dilemma* (Reading, Mass.: Addison-Wesley, 1982). A very clear history and description of American nuclear policy.

Strobe Talbott, *Endgame* (New York: Harper & Row, 1979). An "inside" story of the SALT negotiations.

The Declaration of Independence

When in the Course of human events, it becomes necessary for one people to dissolve the political bands which have connected them with another, and to assume among the Powers of the earth, the separate and equal station to which the Laws of Nature and of Nature's God entitle them, a decent respect to the opinions of mankind requires that they should declare the causes which impel them to the separation.

We hold these truths to be self-evident, that all men are created equal, that they are endowed by their Creator with certain unalienable Rights, that among these are Life, Liberty and the pursuit of Happiness. That to secure these rights, Governments are instituted among Men, deriving their just powers from the consent of the governed, That whenever any Form of Government becomes destructive of these ends, it is the Right of the People to alter or to abolish it, and to institute new Government, laying its foundation on such principles and organizing its powers in such form, as to them shall seem most likely to effect their Safety and Happiness. Prudence, indeed, will dictate that Governments long established should not be changed for light and transient causes; and accordingly all experience hath shown, that mankind are more disposed to suffer, while evils are sufferable, than to right themselves by abolishing the forms to which they are accustomed. But when a long train of abuses and usurpations, pursuing invariably the same Object evinces a design to reduce them under absolute Despotism, it is their right, it is their duty, to throw off such Government, and to provide new Guards for their future security.—Such has been the patient sufferance of these Colonies; and such is now the necessity which constrains them to alter their former Systems of Government. The history of the present King of Great Britain is a history of repeated injuries and usurpations, all having in direct object the establishment of an absolute Tyranny over these States. To prove this, let Facts be submitted to a candid world.

He has refused his Assent to Laws, the most wholesome and necessary for the public good.

He has forbidden his Governors to pass Laws of immediate and pressing importance, unless suspended in their operation till his Assent should be obtained; and when so suspended, he has utterly neglected to attend to them.

He has refused to pass other Laws for the accommodation of large districts of people, unless those people would relinquish the right of Representation in the Legislature, a right inestimable to them and formidable to tyrants only.

He has called together legislative bodies at places unusual, uncomfortable, and distant from the depository of their Public Records, for the sole purpose of fatiguing them into compliance with his measures.

He has dissolved Representative Houses repeatedly, for opposing with manly firmness his invasions on the rights of the people.

He has refused for a long time, after such dissolutions, to cause others to be elected; whereby the Legislative Powers, incapable of Annihilation, have returned to the People at large for their exercise; the State remaining in the mean time exposed to all the dangers of invasion from without, and convulsions within.

He has endeavoured to prevent the population of these States; for that purpose obstructing the Laws of Naturalization of Foreigners; refusing to pass others to encourage their migration hither, and raising the conditions of new Appropriations of Lands.

He has obstructed the Administration of Justice, by refusing his Assent to Laws for establishing Judiciary Powers.

He has made Judges dependent on his Will alone, for the tenure of their offices, and the amount and payment of their salaries.

He has erected a multitude of New Offices, and sent hither swarms of Officers to harass our People, and eat out their substance.

He has kept among us, in times of peace, Standing Armies without the Consent of our legislature.

He has affected to render the Military independent of and superior to the Civil Power.

He has combined with others to subject us to a jurisdiction foreign to our constitution, and unacknowledged by our laws; giving his Assent to their acts of pretended legislation:

For quartering large bodies of armed troops among us:

For protecting them, by a mock Trial, from Punishment for any Murders which they should commit on the Inhabitants of these States:

For cutting off our Trade with all parts of the world:

For imposing taxes on us without our Consent:

For depriving us in many cases, of the benefits of Trial by Jury:

For transporting us beyond Seas to be tried for pretended offences:

For abolishing the free System of English Laws in a neighbouring Province, establishing therein an Arbitrary government, and enlarging its Boundaries so as to render it at once an example and fit instrument for introducing the same absolute rule into these Colonies:

For taking away our Charters, abolishing our most valuable Laws, and altering fundamentally the Forms of our Governments:

For suspending our own Legislature, and declaring themselves invested with Power to legislate for us in all cases whatsoever.

He has abdicated Government here, by declaring us out of his Protection and waging War against us.

He has plundered our seas, ravaged our Coasts, burnt our towns, and destroyed the lives of our people.

He is at this time transporting large armies of foreign mercenaries to compleat the works

of death, desolation and tyranny, already begun with circumstances of Cruelty & perfidy scarcely paralleled in the most barbarous ages, and totally unworthy the Head of a civilized nation.

He has constrained our fellow Citizens taken Captive on the high Seas to bear Arms against their Country, to become the executioners of their friends and Brethren, or to fall themselves by their Hands.

He has excited domestic insurrections amongst us, and has endeavoured to bring on the inhabitants of our frontiers, the merciless Indian Savages, whose known rule of warfare, is an undistinguished destruction of all ages, sexes and conditions.

In every stage of these Oppressions We have Petitioned for Redress in the most humble terms: Our repeated Petitions have been answered only by repeated injury. A Prince, whose character is thus marked by every act which may define a Tyrant, is unfit to be the ruler of a free People.

Nor have We been wanting in attention to our British brethren. We have warned them from time to time of attempts by their legislature to extend an unwarrantable jurisdiction over us. We have reminded them of the circumstances of our emigration and settlement here. We have appealed to their native justice and magnanimity, and we have conjured them by the ties of our common kindred to disavow these usurpations, which, would inevitably interrupt our connections and correspondence. They too have been deaf to the voice of justice and of consanguinity. We must, therefore, acquiesce in the necessity, which denounces our Separation, and hold them, as we hold the rest of mankind, Enemies in War, in Peace Friends.

We, therefore, the Representatives of the united States of America, in General Congress, Assembled, appealing to the Supreme Judge of the world for the rectitude of our intentions, do, in the Name, and by Authority of the good People of these Colonies, solemnly publish and declare, That these United Colonies are, and of Right ought to be Free and Independent States; that they are Absolved from all Allegiance to the British Crown, and that all political connection between them and the State of Great Britain, is and ought to be totally dissolved; and that as

Free and Independent States, they have full Power to levy War, conclude Peace, contract Alliances, establish Commerce, and to do all other Acts and Things which Independent States may of right do. And for the support of this Declaration, with a firm reliance on the Protection of Divine Providence, we mutually pledge to each other our Lives, our Fortunes and our sacred Honor.

John Hancock,

Josiah Bartlett, Wm Whipple, Saml Adams, John Adams, Robt Treat Paine, Elbridge Gerry, Steph. Hopkins, William Ellery, Roger Sherman, Samel Huntington, Wm Williams, Oliver Wolcott, Matthew Thornton, Wm Floyd, Phil Livingston, Frans Lewis, Lewis Morris, Richd Stockton, Jno Witherspoon, Fras Hopkinson, John Hart, Abra Clark, Robt Morris, Benjamin Rush, Benja Franklin, John Morton, Geo Clymer, Jas Smith, Geo. Taylor, James Wilson, Geo. Ross, Caesar Rodney, Geo Read, Thos M:Kean, Samuel Chase, Wm Paca, Thos Stone, Charles Carroll of Carrollton, George Wythe, Richard Henry Lee, Th. Jefferson, Benja Harrison, Thos Nelson, Jr., Francis Lightfoot Lee, Carter Braxton, Wm Hooper, Joseph Hewes, John Penn, Edward Rutledge, Thos Heyward, Junr., Thomas Lynch, Junor., Arthur Middleton, Button Gwinnett, Lyman Hall, Geo Walton.

The Constitution of the United States

We the people of the United States, in Order to form a more perfect Union, establish Justice, insure domestic Tranquility, provide for the common defence, promote the general Welfare, and secure the Blessings of Liberty to ourselves and our Posterity, do ordain and establish this CONSTITUTION for the United States of America.

ARTICLE I

Section 1. All legislative Powers herein granted shall be vested in a Congress of the United States, which shall consist of a Senate and House of Representatives.

Section 2. The House of Representatives shall be composed of Members chosen every second Year by the People of the several States, and the Electors in each State shall have the Qualifications requisite for Electors of the most numerous Branch of the State Legislature.

No Person shall be a Representative who shall not have attained to the Age of twenty-five Years, and been seven Years a Citizen of the United States, and who shall not, when elected, be an Inhabitant of that State in which he shall be chosen.

Representatives and direct Taxes shall be apportioned among the several States which may be included within this Union, according to their respective Numbers, which shall be determined by adding to the whole Number of free Persons, including those bound to Service for a Term of Years, and excluding Indians not taxed, three fifths of all other Persons. The actual Enumeration shall be made within three Years after the first Meeting of the Congress of the United States, and within every subsequent Term of ten Years, in such Manner as they shall by Law direct. The Number of Representatives shall not exceed one for every thirty Thousand, but each State shall have at Least one Representative; and until such enumeration shall be made, the State of New Hampshire shall be entitled to chuse three, Massachusetts eight, Rhode-Island and Providence Plantations one, Connecticut five, New-York six, New Jersey four, Pennsylvania eight, Delaware one, Maryland six, Virginia ten, North Carolina five, South Carolina five, and Georgia three.

When vacancies happen in the Representation from any State, the Executive Authority thereof shall issue Writs of Election to fill such Vacancies.

The House of Representatives shall chuse their Speaker and other Officers; and shall have the sole Power of Impeachment.

Section 3. The Senate of the United States shall be composed of two Senators from each State, chosen by the Legislature thereof, for six Years; and each Senator shall have one Vote.

Immediately after they shall be assembled in Consequence of the first Election, they shall be divided as equally as may be into three Classes. The Seats of the Senators of the first Class shall be vacated at the Expiration of the second Year, of the second Class at the Expiration of the fourth Year, and of the third Class at the Expiration of the sixth Year, so that one-third may be chosen every second Year; and if Vacancies happen by Resignation, or otherwise, during the Recess of the Legislature of any State, the Executive thereof may make temporary Appointments until the next Meeting of the Legislature, which shall then fill such Vacancies.

No Person shall be a Senator who shall not have attained to the Age of thirty Years, and been nine Years a Citizen of the United States, and who shall not, when elected, be an Inhabitant of that State in which he shall be chosen.

The Vice President of the United States shall

be President of the Senate, but shall have no vote, unless they be equally divided.

The Senate shall chuse their other Officers, and also a President pro tempore, in the absence of the Vice President, or when he shall exercise the Office of the President of the United States.

The Senate shall have the sole Power to try all Impeachments. When sitting for that purpose, they shall be on Oath or Affirmation. When the President of the United States is tried, the Chief Justice shall preside: And no person shall be convicted without the Concurrence of two thirds of the Members present.

Judgment in Cases of Impeachment shall not extend further than to removal from Office, and disqualification to hold and enjoy any Office of honor, Trust, or Profit under the United States: but the Party convicted shall nevertheless be liable and subject to Indictment, Trial, Judgment, and Punishment, according to Law.

Section 4. The Times, Places and Manner of holding Elections for Senators and Representatives, shall be prescribed in each state by the Legislature thereof; but the Congress may at any time by Law make or alter such Regulations, except as to the Places of Chusing Senators.

The Congress shall assemble at least once in every Year, and such Meeting shall be on the first Monday in December, unless they shall by Law appoint a different Day.

Section 5. Each House shall be the Judge of the Elections, Returns and Qualifications of its own Members, and a Majority of each shall constitute a Quorum to do Business; but a smaller number may adjourn from day to day, and may be authorized to compel the Attendance of absent Members, in such Manner, and under such Penalties, as each House may provide.

Each House may determine the Rules of its Proceedings, punish its Members for disorderly Behavior, and, with the Concurrence of two thirds, expel a Member.

Each House shall keep a Journal of its Proceedings, and from time to time publish the same, excepting such Parts as may in their Judgment require Secrecy; and the Yeas and Nays of the Members of either House on any question shall, at the Desire of one fifth of those Present, be entered on the Journal.

Neither House, during the Session of Congress,

shall, without the Consent of the other, adjourn for more than three days, nor to any other Place than that in which the two Houses shall be sitting.

Section 6. The Senators and Representatives shall receive a Compensation for their Services, to be ascertained by Law, and paid out of the Treasury of the United States. They shall in all Cases, except Treason, Felony, and Breach of the Peace, be privileged from arrest during their Attendance at the Session of their respective Houses, and in going to and returning from the same; and for any Speech or Debate in either House, they shall not be questioned in any other Place.

No Senator or Representative shall, during the Time for which he was elected, be appointed to any civil Office under the Authority of the United States, which shall have been created, or the Emoluments whereof shall have been increased, during such time; and no Person holding any Office under the United States shall be a Member of either House during his continuance in Office.

Section 7. All Bills for raising Revenue shall originate in the House of Representatives; but the Senate may propose or concur with Amendments as on other bills.

Every Bill which shall have passed the House of Representatives and the Senate, shall, before it become a Law, be presented to the President of the United States; If he approve he shall sign it, but if not he shall return it, with his Objections, to that House in which it shall have originated, who shall enter the Objections at large on their Journal, and proceed to reconsider it. If after such Reconsideration two thirds of that House shall agree to pass the bill, it shall be sent, together with the objections, to the other House, by which it shall likewise be reconsidered, and if approved by two thirds of that House, it shall become a Law. But in all such Cases the Votes of both Houses shall be determined by Yeas and Nays, and the Names of the Persons voting for and against the Bill shall be entered on the Journal of each House respectively. If any Bill shall not be returned by the President within ten Days (Sundays excepted) after it shall have been presented to him, the Same shall be a Law, in like Manner as if he had signed it, unless the Congress by their Adjournment prevent its Return, in which Case it shall not be a Law.

Every Order, Resolution, or Vote to which the Concurrence of the Senate and House of Representatives may be necessary (except on a question of Adjournment) shall be presented to the President of the United States; and before the Same shall take Effect, shall be approved by him, or being disapproved by him, shall be repassed by two thirds of the Senate and House of Representatives, according to the Rules and Limitations prescribed in the Case of a Bill.

Section 8. The Congress shall have Power To lay and collect Taxes, Duties, Imposts and Excises, to pay the Debts and provide for the common Defence and general Welfare of the United States; but all Duties, Imposts and Excises shall be uniform throughout the United States;

To borrow money on the credit of the United States;

To regulate Commerce with foreign Nations, and among the several States, and with the Indian Tribes;

To establish an uniform Rule of Naturalization, and uniform Laws on the subject of Bankruptcies throughout the United States;

To coin Money, regulate the Value thereof, and of foreign Coin, and fix the Standard of Weights and Measures;

To provide for the Punishment of counterfeiting the Securities and current Coin of the United States;

To establish Post Offices and post Roads;

To promote the Progress of Science and useful Arts, by securing for limited Times to Authors and Inventors the exclusive Right to their respective Writings and Discoveries;

To constitute Tribunals inferior to the Supreme Court;

To define and punish Piracies and Felonies committed on the high Seas, and Offences against the Law of Nations;

To declare War, grant Letters of Marque and Reprisal, and make Rules concerning Captures on Land and Water;

To raise and support Armies, but no Appropriation of Money to that Use shall be for a longer Term than two Years;

To provide and maintain a Navy;

To make Rules for the Government and Regulation of the land and naval forces;

To provide for calling forth the Militia to execute the Laws of the Union, suppress Insurrections and repel Invasions;

To provide for organizing, arming, and disciplining the Militia, and for governing such Part of them as may be employed in the Service of the United States, reserving to the States respectively, the Appointment of the Officers, and the Authority of training the Militia according to the discipline prescribed by Congress;

To exercise exclusive Legislation in all Cases whatsoever, over such District (not exceeding ten Miles square) as may, by Cession of particular States, and the acceptance of Congress, become the Seat of Government of the United States, and to exercise like Authority over all Places purchased by the Consent of the Legislature of the State in which the Same shall be, for the Erection of Forts, Magazines, Arsenals, dock-Yards, and other needful Buildings;—And

To make all Laws which shall be necessary and proper for carrying into Execution the foregoing Powers, and all other Powers vested by this Constitution in the government of the United States, or in any Department or Officer thereof.

Section 9. The Migration or Importation of such Persons as any of the States now existing shall think proper to admit, shall not be prohibited by the Congress prior to the Year one thousand eight hundred and eight, but a tax or duty may be imposed on such Importation, not exceeding ten dollars for each Person.

The privilege of the Writ of Habeas Corpus shall not be suspended, unless when in Cases of Rebellion or Invasion the public Safety may require it.

No Bill of Attainder or ex post facto Law shall be passed.

No capitation, or other direct, Tax shall be laid unless in Proportion to the Census or Enumeration herein before directed to be taken.

No Tax or Duty shall be laid on Articles exported from any State.

No Preference shall be given by any Regulation of Revenue to the Ports of one State over those of another: nor shall Vessels bound to, or from, one State, be obliged to enter, clear, or pay Duties in another.

No Money shall be drawn from the Treasury, but in Consequence of Appropriations made by Law; and a regular Statement and Account of the Receipts and Expenditures of all public Money shall be published from time to time.

No Title of Nobility shall be granted by the United States: And no Person holding any Office of Profit or Trust under them, shall, without the Consent of the Congress, accept of any present, Emolument, Office, or Title, of any kind whatever, from any King, Prince, or foreign State.

Section 10. No State shall enter into any Treaty, Alliance, or Confederation; grant Letters of Marque and Reprisal; coin Money; emit Bills of Credit; make any Thing but gold and silver Coin a Tender in Payment of Debts; pass any Bill of Attainder, ex post facto Law, or Law impairing the Obligation of Contracts, or grant any Title of Nobility.

No State shall, without the Consent of the Congress, lay any Imposts or Duties on Imports or Exports, except what may be absolutely necessary for executing its inspection Laws: and the net Produce of all Duties and Imposts, laid by any State on Imports or Exports, shall be for the Use of the Treasury of the United States; and all such Laws shall be subject to the Revision and Control of the Congress.

No State shall, without the Consent of Congress, lay any duty of Tonnage, keep Troops, or Ships of War in time of Peace, enter into any Agreement or Compact with another State, or with a foreign Power, or engage in War, unless actually invaded, or in such imminent Danger as will not admit of delay.

ARTICLE II

Section 1. The executive Power shall be vested in a President of the United States of America. He shall hold his Office during the Term of four years, and, together with the Vice President, chosen for the same Term, be elected, as follows:

Each State shall appoint, in such Manner as the Legislature thereof may direct, a Number of Electors, equal to the whole Number of Senators and Representatives to which the State may be entitled in the Congress; but no Senator or Representative, or Person holding an Office of Trust or Profit under the United States, shall be appointed an Elector.

The Electors shall meet in their respective States, and vote by Ballot for two persons, of whom one at least shall not be an Inhabitant of the same State with themselves. And they shall make a List of all the Persons voted for, and of the Number of Votes for each; which List they shall sign and certify, and transmit sealed to the Seat of the Government of the United States, directed to the President of the Senate. The President of the Senate shall, in the Presence of the Senate and House of Representatives, open all the Certificates, and the Votes shall then be counted. The Person having the greatest Number of Votes shall be the President, if such Number be a Majority of the whole Number of Electors appointed; and if there be more than one who have such Majority, and have an equal Number of Votes, then the House of Representatives shall immediately chuse by Ballot one of them for President; and if no Person have a Majority, then from the five highest on the List the said House shall in like Manner chuse the President. But in chusing the President, the votes shall be taken by States, the Representation from each State having one Vote; a quorum for this Purpose shall consist of a Member or Members from two-thirds of the States, and a Majority of all the States shall be necessary to a Choice. In every Case, after the Choice of the President, the Person having the greatest Number of Votes of the Electors shall be the Vice President. But if there should remain two or more who have equal votes, the Senate shall chuse from them by Ballot the Vice President.

The Congress may determine the time of chusing the Electors, and the Day on which they shall give their Votes; which Day shall be the same throughout the United States.

No person except a natural-born Citizen, or a Citizen of the United States, at the time of the Adoption of this Constitution, shall be eligible to the Office of President; neither shall any Person be eligible to that Office who shall not have attained to the Age of thirty-five years, and been fourteen Years a Resident within the United States.

In Case of the Removal of the President from Office, or of his Death, Resignation, or Inability to discharge the Powers and Duties of the said Office, the same shall devolve on the Vice President, and the Congress may by Law provide for the Case of Removal, Death, Resignation, or Inability, both of the President and Vice President, declaring what Officer shall then act as President, and such Officer shall act accordingly, until the disability be removed, or a President shall be elected.

The President shall, at stated Times, receive for his Services a Compensation, which shall neither be increased nor diminished during the Period for which he shall have been elected, and he shall not receive within that Period any other Emolument from the United States, or any of them.

Before he enter on the execution of his Office, he shall take the following Oath or Affirmation:— "I do solemnly swear (or affirm) that I will faithfully execute the Office of President of the United States, and will, to the best of my Ability, preserve, protect, and defend the Constitution of the United States."

Section 2. The President shall be Commander in Chief of the Army and Navy of the United States, and of the Militia of the several States, when called into the actual Service of the United States; he may require the Opinion, in writing, of the principal Officer in each of the executive Departments, upon any subject relating to the Duties of their respective Offices, and he shall have Power to Grant Reprieves and Pardons for Offences against the United States, except in Cases of Impeachment.

He shall have Power, by and with the Advice and Consent of the Senate, to make Treaties, provided two thirds of the Senators present concur; and he shall nominate, and by and with the Advice and Consent of the Senate, shall appoint Ambassadors, other public Ministers and Consuls, Judges of the supreme Court, and all other Officers of the United States, whose Appointments are not herein otherwise provided for, and which shall be established by Law: but the Congress may by Law vest the Appointment of such inferior Officers, as they think proper, in the President alone, in the Courts of Law, or in the Heads of Departments.

The President shall have Power to fill up all Vacancies that may happen during the Recess of the Senate, by granting Commissions which shall expire at the End of their next Session.

Section 3. He shall from time to time give to the Congress Information of the State of the Union, and recommend to their Consideration such Measures as he shall judge necessary and expedient; he may, on extraordinary occasions, convene both Houses, or either of them, and in Case of Disagreement between them, with respect to the Time of Adjournment, he may adjourn them to such Time as he shall think proper; he shall receive Ambassadors and other public Ministers; he shall take Care that the Laws be faithfully executed, and shall Commission all the Officers of the United States.

Section 4. The President, Vice President and all civil Officers of the United States, shall be removed from Office on Impeachment for, and Conviction of, Treason, Bribery, or other high Crimes and Misdemeanors.

ARTICLE III

Section 1. The judicial Power of the United States, shall be vested in one supreme Court, and in such inferior Courts as the Congress may from time to time ordain and establish. The Judges, both of the supreme and inferior Courts, shall hold their Offices during good Behaviour, and shall, at stated Times, receive for their Services, a Compensation, which shall not be diminished during their Continuance in Office.

Section 2. The judicial Power shall extend to all Cases, in Law and Equity, arising under this Constitution, the Laws of the United States, and treaties made, or which shall be made, under their Authority;—to all Cases affecting ambassadors, other public ministers and consuls;—to all cases of admiralty and maritime Jurisdiction;—to Controversies to which the United States shall be a Party;—to Controversies between two or more States;—between a State and Citizens of another State;—between Citizens of different States,—between Citizens of the same State claiming Lands under Grants of different States, and between a State, or the Citizens thereof, and foreign States, Citizens or Subjects.

In all Cases affecting Ambassadors, other public Ministers and Consuls, and those in which a State shall be Party, the supreme Court shall have original Jurisdiction. In all the other Cases before mentioned, the supreme Court shall have appellate Jurisdiction, both as to Law and Fact, with such Exceptions, and under such Regulations as the Congress shall make.

The trial of all Crimes, except in Cases of Impeachment, shall be by Jury; and such Trial shall be held in the State where the said Crimes shall have been committed; but when not committed within any State, the Trial shall be at such Place or Places as the Congress may by Law have directed.

Section 3. Treason against the United States, shall consist only in levying War against them, or in adhering to their Enemies, giving them Aid and Comfort. No Person shall be convicted of Treason unless on the testimony of two Witnesses to the same overt Act, or on Confession in open Court.

The Congress shall have power to declare the Punishment of Treason, but no Attainder of Treason shall work Corruption of Blood, or Forfeiture except during the Life of the Person attained.

ARTICLE IV

Section 1. Full Faith and Credit shall be given in each State to the public Acts, Records, and judicial Proceedings of every other State. And the Congress may by general Laws prescribe the Manner in which such Acts, Records and Proceedings shall be proved, and the Effect thereof.

Section 2. The Citizens of each State shall be entitled to all Privileges and Immunities of Citizens in the several States.

A Person charged in any State with Treason, Felony, or other Crime, who shall flee from Justice, and be found in another State, shall on demand of the executive Authority of the State from which he fled, be delivered up, to be removed to the State having Jurisdiction of the crime.

No Person held to Service or Labour in one State, under the Laws thereof, escaping into another, shall, in Consequence of any Law or Regulation therein, be discharged from such Service or Labour, but shall be delivered up on Claim of the Party to whom such Service or Labour may be due.

Section 3. New States may be admitted by the Congress into this Union; but no new State shall be formed or erected within the Jurisdiction of any other State; nor any State be formed by the Junction of two or more States, or parts of States, without the Consent of the Legislatures of the States concerned as well as of the Congress.

The Congress shall have Power to dispose of

and make all needful Rules and Regulations respecting the Territory or other Property belonging to the United States; and nothing in this Constitution shall be so construed as to Prejudice any Claims of the United States, or of any particular State.

Section 4. The United States shall guarantee to every State in this Union a Republican Form of Government, and shall protect each of them against Invasion; and on Application of the Legislature, or the Executive (when the Legislature cannot be convened) against domestic Violence.

ARTICLE V

The Congress, whenever two-thirds of both Houses shall deem it necessary, shall propose Amendments to this Constitution, or, on the Application of the Legislatures of two-thirds of the several States, shall call a Convention for proposing Amendments, which, in either Case, shall be valid to all Intents and Purposes, as part of this Constitution, when ratified by the Legislatures of three-fourths of the several States, or by Conventions in three-fourths thereof, as the one or the other Mode of Ratification may be proposed by the Congress; Provided that no Amendment which may be made prior to the Year One thousand eight hundred and eight shall in any Manner affect the first and fourth Clauses in the Ninth Section of the first Article; and that no State, without its Consent, shall be deprived of its equal Suffrage in the Senate.

ARTICLE VI

All Debts contracted and Engagements entered into, before the Adoption of this Constitution, shall be as valid against the United States under this Constitution, as under the Confederation.

This Constitution, and the Laws of the United States which shall be made in Pursuance thereof; and all Treaties made, or which shall be made, under the Authority of the United States, shall be the supreme Law of the Land; and the Judges in every State shall be bound thereby, any Thing in the Constitution or Laws of any State to the Contrary notwithstanding.

The Senators and Representatives before mentioned, and the Members of the several State

Legislatures, and all executive and judicial Officers, both of the United States and of the several States, shall be bound by Oath or Affirmation to support this Constitution; but no religious Test shall ever be required as a qualification to any Office or public Trust under the United States.

ARTICLE VII

The Ratification of the Conventions of nine States shall be sufficient for the Establishment of this Constitution between the States so ratifying the same.

Done in Convention by the Unanimous Consent of the States present the Seventeenth Day of September in the Year of our Lord one thousand seven hundred and Eighty seven, and of the Independence of the United States of America the Twelfth. In Witness whereof We have hereunto subscribed our Names.

Go. Washington, *President and deputy from Virginia; Attest* William Jackson, *Secretary; Delaware:* Geo. Read,* Gunning Bedford, Jr., John Dickinson, Richard Bassett, Jaco. Broom; *Maryland:* James McHenry, Daniel of St. Thomas' Jenifer, Danl. Carroll; *Virginia:* John Blair, James Madison, Jr.; *North Carolina:* Wm. Blount, Richd. Dobbs Spaight, Hu Williamson; *South Carolina:* J. Rutledge, Charles Cotesworth Pinckney, Charles Pinckney, Pierce Butler; *Georgia:* William Few, Abr. Baldwin; *New Hampshire:* John Langdon, Nicholas Gilman; *Massachusetts:* Nathaniel Gorham, Rufus King; *Connecticut:* Wm. Saml. Johnson, Roger Sherman;* *New York:* Alexander Hamilton; *New Jersey:* Wil. Livingston, David Brearley, Wm. Paterson, Jona. Dayton; *Pennsylvania:* B. Franklin,* Thomas Mifflin, Robt. Morris,* Geo. Clymer,* Thos. FitzSimons, Jared Ingersoll, James Wilson, Gouv. Morris.

Articles in Addition to, and Amendment of, the Constitution of the United States of America, Proposed by Congress, and Ratified by the Legislatures of the Several States, Pursuant to the Fifth Article of the Original Constitution.

---

* Also signed the Declaration of Independence

AMENDMENT I [1791]

Congress shall make no law respecting an establishment of religion, or prohibiting the free exercise thereof; or abridging the freedom of speech, or of the press; or the right of the people peaceably to assemble, and to petition the Government for a redress of grievances.

AMENDMENT II [1791]

A well regulated Militia, being necessary to the security of a free State, the right of the people to keep and bear Arms shall not be infringed.

AMENDMENT III [1791]

No Soldier shall, in time of peace, be quartered in any house, without the consent of the Owner, nor in time of war, but in a manner to be prescribed by law.

AMENDMENT IV [1791]

The right of the people to be secure in their persons, houses, papers, and effects, against unreasonable searches and seizures, shall not be violated, and no Warrants shall issue, but upon probable cause, supported by Oath or affirmation, and particularly describing the place to be searched, and the persons or things to be seized.

AMENDMENT V [1791]

No person shall be held to answer for a capital or otherwise infamous crime, unless on a presentment or indictment of a Grand Jury, except in cases arising in the land or naval forces, or in the Militia, when in actual service in time of War or public danger; nor shall any person be subject for the same offence to be twice put in jeopardy of life or limb; nor shall be compelled in any criminal case to be a witness against himself, nor be deprived of life, liberty, or property, without due process of law; nor shall private property be taken for public use, without just compensation.

AMENDMENT VI [1791]

In all criminal prosecutions, the accused shall enjoy the right to a speedy and public trial, by an impartial jury of the State and district wherein the crime shall have been committed, which district shall have been previously ascertained by law, and to be informed of the nature and cause of the accusation; to be confronted with the witness against him; to have compulsory process for obtaining witnesses in his favor, and to have the Assistance of Counsel for his defence.

AMENDMENT VII [1791]

In suits at common law, where the value in controversy shall exceed twenty dollars, the right of trial by jury shall be preserved, and no fact tried by a jury, shall be otherwise reexamined in any Court of the United States, than according to the rules of the common law.

AMENDMENT VIII [1791]

Excessive bail shall not be required, nor excessive fines imposed, nor cruel and unusual punishments inflicted.

AMENDMENT IX [1791]

The enumeration in the Constitution, of certain rights, shall not be construed to deny or disparage others retained by the people.

AMENDMENT X [1791]

The powers not delegated to the United States by the Constitution, nor prohibited by it to the States, are reserved to the States respectively, or to the people.

AMENDMENT XI [1798]

The Judicial power of the United States shall not be construed to extend to any suit in law or equity, commenced or prosecuted against one of the United States by Citizens of another State, or by Citizens or Subjects of any Foreign State.

AMENDMENT XII [1804]

The Electors shall meet in their respective States and vote by ballot for President and Vice-President, one of whom, at least, shall not be an inhabitant of the same State with themselves; they shall name in their ballots the person voted for as President, and in distinct ballots the person voted for as Vice-President, and they shall make distinct lists of all persons voted for as President, and of all persons voted for as Vice-President, and of the number of votes for each, which lists they shall sign and certify, and transmit sealed to the seat of the government of the United States, directed to the President of the Senate;—The President of the Senate shall, in the presence of the Senate and House of Representatives, open all the certificates and the votes shall then be counted;—The person having the greatest number of votes for President, shall be the President, if such number be a majority of the whole number of Electors appointed; and if no person have such majority, then from the persons having the highest numbers not exceeding three on the list of those voted for as President, the House of Representatives shall choose immediately, by ballot, the President. But in choosing the President, the votes shall be taken by states, the representation from each state having one vote; a quorum for this purpose shall consist of a member or members from two-thirds of the states, and a majority of all the states shall be necessary to a choice. And if the House of Representatives shall not choose a President whenever the right of choice shall devolve upon them, before the fourth day of March next following, then the Vice-President shall act as President, as in the case of the death or other constitutional disability of the President.—The person having the greatest number of votes as Vice-President, shall be the Vice-President, if such number be a majority of the whole number of Electors appointed, and if no person have a majority, then from the two highest numbers on the list, the Senate shall choose the Vice-President; a quorum for the purpose shall consist of two-thirds of the whole number of Senators, and a majority of the whole number shall be necessary to a choice. But no person constitutionally ineligible to the office of President shall be eligible to that of Vice-President of the United States.

AMENDMENT XIII [1865]

Section 1. Neither slavery nor involuntary servitude, except as a punishment for crime whereof the party shall have been duly convicted, shall exist within the United States, or any place subject to their jurisdiction.

Section 2. Congress shall have power to enforce this article by appropriate legislation.

AMENDMENT XIV [1868]

Section 1. All persons born or naturalized in the United States, and subject to the jurisdiction thereof, are citizens of the United States and of the State wherein they reside. No State shall make or enforce any law which shall abridge the privileges or immunities of citizens of the United States; nor shall any State deprive any person of life, liberty, or property, without due process of law; nor deny to any person within its jurisdiction the equal protection of the laws.

Section 2. Representatives shall be apportioned among the several States according to their respective numbers, counting the whole number of persons in each State, excluding Indians not taxed. But when the right to vote at any election for the choice of electors for President and Vice-President of the United States, Representatives in Congress, the Executive and Judicial officers of a State, or the members of the Legislature thereof, is denied to any of the male inhabitants of such State, being twenty-one years of age, and citizens of the United States, or in any way abridged, except for participation in rebellion, or other crime, the basis of representation therein shall be reduced in the proportion which the number of such male citizens shall bear to the whole number of male citizens twenty-one years of age in such State.

Section 3. No person shall be a Senator or Representative in Congress, or elector of President and Vice-President, or hold any office, civil or military, under the United States, or under any State, who, having previously taken an oath, as a member of Congress, or as an officer of the United States, or as a member of any State legislature, or as an executive or judicial officer of any State, to support the Constitution of the United States, shall have engaged in insurrection or rebellion against the same, or given aid or comfort to the enemies thereof. But Congress may by a vote of two-thirds of each House, remove such disability.

Section 4. The validity of the public debt of the United States, authorized by law, including debts incurred for payment of pensions and bounties for services in suppressing insurrection or rebellion, shall not be questioned. But neither the United States nor any State shall assume or pay any debt or obligation incurred in aid of insurrection or rebellion against the United States, or any claim for the loss or emancipation of any slave; but all such debts, obligations, and claims shall be held illegal and void.

Section 5. The Congress shall have the power to enforce, by appropriate legislation, the provisions of this article.

AMENDMENT XV [1870]

Section 1. The right of citizens of the United States to vote shall not be denied or abridged by the United States or by any State on account of race, color, or previous condition of servitude—

Section 2. The Congress shall have power to enforce this article by appropriate legislation.

AMENDMENT XVI [1913]

The Congress shall have power to lay and collect taxes on incomes, from whatever source derived, without apportionment among the several States, and without regard to any census or enumeration.

AMENDMENT XVII [1913]

The Senate of the United States shall be composed of two Senators from each State, elected by the people thereof, for six years; and each Senator shall have one vote. The electors in each State shall have the qualifications requisite for electors of the most numerous branch of the State legislatures.

When vacancies happen in the representation of any State in the Senate, the executive authority of such State shall issue writs of election to fill such vacancies: *Provided,* That the legislature of any State may empower the executive thereof to make temporary appointments until the people fill the vacancies by election as the legislature may direct.

This amendment shall not be so construed as to affect the election or term of any Senator chosen before it becomes valid as part of the Constitution.

AMENDMENT XVIII [1919]

Section 1. After one year from the ratification of this article the manufacture, sale, or transportation of intoxicating liquors within, the importation thereof into, or the exportation thereof from the United States and all territory subject to the jurisdiction thereof for beverage purposes is hereby prohibited.

Section 2. The Congress and the several States shall have concurrent power to enforce this article by appropriate legislation.

Section 3. This article shall be inoperative unless it shall have been ratified as an amendment to the Constitution by the legislatures of the several States, as provided in the Constitution, within seven years from the date of the submission hereof to the States by the Congress.

AMENDMENT XIX [1920]

The right of citizens of the United States to vote shall not be denied or abridged by the United States or by any State on account of sex.

Congress shall have power to enforce this article by appropriate legislation.

AMENDMENT XX [1933]

Section 1. The terms of the President and Vice-President shall end at noon on the 20th day of January, and the terms of Senators and Representatives at noon on the 3d day of January, of the years in which such terms would have ended if this article had not been ratified; and the terms of their successors shall then begin.

Section 2. The Congress shall assemble at least once in every year, and such meeting shall begin at noon on the 3d day of January, unless they shall by law appoint a different day.

Section 3. If, at the time fixed for the beginning of the term of the President, the President elect shall have died, the Vice-President elect shall become President. If a President shall not have been chosen before the time fixed for the beginning of his term, or if the President elect shall have failed to qualify, then the Vice-President elect shall act as President until a President shall have qualified; and the Congress may by law provide for the case wherein neither a President elect nor a Vice-President elect shall have qualified, declaring who shall then act as President, or the manner in which one who is to act shall be selected, and such person shall act accordingly until a President or Vice-President shall have qualified.

Section 4. The Congress may by law provide for the case of the death of any of the persons from whom the House of Representatives may choose a President whenever the right of choice shall have devolved upon them, and for the case of the death of any of the persons from whom the Senate may choose a Vice-President whenever the right of choice shall have devolved upon them.

Section 5. Sections 1 and 2 shall take effect on the 15th day of October following the ratification of this article.

Section 6. This article shall be inoperative unless it shall have been ratified as an amendment to the Constitution by the legislatures of three-fourths of the several States within seven years from the date of its submission.

AMENDMENT XXI [1933]

Section 1. The eighteenth article of amendment to the Constitution of the United States is hereby repealed.

Section 2. The transportation or importation into any State, Territory, or possession of the United States for delivery or use therein of intoxicating liquors, in violation of the laws thereof, is hereby prohibited.

Section 3. This article shall be inoperative unless it shall have been ratified as an amendment to the Constitution by conventions in the several States, as provided in the Constitution, within seven years from the date of the submission hereof to the States by the Congress.

AMENDMENT XXII [1951]

No person shall be elected to the office of the President more than twice, and no person who has held the office of President, or acted as President, for more than two years of a term to which some other person was elected President shall be elected to the office of the President more than once.

But this Article shall not apply to any person holding the office of President when this Article was proposed by the Congress, and shall not prevent any person who may be holding the office of President, or acting as President, during the term within which this Article becomes operative from holding the office of President or acting as President during the remainder of such term.

AMENDMENT XXIII [1961]

Section 1. The District constituting the seat of Government of the United States shall appoint in such manner as the Congress may direct:

A number of electors of President and Vice President equal to the whole number of Senators and Representatives in Congress to which the District would be entitled if it were a State, but in no event more than the least populous State; they shall be in addition to those appointed by the States, but they shall be considered, for the purposes of the election of President and Vice President, to be electors appointed by a State; and they shall meet in the District and perform such duties as provided by the twelfth article of amendment.

Section 2. The Congress shall have power to enforce this article by appropriate legislation.

AMENDMENT XXIV [1964]

Section 1. The right of citizens of the United States to vote in any primary or other election for President or Vice President, for electors for President or Vice President, or for Senator or Representative in Congress, shall not be denied or abridged by the United States or any State by reason of failure to pay any poll tax or other tax.

Section 2. The Congress shall have the power to enforce this article by appropriate legislation.

AMENDMENT XXV [1967]

Section 1. In case of the removal of the President from office or his death or resignation, the Vice President shall become President.

Section 2. Whenever there is a vacancy in the office of the Vice President, the President shall nominate a Vice President who shall take the office upon confirmation by a majority vote of both houses of Congress.

Section 3. Whenever the President transmits to the President pro tempore of the Senate and the Speaker of the House of Representatives his written declaration that he is unable to discharge the powers and duties of his office, and until he transmits to them a written declaration to the contrary, such powers and duties shall be discharged by the Vice President as Acting President.

Section 4. Whenever the Vice President and a majority of either the principal officers of the executive departments, or of such other body as Congress may by law provide, transmit to the President pro tempore of the Senate and the Speaker of the House of Representatives their written declaration that the President is unable to discharge the powers and duties of his office, the Vice President shall immediately assume the powers and duties of the office as Acting President.

Thereafter, when the President transmits to the President pro tempore of the Senate and the Speaker of the House of Representatives his written declaration that no inability exists, he shall resume the powers and duties of his office unless the Vice President and a majority of either the principal officers of the executive departments, or of such other body as Congress may by law provide, transmit within four days to the President pro tempore of the Senate and the Speaker of the House of Representatives their written declaration that the President is unable to discharge the powers and duties of his office. Thereupon Congress shall decide the issue, assembling within 48 hours for that purpose if not in session. If the Congress, within 21 days after receipt of the latter written declaration, or, if Congress is not in session, within 21 days after Congress is required to assemble, determines by two-thirds vote of both houses that the President is unable to discharge the powers and duties of his office, the Vice President shall continue to discharge the same as Acting President; otherwise, the President shall resume the powers and duties of his office.

AMENDMENT XXVI [1971]

Section 1. The right of citizens of the United States, who are 18 years of age or older, to vote shall not be denied or abridged by the United States or any state on account of age.

Section 2. The Congress shall have the power to enforce this article by appropriate legislation.

Notes

Chapter 1

1. Robert G. Kaiser, "The End of the Soviet Empire: Failure on a Historic Scale," *Washington Post National Weekly Edition*, January 1–7, 1990, p. 23.

2. *New York Times*, December 31, 1989, p. 11E.

3. *Congressional Quarterly Weekly Report*, January 21, 1989, p. 412.

4. Harold Lasswell, *Politics: Who Gets What When How* (Cleveland, Ohio: Meridian Books, 1958).

5. Thomas Hobbes, *Leviathan* (Indianapolis, Ind.: Bobbs-Merrill, 1958), p. 106.

6. David Easton, *The Political System* (New York: Knopf, 1965), p. 129.

7. Robert Dahl, *Who Governs?* (New Haven, Conn.: Yale University Press, 1961), p. 305.

8. This idea is embedded in the writings of several pluralists. See, for example, Bernard Berelson et al., *Voting* (Chicago: University of Chicago Press, 1954), chap. 14; and John C. Harsanyi, "Democracy, Equality, and Popular Consent," in *Power, Inequality, and Democratic Politics*, ed. Ian Shapiro and Grant Reeher (Boulder, Colo.: Westview Press, 1988), pp. 281–283.

9. Robert Dahl, *Political Analysis*, 4th ed. (Englewood Cliffs, N.J.: Prentice-Hall, 1984), pp. 24–26.

10. Robert Dahl, "Critique of the Ruling Elite Model," *American Political Science Review* 52 (June 1958):463–469.

11. Robert A. Dahl, *Dilemmas of Pluralist Democracy* (New Haven, Conn.: Yale University Press, 1982), pp. 16–29.

12. *Webster* v. *Reproductive Health Services*, 109 S.Ct. 3040 (1989).

13. Joseph Schumpeter, *Capitalism, Socialism, and Democracy*, 3rd ed. (New York: Harper & Row, 1950), p. 269.

14. See, for instance, Giovanni Sartori, *Democratic Theory* (Detroit: Wayne State University Press, 1962).

15. This account is based on Norman J. Ornstein and Shirley Elder, *Interest Groups, Lobbying and Policymaking* (Washington, D.C.: Congressional Quarterly Press, 1978), chap. 7; and Nick Kotz, *Wild Blue Yonder: Money, Politics, and the B-1 Bomber* (New York: Pantheon, 1988).

16. Quoted in Nicholas Wade, "Death of the B-1: The Events Behind Carter's Decision," *Science*, August 5, 1977, p. 536.

17. E. E. Schattschneider, *The Semi-Sovereign People* (New York: Holt, Rinehart and Winston, 1960), p. 35.

18. Nick Kotz, "Money, Politics, and the B-1 Bomber," *Technology Review*, April 1988, pp. 31–40.

19. See, for example, Dahl, *Dilemmas of Pluralist Democracy*; and Charles Lindblom, *Politics and Markets* (New York: Basic Books, 1977).

20. Peter Bachrach, *The Theory of Democratic Elitism* (Boston: Little, Brown, 1967).

21. Lane Davis, "The Costs of Realism: Contemporary Restatement of Democracy," *Western Political Quarterly* 17 (March 1964):43.

22. Thomas Dye, *Who's Running America? The Conservative Years*, 4th ed. (Englewood Cliffs, N.J.: Prentice-Hall, 1986). It should be mentioned that Professor Dye does not necessarily subscribe to all aspects of the elite theory described in this chapter. Also see Gabriel Kolko, *Wealth and Power in America* (New York: Praeger, 1962); and G. William Domhoff, *The Powers That Be* (New York: Random House (Vintage Books), 1979).

23. Dye, *Who's Running America?*, p. 12.

24. Ibid., chaps. 3 and 4.

25. C. Wright Mills, *The Power Elite* (New York: Oxford University Press, 1959), chap. 1.

26. Mills, *The Power Elite*, chaps. 12 and 14. Also see Ralph Miliband, *The State in Capitalist Society* (New York: Basic Books, 1969), pp. 70–72.

27. Dye, *Who's Running America?*, p. 191.

28. Mills, *The Power Elite*, p. 285.

29. Ibid., p. 255.

30. On the importance of the agenda in determining political power, see Peter Bachrach and Morton S. Baratz, "Decisions and Non-Decisions," *American Political Science Review* 57 (June 1963):632–642.

31. Quoted in Robert Donovan, *Conflict and Crisis* (New York: Norton, 1977), p. 374.

Chapter 2

1. Harold Lasswell, *Politics: Who Gets What When How* (Cleveland, Ohio: Meridian Books, 1958).

2. U.S. Bureau of the Census, Current Population Reports, Series P-25, No. 1018, *Projections of the Population of the United States, by Age, Sex, and Race* (Washington, D.C.: Government Printing Office, 1989), p. 4. (Middle series projections cited.)

3. U.S. Senate Special Committee on Aging, *Aging America: Trends and Projections, 1987–88 Edition* (Washington, D.C.: Department of Health and Human Services, n.d.), chap. 6.

4. Paul Taylor, "Remember the Generation Gap," *Washington Post National Weekly Edition*, January 20, 1986, p. 23.

5. Cited in ibid.

6. Henry Aaron, "When Is a Burden Not a Burden? The Elderly in America," *Brookings Review*, Summer 1986, pp. 17–24; and Roger L. Conner, "Answering the Demo-Doomsayers," *Brookings Review*, Fall 1989, pp. 37–38.

7. U.S. Bureau of the Census, Current Population Reports, Series P-20, No. 438, *Marital Status and Living Arrangements: March 1988* (Washington, D.C.: Government Printing Office, 1988), pp. 59–60.

8. U.S. Bureau of the Census, *Statistical Abstract of the United States: 1989* (Washington, D.C.: Government Printing Office, 1989), p. 41.

9. U.S. Department of Labor, Bureau of Labor Statistics, *Handbook of Labor Statistics* (Washington, D.C.: Government Printing Office, 1985), p. 6; and *Monthly Labor Review* 112 (March 1989):64. The proportion of women in the labor force is much higher if one considers the age group 25 to 54. Susan E. Shark, "Women and the Labor Market: The Link Grows Stronger," *Monthly Labor Review* 111 (March 1988):3.

10. U.S. House of Representatives, Committee on Ways and Means, *Background Material and Data on Programs Within the Jurisdiction of the Committee on Ways and Means* (Washington, D.C.: Government Printing Office, 1989), p. 848.

11. U.S. Bureau of the Census, Current Population Reports, Series P-60, No. 162, *Money Income of Households, Families, and Persons in the United States: 1987* (Washington, D.C.: Government Printing Office, 1989), pp. 104–105; and Frank Levy, *Dollars and Dreams* (New York: Russell Sage, 1987), p. 141.

12. Committee on Ways and Means, *Background Material and Data*, p. 859.

13. *New York Times*, April 17, 1989, p. 16.

14. *New York Times*, April 14, 1984, p. 24.

15. U.S. Bureau of the Census, *Statistical Abstract of the United States: 1987* (Washington, D.C.: Government Printing Office, 1987), p. 25.

16. U.S. Bureau of the Census, *State and Metropolitan Area Data Book: 1986* (Washington, D.C.: Government Printing Office, 1986), table B.

17. *Washington Post National Weekly Edition*, February 20–26, 1989, p. 11; and U.S. Bureau of the Census, Current Population Reports, Series P-25, No. 1017, *Projections of Population of States by Age, Sex, and Race: 1988–2010* (Washington, D.C.: Government Printing Office, 1988), pp. 3–4.

18. *New York Times*, December 13, 1982, p. 1.

19. U.S. Bureau of the Census, *Money Income of Households, Families, and Persons in the United States: 1987*, p. 3.

20. Donald J. Bogue, *The Population of the United States* (New York: Free Press, 1985), pp. 567–568.

21. Quoted in E. J. Kahn, Jr., *The American People* (Baltimore: Penguin Books, 1973), p. 177.

22. U.S. Immigration and Naturalization Service, *Statistical Yearbook of Immigration and Naturalization Service, 1986* (Washington, D.C.: Government Printing Office, 1987), p. 1.

23. U.S. Bureau of the Census, *Money Income of Households, Families, and Persons in the United States: 1987*, p. 10. The median household net worth—assets minus debts—of whites is about $39,000 versus $3,400 for nonwhites. U.S. Bureau of the Census, *Statistical Abstract of the United States: 1988* (Washington, D.C.: Government Printing Office, 1988), p. 440.

24. Andrew Hacker, *U/S A Statistical Portrait of the American People* (New York: Viking Press, 1983), p. 36; and U.S Bureau of the Census, Current Population Reports, Series P-20, No. 434, *The Hispanic Population of the United States: March 1986 and 1987* (Washington, D.C.: Government Printing Office, 1988), p. 7.

25. U.S. Bureau of the Census, *The Hispanic Population of the United States*, pp. 22–23.

26. U.S. Bureau of the Census, *Money Income of Households, Families, and Persons in the United States: 1987*, pp. 32–33; and U.S. Bureau of the Census, *The Hispanic Population of the United States: March 1986 and 1987*, pp. 5, 15.

27. *New York Times*, February 8, 1990, p. 10B.

28. Wilmington, Delaware *Morning News*, September 8, 1988, p. 16.

29. Bureau of Economic Statistics, *Employment and Earnings* 36 (January 1989):35.

30. U.S. Bureau of the Census, *Statistical Abstract: 1988*, p. 523.

31. Andrew Levison, *The Working-Class Majority* (Baltimore: Penguin Books, 1974), chaps. 1–3.

32. U.S. Bureau of the Census, *Statistical Abstract: 1989*, p. 131.

33. U.S. Bureau of the Census, *Statistical Abstract of the United States: 1981* (Washington, D.C.: Government Printing Office, 1981), pp. 141, 143, 158, and U. S. Bureau of the Census, *Statistical Abstract: 1989*, pp. 127, 149.

34. U.S. Bureau of the Census, *Statistical Abstract: 1989*, pp. 130–131.

35. *New York Times*, January 3, 1984, p. 3C.

36. National Assessment of Educational Progress, *Reading Comprehension of American Youth* (Denver: Educational Commission of the States, July 1982), p. 57.

37. Department of Education, Center for Educational Statistics, *The Condition of Education*, 1987 ed. (Washington, D.C.: Department of Education, 1987), p. 30.

38. Quoted in Richard Parker, *The Myth of the Middle Class* (New York: Harper & Row, 1972), p. 6.

39. *New York Times*, March 23, 1989, p. 1.

40. Elliott Currie and Jerome Skolnick, *America's Problems* (Boston: Little, Brown, 1984), p. 109, table 4.2. Also see Lars Osberg, *Economic Inequality in the United States* (Armonk, N.Y.: M. E. Sharpe, 1984), pp. 38–47.

41. U.S. Bureau of the Census, Current Population Reports, Series P-60, No. 7, *Household Wealth and Asset Ownership: 1984* (Washington, D.C.: Government Printing Office, 1986), pp. 2, 16–17.

42. "Household Wealth and Asset Ownership," *Family Economics Review* no. 2 (August 1987):10–12.

43. Michael Harrington, *Decade of Decision* (New York: Simon & Schuster, 1980), p. 155.

44. Lester Thurow, *The Zero Sum Society* (New York: Basic Books, 1980), p. 161.

45. Barbara Ehrenreich, "Is the Middle Class Doomed?" *New York Times Magazine*, September 7, 1986, p. 44.

46. Ibid., pp. 44, 50.

47. Ibid., p. 50. Also see Michael W. Horrigan and Steven E. Haugen, "The Declining Middle-Class Thesis: A Sensitivity Analysis," *Monthly Labor Review* 111 (May 1988): 3–13.

48. U.S. Bureau of the Census, Current Population Reports, Series P-60, No. 166, *Money Income and Poverty Status in the United States: 1988* (Washington, D.C.: Government Printing Office, 1989), p. 5.

49. Isabel V. Sawhill, "Poverty and the Underclass," in *Challenge to Leadership*, ed. Isabel V. Sawhill (Washington, D.C.: Urban Institute Press, 1988), p. 218; and Sheldon Danziger, "Alternative Measures of the Recent Rise in Poverty," *Discussion Paper No. 740–83* (Madison, Wis.: Institute for Research on Poverty, 1983), p. 6.

50. U.S. Bureau of the Census, *Statistical Abstract: 1987*, p. 442; and U.S. Bureau of the Census, *Money Income and Poverty Status in the United States: 1988*, p. 12.

51. U.S. Bureau of the Census, *Money Income and Poverty Status in the United States: 1988*, p. 12.

52. U.S. Bureau of the Census, Current Population Reports, Series P-60, No. 163, *Poverty in the United States: 1987* (Washington, D.C.: Government Printing Office, 1989), p. 29.

53. Harrington, *Decade of Decision*, p. 226.

54. Committee on Ways and Means, *Background Material and Data*, pp. 947–948.

55. U.S. Bureau of the Census, *Money Income and Poverty Status in the United States: 1988*, p. 57; and Committee on Ways and Means, *Background Material and Data*, p. 944.

56. U.S. Bureau of the Census, *Money Income and Poverty Status in the United States: 1988*, p. 68.

57. Creel Froman, *The Two American Political Systems* (Englewood Cliffs, N.J.: Prentice-Hall, 1984), p. 59.

58. U.S. Bureau of the Census, Current Population Reports, Series P-20, No. 440, *Voting and Registration in the Election of November 1988* (Washington, D.C.: Government Printing Office, 1989), p. 65.

59. U.S. Bureau of the Census, *Statistical Abstract: 1989*, p. 335.

60. Office of Management and Budget, *Budget of the United States Government Fiscal Year 1991* (Washington, D.C.: Government Printing Office, 1990), p. A-116.

61. Eli Ginzberg, *Good Jobs, Bad Jobs, No Jobs* (Cambridge, Mass.: Harvard University Press, 1979), p. 11.

62. *New York Times*, September 27, 1984, p. 10B.

63. Nell Henderson, "It's Not a Subsidy Exactly; It's Technical Assistance," *Washington Post National Weekly Edition*, July 7, 1986, p. 32.

64. *The Book of the States* (Lexington, Kentucky: The Council of State Governments, 1988), pp. 234–235.

65. U.S. Bureau of the Census, *Statistical Abstract: 1989*, p. 516.

66. Ibid.

67. Internal Revenue Service, *Statistics of Income—Corporate Income Tax Returns* (Washington, D.C.: Government Printing Office, 1985). Also see Douglas F. Greer, "The Concentration of Economic Power," in *Market Power and the Economy*, ed. Wallace C. Peterson et al. (Boston: Kluner Academic Press, 1988), pp. 53–81.

68. Lester Thurow, "The Leverage of Our Wealthiest 400," *New York Times*, October 11, 1984, p. 27.

69. U.S. Bureau of the Census, *Statistical Abstract: 1988*, pp. 387–388.

70. Wilmington, Delaware *Morning News*, February 18, 1985, p. 8C.

71. Eric D. Larson, Marc H. Ross, and Robert H. Williams, "Beyond the Era of Materials," *Scientific American*, June 1986, pp. 34–41.

72. Eli Ginzberg and George J. Vojta, "The Service Sector of the US Economy," *Scientific American*, March 1981, p. 55.

73. *Survey of Current Business* 60 (August 1989): 10.

74. *Washington Post National Weekly Edition*, January 28, 1985, p. 21.

75. U.S. Bureau of the Census, *Statistical Abstract: 1989*, p. 387.

76. *Monthly Labor Review* 112 (March 1989):65.

77. Ibid., p. 73.

78. Barry Bluestone and Bennett Harrison, "The Great American Job Machine" (Washington, D.C.: Joint Economic Committee of Congress, 1986), pp. 5–7.

79. U.S. Bureau of the Census, *Statistical Abstract: 1988*, p. 379; and U.S. Bureau of the Census, *Historical Statis-*

tics of the United States, Colonial Times to 1970 (Washington, D.C.: Government Printing Office, 1975), Part 1, Series K, p. 468.

80. U.S. Bureau of the Census, *Statistical Abstract: 1989*, p. 416.

81. U.S. Congress, Office of Technology Assessment, *Paying the Bill: Manufacturing and America's Trade Deficit*, OTA-ITE-390 (Washington, D.C.: Government Printing Office, 1988), p. 1; and Charles F. Stone, "International Trade," in *Challenge to Leadership*, Sawhill, ed., p. 111.

82. U.S. Bureau of the Census, *Statistical Abstract: 1989*, p. 786; and *Survey of Current Business*, (August 1989):11.

Chapter 3

1. *New York Times*, March 25, 1986, p. 2B.

2. Ibid., March 26, 1911, p. 1. The most gripping account of the fire and its aftermath is contained in the pages of the *New York Times*, which in a prose style not commonly found in contemporary journalism, depicts the outrage and sorrow the tragedy produced.

3. Theodore J. Lowi, *The End of Liberalism*, 2nd ed. (New York: Norton, 1979), p. 3.

4. Louis Hartz, *The Liberal Tradition in America* (New York: Harcourt Brace Jovanovich, 1955).

5. In combining general welfare with liberalism, we are borrowing part of Sidney Fine's title from his seminal book *Laissez-Faire and the General-Welfare State* (Ann Arbor: University of Michigan Press, 1956).

6. Bernard Bailyn, *The Origins of American Politics* (New York: Random House (Vintage Books), 1967), chap. 1.

7. "The Federalist No. 10," *The Federalist Papers*, 2nd ed., ed. Roy P. Fairfield (Garden City, N.Y.: Doubleday (Anchor Books), 1966), p. 22.

8. Hugh Heclo, "General Welfare and Two American Traditions," *Political Science Quarterly* 101 (1986):185.

9. Hartz, *The Liberal Tradition in America*.

10. J. A. G. Pocock, *The Machiavellian Moment: Florentine Political Thought and the Atlantic Republican Tradition* (Princeton, N.J.: Princeton University Press, 1975). For a critique of Pocock's work, see John P. Diggins, *The Lost Soul of American Politics* (New York: Basic Books, 1984), which discusses early American political thought in detail.

11. Issac Kramnick, "Republican Revisionism Revisited," *American Historical Review* 87 (1982):630. Kramnick, we should add, does not reject Locke's influence on American thought; he is simply describing how some of his fellow historians see the matter.

12. "The Federalist No. 51," p. 160.

13. Robert E. Shalhope, "Republicanism and Early American Historiography," *William and Mary Quarterly*, 1986,

p. 346. Also see Joyce Appleby, "The Social Origins of American Revolutionary Ideology," *Journal of American History* 64 (1978):935–958.

14. Shalhope, "Republicanism and Early American Historiography," p. 350.

15. Fine, *Laissez-Faire and the General-Welfare State*, pp. 30–31.

16. Herbert Spencer, *Social Statics* (London, 1851). Quoted in ibid., p. 38.

17. U.S. Bureau of Labor Statistics, "Summary Report on Women and Child Wage Earners," *Monthly Review* 11 (March 1916):36.

18. Steven Pavser and George Clark, "OSHA's Ancestors: Previous Laws of the Work Place," *Job & Safety Health* 2 (U.S. Department of Labor, Occupational Safety and Health Administration) (April 1974):19.

19. W. F. Willoughby, "Accidents to Labor as Regulated by Law in the United States," *Bulletin of the Department of Labor* no. 32 (January 1901):8.

20. Ibid., p. 16.

21. Fine, *Laissez Faire and the General-Welfare State*, chaps. 6–8.

22. *New York Times*, December 1, 1986, p. 14.

23. A list of writers on this topic would fill dozens of pages. Among the most famous are Karl Marx and Friedrich Engels, who spent many hours wondering why capitalism in the United States was never overthrown. Another well-known student of the question is Werner Sombart, *Why Is There No Socialism in America?* (London: Macmillan, 1976) (first published in German in 1906). An excellent collection of essays is John H. M. Laslett and Seymour Martin Lipset, eds., *Failure of a Dream? Essays in the History of American Socialism*, rev. ed. (Berkeley, Calif.: Univ. of California Press, 1984).

24. Seymour M. Lipset, "Radicalism or Reform: The Sources of Working Class Politics in the U.S.," *American Political Science Review* 77 (March 1983):1–2.

25. C. W. Mills, *White Collar* (New York: Oxford University Press, 1936), p. 325.

26. Joan Huber and William H. Form, *Income and Ideology* (New York: Free Press, 1973), chap. 5.

27. Sidney Verba and Kay Lehman Schlozman, *Injury to Insult* (Cambridge, Mass.: Harvard University Press, 1979), pp. 116–117.

28. Ibid., p. 118. Nearly two-thirds of the workers did say that workers are better off sticking together rather than trying to get ahead on their own. But this attitude probably reflects the advantages of cooperation rather than feelings of class solidarity.

29. Huber and Form, *Income and Ideology*, p. 218.

30. Verba and Schlozman, *Injury to Insult*, p. 231.

31. Philippe C. Schmitter discusses more fully the meaning of the term *welfare state* in "Five Reflections on the Future of the Welfare State," *Politics and Society* 16 (December 1988):503–515.

32. Lawrence J. Haas, in "The Terrifying T-Word," *National Journal*, June 3, 1989, p. 1355, says differences of this sort "reflect a far more egalitarian approach to government in Europe."

33. Charles F. Andrain, *Social Policies in Western Industrial Societies* (Berkeley, Calif.: Institute for International Studies, 1985), p. 10. Also, Richard Rose, "How Exceptional Is the American Political Economy?" *Political Science Quarterly* 104 (Spring 1989):91–111.

34. Heclo, "General Welfare and Two American Traditions," pp. 182–186.

35. Quoted in *Government Executive*, January 1988, p. 11.

36. *New York Times*, November 12, 1984, p. 10B.

37. Wilmington, Delaware *News Journal*, May 22, 1989, p. 9.

38. Governor Mario Cuomo, Democrat of New York, quoted in *New York Times*, January 26, 1986, p. 6E.

39. *New York Times*, September 17, 1986, p. 10.

40. An excellent discussion of this point is Hugh Heclo, "The Political Foundations of Antipoverty Policy," in *Fighting Poverty*, ed. Sheldon Danziger and Daniel H. Weinberg, (Cambridge, Mass.: Harvard University Press, 1986) pp. 326–332.

41. *New York Times*, August 1, 1977, p. 1.

42. "Socialist Platform 1980," in *National Party Platforms*, compiled by Donald Bruce Johnson (Urbana: University of Illinois Press, 1982), p. 221.

43. "Libertarian Platform," ibid., p. 91.

44. "Citizens Party Platform 1980," ibid., pp. 21–22.

45. "Communist Party Platform," ibid., pp. 36–37.

46. Philip Converse and Georges Dupeux surmised that in France, where a political party represents virtually every point along the political spectrum, the "proliferation of choices" was too difficult "to be managed comfortably by citizens whose political involvement is average or low." Philip E. Converse and Georges Dupeux, "Politicization of the Electorate in France and the United States," in Angus Campbell et al., *Elections and the Political Order* (New York: Wiley, 1966), p. 291.

47. Sidney Verba and Gary Orren, *Equality in America* (Cambridge, Mass.: Harvard University Press, 1985), pp. 9–19.

48. Robert Lane, *Political Equality* (New York: Free Press, 1962), chap. 5.

49. Ibid., p. 73.

50. Ibid., p. 77.

51. Verba and Orren, *Equality in America*, p. 253.

52. Grant McConnell, *Private Power and American Democracy* (New York: Random House, Vintage Books, 1966), p. 119.

53. *New York Times*, January 21, 1989, p. 10.

54. McConnell, *Private Power and American Democracy*, chap. 5; and Lowi, *The End of Liberalism*.

55. President Reagan's 1986 economic report to Congress quoted in *New York Times*, February 7, 1986, p. 4D.

56. *New York Times*, January 21, 1989, p. 10.

57. *New York Times*, July 29, 1986, p. 18B.

Chapter 4

1. Barbara Hinkson Craig, *Chadha: The Story of an Epic Constitutional Struggle* (New York: Oxford University Press, 1988), p. 25.

2. *Immigration and Naturalization Service* v. *Chadha*, 462 U.S. 919 (1983).

3. Ibid.

4. Craig, *Chadha*, p. 226.

5. James Madison, *Federalist 51*, in Alexander Hamilton, John Jay, and James Madison, *The Federalist* (New York: Random House (Modern Library), n.d.), p. 337. All of the following *Federalist* citations are to this edition.

6. Max Farrand, *The Framing of the Constitution of the United States* (New Haven, Conn.: Yale University Press, 1972), pp. 9–10. Thomas G. Walker, *American Politics and the Constitution* (North Scituate, Mass.: Duxbury Press, 1978), pp. 11–13 was the source of some of the information in this account.

7. Farrand, *The Framing of the Constitution*, p. 128.

8. Hamilton, *Federalist 15*, p. 91.

9. Annapolis Resolution, in Melvin I. Urofsky, *A March of Liberty: A Constitutional History of the United States*, vol. I (New York: Knopf, 1988), p. 89.

10. Forrest McDonald, *A Constitutional History of the United States* (New York: Franklin Watts, 1982), pp. 26–27.

11. Leonard W. Levy, *Essays on the Making of the Constitution* (New York: Oxford University Press, 1987), p. xxxi.

12. Carl Van Doren, *The Great Rehearsal: The Story of the Making and Ratifying of the Constitution of the United States* (Baltimore: Penguin Books, 1986), p. 161.

13. Levy, *Essays on the Making of the Constitution*, p. xxvii.

14. Van Doren, *The Great Rehearsal*, pp. 126–127.

15. Amos Singletary, a delegate to the Massachusetts convention, quoted in Alfred Young, "Conservatives, the Constitution, and the 'Spirit of Accommodation,'" in *How Democratic Is the Constitution*, ed. Robert A. Goldwin and William A. Schambra (Washington, DC: Brookings Institution, 1980), p. 140.

16. Jackson Turner Main, *The Antifederalists* (Chapel Hill: University of North Carolina Press, 1961).

17. Michael Parenti, "The Constitution as an Elitist Document," in Goldwin and Schambra, *How Democratic*, p. 55.

18. Charles Beard, *An Economic Interpretation of the Constitution of the United States* (New York: Free Press, 1965), pp. 242ff.

19. Hamilton, *Federalist 22*, pp. 140–141.

20. Ann Stuart Diamond, "Decent, Even Though Democratic," in Goldwin and Schambra, *How Democratic*, p. 37.

21. Jonathan Elliot, ed., *The Debates of the Several State Conventions on the Adoption of the Federal Constitution* (Philadelphia: Lippincott, 1876), vol. 2, p. 69.

22. Madison, *Federalist 39*, pp. 243–244.

23. Michael Parenti, "The Constitution as an Elitist Document," in Goldwin and Schambra, *How Democratic*, p. 39.

24. Richard Hofstadter, *The American Political Tradition* (New York: Knopf, 1962), p. 13.

25. Andrew Hacker, "Introduction," *The Federalist Papers* (New York: Washington Square Press, 1976), p. xiii.

26. Frank M. Coleman, *Politics, Policy, and the Constitution* (New York: St. Martin's Press, 1982), p. 32.

27. Madison, *Federalist 10*, p. 56.

28. Gordon S. Wood, "Democracy and the Constitution," in Goldwin and Schambra, *How Democratic*, p. 11.

29. Beard, *An Economic Interpretation of the Constitution of the United States*, pp. 15–16, 149–150.

30. Madison, *Federalist 10*, pp. 59 and 60.

31. Madison, *Federalist 10*, p. 62.

32. Gordon Wood, *The Creation of the American Republic 1776–1787* (New York: Norton, 1972), p. 513.

33. Parenti, "Constitution as Elitist Document," p. 58.

34. *Immigration and Naturalization Service* v. *Chadha*, 462 U.S. 1919 (1983).

35. *McCulloch* v. *Maryland*, 4 Wheat. 316 (1819). All of the quotations from Marshall in this section are from his opinion in this case.

36. The quotations from Black, Frankfurter, and Marshall are in Gerald Gunther, *Constitutional Law*, 11th ed. (Mineola, N.Y.: Foundation Press, 1985), pp. 95n, 94n, and 91, respectively.

37. Madison, *Federalist 39*, pp. 242–243.

38. Hamilton, *Federalist 22*, p. 134.

39. Joseph M. Bessette, "Deliberative Democracy: The Majority Principle in Republican Government," in Goldwin and Schambra, *How Democratic*, p. 102.

40. Madison, *Federalist 10*, p. 59.

41. *Luther* v. *Borden*, 48 U.S. 1 (1849).

42. Arend Lijphart, *Democracies: Patterns of Majoritarian and Consensus Government in Twenty-One Countries* (New Haven, Conn.: Yale University Press, 1984), pp. 30–36.

43. Hamilton, *Federalist 84*, pp. 560–561.

44. The landmark contract case is *Dartmouth College* v. *Woodward*, 4 Wheat. 518 (1819). The individual right to interstate travel was based partly on the commerce clause in *Edwards* v. *California* 314 U.S. 160 (1941) and continues to be of importance in some contemporary civil liberties cases (e.g., *New Hampshire* v. *Piper* (1985)).

45. *Herbert* v. *Louisiana* 272 U.S. 312 (1926).

46. Steven V. Roberts, "Of Fairy Tales, Wish Lists and Balanced Budgets," *New York Times*, June 6, 1985, p. B14; and Nadine Cohodas, "Balanced Budget Amendment Advances Here, Loses There," *Congressional Quarterly Weekly Report*, May 18, 1985, pp. 933–934.

47. Gerald Gunther, *Constitutional Law*, 11th ed., p. 246n.

48. Nadine Cohodas, "Balanced Budget Amendment Advances Here, Loses There," *Congressional Quarterly Weekly Report*, May 18, 1985, p. 934.

49. Citizens to Protect the Constitution, quoted in Nadine Cohodas, "Congress Under New Pressure on Balanced Budget Measure," *Congressional Quarterly Weekly Report*, August 1, 1984, p. 1887. *Federalists 49 and 50* provide interesting arguments against easy amendment of the Constitution and the "ticklish nature" (p. 329) of constitutional conventions.

50. Woodrow Wilson, *Constitutional Government in the United States* (New York: Columbia University Press, 1908 and 1961), p. 173.

Chapter 5

1. "Excerpts from President's News Session on Foreign and Domestic Issues," *New York Times*, April 8, 1989, p. 8A.

2. Gerry Studds quoted in Matthew L. Wald, "Liability for Exxon Oil Spill: Untested Waters," *New York Times*, April 7, 1989, p. 5B.

3. Governor Bill Sheffield, "Letter of May 6, 1985, to Hon. Gerry E. Studds," in U.S. Congress, "Hearing Before the Subcommittee on Coast Guard and Navigation of the Committee on Merchant Marine and Fisheries, House of Representatives," March 27, 1985, Serial No. 99–2, p. 171.

4. Arend Lijphart, *Democracies: Patterns of Consensus Government in Twenty-One Countries* (New Haven, Conn.: Yale University Press, 1984), pp. 171 and 188.

5. Bruce E. Johansen, *Forgotten Founders* (Ipswich, Mass.: Gambit Publishers, 1982).

6. Robert A. Gross, *The Minutemen and Their World* (New York: Hill & Wang, 1976), p. 165.

7. Peter S. Onuf, *The Origins of the Federal Republic* (Philadelphia: University of Pennsylvania Press, 1983), p. 20.

8. James Madison, *Federalist 39*, in Alexander Hamilton, John Jay, and James Madison, *The Federalist Papers* (New York: Washington Square Press, 1976).

9. *McCulloch* v. *Maryland* 17 U.S. (4 Wheat.) 316 (1819).

10. Bruce Babbitt, quoted in John Herbers, "High Court Ruling Source of Dismay to Local Officials," *New York Times*, February 21, 1985, p. A1.

11. *Dred Scott* v. *Sandford*, 60 U.S. 393 (1857).

12. *U.S.* v. *E.C. Knight*, 156 U.S. 1 (1895).

13. *Wickard* v. *Filburn*, 317 U.S. 111 (1942).

14. *National League of Cities* v. *Usery*, 426 U.S.833 (1976).

15. *Garcia* v. *San Antonio MTA*, 469 U.S. 528 (1985).

16. John Holusha, "Chairman Defends Exxon's Efforts to Clean Up Oil," *New York Times*, April 19, 1989, p. 21.

17. Martin Tolchin, "States Not Using U.S. Antidrug Money," *New York Times*, April 17, 1989, p. 14.

18. Senator Moynihan quoted in Clifford D. May, "Federal Funds to Spend, New York Legislators Find," *New York Times*, March 17, 1989, p. B2.

19. Morton Grodzins, "The Federal System," in *Goals for Americans: The Report of the President's Commission on National Goals* (Englewood Cliffs, N.J.: Prentice-Hall, 1965), p. 265.

20. This discussion of federal assistance draws on Donald Axelrod, *A Budget Quartet* (New York: St. Martin's Press, 1989), pp. 135–143.

21. Catherine Lovell and Charles Tobin, "The Mandate Issue," *Public Administration Review* 41, no. 3 (May/June, 1981):319–332, cited in Axelrod, *A Budget Quartet*, p. 144.

22. Axelrod, *A Budget Quartet*, p. 142.

23. Ronald Reagan quoted in Timothy Conlan, *New Federalism* (Washington, D.C.: Brookings Institution, 1988), pp. 223–224.

24. George E. Peterson, "Federalism and the States," in *The Reagan Record*, ed. John L. Palmer and Isabel V. Sawhill (Cambridge, Mass.: Ballinger, 1984), p. 222.

25. John E. Chubb, "Hopes, Fears, and Federalism," paper prepared for presentation at the Constitutional Bicentennial Conference, Nelson A. Rockefeller Center, Dartmouth College, Hanover, N.H., October 21, 1986, p. 6.

26. Assistant Attorney General Charles J. Cooper, quoted in Robert Pear, "Dialogue: The Uncertain Status of Federalism," *New York Times*, November 6, 1986, p. 5E.

27. National Republican Congressional Committee, "Does Washington Know Best—Or Did Jefferson?," *New York Times*, September 26, 1983, p. 21.

28. Richard Higgins, "On a Losing Course," *Boston Globe*, March 23, 1989, p. 1.

29. Sheldon Glashow, quoted in ibid, p. 190.

30. Thomas Jefferson, letter to Samuel Kercheval, July 12, 1816, in Andrew A. Lipscomb, ed., *The Writings of Thomas Jefferson* (Washington, D.C.: Thomas Jefferson Memorial Association, 1904), vol. 15, p. 38.

31. George Gallup, "Reagan's 'New Federalism' Strikes Responsive Chord with Public," *The Gallup Poll*, October 18, 1981.

32. Justice Lewis Powell, dissenting opinion, *Garcia* v. *San Antonio MTA* 469 U.S. 528 (1985).

33. Richard Leach, *American Federalism* (New York: Norton, 1970), p. 5.

34. Paul E. Peterson, Barry G. Rabe, and Kenneth K. Wong, *When Federalism Works* (Washington, D.C.: Brookings Institution, 1986), p. 7.

35. Bernard L. Weinstein, quoted in Kenneth Weiss, "States Circle Their Wagons for the Money Wars," *New York Times*, April 25, 1989, p. 24.

36. Rep. Charles E. Schumer, quoted in Clifford May, "Federal Funds Hard to Spend, New York's Legislators Find," *New York Times*, March 17, 1989, p. 1.

37. Sen. Daniel Patrick Moynihan, quoted in ibid.

38. Timothy Conlan, *New Federalism* (Washington, D.C.: Brookings Institution, 1988), pp. 40–43.

39. Peterson, Rabe, and Wong, *When Federalism Works*, pp. 219–229.

40. John E. Chubb, "Federalism and the Bias for Centralization," in *The New Direction in American Politics*, ed. John E. Chubb and Paul E. Peterson (Washington, D.C.: Brookings Institution, 1985), pp. 301–302.

Chapter 6

1. Boston Mayor Ray Flynn quoted in Allan R. Gold, "Dead Officer, Dropped Charges: A Scandal in Boston," *New York Times*, March 20, 1989, p. A12; family friend Diane Wall quoted in Mark Morrow, "Family Devastated and Outraged," *Quincy Patriot Ledger*, March 30, 1989, p. 8.

2. Boston police patrolman's union president, Robert Guiney, quoted in Morrow, "Family Devastated."

3. Boston Bar Association president, Edward Hines, quoted in Gold, "Dead Officer."

4. Leonard W. Levy, *Original Intent and the Framers' Constitution* (New York: Macmillan, 1988), p. 239.

5. Gold, "Dead Officer."

6. *United States* v. *Rabinowitz*, 339 U.S. 56 (1950).

7. *Schenck* v. *United States*, 249 U.S. 47 (1919). For more on this point see Thomas L. Tedford, *Freedom of Speech in the United States* (New York: Random House, 1985), pp. 40–63.

8. Robert A. Rutland, "How the Constitution Protects Our Rights: A Look at the Seminal Years," in *How Does the*

Constitution Secure Rights? ed. Robert A. Goldwin and William A. Schambra (Washington, D.C.: American Enterprise Institute, 1985), p.11.

9. *Barron* v. *Baltimore*, 32 U.S. 243 (1833).

10. Lawrence Baum, *The Supreme Court*, 3d ed. (Washington, D.C.: CQ Books, 1989), pp. 166 and 179.

11. Henry J. Abraham, *Freedom and the Court*, 5th ed. (New York: Oxford University Press, 1988), p. 61.

12. *Slaughterhouse Cases*, 83 U.S. 36 (1873).

13. John Hart Ely, *Democracy and Distrust* (Cambridge, Mass.: Harvard University Press, 1980), pp. 22–23.

14. *Gitlow* v. *New York*, 268 U.S. 652 (1925).

15. Abraham, *Freedom and the Court*, pp. 113–117.

16. *Palko* v. *Connecticut*, 302 U.S. 319 (1937).

17. Martin Shapiro and Douglas Hobbs, *American Constitutional Law* (Cambridge, Mass.: Winthrop, 1978), p. 395; and Gerald Gunther, *Constitutional Law*, 11th ed. (Mineola, N.Y.: Foundation Press, 1985), p. 972.

18. *Schenck* v. *United States; Dennis* v. *United States*, 341 U.S. 494 (1951); *Gitlow* v. *New York*, 268 U.S. 652 (1925); and *Yates* v. *United States*, 355 U.S. 66 (1957).

19. Justice Frankfurter in *Dennis* v. *United States*, and *Adderley* v. *Florida*, 385 U.S. 39 (1966).

20. *Shuttlesworth* v. *Birmingham*, 394 U.S. 147 (1969); *Thornhill* v. *Alabama*, 310 U.S. 88 (1940); *Shelton* v. *Tucker*, 364 U.S. 479 (1960); and *New York Times* v. *United States*, 403 U.S. 713 (1971).

21. *Schenck* v. *United States*.

22. *Dennis.* v. *United States*.

23. *New York Times* v. *Sullivan*, 376 U.S. 254 (1964).

24. *Buckley* v. *Valeo*, 424 U.S. 1 (1976).

25. *Federal Election Commission* v. *National Conservative Political Action Committee*, 470 U.S. 480 (1985).

26. Harry Kalven, Jr., "The New York Times Case: A Note on the Central Meaning of the First Amendment," *Supreme Court Review, 1964*, (Chicago: University of Chicago Press, 1964), pp. 191–221.

27. Robert Bork, "Neutral Principles and Some First Amendment Problems," *Indiana Law Review*, 1971, quoted in U.S. Congress, *Hearings Before the Committee on the Judiciary, U.S. Senate, on the Nomination of Robert H. Bork to be Associate Justice of the Supreme Court of the United States* (Washington, D.C.: Government Printing Office, 1989), part I, p. 268. Italics added.

28. Melvin I. Urofsky, *A March of Liberty: A Constitutional History of the United States* (New York: Knopf, 1988), p. 805.

29. Roger A. Simpson, "Freedom of the Press: The Press and the Court Write a New First Amendment," in *Judging the Constitution*, ed. Michael W. McCann and Gerald L.

Houseman (Glenview, Ill.: Scott, Foresman, 1989), p. 374.

30. Edwin Meese quoted in Stuart Taylor, "Meese, in Bar Group Speech, Criticizes High Court," *New York Times*, July 10, 1985, p. A13.

31. Richard E. Morgan, *The Supreme Court and Religion* (New York: Free Press, 1972), pp. 28–29.

32. *Lemon* v. *Kurtzman*, 403 U.S. 602 (1971).

33. *Grand Rapids* v. *Ball*, 473 U.S. 373 (1985).

34. *Larkin* v. *Grendel's Den, Inc.*, 454 U.S. 116 (1982).

35. M. Glenn Abernathy, *Civil Liberties Under the Constitution*, 4th ed. (Columbia: University of South Carolina Press, 1985), p. 247.

36. Gold, "Dead Officer," p. A12; and Doris Sue Wong, "Judge Refuses to Revive Charge in Officer's Killing," *Boston Globe*, March 30, 1989, p. 18.

37. Justice Cardozo in *People* v. *Defore*, 242 N.Y. 13 (1926); and Chief Justice Burger in *Bivens* v. *Six Unknown Agents of the Federal Bureau of Narcotics*, 403 U.S. 388 (1971).

38. Justice Holmes in *Olmstead* v. *United States*, 277 U.S. 438 (1928); and Justice Brennan in *United States* v. *Leon*, 468 U.S. 897 (1984).

39. *Mapp* v. *Ohio*, 367 U.S. 643 (1961).

40. *United States* v. *Leon*.

41. Samuel Walker, *Sense and Nonsense About Crime*, 2d ed. (Belmont, Calif.: Wadsworth, 1989), p. 121.

42. For more on these exceptions, see Joel B. Grossman and Richard S. Wells, *Constitutional Law and Judicial Policy Making*, 3d ed. (New York: Longman, 1988), pp. 461–465.

43. Ibid., p. 502; and Abraham, *Freedom and the Court*, p. 162n.

44. *Miranda* v. *Arizona*, 384 U.S. 436 (1966).

45. Abraham, *Freedom and the Court*, pp. 159–163.

46. U.S. Department of Justice, *Sourcebook of Criminal Justice Statistics* (Washington, D.C.: Government Printing Office, 1979), p. 300.

47. Walker, *Sense and Nonsense About Crime*, p. 125.

48. *New York* v. *Quarles*, 467 U.S. 649 (1984).

49. *Anti-Fascist Refugee Committee* v. *McGrath*, 341 U.S. 123 (1951).

50. Jean Bethke Elshtain, "Issues and Themes in the 1988 Campaign," in *The Elections of 1988*, ed. Michael Nelson (Washington, D.C.: CQ Press, 1989), pp. 120–121.

51. New York Times/CBS New Poll, *New York Times*, April 26, 1989, p. 1.

52. *Roe* v. *Wade*, 410 U.S. 113 (1973).

53. *Webster* v. *Reproductive Health Services*; 109 S.Ct. 3040 (1989).

54. *Griswold* v. *Connecticut*, 381 U.S. 479 (1965).

55. Levy, *Original Intent and the Framers' Constitution*, p. 267.

56. *Roe* v. *Wade*.

57. U.S. Congress, *Hearings on the Nomination of Robert Bork*, pp. 1269 and 1667.

58. Ibid, p. 862.

59. Herbert McClosky and Alida Brill, *Dimensions of Tolerance: What Americans Believe About Civil Liberties* (New York: Russell Sage, 1983), p. 92.

60. *West Virginia State Board of Education* v. *Barnette*, 319 U.S. 624 (1943).

61. privacy: *Griswold* v. *Connecticut*, 381 U.S. 479 (1965); voting: *Harper* v. *Virginia Board of Elections*, 383 U.S. 663 (1966); travel: *Shapiro* v. *Thompson*, 394 U.S. 618 (1969); interstate travel as more fundamental than foreign travel: *Califano* v. *Aznavorian*, 439 U.S. 170 (1978); marriage: *Skinner* v. *Oklahoma*, 316 U.S. 535 (1942); and child rearing: *Pierce* v. *Society of Sisters*, 268 U.S. 510 (1925).

62. *United States* v. *Carolene Products Co.*, 304 U.S. 144 (1938).

63. Ely, *Democracy and Distrust*, especially p. 103. Also see Jesse Choper, *Judicial Review and the National Political Process* (Chicago: University of Chicago Press, 1980); and Michael J. Perry, *The Constitution, the Courts, and Human Rights* (New Haven, Conn.: Yale University Press, 1982).

64. McClosky and Brill, *Dimensions of Tolerance*,, p. 273.

65. *Federalist 63*, in Alexander Hamilton, John Jay, and James Madison, *The Federalist* (New York: Modern Library, n.d.), p. 413.

66. Leonard Levy, ed., *Freedom of Speech and Press in Early American History: Legacy of Suppression* (New York: Harper & Row, 1963); and John Roche, "American Liberty: An Examination of the Tradition of Freedom," in *Aspects of Liberty*, ed. Milton Konvitz and Clinton Rossiter (Ithaca, N.Y.: Cornell University Press, 1958).

67. John Brigham, *Civil Liberties and American Democracy* (Washington, D.C.: Congressional Quarterly, 1984), pp. 43–50.

68. Ibid., p. 257.

69. Edward S. Greenburg, *The American Political System: A Radical Approach*, 3d ed. (Boston: Little, Brown, 1983), p. 77.

Chapter 7

1. Joseph Berger, "Campus Racial Strains Show Two Perspectives on Inequality," *New York Times*, May 22, 1989, p. 1.

2. Canetta Ivy, Council of Student Presidents, Stanford, quoted in Felicity Barringer, "Drives by Campuses to Curb Race Slurs Pose a Speech Issue," *New York Times*, April 25, 1989, p. 20.

3. Wisconsin Rep. D. Spencer Coggs, quoted in ibid.

4. Ira Glasser, quoted in ibid.

5. John Hope Franklin, "The Moral Legacy of the Founding Fathers," *University of Chicago Magazine*, Summer 1975, p. 13.

6. Thomas Jefferson, initial draft of the Declaration of Independence, quoted in Ralph A. Rossum and G. Alan Tarr, *American Constitutional Law* (New York: St. Martin's Press, 1983), p. 560.

7. Herbert J. Storing, "Slavery and the Moral Foundations of the American Republic," in *The Moral Foundations of the American Republic*, ed. Robert H. Horwitz (Charlottesville: University Press of Virginia, 1979), p. 221.

8. Leonard Levy, *Original Intent and the Framers' Constitution* (New York: Macmillan, 1988), p. 277.

9. Franklin, "The Moral Legacy of the Founding Fathers," p. 13.

10. *Dred Scott* v. *Sanford*, 60 U.S. 393 (1857).

11. Don E. Fehrenbacher, *Slavery, Law, and Politics* (New York: Oxford University Press, 1981), p. 298.

12. The Civil Rights Act of 1866, in Richard Bardolph, *The Civil Rights Record* (New York: Crowell, 1970), p. 46.

13. Judith A. Baer, "The Fruitless Search for Original Intent," in *Judging the Constitution*, ed. Michael McCann and Gerald Houseman (Glenview, Ill: Scott, Foresman, 1989), pp. 55, 56.

14. Henry Abraham, *Freedom and the Court*, 5th ed. (New York: Oxford University Press, 1988), p. 41.

15. *Jett* v. *Dallas Independent School District*, 109 S.Ct. 2702 (1989) (state and local governments); and *Patterson* v. *McLean Credit Union*, 109 S.Ct. 2363 (1989) (discrimination on the job).

16. Justice Anthony Kennedy, *Patterson* v. *McLean Credit Union*.

17. NAACP attorney Eric Schnapper, quoted in Linda Greenhouse, "The Court's Shift to Right," *New York Times*, June 7, 1989, p. 22.

18. Linda Greenhouse, "A Changed Court Revises Rules on Civil Rights," *New York Times*, June 18, 1989, p. 1E.

19. Civil Rights Act of 1866, in Bardolph, *The Civil Rights Record*, p. 46.

20. Howard N. Meyer, *The Amendment that Refused to Die* (Boston: Beacon Press, 1978), p. XIX.

21. Jay Sigler, *American Rights Policies* (Homewood, Ill.: Dorsey Press, 1975), p. 130.

22. Meyer, *The Amendment that Refused to Die*, p. 91.

23. The date when a system of rigid, legally enforced segregation began remains a subject of debate among historians. See, for example, C. Van Woodward, *The Strange Career of Jim Crow* (New York: Oxford University Press,

1974), pp. 31–109; and Charles Lofgren, *The Plessy Case* (New York: Oxford University Press, 1987), pp. 8–9.

24. Thomas Jefferson to Rep. John Holmes, a Republican from Maine, April 22, 1820, quoted in Dumas Malone, *Jefferson and His Time*, vol. 6, *The Sage of Monticello* (Boston: Little, Brown, 1981), p. 336.

25. Storing, "Slavery and the Moral Foundations of the American Republic," pp. 226–227; and Lofgren, *The Plessy Case*, pp. 23–25.

26. Acts of Tennessee, 1875, in Bardolph, *The Civil Rights Record*, p. 82.

27. Charles E. Silberman, *Crisis in Black and White* (New York: Random House, 1964), p. 24.

28. Gerald Gunther, *Constitutional Law*, 11th ed. (Mineola, N.Y.: Foundation Press, 1985), p. 932.

29. Silberman, *Crisis in Black and White*, p. 23.

30. Civil Rights Act of 1875, in Bardolph, *The Civil Rights Record*, p. 55.

31. *Civil Rights Cases* 109 U.S. 3 (1883).

32. Ibid.

33. Justice Harlan, dissent in ibid.

34. Lofgren, *The Plessy Case*, p. 26.

35. Acts of Louisiana, 1890, in Bardolph, *The Civil Rights Record*, p. 132. The title of the act is mentioned in Abraham, *Freedom and the Court*, p. 410.

36. *Plessy* v. *Ferguson*, 163 U.S. 537 (1896).

37. Justice Harlan, dissent in ibid.

38. Abraham, *Freedom and the Court*, p. 413.

39. Joel B. Grossman and Richard S. Wells, *Constitutional Law and Judicial Policy Making*, 3d ed. (New York: Longman, 1988), p. 298.

40. *Sweatt* v. *Painter*, 339 U.S. 629 (1950).

41. *Brown* v. *Board of Education*, 347 U.S. 483 (1954).

42. *Brown* v. *Board of Education*, 349 U.S. 294 (1955).

43. *Alexander* v. *Holmes County Board of Education*, 396 U.S. 19 (1969).

44. *Swann* v. *Charlotte-Mecklenburg Board of Education*, 402 U.S. 1 (1971).

45. *Milliken* v. *Bradley*, 418 U.S. 717 (1974).

46. Walter Goodman, "Brown v. Board of Education: Uneven Results 30 Years Later," *New York Times*, May 17, 1984, p. 18B.

47. Ibid.

48. *Gayle* v. *Browder*, 352 U.S. 903 (1956).

49. John Brigham, *Civil Liberties and American Democracy* (Washington, D.C.: Congressional Quarterly, 1984), p. 222.

50. Charles Whalen and Barbara Whalen, *The Longest Debate* (New York: New American Library, 1985), pp. 27–28.

51. Robert Kennedy, "Hearings Before the Senate Committee on Commerce," in Gunther, *Constitutional Law*, p. 159.

52. *Heart of Atlanta Motel* v. *United States*, 379 U.S. 241 (1964).

53. Melvin Urofsky, *A March of Liberty* (New York: Knopf, 1988), pp. 793–794.

54. Grossman and Wells, *Constitutional Law and Judicial Policy Making*, p. 320.

55. Carl Van Doren, *The Great Rehearsal* (Baltimore: Penguin Books, 1986), p. 141.

56. *Minor* v. *Happersett*, 88 U.S. 162 (1875).

57. Justice Department figures cited in the Supreme Court decision upholding the Voting Rights Act, *South Carolina* v. *Katzenbach*, 383 U.S. 301 (1966).

58. Urofsky, *A March of Liberty*, p. 795.

59. Grossman and Wells, *Constitutional Law and Judicial Policy Making*, p. 329. Nationwide, there were 6000 elected black officials in 1989, compared to a few hundred in 1965. *New York Times*, July 2, 1989, p. 16.

60. Temple University White Students Union President Michael Spletzer and American Council on Education Scholar Reginald Wilson quoted in Joseph Berger, "Campus Racial Strains Show Two Perspectives on Inequality," *New York Times*, May 22, 1989, pp. 1 and 15.

61. Department of Labor, Revised Order Number 4, in Allan P. Sindler, *Bakke, DeFunis, and Minority Admissions* (New York: Longman, 1978), p. 18.

62. President Lyndon Johnson, quoted in James Curry, Richard Riley, and Richard Battistoni, *Constitutional Government: The American Experience* (St. Paul, Minn.: West, 1989), p. 381.

63. "The Decision Everyone Won" was a *Wall Street Journal* headline, cited in Abraham, *Freedom and the Court*, p. 520. Allan Sindler's short summary is in his *Bakke, DeFunis, and Minority Admission*, p. 317.

64. *Richmond* v. *Croson*, 109 S.Ct. 706 (1989).

65. *Martin* v. *Wilks*, 109 S.Ct. 2180 (1989).

66. Professor Derrick Bell, quoted in Derrick Z. Jackson, "Supreme Court Rulings Spell End of an Era for Affirmative Action," *Boston Globe*, July 2, 1989, p. A14.

67. "Michigan U. Is Sued over Anti-bias Policy," *New York Times*, May 27, 1989, p. 8 (no byline).

68. *Minor* v. *Happersett*, 88 U.S. 162 (1874).

69. *Frontiero* v. *Richardson*, 411 U.S. 677 (1973).

70. Brigham, *Civil Liberties and American Democracy*, p. 240; and Andrea Bonnicksen, *Civil Rights and Liberties* (Palo Alto, Calif.: Mayfield, 1982), p. 174.

71. Elizabeth Cady Stanton, quoted in Deborah L. Rhode, "Equal Protection: Gender and Justice," in McCann and Houseman, *Judging the Constitution*, p. 266.

72. Gilbert Steiner, *Constitutional Inequality* (Washington, D.C.: Brookings Institution, 1985), p. 13.

73. Jo Freeman, "Women and Public Policy: An Overview," in Ellen Boneparth, *Women, Power and Policy* (Elmsford, N.Y.: Pergamon Press, 1983), pp. 52–53.

74. Mary Francis Berry, *Why ERA Failed* (Bloomington: Indiana University Press, 1986); Jane Mansbridge, *Why We Lost the ERA* (Chicago: University of Chicago Press, 1986); and Gilbert Steiner, *Constitutional Inequality*.

75. Myra Bradwell, quoted in Karen Berger Morello, *The Invisible Bar* (Boston: Beacon Press, 1986), p. 18. Andrea Bonnicksen agrees: "Blacks point to the *Dred Scott* decision, a decision in which the Court declared blacks not to be citizens in the meaning of the Constitution, as a symbol of their sorry history of discrimination. An analogous nineteenth-century decision for women was *Bradwell* v. *Illinois*, in which the Court upheld a law denying women the right to practice law in the state of Illinois," *Civil Rights and Liberties*, p. 158.

76. *Bradwell* v. *Illinois*, 83 U.S. 130 (1873).

77. *Hoyt* v. *Florida*, 368 U.S. 57 (1961). The Supreme Court effectively overruled this decision in *Taylor* v. *Louisiana*, 419 U.S. 522 (1975).

78. Mansbridge, *Why We Lost the ERA*, p. 50.

79. *Craig* v. *Boren*, 429 U.S. 190 (1976).

80. Justice Louis Brandeis, dissenting opinion, *Olmstead* v. *United States*, 277 U.S. 438 (1928).

81. Rhonda Copelon, "Beyond the Liberal Idea of Privacy: Toward a Positive Right of Autonomy," in McCann and Houseman, *Judging the Constitution*, p. 299.

82. Virginia Apuzzo, quoted in James Barron, "Homosexuals See Two Decades of Gains, but Fear Setbacks," *New York Times*, June 25, 1989, p. 25.

83. Henry Hampton, quoted in Derrick Jackson, "Supreme Court Rulings Spell End of an Era for Affirmative Action," Boston *Globe*, July 2, 1989, p. 44.

84. Whalen and Whalen, *The Longest Debate*, pp. 24, 157, 206.

85. Mansbridge, *Why We Lost the ERA*, p. 14.

86. Ibid., p. 20. Mansbridge reports that when she showed ERA activists poll data and asked if they could explain why a majority of the people who agreed that "a women's place is in the home" supported the ERA, she got responses like: "Jesus, that's incredible!" and "I don't know . . . I don't know" (ibid., p. 22).

87. Herbert Parmet, *JFK: The Presidency of John F. Kennedy* (Baltimore: Penguin Books, 1984), p. 273.

88. John Kennedy, Special Message to Congress, June 19, 1963, quoted in Bruce Miroff, *Pragmatic Illusions* (New York: McKay, 1976), pp. 258–259.

89. Ibid., pp. 223–270.

90. Frances Fox Piven and Richard A. Cloward, *Regulating the Poor* (New York: Random House, 1971), p. 230.

91. Gerald D. Jaynes, quoted in Julie Johnson, "Blacks Found Lagging Despite Gains," *New York Times*, July 28, 1989, p. 6A.

92. Stuart Scheingold, "Constitutional Rights and Social Change: Civil Rights in Perspective," in McCann and Houseman, *Judging the Constitution*, p. 76.

93. Reverend Jesse Jackson, quoted in Ronald Smothers, "Blacks Discussing Routes to Power," *New York Times*, April 24, 1989, p. 12A.

Chapter 8

1. Transcribed from a videotape supplied by the Public Agenda Foundation, which bears no responsibility for any interpretation given herein.

2. Alexander Hamilton, "Speech on the Constitutional Convention on a Plan of Government," in *Selected Writings and Speeches of Alexander Hamilton*, ed. Morton J. Frisch (Washington, D.C.: American Enterprise Institute, 1985), p. 108.

3. Quoted in Gerald Stourzh, *Alexander Hamilton and the Idea of Republican Government* (Stanford, Calif.: Stanford University Press, 1970), p. 40.

4. Walter Lippmann, *The Public Philosophy* (Boston: Little, Brown, 1955), pp. 20, 27.

5. Ibid., p. 27.

6. Quoted in Saul K. Padover, ed., *Democracy* (New York: Greenwood Press, 1939), p. 56.

7. V. O. Key, Jr., *Public Opinion and American Democracy* (New York: Knopf, 1964), p. 557.

8. Joseph A. Schumpeter, *Capitalism, Socialism, and Democracy*, 3rd ed. (New York: Harper & Row, 1975), pp. 260–261.

9. For an argument along these lines but expressed in a far more sophisticated manner, see Gabriel Almond and Sidney Verba, *The Civic Culture* (Princeton, N.J.: Princeton University Press, 1963), pp. 479–487.

10. Gabriel Almond, *The American People and Foreign Policy* (New York: Praeger, 1960), p. 53. (Originally published by Harcourt, Brace, and Company, Inc., 1950.)

11. Ibid., p. 76.

12. Ibid., p. 53.

13. George Kennan, *American Diplomacy 1900–1950* (New York: New American World, 1959), p. 59.

14. Quoted in Daniel Yergin, *The Shattered Peace* (Boston: Houghton Mifflin, 1977), p. 172.

15. Charles W. Kegley and Eugene R. Wittkopf, *American Foreign Policy*, 2nd ed. (New York: St. Martin's Press, 1982), pp. 272–273.

16. Benjamin I. Page and Robert Y. Shapiro, "Changes in America's Policy Preferences, 1935–1979," *Public Opinion Quarterly* 46 (Winter 1982):34.

17. William Caspary, "The 'Mood Theory': A Study of Public Opinion and Foreign Policy," *American Political Science Review* 64 (June 1970):546. Also John E. Mueller, *War, Presidents and Public Opinion* (New York: Wiley, 1973).

18. This section presents a very general framework for analyzing attitudes. Although it relies heavily on the work of a social psychologist, Martin Fishbein, similar approaches have been adopted by innumerable other social scientists. See Martin Fishbein, "A Theory of Reasoned Action," in *Nebraska Symposium on Motivation, 1979*, ed. Herbert Hawe and Monte M. Page (Lincoln: University of Nebraska Press, 1980), pp. 65–116; and Icek Ajzen and Martin Fishbein, "Attitude-Behavior Relations," *Psychological Bulletin* 84 (June 1977):888–918.

19. Icek Ajzen, "Attitude Structure and Behavior," in *Attitude Structure and Function*, ed. Anthony R. Pratkanis, Steven J. Breckler, and Anthony G. Greenwald (Hillsdale, N.J.: Lawrence Earlbaum, 1989), pp. 241–242.

20. See, for example, Susan E. Howell, "Candidates and Attitudes: Revisiting the Question of Causality," *Journal of Politics* 48 (May 1986):450–464; and Benjamin Page and Calvin Jones, "Reciprocal Effects of Policy Preferences, Party Loyalties, and the Vote," *American Political Science Review* 73 (December 1979):1071–1089.

21. *New York Times*, February 14, 1982, p. 31.

22. Richard Dawson and Kenneth Prewitt, *Political Socialization* (Boston: Little, Brown, 1969), p. 19.

23. David Easton and Jack Dennis, *Children in the Political System* (New York: McGraw-Hill, 1969), chap. 1.

24. Fred I. Greenstein, *Children and Politics* (New Haven, Conn.: Yale University Press, 1965), pp. 158ff.

25. Timothy E. Cook, "The Bear Market in Political Socialization and the Costs of Misunderstood Psychological Theories," *American Political Science Review* 79 (December 1985):1079–1093.

26. From the book *The Political Life of Children*; copyright © Robert Coles (New York: Atlantic Monthly Press, 1986), p. 43.

27. See, for example, Robert D. Hess and Judith V. Torney, *The Development of Political Attitudes in Children* (Garden City, N.Y.: Doubleday (Anchor Books), 1968), chap. 2.

28. Reinhold Niebuhr, "After Capitalism—What?" *The World Tomorrow*, vol. VXVI (1933), quoted in *New Deal Thought*, ed. Howard Zinn (Indianapolis: Bobbs-Merrill, 1966), p. 21.

29. Greenstein, *Children and Politics*, pp. 38–40.

30. Her autobiography of her later years reveals the passion of her social and economic philosophy. Helen Keller, *Midstream My Later Life* (1929; reprint ed., New York: Greenwood Press, 1969), pp. 330–337.

31. Quoted in Jonathan Kozol, *The Night Is Dark and I Am Far from Home* (Boston: Houghton Mifflin, 1975), p. 68.

32. Timothy E. Cook, "The Newbery Award as Political Education," *Polity* 17 (Spring 1985):421–445.

33. Ibid., p. 443. Cook's earlier study of books written by Dr. Seuss and L. Frank Baum arrived at essentially the same conclusion: "Another Perspective on Political Authority in Children's Literature," *Western Political Quarterly* 36 (June 1983):326–336.

34. Fred Greenstein, "The Benevolent Leader Revisited," *American Political Science Review* 69 (December 1975):1396–1397. But see F. Christopher Arterton, "The Impact of Watergate on Children's Attitudes Toward Political Authority," *Political Science Quarterly* 89 (June 1974):269–288.

35. Coles, *The Political Life of Children*, pp. 38–39.

36. See, for example, Dean Jaros, Herbert Hirsch, and Frederic J. Fleron, Jr., "The Malevolent Leader," *American Political Science Review* 62 (June 1968):564–575.

37. Greenstein, "The Benevolent Leader Revisited," p. 1386.

38. Edward G. Carmines et al., "Unrealized Partisanship: A Theory of Dealignment," *Journal of Politics* 49 (June 1987):377–399.

39. Robert C. Luskin, John P. McIver, and Edward G. Carmines, "Issues and the Transmission of Partisanship," *American Journal of Political Science* 33 (May 1989):440–452.

40. Richard Flacks, "The Liberated Generation: An Exploration of the Roots of Student Protest," *Journal of Social Issues* 23 (1967):52–75.

41. M. Kent Jennings and Gregory B. Markus, "Partisan Orientation over the Long Haul," *American Political Science Review* 78 (December 1984):1000–1018. Also see M. Kent Jennings and Richard G. Niemi, *Generations and Politics* (Princeton, N.J.: Princeton University Press, 1981), pp. 205–206.

42. Cook, "The Newbery Award as Political Education," p. 422. (Author's italics.) He bases this remark on M. Kent Jennings and Richard G. Niemi's classic study, *The Political Character of Adolescence* (Princeton, N.J.: Princeton University Press, 1974).

43. William H. Flanigan and Nancy H. Zingale, *Political Behavior of the American Electorate*, 6th ed. (Dubuque, Iowa: Brown, 1988), pp. 18–20, 104–106; and Michael Corbett, *Political Tolerance* (New York: Longman, 1982), pp. 124–125.

44. Edgar Litt, "Civic Education, Community Norms, and Political Indoctrination," *American Sociological Review*

28 (February 1963). Reprinted in Richard Flacks, ed., *Conformity, Resistance, and Self-Determination* (Boston: Little, Brown, 1973), pp. 136–141.

45. Ibid., p. 140.

46. Richard Merelman, "Democratic Politics and the Culture of American Education," *American Political Science Review* 74 (June 1980):319. Note that although Merelman coins the term *hidden curriculum*, he does not accept all of the features that others have attributed to it.

47. Robert D. Hess and Judith V. Torney, *The Development of Political Attitudes in Children* (Garden City, N.Y.: Doubleday (Anchor Books), 1968), p. 248.

48. Samuel Bowles and Herbert Gintis, *Schooling in Capitalist America* (New York: Basic Books, 1976), pp. 44–48. A very good and interesting account of how colleges and universities were co-opted by business and management interests is David Noble, *America by Design* (New York: Oxford University Press, 1977), esp. chaps. 8 and 9.

49. Pearl M. Kamer, *The U.S. Economy in Crisis* (New York: Praeger, 1988), p. 108.

50. Henry Giroux makes this observation in "Public Philosophy and the Crisis in Education," *Harvard Education Review* 54 (May 1984):186–194.

51. Herbert Asher, *Polling and the Public* (Washington, D.C.: Congressional Quarterly Press, 1988), pp. 58–64.

52. President John F. Kennedy reputedly admitted after the Bay of Pigs fiasco, "The worse I do, the more popular I get." Quoted in Samuel Kernell, "Explaining Presidential Popularity," *American Political Science Review* 72 (June 1978):512.

53. *Washington Post National Weekly Edition*, May 12, 1986, p. 37.

54. Howard Schuman and Stanley Presser, *Questions and Answers in Attitude Surveys* (New York: Academic Press, 1981).

55. *New York Times*, August 18, 1980, p. 15.

56. Robert Erikson et al., *American Public Opinion*, 3rd ed. (New York: Macmillan, 1988), pp. 40–55.

57. Ibid., pp. 44–45.

58. Key, *Public Opinion and American Democracy*, p. 411.

59. Warren Miller and Donald Stokes, "Constituency Influence in Congress," *American Political Science Review* 57 (March 1963):45–56.

60. An excellent collection of articles on the linkage between mass attitudes and decision making is contained in Norman R. Luttbeg, ed., *Public Opinion and Public Policy*, 3rd ed. (Itasca, Ill.: Peacock, 1982).

61. See, for example, James Kuklinski and Donald McCrone, "Electoral Accountability as a Source of Policy Preferences," in Luttbeg, *Public Opinion and Public Policy*, pp. 320–341.

62. See, for example, the articles in Luttbeg's collection.

63. Charles Steinberg, *The Information Establishment* (New York: Hastings, 1980).

64. Paul Boyer, *By the Bomb's Early Light* (New York: Pantheon Books, 1985), p. 295.

65. Ibid., p. 296.

66. Ibid., p. 296.

67. Ibid., p. 112.

68. Ibid., pp. 296–297.

69. *The Gallup Poll: Public Opinion 1935–1971* (New York: Random House, 1972), vol. 1, p. 767; vol. 2, pp. 1400–1401. Also see Stanley Rothman and S. Robert Lichter, "The Media and the Public," *Public Opinion*, August/September 1982, p. 47.

70. *Washington Post National Weekly Edition*, May 19, 1986, p. 37. Also see *The Gallup Poll: Public Opinion 1972–1977* (Wilmington, Del.: Scholarly Resources, 1978), p. 796.

71. *The Gallup Poll*, vol. 3, p. 141.

72. Murray Edelman, *The Symbolic Uses of Politics* (Urbana: University of Illinois Press, 1964).

73. Ibid., p. 19.

74. Murray Edelman, "Symbols and Political Quiescence," *American Political Science Review* 54 (September 1960):696–698.

75. Quoted in Michael Weisskopf, "A Qualified Failure," *Washington Post National Weekly Edition*, June 19–25, 1989, p. 10.

76. *Clean Air Facts*, March 15, 1989, p. 3.

77. Weisskopf, "A Qualified Failure," p. 10.

Chapter 9

1. Martin Kramer, "Hezbollah Held Hostage," *New York Times*, August 8, 1989, p. 19.

2. Wilmington, Delaware *News Journal*, August 2, 1989, p. 5.

3. Innumerable scholars have complained that American journalism seldom provides a complete picture of foreign policy, particularly in the Middle East and other Third World countries. See Barry Rubin, *Paved with Good Intentions* (Baltimore: Penguin Books, 1981), app. A; James Bill, "Iran and the Crisis of '78," *Foreign Affairs*, Winter 1978–1979, pp. 323–324; and William A. Dorman and Mansour Farhang, *The U.S. Press and Iran* (Berkeley: University of California Press, 1987).

4. Quoted in *Newsweek*, December 6, 1982. Also see Harvey Molotch and Marilyn Lester, "Accidents, Scandals, and Routines: Resources for Insurgent Methodology," in *The TV Establishment*, ed. Gaye Tuchman (Englewood Cliffs, N.J.: Prentice-Hall, 1974), p. 53.

5. Michael W. Suleiman, *The Arabs in the Mind of America* (Brattleboro, Vt.: Amana Books, 1988), chaps. 7–8.

6. Benjamin I. Page, Robert Y. Shapiro, and Glenn R. Dempsy, "What Moves Public Opinion," *American Political Science Review* 81 (March 1987):24. Also see Shanto Iyengar and Donald R. Kinder, *News that Matters* (Chicago: University of Chicago Press, 1987), p. 119.

7. U.S. Bureau of the Census, *Statistical Abstract of the United States: 1989* (Washington, D.C.: Government Printing Office, 1989), p. 523.

8. National Opinion Research Center, *General Social Surveys 1972–1988, Cumulative Codebook* (Chicago: NORC, 1988), p. 256.

9. *New York Times*, May 20, 1980, p. 1C.

10. U.S. Bureau of the Census, *Statistical Abstract: 1989*, p. 541.

11. Ibid., pp. 223, 549.

12. Ben Bagdikian, *The Media Monopoly* (Boston: Beacon Press, 1983), pp. 4–7.

13. *New York Times*, February 2, 1985, p. 7.

14. Benjamin M. Compaine, "Newspapers" in *Who Controls the Media*, ed. Benjamin M. Compaine et al. (White Plains, N.Y.: Knowledge Industry Publications, 1982), p. 37; and Robert M. Entman, *Democracy Without Citizens* (New York: Oxford University Press, 1989), p. 91.

15. *Forbes*, May 1, 1989, p. 251.

16. Ibid.

17. Ibid., p. 266.

18. *New York Times*, March 5, 1989, p.1.

19. Geraldine Fabrikant, "Time-Warner Merger Raises Concerns on Power of a Giant," *New York Times*, March 3, 1989, p. 1.

20. Bagdikian, *The Media Monopoly*, p. 23.

21. Bernard A. Weisberger, "Does the Fourth Estate Dance to the Company Tune?" *Washington Post Book World*, June 26, 1983, p. 4.

22. Bagdikian, *The Media Monopoly*, p. 6.

23. Ralph Miliband, *The State in Capitalist Society* (New York: Basic Books, 1969), chap. 8.

24. Stanton quoted in Edward Jay Epstein, *News from Nowhere* (New York: Random House (Vintage Books), 1974), pp. 13–14.

25. Wilmington, Delaware *News Journal*, August 1, 1989, p. 4. The article contained five paragraphs, two of which have been omitted because they dealt with a side issue.

26. Walter Lippmann, *Public Opinion* (New York: Macmillan, 1960, first published in 1920), p. 358.

27. Herbert J. Gans, *Deciding What's News: A Case Study of CBS Evening News, NBC Nightly News, Newsweek & Time* (New York: Pantheon Books, 1979).

28. Gaye Tuchman, *Making News: A Study in the Construction of Reality* (New York: Free Press, 1978).

29. Quoted in Epstein, *News from Nowhere*, p. 101.

30. W. Lance Bennett, *News: The Politics of Illusion* (New York: Longman, 1983), p. 7.

31. Ibid., p. 53. The study is Leon V. Sigal, *Reporters and Officials: The Organization and Politics of Reporting* (Lexington, Mass.: Heath, 1973), p.124.

32. Bennett, *News*, pp. 53–54. Also see Allan Rachlin, *News as Hegemonic Reality* (New York: Praeger, 1988), chap. 3.

33. Jane Delano Brown et al., "Invisible Power: Newspaper News Sources and the Limits of Diversity," *Journalism Quarterly* 63 (Spring 1987):53.

34. Todd Gitlin, *The Whole World Is Watching* (Berkeley: University of California Press, 1980).

35. Quoted in Edward J. Epstein, *Beyond Fact and Fiction* (New York: Random House (Vintage Books), 1975), p. 215.

36. Daniel C. Hallin, "The Media, the War in Vietnam, and Political Support: A Critique of the Thesis of an Oppositional Media," *Journal of Politics* 46 (February 1984):2–24.

37. Michael Parenti, *Inventing Reality: The Politics of the Mass Media* (New York: St. Martin's Press, 1986), p. 89.

38. Benjamin Ginsberg, *The Captive Public* (New York: Basic Books, 1986), p. 227.

39. *New York Times Co.* v. *United States*, 403 U.S. 713 (1971).

40. Bennett, *News*, p. 21. Also Iyengar and Kinder, *News that Matters*, pp. 120–122.

41. Bennett, *News*, pp. 7–12.

42. David L. Paletz and Robert M. Entman, *Media Power and Politics* (New York: Free Press, 1981), pp. 16–17.

43. Frank Mankiewicz "The Political Costs of a TV Wasteland," *Washington Post*, January 2, 1977, p. 2C.

44. Quoted in William V. Shannon, "The Network Circus," *New York Times*, September 13, 1975, p. 35.

45. *New York Times*, January 19, 1987, p. 12.

46. "CBS Evening News," February 3, 1983. Quoted in *New York Times*, February 4, 1984, p. 5B.

47. See, for example, Tony Atwater, "Network Evening News Coverage of the TWA Hostage Crisis," *Journalism Quarterly* 64 (Summer/Autumn 1987):520–525.

48. Epstein, *News from Nowhere*, p. 255.

49. Thomas Patterson, *The Mass Media Election* (New York: Praeger, 1980), p. 119.

50. Ibid., p. 21.

51. See, for example, Michael Robinson and Margaret Sheehan, *Over the Wire and on TV* (New York: Russell Sage, 1983), pp. 147–148.

52. Mark Hertsgaard, *On Bended Knee* (New York: Farrar, Straus & Giroux, 1988), p. 239.

53. Similar data are presented in Harold W. Stanley and Richard G. Niemi, *Vital Statistics on American Politics* (Washington, D.C.: Congressional Quarterly Press, 1988), p. 50; Doris Graber, *Processing the News*, 2nd ed. (New York: Longman, 1988), p. 78; and Marjorie Randon Hershey, "The Campaign and the Media," in *The Election of 1988*, ed. Gerald Pomper (Chatham, N.J.: Chatham House, 1988), pp. 96–100.

54. Alfred B. DelBello, "Campaign Reporting," *New York Times*, March 22, 1984, p. 23.

55. Patterson and Richard Davis found that a newspaper as prestigious as the *New York Times* spent nearly a third of its coverage of the last week of the 1984 presidential election on polls; Thomas Patterson and Richard Davis, "The Media Campaign," in *The Election of 1984*, ed. Michael Nelson (Washington, D.C.: Congressional Quarterly Press, 1985), p. 124. Also see S. Robert Lichter, Stanley Rothman, and Linda S. Lichter, *The Media Elite* (Bethesda, Md.: Adler and Adler, 1986), p. 111.

56. Richard Joslyn, "The Content of Political Spot Ads," *Journalism Quarterly* 57 (Spring 1980):94.

57. Quoted in Jack W. Germond and Jules Witcover, *Whose Broad Stripes and Bright Stars?* (New York: Warner Books, 1989), p. 403.

58. Quoted in ibid., p. 404.

59. *New York Times*, October 3, 1984, p. 24.

60. David Halberstam, "How Television Failed the American Voter," *Parade*, January 11, 1981, p. 7.

61. Kathleen Hall Jamieson and David S. Birdsall discuss the promise and reality of formal debates in *Presidential Debates* (New York: Oxford University Press, 1988), especially pp. 3–15.

62. Elizabeth Drew, *Election Journal* (New York: Morrow, 1989), pp. 283–284; and Germond and Witcover, *Whose Broad Stripes and Bright Stars?* pp. 425–429.

63. Richard A. Joslyn, "Candidate Appeals and the Meaning of Elections," in *Do Elections Matter?*, ed. Benjamin Ginsberg and Alan Stone (Armonk, N.Y.: Sharpe, 1986), p. 107. Other studies of debates also show that the press tends to ignore whatever programmatic issues are raised. See, for example, David O. Sears and Steven H. Chaffee, "Uses and Effects of the 1976 Debates: An Overview of Empirical Studies," in Sidney Klaus, *The Great Debates: Carter vs. Ford, 1976* (Bloomington: Indiana University Press, 1979), p. 229.

64. Germond and Witcover, *Whose Broad Stripes and Bright Stars?* pp. 434–435.

65. Joseph Klapper, *The Effects of Mass Communications* (New York: Free Press, 1960). Klapper, it should be noted, wrote about the media in general, not political debates. For a more recent discussion of attitude change, see William J. McGwire, "Attitudes and Attitude Change," in *Handbook of Social Psychology*, vol. 2, 3rd ed., ed. Gardner Lindzey and Elliot Aronson (New York: Random House, 1985).

66. *Gallup Report*, October 1988, p. 13.

67. Arthur Miller and Michael MacKuen, "Learning About the Candidates: The 1976 Presidential Debates," *Public Opinion Quarterly* 43 (Fall 1979):326–348.

68. See, for example, Michael Robinson, "Public Affairs Television and the Growth of Political Malaise," *American Political Science Review* 70 (1976):409–432; Arthur Miller, Lutz Ebring, and Eddie Goldenberg, "Type-set Politics: Impact of Newspapers on Public Confidence," *American Political Science Review* 73 (1979):67–84; and S. Robert Lichter and Stanley Rothman, "Media and Business Elites," *Public Opinion*, October/November 1981, pp. 42–46, 59–60.

69. Samuel Huntington, *American Politics: The Promise of Disharmony* (Cambridge, Mass.: Harvard University Press, 1981), pp. 217–219.

70. Quoted in Herbert J. Gans, "Are U.S. Journalists Dangerously Liberal?" *Columbia Journalism Review*, November/December 1985, p. 29.

71. Lichter, Rothman, and Lichter, *The Media Elite*, pp. 28–33. Also William Schneider and I. A. Lewis, "Views on the News," *Public Opinion* 8 (August/September 1985):7.

72. See Lichter, Rothman, and Lichter, *The Media Elite*, table 2, p. 29.

73. In the last dozen presidential races, for example, the majority of newspaper editorials supported the Republican candidate or remained neutral. Relatively few backed the Democrat. See Harold W. Stanley and Richard G. Niemi, *Vital Statistics on American Politics* (Washington, D.C.: Congressional Quarterly Press, 1990), pp. 71–72.

74. Doris Graber, *Mass Media and American Politics* (Washington, D.C.: Congressional Quarterly Press, 1980), p. 83.

75. John W. C. Johnstone, "Review Essay: Who Controls the News," *The American Journal of Sociology* 87 (March 1982):1179; Hallin, "The Media, the War in Vietnam, and Political Support," pp. 18–23; and Iyengar and Kinder, *News that Matters*, p. 133.

76. Marc Howard Ross and Richard Joslyn, "Election Night Coverage as Political Ritual," *Polity* 21 (Winter 1988):315–319.

77. Epstein, *News from Nowhere*, p. 261.

78. John Hart, "Marketing Wins, News Loses, on TV," *New York Times*, May 30, 1981, p. 23.

79. Iyengar and Kinder, *News that Matters*, p. 124.

80. William Dorman, "Journalism in the Third World," *World Policy Journal* 3 (Summer 1986):421.

81. Ibid.

82. Graber, *Processing the News*, p. 265.

83. *Washington Post National Weekly Edition*, September 3, 1984, p. 37.

84. This point has been convincingly made by Hertsgaard, *On Bended Knee*, chaps. 13–14.

85. *New York Times*, March 4, 1987, p. 15.

86. Eleanor Randolph, "The Story the Press Didn't See," *Washington Post National Weekly Edition*, November 30, 1987, p. 6.

87. Graber, *Mass Media and American Politics*, p. 82.

88. Bagdikian, *The Media Monopoly*, p. 210.

89. Bennett, *News*, p. 13.

Chapter 10

1. This account is based on personal observations by one of the authors and stories in the Wilmington, Delaware *News Journal*.

2. Samuel H. Barnes and Max Kaase, *Political Action* (Beverly Hills, Calif.: Sage, 1979), chap. 2.

3. Sidney Verba and Richard A. Brody, "Participation, Policy Preferences, and the War in Vietnam," *Public Opinion Quarterly* 34 (Spring 1970):326. Other polls taken at the time reveal that not only did most Americans hesitate to get involved in antiwar demonstrations, but they also had very negative feelings about the participants and their methods. A mere 20 percent of a 1968 survey supported *lawful* protest marches while just 8 percent approved of efforts to "disrupt" the government. Center for Political Studies, *1968 American National Election Study Codebook* (Ann Arbor, Mich.: Inter-university Consortium for Political Research, 1973), pp. 277–278.

4. James W. Trent and Judith L. Crasie, "Commitment and Conformity in the American College," *Journal of Social Issues* 23 (Summer 1967):33–36.

5. *New York Times*, June 6, 1989, p. 14.

6. Ibid., June 23, 1989, p. 23.

7. Patrick Fenton, "Lots of Guys at Farell's Don't Vote," *New York Times*, March 3, 1988, p. 27.

8. U.S. Bureau of the Census, *Statistical Abstract of the United States 1989* (Washington, D.C.: Government Printing Office, 1989), p. 258; and U.S. Bureau of the Census, "Voting and Registration in the Election of November 1988 (Advanced Report)," Series P-20, No. 435 (Washington, D.C.: Government Printing Office, 1989), pp. 3–4.

9. U.S. Bureau of the Census, *Voting and Registration in the Election of November 1986* (Washington, D.C.: Government Printing Office, 1987).

10. Robert D. Marcus, *Grand Old Party* (New York: Oxford University Press), pp. 13–15.

11. Richard Jensen, *The Winning of the Midwest* (Chicago: University of Chicago Press, 1971), pp. 38–39.

12. Morton Keller, *Affairs of State* (Cambridge, Mass.: Harvard University Press, 1977), p. 524.

13. Philip Converse discusses the relationship between corruption and turnout in "Change in the American Electorate," in Angus Campbell and Philip E. Converse, *The Human Meaning of Social Change* (New York: Russell Sage, 1972), pp. 263–337.

14. See, for example, the exchange of views between Walter Dean Burnham, Philip Converse, and Jerrold Rusk in *American Political Science Review* 68 (September 1974):1002–1057.

15. The most persuasive advocate of this interpretation of the decline in turnout is Walter Dean Burnham. See his *Critical Elections and the Mainsprings of American Politics* (New York: Norton, 1970) and *The Current Crisis in American Politics* (New York: Oxford University Press, 1982).

16. Marcus, *Grand Old Party*, pp. 14–16.

17. The classic statement of the politically unhealthy effects of one-party politics is V. O. Key, Jr., *Southern Politics* (New York: Knopf, 1949). For a more recent statement, see Michael E. McGerr, *The Decline of Popular Politics* (New York: Oxford University Press, 1986).

18. Walter Dean Burnham, "The Turnout Problem," in *Elections American Style*, ed. A. James Reichley (Washington, D.C.: Brookings Institute, 1987), pp. 97–133; and Frances Fox Piven and Richard A. Cloward, *Why Americans Don't Vote* (New York: Pantheon Books, 1988), chaps. 2–3.

19. McGerr, *The Decline of Popular Politics*, p. 135.

20. John R. Petrocik, "Voter Turnout and Electoral Preference: The Anomalous Reagan Election," in *Elections in America*, ed. Kay Lehman Schlozman (Boston: Allen & Unwin, 1987), p. 253.

21. Raymond Wolfinger and Steven Rosenstone, *Who Votes?* (New Haven, Conn.: Yale University Press, 1980), pp. 90–91.

22. Burnham, "The Turnout Problem," pp. 97–133.

23. Angus Campbell et al., *The American Voter* (New York: Wiley, 1960), pp. 121–128.

24. Bruce E. Keith et al., "The Partisan Affinities of Independent 'Leaners,'" *British Journal of Political Science* 16 (1986):155–186; and Jack Dennis, "Political Independence in America, Part I," *British Journal of Political Science* 18 (1988):77–110.

25. Angus Campbell et al., *The Voter Decides* (Westport, Conn.: Greenwood Press, 1971; originally published in 1954), p. 187.

26. Paul R. Abramson and John Aldrich, "The Decline of Electoral Participation in America," *American Political Science Review* 76 (September 1982):502–521. Carol A. Cassel and Robert C. Luskin, however, call into question these generalizations about partisanship and efficacy. "Simple Explanations of Turnout Decline," *American Political Science Review* 82 (December 1988):1321–1330.

27. *Dunn* v. *Blumstein*, 405 U.S. 330 (1972).

28. Wolfinger and Rosenstone, *Who Votes?*, pp. 68–69.

29. *Washington Post*, February 6, 1983, p. 1C.

30. The Council of State Governments, *The Book of the States*, vol. 27 (Lexington, Ky.: Council of State Governments, 1988), p. 211.

31. Wolfinger and Rosenstone, *Who Votes?*, chap. 4.

32. Robert W. Jackman, "Political Institutions and Voter Turnout in the Industrial Democracies," *American Political Science Review* 81 (June 1987):414–416.

33. *New York Times*, April 18, 1977, p. 27; May 31, 1987, p. 4E; and May 7, 1989, p. 33.

34. Robert Kuttner describes the politics of registration in *The Life of the Party* (New York: Viking Press, 1987), pp. 128–144.

35. Eugene C. Lee, *The Politics of Nonpartisanship* (Berkeley: University of California Press, 1960). Cited in Willis D. Hawley, *Nonpartisan Elections* (New York: Wiley, 1973), p. 36.

36. Campbell et al., *The American Voter*, chap. 11.

37. Barnes and Kaase, *Political Action*, p. 168.

38. Jack H. Nagel, *Participation* (Englewood Cliffs, N.J.: Prentice-Hall, 1987), p. 58; Lester W. Milbrath and M. L. Goel, *Political Participation* (Skokie, Ill.: Rand McNally, 1977), p. 92.

39. Jo Freeman, *Social Movements of the Sixties and Seventies* (New York: Longman, 1983) contains numerous examples.

40. *New York Times*, July 2, 1989, p. 1.

41. See, among others, Anthony Lewis, *Portrait of a Decade* (New York: New York Times Books, 1964); James Farmer, *An Autobiography of the Civil Rights Movement* (New York: Arbor House, 1985); and Stephen B. Oates, *Let the Trumpet Sound* (New York: Harper & Row, 1982).

42. Quoted in Howell Raines, *My Soul Is Rested* (New York: Putnam, 1977), p. 321.

43. V. O. Key, Jr., *Southern Politics*, chap. 1.

44. James McGregor Burns, *The Crosswinds of Freedom* (New York: Knopf, 1989), pp. 359–360.

45. Joyce Gelb and Marian Lief Palley, *Women and Public Policies*, rev. ed. (Princeton, N.J.: Princeton University Press, 1987), pp. 13–14. Also see Robert Salisbury, "An Exchange Theory of Interest Groups," *Midwest Journal of Political Science* 13 (February 1969):1–32.

46. Jane Mansbridge, *Why We Lost the ERA* (Chicago: University of Chicago Press, 1986), pp. 4–6.

47. Douglas C. Waller, *Congress and the Nuclear Freeze* (Amherst: University of Massachusetts Press, 1982).

48. Gelb and Palley, *Women and Public Policies*, p. 7.

49. Center for Political Studies, *The CPS 1970 National Election Study Codebook* (Ann Arbor, Mich.: Inter-university Consortium for Political Research, 1972), p. 64.

50. Robert J. Goldstein, *Political Repression in Modern America* (Cambridge, Mass.: Schenkman, 1978).

51. United States Senate, *Hearings Before the Select Committee to Study Governmental Operations with Respect to Intelligence Activities*, 94th Congress, 1st Session (Washington, D.C.: Government Printing Office, 1976), vol. 2, p. 154. (Cited as *Hearings* hereafter.)

52. *Hearings*, vol. 2, p. 146.

53. Goldstein, *Political Repression in Modern America*, p. 440.

54. *Hearings*, vols. 2, 3, 4, and 6.

55. Ibid., vol. 3, p. 2.

56. Ibid., vol. 4.

57. Taylor Branch, *Parting the Waters* (New York: Simon & Schuster, 1988), pp. 360–362; and Oates, *Let the Trumpet Sound*, pp. 312–318.

58. Cited in Loch K. Johnson, *A Season of Inquiry* (Lexington: University Press of Kentucky, 1985), pp. 126–127.

59. John Stuart Mill, *An Essay on Representative Government*, quoted in Carole Pateman, *Participation and Democratic Theory* (New York: Cambridge University Press, 1970), p. 70.

60. Dennis F. Thompson, *The Democratic Citizen* (New York: Cambridge University Press, 1970), chap. 3. Also, Benjamin R. Barber, *Strong Democracy: Participatory Politics for a New Age* (Berkeley: University of California Press, 1984).

61. Pateman, *Participation and Democratic Theory*, p. 43. In addition, see Robert Dahl, *A Preface to Economic Democracy* (Berkeley: University of California Press, 1985). Jack Nagel reviews the arguments for workplace democracy in *Participation* (Englewood Cliffs, N.J.: Prentice-Hall, 1987), chap. 11.

62. Giovanni Sartori, *Democratic Theory* (Detroit: Wayne State University Press, 1962), p. 90.

63. Many social scientists have made this case, including Harry Eckstein, *A Theory of Stable Democracy* (Princeton, N.J.: Princeton University Press, 1961); and Gabriel Almond and Sidney Verba, *The Civic Culture* (Princeton, N.J.: Princeton University Press, 1963).

64. C. Wright Mills, *The Power Elite* (New York: Oxford University Press, 1959), chap. 13.

Chapter 11

1. For a discussion of the pros and cons of changing the electoral college, see Neil R. Pierce and Lawrence D. Longley, *The People's President: The Electoral College in American History and the Direct Vote Alternative*, rev. ed. (New Haven, Conn.: Yale University Press, 1981).

2. *Baker* v. *Carr*, 369 U.S. 186 (1962); and *Wesberry* v. *Sanders*, 376 U.S. 1 (1964).

3. *Newsweek*, November 21, 1988, pp. 50, 58.

4. *New York Times*, May 1, 1988, p. 30.

5. Ibid.

6. *Washington Post National Weekly Edition*, September 19–25, 1988, p. 10.

7. Ibid.

8. Ibid.

9. *New York Times*, October 11, 1988, p. 11.

10. *Washington Post National Weekly Edition*, January 3, 1988, p. 8.

11. *Washington Post National Weekly Edition*, September 19–25, 1988, p. 10.

12. V. O. Key, Jr., *The Responsible Electorate* (Cambridge, Mass.: Harvard University Press, 1966), p. 7.

13. The classic work linking social status and voting is Paul Lazarsfeld et al., *The People's Choice* (New York: Duell, Sloan, Pearce, 1944).

14. Chapter 12 takes up the realignment concept in more detail. Also see John R. Petrocik, "Realignment: New Party Coalitions and the Nationalization of the South," *Journal of Politics* 49 (May 1987):347–375; and James L. Sundquist, *Dynamics of the Party System* (Washington, D.C.: Brookings Institution, 1983).

15. Everett Carll Ladd, "On Mandates, Realignments, and the 1984 Presidential Election," *Political Science Quarterly* 100 (Spring 1985):22.

16. See Angus Campbell et al., *The American Voter* (New York: Wiley, 1960); and Norman H. Nie, Sidney Verba, and John R. Petrocik, *The Changing American Voter*, enlarged ed. (Cambridge, Mass.: Harvard University Press, 1979), pp. 331–337.

17. James L. Sundquist, *Constitutional Reform and Effective Government* (Washington, D.C.: Brookings Institution, 1986), pp. 75–78.

18. William H. Flanigan and Nancy H. Zingale, *Political Behavior of the American Electorate*, 6th ed. (Dubuque, Iowa: Brown, 1988), pp. 37–42.

19. Anthony Downs, *An Economic Theory of Democracy* (New York: Harper & Row, 1959), chaps. 11–14.

20. Edward G. Carmines and James A. Stimson, "The Two Faces of Issue Voting," *American Political Science Review* 74 (March 1980):80–81.

21. Ibid., p. 85.

22. Nie, Verba, and Petrocik, *The Changing American Voter*, pp. 165–167.

23. The concept of proximity or closeness has a long history in political research. It is well explained in David M. Kovenock, James W. Prothro, and associates, *Explaining the Vote: Presidential Choices in the Nation and the States, 1968*, part I (Chapel Hill, N.C.: Institute for Research in Social Science, 1973).

24. See, for example, Stanley Kelley Jr., and Thad W. Mirer, "The Simple Act of Voting," *American Political Science Review* 68 (June 1974):572–591.

25. Gregory B. Markus and Philip E. Converse, "A Dynamic Simultaneous Equation Model of Electoral Choice," *American Political Science Review* 73 (September 1979):1055–1070.

26. Morris Fiorina, *Retrospective Voting in American National Elections* (New Haven, Conn.: Yale University Press, 1981). Also see Arthur H. Miller and Martin P. Wattenberg, "Throwing the Rascals Out: Policy and Performance Evaluations of Presidential Candidates, 1952–1980," *American Political Science Review* 78 (March 1984):359–372.

27. Fiorina, *Retrospective Voting in American National Elections*, p. 25.

28. Campbell and others, *The American Voter*, pp. 45–59.

29. Ibid., pp. 68–75.

30. Arthur H. Miller and Martin P. Wattenberg, "Throwing The Rascals Out: Policy and Performance Evaluations of Presidential Candidates, 1952–1980," *American Political Science Review* 79 (June 1985):359–372.

31. Arthur H. Miller, Martin P. Wattenberg, and Oksana Malanchuk, "Schematic Assessments of Presidential Candidates," *American Political Science Review* 80 (June 1986):528–529.

32. Richard A. Brody and Benjamin I. Page, "The Assessment of Policy Voting," *American Political Science Review* 66 (June 1972):450–458; and Benjamin I. Page, *Choices and Echoes in Presidential Elections* (Chicago: University of Chicago Press, 1978).

33. An excellent summary of research on voting behavior is contained in Richard G. Niemi and Herbert F. Weisberg, eds., *Controversies in Voting Research*, 2nd ed. (Washington, D.C.: Congressional Quarterly Press, 1984), especially pp. 89–105.

34. This account is based on a story in the *Washington Post*, November 7, 1982, pp. 1, 6.

35. Ibid., p. 6.

36. *Newsweek*, November 21, 1988, p. 100. Also see the discussion among campaign managers about how this and other themes developed in *Campaign for President: The Managers Look at '88*, edited by David R. Runkel (Dover, Massachusetts: Auburn House, 1989), pp. 109–129.

37. *New York Times*, May 24, 1987, p. 6F.

38. Ibid.

39. Sidney Blumenthal, "Marketing the President," *New York Times Magazine*, September 13, 1981, p. 114.

40. *New York Times*, November 1, 1988, p. 1.

41. See Larry Sabato, *The Rise of Political Consultants* (New York: Basic Books, 1981).

42. *Washington Post National Weekly Edition*, October 10–16, 1988, p. 14.

43. Richard Scammon and Ben Wattenberg, *The Real Majority* (New York: Coward, McCann & Geoghegan, 1970).

44. Benjamin I. Page, "The Theory of Political Ambiguity," *American Political Science Review* 70 (September 1977):742–752.

45. *New York Times*, May 5, 1977, p. 1.

46. Ibid., October 15, 1976, p. 5B.

47. *Washington Post National Weekly Edition*, January 30–February 15, 1988, p. 13.

48. *New York Times*, April 24, 1988, p. 24, and July 11, 1988, p. 15.

49. Mark P. Petracca, "Political Consultants and Democratic Governance," *PS*, March 1989, pp. 11–14.

50. *Washington Post National Weekly Edition*, March 21–27, 1988, p. 4, and March 20–26, 1989, p. 4.

51. *Washington Post National Weekly Edition*, February 13–19, 1989, p. 7.

52. Jack W. Germond and Jules Witcover, *Wake Us When It's Over* (New York: Macmillan, 1985), p. 540.

53. *New York Times*, November 6, 1988, p. 43.

54. Page, "The Theory of Political Ambiguity," pp. 742–752, explores the logic and justification of this thinking.

55. See Sabato, *The Rise of Political Consultants*; and Sidney Blumenthal, *The Permanent Campaign* (Boston: Beacon Press, 1980).

56. *Washington Post National Weekly Edition*, April 11–17, 1988, p. 4.

57. *New York Times*, October 16, 1989, p. 1B.

58. Quoted in *Washington Post National Weekly Edition*, February 19, 1988, p. 15.

59. *New York Times*, October 10, 1988, p. 6B.

60. Walter Dean Burnham, "American Politics in the 1970s: Beyond Party?", in *Parties and Elections in an Anti-Party Age*, ed. Jeff Fishel (Bloomington: University of Indiana Press, 1978) p. 340. Whether or not Burnham's ideas hold water would make an interesting topic for a paper: To what extent do elections give voters meaningful choices?

61. Stephen A. Salmore and Barbara G. Salmore, "Candidate-Centered Parties: Politics Without Intermediaries," in *Remaking American Politics*, ed. Sidney M. Milkis (Boulder, Colo.: Westview Press, 1989), pp. 215–238.

62. Quoted in William Crotty, *Political Reform and the American Experiment* (New York: Crowell, 1977), p. 103.

63. *New York Times*, August 27, 1989, p. 23.

64. Federal Election Commission news release, February 24, 1989.

65. Ibid.

66. Ibid.

67. *New York Times*, July 18, 1989, p. 1.

68. *New York Times*, December 11, 1988, p. 43.

69. *Buckley* v. *Valeo*, 424 U.S. 1 (1976).

70. *New York Times*, November 3, 1988, p. 23.

71. *Washington Post National Weekly Edition*, November 28–December 4, 1988, p. 15.

72. Federal Election Commission, press release, September 28, 1988.

73. See *Washington Post National Weekly Edition*, March 13–19, 1989, p. 12.

74. Elizabeth Drew, "Politics and Money—II", *New Yorker*, December 13, 1982, pp. 85–91.

75. Quoted in Richard Cohen, "Giving Till It Hurts," *National Journal*, December 18, 1982, pp. 2144, 2149.

76. Ibid., p. 2144.

77. Drew, "Politics and Money," p. 75.

78. *National Journal*, December 2, 1989, p. 2956.

79. Gary C. Jacobson, "Enough Is Too Much: Money and Competition in House Elections," in *Elections in America*, ed. Kay Lehman Schlozman (Boston: Allen & Unwin, 1987), p. 180.

80. *Washington Post*, June 28, 1981, p. 1D.

81. Jude Wanniski, "To Aid the Poor, Cut Capital Gains Taxes," *New York Times*, July 25, 1989, p. 23.

82. Everett Carll Ladd, "The Brittle Mandate: Electoral Dealignment and the 1980 Presidential Election," *Political Science Quarterly*, Spring 1981, p. 24.

83. *Washington Post*, June 28, 1981, p. 5D.

84. Ibid. Also see Warren E. Miller and J. Merrill Shanks, "Policy Directions and Presidential Leadership," *British Journal of Political Science* 12 (1983):299–356; and Chapter 8.

85. Robert Dahl, *Preface to Democratic Theory* (Chicago: University of Chicago Press, 1956), explores some of these points in greater detail.

Chapter 12

1. President George Bush, quoted in Andrew Rosenthal, "President Mends Some GOP Fences in Providence and Chicago," *New York Times*, November 21, 1989, p. 18.

2. Ibid.

3. Text of Republican platform, *Congressional Quarterly Weekly Report*, August 20, 1988, p. 2378.

4. Governor Thomas Kean, quoted in Dan Balz, "GOP Governors Urge Party to Ease Antiabortion Stance," *Washington Post*, November 14, 1989, p. 1.

5. Text of November 7, presidential news conference, *Congressional Quarterly Weekly Report*, November 11, 1989, p. 3107.

6. Rosenthal, "President Mends Some GOP Fences," p. 18.

7. Ibid.

8. Maureen Dowd, "GOP Congresswomen Hopeful After Bush Meeting on Abortion," *New York Times*, November 15, 1989, p. 18.

9. Frank J. Sorauf and Paul Allen Beck, *Party Politics in America*, 6th ed. (Glenview, Ill.: Scott, Foresman, 1988), p. 8.

10. Edmund Burke, "Thoughts on the Cause of the Present Discontents" (1770), in *Edmund Burke: Selected Writings and Speeches*, ed. Peter J. Stanlis (New York: Anchor Books, 1963), p. 143.

11. Larry J. Sabato, *The Party's Just Begun* (Glenview, Ill.: Scott, Foresman, 1988), p. 26; and Sorauf and Beck, *Party Politics in America*, p. 8.

12. Hugh L. LeBlanc, *American Political Parties* (New York: St. Martin's Press, 1982), p. 3.

13. William Chambers and Walter Dean Burnham provided the basic framework of five party systems in *The American Party Systems: Stages of Development*, 2nd ed. (New York: Oxford University Press, 1967).

14. Paul Goodman, "The First American Party System," in Chambers and Burnham, *The American Party Systems*, p. 59.

15. Samuel J. Eldersveld, *Political Parties in American Society* (New York: Basic Books, 1982), pp. 204–205.

16. Paul Abramson, John Aldrich, and David Rohde, *Change and Continuity in the 1984 Elections* (Washington, D.C.: Congressional Quarterly Press, 1986), pp. 116–117.

17. William Flanigan and Nancy Zingale, *Political Behavior of the American Electorate*, 5th ed. (Boston: Allyn & Bacon, 1983), pp. 78–79.

18. Joseph Schlesinger, "Political Party Organization," in *Handbook of Organizations*, ed. James March (Skokie, Ill.: Rand McNally, 1965).

19. Eldersveld, *Political Parties in American Society*, p. 95; and Sorauf and Beck, *Party Politics in America*, p. 79.

20. Sorauf and Beck, *Party Politics in America*, p. 79.

21. Charles L. Clapp, *The Congressman: His Work as He Sees It* (Garden City, N.Y.: Doubleday (Anchor Books), 1964), p. 397.

22. Gary C. Jacobson, *The Politics of Congressional Elections*, 2nd ed. (Boston: Little, Brown, 1987), pp. 19–20. See also Linda L. Fowler and Robert D. McClure, *Political Ambition: Who Decides to Run for Congress* (New Haven, Conn.: Yale University Press, 1989), p. 197.

23. Sorauf and Beck, *Party Politics in America*, p. 92.

24. David R. Mayhew, *Placing Parties in American Politics* (Princeton, N.J.: Princeton University Press, 1986), pp. 329–330.

25. Eldersveld, *Political Parties in American Society*, p. 412.

26. Cornelius P. Cotter, James Gibson, John F. Bibby, and Robert Huckshorn, *Party Organization in American Politics* (New York: Praeger, 1984); and Samuel J. Eldersveld, "Research on Local Party Activists and Organizations," a paper prepared for the Annual Meeting of the American Political Science Association, Washington, D.C., August 29, 1986.

27. Robert J. Huckshorn and John F. Bibby, "State Parties in an Era of Political Change," in *The Future of American Political Parties*, ed. Joel L. Fleishman (Englewood Cliffs, N.J.: Prentice-Hall, 1982), pp. 93–96.

28. Nelson W. Polsby, *Consequences of Party Reform* (New York: Oxford University Press, 1983), p. 176.

29. Cornelius Cotter and Bernard C. Hennessey, *Politics Without Power* (New York: Atherton, 1964), p. 3.

30. Charles Longley, "Party Reform and Party Nationalization: The Case of the Democrats," in *The Party Symbol*, ed. William Crotty (San Francisco: Freeman, 1980), p. 375.

31. *Congressional Quarterly Weekly Report*, April 1, 1989, p. 718.

32. Polsby, *Consequences of Party Reform*, pp. 183 and 184.

33. *Congressional Quarterly Weekly Report*, July 3, 1982, p. 1591.

34. Sorauf and Beck, *Party Politics in America*, pp. 116–121; and Eldersveld, *Political Parties in American Society*, pp. 171–174.

35. Helmut Norpoth and Jerrold G. Rusk, "Partisan Dealignment in the American Electorate: Itemizing the Deductions Since 1964," *American Political Science Review*, September 1982, p. 535.

36. Polsby, *Consequences of Party Reform*, p. 140.

37. Hamilton Jordan, quoted in Larry Liebert, "Democrats Warned Not to Make Too Many Promises," *Boston Globe*, May 22, 1983, p. 16.

38. James Hunt, quoted in Rhodes Cook, "New Democratic Rules Panel: A Careful Approach to Change," *Congressional Quarterly Weekly Report*, December 26, 1981, p. 2565.

39. Vin Weber, Republican congressman from Minnesota, quoted in Chuck Alston, "Rules of Political Navigation Altered by Bush Centrism," *Congressional Quarterly Weekly Report*, May 6, 1989, p. 1019.

40. E. E. Schattschneider, *Party Government* (New York: Holt, Rinehart and Winston, 1942), pp. 131–132.

41. David W. Brady, Joseph Cooper, and Patricia Hurley, "The Decline of Party in the U.S. House of Representa-

tives, 1887–1968," *Legislative Studies Quarterly*, August 1979, pp. 381–406; Glenn R. Parker, *Characteristics of Congress* (Englewood Cliffs, N.J.: Prentice-Hall, 1989), pp. 190–191; and John R. Cranford, "Party Unity Scores Slip in 1988, but Overall Pattern Is Upward," *Congressional Quarterly Weekly Report*, November 19, 1988, pp. 3334–3342.

42. Ronald D. Elving, "House Partisanship Scores Rise; Senate Goes Other Direction," *Congressional Quarterly Weekly Report*, December 30, 1989, pp. 3546–3550; and Cranford, "Party Unity Scores Slip in 1988," p. 3338.

43. Rhodes Cook, "Key to Survival for Democrats Lies in Split-Ticket Voting," *Congressional Quarterly Weekly Report*, July 8, 1989, p. 1710.

44. National poll by Richard B. Wirthlin, reported in John Kenneth White, *The New Politics of Old Values* (Hanover, N.H.: University Press of New England, 1988), p. 97.

45. Les AuCoin, Democratic representative from Oregon, quoted in Mary McGrory, "But the Doubts Won't Go Away," *Boston Globe*, June 22, 1983; and President Harry Truman, quoted in Robert Kuttner, *The Life of the Party* (Baltimore: Penguin Books, 1987), p. 5.

46. Sabato, *The Party's Just Begun*, p. 142.

47. Ibid.

48. Gerald M. Pomper, *Elections in America* (New York: Longman, 1980).

49. Benjamin Ginsburg, "Elections and Public Policy," *American Political Science Review*, March 1976, pp. 41–49.

50. Cornelius Cotter and his associates used the "death watch" description in *Party Organization in American Politics*, p. 168.

51. Arthur Schlesinger, Jr., quoted in Howard L. Reiter, *Parties and Elections in Corporate America* (New York: St. Martin's Press, 1987), p. 69.

52. Schattschneider, *Party Government*, p. 1.

53. Gary R. Orren, "The Changing Styles of American Party Politics," in Joel L. Fleishman, *The Future of American Political Parties* (Englewood Cliffs, N.J.: Prentice-Hall, 1982), p. 5.

54. Walter Dean Burnham, "The Turnout Problem," in *Elections American Style*, ed. A. James Reichley (Washington, D.C.: The Brookings Institution, 1987), pp. 131–132.

55. Robert W. Merry, "Status Quo May Really Be Calm Before Storm," *Congressional Quarterly Weekly Report*, November 12, 1988, p. 3239.

56. John F. Kennedy, quoted in Rhodes Cook, "Turnout Hits 64-Year Low in Presidential Race," *Congressional Quarterly Weekly Report*, January 21, 1989, p. 138.

57. Tommy Robinson, Republican congressman from Arkansas, quoted in John W. Mashek, "Bush Welcomes Defecting Democrat," *Boston Globe*, July 29, 1989, p. 3.

58. Sabato, "A World Without Parties," in *The Party's Just Begun*, pp. 20–24.

59. Robert Benchley, quoted in Reiter, *Parties and Elections in Corporate America*, p. 262.

60. Ibid., p. 302.

61. Bernard Sanders, "This Country Needs a Third Political Party," *New York Times*, January 3, 1989, p. A19.

62. Michigan Rep. Maxine Berman, quoted in E. J. Dionne, Jr., "Women's Caucus Is Focusing on Abortion Rights," *New York Times*, August 6, 1989, p. 18A.

Chapter 13

1. Quoted in Elizabeth Drew, "Charlie," *New Yorker*, January 9, 1978, p. 40.

2. Ibid., p. 45. The "problem," it turned out, was raised by George Shultz, former secretary of the treasury under President Ford and later secretary of state, but at the time president of Bechtel Corporation, a multinational construction and engineering firm.

3. Leon Epstein, *Political Parties in the American Mold* (Madison: University of Wisconsin Press, 1986), pp. 21–22.

4. Arthur C. Close, ed., *Washington Representatives 1989* (Washington, D.C.: Columbia Books, 1989), pp. 2–3.

5. Kay Lehman Schlozman, "What Accent the Heavenly Chorus? Political Equality and the American Pressure System," *Journal of Politics* 46 (1984):1011.

6. Alexis de Tocqueville, *Democracy in America*, vol. 1 (New York: Random House (Vintage Books), 1945), p. 198.

7. Mancur Olson, "The Political Economy of Comparative Growth Rates," in *The Political Economy of Growth*, ed. Dennis C. Miller (New Haven, Conn.: Yale University Press, 1983), chap. 1.

8. Jeffrey H. Birnbaum and Alan S. Murray, *Showdown at Gucci Gulch* (New York: Random House, 1987), app. B.

9. On the distrust of authority see Samuel P. Huntington, *American Politics: The Promise of Disharmony* (Cambridge, Mass.: Harvard University Press, 1981), chap. 2.

10. Gabriel Almond and Sidney Verba, *The Civic Culture* (Princeton, N.J.: Princeton University Press, 1963), p. 184n.

11. Ibid., table 4 (p. 191) and table 6 (p. 203).

12. Ibid., p. 195.

13. Tocqueville, *Democracy in America*, vol. 1, p. 201.

14. Robert Dahl, *Dilemmas of Pluralist Democracy* (New Haven, Conn.: Yale University Press, 1982).

15. Grant McConnell describes the cycles of scandal and outrage that have occurred throughout American history in *Private Power and American Democracy* (New York: Random House (Vintage Books), 1966), chap. 1.

16. Jervis Anderson, "An Extraordinary People," *New Yorker*, November 12, 1984.

17. *Washington Post National Weekly Edition*, September 26–October 2, 1988, p. 15.

18. Jamie Manlanowki, "Monkey-Wrenching Around," *Nation*, May 2, 1986, p. 568.

19. Wilmington, Delaware *News Journal*, September 2, 1989, p. 1.

20. Gregory A. Calderia and John R. Wright, "Organized Interests and Agenda Setting in the U.S. Supreme Court," *American Political Science Review* 82 (December 1988):1110–1111.

21. *New York Times*, July 1, 1985, p. 8B.

22. Quoted in Charles R. Babcock, "Get Elected to Congress and Win a Free Vacation!" *Washington Post National Weekly Edition*, February 10–12, 1989, p. 13.

23. Ibid.

24. Charles R. Babcock and Bob Woodward, "John Tower, Advocate," *Washington Post National Weekly Edition*, February 20–26, 1989, p. 31.

25. *New York Times*, July 14, 1983, p. 28.

26. Dan Clawson and Alan Neustadtl, "Interlocks, PACs, and Corporate Conservatism," *American Journal of Sociology* 4 (January 1989):767.

27. *New York Times*, October 20, 1986, p. 8B.

28. Lester M. Salamon, "Rethinking Public Management: Third-Party Government and the Changing Forms of Government Action," *Public Policy* 29 (Summer 1981):255–275.

29. Steve H. Hanke, "Privatization Versus Nationalization," *Proceedings of the Academy of Political Science* 36 (1987):2.

30. *National Journal*, July 7, 1985, pp. 1564–1567.

31. *Washington Post National Weekly Edition*, May 13, 1985, p. 7.

32. Salamon, "Rethinking Public Management," p. 259.

33. Ibid., p. 141.

34. Ibid., p. 146.

35. Clement E. Vose, *Caucasians Only* (Berkeley: University of California Press, 1959), pp. 250–252. Chapter 7 describes the legal struggle for civil rights in greater detail.

36. Wilmington, Delaware *News Journal*, October 30, 1983, p. 4.

37. *Washington Post National Weekly Edition*, October 28, 1985, p. 4.

38. Quoted in *New York Times*, April 24, 1983, p. 25.

39. *New York Times*, March 17, 1981, p. 11D.

40. Larry Sabato, *PAC Power: Inside the World of Political Action Committees*, rev. ed. (New York: Norton, 1985), pp. 122–159.

41. Representative Joe Bryant of Texas quoted in *Washington Post*, August 21, 1983, p. 16.

42. Quoted in Gary J. Anders, "Business Involvement in Campaign Finance," *PS*, Spring 1985, p. 213.

43. Schlozman, "What Accent the Heavenly Chorus?" p. 1029n.

44. *Washington Post National Weekly Edition*, March 26, 1984, p. 6.

45. Ibid.

46. Robert Michels, *Political Parties*, trans. Eden and Cedar Paul (New York: Free Press, 1949), p. 14.

47. Quoted in John Tierney, "Old Money, New Power," *New York Times Magazine*, October 23, 1988, p. 102. The iron-law-of-oligarchy problem is discussed in David Truman, *The Governmental Process* (New York: Knopf, 1962), pp. 139–155.

48. T. R. Reid, "Public Trust, Private Money," *Washington Post Magazine*, November 26, 1978, p. 17.

49. McConnell, *Private Power and American Democracy*, chap. 5.

50. John R. Wright, "PACs, Contributions, and Roll Calls," *American Political Science Review* 79 (June 1985): 403–404.

51. For a discussion of these problems, see Paul Starr, "The Limits of Privatization," *Prospects for Privatization: Proceedings of the Academy of Political Science* 36 (1987): 124–137.

52. Alan Ware, "United States: Disappearing Parties?" in *Political Parties*, ed. Alan Ware (Oxford: Basil Blackwell, 1987), pp. 117–136.

53. John Brademas, "Special Interests Overshadow Political Parties," Wilmington, *Delaware Sunday News Journal*, October 31, 1982, p. 4H.

54. A. Lee Fritschler, *Smoking and Politics*, 3rd ed. (Englewood Cliffs, N.J.: Prentice-Hall, 1983), chap. 1.

Chapter 14

1. Jeffrey H. Birnbaum and Alan S. Murray, *Showdown at Gucci Gulch* (New York: Random House, 1987), pp. 231–232.

2. J. W. Peltason, *Understanding the Constitution*, 11th ed. (New York: Holt, Rinehart and Winston, 1988), p. 36.

3. Unidentified House member, quoted in John Bibby, ed., *Congress Off the Record* (Washington, D.C.: American Enterprise Institute, 1983), p. 40.

4. James Madison, *Federalist 52*, in Alexander Hamilton, James Madison, and John Jay, *The Federalist* (1788; reprint, New York: Random House (Modern Library), n.d.), p. 343.

5. Representative Silvio Conte, Republican from Massachusetts, remarks, in *The United States Congress: Pro-*

ceedings of the Thomas P. O'Neill, Jr., Symposium, ed. Dennis Hale (Chestnut Hill, Mass.: Boston College, 1982), p. 87.

6. Richard F. Fenno, Jr., *Home Style: House Members in Their Districts* (Boston: Little, Brown, 1978), p. 241.

7. Unidentified representative, quoted in Bibby, *Congress Off the Record,* pp. 43–44.

8. "Congress: The First and the 100th," *New York Times,* January 5, 1987, p. A14.

9. Silvio Conte, Republican representative from Massachusetts, quoted in Elizabeth Wehr, "Congress Clears $576 Billion Spending Measure," *Congressional Quarterly Weekly Report,* October 18, 1986, p. 2584.

10. Fenno, *Home Style,* p. 246.

11. Philip Brenner, *The Limits and Possibilities of Congress* (New York: St. Martin's Press, 1983), p. 180.

12. Former Rep. John Brademas, remarks, in Hale, *The United States Congress,* p. 92.

13. David Vogler and Sidney Waldman, *Congress and Democracy* (Washington, D.C.: Congressional Quarterly Press, 1985).

14. Louis Fisher, quoted in Martin Tolchin, "The Legislative Veto, an Accommodation that Goes On and On," *New York Times,* March 32, 1989, p. 11.

15. Louis Fisher, *The Politics of Shared Power: Congress and the Executive* (Washington, D.C.: Congressional Quarterly Press, 1981), p. 79.

16. Martin Tolchin, "Between Constituencies at Capitol and at Home," *New York Times,* April 2, 1983, p. 6.

17. Woodrow Wilson, *Congressional Government* (1885; reprint ed., New York: Harcourt Brace Jovanovich, 1967), p. 195.

18. Joel Pritchard, Republican representative from Washington, statement in U.S. Congress, House, Administrative Reorganization and Legislative Management, Hearings Before the Commission on Administrative Review, 95th Congress, 1st Session, June 2, 1977, p. 62.

19. John Johannes, *To Serve the People: Congress and Constituency Service* (Lincoln: University of Nebraska Press, 1984), pp. 19–20 and 35.

20. Unidentified representative quoted in Charles L. Clapp, *The Congressman: His Work As He Sees It* (Garden City, New York: Doubleday, 1963), p. 375.

21. Benjamin Taylor, "New England's Three Freshmen Weigh Roles in New Congress," *Boston Globe,* December 11, 1982, p. 2.

22. Unidentified representative, quoted in Fenno, *Home Style,* p. 216.

23. Norman J. Ornstein, Thomas E. Mann, and Michael J. Malbin, *Vital Statistics on Congress, 1989–1990* (Washington, D.C.: Congressional Quarterly Press, 1990), p. 61.

24. Rhodes Cook, "Is Competition in Elections Becoming Obsolete?" *Congressional Quarterly Weekly Report,* May 6, 1989, p. 1060.

25. Linda L. Fowler and Robert D. McClure, *Political Ambition: Who Decides to Run for Congress* (New Haven, Conn.: Yale University Press, 1989), pp. 118–121.

26. May 1, 1989, Fact Sheet, Center for American Women and Politics, Eagleton Institute of Politics, Rutgers University.

27. Fowler and McClure, *Political Ambition,* p. 120.

28. Burdett Loomis, *The New American Politician* (New York: Basic Books, 1988), p. 137.

29. Based on FEC data cited in David Boren, "Capitol Hill or Capital Hill?" *New York Times,* May 29, 1989, p. 23.

30. Barbara Hinckley, *Congressional Elections* (Washington, D.C.: Congressional Quarterly Press, 1981), pp. 51 and 23.

31. Boren, "Capitol Hill or Capital Hill?"; and Alan I. Abramowitz, "Finance House Campaigns," *New York Times,* June 27, 1989, p. 23.

32. Gary C. Jacobson, "Congress: A Singular Continuity," in *The Elections of 1988,* ed. Michael Nelson (Washington, D.C.: Congressional Quarterly Press, 1989), p. 136.

33. Gary C. Jacobson, *Money in Congressional Elections* (New Haven, Conn.: Yale University Press, 1989), p. 49.

34. Thomas E. Mann and Raymond E. Wolfinger, "Candidates and Parties in Congressional Elections," *American Political Science Review,* September 1980, p. 620; Hinckley, *Congressional Elections,* p. 69; and Robert S. Erikson and Gerald C. Wright, "Voters, Candidates and Issues in Congressional Elections," in *Congress Reconsidered,* ed. Lawrence C. Dodd and Bruce I. Oppenheimer (Washington, D.C.: Congressional Quarterly Press, 1989), pp. 92–93.

35. Rhodes Cook, "Key to Survival for Democrats Lies in Split-Ticket Voting," *Congressional Quarterly Weekly Report,* July 8, 1989, p. 1710.

36. Hinckley, *Congressional Elections,* p. 109.

37. Glenn R. Parker, *Characteristics of Congress* (Englewood Cliffs, N.J.: Prentice-Hall, 1989), pp. 55–60.

38. For an interesting discussion of this and other aspects of "the myth of constituency control," see Robert A. Bernstein, *Elections, Representation, and Congressional Voting Behavior* (Englewood Cliffs, N.J.: Prentice-Hall, 1989).

39. Fenno, *Home Style,* pp. 1–30.

40. Richard Fenno, *The United States Senate: A Bicameral Perspective* (Washington, D.C.: American Enterprise Institute, 1982), p. 14.

41. Fenno, *Home Style,* p. 19.

42. Elizabeth Drew, *Politics and Money: The New Road to Corruption* (New York: Macmillan, 1983), p. 97.

43. Unnamed representative, quoted in David Rosenbaum, "For Congress, Money Is the Root of Evil and Reelection," *New York Times*, June 4, 1989, p. 1E.

44. Richard L. Berke, "Realtors' Political Arm Offers Lessons on Strength of PACs," *New York Times*, June 29, 1989, p. 1.

45. Abramowitz, "Finance House Campaigns," p. 23.

46. Larry Sabato, quoted in David S. Cloud, "Big Bucks and Victory Often Go Hand in Hand," *Congressional Quarterly Weekly Report*, November 12, 1988, p. 3271.

47. "How PAC Money Flows to Party Leaders," *New York Times*, June 29, 1989, p. 7B; and Larry Sabato, *PAC Power* (New York: Norton, 1985).

48. William Thompson, quoted in Berke, "Realtors' Political Arm," p. 6B.

49. Morris P. Fiorina, *Congress: Keystone of the Washington Establishment*, 2nd ed. (New Haven, Conn.: Yale University Press, 1989), p. 129.

50. Les AuCoin, Democratic representative from Oregon, quoted in Rosenbaum, "For Congress, Money Is the Root," p. 1E.

51. Representative Tony Coelho, quoted in Chuck Alston and Janet Hook, "An Election Lesson: Money Can Be Dangerous," *Congressional Quarterly Weekly Report*, November 19, 1988, p. 3366.

52. *Congressional Quarterly Weekly Report*, July 8, 1989, pp. 1678–1679, and August 12, 1989, p. 2112.

53. Patricia Schroeder, Democratic representative from Colorado, quoted in Robin Toner, "As Foley Steps in, the House Needs Serious Repairs," *New York Times*, June 11, 1989, p. 1E; poll results in *Congressional Quarterly Weekly Report*, July 15, 1989, p. 1810.

54. Robert Walker, Republican representative from Pennsylvania, quoted in Chuck Alston, "Once-Soft Ethics Committee Hardens Its Standards," *Congressional Quarterly Weekly Report*, May 27, 1989, p. 1233; and Otis Pike, former Democratic representative from New York, quoted in Robin Toner, "New Fallout over Ethics," *New York Times*, May 27, 1989, p. 9.

55. Norman J. Ornstein quoted in Rosenbaum, "For Congress, Money Is the Root," p. 1E.

56. Fiorina, *Congress: Keystone of the Washington Establishment*, p. 129.

57. Thomas Jefferson, "First Inaugural Address," in James D. Richardson, *A Compilation of the Messages and Papers of the Presidents*, vol. I (New York: Bureau of National Literature, 1897), p. 312; Wilson and Kennedy, quoted in Thomas E. Cronin, *The State of the Presidency* (Boston: Little, Brown, 1980), p. 75.

58. Vogler and Waldman, *Congress and Democracy*, p. 40.

59. Paul Light, *Artful Work* (New York: Random House, 1985); and Birnbaum and Murray, *Showdown at Gucci Gulch*.

60. George C. Edwards III, *At the Margins: Presidential Leadership of Congress* (New Haven, Conn.: Yale University Press, 1989), p. 7.

61. Ibid., p. 38.

62. Ibid., p. 124. See also George C. Edwards, *The Public Presidency* (New York: St. Martin's Press, 1983); Samuel Kernell, *Going Public* (Washington, D.C.: Congressional Quarterly Press, 1986); and Theodore J. Lowi, *The Personal President* (Ithaca, N.Y.: Cornell University Press, 1985).

63. Edwards, *At the Margins*, p. 105; Roger Davidson and Walter Oleszek, *Congress and Its Members*, 3rd ed. (Washington, D.C.: Congressional Quarterly Press, 1990), p. 244; Vogler and Waldman, *Congress and Democracy*, pp. 48–49.

64. Edwards, *At the Margins*, p. 187.

65. President Ronald Reagan, quoted in Martin F. Nolan, "Reagan's Luck Dazzles the Capital, but November Is Still Far Away," *Boston Globe*, February 1, 1984, p. 15.

66. Speaker Thomas P. O'Neill, quoted in Steven V. Roberts, "Democrats Want President to Move First on Budget Gap," *New York Times*, January 27, 1984, p. 1.

67. Randall B. Ripley, *Congress: Process and Policy*, 4th ed. (New York: Norton, 1988), pp. 366–368; also see Parker, *Characteristics of Congress*, pp. 45–64.

68. Representatives Ben Jones, Democrat from Georgia, and Dale Kildee, Democrat from Michigan, quoted in Janet Hook, "Rout of Democratic Leaders Reflects Fractured Party," *Congressional Quarterly Weekly Report*, September 30, 1989, pp. 2530–2531.

69. Unnamed Democratic congressman, ibid., p. 2531.

70. Ripley, *Congress: Process and Policy*, pp. 213–217.

71. Stanley Bach and Steven Smith, *Managing Uncertainly in the House of Representatives* (Washington, D.C.: Brookings Institution, 1988).

72. Representative Norman Mineta, quoted in Loomis, *The New American Politician*, p. 177.

73. Representative Bill Frenzel, quoted in Susan F. Rasky, "Congress Courts the Dangers of Living for the Moment," *New York Times*, October 1, 1989, p. 4E.

74. Lawrence C. Dodd and Richard L. Schott, *Congress and the Administrative State* (New York: Wiley, 1979), p. 124.

75. Lawrence Dodd and Bruce Oppenheimer, *Congress Reconsidered* (Washington, D.C.: Congressional Quarterly Press, 1989), pp. 443–449.

76. Davidson and Oleszek, *Congress and Its Members*, pp. 207–209.

77. Richard F. Fenno, Jr., *Congressmen in Committees* (Boston: Little, Brown, 1973).

78. For an interesting discussion of the effects of this on conference bargaining, see Lawrence D. Longley and

Walter J. Oleszek, *Bicameral Politics* (New Haven, Conn.: Yale University Press, 1989).

79. Donald R. Matthews, *U.S. Senators and Their World* (New York: Random House (Vintage Books), 1960), pp. 92–117; Norman J. Ornstein, Robert L. Peabody, and David W. Rohde, "Change in the Senate: Toward the 1990s," in Dodd and Oppenheimer, *Congress Reconsidered*, pp. 17–21; and Dodd and Oppenheimer, "Consolidating Power in the House," ibid., p. 42.

80. For an excellent analysis of the impact of activist new members, see Loomis, *The New American Politician*.

81. Harold D. Stanley and Richard G. Niemi, *Vital Statistics on American Politics*, 2nd ed. (Washington, D.C.: Congressional Quarterly Press, 1990), p. 242; Ornstein, Mann, and Malbin, *Vital Statistics on Congress 1989– 1990*, p. 125.

82. Democratic Senators Ernest Hollings from South Carolina and Herman Talmadge from Georgia, quoted in Harrison W. Fox, Jr., and Susan Webb Hammond, *Congressional Staffs: The Invisible Force in American Lawmaking* (New York: Free Press, 1977), pp. 4–5.

83. Ibid., p. 143.

84. Ornstein et al., *Vital Statistics on Congress 1989–90*, pp. 134–135.

85. Michael J. Malbin, *Unelected Representatives: Congressional Staff and the Future of Representative Government* (New York: Basic Books, 1980).

86. Ibid., p. 243.

87. The major studies of congressional voting on which this discussion is based are: Aage Clausen, *How Congressmen Decide* (New York: St. Martin's Press, 1973); John Kingdon, *Congressmen's Voting Decisions*, 2nd ed. (New York: Harper & Row, 1981); Jerrold Schneider, *Ideological Coalitions in Congress* (Westport, Conn.: Greenwood Press, 1979); and Barbara Sinclair, *Congressional Realignment, 1925–78* (Austin: University of Texas, 1982).

88. Ornstein et al., "Change in the Senate"; and Dodd and Oppenheimer, "Consolidating Power in the House," in Dodd and Oppenheimer, *Congress Reconsidered*, pp. 16–17 and 41-42.

89. Julie Rovner, "Conservative Coalition Is Still Dormant as Force on Floor," *Congressional Quarterly Weekly Report*, December 30, 1989, p. 3551.

90. Unidentified U.S. representative, quoted in Bibby, *Congress Off the Record*, pp. 22–23.

91. Donald R. Matthews and James A. Stimson, *Yeas and Nays: Normal Decision-Making in the U.S. House of Representatives* (New York: Wiley, 1975), p. 124.

92. Alexander Hamilton, "New York Ratifying Convention Remarks" (27 June, 1788), in *The Papers of Alexander Hamilton*, vol. V, ed. Harold C. Syrett (New York: Columbia University Press, 1962), p. 95.

93. James Madison, *Notes of Debates in the Federal Convention of 1787* (New York: Norton, 1969), p. 39.

94. Bernstein, *Elections, Representation, and Congressional Voting Behavior*, p. 104.

95. Amihai Glazer and Bernard Grofman, "Two Plus Two Plus Two Equals Six: Tenure in Office of Senators and Representatives, 1953–1983," *Legislative Studies Quarterly*, November 1987, pp. 555–564

96. Vogler and Waldman, *Congress and Democracy*.

97. William J. Keefe and Morris S. Ogul, *The American Legislative Process* (Englewood Cliffs, N.J.: Prentice-Hall, 1985), p. 380.

98. Birnbaum and Murray, *Showdown at Gucci Gulch*, pp. 240–288.

99. Parker, *Characteristics of Congress*, p. 212.

100. Johannes, *To Serve the People*, pp. 31 and 227.

101. Unidentified representatives, quoted in Alan Ehrenhalt, "Influence on the Hill: Having It and Using It," *Congressional Quarterly Weekly Report*, January 3, 1987, p. 3.

102. Howard Reiter, *Parties and Elections in Corporate America* (New York: St. Martin's Press, 1987), p. 209.

103. Mark Green, *Who Runs Congress?* (New York: Dell, 1984), pp. 159–160.

104. Thomas R. Dye, *Who's Running America?* 3rd ed. (Englewood Cliffs, N.J.: Prentice-Hall, 1983), p. 106.

Chapter 15

1. President Ronald Reagan, "Text of March 4 Televised Address," *Congressional Quarterly Weekly Report*, March 7, 1987, p. 440.

2. President John Kennedy, quoted in Arthur M. Schlesinger, Jr., *A Thousand Days: John F. Kennedy in the White House* (Boston: Houghton Mifflin, 1965), pp. 270–271; and in Thomas Powers, *The Man Who Kept the Secrets: Richard Helms and the CIA* (New York: Knopf, 1979), p. 115.

3. Jimmy Carter, quoted in Godfrey Hodgson, *All Things to All Men: The False Promise of the Modern American Presidency from Franklin Roosevelt to Ronald Reagan* (New York: Simon & Schuster, 1980), p. 25.

4. Theodore J. Lowi, *The Personal President* (Ithaca, N.Y.: Cornell University Press, 1985), p. 181.

5. For the various statements, Roosevelt: see Richard E. Neustadt, *Presidential Power*, 3rd ed. (New York: Wiley, 1980), p. 134; Kennedy: Theodore C. Sorensen, *Kennedy* (New York: Harper & Row, 1965), p. 346; Johnson: Hugh Sidey, *A Very Personal Presidency: Lyndon Johnson in the White House* (New York: Atheneum, 1968), p. 260; Truman: Harry S. Truman, letter to Mary Jane Truman, November 14, 1947, in *Off the Record: The Private Papers of Harry S. Truman*, ed. Robert H. Ferrell (New York: Harper & Row, 1980), p. 119

6. Michael Deaver, quoted in Maureen Dowd, "Bush's News Conference: A Revision in Strategy," *New York Times*, June 10, 1989, p. 11.

7. Patrick Buchanan, in ibid.

8. "Text of Presidential News Conference," June 8, 1989, *Congressional Quarterly Weekly Report*, June 10, 1989, p. 1429.

9. Lowi, *The Personal President*, p. 151.

10. Edward Rollins, quoted in Dowd, "Bush's News Conference," p. 11.

11. *In re Neagle*, 135 U.S. 1 (1890).

12. *Youngstown Sheet and Tube* v. *Sawyer*, 343 U.S. 579 (1952); and *U.S.* v. *Nixon*, 418 U.S. 683 (1974).

13. See, for example, Michael L. Mezey, *Congress, the President, and Public Policy* (Boulder, Colo.: Westview Press, 1989), pp. 35–36.

14. Harold W. Stanley and Richard G. Niemi, *Vital Statistics on American Politics*, 2nd ed. (Washington, D.C.: Congressional Quarterly Press, 1990), p. 253.

15. Thomas Jefferson, quoted in Gerald Gunther, *Constitutional Law*, 11th ed. (Mineola, N.Y.: Foundation Press, 1985), p. 418.

16. U.S. Department of State memo, in Larry Berman, *The New American Presidency* (Boston: Little, Brown, 1987), p. 92.

17. Chuck Alston, "Bush Tests His Pocket-Veto Power," *Congressional Quarterly Weekly Report*, December 2, 1989, p. 3285; and Robert Pear, "Pocket Veto Dispute: President Calls a Truce," *New York Times*, December 7, 1989, p. 28.

18. George C. Edwards III, *Presidential Influence in Congress* (San Francisco: Freeman, 1980), p. 22.

19. Mezey, *Congress, the President, and Public Policy*, p. 61.

20. John Marshall, quoted in Edward S. Corwin, *The President: Office and Powers* (New York: New York University Press, 1957), p. 177; and Corwin, p. 184.

21. *United States* v. *Curtiss-Wright Export Corp.*, 299 U.S. 304 (1936).

22. President Lyndon Johnson, quoted in Louis W. Koenig, *The Chief Executive* (New York: Harcourt Brace Jovanovich, 1986), p. 13.

23. John Locke, *The Second Treatise of Government* (Indianapolis: Bobbs-Merrill, 1952), p. 92.

24. Stephen J. Wayne, "Great Expectations: What People Want from Presidents," in *Rethinking the Presidency*, ed. Thomas E. Cronin (Boston: Little, Brown, 1982), pp. 185–199; and Bruce Buchanan, *The Citizen's Presidency* (Washington, D.C.: Congressional Quarterly Press, 1987), pp. 35–40.

25. Arthur M. Schlesinger, Jr., *The Imperial Presidency* (Boston: Houghton Mifflin, 1973); Lester M. Salamon, "Be-
yond the Presidential Illusion—Toward a Constitutional Presidency," in *The Illusion of Presidential Government*, ed. Hugh Heclo and Lester M. Salamon (Boulder, Colo.: Westview Press, 1981), pp. 289–290; and Alan Wolfe, "Presidential Power and the Crisis of Modernization," in Cronin, *Rethinking the Presidency*, p. 144.

26. Neustadt, *Presidental Power*, p. 10.

27. Polls rating presidents, including polls of scholars and the general public, from 1948 to 1982 can be found in Stanley and Niemi, *Vital Statistics on American Politics*, pp. 237–238.

28. Stephen Hess, *The Presidential Campaign* (Washington, D.C.: Brookings Institution, 1988), pp. 16–27

29. Marcia Lynn Whicker and Raymond A. Moore, *When Presidents Are Great* (Englewood Cliffs, N.J.: Prentice-Hall, 1988).

30. Lowi, *The Personal President*, p. 32.

31. Barry Schwartz, *George Washington: The Making of an American Symbol* (New York: Free Press, 1987), p. 38.

32. Edward Pessen, *The Log Cabin Myth* (New Haven, Conn.: Yale University Press, 1984), p. 69.

33. Paul Abramson, John Aldrich, and David Rohde, *Change and Continuity in the 1984 Elections* (Washington, D.C.: Congressional Quarterly Press, 1986), pp. 15–16.

34. Hess, *The Presidential Campaign*, p. 113.

35. *Congressional Quarterly Weekly Report*, November 7, 1987, p. 2732.

36. Quoted in Gary Orren, "The Nomination Process: Vicissitudes of Candidate Selection," in *The Elections of 1984*, ed. Michael Nelson (Washington, D.C.: Congressional Quarterly Press, 1985), p. 27.

37. Arthur Hadley, *The Invisible Primary* (Englewood Cliffs, N.J.: Prentice-Hall, 1976).

38. Rhodes Cook, "The Nominating Process," in Michael Nelson, *The Elections of 1988* (Washington, D.C.: Congressional Quarterly Press, 1989), p. 32; and Federal Election Commission, "Presidential Primary Spending at $200 Million Mark," August 18, 1988, press release.

39. Gerald Pomper, "The Presidential Nominations," in Gerald Pomper, *The Election of 1988* (Chatham, N.J.: Chatham House, 1989), p. 33.

40. William R. Keech, "Selecting and Electing Presidents: 1936–1980," in Cronin, *Rethinking the Presidency*, pp. 32–35.

41. George Mason, quoted in Max Farrand, *The Framing of the Constitution of the United States* (New Haven, Conn.: Yale University Press, 1972), p. 116.

42. Neustadt, *Presidential Power*, p. 133.

43. Whicker and Moore, *When Presidents Are Great*, p. 201.

44. Wilson Carey McWilliams, "The Meaning of the Election," in Pomper, *The Election of 1988*, p. 192.

45. Fred Kaplan, "Juror Likens North Case to 'Mission Impossible,'" *Boston Globe*, May 8, 1989, p. 8.

46. Marlin Fitzwater, quoted in John W. Mashek, "President Is a Telephone Operator," *Boston Globe*, April 22, 1989 p. 2; Gerald M. Boyd, "The Bush Style of Management," *New York Times*, March 19, 1989, p. 1.

47. Budget official Roger Jones, quoted in Salamon, "Beyond the Presidential Illusion," p. 288.

48. Bernard Weinraub, "Unlikely Alliance Atop Bush's Staff," *New York Times*, June 19, 1989, p. 14.

49. Thomas E. Cronin, *The State of the Presidency* (Boston: Little, Brown, 1980), pp. 276–286.

50. Nelson W. Polsby, *Consequences of Party Reform* (New York: Oxford University Press, 1983), pp. 95-105.

51. Jesse Jones, quoted in Elliot Richardson and James Pfiffner, "Our Cabinet System Is a Charade," *New York Times*, May 28, 1989, p. 15E.

52. Charles Dawes, quoted in Richardson and Pfiffner, "Our Cabinet System," p. 15E.

53. Bernard Weinraub, "White House," p. 14.

54. Ben W. Heineman, Jr., and Curtis A. Hesler, *Memorandum for the President* (New York: Random House, 1980), pp. 176–177.

55. George E. Reedy, *The Twilight of the Presidency* (New York: Harcourt Brace Jovanovich, 1970), p. 4.

56. Laurence I. Barrett, *Gambling with History* (Garden City, New York: Doubleday, 1983), p. 75.

57. Jack Valenti, quoted in Berman, *The New American Presidency*, p. 114.

58. Neustadt, *Presidential Power*, p. 201.

59. Richard Darman, quoted in Barrett, *Gambling with History*, p. 399.

60. Schlesinger, *The Imperial Presidency*, p. 474.

61. Thomas E. Cronin, "Rethinking the Vice Presidency," in Cronin, *Rethinking the Presidency*, p. 337.

62. Maureen Dowd, "Quayle in the Spotlight: A New Model for Number 2," *New York Times*, April 24, 1989, p. 14.

63. Edwards, *Presidential Influence in Congress*, pp. 86–100.

64. Abraham Lincoln, quoted in George C. Edwards III, *The Public Presidency* (New York: St. Martin's Press, 1983), p. 1.

65. Michael Oreskes, "Approval of Bush, Bolstered by Panama, Soars in Poll," *New York Times*, January 19, 1990, p. 20.

66. Edwards, *Presidential Influence in Congress*, pp. 86-100.

67. Samuel Kernell, *Going Public* (Washington, D.C.: Congressional Quarterly Press, 1986).

68. Whicker and Moore, *When Presidents Are Great*, p. 87.

69. John Mueller, *War, Presidents and Public Opinion* (New York: Wiley, 1973), p. 220.

70. Steven V. Roberts, "Reagan's Final Rating Best of Any President Since 40's," *New York Times*, January 18, 1989, p. 1.

71. Michael Oreskes, "Approval of Bush, Bolstered by Panama, Soars in Poll," *New York Times*, January 19, 1990, p. 20.

72. Lyndon Johnson, quoted in Jack Valenti, *A Very Human President* (New York: Norton, 1975), p. 144.

73. Fred Greenstein, quoted in Rhodes Cook, "Approval of Bush Is High, but Ratings Are Slippery," *Congressional Quarterly Weekly Report*, November 11, 1989, p. 3098. See also Fred Greenstein, *The Hidden-Hand Presidency: Eisenhower as Leader* (New York: Basic Books, 1982).

74. Unnamed Republican strategist, quoted in Walter Robinson, "Poll Shows Surge in Bush Ratings," *Boston Globe*, January 11, 1990, p. 3.

75. Barrett, *Gambling with History*, p. 442.

76. Lloyd Cutler, "The Evening News: A 'Galvanizing Force,'" *New York Times*, July 7, 1983, p. B6. See also Martin Linsky, *Impact: How the Press Affects Federal Policymaking* (New York: Norton, 1986).

77. Reedy, *The Twilight of the Presidency*, pp. 41–42.

78. Salamon, "Beyond the Presidential Illusion," p. 292.

79. Hendrick Smith, "The President as Coalition-Builder: Reagan's First Year," in Cronin, *Rethinking the Presidency*, p. 276.

80. Sorenson, *Kennedy*, p. 392.

81. Polsby, *Consequences of Party Reform*, p. 89.

82. Charles O. Jones, *The Trusteeship Presidency* (Baton Rouge: Louisiana State University Press, 1988), pp. 93–98.

83. Lester W. Seligman and Cary R. Covington, *The Coalitional Presidency* (Homewood, Ill.: Dorsey Press, 1989), p. 162.

84. Nelson, *The Elections of 1988*, p. 128.

85. Quoted in Robin Toner, "Congress Still Purring as Bush Applies the Right Strokes," *New York Times*, January 31, 1989, p. 20.

86. Irving Janis, *Victims of Groupthink* (Boston: Houghton Mifflin, 1972).

87. The discussion here relies primarily on chaps. 6 and 11 of Alexander L. George, *Presidential Decisionmaking in Foreign Policy: The Effective Use of Information and Advice* (Boulder, Colo.: Westview Press, 1980).

88. Paul Light, *Artful Work* (New York: Random House, 1985), p. 233.

89. Buchanan, *The Citizen's Presidency*.

90. Alexander Hamilton, *Federalist 70*, in Alexander Hamilton, John Jay, and James Madison, *The Federalist* (New York: Random House (Modern Library), n.d.), p. 455.

Chapter 16

1. Former Representative Elliott Levitas, quoted in Mary Russell, "Hill Increasingly Taking Veto Weapon into Its Own Hands," *Washington Post,* September 5, 1976, p. 10A.

2. Norman J. Ornstein, Thomas E. Mann, and Michael J. Malbins, *Vital Statistics on Congress 1989–1990* (Washington, D.C.: Congressional Quarterly Press, 1990), p. 160.

3. Marjorie Hunter and Warren Weaver, Jr., "Washington Talk: Briefing," *New York Times,* July 29, 1985, p. 10.

4. Harold Seidman and Robert Gilmour, *Politics, Position, and Power,* 4th ed. (New York: Oxford University Press, 1986), pp. 131–132; and Peter Benda and Charles H. Levine, "Reagan and the Bureaucracy," in *The Reagan Legacy,* ed. Charles O. Jones (Chatham, N.J.: Chatham House, 1988), p. 119.

5. Robert Rothman, "White House Outlines Year's Regulatory Program," *Congressional Quarterly Weekly Report,* August 10, 1985, pp. 1602–1603, and "Reagan's Regulatory Message to Congress," ibid., p. 1611.

6. Francis E. Rourke, *Bureaucracy, Politics and Public Policy,* 3rd ed. (Boston: Little, Brown, 1984), p. 16.

7. Ralph P. Hummel, *The Bureaucratic Experience* (New York: St. Martin's Press, 1977), p. vii.

8. John Kenneth White, *The New Politics of Old Values* (Hanover, N.H.: University Press of New England, 1988), p. 133.

9. David Nachmias and David Rosenbloom, *Bureaucratic Government USA* (New York: St. Martins Press, 1980), pp. 12–13.

10. Randall B. Ripley and Grace A. Franklin, *Bureaucracy and Policy Implementation* (Homewood, Ill.: Dorsey Press, 1982), pp. 29–40.

11. Herbert Kaufman, *Are Government Organizations Immortal?* (Washington, D.C.: Brookings Institution, 1976), p. 34.

12. Max Weber, "Bureaucracy," (1920) in *From Max Weber: Essays in Sociology,* ed. H. H. Gerth and C. Wright Mills (New York: Oxford University Press, 1958), p. 214.

13. President Franklin Roosevelt, Memorandum for the Director of the Bureau of the Budget, July 20, 1939, in Seidman and Gilmour, *Politics, Position, and Power,* p. 89.

14. Ibid., pp. 145–158.

15. The discussion of the structural characteristics of bureaucracies is based on Douglas Yates, *Bureaucratic Democracy* (Cambridge, Mass.: Harvard University Press, 1982), pp. 121–139.

16. Nathaniel Nash, "Government Intramurals Entangle the Rescue of the Savings Industry," *New York Times,* August 28, 1989, p. 1.

17. Quoted in Joseph A. Davis, "Grace Panel Blames Congress for Wasted Federal Spending," *Congressional Quarterly Weekly Report,* January 14, 1984, p. 47.

18. This account of the Grace Commission and subsequent studies is based on Davis, "Grace Panel Blames Congress," pp. 47–48; Robert Rothman, "Few Grace Commission Suggestions Adopted," *Congressional Quarterly Weekly Report,* November 24, 1984, p. 2990, and "Grace Commission Recommendations Reviewed," May 11, 1985, p. 911; and Bernard Rosen, "Civil Service Reform: Are the Constraints Impenetrable?" in *The Unfinished Agenda for Civil Service Reform: Implications of the Grace Commission Report,* ed. Charles H. Levine (Washington, D.C.: Brookings Institution, 1985), pp. 102–114.

19. The Grace Commission critique was by Public Citizen, as discussed in Robert D. Hershey, Jr., "Grace Study on Federal Spending Called Assault on Social Programs," *New York Times,* August 29, 1985, p. D23.

20. *New York Times,* January 4, 1990, p. 22.

21. Lipset and Schneider, *The Confidence Gap* (New York: Macmillan, 1983), pp. 348–349.

22. Eric Nordlinger, *On the Autonomy of the Democratic State* (Cambridge, Mass.: Harvard University Press, 1981), pp. 152–153.

23. Robert A. Dahl, *A Preface to Democratic Theory* (Chicago: University of Chicago Press, 1956), p. 145.

24. Lawrence C. Dodd and Richard L. Schott, *Congress and the Administrative State* (New York: Wiley, 1979), p. 27.

25. A good overview of the subgovernment phenomenon can be found in Randall B. Ripley and Grace A. Franklin, *Congress, the Bureaucracy, and Public Policy,* 4th ed. (Homewood, Ill.: Dorsey Press, 1987).

26. Nordlinger, *On the Autonomy of the Democratic State,* p. 152.

27. C. Wright Mills, *The Power Elite* (New York: Oxford University Press, 1956), p. 229. Mills argues that the United States lacks a genuine bureaucracy and that the "pseudo-bureaucracy" found in this system is actually controlled by political outsiders. See especially pp. 235–241.

28. Thomas R. Dye, *Who's Running America?*, 3rd ed. (Englewood Cliffs, N.J.: Prentice-Hall, 1983), p. 91.

29. Hummel, *The Bureaucratic Experience,* p. 219.

30. Morris P. Fiorina, *Congress: Keystone of the Washington Establishment,* 2nd ed. (New Haven, Conn.: Yale University Press, 1989), p. 47.

31. Patrick S. Korten, executive assistant director for policy and communication, U.S. Office of Personnel Management, quoted in Peter T. Kilborn, "Hail to the Senior

General Deputy Assistant Chief," *New York Times*, April 26, 1984, p. B10.

32. Anthony Downs, *Inside Bureaucracy* (Boston: Little, Brown, 1967), pp. 16–18.

33. William Niskanen, *Bureaucracy and Representative Government* (Chicago: Aldine-Atherton, 1971).

34. Rourke, *Bureaucracy, Politics and Public Policy*, p. 195.

35. Richard Nixon, quoted in Richard P. Nathan, *The Administrative Presidency* (New York: Wiley, 1983), p. 53.

36. Larry Berman, *The New American Presidency* (Boston: Little, Brown, 1987), p. 261.

37. James Madison, *Federalist 51*, in Alexander Hamilton, John Jay, and James Madison, *The Federalist* (New York: Random House, (Modern Library), n.d.), p. 337.

38. Rourke, *Bureaucracy, Politics and Public Policy*, p. 31.

39. Jerry L. Mashaw, *Bureaucratic Justice* (New Haven, Conn.: Yale University Press, 1983), pp. 18 and 60.

40. Robert A. Dahl, *Dilemmas of Pluralist Democracy* (New Haven, Conn.: Yale University Press, 1982), pp. 202–203.

41. Andrew Rosenthal, "The Man Who Got the Pentagon's Attention," *New York Times*, April 5, 1989, p. 22.

42. HUD Inspector General Paul Adams, quoted in Phil Kuntz and Joan Biskupic, "New Investigations Launched as HUD Scandal Widens," *Congressional Quarterly Weekly Report*, June 17, 1989, p. 1477; Former HUD Secretary Samuel Pierce, quoted in Phil Kuntz, "Former HUD Secretary Grilled on Influence-Peddling Scam," *Congressional Quarterly Weekly Report*, May 27, 1989, p. 1260.

43. Gary Bauer, deputy under secretary of education, quoted in Robert Pear, "Reading, Writing, Roping Liberals," *New York Times*, December 4, 1984, p. B8.

44. George Hager, "OMB Tampering of Testimony Hurts Bush's Credibility," *Congressional Quarterly Weekly Report*, May 13, 1989, p. 1112.

45. Stuart Eizenstat, quoted in Peter Kilborn, "Tight White House Control Marks Bush Economic Policy," *New York Times*, March 26, 1989, p. 22.

46. Michael Boskin, chairman of the Council of Economic Advisers, quoted in ibid.

47. Rourke, *Bureaucracy, Politics and Public Policy*, p.208. A brief comparative discussion of representative bureaucracy is B. Guy Peters, *The Politics of Bureaucracy* (New York: Longman, 1978), pp. 76–78.

48. These three dimensions and much of the following discussion are based on Samuel Krislov and David H. Rosenbloom, *Representative Bureaucracy and the American Political System* (New York: Praeger, 1981), pp. 22–26.

49. Ibid., p. 23.

50. Hugh Heclo, *A Government of Strangers: Executive Politics in Washington* (Washington, D.C.: Brookings Institution, 1977), p. 114.

51. Theodore J. Lowi, *The End of Liberalism*, 2nd ed. (New York: Norton, 1979), pp. 91 and 77.

52. Fiorina, *Congress: Keystone of the Washington Establishment*, pp. 122–123; and Roger Davidson and Walter Oleszek, *Congress and Its Members*, 3rd ed. (Washington, D.C.: Congressional Quarterly Press, 1990), p. 293.

53. Seidman and Gilmour, *Politics, Position, and Power*, p. 298.

54. Ibid., p. 296.

55. Mills, *The Power Elite*, p. 241. His comments on efficiency and political neutrality are on p. 236.

56. B. Guy Peters, "Administrative Change and the Grace Commission," in Levine, *The Unfinished Agenda for Civil Service Reform*, p. 39.

57. Mark Green and John Berry, *Challenge of Hidden Profits* (New York: William Morrow, 1985).

58. Rourke, *Bureaucracy, Politics and Public Policy*, pp. 189–215.

Chapter 17

1. J. Anthony Lukas, *Common Ground* (New York: Random House, 1985), p. 250.

2. Ibid., p. 606.

3. Ibid., p. 244.

4. Ibid., p. 317.

5. James Madison, *Federalist 51*, in Alexander Hamilton, John Jay, and James Madison, *The Federalist* (New York: Random House (Modern Library), n.d.), p. 337.

6. Republican party platform, 1988, *Congressional Quarterly Weekly Report*, August 20, 1988, p. 2379.

7. Democratic party platform, 1988, *Congressional Quarterly Weekly Report*, July 16, 1988, p. 1968.

8. George Bush, quoted in Robert A. Carp and Ronald Stidham, *Judicial Process in America* (Washington, D.C.: Congressional Quarterly Press, 1990), p. 239.

9. Harold W. Stanley and Richard G. Niemi, *Vital Statistics on American Politics*, 2nd ed. (Washington, D.C.: Congressional Quarterly Press, 1990), pp. 281 and 277.

10. Carp and Stidham, *Judicial Process in America*, pp. 12–13.

11. Lawrence M. Friedman, *American Law* (New York: Norton, 1984), p. 131.

12. Ibid., p. 132.

13. David M. O'Brien, "The Reagan Judges: His Most Enduring Legacy?" in *The Reagan Legacy*, ed. Charles O. Jones (Chatham, N.J.: Chatham House, 1988), pp. 96–97.

14. Neil A. Lewis, "Florida Court Rules Against Abortion Curbs," *New York Times*, October 6, 1989, p. 15.

15. Richard Morin, "Poll Finds High Court Has Low Recognition," *Boston Globe*, June 24, 1989, p. 6.

16. Henry J. Abraham, *The Judiciary*, 7th ed. (Dubuque, Iowa: Wm C. Brown, 1987), p. 66.

17. Lawrence Baum, *The Supreme Court*, 3rd ed. (Washington, D.C.: Congressional Quarterly Press, 1989), p. 179.

18. *Marbury* v. *Madison*, 5 U.S. 137 (1803).

19. Quoted in Sheldon Goldman, *Constitutional Law: Cases and Essays* (New York: Harper & Row, 1987), p. 25.

20. Baum, *The Supreme Court*, p. 178.

21. *Marbury* v. *Madison*.

22. *Federalist 22*, in Hamilton, Jay, and Madison, *The Federalist*, pp. 140–141.

23. *Marbury* v. *Madison*.

24. Max Farrand, *The Framing of the Constitution of the United States* (New Haven, Conn.: Yale University Press, 1972), p. 157.

25. Alexander Hamilton, *Federalist 78*, in Hamilton, Jay, and Madison, *The Federalist*, p. 505.

26. William W. Crosskey, *Politics and the Constitution in the History of the United States* (Chicago: University of Chicago Press, 1953). Gerald Gunther gives a short summary of this debate in *Constitutional Law*, 11th ed. (Mineola, N.Y.: Foundation Press, 1985), pp. 15–18, including Edward Corwin's conclusion: "The people who say the framers intended (judicial review) are talking nonsense, and the people who say they did not intend it are talking nonsense" (p. 18).

27. Charles A. Johnson and Bradley C. Canon, *Judicial Policies: Implementation and Impact* (Washington, D.C.: Congressional Quarterly Press, 1984), p. 251.

28. Stuart A. Scheingold, *The Politics of Law and Order* (New York: Longman, 1984), pp. 43–45. Scheingold discusses the variability and public suggestibility reflected in these public opinion polls on crime. The public's fear of crime and relative position of the crime issue on the political agendas of American cities is also discussed in Herbert Jacob, *The Frustrations of Policy: Responses to Crime by American Cities* (Boston: Little, Brown, 1984), pp. 3 and 18–24.

29. Crime Rates, 1960–1987, in Stanley and Niemi, *Vital Statistics*, p. 372.

30. *New York Times*, April 24, 1989, p. 12.

31. Lawrence Baum, *American Courts: Process and Policy*, 2nd ed. (Boston: Houghton Mifflin, 1990), p. 199.

32. Carp and Stidham, *Judicial Process in America*, p. 144.

33. Steven Phillips, *No Heroes, No Villains* (New York: Random House (Vintage Books), 1978), p. 99.

34. John Kaplan and Jerome H. Skolnick, *Criminal Justice: Introductory Cases and Materials*, 4th ed. (Mineola, N.Y.: Foundation Press, 1987), p. 454.

35. Phillips, *No Heroes, No Villains*, pp. 98–101; and Kaplan and Skolnick, *Criminal Justice*, pp. 444–491. The latter includes a San Francisco case that illustrates how a guilty plea is the rational choice of two men who, in fact, are not guilty of a crime. A guilty plea led to their release after one night in jail, whereas they would have been in jail 10 to 30 days awaiting a trial.

36. W. Boyd Littrell, *Bureaucratic Justice* (Beverly Hills, Calif.: Sage, 1979).

37. Stuart Nagel, Erika Fairchild, and Anthony Champagne, *The Political Science of Criminal Justice* (Springfield, Ill.: Thomas, 1983), p. 68; and Johnson and Canon, *Judicial Policies*, pp. 255–256.

38. Herbert Jacob, *The Frustrations of Policy: Responses to Crime by American Cities* (Boston: Little, Brown, 1984), pp. 1–5.

39. James Calvi and Susan Coleman, *American Law and Legal Systems* (Englewood Cliffs, N.J.: Prentice-Hall, 1989), p. 31.

40. Jethro K. Lieberman, *The Litigious Society* (New York: Basic Books, 1983), p. 4.

41. Stuart Taylor, Jr., "Justice System Stifled by Its Costs and Its Complexity, Experts Warn," *New York Times*, June 1, 1983, p. 1.

42. Joseph M. Harvey and Jean Caldwell, "Towns Liable If Police Let Drunks Drive—SJC," *Boston Globe*, August 16, 1984, p. 8.

43. Michael K. Brown, *Working the Street: Police Discretion and the Dilemmas of Reform* (New York: Russell Sage Foundation, 1981), p. 4.

44. William K. Muir, Jr., *Police: Streetcorner Politicians* (Chicago: University of Chicago Press, 1977), p. 271.

45. Samuel Walker, *Sense and Nonsense About Crime*, 2nd ed. (Monterey, Calif.: Brooks/Cole, 1989), p. 19; and Carp and Stidham, *Judicial Process in America*, p. 144.

46. Jerome K. Skolnick and David H. Bayley, *The New Blue Line* (New York: Macmillan, 1988), p. 85.

47. Ibid., pp. 4–5.

48. Howard Abadinsky, *Law and Justice* (Chicago: Nelson-Hall, 1988), p. 74; and Carp and Stidham, *Judicial Process in America*, p. 89.

49. Abraham S. Blumburg, *Criminal Justice: Issues and Ironies*, 2nd ed. (New York: New Viewpoints, 1979), p. 230.

50. Taylor, "Justice System Stifled," p. 1.

51. Ibid. A 1974 survey reported in Kaplan and Skolnick, *Criminal Justice*, p. 344, found that 65 percent of all defendants charged with felony offenses and 47 percent of all those charged with misdemeanors could not afford legal representation.

52. Taylor, "Justice System Stifled."

53. Herbert Jacob, *Justice in America*, 4th ed. (Boston: Little, Brown, 1984), pp. 12–13.

54. Scheingold, *The Politics of Law and Order*, p. 229.

55. Blumberg, *Criminal Justice: Issues and Ironies*, pp. 228 and 245.

56. Ibid., p. 222.

57. Richard Neely, *How Courts Govern America* (New Haven: Yale University Press, 1981), pp. 204–205.

58. Dennis DeConcini, Democratic senator from Arizona, in Committee on the Judiciary, U.S. Senate, *Hearings on the Nomination of Robert H. Bork to Be Associate Justice of the Supreme Court of the United States*, September 15, 1987, p. 52.

59. Justice Lewis Powell, quoted in Baum, *The Supreme Court*, p. 149.

60. David M. O'Brien, *Storm Center: The Supreme Court in American Politics*, 2nd ed. (New York: Norton, 1990), p. 252.

61. Henry J. Abraham, *Freedom and the Court*, 5th ed. (New York: Oxford University Press, 1988), p. 286.

62. Ibid., p. 150.

63. Neil Skene, "O'Connor Becoming the New Powell," *Congressional Quarterly Weekly Report*, September 30, 1989, p. 2598.

64. Baum, *The Supreme Court*, p. 158.

65. Henry J. Abraham, *Justices and Presidents: A Political History of Appointments to the Supreme Court*, 2nd ed. (New York: Oxford University Press, 1985), p. 341.

66. Baum, *The Supreme Court*, p. 142.

67. Carp and Stidham, *Judicial Process in America*, p. 270.

68. David M. O'Brien, "The Reagan Judges," pp. 96–97; Sheldon Goldman, "Reagan's Judicial Legacy: Completing the Puzzle and Summing Up," *Judicature*, April–May 1989, p. 329.

69. Professor A. E. Dick Howard, quoted in O'Brien, "The Reagan Judges," p. 83.

70. Goldman, "Reagan's Judicial Legacy," p. 330.

71. David Johnston, "Bush Appears Set to Follow Reagan by Putting Conservatives on Bench," *New York Times*, May 31, 1989, p. 5B.

72. Frank M. Coleman, *Politics, Policy, and the Constitution* (New York: St. Martin's Press, 1982), pp. 19–20.

73. John Hart Ely, *Democracy and Distrust* (Cambridge, Mass.: Harvard University Press, 1980), pp. 4–5.

74. Jesse H. Choper, *Judicial Review and the National Political Process* (Chicago: University of Chicago Press, 1980), p. 4.

75. Neely, *How Courts Govern America*, p. xi.

76. Johnson and Canon, *Judicial Policies*, pp. 230–234; and Baum, *The Supreme Court*, pp. 174–190.

77. *United States v. Carolene Products Co.*, 304 U.S. 144 (1938).

78. Jacob, *Justice in America*, p. 45.

79. *NAACP v. Button*, 371 U.S. 415 (1963).

80. *Firefighters Local Union No. 1784 v. Stotts*, 467 U.S. 561 (1984).

81. Baum, *The Supreme Court*, p. 221.

82. Jacob, *Justice in America*, p. 7.

83. Carp and Stidham, *Judicial Process in America*, pp. 359 and 208.

84. Scheingold, *The Politics of Law and Order*, pp. 164–169.

Chapter 18

1. *New York Times*, October 7, 1979, pp. 1 and 35.

2. Timothy B. Clark, "The Politics of Money Could Determine Volcker's Fate as Chairman of the Fed," *National Journal*, June 11, 1983, p. 1214.

3. Charles Stone and Isabel Sawhill, *Economic Policy in the Reagan Years* (Washington, D.C.: Urban Institute, 1984). Cited in Paul Peretz, "Economic Policy in the 1980s," in *The Politics of American Economic Policy*, ed. Paul Peretz (Armonk, N.Y.: M. E. Sharpe, 1987), p. 441.

4. Brenner's conclusions are cited in Robert Gordon, *Macroeconomics*, 2nd ed. (Boston: Little, Brown, 1981), pp. 323–324. For more details, see Joint Economic Committee, "Estimating the Effects of Economic Changes on National Health and Social Well-Being," 98th Congress, 2nd Session, June 15, 1984 (Washington, D.C.: Government Printing Office, 1984); M. Harvey Brenner, "Economic Change, Alcohol Consumption and Heart Disease Mortality in Nine Industrialized Countries," *Social Science and Medicine* 25 (1987):119–132; and Steven Platt, "Unemployment and Suicidal Behaviour," *Social Science and Medicine* 19 (1984):93–115.

5. U.S. Bureau of the Census, *Statistical Abstract of the United States: 1989* (Washington, D.C.: Government Printing Office, 1989), p. 303.

6. Allen Schick, "The Distributive Congress," in *Making Economic Policy in Congress*, ed. Allen Schick (Washington, D.C.: American Enterprise Institute, 1983), p. 264.

7. Allen Schick, *Congress and Money* (Washington, D.C.: Urban Institute Press, 1980), p. 24.

8. John W. Ellwood, "The Great Exception: The Congressional Budget Process in an Age of Decentralization," in *Congress Reconsidered*, 3rd ed., ed. Lawrence C. Dodd and Bruce I. Oppenheimer (Washington, D.C.: Congressional Quarterly Press, 1985), p. 320.

9. Council of Economic Advisors, *Economic Report of the President 1989* (Washington, D.C.: Government Printing Office, 1989), p. 373.

10. Stanley Collender, *The Guide to the Federal Budget Fiscal 1987* (Washington, D.C.: Urban Institute Press, 1986), p. 2.

11. Congressional Budget Office, *The Economic and Budget Outlook: Fiscal Years 1990–1994* (Washington, D.C.: Government Printing Office, 1989), p. 139.

12. Rudolph G. Penner and Alan J. Abramson, *Broken Purse Strings* (Washington, D.C.: Urban Institute Press, 1988), pp. 49–50.

13. Office of Management and Budget, *Economic Report of the President 1989* (Washington, D.C.: Government Printing Office, 1989), p. 338.

14. Alan S. Blinder, "The Policy Mix," *Economic Outlook USA*, First quarter 1986, pp. 3–4. Blinder also points out that once inflation is taken into account, the budgets in the early Reagan years were not as out of balance as they appeared and, therefore, government spending did not stimulate the economy.

15. Council of Economic Advisors, *Economic Report of the President 1989*, pp. 373–375.

16. James Tobin, "How to Think About the Deficit," *New York Review of Books*, September 25, 1986, p. 44.

17. The poverty level jumped to more than 15 percent in 1983 and remained above 13 percent throughout Reagan's two terms. Bureau of the Census, *Statistical Abstract of the United States: 1989*, p. 452.

18. *New York Times*, January 26, 1990, p. 16.

19. *New York Times*, January 27, 1990, p. 13.

20. Joseph A. Pechman, *Who Paid the Taxes, 1966–1985* (Washington, D.C.: Brookings Institution, 1985), p. 80.

21. Sheldon Danziger, "Tax Reform, Poverty, and Inequality," Institute for Research on Poverty, Madison, Wisconsin, Discussion Paper No. 129–87.

22. *New York Times*, January 21, 1990, p. 4E.

23. Lawrence Summers, "A Fair Tax Act That's Bad for Business," *Harvard Business Review*, March/April 1987, p. 57.

24. *New York Times*, September 25, 1989, p. 3D.

25. Office of Management and Budget, *Budget of the United States Government Fiscal Year 1991* (Washington, D.C.: Government Printing Office, 1990), p. 2.

26. Boyce Rensberger, "$1,000,000,000,000—We're Talking Real Money," *Washington Post National Weekly Edition*, January 19, 1987, p. 32.

27. *New York Times*, October 25, 1989, p. 31.

28. Robert Eisner, *How Real Is the Federal Deficit?* (New York: Free Press, 1986), chap. 3. Eisner notes that if businesses kept their books the way the federal government does, most would appear on the brink of bankruptcy since they would show no capital assets to counterbalance their debts. Also see Edward Nell, *Prosperity and Public Spending* (Boston: Unwin Hyman, 1988), pp. 50–55.

29. Eisner, *How Real Is the Federal Deficit?* p. 17.

30. Robert Eisner and Paul J. Pieper, "How to Make Sense of the Deficit," *The Public Interest*, 78 (Winter 1985):102.

31. Robert Heilbroner and Lester Thurow, *Economics Explained* (New York: Simon and Schuster, 1982), p. 96.

32. Charles L. Schultze, "Of Wolves, Termites, and Pussycats," *The Brookings Review* 7 (Summer 1989):29.

33. Benjamin M. Friedman, *Day of Reckoning* (New York: Random House, 1988), pp. 28–30.

34. Penner and Abramson, *Broken Purse Strings*, chap. 2.

35. *New York Times*, October 9, 1989, p. 11.

36. *New York Times*, December 19, 1987, p. 20.

37. William C. Melton, *Inside the Fed* (Homewood, Ill.: Dow-Jones Irwin, 1985), chap. 5.

38. See, for example, Kevin B. Grier, "On the Existence of a Political Monetary Cycle," *American Journal of Political Science* 33 (May 1989):376–389.

39. See, for example, Nathaniel Beck, "Elections and the Fed: Is There a Political Monetary Cycle?" *American Journal of Political Science* 31 (February 1987):193–216; and John T. Wooley, "The Federal Reserve and the Politics of Monetary Policy," in James P. Pfiffner ed., *The President and Economic Policy* (Philadelphia: Institute for the Study of Human Issues, 1986), pp. 240–263.

40. Quoted in Jonathan Rauch, "Sidestepping on a Ledge," *National Journal*, September 5, 1987, p. 2201. Also note that John T. Wooley doubts that the Fed's actions were motivated primarily by partisan political considerations. See his *The Federal Reserve and the Politics of Monetary Policy* (New York: Cambridge University Press, 1984).

41. Wooley, "The Federal Reserve and the Politics of Monetary Policy," p. 255.

42. Morris Fiorina, *Retrospective Voting in American National Elections* (New Haven, Conn.: Yale University Press, 1981). Also see Arthur H. Miller and Martin P. Wattenberg, "Throwing the Rascals Out: Policy and Performance Evaluations of Presidential Candidates, 1952–1980," *American Political Science Review* 78 (March 1984):359–372.

43. *Washington Post National Weekly Edition*, October 12, 1987, p. 31. Some statistical evidence also backs up the PBC argument. See Edward R. Tufte, *Political Control of the Economy* (Princeton, N.J.: Princeton University Press, 1978), p. 26; Gerald Kramer, "Short-Term Fluctuations in U.S. Voting Behavior, 1896–1964," *American Political Science Review* 65 (March 1971):131–143; and Robert S. Erikson, "Economic Conditions and the Presidential Vote," *American Political Science Review* 83 (June 1989):568–573.

44. Henry Chappell and William Keech, "A New View of Political Accountability for Economic Performance,"

American Political Science Review 79 (March 1985):10–27.

45. See, for example, Beck, "Elections and the Fed," p. 196; Thad A. Brown and Arthur A. Stein, "The Political Economy of National Elections," *Comparative Politics*, July 1982, pp. 479–497; Paul Peretz, "Economic Policy in the 1980s," in *The Politics of American Economic Policy Making*, ed. by Paul Peretz (Armonk, N.Y.: M. E. Sharpe, 1987), p. 450; and Douglas H. Hibbs, *The American Political Economy* (Cambridge, Mass.: Harvard University Press, 1987), pp. 277–278.

Chapter 19

1. Richard A. Knox, "Catastrophic Care Bill's Repeal Clouds Future of Social Programs," *Boston Globe*, October 8, 1989, p. 20.

2. D. Lee Bawden and John L. Palmer, "Social Policy," in *The Reagan Record*, ed. John L. Palmer and Isabel V. Sawhill (Cambridge, Mass.: Ballinger, 1984), p. 188; and David Stockman, *The Triumph of Politics* (New York: Avon Books, 1986), p. 9.

3. Hugh Heclo, *The Welfare State in Hard Times* (Washington, D.C.: American Political Science Association, 1985), pp. 4–6.

4. Quoted in Joseph Berger, "Bishops Reiterate Concern for Poor but Add Emphasis on Middle Class," *New York Times*, October 7, 1985, p. 24.

5. Office of Management and Budget, *The United States Budget in Brief, 1990* (Washington, D.C.: Government Printing Office, 1989), p. 79; and Paul Light, *Artful Work: The Politics of Social Security Reform* (New York: Random House, 1985), pp. ix and 34. Much of the discussion of Social Security in this section is drawn from Light's book.

6. Ibid., p. 33. The political appeal of the Social Security program is discussed in Martha Derthhick, *Policymaking for Social Security* (Washington, D.C.: Brookings Institution, 1979).

7. Thomas Oliphant, "After 50 Years, Social Security Prevailing," *Boston Globe*, August 14, 1985, p. 3.

8. Kirk O'Donnell (counsel to Speaker Thomas P. O'Neill), quoted in ibid.

9. Light, *Artful Work*, p. 3.

10. Ronald D. Elving, "Moynihan Seeks to Roll Back Social Security Tax Rate," *Congressional Quarterly Weekly Report*, January 6, 1990, pp. 32–33.

11. Janet Hook, "Medicare: The Promise and the Reality," *Congressional Quarterly Weekly Report*, March 30, 1985, p. 578; and U.S. House of Representatives, Committee on Ways and Means, *Background Material and Data on Programs Within the Jurisdiction of the Committee on Ways and Means* (Washington, D.C.: Government Printing Office, 1989), pp. 1127–1153.

12. Ibid., pp. 844–846; and Julie Johnson, "Congress Shows Signs of Spending to Fight Infant Deaths," *New York Times*, May 21, 1989, p. 4E.

13. Julie Rovner, "The Catastrophic-Costs Law: A Massive Miscalculation," *Congressional Quarterly Weekly Report*, October 14, 1989, p. 2715; and Martin Tolchin, "A Plan to Protect the Elderly Against Catastrophe Has Backfired on Stunned Lawmakers," *New York Times*, August 30, 1989, p. 18.

14. Phoebe H. Cottingham and David T. Ellwood, eds., *Welfare Policy for the 1990s* (Cambridge, Mass.: Harvard University Press, 1989), pp. 44-47.

15. Nicki Wiesensee, "In Congress This Week, a Health Fund Is Threatened," *Boston Globe*, October 2, 1989, p. 3; and Martin Tolchin, "How the New Medicare Law Fell on Hard Times," *New York Times*, October 9, 1989, p. 10.

16. Brian Donnelly, quoted in Wiesensee, "In Congress This Week."

17. Theodore Lowi, *The End of Liberalism*, 2nd ed. (New York: Norton, 1979), pp. 229–230.

18. James E. Anderson, David W. Brady, and Charles Bullock III, *Public Policy and Politics in America* (North Scituate, Mass.: Duxbury Press, 1978), p. 145.

19. Committee on Ways and Means, *Background Material*, pp. 1120–1125.

20. Cottingham and Ellwood, *Welfare Policy for the 1990s*, p. 13.

21. Anderson, Brady, and Bullock, *Public Policy and Politics in America*, p. 111. For a discussion of the "welfare explosion," see James T. Patterson, *America's Struggle Against Poverty* (Cambridge, Mass.: Harvard University Press, 1981), p. 171.

22. Committee on Ways and Means, *Background Material*, p. 560.

23. Cottingham and Ellwood, *Welfare Policy for the 1990s*, p. 13.

24. *Boston Globe*, May 1, 1989, p. 3.

25. Cottingham and Ellwood, *Welfare Policy for the 1990s*, p. 5.

26. Ibid., p. 271.

27. Julie Rovner, "Congress Clears Overhaul of Welfare System," *Congressional Quarterly Weekly Report*, October 1, 1988, p. 2699.

28. Senator Moynihan, quoted in Cottingham and Ellwood, *Welfare Policy for the 1990s*, p. 146.

29. Committee on Ways and Means, *Background Material*, p. 829.

30. John E. Schwartz, *America's Hidden Success* (New York: Norton, 1983), pp. 32–33.

31. Charles Murray, *Losing Ground* (New York: Basic Books, 1984), p. 58.

32. Felicity Barringer, "Number of Nation's Poor Remains at 32 Million for a Second Year," *New York Times*, October 19, 1989, p. 24.

33. Robert Pear, "U.S. Poverty Rate Dropped by 1.4% in 1984, Bureau Says," *New York Times*, August 28, 1985, p. 1.

34. Barringer, "Number of Nation's Poor," p. 24; and Committee on Ways and Means, *Background Material*, p. 944.

35. Ibid.

36. Martin Tolchin, "Study Shows Growing Gap Between Rich and Poor," *New York Times*, March 23, 1989, p. 1.

37. Hugh Heclo, *The Welfare State in Hard Times* (Washington, D.C.: American Political Science Association, 1985), pp. 13–14.

38. Gary Burtless, "Public Spending for the Poor: Trends, Prospects, and Economic Limits," in *Fighting Poverty: What Works and What Doesn't*, ed. Sheldon H. Danziger and Daniel H. Weinberg (Cambridge, Mass.: Harvard University Press, 1986), p. 27.

39. "A Stunning Win, or Loss, for the Poor," *New York Times*, December 12, 1985, p. A30.

40. Anderson, Brady, and Bullock, *Public Policy and Politics in America*, pp. 403–405.

41. Michael B. Katz, *In the Shadow of the Poorhouse: A Social History of Welfare in America* (New York: Basic Books, 1986), p. 278.

42. Paul E. Peterson and Mark Rom, "Lower Taxes, More Spending, and Budget Deficits," in *The Reagan Legacy*, ed. Charles O. Jones (Chatham, N.J.: Chatham House, 1988), p. 233.

43. Former HEW Secretary Joseph Califano, quoted in Tom Joe and Cheryl Rogers, *By the Few for the Few: The Reagan Welfare Legacy* (Lexington, Mass.: Heath, 1985), p. xiii.

44. Representative George Miller, quoted in Julie Rovner, "Fast Track, Slow Crawl: A Tale of Two Bills," *Congressional Quarterly Weekly Report*, June 27, 1987, p. 1414.

45. Light, *Artful Work*, p. ix.

46. Richard M. Coughlin, *Ideology, Public Opinion and Welfare Policy* (Berkeley: Institute of International Studies, University of California, 1980), p. 15.

47. Patterson, *America's Struggle Against Poverty*, p. 171.

48. "Public Opinion and Government Spending," *National Journal*, April 29, 1989, p. 1076; and "Support for Government Spending on Various Programs, Selected Years, 1973–1988," National Opinion Research Center, *General Social Surveys, 1972-1988*.

49. Hugh Heclo, "The Political Foundations of Antipoverty Policy," in Danziger and Weinberg, *Fighting Poverty*, pp. 327-332.

50. Ibid., p. 331.

51. Vincent Blasi, ed., *The Burger Court* (New Haven, Conn.: Yale University Press, 1983), pp. 46–61.

52. Heclo, *The Welfare State in Hard Times*, pp. 23–24.

53. This discussion draws on material in Allan J. Cigler and Burdett A. Loomis, eds., *Interest Group Politics* (Washington, D.C.: Congressional Quarterly Press, 1983), p. 13; and Light, *Artful Work*, pp. 75–79.

54. Theodore J. Lowi, *The End of Liberalism* (New York: Norton, 1979), p. 51.

55. Ibid., p. 200.

56. See, for example, the essays in Peter Flora and Arnold J. Heidenheimer, eds., *The Development of Welfare States in Europe and America* (New Brunswick, N.J.: Transaction Books, 1981).

57. James O'Connor, *The Fiscal Crisis of the State* (New York: St. Martin's Press, 1973), p. 7.

58. Frances Fox Piven and Richard A. Cloward, *Regulating the Poor: The Functions of Public Welfare* (New York: Pantheon Books, 1971), and *The New Class War: Reagan's Attack on the Welfare State and Its Consequences* (New York: Pantheon Books, 1982).

59. Charles Murray, *Losing Ground*. As Murray himself observes, "it is interesting how many of Piven's and Cloward's points, made in support of a left-radical critique of social policy, coincide with those in critiques from the other end of the political spectrum" (p. 296n).

60. Ibid., p. 42.

61. Heclo, *The Welfare State in Hard Times*, p. 27.

Chapter 20

1. *New York Times*, February 1, 1990, p. 22D.

2. *New York Times*, December 3, 1989, p. 1E.

3. C. Wright Mills, *The Power Elite* (New York: Oxford University Press, 1959), p. 20.

4. John Lewis Gaddis, *The Long Peace* (New York: Oxford University Press, 1987), chap. 2.

5. James A. Nathan and James K. Oliver, *United States Foreign Policy and World Order*, 4th ed. (Glenview, Ill.: Scott, Foresman, 1989), chaps. 3–7.

6. Quoted in Walter LaFeber, *America, Russia, and the Cold War*, 5th ed. (New York: Knopf, 1985), p. 82.

7. Quoted in ibid., p. 162.

8. "A Report to the President (NSC 68)," reprinted in *Foreign Relations of the United States, 1950*, vol. 1 (Washington, D.C.: Government Printing Office, 1977), pp. 238–285.

9. McGeorge Bundy, *Danger and Survival* (New York: Random House, 1988), p. 229.

10. Richard Smoke, *National Security and the Nuclear Dilemma* (Reading, Mass.: Addison-Wesley, 1984), p. 131.

11. Quoted in Townsend Hoopes, *The Devil and John Foster Dulles* (Boston: Little, Brown, 1973), p. 126.

12. The issue is forcefully raised by Jonathan Schell in *The Fate of the Earth* (Boston: Houghton Mifflin, 1982).

13. Deputy Assistant Secretary of Defense Alain C. Enthoven, quoted in Wesley Posvar et al., eds., *American Defense Policy* (Baltimore: Johns Hopkins University Press, 1965), p. 314. Italics added.

14. Bundy, *Danger and Survival*, p. 544.

15. John Lewis Gaddis, *Strategies of Containment* (New York: Oxford University Press, 1982), p. 289.

16. Ibid., chaps. 9–10.

17. *New York Times*, January 28, 1987, p. 16.

18. Ibid., March 9, 1983, p. 18.

19. Ibid., February 24, 1986, p. 20.

20. Office of Management and Budget, *Budget of the United States Government Fiscal Year 1991* (Washington, D.C.: Government Printing Office, 1990), pp. A293–294.

21. Secretary of Defense Caspar Weinberger explained the mission of these forces: "To deter aggression . . . against the United States and its allies, friends, and vital interests"; and "Should deterrence fail, to seek the earliest termination of conflict on terms favorable to the United States. . . ." *Report of the Secretary of Defense Caspar W. Weinberger to the Congress*, February 4, 1985 (Washington, D.C.: Government Printing Office, 1985), p. 25.

22. Lloyd Grove, "Elliot Abrams: The Contras' Patron," *Washington Post National Weekly Edition*, February 2, 1987, p. 6.

23. *New York Times*, January 20, 1987, p. 10.

24. *Arms Control Today* 18, Supplement (January/February 1988):1–16.

25. *New York Times*, March 8, 1990, p. 24.

26. Many of these feats are retold in Thomas Powers, *The Man Who Kept the Secrets* (Boston: Houghton Mifflin, 1979); Penny Lernoux, *Cry of the People* (Baltimore: Penguin Books, 1983), chap. 8; and Loch Johnson, *America's Secret Power* (New York: Oxford University Press, 1989).

27. Quoted in Godfrey Hodgson, *All Things to All Men* (New York: Simon & Schuster, 1980), p. 92.

28. Strobe Talbott, *Endgame: The Inside Story of SALT II* (New York: Harper & Row, 1979), p. 34.

29. Charles W. Kegley, Jr., and Eugene R. Wittkopf, *American Foreign Policy*, 2nd ed. (New York: St. Martin's Press, 1982), p. 394.

30. Robert J. Art, "Congress and the Defense Budget," *Political Science Quarterly* 100 (Summer 1985):227–248.

31. Ibid., pp. 227–228.

32. Ibid., p. 235.

33. Jacques S. Gansler, *Affording Defense* (Cambridge, Mass.: MIT Press, 1989), pp. 107–121.

34. James L. Sundquist, *The Decline and Resurgence of Congress* (Washington, D.C.: Brookings Institution, 1981), chap. 10.

35. John H. Aldrich, John L. Sullivan, and Eugene Borgida, "Foreign Affairs and Issue Voting," *American Political Science Review* 83 (March 1989):123–125.

36. Richard Barnet, "The Search for National Security," *New Yorker*, April 27, 1981, p. 96.

37. Jerry W. Sanders, *Peddlers of Crisis* (Boston: South End Press, 1983), p. 9.

38. Barnet, "The Search for National Security," pp. 102–103. Barnet is citing information in Sanders, *Peddlers of Crisis*, which is a fascinating if biased account of the Committee on the Present Danger.

39. Barnet, "The Search for National Security," p. 94.

40. Thomas R. Dye, *Who's Running America*, 4th ed. (Englewood Cliffs, N.J.: Prentice-Hall, 1986), p. 149.

Glossary

Note: Numbers in parentheses following the definition give the principal chapters in which the term is used.

Accountability the principle that public officials are answerable or responsible to citizens, who are the ultimate source of power. (1)

Activist press media sources used by politically active and influential individuals. (See also *popular press*.) (9)

Actual power the ability to compel persons to do something they would not otherwise do of their own free will. (See also *potential power*.) (1)

Administrative oversight the process by which Congress seeks to assure that laws are being implemented as Congress intended; a function of Congress that is carried out through investigative hearings, legislative vetoes, and control over agencies' appropriations. (14)

Adversary proceedings a system for achieving justice in which the opposing sides directly confront one another, with each side arguing its own case and refuting the arguments and evidence of the other side. (17)

AFDC Aid to Families with Dependent Children. A social policy established in the Social Security Act of 1935 that provides assistance to needy families with children under the age of 18. (19)

Affirmative action programs that seek to remedy the effects of past discrimination and to prevent it in the future by obtaining a broad representation of all groups and racial and cultural diversity in employment and education. (7)

Agents of socialization institutions such as the family, school, community, peers, and mass media that transmit social, economic, and political values, beliefs, and skills. (See also *socialization*.) (8)

American exceptionalism the concept that despite the existence of actual social classes in the United States, there is relatively little class conflict and no widespread acceptance of socialism in the United States. (3)

Amicus curiae brief a statement and supporting documentation submitted to a court by "a friend of the court," that is, someone not directly involved in the litigation, with the intention of influencing the decision. (13)

Appointing power the president's power to appoint, with the Senate's consent, important officials of the executive branch, judges, and ambassadors; one of the core powers of the presidency. (15)

Appropriation legislation that actually allocates money to a previously authorized program. (See also *authorization*.) (18)

Attitude a predisposition or tendency to favor or disfavor an object, such as a person or policy. (See also *attitude object*.) (8)

Attitude object the subject of a person's attitude or opinion. (8)

Australian ballot a ballot printed at public expense that lists the names of all candidates for office and is cast in secret. (10)

Authorization legislation that establishes a program, identifies its goals, and determines its spending limits but does not actually allocate any money. (See also *appropriation*.) (19)

Balance of trade the value of a country's exports minus the value of imports. (2, 18)

Belief that which a person thinks is true about someone or something. (See also *attitude*.) (8)

Benevolent leader the tendency of many children to see political authorities such as presidents, mayors, and police officers as kind, all-powerful, and caring people. (8)

Bill of Rights the first ten amendments to the Constitution, which establish fundamental civil liberties. (4)

Bipartisan coalition a group of policymakers from both major parties that works together to propose or enact a government policy or series of policies. (12)

Black Code a collection of laws adopted in southern states after the Civil War that restricted the living and working conditions of freed blacks nearly as severely as slave codes had before the Civil War. (7)

Block grants programs that provide federal assistance in a general area such as health or education and leave it to the recipient states or local governments to decide how the funds will be used within the general area. (See also *categorical grants*.) (5)

Budget resolution legislation (not requiring the president's signature) that spells out Congress's economic goals, sets revenues and spending limits, and instructs various committees to adjust programs within their jurisdictions to the resolution's targets. (18)

Bureaucracy a formal organization in which specialists organized in a hierarchy carry out policies by using standardized procedures. (16)

Bureaucratic justice an administrative process by which the criminal justice system seeks to achieve the goals of justice and efficiency; it is a process based on a presumption of guilt and a commitment to fairness. (17)

Cabinet the group of advisers and department heads selected by the president to assist in making decisions and running the government. (15)

Calendars a list of bills in the Senate and House of Representatives that shows, in chronological order, the names of all bills and resolutions introduced that session and awaiting consideration in committee or on the chamber floor. (14)

Campaign hoopla the relatively trivial aspects of election campaigns, such as the size of crowds, candidates' mistakes, their standings in the polls, and who has endorsed them. (9)

Categorical grants assistance programs that provide federal funds for specific purposes and restrict use of the funds to a particular program or specific function of government such as vocational rehabilitation or wastewater treatment. (See also *block grants*.) (5)

Caucus a closed meeting of party leaders or rank-and-file members to select candidates. Once the chief method for nominating candidates during the first party system (1790–1824), they are used today mostly to select delegates to state and local party conventions. (12)

Checks and balances a fundamental principle of the Constitution, which provides that the separate branches and levels of government can offset the powers of other branches or levels of government. Instruments of checks and balances include the presidential veto and congressional override powers, the presidential appointment of judges with Senate approval, the Supreme Court's judicial review powers, and the role of the states in amending the Constitution. (4)

Civic virtue the idea that a nation can be free only if its leaders exhibit statemanship, honesty, personal sacrifice, wisdom, prudence, and commitment to the common good. (3)

Civil cases court cases in which one party sues another to recover damages or to change another's behavior. (See also *criminal cases*.) (17)

Civil liberties guarantees against arbitrary government interference with people, opinions, and property that are usually spelled out in a constitution or a bill of rights. Civil liberties protect individual freedom by saying what the government cannot do. (See also *civil rights*.) (1, 6)

Civil rights guarantees that protect individuals and groups from arbitrary treatment by the government and by private groups in the society. Civil rights may require government action to provide equal protection in politics and in the broader society. (See also *civil liberties*.) (6, 7)

Class consciousness the feelings of solidarity with one's own social or economic peers and the belief that one's class interests are incompatible with those of other classes. (3)

Classical liberalism a philosophy that emphasizes personal freedoms, political equality, the dignity of the individual, private property rights, limited government, and faith in human progress. (3)

Cohorts members of a particular age group; people born in the same time period. (2)

Collectivism a belief that the rights and welfare of the group constitute the chief value of society and that government programs are necessary to correct economic and political decisions that benefit some citizens at the expense of others. (19)

Command posts directorships of political, corporate, financial, social, civic, educational, and cultural institutions that give their holders potential power. (1)

Community-oriented policing a contemporary form of police professionalism found in many American cities, in which police officers form a partnership with the community in preventing crime. (17)

Comparable worth a doctrine of economic equality advanced by feminists that says a person's salary should be based on his or her job's value to society rather than whether the person in that job is usually a man or a woman. (7)

Congressional norms the customs or informal guidelines of behavior in the House or Senate that members need to follow in order to get ahead and that help the institution perform its functions in the American political system. (14)

Constituent service intervention by legislators and their staffs to help constituents having problems because of government action or inaction; also known as casework. (14)

Containment the policy of using diplomatic, economic, and military means to prevent the expansion of Soviet power and influence. (1, 20)

Contingent influence the theory that the effect of public opinion on public policy depends on certain conditions, such as how much people know or care about an issue. (See also *direct influence*, *symbolic influence*, and *top-down influence*.) (8)

Convention a meeting of party delegates at the local, state, or national level, which endorses a platform of party issue positions and, in some cases, nominates candidates for political office. (12)

Cooperative federalism a modern form of federalism under which the different levels of government share resources and program administration. (5)

Criminal cases court cases in which the government charges someone with violating a law. (See also *civil cases*). (17)

Cue network those legislative colleagues that senators and representatives regularly look to for information and advice on how to vote. (14)

Delegate a role in which a legislator or other elected official represents the majority constituency opinion even if he or she disagrees with that opinion. (See also *trustee*.) (14)

Demobilization a general decline in voting turnout in presidential and congressional elections, as seen in the United States since the early 1900s. (10)

Democratic party one of the two major political parties in American politics today and the first mass-based party organization in the United States. (12)

Détente a period in the 1970s when the United States and the Soviet Union attempted to find areas of common agreement in order to reduce tensions and the chances of armed conflict. (20)

Direct (participatory) democracy a system of government in which the citizens themselves, rather than elected representatives, make decisions. (See also *representative democracy*.) (1)

Direct influence the theory that public opinion does or should have a direct impact on the making of public policy. (See also *contingent influence, symbolic influence,* and *top-down influence*.) (8)

Direct primary an election in which the voters themselves, rather than party bosses, select the candidates to run on the party label in the general election. (12)

Discretion the freedom or authority to choose among different courses of action or inaction, as exercised by officials in a public bureaucracy in administering laws and implementing policies passed by Congress. (16)

Disjointed incrementalism the practice of increasing spending on existing programs each year without following any comprehensive budget plan. (18)

Distributive policy a policy that provides benefits to one group but not at the expense of others. (18)

Domino analogy President Dwight Eisenhower's belief that a Communist takeover in one nation would lead to the fall of a neighboring country, so that countries would consecutively come under Communist domination. (20)

Dual court system the structure of the court system in the United States, which is characterized by a parallel system of state and federal courts that converge at the highest level of the U.S. Supreme Court. (17)

Dual federalism a state-centered view of federalism, under which the state and national governments had distinct spheres of governing and each level was supreme in its own sphere; the prevailing view on the Supreme Court from 1835 to about 1935. (5)

Efficiency a standard of evaluating government bureaucracies that measures the ability of departments and agencies to produce a desired effect with the minimum amount of effort, cost, or waste. (16)

Elastic clause the clause at the end of Article I, Section 8 of the Constitution, which gives Congress the power to make all laws "necessary and proper" for carrying out its specific powers listed earlier and all other powers vested by the Constitution in the national government. It is known as the elastic clause because it has been used to stretch the powers of the national government. (5)

Electoral coalition an interdependent set of groups that support a particular candidate or party in a nominating process or in a general election. (See also *governing coalition*.) (15)

Electoral college the institution established by the Constitution for selecting a president and vice-president. It consists of electors from each state who meet after the general election and cast ballots for president and vice-president. Each state has as many electors as it has representatives in both houses of Congress. (4, 11, 15)

Entitlement social policies that provide a benefit that has been earned, such as Social Security and Medicare. An entitlement requires the federal government to pay benefits to those who qualify and is not subject to the normal congressional appropriations process. (18, 19)

Equal protection a guarantee of the Fourteenth Amendment which forbids any state law that arbitrarily discriminates against a person or group. (7)

Equal Rights Amendment (ERA) a proposed amendment to the Constitution stating that equality of rights under the law should not be denied or abridged by the United States or by any state on account of sex. The proposed amendment died three states short of ratification in 1982. (7)

Establishment clause First amendment guarantee against the government "establishing" a religion by recognizing a church or religion as the official church or religion of that state or nation. (6)

Evaluation a judgment about a belief pertaining to an attitude object. (See also *belief*.) (8)

Exclusionary rule a rule stating that a state or the federal government may not use evidence in a trial if that evidence has been illegally obtained as a result of violations of the Fourth or Fifth Amendments. (6)

Executive agreement an international ageement between the president and foreign heads of state that does not need Senate approval, as a treaty does. (15)

Executive branch the branch of the government headed by the president whose job it is to propose policies and work for their passage in Congress and to implement policies once they are passed. (4)

Executive Office of the President an organization established in 1939 to assist presidential policymaking, which today includes such key staff agencies as the Office of Management and Budget, the National Security Council, the Council of Economic Advisers, and the White House Office. (15)

Executive prerogative the right that is attached to the executive office to perform certain functions without the requirement of public or legislative approval, particularly in time of domestic or international crisis. (15)

Executive power the constitutional grant of power to the president in Article II, which is not limited to implementing specific laws passed by Congress or to other specific presidential powers in the Constitution. (15)

Extended republic James Madison's term for a nation large and diverse enough that multiple interests would inevitably check and balance one another. (3)

Federalism a fundamental principle of the Constitution that divides government responsibility between a national and smaller component governments, and ensures that component governments are represented in the larger one. (4)

Federalists supporters of ratification of the Constitution in 1787–1789 who took the reins of government in the Washington and Adams administrations (1789–1800) and supported a strong national government and economic development programs. (12)

Federal system a system of government in which the responsibility for governing is divided between a national government and smaller component governments and the component governments are represented in the national government. (See also *unitary system*.) (5)

Feminization of poverty a general term for the high and increasing incidence of poverty among female-headed single-parent families in the United States. (19)

Filibuster a parliamentary device by which a minority in the Senate is able to slow down or stop action by a majority by holding the floor with long speeches or other delaying tactics. (The term comes from the Spanish word for a freebooter, a military adventurer who conducted unauthorized warfare against a nation with which his own nation was at peace.) (14)

Fiscal policy the attempt by the federal government to stimulate or slow down aggregate economic demand by raising or lowering taxes and/or public spending. (See also *monetary policy*.) (18)

Flat tax a tax rate according to which people are taxed the same percentage, regardless of their income levels. (See also *progressive tax*.) (18)

Focus group a dozen or so randomly selected citizens brought together for an in-depth probe of their opinions about issues, campaign events, or radio and television commercials. (11)

Food stamps a major nutritional social policy by which the government sells food stamps to needy individuals and families who then use the stamps to buy food at a higher value than the purchase price of the stamps. (19)

Free exercise clause First amendment guarantee that protects individuals and groups from government interference in their right to worship. (6)

Functional illiteracy the inability to read and comprehend practical information, such as a loan application or a ballot. (2)

Fundamental rights those guarantees of the Bill of Rights that are so important they must prevail over state interests unless those interests are compelling. (6)

General-welfare liberalism the philosophy that government has a positive role to play in stabilizing the economy and protecting the safety and welfare of its citizens, while at the same time respecting political rights. (3)

Generation gap young people's rejection of their parents' political values, norms, or loyalties. (8)

Geographic constituency the physical location and boundaries of a representative's congressional district. (See also *personal constituency*, *primary constituency*, and *reelection constituency*.) (14)

Gerrymandering the practice of drawing election districts in such a fashion as to favor one political party over another. (The term originated with an early nineteenth-century Massachusetts congressional district that was drawn in a way that favored the party of Governor Elbridge Gerry, but looked to a political cartoonist like a salamander.) (11)

Governing coalition an interdependent set of groups that support particular officeholders and their programs or policies. (See also *electoral coalition*.) (15)

Gramm-Rudman-Hollings Act named after its sponsors Senators Phil Gramm, Warren Rudman, and Ernest Hollings, this law requires the Congress and president to agree on budgets that will steadily reduce the federal deficit to zero. If, in any year, no agreement is reached, cuts in both defense and domestic spending are to be made automatically according to a fixed formula. (18)

Grass roots movement the activities of a group of citizens organized on a local level to promote or attain a political objective..(10)

Gross national product (GNP) the total value of all goods and services produced by the economy. (2)

Groupthink the tendency of any small, cohesive, decision-making group to arrive at a group consensus without considering a number of options and dissenting opinions. (15)

Independent committees groups that solicit and spend money on behalf of a presidential candidate while working independently of the candidate's official campaign headquarters. (11)

Individualism the belief that the freedom and well-being of the individual is the chief value of society and that government intervention in the private economic market should be limited. (19)

Inflation a condition in which the value of money decreases as prices rise. (18)

Initiative an instrument of direct democracy by which a certain number of citizens sign a petition to place proposed legislation or a constitutional amendment on the ballot for the voters to approve or disapprove. (See also *referendum*.) (4)

Institutional presidency those officials and staff members who assist the president in information gathering, decision making, and the implementation of decisions. (See also *Executive Office of the President*.) (15)

Interest group litigation the process whereby a group that is denied access to the executive and legislative seeks to influence policy by initiating or sponsoring cases in the courts. (17)

Interest groups private organizations that try to influence public policy; sometimes called *pressure groups* or *special interests*. (13)

Interposition a doctrine providing that states have a right to interpose themselves between an unconstitutional law and the people of that state and to nullify that law. Associated with the state-centered, or compact theory, view of federalism. (5)

Investigative hearings a fact-finding process carried out by a congressional committee or subcommittee to assist legislators in administrative oversight and lawmaking. (14)

Iron law of oligarchy the tendency of organizations and political parties to become dominated by self-perpetuating leaders. (13)

Iron triangles See *subgovernments*.

Isolationism before World War II, the American tradition of neutrality and noninvolvement in the affairs of countries outside the Western Hemisphere. (20)

Jeffersonians the political faction or early party developed under the leadership of Thomas Jefferson and James Madison around the principle of states' rights and in opposition to Federalist programs in the 1790s; also known as Republicans and Democratic-Republicans. (12)

"Jim Crow" laws statutes in southern states that enforced segregation by requiring separate facilities for blacks and whites during the era of segregation (1880s–1954). Named after a derogatory term for a black person used in minstrel shows. (7)

Judicial activism a pattern of judicial behavior whereby judges actively promote certain social goals by overturning legislative and executive policies they consider contrary to those goals. (See also *judicial restraint*.) (17)

Judicial branch the branch of government responsible for settling disputes and for the administration of justice in society. (4)

Judicial restraint a pattern of judicial behavior whereby judges defer to the elected political branches of government and keep their personal political beliefs out of their decisions. (See also *judicial activism*.) (17)

Judicial review the power of the Supreme Court to declare any law or any action by a public official unconstitutional and therefore unenforceable. The Constitution does not specifically list judicial review among the powers of the judiciary, but the Supreme Court asserted it as a constitutional power in *Marbury* v. *Madison* (1803). (17)

Keynesian theory the theory propounded by the British economist John Maynard Keynes that governments can stimulate national economies by manipulating spending and taxes. (See also *fiscal policy*.) (18)

Laissez faire the doctrine that government interference in the economy is unjust and inefficient and should be restricted to protecting property rights. (3)

Lawmaking the process of considering and passing legislation; a central function of the Congress in the American political system. (14)

Legislative branch the branch of government consisting of the House of Representatives and the Senate. Article I of the Constitution makes Congress the central lawmaking institution of the federal government. (4)

Legislative powers constitutional powers given to the president to recommend legislation to Congress, call special sessions, and veto legislation. These legislative powers form the basis of the president's ability to influence Congress and have been considerably augmented by custom and statutes. (15)

Legislative veto a resolution passed by the House, Senate, or both chambers that overrules or prohibits a decision made in the executive branch. In 1983 the Supreme Court declared specific types of legislative vetoes unconstitutional, but they continue to be an important instrument of administrative oversight. (14)

Literacy tests state tests that required voters to demonstrate an ability to read, write, and in some cases interpret the meaning of laws or the Constitution as a qualification to vote. One of several methods of voting restrictions used to deny blacks the right to vote during the era of segregation (1880s–1954). (7)

Lobbying any effort by a group or individual to influence government's policies and actions. (13)

Macroeconomic policy government policy that attempts to stabilize the economy by controlling the amount of money in circulation (see also *monetary policy*) and increasing and decreasing total demand for goods and services through spending and taxation policies. (See also *fiscal policy*.) (2, 18)

Majority leader the floor leader of the majority party in a legislative body. The Senate majority leader is chosen by the members of the majority party and is the top majority party official; the house majority leader is chosen by majority party legislators and is the number-two party strategist after the Speaker of the House. (14)

Majority rule the principle that when a dispute arises the preference of a majority of the participants wins. (1)

Malapportionment a situation in which certain election districts in a state contain too few or too many residents compared to other districts in the state. (11)

Mandate an authorization from voters to a winning candidate to enact or carry out a particular policy or program. (11)

Marshall Plan a program of American economic assistance to Europe in the late 1940s designed to help rebuild European economies, thereby making the countries less susceptible to Communist subversion; named after Secretary of State George Marshall. (20)

Massive retaliation the strategic doctrine developed in the Eisenhower administration calling for nuclear retaliation against the Soviet Union in the event the Russians or that country's puppets launched a conventional or nuclear military attack against the United States or its allies. (20)

Mass media channels of public communication such as newspapers, television, radio, magazines, and books. (9)

Means-tested programs social policies in which benefits are restricted to those without the means to acquire them on their own and funding is based on general government revenues rather than previous contributions by recipients; an example is the Food Stamp program. (19)

Medicaid a joint federal-state program to give medical care to the poor. The federal government provides some funding and establishes health care standards, but the primary responsibility for administering the program rests with state governments. (19)

Medicare a federal program that provides health insurance for the aged and disabled and is funded through a payroll tax. (19)

Merchandise trade deficit the value of manufactured goods and agricultural products imported from overseas minus the value of exports. (2, 18)

Minority leader the top party official selected by the minority members of a legislature who serves as the chief strategist and spokesperson for the minority legislative party. (14)

***Miranda* rule** a rule to protect persons against self-incrimination that requires police, before questioning suspects, to advise them of their rights. (6)

Mirror metaphor the notion that newspapers and television describe events exactly as they happen without distortion. (9)

Mixed economic system an economic system characterized

by private ownership, open markets, free enterprise, *and* government management and regulation of economic activity. (2)

Monetary policy the attempt to manage a nation's level of economic activity by controlling the amount of money in circulation or the cost and availability of credit. (See also *fiscal policy*.) (18)

Multiple advocacy a type of presidential decision-making structure in which the president actively participates in and regulates the advisory system, and in which participants are relatively equal in their competence and expertise, the information available to them, their staff support, their status with the president, and their bargaining skills. (15)

Mutual assured destruction (MAD) the situation in which the United States and the Soviet Union maintain sufficient numbers of invulnerable nuclear weapons so that neither side can prevent total destruction of the other in the event of a nuclear war. (20)

National committees standing committees in each major party whose membership represents all the state parties and whose job it is to provide party leadership and continuity between national conventions. (12)

National convention a meeting of delegates held every four years by each of the major parties to nominate presidential and vice-presidential candidates, vote on the party platform, and pass rules governing the structure and procedures of the national and state parties. (12)

National security state a government so preoccupied with national security that it devotes an extraordinary amount of its resources to military preparedness. (20)

National supremacy a fundamental principle of the Constitution that states that any lawful exercise of power by the national government takes precedence over any conflicting action by a state government. (See also *supremacy clause*.) (4)

Nation-centered federalism a theory of federalism that views the American people, rather than the states, as the source of national authority under the Constitution. The wording of the preamble of the Constitution ("We the people") and the supremacy clause of Article VI form the basis of this theory of federalism. (See also *state-centered federalism*.) (5)

Natural rights innate liberties deriving from human existence that government should not deny to individuals. (3)

Negative campaigning campaigning in which personal attacks, not public policy, characterize campaign messages. (11)

New Deal the set of laws and programs enacted during Franklin Roosevelt's administration in the 1930s that attempted to revitalize industry and agriculture, stabilize banking, and reduce unemployment and poverty. (18)

"New Federalism" a term used in both the Nixon and Reagan administrations for the consolidation of categorical grant programs into broader categories of revenue sharing (Nixon) or block grants (Nixon and Reagan)

in order to give states and localities more discretion in how the federal funds would be spent. (5)

New welfare social policies in the 1960s, shaped by interest group liberalism, that treated poverty as a human characteristic or "interest" and sought not just to mitigate the effects of poverty but to eliminate poverty altogether. An example is the Economic Opportunity Act of 1964. (See also *old welfare*.) (19)

Nonpartisan elections elections in which only candidates' names, not their party affiliation, are listed on the ballot. (10)

NSC 68 a report by the National Security Council written in 1950 concluding that because the Soviet Union threatened America's national security interests, the United States had to strengthen its military capability. (20)

Nuclear deterrence threatening nuclear retaliation against a nation that attacks what a country perceives to be its vital interests. (20)

Objectivity the belief that journalists report the news accurately, truthfully, completely, and without bias. (9)

Official point of view the idea that most news stories originate from public officials and hence reflect their attitudes and beliefs about political matters. (9)

Old welfare social policies that treated poverty as an economic problem affecting people randomly and that sought to remedy the problem by establishing categories of relief and delivering benefits to people within those categories. An example is the original Social Security program of 1935. (See also *new welfare*.) (19)

Opinion intensity the degree or amount of conviction with which an attitude or opinion is held. (8)

Optimists social scientists and philosophers who believe that most citizens have the innate intelligence and desire to govern themselves responsibly. Whatever civic inadequacies people exhibit stem not from inborn character defects but from flawed social and political institutions that limit information and discourage participation. (See also *skeptics*.) (8)

Partisanship See *party identification*.

Party activists individuals within the party who regularly engage in campaign work or other party activities at the national, state, and/or local levels and who expect to have some influence on decisions made by those they help put in office. (12)

Party identification the feeling of closeness or attachment to a political party; also called partisanship. (10, 11, 12)

Party-in-government those people who have been elected to office and are identified as Democrats, Republicans, or members of another party. (12)

Party-in-the-electorate those people who are not active in the party but who think of themselves as Democrats or Republicans and who vote that way at least some of the time. (12)

Party organization those people who hold formal party positions at the local, state, or national level of the party and all the volunteers who help run campaigns and engage in other party activities. (12)

Patronage the power to give material rewards such as appointments to office and contracts to political supporters. The Jackson administration introduced an extensive patronage system to national politics in 1829 that was known as the "spoils system" from the expression "to the victors belong the spoils." (12)

Personal constituency a representative's innermost circle of political and personal friends whom she or he trusts completely. (See also *geographic constituency*, *primary constituency*, and *reelection constituency*.) (14)

Personalization the emphasis in news reporting on the personal aspects of a story, such as who appeared to have won or lost a political battle, rather than the substance of the issue. (9)

Plea bargaining negotiations between prosecutors and persons accused of a crime or their lawyers that result in those accused of a crime pleading guilty in return for a lesser charge or sentence. (17)

Pluralism the theory that groups, not the people as a whole, govern. (1)

Plurality a number of votes for a candidate that exceeds the number cast for any other candidates; when more than two candidates are running, a plurality need not be more than half the votes cast. (11)

Political action committees (PACs) organizations that solicit and distribute contributions to candidates who sympathize with their own purposes, interests, or ideology. (11)

Political business cycle (PBC) the theory that presidents attempt to manipulate fiscal policy in order to stimulate the economy during election years. (18)

Political efficacy the belief that one's political participation can and does influence decision makers and is thus worthwhile. (10)

Political entrepreneurs individuals who build their own election organizations and do not depend on party support to get elected. (13)

Political equality the principle that each citizen's preference or opinion counts the same in making public decisions. (1)

Political monetary cycle (PMC) the theory that the Federal Reserve System manipulates the money supply to benefit the president's party during an election year and then reverses direction after the election is over. (18)

Political participation any activity intended to affect the making and content of public policy. (10)

Political party a group of people with a shared ideology who seek to determine public policy by winning elections and governing. (12)

Political recruitment the process by which persons seek to become and are selected to be members of government or to fill positions where they can influence government decisions. Political recruitment is a central function of political parties. (12)

Political resources assets such as wealth, prestige, skill, and organizational strength that can be used to make others do what one wants. (1)

Popular press media sources that typical citizens read, watch, and listen to. (See also *activist press*.) (9)

Popular sovereignty the doctrine that political power is ultimately vested in the people. (1)

Potential power the *possibility* of turning political resources into actual or real power. (See also *actual power*.) (1)

Precinct the smallest unit in the political party organization or election system, containing between 200 and 1,000 voters. (12)

Presidential primaries Statewide elections for directly selecting delegates to a national party convention and indirectly selecting the party's candidates for the presidency. (12)

Primary constituency a group of people within a representative's geographic constituency who have demonstrated intense and durable support over a number of elections and who often helped to recruit the representative for her or his first campaign. (See also *geographic constituency*, *personal constituency*, and *reelection constituency*.) (14)

Progressive tax a tax rate that increases progressively with wealth; the rich pay a higher percentage of their incomes than the poor. (See also *flat tax*.) (18)

Protectionism the use of tariffs, quotas, surcharges, and other trade barriers to protect American industry from foreign imports. (2)

Proximity the closeness of a voter's position on an issue to where he or she believes the candidate stands on the matter. (11)

Public interest groups organizations that claim to speak for the public as a whole or significant parts of it. (13)

Public opinion the aggregation of millions of individual attitudes or opinions. (8)

Public opinion poll a survey of political attitudes based on a representative sample of individuals. (8)

Reagan Doctrine President Ronald Reagan's policy of providing military, diplomatic, and economic assistance to groups attempting to overthrow Communist or Soviet-supported governments. (20)

Reaganomics President Ronald Reagan's economic program that included across-the-board cuts in income tax, reductions in domestic spending, curtailment of federal regulation of business, a balanced federal budget, and increases in military spending. (18)

Realignment a fundamental change in party loyalties and voting behavior in the electorate that produces a new political party or a new coalition of support for one of the major political parties. (12)

Recession a period of greatly reduced economic activity. (18)

Reconstruction amendments the Thirteenth, Fourteenth, and Fifteenth Amendments, which changed the relationships between the national government and the states and are sometimes called a second American Constitution. The Thirteenth Amendment outlawed slavery, the Fourteenth spelled out the protections given all citizens, and the Fifteenth guaranteed the right to vote to blacks. (7)

Reelection constituency a group within the geographic constituency consisting of those people who a representative feels supported him or her in the last election. (See also *geographic constituency*, *personal constituency*, and *primary constituency*). (14)

Referendum an instrument of direct democracy that permits voters to veto legislation passed by the legislature; a petition places the measure on the ballot for voters to approve or disapprove within a fixed period of time. (See also *initiative*.) (4)

Registration the process of establishing one's eligibility to vote in an election by meeting the necessary age and residency requirements. (10)

Reindustrialization the effort to rebuild and streamline American industry with public funds and the cooperation of government, labor, and management. (2)

Representation the process by which elected officials speak for and act in the interests of constituents or other individuals and groups in the policymaking process; one of the central functions of Congress. (14)

Representational federalism a theory of federalism that says the agreement or formal arrangement of the Constitution is among the people, who are represented in *both* the national and state governments. The nature of representation in the political system, rather than the precise language of the Constitution, provides answers to questions about who should govern in particular policy areas. (5)

Representative bureaucracy a government bureaucracy that mirrors society in its social, economic, and cultural composition. (16)

Representative democracy a form of government in which citizens choose agents who act on their behalf; the people do not govern directly. (See also *direct democracy*.) (1)

Republic a system of government in which power is exercised by elected officials, not by the people themselves. (1)

Republican party one of the two major political parties in contemporary American politics. (12)

Responsible electorate voters who are active, alert, and informed and who choose among candidates on rational grounds. (11)

Retrospective voting the theory that voters choose candidates on the basis of how the country, particularly the economy, has fared in the past. (11, 18)

Revenue sharing a form of federal assistance from 1972 to 1986, under which the federal government distributed funds to state and local governments without requiring that the money be spent on particular programs or even for certain broad functions like education or health. (5)

Revolving door the practice of former public officials or lawmakers going to work for private groups having business with the government or, conversely, members of these private concerns going to work for the government. (13)

Right of privacy a broad guarantee against governmental interference in a person's life, which includes a right of abortion, and is implicit in specific guarantees of the Bill of Rights, such as the First Amendment's freedom of association, the Fourth Amendment's protection against unreasonable searches and seizures, and the Fifth Amendment's guarantee against self-incrimination. (6)

Rights of the accused the procedural guarantees contained primarily in the Fourth, Fifth, Sixth, and Eighth Amendments, which require the government to follow certain procedures in investigating, prosecuting, trying, and punishing crimes. (6)

SALT negotiations an acronym for *Strategic Arms Limitation Talks*, discussions between the United States and the Soviet Union in the 1970s that led to the signing of treaties limiting strategic nuclear weapons and antimissile defenses. (20)

Scope the range of issues or areas over which someone exerts political power. (1)

Segregation the separation of blacks and whites in public and private places. (7)

Selective incorporation the process by which the Supreme Court has extended the Bill of Rights to the states by including specific guarantees of the Bill of Rights in the due process clause of the Fourteenth Amendment as restrictions on state governments as well as the national government. (6)

Selective perception the tendency to see, hear, or remember what one wants to see, hear, or remember. (8)

Separate but equal the doctrine upholding segregation laws on the grounds that blacks were not being denied equal protection under laws that provided facilities that were racially separate but equal. (7)

Separation of powers a fundamental principle of the Constitution by which the political system is divided top to bottom and side to side into competing jurisdictions in order to prevent the accumulation of too much power by one branch or institution. (4)

Shared government the practice of private groups and businesses acting as agents of or partners with government in creating, administering, and enforcing public policy. (13)

Single-issue voters people who choose a candidate solely on the basis of that candidate's stand on a particular issue. (11)

Single-member plurality an election in which the candidate with the most votes represents the district; parties do *not* share representation according to the percentage of the votes they received. (11)

Skeptics social scientists and philosophers who maintain that human frailties, such as lack of interest and knowledge about government, make mass participation in politics both impractical and undesirable. (See also *optimists*.) (8)

Social class a segment of society defined by such characteristics as occupation, education, or income. (2)

Socialization the process of learning a society's norms, values, customs, and roles. (8)

Social policy a general term used for government attempts to improve the welfare of people who would otherwise be hurt by unregulated social and economic forces. (19)

Social Security a social program that includes a pension system for retired workers, an unemployment compensation program for those out of work, and an assistance program for the elderly, the blind, and needy children. The basic program was established in 1935 and has since been expanded to include disability, health insurance, and medical assistance programs. (19)

Soft money donations made to state parties ostensibly for local activities such as registration and get-out-the-vote drives, but which in fact benefit presidential candidates; viewed as a way to circumvent spending limits imposed by federal campaign finance laws. (11)

Sound bites short, easily understood statements or slogans uttered by candidates or their advisers primarily for media use. (9)

Speaker the presiding officer in the House of Representatives who is formally elected by the entire membership of the House (in a vote that follows strict party lines) but is actually selected by the majority party caucus. (14)

Stagflation a period of both high unemployment and high prices. (18)

Standing a legal concept that determines who has the ability to bring a case into court. To achieve standing, a person or group must demonstrate a personal stake in the outcome or show that the person or group is representative of those with such a personal stake. (17)

State action an official act by a state or local government official or agency. The Fourteenth Amendment prohibits state actions that discriminate against persons or groups and deny them due process and equal protection but it does not prohibit discrimination carried out by private individuals. (7)

State-centered federalism a theory of federalism that views the Constitution as a compact drawn up by independent and sovereign states, which limits the authority of the national government to those powers conceded by the states in the Constitution. Also known as the compact theory of federalism. (See also *nation-centered federalism*.) (5)

Straight-ticket ballots ballots that permit a voter to select a party's entire slate by marking one box or column. (10)

Strategic Defense Initiative (SDI) President Ronald Reagan's plan to defend the United States with a sophisticated and impenetrable space-based antimissile shield. (20)

Strategy of political ambiguity the practice of candidates' avoiding clear statements of their positions on major issues. (11)

Subgovernments an autonomous and enduring relationship among a government agency, key interest groups in a policy area, and members of a congressional committee or subcommittee with jurisdiction in that area. Also known as iron triangles, these subgovernments are often said to control policymaking in their areas to the benefit of all the involved parties. (16)

Suffrage the right to vote. (10)

Supply-side economics the doctrine that tax cuts stimulate investment, employment, and productivity, and thus pay for themselves in the long run by leading to greater savings, output, and profits and hence higher tax revenues. (18)

Supremacy clause the second section of Article VI of the Constitution, which says that the Constitution, national laws made in pursuance of the Constitution, and all treaties shall be the supreme law of the land and take precedence over any conflicting sections of state constitutions or state statutes. The clause supports the expansive view of national powers seen under nation-centered federalism. (4, 5)

Symbolic influence the theory that political participation reassures people that their efforts are worthwhile when in fact it has little real impact on policymaking. (See also *contingent influence, direct influence,* and *top-down influence.*) (8)

Top-down influence the theory that political leaders sell policies to the public rather than respond to what the people want. (See also *contingent influence, direct influence,* and *symbolic influence.*) (8)

Treaty power the president's power to make treaties, with the advice and consent of the Senate and with the concurrence of two-thirds of the Senate. (15)

Triad a trio of three weapons systems—bombers, land-based intercontinental missiles, and submarine-launched missiles—to implement nuclear deterrence. (20)

Trunk decisions basic policies that determine the general determination and content of public policy in a broad area such as foreign affairs. (1)

Trustee a role in which the legislator or other elected official acts in what he or she believes to be the long-term interests of constituents, regardless of the current opinion of a majority of the constituency. (See also *delegate.*) (14)

Unitary system a centralized system of government in which the national government has the ultimate responsibility for policymaking in all areas. (See also *federal system.*) (5)

War power the authority for protecting the nation from its enemies. The Constitution divides the war power between Congress and the president. (15)

Welfare state a form of government that provides income, social security, unemployment compensation, job training, medical and hospital care, and other benefits to its citizens in order to ensure them a minimal level of well-being. (3)

Whig party a political party formed in 1834 by defecting conservative southern Democrats who opposed the nationalism of the Democratic party. (12)

Whip a legislative party official who serves as an assistant floor leader and whose chief responsibility is to get legislators to vote with their party leaders. (The term comes from the strong party organizations of the British parliament in the eighteenth century and the English term "whipper-in," the person responsible for keeping the hounds together in a fox hunt.) (14)

White House Office a staff agency in the Executive Office of the President that includes the president's personal assistants and key advisers who provide information and advice as part of the routine, everyday decision-making process. (15)

White primary a method used to deny blacks a right to vote by outlawing black participation in the Democratic primary (the only election that mattered in most southern states) under the guise that the Democratic party was a private group. The Supreme Court outlawed the white primary in 1944. (7)

Workfare the notion that welfare recipients should be required to accept job training and employment as a condition of receiving public assistance. (3)

World view a set of values, beliefs, and attitudes shared by top leadership echelons concerning the proper form of the economy, the government, and the United States's role in world affairs. (1)

Zero-sum games controversies characterized by the fact that if one side wins, the other side inevitably loses; there is no way for both sides to win something. (10)

Photo Credits

Index